CHINESE CHARACTERS

THEIR ORIGIN, ETYMOLOGY, HISTORY, CLASSIFICATION AND SIGNIFICATION. A THOROUGH STUDY FROM CHINESE DOCUMENTS

by Dr. L. WIEGER, S.J.

Translated into English by L. Davrout, S.J.

Second Edition, enlarged and revised according to the 4th French edition

PARAGON BOOK REPRINT CORP., NEW YORK
DOVER PUBLICATIONS, INC., NEW YORK

This edition, first published in 1965, is an unabridged and unaltered republication of the second edition, published by the Catholic Mission Press in 1927. The first edition of *Chinese Characters* was published in 1915.

This edition is a joint publication of Paragon Book Reprint Corp. and Dover Publications, Inc.

Standard Book Number: 486-21321-8
Library of Congress Catalog Card Number: 64-18441

Manufactured in the United States of America

Paragon Book Reprint Corp.
140 East 59th Street
New York 22, N.Y.

Dover Publications, Inc.
180 Varick Street
New York 14, N.Y.

CHINESE CHARACTERS

THEIR ORIGIN, ETYMOLOGY, HISTORY, CLASSIFICATION AND SIGNIFICATION. A THOROUGH STUDY FROM CHINESE DOCUMENTS

PREFACE.

The end aimed at by the Author has been to analyse the ancient forms of the Chinese characters, to extract from them their primitive constituents, and then to group them together according to these primitive elements, in an order both logical and synoptical.

The materials, figures and interpretations, were gathered from the works of the Chinese epigraphers and philologues. After having eliminated the useless characters, the Author picked out, among the usual characters, 224 Primitives. Around these elements were grouped about 1500 logical aggregates and phonetic complexes, from which all the other characters are derived. Then the whole matter was divided into 177 *Lessons*. After many experiences, this disposition seemed to be the most advantageous for study.

The *Introduction* is designed to furnish some necessary explanation respecting the history, the categories, the analysis and the different classifications of the Chinese characters.

The *Graphies* are fac-similes of the oldest specimens of Chinese writing, cast, not engraved, upon bronze bells and vases.

The *Phonetic Series*, are a natural complement of the Lessons.

Two *Lexicons* showing the characters arranged by order of Sounds and Radicals, complete the work.

The *Romanisation* adopted by the Translator, was according to the Wade system.

L. Davrout S.J.

CHINESE CHARACTERS.

INTRODUCTORY.

I. HISTORICAL SKETCH.

Tradition ascribes the idea of the characters to 伏 羲 **Fu-hsi**, and their first drawing to 倉 頡 **Ts'ang-hsieh**, two worthies of the prehistoric age. The systematisation of the Chinese writing, is attributed to 黃 帝 **Huang-ti**, the founder of the Chinese empire, 25th century B.C. Some texts of the *Annals*, may have been written earlier than the 22th century B.C. — In the beginning, writing was used only for matters of government and administration. By its means, the Emperor was given information, and his orders were transmitted to the mandarins and to the people. The 史 **shih**, recorders, registrars, scribes, were trained up in official schools, under the direction of a 太 史 **t'ai-shih** grand-recorder.

The oldest 古 文 **ku-wên** graphies that have come down to us in their original form, are traced back to the 18th century B.C. Their study reveals the fact, that while their making was well defined, their form varied much. Towards the year B.C. 800, the grand-recorder 籀 **Chou** drew up, for the use of the official scribes, a catalogue of the then existing characters, and fixed their standard shape. Those *ku-wên* are called by Chinese philologists 籀 文 **chou-wên**, or 大 篆 **ta-chuan** greater seal characters, or 蝌 蚪 字 **k'o-tou-tzŭ** tadpoles. The origin of the latter appellation is thus recorded. In the 2d century B.C., when the house in which

Confucius had dwelt was pulled down, old books written in ancient characters were discovered in a hiding-place. At the sight of the big heads and the slender tails, 恭 **Kung** prince of 魯 **Lu** who was not a learned man, exclaimed: these are tadpoles!.. The name has stuck to them ever since.

As the decay of the 周 **Chou** Dynasty grew worse, studies were neglected and the scribes became more and more ignorant. When they did not remember the genuine character, they blunderingly invented a false one. Those non-genuine characters, copied out again by other ignorant writers, became usual. Confucius himself made this statement. Towards the year B. C. 500, he uttered this complaint: «When I was young, I still knew some scribes who left blank the characters which they could not write; now there are no more such men!» Consequently the 奇 字 **ch'i tzŭ** «odd characters» were multiplied without restraint, to the great prejudice of etymology.

Towards the year B. C. 213, under the Emperor 秦 始 皇 **Ch'in-shih-huang** who destroyed the classical books, 李 斯 **Li-ssŭ**, his prime-minister, published a new official index of the characters, and fixed a way of writing which became obligatory for scholars. His collection, entitled 三 倉 **San-ts'ang**, contained 3300 characters. This new form of writing was known as the 小 篆 **hsiao-chuan**, lesser seal characters. — The study of the work of **Li-ssŭ** discloses two facts:.. 1. He did not create any new primitive, but he contented himself with composing, by means of preexisting elements, the names for objects which were unknown before. Therefore the evolution of characters was certainly closed before the times of **Li-ssŭ**, probably many centuries before him... 2. Deceived by the 奇 字 **ch'i-tzŭ**, then so numerous, **Li-ssŭ** wrongly interpreted some characters, and fixed them for posterity under a wrong shape. Many instances of these mistakes of **Li-ssŭ** will be seen in the *Etymological Lessons*.

A few years after the catalogue of Li-ssŭ was edited, a new era was opened in the study of characters. Two facts are peculiar to this change: an excessive *multiplication*; a gradual *transformation*. Let us briefly state the causes of these philological phenomena:

1. Causes of the excessive multiplication of characters... First, the ignorance of scribes who continually brougt to light faulty forms which were stupidly reproduced by posterity; then, the need felt to give names to new things. The Empire was growing, learning was spreading; writing had become a public thing; the process 形聲 **hsing-shêng** (see page 10) being an easy one, all took to it. From this disorderly fermentation, without direction, without control, without criticism, sprang up, together with useful characters, thousands of useless doubles. Things could not well be otherwise, when one remembers that the centres of fabrication were multiplied, and that the local idioms were very different. The index of **Li-ssŭ** contained 3300 characters. In the space of two centuries, it was completed seven times, and the 7th edition, published at the beginning of the Christian era, contains 7380 characters. Two centuries later, there were 10.000. Now the dictionary of 康熙 **K'ang-hsi** (A.D. 1716), contains 40,000 characters that may be plainly divided as follows: 4000 characters in common use; 2000 proper names and doubles of limited use; 34.000 monstrosities of no practical use. We are far from the legendary number of 80.000 usual characters, ascribed to the Chinese language.

2. Causes of the gradual transformation of characters. — The first to be noticed, is the complete change in the instruments and material used for writing. The ancient wrote with a sort of fountain-pen, upon small laths of bamboo or smooth wooden tablets. Hereby the figure of the fountain-pen of old, as it has been transmitted to us on a bronze of the 2d dynasty. Above, the reservoir holding the fluid, presumably a black varnish. The narrow bamboo tube contained probably a wick, to regulate the flowing of the ink. Such an instrument traces lines any way it is moved, either backwards or forwards, straight or curved, as one likes, but all equally thick. Therefore in the 篆 **chuan**, greater or lesser seal characters of all ages, there are figures of every shape, round, oval, sinuous, the lines being all uniformly thick. — Not long after the catalogue of **Li-ssŭ** was edited, 程邈 **Ch'êng-miao** invented a pencil of soft wood, ending in a fibrous point, which being dipped in the black varnish, was used for writing on silk strips. Traced with this coarse instrument on a rough material, the rounded figures became square, the curved lines were broken at right angles. But this ungraceful writing being quicker than with the fountain-pen, the wooden pencil was adopted for public deeds, and the 隸字 **li-tzŭ** or official hand, became the current writing, while the lesser seal characters remained the classical writing.

As it commonly happens, the way being opened, inventions succeeded one another. During his campaigns against the Huns, the general 蒙恬 **Mêng-t'ien** is said to have invented or improved the writing-brush, the ink and the paper. This invention was fatal to the characters. — A writing-brush cannot trace lines against the hair, therefore many characters could not be written and were replaced by arbitrary and fanciful sketches. — The materials used further helped to increase the confusion. Paper is absorbent: hence came the thick strokes, the thin strokes and the slabbery letters, which were all unknown to the ancients. — A writing-brush, made with stiff and elastic hair, flattens out when pressed down, twists when turned, projects its point when raised up; hence the swellings, the joints, the crooks, which are not intentional, but are due to the instrument itself. — Therefore the actual classical writing 楷子 **chieh-tzŭ**, represents the 小篆 **hsiao-chuan** as transformed by the writing-brush.

There is more. The writing-brush galloping, the strokes were connected up, giving birth to the 連筆字 **lien-pei-tzŭ**; then it flew, throwing on the paper misshapen figures, which are called 草字 **ts'ao-tzŭ**. The fancy for these novelties became a rage. At the beginning of the Christian era, a man believed himself dishonoured if he wrote in a legible way. In this crisis, the initiative of a private scholar saved what could still be saved.

Towards the year A.D. 200, after long travels undertaken to get the authentic originals, a literate of renown 許愼 **Hsü-shên** or 許叔重 **Hsü shu-chung**, vulgo 許氏 **Hsü-shih**, published the lexicon 說文解字 **Shuo-wên chieh-tzŭ**. It was the collection of **Li-ssŭ**, controlled, amended, explained and classified under 540 rational keys. The aim of **Hsü-shên** was to impede any ulterior alteration of the characters, by setting their authentical form before the eyes of all scholars. His book contains 9353 simples and 1163 doubles, which makes 10.516 in all. It was not less useful to the nation, the admirers say, than the canals of the great 禹 **Yü** It remained, from that time, the canon of the 字 **tzŭ**, the authority consulted in all doubts, by Chinese philologists. All the dictionaries published for the last 17 centuries, boast of their having followed the **Shuo-wên**, 以說文爲本.

But the work of **Hsü-shên** had a more far reaching effect than the mere conservation of the **hsiao-chuan**. It was the origin of archeological researches which brought to light more of the antique **ku-wên**, and of philological studies which explained them. These successive discoveries were published, according to the Chinese way, in enlarged and annotated editions of the primitive **Shuo-wên**. See 說文通訓定聲 — Later on, under each key of **Hsü-shên**, were ranged a chronological series of ancient forms, copied either from stones or bronzes that were discovered, or from books that were extracted from tombs or other hiding places, throughout the Empire. See 六書統. — Published in fine books, carefully analysed, learnedly explained, these *Series* give the genealogy of the actual characters. Their study enabled the critics to rectify the errors and mistakes of **Li-ssŭ** and of **Hsü-shên**. It gave the material for the *Etymological Lessons* contained in this volume.

For instance, Series of the character 君 **chün**, prince, through 45 centuries.

1. The primitive form, **ku-wên**. A cap with horns, to inspire awe. Two arms, the executive power. A mouth, the legislative power.

2. A mere graphic variety. The elements are the same, but their form is different.

3. Another variety. The same elements, a different form; It is so with all the **ku-wên**; the idea is determined, the form varies.

Then came a fanciful scribe who gave to the cap a curious form; whence the **k'i-tzŭ** 4, the elements being still the same.

The next writer, an ignoramus, thought he saw two hands, instead of the horns on the cap, and he invented the **ch'i-tzŭ** 5. The hands figure the power, the mouth makes law; the idea is still the same, but the graphic elements are partially different.

An idle writer, for the sake of abbreviation, replaced one of the hands by a simple stroke, which gave the **ch'i-tzŭ** 6.

This last character, being in use at the end of the **Chou** Dynasty, **Li-ssŭ** interpreted it: a *hand* which acts, a mouth which *makes law*. Thus was fixed the **hsiao-chuan** 7.

The wood-pencil made with this **hsiao- chuan**, the **li-tzŭ** 8 and 9.

The writing-brush changed the **li-tzŭ** into the **chieh-tzŭ** 10, which is still classic in our days.

The latter being connected together, became the **lien-pei-tzŭ** 11, the successive abbreviations of which gave the **ts'ao-tzŭ** 12, 13, 14.

It is all about the same for the other Series.

II. 六書 LIU-SHU.

Six Categories of Characters.

The Chinese philologists divide the characters into two great classes: the 文 **wên**, simple *figures*, and the 字 **tzŭ**, compound *letters*.

The *figures* are subdivided into 像 **hsiang** or 像形 **hsiang-hsing**, imitative drafts; and 指事 **chih-shih**, indicative symbols.

The compound *letters* are subdivided into 會意 **hui-i**, logical aggregates, in which all parts have a meaning; and in 形聲 **hsing-shêng** or 諧聲 **hsieh-shêng**, phonetic complexes, in which one part has a meaning, while the other points out the pronunciation.

Let us summarise the matter, with a few details and instances.

First category. *Imitative drafts*, rough sketches representing the object; 畫成其物、隨體詰詘。The **Shuo-wên** contains 364 imitative drafts. Example: ㇌ the right hand.

Second category. *Indicative symbols.* A figure that suggests the meaning; 視而可識、察而見意。The **Shuo-wên** contains 125 indicative symbols. Example: 亅 action of the authority which exerts itself from up down. Those symbols often suggest an idea of motion.

Third category. *Logical aggregates.* They are made with two or several characters more simple. Their signification results from the meanings of the different elements; 比類合誼、以見指撝。The **Shuo-wên** contains 1167 logical aggregates. Example: 占, composed of 口 mouth and 卜 divination; the outcome is **chan**, to consult fortune-tellers, to cast lots.

Fourth category. *Phonetic complexes.* They are made with two or more simple characters. One of them gives the meaning; the other is not a «meaning element», but gives to the complex its pronunciation; 以事爲名、取譬相成。The **Shuo-wên** contains 7697 phonetic complexes. Example: 沾. The first part 氵, water, gives the meaning; the second 占, **chan**, gives the sound. The compound means, to tinge, to moisten, and is pronounced **chan**.

To complete the study of the 六書 **liu-shu**, there are two more categories to be studied, the 轉注 **chuan-chu** and the 假借 **chia-chieh**. The above four categories are based upon the *composition* of characters. The last two are based upon their *use*.

Fifth category. **Chuan-chu**. Acceptation of the character in a meaning more extended, derived, generalised, metaphorical, analogous, adapted, figurative, etc.

Example: 网 picture of a fishing-net. By extension of the primitive sense, any net-work, cobweb, reticulate design; to catch with a net, to catch in general, to envelop, to gather, etc. All these meanings are **chuan-chu**. i. e. begot by successive *turns* in the *interpretation*. Nearly all the primitive characters refer to concrete objects. As the ideas became broader, the signification of characters spread in the same proportion. The abstract terms are commonly **chuan-chu** of concrete characters.

Sixth category. **Chia-chieh**. A mistake, lit. *false borrowing*. Use of a character in a sense which is not its own, either 1. By error, for an other existing character; or 2. By convention, to designate an object which has its name in the spoken language, but which has no special character. Examples:

1. In the first paragraph of the Analects of Confucius, one may find the character 說 meaning *to rejoice*. Now 說 means *to speak*, and *to rejoice* is written 悅. Once a scribe wrote 說 for 悅. It was a mistake, a **chia-chieh**, which was not amended, on account of the superstitious respect for the classical text.

2. Formerly, in some time, in some place, the *elder brother* was called **ko**. This word was used in the spoken language only. None among the then existing characters **ko**, had that meaning. Instead of making a new one, it was agreed that 哥 **ko**, to sing, should be used also to mean, *elder brother*. Though this meaning be unconnected with the composition of the character, however it was admitted. This was a **chia-chieh**, an arbitrary character. — Not a few usual characters were thus given artificial meanings, besides their own meaning and their different meanings **chuan-chu**. Other characters, either names of lost things, or useless doubles, first disappeared and then appeared again with a meaning quite new and in absolute contrast with their composition. Thus the foreign student is quite puzzled when he sees the figure of a scorpion meaning also *a myriad*, and he wonders how any relation may be found between the two terms? The answer is very easy. There was not a proper character to mean *a myriad*, which was said **wan** in the spoken language. On the contrary, there were many characters to write *scorpion* and one among them was just pronounced **wan**. It was dispossessed, installed in its new functions, and from that time, *myriad* is written with two claws and a tail. See, in the *Lessons*, the numbers 47 X, 49 H, 50 O, 71 Q, etc.

Those **chia-chieh** are the very reason why the interpretation of the Chinese characters, which was primitively simple and easy, became so intricate and so difficult. They obscure many texts, fill up the lexicons, overburden the memory, and exasperate the students. These sad results spring not from a vice inherent to the Chinese characters, but from their antiquity and from the carelessness of their successive keepers.

Notice. **In the *Lessons*, for the sake of brevity, we shall not say in English, about each character; this is «an imitative draft,» that is «an indicative symbol,» or a «logical aggregate,» or a «phonetic complex.» More commonly we shall**

content ourselves with the Chinese definition given in Chinese characters. The ordinary formulas for these definitions are thus given:

彐, 像 or 像形 **hsiang or hsiang-hsing.** Lit. *imitative draft* of the right hand.

丿, 指事 **chih-shih.** Lit. shows the thing, *indicative symbol,* to act, action.

尹, 从彐像, 从丿指事, 會意, 治也。Lit. from 彐 hand, *draft*; from 丿 to act, *symbol;* by the fusion of meanings, to govern. This is a *logical aggregate.*

支, 从彐, 从卜, 會意, 擊也。Lit, from 彐 hand, from 卜 rod; by a fusion of meanings, to strike. A *logical aggregate.*

固, 从口, 古聲, 四塞也。Lit. from 口, to enclose; 古 gives the sound; closed on the four sides, shut up hermetically. It is a *phonetic complex.*

As for the *derived* or *arbitrary* meanings, we shall be satisfied with indicating them by the words **chuan-chu** or **chia-chieh**, inserted in the text. The most important **chuan-chu** have been indicated, but not all the **chia-chieh**. The latter are to be looked for in the larger dictionaries, which are absolutely necessary on their account.

III. COMPOSITION AND DECOMPOSITION.

Primitives. Radicals. Phonetics.

From the calligraphic stand-point, the Chinese characters are all reduced into simple strokes. These material elements amount, for the modern writing, to nine in theory, and to about seventeen in practice. Their form is ascribed to the nature of the writing brush, as explained previously. The strokes are:

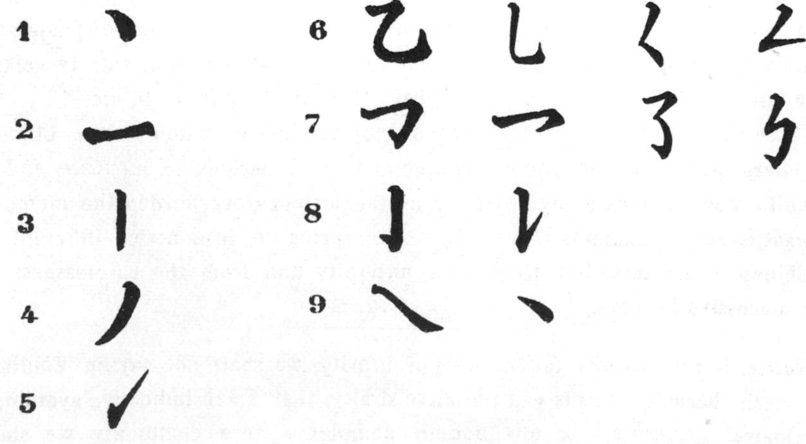

Note well and do not forget that this reduction into *simple strokes*, into ***material elements***, has no connection whatever with the etymological study of the characters.

From the *logical, etymological* point of view, the compounds are made, not with strokes, but with characters more simple, having their own use and meaning. These simple characters are what we call «elements», when we speak of compositions and decompositions. The more intricate character was formed by their association, and the analysis must end when it has separated and isolated these *formal elements*. To go further, to decompose into strokes, would add nothing to knowledge. Just as, in systematic botany, the study of a plant is ended when one has determined its specific organs. The ulterior decomposition of these formal elements into cells and fibres, belongs to histology, and is of no interest for classification purposes. Examples:

歸, a logical aggregate, is decomposed into 𠂤。止。帚。

欄, a phonetic complex, is decomposed into 木 and 闌。

If one says that 帚 and 闌 which are given as elements, are evidently themselves compounds, we answer: no doubt, if it is a question of *material* analysis, one should decompose 帚 into 彐 冖 巾, and 闌 into 門 and 柬. But here, this is not the question. What we look for, is the *logical etymological* analysis. Now, in the logical aggregate 歸, the element 帚 gives the *meaning*; it is therefore a *formal element*. In the phonetic complex 欄, 闌 gives the sound; it is therefore a *formal element*. The etymological decomposition ends there.

It may be asked how numerous are those relatively simple characters or *formal elements*, which are used to compose the more intricate characters? — Before answering, one must distinguish two categories, indicated previously: the *meaning elements* and the *phonetic elements*.

1. *Meaning elements.* — *Theoretically*, any simple character could be used for the composition of a logical aggregate. The ancient writers used those they wanted. — *Practically*, how many of those elements did they use? Relatively very few. Indeed, the research of those elements had to be made among the ancient regular forms, and not among the modern corrupted forms. Different Chinese authors numbered from about five to six hundred elements, but their choice was imperfect because there were compound forms, either multiples or inverted, which were kept without reason. The first European who studied the question, J.-M. Callery, suggested the number of 300. J. Chalmers who resumed this study, gave also 300 as a rough estimate Our own researches deliberately circumscribed in the *practical* domain led us to give 224 meaning elements, the list of which may be found at the head of the *Lessons*.

As said above, we call *primitives* the elements of the logical composition called by the Chinese 建首 **chien-shou,** *fundamental heads.* The definition of this term is to be noted well. ***Primitive***, formal meaning element that cannot admit of an ulterior decomposition into meaning parts; or, more shortly, ***ideographic minimum***. In other words, the primitives are characters relatively simple, having sound and meaning, and which are not formally resolved into *figures* having sound and meaning. Materially, they may be reduced into *strokes*, but this is without any use for the analysis. Just as a simple chemical body, or a bar of sulphur, or an iron ingot, can be smashed with a hammer, and yet this is not a decomposition, but a breaking up. — In a few characters, strokes or dots were added to extend or to modify the meaning. We call those characters *partial primitives.* They are primitives, relatively to the graphical details superadded. See, as examples, the nipples in 母, Lesson 67 O; the thorns in 朿, Lesson 120 H; the grains of salt in 鹵, Lesson 41 D; etc.

2. *Phonetic elements.* — *Theoretically,* the Chinese sounds not being numerous, four hundred characters would have been sufficient to compose á phonetic scale. — *Practically*, the Chinese used as phonetic elements, a greater number of characters; the reason of this will be given below. Some Chinese authors numbered one thousand of them, which they called the *thousand mothers of sounds.* **J.-M.** Callery who made a special study of these characters and found in them a key to his system, numbers 1040. Our researches, circumscribed in the *practical* domain, gave 858 phonetic prolific elements. This list may be seen at the head of the ***Phonetic Series.*** In the choice of these phonetic elements, the Chinese cared only about the sound and not about the character. They employed, from 乚 which has one stroke only, till 靈 which has twenty-four.

The inflected words of European languages are decomposed into *radical* and *termination*. The radical gives the meaning; the termination indicates case, time, mood. The first sinologists applied those grammatical terms belonging to inflected languages, to the Chinese language which is not an inflected one. In the phonetic complexes, they called *radical* the meaning part. They dared not call *termination* the phonetic part, and with reason, for it would have been a mistake. They called that part *phonetic.* We make ours those two terms, radical and phonetic, but strictly in the sense above given, viz. *Radical,* formal element which gives the meaning. *Phonetic,* the formal element which does not give the **meaning,** but indicates the sound.

Why do we insist thus upon the definition of these terms?.. The reason is this: in sinology, they were often used in an equivocal sense. — Some divided the characters into categories, stating that such a one is a radical, and such a one a phonetic, while any character may be, in composition, either a radical, or a phonetic, according to the part it has to act. — Others reduced the extension of the term ***radical*** **to the keys of the dictionaries, and gave as radicals only the 214 keys of K'ang-hsi;**

they called *phonetic* any character which was not radical. — Hence arose ways of speaking, improper, equivocal and false. For example: because 木 is the 75th key of *K'ang-hsi*, some say: the radical 木 is phonetic in 沐, instead of saying: 木 is phonetic in 沐, and radical in 柏. Because 占 is the 190th key of Callery, some say: the phonetic 占 is radical in 乩, instead of saying: 占 is radical in 乩, and phonetic in 沾. — To avoid such a confused and inexact way of speaking, one must remember that *radicals* and *phonetics* are not two categories of characters specifically distinct. They are two categories of a certain number of characters which, being neuter or indifferent by nature, are used in composition, either as radicals, or as phonetics, according to the cases. Even the *primitives* are, in composition, radicals or phonetics, according to the cases. They form a class by themselves only as elements formally indivisible; elements which, being not composed, compose all the others.

Why did they use one thousand characters, when four hundred could do? — It was to avoid confusion. In certain categories, there were to be placed objects of different kinds, but having the same sound. The radical proper to the category could not be changed and consequently the phonetics had necessarily to be changed, in order to get different characters. Example: In the category of trees, the radical of which is 木, the phonetic 古 had given the phonetic complex 枯 *k'u*, dead tree. Now there is a kind of elm which is also pronounced *k'u*. For this elm, the character 橭 k'u was made, in which 辜 is used as phonetic; and so on for many others. — As above stated, the new characters are selected, for more than twenty centuries, exclusively among the phonetic complexes. Out of the ten thousand characters that constitute the main part of the big dictionaries, about seven thousands of them are phonetic complexes. Some variety in their composition was of absolute necessity, to form a way of distinguishing one from another.

In which sense must we understand the assertion that the phonetics give their sounds to the phonetic complexes? — To answer the question, one must presuppose the following facts which are so evident that they need no proof. The Chinese language is spoken for tens of centuries past, in an immense territory. Its sounds are not numerous, and may be easily confounded. Hence arose a great number of dialectic differences. A Chinese proverb says that at a distance of one hundred *li*, people cannot understand each other. This assertion is exaggerated, but it is right to say that, at a distance of one hundred *li*, there are perceptible dialectic differences; that, at a distance of one thousand *li*, only a half of the things said are understood: and that, at a distance of two thousand *li*, nothing is understood. Further, the dialect of the same district varied in the course of ages. — That fact being granted, let us take as example 占. In the place and time when 占 was first chosen to be used as a phonetic, this character was pronounced *chan*. Its compounds, made after the same phonetic, were all pronounced *chan*, and being put in circulation with that sound, went to the North and to the South. Now the Chinese philologists say that the North is known as corrupting the finals in the words, while the South alters the initials. Thus when passing over in the Northern dialects, 砧 had its final **an** transformed into **ên**; 店 was ended into **yen** and 帖 into **yeh**: which are dialectic differences of a common origin. In a Southern dialect, the **ch** of 占 became **t** in 玷, and **n** in 黏: which are also differences of a common origin. At the same time, the tones and aspirates, special to different places, stuck to the former as well as to the latter. Then at last when, in the making of a big dictionary, 司 馬 光 **Ssŭ-ma kuang** for instance, gathered under the mother word 占 its roving brood, it was diversified with odd colours; there were characters pronounced **chan, chên, tien, nien** and **t'ieh**. The compiler neither made a choice, nor criticised, nor tried to restore the primitive pronunciation, nor returned to a unique dialect, but simply set down what was then used, and posterity was told by him, once for all, that 沾 was pronounced **chan**, that 帖 was pronounced **t'ieh**, and that 占 was their common phonetic. — Upon the whole, with regard to the phonetic series, note the three following points: 1. The sound was well determined in the beginning... 2. There were dialectical corruptions... 3. The sound was finally, and without any critical study, fixed by insertion in the dictionaries.

But then when one says that the phonetics determine the sound of compounds, is this determination practically reduced to something rather vague? — It is much to be regretted that it is often so. The determination is somewhat vague for the final (vowel), still more vague for the initial (consonant), and nearly non-existing for the tone aud aspiration.

But then is the study of phonetics useless? — It is an exaggeration to say so. The study of phonetics and of the phonetic series is useful. For, after all, the sounds, initials and finals of each series varied only to a certain extent and according to certain dialectic rules. Therefore the knowledge of phonetics allows, after a certain use, to guess *approximatively* the sound of compound characters. It helps also to fix those characters in the memory. Further, the study of characters, made by following the phonetic series, is more attractive and more useful than by following the series by radicals or by sounds. It is the reason why we add to this volume a lexicon by phonetic series.

IMPORTANT NOTICES.

1. *Use of a compound instead of a simple, as a radical.* The same need of variety, of distinction, that multiplied the phonetics (as above stated), impelled the use sometimes, as a radical, of a compound, instead of a simple character. Item, an inverted character was used instead of the straight form, etc. For example 卜 for 亅, 支 or 丑 or 寸 for 彐, 㡀 for 巾, 來 for 从, 𠫓 for 子.

2. *Phonetic-Radicals.* — In some ancient characters, an element which is *radical* gives also its *sound* to the compound, being thus together radical and phonetic. For ex. 冰。从水，从冫。冫亦聲。Lit. 冰 **ping** ice, from 水 **shui** water, from 冫 **ping** to freeze; 冫 **ping** is thus both radical and phonetic, Those characters are like a link between the logical aggregates and the phonetic complexes.

3. *Radical or phonetic redundancies.* — 1. The ancient characters were relatively simple. When the systematic classifications begun to be made, then without change in the meaning of those characters, *a meaning element* was super-added to many of them. This was a new radical, well chosen, but useless, under which the character was classified in the new dictionaries. Thus, to 𡥉 **chiao**, to teach, which nicely figured the action 爻 of the master descending upon the disciple, 攴 a hand was added, holding a rod, symbol of the master's authority. This addition was the cause why 教 was classified under the 66th radical in **K'ang-hsi**. Thus the old characters happened to have, nearly all, synonym compounds, and it is the compound that is used now, while the primitive character remains in the dictionaries with the mention 古文 **ku-wên**, ancient form. This is why one may often read in the *Lessons* the words « *it is now written.* » For ex., 匧, now 篋; the ancient form was enriched with the radical 竹, the rest being quite the same. — 2. The ancient drafts, or symbols, or logical aggregates, had no phonetic element, and nothing helped the memory to remember the sound. Later on, specially in the time of **Li-ssŭ**, *a phonetic element* was added to some ancient characters, without changing anything in the sense. For ex., to the character 㱕 **kui**, was added 𠂤 **tui**, to recall the sound **ui**, which gave 歸 Those embellished logical aggregates differ from the phonetic complexes in this, that they cannot be adequately decomposed into two elements, one being a radical, the other a phonetic... Another example: 処 **ch'u** was added with the phonetic 虍 **hu**, which gave 處 **ch'u**... Now 㱕 and 処 are no longer used. They are found in the dictionaries, with the mention 古文 **ku-wên**, ancient forms of 歸 and 處.

4. *Phonetics and Radicals contracted.* — See the phonetic Series 469, 腦 惱 瑙, etc. It seems to come from 囟 **hsin**, but it ends in **ao**. Its phonetic is not **hsin**, but 𡿺 **nao**, a logical aggregate made from **hsin**. But **nao** having already a lateral radical 匕, the addition of the radical of phonetic complexes would make ugly characters. To avoid this, 𡿺 is contracted, that is: its 匕 is suppressed, and in its place the radical of the complex is substituted. It the series 469, **nao** contracted is the phonetic, 从𡿺省聲. — The same happens in the series 119, under 去 **ch'ü**, where one may find compounds in **ieh**. Their phonetic is 劫 **chieh** contracted, in which 力 gave place to another radical. — Remember well this remark, it is very important in practice. One may often read, in the *Lessons*, the expression 省聲 «contracted phonetic.» — In the logical combinations some radicals are abbreviated in the same way. Thus 尾 becomes [illegible] or 尸. See 隶 and 雪, L. 44 E,J. — The scribes definitively contracted several intricate ancient forms, for example:

靃霍 雧集 𣡕栗

5. *Phonetics mixed.* — Under some numbers of the phonetic Lexicon, one may find two series written in the same way, but of different sound. The reason is that in the modern writing, two ancient phonetics were mixed. Thus one writes to-day in the same way two series utterly distinct in the ancient writing. See, for example, the Series 227, 284, 359-549.

6. *Synonyms.* — The great number of phonetic complexes, different in form and in sound, but perfectly synonymous, is explained by the fact that they sprung from many different places, in the modern times, after **Li-ssŭ**. Some double logical aggregates probably owe their origin to the same cause, v.g. 仁 𡰥 LL. 2 B and 32 B. There were differences between the rival states and the jealous literati of those times.

7. ***Multiples.*** — An element reproduced two or several times, figures graphically the great number, or the great intensity. For example: Two 木 trees make a 林 forest. Two 火 fires 炎 means to blaze. Three 人 men 众, a multitude. Three 車 chariots 轟, a rolling, a big rumbling.

8. *Figures straightened.* — Certain figures, broader than high, as 罒, are often straightened 目 in the compounds, to take less place. See 壬 L. 82 C, 舟 L. 66, 車 L. 167, 目 L 158, etc.

Conclusion. — The knowledge of the Chinese characters consists in mastering less than 300 primitives, and about 1500 principal compounds made with the primitives, that is less than 2000 characters. All the others are derived from them. Those are the elements and groups that are treated in the *Etymological Lessons*, and collected in the *Index of usual Groups*. When the student knows them, he may explain to himself all the compounds. The *Lessons* explain the *logical aggregates* under their principal primitive. Each paragraph refers to the phonetical series which contains the *phonetic complexes* derived from the same element. The paragraph and the series form a whole, that exhausts *practically* the study of an element.

IV. CLASSIFICATION OF CHARACTERS.

A. Chinese classifications.

1. *Natural classification.* — The first classifications were encyclopedias of things, after the manner of the present 類書 **lei-shu**. The prototype of those compilations is the 爾雅 **Erh-ya**, the first sketch of which is ascribed to 周公 **Chu-kung** (11th century B.C.). Remodelled in the 5th century B.C. by a disciple of Confucius, 子夏 **Tzŭ-hsia**, it took its actual shape from 郭璞 **Kuo-p'u**, circa

A.D. 280. The things of this world were distributed under 16 sections: kindred, houses, utensils, music, heaven, earth, mounds, hills, waters, plants, trees, insects, fishes, birds, wild and domestic animals. In the actual 類書 **lei-shu**, the headings are more numerous.

2. *Logical classification, by Radicals.* — Starting from the *meaning element* of the phonetic complexes, or from one among the meaning elements in the logical aggregates, the characters were disposed by *logical* series, under keys called *Radicals*, according to the number of strokes. The 說文 **shuo-wên** was the first lexicon, thus disposed. It contains 540 keys, some of them being very abundant, and some very poor, according to the notion expressed by them. Later on, for the sake of simplification, the latter keys were suppressed. This reduction brought about the placing of the characters that had belonged to the keys left out, under other keys, with which the former had some analogy of figures, but no real relation. The classification thus became half logical, half arbitrary. Under the 明 **Ming**, the number of keys was reduced to 214; which meant that the characters belonging to more than 300 ancient keys, were arbitrarily placed where they should not be. The dictionary of **K'ang-hsi** 康熙字典, is based upon these 214 keys. This dictionary is easy enough to consult and precise in its definitions. But one must avoid to use it for any study of etymology or of classification, under pain of committing the worst blunders. We shall indicate, in the *Lessons*, a certain number of these mistakes, for which the compilers are not personally answerable, because the system of keys used by them was composed before their time. — Recently the 商務印書館 **Commercial Press** of *Shang-hai* has printed a very good 新字典 abbreviated **K'ang-hsi**.

3. *Phonetic classification, by Rhymes.* — Towards the year A. D. 500, 沈約 **Shên-yao** introduced the system 反切 **fan-ch'ieh**, which consists in associating, for the expression of a sound of any unknown character, two other known characters, the first of which gives the initial consonant, and the second the final vowel. Examples: **p'an** and **nieh** make **p'ieh**; **li** and **mo** make **lo**; etc. — The **fan-ch'ieh** was devised by Indian Buddhist Monks, in order to render approximately, in Chinese, the Pali or Sanskrit syllables. — It was according to this system, that dictionaries called 韻府 **yün-fu** were made. In the beginning, they were nearly dictionaries by sounds, the finals being very numerous: under the 唐 **T'ang**, there were 206 finals for 36 initials. Later on, the number of finals was reduced, by gathering in the same category all those that rhymed according to the Chinese prosody; so that now **ên, in, ün, un**, are mingled; **an, uan, ien**, form a same category, etc. — The 韻府 **yün-fu** have all five volumens, one for each tone. To find a character, one must know first its tone, then its prosodical category; lastly one must seek in the latter, following the order of initials. The largest Chinese dictionary, the 佩文韻府 **P'ei-wen-yün-fu**, was composed after this type. We join here the usual table of rhymes.

Table of Rhymes.

平聲	上聲	去聲		入聲	
東	董	送		屋	
冬	腫	宋	Ung.	沃	U, ü, iü, etc.
江	講	絳	Iang.	覺	
支	紙	寘	Ih.		
微	尾	未	Ei.	質	
魚	語	御	Ü.	物	Ih, ei, i, ê, etc.
虞	麌	遇	U.	月	
齊	薺	霽	I.		
佳	解	泰	Ai, uai, yeh.	曷	Ê, o, ai.
灰	賄	隊	Ei, uei.	黠	A, ia.
眞	軫	震	Ên, in, ün, un.	屑	Ê, ieh, üeh.
文	吻	問		藥	Iao, ieh, o, uo, ao.
元	阮	願			
寒	旱	翰		陌	
刪	潸	諫	An, uan, yen.	錫	Ai, ei, ê, i, ieh,
先	銑	霰		職	ih, o, uo, ü.
蕭	篠	嘯		緝	I, ih.
肴	巧	效	Ao, iao.	合	A, ia, o, uo.
豪	皓	號			
歌	哿	箇	Ê, o.	葉	Ieh, yeh.
麻	馬	禡	A, ai, ya, ua.	洽	
陽	養	漾	Ang, iang, uang.		
庚	梗	敬			
青	迥	徑	Êng ing, iung.		
蒸	○	○			
尤	有	宥	Iu, ou.		
侵	寢	沁	Ên, in, un.		
覃	感	勘			
鹽	琰	豔	An, ien.		
咸	豏	鑑			

4. *Phonetic classification, by sounds.* — Basing himself upon the system **反切 fan-ch'ieh**, a certain 樊 騰 風 **Fan t'êng-fêng** invented, towards the year 1700, a combination of 20 initials and 12 finals, that is nearly as easy as the European alphabetical order though it does not attain it, for sounds like **i, ih, ü ei,** are still confounded. Instead of being capital, the division by *tones* is accessory. This classification is far more convenient than the dictionaries by *rhymes*. Therefore the 五 方 元 音 **Wu-fang-yüan-yin** was a great success. It was the most common dictionary in the days of the 清 **Ch'ing** dynasty. Its key is thus given:

Initials		Finals
梆 **P**	石 **Sh**	天 **ien, an, uan.**
匏 **P'**	日 **J**	人 **ên, in, unn, ün.**
木 **M**	剪 **Ch**	龍 **ung, ing, êng, iung.**
風 **F**	鵲 **Ch'**	羊 **an, iang, uang.**
斗 **T**	系 **Hs**	牛 **iu, ou.**
土 **T'**	雲 **Y**	獒 **ao, iao.**
鳥 **N**	金 **K**	虎 **u.**
雷 **L**	橋 **K'**	駝 **uo, iao, o.**
竹 **Ch**	火 **H**	蛇 **ê, ieh, üeh.**
虫 **Ch'**	蛙 **W**	馬 **a, ia, ua.**
		豺 **ai, uai.**
		地 **i, ei, ui, ih, êrh, ü, iü.**

5. The 字 學 舉 隅 **Tzŭ-hsiao-chü-yü** that will be occasionally mentioned in the *Lessons*, is a small book that gives the form of the modern characters, as it was required for the official examinations, till A.D. 1905, with an index of the wrong characters. It contains some mistakes.

B. European classifications.

1. *By radicals.* The dictionary by radicals of **K'ang-hsi** was translated, abridged or enlarged, a *figuration* replacing the original **反切 fan-ch'ieh.** For ex., the «*Dictionnaire classique de la langue chinoise, du P.S. Couvreur S J., Ho-chien-fu, 1904*». These dictionaries partake of the advantages and drawbacks of the **K'ang-hsi's** dictionary.

2. *By phonetics.* The characters were gathered according to the phonetic series. The type of the kind is the «*Systema phoneticum scripturae sinicae, auctore J.-M. Callery, C. Miss., Macao, 1841.*»

3. By sounds. Being given a system of figuration, the characters were classified according to the European alphabetical order. The big English dictionaries of ***Williams*** and *Giles*, and the big «***Dictionnaire chinois-francais du P.S. Couvreur S.J.***, *Ho-chien-fu, 1890*», are made after this method.

Use of the dictionaries. — To find a character the sound and meaning of which are unknown, one must refer to a dictionary by radicals, which supposes the knowledge of the **214** keys of **K'ang-hsi**. — If the sound is known, with the help of a Chinese master, or otherwise, then the shorter method is to use a dictionary by sounds, supposing that one is well acquainted with its figuration. — The phonetic series are the most useful for study, but they are not very useful as a dictionary, unless one is already far advanced in the study of Chinese.

ETYMOLOGICAL LESSONS.

LIST OF THE 224 PRIMITIVES.

Modern form. The ancient form may be found at the number given.

1

- 乁 **Chi^{4}.** 11.
- 丶 **Chu^{3}.** 4.
- 𡿨 **Chüan^{3}.** 12.
- 亅 **Chüeh^{2}.** 6.
- 一 **I^{1}.** 1.
- 𠂆 **I^{4}.** 8.
- 乙 **I^{1}.** 9.
- 丨 **Kun^{3}.** 6.
- 丿 **P'ieh^{1}.** 7.
- 乛 **Ya^{2}.** 9.
- 乚 **Yin^{3}.** 10.

2

- 几 **Chi^{1}.** 20.
- 七 **Ch'i^{1}.** 33.
- 丂 **Ch'iao^{3}.** 58.
- 九 **Chiu^{3}.** 23.
- 丩 **Chiu^{1}.** 54.
- 冂 **Chiung^{3}.** 34.
- 厶 **Ch'ü^{1}.** 38.
- 𠆢 **Ch'uei^{2}.** 13.
- 匚 **Fang^{1}.** 51.
- 𢎘 **Han^{3}.** 55.
- 厂 **Han^{4}.** 59.
- 乂 **I^{4}.** 39.
- 人 **Jên^{2}.** 25.
- 入 **Ju^{4}.** 15.
- 凵 **K'an^{3}.** 38.
- 厶 **Kung^{1}.** 38.
- 力 **Li^{4}.** 53.
- 冖 **Mi^{2}.** 34.
- 乃 **Nai^{3}.** 19.
- 八 **Pa^{1}.** 18.
- 匕 **Pi^{3}.** 26.
- 冫 **Ping^{1}.** 17.
- 卜 **Po^{3}.** 56.
- 十 **Shih^{2}.** 24.
- 𠘧 **Shu^{2}.** 22.
- 厶 **Ssŭ^{1}.** 89.
- 刀 **Tao^{1}.** 52.
- 丁 **Ting^{1}.** 57.
- 乂 **Wu^{3}.** 39.
- 㕚 **Yu^{4}.** 43.

3

屮 Ch'ê^{4}. 78.
彐 Chi^{4}. 68.
几 Chi^{1}. 70.
己 Chi^{3}. 84.
亼 Chi^{2}. 14.
夂 Chih^{3}. 31.
彳 Ch'ih^{4}. 63.
巾 Chin^{1}. 35.
久 Chiu^{3}. 31.
夊 Chung^{1}. 17.
凡 Fan^{2}. 21.
夕 Hsi^{4}. 64.
丮 Hsün^{3}. 11.
弋 I^{4}. 71.
已 I^{3}. 85.
干 Kan^{1}. 102.
个 Ko^{4}. 77.
口 K'ou^{3}. 72.
工 Kung^{1}. 82.
弓 Kung^{1}. 87.
巾 Liang^{3}. 35.
宀 Mien^{2}. 36.
女 Nü^{3}. 67.
彡 Shan^{1}. 62.
山 Shan^{1}. 80.
勺 Shao^{2}. 54.
巳 Ssŭ^{4}. 85.
夊 Sui^{1}. 31.
大 Ta^{4}. 60.
乇 T'o^{1}. 33.
土 T'u^{3}. 81.
才 Ts'ai^{2}. 96.
子 Tzŭ^{3}. 94.
囗 Wei^{2}. 74.
也 Yeh^{3}. 107.

4

气 Ch'i^{4}. 98.
爿 Ch'iang^{2}. 127.
丯 Chieh^{4}. 97.
欠 Ch'ien^{4}. 99.
止 Chih^{3}. 112.
斤 Chin^{1}. 128.
井 Ching^{3}. 115.
犬 Ch'üan^{3}. 134.
中 Chung^{1}. 109.
方 Fang^{1}. 117.
丰 Fêng^{1}. 97.
互 Hu^{4}. 68.
戶 Hu^{4}. 129.
火 Huo^{3}. 126.
心 Hsin^{1}. 107.
日 Jih^{4}. 143.
凵 Ku^{3}. 106.
毛 Mao^{2}. 100.
木 Mu^{4}. 119.
牛 Niu^{2}. 132.
巴 Pa^{1}. 55.
片 P'ien^{4}. 127.
不 Pu^{2}. 133.
氏 Shih^{4}. 114.
手 Shou^{3}. 48.
水 Shui^{3}. 125.
丹 Tan^{1}. 115.
斗 Tou^{3}. 98.
文 Wên^{2}. 61.
勿 Wu^{4}. 101.
午 Wu^{3}. 130.
牙 Ya^{2}. 147.
王 Yü^{4}. 83
予 Yü^{2}. 95.
月 Yüeh^{4}. 64.
云 Yün^{2}. 93.

5

冊 Ch'ai^{2}. 156.
甲 Chia^{3}. 152.
且 Ch'ieh^{3}. 20.
卯 Ch'ing^{1}. 55.
宁 Chu^{4}. 57.
弗 Fu^{4}. 87.
禾 Ho^{2}. 121.
回 Hui^{2}. 76.
冉 Jan^{3}. 116.
肉 Jou^{3}. 23.
瓜 Kua^{1}. 162.
丱 Kuan^{3}. 108.
毋 Kuan^{4}. 153.
虫 K'ui^{4}. 111.
矛 Mao^{2}. 95.
民 Min^{2}. 114.
皿 Min^{3}. 157.
目 Mu^{4}. 158.
丙 Ping^{3}. 41.
矢 Shih^{3}. 131.
四 Ssŭ^{4}. 42.
歺 Tai^{3}. 118.
田 T'ien^{2}. 149.
它 T'o^{1}. 108.
曾 Tsêng^{4}. 154.
瓦 Wa^{3}. 145.
由 Yu^{2}. 151.

6

[illegible] Ch'i². 70.
幵 Ch'ien¹. 115.
至 Chih⁴. 133.
臼 Chiu⁴. 139.
舟 Chou¹. 66.
曲 Ch'ü¹. 51.
耳 Erh³. 146.
而 Erh². 164.
缶 Fao³. 130
甶 Fu⁴. 40.
覀 Hsi¹. 41.
襾 Hsia⁴. 41.
囟 Hsin⁴. 40.
虍 Hu¹. 135.
虫 Hui¹. 110.
衣 I¹. 16.
肉 Jou⁴. 65.
冎 Kua³. 118.
米 Mi³. 122.
尗 Shu². 124.
㐁 T'ien⁴. 41.
自 Tzŭ⁴. 159.
羊 Yang². 103.
㫃 Yen³. 117.

7

車 Ch'ê¹. 167.
角 Chiao³. 142.
豸 Chih⁴. 166.
囧 Chiung³. 42.
串 Ch'uan⁴. 153.
囱 Ch'uang¹. 40.
𦣝 I². 82.
[illegible] K'uai³. 156.
呂 Lü³. 90.
𠦒 Pan¹. 104.
貝 Pei⁴. 161.
釆 Pien⁴. 123.
身 Shên¹. 148.
豕 Shih³. 69.
𦣻 Shou³. 160.
弟 Ti⁴. 87.
豆 Tou⁴. 165.
酉 Yu³. 41.

8

長 Ch'ang². 113.
金 Chin¹. 14.
叕 Cho⁴. 43.
隹 Chui¹. 168.
非 Fei¹. 170
阜 Fu⁴. 86.
易 I⁴. 101.
丽 Li⁴. 163.
朋 P'êng². 64.
兔 T'u⁴. 106.
甾 Tzŭ¹. 150.

9

㲋 Ch'ao¹. 106.
者 Chê³. 159.
韭 Chiu³. 170.
耑 Chuan¹. 164.
泉 Ch'üan². 125.
飛 Fei¹. 11.
革 Ko². 105.
卣 T'iao². 41.
昜 Yang². 101.

10

鬲 Ko². 155.
冓 Kou⁴. 104.
馬 Ma³. 137.
𢊁 Ssŭ⁴. 136.
丵 Tsao². 102.

11

殸 Ch'ing⁴. 173.
鹿 Lu⁴. 136.
鳥 Niao³. 138.
[illegible] T'ou³. 82.
寅 Yin². 172.
魚 Yü². 142.

12 &

齊 Ch'i². 174.
爵 Chiao² 176.
齒 Ch'ih³. 175
萈 Huan¹. 106.
龜 Kui¹. 108.
龍 Lung². 140.
黽 Min³. 108.
壽 Shou⁴. 144.
蜀 Shu³. 54.
鼠 Shu³. 139.
樂 Yao⁴. 88.
燕 Yen⁴. 141.

LESSON 1.

About the primitive 一, a single stroke.

A 一 一

I[1] represents the unity, principle of numeration; **爲記數之始。** It figures the primordial unity, source of all beings; **惟初太始、道立於一、造分天地、化成萬物。一也者、萬物之本也。** — It is the 1st radical in **K'ang-hsi's** dictionary.

In composition, says the **Shuo-wên**, 一 is most commonly symbolic; **凡从一之字、多指事。** Its different symbolic meanings may be summed up under four principal categories.

Firstly, when written on top of the compound, 一 represents either heaven, or a roof, or any cover. Example:

B 雨 雨

Yü[3]. The rain. Drops of water falling from a 冂 cloud that hangs to 一 heaven; 亅 means the vertical falling; **一像天。冂像雲。水从雲下也。** — It is the 173th radical in **K'ang-hsi**.

C 天 天

T'ien[1]. Heaven, the vast 一 extent of space that is above 大 men, the highest of things; **天顛也。至高無上、从一大會意。按大猶人也。天在人上、仰首見之。一指事。** Note that **大** (L. 60) means *man* and not *great*; therefore do not translate **一大** *the unique great*. The derived idea, as explained by all the commentators, is that of physical or moral *superiority*. The **春秋 Ch'un-ch'iu** says: **天之言鎮也。居高理下、爲人經緯。故其字一大以鎮之也。** Placed above them, heaven governs men... According to this fundamental notion, any superior, says the **爾雅 Erh-ya**, is the **天** of his inferior; **天君也。凡至尊重者皆是。故臣於君、子於父、妻於夫、皆曰天。** — For the compounds of **天**, see Lesson 60 C.

D 末 末

Mo[4]. The outmost twigs, the 一 top of a **木** tree; **木上曰末。从木、一在其上。指事。** — Phonetic series 138.

Secondly, placed below the compound, — represents the foundation, the base, or any support. Examples:

E 旦

Tan⁴. The dawn, the beginning of the day. The 日 sun above a — line, viz. the horizon; 明也。从日見一上。一地也。— Phonetic series 162.

F 立

Li⁴. To stand, to be erected. A man 大 (L. 60) standing upon — the ground. This character is the reverse of 天, above C. 从大立一之上、會意。大人也、一地也、指事。It forms the 117th radical in **K'ang-hsi**. Phonetic series 134.

G 本

Pên³. The trunk of a tree. The part of a 木 tree above the — earth. This character is the reverse of 末, above D 木下日本。从木、一在其下、指事。— Phonetic series 147.

Thirdly, — represents a barrier, a hindrance. Examples:

H 閂

Shuan¹. A beam — used to bolt a 門 door.

I 丂

Ch'iao³. Difficulty in breathing, oppression; 气欲舒出、上礙於一也。按ㄅ像气形、一指事。The line bent up represents the breath that tries to go out, but is checked by the transversal barrier. See L. 58. — Phonetic series 3.

Fourthly, — represents something contained. Example:

J 血

Hsüeh³. Blood. A 皿 vase containing — something. This character primitively meant the oblation of the blood of the victim in the sacrifices; 从皿、一指事。祭所薦牲血也。See the 詩經、Legge's edition, Part II, Bk VI, Ode VI, 5, 取其血膋。箋血以告殺也。The modern signification, *blood*, is a derivative, **chuan-chu**. See Lesson 157. — It forms the 143th radical in **K'ang-hsi**. — Phonetic series 208.

LESSON 2.

About the character 二, two strokes, and some of its derivatives.

A 二 二 **Erh**[4]. Two. The number of the earth, because it makes the pair with heaven. The number of the two principles **yin** and **yang**. 地之數也。陰陽之數也。 — It is the 7th radical in **K'ang-hsi**.

In composition, 二 has three different uses.

Firstly, 二 means *two*. Example:

B 仁 𡰥 **Jên**[2]. The fundamental virtue of Confucianism, which the **Shuo-wên** defines: 親也。从人、从二、會意。相親謂之仁、to love each other. The benevolence that must link each 亻 man with 二 his neighbour; 二 two, mutual, reciprocal. From 仁 is derived

C 佞 **Ning**[4]. Coaxing, flattery; 巧諂也; the 仁 of 女 women.

Secondly, 二 represents two terms, two extremes. Examples:

D 亟 亟 **Chi**[2]. Activity, working up of faculties, struggle for life. A 人 man who acts, who struggles, with his 口 mouth and his 又 hand, between 二 heaven and earth, to gain his point; 从人、从口、从又、會意。从二、天地也、指事。。。人生天地間、手口並作敏疾成事也。 — Phonetic series 325.

E 亙 亙 **Kên**[4] or **Kêng**[4]. Idea of passage, of crossing, of duration, between two terms. It represents a 舟 passage-boat, that crosses 二 from one bank to the other: 从二、从舟、會意．兼指事。二者上下岸也。 See 舟 L. 66. — In the modern writing, 亘 (L. 76 H) is often used for 亙. It is a mistake. Note the compound

F 恆 恆 **Hêng**. Constancy, perseverance. The heart 忄 (the will) crossing from the beginning till the end, as a 舟 boat does from 二 one bank to the other; the moral trip continued till one reaches the harbour. Rather a well found simile. 常也。从心．从舟、在二之間．上下一．必似舟旋航也。

G **Thirdly**. 二 is an old form of 上 **shang**[4], high; and 二 reversed, an old form of 下 **hsia**[4], low. See L. 5. — This remark is to be remembered; there will be many applications of it. See, for instance, 示 L. 3 D, 元 L. 29 H, etc... 上 is sometimes reduced to a single stroke, as in 吏 L. 43 N, 票 L. 50 O, etc.

LESSON 3.

About 三, three strokes, and its derivatives.

A 三 三 **San**[1]. Three; 天地人之數也。The number of heaven earth and humanity; the 三才 **san**[1] **ts'ai**[2], three Powers. Hence

B 王 王 **Wang**[2]. King. 古之造文者、三畫而連其中、謂之王。三者、天地人也、而參通之者、王也。孔子曰、一貫三爲王. According to the ancients, the 王 king is 丨 the one, the man who connects together 三 heaven earth and humanity. See L. 83 C. — Phonetic series 87.

三 represents boundary lines, limits, in

C 畺 畺 **Chiang**[1]. Bounds. The 三 partitions that divide and limit two 田 fields; 从畕, 三其界畫也。— Phonetic series 724.

三 straightened 川, forms a part of

D 示 示 礻 **Shih**[4]. Influx coming from heaven; auspicious or inauspicious signs, by which the will of heaven is known to mankind; 天垂像. 見吉凶、所以示人也。The two horizontal lines 二 are the old form of the character 上 **shang**[4], high, superior (L. 2 G); here they mean *heaven*; 二、古文上字。The three vertical lines 川 represent what is hanging from heaven, viz. the sun, the moon and the stars, the mutations of which reveal to men the transcendent things; 三垂、日月星也。觀乎天文以察時變、示神事也。The actual meaning, to *teach*, is **chuan-chu**. — 示 forms the 113th radical of characters relating to transcendental matters. Note 礻, its modern contracted form, that is easily mistaken for 衤, the contracted form of 衣 garments (L. 16 A).

E 祘 F 蒜

示 doubled forms 祘 **hsüan**[4]. It is believed that this character figures the primitive abacus, and has nothing to do with 示。See 算 and 筭, L. 47 G, F. Anyhow from 祘 is derived the phonetic compound 蒜 **hsüan**[4], garlic.

LESSON 4.

About the 丶 dot.

A

Chu[5]. A dot, a sign of punctuation, etc. Formerly the dot was round; it is now piriform, on account of the writing-brush that writes thus. It is the 3d radical in **K'ang-hsi**.

丶 is found in the following characters:

B 主

Chu[3]. The inferior part represents a lamp, the flame of which is 丶: 王 像 燈、丶 像 火。One writes now 炷 to mean a *lamp*, the character 主 signifying (**chuan-chu**) *prince, master*. Because, say the interpreters, 首 出 庶 物、萬 民 所 望 之 意 the prince rises above the multitude and is seen by all, as the flame rises and shines over the lamp. — Phonetic series 115.

C 丹

Tan[1]. Cinnabar. The 丶 is supposed to represent the red mineral, and 井 the mine where it is found; 採 丹 井。丶 像 丹 形。The ancient characters suggest a different interpretation. They represent the crucible of the Taoist alchimists, with 丶 cinnabar in it. Decompose and recompose cinnabar, was their chief practice. See L. 115 D. — Phonetic Series 83. Compare 金 (L.14 T.)—Two old characters express the 匕 (L.30 D) transformation of mortal men into immortal genii, by means of 丹 alchemy and 卜 divination (L. 56 A.)

D **N.B.** —In the modern writing, many characters, for instance 亠 衣 言 辛, are surmounted with a dot, that replaces elements which are very different in the ancient writing. It is the same with the dot introduced inside some of the characters, for example 丸 小 心 The writing-brush is the cause of it. — Note by the way that 亠 the 8th radical, is but a corruption of 入 the 11th radical.

LESSON 5.

We saw (L. 1, 1° ond 2°) — used as meaning an horizontal line. From this acception are derived the following characters;

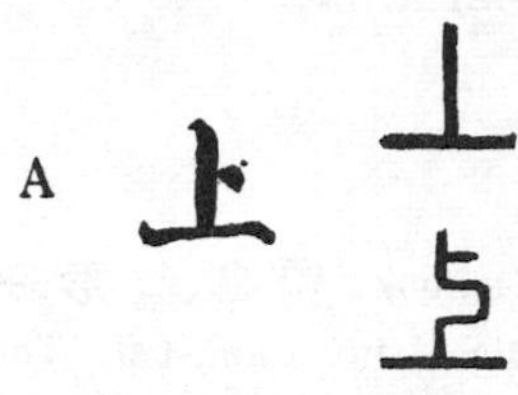

A **Shang⁴**. Up, upon, superior, to mount. A sign 丨 placed *above* the fundamental line 一, signifying *above* the level; 从一、从丨、所謂引而上行。指事。The ancient form of this character was 二 (L. 2 G), the smaller top line being usep as a sign relatively to the longer bottom line. In the more recent forms, the sign became more and more intricate. — In the modern writing, 上 kept up its ancient form 丄 at the top of many characters, for example, 辛帝旁. It is to be distinguished from 亠, the fictitious 8th radical in **K'ang-hsi**. (See L 4 D).

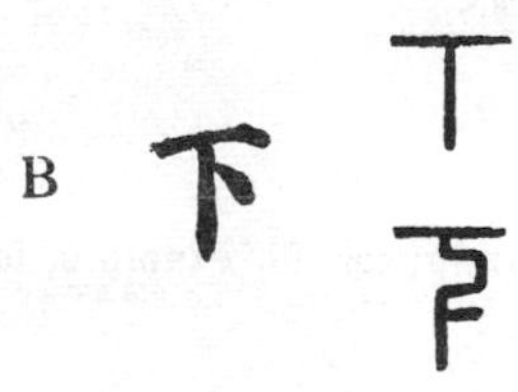

B **Hsia⁴**. Below, to descend, inferior. A line 丨 traced *below* the fundamental line 一, signifying *below* the level; 从丨在一之下、指事。— The ancient form of this character was 二 (L. 2 G), the shorter bottom line being used as a sign relatively to the longer top line.

LESSON 6.

About two primitives, 丨 and 亅

Firstly, 丨 **kun³.**

A **Kun³**. A vertical stroke, a perpendicular; 上下通也。指事。— It forms the 2d radical in **K'ang-hsi**. It is found in many characters, in which it has generally a symbolic signification.

It represents the trunk, in
Mu⁴. Tree. See L. 119 A.

It represents a man standing, in
Shên¹. To gird up (with both hands). See L. 50 C.

It represents an arow fixed in a target, in
Chung¹. Middle, centre. L. 109 A.

It represents a spindle running through two objects, in **Ch'uan**^{4}. To string together. See L 153 B.

It represents a bow-string, in **Yin**^{3}, to draw a bow; See L. 87 A. Etc.

Secondly, 亅 *chüeh*^{2}.

B 

Chüeh^{2}. A crooked stroke, a hook; 鉤也。像形。— It is the fictitious 6th radical in **K'ang-hsi**. The **Shuo-wên** gives no derivatives from this primitive. However, in the modern characters, 亅 occurs very frequently. The reason of the fact is that, with the writing-brush, it is easier to trace 亅 than 丨 Consequently:

1. 亅 replaced 丨 in many characters, for example:

Hsiao^{3}. See L. 18 H.

2. 亅 is arbitrarily written, as an abbreviation of different figures, for example, for the longer line of 彐 in

Ts'un^{4}. See L. 45 B.

N. B. — 亅 inverted gives

C  

Chüeh^{2}. A hook, 鉤也、从反亅. that is found in

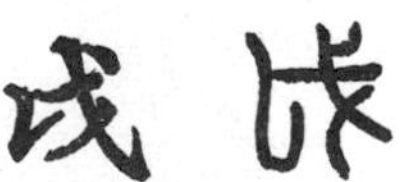

Yüeh^{4}. A halberd with a hook. See L 71 L.

LESSON 7.

About the primitive 丿

A 

P'ieh^{1}. An oblique line from righ to left; 右戾也、像。General idea of action, of motion. — It is the fictitious 4th radical in **K'ang-hsi**. Nearly all the modern 丿 are abbreviations for other signs, while the true 丿 are hardly recognized in the modern writing. For example:

升 **Shêng**[1]. The tenth part of a bushel. Composed of 斗 bushel, and of 丿 which figures that a tenth part of it is taken out. See L. 98 B.

眉 **Mei**[2]. Eye-brow; 丿 represents the curve of the orbita; the lines on the top represent the hairs; 目 is the eye. — Phonetic series 463.

丿 inverted gives

B 

Fu[2], an oblique line from left to right. 左戾也。从反丿、指事。This stroke that seldom occurs in the ancient writing, is now frequently used as an abbreviation.

丿 and ㇏ combined, give

C 

I[4]. To cut down with scissors, to mow. See L. 39 B.

LESSON 8.

About the primitive 𠂆.

A 

I[4]. To draw, to drag; 像、引之形。Forms several compounds, for ex.

I[4]. A crooked arrow, a dart, kept by a thread, to kill birds. In the modern writing, the hook was changed into a point; and 𠂆 that represents the thread or the action of drawing the arrow back, became 一. It forms the 56th radical in **K'ang-hsi**.

I[4]. To draw. See L. 50 F. — Phonetic series 213.

The same in 虒 **ti**[4], L. 135 G. — in 犮 **pa**[2], L. 134. A. — In 系 **hsi**[1], L. 92 B. — In 爭 **chêng**[1], L. 49 D, where 𠂆 became 亅 in the modern writing.

𠂆 inverted gives

B 乀

I[4]. To drag; 从反𠂆、指事。Is found in

臾 **Yü**[2]. To drag, to trail. See L. 50 G.

LESSON 9.

About the primitives 乙 i[1] and 乞 ya[2].

A 乙

I[1]. Germination; it represents the germ that strives to get out; 草木冤曲而出也。像形。Hence, general notion of movement, of effort. Cyclical character. To be distinguished from B; 於燕乞字、音意皆別、— It is the 5th radical. Among its derivatives, note 亂 L. 90 B, 尼 L. 129 A, and

失

Shih[1]. To let 乙 slip from the 手 hand, to lose. See L. 48 B. — Phonetic series 155.

B 乞

Ya[2]. Swallow, 燕也。It represents the jerking flying of this bird, 飛之形。To be distinguished from A; 於甲乙字別。— Phonetic series 1. Logical aggregates, 孔, 乳, L. 94 A, B, etc. The modern writing is

Ya[2] Swallow, the jerking bird. See L. 138.

Note: The scribes often write 乚 as an abbreviation of intricate compounds. In that case, it is neither **i**[1] nor **ya**[2], but a conventional sign. For instance, 礼 for 禮, etc.

LESSON 10.

About the primitive 乚 and its two important compounds, 匚 and 亾, with their series; then about the derivatives 直 眞 悳, a group apart.

A 乚

Yin[3]. Curve; to cover, to conceal; 曲也。像。隱蔽之形。

First series: 乚 combined with 一 (L. 1), gives

B 匚

Hsi[3]. Chest, trunk, box; 从乚、上有一覆之、指事。Therefore 一 represents the cover, 乚 the chest or the action of containing. — It is the 23th radical. — Note the next derivatives:

C 陋 **Lou⁴**. Shut up, in a confined space; 从匸. 从內. 會意。 As 內 in a 匸 chest. It forms the compound 陋, mean, ugly; perhaps 陋 cave-dwelling 阝 mountaineers (L. 86 A). — As the engravers often take off a part of 乚, to make room for 阝, this character might seem to be derived from 丙 (L. 41 A), which it is not.

D 匿 **Ni⁴**. To hide, to abscond; 从匸、从若、會意。— 若 (L. 46 G) meaning to *collect, to gather*, the aggregate means, to gather and to hide in a chest. Phonetic series 639.

Note. The derivatives of **Hsi**, the **23**th radical, are to be distinguished from those of **Fang**, the **22**th radical. In the ancient writing, the two series were distinct; in the modern writing, they are mingled together. See L. 51 A, and the Lexicon by order of Radicals.

Second series: 乚 combined with 入 (L. 15), gives

E 亡 **Wang²**. Primitive meaning, to *hide*; 从入.从乚、會意。Now 入 meaning to *enter*, 亡 means to enter into a hiding place. Derived meanings, to die, to perish, to vanish. — Phonetic series 35.

F 乍 **Cha⁴**. 从亡、从一、指事。It is 亡, plus 一. But the line — representing an obstacle, as in 丂 (L. 1, I), the meaning of **cha** is, to try to hide one's self and to be hindered. Hence the modern meanings **chuan-chu**, suddenly, unexpectedly. — Phonetic series 102. See L. 37 G.

G 匃 匄 丐 **Kai⁴**. To beg, a beggar; 从人、从亡。會意。A wandering 人 man, who 亡 seeks a refuge in a foreign country, begging alms for his livelihood; 亡逃之人.求食於他鄉也. See 勹 L. 54 A. In the old form, 人 and 亡 were in juxtaposition; then 人 covered 亡. Note the fanciful modern contractions of this character. — It forms an important compound 曷. See L. 73 A.

H 喪

Sang[1]. 从哭、从亾。會意。Etymologically, 哭 to weep over the 亾 dead; funerals. This compound is a typical picture of the Chinese thing which it means: to howl with several 口 mouths, as 犬 dogs do, over a 亾 dead person. Meanings **chuan-chu**, to die, to destroy. Note the contraction of the lower part of the modern character.

I 無

J

Wu[2]. 从林、从大、从卌、會意。A multitude 卌 (L 24 H) of 大 men, acting upon a 林 forest, felling the trees, clearing of wood a tract of land. In the old form J, 亾 stated that the wood had vanished. Hence **chuan-chu** the general abstract notions of vanishing, defect, want, negation. — Phonetic series 718.

Note. The study of this second series, E F G H I J, proofs with evidence that it is impossible to understand the characters, if one attends only to the modern forms.

Third series: 乚 combined with 十 ten (L. 24), and 目 eye (L. 158), gives the interesting following compounds:

K 直

Chih[2]. Perfectly right, not curved in the least; 从乚、从十、从目、會意。The eyes having looked at something, did not discover any deviation. — Phonetic series 335. — Note the right way of writing this character. The modern engravers cut 乚, so that one may believe it is composed of two strokes 直. The scribes often change it into a single horizontal line 直, etc.

L 眞

Chên[1]. Perfectly true; 从直、从丌、會意。Something having been exposed on a pedestal, 直 ten eyes could not find any fault in it... The — of the pedestal was mingled with the lower part of 乚. — Perfect genuineness of nature being the characteristic of the Taoist 眞人 Genii, the scope at which the Taoist transformation 匕 (L. 30 D) of man aims, the Taoists replaced 十 by 匕 at the top of **chên** (contraction). 从匕、从直、从丌、會意。The calligraphic remarks made about 直, are to be made here also. — Phonetic series 509.

O 悳 𢛳

Te². 从直.从心.會意. The 直 rectitude of the 心 heart. In modern writing, the 目 was bent down to gain room (L. 158 A), the 乚 is often reduced to a small horizontal stroke. — It forms the compound

德

德 te², moral 彳 conduct (L. 63 A) directed by a righteous heart, righteousness, virtue. — Another compound is

聽

T'ing¹. 从耳.从悳.會意.壬聲. Rectification of the heart 悳 heart of a 壬 disciple (L. 81 O) or an auditor, by his 耳 ear (L. 146 A). To hear, to listen, to be attentive, to conform to instruction, to obey... 壬 t'ing is also phonetic. — It forms the compound

廳

T'ing¹. From 广 shelter and 聽 to hear. An open hall, used for meetings, teaching, official proclamations (L. 59 J).

Note: 県

Hsiao¹ has nothing in common with this series. See LL. 12 N, and 160 A.

Lesson 11.

about 卂, 丮, 丸, three series perfectly distinct in the ancient writing, but mingled together in the modern writing.

First series: 卂 **hsün⁴**. Before studying this primitive, one must explain

A 飛

Fei¹. To fly. A primitive. It represents a crane (very common in China) seen from behind. Upwards, the head and the neck bent up, as when the cranes are flying. Below, the tail. On both sides, the wings fluttering. The small strokes represent the quills separated when the bird is flying. 鳥翥也.像.張翼之形. — It is the 183th radical in **K'ang-hsi**. That being granted, one may now explain

B 卂

Hsün⁴. To hover. A primitive. Compare with A. The crane is hovering; its wings do not flutter. The feathers being close together, are not visible; 疾飛也.从飛而羽不見.指事. — Phonetic series 20. Note the compound

C 蝨 虱

Shih^1. Formerly, it meant the mosquito, the hovering 丮 insect, forming 䖵 swarms, that bites men; 齧人蟲也。Now this character means a *louse*. Note its abbreviated form 虱 that it commonly called 半風 **pan^4 fêng^1**, half 風 wind. However 風 (L. 21 B) has nothing in common with 丮. See also 夙 **hsü^4**, below G.

Second series: 丮 **Chi^4**. Is derived from the primitive

D

Chi^4. To catch. This primitive is found only in one compound, with 手 the hand (L. 48), which gives

E 丮

Chi^4. To do, to hold. It represents the hand doing or keeping something; 像。手有所據也。。丮 forms important compounds in which it is nearly always wrongly shaped. The scribes write 丮 (as above B), or 丸 (as below J), or 凡 (L. 21), etc. See 孰 **shu^2**, L. 75 E; 埶 **i^4**, L. 79 K; 執 **chih^2**, L. 102 G; 羸 **lo^3**, L. 74 B; etc.

F 巩

K'ung^3. To do a work 工 (L. 82 A), by pressing or knocking; 加手、从丮、工聲、 Notice the compounds 恐 **k'ung^3**, pulsations of the 心 heart, fear; and 築 **chu^2**, to build a clay-wall by battering mud betwen 木 boards and 竹 mats. — Phonetic series 226, under its modern form.

G 夙

Hsü^4. The end of the night, before dawn; the time for oblations and sacrifices; 从夕、从丮、會意。早敬者也。Lit. To present one's self before dawn, when it is still 夕 night, while 丮 holding one's offering for sacrifice. — In the modern form, 丮 mutilated covers 夕 Compare with 風 **fêng^1** denived from 凡 **fan^2**,L. 21 B.

Inverted, 丮 forms

H 

Chü^2. To seize, to hold; 持也。从反丮。指事。 This ancient form is no longer nsed and was replaced by 挶.

Both combined form

I 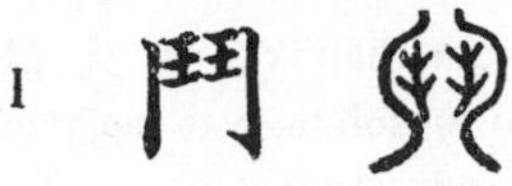

Tou[4]. To seize each other, to fight; **从 丮 正 反。相 持。會 意。** — It is the 191th radical in **K'ang-hsi, not** to be confounded with **門** the 169th radical.

Third series: 丸 wan[2].

J 

Wan[2]. A pill, anything round. Often used for the preceding **丮**. It is 仄 **chai**[3] inverted **(L. 59 E)**. — The derivatives of **丸** (phonetic series 34) are to be distinguished from those of **凡** (L. 21; phonetic series 19). It is sometimes difficult to make the distinction.

LESSON 12.

This lesson contains three series, **巜**, **巜**, **巛**, and an appendix.

First series: **〈** **chüan**[3].

A 〈

Chüan[3]. Small water course, rivulet; **水 小 流 也。像 形。** A primitive. Forms some important compounds, as:

B 水

Shui[3]. Water, small river; **像 形。** The four strokes added to the rivulet represent the waves of the water. See L. 125. — It is the 85th radical in **K'ang-hsi.**

C 攸

Yu[1]. Primitive meaning, to sound a ford. A man **亻** crossing **〈** water, holding with the **彐** hand a **卜** stick (**攴** L. 43 D), sounding the river with a stick; **从 人、从 〈、从 攴。會 意。** An ancient form is simply composed of **水** water and **攴** to sound. — **Chuan-chu** the place where one is going. Often used **chia-chieh** as a relative pronoun. — Phonetic series 318, in which the radical is placed under **攵、脩 修 絛 倏 條 儵**, etc. In these compounds. **亻** may be easily taken for the radical; in reality **亻** is but a part of the phonetic. The small stroke at the right of **亻** is what remains of **〈** in the modern writing. — Note that **偹** has no relation with this character; it is an arbitrary abbreviation of **備 pi**[4], **pei**[4] **(L. 54 G)**.

Second series: 巜 **kuai**⁴. It is 〈 doubled.

D 巜

Kuai⁴. A river, a stream larger than 〈. 水大流也。像形。This character, now obsolete, was replaced by 澮. — Forms some compounds, for instance

Lin². A torrent (L. 126 D).

Yü². A boat (L. 14 F).

Note that engravers substitute for 巜 the character 刂, easier to be engraved. But 刂 being also an abbreviation for 刀, the 18th radical, this double employ of the same sign brings confusion.

Third series: 巛 **ch'uan**¹. It is 〈 repeated thrice.

E 巛 川

Ch'uan¹. A river, a big stream formed by the junction of several others; 〈 巜 之 水 會 爲 巛 也。Note the differences in the modern writing. — It is the 47th radical. Phonetic series 18. Note the following compounds:

F

Lieh⁴. Bubbles; 从川。歺 聲。The phonetic is not 夕 **hsi**⁴ (the 36th radical), as the modern character might suggest; it is 歺 **tai**³ (the 78th radical) contracted. It forms the important compound 列 **lieh**⁴ (L. 52 D).

G 邕

Yung¹. Moats. 从 巛、从 邑、會 意。城 池 也。In the writing **ta-chuan**, instead of 邑 **i**⁴, city (L. 74 C), there was 吕, representing circumvallations (L. 90 G); 从 巛、吕、像 形。— It forms the compound

雝 雍

Yung¹. Wagtail; the 隹 bird that likes the sides of moats 邕. This character is the important phonetic 769, under its modern contracted form 雍 (今 字 譔 作 雍)。亠 takes the place of 巛, and 乡 of 邑. See L. 74 C, and the series 鄉 **hsiang**¹, L. 26 M.

H **Ching**[1]. The underground water courses, so important in the Chinese geomancy 風水 **fêng-shui**. 水脈也。从巛在一下。會意。一地也。壬聲。The currents of water 巛 that flow under 一 the surface of the ground (L. 1. 1). The phonetic is not 工 **kung**[1] (L. 82), as the modern character might induce one to believe, it is 壬 **t'ing**[2] (L. 81 D). The primitive meaning was perhaps 壬 to examine the underground veins. — Phonetic series 262.

I **Tsai**[1]. Actual meaning **chuan-chu**, calamity, misfortune; 害也. Primitive sense, 从巛、一壅之、指事。A river 巛 barred 一 (L. 1, 3), which causes the *calamity* of inundation. The character now used to mean *calamity*, is the compound 災, that represents indifferently either a flood (巛 water), or a fire (火 fire). Note moreover the next compound:

Tzŭ[1]. Grounds 田 uncultivated, exposed to 巛 floods; 不耕田也。One writes now 菑. — The character 甾 **tzŭ**[1] must be carefully distinguished from 甾 **tzŭ**[1] (L. 150) that forms the phonetic series 406. The two have no connection whatever. The engravers often cut 巛, instead of 巛, because it is easier; hence the confusion of series.

J 巟 **Huang**[1]. Devastation, 亾 ravage caused by the 川 rivers; 水廣也. See L 10 E. — It forms.

荒 **Huang**[1]. Wild, barren, drought, a consequence of inundations for 艹 the plants. Phonetic series 536.

K 侃 **K'an**[3]. Incorruptible uprightness, inflexible rigidity of principles; 剛直也。从川、取其不舍晝夜。从㐰、古文信字會意。Fidelity (㐰, an ancient form of 信) to one's principles, constant as the 川 current of a river. See L. 25 H.

L 州 **Chou**[1] Main lands inhabitable (iles or continents), surrounded by waters. The lands are represented by three points in the modern writing, and by three rounds in the old writing. This character was composed of two 巛 superposed. 水中可居曰州。从重川。會意。— Phonetic series 187.

Appendix: In all the following characters, 巛 is not **ch'uan**, but it represents the hair. Nevertheless they are nearly all classified under the 47th radical.

See L. 40 B.

M **Tzŭ**³. Different writing of 子, a child born with hair. See L. 94 A.

T'u². The last inverted. Primitive sense, *partus cephalicus*, the hairy head coming first. See L. 94 F.

N 首 **Shou**³. A hairy head. See L. 160 A.

県 **Hsiao**¹. The last inverted. Head of a *criminal* hung up, as a lesson; the hair hangs down. See LL. 160 A, 119 K.

O 巢 巢 **Ch'ao**². A bird's nest upon a tree, the bird covering it; 鳥在木上曰巢。从木。像形。The 臼 at the top of 木 a tree is the nest (a primitive, and not both hands (L. 50, A); 巛 represents the feathers of the bird brooding on the nest. Note that this character has nothing in common with 果 **kuo**³ (L. 110 F), though the engravers always cut it in that way. — Phonetic series 594.

LESSON 13.

About the primitive

A  **Ch'ui**². An object suspended, a pendant; with its multiples 𠆢𠆢 亽 仌.

First series: 𠆢 doubled 𠆢𠆢. It is found in

B 夾 **Shan**³. 盗竊懷物也。从大。有所持。指事。 A thief bringing under his arms stolen things (大 a man, L. 60 A). It forms the compound

陜 **Shên**³, the name of the Province of 陝西 **Shên-si**.

C 

Lai². 𠆢𠆢 represents bearded ears of corn hanging down, 𠆢𠆢像、芒束之形; the other part of the character is a primitive representing the plant. A sort of bearded barley, which constituted the main food of the people under the 周 Dynasty. This character now means **chia-chieh** to come, the contrary of 去 to go.— Phonetic series 374. Note the following derivatives:

Mai⁴. It is composed of 來 and of 夊 (the 35th radical) to advance; ripening corn. Now, either barley or wheat, according to the times, the places, or the epithet added to it. — It is the 199th radical of a group of characters relating to corn.

Shê⁴. Primitive sense, 來 corn gathered in the 㐭 barn; 从來、从㐭、會意。來者㐭而藏之; this character is now written 穡. Meaning **chuan-chu**, thrift, parsimony; for the countrymen are not inclined to waste corn that cost them so much labour. — Note how, in the modern character, the bottom of 來 and the top of 㐭 were blended into a 一... Phonetic series 755.

Yin⁴. 从犬、从來、會意。A logical aggregate. A dog (犬 L. 134) that shows his teeth, the points of which are represented by 來 instead of 𠆢𠆢 (page 16, notice 1). It forms the phonetic compound 憖 **yin**⁴, to desire, to ask, etc.

Note: 夾 **chia**¹, to pinch (L. 27 F); 卒 **tsu**², soldier (L. 16 M); as well as different others (27 B C D E), have nothing in common with the primitive 𠆢 which is spoken of here.

Second series: 𠆢 repeated twice and superposed 仌. It represents the hair of the eye-brows, in / the hanging fruits in

D 眉 𥃩

Mei², eye-brow, L. 7 A.

T'iao², to bear fruit, L 41 E.

Third series: ⋀ repeated four times 𠂹. Note the arbitrary deformation of the modern forms in this series

E 𠂹 **Ch'ui**[2]. A bough loaded with leaves and drooping flowers; 草木華葉下垂。像形。This character, now obsolete, was superseded by the next compound, its synonym and homophone

垂 **Ch'ui**[2]. To hang, to be suspended from. It is the last character combined with 土 **t'u**[3], the earth (L. 81), the leaves hanging down towards the earth. — Phonetic series **435**.

F 華 花 **Hua**[1]. Flower; 草木華也。从𠂹、从亏。今俗作花。The vernal expansion 亏 (L. 58 E) of 𠂹 leaves and flowers. In the second ancient character, 艸 is a radical redundance (L. 78 B). — Phonetic series 687. — The modern character 花, means the term of 艹 vegetal 化 evolution, the flower (L. 30 D).

G 差 **Ch'a**[1]. Divergency, error, etc. It is a logical aggregate. See L. 46 C, where this character was fully explained. — Phonetic series 506.

H 素 **Su**[4]. Pongee, 糸 silk obtained from the cocoons of wild silkworms, collected on the 𠂹 boughs of mulberries. Chuan-chu, natural, simple. — Phonetic series **568**.

I **Kuai**[1]. It represents the torso, back view. The vertical line is the spine, 𠂹 represents the muscles on each side, 一 represents the waist; 背呂也。脅肋也。像。按丨像背脊。𠂹像兩旁肉形。一爲腰指事。— It forms

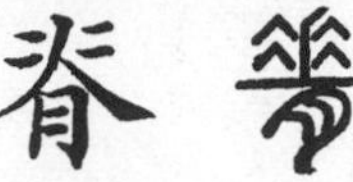 **Chi**[2]. Spine, back (月 L. 65).

So far, all is right. But there wat another

Kuai[1]. Odd, singular, irregular. See L. 103 C.

The scribes confounded these two **kuai**[1], so well defined and distinct in the ancient writing, and they formed the single modern character 乖, which resembles neither of them. Now one may read in **K'ang-hsi**, under the arbitrary radical 丿, 乖 **kuai**, spine, odd, irregular.

Who is to blame, if the students not forewarned, find Chinese characters absurd and inexplicable?

LESSON 14.

About the primitive 亼 and its more important derivatives.

Three series, 亼, 今. 金

A

Chi[2]. Notion of union, of assemblage, of a junction of different elements, represented by three lines. Three is used to mean many; 三合也. 像. A primitive, which is now commonly superseded by the character 集 **chi**[2] (L. 119 G). It forms

First series;

B

Ho[2]. Union, agreement, harmony; 亼口也。从亼、从口、會意。三口相同爲合。Etymologically, many (three) 口 mouths (L. 72) speaking together; good understanding. — Phonetic series 198. — Note the two following compounds:

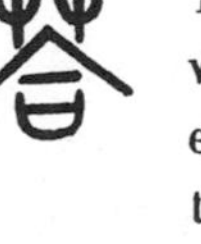

Ta[2]. Vetch, pea, vegetables 艸, whose boughs are joined, get entangled. **Chuan-chu**, to join, to adapt, to answer. In the last sense, this character is now written 答, which is unauthorised. — Phonetic series 570.

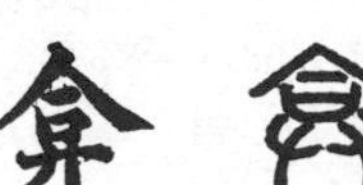

Yen[3]. To join 合 the hands 廾 to cover something; to cover. See L. 47 L — Phonetic series 496.

C 舍 舍

She[1]. A shed, a booth; 从口像築。从亼屮像屋也。廬也。Joining of 口 walls in beaten earth and of 屮 thatch (LL. 74 and 78). In its modern form, this character seems to be derived from 舌 (L. 102 C, 135th radical), under which it was classified by **K'ang-hsi**. But there is no relation whatever between both. It forms the compound 捨 **shê**[3], to part with, to reject, and the logical aggregate

Yü[2]. I, me; 我也。自稱發聲之詞。Composition: 从八 to distinguish (L. 18); 从舍 contracted, 口 being replaced by 八. The Chinese custom requires that anyone entering a 舍 house, 八 should make known his presence and distinguish himself from any other person by crying out: It is I, so and so, who comes for such and such a purpose.».. A man entering a house and keeping silence, is liable to suspicion. — Phonetic series 319. It forms the phonetic complex

Ch'a[2]. Tea; 从艸,余聲。The modern scribes mutilated the ancient form.—Phonetic series 507.

D 會 會

Hui[4]. To gather, a meeting; 合也,聚也。从亼,从曾省,會意. To order 亼, to add 曾 (contracted, L. 40 D). The ancient character was simpler; 古文,从合,从彡,會意。按彡,衆多意。To assemble 合 a multitude represented by 彡 three. — Phonetic series 736.

E 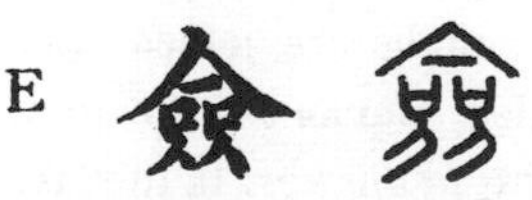

Ch'ien[1]. Meeting, together; 皆也. From 亼 to gather, from 人 人 several men, from 口 口 several mouths. It is a well known fact that a Chinese crowd cannot keep silent. — Phonetic series 726.

F 兪 兪 俞

Yü[2]. A small boat, a primitive barge; 舟之始也。从亼,从巜,从舟,會意。Junction of a few planks, forming a boat 舟, to go up the river 巜 (L. 12 D). Note 月 for 舟 (L. 66). Note also that the engravers often cut 刂 instead of 巜, which wrongfully reminds of the 18th radical (L. 52). — Phonetic series 501.

G 侖 **Lün²**. To gather 亼 documents 冊 (L. 156), to compare, to meditate, to develop them; 思也。从亼，从冊，會意。— Phonetic series 380.

H 龠 **Yao⁴**. This character, which is much like the preceding, is not derived from it. 从品，从亼，从冊，會意。亼合也。冊像編竹形，三口三孔也。A flute, a pandean pipe. Assemblage 亼 of several bamboos, the 口 holes of which are disposed in a row, and that gives sounds together; 竹管以和眾音。Now, accord, harmony, in general. — It is the 214th radical of characters relating to pipes and similar instruments. — Phonetic series 835.

I 令 命 Note the two following characters: 令 **ling⁴**, decree; and its compound by the addition of a 口 mouth, 命 **ming⁴**, order. There is a difference between them. 令，从亼，从卩，會意: to fix 亼 *upon a written order* the seal 卩 (L. 55 B) which makes it a writ of execution. 命，从口，从令，會意; an order 令 given 口 orally. 在事爲令。在言爲命。— In the philosophical language, 命 means the decree by which heaven calls men to life and determines their fate. Two ancient characters express this meaning well: 口 mouth *of heaven* dictating to a man his destiny between 二 heaven and earth (L. 2 D)... 亼 combining of the destiny of a 人 man. 命者、天之令也。。。天命之謂性，注謂天所命生人者也。— Phonetic series 135.

J **Note**. In the modern writing, 亼 may be easily confounded with 入 11th radical, L 15), 八 (12th radical, L 18), 人 (9th radical, L. 25) placed on the top of a compound K'ang-hsi arbitrarily classified 俞 under 入, 今 余 命 僉 under 人, etc. But the horizontal line of 亼, some vestige of which generally remains, is the test that manifests the mistake. Its presence is indicative of a derivative from 亼. — See 全 L. 15 B.

Second series; 今. This character is put apart from the derivatives of 亼, on account of its many and important sub-derivatives.

K 

Chin1. The actual moment; notion of actuality, of presence; 是時也。从亼、从乛、會意。乛、古文及字。The composition is tautologic; 亼 union, 乛 contact. Note that 乛 is often written ㇀. For the old forms of 及 **chi**2, see L. 19 E — Phonetic series 17. It forms

L 

Han2, **hên**2. To hold in the mouth (to have actually 今 in the 口 mouth); 从口从今. 今亦聲。 Meaning **chuan-chu**, to contain, to shut up. — Phonetic series 272. — It is distinct from 吟 **yin**2, to mutter, which is composed of the same elements.

M 

T'an1. To covet; 欲物也、从今、从貝、今亦聲。 The feeling moved by the presence 今 of a 貝 precious object. Its phonetic compounds are unimportant.

N 

Nien4. To remember, to think again of; 常思也。从心、从今。今亦聲、To make 今 actually present to the 心 heart, to the mind, a fact of the past. Derived meanings, to speak of, to recite, to read; these actions reviving, making actual, the idea of a thing passed or absent. — Phonetic series 385.

O 酓

Yin3. 酉 wine (L. 41 G), 今 new. It forms

㱃

Yin3. To drink; to water. This character is now written 飲, a wrongly chosen compound, for it means 欠 to wish for 食 food. There were formerly three characters

1

Yin3. To have water 水 in one's presence 今; to drink.

2

Yin3. To have food 食 at one's disposal 今; to eat.

3

Yin3. To 欠 wish for 酓 wine; to drink.

The first character, which was the right one, became obsolete. An element was taken from each of the last two. Thus was made the irregular character 飲。

P 侌

Yin[1]. Cloudy weather; 雲覆日也从云。从今。云。古文雲字。Lit. There are actually 今 clouds 云 (L 93 A). In the dualist system, 侌 **yin** denotes the inferior principle (obscurity), by opposition to 昜 **yang** the superior principle (light). The compounds 陰 and 陽 are now used. 陰 **yin**[1], the shady Northern watershed 阝 of a valley; 陽 **yang**[2], the sunny South watershed 阝. See L. 86 A.

Q 

Ch'ên[1]. The sharp pike of a 山 mountain (L. 80). It is a phonetic complex; 从山、今聲。— Phonetic series 253.

R 禽

Ch'in[2]. A phonetic complex. See L. 23 E.

S 琴

Ch'in[2]. A phonetic complex. See L. 83 B. Note the contraction.

Third series: 金.

T 金

Chin[1]. Metal. According to the Chinese geology, the metals are born from the earth. 金生於土。Hence the etymology: 从土。左右注像。金在土中形。今聲。In the bosom of the earth 土, two grains or nuggets of gold; 今 is phonetic. The bottom stroke of 今 is combined with the top of 土, and is sometimes inverted, as stated above K. This interpretation was made by **Li-ssŭ**. — The old character was composed of four nuggets, of horizontal lines denoting the stratification of the metalliferous layer, and lastly of a cover which meant that the whole was conceiled under the earth. Evidently a primitive. 古文像形。— It is the 167th radical of a group of characters describing metals and their uses.

LESSON 15.

About the primitive 入 and its derivatives.

A 

Ju[4]. To enter, to put in, to penetrate into; 内也。像。艸木根入地形。The character represents the penetration of roots into the earth; the vertical line representing the plant, the two descending lines denoting the roots. It is the reverse of 出 **ch'u**[1], to go out (L. 78 E), that represents a plant growing upwards; 於出爲對文。— It is the 11th radical.

B

Ch'üan[2]. Complete, entire, perfect. The etymologists give two different interpretations of this character:

1. The old one: 从亼、从工、會意。The work 工 (L. 82) is ordered 亼, finished, complete, perfect. According to this etymology, 仝 is derived from 亼 (L. 14) and not from 入 The bottom stroke of 亼 is combined together with the top stroke of 工.

2. The modern one: 从王、㫃省聲。純玉曰全。A 王 jade (L. 83) spotless, perfect; 入 would be an abbreviation of 㫃 **yen**[3] (L. 117 B), used as a phonetic. This unlikely supposition is of **Li-ssŭ**.

Phonetic series 192, under its present form.

C

Nei[4]. To enter, interior, into; 从冂、从入、會意。自外而入也。See 冂 **chiung**[3], the outside, L. 34 A. — Phonetic series 74. It forms

O[4]. **Na**[4]. To speak in a whisper, as it were 內 into one's 口 mouth. 言之訥也。从口、从內、會意。Note the modern form contracted. Taken for 內 (the compound for the simple, p. 16, 1), it forms the two following characters:

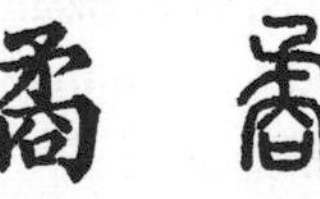

Yü[4]. To penetrate into 㕯, to pierce with a 矛 sharp instrument (L. 95 C). — Phonetic series 720.

Hsi[1]. Swallow; 燕也。从隹、从㕯、屮像其冠也。A bird 隹 that builds its nest within 㕯 the dwellings (a thing common in China); 屮 (and not 山, as the modern character might induce to believe) represents the head (L. 78 A), says the Glose. It may be so; it seems probable however that 屮 represents the grass with which the swallow stuffs its nest. — Phonetic series 840. 嶲 is a wrong abbreviation of this character (see L. 87 C).

The following character is derived from 內, and not from 商. It is formed by combination and fusion of 言 and 內. The mouth 口 at the bottom of the compound, belongs to 言 (L. 73 C).

D 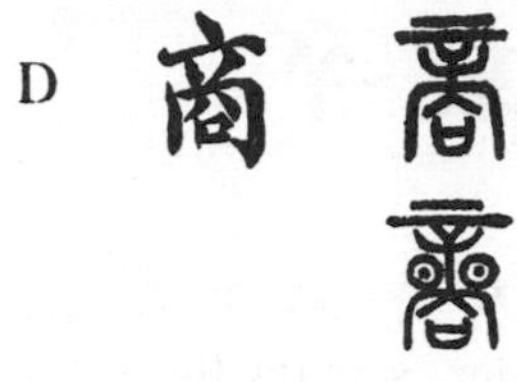

Shang[1]. To give advice, to consult, to deliberate; 从言、从內。To express 言, one's 內 interior feelings. In the old character there were two 日 days added, which proves that the 商量 deliberations of old, were not shorter than the present time ones; they probably took place during the night, between two days, just as now; 古文、从言、从內、从二日。— In the sense of trade, 商 is **chia-chieh** for its compound with 貝 (L. 161, cowry, the money of the ancients), trade being made with 商 talk and 貝 money. The Glose says so.

E In the modern writing, 入 became 亠 on the top of 亡 **wang**[2] (L. 10 E), 亩 **lin**[3] (L. 76 B); and 𠂉 in 㣇 **êrh**[3] (L. 18 O). — Two 入 are a part of the character 兩 **liang**[3] (L. 35 H I).

LESSON 16.

About the primitive 衣.

A 

I[1]. Clothes, a cover, cloak. The summary outlines of clothing. On the top, the upper garments and sleeves, 上像兩袖。At the bottom, the robes waving and draggling, 下像衣𧘇之形。— It is the 145th radical of a large group of characters relating to garments. The phonetic complexes are not important; note 依 **i**[1], to rely on, to trust to. Note the modern contracted form, and compare it with that of 示 113th radical (L. 3 D).

Note. In composition, 衣 has three positions. — 1. One the left side of the character. It is then contracted under the form 衤. — 2. on the top or at the bottom, it is then unchanged. — 3. Cut into two halves, 亠 on the top, 𧘇 at the bottom, the phonetic being introduced between the two. These characters are not to be confounded with those belonging to the 8th radical 亠; 𧘇 is the test; any time one sees 𧘇 at the bottom of a compound, then it is a derivative of 衣 145th radical, not of 亠 8th radical. — 4. Note also that in some characters, as a consequence of the fusion with an element placed on the top, the upper part of 衣 is quite altered in the modern forms. The lower part has also been altered in the character 卒 (L. 16 M).

Examples of the four remarks.

1° 衫袍褐禨　　3° 褭褒褻袤

2° 裂裴裔卒　　4° 表袁卒

Note the following derivatives;

B 初 — **Ch'u**[1]. Beginning; 始也。从刀 从衣、會意。A 刀 knife and 衣 garments; for, says the Glose, the cutting is the first thing required to make clothes. 裁者衣之始也. This is quite true!

C 哀 — **Nai**[1]. To bewail, to lament; 从口、从衣、會意。Howling 口 of the mourners clad in mourning 衣 dress.

D 衰 — **Shuai**[1]. **So**[1]. Straw-clothes against rain; 艸雨衣也。从衣、𠂹像、(See L. 116). This character is now written 蓑 — The modern meaning, decay, is **chia-chieh** for 㾙, cachexy from malaria, slow exhaustion caused by the marsh-fever, the 疒 disease of the rainy 衰 countries. — Phonetic series 563, under its modern form.

E 衷 — **Chung**[1]. Primitive sense, the under-garments: 衣 clothes, 中 inside (L. 109); 从衣, 从中, 裏褻衣也 Then, by extension, the inside of man, the feelings of his heart, fidelity.

F 衮 袞 — **Kun**[3]. Official 公 robe 衣 of the Emperor, adorned with dragons; 从公,从衣、會意. See 公 L. 18 C. Note the modern form. — Its phonetic complexes are not important, v. g. 滚 kun[3], to bubble.

The two following characters are to be carefully distinguished:

G 裏 — **Li**[3]. The inside, the lining of clothes, 衣內也。从衣、里聲。Then, in general, interior, inside. 裡 is a synonym. See 里 L. 149 D.

H 裹 — **Ko**[3]. To tie up. 纏也。从衣、果聲。Note that 裸 lo[3] naked, composed of the same elements, is neither an homophone nor a synonyme. See 果 L. 120. F.

I 襄

Hsiang[1]. To take off one's 衣, robe 解衣耕謂之襄, in order to work in common, to help the others. See (L. 72 H) the radical **nang**[2], intricate and unrecognisable in the modern writing. — Phonetic series 831.

J 褱

Huai[2]. To tie the clothes tight round the body; to hide in one's bosom; 夾也 See (L. 100 C) the phonetic **tai**[4]. — Phonetie series 820.

K 表

Piao[3]. The outside of the clothes (compare above G). The first garments 衣 were beasts'skins worn with the 毛 hair outside; 古者衣。以毛爲表。皆外毛。oo 表，衣外也。从衣、从毛、會意。 See 毛 L. 100. — Phonetic series 389.

L 袁

Yüan[2]. Trailing robe; 長衣也。从衣、叀省聲。 About 叀, contracted and combined with 亠, see L. 91 E. — Phonetic series 587. It forms the phonetic complex

瞏 睘

Huan[2]. Timid looks; 目驚視也。从目，袁聲。 See 目 L. 158. — Phonetic series 734, under its modern contracted form.

M 卒 卒

Tsu[2]. Soldier, satellite; 从衣 从一。指事。 A garment 衣, marked with a — sign. The uniform of the ancient Chinese soldiers, viz. an ordinary garment with an indicative mark; 衣有題識者。 Then, by extension, the man who wears the uniform, a soldier, a satellite. Lastly, a sudden and unexpected accident, end, death; the soldiers, says the Glose, being unceasingly laid open to surprises and to death in their fights against the enemies and against the wild beasts. — Note the alteration of the two modern forms. — Phonetic series 403.

LESSON 17.

About the primitive 冫 and, in an appendix, about some characters that might seem to be derived from it, but that do not do so in reality.

A 冫

Ping[1]. To freeze, ice; 凍也。像。水凝之形。按水始凝文理似之。It represents the rays that appear by crystallisation at the surface of water when it is freezing. — It is the 15th radical of characters referring to cold, freezing, and ice. It forms.

B 冰 氷

Ping[1]. Ice; 水 water 冫 crystallised; 水堅也。从冫、从水、會意、冫亦聲。— The scribes often write 氷, which is an unauthorised form. This is not to be confounded with 永 **yung**[3] (L. 125 D).

C 冶

Yeh[3]. To fuse metals, solidification 冫 of the melted metals; 銷也。从冫。台聲。金遭熱卽流、遇冷卽合、似之、古从冫。See 台 L. 85 E.

D 凋

Tiao[1]. Taken by 冫 frost, exhausted, fading, dying; 从冫、周聲。See 周 L. 109 C.

E 馮

憑

This character suffered from many fanciful alterations in the course of ages. Its true sound is **p'ing**[2]. It means a 馬 horse slipping on 冫 ice, nervous, anxious. It forms the homophone derivative

P'ing[2]. Anxiety 馮 of the 心 heart.

Now 1. The first of these two characters was misused, as an abbreviation, for the family name 鄷 **fêng**[2]. 2. The second was misused and written (**chia-chieh**) for 凭 **p'ing**[2], proof, evidence, to lean upon. Then the scribes semi-repaired the mistake, which change gave birth to the new character 凴 **p'ing**[2], proof, etc.

F 冬 **Tung**^{1}. Winter. It forms 終 **chung**^{1}, end, extremity, term.

Before explaining these characters, the primitive 夂 must be dealt with.

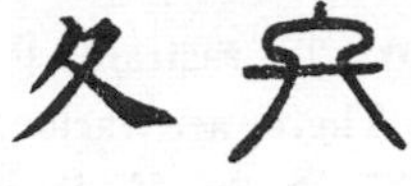

Chung^1. 像絲一束之形。It represents a thread skein, the extremity of which is fixed by a tie or a brooch, to keep it closed. Hence two notions, *end* and *fixation*. — Compare L. 83 B. This character, in its modern form, is to be distinguished from the 34th, 35th, 36th, 66th radicals of **K'ang-hsi**. Now let us come back to

Tung^1. Winter 四時盡也。从冫、从夂、會意。The 冫 frozen 夂 end of the year. The old character meant 夂 cessation of the solar 日 action, confinement of the sun; 古文、从日、从夂、於牢同形 For, says the Glose, 夂 must be interpreted as in

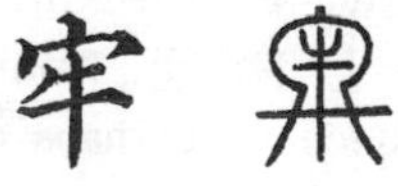

Lao^2, a paddock: 牛 oxen 夂 confined. In the modern writing, 夂 was changed into 宀 by the scribes.

Now 終 **Chung**^{1} replaced the primitive 夂, in the sense of *end*, *extremity*, *term*.

Appendix

In the following characters, 仌 is a special primitive, that has nothing in common with 冫. It means thongs, folds, in G H I J; scales, streaks, in K.

G  

Ju^4, **jou**^{4}. Meat, flesh. 胾肉、像形. Thongs 仌 of dried meat, made up into a 勹 bundle (L. 54). The ancient Chinese were used to dry-salt meat, without smoking it. The pay of a school-master is still called 束脩 **shu-hsiu**, because he was formerly paid with dried meat. See L. 65. — It is the 130th radical of many characters relating to meat and food. Note the derivative

俎

Tsu^3. Credence-table charged with meat, that was offered in the sacrifices; 胾肉在且上、會意。See L. 20 D. **K'ang-hsi** wrongfully classified this character under the 9th radical 人.

H 谷

Ch'iao^{4}. The top lip. 仌 flesh above the 口 mouth 口上肉也、像。It forms the phonetic complex

卻 **Ch'iao^{4}**. To restrain 卩 on'es desires. There are various **chia-chieh**. 節欲也。从卩節意。谷聲 See L. 55 B This character is now written 却; it is a licence. It forms the phonetic complex 腳 脚 **chiao^{3}** the feet. — Distinguish 谷 **ch'iao^{4}** from 谷 **ku^{3}** (L. 18 E); the modern writing of both is identic.

I 㐫

T'ien^{4}. This character matches with the preceding. It means the chin, 仌 flesh below 一 the mouth (a line between the two lips closed). 口下肉也、像。The circle depicts the chin-dimple. See L. 41 B.

J 昔

Hsi^{2}. Thongs 仌 of flesh drying or dried in 日 the sun; 乾肉也、像。殘肉、日以晞之。**Chia-chieh**, formerly, in days of old, ancient; or perhaps **chuan-chu**, the dried meat being *old*, if compared with the fresh meat. The second ancient form, which is incorrect, recalls 丫 (L 103 C). The modern form is contracted. — Phonetic series 358. It forms the phonetic complex

耤 **Chi^{2}**. Field ploughed by the Emperor. Appanage. Property.— Phonetic series 770.

K 魚

Yü^{2}. Fish. See L. 142 A. Here 仌 represents the scales. A sharp head, a scaly body, a tail represented by 火 (L. 126 C), make up a fish. The modern character is contracted. — It is the 195th radical of names and parts of fish.

L 角

Chiao^{3}. Horn. See L. 142 B. It would be the preceding, less the 火 tail. For, says the Glose, a horn resembles a fish. It seems rather to be that 角 is a primitive, 仌 representing the streaks of the horns. — It is the 148th radical.

LESSON 18.

About the primitive 八, and its derivative 小, which forms an important group.

First series: 八.

A 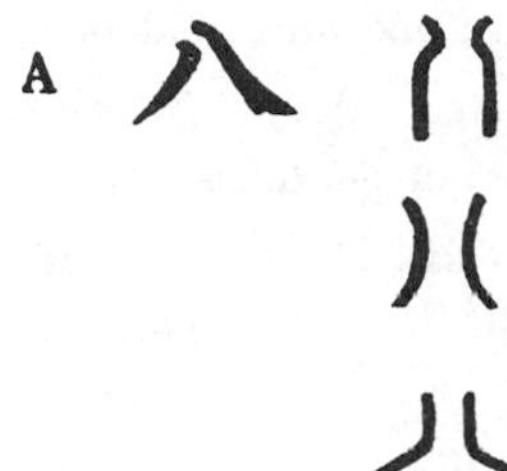

Pa[1]. Etymological sense, to divide, to partake. It is a primitive representing the division in two parts, the separation; 別也。像。分別之形。This character now means *eight*, this number being easily divided into two equal parts (note that four, a square, is a kind of unity in the Chinese reckoning). — It is the 12th radical. Phonetic series 8. — In the compounds, 八 placed *on the top* of the character, is sometimes reduced to two points in the modern writing, v.g. 曾 for 曾. Most of the characters having 八 *at the bottom* in the **K'ang-hsi** dictionary, as 共 兵 其 具 典, have really nothing in common with this primitive. — Note the following derivatives:

B 分

Fên[1]. To divide, to separate, to partake; 別也。从八。从刀。會意。刀以分別物也。A 刀 knife (L 52) that 八 divides. Phonetic series 58. It forms

P'in[2]. Poverty, pecuniary difficulties. That to which leads the 分 partition of 貝 goods; 財分。少也 从貝。从分。會意。。。貝 was the money of the ancients (L. 161). The ancient form is still more expressive; 古文。从宀 dwellings, 从分 to partake. Note that the heritage being equally divided among the male offspring, and the Chinese families counting many members, poverty follows the partition.

C 公

Kung[1]. Common. Division and distribution 八 of private 厶 goods (L. 89 A); 从八。从厶。會意。分其厶以與人。爲公。By extension, *justice*, implying a treatment equal for all; while 義 (L. 71 Q) means *justice* in the sense of a kind, decent treatment. — Phonetic series 68. It forms the phonetic complexes

松 松

Sung^1. The fir-tribe; 松木也。从木、公聲。— Phonetic series 394.

翁 翁

Wêng^1. 頸毛也。从羽、公聲。Hairs or feathers in the neck. The modern meaning, old man, sir, is a **chia-chieh**; the characters 公 and 翁 were chosen to denote appellations of politeness which existed before; 尊老謂之公。或謂之翁。Phonetic series **581**. See 袞 **kun**^{2}, L. 16 F, etc.

D 半 半

Pan^4. To divide in two by the middle, equally; a half; 物中分也。从八、从牛、會意。Etymologically, 八 to divide an 牛 ox in two parts, in all its length, as the butchers do, before the cutting up. — Phonetic series **144**. **K'ang-hsi** wrongly classified this character under the radical 十.

E 㕣 㕣

船

Yen^3. The ravines, on the mountains' ridges; separation 八 and flowing 口 of waters; 从口、从八、會意. — Phonetic series **169**. Note the phonetic complex 船 **ch'uan**^{2}, a boat. Distinguish 船 from 般 **pan**^{1}, L. 66 B. See 㕣 L. 29 D.

谷 谷

Ku^3. A deep hollow, a gorge, a torrent; 山之瀆、一有水、一無水者、名曰谷。— It is the 150th radical. Phonetic series **284**. Distinguish 谷 **ku**^{3} from 谷 **ch'iao**^{4}, L. 17 H. The two are identic in the modern writing. — It forms

Jung^2, **yung**^{2}. To contain, to shut up; 盛也. From 宀 to cover, and 谷 hollow, a recipient; 會意. **Chuan-chu,** to endure, to bear, to compose one's demeanour, a mask, a face made to 宀 disguise the 谷 depths of the heart. — Phonetic series **542**.

Hsün^4. **A ravine, a torrent. See L. 118 D.**

F 介 **Chieh^4**. Boundaries, limits; the *lines* that 八 separate 人 men. 从八，从人，會意。人各有介。按八者分也。— Phonetic series 42.

G 必 **Pi^2**. Certainly, necessarily. An arrow 弋 that divides 八, that solves *a doubt, a dilemma*; 从八，从弋，會意。弋者，介分也。It seems to have primitively been a kind of interjection pointing out a strict order; 發聲之詞。There are different meanings derived from it. **K'ang-hsi** wrongly classified this character under the radical 心. — Phonetic series 148. It forms the phonetic complex •

Mi^4. A quiet 宀 retreat (L. 36), close, still, silent; 安也. — Phonetic series 383. It forms

Mi^4. A grotto, secret, mysterious (L. 80); 山如堂也。Etc.

Second series: 小

H 小 **Hsiao^3**. Small, trifling, mean; 物之微也。This idea is represented by the 八 partition of an object 丨 already small by its nature; 从丨，而八分之。會意。— It is the 42th radical. It forms

I 尖 **Chien^1**. Point, sharp. A 大 big object (L. 60) that becomes 小 small on its top. It is a 俗字 vulgar modern character.

J 肖 **Hsiao^4**. To be like one's father, not degenerate; 骨肉相似也。Small 小 flesh 肉, offspring, like the big flesh, one's parent... 不肖 pu-hsiao, to be degenerate; 不似其先。故曰不肖也。— Phonetic series 277. In the modern writing, some derivatives of 肙 (L. 65 D) v.g. 屑, seem to be derived from 肖; the scribes are the cause of this mistake, as of so many others.

K 貨 **So^3**. A small 小 object, not larger than the 貝 (L. 161) cowries used as money by the ancients. 从小，从貝，會意。爲細碎之辭。In that sense, this character is now written 瑣. — Phonetic series 566.

L 糹 糹 隙 𤔔 㣎 穆

Hsi[4]. Chink, fissure 小 小 very small, that leaves passage for a slender 白 light (L. 88); 从白。上下小。會意。際見之光一線而已。Note how the top of 白 disappeared, by its fusion with the upper 小. This character is now replaced by the compound 隙 **hsi**[4], chink, fissure.

Mu[4]. Striped; 細文也。从彡、从貨省。會意。This character is derived from the preceding; the 小 on the top was suppressed, and replaced by 彡 (L. 62 A) stripes, added at the bottom. It forms 穆 **mu**[4], the waving of grain; **chuan-chu,** grace, amenity.

M 少

Shao[3]. Little, few, wanting; 不多也。It comes from 丿 to diminish that which is already 小 small; 从小、从丿、會意。丿之言擊也、盡分之意。See L. 7 A **shêng**[1]. — Phonetic series 80 It forms

沙 **Sha**[1]. Sediment, gravel or sand deposed by water. 水中散石也。从水、从少、會意。水少、沙見。That which appears, when 水 water 少 decreases. — Phonetic series 302. It forms

眇 **Miao**[3]. To contract 少 the 目 eyelids, or to use one eye 目 only, in order to examine attentively a subtile object. 㬥目綱視也。會意 By extension, subtle, confused — Phonetic series 465.

N 雀

Chiao[3]. Is derived from 小, and not from 少. A sparrow. 依人小鳥也。从小、从隹、會意。Lit. the small 小 bird 隹 that lives from the superfluity of men; and, by extension, any small bird. Note that the 丿 that reminds of 少, belongs to 隹. See an analogous case in 隺 (冖 隹 L. 34 F). — 雀 forms the following compound, in which 小 passed through a still more singular alteration in the modern writing.

截 截 **Chieh**[2]. To cut off; 斷也 从戈。雀聲。See 71 F. Not to be confounded with the 𢦏 derivatives of 才, L. 96 B.

For 省 **hsing**[3], see L. 158 D.

Appendix: The following characters have nothing in common with 小 nor with 少. See 尙 L. 36 E, 㡀 L. 35 F, 系 L 92 A, 赤 L. 124 A, 京 L. 75 C, 示 L. 3 D, 原 L. 59 C, 尞 L. 126 E, 步 歲 賓 L. 112 G, L, etc. The following is derived from 八 and not from 小.

O 尒 尒 尒 尔 你

Erh[3]. A final used as a full stop, equivalent to a *there now, that is done*; 猶云如此而已也。At the end of a phrase, the voice is 入 drawn in, and the 丨 reserve of breathing is 八 sent forth; 从入丨八。會意。八者气之分也。It is now used (**chia-chieh** for 爾 L. 35 L) as a personal pronoun, thou, you. The modern compound 你 is used for the same purpose.

LESSON 19.

About the two series 乃 and 及.

First series; 乃.

A 乃

Nai[3]. A primitive. A difficulty of breathing; any difficulty in general; 像。气之出難. It is intended to represent the air curling to make its way through the wind-pipe. A sigh, a cry. This character, or rather the sound that is written 乃, is in style an important connective particle, a 發聲之詞, as say the Chinese etymologists; the conjunctions being not *meaning* characters, but *exclamations* to make the hearer understand, how that which one is to say, is connected with that which one has just said — Phonetic series 7. In reality, 乃 does not form a series. Among the derivatives ascribed to it, 1 Those in **nai** are arbitrary abbreviations of more intricate forms, e. g. 奶 for 嬭 **nai**[3], milk. 2 Those in **êng** and **ing** belong to the phonetic 西 (later on 迺) **jêng**[1], for which 乃 was written from immemorial time. 西 meant the shrieking cry of a bird surprised on its nest, a meaning analogous to that of 乃 (See 西 L. 41 D, and 乚 L. 10 A). Now 乃 and 迺 being both read **nai**, are used one for another, and 乃 is the graphic radical of a series that has no relation whatever with it.

To this character 乃 combined with 夂 chih3 (L. 31 B), is ascribed the compound

B 夃  Ying². Note the fusion of the 丿 from 夂, with the 丿 from 乃. Success, happy issue. To get 夂 well out of a 乃 difficullty; 舒難之意. It forms with the dish 皿 (L. 157), the compound

盈  Ying². 从皿. 从夃. 會意. 滿器也. The abundance that comes to one when, by one's efforts, one 夃 arrived to fill with provisions 皿 one's vessels.

The etymologists give also as a derivative of 乃

C 孕 Yün⁴. To be with child, 懷子也. This derivation is a fancy one, as the commentators admit. In this character, 乃 is a primitive, that represents the closing in of the 子 (L. 94 A) fœtus by the womb.

Note. 朵 L. 22 C, and 秀 L. 23 B, have nothing in common with 乃.

Second series: 及.

D 及  Chi². To reach, to seize, to catch; 逮也. 从又、从人、會意. A 彐 hand that seizes a 人 man. Not connected with 乃. — Phonetic series 40. Note the compound

急  Chi². An emotion 及 of the 心 heart; with that which occasionally ensues, haste, zeal, impatience, hatred, etc. Note how the old form of 及 was preserved in the modern character.

E **Note**: 及 had old forms, primitives, now obsolete, but that may be still found in compounds. Those forms are

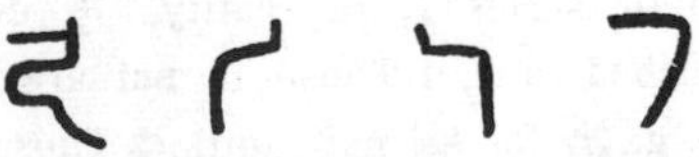

For instance at the bottom of

今  市 

Chin¹. L. 14 K. **Shih⁴**. L. 34 D.

LESSON 20.

About the primitive 几, and its derivative 且 that forms important compounds.

First series: 几.

A 几

Chi^1. A seat, a stool; 坐所以凭也。像形。— It forms the artificial 16th radical. Phonetic series 4. Derivatives

B 処 處

Ch'u^3, ch'u^4. To stop in a place, to sojourn; a place; 从几、从夂、會意。夂几而止。The primitive idea is 夂 to have found a 几 seat, a place of rest. In the modern character, 虍 **hu** is a phonetic redundancy. Compare 尻 L. 32 C.

C 凭

P'ing^2. To lean up, to sit down; 依几也。从几。从任 (L. 82 C). To lean 任 one's self on a 几 stand. By extension, moral help, proof, evidence. This character is now written 憑 or 凴 L. 17 E.

Note: 几 is written as an arbitrary abreviation of more intricate phonetics, e.g. 飢 **chi^1** for 饑 dearth, famine.

Second series: 且.

D 且

Ch'ieh^3. A partial primitive. It was formerly pronounced **tsu^3** or **chü^3**. It represents a small 几 square stand, with 二 shelves superposed; this utensil, so common in China, was primitively used at sacrifices; the — lower stroke represents the earth. See 俎 L. 17 G, the modern form more explicit (且 the stand, 肉 the meat placed upon it); 从几、有二横、一其下地也。卽俎字之古文。Now 且 changed its meaning and became (**chia-chieh**) an important conjunction, 發聲之詞。— Phonetic series 110. It forms the phonetic complexes

E 助 助

Chu^4. To help; 从力。且聲。To exert one's strength (L. 53) for others. The fanciful ways of engravers are the cause why this character is often mistaken for a compound of the 109th radical. See the lead cut character here joined. — Phonetic series 264.

F 

Ch'a^{2}. A proper name; 从 木。且 聲。**Chia-chieh** for 察, to examine, to search. — Phonetic series 420. See below, *note*.

G 

Cha^{1}. A proper name; 从 虍、且 聲。— Phonetic series 589. See below *note*.

Note. The engravers fancifully cut the two preceding characters, F and G, as here joined, which leads one to mistake them for derivatives from 且 L. 143 B. — These characters, with their series, would, according to the Chinese etymologists, originate from the **Kiang-su.** Hence their anomalous pronunciation. It is an effect of the dialect. See pp. 15 and 16.

LESSON 21.

About the primitive 凡 **fan**^{2}.

A 凡

Fan^{2}. Idea of generality, of universality; 數 之 總 名 也。This character was differently explained by the philologists. — Some, starting from an ancient form that was probably but an abbreviation, explain: 从 及 (an old form, L. 19 E), 从 二、會 意。The number 二 of heaven and earth, generalised by 及; all beings existant. — The classical form of the character seems to denote a more natural explanation: — the unity, the origin of beings and numbers (L. 1 A), contained in a kind of primitive, which denotes the generalisation of a particular case. It is the true notion of 凡. — Phonetic series 19. The scribes often write 凡 instead of 丮 or 丸 (L. 11 E J). See also 夙 (L. 11 G).

B 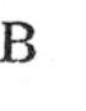

Fêng^{1}. The wind; 从 蟲 省。凡 聲。For, says the Glose, when the wind blows, insects are born; 風 動、生 蟲, This composition and interpretation are in the manner of **Li-ssŭ.** —The ancient character was derived from 日 sun, 丿 motion (L. 7 A), 凡 extension, expansion. All this seems to mean that the atmospheric currents are produced by the action of solar rays; which is true for some winds. — It is the 182th radical of a group of characters relating to storms, etc. Phonetic series 439. See 䖝 (L. 11 C).

C 

Fêng4. The male phœnix. A modern character; 从鳥、凡聲。See the old character, L. 64 I.

D **P'ei**4. Small ornaments made of jade or ivory, scent-cushions, hanging from the girdle, when full dress is worn. 从人、从凡、从巾。會意。玉也。Anything 凡 worn by a 人 man on the 巾 piece of linen which, being rolled up, makes a girdle (L. 35 A). This character seems to be of a relatively modern origin.

LESSON 22.

About the primitive 几, and its derivative 殳.

First series: 几.

A **Shu**2, **ch'u**2. The jerky flapping of a short wing; 鳥之短羽飛几几也。像形。Then, in general, any rhythmical and jerky motion. The derivatives of 几 must be carefully distinguished from those of 乃 L. 19, and 儿 L. 20; in the modern writing, this distinction is not easy to be made. Forms

B **Fu**2. A wild duck; the bird 鳥 which flies 几 heavily; 野鴨也。从鳥、从几、會意。鴨羽短、飛几几也。

C **To**3. The balancing of twigs and flowers. It is used as a specificative of flowers, 一朶花 **i-to hua.** — Phonetic series 240. Note the modern form 朵.

Second series: 殳.

D **Shu**2, **ch'u**2. The right hand 彐 making a jerky 几 motion; to strike; 以杖殊人也. By extension, a stick, a ferule. — It is the 79th radical. Phonetic series 51. Note the following derivatives

Shan4; 刈艸也。从艸、从殳、會意。Jerky motion of the scythe that cuts the grass; to mow.

股 **Ku**[3]; 从肉,从殳. The upper part of the thigh, the fleshy 肉 part of man's body, upon which the mandarins of old bestowed the 殳 ferule bountifully.

殿 **Tien**[4]; 从屍,从殳. The great hall of a tribunal, where flogging 殳 was given on the 屍 breech; a realistic but exact description. The modern scribes write 殿. See L. 32 A.

設 **Shê**[4]. 使人也。施陳也。 To notify an order; to set in order, in the Asiatic way, with many 言 cries and 殳 strokes; 从言,从殳,會意。按言以口使,殳以手使。

役 **I**[4]. The satellites; those who, being armed 殳 with a whip or a bamboo, 彳 prowl about every where, looking for a victim; 从殳,从彳,會意。執殳巡行也。

Other important derivatives will be explained elsewhere, e. g. 段 **tuan**[4] L. 164 D, 殸 **ch'ing**[4] L. 173, 般 **pan**[1] L. 66 B. Etc.

LESSON 23.

About the two primitives 九 and 㕤.

First series: 九.

A 九 **Chiu**[3]. Nine; a numerical sign, without any other signification; 無意可會.指事. — Phonetic series 5. It forms

B 秀 **Hsiu**[4]. This character was made, they say, to be used as the name of the founder of the 後漢 **Hou-han** Dynasty, 劉秀 **Liu-hsiu**. At his birth, 有嘉禾一莖九穗,因名秀 a story says there were found, hanging down from one only 禾 stalk, 九 nine beautiful ears. This phenomenon was regarded as a presage of the Emperor's future elevation. Hence 秀,从禾,从九。會意 This auspicious character was used to designate the bachelors 秀才 **hsiu-ts'ai**, in imperial times. In the modern writing, 九 was changed into 乃 (See L. 19). — Phonetic series 278.

Second series: 禸.

C 内

Jou³. The hind legs and tail of an animal; the track of an animal's paws and rail; a step; 獸足蹂地也像形。It is a primitive that has nothing in common with 九. — It is the 114th radical. Found in

D 禹

Yü². It represents an insect with a big tail, probably the scorpion. 蟲也。像形。Name of the celebrated Emperor who was the founder of the 夏 **Hsia** Dynasty, 1989 B.C. See our *Textes Historiques*, p. 38. — Phonetic series 504.

E 禺

Yü³. Monkey; 猴也。从由,从禸,會意。Its head, says the Glose, resembles that of the demons (L. 40 C), and its tail is a prehensile one. Cf. 爲 L. 49 H. — Phonetic series 503. Note the successive following compounds

离

Li². A yak; the 禸 paws and the big tail; 凶 is an abbreviation of 由 L. 40 C, the head; 屮 changed into 亠 in the modern writing, represents the horns (Cf. 鹿 L. 136). — Phonetic series 628.

Ch'in². It is 离, the horns 屮 being replaced by the phonotic 今 chin¹ (L. 14 K). Wild animals 野獸總名, by opposition to domesticated animals 嘼 (below I). — Phonetic series 728.

F

Fei⁴. A big ape. The character represents the 由 head, the four hands, and 禸 the tail. Note the successive abbreviations. A contraction of the last 萬, is considered as the central part of the compound 舝 hsia².

G 禼

Hsieh⁴. The white ant; 蟲也。像形。it forms

竊

Ch'ieh; 蟲私取米食也。从禼,从廿,从穴,从米,會意。A swarm of termites 禼 stealing 米 grain in a 穴 storehouse, to eat it. To steal, to act by stealth, etc. The scribes write in different manners this intricate character. Note that the form authorised by the 字學舉隅 is also mutilated. From 廿 (L. 24 H) there remains only a 丿, which leads to confound 米 with 釆 (L. 123).

H 

Wan⁴. A scorpion, 像形。The claws 𦥑, the head 由, the tail 禸. This character is now used to write the number 10000 (**chia-chieh**); see page **11**. 託名標識字、古用以紀數。十千謂之萬。It has nothing in common with the 140th radical, under which it was classified by **K'ang-hsi**. It is not derived from 禺 **yü²** (above E), but from 蠆 **ch'ai⁴** L. 47 X. — Phonetic series 765, that must not be confounded with the series of 禺. The sound of the compounds is derived from **ch'ai⁴**, and not from **wan⁴**; e.g. 邁 **mai⁴**. Note

Li⁴. A scorpion 萬 crouched down under a 厂 stone (L. 59 A). Pricking, sharp, bad, cruel, and other **chuan-chu**. — Phonetic series 804.

嘼

Shou⁴. The domesticated animals, by opposition to 禽 **ch'in²** wild (above E); 六牲。馬牛羊雞犬豕也。像耳頭足之形。On the top two ears, in the middle 由 the head, at the bottom 禸 the paws and tail. The second ancient character from which came the modern one, is an abbreviation. It forms the compound 獸 **shou⁴**, flocks or herds guarded by 犬 dogs. But 鼉 **t'o²**, crocodile, has another origin. See L. 72 E.

LESSON 24.

About the primitive 十 and its multiples 廿 卅 卌.

First series: 十.

A 十 十

Shih². Ten 數之具也。一爲東西。丨爲南北。則四方中央備矣。The number that contains all the other simple numbers (decimal numeration). Symbol of extent (two dimensions) and of the five cardinal points (East, West, South, North, Centre). — It is the 24th radical. Phonetic series 10. Note the derivatives

B 計

Chi⁴. To know how to calculate; 會算也。从言、从十、會意。To know how to enounce 言 the ten numbers 十 of the decimal system. By extension, to reckon, to plan, a scheme.

C 士

Shih^{4}. An affair, a thing; 事也。从一、从十、會意。推十合一.推一合十.爲士。Because, says the Glose, all things are comprised between the two terms of numeration, 一 and 十. By extension, a sage, a man pointed out, by his learning, to become an official (now 仕). — It is the 33th radical. It forms

吉 **Chi**^{2}. Speach 口 of a 士 sage, bringing luck; good, auspicious, happy; 善也、祥也。从口、从士、會意。Compare 凶 **hsiung**^{1}, inauspicious, L. 38 D. — Phonetic series 180. See 壹 L. 38 G. Compare 壴 L. 165 B, 臺 L. 75 B, etc. Note

頡 **Chieh**^{2}. A phonetic complex. To keep one's head 頁 straight; 吉 is phonetic. — Phon. ser. 797.

D 千

Ch'ien^{1}. A thousand; 十百也。从十、人聲。Ten times one hundred. The hundred is not represented in the character. The 丿 on the top, an abbreviation of 人 (L. 28), is phonetic says the Glose. 千 is perhaps an old primitive. — Phonetic series 16. Forms

年 **Nien**^{2}. The crop, the harvest; 年成也。从禾、从千。The thousand grains. By extension, a year, the time required for a harvest. The modern character is an incongruous contraction.

E 丈

Chang^{4}. A lenght of ten spans, now of ten feet; 十尺也、从又持十、會意。A hand 彐 and 十 ten See L. 43 L. — Phonetic series 13.

F 古

Ku^{2}. Old; 故也。从十、从口、會意。十口相傳爲古。That which passed through 十 ten 口 mouths, i.e. a tradition dating back ten generations.— 叶 **hsieh** composed of the same elements means *unanimity*, ten mouths speaking in unison; 十口並協爲叶。— Phonetic series 132. It forms

固 **Ku**^{4}. Hermetically closed 囗 on all sides (L. 74). 四塞也。从囗、古聲。— Phonetic series 368.

胡 **Hu**^{2}. The fetlock of an ox; 从肉、古聲。牛頷垂也。It is now used as an interrogative particle, **chia-chieh** for 曷, — Phonetic series 450.

Note: 啇 **ti**^{2} is not derived from 古. See L. 120 H.

G 直 直

Chih². Straight; 从乚、从十、从目、會意。When ten eyes have seen to it, the line must be straight. See L. 10 K, where this character was fully explained. — Phonetic series 335.

Note: **K'ang-hsi** incorrectly classified under 十, 卑 L 46 E, 卒 L 46 M, 半 L. 18 D, etc.

Second series: 十 repeated twice 卄, 廿.

H 卄 廿 廿

Nien⁴. Erh⁴-shih². Twenty; 二十并也、會意。The tens added one to another. In composition, it often means a multitude (L. 10 I). It is liable to be confounded with 甘 **kan¹** (L. 73 B). It forms.

I 共

Kung⁴. An action done in common, all taking part in it, represented by 廿 twenty 𦥑 pairs of hands; 从廿. 从𦥑. 會意 See L 47 Q — Phonetic series 225.

J 光

Kuang¹. Light, luster. 明也。古文、从廿、从火、會意。Primitively twenty 廿火 fires (L. 126). The modern form represents 人上火, a man with fire (L. 29); probably a man carrying a torch. The ancient form was maintained in a few compounds (below L) — Phonetic series 222. It forms

K 晃

Huang³. Brightness 光 of the 日 sun, to dazzle: 暉也、从日、从光、會意。— Phonetic series 537.

L 黃

Huang². Yellow, the 光 hue of the ploughed earth 田 (L. 149); 地之色也。从田、从古文光。Note how 田 and 火 are mixed up. See the derivatives, L. 171. — It is the 201th radical Phonetic series 688.

M 庶 㡿 **Shu**⁴. All 廿 the inhabitants of a 广 dwelling, gathered around the 火 hearth (L. 126); among the ancients, the hearth gave light and heat; 屋下眾也。从广,从古文光,會意。Meanings **chuan-chu** 眾也 the familial flock, concubines and children; the human herd, the people. Various **chia-chieh**. — Phonetic series 645. — Note the following logical aggregates, in which 灬 was replaced by the radical.

度 度 **Tu**⁴. To measure, a rule, a degree; 取法也。从又,从庶。A hand which counts or measures 庶 a quantity. — Phonetic series 484.

席 席 **Hsi**³. A mat, a meal; because, in the olden times, 庶 people used to eat, while sitting on mats, the dishes being placed on a mat. 籍也。从巾,从庶。See 巾, a napkin, L. 35 A.

Third series: 十 repeated three times; 卅.

N 卅 卅 **San**¹**-shih**². Thirty; 三十并也,會意。It forms

O 世 世 世 **Shih**⁴. A period of thirty years; duration of a man's active life; an age, a generation; 三十年爲一世,从卅而曳長,指事。The vertical stroke of 十 on the left side is lenghtened, to denote the prolongation and duration of life. — Phonetic series 157. It forms

業 枼 **Yeh**⁴. The 世 successions *of leaves* upon the 木 trees; a leaf (now 葉); by extension, a thin plate of metal or gold; 从世,从木。世亦聲。古葉字。薄也。— Phonetic series 494. Compare 業 L. 104 A.

Fourth series: 十 repeated four times, 卌.

P 卌 卌 **Ssŭ⁴-shih²**. Forty; 二廿幷也。會意。 Twice twenty. Some etymologists think this 卌 to be the top part of the following character

Q 帶 帶 **Tai⁴**. A girdle, to take along as if worn at the girdle, to wear; 紳也。This derivation is an arbitrary one, calligraphic, not etymological. 卌 is a primitive, while — means the girdle, and the other part represents the trinkets 佩 (L. 21 D) hanging from the girdle; 上像。At the bottom, the robes are represented by two 巾 (L. 35), one above the other; 从重巾。— Phonetic series 648.

R 無 無 **Wu²**. See L. 10 I, where this character was fully explained. A luxuriant 林 forest destroyed by 卌 a great number of 大 men. It is now an adverb of negation; no, none, no more. — Phonetic series 718.

LESSON 25.

Note: The primitive 人 jên², a man, being written in different manners; several lessons are devoted to it. Here is a list of them.

人 jên² standing, or 亻 put on the side.	L. 25
匕 jên² inverted.	L. 26
Multiples of 人 and 匕.	L. 27
人 jên² on the top of the compounds, curtailed.	L. 28
儿 jên² at the bottom of the compounds.	L. 29
𠂆 jên² bent down.	L. 30 A
尸 jên² sitting down.	L. 32
㔾 jên² overturned.	L. 30 D
勹 jên² doubled up.	L. 54
夂 夊 夊 jên² moving on.	L. 31
大 jên² with arms.	LL. 60, 61

About the primitive 人 under its two forms, 人 and 亻.

A 人 亻

Jên[2]. A man, represented by his legs; the one who stands upright. Compare 大 (L. 60): 像。臂脛之形。人、天地之性最貴者也、五行之秀氣也。— It is the 9th radical of characters relating to man. It forms

B 囚

Ch'iu[2]. A prisoner, to emprison; 从人在口中、會意。A man 人 in an 口 enclosure, L. 74. See 盈 L. 157 C.

C 閃

Shan[3]. 从人在門中、會意。A man 人 in a door 門 (L. 129 C), moving sideways to give way to others; by extension, a sudden and quick motion in general.

D 戍

Shu[4]. To guard the frontiers; 人 a man with 戈 a spear (L. 71 F); 守邊也。从人持戈、會意。See the compound 幾 (L. 90 D).

E 伏

Fu[2]. From 人 man and 犬 dog (L. 134). A man imitating the dog, or making others imitate it. To crouch, to fall or lie prostrate, to hide, to humble, to subject, etc. — Phonetic series 196.

F 位

Wei[4]. The place where a 人 man is 立 standing erect; the place assigned, according to his dignity, to each official; 从人、从立、會意。列中廷之左右謂之位。By extension, seat, rank, person. See 立 (L. 60 H).

G 仁

Jên[2]. The virtue that must unite men to men; 親也。从人、从二、會意。See L. 2 B, where this character was explained.

H 信

Hsin[4]. True words, and, by extension, the effect produced by these words upon others, truthfulness, faith, confidence; 誠也。从言、从人、會意。古文、从人、从口。A man 人 and a 言 word. In the old form, a 人 man and a 口 mouth. In still more ancient form, a word 言 and a 心 heart; words coming from the heart and appealing to it.

I 僊 僊 仙 屳 — **Hsien**[1]. The taoist Genii; 从人、从䙴。會意。䙴，升高也。長生不死曰僊。今俗作仙。 According to the legends, they live on the mountains, hence the modern character 仙, man and mountain. The etymological meaning is 亻 a man who 䙴 rose, by the taoist practices, above mortals. (See L. 50 P, L. 10 L).

LESSON 26.

About the 人 inverted which is now written 匕. (Compare with the old forms, L. 25 A and 26 B).

Preliminary note: The modern 匕. corresponds to two old primitives. — 1. 𠤎 represents an old instrument, a kind of scraper, of spoon. 像形，挹鼎之器。 This character became soon obsolete. In the derivatives that remained after it (匙、鬯, etc.) it was written 匕 even before the reform of **Li-ssu**. This explains how, in the series 匕, one may find several characters that mean *utensils* (below C, D, M). — 2. 人 inverted, over-turned. Hence the significations derived from the origin of this character; to turn round, to invert, to compare, to join, to match, to pair (right side and reverse).

A

B 匕 — **Pi**[3]. To turn one's self round, etc. 从反人。— It is the 21th radical.

First series: Compounds in which 匕 means an object.

匙 — **Shih**[2]. A spoon, a key. (Phon. 是 L. 112 I).

C 鬯 — **Ch'ang**[4]. A special liquor, used in the sacrifices, to induce the 神 **shên**[2] to come down; 以秬釀鬱艸芬芳攸服以降神也。从凵器也。中像米。匕所以扱之。 A vase 凵 (L. 38E) full of 米 grain which, when fermented, produced the liquor; at the bottom, 匕 the spoon with which people drew up the liquor from the vessel. Compare below M. — It is the 192th radical. It forms

Yü[4]. Oblation of the liquor 鬯. See L. 130 E.

D 兂 旡 **Tsan**^{1}. A forked brooch used to fix the hair. Now 簪 The character represents a man 人, with a 匕 brooch on the top. 从古文人。匕像、簪形。所以持冠。首笄也。 Note the alteration of the modern character and try do distinguish it from 无 **wu**^{2} L. 61 C, and from 旡 **chi**^{4} L. 99 E. Repeated twice, **tsan**^{1} is phonetic in **hsün**^{2}, a caldron (L. 155), and in

朁 **Tsan**^{1}. To murmur; 民勞曰朁。从曰、重兂聲。 See L. 73 A. Not to be confounded, either with 替 t'i (L. 60 L) as many scribes do, or with 贊 L. 79 B. — Phonetic series 709. Note

昝 **Tsan**^{2}. I, we. This modern character is an arbitrary abbreviation of 朁. It is used, regardless of the sense, to write the sound **tsan**^{2}, a personal pronoun used by common people in the provinces of the North. Its derivatives 偺 and 喒, much used in the books written in spoken language, have no more value than 昝 itself. 今北方人稱我曰昝、卽朁字之轉也。— 昝 must be distinguished from 咎 **chiu**^{1}, L. 31 B.

Second series: Compounds in which 匕 means man, etc.

E **Pao**^{3}. A tithing of 十 ten 匕 men. It forms some phonetic compounds, e g. 鴇 **pao**^{3}, a bustard, etc.

F 尼 **Ni**^{2}. Near, in contact; 近之也。 Morally, intimity. Etymology, 从尸、从匕、會意。 But 尸 (L. 32) means also, a man. Therefore ni means, two men near one another. Phonetic series 140.

G 卬 **Nang**^{2}. A high 卩 dignity, towards which rise the eyes and desires of 匕 men; exalted, to desire; 从匕、从卩、會意。卩者、望之處。望欲有所庶及也。— Phonetic series 73. Compare 印 **yin**^{4}, L. 49 I.

H 死 **Ssŭ**^{3}. Dead, to die; 从歺从人、會意。人之終也。 A 人 man, 歺 dead (L. 118 C). Note 1. In the modern character, the top stroke of 歺 is prolonged and covers 匕. 2. In the ancient form, instead of 匕, the inverted form, there is 人, the straight form.

I 牝

P'in^3. Etymologically, the cow that makes 匕 the pair with the 牛 bull. Now 牡 **mu**^{3} means the male, and 牝 **p'in**^{3} the female of all kinds of animals. Note the analogous compound 麀 **yu**^{1}, hind, female of the 鹿 **lu**^{4}, stag.

J 頃

Kêng^3. Etymologically 匕 to turn 頁 the head. Then, to turn over, to overthrow, in general; **从匕、从頁、會意。** There are also a few unusual phonetic complexes; for these, see **此 tsŭ**^{3}, L. 1[illegible]; and **比 pi**^{3}, L. 27 I.

Third series: A special series is ascribed to the following compounds of 匕, on account both of the singular forms which were given to them in the modern writing, and of the importance of their derivatives. In the old writing, those characters were perfectly regular.

K

Yao^3. **从日、从匕、會意。** To turn one's back 匕 to the 日 sun; obscure, hidden. It forms 窅 **yao**^{3}, dark as in a 穴 cavern; 官 **yao**^{3}, the South-East angle, the most retired place in a 宀 house; etc. In its modern form, the next seems to be a compound of the same elements; it is not so.

旨

Chih^3. The old form is composed of 舌, the tongue (L. 102 C), and of 一, a sweet thing (L. 1, 4°); good, agreeable to the taste; **古文、从舌含一、指事。** After **Li-ssŭ**, the character was composed of **甘 kan**^{1} sweet (L. 73 B), and of 匕 Phonetic; **从甘、匕聲。** **Chuan-chu**, an edict of the Emperor who is supposed to speak in soft words. — Phonetic series 186. It forms 嘗 **ch'ang**^{2} (L. 36 E), 耆 **ch'i**^{2} (L. 30 E), 稽 **chi**^{1} (L. 121 M).

L 艮

Kên^4. **从目、从匕、會意。狠視也。** To turn suddenly round 匕, in order to 目 look a man full in the face, haughtily; anger, defiance. — It is the 138th radical. Phonetic series 219 and 741.

Note. 良 **liang**^{2} has another origin. See L. 75 F.
Item 退 **t'ui**^{4}. See L. 31 C.

M 皀 皀 良

Hsiang[1] Boiled grain, the Chinese soup 飯 **fan**[4]- It is composed as 皀 (L. 26 C). A 白 vase (primitive); — its contents (L. 1. 4°); 匕 the spoon to draw up (L. 26 A). 像。米在鍋中之形。匕所以扱之。 Its contracted form must be distinguished from 艮 liang (L. 75 F). It forms the following characters:

鄉 鄕

Hsiang[1]. The 皀 grain producing country, between the walled cities, represented by two 邑、one of them being straight, the other being inverted and abbrevia-ted in the modern writing (L. 74 C). 从邑正反。皀亦聲。— Phonetic series 682.

卿 卿

Ch'ing[2]. Ministers. Those who were present at the imperial 皀 meals, standing in two opposite rows, holding the 卩 卩 sceptres, badges of their dignity; 从正反卩、皀亦聲。See L. 55 A.

卽 即 卽

Chi[2]. The convenient 卩 measure (L. 55 B) of 皀 soup; temperance, moderation; now 節. — **Chi**[2] is widely used **chia-chieh** as a conjunction expressing the logical consequence. — Phonetic series 424. It forms the phonetic complex.

節

Chieh[2]. A segment of the bamboo, between two nodes. **Chuan-chu**, an article, a limit of time, a term. **Chia-chieh** for **chi**[2], temperance, moderation. — Phonetic series 798.

旣 既

Chi[4]. To suck up, to swallow; (L. 99 E). **Chuan-chu**, already passed, as 旡 swallowed 皀 soup; finished, alrea-dy, since; 盡也畢也、定也。— Phonetic series 596.

Shih[2]. **ssŭ**[4]. Food, to eat, to feed; 从 皀, 从 亼, 會 意。 See L. 14, 亼 union, together; 皀 grain, food. Because, says the Glose, it is by mixing the different (six) kinds of grain that the human food is prepared; 按 六 穀 之 飯 曰 食。Note the top stroke of 良, a contraction of 皀, is confounded with the lower stroke of 亼. — It is the 184th radical of characters relating to food. It forms

Shih[2]. To nourish; to give 食 food to a 人 man; 从 食、从 人、會 意。以 食 食 人 也。It forms the phonetic complexes 飾 **shih**[4], **to adorn, and** 飭 **ch'ih**[4], an order, injunction. See L. **28.**

Ts'ang[1]. A granary, government storehouse. In this character, 食 is mutilated, to make room beneath for 口 (L. 74): 从 食 省。口 像、穀 藏 也。— Phonetic series **575.**

N **Chiu**[4] is not derived from 皀. The modern forms are corrupt. Compare the ancient forms with L. **117 B.** The rearing of cattle, under trees, in the steppe. Hence now 廄 **chiu**[4], a stud, a stable.

O **N. B.** — Let us recall — 1. That 艮 is the classical abbreviation of 皀 **kên**[3] (**26 L**), but that it is also used for other compounds. — **2. That** 良 is the classical abbreviation of 皀 **hsiang**[1] **(26 M)**. By the principle of the *least effort*, the scribes often write 艮 instead of 良. — 3. That these abbreviations are to be distinguished from the derivatives of 良 **liang**[2] (**75 F**); a thing easier to say than to do. — 4. That the engravers, following the scribes, cut in fanciful ways, several characters of this series, as one may have noticed. — See also 退, L. 31 C.

LESSON 27.

About the multiples of 人.

First series: 人 repeated twice (the straight form, L. 25).

A 从 — **Ts'ung^{2}**. A man walking after another; to follow, to obey. It is the opposite of 北, L. 27 C. 相聽也。从二人、會意。二人相順爲从、二人相背爲北。Chuan-chu, a preposition, as the Latin *ab, ex;* it is in this sense that 从 is so often used in this work, for the analysis of characters. It is now practically superseded by the next homophone and synonym compound

從 — **Ts'ung^{2}**. Note the curious form of the modern character. It is composed of 从, and of 辵 (Rad. 162; L. 112 E) dislocated; the three 彡 placed on the left side simulate 彳, the 60th radical, under which K'ang-hsi wrongfully classified 從 and its similes; the lower part 止 is placed under 从. In the ancient character, there is simply a juxtaposition of the elements. — Phonetic series 657.

B 㦰 — **Ch'ien^{1}**. To cut. Two men and a halberd; 絕也。从二人持戈、會意。See L. 71. Compare 成 L. 25 D, and 戒 L. 47 E. — It forms

韱 — **Ch'ien^{1}**. The wild garlic; 山韭也。从韭、㦰聲。See L. 170 B. — Phonetic series 829.

C 僉 — **Ch'ien^{1}**. Reunion, meeting. By extension, together. 皆也。从亼 (L. 14), 从吅、會意。A meeting 亼 of several 人 men, who 口 speak. — Phonetic series 726.

Second series: Two 人 turned face to face.

D 坐 — **Tso^{4}**. To sit down, to be seated; 从土、从二人對坐、會意。Two 人 men sitting on the 土 ground, in the old fashion, and facing each other to talk. — Phonetic series 309.

E 巫

Wu[1]. The work 工 (L. 82) of 从 witches; magic, incantations. Two witches who dance to obtain rain 祝也。女能以舞降神者也。像。从工、兩人舞形。It forms

筮 **Shih**[1]. The stalks 𥫗 of *Achillea Sibirica* 蓍, that were used by the wizards 巫 to divine. 易卦用蓍也。从竹、从巫、會意。It forms the phonetic complexes 噬 **shih**[4], to bite, to gnaw; 澨 **shih**[4], bank, quay.

See 靈 **Ling**[2], L 72 K. Distinguish 巫 from 𠦒 L. 16 M, and from 來 contracted in 嗇 L. 13 C, etc.

F 夾

Chia[1]. A man 大 (L. 60) who clasps two 从 others in his arms: to press, to squeeze, to pick up, to fix; 持也。从大挾二人、會意。— Phonetic series 257. To be distinguished from 夾 **shan**[3] (L. 13 B), and from 來 **lai**[2] (L. 13 C). It forms the phonetic complex

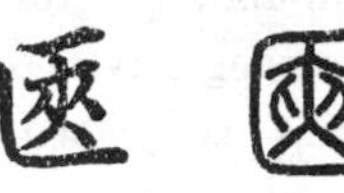

Ch'ieh[4]. Box, casket, 从匚 (L. 10. B), 夾聲。It is now written 篋.

Third series: Two 人 turned one against another.

G 北

Pei[3]. The opposite of 从 (L. 27 A). Not to follow each other, to turn one's back, disagreement; 从二人相背、指事。二人相順爲从、二人相違爲北。Derived meaning, the back 背也; and, by extension, the North 北方也, the cardinal point towards which one turns one's back when sitting down facing the South, according to custom. — The modern scribes write 北 for different more intricate characters. See 乖 **kuai**[1], L. 103 C; 乘 **ch'êng**[2], L. 31 E, etc.

H 丠 丘

Ch'iu[1]. A hill, a mound; 从北、从一、指事。一地也。The Glose is summed up thus: — represents the top of a height. On the top, 北 two men turned one against another, instead of four men whom it would have been too difficult to depict. The meaning is that, from the top one may see towards the four directions i. e. towards all directions; a culminating point. — Phonetic series 113. — Note that 兵 ping^{1} (L. 47 D) is unconnected with 丘... Item, the kind of primitive 岳 (L. 80 B)... But 丘 forms

虛 虚

Hsü^{1}. A high upland; 大丘也。从丘、虍聲。These uplands being generally wild and barren, hence **chuan-chu**, empty, that which contains nothing; 大丘空曠、故虛閒也、空也。— Phonetic series 685, under its modern corrupt form.

Fourth series: 匕 repeated twice (人, inverted form, L. 26).

I 比

Pi^{4}. It is 从 inverted (27 A), 从二匕、會意。To effect a union, to follow, to cooperate, to plot.

Pi^{3}. Meanings derived from the inversion (See L. 26 A, 2°), to draw a parallel between, to compare, rank.— It is the 81th radical. Phonetic series 77. It forms

坒

Pi^{3}. A synonym of the preceding. The two men are placed upon 土 (L. 81) the earth. — Phonetic series 299.

皆

Chieh^{1}. Together, all; 同也。从自、从比、會意。Several 比 men 自 (L. 169 A contracted) acting in concert. — Phonetic series 428. K'ang-hsi erroneously classified this character under the radical 106 白.

昆

K'un^{1}. A number 比 or men under the 日 sun (L. 143); multitude, generality; 同也。从日、从比、會意。**Chuan-chu** of different kinds; 後也, a posterity, those who will succeed in life, under the sun; 蟲也, the multitude of insects that the sun is supposed to bring forth... **Chia-chieh** 兄也, an elder brother; compare ko^{1}, p. 11. — Phonetic series 371.

毘 毗

P'i^{2}. The navel which is supposed to be in communication with the head 囟 (L. 40 A) through channels in which circulate the 气 vital spirits. 人臍也。从囟。取气通也。比聲。So the lower part would not be 比, but a kind of primitive, representing the channels. Instead of 囟, the scribes write 田, hence the erroneous character here joined. — Phonetic series 557.

Note 1: 比 is intended to delineate the feet in some characters that represent animals, e. g.

毚 **Ch'ao**[4], jerboa, L. 106 C. 鹿 **Lu**[4], antelope. L. 136 A.

Note 2: Two 比, one above the other, represent also the feet in the following series

J 能

Nêng[2], formerly **Nai**[4], which explains the sound of some derivatives. The great brown bear. After **Li-ssŭ**, this character was explained thus: two 匕 paws, 月 the body, 厶 the growling of the angry bear. (L. 85 E). But the study of the old forms reveals a special primitive delineating a head, a hairy body standing, and claws. (L. 146 H). The bear is the symbol of bravery; hence the meanings **chuan-chu**, valour, an officer; 才能之意。— Phonetic series 554. It forms

態 **T'ai**[4]. Martial attitude. 从心.从能.會意。— The outward of the 心 interior 能 valour.

熊 **Hsiung**[2]. The small black 能 bear; 灬 represents the feet (L. 126 C), a graphic redundancy.

罷 **Pa**[4]. A 能 bear, figuratively an officer taken in a 网 net (L. 39 C); to dismiss, to resign, to cease, and other **chuan-chu**. The Glose explains that the net means calumnious accusations. Compare 置 L. 39 F.

Fifth series: 人 repeated thrice.

K 㐺

Chung[4]. Gathering, meeting. *Tres collegium faciunt*; 从三人.會意。The next compound, a synonym and homophone, is now used instead.

L 眾

Chung[4]. A crowd; 从三人.从目.會意。Note that 罒 is not 网 (as above, in 罷), but the eye 目 (L. 158) depicted horizontally. The visual 目 space full of 人 men; all the men taken in at a glance; crowd, all, etc. The scribes fancifully and strangely altered this character, as one may see by the two specimens here joined.

聚 **Chü**[4]. To meet; 取 a reunion of 㐺 men; 會也、从三人.从取。取亦聲。See L. 146 F. — Phonetic series 775.

LESSON 28.

About some peculiar forms of 人, curtailed in the modern writing, either through want of space, or through a partial fusion with a phonetic; 人 is reduced to 丿, 卜, etc. In the ancient writing, 人 has its normal form.

A 及

Chi^{2}. To attain, to seize upon. A 彐 hand that seizes a 人 man. This character was explained, L. 19 D. — Phonetic series 40.

B 臽

Hsien^{4}. A trap, a pit; 小穽也。从人在臼上、會意。臼即坎也。A man 人 who falls into a 臼 pit (L 139). Cf. L. 38 D. — Phonetic series 360.

C 負

Fu^{4}. 1. Morally, a 人 man who has 貝 cowries, money (L. 161); the pride caused by fortune; insubordination, disdain; 从人守貝有所恃也。— 2. Physically, a 人 man who bears a load on his back, in order to gain 貝 cowries; to toil hard, to suffer; 凡从背任物曰負。

D 色

Shê^{4}. Primitive sense, the flush of the face; 顔气也。从人、从卩、會意、根心生色、若合符卩也。The composition of this character is typical; 人 a man, and 卩 (L. 55) a seal; because, says the Glose, the colour of the face corresponds with the feelings of the heart, as the stamp reproduces the seal. By extension, the flush arising from passion, sexual pleasure, colour in general — It is the 139th radical.

E 厃

Wei^{2}. A man 人 looking from up a 厂 steep cliff (L. 59); a perilous situation, danger; 仰也、从人在厂上會意。There are important compounds, about which see L. 59 H.

F 千

Ch'ien^{1}. One thousand. This anomalous character was explained L. 24 D. 人 on the top is phonetic; 十 is for 十百也、ten times one hundred, says the Glose. — Phonetic series 16.

G 壬

T'ing^{2}. Upright, raised, attentive; 从人立土上、會意。挺立也。於立同意。A man 人 on the 土 ground (L. 81). Not to be confounded with 壬 jên^{4} (L. 82 C). In the modern writing, the two characters are almost identical.

H 弔

Tiao^4. Actual meaning, to mourn for one dead, in order to console his family. Composition: a man 人 who carries a bow 弓 (L. 87) over his shoulders. The Chinese of olden times did not bury their dead. The corpse was packed up in a bundle of grass (L. 78 G), and left to rot away in some remote place. The rite of condoling, at that time, consisted in offering one's self with a bow, to protect the corpse against wild beasts. 問終也。古之葬者、厚之以薪。从持弓敺禽、會意。 The meaning, to hang up, to suspend, comes from the fact that the bow was carried hanging across the shoulder, which is represented by the old character.

I 

Chiu^1. Primitive sense, egotism hurting one's neighbour; a man 人 who does not look for his own 各 (L. 31 B) benefit; 从人、从各、會意。各者相違也。 By extension, offence, fault, mistake; 過也。— Phonetic series 338.

J 

Shên^1. Body, person. It is 人 with a big belly and a leg. See L. 148. — It is the 158th radical of characters relating to the shapes of the body.

Note: The head (sharp snout) of some animal figures, is like 人 in the ancient writing. The resemblance is merely a graphical one. For instance:

T'u^2, hare, L. 106 B.

Yü^2, fish, L. 142 A.

LESSON 29.

About 儿, the form taken by 人, when placed at the bottom of the characters.

A 儿

Jên^2. A man (two legs). It sometimes means, feet, support. 古文人像。— It is the 10th radical.

B 兒

Erh^2. An infant: 孺子也、从儿、从囟、會意。儿古文人像、囟小兒頭。 A body 儿 and a head 囟 (L. 40 C) opened in the form of 臼, representing a skull, the fontanels of which are not yet closed. — Phonetic series 352.

C 皃

Mao^{4}. The face; 从人、从白。像。人面形 From 儿 man and 白 (L. 88), white, colour or form of the face. Instead of this, the synonym and homophone compound 貌 is now used.

D 兄

Huang^{4}; 从口在儿上、會意。A 口 mouth on the top of a 儿 man; to speak strongly, emphatically, authoritatively. Note the two modern **chuan-chu**, with change of sounds

1. **K'uang**^{4}. An emphatic conjunction, so much the more, *a fortiori*. The scribes write 兄 況 况, but their writing is rejected by the critics, 正作兄.

2. **Hsiung**^{1}. The eldest among several brothers; the one who must 口 exhort and correct his brothers.— Phonetic series 123. Note also the compounds

祝 **Chu**^{4}. An 兄 oration that goes with the oblation of a 示 sacrifice, and that touches the 神 **shên**; 从示儿口、會意。祭文也。所以悅神。

呪 **Chou**^{4}. A modern character. The 口 added is a redundancy. Adjuration, imprecation; 祈也。 This character is often erroneously written 咒.

兑

Yüeh^{4}. Good words that dispel grief and rejoice the hearer; hence the two meanings, to speak, to rejoice. It is 兄 added with a 八 (L. 18), that means, dissipation; 从儿口八、會意。八像、氣之散者。說也。喜也。It is unconnected with 台 (L. 18 E.). It is used as a modern arbitrary **chia-chieh** to mean, exchange, delivery in the commercial transactions; it is then pronounced **tui**^{4}; 今俗書兌、換字。— Phonetic series 313.

E 允

Yün^{3}. To consent, to grant. A man 儿 who 厶 says *yes*; 准也。从儿、从厶。會意。To make out one's assent, by breathing forth a *yes*. See L. 85 E. — Phonetic series 100. Note the phonetic complex

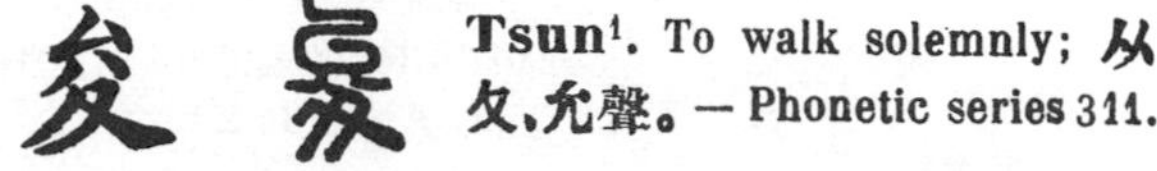

Tsun^{1}. To walk solemnly; 从夊、允聲。— Phonetic series 311.

F 充

Ch'ung^{1}. To nourish a 𠫓 child, from its birth till, knowing how to 儿 walk, it has become a man; 从𠫓、从儿. 會意。育子長大成人也。To feed, to fill, full, etc. **Chuan-chu** and **chia-chieh** of different kinds. — Phonetic series 189.

G 頁

Yeh^{4}. The head; 頭也。从百在儿上。像。百者古文首字也。A head 百 (L. 160) upon a body 儿 Note the contraction of 儿 in the modern character. — It is the 181th radical of a group of characters relating to the head, neck, etc.

H 元

Yüan^{2}. That which is 上 on the top, upon 儿 man. Head, principle, origin; as *caput* in latin; 始也、首也。从古文人. 古文上。首於人體最上、故从人、上、會意。See 二, an ancient form of 上, L. 2 G. — Phonetic series 97. Note the compounds

Kuan^{1}. The man's cap, then caps and hats in general; 弁冕之總名也。从冖、从元、會意。。。寸 (L. 45 B) stands for 彐。The meaning is, 冖 what is placed 彐 on the 元 head, to cover it.

完

Wan^{2}. Entire, finished, done; 全也。从宀、元聲。The putting up of the 宀 roof completes a building. — Phonetic series 314. It forms

K'ou^{4}. Robbers, to loot. The man who armed with 攴 a stick (L. 43 D) threatens the 完 dwelling-places; 从攴、从完、會意。與賊同意。

I 光

Kuang^{1}. Light. The old form of this character was explained L. 24 J. This is the modern form, 儿上火、probably, a man carrying a torch. — Phonetic series 222.

J 宂

Jung^{3}. Inaction, to remain inactive; 从宀、从儿、會意。人在屋下無田事也。A 儿 man in his 宀 house, because he has no work to do in the fields. Not to be confounded with 冘 **yin**^{3}, composed of 冖 and 人 (L. 34 E).

K 兀 **Wu**⁴. A stool. A plane surface — upon a 儿 support; 高而上平也。从一在儿上。一者平也。指事。— Phonetic series 36.

LESSON 30.

About 尸 (人 who bends forward), and 匕 (人 inverted, the feed being turned up).

First series: 尸.

A 

Jên². A man who leans, who bends up; 像。人之形。It forms

B 辰 **Ch'ên**². 从尸、从丏、會意。尸像人之形、伏而蔽有所恥也。A woman 尸 who bends forward to conceal 丏 her shame, says the Glose; probably her menses (not her pregnancy L. 112 L). Hence **chuan-chu** time, epoch, period. — It is the 161th radical. — Phonetic series 254. — The primitive meaning has been preserved in the compound

Ju⁴. To shame, to insult; 从寸、从辰、會意。To reveal 寸 (for 又, L. 43 A) a shameful 辰 situation or thing. — Phonetic series 541.

C 后 **Hou**⁴. A prince (by extension, a princess). 君后也。从尸。从口、會意。於君同意。按口發號者。The man who notifies 口 his orders, 尸 bending towards the people. This composition is analogous to that of 君 **chūn**², a prince, See page 9. — Phonetic series 199. — 后 inverted, forms

司 **Ssŭ**⁴. The government, the administration, that is like the reverse of the prince; 从反后、指事。— Phonetic series 159.

Second series: 匕.

D 匕 **Hua**⁴. A man tumbled head over heels; 从倒人、指事。The primitive sense was, to die; 倒人爲匕、死也。Derived meanings, to overthrow, to transform; 變也 It forms

化 𠤎

Hua^4. To change, to convert 匕 men 亻 by teaching them; 教行也。从匕、从亻。會意。-- Phonetic series 64. It forms 花 **hua^1**, flowers, the term of the 化 evolution of 艹 plants. See L. 13 F.

眞

Chên^1. Transformation by the Taoist practices. See, L. 10 L.

E 老

Lao^3. Old, venerable, a septuagenarian. A man 人 whose hair and beard 毛 (L. 100) change 匕, grow white; 从人毛匕、會意。言須髮變白也。七十日老。Note the strange modern contraction of 人 and of 毛. — It is the 125th radical. This character forms important compounds, in which 匕 was suppressed to give room to the radical or to the phonetic. For instance:

Ch'i^2. Sexagenarian; 老 old man who 旨 needs a better food. See 旨 L. 26 K. — Phonetic series 513.

K'ao^3. Old age; 丂 represents the asthma of old men (L. 1, l). By extension, to examine, to interrogate pupils and candidates, which are attributes of worthies. — Phonetic series 218.

Hsiao^4. Filial piety; the thing which the 子 children owe to the 老 aged persons in general, and to their parents in particular; 善事父母者。从老省。从子、會意。— Phonetic series 276. But 教 **chiao^1**, to teach, has nothing in common with 孝. This character, whose exact form is given here, will be explained L. 39 H.

者

Chê^3. This character is not derived from 老. See L. 159 B.

LESSON 31.

About three derivatives of 人, partial primitives, viz.: 久 **chiu^3**, 夂 **chih^3**, 夊 **sui^1**.

First series: 久.

A 

Chiu^3. A man hindered while walking, by a kind of train; 行遲也。从人、像、後有迫而止之者。乀指事。Hence the notion of slowness, of duration. — Phonetic series 17.

Second series: 夂.

B 夂

Chih[3]. To follow, to pursue a man who walks; 從後至也。从人、像、乀指事。— It is the 34th radical, ordinarily placed on the top of compounds. It forms

各

Ko[3]. To 夂 go on one's way, without hearing the 口 advice of others; 行而不相聽也。从夂、从口、會意。Separated, distinct, particular, other. The individual described by his self-love, his own way. — Phonetic series 220. It forms

咎

Chiu[1]. A man 人 attached to his 各 own opinion, who cares only for his own interests, and who consequently offends against others. By extension, offence, fault; 从人、从各、會意。各者相違也。 See L. 28 I. Note the contraction of the modern character. — Phonetic series 338.

路

Lu[4]. Way, road; 从足、从各; through which 各 each one 足 trespasses. — Phonetic series 748.

客

K'o[4]. **Ch'ieh**[4]. A guest, a traveller; 从宀。从各; to stay for a time in a 宀 house not 各 one's own.

畧

Liao[4]. Boundary that 各 divides the 田 fields. **Chuan-chu**, to partition, to shorten, a little, etc. It forms 擥 liao[4], to lay down, to depose.

洛

Lao[4]. Old meaning: a trench to irrigate; 氵 water used by 各 everybody. It forms 落 lao[4], the fall of the leaves, to sink.

See 夆 **hai**[4], L. 97 H; 夆 **fêng**[1] L. 97 A; and 冬 **tung**[1] L. 17 F.
The 34th radical 夂 **chih**[3] (three strokes) must be carefully distinguished from the 66th radical 攵 **p'u**[1] (four strokes), and from the 36th radieal 夕 **hsi**[4].

Third series: 夊

C 夊

Sui[1]. A man who goes on, despite of shackles; 行遲也、像。人兩脛有所躧之形。To be distinguished from analogous forms, as stated above. — It is the 35th radical, ordinarily placed at the bottom of the compounds. It forms

致 **Chih**⁴. To 夊 reach or make others reach 至 the aim, despite of difficulties; 从夊.从至.會意 See L. 133 B.

退 **T'ui**⁴. To have 夊 walked with difficulty all the day 日 long, and consequently, to *refuse* to advance more, or to *go backwards*, on account of the difficulties of the road. To refuse, to retreat. — 日行遲也。从日.从夊.會意。The 辵 added is a radical redundancy (L. 112 E). Note the contraction of the modern character, and read again the note L. 26 O. — Phonetic series 578.

oSee 夋 L. 29 E; 夌 L. 79 K; 嵏 L. 38 D; etc.

夊 **inverted**, forms

D **K'ua**⁴ To overcome an obstacle represented by 亅; 从反夊.指事。跨步也。The modern character kept the old form. Phonetic in 鈄 ko¹, a pot.

夊 **straight** and **inverted**, forms

E 舛 **Ch'uan**³. It is composed of 夊, the straight and the inverted form, back to back; 从夊正反相背.會意. To go in contrary directions; opposition, contradiction, offence, error; 舛錯也。Compare L. 27 G. — It is the 136th radical. In the compounds, 舛 represents two men back to back Note the following

Wu³. A dance with gestures, performed by two groups opposing each other (See L. 65 D); 舛 the dancers back to back, 無 a phonetic contracted (L. 10 I); 樂也。用足相背。从舛.無聲。

桀 **Chieh**². Primitive sense: 木 tree, on which criminals were hung, 舛 back to back; the gallows of old. This character now means a roost, for fowls to rest on; 雞棲也,从舛在木上.會意。舛雞像。— Phonetic series 518. It forms the following

Shêng⁴, **ch'êng**². A warriors' car, a sort of roost for men standing back to back, on two ranks; the top represents a roof. The modern form does credit to the ingenious scribes. — Phonetic series 512.

See also 舜, and 粦 L. 126 D; etc.

F 夅 **Chiang**^{4}. From 夊, the straight and the inverted form one above the other; 从夊㐄相承會意。服也。Two men, one of them (the inferior) is subject to the other (the superior). This character is now written 降, and the pronunciation is different according to the two different meanings. **Hsiang**^{4}, to subject, to submit (the inferior). **Chiang**^{4}, to descend, to send down, to degrade, to grant (the superior). — Phonetic series 182. — 降 contracted is phonetic in 隆 **lung**^{2}, L. 79 F; 夅 being reduced to 夂。

G Another form of 夊 straight and inverted, one above the other. It is found only in the compound

韋 **Wei**^{2}. Refractory opposition: two men who pull at the same object in contrary directions; 相背也。从夊㐄。口亦聲。(L. 74). This character is now written 違 — Phonetic series 487. See 羍 L. 23 F.

LESSON 32.

About a peculiar form of 人, 尸 **shih**^{1}, analogous to 𠂆, which was explained L 30 A.

A 尸 **Shih**^{1}. A seated man. The living person who anciently represented the dead; by extension, a dead person. The Glose says: The sons, not seeing the deceased ancestor whom they worshipped, invented the 尸 to impersonate him; 尸、主也、孝子之祭。不見親之形像。心無所繫、立尸而主意焉。— It is the 44th radical of characters relating to parts and positions of bodies. It forms

屍 **Shih**^{1}. Corpse; 尸 a man, 死 dead (L. 26 H).

尼 **Ni**^{2}. Two men near each other (L. 26 F).

𡱂 **T'un**^{2}. The lower part of 尸 the body; the part seated 几 (L. 20 A); 丌 represents this part; 从尸、下丌、居几、會意、人之下基也、坐得几而安。Hence 殿 **tien**^{4}, the flogging on the buttocks (L 22 D). Instead of 丌, the scribes write 共, which makes one more false character.

B 㕻 **I²**. It is composed as 仁 (L. 2 B), the feeling that must bind man to man (二 two, 𡰣 men). Is phonetic in

㷉 **Wei⁴**. To smooth cloth, the ⺕ hand holding a 火 hot iron. By extension, to make even, to sweeten; 从㕻聲。从⺕持火以伸繒也會意。轉注、安之也。It forms 慰 wei⁴, to soothe, to console, to iron the wrinkles of 心 the heart. Note how the scribes changed 火 into 小, and 又 into 寸。㷉、俗字作尉。— Phonetic series 658.

尉

C 凥 居 **Chü¹**. A place, a spot, an abode. Etymologically, 尸 a man who found 几 a seat. Its composition is analogous to that of 屍, above A; 處也。从尸得几而止、會意。This character was arbitrarily changed by the scribes into 居; 从尸、古聲。Compare L. 20 B. — Phonetic series 345.

D 尾 𡰪 **I³. Wei³**. Tail. The 毛 hair at the end of 尸 the body. Contracted into 𡰪, and sometimes into 尸, 尾 forms important compounds (See L. 100 B). The **Shuowên** tells us that the old Chinese put on a false tail, in order to be as beautiful as animals; 从到毛在尸後、按禽獸後也。古人或飾系尾。

E 尿 **Sui¹. Niao⁴**. Urine, 水 water coming from under the tail, for 尸 is 尾 contracted.

屎 **Shih³**. Excrement; the residue of 米 grain similarly ejected; 尸 is 尾 contracted. This character is a modern one and superseded the old 菌. See L. 122 C.

F 尺 **Ch'ih³**. The span of a 尸 man, of a male adult's hand. This span was, under the 周 Dynasty, the unity of length and measured about twenty centimeters. The 尺 grew longer, after that time, up to thirty centimeters. The Europeans call it a *foot*. In China it is a *hand*; 十寸也。从尸从乙、指事。The 乙 (L. 9 A), says the Glose, represents the opening of the hand, from the thumb to the little finger. See 寸 (L. 45 B). It forms

局

Chü². To fit up, workshop where things are fitted up. This end is obtained by using both 口 mouth and 尺 hands (span, used for the hand); 从口。从尺。會意。尺猶手也。手口所以分部之。— Phonetic series 266.

G 屋

Wu¹. Abode, lodgings. Place where a man 尸 being arrived 至 (L. 133 B), takes rest. 居也。从尸。人所住也。从至。人所止也。Compare 室 **Shih⁴** (L. 133 B), which is a synonym. — Phonetic series 490. It is contracted into 尸 in several characters; for instance

屚

Lou⁴. The rain 雨 passing through the roof of a house 尸; to leak; 屋穿水下也。从雨在尸下。會意。尸者。屋省。See L. 125 B.

LESSON 33.

About the two primitives, 七 and 乇

First series: 七.

A 七

Ch'i¹. Seven. A numerical sign, without any other signification: 以紀數。本無意。It is radical in 齔 **ch'ên³**, second 齒 teething, about the age of seven 七 years. It is phonetic in 叱 **ch'ih⁴**, to cry out at, to scold; and in

Ch'ieh¹. To cut; 刀 knife, L. 52. — Phonetic series 43.

Second series: 乇.

B 乇

T'o¹. A partial primitive. It represents a small plant sinking its root into the ground. The ground —, the root beneath, the stalk and a small ear above; 草也。从垂穗上貫一。下有根。像形。— Phonetic series 29. It forms

宅

Chai². Habitation, abode; 居也。从宀。从乇。會意。The place where a man 乇 takes root, fixes his 宀 dwelling. — Phonetic series 177.

LESSON 34.

In this number we distinguish the series of two primitives, 冂 and 冖, wantonly mingled together by the scribes, and mixed up by **K'ang-hsi**.

First series:

A 冂

Chiung^3. The suburbs, the country, the space. The two vertical strokes delineate the limits; the horizontal stroke represents the interval between them, the void space; 邑外謂之冂。像。遠界也。 — It is the 13th radical. Note the derivatives

B 冋

Chiung^3. A synonym of the preceding. The representation is more explicit; 口 (L. 74) delineating the walled town in the middle of the country. — Phonetic series 114. The derivatives of 冋 are to be distinguished from those of 囘 (L. 76 G), e. g. 迥 **chiung**^{3}, to go in remote places; 迴 **hui**^{2}, to return. Distinguish also 冋 **chiung**^{3} from 向 **hsiang**^{4} and 尙 **shang**^{4} (L. 36 E); from 㕯 **o**^{4} (L. 15 C); from 囧 **chiung**^{3} (L. 42 B).

C 内

Nei^4. The interior; to enter 入 in a 冂 void space, in the interior. This character was explained L. 15 C. Note how in the old form here joined, 冂 is already mistaken for 冖 (34 H), while the Glose gives the true explanation. — Phonetic series 74.

D 市

Shih^4. A market. The 㞢 grass-grown 冂 space out of the city, where people go and get ㇏ (L. 19 E) what they are in need of; 買賣所之也。从冂。从古文及、會意。物相及也。㞢 (L. 79 B) 亦聲。 This character has nothing in common with 巾 (L. 35), under which it was erroneously classified by **K'ang-hsi**. It must be carefully distinguished from 市 **fu**^{4} (35 B), and from 巿 **fei**^{4} (L. 79 G). There are a few insignificant compounds. Note the logical aggregate 鬧 **nao**^{4}, to bustle; 鬥 (L. 11 I) to quarrel as in the market place 市; the noisy wrangling and confusion of a market, so dear to the Chinese.

E 冘

Yin^2. To go away, to withdraw. A 人 man who walks in order to go out of a 冂 space; 行皃。从人出冂、會意。 — Phonetic series 94. Not to be confounded with 宂 **jung**^{3}, L. 29 J.

F 隺 **Hao⁴**. To rise up, high. A bird 隹 that rises up in the 冂 space; 从隹上、欲出冂。會意。When this character is not well engraved, one might believe it is topped by a 宀 (L. 36); in reality it is the 丿 of the left side of 隹, that crosses 冖, just as 人 crosses 冖 in the preceding. — Phonetic series 531.

G 冥 **Ming²** Obscurity, darkness; 从冂、从日、从六、會意。The six 六 Chinese hours (half a day) during which the 冂 space is in darkness, the 日 sun being absent. — Phonetic series 553.

Note. One may see how, in the modern forms, 冂 and 冖 are absolutely mixed together.

Second series: 冖.

H 

Mi². To cover. A line that falls at both ends, to cover; 覆也。从一下垂。像形。— It is the 14th radical of a few characters meaning, to cover. Note the following derivatives

鼏 **Mi²**. A trivet 鼎 covered 冖 (L. 127 D).

冠 **Kuan¹**. To cover 冖 the head 元; a cap. See L. 29 H.

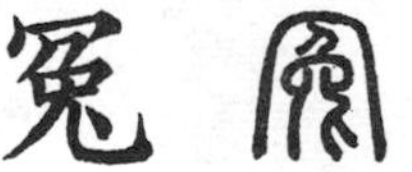

Yüan¹ Ill-use without motive, wrong, grievance. Etymologically a rabbit 兔 (L. 106 B), trapped 冖. 屈也从兔在冖下、不得走、會意。It forms a few insignificant phonetic complexes. This character is sometimes wrongly written 寃.

冖 is met, with the meaning of physical cover, of moral blindness, in many characters, e.g. 熒 L. 126 F; 爨 L. 154 B; 學 L. 72 D; 學 L. 39 I. But the following are derived from 勹 (L. 54), and not from 冖, as the modern form might induce one to believe, e.g. 冢 L. 69 G; 軍 L. 167 C; etc.

I 𠔼

Mao³. To cover 冂 something 一 (L. 1, 4°); 覆也。从冂、一指事。It forms

同

T'ung². Agreement, union, reunion; 合會也。从𠔼、从口、會意。The primitive meaning is: adaptation of a cover 𠔼 to the orifice 口 of a vase. — Phonetic series 246.

𡉉 㱿

Ch'iao¹. A cover 𠔼 with flowers 㞢 (L. 79 B); 幬也。像。从𠔼、㞢其飾也 (vegetable objects; compare L. 102 I). By extension, the shell of mollusks, of fruits, of eggs, that 𠔼 covers them, and is ornamented with 㞢 fine designs; 凡物之甲在外者曰𡉉。書皆以殼爲之。In these last meanings, this character is now written **chia-chieh** 殼 ch'iao¹, the primitive meaning of which was to *strike*. This character forms the phonetic series 517, in which the radical is placed under 𡉉 contracted; e.g.

穀 榖 轂 觳 縠 㝅

The scribes and the engravers often forget the small stroke of 𠔼. On the other hand, they fancy the different writings 壳 壳 殼, etc.

冡 蒙

Mêng². To cover. Its composition resembles that of 冤 (L. 34 H), a boar 豕 taken in a 𠔼 snare. 从𠔼、从豕、會意。It forms 蒙 **mêng**², the wistaria, a trailing plant that covers; to cover. Phonetic series 784. — The character 冡 **mêng**² is to be distinguished from 冢 **chung**³, L. 69 G

—◆—◆—

J 冃

Mao⁴ A covering for the head; that which 𠔼 covers — the head (L. 1, 4°); 从𠔼、从一、指事、一首也。It is now written 帽. — The scribes write 冃, 彐, 日; so that the derivatives of 冃 **mao**⁴ cannot be distinguished from those of 曰 **yüeh**¹ (L. 73 A). Still improving on the scribes, **K'ang-hsi**, after having classified, under the 14th radical 冖, characters that do not belong to it, placed the true derivatives of 冖, the whole series 冃, under the 13th radical 冂. Such is the value of classifications based upon the modern characters, altered or mingled with others. — It forms the compounds.

冒 **Mao⁴**. To rush on heedless, to act with the eyes 目 covered 冃; imprudence, temerity; 蒙而前也。从冃。从目、會意。— Phonetic series 462. It forms the phonetic complex

Man². To offend by 冒 headless 又 action. The 目 of 冒 is bent (L. 158), to give room to 又. — Phonetic series 635.

𦐇 **T'a⁴**. Birds of passage flying in flock; swarm of 羽 wings 冃 covering the sky; 飛盛皃。从羽。从冃。會意。— Phonetic series 571.

冑 **Chou⁴**. A helmet, the 冃 headgear of soldiers; 由 (L. 151 A) is phonetic; 从冃。由聲。兵冠也。 Not to be confounded with the character 胄 **chou⁴** posterity, that is pronounced and written in the same way (L. 65 B); neither with 胃 **wei⁴** (L. 122 C).

冕 **Mien³**. Official 冃 cap; 免 **mien³** (L. 106 A) is phonetic. Compare 冤 **yüan¹**, L. 34 H.

最 **Tsui⁴**. A meeting 取 under the same 冃 roof. See L. 146 F. — Phonetic series 711.

Appendix. The 冖 repeated twice, is given as being the lower part of the next

K 冂 important compound, though it appears seldom, the modern scribes having changed 冂 into 方.

Yén¹. Disappearance, loss, absence. An object that was at one tine 自 (L. 159 A) in a 穴 store, and became invisible 冂 (a double cover) later on. 从冂。从自、从穴。會意。冖冖不見也。此字形意俱闕也。See L. 23 G. Note the phonetic complex

邊 **Pien¹**. To walk on the edge of a precipice, running the risk of falling into it and disappearing. **Chuan-chu**, bank, edge, margin, a boundary in general; 行垂崖也。从辵。臱亦聲。

LESSON 35.

About two primitives nearly identical in the modern writing, 巾 chin[1], and 㒳 liang[3], with their derivatives.

First series: 巾 chin[1].

A 巾 巾 **Chin[1]**. A small piece of cloth resembling the European handkerchief, that was worn in ancient times, hanging from the girdle, and used for cleaning and dusting. By extension, a bonnet, the ancient Chinese putting on a cloth to cover their heads; cloth in general. 冂 represents the two extremities of cloth hanging from the girdle; 丨 represents the state of suspension; 佩巾也。像。丨系也。— It is the the 50th radical of characters relating to cloth.

Note. The lower part of some ancient characters, v.g. 木 L. 119, 糸 L. 92, accidentally resembles 巾. Note also that 币 (L. 79 C) has nothing in common with 巾. But 佩 (L. 21 D) is derived from it, as are also the following characters

B 市 市 **Fu[4]**. The cloth worn by the ancient Chinese, a kind of skin apron hanging from the waist, down to the knees. It was preserved as a souvenir of ancient custom in the Imperial dress... — represents the girdle, 冂 the piece of cloth, 丨 the hanging of the same; 上古衣獸皮。先知蔽前。繼知蔽後。市像。前蔽。以存古。天子朱市. Compare 帶 tai[4] (L. 24 Q), the construction of which is analogous.

Note. The modern form 市 is used for three characters that must be carefully distinguished; 市 **shih[4]** market, L. 34 D; 市 **fu[4]** apron, L. 35 B; 市 **fei[4]** vegetation, L. 79 G, that forms the important phonetic series 45, whilst the two preceding ones have only a few derivatives.

C 布 布 **Pu[4]**. A piece sf cloth made of hemp, nettles or dolic; the ancient Chinese did not know of cotton. At the bottom 巾, on the top 父 fu[4] (L 43 G) as phonetic. 从巾。父聲。古無棉布。但有麻布葛布。 **Chuan-chu**: to spread out, to display, to explain, etc. — Phonetic series 152.

D 希 希 **Hsi[1]**. The interstices of a woven material, between the crossed threads (L. 39 G); 从巾。从爻。像。 **Chuan-chu**, loose, not close, thinly, scattered, infrequent. Different **chia-chieh**. Now 稀, literally 禾 grain 希 thin-sown. — Phonetic series 275.

E 帚 **Chou**[3]. A dusting-brush. See L. 44 K, L,

㕞 **Shua**[1]. To 彐 wipe one's 尸 body with a 巾 rag; to wipe; 从彐从巾.从尸.會意。It is contracted in the compound

刷 **Shua**[1]. To scrape with 刀 a knife or otherwise, to scrub, to cleanse; 刮也.拭也。从刀.㕞省聲。

F 㡀 **Pi**[4]. Rag, tatters. A 巾 piece of cloth riddled with 八 holes (L. 18 A, division). K'ang-hsi erroneously gives eight strokes to this character, instead of seven. 从巾.像。按上下八指事.巾敗之形。本訓爲敗巾.轉注爲敗衣。It forms the homophone and synonymous compound

敝 **Pi**[4], in which 攴 (L. 43 D) represents the physical action that tore the 巾 cloth into 㡀 shreds.—Phonetic series 641.

G 黹 **Chih**[3]. It is also derived from 㡀. The top is 丵 contracted (L. 102, I), boughs, foliage. 㡀 cloth that has been pierced with needles and so 丵 flowered. Leaves were the first designs used for embroidery; 从㡀.丵省.像,刺文也。—It is the 204th radical.

Second series: 巾 liang[3].

H 巾 **Liang**[3]. It represents scalse in equilibrium. This character is now obsolete, but forms important compounds in which its primitive meaning may be still found. In these compounds, a supperadded element develops the notion of weighing and equilibrium. Thus 二 two, represents the weight and counterpoise; 入 入 to enter-enter (L. 15), means that an equal weight was placed on both sides; 爻 爻 graphically represents the same thing. Etc.

I 㒳

Liang^3. Two weights equal, state of balance; 像, 權衡形。左右相比。Hence

兩 两 両

Leang^3. One ounce. This character is of modern origin. The 一 level beam, is a graphic redundancy. In the sense of *two*, this character is **chia-chieh** for the preceding. — Phonetic series 376. The scribes mutilate 兩 in different ways, as may be seen here

J 再

Tsai^4. A second 二 weighing 巾, equal to the first one. 一 on the top represents the horizontal beam. Twice, again, repeated; 从巾、从二、會意。對耦之詞曰二。重疊之詞曰再。— It has nothing in common with 冉. L. 116 A.

K 爯

Ch'êng^4. This character is formed like the preceding; but instead of 一 a beam, there is 爫 a hand that lifts the balance, in order to let it oscillate; 二 represents the equilibrium of the two scales. 从爫、从巾、从二、會意。To weigh, weighing, scales; now 稱. It is often written 爯 by the scribes.

L 爾

Erh^3. Symmetry, harmony of proportions; 靡麗也。从巾。从㸚、會意。尒聲。A 巾 balance loaded 㸚 equally on both sides. On the top, 尒 êrh (L. 18 O) is phonetic. See L. 39 N. Chia-chieh, personal pronoun, *thou, you*; 發聲之詞。俗字作你。汝也。It is often incorrectly engraved The right form has only 14 strokes. — Phonetic series 776.

M 㒼

Man^2. Before the equilibrium is perfect, the 巾 balance 丫 oscillating hither and thither. Compare L. 103 C. 从丫。从巾會意。The vertical strokes of the two elements are united. The modern scribes commonly write 廿 instead of 丫. It forms.

㒼 **Man**[2]. Equality, equilibrium; 平也。从芇,从㒳. 會意。Compare L. 35 I. — represents the level beam. — Phonetic series 636.

繭 **Chien**[3] The cocoon of the silkworm: from 糸 silk, 虫 the worm, 芇 the regular form of the cocoon; 會意。蠶衣也。The modern character is placed here purposely to show how the engravers transformed the 丫。

LESSON 36.

About the primitive 宀

A 

Mien[1]. It represents a hut, a dwelling; 屋也。像形。— It is the 40th radical of characters relating to dwellings. It forms

宋 **Sung**[4]. A hut 宀 made with 木 wood; 从宀, 从木。居也、

宕 **T'ang**[4]. A cave-dwelling 宀, in the 石 rock; 从宀, 从石。洞屋也。

B 

Tsung[1]. An ancestral hall; 尊祖廟也。从宀、从示、會意。The building 宀 from which emanates 示 (L. 3 D) the influence of the deceased ancestors over their posterity. By extension, ancestors, a clan. — Phonetic series 404.

C 寍 **Ning**[2]. Rest, happiness; the 心 heart of man being satisfied, when he has a 宀 shelter and a full 皿 dish, board and lodging; 安也。从宀、从心、从皿。會意。It is found contracted in

甯 **Ning**[2]. That which one 用 is in need of, to enjoy 寍 rest; 所願也。从用, 寍省亦聲。The 皿 of 寍 was replaced by 用. The scribes often write incorrectly 甯.

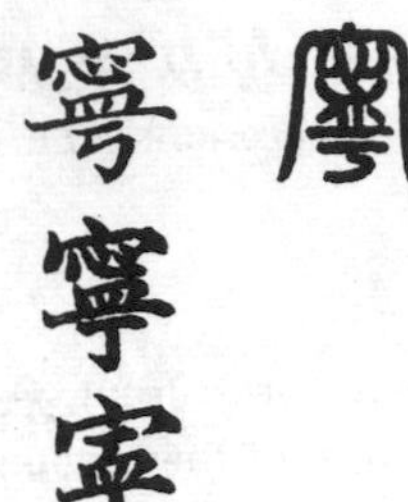

Ning[2]. That which one aspires to 丂, to enjoy 寍 peace. To wish, to prefer; peace, to soothe; 願詞也。从丂、从寍。 The modern writers put 丁 (L. 57) instead of 丂 (L. 58), out of respect for the etymology. — Phonetic series 785, under the modern form 寧. — This character was specially ill-treated by the scribes. See, underneath the right one, some wrong ones invented by them.

Note: 牢 **lao**[2] is not derived from 宀. L. 17 F.

Second series. In some modern characters, instead of being contracted into 宀, **mien**[2] kept its ancient form. Only the dot which represents the top of the roof, sometimes slipped to the left, and was changed into 丿. Examples:

D 奧 粵 See L. 123 F.

E 向 **Hsiang**[4]. A small round window ○ in the Northern wall, under the roof 宀, for ventilation; 北牖也。从宀、从口、按口像。The ○ is the representation of the small window, and not 口 the mouth, 30th radical. **Chuan-chu**, to face, direction. — Phonetic series 200. To be distinguished from the series 122. 冋 **chiung**[3] (L. 34 B). It forms

尚 㕮 **Shang**[4]. Has nothing in common with 小 (L. 18 H), under which it was classified by **K'ang-hsi**. The vertical stroke is the top of 宀 protracted; the two lateral strokes are 八 (L. 18 A), division, separation; 从八、像。气之分散也。The crest or ridge on the roof of Chinese houses, which divides wind and rain, and which is placed last of all. Hence the meanings, to add to, still, elevated, superior, to esteem, etc. — Phonetic series 391, in which 尙 placed above the radical, is contracted into 㕮. In composition, 尙 means a roof or a house.

敞 **Ch'ang**[3]. To knock 攴 (L. 43 D) at a 尙 house door, to open. — Phonetic series 663.

T'ang^{2}. Dry and even 土 soil under a 尙 roof. A hall, a meeting-house, a court. — Phonetic series 649.

Tang^{1}. Value of a 田 field (L. 149), or of a 尙 house. To value, equal to, to compensate, to match, convenient, etc. — Phonetic series 763.

Tang^{3}. A house 尙 which is 黑 smoky or dark. A poor hamlet. To club together in darkness, secretly, a cabal, a conspiracy. — Phonetic series 857.

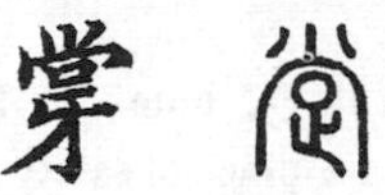

Ch'eng^{1}. To give 足 feet (L. 112 B) to a 尙 house, to prop it up. The scribes altered the ancient form. — Phonetic series 666.

裳 **Shang^{1}.** The flowing garment 衣, robe, which covers the lower part of the body (L. 16); 从衣、尙聲。

賞 **Shang^{1}.** To bestow as a reward 貝 cowries (L. 161), the money of the ancients; 从貝、尙聲。賜有功也。It forms 償 ch'ang^{2}, to pay, to compensate.

掌 **Chang^{3}.** The palm of the 手 hand. **Chuan-chu**, to grasp, to rule (L. 48); 从手、尙聲。

常 **Ch'ang^{2}.** A banner 巾 used to head the troops (L. 35); hence **chuan-chu**, rule, constant way, constantly; 从巾、尙聲。

嘗 **Ch'ang^{2}.** To think 旨 something good, to taste (L. 26 K); 从旨、尙聲。**Chia-chieh** for the last. It is often engraved incorrectly.

LESSON 37.

About 穴, derived from the primitive 宀, explained in the last Lesson.

A 穴 — **Hsüeh**². 室也。从宀，从八。A space obtained by the 八 removal of rock or of earth; a cave, a hole a den. — It is the 116th radical. Phonetic series 125. It forms

B 突 — **T'u**⁴. A 犬 dog (L. 134) that rushes headlong out of its 穴 kennel, to attack an intruder. Chuan-chu, impetuousness, suddenly; 从犬，从穴，會意，犬从穴中出也。

C 竄 — **Ts'uan**⁴. A rat 鼠 (L. 139) in its 穴 hole. To hide one's self, to conceal one's self in a place of safety; 匿也。从鼠在穴中，會意。— Phonetic series 843.

D 穿 — **Ch'uan**¹ To bore 穴, with the teeth 牙 (L. 147). To perforate, to run through, to put on; 通也。从牙，从穴，會意。

E 穵 — **Wa**¹. A hole, to make a hole as the robbers do when they pierce through the walls; 从穴，乙聲 (L. 9 B). 今俗謂之賊穴牆，曰穵。It forms 挖 wa¹, to dig out, to scoop out, to excavate.

F 夐 — **Ch'iung**². A man 人 (L. 28) who 目 looks (L. 158) out from a 穴 cavern, to 攴 hit (L. 43 D) or to catch. To be on the watch for, to spy, to expect, to covet. It is often altered, as are all the intricate compounds; 从旻，从人在穴上，會意。視也，求也。It forms the phonetic compound 瓊 ch'iung², a precious stone. It is a radical contracted in the important compound

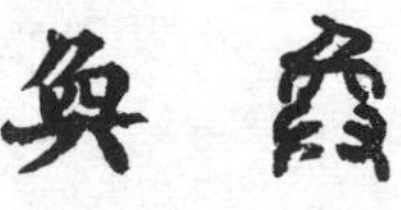

Huan⁴. To exchange, to change; 从廾，从夐，會意。To pass an object from one hand to another, while 夐 examining it attentively, to avoid deception. Now 換. Note the contraction of 廾 into 大, in the modern writing. — Phonetic series 451.

G 窄 — **Chai**³. In a confined space, narrow, as when one is 乍 crouched down in a 穴 hole. See L. 10 F.

LESSON 38.

About the three primitives: 凵 k'an³; ch'ü¹, and kung¹, which are both written 厶 in the modern way.

A **Note**: Two other primitives, i³ (L 85 B) and ssŭ¹ (L. 89) are also written 厶, in the modern running hand: so that 厶 is used for four ancient primitives, which fact does not make the matter clearer.

First series: 凵 k'an³.

B **K'an³**. A hole in the earth, a pit; 坎也。像。地穿。— It is the 17th radical. It forms

C **K'uai⁴**. A clod, a shovelful of 土 earth; there is a hole 凵, where the earth was removed; a furrow, a trench; 从土一掘像形。It forms 屆 chieh⁴, often incorrectly engraved 届; a man 尸 (L. 32) sitting down on the trench which marks the limit of his property, and thus asserting his domain. Boundary, limit.

D **Hsiung¹**. This character represents the fall 乂 (L. 39 B) *of a man* into a 凵 pit; 像。地穿，陷其中也，指事。Chuan-chu, an accident, unfortunate, unlucky. — Phonetic series 62. Note the compounds

Hsiung¹. The thorax, the breast, the heart, the affections. 凶 concealed in a man 勹 (L. 54). — In the second form, 月 (L. 65) represents the flesh enveloping 凶 the interior. For, says the Glose, it is in the heart that the 凶 evil is conceived; 失己、謀失於匈、注猶內也。— Phonetic series 206.

Hsiung¹. A man 儿 (L. 29) under 凶 evil influonces, contemplating or doing evil; 从人在凶下。會意，It forms the phonetic complex

Tsung¹. To move, to shake; 从夊、兇聲 (L. 31 C). — Phonetic series 483.

酗 **Hsü**. Mad 凶 with drink 酉 (L. 41 G).

Second series: 厶 ch'ü^1.

E 厶

Ch'ü^1. Basin, porringer; 飯器也。像。This representation is found in more intricate characters designing different vessels. e. g.

 皿 L 157 A.  鬯 L. 26 C.

F 去

Ch'ü^4. An empty vessel and its cover; 从厶、土其蓋也。像形。The top resembling 土 in the modern writing, and 大 in the old one, is a special primitive. **Chuan-chu**, to empty, to remove, to lay aside, to leave; ideas coming from the removal of a vessel's cover, and of its contents. Compare below 盍. — Phonetic series 119. It forms

Tiu^1. To lose. Falling down 丿 and disappearance 去 of an object; 从丿、从去、會意。Compare 失 L. 48 B.

劫

Chieh^2. To prevent by 力 violence (L. 53) a man from 去 going, as the brigands do; 人欲去、以力止、曰劫。从力、从去、會意。By extension, coercion, violence. The scribes often write 刼, which is a wrong character. The philologists refer to 劫, a contracted phonetic, the compounds of 去 in ieh, as 怯 chieh^4, etc.

The same cover, upon a different vessel, may be found in the ancient forms of the following characters

G 壺

Hu^2. A pot, a jug. The representation of the vessel is a primitive. On the top, the cover. 圓器也。像形。从土像其蓋也。It has nothing in common with 亞 ya^4, L. 82 H. Not to be confounded with 壼 k'un^3, L. 15 A. It forms the next.

I^1. A kind of ritual vase of old. This character, now obsolete in the primitive sense, is used instead of 一 one, in casting up accounts. See 24 C, and 38 D. 壹 was the 吉 auspicious vase; 壺 was the 凶 inauspicious corresponding vase. — Phonetic series 690.

Ho². A dish filled and its cover. To till, to cover. This cover resembles the cover of 去, the vase being represented by 皿 (L 157 A) instead of 厶. In the vase, — represents the contents (L. 1, 4°). 覆也。从皿像。从大蓋形。从一。皿中物也。指事。今作盍。In the modern writing, the scribes contracted the cover and the contents into 去, thus forming an illogical character, for it is made with one cover 土 and *two* vases, 厶 and 皿. It is often **chia-chieh** for 曷, an interrogative particle: 發聲之詞。— Phonetic series 532, under its modern form. Note the compound

蓋 蓋 盖 **Kai**⁴. A 盇 roof made with 艹 coarse grass used for thatching, to put a roof on, to conceal both literally and figuratively; a cover; 苫也。覆星也。弇也。从艸。从盇。會意。The modern form 蓋 is admitted by the critics, but 盖 is an unauthorised character.

Third series: 厶 kung¹.

H 厶 厷 **Kung**¹. It was at first a rudimental representation of the arm bent; 古文像形。肱也。Then the hand 𠂇 (L. 46) was added. The latter forms the phonetic series 69.

LESSON 39.

About the character 乂, which corresponds with two primitives (Series 1 and 2); and about its multiples (Series 3. 4. 5.).

First series: 乂 wu³.

A **Wu**³. Five; a numerical sign, 以紀數。It represents, says the Glose, 五行 the five elements (four sides and the centre; compare 十 L. 24 A). Later on, two strokes were added, to represent heaven and earth, and thus was formed

五 **Wu**³. Five; 五行也。从二。陰陽在天地間。The two principles **yin**¹ and **yang**², begetting the five elements, between heaven and earth. It forms

吾 **Wu**². An appellation to design one's self; I, my, me; 我自稱也。从口。五聲。— Phonetic series 316.

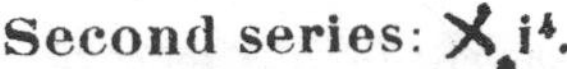

Second series: 乂 i⁴.

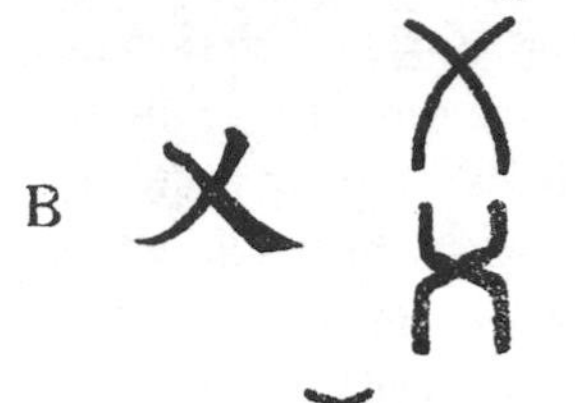

B

I⁴. This character is intended to depict the blades of shears; action of cutting or turning; action or influence of any kind. It is formed of two 丿 (L. 7 C) intercrossed and jointed; 从丿㇏相交。會意。刈草也。To cut grass, to mow. It is found in

Sha¹. To cut 乂 an 朮 ear. See L. 45 J.

Hsiung¹. To roll down 乂 into a 凵 pit. See L. 38 D.

Third series: Two 乂, side by side, represent the meshes in the important character

C

Wang³. A net; to throw down the net, to entangle, to catch. It is derived from 冖 covering (L. 34 H), and 㸚 representing the net; 从冖中像网交文。伏羲所結繩以漁者也。— It is the 122th radical of characters concerning nets. The scribes alter 网, so that it may be mistaken for 目 bent down 罒 (L. 158). It forms

Wang³. To carry off 亡 by a cast of 网 the net (L. 10 E). By extension, disappearance, absence, negation; compare 無 (L. 10 I, J). The scribes wrote 网 in such a way that it resembles the 169th radical 門. — Phonetic series 408. Not to be confounded with the next

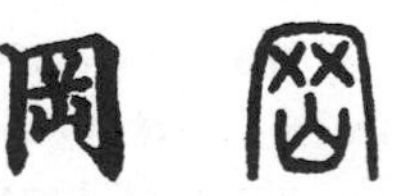

Kang¹. The culminating point of a mountain 山 (L. 80), covered 网 by the clouds; 山脊也。The Glose rejects 崗 as being a graphic redundancy, and gives 罡 as an irregular form of 岡。— Phonetic series 366.

D

Chao⁴. To take a bird 隹 (L. 168) in a 网 net; 从网、从隹、會意。覆鳥、令不飛走也。

Lo². To catch birds 隹 with a 网 net made with 糸 threads (LL. 168 and 92). — Phonetic series 815.

E 詈 **Li⁴** To blame. To entangle 网 a culprit, in the 言 reproaches (L. 73 C) addressed to him; 从网, 从言, 會意网罪人也。

罰 **Fa²**. To punish, a penalty; 从刀、从詈、會意。Railings 詈 and corporal maimings inflicted with a 刀 sword (L. 52).

F 置 **Chih⁴**. The Glose explains this character as follows: to procure the delivery of a 直 just man (L. 10 K), fallen into the net 网 of a slanderous accusation; 从网, 从直, 會意 Chuan-chu, to procure, to dispose.

罷 **Pa⁴**. To dismiss a 能 mandarin, drawn into a 网 snare. To cease, to stop. See L. 27 J.

Fourth series: Two 㐅 superposed.

G 爻 **Yao²**. Mutual action and reaction 交也 (L. 39 B); influence; symmetrical disposition, net-work, etc. — It is the 89th radical. Note the form of 爻 on the top of the compounds.

H 斈 **Hsiao²**. To learn. The disciple 子 (L. 4), improving under the influence 爻 of the master; 卽學之古文。See below 學. — Not to be confounded with 孝 hsiao⁴, filial piety, L. 39 E. — It forms

教 **Chiao¹**. To teach. Here the 攴 (L. 43 D) ferule is joined to the master's influence, for the formation of the 子 disciple; 上所施、下所效也。从攴、从爻、从子、會意。

I 學 𦥯 覺 **Hsiao²**. To learn. This character is more explicit than 斈 (above H). Both hands 臼 (L. 50 A) of the master, 爻 acting from above upon the darkness which covers 冖 (L. 34 H) the mind of 子 the disciple. 覺悟也。从臼、爻、冖、子。冖朦也。— Phonetic series 733, under the contracted form 𦥯, 子 always giving place to the radical. Note 覺 chiao³, to perceive, to feel, which forms some insignificant compounds.

J 

Yao[3]. Meat 肉, cut up 爻 and made ready according to the rules. — Phonotic series 412.

K 

Hsi[1]. Interstices of any material, between the intercrossed 爻 threads; loose, scarce, etc. See L. 35 D. — Phonetic series 275.

L 楙

Fan[2]. Fence, hedge-row. From two 木 trees, bound and interlaced 爻, to form a hedge; 从林。爻像。今俗所謂籬笆是也。See 樊, L. 47 Z.

M 駁

Po[2]. A horse 馬 (L. 137), 爻 dappled, spotted; 馬色不純。雜毛曰駁。By extension, to find fault with, to criticise, to censure, to refute. This character is often incorrectly written 駮.

Fifth series: 乂 repeated four times 㸚, representing symmetry, meaning action, in the following

N 

Erh[3]. Harmony. See L. 35 L. — Phonetic series 776.

O 

Shuang[3]. A man 大 (L. 60) acting 爻 with both arms; active, alert, cheerful; 从㸚，从大，會意。There are different **chia-chieh**. Compare 13 B, and 27 E.

LESSON 40.

About the three series 囟 由 囪, includiug five primitives.

First series: 囟 hsin[4].

A 

Hsin[4]. The skull, the cover of the brain; 𡿺盖也。像。In composition, the head. It is often altered in the modern writing, so that it resembles 田 (L. 119) It forms

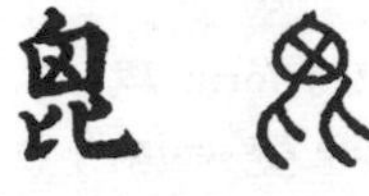

P i[2]. The navel, which is supposed to be in communication with the head 囟, through 比 ducts in which circulate the vital spirits. See L. 27 I. — Phonetic series 557.

Ssŭ^{1}. To think; 从心.从囟.會意。思者、心神通於𡿺.故从囟。When one is thinking, says the Glose, the vital fluid of the 心 heart ascends to the 囟 brain. — Phonetic series 477. It forms

Lü^{4}. To meditate; 謀思也，从思。虍聲，Phonetic series 807.

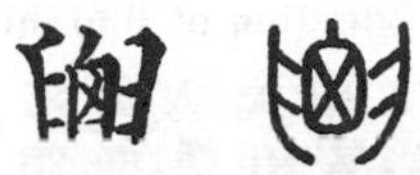

Head 囟 and 臼 hands. It will be explained, with its important series, in the L. 50, M N O P.

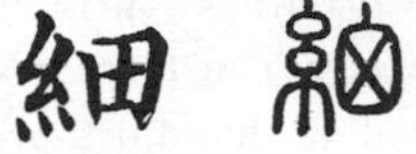

Hsi^{4}. Tenuous, slender, like a thread; 从糸 (L. 92), 从囟。It may be that the primitive sense was *hair*, the 糸 filaments that cover 囟 the head.

Sub-series: 𡿺 hsin^{4}, which is often engraved by the modern writers 𡿺 op 甾。

B

Hsin^{4}. The hairy head; 𡿺蓋也,像。按上其髮也。This was first a special primitive, representing the hair raised up and knotted in a tuft; **then the** 囟 was covered with hair (L. 12 M). The engravers often cutting 田 instead of 囟, the derivatives of 𡿺 **hsin**^{4} are easily confounded wirh those of 甾 **tzŭ**^{1}. See LL. 150 A, and 12 I. — It forms

C 

Nao^{3}. The brain, the marrow of the head, says the Glose; 頭髓也.从匕.从囟.从巛像髮也。會意。The 匕 (L. 26 A, 2°) is intended to mean the symmetrical structure of the brain, bemispheres and lobes. — Note: 𡿺 always contracted into 甾、匕 giving place to the radical, forms the phonetic series 469, 腦 惱 瑙 etc.

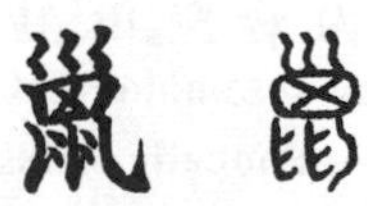

Lieh^{4}. Hairy, bristly, disorderly; 像髮在囟上。The top is the hairy head, as above. The bottom is 鼠 shu^{3}, rat (L. 139 B) contracted; the whiskers and the tail of a rat. — Phonetic series 805.

Fei^{4}. Monkey. See L. 23 F.

Second series: 甶 fu⁴.

C 

Fu⁴. Head of a devil, of a phantom; 鬼頭也。像形。It forms

Kui³. The spirit of a dead man, a manes, a ghost, a spectre. Further, after the introduction of Buddhism, it meant, a devil, a prêta. 古者謂死人爲歸人。人所歸爲鬼。从古文人。从甶像。鬼頭也。 The old character is evidently a primitive representing a human form floating in the air. The more recent forms often show the split head of Buddhist prêtas, and always have an appendage, that was sometimes taken for a tail, but that really represents the whirling made by the ghost, while it moves. — It forms the 194th radical of characters relating to devils. Phonetic series 548. — Now 鬼 is a synonym for horrid, repulsive, malignant.

Wei⁴. To dread, to be in awe, awful, terrible. The character was first composed of the head of a spectre 甶, and of claws 爪 (L. 49). Later on, a man 人 frightened, was added; for, says the Glose, nothing inspires more awe, than the head of a demon, or the claws of a tiger; 古文从甶、从爪、會意。鬼頭而虎爪可畏也。篆文、鬼頭而虎足反爪人也。 Compare the composition of 虐, L. 135 H. The bottom of the modern character is a strange contraction (compare L. 10 H); 甶 lost its 丿; finally Kang-hsi placed this character thus altered under 田, the 120th radical. — Phonetic series 488.

禺 **Yü²**. An ape; 猴也、从甶、从禸、會意。Its 甶 head and its tail and paws 禸; the head resembles that of a demon, 頭似鬼, See L. 23 E — Phonetic series 503.

畀 **Pi⁴**. To agree, to enter into an engagement. 甶 is not a head. It is the pledge, the earnest-money placed upon a 丌 small table (L. 29 K), an act that conclndes a transaction. By extension, to yield (to the conditions), to give (the earnest-money). Classified by

K'ang-hsi under 田 the 102th radical. 賜也,與也相付與之物在閣上也。从由、从丌。會意。 Compare L. 47 R 異 i[4], difference, disagreement. The 廾 hands rejecting 由 the pledge placed upon the table 丌, that is, the affair is not concluded, the bargain is not made. — Pi[4] is phonetic in

鼻 P1[2]. The nose; 从自。畀聲, See 自 (L. 159 A). — It is the 209th radical.

Note: 囱 and 由 much annoyed K'ang-hsi. Finally he classified 囱 under 囗 the 31th radical, and 由 under 田 the 102th radical. It is therefore not easy to see the etymological meanings in the modern series of radicals.

Third series: 囪 ch'uang[1].

This modern character has two ancient forms, each forming a distinct series. Further there will be an appendix for the modern abbreviation 匆.

D 囱 **Ch'uang[1]**. A window, closed by a shutter or by lattices (two forms); 像形。It is now replaced by its compound 窗。

1. Derivatives from the first ancient form. Besides 窗 ch'uang[1] window, and 䆫 shu[1] shutter, note

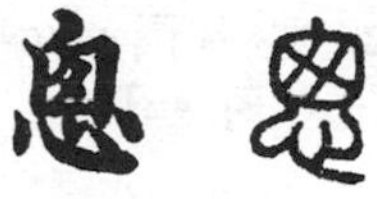

Ts'ung[1]. To feel alarm or agitation; 多遽也。从心、會意。When the 心 heart being restless, one looks through the 囱 window, to see what is coming. — Phonetic series 656.

2. Derivatives from the second ancient form.

Hei[1]. Black. That which the 火 fire deposits around the 囧 aperture through which the smoke escapes; soot; 火所熏之色也。从炎上出囧。囧古文囱字。按謂竈埃也。會意。In the primitive Chinese huts, the smoke found its way through the window. Note the contraction of 炎 (L. 126 D) in the modern character. — It is the 203th radical. Phonetic series 678. It forms

墨 **Mei[4]**. Chinese ink, an earthy 土 substance made with 黑 soot; 从土从黑。會意。

Hsün[1]. Smoke, to fumigate. Black 黑 vapour that 屮 rises from the fire; 屮 (L. 78 A) is used symbolically; 从屮、从黑。會意。按炎上爲煙、其色黑。屮像煙上出形。Note the modern contraction. — Phonetic series 781.

Tang[3]. A meeting 尙 in the darkness 黑; conspiracy. See L. 36 E. — Phonetic series 857.

Tsêng[1], **ts'êng**[2]. The words that people say 曰 to each other, when still at the 囪 door, at the moment of 八 departure; adieu. By extension, still, more, to add. — Phonetic series 710.

Hui[4]. The words that people 曰 say at the 囪 door, when 亼 (L. 14 A) they meet; greeting. By extension, meeting, reunion. — Phonetic series 736.

Note. 柬 Chien[3] does not come from 囪. It is 東 added with 八. See L. 75 A.

3. Appendix. 匆 an abbreviation of 囪, above 40 D, is found in 怱 ts'ung[1] for 悤. Hence 葱 ts'ung[1] onion.

匆怱葱

LESSON 41

The seven series of this Lesson are devoted to seven characters, distinct in the ancient writing, analogous or identical in the modern writing, viz: 1. 丙 ping[3]. — 2. 丙 t'ien[4]. — 3. 襾 hsia[4]. — 4, 5, 6 西 hsi[1], t'iao[2], yao[1]. — 7. 酉 yu[3].

First series: 丙 ping[3].

A 丙

Ping[3]. Fire, calamity. The fire 火 under a 宀 roof, in a house. The more recent form represents the flames rising up and — spreading over the roof; 災也。古文、从火燒宀。會意。今丙、火炎上。— Phonetic series 150 It forms

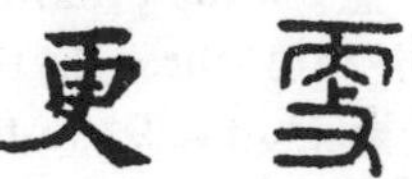

Kêng[1]. To change, to improve; 改也。易也。从攴、从丙、丙亦聲, Intervention of the 攴 armed hand (L. 43 D) in a 丙 fire, in an unhappy situation; change, amendment. Note the contraction of the modern character, and the compound 甦 su[1], to return to 生 life. K'ang-hsi erroneously classified 更 under 曰, the 73th. radical. — Phonetic series 283. It forms

便 㝘 **Pien⁴. Pien²**. A man 人 who settles 更 his affairs well; advantage, convenience, ease: 安也。人有不便,更之。从人,从更,會意. — Phonetic series 474.

Second series: 丙 t'ien⁴.

B 丙 **T'ien⁴**. Chin. A primitive. The second ancient character is considered as an abbreviation of the first, which was explained in the L 17 I. In composition, 丙 is often used for 肉 (L. 17 G), dried meat. It forms the phonetic compound

茜 **Ch'ien⁴**. Rubia cordifolia, a climbing plant with large ovale leaves, used in dyeing.

佰 **Hsü⁴**. A 人 man who eats or offers 丙 (for 肉) dried meat It forms

宿 **Hsü¹. Hsiu³**. A roof 宀 under which a traveller stops, to spend the night; 佰 means, either that he eats the dried meat he brought with him, or rather that he gives the dried meat to pay his host Constellations, the celestial inns. The scribes write 百 for 丙; it is a licence. — Phonetic series 613.

弼 弻 弼 **Pi⁴**. Aid, helper, lieutenant, 輔也。重也。从重弓,从丙,會意。Two 弓 bows, strung on a bamboo with 丙 leather-strongs, to prevent deformation; 丙者,竹上皮也。The idea of helper, of minister, comes from the fact that, in ancient times, bows, like swords, were paired, not single. See L 87 B.

Third series: 襾 hsia⁴

C 襾 **Hsia⁴**. A kind of stopper, of cover; 覆也。指事。A primitive, often engraved 西. — It is the 146th radical of a few common character. It forms

賈 **Chia³. Ku³**. To buy. To 襾 cover an object by its value in 貝 cowries (L. 161), to pay its value.

覆 **Fu²**. To cover. See L. 75 I.

Fourth series: 西 hsi[1].

D 西

Hsi[1]. A primitive not to be confounded with the preceding, under which **K'ang-hsi** wrongly chassified it. Image of a bird sitting on its nest; note the successive contractions; 鳥在巢上。像形。**Chuan-chu**, the West, for the birds go to roost when the sun is setting; 日在西方、而鳥棲。故因以爲東西之西。It forms

Jêng[1]. Cry and flight of a bird caught on its nest; 驚聲也。It is now written 迺. See L. 19 A, where this character was fully explained.

Yin[1]. To destroy, to wall, to dam in; 塞也。从土、从西、會意。See 土 L. 81. It is now written 堙. The primitive idea was probably that of mud nests built by certain birds, v.g. such as the swallows. — Phonetic series 499.

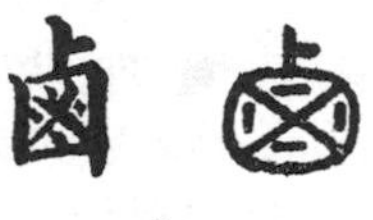

Lu[3]. The rock salt, that was first used by the Chinese, and that comes from the West, says the Glose. Hence the composition: 西 **hsi**[1], West, in its ancient form, and four grains of salt; 西方鹹地也。从古文西、四丶像、鹽形。— It is the 197th radical. It forms the compounds

Yen[2]. Salt obtained by evaporation of the sea-water; 天生曰鹵、人作曰鹽。煮海水謂之鹽。Ancient form 鹵 salt and the 皿 basin (L. 157 A) used to prepare it. Compare 監 L. 82 F.

鹼 **Chien**[3]. Impure carbonate of soda.

Hsien[2]. Salted.

覃 **T'an**[2]. Pickled. See L. 75 G.

Fifth series: 覀 t'iao^2, contraction of 𠧪.

E 𠧪

T'iao^2. Fruits hanging from plants or trees, in ears or in bunches; 草木實垂、像形。A primitive. On the top 卜 the pedicle, at the bottom the ear or the bunch. The ancient form was thrice repeated, to mean the multitude of fruits. Not to be confounded with 卣 a singular form of 酉 yu^3 (L. 41 G). K'ang-hsi wrongly classified this character under 卜, the 25th radical. In composition, in the modern forms, 𠧪 is written 覀, v.g.

Li^4. Chestnut-tree; 从木、其實下垂。See 木 L. 119. — Phonetic series 550.

Su^4. Ears, grains of corn; 从米、穀實也。See 米 L. 122.

Sixth series: 覀 yao^4, contraction of [illegible].

F   要 票 䙴 See L. 50, N, O, P.

Seventh series: 酉 yu^3.

G 酉

Yu^3. A primitive. It represents an ancient vase, a kind of amphora, used for making or keeping the fermented liquors. By extension, fermented liquor, now 酒 chiu^3. 像。釀器形、中有實。There are chia chieh of different kinds. — It is the 164th radical of characters relating to liquors It forms

莤

Yu^2 or **shu^2**. To offer up 酉 libations, in the old way, on a straw bundle 艸; 禮祭束茅加於祼圭而灌鬯酒、是爲莤像神歆之也。从酉、从艸。按酒滲艸下、會意。See page 362.

Chiu^4. Liquor 酉 obtained when the fermentation is over, when the dregs are entirely 八 separated (L. 18 A); spirits that have settled; 从酉、从八、會意。繹酒也。— Phonetic series 432. It forms

Tsun^1. To offer with 廾 both hands, the 酋 wine, to the manes. By extension, to honour, high, noble. See L. 46 E. The scribes replaced 廾 by 寸. — Phonetic series 713.

Tien[4]. Spirits 酋 for the libations, placed upon a small table 丌 (L. 29 K); to offer libations. The scribes often contracted 丌 into 大。It forms the compound

Chêng[4]. Name of a 邑 city.

LESSON 42.

About the two primitives 四 ssŭ[4] and 囧 chiung[3].

First series: 四 ssŭ[4].

A 

Ssŭ[4]. Four. Numerical sign. Even number, which is easily divided into two halves. The old form graphically represents the division of 四 into two halves. — Phonetic series 1 0.

六

Liu[4]. Six. The even number, also easily divisible, that comes after four; 四 marked with a dot. Note that in the other simple even numbers, the divisibility is also indicated; 二 two; 八 eight.

匹

P'i[3]. Half of a whole. The whole is represented by 四. A little more than the half of 四 was kept, so that the character is still recognisable; 分四爲二.也。一夫也。偶也。That which, being joined with its like, forms a pair, a match See the compound 甚 L. 73 B.

Second series: 囧 chiung[3].

B 

Chiung[3]. A window; 窗牖、像形。By extension, light; 明也。光也。Compare 囱 L 40 D, and 西 L 41 G. The modern form is to be distinguished from 冏 L. 15 C. It forms the compounds

莔

Mêng[2]. A liliaceous plant, Fritillaria Thunbergii. A phonetic complex.

C 明 Ming². Brightness, to illustrate. The 月 moon shining through the 囧 window; 照也。从月。从囧。會意。Li-ssŭ read 日 instead of 囧; hence 明. 日 sun and 月 moon, light. — Phonetic series 384. It forms

盟 Mêng². Note in the first place that the radical is not 皿, as the modern character might induce one to believe; it is 血 blood; 从血。从明。明亦聲。歃血誓也。To clear up 明 an obscure affair, by swearing, in the old way, upon a vessel full of 血 blood.

萌 Mêng². To bud, to germinate, to open, to appear in the light; 艸芽也 从艸。从明。明亦聲。See L 78 B.

LESSON 43

The eight following Lessons, 43 to 50, treat about the character representing the human hand. Among the modifications introduced in the modern writing, there were none more deplorable, than the replacing of those very expressive characters, by unrecognisable abbreviations.

In the old writing, the hand is represented in six different ways:

	The right hand in profile. L. 43 seq.		The right hand prone. L. 49.
	The left hand in profile. L 46.		Both hands raised. L. 47.
	The hand facing. L 48.		Both hands hanging L. 50.

A **Note.** The use of a compound, instead of the primitive, is frequent in these series, in order to make easier the distinction between the numerous derivatives from *hand*. See p. 16, note 1.

First series: 又.

B 又

Yu^{4}. The right hand. The Glose explains that the fingers are reduced to three, for the sake of simplification; 右手也。像形。三指者。It is found in a great number of compounds. — It is the 29th radical.

C 支

Chih^{1}. Bough, branch. The right hand holding a bough. The old form represents the hand separating the bough from the stem; 去竹之枝也。从彐持半竹。會意。— It is the 65th radical. — Phonetic series 45.

D 攴 攵

P'u^{1}. To tap; 小擊也。从彐持卜。會意。The right hand holding a rod. Compare 父 L. 43 G. The engravers invented the modern form 攵. — It is the 66th radical of characters relating to strokes and motions. Note the two following compounds

牧 **Mu**^{4}. Shepherd, to feed. The man who 攴 superintends, has oversight of 牛 cattle; 从攴。从牛。會意。

教 **Chiao**^{1}. To teach. The master armed with a 攴 rod, 爻 acting upon his 子 disciple. See L. 89 H. 从攴、从孝。上所施下所效也。

E 反

Fan^{3}. To turn over, inversion. The motion 厂 of the 彐 hand turning over; 反手也、覆也。从彐、从厂像、形彐。— Phonetic series 55.

F 及

Chi^{2}. To reach, to seize. A hand 彐 seizing a 人 man; 从彐、从人、會意。See L. 19 D. — Phonetic series 40.

G 父

Fu^{4}. Father, considered as the chief and instructor of his family. Composed of 彐 hand and | a stick; 家長率教者。从彐舉杖、指事。Compare 教 L. 43 D. — It is the 88th radical. Phonetic series 60

H 皮 𡰪

P'i². To flay; skin. The hand 彐 that flays; 剝取獸革者、謂之皮。The left stroke represents the skin; the stroke above the 彐 hand may represent the knife. These two strokes are a special primitive. — It is the 107th radical of characters relating to skins. Phonetic series 149. It forms

I 叚

Chia³. False, borrowed; 从二皮、會意。To have 二 two 皮 skins, a double skin, a borrowed skin over one's true skin. The modern character reproduces the ancient one. — Phonetic series 427.

J 𠬪

Nan³, nien³. Thin skin. It is an abbreviation of 皮. Not to be confounded with 艮 fu², L. 55 C. It forms 赧 nan³, to blush. Turning 赤 red of the thin skin that covers the cheeks.

Second series:

K In the modern writing, the stroke 丿 of 又 is suppressed, when it coincides with a stroke in the same direction, coming down from the top of the character. In this case, there remains but ㇏ from 又. In the ancient writing, these characters are made like those of the first series.

L 丈

Chang⁴. A line of ten spans (See 尺 L. 32 F). A 彐 hand and 十 ten; 十尺也。从又持十、會意。— Phonetic series 13.

M 史

Shih³. Annalist, scribe, literate. A hand 彐 grasping 中 the fountain-pen (page 7); 記事者也。从彐持中、會意。It forms

N 吏

Li⁴. Those among the 史 literati, who were 上 (L. 2 G) *set over* the instruction and administration of the people; 从一、从史、會意。从一猶从上也。吏者、民之師也。— See 事 L. 44 H.

O 夬

Chüeh². To divide, to partake; 分也。从彐、中像、決形。A hand holding one half of a bilateral 中 object, which was divided into two halves. K'ang-hsi wrongly classified this character under 大, the 37th radical. — Phonetic series 53.

Third series: Multiples of 彐

P 友 **Yu³**. Friend, friendship. The character represents the right hands of two friends, acting in the same direction; for, says the Glose, true friends are those who cooperate; 同志爲友、从二彐、會意。 Compare L. 46 C.

Q 叒 **Jao²**. Three hands 彐 picking herbs; to gather; 擇菜也。 It is an ancient form of 若 L. 46 G The hand represented thrice signifies *activity*. It forms

Sang¹. The mulberry, the 木 tree, the leaves of which are plucked to feed the silkworms; 从叒、从木、會意。— Phonetic series 558.

R 叕 **Cho⁴**. To sew; 綴聯也。像形。 This character has nothing in common with 又 the hand. It is a primitive that represents the stitches encroaching upon one another. Compare 宁 (L. 57 B). – Phonetic series 341.

LESSON 44.

A In this Lesson, we shall examine some characters in which the hand 彐 kept almost its ancient form ⺕ in the modern writing. The ancient forms of these characters resemble those of the last Lesson. Do not confound the hand ⺕, with the 58th radical 彐.

B 丑 **Ch'ou³**. A 彐 hand 丿 bound. To bind, to tie up; 从彐而繫之、指事。 **Chia-chieh**, a cyclical character. Sometimes, in composition, it means the hand (L. 43 A). — Phonetic series 50. It forms.

羞 **Hsiu¹**. To be forced to offer 丑 a sheep 羊 in expiation, as a reparation for wrong. Hence, to feel ashamed, to blush.

C 尹 **Yin³**. A magistrate, to govern. A hand 彐 that exerts 丿 authority; 治也。从彐像。丿握事者也、指事。 It forms 伊 i¹, a proper name; and

君 **Chün¹**. A prince; 从尹、从口、會意。尹出令、治民者也。 See, p. 9, for the story and the interpretation of this character. — Phonetic series 267. But 倉 ts'ang¹ is not derived from 君. See L. 26 M, under 食.

D 聿 肀

Nieh[4]. A hand ⺕ writing upon — a surface. In the ancient form, ⺕ hand | writing upon a 冂 tablet, whose top only is figured.

聿 聿

Yü[4]. A more explicit form. Hand writing — a line on a tablet. The line is horizontal, because it was impossible to trace a vertical one (p. 18, 8). The modern writing-brush is written 筆, because its handle is made of 竹 bamboo. — It is the 129th radical. See its important derivatives, L. 169.

E 隶 隶

Tai[4]. To reach, to seize, to hold. A hand ⺕ that seizes a tail 尾; when running, one seizes from behind; 从⺕、从尾省、會意，⺕持尾者、從後及之也。For 尾 contracted, see L. 100. Compare 求 ch'iu[2], L. 45 K. See also (L. 102 B) 康 k'ang[1], that has nothing in common with 隶. — It is the 171th radical.

F 疌 疌

Chieh[2]. Result, success. The hand ⺕ having reached its 屮 end, 止 ceases from acting. See 止 L. 112, and 屮 L. 78. — Phonetic series 330 It forms

G 妻 妻

Ch'i[1]. Wife. — This form is a relatively modern one; 女 (L. 67) a woman who ⺕ holds 屮 a broom or a duster. For, says the Glose, the woman must take care of the household. Compare 婦 (below K). — A more ancient form gives: 女 daughter, and 肖 price (L. 111 B). The price paid to the parents, for their daughter, by the husband. — Phonetic series 326.

H 事 事

Shih[4]. To serve. **Chia-chieh** any affair. Hand ⺕ acting 屮 with 中 fidelity, is a false interpretation. This character has nothing to do with 史 L. 43 M. It represents the hand of a son inviting the soul of his ancestor. See page 370.

I 秉 𥝌 **Ping**³. Sheaf of grain 禾 hold by a 彐 hand, to bind in sheaves, to hold; 禾束也从彐持禾、會意。

兼 𩠐 **Chien**¹. A hand 彐 that binds up into sheaves two (several) 禾 stalks of grain. By extension, to join several together, a whole. Note the contraction of the two 禾 in the modern form. — Phonetic series 519.

J 彗 𢇍 **Hui**⁴. A broom, bundle of branches 丰丰 held in a 彐; 从彐持丰丰、會意。See L. 97 B. **K'ang-hsi** wrongly classified this character under 彐 the 58th radical. — Phonetic series 617. It forms

雪 䨮 **Hsüeh**³. Snow; 雨 rain solidified, that may be 彗 swept away; 凝雨也。从雨、从彗、會意、雨而可埽者、雪也、今字作雪。The scribes contracted 彗 into 彐.

K 帚 𢂃 **Chou**³. A duster, made with a cloth, fixed by the middle to a handle. Invented in the 21th Century B. C., according to the Glose, it is still used in our days. A 彐 hand, the 丨 handle, and a double cloth 巾 hanging. Compare the bottom of 帶 L. 24 Q. — Phonetic series 343. It forms

婦 **Fu**⁴. A married woman, wife; 从女持帚灑埽也、會意。A woman 女 with a 帚 duster, indicating her household duties. The ancients, says the Glose, gave to this character the sound of fu, to remind the wife that she must be 服 fu, obedient to her husband. Compare 妻 ch'i¹, above G.

𡚁 歸 **Kui**¹. The arrival 止 of the bride at her husband's house, where she will stay as a wife 帚 (婦 contracted); 女嫁也。从止、从婦省、會意。Later on 自 was added as a phonetic. **Chuan-chu**, to belong to, to depend upon; the maried woman belonging to a new family, being submitted to a new authority.

L 㣈 𡠗 **Chin**⁴ To dust A 彐 hand holding a 帚 duster (above K) Pleonastic composition (two 彐). The scribes invented the modern form. — Phonetic series 261. The compound 侵 ch'in⁴, to encroach upon the neighbour's ground, is explained thus: to act gradually and discretely, as with a 帚 dusting-brush, thus gaining on 亻 one's neighbour's ground; 漸進也、若埽之進。

LESSON 45.

A About five derivatives from 彐, that are of a special interest, on account of the series derived from them. These are: 寸 叉 㕛 朮 求。

First series. 寸.

B 寸

Tsun⁴. The Chinese inch. The dot represents the place on the wrist where the pulse is felt, which place is an inch distant from the hand; hence the meaning *inch*; 从彐、一指事。人手卻一寸動𧖴、謂之寸口。By extension, measure, rule. In composition, 寸 is often written instead of 彐; see L. 43 A. — It is the 41th radical. Phonetic series **32**. It forms

C 付

Fu⁴. To give. A hand 寸 that gives up some object to a 人 man; 从寸持物對人。會意。— Phonetic series 420. It forms

府

Fu³. Building 广 where the records, the title-deeds of 付 donations, the diplomas, were kept; 文書藏也。By extension, tribunal, palace. — Phonetic series 355.

D 守

Shou³. A mandarin, a prefect; the man who, in his 宀 tribunal, applies the 寸 law; 从宀、从寸、會意。宀宮也。寸法度也。By extension, to observe, to keep. — Phonetic series **237**.

E 㝵

Tê². To acquire, to obtain; 取也。从見、从寸、會意。寸手也。To lay one's hand 寸 on the thing one had in view 見。The compound 得 is now used instead. — Phonetic series 397. Sometimes 㝵 is used as an abbreviation of 疑, e.g. 碍 for 礙 **nai**⁴; it is a licence. Note the contraction of the modern character.

F 尋

Hsün². To wind, to unravel treads 彡 with 彐 寸 the hands and the 工口; the latter probably representing an instrument used for the winding. 从彐、寸、工口、彡、會意。彡亂也。彐寸分理之。The old character represented the unravelling of threads by two hands 𦥑 holding combs. By extension, to examine, to investigate (the winding requires attention); length, duration (as of a thread winded). The character was altered by the scribes. There are different **chia-chieh**. — Phonetic series 686.

G 肘 **Chou**^{3}. The fore-arm, the elbow; 从肉、从寸、會意。The fleshy 月 part above the 寸 wrist.

紂 **Chou**^{4}. The crupper of a saddle; 馬緧也。The preceding contracted, is supposed to be the phonetic. Now 鞦.

討 **T'ao**^{3}. To rule 寸 by one's 言 words; to chide 治也。从言、从寸、會意。寸、法度也。

Second series: 叉

H 

Ch'a^{1}. To cross, to interlace. The ancient character represented the two hands interlaced. In the modern character, the left hand is represented by 一。手指相錯也。从彐像。按一者指事。By extension, gearings, toothed wheels, etc. — Phonetic series 12.

Third series.: 叉

I 

Chao^{3}. Claws; 手足甲也。Hand or paw with points; 从彐像形。按二者指事。It forms

Tsao^{2}. Flea. The insect 虫 that 叉 irritates men, says the Glose. — Phonetic series 576.

Fourth series: 朮

J 

朮

Shu^{2}. A glutinous grain, rice or millet; 稻稷之黏者也。The idea of glutinousness is represented by the hand 彐, that separates three agglutinated grains. The ancient charater represented the plant. — Phonetic series 158. It forms

Sha^{1}. To decapitate; 戮也。从朮、从乂、會意。The cutting 乂 (39 B) of the ear, upon a stalk of 朮 rice, sorghum or millet. The ancient forms represent: on the top, the hand after the cutting; at the bottom, the stalk beheaded. To behead a man is now said 殺 sha^{1}, 殳 (L. 22 D) representing the sword's stroke.

杀 Note that the modern scribes, leaving off the dot on the top of 术, write 殺 刹 etc., which gives the phonetic 6 strokes, instead of 7, and makes one mistake 术 for 木 (L. 119). It is a licence. K'ang-hsi numbered 6 strokes in 刹, 7 in 殺, then 6 again in 鎩, etc. It is an inconsistency.

Fifth, series: 求.

K  **Ch'iu²**. To search for, to ask, to implore. According to the Glose, the primitive composition and meaning of this character would be like those of 隶 (L. 44 E); 从彐从尾省。會意。於隶同意; to seize, or to hold 彐 by the tail 尾 contracted (L. 100 B). The meaning, to beg, to pray, would come from 求牛 sacrifice of a bull for impetration, as under the 周 Chow Dynasty. Perhaps, in this sacrifice, the offerer held by its tail the offered bull. — It seems rather that the primitive sense was 彐, to offer 氺 hairs (L 100) of the victim, with prayers, as was done in the ancient sacrifices. **K'ang-hi** wrongly classified 求 under 水 water. — Phonetic series 263.

LESSON 46.

A The first Series of this Lesson treats about the left hand 𠂇. In the modern writing, on the top of the compounds, it becomes 𠂇; at the bottom, it becomes 十, etc. It is never written 𠂇 (See LL. 44 and 135 H).

The second Series treats about some compounds, in which the right hand 彐 placed on the top, became also 𠂇 in the modern writing. In their ancient form, those compounds are made just like those given in the LL. 43, 44, 45.

First series: 𠂇 for 𠂇.

B 𠂇  **Tso³**. The left hand; 左手也。像形。Was soon replaced by

左 **Tso³**. Properly, the help 工 given by the left hand to the right, its action; 从𠂇、工、會意。𠂇手所以助彐手者也。

C 𠂇𠃌 𢀩 差 𢀩

Ch'a¹. Variance, and consequently, aberration, failure. Two hands opposite. While the left hand is acting, offering some object, the right one does not move, does not receive, remains hanging. Compare 43 P, 47 B, 47 Y, 50 A, etc. The tracing of the hanging right hand being too difficult with the modern writing-brush, the composition of this character was modified as follows; 𠂇 left hand, making 二 two *with the right one*, not agreeing with it, forsaken by the right that 𠂹 (L 48 E) remains hanging, instead of helping the left; 从𠂇.从二.从𠂹.會意。不相助也。 Finally, a foolish scribe wrote 工 instead of 二, and Li-ssŭ adopted. Conclusion: 差 has nothing in common, either with 左, or with 羊 (L. 103). — Phonetic series 506.

D 隓 隓

To⁴. To build a 阝 (L. 86) line of contravallation, terraces, to besiege a fortified town, according to the Chinese ways; 左 represents the action of the besiegers; *twice repealed*, means their great number; *left*, means that their action is the inverse, the contrary to the action of the besieged; 敗城也。By extension, to destroy. It forms

隋 隋 㣣 㣣 遀 遀

To⁴. Sui². Meat cut up. 裂肉也。 One of the two 左 was replaced by the radical 月 (L. 65). It forms, contracted into 𢀡 in the modern writing, the phonetic series 480. The phonetic complex 遀 sui², to follow, 從也。从辵。隋省聲。 forms the phonetic series 759.

E 卑 卑

Pi⁴. Ordinary, vulgar. This meaning is chuan-chu from the primitive meaning; 从𠂇.从甲.酒器像形 𠂇持之。卽椑之古文。This character represents an ancient drinking vase provided with a handle on the left side (a primitive distinct from 甲 (L. 152), and which was held with 𠂇 the left hand. How came this character to mean common, vulgar? There were, says the Glose, two wine vessels, the 尊 tsun¹ and the 卑 pi¹. The tsun¹ was used for the sacrifices, the pi¹ was used every day. Later on, the two characters were taken in the abstract sense for *noble* and *vulgar*, and the vases were written 樽 tsun¹ and 椑 pi¹; 尊禮器。故爲貴。卑者、常用之器、故爲賤。轉而爲人貴賤之稱 — Phonetic series 388.

Second series: 𠂇 for 彐.

G 右

Yu⁴. It means now, the right hand (**chia-chieh** for 又 L. 43 B), the right side. The primitive meaning was, to 彐 put in the 口 mouth; to help the mouth, as the Glose says; which is a proof that the ancient Chinese used the right hand to eat; 从彐.从口.會意。手口相助也。Hence, to help. Compare L. 46 B. — Phonetic series 172.

若

Jao². Primitive sense, 彐 to pick, 艸 eatable herbs, in order to 口 eat them; 擇菜也。Compare L. 43 Q. — **Jao²** is now (**chia-chieh**) an important conjunction, if, as, etc. See the compound 匿 L 10 D. Phonetic series 454.

H 有

Yu³. Primitive meaning: the phases of the moon 月, its monthly darkening, as if a hand covered it; 从彐、从月。一有、一亡。Or, according to others, eclipse of the moon, the interpretation being the same. The following interpretation: eclipse of the sun, the 月 moon placing the 彐 hand before it, 日食。按掩日者、月也。is rejected by the commentators. — **Yu³** means now (**chia-chieh**) to be, to have. — Phonetic series 250.

I 灰

Hui¹. Ashes, 火 fire that can be 彐 handled; or perhaps that which remains of the 火 fire that was 彐 covered, smothered; 死火也。从火、从彐、會意。— Phonetic series 210.

J 厷

Kung². The arm; 从彐、从𠂇。See L. 38 H. — Phonetic series 69.

K 布

Pu⁴. Linen, cloth. In this character, 𠂇 is not 彐, but 父 fu (L. 43 G) contracted, phonetic. See L. 35 G. — Phonetic series 152.

LESSON 47.

A About 廾 the two hands. The simplification of this character, in the modern writing, made many compounds quite unintelligible. See the examples given below, and you may verify the remark. Any signs are good to replace 廾; 廾、大、八、六、寸、etc.

B 廾 廾 **Kung**³. The two hands joined and held up, as when presenting a thing: 从𠂇、从又、會意。廾者、兩手捧物。It is the 55th radical.

First series.

C  **Tsun**¹. To offer a wine vessel that was held with both hands; 酒器也。从酋、廾以奉之、會意。The scribes changed 廾 into 寸. See, L. 40 E, the origin of the modern **chuan-chu**, noble, high, eminent. — Phonetic series 713.

D 兵 **Ping**¹. Arms, soldiers; 从廾持斤、會意。Two hands brandishing an axe (L. 128).

E 戒 **Chieh**⁴. To daunt, to forbid with threats; 从廾持戈、會意。Two hands holding a halberd (L. 71). — Phonetic series 258.

F 弄 **Lung**⁴, **nêng**⁴. Two hands 廾 playing with a 王 jade ball (L. 83); 玩也。从廾持玉、會意。To hahdle, to make. — Phonetic series 290.

筭 **Hsüan**. To calculate. It has nothing in common with **lung**⁴. It is a different writing of 算, below G, the representation of the abacus being 王 instead of 目.

G 具 **Chü**⁴. To heap up, to hoard up, to prepare. The 貝 is contracted into 目. Two hands 廾 heaping up 貝 cowries (L. 161), the money of the ancients; 古以貝爲貨。如後世之用泉刀。— Phonetic series 347.

算 **Hsüan**⁴. To calculate, to plan. It has nothing in common with **chü**⁴; 數也。从竹、从目、从廾、會意。Two hands 廾 manipulating the Chinese abacus 目 (a primitive) made of 竹 bamboo. Compare above F. — Phonetic series 780, the radical being placed at the bottom, 纂 etc.

H 弁 卞

Pien[4]. Hat; 冠也。从廾、从人、像形。On the top, the hat, a primitive form. At the bottom, two hands, the ritual requiring both hands to be used in covering or uncovering oneself. The form 卞 is a modern contraction. — Phonetic series 78.

I 

Yen[3]. To cover, 蓋也。To join 合 the 廾 hands, in order to cover something; 从廾从合、會意。— Phonetic series 496.

Second series.

In the modern writing, the hands 廾 are often mixed up with the object which they hold. Among these compounds, that are now unrecognisable, some are very important. The two following, J and K, are to be carefully distinguished.

J 

Chêng[4]. Fire 火 that can be 廾 handled, embers, live coal, lit. grain of fire; 火種也。从火、从廾、會意。Compare 灰, L. 46 I. It forms

朕

Chêng[4]. To caulk the seams of a boat (月 for 舟 L 66); or rather, to 廾 curve with 火 fire planks to build 舟 a hull. — Phonetic series 511, in which the radical is inserted at the bottom of 关、勝 滕、etc. — From the year B. C. 221, 朕 was used (**chia-chieh**) to write the personal pronoun **chên** by which the Emperor designated himself.

K 

Chüan[4]. To pick and sort 釆 (L. 123) with the 廾 hands, to choose the best. The top is not 米 (L. 122). — Phonetic series 191, in which the radical is placed at the bottom, 劵、拳、etc. Note the derivative

Chüan[4]. A deed sealed (㔾 L. 55 B), a roll, a scroll, a section or division of a work; 关 is phonetic. — Phonetic series 350.

Third series:

This is another series formed by the 𦥑 hands mixed up with the object which they hold. Though the object is not the same in the ancient characters, the modern contraction 𡗗 is the same. The radical is at the bottom.

L 

Fêng[4]. To hold up (or to receive) respectfully in both hands, as required by the ritual; 獻也。承也。从𦥑,从手,从丯,會意。Note that 手 at the bottom, has only two transversal strokes, as in the ancient character (L. 48). 手 says the Glose, represents the action of presenting 丯 something, while the two hands 𦥑 represent the ritual reverence. —. Phonetic series 354.

M 

Tsou[4]. To inform, a memorandum. To present one's self 夲 (L. 60 F) before a superior, and to offer 𦥑 to him 屮 one's advice; 會意。The 屮 (L. 78 A) is symbolic, 上進之意。— Phonetic series 482.

N 

Ch'ung[1]. To bark the grain by pounding it, 擣粟也。Two hands 𦥑 that raise up the 午 pestle (L. 130), above the 臼 mortar (L. 139); 會意。According to the Glose, the guilty women were condemned to this hard work. Not to be confounded with 春, below P. — Phonetic series 606. The composition of the next is analogous.

Ch'in[2]. A kind of 禾 rice, cultivated in the **Wei** valley; then the name of this valley, and lastly of the **Ch'in** Dynasty. The character represents the barking of this rice. — Phonetic series 522.

O 

T'ai[4]. A 大 man, who 𦥑 struggles, in 水 water; flooded river, inundation. Hence the derived notion, vast, wide-spreading. The modern character is a strange contraction.

P 

Ch'un[1]. Spring. Here the modern 𡗗 has a quite different meaning from that of the preceding characters. Outburst 屯 of the plants 艸, under the influence of the sun 日, at the beginning of the year. See L. 79 A. — Phonetic series 436.

Fourth series. Other modern contractions of 廾.

Q 

Kung[4] Generally, all, altogether. Action in common 同也, symbolised, in the old character, by four hands joined together, and in the more recent form, by twenty 廿 pairs of 廾 hands; 从廿、从廾。會意。See 卷 L. 74 C. — Phonetic series 225.

Note: 殿 L. 22 D, has nothing in common with 共。The same may be said of the two following characters, R and S.

R 異

I[4]. To disagree, discord, variance, difference, heterodox. Two hands 廾, thrust aside 由 the earnest money, from the 丌 small table, upon which it was laid down; the parties do not want to conclude, they disagree. Compare 畀 the agreement, L. 40 C. — Phonetic series 620.

S 

Pao[4]. Insolation, exposure to the sun; 廾 to spread out the grain 米, when the sun 日 is risen 出. By extension, any intense, violent action or influence. — Phonetic series 809.

Fifth series. Other modern contractions of 廾.

T 寒 

Sai[1]. To wall in, to block up, to shut up. An empty place 宀 is filled with 工 bricks, or other materials, that are introduced by the 廾 hands. It is now written 塞. — Phonetic series 530. The top of the compounds, which now resembles the top of the derivatives from 寒 (below U), was different from them in the old writing.

U 

Han[2]. Cold; 凍也。从人在宀下、以茻薦覆之。下有冫、會意。A poor man 人, who tries to protect himself from 冫 frost (L. 17 A), in his 宀 shelter, by burying himself in 茻 straw. — Phonetic series 530, in which the top is the same as in the derivatives from **sai**[1] (above T); 冫 gives room to the radical, v.g.

Ch'ien[5]. To go lame; 从足、寒省聲。

Sixth series. Other modern contractions of 𦥑.

V 

Ch'êng[2]. To aid, to second; a deputy, a minister 翼也。Two hands 𦥑 holding a 卩, the official sceptre, to mean the minister (See L. 55 A, B). A 山 mountain represents the prince who is assisted; for, says the Glose, mountain means *eminence, dignity.* In the modern character, 山 flattened was changed into 一. It forms the phonetic compound

Chêng[1]. To steam, to boil; 从火、丞聲。— Phonetic series 510. Note also

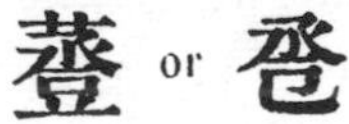

Chin[3]. The symbolical wedding cup, two halves of a same gourd.

W 

Ch'êng[2]. To present, 奉也。从卩、𦥑、手、會意。 See 奉 (above L), the composition and meaning of which are nearly identical; instead of 丰, there is 卩, representing any object whatever.

Seventh series: In the two following characters, 𦥑 represents the claws of a scorpion.

X  

Ch'ai[4]. A scorpion represented by its claws, head and tail; 像形。The legs being added, this character became

Wan[4]. Scorpion; 像形。This character now means **chia-chieh** a myriad. See the Introduction, p. 11, and L. 23 H. Phonetic series 765.

Eighth series: 𠬜 the hands diverging.

Y 

P'an[1]. To discard. Gesture of a man who exerts himself to separate, to repel obstacles, on the right and on the left; 从反𦥑、指事。The modern abbreviation is an unhappy one. It forms

Z 

Fan[2]. Hedge, trellis, obtacle, to stop; 从𠬜、从棥、會意、The hands trying in vain to 𠬜 separate the interlaced branches of a 棥 hedge (L. 39 L). — Phonetic series 801, in which the radical is added at the bottom, 攀, etc.

LESSON 48.

About 手, a special form of the hand.

A 

Shou³. ⺕ is the hand seen half face; 手 is the hand (palm) seen full face; 像形。掌也。The small ∧ in the ancient form, represents the lines of the hand. Now 手 or 扌. — It is the 64th radical of characters relating to the hand. See 𠃨 L. 11 E, and note the following.

B 

Shih¹. To lose, to let 乙 fall from the 手 hand; 从手、从乙。在手而去也。See L. 9 A. The ancient character is hardly recognisable in its modern form. — Phonetic series 155.

C 看

K'an⁴. To look at, to regard carefully. A hand 手 covering an 目 eye; 从手下目。會意。For, says the Glose, in order to see well, one shades the eye with the hand, that stops the rays of the sun; 凡有所望者。常以手加目上、障日也。Compare L. 37 F.

D 折

Chê². Shê². To cut, to break, to burst; 斷也。A 手 hand holding an 斤 axe; 从手、从斤、會意。This is a mistake of Li-ssŭ. The old character represented an 斤 axe. and the two 屮 parts of a cut branch; 从斤、斷屮、會意。— Phonetic series 252.

E 拜

Pai⁴. To honour, to reverence. Two 手 hands that are 丅 held down; 从兩手、下、會意. See 丅 an ancient form of 下, L. 5 B.

LESSON 49.

About the hand, not raised up, but prone.

A 爪 ⺤

Chao³. The right hand, prone, leaning on the palm. By extension, paw, claw; 覆⺕日爪。像形。— It is the 87th radical. Phonetic series 39. On account of its meaning, in the compounds, the normal position of 爪 is on the top of the compound; ⺤ is the contracted form in the modern writing.

B 采 **Ts'ai**[3]. To pluck, with the tip of the 爫 fingers, upon 木 a tree, a flower or a fruit; 捋取也。从木、从爫、會意。Now 採. — Phonetic series 402.

C 寽 **Lüeh**[4]. To draw, to stretch between fingers; 从爫、从彐、从一、指事。Two hands 爫 and 彐; — represents the stretching. Compare below D, E. — Phonetic series 292.

D 爭 **Chêng**[1]. To pull in different directions; to quarrel, to fight. Two hands 爫 彐, and the primitive ʃ (L. 8) that means, to pull; 从爫、从彐、从ʃ、會意。The Glose explains that pulling brings quarrels 曳之爭之道也。— Phonetic series 324.

E 𠬪 **P'iao**[3]. To pass an object downwards, from 爫 one's own hand, to 彐 another's; 物落上下相付也。从爪、从彐、會意。It forms

受 **Shou**[4]. To give or to receive from hand to hand, to confine into a recipent; 相付也。盛也。从爫、从彐、冖舟也。Therefore 冖 is that which remains from 舟 L. 66. One may follow, in the ancient characters, the successive alterations of this element. The character represents a lading; a hand 爫, on the bank, delivers the goods; another 又, in the boat, receives and stows them away. The modern abstract meanings, to receive, to endure, are **chuan-chu**. — Phonetic series 392. Note that 愛 ai[4] (L. 99 F) has nothing in common with 受.

F 爰 **Yüan**[2]. A traction equal on both sides; 爫 action and 彐 reaction, 幵 (L. 115 B contracted) annulling each other; equilibrium, pause, halt. — Phonetic series 505.

G 𢀛 㥯 **Yin**[3]. To enjoy the result of the work 工 of one's hands 爫 彐, of one's toil, of that which one has gathered; a life secure and free from care; 所依據也。从爫、彐、工、會意。It forms 㥯, peace of 心 heart, the man who has what he 𢀛 needs, and who desires nothing else; now 隱. — Phonetic series 794.

H 

Wei⁴. Female monkey, 母猴也 (Compare 禺 L. 23 E). One 爪 on the top, and two others mingled at the bottom; because, says the Glose, among all the animals, the female monkey is the most prone to claw; 其爲禽、好爪。The middle is intended to represent the body of the female monkey. This body is composed of 人 man (on account of the resemblance), and of a coarse representation of the breasts (to signify the female). This last element is a primitive (See 母, L. 67 O) — That is all pure fun. The ancient character represented 𢀸 a hand carding textile fibres. — Now **chuan-chu** to do, **chia-chieh** to be; for, in order to, etc. Note the modern usual abbreviation. — Phonetic series 717.

I 印

Yin⁴. A seal, to seal, to print. A hand 爪, holding a piece of jade 卩, the seal of office (L. 55 B; L. 47 V, W), and using it downwards; 執政所持信也。从爪、从卩、會意。In the modern character, the two elements, instead of overlying each other, are in juxtaposition, which is illogical. — The following is 印 inverted.

抑

I⁴. The contrary idea: stamp, pressure, to compress (positive-negative, compare L 30 C); 按也。从反印、指事。用印、必向下按之。The hand 扌 added further, is a redundancy of radicals. Then 印 lost one stroke, 今課作抑。

LESSON 50.

About the two hands 𦥔 lowered, the invert of 𦥑, L. 47.

A 𦥔

Chü². Hands lowered, giving or taking downwards; 从倒𦥑指事。There are numerous compounds. Note that the modern writers and engravers often draw 臼, which makes the compounds unintelligible, and changes the number of strokes.

B 盥

Kuan⁴. To wash one s hands. Water 水 poured upon the 𦥔 hands, over a 皿 vessel; 操手也。从𦥔水臨皿、會意。

First series: 申 and its derivatives.

C **Shên**[1]. Ancient form: two hands extending a rope; idea of extension, of expansion. Later on, the rope straightened by the scribes was interpreted as being a man standing, who girds himself with both hands; 束身也。从臼自持也。丨身也。指事。 The oldest forms were primitives, figuring the alternate expansion of the two natural powers. — Phonetic series 153. It forms the following.

D 電 **Tien**[4]. Lightning, thunderbolt, the expansion (discharge) 申 towards the earth, of a 雨 stormy cloud. In the modern character, the line 丨 is curved towards the right, in order to take less room. The Glose explains the nature of a thunderbolt as follows: 陽氣之發與地面陰氣格鬥。成光。 The **ch'i**[4] **yang**[2], the male power, rushing on the earth, fights with the **ch'i**[4] **yin**[1], the female power, which gives birth to the lightning. Thus the Chinese, twenty centuries before Franklin.

E 奄 **Yen**[3]. A 大 man (L. 60) who stretches his legs and covers a stride's length; by extension, to cover; 覆也。从大。从申。會意。— Phonetic series 418.

F 曳 **I**[4]. To stretch 申, to pull in ㇓ a direction; 从申。从㇓。會意。See L. 8 A. Now 曳. — Phonetic series 213.

G 臾 **Yü**[2]. To stretch 申, to pull in another ㇏ direction; 从申。从㇏。會意。 See L. 8 B. Now 臾. — Phonetic series 502.

H 陳 **Ch'ên**[2]. Name of a place. The first Capital, the first seat of administration of China, under **Fu-hsi** (See our *Textes Historiques*, p. 19). From 木 L. 119, cutting down of trees; 阝 L. 86, building walls; 申 exercising authority. The vertical lines of 木 and of 申 are joined. Derived notions of antiquity, of a long duration, to dispose, to fit up, etc. It has nothing in common with 東, L. 120 K. Compare 巢 L. 12 O.

Second series: 舁 and its derivatives

I 舁

Yü². To lift up, many hands drawing or pushing; 从𦥑.从廾.會意。共舉也。It forms compounds, in which the radical is inserted on the top, between the two 𦥑; v.g.

Yü². A heavy 車 car (L. 167), a roller drawn or pushed with much trouble.

J 

Yü³ To give. See 与 and the analysis of 與, L. 54 H. — Phonetic series 768, in which the radical is added at the bottom, between the two 廾; v.g.

Chü³. To raise; 从手.與聲。

K 

Hsing¹. To lift up 舁, several men acting 同 together; 从舁.从同.會意。同力也。Not to be confounded with the derivatives of 同 (L. 154) 爨, etc. **Chuan-chu**, animation, success, the results of cooperation and concord; to be in demand, fashionable.

Third series: 學 and its derivatives.

L 

Hsiao². To learn. Was explained L. 39 I. When the hands 𦥑 of the master act 爻 downwards, the darkness that covers the mind of the disciple 子 is dispelled. — Phonetic series 𦥯 733, 子 giving place to the radical.

Fourth series: [illegible] and its derivatives.

M [illegible]

Yao¹. This compound represents a 囟 head and two 𦥑 hands. It means sometimes, head and hands; and sometimes, head and shoulders, the bust. It forms compounds that are important, but unrecognisable in the modern form, on account of the fusion of different elements.

N 要

Yao^{1}. The loins, the waist; 身中也。像。从囟。从𦥑。从女。A head 囟, the two hands 𦥑, that surround a woman's figure, women taking more care of their waist than men. The ancient forms represented a human face, and two hands girding the waist; 上像首。下像足。中像腰。𦥑束腰之形。To mean, loins, waist, this character is now written 腰. The ancient character now means **chia-chieh**, to want, to need, to ask for, etc. — Phonetic series 493.

O 票

P'iao^{4}. Ignis fatuus (*vulgo* 鬼火 phantom-fire) The Chinese fear them. On the top, 𡿺 the bust of the hobgoblin. At the bottom, 火 the flame that takes the place of the body's lower part. In the middle, 一 the waist. The modern meanings of this character, a warrant, a bill, are **chuan-chu** (things that are feared). — Phonetic series 642. — **K'ang-hsi** who might have rightly classified 要 under 女, placed it under 西, which is a mistake. But this is the worst instance, and shows how all his classifications are arbitrary and without foundation: instead of classifying 票 under 西, as he did for 要, he classified it under 示 (113th radical), with which it has nothing in common, the character at the bottom being 火 (86th radical).

P 䙴

Ch'ien^{1}. To rise by climbing up. The head 囟 and four 𦥑 𠬞 hands. The idea is probably taken from the monkeys (quadrumana). By extension, to rise up, to make headway, promotion. The modern form was added with an 卩 official seal, which means promotion in the hierarchy, the seal being the badge of the rank. Now 遷, to be promoted. See L. 25 I 僊, the Immortals, the men who rose above the human condition.

Q 農

Nung^{2}. The husbandman; 耕人也。A head 囟, two hands 𠬞, and 晨 the break of the day contracted, 日 giving place to 囟. The man who works from early dawn; all field-work being done very early in hot countries 耕作必於晨。— Phonetic series 751.

Note: 農 has nothing in common with 曲 ch'ü^{1} L. 51 B, 豊 li^{3} L. 97 B, 曹 ts'ao^{2} L. 120 K. Neither of the last two are derived from 曲.

LESSON 51.

About two primitives, which were united on account of their resemblance in the old writing, 匚 fang^{1} and 曲 ch'ü^{1}.

First series: 匚 fang^{1}.

A

Fang^{1}. The primitive wooden vessel, a log hollowed out; 受物之器。像形。The character is written horizontally. By extension, chest, trunk, box. — It is the 22th radical. To be distinguished from the 23th radical (L. 10 B); the two are much alike. It forms.

Chiang^{4}. The primitive art, the first handicraft, which consisted in hollowing the wood with an 斤 axe, to make the 匚 vessels; carpentry; 匠人 a carpenter; then, by extension, craft, art, in general. 木工也.从匚、从斤。會意。斤所以作器也。

Second series: 曲 ch'ü^{1}.

B

Ch'ü^{1}. Represents a piece of wood that is bent. It was later on replaced by fang^{1} (above A) raised up. By extension, curved, crooked, oblique, not straight. — Phonetic series 190. But 豊 li^{3} L. 97 B, 農 nung^{2} L. 50 Q, 曹 ts'ao^{2} L. 120 K, are not derived from 曲.

LESSON 52.

About the primitive 刀.

A

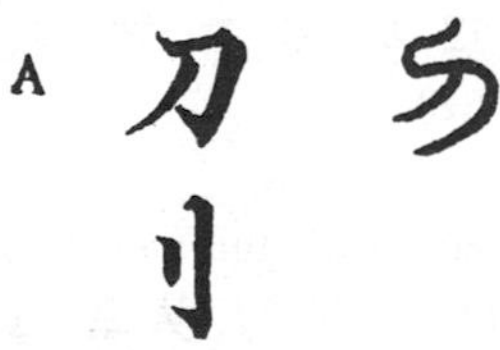

Tao^{1}. Edge-tool, knife, sword; 兵也。像形。The handle is curved, to take less room. The upper hook belongs to the handle, the lower hook is the edge. See page 365 the primitive instrument, of silex, fixed into a curved handle of wood. — Note the contracted form of this character, when it is placed on the side. It is the 18th radical of characters relating to cutting, etc.

This character is not found in the old dictionaries. It is considered as a different writing of 刀。刀字變作刁。It is read tiao^{1}, and means, perverse, caballing.

B 刃

Jên. Edged weapons, the edge, sharp, pointed: 从刀、丶者指事。The character represents a 刀 sword with a dot on the blade, to indicate the place where the instrument cuts. — Phonetic series 21. It forms

忍

Jên^{3}. To bear, to sustain; 从心、刃亦聲。耐也。From heart and a cutting weapon. The heart wounded.

刅

Liang^{2}. Cutting weapon 刀 fixed in the notch it made, action of a cutting weapon; 从刀、从一者、指事。It is found in

梁

Liang^{2}. Primitively, a narrow 一 foot-bridge, made with two 木 trees placed over a 水 brook. Later on, 木 a tree, 刅 barked and planed, placed over a 水 brook. Then, by extension, a beam, a sleeper. It forms by substituting 米 to 木, the character 粱 **liang**^{2}, sorghum.

C 召

Chao^{4}. Primitive meaning, 評也、to judge according to the Chinese way, viz. 口 to chide and to make some 刀 amputation. Compare the similar composition of 言 and 刀, L. 39 E. By extension, to cite, to send for, to call. — Phonetic series 105.

D 列

Lieh^{4}. To divide seriatim, to arrange, to place according to rank or rule; 分解也 从刀、𡿪聲。See L. 12 F. — Phonetic series 228.

E 則

Tsai^{2}. Law, rule to be observed; and the penalties of old, 貝 fines and 刀 mutilations; 从刀、从貝、會意。**Chuan-chu**, consequently. — Phonetic series 481.

賊

Tsei^{2}. In its modern form, this character might be taken for a derivative of 戎 (L. 71 O). This is not so. It is composed of 戈 a halberd, 刀 a sword, 貝 cowries, 會意。To plunder with arms in hand; robbery; a bandit. It derives not from 則。

F 利 ⿰ 秎 ⿰

Li[4]. To cut 刀 the corn 禾; reaping-hook; hence, sharp, acute; 从刀刈禾.會意。**Chuan-chu**, the harvest, the acquisition of the year; hence, gains, profit, interest on money. — An old form was composed of 禾, and 勿 (L. 101) representing the motion of the sickle. In the corresponding modern form, 勿 lost one stroke, as it may be seen above. — The two forms are found in the compounds, the old one being used specially when 利 is placed on the top of the compound, as in 棃, 犂, 黎。This last character is composed of 秎 and 黍, the 202th radical. The 禾 of the radical, and of the phonetic, are mingled together. — Phonetic series 288.

See 分 L. 18 B, 初 L. 16 B, etc.
Do not mistake for 刀, the 人 contracted, e.g. in 色. See the whole Lesson 28.— However 刀 has sometimes, but seldom, this form. See 絕 L. 55 G.

刀 repeated three times is found in

荔

Li[4]. *Nephelium* **li-chih** 荔枝, the fruit so dear to the Chinese. The sound 力 **li**[4] (L. 53) induced the scribes to write 荔, thus making one more wrong character.

LESSON 53.

About the primitive 力.

A 力

Li[4]. Sinew; by extension, strength; 筋也。像形。The top of the middle-line (the sinew) is curved, to take less room. The two side-lines and the transversal stroke represent the fibrous sheath. — It is the 19th radical of characters relating to effort of any kind. It forms

B 劣

Lüeh[3]. Infirm, feeble; from 力 strength and 少 few: 弱也。从力、少.會意。

C 男

Nan[2]. The man, by opposition to the woman, the male. The one who exerts his 力 strength in the work of the 田 field, the woman being busy at home; 丈夫者也。从田、从力。會意。言、男用力於田也。Compare 虜 L. 135 C.

D 加 **Chia**[1]. To add 力 the sinews to the 口 mouth, violence to persuasion; 从力。从口、會意。By extension, to add to, to increase, to insist, to inflict, etc. — Phonetic series 108.

See 助 L. 20 E; 劫 L. 38 F; 幼 L. 90 A.

E 劦 **Hsieh**[2]. Action in common, represented by the union of the 力 strength of three persons; union, concord, cooperation; 从三力、會意。同力也。Compare 共 L. 47 Q. — Phonetic series 201 It forms

協 **Hsieh**[2]. Union, ten 十 persons, i. e. a multitude, joining their efforts; 眾之同和也。會意。See L. 24.

Hsieh[2]. The sides of the chest. Perfect cooperation of the ribs; 兩膀也、會意。

LESSON 54.

In the first part of this Lesson, 勹 a particular form of the primitive 人 (L. 25) will be studied. The second part is devoted to the primitives 丩、勻、蜀、the compounds of which resemble those of 勹 in the modern writing.

First part. 勹.

A 勹 **Pao**[1]. A man 人 who bends to enfold an object; 人曲有所包。像形。褢也。To wrap up, to envelop, to contain; a bundle, a whole. — It is the 20th radical of characters relating to wrapping and enclosing. Note that in a few modern characters, 勹 is written like 冖 (14th radical); v g. 軍 (L. 167 C), 冢 (L. 69 G), etc. The following compounds form important groups.

B 包 **Pao**[1]. Actual meaning: to wrap up, to contain, in general. Primitive meaning: gestation, the fœtus 巳 inwrapped 勹 in the womb; 从勹、从巳、會意。人褢妊也。巳在中像子。未成形也。Compare 辰 L. 30 B. — Phonetic series 145.

C 匋 **T'ao**[2]. A furnace 勹 for burning 缶 (L. 130C) earthenware; 从勹、从缶、會意。瓦器竈也。— Phonetic series 396.

D 

Chü[2]. A handful, to grasp. Primitive meaning: the quantity of 米 grains that can be grasped 勹 by a hand; 从勹、从米、會意。在手曰匊。Now 掬. — Phonetic series 346.

E 匀

Yün[2]. To divide 二 a whole 勹, into parts supposed to be equal; uniform repartition; regularity, equality; 从勹、从二、會意。二猶分也。— Phonetic series 98. It is contracted in the two following

旬

Hsün[2]. A period of ten days; 从日、匀省聲。— Phonetic series 209.

訇

Hung[1]. The noise of a crowd; 从言、匀省聲。— Phonetic series 453.

It seems rather that these two characters are derived directly from 勹, and not from 匀 contracted. — **Hsün**[2]: a whole 勹, a period of ten days. — **Hung**[1]: a whole 勹, a union of 言 voices.
See 匐 L. 38 D; 匈 L. 10 G; 苟 L. 54 G; 肉 L. 17 G, etc.

Second series: 丩, 句, 蜀.

F 丩

Chiu[1]. A primitive, intended to represent the tangle of creeping plants; 瓜瓠相糾繚也。像形。By extension, curved, crooked, entangled. — Phonetic series 5. In the modern writing, 丩 is sometimes replaced by 斗, e.g. 叫 for 叫; it is a licence. From 丩, and not from 勹, comes

句 勾

Kou[1]. Curved, crooked, hook; 曲也。从丩、口聲。The form 勾 is a modern abbreviation; 今俗作勾。... 句 is also read

Chü[4]. A sentence; because, in the Chinese compositions, the end of each sentence, the pause, is indicated, when it is so, by a 乚 hook, which is the equivalent of the European punctuation; 語絕爲句。句者局也。聯字分疆所以局言者也。乚畫以識者也。Phonetic series 131, in which are found the two sounds **kou** and **chü**. 局 (L. 32 F) has nothing in common with 句.

Note: The following, 茍 chi[4], comes from 勹, and not from 句. It must be carefully distinguished from 苟 kou[3] (句 under the 140th radical 艹).

G 茍

Chi[4]. To restrain one's self, self-possession, deferential reserve. Etymologically, 勹 to restrain one's 口 mouth, and to stand quiet 丫 (L. 103 C); 从丫.从口.从勹.會意。自急敕也。勹口猶愼言也。羊於善美同意。It forms

Ching[4]. Deferential behaviour, reverence, reserve, 茍 modesty in the presence of the 攴 authority (the hand holding the rod, L. 43 D). — Phonetic series 192.

Pei[4]. **Pi**[4]. To prepare, to make ready all the things 用 necessary, with 茍 modesty. This is meant for women, on whom devolve the preparations, the care of the household. The 茍 is contracted, 口 giving room to 用. Now 備. The engravers strangely altered this character. Some specimens of their skilfulness may be seen here:

葡 葡 备 備 備 備 偹 俻

H 勺

Shao[2]. A primitive representing a kind of spoon, that was used to draw up; — (L. 1, 4°) represents the contents; 挹取也。像形。中有實。— Phonetic series 27. It forms

与 與

Yü[3]. The full spoon, with an — index meaning that it is being emptied (compare L. 1, 5°). To give (the contents); 賜與也。This character became intricate in course of time. The two hands 廾 of the receiver were first added (L. 47). Then, on the top, the two hands 𦥑 of the giver (L. 50). Under this last form, 與 makes the phonetic series 768, the radical being added at the bottom. See L. 50 J.

I  

Shu^{3}. A primitive, that has nothing in common, either with 勹, or with 罒. It represents a silk-worm moving on. On the top, the head. The curved line represents the body that bends and stretches. At the bottom 虫 (L. 110), radical, was added later on; 桑蟲也。从虫、上頭形、中像其身蜎蜎。— Phonetic series 756. It forms

Shu^{2}. The 尾 tail (L. 100 B), that 蜀 wriggles at the extremity of the body. By extension, 連也 appendix, to stick to (as the tail to the body), to depend from. — Phonetic series 856.

LESSON 55.

About three primitives 卯 ch'ing^{1}, 马 han$_{3}$, 巴 pa^{1}.

First series: 卯 ch'ing^{1}.

A 卯

Ch'ing^{1}. In ancient times the Emperor, when investing the feudatories or officials, handed over to them one half of a piece of wood or of jade diversely cut out; the other half was used to make the proof, as the modern counterfoil. The two pieces gathered are the 卯 ch'ing^{1}. We shall see further (L. 55 B, I) 𠂎 and 卩, the two halves, left and right... When they appeared before the Emperor, or when they held the functions of their office, the feudatories or officials had this kind of sceptre in their hands. It was used also as a seal. — It forms

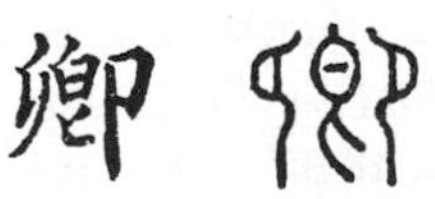

Ch'ing^{2}. This character first meant the 皀 feasts (L. 26 M) of the court, the high personages attending, ranged in 卯 two opposite rows. By extension, ministers, high officials.

Note: The modern form 卯 is not symmetrical, because the writing-brush cannot trace the left half 𠂎 against the grain. Note also that many symmetrical representations, absolutely different in the old writing, nowadays ressemble 卯 ch'ing^{1}. K'ang-hsi classified them under 卩. These are 卬 nang^{2}, L. 26 G; 卯 mao^{3}, L. 129 D; 卵 luan^{3}, L. 108 D; 丣 yu^{3}, L. 129 E.

B 卩 㔾 巴

Chieh². The right half part of 卯, the one committed to the functionary, that was used by him as a badge and as a seal; 瑞信也。像, By extension, dignity, authority, rule, just measure, print; part of a whole, segment, fragment. — See L. 26 M; L. 64 D; L. 47 V, W; L. 49 I. It is the 26th radical.

Note the three different writings of the modern form. The first must be distinguished from 阝, a contracted form of the 163th and 170th radicals — The second form is hardly recognisable from the cursive form of 马 han³ (L. 55 K); as well as from 己 chi³ (L. 84), 已 i³ (L. 85 B), 巳 ssŭ⁴ (L. 85 A). K'ang-hsi did not succeed in distinguishing them; he counted sometimes 㔾 two strokes, and at others 己 three strokes. — The third form is to be distinguished from 巴 pa¹ (L 55 L). — In all this series, it is quite impossible, without recurring to the old forms, to know exactly which element is used.

C 𠬝

Fu². The hand 彐 holding a 卩 sceptre; to impose one's authority; 治也。从彐、从卩、會意。It forms 服 fu², to steer a boat (L. 66 C); and 報 pao⁴, to repress bandits (L. 102 G). But 赧 nan³ is not derived from 𠬝; see L. 43 J.

D 卮 巵

Chih¹. A vessel that was u ed, in the feasts, for pouring wine 卩 with measure; 器也。以節飲食。 The top that ressembles 𠂆 L. 30 A, is intended to represent the vessel, a kind of siphon.

E 肥

Fei². Fleshy 肉, muscular, just 卩 as much as it is proper, for the sacrifices, for the table. The just measure of flesh; 从肉、从卩、會意。

F 色

Shê⁴. The blush of the 人 human face, a mark 卩 of the passions. By extension, colour, passion, lust. See the explanations given L. 28 D. — It is the 139th radical. The following is not derived from 色.

G 絕

Chüeh². To cut 刀 (L. 52) a thread 糸 (L. 92), in 卩 pieces; 斷絲也。从糸、从刀、从卩、會意。 To cut, to cease, to leave, to renounce, etc. See the ancient form L. 90 E Has nothing in common with the last 色.

H Two 卩, with which the scribes made two 弓 (L. 87), are found in

巽 **Hsüan⁴**. To elect, to choose. Two 卩 seals of officials, placed upon a 丌 table (L. 70), to be committed to those who were elected, chosen. Later on, the two hands 𦥑 were added to mean the awarding, the investiture. In the modern character, 𦥑 and 丌 joined together, gave 共, which has nothing in common with 共 kung⁴ (L 47 Q); 从丌、从二卩、从𦥑、會意。This character is seldom seen well written — Phonetic series 535.

I The left half of 卯 (L. 55 A); 合卩之半也。It is found in 抑 i⁴, that means, printing of the 卩 seal. See the explanation given L. 49 I.

Second series: 㔾 han³.

K **Han³**. To bud, to put forth buds, to bloom. A primitive, representing the effort of the blooming, of the springing up. 草木之花發圅然。像形。Note the modern form, identical with the second form of 卩 (L. 55 B); hence confusions. — Phonetic series 6. Note the following compounds, in which there remains something of the primitive idea of 㔾, external manifestation of an interior force, expansion, eruption.

犯 **Fan⁴**. To rush 㔾 like a 犬 dog. To invade, to offend. Compare 突 L. 37 B. In the symbolism of characters, the dog plays a considerable, though not creditable part. 侵也。从犬、从㔾。言犬犯人。轉注爲凡干陵違道之稱。

Han². To withdraw 𢆉 the lolled 㔾 tongue, and hold it in the 口 mouth. Compare 舌 L. 102 C. By extension, to endure in silence. 舌體㔾𢆉。Note the awful modern abbreviation, which became usual.— Phonetic series 356.

Yung^{3}. Blooming 马, opening of flowers; 用 yung^{4} (L. 109 B) is phonetic; 从马. 用聲。— Phonetic series 320. It forms 勇 yung^{3}, bravery, exercice of the 力 manly vigour.

Yu^{2}. To shoot branches, boughs. 木生條也。从马、由聲。Not to be confounded with 甹 p'in^{2} (L. 58 C).

Third series: 巴 **pa.**

L 巴

Pa^{1}. A kind of boa, large and short, found in the Southern Provincos, in 四川 Ssŭ-ch'uan and elsewhere. Its flesh is eaten (蟒肉), and its skin is used to cover the guitars. The character represents the boa raised on its tail; 巴蛇。像形。Compare L 108 A. Not to be confounded with the third form of 卩 (L. 55 B). — Phonetic series 76. Note the compound 琶 pa^{1}, a guitar made from a boa-skin (L. 83 B).

LESSON 56.

About the primitive 卜.

A 卜

Pu^{3}, po^{3}. To divine by looking at the cracks in a tortoise-shell as the heat develops them. The character represents two cracks, one being longitudinal, and the othor transversal; 像。炙龜之形。龜兆之縱橫也。— It is the 25th radical. Phonetic series 9. It froms

B 占

Chan^{1}. To ask 口 about some enterprise, by singeing 卜 a tortoise shell; divination; 視兆問也。从卜。从口、會意。卜以問疑也, Not to be confounded with 叱 chi^{1}, made with the same elements; and synonym. — Phonetic series 104.

C 貞

Chêng^{1}. The salary of a fortune-teller; a sum of 貝 cowries given to the man who singes 卜 the shell; 从卜。問事也。貝以爲贄。會意。The answer received was considered as most certain, most firm, and most immutable, hence the derived meanings: immutability, coustaucy, perseverauce in purpose generally, and specially in the purpose of keeping continence; 爲正、爲定。守節曰貞。言行抱一、謂之貞。— Phonetic series 423.

D 兆 𠬤 **Chao**[4]. Numerous cracks on a tortoise-shell; 像。灸龜坼也。In the middle, 卜 in its ancient form; on each side, two other cracks; the first left crack is confounded with the vertical stroke of 卜. By extension, an omen, a numher, now a million. — Phonetic series 178.

E 卦 卦 **Kua**[4]. The diagrams of the 易經 **I Ching**, the Book of Mutations. It seems that, in the beginning, 卜 the shell was first used to find the hexagram which might resolve the pending difficnlty. Later on, people had recourse, for that purpose, to the 筮 milfoil stalks The 圭 is not **kui**[1] L. 81 B, but represents an hexagram. — Phonetic sories 369.

F 外 外 **Wai**[4]. Composed of 夕 the evening, and 卜 to divine; 卜尙平旦、今夕、卜於事外矣。When the shell was consulted about the meaning of a dream one had during the night, the divination ought to take place in the morning, or during the day, in any case before 夕 the evening. After sunset, the divination 卜 was no longer *ad rem*, being *outside* the ritual limits. Hence the **chuan-chu** meaning of this important character, outside, out of.

Note: Like all the characters simple and easy to write, 卜 is used by the scribes as an arbitrary abbreviation for the most different elements. It represents a bird in 西 (ancient form) L. 41 D; the antennae of an insect 禼 L. 23 G; the peduncle ot a fruit 卤 L. 41 E; a rod 攴 L. 43 D. — Note also that 卞 has nothing in common with 卜; it is a modern contraction of 弁 L 47 H. — **K'ang-hsi** wrongly placed several among those abbreviations under 卜 the 25th radical.

LESSON 57.

About two primitives. 丁 and 宁.

First part: 丁.

A 丁 丁 **Ting**[1]. A nail (head and tack). It is now written 釘… 像形、今俗以釘爲篇。**Ting**[4], to nail; 以丁入物。Is used, on account of its simplicity, as a numeral sign, for unity, and for other different **chia-chieh**. — Phonetic series 11. — It forms the important compounds 亭 **t'ing**[2], L. 75 B; and 成 **ch'êng**[2], L. 71 M. But 寧 **ning**[2] (L. 36 C) comes from 丂 (L. 58 A), and not from 丁. Item, 亍 (L. 63 B) has nothing in common with 丁.

Second part: 宁.

B 宁

Chu⁴. Storehouse, to warehouse. It is now written 貯… 積物也，像形。於貯同. The old character shows the storehouse, well closed on all sides. The modern character is a nonsense. Compare the primitive 叕 (L. 43 R). — Phonetic series 116,

LESSON 58.

About the partial primitive 丂, and its derivatives.

First series: 丂.

A 丂

Ch'iao³. Difficulty or effort of the rospiration, sobbing, hiccup, the breath 丂 fighting against an — obstacle. See L. I, 3°. 气欲舒出，上礙於一也。按丂像形。一指事。Phonetic series 3. It forms

B 号

Hao⁴. To lament, to howl; the 口 mouth uttering 丂 shrieks; 从口、丂。會意。痛聲也。— Phonetic series 122. It forms

號 **Hao⁴.** To call, to cry; 嘑也。叫也。从号、从虎。The strong-voiced tiger 虎 enters into different compounds that mean, cries, roars. It forms 饕 t'ao¹, covetousness; 貪也。从食、號聲。

C 甹

Pin². To make out 由 one's motives with 丂 cries and noise; to quarrel, to reproof; 亟詞也。从丂、从由、會意、See 由 L. 151. Not to be confounded with 甹 yu², L. 55 K. — Phonetic series 300.

D 兮

Hsi¹. A sigh, a sound 丂 used to indicate a 八 pause in the music, in the verses, in the sentences; a kind of phonetic punctuation; 語之分也。从丂、从八、會意。It forms

乎

Hu¹. A sigh that 丿 passe the cæsura, the pause. A particle of varied uses, interrogative, expletive, euphonic, etc. 語之餘也。从兮、丿像越揚之形。It forms

虖 **Hu¹.** The roaring 乎 of the 虍 tiger. To cry, to call for. — Phonetio series 615.

Second series: 亏.

E 亏 亏 于 **Yü²**. The breath 丂 having overcome the 一 obstacle, spreads 一 in liberty. A particle of transition, a preposition; talk, show; 於詞也。像。氣之舒也。从丂,从一。一者其氣平也,指事。Phonetic series 38, under its two forms. It makes

F 平 **P'ing²**. Compare with 乎 L. 58 D; the top is different. 平 is composed of 亏 and of 八 (L. 18) placed between the two top lines, and reinforcing the idea of free expansion on 八 both sides, on all sides. The modern meaning, plane, even, is derived from the last idea; there is no more obstacle; 語平舒也。从亏。从八。八分也。Phonetic series 151.

G 夸 **K'ua¹**. Vanity, boasting; a 大 man who 亏 makes a show of himself. — Phonetic series 221.

H 雩 **Yü²**. Invocations 亏 to obtain 雨 rain. — Phonetic series 662.

Third series: 丂 (L. 58 A) inverted 丆.

I 丆 **Ho¹**. A synonym of 丂。氣之舒也。从反丂、指事。It is now obsolete. It forms the important compound

可 **K'o³**. To send forth 口 a breathing 丆 of approbation. To express one's satisfaction. To be willing, to permit, to consent, to admire; 从口、从丆、會意。許詞也。— Phonetic series 130. It form the following

奇 **Ch'i²**. Extraordinary, surprising, strange; that which impels 大 men to 可 utter exclamations of surprise and admiration; 異也。非常也。— Phonetic series 328.

哥 **Ko¹**. It is 可 repeated twice; 从二可、會意。To sing 歌也、Expression of satisfaction. The primitive singing consisted probably of a succession of cadenced exclamations of joy. This character became (chia-chieh) the appellative of an elder brother; 今以爲稱兄之詞。See p. 11.

Note: Other compounds of 丂 and 亏: 考 L. 30 D; 寧 L. 36 C; 華 L. 13 F; 粵 L. 123 F; 虧 L. 135 F. — But 咢 L. 102 D, has nothing in common with 亏. Item 亟 L. 2 D, does not come from 丂.

LESSON 59.

About the primitive 厂 and its derivatives.

First series: 厂

A 厂 厂 **Han**^{4}. A cliff which projects, a stiff slope; 像形。 On the top, the summit; on the left side, the slope. In composition, the accessories which should be represented on the cliff, are placed at the bottom, to make the compound smaller. This character represents two notions. 1. If the top is considered, it suggests the idea of an elevated place near an abyss, dangerous, exposed to the view. 2. If the side is considered, it suggests the idea of a slide, of a fall. — It is the 27th radical.

B 厓 厓 **Yeh**^{2}. Steep 厂 of a mountain, covered with 圭 earth; rising ground. — Phonetic series 413.

C 原 原 **Yüan**^{2}. A spring 泉 that gushes out from 厂 a hill It is now written 源 spring, while 原 is used in the extended meaning of principle, origin, 本也。 For 泉, see L. 125 F. In the primitive character, there were three 泉. — Phonetic series 588.

D 石 石 **Shih**^{2}. A 口 piece of rock fallen down or taken down from a cliff, rough-stone, shingle, pebble, stone; 口、像形。 Note the alteration of 厂 in the modern writing. — It is the 112th radical of characters relating to stones. — Phonetic series 156.

E 仄 仄 **Chai**^{3}. A man 人 who, while climbing up a stiff slope, bends forward. By extension, inclined, slanting, sloping; 側傾也。 It forms 昃 **chai**^{4}: the 日 sun, 仄 leaning towards the horizon.—Inverted, 仄 becomes 丸.

丸 丸 **Wan**^{2}. A man who tumbles down on a stiff slope, rolling down. By extension, round, pellet, pill; 側傾而轉者。— Phonetic series 34.

F 屵 屵 **Yao**^{4}. Visible from afar, as a 屮 tree (L. 78) over a 厂 rock, standing out in relief against the sky; 遠望而見也。从厂、屮上出之形、會意。

G 屵 — **Nan^{4}**. Stiff slope 厂 of a high 山 mountain (L. 80). It forms 炭 **t'ân^{4}**, charcoal, which is made in the mountains, so cragged that wood cannot be taken away from them.

H 厃 — **Wei^{3}**. A man 人 (L. 28), watching upon a 厂 rock, looking afar; 从人在厂上。會意。仰也。It forms

危 — **Wei^{2}**. A man 人, upon a 厂 rock, who 卩 restrains (L. 55 B) his motions, who takes care not to fall; a perilous situation, danger, fear; 在高而懼也。从厂，从人自止之，會意。— Phonetic series 247.

詹 — **Chan^{1}**. Verbose, tattling; 八 to scatter imprudently 言 one's words (L. 73 C), which is 厃 dangerous; 多言也。— Phonetic series 722.

矦 侯 — **Hou^{2}**. In this character, 厃 has quite another meaning. It represents a 厂 target and 人 a man. An arrow 矢 (L. 131) is fixed in the target. The shooting at a target was used in antiquity, for the election of feudatories and officials. The precision in shooting was supposed to represent the uprightness of the heart, and *vice-versa*. Hence the derived meaning, aristocracy. Note the alteration of the character in the modern writing. The 人 on the top became 亻; 厂 became 丄 or 工; 矢 was unimpaired. — Phonetic series 444. In the compound 候, the 亻 of 侯 was contracted into a small vertical stroke.

Note: 厄 L 129 A, is unconnected with 厂; and so is 彥, L. 61 F.

Second series: 广.

I 广 — **Yen^{3}**. Compare 宀 the hut, L. 36 A. 广 is half of a hut, a shed, a shop. — It is the 53th radical. See 庶 L. 24 M, etc. It forms

庫 — **K'u^{4}**. A shed for the 車 chariots (L. 167); out-house, shop; 兵車藏也。从車在广下。會意。

Note: 庚 **kêng^{1}**, 康 **k'ang^{1}**, 唐 **t'ang^{2}**, 庸 **yung^{1}**, are not derived from 广. See L. 102 B. — Item 鹿 **lu^{4}**, L. 136.

LESSON 60.

About the primitive 大 and its derivatives. In the ancient writing, 大 has two forms, for which we reserve two distinct series.

First series: 大 the first form.

A 大 **Ta⁴** A primitive. A grown up man standing (body, legs and arms); 像。人 形。By extension, **chuan-chu**, the stature of an adult (by opposition to the child's stature), great, tall; 太 也。But in composition, 大 means a *man*, and not *great*. — It is the 37th radical of miscellaneous characters. It forms

B 因 **Yin¹**. To confine 囗 a man 大; 从 囗、从 大。會 意。Compare 囚, L. 25 B. It is now obsolete in that sense, but is much used in the **chuan-chu** meanings, cause, reason, argument; that with which one confines, one catches one's opponent. — Phonetic series 249.

C 天 **T'ien¹**. The heavens, the — firmament which is over 大 men; 至 高 無 上。从 一、大、會 意。按 大 猶 人 也。天 在 人 上、仰 首 見 之、一 指 事。See L. 1 C. It forms the phonetic complexes

忝 **T'ien³**. To outrage; 辱 也。从 心 (L. 107). 天 聲。— Phonetic series 389

吞 **T'un¹**. To gulp down. 咽 也。从 口 (L. 72). 天 聲。

D 夷 **I²**. The men 大 armed with bows 弓; the primitive inhabitants, barbarians, borderers of the Eastern Sea, inhabitants of the South-West countries; 从 大、从 弓、會 意。— Phonetic series 212.

Compare 夾 **shan³** L. 13 B; 夾 **chia¹** L. 27 F; 奭 L. 88 B; 爽 L. 39 O; 無, L 10 I.

1 奞 **Sui¹**. Bird 隹 spreading its wings to fly, as the man stretches out his arms in the character 大; 鳥 張 羽 也。从 大、从 隹、會 意。It is now obsolete, but forms the important compounds.

奪 **To²**. **Chuan-chu**, the modern meaning is: to take by violence, to seize, to carry off. Primitive meaning: to apprehend with 又 the hand, a 奞 bird that flies, that is free. The 寸 for 又 is a modern substitution. See L. 43 A. 从又、从奞、會意，手持隹也。

奮 **Fên⁴**. **Chuan-chu**, the modern meaning is: to excite, to arouse, to exert one's strength. The primitive meaning is: a bird 奞 flying upwards over the 田 fields; 飛也，从奞在田上、會意。

F 夲 **T'ao¹**. To advance, to move forward, to prosper rapidly, as 大 the man who has past his 十 tenth year. Speedy growing. By extension, to enter, to go in gladly; 進也。See 奏 **tsou⁴**, L. 47 M. It forms

皋 **Kao¹**. Growing 夲 clearness 白; light, full day; 白之進也。从夲, 从白、會意。Note the modern altered forms

臯 皐 皋 皐

Second series: 大 the second form.

G 大 **Ta⁴**. Primitive sense: a man standing (head, arms and legs; compare L. 60 A); 古文大也。像，人形。It forms the important following compounds

H 立 **Li⁴**. A man 大 standing on the 一 ground (L. 1, 2°). To stand; 从大在一之上、會意。大人也、像。一地也、指事。– It is the 117h radical of characters relating to position and posture. Phonetic series 134. See the third series, below L. It forms

位 **Wei⁴**. The place upon which a man 人 stands 立 straight; position, dignity, person; 从人，从立、會意、列中廷之左右謂之位。

昱 **Yü¹**. Sun 日, 立 risen. Light, day.

I 亦

I⁴. In its ancient form, this character belongs to the first series. Its modern form induced to place it in the second. The primitive meaning is, the sides. A 大 standing man, whose sides are indicated by 八 two lines or dots; 从大、八像。By extension, a contact, conjunction, and, also, etc. — Phonetic series 214. It forms

Yeh⁴. What is done by 大 men, when the 夕 night comes; to lie down on the right side, in order to sleep. Now, by extension, the night. The modern form of the character is a quaint invention of the scribes. — Phonetic series 415.

J 夫

Fu¹. A grown up 人 man, with a 一 pin in his hair, to show that he is of age; the virile cap is not represented; 丈夫也。从大、一以像簪。人二十而冠。成人也。冠而既簪。— Phonetic series 59.

K 央

Yang¹. A man 大 in the middle of the 冂 space (L. 34 A). Middle, centre. There are different **chia-chieh**. 从大在冂內。大者人也。— Phonetic series 168.

Third series: Multiples of 立 and of 夫. Note the modern contractions and confusions.

L 竝 並

Ping⁴. Two or several men 立 (L. 60 H) standing side by side; together, succession, etc.; 从二立。會意。併也。今作並。Note the modern deformation. It forms

普

P'u³. Succession 並 of the 日 days, course of times, indefinite duration; then, by extension, generality, universality, ubiquity. — Phonetic series 754.

替 

T'i⁴. Succession 並 in a 自 prefixed order, after a list (L. 159); then, by extension, substitution, permutation, in the place of, instead of. The silly scribes changed the two 立 into two 夫, and 自 into 日.

M 扶 㚘 **Pan**[4]. Two 夫 men keeping together; 从二夫並行也。It is found in

輦 輦 **Nien**[3]. Imperial 車 car, drawn by 夫 men. It forms the phonetic complex 撵 **nien**[3], to drive away, to cast out.

Fourth series: In some modern characters, 大 on the top of the compound is written 土; v.g.

N 赤 灻 **Ch'ih**[4]. Composed of 大 and 火 (L. 126), both being contracted in the modern form; 从大,从火,會意。The 大 human 火 fire, blushing through anger. By extension, red colour. — It is the 155th radical. See 赧 **nan**[3] (L. 43 J), to blush through shame.

O 羍 羍 **T'a**[4]. A man 大, who feeds 羊 flocks; 放羊也。It forms

達 達 **Ta**[2]. To lead forward 辵 (L. 112 E) flocks. By extension, a large space in which one moves at ease, as the steppes, 行不相遇也; open way, to attain, to prosper, etc. — Phonetic series 761.

P **Note**: Do not mistake 大 for a certain cover, similar to the first ancient form of 大, which is also written 土 in the modern writing, e.g. in 去, etc. See L. 38 F, G.

LESSON 61.

About the different modifications of 大 (L. 60): 夨、夭、尢、交、亢、with an appendix on the primitive 文.

First series: 夨 chai^3.

A 夨

Chai^3. A man who bows the head behind. It is found in

Wu^2. A man who bows the head behind, to cry 口 louder; to vociferate; 从夨、从口、會意. It became an important proper name. — Phonetic series 315. Note the strange alteration of the mordern character.

Second series: 夭 yao^1.

B 

Yao^1. A man who bends the head forward, in order to run, to jump, to march. By extension, to lean, to to incline, to hang, to rock, to shake. — Phonetic series 92. On the top of the compounds, 夭 sometimes becomes 土 in the modern writing (as 大, L. 60, fourth series), e.g. in 幸 **hsing^4** L. 102, and 走 **tsou^3** L. 112, 喬 **ch'iao^2** L. 75 B. — Note 笑 **hsiao^4**, to laugh. Etymologically, 竹 bamboos 夭 rocked by the wind; 竹得風、如人之笑也。从竹、从夭、會意。 The spasmodic motion of the belly, when a fat Chinese is laughing.

Third series: 尢 wang^1.

C 尢

Wang^1. A 大 man who puts his weight on his 尢 right leg, to make an effort, a spring; 曲脛也。从大、像。而屈其右腿. 指事。 It is often written 尣, or 尪 (a phonetic being added). — It is the 43th radical. It must be distinguished from 尤 yu (L. 134 C). It forms

无

Wu^2. A 大 man who 尢 exerts himself against an 一 obstacle, without surmounting it, unsuccessfully, in vain. By extension, negation, not, no. — It is the 71th radical, a fictitious one, for the whole series belongs to 旡 **chi^4**, L. 99 E.

Fourth series: 交 chiao[1].

D 交

Chiao[1]. A man 大 who crosses his legs, who entwines between his legs; 交脛也。从大。像。To join, to unite, to have intercourse, etc. — Phonetic series 183.

Fifth series: 亢 k'ang[4].

E 亢

K'ang[4]. A man who puts his weight on both legs, stretched apart, to make an effort; 屈左右腿。指事。Compare L. 61 C. The upper part of the body is shortened, to represent that it is the lower part that acts. Derived meanings: exaggerate firmness, obstination, rebellion. — Phonetic series 67.

Appendix. 文 wên[2] has nothing in common with 大.

F 文

Wên[2]. A primitive. Lines that intercross, veins, wrinkles, ripples; sketch, literary, genteel, elegant; 畫也。像。— It is the 67th radical of a few characters relating to ornamentation. Phonetic series 88. It forms

吝

Lin[4]. The wrinkles 文 of an emaciated man, who does not 口 eat enough; parsimony, stinginess.

虔

Ch'ien[2]. The wrinkles 文 caused by terror, in the presence of a 虍 tiger; reverential awe. It is often wrongly written 虔.

彣

Wen[2]. A whole of intricate lines. To the thick lines 文, are added finer lines 彡 (L. 62). It forms

彥

Yen[4]. A collection of lines still more intricate; 文, 彡 and 厂 that has nothing in common with han[4] L. 59 A. The wrinkles of the old men's face. By extension, a venerable person or appearance. — Phonetic series 497. It forms

產

Ch'an[3]. The 彥 wrinkles formed on the body consequent upon child-birth 生. Fecundity, to bear, to produce. — Phonetic series 592.

LESSON 62.

About the primitive 彡, and its derivatives.

First series: 彡.

A 彡 — **Shan**¹. Hair, feathers, lines, etc. 毛飾畫文也。像。— It is the 59th radical of characters alluding to stripes. Phonetic series 26. It forms

B 須 — **Hsü**¹. Beard. The 彡 hair on the chin, beneath the head (L. 160 C); 頁下之毛也。从頁、从彡、會意。Now 鬚。Men, in China, only allow their beards to grow, when the time has come for them to govern their family, to be a master over it. Hence the extended meanings: necessary, requisite, appointed time, etc.

The two following compounds, often confounded in the modern writing, are to be carefully distinguished:

C — **Chên**³. Hair 彡 of a 人 man, says the Glose; 从彡、从人、會意。鬒也。— Phonetic series 106.

Shan¹. A wing 几 (L 22 A) provided with 彡 feathers; 从几、从彡、會意。Flapping, vibration. It forms

Shên¹. **Ts'ân**¹. The three stars in the middle of Orion. They are represented by three 日, of which 厶 is the modern abbreviation. The lower part represents the rays emitted. 三星也。㐱像光大下垂。Compare 星 L. 79 F. — Phonetic series 652, under its modern form

---

Second series. Multiples of 彡 and of 㐱. The Chinese philologists consider, as derivatives from 㐱, the two following, D and E. It seems rather as if there were two other ways of representing a pair of wings, analogous to 㐱.

D 弱 — **Jao**⁴. Slender, fragile, weak. The wings of a young bird, with their first feathers; 新生羽也。The skeleton of the wings resembles two 弓 bows, L. 87. The two wings are represented as torn out; the crook on the top represents the extremity by which they were united to the body; in the modern writing, the crook at the bottom replaces one of the strokes of 彡. — Phonetic series 540.

E 羽 Yü³. Another representation of a pair of wings with feathers; 鳥長毛也。— It is the 124th radical of the characters relating to plumes and feathers. Phonetic series 251. It forms many important compounds We saw 翁 L. 18 C; 弱 L. 34 J; note also

F 翏 Liao⁴. To flutter, to rise while flying; 从羽、从㐱、會意高飛也。— Phonetic series 629.

G 翟 Ti². A pheasant, 从羽、从隹、會意。山雉、尾長者 — Phonetic series 791. See 糶 t'iao⁴ and 糴 ti², L 78 E.

H 翕 Hsi⁴. To gather 合 the wings 羽; union, harmony; 从羽、从合、會意。斂羽也。— Phonetic series 681.

I 扇 Shan⁴ The two sections of a 戶 folding-door (L. 129); 从戶、从羽、會意、門兩傍如羽也。— Phonetic series 559.

LESSON 63.

About the primitive 彳.

A 彳 Ch'ih⁴. To take a step forward with the left foot; 步也。像. By extension, in composition: to walk. — It is the 60th radical of characters relating to walking. See the derivative 役 i⁴, L 22 D.

Inverted, 彳 gives

B 亍 Ch'u⁴. To finish the step, by bringing forward the right foot; 从反彳、指事。步止也。 It has nothing in common with 丁 ting⁴, L. 57 A.

Both together, they form

C 行 Hsing². To march, composed of 彳 one step with the left foot, joined to 亍 one step with the right; to step; 从彳、从亍、會意。人之步趨也。— It is the 144th radical of characters relating to motion. The phonetic is inserted in the middle; e.g. 衍、衛、衙 etc.

D 㣇 彳 **Yin**³. It is 彳 lengthened, to represent long strides; 長行也。从彳而引之、指事、— It is the 54th radical. To be distinguished from the 162th radical 辶, composed of 彳 and 止 (See L. 112 E).

LESSON 64.

About the three primitives, 夕 **hsi**⁴, 月 **yüeh**⁴, 朋 **fêng**⁴, **p'êng**².

First series: 夕 hsi⁴.

A 夕 **Hsi**⁴. The evening, the beginning of night; represented by the moon emerging on the horizon, the lower part of the moon being still invisible. Compare the ancient form of 夕, with that of 月 (L. 64 G); the latter has one stroke more; 暮也。从月半見、指事。— It is the 36th radical and forms

B 名 **Ming**². The name, the personal appellative of a man, from 口 mouth and 夕 evening, because, at dusk, it is necessary to give one's name to be known; 从口、从夕、會意。夕不相見、故以口自名。— Phonetic series 230.

C 飧 **Sun**¹. An 夕 evening 食 meal, supper; 餔也。从夕、从食、會意。

D 夗 **Yüan**¹. Decency, 卩 (L. 55 B) modesty during 夕 night. It is not decent 寢不尸 to lie like a corpse, says Confucius. Good behaviour, good bearing, 从夕、从卩、會意。臥有節也。Compare L. 60 I. — Phonetic series 174. It forms

宛 **Wan**³. In the 宀 house, 夗 good behaviour. To comply with the demands of others; hence the derived meaning, to bend. — Phonetic series 407.

E 多 **To**¹. Two 夕, meaning symbolically, reduplication, multiplication, multitude, many. The old character (two nights) was used **chia-chieh** in this sense, on account of its simplicity; 重也。Compare 72 L, and 147 F *note*. — Phonetic series 239. It forms

F 

I^{2}. Idea of the good ordering of all the 多 objects contained in a house, between the 宀 roof and the 一 ground. The 夕 unique is supposed to be 多 contracted. By extension, fit, right, harmonious, proper; 所安也。从多在宀之下、一之上。會意。指事。— A more simple explanation is at hand: in the 宀 house, 一 to spread out, in good order, the mats and bed cover for 夕 night. Regular stir at night. We are indebted to the scribes for 宜, the modern form. Compare pei^{4}, L. 54 G.
Other derivatives from 夕: see 外 wai^{4}, L. 56 F; 夜 yeh^{4}, L. 60 I; 夙 hsü^{4}, L. 11 G; 夢 mêng^{4}, L. 158 F; etc.

Second series: 月 yüeh^{4}.

G 月

Yüeh^{4}. The moon's crescent, completely visible (compare 夕 hsi$_{4}$, L. 64 A); 太陰之像。弦闕形。— It is the 74th radical of characters relating to the moon. It forms

H 閒 間

Hsien^{2}. From 門 door and 月 moon; the moonlight streaming in through the crackles of the door Interstice, idle, empty, leisure, and other **chuan-chu**; 隙也。从門中見月、會意。The modern scribes often write incorrectly 間. Phonetic series 684.

Other derivatives from 月: see 有 yu^{3}, L. 46 H; 明 ming^{2}, L. 42 C; 朔 sho^{4}, L. 102 D; 望 wang^{4}, L. 81 G; etc. But 朝 chao^{1} does not come from 月; see L. 117 D.

Third series 朋. Has nothing in common with 月 yüeh^{4}.

I 朋

The ancient character, a primitive, represents the *tail* of the fabulous and felicitous bird **Fêng^{4}**, the phœnix; by extension, the phœnix *complete*. Was the phœnix called **P'êng^{2}** in certain Provinces, or was the **p'êng^{2}** another auspicious bird? We do not know. Anyhow, two new characters were made: 鳳 **fêng^{4}**, the phœnix; and 鵬 p'êng^{2} a monstrous bird, like the *rukh* or *roc* of Arabian story (according to European definitions). — From that time, 朋 is no more read **fêng**[4], and does not mean *phœnix*. It is read **p'êng**[2], and means, *friend*, friendship; for, says the Glose, when the phœnix flies, it draws all other birds after it, by sympathy; hence the idea of affection, friendship, association; 朋．神鳥也。古文鳳．像形。鳳飛．羣鳥隨以萬數．故以爲朋黨字。— Phonetic series 387. But 蒯 does not come from 朋; see L. 156 H.

LESSON 65.

About the partial primitive 肉. See 仌, L. 17, G, H, I, J. Note also that, in its contracted form 月, 肉 is easily confounded with 月 **yüeh**[4] (the moon, L. 64 G), and with 月 for 舟 **chou**[1] (boat, L. 66 A).

A 肉 月

Ju[4]. **Jou**[4]. Pieces 仌 of dry meat 冂 gathered in bundle; 胾肉，像形; meat smoke-dried in the old fashion; now, meat in general. See L. 17 G. — It is the 130th radical of a large group of characters relating to meat and food. See 肴 L. 39 J, 肖 L. 18 J, 育 L. 94 E. 脊 L. 46 D, 脊 L. 13 I, 胃 L. 122 C, etc. Note 筋 **chin**[1], the sinews; the parts of the flesh 月, elastic like bamboo 𥫗, that give 力 strength; 會意。肉之力也。

B 胄

Chou[4]. Compare the composition of this character with that of 肖, L. 18 J. Flesh 月 coming from its 由 principle; posterity, offspring. Do not confound this character with 胄 helmet, L. 34 J. The modern forms are identical; the ancient ones differ.

C 肎 肯

K'ên[3]. The flesh 月, by opposition to the 冎 skeleton, (L. 118 A) The top of 冎 was already missing in the **hsiao-chuan** writing. The modern scribes replaced it by a 止, which is a nonsense, **k'ên**[3] having nothing in common with 止 (L 112 A); 著骨肉也。从肉．从冎省．會意。今俗字譌作肯。The flesh being soft and flexible relatively to the bones that are tough and rigid, hence the derived meanings, to model one's self, to yield, to follow, to be easy tempered, to be inclined, prone to. — Phonetic series 367, under its modern form.

D 佾 屑 — I⁴. The antique dance. The pantomimists dancing 八 on two ranks, back-to-back 背 (contracted into 月). Now 佾。。 佾 舞 佾 也。从 背 省。从 八 會 意。It forms 屑 hsieh⁴, which the scribes changed into 屑。 Resting 尸 of dancers 佾, after the dance; they received then small gifts. Hence the extended meaning, of small value, of little importance, insignificant.

E 肙 — Yüan⁴. Larvæ 月 fleshy without skeleton, that can ◯ double themselves up, like mosquito and ephemera larvae, that swarm in summer, even in the wells; 井中赤蟲也。从肉無骨也。◯ 像、首尾可按之形。— Phonetic series 321.

F 肩 — Chien¹. Shoulder; 髆 也。从 肉、像 形。In the ancient characters, 肉 represents the whole of the pectoral and the scapulary muscles, the line that springs from them representing the arm. In the modern character, the shoulder-blade is outlined. The scribes strangely contracted it into 戶. It is unconnected with 戶, L. 129. See 克, L. 75 K

G 肰 — Jan². Meat 月 of 犬 dog (L. 134); 犬 肉 也。从 肉、从 犬、會 意。It forms

猒 厭 — Yen⁴. To be satiated; 飽 也, To be glutted 甘 (changed by the scribes into 日), with 月 meat of 犬 dog. This satiety seems to have been the ideal one. It went, in an ancient form, till belching 㠯 took place (L. 85 C). By extension, disgust, aversion. It is now replaced, in this sense, by the compound 厭 yen⁴, 厂 representing the retreat from eating. Phonetic series 793.

然 — Jan³. To roast 火 flesh 月 of dog 犬 By extension, to roast, to burn, to light. It is now also used, **chia-chieh**, as a conjunction, an adverbial particle, etc. — Phonetic series 691.

H 祭 — **Chi**[4]. Oblation, sacrifice; **祀也。从示、从⺕持肉會意。** Offering ⺕ of meat 月, that brings down the 示 influences from heaven (L. 3 D) — Phonetic series 595. — There is an analogous composition in 登 **têng**[1] (a 豆 vase in which 月 meat is ⺕ offered). But 望 **wang**[4] is derived from 月 **yüeh**[4], moon, and not from 月 **jou**[4]. See L. 81 A.

LESSON 66.

About the primitive 舟 **chou**[1]. Its contracted form 月 is to be distinguished from 月 **yüeh**[4], L. 64; and from 月 **jou**[4], L. 65.

A 舟 — **Chou**[1]. Canoe, vessel, boat of any sort. The first canoes, says the Glose, were trunks of trees hollowed out; **船也。像形。古者鼓貨、刳木爲舟、剡木爲楫、以濟不通。** It represents a kind of canoe, straightened, to take less room. Turned up bow, deck propped up by a pivot that represents the internal wood-work; an oar on front, a helm behind the boat, which is opened, to mean that the helm goes beyond. — It is the 137th radical of characters relating to vessels. It forms

B 般 — **Pan**[1]. To make a boat 舟 move along, by repeated 殳 strokes of the oar (L. 22 B); **从舟、从殳、會意。舟之旋。殳所以旋也。** The action of the oars must he equal and regular; hence, the derived meanings, regular way, manner, equally. Do not confound this character with 船 **ch'uan**[2], boat, L. 18 E. — Phonetic series 555.

C 服 — **Fu**[2] To govern 𠬝 (L. 55 C) a 舟 boat, that obeys; **舟人行舟者。从舟、从𠬝、會意。** **Chuan-chu**, to obey, to yield to; mourning clothes as coarse as the clothes of sailors; clothes in general, etc. **K'ang-hsi** incorrectly classified 服, as well as 朕 (L. 47 J), under the 74th radical 月, the moon.

D 前 — **Ch'ien**[2]. To advance, forward, before, formerly, etc. A boat 舟 advancing towards the harbour, where it will 止 stop. The modern character is a strange invention of a scribe; **从止在舟上、會意。進也、先也。今俗作前。** — Phonetic series 431.

Other characters derived from 舟: 朕, L. 47 J; 亙, L. 2 E; 兪, L. 14 F; 受, L. 49 E; 朝, L. 117 D.

LESSON 67.

About the **primitive** 女 **nü**^{3}.

First series: 女 and its multiples.

A 女 **Nü**^{3}. A girl; 像 形, The character **hsiao-chuan** is already a cursive modification of the ancient character, that was uneasy to write, on account of the perfectly symmetrical lines. The right part was altered. — The ancient character represented the ritual bearing of the Chinese women, the arms hanging down, and crossed over the body. The head was not represented. The shoulders, arms, chest and legs were outlined. Compare L. 67 O. — It is the 38th radical of characters relating to women. When meaning *thou, you*, 女 and 汝 are mere **chia-chieh**, adaptation of a sound.

B 好 **Hao**^{3}. **Hao**^{4}. What is good, what one loves: 女 wife and 子 children. By extension, good, to love; 美 也。愛 也。从 女、子、會 意。

C 奴 **Nu**^{2}. Female slave. Women 女 under the hand 彐 of a master; a guilty woman, condemned to pound the rice (see 舂 L. 47 N). 从 彐、从 女、會 意。奴 婢 皆 古 之 罪 人 也。— Phonetic series 141.

D 如 **Ju**^{2}. To 口 speak like a 女 woman, with a womanly skill, in conformity with the circumstances, and the dispositions of the man one desires to wheedle. Extended meaning, as, like, according to. 从 女、从 口、會 意。— Phonetic series 216.

E 妾 **Ch'ieh**^{4}. Daughter of a culprit, reduced to servitude, according to the old way; by extension, a concubine; 从 辛 (L. 102 E), 从 女。會 意。有 罪 女 子。— Phonetic series 331.

F 妥 **T'o**^{3}. Security, tranquillity. When 爫 the hand is firmly placed upon 女 women; 安 也。从 爫。从 女。會 意。— Phonetic series 306. It forms 綏 **sui**^{1}, 糸 a thread that 妥 attaches, that makes sure.

G 安 **Nan**^{1}. Good order, peace. When the 女 women are well enclosed in the 宀 house; 靖 也。从 女 在 宀 中、會 意。— Phonetic series 176.

H 晏

Yen⁴. Visit during the 日 day, to the 女 gynecium; siesta, mid-day nap; 从女、从日、會意。 It forms 宴 **yen**⁴, recreation, feast, banquet; and the phonetic compound

匽 **Yen**³. To hide; 匿也。从匸 (L. 10 B), 晏聲。— Phonetic series 495.

Other derivatives from 女; see 妻 ch'i¹, L. 44 G; 要 yao¹, L. 50 N; etc.

I 奻 **Chien**¹. Quarrelling, mutual slandering. For, says the Glose, not without melancholy, two women cannot be on good terms; 訟也。从二女、會意。二同居、其志不同。

J 姦 **Chien**¹. Amours and intrigues among and with women; traitorous; for, says the Glose, a man who debauches women, is a traitor to his fellow-men; 私也。从三女、會意。

Second series: 毋 **wu**². A series is reserved to this derivative from 女, because it forms a group. Note the malformation of the modern character.

K. 毋 **Wu**². A woman placed under lock and key — (L. I, 3) for misbehaviour. Prison of the guilty women. Each palace had a place reserved for that purpose. The persons thus confined were utterly unemployed, and saw nobody. Hence the derived meanings, to avoid, to abstain, inutility, nothingness; 禁止之也。从女、像、有姦之者。一、以止之、指事。 — It is the 80th radical.

L 毐 **Ai**³. A man 士 (24 C) who behaves badly; 毋 confined, or worth to be so; a debauchee; 士無行也。从士、从毋、會意。

M 毒 **Tu**². The poisonous vegetables that 生 grow here and there, and that must be 毋 avoided; poison, venom; 害人之草、往往而生。从生、从毋以止之、會意。

N 婁 **Lou**². Woman 女 confined, enclosed 中 in the 毋 prison of the gynecium; for ever idle; useless, etc; 毋中女、空虛之意也。— Phonetic series 631. It forms

數 **Shu**³. **Shu**⁴. Formerly, it meant 攴 to govern the 婁 confined women. Now, it means, to count, a number; 計也。— Phonetic series 812.

Third series: 毋 mu^{3}. It is another derivative from 女, forming a group.

O 

Mu^{3}. A woman who has become a mother. This is represented by the addition of two breasts to the character 女. She suckles a child, says the Glose; 从女.像。兩點像。乳形。乳子也。 Idea of fecundity, of multiplication. — Phonetic series **139.** It forms

P 

Mei^{3}. Grass 屮 (L. 78), 毋 prolific; 从屮、从毋。草盛也。 The actual meaning of this character, every, each, is **chia-chieh.** — Phonetic series **294.** It forms.

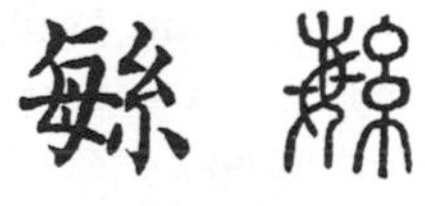

Fan^{2}. Luxuriant vegetation, the 每 plants 糸 twisting into a tangle; 从每、从糸、會意。Now 繁, on account of a mistake made by the scribes, says the Glose; 誤作繁。

毓

Yü^{4}. See L. 94 F.

LESSON 68.

About the primitive 彐 chi^{4}. An appendix is reserved for a few analogous forms. In the modern writing, 彐 has different forms and is easily mistaken for 彐 the hand (L. 44).

First series; 彑 chui^{4} and 互 hu^{4}.

A 彑 彑 彑 彐 彐

Chi^{4}. A primitive. It is intended to represent a boar's or a hogs snout; 豕之頭也。像。 The representation, wich is lifted up, is very rough. The top stroke represents the nose flattened. The bottom stroke represents the neck. The left stroke is a boar's tusk, the point being forward. — The boar and the hog played a very important part in the Chinese hunting and cattle-breeding, therefore they gave birth to many characters. — It is the 58th radical of characters, mostly relating to swine. It is unconnected with the following.

B 互 互

Hu^{4}. A primitive. Represents the twisting of two or several strands, to make a rope; 所以糾繩也。像。 By extension, reciprocity, relation, connection, communication.

Second series: Derivatives from 彐 chi⁴.

C **Chih⁴**. Boar 彐, wounded by an 矢 (131 A) arrow, under the neck, between the two 比 (27 I, note 1) fore-legs; killed at the hunting.

D **I²**. Offerings to the manes of ancestors; 宗廟祀也。从糸、从米、从彐、从廾、會意。A 彐 boar's head, 米 grain, 糸 silk, the whole being offered with 廾 the hands.

E **I⁴**. Boar, a bristle-covered animal. The head, the bristles, the 巾 hind-legs and tail. Compare 肉 L. 23 C; 从彐、下像毛足。It forms

Wei⁴. Hui⁴. This character, utterly altered in the modern writing, first meant, the hedgehog, the snout of which resembles the hog's; 彙蟲也。似豬而小、毛刺。The animal is specified by 胃 (ancient form, L. 122 C) the stomach, on account of its extraordinary voracity. In the modern character, on the top 彐; then ⺈ the two long bristles of the third ancient form; then 田 for the ancient form of 胃; lastly 木 for the hind-legs and tail of 希. To mean *hedgehog*, the character is now written 蝟; while 彙 hui⁴ is used chuan-chu to mean *collection*. The idea is taken from the collection of sharp points that cover the back of a hedgehog.

Appendix. According to their modern writing, the four following compounds seemingly come from 彐; but the two first ones are certainly not derived from it.

F **Lu⁴**. To behead, to trim and to bark a tree (the stump being upright). On the top, an axe of a special form, the haft of which bends to the right; 丿 its action; 丨 the tree 一 beheaded; four small strokes represent the branches and the bark cut. Now 剝. — Phonetic series 461. — The ancient character simply represented the cutting off the trunk, the branches falling on both sides, and the shreds of the bark torn out. Compare L. 45 J. 刻木也。像形。

G

Mei[4]. A modification of the preceding The axe's handle is not represented. Ancient form: a head of 鬼 (L. 40 C) upon a trunk cut down. Now 鬽 Spirit of a dead tree; supposed, to be malignant; 老物精也。物神謂之鬽。

The two following characters, of identical composition, 彑 head, and 豕 body of a hog, have probably been fabricated in two different centres (see page 7).

They differ only by one stroke, the head being separated in the first, and joined with the rest in the latter.

H

Shih[3]. Pig. The scribes write it, as the following, in its derivative 蠡 li[3], bristle-covered larvæ that eat away the tissues and the books.

I

T'uan[3]. Usual meaning, pig's bristles. Derived meaning, commentaries, accessories to the text as the bristles are accessory to the pig. — Phonetic series 577.

LESSON 69.

About the primitive 豕 **shih**[3]. An appendix will treat abont 亥 **hai**[4] and 象 **hsiang**[4].

A

Shih[3]. Boar, hog. The head is replaced by a line; on the left side, the belly and the paws; on the right side, the back and the tail; 彘也。像。頭、足、而後有尾。 It has many compounds, e. g. 逐 **chu**[2], to drive or push out pigs, to expel in general. — It is the 152th radical of characters mostly referring to swine.

B

Hun[4]. Inclosure 囗 of 豕 pigs, a sty, a privy: the pigs in China eating fecal matters; 厠也。— Phonetic series 538.

C

Chia[1]. Human dwelling, says the Glose. By extension, family. 从宀、从豕、會意。古文从豩。人所居室、The pigs live around the houses of the Chinese countrymen, and even enter in them, as well as the dogs. The street-cleaning and privy-emptying are left to these two animals. — Phonetic series 516.

D 豦 豦

Chü[4]. To fight with rage, as a 豕 boar that defends itself against 虍 a tiger; 从豕、从虍、會意。豕虍相鬥、不解也。— Phonetic series 731.

E 豚 豚

T un[2]. A sucking pig. It was offered in some sacrifices, hence the ancient form, 豕 a pig, the 月 flesh of which is 又 offered. Compare 祭 **chi**[4], L. 65 H. 古文、从豕、从又持肉、以給祠祀、會意。

F 㒸 㒸

Sui[2]. To partake 八 (18) the 豕 pigs, in bands, in flocks: 从豕、从八、散也。It forms

遂 遂 **Sui**[2]. A band of pigs marching, following their leader; hence, to follow in general; 順也。— Phonetic series 758.

隊 **Tui**[4]. Troops; garrison that guards the 阝 walls. It forms the phonetic compound 墜 **chui**[4], to fall, 落也。

G 豖 豖

Cho[2]. A pig 豕 having two feet 丶 trammelled; 从豕繫二足。按丶指事。— Phonetic series 340 It forms

冢 冢 **Chung**[3]. Tumulus, knoll, tomb, **chia-chieh** of an ancient character used in hunting; 高墳也。Compare 冢 L 34 I, the composition of which is similar. — Phonetic series 527.

H 豙 豙

I[2]. Boar 豕 that 辛 attacks (L. 102 E); 从豕、从辛、會意。辛犯之意。Bravery, heroism. In this sense, the compound 毅 i[4] is now used.

I 彖 彖

Shih[3] and **T uan**[3]. See L. 68 H, I.

J 豩 **Pin¹**. A flock of pigs; *two* being taken for a multitude. It forms

豳 **Pin¹**. A district in the mountains 山 of 陝西 Shensi, where boars 豕 formerly abounded.

燹 **Hsien³**. To burn brush-wood, in order to drive out the boars.

Appendix: 亥 **hai⁴** and 象 **hsiang⁴**.

K 亥 **Hai⁴**. The hog 豕 (L. 69 A), with one stroke added to the tail; 古文豕字。加尾。 It is used, in the horary cycle, to designate the time 9 to 11 p. m.. This time, says the Glose, is the most propitious for the conception. Hence numerous different figures, that represent two persons, sometimes a man and a woman (L. 67 O), under 二 heaven (L. 2 G), that is to say, cooperating with the productive action of heaven, by begetting chidren. — Phonetic series 197.

L 象 **Hsiang⁴**. Elephant. A primitive, representing the characteristic parts of this animal. On the top, the trunk; then a bow representing the tusks. The legs and tail look like those of the 豕 pig. 南方大獸。長鼻牙。像鼻牙。四足尾之形。— Phonetic series 683.

LESSON 70.

About two primitives, 甘 chi² and 丌 chi¹. The latter is to be distinguished from 兀 wu⁴ (L. 29 K); as well as from 八 or 廾 at the bottom (LL. 18 and 47).

A 甘 **Chi²**. Sieve, riddle. It represents the object; 像形。

B 丌 **Chi²**. Prop, stool; 下基也。像形。 Both being combined form

C 其 **Ch'i²**. Sieve placed upon its support; 从甘。像形。下其丌也。 The old utensil being no longer used, the character has become chia-chieh a demonstrative pronoun; 助語之詞. — Phonetic series 327.

丌 **Chi¹** is found in 典 L. 156 C; 奠 L. 41 G; 畀 L. 40 C; 巽 L. 55 H.

LESSON 71.

About the primitive 弋 i⁴. Special series are reserved for the important derivative 戈 ko¹, and its numerous family.

First series: 弋 i⁴.

A 弋

I⁴. Primitive. Some see, in this figure, a hook driven in the wall, to suspend objects; others see an arrow with a thread; others, see in it a fish or pin that was used to count, to mark, to order, to decide. — Note for the understanding of this Lesson, that the ancient weapons were varied. Each one had its own representation. Later on, many of them disappeared, and their characters were used for other purposes. It is the 56th radical, and forms

B 代

Tai⁴. Order 弋 of succession, substitution of 亻 men, and by extension, of things; instead of, in place of; 凡以此易彼、以後續前、皆曰代。— Phonetic series 161, Not to be confounded with 伐 fa¹, L. 71 G.

C 式

Shih⁴. Work 工 done after 弋 indications, after a pattern; a model, to imitate; 法也。 — Phonetic series 236.

D 弍

Erh⁴. Two pins, two. There is an old analogous form 弌 for 一 one. It forms

貳

Erh⁴. Profit; a second 二 sum 貝 (L. 161) added to the first, to the capital; 副益也。从貝、从弍、會意。It is now used for security in accounts, instead of 二 that may be easily changed into 三 or 五. — Phonetic series 674.

E 必

Pi. A thing certain, decided. An arrow or a fish 弋 that divides 八, that solves a doubt, a dilemma; 从弋、从八、會意。弋者.介分也。See L. 18 G. **K'ang-hsi** erroneously classified this character under 心 the heart. — Phonetic series 148.

Note that 武 does not come from 弋. See below K.

Second series: 戈 kuo^{1}.

F 戈

Kuo^{1}. A kind of halberd, formerly much used. A hook or crescent on the top, then a cross-bar, and a halter hanging; 平頭戟也。像形。— It is the 62th radical of words relating to spears and arms. It forms

G 伐

Fa^{1} To destroy, to cut down. A man 人 who receives from behind a stroke with a 戈 halberd; 擊也。敗也。會意。— Phonetic series 195, To be distinguished from 代 tai^{4}, L. 71 B.

H 𢦏

Ts'ai^{2}. At the bottom, 戈. On the top, the phonetic ts'ai^{2} 才 (L. 96), contracted into 十 in the modern writing. To wound with weapons; 傷也. 从戈、才聲. — Phonetic series 241.

戔

Ch'ien^{1}. See L. 27 B.

I 戠

Chih^{4}. The ancient chiefs or officials. They held a 戈 weapon, when they made known their 意 (L. 73 E, contracted) will to their people 古職字。古之職役、皆執干戈。Note the combination of the bottom stroke of 立, with the horizontal stroke of 戈, which gives one stroke less to the phonetic series 671.

J 或

Yü^{4}. A primitive appanage, a post, a centre; the 一 land that a landlord defended with 戈 the weapons of his men; 口 represents his residence, castle or town; the limits are not indicated, because there were none; 邦也。从口、从戈以守一、會意。一地也。—

Huo^{4}. Extended meaning of the preceding, an indeterminate person, whose name is not given, known only to be from such a principality; a vague determination. — Phonetic series 364. It forms

Kuo^{3}. An estate, well 口 defined and surrounded with marks, as they were later on. Extended meaning, a state, a country; 从口、从或。會意。— Phonetic series 625.

𢧢

Po^{4}. Anarchy, revolution. When the fiefs are upset; one 或 being straight up, the other upside down; 亂也。从二或相對。

K 武 **Wu³**. The army, soldiers. The 戈 lances that 止 stop the hostile incursions, thus allowing the people to prosper, says the Glose; 从止、从戈。會意。 Note that, in the modern character, by a singular exception, the 丿 of 戈 was placed on the top of the compound. — Phonetic series 410.

Third series. Characters derived from 戈 and easily confounded.

L 戉 **Yüeh⁴**. A halberd 戈 with a 𠄌 hook; 兵也。从戈. 从𠄌. 像形。Phonetic series 175.

M 戊 **Wu⁴**. Halberd with a crescent; 兵也。从戈、从丿, 像形。See below P, the series 戌 derived from it. It forms the phonetic complex

茂 **Mao⁴**. Flourishing, blooming; 从艸、戊聲、艸豐盛也。On its side, 茂 contracted forms

成 **Ch'êng²**. To grow, to prosper, to attain, to end; 丁 (L. 57) is phonetic; 从茂省。丁聲。就也。畢也。— Phonetic series 179. 丁 is abbreviated in the modern writing.

N 戍 **Shu⁴**. The 人 men armed with 戈 lances, who defend the frontiers; 守邊也。从人持戈、會意。 See the derivative 幾, 90 D.

O 戎 **Jung²** Arms in general, war. From 戈 arms for the offensive, and 甲 (L. 152) armour for the defensive; the latter character is reduced to two strokes in the modern writing; 兵也。从戈、从甲、會意。— Phonetic series 217.

P 戌 **Hsü¹**. To attack, to wound, to kill. A halberd 戊 and 一 a wound; 从戊、一指事、識其殺傷處。 It forms

烕 **Mieh⁴**. To extinguish; 戌 to destroy the 火 fire; 火死曰烕。This character is now written 滅.

威 **Wei¹**. Fear; the awe felt by 女 women menaced with 戌 death; 畏也。从女、从戌、會意。 **By extension, a stern composure, an exterior that inspires awe; dignity, majesty.**

Hsien². To bite; to wound 戌 with the 口 mouth; 从戌.从口.會意.戌傷也. The modern meaning, all, together, 皆也, is **chia-chieh** for 僉 or 兼.— Phonetic series 446. It forms

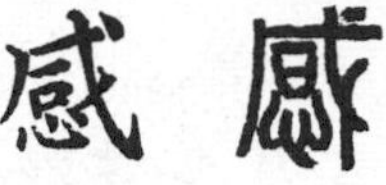

Kan³. Heart 心 bitten 咸 by a passion, an emotion. — Phonetic series 740.

Sui⁴. Jupiter, 木星也. the 步 planet that indicated whether 戌 an attack was to be made, or not. See L. 71 P, L. 112 G The 步 is broken up, a half being on the top, a half at the bottom. — The ancients had also, for the computation of time, a cycle of twelve *years* based upon the revolution of Jupiter. Hence, later on, the extended and adapted meaning, a period of twelve *months*, a solar year; 越二十八宿.十二年一次.年也.取木星行一次也.四時一絡曰歲. Note that 歲 is a modern and wrong form.— Phonetic series 760.

Fourth series: 戈 doubled, in opposite directions; 我 o².

Q

O². **Ngo**². Two 戈 weapons in conflict, two rights that oppose one another, my right, and, by extension, my *Ego*, my own person; personal pronoun, I, me. This character being uneasy to write, was soon changed into 我.— Phonetic series 297. It forms

I⁴. Harmony, good 羊 understanding (L. 103), peace restored after 我 a conflict; convention concluded after a disagreement, restoring concord and giving satisfaction to the interested parties. Hence all the derived meanings of this important character; the bottom of an affair, truth, right; conventional, just, equitable, proper, etc. Compare 善 L 73 D, and 苟 L 54 G.— Phonetic series 737. It forms

Hsi¹. The imprecations 兮 (L. 53 D) that accompanied the conclusion 義 of a treaty. They were made upon immolated animals. Hence the extended meaning, victim; now 犧. Phonetic series 830.

Fifth series: 戈 doubled, in the same direction; 戔 chien¹.

R  

Chien¹. To exterminate, to destroy. The common work of two (many) halberds; 从二戈.會意.— Phonetic series 333.

LESSON 72

About the primitive 口 k'ou³, and its multiples.

First series: 口 simple.

A 口 **K'ou³**. It represents the mouth. Mouth, entrance. 人所以言食也。像形。— It is the 30th radical. Phonetic series 23. — This primitive is found in many compounds. Let us recall 古 L. 24 F; 吞 L. 60 C; 台 L. 18 E; 名 L 64 B; 亟 L. 2 D; etc It is to be distinguished from 囗 wei² L. 74, and from other primitive analogous characters; 石 L. 59 D; 吕 L. 90 F; 中 L 109 A; etc. Note the derivatives

只 **Chih³**. But, however. The Glose explains this particle as follows: When a sentence is over, the breath issues from the 口 mouth, in two puffs, that connect what follows with what precedes. But what follows is written below, in the vertical Chinese lines, therefore the two strokes are turned downwards... All the particles are intonations or finals, rather *musical* than *significative*, an interpunctuation that is read; 語巳也。从口、像、气下引之形。— Phonetic series 111.

吠 **Fei⁴**. From 犬 dog and 口 mouth. The bark of the dog; to howl; 犬鳴也。从口、从犬、會意。(L. 134).

吹 **Ch'ui⁴**. From 口 mouth and 欠 to puff; to blow, to grumble. 从口、从欠、會意。气急日吹。(L. 99).

Second series: 口 doubled, 吅.

B 吅 **Hsüan¹**. Clamours. Two 口 mouths expressing the intensity of the action of the mouth ; 从二口、會意

C 哭 **K'u¹**. To lament. To wail, as with many mouths, after the 犬 dogs manner; 从犬、从二口、會意。按犬哀聲也。It forms

喪 **Sang¹**. Funerals. To wail 口, as dogs 犬, over a 亾 dead body; 从哭、从亾、會意。See L. 10 H. — These two characters vividly depict the Chinese thing that they mean.

D 喌

Chu[1]. Repeated cries 吅 to call the hens; 州 is phonetic.

斝

Chia[3]. Large 斗 cup, with a 冖 cover; a hanap passing round, 吅 all mouths drinking out of the same.

E 單

Tan[1]. To assault somebody, with 吅 cries and a pitchfork 𢆉 (L. 104). Compare L 72 F. — The primitive meaning of this character is obsolete. It now means, single, thin, a check, a bill, only, etc. These are mere **chia-chieh.** — Phonetic series 705 It has nothing in common with

鼉

T'o[2]. A crocodile, whose skin was used for making drums; 水蟲。似蛟而大。It represents the monster. The top part resembles 罒 L. 23 I. For the bottom, see 黽 L. 108 C. It is unconnected with **tan**[1].

F 咢

噩

O[4]. To accuse somebody with great cries. Two mouths, and 屰 (L. 102 D) to attack; 譁訟也。Note the modern form imagined by the scribes. — Double phonetic series 470, under its two forms.

G 嚴

Yen[2]. Cries 吅 that 厰 inspire awe. See L. 141 H. Severe, stern, majestic. — Phonetic series 858.

H

Nang[2]. Cries 吅, and 乂 agitation, that accompany the 𤕦 execution of a common 工 work; cooperation, working in common. Here again, the Chinese at work are well described. By extension, big disorder; 亂也。从𤕦、工、乂、吅、四字會意。See LL. 39 B, 39 G, 82 A. In the modern form, 乂 was changed into 己, by a fancy of some scribe. It forms

襄

Hsiang[1]. Composed of the last and of 衣 clothes, L. 16 A. To disrobe, in order to plough, or to work, or to help others. To work, to cooperate, to help. Note the modern contraction. — Phonetic series 831.

Nang[2] A satchel, a recipient (L. 74 A), in which are, or may be 口 enclosed pell-mell any objects whatever; a bag, a sack. — Phonetic series 854.

I 

Ch'ien[1]. Meeting, together. Men 人 gathered 亼 who 口 chat. See L. 14 A and E — Phonetic series 726.

J 

Kuan[4]. The heron Bird 隹 with a 丫 crest (L. 103 C), and 吅 clamorous. — Phonetic series 841.

Note: 咒 chou[4] L. 29 D, and 嚚 shou[4] L. 23 I, are not derived from 吅.

Third series: 口 repeated three times in the same line, 㗊.

K 㗊

Ling[2]. Noise of voices; 从三口、會意。The two following characters are not derived from 㗊, though they have a figure of the same kind.

Yao[4]. A Pandean flute. The three 㗊 represent the holes of the 冊 pipes united together 亼 in a straight row. See L. 14 H — It is the 244th radical. Phonetic series 835.

Ling[2]. Falling of 雨 rain in 㗊 big drops; 从雨、㗊像。Formerly, it made a phonetic series, in which is now written the compound

Ling[2] To offer to heaven 玉 jade (L. 83 A), or certain 巫 dances (L. 27 E), in order to get rain 霝. Compare L. 58 H. It was the first thing asked from the magicians and sorcerers, by a people whose life depended upon rain. By extension, spiritual, mysterious, supernatural power or effect, transcendent, marvellous.— Phonetic series 853.

Sub-series: 口 repeated three times in a pyramidical form, 品.

L 品 品

P'in[3]. Disposition by order and degrees, graphically represented by the disposition of three elements, taken for a multitude. 口 is used as a sign and has no meaning.

喦 嵒 **Yen**^{2}. Rocks scattered upon a 山 mountain. The three 口 are used as signs and have no meaning.

區 區 **Ch'ü**^{1}. To dispose, to stow away 品 things in a 匸 box; 从品在匸中、會意。By extension, lodging, place, site; 四方也。— Phonetic series 607.

But, in the two following characters, the three 口 mean mouths.

Nieh^1. Three mouths 口 joined by lines. To be distinguished from 喦 yen^2, above. To cabal, to plot; 从三口相連、指事。Now 囁 nieh^1, a mouth 口 that pours its words into three 耳 ears.

Tsao^4. Singing 品 of the birds on 木 trees; 从品在木上、會意。鳥羣鳴也。— Phonetic series 764.

Fourth series: 口 repeated four times, 㗊.

M 㗊 **Ch'i**^{1}. Many mouths, clamours; 从四口、會意。— Four mouths may be seen in different characters, e.g.

器 **Ch'i**^{4}. The vessels for the 口 mouths, used for eating. In the middle, a 犬 dog that cleans them. It was not very refined, therefore 工 (work, utensil) was substituted for 犬; but this form was not admitted by the critics. A very old form shows a hand and three pots. The primitive meaning was probably, earthenware, clay vessels, made by the potter. By extension, any utensil.

囂 **Hsiao**^{4}. A 頁 man with four mouths. To vociferate, to clamour; 从㗊、从頁、會意。

嚚 **Yin**^{2}. An 臣 officer with four mouths. To speak loud; 从㗊、从臣、會意。

嘂 **Chiao**^{4}. Union 丩 of several mouths. Cries, appeals (L. 54 F).

噩 **O**^{4}. A modern form of 咢. See L. 72 F. — Phonetic series 470.

LESSON 73.

About three derivatives of 口: 曰 yüeh[1], 甘 kan[1], 言 yen[2], that form important series.

First series: 曰 yüeh[1].

A 

Yüeh[1]. To speak, to tell. The mouth 口 that exhales ㇗ a breath, a word; 言也。从口.㇗像。口气出也。Sometimes, by derivation; exhalation, emanation. — It is the 73th radical. In the compounds, 曰 is to be accurately distinguished, from 日 jih[4] L. 143, and from 冃 mao[4] L. 31 J, which is written 曰 by the modern scribes. — Note a more ancient and more evolved form of 曰: the breath forming like a volute of vapour before the mouth, as when condensed in winter. See L. 76 K.

Ho[2]. A stranger 匃, a beggar, who 曰 speaks, in order to ask his way or to beg By extension, to ask, where? why? how? See L 10 G. — Phonetic series 443.

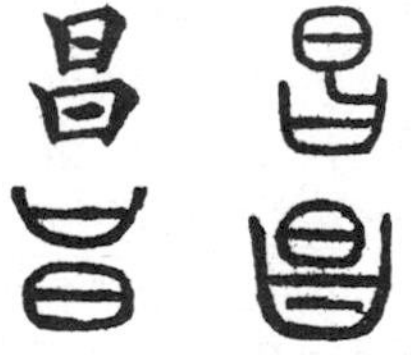

Ch'ang[1] Emanation 曰, swarming, under the 日 sun's heat (L 143); by extension, prosperity, splendour, glory. — The old forms figure 日 sun and 月. moon, light and life. — Phonetic series 322.

Ta[2]. Flow 水 of 曰 words (L 125). — Phonetic series 395.

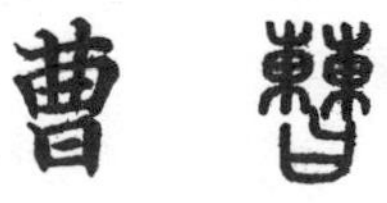

Ts'ao[2]. Judges. Primitively two worthies who sat and pronounced 曰 judgment in the 東 East halls. See L. 120 K. Note the ugly modern contraction.— Phonetic series 653.

替 會 曾 See LL. 26 D; 40 D.

Second series : 甘 kan¹.

B 甘 — **Kan¹**. Sweetness of something — held in the 口 mouth (L. 1, 4°); good, sweet; by extension, satisfaction, affection; 美也。从口含一，會意。一者味也。— It is the 99th radical of few characters relating to sweetness. Phonetic series 129 It forms

某 — **Mu³**. The thing 甘 sweet to the taste, the fruits that grow on 木 trees; 果也。从木、从甘、會意。It is used now, by a mere conventional **chia-chieh**, to mean, a certain person whose name is unknown, or respect or caution forbids to use, 某人 **mu-jên**; 發聲之詞，名也。Phonetic series 467.

甚 — **Shên⁴** In the more ancient form, 匹 what was agreeable to the 口 taste. In the more modern form, affection 甘 for the being 匹 that makes the pair (sexual) See L. 42 A. This affection being very great, says the Glose, hence the extended meaning, superlative, very, extremely, excessive. 古文从口从匹。今从甘从匹。匹偶也。會意。安樂也。男女之大欲存焉。— Phonetic series 475.

香 — **Hsiang¹**. Savour or odour 甘 agreeable, of the 黍 (contracted, L. 121 I) fermented grain, of the arack; 从黍。从甘、會意，芳也。酒之臭曰香。By extension, fragrant, odoriferous. — It is the 186th radical.

旨 — **Chih³**. Formerly, the tongue 舌 (L. 102 C), in contact with a sweet thing — (L. 1 4°). Now 甘 sweet; 匕 is the phonetic (L. 26 K). By extension, edict of the Emperor that is supposed to be couched in sweet words. — Phonetic series 185.

甛 — **Tien²**. Sweet 甘 to the 舌 tongue; it is from this phonetic contracted, that are derived, in the phonetic series 227 舌, the compounds in **ien**. See L. 102 C. 舌知甘者、會意。

猒 — **Yen⁴**. Satiated. Glutted 甘 with the 月 meat of a 犬 dog. See 肰 L. 65 G. In the modern character, 甘 became 曰, as in 香 and 旨 above. It forms 厭 **yen⁴**, L. 65 G.

Third series: 言 yen².

C 言

Yen². To speak, to tell; speech, word. Words issuing 䇂 (L. 102 E) from the 口 mouth. The sounds of the heart, says the Glose; 心聲也。— It is the 149th radical of characters relating to speech. It forms

計

Chi⁴. To compute, to calculate. To know how to 言 enunciate the numbers till 十 ten, i.e. all the numbers. See L. 24 B.

討

T'ao³. To rule 寸 by one's 言 words; to chide; 治也。See L. 45 B.

信

Hsin⁴. Sincerity; the quality that the 言 words of every man 人 should have. Faith, truthfulness, the effect produced upon a 人 man by the 言 words of another. See L. 25 H.

衙

Hsüan⁴. To go here and there 行, while offering and praising 言 one's goods, as the pedlars do. To praise up one's self.

䜌

Luan⁴. See L. 92 D.

商

Shang¹. See L. 15 D.

Fourth series: 言 doubled 誩.

D 誩 競 競 競

Ching⁴. Primitively, 言 words against words, dispute; 从二言、會意。Then the two 儿 men (L. 29 A) were added; 从二儿、二言、會意。Lastly, the scribes contracted this character into 競, and **K'ang-hsi** wrongly classified it under the 117th radical 立. Not to be confounded with 兢 L. 97 I.

譱 善

Shan⁴. Harmony, good understanding 羊 (L. 103), peace made again after an 誩 altercation By extension, amenity, pleasantness, sweetness, good, well; 从誩、从羊、會意、於義同意。Compare 義 L. 71 Q. This character being uneasy to trace, the scribes altered it in a strange way. — Phonetic series 702.

Fifth series: 音 yin[1]. A series is reserved to this derivative of 言, on account of its important compounds.

E 音 — **Yin**[1]. Utterance 言 of a 一 sound. A sound, tone, phonation, modulation; 聲也。从言含一、會意。 Compare the composition of **kan**[1] and **chih**[3], L. 73 B. — It is the 180th radical. Phonetic series 498. It forms

章 — **Chang**[1]. A strain in music 音, or an essay in literature, 十 perfect (ten representing the finishing, the perfection); 从音、从十、會意。 — Phonetic series 593. It forms

竷 — **Kan**[4] Music 章, that ruled the evolutions of the dancers in ancient times (see 舛 and 舞 L. 31 E). It forms, by adding the radical 貝

贛 — **Kan**[4]. **Kung**[4]. The 貝 gratification (L. 161) given to the musicians. Compare 屑 L. 65 D. The scribes changed 牛 into 工, therefore this character is now written 贛。— Phonetic series 850.

竟 — **Ching**[4]. Limits, boundaries; where the 音 languages or dialects of 儿 men change. By extension, end; 从音、从人、會意。 **K'ang-hsi** who took 音 for his 180th radical, arbitrarily classified 竟 under 立. — Phonetic series 603.

意 — **I**[4]. The intention 心 of the man who speaks, manifested by the sounds 音 he utters; 志也。By extension, the meaning, the signification that the 心 intelligence of the hearer perceives in the 音 words of the speaker; 从心、从音、會意。心察音而知意也。— Phonetic series 739. It became, by contraction, 音 in the compound

Chih[4]. **Officer. See L. 71 I. — Phonetic series 671.**

Note: In the phonetic series 意 739, are enclosed some derivatives of another compound, which the scribes confounded with 意。

I^{4}. Pleasure, cheerfulness, caused by a 言 word, that hit the point 中 (L. 109); 快也。从言，从中、會意。。。言 is divided, a half being on the top, a half at the bottom; 中 is in the middle. With 心 at the bottom, we have a compound which is also written 意 It meant, pleasure. This sense became obsolete, and the character now means 100.000. It is written 億 Compare L. 47 X. — Conclusion: in modern characters, the series is uniform; written in ancient characters, it is decomposed into two distinct series.

LESSON 74.

About the primitive 囗 **wei**^{2}. See 回 L. 76.

A 囗 ○ **Wei**^{2}. A round, a circumference, an inclosure, to contain; 圓 周 也。像。— It is the 31th radical of characters relating to enclosures. To be distinguished from the 30th radical 口, mouth. Different compounds of 囗 **wei**^{2} were already explained. Let us recall

肙 **Yüan**^{4}. Larvæ 月 without skeleton, that can bend in round ○. See L. 65 E.

員 **Yüan**^{2}. Cowries 貝 of a ○ round form. See L. 161 B.

舍 **Shê**^{4}. Dwelling made with walls. See L. 14 C.

倉 **Ts'ang**^{1}. A granary to 囗 keep the 食 provisions. See L. 26 M.

囚 **Ch'iu**^{2}. A man 人 imprisoned 囗 See L. 25 B.

因 **Yin**^{1}. A man 人 enclosed, knowing not what to say. See L. 60 B

圂 **Hun**^{4}. A sty 囗 for 豕 pigs. See L. 69 B.

B 𣎆

Lo^3. Penning, cattle-breeding, fattening. To 丮 catch and inclose 亡 an animal in a 口 pen, in order, later on, to get its 月 flesh; 多肉獸也。See LL. 10 E, 11 E, 65 A. The scribes changed 丮 into 凡. — Phonetic series 747, the radical being inserted at the bottom, betveen 月 and 丮.

羸

Lei^2. A 羊 sheep that needs to be fattened. Lean, feeble, meagre.

贏

Ying^2. To feed one's purse (貝 cowries). To gain at a game or in doing commerce. Is phonetic contracted in the compounds in **ing** of the phonetic series 747.

C 邑

I^4. Seat 口 of the government's authority 卩 (L. 55 B). Capital of a district, of a fief. Walled city; 从口、从卩、會意. 國都也。— It is the 163th radical of characters denoting towns. Let us recall the compounds

邕

Yung^1. The moat around a city L 12 G.

雝

Yung^1. The wagtail, the bird 隹 that likes the moats. L 12 G.

Note: 邑 straight or turned, when abbreviated, becomes 阝 on the right, 乡 on the left. Hence the following

雍

Yung^1. The wagtail, as above; 亠 is for 巛, 乡 is for 邑. — Phonetic series 769.

鄉

Hsiang^1. The country, the space between the cities 乡 and 阝, where the grains 皀 are growing See L. 26 M — Phonetic series 682.

Lastly, in the next, 邑 is reduced to 巳 (L. 55 B).

巷

Hsiang^4. Composed of 共 (L 47 Q) and of two 邑, later on reduced to one, and then to 巳. What is of a common 共 use in the cities 邑, i.e. the streets, the paths; 从共。从邑。會意。在邑中所共也。道也。

LESSON 75.

About several series derived from 口 wei², viz. 東、高、亯、享、克、etc , that are important and difficult.

First series: 東 shu⁴.

A 

Shu⁴. To bind, to tie, 口 to inclose a 木 tree, taken here as meaning any object; 縛也。从口，从木，會意。— Phonetic series 303. It forms

Su⁴, sou⁴. To clear the throat, to cough; 从欠 (L. 99) 東聲。— Phonetic series 647.

Chien³. To select; to choose in a 東 bundle previously 八 opened; 从東.从八，會意。分別也。Not to be confounded with the compounds of 㓁, L. 40 D. — Phonetic series 429.

This is a singular compound, that forms an interesting series. It is composed of 東, with a second 口 greater, inserted half way up the tree The radical, or sometimes the phonetic, is introduced in this frame. The general idea of this now obsolete character was, a recipient, a case, a bag, placed high, out of reach. The scribes altered it in many ways. The large 口 is generally reduced to 冖, and the foot of the tree 木 to 小. Some compounds are given here :

Kao¹. Quiver, a case for arrows; 咎 is phonetic.

T'o³. A bag; 石, stone, represents the contents. See the ancient character above. It forms

Tu⁴. Worms 虫 in cases, books or clothes, moths, book-worms.

Nang². A sack. Explained L 72 H. — Phonetic series 854.

The philologists attribute also to this compound, taken in the sense of enclosure, the intricate forms of k'un³. See below, the different writings of this character. It means the path in the shape of a 十, which cuts the 口 square yards of the

Chinese palaces, giving in the angles four 口 spaces, planted with flowers; 宮中道也。像。The first ancient form graphically represented this idea, which was darkened by successive additions. The contractions were made by the scribes. Not to be confounded with 壺 hu², L. 38 G. It has nothing in common with 亞 ya⁴, L. 82 H.

囲 𡎡 壸 壺

Second series: 高 kao¹.

B 高 高

Kao¹. A kind of pavilion 古, raised upon a 冂 substructure; 口 represents the hall in this under building; 像。臺觀高之形。An elevated place; high, lofty, eminent. — It forms the 189th radical. Phonetic series 544. When it is variously contracted, or overturned, or when its strokes are mingled, it forms the singular following series.

亭 亭

T'ing². The phonetic 丁 ting¹ (L. 57 A) replaced the 口 at the bottom. In the modern writing, 冂 became 冖. Pavilion, terrace; 樓也。从高省。丁聲。— Phonetic series 479.

亳

Po⁴. An old city, 乇 (L. 33 B) root of the 商 Shang dynasty, built upon a 高 height.

豪 豪 毫

Hao². An angry 豕 boar (L. 69) bristling up; 高 contracted is phonetic. Extended meanings, bravery; compare L. 69 D. IL.. or bristles, a hair, anything very minute. Hence the modern form 毫, which is not classical (毛 mao², hair, L. 100) — Recently the character has been adapted to the porcupine, common in the West of China. It is supposed to be very brave, and to shoot out its quills, like arrows. — Phonetic series 777.

喬 喬

Ch'iao². In this character, it was the top 亠 of 高 that disappeared, to make room for 夭 yao¹, L. 61 B; 高而曲也。从夭、从高省、會意。Something 高 high, a tree for instance, the top of which bends down, overhangs. — Phonetic series 670. K'ang-hsi wrongly classified this character under 口 the mouth.

T'ai². A high place, a lofty terrace, a look-out. Here 高 is reduced to 口 and 冖. The 口 of the bottom was replaced by 至, L 133 which means that the birds alight there. The 亠 on the top, is replaced by 㞢 L 79, which indicates the summit, as in 岁 L. 59 F. 觀四方而高者、从至、从㞢、从高省、會意。 By extension, any elevated place, staging, tower, observatory. — Phonetic series 790.

Third series: 京 ching¹, derived from 高.

C 京

Ching¹. It is 高, the bottom part of which is replaced by a pivot (L. 6 A); idea of loftiness, of centrality. The capital or metropolis, centre of the Empire. 从高省、从丨引而上、指事也。The scribes altered the bottom in the modern character. It is unconnected with 小、 — Phonetic series 336. It forms

就 **Chiu**⁴ Admiration 尤 (L. 134 C), before something 京 exalted. By extension, to go towards, to follow, consequently.

景 **Ching**³. The sun 日 very 京 high; brightness; a vista, a prospect. Forms 影 ying³, shade caused by an object, intercepting 彡 light. — Another explanation: the sun 日 at the capital 京. Prognostics given by it about the affairs of the Empire. state of things, circumstances — Phonetic series 672.

亮 **Liang**⁴. The 人 men of the 京 capital, more enlightened than those of the provinces, advisors to the Government, etc. By extension, clear, illumined. The actual form is relatively modern.

Fourth series: 亯 **hsiang**³; modern form 享, derived from 高.

D Before studying this series, that was specially distorted by the scribes, let us note — 1. That 享 is an arbitrary abbreviation of 亯, which has nothing in common with 子 L. 94 — 2. That the scribes used the same 享 as an abbreviation of two compounds of 亯 ch'un² and kuo¹ (below E and H), that form series. If therefore the group 享 is gathered, one gets a mixture of **yang**, **un**, **wu**, **uo**, etc. This phonetic confusion betrays a primitive diversity of characters which cannot be distinguished in the modern writing, but is manifest in the ancient forms.

Hsiang^{3}. To offer a 曰 gift to a superior 古 (高 contracted); 曰 represents the object offered; it is a modern primitive, distinct from 曰 **yüeh**^{1} L. 73, and from 日 **jih**^{4} L. 143. 獻也。从高上下相向省。— The ancient form was composed of two 高 abbreviated, one being straight, the other inverted; one offering, the other receiving; 二高上下相向省。Hence two meanings; to *treat with favour* (now 亨 **hêng**^{1}), or to *enjoy the favour received* (now 享 **hsiang**^{3}). Compare L. **75** G. — Phonetic series **274** and **359**; the latter is almost completely attributed to the compounds **ch'un**^{2} and **huo**^{1}, below E, H.

Fu^{2}. Abundance. According to some interpreters, this character is composed of 亯 gifts received, and of 丨 that divides in four parts 曰, this division implying that all the corners are filled; 滿也。从亯.加丨.像,四塞也、指事。— A more ancient explanation, though less commonly admitted, seems to be the true one. According to this, the character means 高 (contracted), the heaping up of the productions of the 田 fields, goods of the earth Abundance, prosperity, Then the character is derived directly from 高, and not from 亯. — Note the modern deformation, and the compounds 富 **fu**^{4}, houses filled, wealth; 福 **fu**^{2}, a transcendent influence that brings luck; 百順之名也。— Phonetic series 441.

E

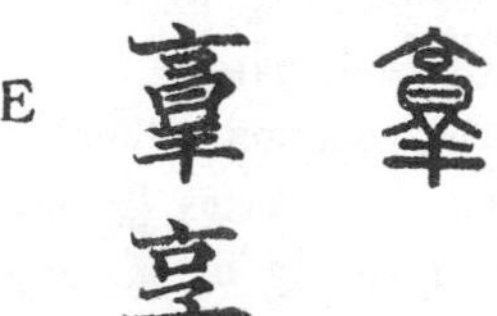

Ch'un^{2}. A lamb 羊 grown up, big and nice enough to be offered 亯 as a present; 从亯、从羊、會意。— Is altered into 享, as it was explained above D. — Phonetic series 359. It forms

Shu^{2}. To take 丮 (L. 11 E) a lamb 享 acceptable, to be roasted; 丮而食之。Note the compound 熟 **shu**^{2}, **shou**^{2}, the lamb roasted (灬 L. 126); by extension, well cooked, ripe. — Phonetic series 644. Now 孰 is used **chia-chieh**, as an interrogative pronoun.

Tun^{1}. Meek-minded, honest, simple as a 享 lamb, that is beaten 攴 and does not cry; to bear, to beat, etc. — Phonetic series 715.

F 良 

Liang^{2}. The evolution of this character parallelled the evolution of Chinese moral philosophy. Primitively the gift 曰 (as in 亯 L. 75 D), the capital gift, the nature heavenly received. In the second ancient character, the coming down from heaven of the gift, is shown graphically (school of **Mêng-tzŭ**, good nature). In the third ancient character, 二 good and evil (school of **Tung chung-shu**). Finally, the gift has been 亾 lost (school of **Li-ssu** and **Hsün-tzŭ**, bad nature). — Anyhow, the primitive meaning has been preserved: 良, original qualities, nature, natural, inborn, good. The actual character is an arbitrary contraction. See L. 26 O. — Phonetic series 289. It forms

郎

Lang^{2}. Name of an old 邑 city. **Chia-chieh**, a title. — Phonetic series 460.

量

Liang^{2}. Measure, weight, to measure, to weigh. Composed of 重 (L. 120 K) weight, 良 natural; the weight of things according with their nature. Note the contractions. It has nothing in common either with 里 L. 149 D, or with 旦 L. 143 B. It forms 糧 **liang**^{2}, rations, food, provisions; the quantity of 米 grains required for food.

G 亯 inverted, and contracted, forms

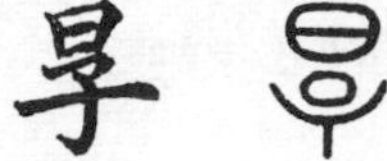

Hou⁴. Liberality, generosity. The reverse of 亯, L 75 D. The inferior receives a gift 日; 从反亯。 It is now written

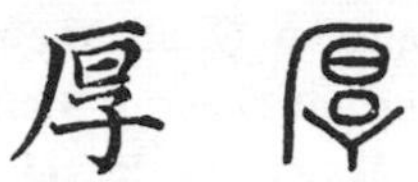

Hou⁴. Liberality, generosity. The 厂 represents the coming down of the gift, from upwards. By extension, thick, large (qualities of a generous gift). The modern character is an arbitrary abbreviation.

T'an². Abundance 㫗 of 鹵 salt (L. 41 D); salting, pickling; by extension, different macerations; various **chia-chieh**. After many contractions, the bottom of the character became 十. — Phonetic series 706.

Fifth series: 享 **kuo**, derived from 高.

H 享

Kuo¹. Walls, fortifications. The fence 囗 (L. 74) simple, or doubled 回 (L. 76) of the ancient cities, with two (four) doors opposite, each surmounted with a 古 look-out. The 古 is 高 contracted. For the modern abbreviation 享, see the note, L. 75 D. — Phonetic series 349. It forms

Kuo¹. Walls (邑 city); it is now used for the last character. — Phonetic series 549.

I

Fu⁴. This character is derived from **kuo¹** (above, the second ancient form, with a simple 囗), taken in the sense of city, place. The 古 turned up was replaced by the radical 夊 (L. 31 B), to march, to go. To go in a city, to market. By extension, to go where one already often went, to return for a second time, reiteration, repetition, etc. 从夊、从享、會意。凡重再意。 Note the absurd modern contraction. — Phonetic series 442. It forms

Fu⁴. A synonym of the last; it is now used for the simple form; 往來也。从彳、复聲。 See below J.

Note. We incidently treat here about an important compound, 履 li³, shoes, to walk; it is seemingly derived from 復, but in reality, it has no connection whatever with that character. Its story is thus given: primitively it was

[illegible]
[illegible]
[illegible]
履

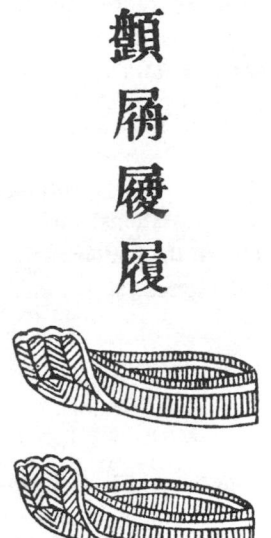

Li³. The boats 舟 (L. 66), that men 頁 put their 足 feet in (L. 112). In fact, the ancient shoes of Chinese much resembled a small boat; 从頁、从足、从舟。 Then 彳 (L. 63), to walk, was substituted for 足 feet; and 尸 a man (L. 32) for 頁. Later on, the character was increased with 夂, to march (L. 31 C); this was a mere redundancy. Lastly the scribes contracted 舟 and 夂 into 复, the bottom of the character thus becoming identical to 復 fu⁴ (L. 75 I). 足所依也。从彳、从夂、會意，舟省像。尸聲。 Finally, this compound became like a radical of shoes, 复 being replaced by different phonetics. For instance:

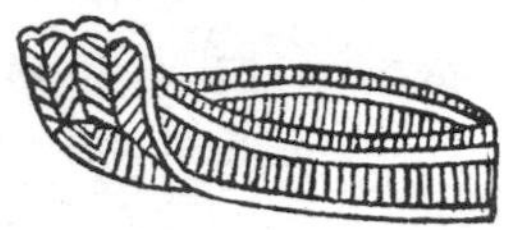

屐	屨	[illegible]	屩
Chi⁴, clog.	**Chü⁴**, shoe	**Hsüeh¹**, boot	**Chiao¹**, shoe.

Sixth series: 克 **k'o¹**, derived from 高.

K 克 [illegible]

K'o¹. To overcome, to prevail over, to repress, to subdue, etc. The top part is 高 contracted, that means, pressure from upwards, a weight that hangs heavily. Some say, the bottom is 肩 (L 65 F) shoulder, contracted. A load that weighs heavy upon the shoulders; 以肩任物曰克。物高於肩，故从高省。下像肩形。 The lower part seems rather to be a primitive, representing the idea of bending under 古 a load Note that, among the three compounds 勊、剋 尅 k'o¹, to be able of supporting, of mastering, the first is the right one, though it is now used the least; 从克、从力、能也。 To have the 力 strength of 克 supporting, of subduing.

兢 does not come from 克. See L. 97 I.

LESSON 76.

The first series of this Lesson is about 回, which is 囗 wei^{2} L.74, doubled. The second series is about the primitive 囘 **hui^{2}**, that is often written 回 by the modern scribes. To be distinguished from the series 冋 **chiung^{3}**, L. 34 B.

First series: 回.

A 回 — **Wei^{2}. Hui^{2}.** Double fence (see **kuo^{1}**, L. 75 H); a vase hermetically closed. It forms very important radical compounds, but no phonetic compounds. Those that are sometimes attributed to it, belong to 囘, below G.

B 㐭 — **Lin^{3}.** A 回 depot, to 入 put in (L. 15) the grains; 倉也。从入，回像。屋形。 It is now written 廩 and forms

C 稟 — **Lin^{3}.** A depot 㐭 for 禾 grains, a storehouse; distribution of grain to the poor; gift, favour. — Phonetic series 746. Note that

禀 **Ping^{3}**, is a modern character, that is not found in the ancient dictionaries; 示 to let know to the authorities the poor that must be 稟 (contracted) helped; to warn, to inform.

D 亶 — **T'an^{2}.** Granary 㐭 that may be examined at the 旦 (L. 143 B) day's light; all the grain that must be there, is really there; sincerity, honesty. — Phonetic series 762.

E 嗇 — **She^{4}.** Grains 來 enclosed in a 㐭 grange. When one has grains, he does not spoil them; thrift, parsimony. See L. 13 C. In the modern character, the bottom of 來, and the top of 㐭, are mingled together. — Phonetic series 755.

F 啚 — **Pei^{3}. Pi^{3}.** To have a small heap of grains 口, an overplus that cannot be received in the 㐭 granary. Superabundant, and hence, not precious. It forms

鄙 **Pi^{3}.** Vulgar, low (extended meaning of the simple character). Primitively, the 阝 small garrisons on the barbarian borders; 界上邑。

T'u². The plans to be made to order one's 口 granary, when there are 啚 too many grains to be received therein. By extension, to plan, to scheme, to calculate, long for, etc. 畫計難也。謀也。从口、从啚、會意。There are four 口 in this character.

Second series: 回.

G 

Hui². Image of an object (clouds, volutes of the smoke) that turns, that rolls, that revolves; 轉也。像, Abstract notion of revolving, of return. The scribes often write 回 (L. 76 A). — Phonetic series 211. It forms

H 

Hsüan¹. To make a complete 二 revolution, either on ones self, or through and through, or from one end to the other. See 二 L. 2 D E F. To revolve, to go through, completely. — Phonetic series 207. The modern scribes changed 回 into 日. It forms

Hsüan¹. A palace; 大室也。从宀, 亘聲。— Phonetic series 449.

I 

Mu². To dive, while 回 turning on one's self, in order to get 彐 something under water, the head being below; 入水有所取也。从彐在回下、會意。By extension, to disappear, to be no more. — Phonetic series 72. The modern scribes changed 回 into 刀.

The primitive 回 is found also, more or less modified, in the old form of 云 **yün**² cloud (L. 93 A); in an old form of 日 **yüeh**¹ (L. 73 A); in the old form of 雷 **lei**² (L. 93 D), thunder rolling above 田 the fields.

LESSON 77.

About the primitive 个 **ko**⁴.

A 

Ko⁴. A twig of bamboo, with a knot, and the whorl of pending branches inserted in the knot; 竹枝也。像形, It is now written 箇, or 個. By extension, an article. Specificative of unities. Let us recall the compound

Chih¹. The 彐 hand, breaking a bamboo sprig between two 个 knots; or, in the more modern form, the hand holding a bamboo sprig. A branch, a twig, to hold. — It is the 65th radical. Phonetic series 45.

B 竹 𥫗 **Chu**². Bamboo, the twigs of which are not 艸 raised up, but 𥫗 drooping; 像形。下 垂 者。It is now written 竹. Contracted form 𥫗. — It is the 118th radical of characters mostly referring to the many kinds or articles of bamboo. It is phonetic in some characters, e.g.

竺 **Chu**⁴. A multitude of bamboos. The common name of India in Buddhist books.

筑 **Chu**². A kind of rude harp, composed of thirteen strings that were struck with hammers. It forms

篤 **Tu**³. To advance. Firm, resolute.

LESSON 78.

About the primitive 屮 and its multiples. The complete series of the compounds derived from this important element will be treated in the L. 78.

First series: 屮 simple.

A 屮 **Ch'ê**⁴. A plant that sprouts from its grain; the minimum of a plant; at the bottom, the root; on the top, the culm; on each side, one leaf; 草木初生也。像,草出形。It is often used as a symbol, either to represent any object (L. 44 H), or to mark a point (L. 59 F). — It is the 45th radical of characters mostly referring to springing plants. In the modern writing, the scribes disfigured this element in the most fanciful ways. See, for instance, 舍 L. 14 C, 奏 L. 47 M, 巂 L. 15 C, 事 L. 44 H, etc.

𠬶 **T'ao**¹. To hold. A hand 彐 holding an 屮 object; 从 彐。从 屮、取 也。Forms 弢 t'ao¹, a bow-case, a scabbard, etc.

𧈧 **Ch'ên**³ An 虫 insect that crawls (L. 110), the 屮 head being raised (屮 beak and feelers). There are unimportant compounds. Not to be confounded with 蚩 ch'ih¹, L. 79 B.

Second series: 屮 repeated horizontally.

B 艸 芔

Ts'ao³. Plants 屮 with herbaceous stems. The repetition means their multiplicity; 百卉也。从二屮。會意。— It is the 140th radical of characters relating to plants. Modern contracted form 艹. The scribes contracted in the same way a few very different elements, e.g. 𦥑 in 萬 L. 23 H; 𠂉 in 敬 L. 54 G; etc.

Third series: 屮 repeated vertically, 𡳿 not united.

C 㪿

Chê³, **shê**². To cut, to break; 斷也。An axe 斤, and the two 屮 stumps of a branch cut. It is now written **折**. See L. 48 D. — Phonetic series **252**.

D 芻

Ch'u². Grass 屮 bound in 勹 sheaves (L. 54); 像。包束艸之形、以餧馬牛者也。**By extension**, vulgar, of small value, as the grass. Compare **L. 44 I**. — Phonetic series **524**.

Fourth series: 屮 repeated vertically, 出 united.

E 出

Ch'u¹. Springing of plants; the small plant 屮 (L. 78 A) formed a second pair of leaves, and thrusts itself out; 艸木進也。像。上出達之形。To issue, to go out, to spring from, to manifest, and other **chuan-chu**. It is often disfigured by the scribes, so that it becomes 土, etc. — Phonetic series 117. It forms

屈

Ch'ü¹. 尸 is 尾 tail contracted (L. 100 B). To go away 出, the tail 𡰣 lowering; 从出、从尾省。服也。By extension, depression, grievance, bent down. Compare li⁴, L. 129 A. — Phonetic series 348.

敖

Nao². To go out 出 in order to 放 saunter (L. 117 A); 出游也。从出、从放、會意。Now 遨 By extension, excessive relaxation, pride, insolence. — Phonetic series 638. The scribes contracted 出 into 土、

Mai^4. To sell. This part of 買 business (L 161 D) which consists in 出 exporting goods; to sell them; 出貨也。从出。从買。會意。The scribes contracted 出 into 土. Note that 賣 mai^4 does not form phonetic compounds; the phonetic series in 賣, has another origin. See L. 79 J.

Pao^4. To spread 廾 the 米 grain, in order to dry it, when the 日 sun is 出 rising. See L. 47 S. The modern contraction is a strange one — Phonetic series 809.

祟 **Sui**^{4}. Unpropitious 示 transcendent 出 emanation. Bad omen, noxious influence; 神禍也。Not to be confounded with 崇 ch'ung^2, to revere.

糶 糴 **T'iao**^{4}. To sell 出 grain 米; and its correlative **Ti**^{2}. To buy 入 grain 米; 翟 (L. 62 G) is phonetic... 出 to go out; 入 to enter.

Fifth series: 屮 repeated three times, and contracted 卉.

F 卉 

Hui^3. Vegetables, plants in general; the three 屮 representing the multitude; 草之總名也。按三屮。衆多意。The modern form is to be distinguished from 卅 thirty, derived from 十, L. 24 N. It forms

Pên^4. A man 大 (L. 60) who walks in the 卉 grass. To stride, 大走也。In the ancient character, there is 夭 for 大 (L. 61 B). — Phonetic series 472.

Fên^4. Ornaments, 飾也。从貝。从卉。Shells 貝 and 卉 plants. These were the first motives of decoration, being easier to be traced than others. See L. 35 G. — Phonetic series 732.

Sixth series: 屮 quadrupled 茻.

G 茻 茻 **Mang**^{3}. High plants, luxuriant vegetation; 衆草也。从四屮。會意。Note the modern abbreviation. In the compounds, the added part is inserted between the 艹 on the top. and the 廾 at the bottom, the latter being often changed by the scribes into 廾, 大, etc.

Mang³. A hound 犬 frisking about in the 茻 thickets. A kind of greyhound; 从犬、从四屮、會意。犬善逐兎艸中爲莽、Phonetic series 698.

Mo⁴. The 日 sun fading away at the horizon, in the 茻 plants. Sunset; now 暮. By extension, to disappear, to be no more, negation. — Phonetic series 637, in which the radical is often placed at the bottom, between the two down strokes of the lower 艹, changed into 大; e g. 幕, 墓, etc.

Tsang⁴. The ancient burial; to tie 一 a corpse 死 in a bundle of grass. See L. 28 H. The tie 一 has disappeared from the modern character. 从死在茻中、會意。一其中所以束之。指事。易曰。古之葬者、厚衣之以薪、故从茻。

Han². Cold. A man 人 who tries to protect himself against cold 冫, in a 宀 shelter, by burying himself in 茻 straw. See L 47 U. — Phonetic series 530.

LESSON 79.

This Lesson, one of the most intricate, is reserved for the important series that are derived from 屮 (L. 73), viz.: 屯、之、生、市、朮、夫、 etc.

First series: 屯 t'un².

A 屯

T'un². The underground germination. The two cotyledons part from each other; the curved line represents the struggles of the young plant in order to take root; the plumula rises above the — earth, and is brought to light; 像。草木之初生、屯然而難。从屮貫一尾曲。一地也指事。By extension, the difficult beginning of an establishment, a foundation, a village, a camp. — Phonetic series 85. It forms

Ch'un¹. Spring. Germination 屯 and pullulation of 艸 plants, by the effects of the 日 sun. — Phonetic series 436. The modern character is another strange alteration made by the scribes.

Second series: 之 chih.

B 之 Ψ 㞢 **Chih**[1]. A small plant Ψ ascending from the — ground; to grow; idea of development, of progress, of continuity; 出也。像一者地也。指事。It is now used (chia-chieh) as the sign of the genitive, as an expletive, etc. 助語之辭。Not to be confounded with 乏 fa[2], L. 112 K. In the modern compounds, 之 either has its ancient form, or is contracted into 土, or otherwise. Note the derivatives

蚩 **Ch'ih**[1]. A scarab, large black 虫 beetle, Ψ boring through — the hard soil, coming to light. Chuan-chu, clumsy, stupid. Compare ch'ên[3], L. 78 A. — Phonetic series 520.

旹 時 **Shih**[2]. The time, succession of the annual 㞢 sprouting periods of plants, under the action of the 日 sun; compare L. 24 D, L. 79 A. Constancy. Later on, the character was erroneously connected with 寺。— Phonetic series 562.

寺 **Ssŭ**[4]. Court, temple. The place where the law or the rule 寸 are applied, in a 㞢 constant manner; 官舍也。有法度者也。— Phonetic series 238.

志 **Chih**[4]. The will; a 心 purpose that is fixed, that develops 㞢 itself; 意存在心爲志。The heart is, according to the Chinese, the seat of the intellect and of the will. — Phonetic series 260.

先 **Hsien**[1] To advance; to progress 㞢 with one's 儿 feet (L 29); 从儿、从㞢．會意。前進也。— Phonetic series 202. Repeated in

兟 **Shên**[1]. To advance, to present one's self, in order to give one's advice. It forms

贊 **Tsan**[4]. To pay a visit 兟, in order to give an advice; 貝 presents offered, or, more probably, received; 从貝、兟．會意。貝也．見必有贊。故从貝。— Phonetic series 849.

市 𢆶

Shih[4]. A market. The 㞢 grass grown place 冂 (L. 34 A), where one ㇏ gets what one is in need of (L. 19 E)... 㞢 instead of 屮, the down stroke being mingled with the horizontal stroke of 冂. Compare 舍 L 14 C. The modern form is not to be confounded, either with 市 **fu**[4] (L 35 B), or with 市 **fei**[4] (L. 79 G). It forms 柿 **shih**[4], the kaki (phonetic complex); and 鬧 **nao**[4] (logical aggregate), to wrangle 鬥 as on the market, to quarrel, to scold, etc.

㞢 **inverted** forms

C 帀 帀

匝

Tsa[1]. To go round; to perform a circuit or entire revolution; as 屮 which turned on its — axis; 周 也。从 反 㞢 而 帀 也。 In the modern times, this character was changed by the scribes into 匝; 俗 誤 作 匝。

帀 is found in 師 **shih**[1], L. 86 B; and in 衞 **wei**[4], to escort, a different writing of 衛, in which 帀 replacing the 中 of the phonetic 韋, means perhaps the ***return***, while 行 means the *going*.

Sub-series 𡈼 and 王... 㞢 combined with 土 **t'u**[3] (L 81) forms

D 㞷 㞷

主

王

Wang[3]. Luxuriant vegetation, that 㞢 sprouts from the 土 earth, here and there; rambling, wandering; 草 木 妄 生 也。从 㞢 在 土 上、會 意。 *Note*. In its modern contracted forms, **wang**[3] might be confounded with 主 **chu**[3], master, L. 83 D; and with 王 **wang**[2], king, L. 83 C. In the first case, the sound prevents any mistake. In the second case, the distinction is not easy, the two phonetics being homophonous. See phonetic series 87 and 115. Note the derivatives

往 𨑧

Wang[3] To stray, to go away; 从 彳、从 㞷。

狂 𤞑

K'uang[2]. A mad dog that roves; 瘋 狗 也。从 犬、从 㞷 — Phonetic series 285.

匡 匩

K uang[1] A regular assemblage. It is supposed to come from 匚 (L. 51 A), and 㞷 already contracted in the writing **hsiao-chuan**. It seems rather that 王 is a primitive, representing a regular ordering. Compare **hsüan**[4], L. 47 F. — Phonetic series 223.

Sub-series 封, another combination of 㞢 with 土 t'u^{3}, (L. 81).

E 封

Fêng^{1}. Fields 土 and meadows 㞢, under the authority 寸 of a feudatory; an appanage, a domain, a tenure; 諸侯之土也。从㞢、从土、从寸、守其制度也。This explanation seems to be erroneous. The ancient character first represented a 木 tree upon a 土 tumulus; 寸, the authority, was added later on. It is composed like 社, in which 示 was also added later on. A knoll surmounted with a tree, represented the Imperial possession of the land. A similar knoll, but smaller, was erected in the fief granted by the Emperor to a feudatory. Symbol of the jurisdiction; fictitious principle of propitious influences; etc. By extension, to raise a tumulus, to invest a noble, to appoint to office, to seal, to close, etc. The modern forms are contracted. Nothing in common with 圭 (L. 81 B). — Phonetic series 440.

Third series: 生 **shêng**, often contracted into 主.

F 生

Shêng^{1}. A plant that grows more and more. A whorl was added to 㞢 L. 79 B; 草木進於㞢也。By extension, to bear, to spring, to live, to grow. — It is the 100th radical. Phonetic series 154. Note the derivatives

青

Ch'ing^{1}. Green. The 丹 hue of growing 生 plants, the light green of sprouting plants; 草木始生其色。But 丹 (L. 115 D) means *red*! Was the inventor of 青 a Daltonian? — It is the 174th radical. Phonetic series 337.

星

Hsing^{1} The stars; the quintessence of sublimated matter, that 生 ascended and crystallised into stars; 萬物之精上爲列星。The three top elements of the ancient character are a primitive, representing the stars. The modern character is a contraction of the same. — Phonetic series 447.

產 **Ch'an**³. The 彥 signs of 生 parturition. See L. 61 F. — Phonetic series 592.

隆 **Lung**². Prosperity, abundance. What descends 降 (contracted) from heaven; what is produced 生 on earth; all goods. See L. 31 F.

毒 **Tu**². The noxious weeds that grow 生 everywhere, and that must be 毋 avoided. Poison, venom. See L. 67 M.

甦 **Su**¹. This character does not mean to rise from the dead, but to change 更 (L. 41 A) one's 生 existence, in the Taoist or Buddhist sense.

性 **Hsing**⁴. The natural disposition, temper, spirit, the qualities and propensities; the 心 heart of a man, at his 生 birth.

姓 **Hsing**⁴. The place where the clan-chiefs of old, were 生 born from a 女 woman impregnated by heaven. They were surnamed after that place; hence the extended meaning, 姓 family surname.

甡 **Shêng**¹. A multitude, a great number of 生 beings.

屮 combined with 八 (L 18) forms the two series 4 and 5.

Fourth series. 朩 **fei**⁴.

G 朩 **Fei**⁴. The branching 屮 plants, that do not 业 stand, but creep, and whose bough's-multiply indefinitely; by extension, multiplication, fibres; 从屮、从八、會意，枝葉分布也。— Phonetic series 57 The modern form is to be distinguished from 市 **shih**⁴, L. 34 D, and from 朩 **fu**⁴, L. 35 B... **Fei**⁴ is, sometimes, used also under the contracted forms 𠂋 and 𡿨. Note the derivatives

孛 **Po**⁴. The multiplication, the human procreation (子 child, L. 94). — Phonetic series 301.

索 **So**³. Fibres 糸 (L. 92) 𡿨 of the plants; to tie up; a cord. 从糸、从𡿨、會意。— Phonetic series 565.

南 𡴭 **Nan²**. The South. Regions in which the 𢆉 luxuriant (L. 102 F) vegetation 冂 expands everywhere. The country of lianas. — Phonetic series 468.

𠂔 𣎵 **Tzŭ³**. A stop 一 (L. 1. 3°), in the 𣎵 development of vegetation. To stop. The modern form was invented by the scribes; 止也、从𣎵成而一橫止之也。— Phonetic series 86.

Fifth series: 朩 p'an⁴.

H 朩 朩 **P'an⁴**. To strip hemp and 八 divide the fibres from the 屮 stalk; 分枲莖皮也。从屮像。八分也。 The modern form is to be distinguished from 木 **mu⁴**, tree, L 119; and from 朮 **shu²**, L. 45 J. **P'an⁴** (and not **mu⁴**) is the radical in 枲 **hsi³**, hemp. It forms

𣏟 𣏟 **P'ai⁴**. Textile fibres Not to be confounded with 林 **lin²**, that comes from 木 **mu⁴**, L. 119 L. It forms

麻 麻 **Ma₂**. Prepared hempen tow, kept under a shelter 广 (L. 59 I). — It is the 200th radical. Phonetic series 634. It forms

靡 靡 **Mei²**. Bad tow, 从非 (L. 170), bad; negation.

𣗥 𣗥 **San⁴**. Striking 攴 of the fibres, to dissociate them; to separate; 分離也。从攴。It forms

𢿣 𢿣 散 **San⁴**. To strike 攴 meat 月 and to reduce it into filaments, in the Chinese way; 𢿣肉也。 The modern form contracted is now used for the last; to scatter, to separate, to disperse, to break up, etc. — Phonetic series 701.

Sixth series. 坴 lu⁴. From 屮 and 大 (L. 60).

I 坴 坴 **Lu⁴**. Mushroom. A plant 屮 that stands as a 大 man; 从屮、从大、會意。菌也。 The 大 is contracted. It forms

Ch'iu^4. The tadpoles that swarm like mushrooms. Hence the phonetic compound

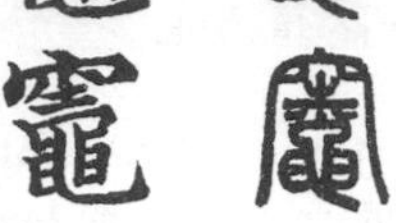

Tsao^4 A stove for cooking; 炊穴也。— In these intricate characters, 夫 is often contracted into 土, to give room. See 黽 L. 108 C.

J 

Mu^4. A benevolent 目 look; 夫 is phonetic. Friendliness. Now 睦, lu^4 坴 (below) being the phonetic. It forms

Yu^4. To chaffer; to haggle about 貝 the price in friendly 夫 terms. 夫 is contracted into 土, so that the modern form of this character is identical to 賣 **mai**^{4}, to sell, L. 78 E. — Phonetic series 817.

K 坴

Lu^4. Earth, soil, a mound; 土塊也。从土、夫聲。— Phonetic series 379. It forms

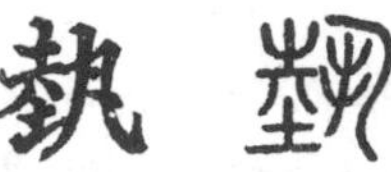

I^4 To cultivate the ground; 種也。从坴、从丮、會意。See L. 11 E. — Phonetic series 619.

The following is considered as a derivative from 坴 contracted:

夌

Ling^2 To stumble, to 夂 knock against an 坴 obstacle; a tumulus, a hillock. — Phonetic series 378.

L 壴 豈

For these two forms, see L. 165 B.

LESSON 80.

About the primitive 山 **shan**^{1}.

A 山

Shan^1. Mountain. On the top, three rocks; 土有石而高。像形。— It is the 46th radical of characters relating to hills. Phonetic series 25. — This character is to be distinguished from certain modern contractions, e.g. 耑 L. 164 B, 豈 L. 165 B, etc. See L. 25 I, 仙 **hsien**^{1}, the genii, the 人 men who dwell on the 山 mountains. Sometimes a symmetrical phonetic is introduced in the radical 山, e.g. 幽 L. 90 D, 幽 L. 69 J.

Note the development of the image in the following

B 岳

Yao[4]. The highest peaks of mountains (4, then 5), where the Emperors worshipped when visiting their empire (*Textes Historiques*, p. 32). The ancient character represents the rows superposed; the modern character is a fanciful deformation made by the scribes; 古文从山像.高形、王者巡狩所至。今作岳.作嶽。It is used also **chia-chieh**, as a term of respect.

LESSON 81.

About the primitive 土 t'u[3], and its multiples. A special series is reserved for 壬 t'ing[3].

First series: 土 t'u[3].

A 土 土

T'u[3]. Earth, soil, ground. The 二 earth that produces all 丨 things. The top line represents the surface, the soil; the down line represents the subsoil, the rock; 地之生、萬物者也。从二、像。丨、物出形。— It is the 32th. radical of characters relating to earth. Phonetic series 32.

— See 由 L. 38 C; 坐 L. 27 D; 封 生 L. 79 E, F; etc. Note the following

圣

Kuai[4]. To 又 clear 土 land, changing thus his appearance; new, strange; 致力於地曰圣。从土、从又。會意。Forms 怪 **kuai**[4], 心 moral 圣 singularity; singularity in general; 異也。从心、圣亦聲。

垔 涅

Nieh[1]. Clay 土 exposed to the 日 sun. Hence 土 clay 氵 watered, then hardening when exposed to the 日 sun. To mould earthenware, bricks, etc. — Phonetic series 296.

皇

Nieh[1] (mistaken for the precedent)

Hui[3]. The primitive 臼 mortar to pound rice, a hole dug in 土 the hard soil, or perhaps a hollow brick. Hence

毀 毀 **Hui^3**. To 殳 pound (L. 22 D) in the 臼 mortar, to grind to dust. **Chuan-chu**, to destroy utterly. — 臼 is a vicious form. — Phonetic series 735.

Note: 土 t'u^3 is to be distinguished from 大 (L. 60) or 夭 (L. 61) on the top of 幸、奉、走、etc; and from 屮 or 㞢 (L. 79) on the top of 寺、志、壴、etc. In composition, 土 t'u^3 is ordinarily at the bottom, or on the left side of the compound.

Second series: Multiples of 土.

B 圭 圭 **Kui^1**. Lands; 从重土、會意、Appanages of the ancient feudatories. By extension, the different sceptres given to nobles by the Emperor, when they were invested with their fief. — Phonetic series 224. For 封 that is not derived from 圭, see L. 79 E.

C 垚 **Yao^2** Earth heaped up; 土高也。从三土。會意。It forms

堯 堯 **Yao^2**. Knoll, mound. From 土 earth heaped up on a 兀 high base; 高也。从三土在兀上。會意。Name of the celebrated Emperor **Yao^2** (22 Centuries B. C.). — Phonetic series 719.

Third series: 𡈼 t'ing^2, composed of 人 and 土.

D 𡈼 𡈼 **T'ing^2**. A man 人 standing on the 土 ground; 从人立土上、會意。挺立也。Compare 立 L. 60 H. To be distinguished from 壬 **jên^2** (L. 82 C). It forms

E 㸒 㸒 **Yin^2**. Idea of encroachment, of usurpation, of outrage, of violence; 挺立於此而欲爪取於彼。从爪、从𡈼、會意。Lit, while standing 𡈼 on one's rights, to encroach 爫 on another's rights. The compound 淫 **yin^2**, that is now used to mean lewdness in general, is in that meaning **chia-chieh** for 婬 rape.

F 廷 𢓊 **T'ing**². To go 廴 to the court, to stand 壬 at one's place, for an imperial audience: 朝也。古朝、皆不屋。君立於門中、臣立於廷中、延之左右謂之位。The Emperor sat on his throne before the inner door, the ministers were standing in two lines, on the left and the right side, in the court-yard. Each of them held in his hands the sceptre, sign of his dignity. See LL. 55 A, B; 25 F; 81 G. — Phonetic series 305.

G 𦣞 **Ch'ên**². A minister who, when 壬 standing at his place, bows down profoundly. See 臣 (L. 82 F). Forms, by adding 月 moon (L. 64 G), the quaint compound

𦣠 **Wang**⁴. A solemn imperial audience The ministers reflecting the splendour of the Emperor, as the moon reflects the light of the sun; 从月、从臣、从壬、會意。朝廷也。月滿於日相望、似朝君也。月本無光、借日之光以爲光。Forms by substituting 亡 to 臣:

望 𦣠 **Wang**⁴. This character has two different meanings.— 1. The full of the moon, after which the 月 moon 亡 decreases. — 2. To look at, or forward, or towards, to desire; in this sense, it is chia-chieh for the last.

H 呈 𡈼 **Ch'êng**². To speak 口, while standing at one's 壬 place; to notify, to lay before a superior. — Phonetic series 255. It forms

聖 𦔻 **Shêng**⁴. Those who 耳 listened to and understood the 呈 advices given, and therefore became wise; wise, perfect; 通也。从耳、从呈。按耳順之謂聖。

戜 𢧐 **Tieh**⁴. Notification 呈 made with 戈 menaces (L. 71 F). It became by the redundant addition of 大 contracted into 十

䥫 𢧁 **Tieh**⁴. Hence the phonetic complex 鐵 t'ieh, iron, 黑金也。

Other derivatives of 壬 explained elsewhere: 巠 L. 12 H; 聽 L. 1) O; 重 L. 120 K.

LESSON 82.

About the primitive 工 kung¹, and its important derivatives, 壬 jên², 巨 chü⁴, 臣 ch'ên², 亞 ya⁴. Two other primitives, 𦣝 i², and [illegible] t'ou³, will be incidentally explained.

First series: 工 and its multiples.

A 工 — **Kung¹**. It represents the ancient square. By extension, work, skill, labour, any ornament requiring skill. For, says the Glose, the square gives the shape to all things; it forms the right angle that forms the squares, that form the circles, etc. In an ancient form, 彡 represents the parallel lines traced with the square; 規矩也、像、古文㺬从彡指事。凡工之事以規矩盡之。— It is the 48th radical. Phonetic series 24.

Different compounds of 工 were explained elsewhere. See 巫 L. 27 E; [illegible] L. 49 G; 左 L. 46 B; 式 L. 71 G; 巩 L. 11 F. But 差 is not derived from it. Note the following:

功 — **Kung¹**. A work 工 that requires 力 (L. 53 A) strength, and therefore meritorious; work done, achievements, merit; 从力、从工、會意。

項 — **Hsiang⁴**. The nape, 頭後也。The part behind the 頁 head, on which the 工 loads are carried (L. 160),

貢 — **Kung⁴**. Cowries 貝 paid for a 工 work done; salary, contributions, taxes; 獻也从貝 (L. 161).

空 — **K'ung¹**. Artificial 工 excavation 穴 (L. 37); a cavern, a hole, an opening, empty: 竅也。从穴。— Phonetic series 372.

B 㠭 — **Chan³** Symmetrical and intricate ordering or drawing, for which the square 工 was much used; 从四工會意 It forms

襄 — **Chan³** Gowns 衣 (L. 16) embroidered with ornaments, worn by the ladies at the court. Contracted in

展 𡱵 **Chan**[3]. The skirt of that gown, the train which unrolls itself from the lower part of 尸 the body; 从尸.轉也。By extension, to open out, to unroll, to expand, to exhibit Now 輾 The modern contraction was made by the scribes. — Phonetic series 508.

寒 𡨄 **Sai**[1]. To fill or stuff a hole, to stop up, to obstruct. Two hands 廾 pile up 工 bricks or other materials, in an 宀 opening: 从四工、从廾、从宀、會意, Now 塞 — Phonetic series 350.

Second series: 壬 jên[2].

C 壬 壬 **Jên**[2]. Not to be confounded witd 壬 t'ing[2], L. 81 D. A man 丨 (as in 申 L. 50 C) who carries a 工 load; the Chinese carrying bamboo pole with a load hanging at each end. The figure is couched, to take less place; see page 18-8. A loan, a burden; to bear, to endure, etc. This character was used to mean the ninth of the ten stems in the cycle, and the compound 任 was made to replace it 擔也。上下物也、指事、中像、人擔之形。古像形字、若舟車、若目馬之類、横作豎作同也。— Phonetic series 66.

任 任 **Jên**[4]. A burden, a charge, to bear, etc. It is used for 壬. The tone was changed: 从人、壬聲。— Phonetic series 215.

Third series. 巨 chü.

D 巨 巨 巨 **Chü**[4]. A greater square (工 L. 82 A), for longer measures, either agrarian or others. It had a handle or a tie, to be handled. Now 矩. By extension, big. — Phonetic series 118.

渠 渠 **Ch'ü**[2]. A drain, a canal, a place for 氵 water to run into; 水所居。It comes from 榘, a kind of wooden square or level, used to make the aqueducts. There are different **chia-chieh**.

Fourth series: 臣 ch'ên².

E 臣 臣

Ch'ên². Minister, attendant on a prince. The character, straightened in modern writing (see page 18-8), represents the minister prostrate before his master; 事君者也、像屈服之形、— It is the 131th radical It forms

宦

Huan⁴. Minister 臣 at the 宀 palace; an official, an eunuch. Compare 官 **kuan¹**, L. 86 C.

臧

Tsang¹. Compliance, the virtue of the 臣 ministers. Phonetic 戕 (LL. 127 B, 71 F). There are different **chia-chieh** — Phonetic series 792.

臤

Chien¹. To have hold 又 of one's men 臣; firm, solid; 掔持之固也。Now 堅. — Phonetic series 332.

F 臥

Wo⁴. To resalute 从 kindly the saluting 臣 minister; 伏也。从人、从臣、會意。It forms

臨

Lin². To treat 人 kindly the different classes 品 of officials 臣 (L. 72). By extension, to be condescending, amicable; 以高視下也、以尊適卑、曰臨。

監

Chien¹. To bend 臥 over a full vase 皿 (L. 157), to see its contents. To examine carefully, to watch over; places under watch, as an office, a bureau, a prison, etc. 視也。察也。— Note how, in the modern character, the 人 contracted received between its two strokes, the 丿 of 皿 dislocated. In the compounds, when a radical is added at the bottom, 皿 placed on the top, on the right side, becomes 皿; see the following **lan³**. — Phonetic series 772. Compare 鹽 L. 41 D.

覽

Lan³. To examine carefully, to consider; 觀也、視也、从見从監、會意。— Phonetic series 852.

The derivatives of 臣 are to be distinguished from those of the primitive

G 臣 — I². This character, a straightened figure (page 18-8), rudely represents the face and projecting chin; 頷也、像形。Compare L. 41 B. — Phonetic series 279. See 熙 L. 85 A.

Fifth series: 亞 ya⁴.

H 亞 — Ya⁴. A work 工 deformed; ugly, as a hunchback. The vertical line is doubled, to show a deformation in different directions. The meaning *second*, derived from 二, is **chia-chieh**. — Phonetic series 411. It forms

惡 — O⁴. Wu⁴. The moral evil, deformation 亞 of the 心 heart (o⁴), and the repulsion which it causes (wu⁴); to detest, to hate.

Note: in the modern writing, several characters contain a 亞 that has no relation whatever with the ya⁴ of this Lesson; e.g. 壺 L. 38 G, 壼 L. 75 A. Item, the next primitive has nothing in common with 亞.

I 𠀃 — T'ou³. A wine vessel, probably wooden made; 酒器也。像形。Is found in

斲 — Cho² To cut, to scoop out; 斫也。从斤。The scribes write 斵, which is a wrong form.

鬭 — Tou₄. To quarrel (L. 11 I).

LESSON 83.

About the primitive 王 yü⁴, jade; and incidently, about the analogous characters 王 wang² and 主 chu³.

First series: 王 yü⁴, often written 玉

A 玉 王 — Yü⁴. The half-translucid minerals, milky or coloured, as jade and others, of which the Chinese are so fond; 石之美者。They ascribe to it different effects, and make with it articles worn at the girdle. The character 王 represents three pieces of jade | threaded; 三玉之連，| 其貫也。The addition of a dot 玉 is modern, and made in order to distinguish yü⁴ from wang². — It is the 95th radical of characters relating to gems It is found in many compounds, e.g. 弄 lung⁴, nêng⁴, to handle 廾 an object made with jade 王, L. 47 F.

B 玨 玉 doubled, forms the next two:

斑 **Pan**[1]. Veined 文 (L. 61 F), like certain nice 王 stones.

班 **Pan**[1]. Division of charges, of offices. The middle is 刂, 刀 (L. 52) in the sense of 分 (L. 18) to divide. The two 王 are two jade sceptres, signs of dignities. L. 55 H. 分瑞玉也。从二王。从刀、會意。

琴 琴 **Ch'in**[2]. Harpsichord of soniferous 玉 stones, hanging from a string. See *Textes Historiques*, p. 82 (one stone). The ancient character represents two stones, and the suspension string (a primitive). Compare L. 17 F — The following characters are said to be derived from **ch'in**[2] (radical contracted; the phonetic is at the bottom): 琴 **ch'in**[4], 瑟 **shê**[4], 琵 **p'i**[2], 琶 **pa**[1], etc., different kinds of citharas or harpsichords.

Second series: 王 **wang**[2].

C 王 王 **Wang**[2]. A king; the man 丨 who connects 三 heaven, earth and man. See L 3 B, where this character was fully explained. — Phonetic series 87. It forms

皇 皇 皇 **Huang**[2]. Originally, it meant the three most renowned rulers of antiquity, 伏羲 **Fu-hsi**, 神農 **Shên-nung**, 黃帝 **Huang-ti**; those who were 王 kings, in the beginning 白 (a contraction of 自 L. 159) 从自、从王、會意。自。始也。始王者、三皇大君也。It was used to designate the modern Emperors, from the year 221 B.C See *Textes Historiques*, p. 209. The 獨斷 gives this definition: «light of the Empire». 皇者煌也。盛德煌煌、無所不照。Compare with the definition of 主, below D. — Phonetic series 452.

閏 閏 **Yün**[4]. **Lün**[4]. Intercalary moon, supplementary. Two explanations of this character are given. — 1. Formerly, in the plenary audience at the Court, when the moon was intercalary, the Emperor 王 sat at the door 門, not in his ordinary place; 天子居明堂、閏月居門中。— 2. Once 丨, every three 三 years, a moon must be intercalated; 門 is phonetic; 三年一閏也、从丨猶一也、指事。从三。無王字。In that case, 閏 is not derived from 王, but directly from 三 L. 3, as 王.

Third series: 主 **chu³**.

D 主 𡳾 **Chu³**. A lamp-stand with the flame rising. By extension, a man who spreads light, a lord, a master. See L. 4 B, where this character was fully explained. — Phonetic series 115.

Note. Do not confound with the derivatives of 王 and of 主, those of 𡉚 L. 79 D; 狂, 往, etc This is more easily said than done.

LESSON 84.

About the primitive 己 **chi³**, to be distinguished from 巳 **i²**, and from 巳 **ssŭ⁴**, L. 85.

A 己 **Chi³**. The ancient character represented the threads of the weft, on the weaving-loom. On the top, two threads transversal, one thread longitudinal; at the bottom, the thread in the shuttle. The character was simplified later on. 古文像．別絲之形。二橫一縱。絲相別也。When 己 was chosen, on account of its simplicity, to become a cyclical character (the sixth of the ten stems), it was replaced by 紀. It means also, **chia-chieh**, a person, one's self, I, myself; 又借爲台。— It is the 49th radical. Phonetic series 14. Note the compounds:

紀 **Chi⁴**. Used for the last: 己 to sort 糸 threads. By extension, 埋也、緒也、arrangement, disposition, set, succession.

記 **Chi⁴**. To 言 tell the succession 己 of facts, either by speaking, or by writing.

起 **Ch'i³**. To rise; to put one's self 己 in motion 走.

妃 **Fei¹**. Women 女 secured for 己 one's own self; 匹也。从女儷己．會意。The secondary wives or concubines of an emperor. Its original meaning, to match, to suit, was given to the next.

配 **P'ei⁴** The wine 酉 drunk at the wedding-feast 妃 (contracted). See L. 47 V. To pair, to mate, marriage.

忌 **Chi⁴**. The series 己 of events or times that are kept in memory 心; death of great men, of parents; 忌日、anniversary day of the death. By extension. because on such days, music, spirits, meat, etc. were avoided, the character meant, to shun, to abstain from. — Phonetic series 256.

Note. The derivatives of 己 **chi³** are often scarcely distinguishable from those of 巳 **ssŭ⁴** and 㠯 **i³** (L. 85), when these are wrongly shaped; as well as from those of 㔾 (for 卩 L 55), as in 巽. **K'ang-hsi** wrongly classified this character under **chi³**. On their side, the scribes commonly maltreated those series, as may be seen by the characters given above.

LESSON 85.

About two primitives, 巳 **ssŭ⁴** and 㠯 **i³**, to be distinguished from 己 **chi³**, L. 84. **K'ang-hsi** gathered under the 49th radical 己, all those heterogeneous elements.

First series: 巳 **ssŭ⁴**.

A 巳

Ssŭ⁴. The figure of an embryo, a fœtus See 包 **pao¹**, L. 54 B. — In the maternal womb, the child is 巳 or 包; at birth, 𠫓 or 㐬 L. 94 E, F; when swaddled, 子 L. 94 A; when it begins to walk, 兒 29 B. — **Ssŭ⁴** is used as a cyclical character. — Phonetic series **28**. Note the derivatives

祀 **Ssŭ⁴**. Sacrifice 祭也、从示、巳聲，國之大事也。See 示 L. 3 D.

𦣞 **I²**. The chin; 从 𦣝 (L. 82 G), 巳 聲。It forms

熙 **Hsi¹**. Bright, splendid, glorious.

Second series: 㠯 **i³**.

B 㠯 已 厶 目 以

I³. This very ancient character is supposed to represent the exhalation of the breath, the virtue that emanates from any object, its action, its use. By extension, use till exhaustion, to terminate, to decline, to have done with, to be no more, passed; 像形，物之實也。用也。Compare L. 73 A, and L. 76 G.

Note: 㠯 is uniform in the ancient writing. In the modern writing, it is written by the scribes in four different ways, 巳、目、厶 and 以, that we shall explain successively

C 1. 㠯 written 巳, e.g.

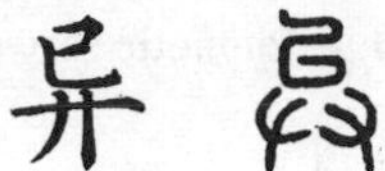

I². To extract 人 from a thing 㠯 all that can be extracted from it, *then*, to stop, to finish.

Kai³. To treat a person or a thing 攴 (with hand and rod), so that amendment is 㠯 produced; to change, to alter, to reform, to correct.

D 2. 㠯 written 目, e.g.

相

Ssŭ⁴. Plough-beam and handle; the 木 wood that 㠯 fertilizes the fields. It is unconnected with 𠂤 L. 86 B.

E 3. 㠯 written 厶 in the following series. (Note that 厶 is used as an abbreviation for three other primitives, L.L. 38 E, 38 H, 89 A; hence an easy confusion).

台

I². The mouth 口 exhaling a 㠯 breath. By extension, to speak in order to make one's self known; I, one's self; 說也。It is used as an arbitrary abbreviation of 臺 t'ai² (L. 75 B). — Phonetic series 127.

允

Yün³. To manifest one's consent, one's approbation. A 儿 man who 㠯 says *yes*. See L. 29 E. — Phonetic series 99. Forms the phonetic complex

Tsun¹. To walk 夂 with dignity — Phonetic series 311.

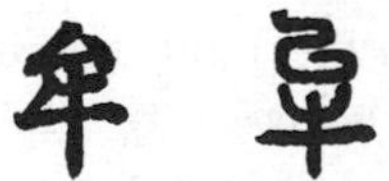

Mou². To low, to bellow. An 牛 ox that exhales its 㠯 breath; 牛鳴也。从牛、㠯像其聲。气從口出。See L. 132. — Phonetic series 231.

I³. A final particle denoting that one has 矢 finished to 㠯 speak; 語已詞也。The 矢 dart (L. 131) means that the action is ended, fixed, as when the arrow has hit the mark. Compare 必 L. 71 E. — Phonetic series 280.

能 䏻 **Nêng**². Here 㠯 represents the roaring of the angry bear, that stands up ready for a fight (月 the fleshy body, two 匕 claws). See L. 27 J. — Phonetic series 554.

F 4. 㠯 written 以. By, with, to use, by means of; 用也。**K'ang-hsi** counts five strokes for this character, that really has four only. — Phonetic series 65. It forms

似 佀 **Ssŭ**⁴. A 亻 man who has the same 㠯 virtue as another. By extension, 像也。類也。equivalent, like, similar, to resemble in general

LESSON 86.

About two primitives, that really form only one, because they differ only by plus or minus strokes of the same kind; 𠂤 **fu**⁴, and 𠂤 **tui**¹.

First series: 𠂤 **fu**⁴, now 阜.

A 𨸏 𨸏 𠂤 阜 阝 **Fu**⁴. Compare 厂 L. 59 A. Declivity with successive rows superposed. The steps are placed under 厂, so that the compounds may not be too large. In the first ancient form, the three small rounds represent a forest on the top. The scribes invented the modern arbitrary abbreviations. By extension, big earthworks, embankments, dams. — It is the 170th radical and distinguished from the 163th radical 邑 (also contracted into 阝), by the fact that 阝 is on the left side in the Series 170, while it is on the right side in the Series 163 Note the two derivatives, 陰 **yin**¹, the shady side of a hill (North); and 陽 **yang**², the sunny side of a hill (South). It is now used to mean the dual powers, day and night, life and death, male and frmale, etc.

陰 陽

Second series: 𠂤 tui[1].

B

Tui[1]. A lighter declivity; two steps only. By extension, ramparts, city, troops that keep it, a legion. The 𠂤 lost its 丿 in some modern compounds; it is then to be distinguished from 㠯 i[3] (L. 85 D). — Phonetic series 245. Note the derivatives

Shuai[4]. To lead 巾 a 𠂤 legion; a general; 从巾、將軍也。The 巾 (L. 35 A) is the guidon of the commander. Compare the following

Shih[1]. It is — the first 巾 banner, that staid at 𠂤 the capital; the guards, whose commander was commander-in-chief, the one above the others. Hence, by extension, capital, army, multitude, master, etc. — The old forms are made of a primitive that means waving, and 帀 tsa[1] (L. 79 C) that means rolling. A waving and rolling mass; the people or the army. — Phonetic series 561.

Chui[1] Legion 𠂤 in march 辵; 逐也。to pursue. — Phonetic series 526

Nieh[4]. A 屮 plant that grows on a 𠂤 declivity. Compare L. 59 F Notion of visibility, of notoriety. It forms

Nieh[4]. Evil deed, sin; scandal; 从辛 (L. 102 H), 罪也。This character not being easy to write, the scribes replaced it by the derivative contracted 薛 (properly hsieh[1], hsüeh[1]), in the phonetic compound 孽, son 子 of sin, child born in adultery. The 字學舉隅 admitted the change.

Kui[1]. The arrival 止 of the bride in her husband's family, to which she will belong as a wife 婦 (contracted). See L. 44 K. The 𠂤 is a modern phonetic redundancy.

C 

Kuan^1. Primitive meaning, the residence of a mandarin who presides over a city, the 宀 hall of the 𠂤 city, (𠂤 is the modern abbreviation) By extension, the mandarin, the government. — Phonetic series 370.

LESSON 87.

About the primitive 弓 **kung^1**, and incidentally about the primitives 弗 **fu^4** and 弟 **ti^4**, that resemble it in the modern writing.

First series: 弓 kung^1.

A 弓

Kung^1. It represents a Chinese bow, with its handle in the middle; 兵也。所以發矢。像。The ancient forms represent the bow bent or vibrating. — It is the 57th radical. We have seen it already, in 弔 L. 28 H, 夷 L. 60 D, etc. For 躬, see L 90 L, 强 L. 110 B. Note the following

引

Yin^3. To draw the 丨 string of the 弓 bow; 開弓也。从弓、从丨、會意。Chuan-chu, to attract, to lead, to induce, to seduce. — Phonetic series 93.

B 弜

Ch'iang^2. Muscular strength. To have the strength to bend a kind of 弓 bow, the resistance of which is equal to the resistance of *two* ordinary bows. In the military competitions, such exercises took place.

Note 1. The bows were kept by pairs, fixed upon a stiff piece of wood, in a sheath. Hence it comes that, sometimes, in composition, two 弓 mean a pair, or that which makes the pair, a second; as in

弼 **Pi^4**. Auxiliary, minister. See L. 41 B.

Note 2. In the following, the scribes fancifully wrote 弓 for another thing.

弱 **Jao^4**. Feeble, fragile, slender. Wings of a young bird. See L. 62 D.

Li^1. A caldron 鬲 (L. 155) steaming (the two side-lines undulating represent the steam).

Chou^1. Rice water or gruel; 米 grain that boils in a 鬲 caldron. This last character is now contracted into 粥.

C The bow 弓 is kept horizontally, in the following, as it is natural, to shoot a bird that flies above the bowman.

Tsun4. To shoot a bird on the wing; 从弓所以射隹。會意。— Phonetic series 714.

Note: 隽 is a wrong form of **tsun**4.

雟 is a wrong abbreviation of 巂 **hsi**1, L. 15 C.

Second series. 弗 **fu**4. Primitive.

D 

Fu4. To act against an obstacle. Two divergent rods which one seeks to tie together; 从丿、从乀像。束之形 Opposition, prohibition, negation. — Phonetic series 121

Third series. 弟 **ti**4. Primitive.

E 

Ti4. A thread that is wound on a spool, having a catch on the top, and a winch at the bottom. Primitive instrument, reef and bobbin. Compare 庚 L. 102 B. — **Chuan-chu**, succession of brothers, elder, younger; succession; younger brothers; 弟也。相次弟而生也。— Phonetic series 304.

Note. 㢴 **tzŭ**3 that is like 弟 **ti**4, has nothing in common with it, nor with 弓. See L. 79 G.

LESSON 88.

About the partial primitive 白, and incidentally about 樂,

First series. 白 **pai**2.

A  

Pai2. The 日 sun (L. 143) that just appears. This meaning is represented by a small point (primitive) on the top of the sun. The dawn, when the Eastern sky becomes white 白. Clear, white, bright, etc. 像。日未出。初生微光。— It is the 106th radical. Phonetic series 143.

We saw already 白 in the compounds 皃 L. 29 C; 貟 L. 18 L; 臬 L. 60 F, etc. Note the following:

Pai^{2}. From 巾 cloth, and 白 white. See 緜 **mien^{2}**, L 92 B. — Phonetic series 386.

B 百

Pai^{3}. One hundred; 从一，白聲。百亦一也。故从一。One hundred is the — unity of hundreds; 白 is phonetic. Other commentators, judging from an ancient writing, consider 白 as a 自 contracted (L. 159); but 自 meaning the beginning, the interpretation is the same. It is to be noted that all the great unities of the Chinese numeration, hundred, thousand, myriad, are designated by borrowed characters. See 24 D, 17 X. — Phonetic series 233. It is repeated in 奭 **shih^{4}**, abundance, wealth A man 大 with one hundred 百 under each arm ; 盛也。

Second series, 樂 **yao^{4}**, **lao^{4}**, a special partial primitive.

C 樂

Yao^{4} It represents a wooden 木 support on which 白 a drum and 幺 bells are hung. Therefore 白 is not **pai^{2}**, and 幺 is not **yao^{1}** (L. 90). — The orchestrion of old **Yao^{4}**, music in general. When read **lao^{4}**, it means the effect produced by music, pleasure, joy. Phonetic series 815.

LESSON 89.

About the primitive 厶 **ssŭ^{1}**. See the Note, below B. Compare LL. 90, 91, 92.

A 厶

Ssŭ^{1}. A cocoon. It represents a silkworm that coils itself up, and shuts itself in its cocoon. By extension, selfish, to care only for one's self, separation, private, particular; 蠶自環者謂之厶。自營爲厶。— It is the conventional 28th radical. The following compound replaced 厶 in the modern writing

私

Ssŭ^{1}. Etymological meaning, my 厶 share of 禾 grains. By extension, private, personal, partial, selfish; 反公爲私。— Note also

篡 **Ch'uan^4**. To calculate 算 (L. 47 G) one's own 厶 advantage (at the others' expense). To embezzle, to assume, to usurp. 逆而奪取曰簒。

B **Note**. The scribes used 厶 as an abbreviation for three other primitives (LL. 38 E, 38 H, and 85 E), which makes four in all; hence an easy confusion between them. Further, the scribes still use arbitrarily 厶 for other intricate characters, in which case 厶 is an abbreviation, and not a primitive. Note the following

壘 垒 **Lei^3**. To build a wall. L. 149 E.

曑 叅 **Shên^1**. Orion. L. 62 G.

齊 亝 **Ch'i^2**. A regular assemblage. L. 174.

LESSON 90.

About 厶 doubled 幺, and its multiples; incidentally about 呂.

First series. 幺 yao^1.

A 幺  **Yao^1**. The lightest thread, as it is obtained by the simultaneous winding of two ○ cocoons. By extension, thread, slender, tender, 細小也。— It is the 52th radical. Note the compounds

麼 **Ma^1, mo^1**. Vegetable 麻 fibre 幺 (L. 79 H). It is now used, by convention, as an interrogative particle.

幼  **Yu^4**. Young, slender, who has very 幺 slender 力 tendons. Not to be confounded with 幻 **huan^4**, false, L. 95 B. — Phonetic series 171.

後  **Hou^4**. To march 彳 (63 A), while stretching a 幺 thread behind. The 夊 is a radical redundancy added later on. By extension, to follow, behind, posterior, after.

B 亂 辭

Luan^4. An embroiled 幺 thread, that is disentangled by two hands 彡 彐; 冂 (L. 34 A) means separation; 會意。理也。治也。Confusion, disorder. Note the alteration of the modern character. It forms

Luan^4. A synonym of the last; 乙 representing the thread that is drawn 指事, is a radical redundancy.

Ts'ŭ^2. To clear one's self from a 辛 sin (L. 102 H); to excuse one's self; 猶理辜也。

C 胤

Yin$_4$. A line of posterity, heirs, generation Transmission 幺 of the 月 (L. 65) ancestors' substance, that is 八 divided into branches. The continuous succession, in a family, of one generation after another; 从肉、从八、猶分祖父之遺體也。从幺、如之繼絲續也。會意。

Second series. 幺 doubled.

D 𢆶

Yu^1. It is the meaning of 幺 reinforced. Very slender, almost invisible; 从二幺、會意。微也。It forms

幽

Yu^1. The most shady 𢆶 recesses in the 山 hills (L. 80); 山之隱處也。

幾

Chi^1. A guard of soldiers on the frontiers 戍 (**shu**^{4}, L. 25 D), who are attentive to the least 𢆶 movement, to the smallest event. Hence the derived meanings, to examine into, subtle, hidden, small, a few; 微也。从𢆶、从戍、會意。— Phonetic series 667.

茲

are derived from 絲 contracted. See L. 92 F, G.

Third series. 幺 quadrupled. In

E

Chüeh^2. To cut short a thread, to interrupt, to sunder, to break off, to cease. Four threads 幺 cut short, divided by the two 𠃊; 像。不連體。絕二絲拔𠃊者、指事。This ancient character was replaced, when the writing-brush was invented, by 絕 **chüeh**^{2}, that is synonym; 刀 to cut a 糸 thread in 卩 pieces. See L. 55 G. It forms

斷 𣃔 **Tuan⁴**. To cut, to break off, to interrupt; 截也。From an 斤 axe, and 𢇍 to cut, 會意。The ancient character 𢇍 could not be traced with the writing-brush; it was therefore written 㡭 **chi⁴** in the modern writing, hence 斷 instead of 𣃔, which is graphically wrong. Note the modern junction of the two ㇄.

㡭 繼 **Chi⁴**. It means the contrary of 𢇍 **chüeh²**, because it is **chüeh²** inverted. Later on, the 糸 was added, which was quite useless. To connect as with threads; a line of succession; 續也。反𢇍爲㡭。

Appendix. 呂 lü³, almost similar to 幺 in its ancient form.

F 呂 **Lü³**. The spinal vertebrae. A primitive character that represents the body of two vertebrae, and the disk that joins them; or rather, two spinal apophysises, with the ligament between them. 脊骨也。像形。By extension, tones in music, on account of their succession. — Phonetic series 291. It forms

躬 **Kung¹**. To bend, to bow one's body 身, so that the spinal apophysises 呂 stand out along the rachis. Later on, 弓 replaced 呂, the meaning remaining the same; 弓 to bend one's body 身. By extension, body, person. — It forms 窮 **ch'iung²**, to be at bay, exhausted, driven into a corner (穴 cavern); misery; limits, end.

Note. The ○ in the following characters are probably primitives unconnected with 呂.

G **Yung¹**. An old form of 邕. Moats 巛 of a 呂 city (two walls or buildings). L. 12 G.

營 **Ying¹**. Encampment, a primitive settlement. In the more ancient form, there are two (several) tents or huts. In the modern form, there are huts with a fence, and two 火 fires, for the kitchen, or to frighten away the wild beasts. By extension, to measure, to scheme, to regulate. Compare 34 B, 126 F.

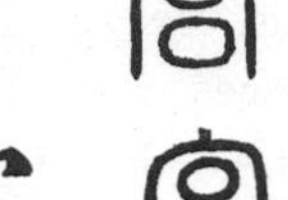

Kung¹. A big building. Several ◯ rooms under the same 宀 roof. This character is used to designate the Imperial private residence, from the 秦 **Ch'in**² Dynasty. Now, in 宮 and 營, it is written 呂 and not 吕.

LESSON 91.

About two compounds of 幺 (L. 90), 玄 and 叀, that form important series.

First series. 玄 hsüan².

A

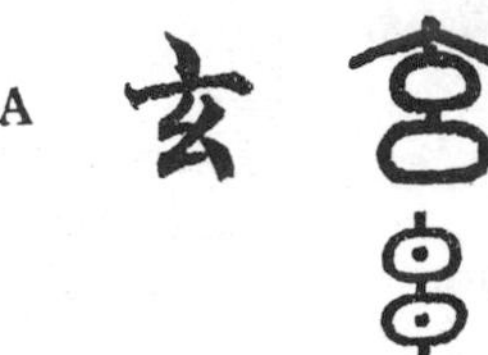

Hsüan². To put 入 (L. 15) the thread 幺 in the dye; dyed thread; *green* colour (later on, the *black* one, on account of certain Taoist theories). Under the 淸 **Ch'ing** Dynasty, the 丶 of 玄 was suppressed, because this was the personal name of the Emperor **K'ang-hsi**. An ancient form was composed of 糸 thread (L. 92), and of two points that mean the dyeing; 指事。— It is the 96th radical. Phonetic series 124. — In composition, 玄 means, either *green*, or a *string* (probably because the thread was dyed by big hanks). Note the derivatives

弦 絃

Hsien². The string of a bow 弓. Stringed instruments in general. 玄 is altered, as stated above.

B 畜

Ch'u⁴. **Hsü**⁴. The 田 fields (L. 149) 玄 green, covered with grass; meadows, pasture-lands where the cattle graze. Hence two meanings, and two sounds: **ch'u**⁴ 爲 嘼 cattle; **hsü**⁴ 爲 養 to feed. — Phonetic series 525.

C

Ch'ien¹. To haul along an ox 牛 by a rope 玄; 冖 represents the traction or the resistance; 从牛、从玄、冖像。引牛之縻也。— Phonetic series 600.

D

Shuai⁴. It represents a net with a frame, such as birds are snared with, and a 玄 rope by meaas of which the trap is made to fall. By extension, to draw, to lead, to follow; together (the birds taken); suddenly (the falling of the net). — Phonetic series 646.

Second series. 叀 ch'uan[1].

E 叀

Ch'uan[1]. Some commentators say that this character is a contraction of 牛 and 幺; it seems unlikely. «It is an ox led by a ring passed through the nose», says the Glose; why then is this ring marked at the tail? More seemingly, the transversal piece fixed behind the horns represents the yoke or the collar of the ox, and the one trace passing under the animal is the primitive harness; extremity curved to diminish the length. By extension, to attach, to draw, traction, resistance, to master. — It forms

F 專

Chuan[1]. A writing tablet that was worn 叀 attached to the 寸 wrist; 从叀。从寸、手版也。— Phonetic series 605, that must be distinguished from the series 尃 fu[1] 528.

G 惠

Hui[4]. It has two meanings: to let one's self be 心 willingly 叀 attracted; kind, compliant: what wins 叀 the 心 hearts; benevolence. — Phonetic series 689.

H 袁

Yüan[2]. A long robe 衣 with a 叀 trail, that hinders and slakens the walk; length, hesitation. Here 叀 lost its middle-part and is gone through by the cover 亠 of 衣. — Phonetic series 587. It forms

瞏 睘

Huan[2]. Eyes 罒 (L. 158) anxious, and gait 袁 hesitating; fear, trouble, strait. The modern form is contracted. — Phonetic series 734. See L. 16 L.

I 疐

T'i[4]. Traction 叀 interrupted by a ⊢ resistance; 从叀引而止之也。礙不行也。Compare L. 91 C. The modern character is a contraction. K'ang-hsi wrongly classified it under 疋. — It forms

嚏 𪖐

T'i[4]. Sneezing. A victory won against the obstruction of the 鼻 nose (or of the 口 mouth, a different writing); 悟解氣也。

LESSON 92.

About the partial primitive 糸, and its derivatives. See again the whole series, after 厶 **ssŭ**^{1}, LL. 89, 90, 91, **92.** The textile matters, chiefly the silk, interested the Chinese from the remotest antiquity; hence the importance given to these elements in their writing.

First series. 糸 mi^{4}.

A 糸

Mi^{4}. A strong thread; 絲綫也。像。The bottom of this character (a primitive) represents the twisting of several small threads into a big one (L. 90 A). — It is the 120th radical of characters relating to textile matters or tissues.

We saw that element in 細 L. 40 A; 絕 L. 55 G; 終 L. 17 E; 素 L. 13 H; 索 L. 79 G; 繁 L. 67 P; 羅 L. 39 D; 繭 L. 35 M; etc.

B 系

Hsi^{1}. Drawing out of the thread. Primitively, 爪 a hand drawing out threads 糸. Later on, 丿 the action of drawing out a 糸 thread. By extension, thread, line, succession, relation, to tie again, to fasten; 連也。續也。統於上而屬於下、謂之系。The compound 係 is used instead now. Note the derived following radicals

緜

Mien^{2}. Fibres 系 raw 帛 (L. 88 A), raw floss. It is contracted phonetic in 綿 **mien**^{2}, cotton; and in 棉 **mien**^{2}, the cotton plant. These are modern characters. See phonetic series 386.

孫

Sun^{1}. A grandson, posterity. The connecting 系 line of the 子 offspring; 子之子曰孫。从子、从系、會意。系續也。— Phonetic series 569. It is phonetic contracted in 鯀 **kun**^{3}, big fish.

繇

Yu^{2}. Succession, sequel, causality, relation; 从系。䍃聲。隨從也。歸也。Winding of the effects from a cause; moral threads.

縣

Hsien^{4}. **Hsüan**^{2}. The chief-town of a district, **hsien**^{4}, where the executions take place, and where are hung, upside down, the 県 (L. 12 N) heads of the men beheaded because 系 they committed crimes. By extension, **hsüan**^{2}, to bind, to suspend, to be suspended. Now, the compound 懸, to be in suspense 心 morally, is also used for the simple in the sense, to hang, to be suspended,

C 奚

Hsi[1]. Primitively, the guilty women condemned to spinning and weaving in the official prisons, 官婢。 It is explained thus: 大 persons (L. 60), 彡 working (L. 49) the thread 糸 (contracted). It seems rather that 大 is a corruption of the bottom of 糸, and that the primitive composition was 彡 糸, a spinster. This punishment having ceased, this character's meaning was altered, and it became an interrogative particle, what? how? why? — Phonetic series 533.

Second series. 絲 ssŭ[1].

D 絲

Ssŭ[1]. The silk-threads, that the silk-worms are supposed to spit out; 蠶所吐也。从二糸、會意。 By extension, according to the compound, thread, link, intricacy, etc. Note the following derivatives often contracted:

轡

P'ei[4]. The two 糸 reins of a bridle passed in the 口 mouth of the animal that draws a 車 car; 縻也。會意。

䜌

Luan[4]. Primitively, a hand 彡 busy in disentangling three 糸 threads, the common main stem of which is contracted into 十... 紊像、彡分理之。Intricacy. This action of disentangling any intricate matter, when done in common, leads to impatience and quarrelling, hence the character became later on 絲, increased with 言; general meaning, disorder, quarrelling, trouble, discord; 會意。亂也、煩也。 — Phonetic series 846.

E 㬎

Hsien[3]. Two 糸 silk threads exposed to the sunlight 日, where they become visible; 从日中視絲。會意。 By extension, to be visible, to appear, remarkable, evident, bright. Note the modern contraction at the bottom of the character. — Phonetic series 778. It forms

顯 **Hsien**[3]. A tuft that makes the 頁 head 㬎 conspicuous. 會意。首飾之光明也。It is now used for 㬎, to appear. The latter is contracted in

溼 **Shih**[1]. A marsh, marshy, wet, humid; 氵 water in which the 土 earth appears; 一 is for 日; the 幺幺 were suppressed, to give room to 土.

F 兹

Tzŭ[1]. The 絲 velvety appearance made by 艸 the herbs and grass on the surface of the earth; the vegetation; 艸多意也。从艸。从絲省。Contraction of 絲 into 丝。 Compare L. 91 B. This character became obsolete in that sense, and is now used as a demonstrative particle. — Phonetic series 579.

G

Kuan[1]. To weave. The two 絲 (contracted into 丝) represent the threads of the warp. The down strokes (a primitive) represent the action of the shuttle, that goes through and through, making the woof. Compare L. 84 A. By extension, to join, to fix, transversal, etc. It forms

關 **Kuan**[1]. The cross-bar of a gate, to shut up; 以木横持門戶也。

聯 **Lien**[2]. To connect, to join, to link together.

LESSON 93.

About the primitive 云.

A 云

Yün[2]. Clouds. The ancient form, that represents vapours curling and rising, is a primitive. The more recent form is composed of 二 (上, L. 2 G) the skies, and of the same primitive. — Phonetic series 99. Now the meaning *clouds* is given to the following, while 云 means chia-chieh, to *speak*, to *enumerate*, etc. 言也。曰也。助語之詞。

B 雲

Yün[2]. Clouds; 从雨。从云。會意。凡地面溼熱之氣。上騰至冷際。則散爲雨。When the humid and warm vapours have reached the colder regions, they are condensed there. Not a bad explanation of the production of clouds.

C 侌

Yin[1]. Cloudy weather; 从今。从云。會意。雲覆日也。Actually 今, there are 云 clouds. See L. 14 P.

D

Clouds rolling over the 田 fields; an ancient form of 雷 storm, L. 149 F. Compare the old form of 日 L. 73 A, 回 L. 76 G, 㠯 L. 85 B, etc.

LESSON 94.

About the important primitive 子 straight, 𠫓 inverted.

First series. 子 **tzŭ**³ straight.

A 子

Tzŭ³. A new-born child, swathed up; it is the reason why the legs are not visible, says the Glose; 像形。兒在襁褓中。足併也。In an ancient form, the child has hair; 古文从巛。像髮也。By extension, disciple; *then*, a sage, a teacher, because the ancient Emperors, in order to honour them, call them 子 *sons*. 古者士通曰子、尊之也。— It is the 39th radical of characters mostly relating to children. Phonetic series 33. We saw already 子 in 孫 L. 92 B; 孝 L. 30 E; 孶 L. 39 H; 學 L. 39 I; 李 L. 79 G; etc. Add the following:

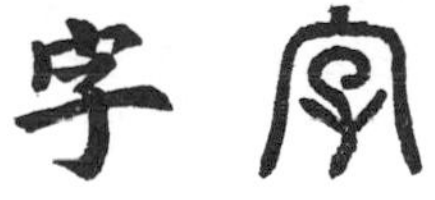

Tzŭ⁴. To bear and nurse; to have 子 children in one's 宀 house; 會意。By extension, the compound characters (by opposition to the simple 文 figures), *begotten* by the process of composition 會意 and 諧聲 (see p. 10). The 文 made by their authors gave birth to the 字、says the Glose.

孔

K'ung³. The swallow 乚 (L. 9 B) which in China rears its 子 broods in the fissures and holes of the Chinese mud houses; 从乚、从子、會意。By extension, a hole, an orifice, an opening. Compare 乳 L. 94 B.

汓

Fu². A man 子 who swims 氵. There is 子, and not 大 or 人, because the legs of the swimmer are concealed by the water, as those of the child are concealed by its long clothes. It is now written 浮, which is a nonsensical compound; 行水上也。从水、从子、會意。Forms 游 yu², to float, 117 B. Note its dissociation into 氵 and 子, on the both sides of 㫃.

李

Li³. A prune, a plum-tree; 木 the tree, the 子 children are fond of; 从木、从子、李果也。

季

Chi⁴. Infant; 从子、从稚省、會意。幼也。The most 稚 (contracted) delicate among the children 子, the youngest, the last. By extension, the last month of each quarter of the year, that ends the season; hence the derived meaning, season.

B 呆

Pao³. A bird which 八 spreads its wings to cover its nest 子; to hatch, to protect. It is now written 呆, that is to be distinguished from 呆 **tai¹**, a modern invention of the scribes. It forms

保 **Pao³.** To protect, to feed, to keep safe, 人 a man; 養也。— Phonetic series 471.

孚 **Fu².** A hen-bird covering with her legs 爫 her 子 little ones; to hatch. — Phonetic series 270. It forms

乳 **Ju³.** The swallow 乙 (L. 9 B) sitting on its 孚 nest. See 孔 L. 94 A. Now, in general, what is required to rear the offspring of men, or the little ones of animals: to feed, to suckle, etc. 養子曰乳。

This is another character, containing the elements of **fu²** and of **pao³**. The hen-bird covers her nest 子, with her 爫 legs, and her 八 wings. It forms the next two:

Pao³. Another way of writing 保.

Pao¹. A phonetic compound. Long robes such as the Emperors give; favour, distinction. The scribes altered this character in many fanciful ways, 褒 褎 褏 襃, etc.

C 

Luan². To bear twins. Formerly, there were two 子; then the scribes wrote but one; 䜌 (L. 92 D) represents the encumbering, the difficulty in the bearing and rearing of twins.

D 孨

Ch'uan¹. Many sons. It forms

Ch'uan¹. A numerous family filling the house; 从三子. 从尸猶从屋也。窄也。 By extension, poverty, misery. See L. 32 G.

Second series. 𠫓 t'u^{2}, which is 子 inverted.

E 𠫓

T'u^{2}. Birth of a child 子, the head forward, in the most favourable conditions; hence the extended meaning 順之意, a thing that goes on fluently; natural, regular, easy, fluent. The hairy form (compare 子, above A), makes a special group (below F). Note the derivatives

充

Ch'ung^{1}. To feed, to rear a child, from its 𠫓 birth till when it 儿 stands, and becomes a man. By extension, to fulfil, to satiate, to carry out, perfect, etc. See L 29 F. — Phonetic series 189.

育

Yü^{4}. To satisfy, to feed a 𠫓 child (or an animal), so that it becomes 月 fleshy (L. 65), strong, fat. The physical breeding. It forms

Chê^{4}. Education, both 育 physical and 攴 moral. We know that the rod is the instrument used for the latter. Compare 教 L. 39 H. — Phonetic series 665.

F 㐬

T'u^{2}. A synonym of 𠫓, with the hair added; 巛像髮也。— Phonetic series 312. Note the following radical compounds:

流

Liu^{2}. The flowing 㐬 (natural and easy) of 氵 water. There were primitively two 水, one on each side; the scribes left out one of them; 水行也。

疏

Shu^{1}. Birth of a child 㐬, the feet 疋 (L. 112 C) coming forwards. See 𠫓 (L. 94 E). By extension, unnatural, uneasy; anomaly, difference, distance, etc.

毓

Yü^{4}. Rise 㐬 and growing of 每 plants (L. 67 P); 生養草木也。

醯

Hsi^{1}. Sour, vinegar. Wine 酉 in a 皿 vase, in which 㐬 appear animalculæ 醯雞, the sign that the wine turns into vinegar.

G 棄

Ch'i^{4}. To push aside, to cast away, to abandon. An ancient form represents two hands repulsing a new-born. A more recent form represents two hands, armed with a fork or a shovel, that throw away a new-born. An allusion to the Chinese infanticide. This character was used to name 后稷 **Hou-chi**, who was cast away by his mother 姜原 **Chiang-yüan**. See the **Shih-Ching**, Legge's edition, p. 465.

Third series. 子 altered.

H 孑 **Chieh**². One-armed person; 从子像、缺右臂指事。 Here it is the right arm that is taken off. The symmetrical character in which the left arm was taken away, existed formerly; it is now obsolete.

了 **Liao**³. A child without arms, mutilated; 从子無臂、指事。 This character, being very easy to write, and of no use, had its primitive meaning changed into different arbitrary ones. It is now used specially to write the suffix **liao**³, so frequent in the spoken language. Note the philological definition of the part it plays in that case; 發聲之詞、猶言結; emission of a sound, in order to knot, to end a sentence.

LESSON 95.

About two primitives 予 and 矛, joined here together on account of their resemblance in the modern writing.

First series. 予 yü².

A 

Yü². To pass from hand to hand, to hand down, to give, communication, connexion; 像、相與之形。 The character represents the palm of two hands, one of them giving, and the other receiving. The modern form is not a credit to the scribes. Compare 與 L, 54 H. **Chia-chieh**, I, we, myself. Phonetic series 96. It forms

Chu¹. The shuttle of the weaver; the 木 wood that passes 予 from one hand to the other. The second form is to be distinguished from 柔 **jou**², below C.

Shu¹. To give out 予 one's goods 舍 to the others (L. 14 C). By extension, to unroll, to expand, at ease.

Yü⁴. An elephant 象 that 予 passes backwards and forwards, that frolics. Derived meanings, indecision, uncertainty; to frolic; in advance, to prepare.

Hsü⁴. The East and West halls of the Chinese houses, in which traditional instruction 予 was given, and where the transactions took place. These halls were connected with the principal buildings; hence the derived meaning, a series, order, preface to a book in which the subjects are stated in order, etc.

壄 野 野

Yeh^3. In the primitive 國 fiefs established in wild regions, **yeh**^{3} was the intermediate zone between the cleared 郊 centre, and the forest 林 all around; the zone where cultivation of the 土 soil began. It was in that zone, that the communications 予 took place with the barbarians. Later on, when the clearing of forests was finished, the character became 里 settlements (L. 149 D), where the 予 exchanges are made. Actual meaning, the country, rustic, wild. Compare 樊 L. 47 Z.

B 幻

Huan^4. Fraud, deceiving, false. It is 予 inverted. To give things *differing* from those expected, or to give an *empty* hand, to deceive, to frustrate. The frustration of the beggar's hopes is graphically represented by 予 inverted. 相詐惑也。从到予、指事。The modern abbreviation is absurd. Not to be confounded with 幼 **yu**^{4}, L. 90 A.

Second series. 矛 **mao**^{2}.

C 矛 

Mao^2. A kind of halberd, with a very long staff, such as were used on chariots, to hook fighting men. 像形。Compare 戈 L. 71 F. **Chuan-chu**, arms, weapons sharp or cutting, a long and slender pole. — It is the 110th radical. It forms

矜

Ching^1. The handle of a 矛 spear; 矛柄也。今聲。By extension, to pity, to spare. It represents probably the warrior who surrenders, by offering the handle of his spear.

矞 矞

Yü^4. To pierce 冏 with a 矛 sharp instrument (L. 15 C). — Phonetic series 720.

柔 柔

Jou^2. A 矛 slender 木 stem, flexible, elastic, pliant; 木曲直也。— Phonetic series 455.

楙 楙

Mao^4. Trees 林 shooting forth 矛 branches, many shoots, luxuriant, to strive. Forms 懋 **mao**^{4}, moral effort, to exert one's self, merit, glory.

敄 **Wu**[4]. To display one's skill in 攴 wielding 矛 arms. Now 務, a radical redundancy, to exert one's 力 strength, one's talents, to strife after. — Phonetic series 491.

LESSON 96.

About the primitive 才 ts'ai[2].

A 才 **Ts'ai**[2]. This character represents the stem of a plant forcing its way above the ground. (Compare 屯, 㞢、生, L. 79 A, B, F, etc). | represents the stem; on the top, 一 represents its branches; at the bottom, 一 represents the ground; 草木之初也。从丨引而上行也，上卽草之枝葉也。下地也。會意。By extension, strength of expansion, natural activity, mental capacity, power, talents, endowments or gifts; the substance of a thing. — Phonetic series 30. It forms

材 **Ts'ai**[2]. Materials 才 of which things are made. From 木 wood and 才 talent, the wood being the first material worked by men.

財 **Ts'ai**[2]. Property, precious things, wealth; the 貝 cowries 才 acquired by a man.

豺 **Ch'ai**[2]. The wolf, an animal (豸 or 犭) very clever 才, say the Chinese.

B 𢦏 **Ts'ai**[2]. Skilfulness in 才 wielding 戈 weapons (L. 71 F); to wound with weapons, to injure; ts'ai[2] is also a phonetic. — Phonetic series 241.

C 閉 **Pi**[4]. To shut a 門 door; 才所以歫門也。像形。Here 才 represents a system of bars to shut the door. Compare 門 L. 1 H.

D 在 **Tsai**[4]. To exert one's activity 才 on the 土 earth; presence in a 土 place, manifested by one's 才 activity. By extension, to be in or at, to be present, to live, to act; 於亡。爲對文。— The following is derived from 在, the 子 being substituted for 土.

存 **Ts'un**[2]. To continue to be 在, present by one's 子 offspring. By extension, to maintain, to preserve, to continue.

LESSON 97.

About the primitives 丰 fêng¹ and 丯 chieh⁴. Not to be confounded with 手 (L. 48), nor with 毛 (L. 100).

First series. 丰 fêng¹.

A 丰

Fêng¹. Some philologists say that this character is 生 (L. 79 F), that strikes down its tap root; 从生上下達、指事。The study of the compounds makes this opinion improbable. 丰 is a primitive, representing a leafy bough. By extension, bush, brushwood, hedge. It forms

奉

Fêng⁴. At the bottom a 手 hand, offering a 丰 branch (a symbol for any object), while two hands 𠬞 salute respectfully. Now the top part is strangely altered. To offer, to receive. See L. 47 L. — Phonetic series 354.

夆

Fêng¹. To 夂 walk in the 丰 brushwoods. By extension, to meet opposition; to meet; 遇也、啎也。— Phonetic series 269. Now

Fêng¹. A synonym of the last; 辶 is a radical redundancy. To meet with one, to come across, etc. — Phonetic series 608.

邦

Pang¹. A fief, a country; 邑 the central city; 丰 represents probably the bushy outskirts.— The scribes often write this character 邦.

Sub-series. 丰 doubled. The ancient form has different writings.

B

Fêng¹. Boughs, shoots, vitality, prosperity, abundance. It forms

彗

Hui⁴. A broom. A hand 彐 that holds a bundle of 丰丰 branches. See the explanation, and the derivative 雪, L. 44 J. — Phonetic series 617.

豐

Li⁴. A vessel used in sacrificing; 行禮之器也。从豆 (vessel, L. 165), 像形。二丰、像，滿形。The top has nothing in common with 曲 (L. 51 B); it is a cup (L. 38 E), in which is pricked a bunch of green branches for decoration; symbol of plenty. — Phonetic series 744.

豐

Fêng[1]. Prosperity, plenty. It seems that the ancient character represents the Chinese threshing-floor, at the harvest-time, as it still appears in our days. On the ground — levelled, grains are heaped together, and all around 丰丰 the corn-sheaves are ranged... In the modern character, at the bottom, 豆 (L. 165) represents a cup; on the top, 丰丰 represents boughs, a symbol of plenty. The cup 凵 became 山. Idea of greatness, of multitude; mountains of grain, say the philologists; 取其高大也。 It seems rather that 山 is a graphical difference of 凵. — Phonetic series 839. It forms

豔 豓

Yen[4]. Prosperity, abundance. Radical redundancy, for 盇 is a synonym of 豐. See L. 38 G.

艷

Yen[4]. The 色 colour, the appearance, the looking of 豐 prosperity. Gracious, handsome. See L. 28 D.

Second series. 丯 chieh[4].

C 丯

Chieh[4]. The first mnemonic way invented after the knotted strings; the first writing, or rather the first engraving. Notches 彡 cut in a 丨 bamboo lath. By extension, deed, document, record, proof; 丨像竹木，彡像齒形，刻竹木爲識也。上古未有書契，刻齒於竹木，以記事。 It forms

D 㓞

Ch'i[4]. To cut a notch with a 刀 knife, in a lath that will be used as a 丯 record, a document, or a proof; 从刀，从丯，會意。刻之爲㓞。 — Phonetic series 181. It forms

契

Ch'i[4]. The title deeds 㓞 of a 大 man; 从大，从㓞。會意。 A covenant, an agreement, a bond, a contract. — Phonetic series 426.

絜

Hsieh[2]. To measure 糸 before making a 㓞 contract; land-measuring.

E 害

Hai[4]. To injure, to hurt, to damage; 口 to speak, 丯 to write, 宀 under a shelter, by stealth, *against somebody*; 从口，从丯、會意。傷也。 — Phonetic series 529.

F  **Hsien**^{4}. To apply, in one's 宀 study, one's 心 heart and one's 罒 eyes, to the study of 丯 documents. By extension, to draw up laws, a constitution, rules, etc.

G **Lei**^{3}. A harrow. A piece of wood 木 with 丯 dents, says the Glose; 从木、丯像、刻齒。The modern form has one dent less. — It is the 127th radical of characters pertaining to tillage.

H **Hai**^{4}. To be 夂 entangled in 丯 litigations. Compare 夆 **fêng**^{1}, above A.

I **Ching**^{1}. It has nothing in common, either with 克 (L. 75 K), or with 競 (L. 73 D). Two brothers 兄 (L. 29 D) holding each one their sharing contract 丯; mutual respect of rights; deference, good understanding; 从二兄、各執一丯。The modern form is contracted.

LESSON 98.

About two primitives, 气 and 斗, that are not connected together.

First series. 气 **ch'i**^{4}.

A 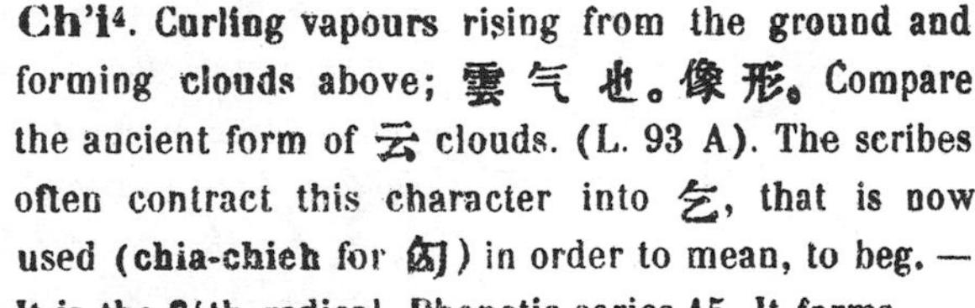
Ch'i^4. Curling vapours rising from the ground and forming clouds above; 雲气也。像形。Compare the ancient form of 云 clouds. (L. 93 A). The scribes often contract this character into 乞, that is now used (**chia-chieh** for 匃) in order to mean, to beg. — It is the 84th radical. Phonetic series 15. It forms

Ch'i^4. Vapour 气 ascending from boiling 米 rice. This character was practically substituted to the last. It plays an important part in Chinese philosophy. — Phonetic series 515.

Second series: 斗 tou^{3}.

B 斗 升

Tou^{3}. A measure of 十 ten 勺 ladles or 升 pints; a peck; 十升也。像形。勺也。有柄。The ancient forms represent a 勺 ladle and 十 ten. The modern forms are mutilated. — The scribes sometimes write 斗 for 丩, e.g. 呌 for 叫; it is a licence. — It forms the 68th radical. Phonetic series 84. It forms

料 **Liao^{4}.** To measure grain 米 with a peck 斗; 會意。**Chuan-chu**, grain, substance, to calculate.

科 **K'o^{1}.** To measure corn 禾 with a 斗 peck; 會意。By extension, a class, a rank; gradation, examination; 品也。Each degree received a fixed quantity of grain.

斝 **Chia^{3}.** A hanap of the size of a 斗 peck, in order to drink 吅 together.

升 **Shêng^{1}.** A measure ot 十 ten 㪅 handfuls, a pint. The modern forms are arbitrary contractions. **Chia-chieh** 升 and 昇 mean, to rise in office. Cf. 科 above. — Phonetic series 81.

LESSON 99

About the partial primitive 欠, both straight and inverted.

First series. 欠 straight, **ch'ien^{4}.**

A 欠

Ch'ien^{4}. To breathe. A man 儿 (L. 29) who breathes 彡. This latter element, a synonym of 气 (L. 98 A), says the Glose, somewhat differs graphically from it, therefore 欠 is a special partial primitive; 从儿、彡像、气從人上出之形。By extension, to get out of breath, to be exhausted, to owe money, deficiency. — It is the 76th radical. Phonetic series 44. It forms

吹 **Ch'ui^{1}.** To blow, to puff, to scold; 从口、从欠、會意。出气急曰吹。

B 次

Ts'ŭ^{4}. Idea of succession 第也。represented by 二 two successive 欠 breathes, inspiration and expiration; 从二、从欠、會意。— Phonetic series 244.

C 次

Hsien[4]. The saliva 氵 that flows in the mouth, when something good to eat is smelt. 欠; 慕欲口液也。从欠、从水、會意。To desire, to covet. It forms

羡 **Hsien**[4]. To covet; an overplus, an excess; 貪欲也。餘也。The 羊 is supposed to be 㳄 contracted.

盜 **Tao**[4] A robber, to plunder; 賊也。Those who 次 covet the goods 皿 of their neighbour; 私利物也。从次欲皿者。會意。

D 欵 款 款 欵

K'uan[3]. Primitively, 欠 to blow against a malignant influence 祟, as the pagans still do, in order to preserve from it either on'es self or others. By extension, affection, care, etc. The scribes found out many ways of writing this character. The third of them is now classic, the last is unauthorised. Not to be confounded with 疑 i[2], L. 131 G.

Second series. 欠 inverted, 旡 **chi**[4].

E 旡

Chi[4]. To breathe into, to swallow. It is the reverse of 欠, composed also of 儿 and of 彡, but inverted; 从反欠、指事。The second ancient form is a mere abbreviation, not to be confounded with **tsan**[1] (L. 26 D). — It is the 71th radical. See 旣 **chi**[4] (L. 26 M) It forms

F 炁 愛

Ai[4]. To swallow 旡 down in one's 心 heart, to love, to be fond of, kindness, favour. Now this character, joined with 夊, made 愛, that has **chia-chieh** the same meaning as the radical had before. Primitively it meant, gracious gait; 行皃。— Phonetic series 721.

LESSON 100.

About the primitive 毛 mao², both straight and inverted. Not to be confounded with 手 (L. 48)

First series. 毛 straight.

A 毛

Mao². Hair, fur, plumage; 獸毛也。像形。By extension, feathers. It is the 82th radical of characters relating to hair and feathers. Phonetic series 70. It forms

老

Lao³. Old, to grow old, seventy years old. A man 人 whose 毛 hair transforms 匕 itself, changes to white. See L. 30 E. Note the contraction of the modern character. — It is the 125th radical of a few characters mostly relating to age.

Piao³. The outer surface of garments. The first 衣 garments were skins worn with the hair 毛 outside. See L. 16 K. The modern form is contracted. — Phonetic series 389.

Ts'ui⁴. From 毛 thrice repeated, to denote its fineness. Hair thick and soft, fine furs; 獸細毛也。从三毛､會意, — Phonetic series 712.

Second series. 毛 inverted 𠂔, in

B

尾

I³. Wei³. The tail of animals. From 尸 body and 𠂔 the hair at the lower part. In the modern recent form, the scribes wrote 毛 instead of 𠂔. See L. 32 D. It is often compressed 尾, or contracted, reduced to 尸 or to 𠂔, in the compounds. It forms

尿

Sui¹. Niao⁴. Urine. From tail and water. See L. 32 E. The modern form is contracted.

屈

Ch'ü¹. Oppression, vexation, curved. Composed of 尾 and 出, L. 78 E. The modern form is contracted. — Phonetic series 348.

犀

Hsi¹. The Thibetan yak. 牛 ox with a long hairy 尾 tail. The tail of the yak was used in old China to make military standards. — Phonetic series 679.

C 隶

Tai⁴. To hold 彐 by the tail 尾 (contracted into 𠂔, and altered in the modern form). See L. 44 E. — It is the 171th radical. It forms (contracted into 𠂔)

眔

Tai^4. To wink, to catch 隶 with 目 the eyes, says the Glose. This explanation seems improbable. The character is composed of 罒 eye and of 氺 eyelashes. The covering of the eye-ball by the eyelashes, could not be represented in the elementary design. It forms

Huai^2. To hide in one's 衣 clothes, to carry in one's bosom. L. 16 J. — Phonetic series 820.

D 

Ch'iu^2. It is explained like 隶 **tai^4**, to hold 彐 by the tail 尾 (contracted); to ask, to implore. See L. 45 K. It was altered in the modern writing, and wrongly classified by K'ang-hsi under 水 (L 125). — Phonetic series 263. Compare **lu^4**, L. 68 F.

LESSON 101.

About two primitives 勿 and 昜.

First series. 勿 **wu^4**.

A 勿

Wu^4. Three pennons attached to a stick; a flag; 旗也。像形。By extension, 1. Jerky motions, as that of pennons agitated by the wind (L. 52 F); 2. A decree, a prohibition, a defence, an order made to soldiers with a flag; 3. Objects laciniated or foliated; sudden rays. **K'ang-hsi** wrongly classified this primitive under 勹. — Phonetic series 90. It forms

Hu^1. Jerking 勿 of the heart 心, emotion, surprise; 从心从勿、會意。

刎

Wên^3. To cut the throat; 刀 a knife, and 勿 the blood that gushes out from the severed arteries of the neck.

吻

Wên^3. The lips: 勿 strips (of flesh) that close the mouth

笏

Hu^1. A small book made from 勿 strips of 竹 bamboo.

物

Wu^4. A thing, a being, an article. An ox 牛; 勿 is a mere phonetic. The oxen were the most valued things in ancient times. 萬物也。牛爲大物。勿聲。

B 昜

Yang^2. The sun 日 above the horizon, 勿 shooting its rays; light, solar action, etc. — Phonetic series 492. Note the following phonetic complexes that form series.

湯

T'ang^1. Water, infusion, hot decoction; 熱水也。从水、昜聲。— Phonetic series 707.

Shang^1. To wound with 矢 an arrow; 傷也。从矢 (L. 131), 昜聲。In the compounds, 矢 is reduced to 𠂉 placed on the top of 昜; the radical is placed on the left side, instead of 矢, e g. 傷, 殤, etc. — Phonetic series 643.

Second series. 易 i^4.

C 易

I^4. It represents a lizard, probably the chameleon. A primitive. On the top, the head; at the bottom, the light feet of the reptile; 像形。By extension, alert, easy, to change, to transform. — Phonetic series 365.

LESSON 102.

About the primitive 干 kan^1, and the important series derived from it. An appendix will treat about the primitive 丵 tsao^2.

First series. 干 kan^1, 庚、舌。

A 干

Kan^1. It represents a pestle. Compare L. 130. By extension, to grind, to destroy; morally, to oppose, to offend against; blunt arms, offence, injury, etc. — It is the 51th radical of a few unassorted characters. Phonetic series 22. It forms

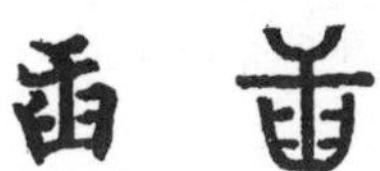

Ch'a^2. The 干 pestle in the mortar 臼 (L. 139). To pound, to pierce, to drive into or stick in. — Phonetic series 421.

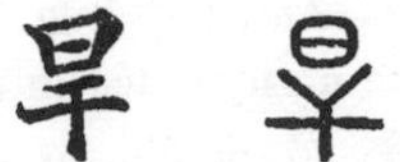

Han^4. The torrid and destroying 干 effect of the sun 日; drought, dryness.

B 庚

Kêng[1]. To bark the rice by pounding it in a mortar. This was the main daily domestic work among the ancients. Compare L. 47 N.

康

K'ang[1]. To 庚 decorticate 米 rice. **Chuan-chu: 1.** The chaff detached from the pounded grain, now 糠; 2. The repose that follows this hard work. — Phonetic series 623. It has nothing in common with 隶 L. 44 E.

庸

Jung[1]. Ordinary, common, as the 庚 decortication of rice, 用 for every-day use. — Phonetic series 621.

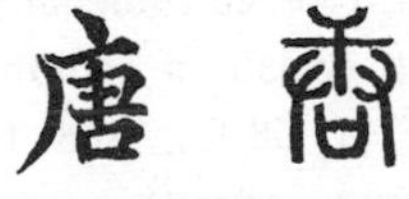

T'ang[2]. The 口 words that accompany the 庚 pounding of rice; idle gossip, noisy wrangle. — Phonetic series 572.

C 舌

Shê[2]. The tongue 干 stretched out of the mouth 口. Here 干 represents the tongue, and is a partial special primitive, that is not derived from **kan**[1], L. 102 A. Compare, L. 55 K, **han**[2], the tongue drawn back into the mouth. Compare the ancient forms given here 1. The tongue held out of the mouth **shê**; 2. The tongue retiring into the mouth; 3. The tongue enclosed in the mouth **han**[2]. — It is the 135th radical. Note the compound 甜 **t'ien**[2] (L. 73 B); what is sweet 甘 to the 舌 tongue; sweet.

Note: 舌 **shê**[2] does not form a phonetic series. The one that is sometimes attributed to it (Cf. Callery, N° 262), belongs to the character 昏 **kuo**[2] (L. 114 C), contracted by the scribes into 舌, and often into 舌. To add to the confusion, 甜 **t'ien**[2] forms phonetic complexes in which it is contracted into 舌 These compounds may be found in the series 227, derived from **kuo**[2]; they may be recognised by their sound **ien**. Examples:

恬 — **T'ien**[2], from 甜 contracted.

活 — **Huo**[2], from 昏.

Second series. 逆 I⁴, ni⁴.

D

I⁴. This character, says the Glose, is 干 doubled (though incompletely) to mean that the attack was repeated, because it met with resistance. Hence the derived meanings, to attack,. to resist, opposition, obstacle. Now 逆。It forms

Ch'ih⁴. To attack 屰 a man in his 广 house; to expel, to turn out of the house, to scold, to strike or cuff. Note the modern abbreviation, the only one used now. — Phonetic series 112.

O⁴. To resist to somebody, to check 屰 him openly with 吅 cries and scoldings. The scribes changed 屰 into 亏 (L. 58 E), and this strange alteration was commonly admitted. See L. 72 F. — Phonetic series 470.

Shuo⁴. The new moon; when the 月 moon being 屰 opposite to the sun, refuses to receive its light; 从月、从屰、會意。— Phonetic series 564.

Chüeh¹. To have hiccup, suffocation, asthma, cough; 屰 an obstacle that impedes 欠 breathing (L. 99). It forms

Ch'üeh². A steep acclivity 厂 (L. 59), the ascension of which 欮 puts out of breath. This character lost that meaning, and is now used as a demonstrative pronoun; 發聲之詞。— Phonetic series 673.

Hsing⁴. Fortunate, lucky. A man 夭 (L. 61 B, written 土), who gets over 屰 opposition, who triumphs over resistance; 从屰、从夭、會意。吉而免凶也。— Phonetic series 361. Not to be confounded with 㚔 nieh⁴, below G.

Third series. 辛 ch'ien².

E 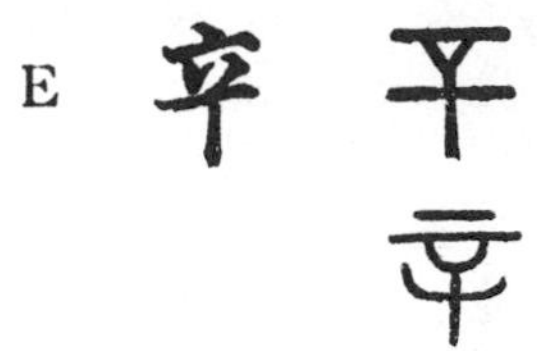

Ch'ien². To offend 干 (L. 102 A) a superior — or 二 (L. 2 G); offence, fault, crime; 干上爲辛。罪也。In the modern writing, 辛 on the top of different compounds is reduced to 立, that must be distinguished from 立 li⁴, L. 60 H. By extension, to attack, to face, etc. It forms

Ch'ieh⁴. A guilty 辛 woman 女, or a culprit's daughter enslaved according to the ancient custom; 有罪女子。从辛、从女、會意。See L. 67 E. Now it means, a concubine, an accessory wife. — Phonetic series 331.

T'ung². The counterpart of the last. A boy, a lad under 15 years, who became a slave for a great 重 crime 辛 committed by his parents. — Phonetic series 716.

I⁴. An angry boar 豕 that assumes 辛 the offensive; bravery. 从豕、从辛、會意。辛、犯之意, See L. 69 H. — See also 言 L. 73 C, and 商 L. 15 G.

Fourth series. 羊 jên³.

F 羊 羊 羊

Jên³. This character is composed nearly as 屰 (L. 102 D). It is 干 (L. 102 A) increased by one stroke. The idea is that of an offence repeated or aggravated, 犯之甚也。Derived meanings, relapse, recidivation, obduracy. See 南 nan², L. 79 G. It forms the two important sub-series 幸 nieh⁴ and 辛 hsin¹ (below).

Sub-series. 幸 nieh⁴.

G 

Nieh⁴. A man 大 (L. 60) who committed a 羊 crime; a criminal; 从大、从羊、會意。罪也。Not to be confounded with 幸 hsing⁴ (L. 102 D); both are now written in the same way. Not to be confounded with 幸 t'a⁴ (L. 60 C). Note the derivatives

執

Chih^{2}. To apprehend 丮 (L. 11 E) a 幸 criminal; 捕罪人也。从丮、从幸、會意。By extension, to seize, to maintain, etc. — Phonetic series 601.

報

Pao^{4}. To repress 𠬝 (L. 55 C) 幸 evil-doers; 从幸、从𠬝、會意。攩罪人也。By extension, to denounce them, to state, to inform; hence the modern meanings, a report, an announcement, a gazette.

睪

I^{4}. To keep a watchful 目 eye (L. 158), over the 幸 criminals; vigilance; 从橫目。从幸、會意。令吏將目捕罪人也。— Phonetic series 738.

圉

Yü^{3}. A prison. The inclosure 囗 where criminals 幸 are confined; 所以拘罪人。从囗、从幸、會意。

盩

Chou^{1}. To flog 攵 (L. 43 D) a 幸 criminal till he is 血 bleeding (L. 157). The scribes substituted 丸 to 攵, and suppressed the 丿 of 血; then **K'ang-hsi** classified this character under 皿.

𥷚

Chü^{2}. To convict a criminal 幸, in the Chinese way, by dint of rattan strokes ⺮ (L. 77 B), and of 訇 cries (L. 54 E).

Sub-series 辛 hsin^{1}.

H 辛

Hsin^{1}. Composed of 䇂 and 上 (ancient form 二 or 丄 L. 2 G); to offend 䇂 one's 上 superior; and the consequence of it, chastisement, pain, bitterness; 大罪也。从䇂、从上、會意。The ends of the first horizontal lines are generally turned up, the scribes deeming is to be more gracious in that way. — It is the 160th radical. It forms

宰

Tsai^{3}. A criminal 辛 at the 宀 tribunal, judged and chastised; 从宀、从辛、會意。屋下制治罪人、謂之宰。By extension, to govern, to judge, to order the legal tortures, to slaughter. — Phonetic series 574. — **Tsai**^{3} 宰 contracted into 辛 is phonetic in 梓 **tzŭ**^{3}, *Rottlera japonica*, a hard wood, instruments for torturing were made of.

辟 𨐨 **Pi⁴**. The man who 口 states 卩 authoritatively about the 辛 criminals (L. 55 B; 从口用法者也。从卩、从辛節制其罪也，會意。Prince, law, chastisement, etc. The scribes changed 卩 into 尸. — Phonetic series 752.

亲 𣓀 **Chên⁴**. The Chinese hazel, wood 木 for the 辛 criminals, because the rods were made of it. It is phonetic in

親 親 **Ch'in¹**. Those who are 見 seen habitually; one's self, one's kindred; by extension, to love, to embrace; 近也。屬也。愛也。It lost one stroke in the junction. — Phonetic series 818.

新 **Hsin¹**. To cut 斤 (L. 126) small 亲 branches (of the hazel); shoots of the year; hence the meaning, recent, new. Now 薪 fuel, wood cut for the fire, brush-wood.

辥 辥 **Nieh⁴**. Offence, sin For the phonetic, see L. 86 B. The meaning is probably 辛 an offence 㠯 visible, evident, public.

辭 辭 **Ts'ŭ²**. To rid 𤔔 of an 辛 accusation, to clear one's self, to excuse one's self. See L. 90 B.

犀 犀 **Hsi¹**. A contraction of 犀 hsi¹, yak, L 100 B, now commonly used, e.g. in 穉 chih⁴, etc.

辠 辠 **Tsui⁴**. To commit 自 a crime 辛 (L. 159); 犯法也。It appears that some malicious literati substituted this character to the 皇 of their enemy, the First Emperor 秦始皇 Ch'in-shih-huang This Emperor not over flattered to be called the «first sinner», ordered by an Imperial decree that in future *sin* should be written 罪, the ancient character 辠 becoming taboe; 秦以辠以皇字。改用罪。This 罪 primitively meant a 网 net (L. 39 C); 非 (L 170) being phonetic.

辡 辡 辦 **Pien⁴**. Two criminals 辛 impeaching each other; 罪人相與訟也。从二辛會意. It forms interesting compounds in which the radical is inserted between the two 辛: 辨, 辯, 辮, etc. — Phonetic series 786.

Appendix. The primitive 丵 **tsao**².

I 丵

Tsao². This character is unconnected with the preceding ones, 羊, etc. It is a primitive representing the successive division and sub-division of a tree's branches, the boughs, the twigs; 像。Hence, arborisation, emanation, multitude, faggot, collection. It forms

業

Yeh⁴. A tree 木 crowned with its 丵 foliage. The moral foliage, the deeds of a man, the affairs upon which he exerts his activity, and what he acquires by his doings, viz. merits, goods, titles, etc.

菐

P'u². To gather with one's 𦥑 hands twigs 丵, in order to make with them a faggot. — Phonetic series 700. The compound 僕 forms an unimportant sub-series.

叢

Ts'ung¹. To gather 取 bushes 丵. A bushy place, crowded; a collection, to collect. See L. 146 F.

對

Tui⁴. To confront, to compare, and, by extension, to correspond to; 从口、从丵、从寸、會意。To apply a 寸 measure to the 丵 luxuriant vegetation of the 口 mouths, viz. to the testimonies of men, to see whether they agree or not. Compare the composition of 言 (L. 73 C). To recall to his officials that one must not rely on every 口 mouth's testimony, but only on the testimony of the 士 sages, which alone deserves to be 寸 examined, the Emperor 文帝 **Wên-ti** of the first **Han**⁴ changed by decree 口 into 士, thus making the modern character, which was contracted by the scribes.

黹

Chih³. Delicate leaves 丵, embroidered 㡀 upon linen, 丵 is contracted; 从㡀丵省。像刺文也。See L, 35 G. — It is the 204th radical.

鑿

Tsao². To chisel, by delicate 𣪘 cuts, with a chisel, in 金 metal, so that 丵 designes of leaves and branches be reproduced. Chiselling in general. Compare (L. 81 A) 毇 to pound grain, 毀 to grind.

LESSON 103.

About the primitive 羊 yang[2].

First series. 羊 and its multiples.

A 羊 **Yang**[2]. A sheep seen from behind; the horns, the head, the feet and the tail of a sheep. The tail is often curtailed, to make room for a phonetic; 像，頭角足尾之形。Idea of sweetness, of peace, of harmony. — It is the 123th radical. Phonetic series 248. It forms

羌 **Ch'iang**[1]. From 儿 men and 羊 sheep. Nomadic shepherds living in the Western steppes; the Thibetans. 西戎牧羊人也。从儿、从羊、會意。

美 **Mei**[3]. A man 人 resembling to the 羊 lamb, sweet, gentle, good; 从羊、从大、會意。於善同意。

羔 **Kao**[1]. A lamb 羊 that begins to 灬 walk. The feet being already represented in 羊, there is a radical redundancy. By extension, the little ones of different animals.

姜 **Chiang**[1]. The clan (see 姓 L. 79 F) of the Emperor 神農 Shên-nung; 羊 is phonetic.

養 **Yang**[3]. To nourish (L. 26 M); 羊 is phonetic. — Phonetic series 814.

羕 **Yang**[4]. The unceasing flow of water. See 永 L. 125 D; 羊 is phonetic. By extension, uniformity, model, tediousness. — Phonetic series 659.

鮮 **Hsien**[1]. Composed of 魚 fish and 羊 sheep, the two kinds of flesh that were eaten *fresh* by the ancients, while they cured the other meats. By extension, fresh (neither salted, nor dried, nor smoked). — Phonetic series 832.

羹 **Kêng**[1]. A thick broth, soup. Composed of 羔 and 美, a modern abbreviation invented by the scribes. Primitively, 羔 a lamb stewed on a 鬲 caldron; on both sides, the 弜 vapour that rises. See **li**[1], **L. 87 B.** — See again 羍 L. 60 O; 羞 L. 44 B; 義 and 羲 L. 71 Q; 善 L. 73 D. — See also 差 L. 46 C, that is unconnected with 羊.

B 羴 **Shan**[1]. Three 羊 sheep, a flock of sheep. By extension, the rank odour of sheep or goats. It forms the following.

羼 **Ch'an**[3]. A sheep-fold; 从羴在尸下。尸屋也。 (L. 32 G) By extension, crowd, press.

Second series. 𦫳 **kuai**[1].

C 𦫳 **Kuai**[1]. Horns of the ram. It is 羊 without the feet; 羊角也。像形。It figures in different compounds, as a symbol; see L. 35 M, 54 G. The modern scribes often change it into 艹.

乖 **Kuai**[1]. Ramified (twice 八 L. 18, division) ram's horns 𦫳; odd, singular; 从𦫳、从重八、分也。 The modern character is absurd. It forms the two phonetic compounds

雈 **Huan**[1]. A big 隹 owl, the Grand-duke, with 𦫳 feather-horns, egrets; 从隹、从𦫳、會意。有毛角。 Forms the three following characters

舊 **Chiu**[4]. A sort of 雈 owl, 臼 (L. 139) is phonetic. It now means, **chia-chieh**, old, worn out, formerly.

蒦 **Huai**[2]. **Huo**[1]. To seize (an owl) with the 彐 hand. — Phonetic series 782.

雚 **Kuan**[4]. The heron, a screeming 吅 bird 隹 with an egret 𦫳. — Phonetic series 841.

K'ui². A demon that wanders through the mountains. It is said to have 丫 horns. This is a false interpretation resulting from the ill-formed modern character. See the ancient form: a face of demon, two arms, a belly, a tail, and two feet (L. 27 I, note 1).

Chi⁴ and **Man**². See L. 35 M, L. 54 G.

D 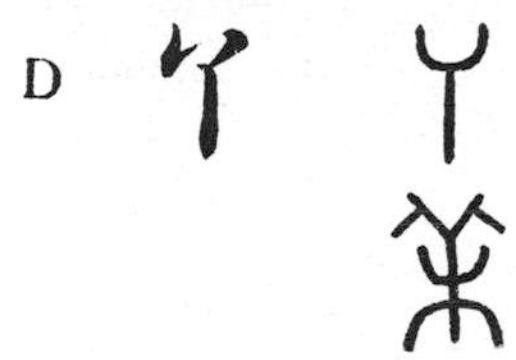

Ya¹. A fork, crooked. Now, appellative of girls, ya-t'ou, on account of their two tufts of hair. — Some interpreters consider 丫 as an abbreviation of the ancient character 木 a tree whose branches are 丫 forked. It is the reason why it is given here.

LESSON 104.

About the primitive 𠦒 pan¹.

A 

Pan¹. A sort of fork, or shovel, which it represents; 像形。所以推棄之器也。It was altered in different ways by the modern scribes. It forms

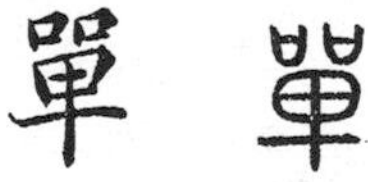

Tan¹. To assault a man with 吅 cries and a 𠦒 fork. See L. 72 E. — Phonetic series 705.

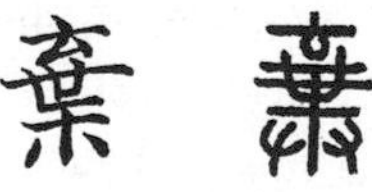

Ch'i⁴. To repulse, to expulse. Two hands 𦥑 with a 𠦒 shovel, casting a 𠫓 child away. See L. 94 G. Note the modern alteration.

Fên⁴. The modern character is totally distorted. The top is not 米, but 釆 (L. 123) Ordure, filth. Two hands 𦥑 removing with a shovel 𠦒 the 釆 dung of animals; 从𦥑推𠦒棄釆也。會意。

Pi[2]. This character represents two ancient instruments: 1. A shovel upon which was offered the meat 田 at the *end* of the sacrifice, hence the derived meaning, to *end*, which is still used in our days; 2. A racket 苹 with a 田 net, resembling the butterflies net, to catch small animals. This character has those two meanings in very ancient texts. — Phonetic series 640.

B 

Kou[4]. Some consider this character as being composed of two 苹, one being straight, the other inverted, while the stroke at the bottom was suppressed for simplification's sake. This explanation seems to be far fetched. **Kou**[4] is a primitive, whose straight and crossed lines represent graphically the timbers in the framework of a house, as they interlock and cross each other; hence the idea of a net-work, an ordering, a combination. This notion is hinted in the compounds, 構, etc. 取横直交加之像。— Phonetic series 546.

LESSON 105

About the primitive 革 **ko**.

A

Ko[2]. The raw skin of a flayed sheep, as it is stretched out. To skin. The fork in the middle is 羊 or 𦍌 a sheep, contracted (L. 103); the two horizontal lines 二 mean that the skin is stretched out, two hands or scrapers 臼 working it. The second ancient character is already contracted; 羊皮、治去其毛、日革。古文像。By extension, to *skin* an officer, to degrade him from office with a fine or a confiscation. — It is the 177th radical. It forms

B 

Pa[4]. Leather 革 drenched by the 雨 rain, that stretches out when it is drawn. It forms

Pa[4]. Lengthening 霸 of the moon 月, in the first fortnight of the month; growing, prosperity. This character was used to designate the feudal princes in ancient times; double idea of *growing* in glory, and of glory *borrowed* by them from the Emperor, as the moon borrows its light from the sun. — Phonetic series 355.

Chi[1]. Trammels. Leather 革 to trammel 网 a horse 馬. In the primitive form, the leather was not represented; 中 represented the trammel put to the feet of the horse, and the peg to tie it up. The leather was added later on. Then 中 was suppressed.

LESSON 106.

About several representations of animals or other beings, primitives either complete or partial, gathered here on account of their resemblance.

First series. 冂 swelling on both sides, in

A 兆

Ku³. A man 儿 (L 29) whose 冂 sides are swollen, because he makes an effort; 从儿、左右皆鼓形。

免 **Mien³.** A man 亻 (L. 25) whose sides 冂 are swollen, whose legs are propped; to *make an effort* to get some good or to avoid some evil; 从亻、从冂、會意。— Phonetic series 295.

兜 **Tou¹.** A kind of helmet with 冂 appendixes on both sides to cover the cheeks; a helmet, a cowl; 皃 **mao⁴** (L. 29 C) represents a man, 白 head and 儿 legs; 从皃像.白人頭也。冂形。By extension, to cover, to envelop. — Phonetic series 651.

Second series. 兔 t'u⁴, a hare or rabbit.

B 兔

T'u⁴. It represents a hare when it is squatting, with its tail perked up; 獸像。後其尾形。It forms

冤 **Yüan¹.** A hare 兔 under a covert 冖, whence it is unable to run. Derived meanings, to injure, to ill-use without cause, grievance, oppression, the hare being an inoffensive animal; 屈也。从兔在冖下、會意。See L. 34 H.

娩 **Mien³.** The female of the hare, 會意。By extension, to bear, by allusion to the fecundity of the doe-hare.

逸 **I⁴.** A hare that runs away, 會意。By extension, to live like a hare, to lead an idle and licentious life; the hare being looked upon in China as the type of profligacy, and very ill-reputed.

Third series. 㲋 ch'ao⁴.

C 㲋

Ch'ao⁴. It represents some animal resembling the hare; 獸也。似兔而大、像形。This character, combined with 兔 (L 106 B), forms

毚 **Ch'an².** The numerous tribe ot the rodents. — Phonetic series 828.

Fourth series. 萈 **huan**[1].

D

Huan[1]. A sort of antelope; 山羊。細角者。On the top, the horns (L. 103 C); 目 represents the head; at the bottom there are paws and a tail, which is often omitted in the modern character. This was wrongly classified by **K'ang-hsi** under 艹 vegetals. — It forms

寬 **K'uan**[1]. Large, spacious, ample in the physical sense; broad-mindedness, indulgence in the moral sense. This idea may come from the width of the 宀 paddocks reserved for the breeding of these animals.

LESSON 107.

About two primitives 心 and 也, much alike in the ancient writing.

First series. 心 **hsin**[1].

A 心

Hsin[1]. It represents the heart; 人心也。像形。On the top, the pericardium opened; in the middle, the organ; at the bottom, a summary delineation of the aorta. The extended meanings are very numerous. There are modern abbreviations as here joined. — It is the 61th radical of characters relating to the feelings. Phonetic series 61.

Many derivatives from 心 were already explained, e.g. 惡 o[4], **wu**[4], L. 82 H; 寧 **ning**[2], L. 36 C; 急 **chi**[2], L. 19 D. 念 **nien**[4], L. 14 N; 悳 **tê**[2], L. 10 O; 思 **ssŭ**[1], L. 40 A; etc. Let us recall here that 必 **pi**[2] (L. 18 G), has nothing in common with 心 — Note the following multiple:

Jui[3]. The heart 心 of the flowers; 花心也。It is now written 蕊.

Second series. 也 **yeh**[3].

B 也

Yeh[3]. It represents an ancient utensil, either a funnel or a rhyton; 器也。像形。— Phonetic series 37.

Note: The scribes introduced the most regrettable confusion between the derivatives of 也, and those of 它 (L. 108). The **Shuo-wên** ascribes to 也: 匜、貤、灺、弛、地、酏。。。and to 它: 池、迆、杝、馳、阤、etc. The cause of the confusion was that 它 was and is still sometimes written 㐌。The 𠂉 was placed where it was not required, and omitted where it was required; then the dictionaries set down all those errors of orthography.

LESSON 108.

About the primitives 它、龜、黽、卵 and 丱.

A 

T'o^{1}. A snake (See 虫 L. 110) that stands on its tail, distends its neck and darts its tongue out; 像。 It is often written 㐌, and sometimes 也。See L. 107 B, note. — Phonetic series 165 and 126. — In the ancient writing, the head of the two following is alike.

B 

Kui^{1}. A tortoise, which is described by the Glose as an animal having its flesh inside and its bones outside; 外骨內肉者也。The character represents the head, the claws, the shell and the tail A more ancient character represented the tortoise-shell ornamented with stripes, and a summary delineation of the head and of the tail. — It is the 213th radical. It forms

Chiu^{1}. A contest 鬥 (L. 11 I) settled by divination. A singed 龜 tortoise-shell was formerly used for that purpose. See L. 56.

C 

Min^{3}. The soft turtle. The character was then applied to mean a tadpole; the head, the gills, and a tail (L. 79 I). It is the 205th radical. Phonetic series 749.

D 

Luan^{2}. A primitive representing the ovaries and the oviduct of the female, the testicles and cords of the male.

E 丱

Kuan^{1}. Another primitive, and not an abbreviation of luan^{3}. It represents the shuttle, that passes and repasses, inserting the transversal thread of the woof between the longitudinal threads of the warp. See L. 92 G.

LESSON 109.

About the primitive 中; about 用 and its important series.

First series. 中 **chung[1].**

A 中

Chung[1]. The centre. **Chung[4].** To hit the centre, to attain. It represents a square target, pierced in its centre by an 丨 arrow. Later on, the target was contracted by the scribes and changed into a form somewhat like 口 (L 72); but the primitive form is still maintained in the series 用. To represent, in a design without perspective, the perforation of the target, the two extremities of the arrow were marked with 二 a sign, or the extremity that passed through was curved; these are mere graphic tricks; 从口、丨上下通。 — Phonetic series 52.

Different compounds of 中 were explained elsewhere, 衷 L. 16 E; 婁 L. 67 N; 啻 L. 73 E; etc. Compare 串 L. 153. See also 史 and 吏 L. 43 M. N.

Second series. 用 **yung[4]** and its derivatives.

B 用

Yung[4]. This character primitively represented the bronze ex-voto offered to the Ancestors, placed in the temple as a memorial for their offspring. Afterwards it was given the shape of a bronze tripod The vessel was used for the offerings to the Manes, hence **chuan-chu** to use, usage. The offerings brought blessing, hence **chuan-chu** aptitude, efficacity, utility, etc. — It is the 101th radical of a few incongruous characters.

C 周

Chou[1]. 用 aptitude 及 (the old form ㇇ L. 19 E) extending to every thing, general, universal; hence the derived meanings, propagation, universality; totality; 从用,从古文及。The scribes arbitrarily changed ㇇ into 口. — Phonetic series 342

D 甫

Fu[3]. Aptitude 用 for founding and 父 governing a family (L 43 G), the manhood. Then a definitive appellation was taken by men. Hence the extended meaning, I, myself. — Phonetic series 271. It forms

尃 　**Fu**[1]. The hand 寸 (for 又 L. 45 B) of a grown up 甫 man. Derived meanings, action, amplitude. — The modern scribes imagined to write 専, and this faulty writing became classical in the character 敷 **fu**[1], to spread out, to promulge. — Phonetic series 528. It forms

溥 　**P'u**[3]. A wide 尃 expanse of 氵 water. By extension, large, general, universal, etc. — Phonetic series 753.

See 甬 L. 55 K; 庸 L 102 B; 蒲 L. 54 G; etc.

LESSON 110.

About the primitive 虫, and its derivatives.

A 虫 　**Hui**[1]. All kind of crawling animals, snakes, worms, etc.

Compare L. 108 A. — It is the 142th radical. See 蚤 L. 45 I, and 風 L. 21 B. Note further

B 強 強 　**Ch'iang**[2]. A bow 弓 (L. 87 A) that shoots its arrow above several 畺 acres of land (L. 3 C), a strong bow. By extension, strong, good. This character being difficult to write, was replaced by 強, a name of the same sound which represents an insect, *Elater* the snapping beetle, that unbends like a bow 弓 when it fell on its back; 虫 represents the insect, 厶 its head, which was arbitrarily changed into 口 by the scribes. — Phonetic series 668.

C 䖵 　**K'un**[1]. Insects that are numerous at certain times of the year (*two* to intimate the great number); e.g. 蝨 **shih**[1], formerly fly, and now louce; 螽 **chung**[1]. locusts; 蟁 **wên**[2], mosquitoes; 蠡 **li**[3], book-worms; 蠶 **ts'an**[2], silk-worms; etc.

D 蟲 **Ch'ung²**. An ancient term for all crawling and swarming animals, insects, etc. It is found in

蠱 **Ku³**. Chronic diseases, the etiology of which escapes the Chinese, as tuberculosis, syphilis, etc. — Some suppose that 蟲 worms corrode the interior of the 皿 body; 腹中蟲也。从蟲，从皿，會意。— Others explain that these diseases are caused by the venom of animals, swallowed with food and drink Hence the dreadful fear of the Chinese for the urine of the gecko (a lizard found in all the houses); also for rain-water that has filtered through a roof, because it is supposed to be soiled by the venom of scorpions that live there; etc. This etymology seems to be the right one, because it explains better the word 皿 vessel; poison of the 蟲 worms taken with 皿 food; 皿物之用也，按凡蟲行毒飲食中殺人。人不覺。— Moreover, there are who say that the magicians make a poison slow and sure, by grinding in a vessel 皿 different sorts of venimous 蟲 worms. This seems to be rather a legend.

LESSON 111.

About the primitive 虫, and its compounds.

A 臾 臾 虫 **K'ui⁴**. It represents an ancient recipient, either a basket or a bag. 器也。像形。Note the modern abbreviation. It forms

B 貴 貴 **K'ui⁴**. Not mean, or cheap; a whole 虫 basket of 貝 cowries; 物不賤也。The ancient form is unexplained, 未詳。It appears in the ancient character 𡚶 L. 44 G. It is perhaps an abbreviation of the last — Phonetic series 693.

C 𦣻 𦣻 **Ch'ien³**. To carry soil in 虫 baskets, in order to erect a wall, a dike, as it is still done in China (L. 86 B). It is phonetic in

遣 遣 **Ch'ien³**. To commission, to depute. — Phonetic series 773.

LESSON 112.

About the primitive 止, and its important derivatives

First series, 止 **chih**^{3}, its compounds and multiples.

A 止

Chih^{3} A coarse representation of a foot, or of the footprint; on the left side, the heels; on the right side, the toes; on the top, the ankle; 足止像形也。Derived meanings, to march (the feet moving); to halt, to stop (the feet being still), etc. — It is the 77th radical. Phonetic series 46. We saw the derivatives 走 L. 44 F; 歸 L. 44 K; 前 L. 66 D. Add the following:

企

Ch'i^{4}. A man 人 rising on his 止 heels; 从人、从止、會意。立也。

此

Ts'ŭ^{3}. To turn one one's heels (匕 L. 26). Now chia-chieh used as a demonstrative pronoun, this. — Phonetic series 242.

㢟

Ch'ên^{2}. A firm 廴 gait, by posing well the 止 foot (L. 63 D); 从廴、从止、會意。It forms

延

Yen^{2}. A gait 廴 firm 止 an 丿 steady (L. 7); 長行也。Phonetic series 417. Not to be confounded with the derivatives of 正 below I.

止 quadrupled, two being straight, and two inverted (altered in the modern writing), forms

歰

Shih^{4}. Rough, rugged. An irregular surface, that obliges to many steps 止 in different directions. The modern contractions 澁 澀, now replace the ancient form difficult to write. 不滑也。从四止、會意。

Second series. 足 tsu^4 and 疋 shu^2, both being composed of 止 the foot, increased with a symbol 指事。

B 足 𧾷 𤴓 — **Tsu^4**. A foot 止 at rest. By extension, feet in general. The stillness is represented by the closed ○. Compare below C. 脛止則爲足。行則爲疋。ς動像。○靜像也。 It is the 157th radical (two modern forms). Phonetic series 310.

C 疋 𤴔 𤴔 — **Shu^2**. Foot 止 in motion, to turn. The motion is represented by the open ς. Compare above B. 上像。下从止。按足者靜像，疋者動像。 The reading p'i^3, in the sense of *rolled up piece,* is a modern **chuan-chu.** — It is the 103th radical (two modern forms). — It forms

疏 — **Shu^1**. Birth 㐬, the feet 疋 coming first, Different extended meanings. See L. 94 F.

旋 — **Hsüan^2**. To turn on one's 疋 heels; 㫃 (L. 117) is phonetic. — Phonetic series 614.

楚 — **Ch'u^3**. A 林 woody land; 疋 is phonetic.

胥 — **Hsü^1**. Gravy 月; 疋 is phonetic. Phonetic series 448.

蛋 — **Tan^4**. The ball 疋 rolled by the 虫 dung-beetle. By extension, egg.

Third series. 走 tsou^3.

D 走 — **Tsou^3**. To march. A man 夭 who bends (L. 61 B) to walk quickly and with hasty strides; to go, to travel, to sail; 趨也。从夭，从止，會意。 — It is the 156th radical of characters relating to modes of going.

Fourth series. 辵 cho⁴.

E 辵 辵 辶 辶

Cho⁴. To go step by step. It is composed of 止 and 彳 (L. 63 A), say some philologists. It seems more probable that 彡 are three 止 footprints. Not to be confounded with 廴 (L. 63 D). — It is the 162th radical of a large group of characters relating to movements, e.g. 進 chin⁴. to advance, 退 t'ui⁴ to move back, etc.

Note: In some modern characters, the scribes divide 辵; 止 is placed on the right side, underneath the phonetic; 彡 is placed on the left side. **K'ang-hsi** classified those characters under 彳 the 60th radical. Examples:

徒 辻 **T'u²**. To go; 从辵。土聲。

從 逊 **Ts'ung²**. To follow; 从辵。从聲。

徙 𨑨 **Hsi³**. To move one's abode. 从辵。止聲。— Phonetic series 611.

Fifth series.

F 少 㐅

止 inverted is not used alone, but forms, when combined with 止 straight, two important series. In the first, G, the two forms are superposed, and 止 inverted is now written 少 (not to be confounded with 小, nor with 少, L. 18 H, M). In the second, H, the two forms placed in juxtaposition are now written 癶.

G 步 步

Pu⁴. A step, to take a step, to march; 行也。The character represents the succession in the steps (compare 行 L. 63 C). By extension, the planets, stars that move. It forms

涉 涉 **Shê⁴**. To step 步 in 氵 water, to ford, to wade over. Hence

頻 頻 **Pin²**. A man 頁 (L. 160) who wades 涉 through water; uneasiness. In the ancient character, 氵 was introduced between the two 止, to gain room. In the modern character, 氵 was suppressed. — Phonetic series 825.

Chih^{4}. To ascend 步 step by step an 阝 acclivity (L 86); 登也。从阝。从步，會意。It forms 隲 **chih**^{1}, merit, to promote.

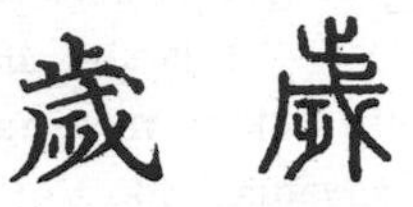

Sui^{4}. The planet 步 Jupiter, that presided over 戌 the wars. See L. 71 P. — Phonetic series 760.

H **Po**^{4}. Two 止 in contrary directions; idea of two feet; or of separation, divergence, letting loose. — It is the 105th radical. Note the derivatives

P'o^{2}. To stamp 殳 with the two 癶 feet, to trample. It is now a part of

Fa^{1}. To shoot an arrow, and, by extension, any expansion, any manifestation of a latent energy. The modern form (to trample with a bow) is a nonsense. In the ancient primitive character, there was 矢 an arrow, instead of 殳; shooting 癶 of the 矢 arrow by the 弓 bow. — Phonetic series 675.

Têng^{1}. To ascend 癶 upon a 豆 pedestal, firstly with one foot, then with the other. By extension, to ascend, to go up, in general. — Phonetic series 708.

Kui^{3}. The nicely disposed grass, on which the Ancients poured the libations offered to the Manes; see Graphies, page 362. This character, not easily written, was replaced, in the days of **Li-ssŭ**, by 癶 plus 矢, probably the primitive form of **fa**^{1} (above). The modern form has been arbitrarily mutilated by the scribes. Now **chia-chieh** a cyclical character. — Phonetic series 458.

Sixth series. 正 **chêng**^{4}. A special series is reserved for this compound of 止, on account of its important derivatives.

I **Chêng**^{4}. To be arrived and 止 to stop at the — line, at the limit, where one had to reach, without going astray; 从一、从止、會意。By extension, correct. straight, regular. — Phonetic series 107. It forms

定 **Ting**^{4}. Order 正 in the 宀 house, and, consequently, tranquillity, peace; 安也。从 正、从 宀。會 意。 By extension, fixed, certain, decided. — Phonetic series 400.

是 **Shih**^{4}. What was 正 controlled at 日 sun's light; 从 日、从 正。會 意。 The Glose compares this etymology with the etymology of 直 **chih**^{2}, L. 10 K. Extended meanings, truthfulness, reality, existence. — Phonetic series 476

歪 **Wai**^{1}. Deflected from the perpendicular, aslant; what is not 不 correct 正. This character is a modern one.

K 乏 **Fa**^{2}. It is 止 turned to the left. The inversion means that one did not reach 止 the line 一, the point where one had to reach; a defect, to be in want of, exhausted. The modern character is a fanciful abbreviation that has nothing in common with 之 **chih**^{1} (L. 79 B). — Phonetic series 54.

L 丏 **Mien**^{4}. This character is considered by some philologists as a derivative of 正. This is a mistake. It is a primitive, representing a woman sitting; — is the girdle; on the left, the seat; on the right, an apron that hides the fore and lower part of the body. By extension, to conceal, to hide, retreat, confinement, screened, out of view. — Phonetic series 71. It forms

Ch'ên^2. From 丏 and 厂. See L. 30 B.

Min^1. The retreat 丏 in a 宀 house, the home, a dwelling. It forms

Pin^1. A present 貝 offered to a man 𡧍 received in one's house 所 敬 也。賓 禮。 By extension, a guest. The scribes arbitrarily altered the primitive character to the two forms here joined. — Phonetic series 787.

LESSON 113.

About the primitive 長.

A 長 長 — **Chang**³, to grow. **Ch'ang**², long. The primitive form indicates locks of hair so long that they must be tied by a 一 hand and a brooch (the fork on the right); 像。一 束 之 形。Later on, 匕 was added, which made the composition of 長 analogous to the one of 老 (L. 30 E); manhood, when the hair is long By extension, long in time or distance. The modern form is an arbitrary contraction. — It is the 163th radical. Phonetic series 323. It forms

B 

Pao¹. Long 長 locks 彡 (L. 62); 長 髮 也。从 長、从 彡、會 意。— It is the 190th radical.

肆 — **Ssŭ**⁴. To expand 聿 to the utmost 長, to exhibit, unrestrained. See L. 169.

套 — **T'ao**⁴. A modern character. To suit what is of the same 大 height and 長 length. Assortment, to unite, etc.

LESSON 114.

About the two primitives 氏 and 氐.

A 氏 — **Shih**⁴. A floating plant, without roots, that ramifies and grows, like the nymphæaceæ so common in China, *Euryale ferox* and others, that spring up from a grain, float first, then fix themselves and acquire in a short time a prodigious development. By extension, development, multiplication; a wandering hord of the primitive times, a clan, a family — It is the 83th radical Phonetic series 82. It forms

B 氐 — **Ti**³. A development of the last. The floating plant 氏 sprouts to the bottom 一 of water, to be fixed and rooted there. By extension, bottom, foundation, to sink down; 加 一 以 像 地。— Phonetic series 163. It forms

Hun¹. Dusk, twilight; when the 日 sun has plunged 氐 below the horizon. The — of 氐 was suppressed; 从日、从氐省。會意。— Phonetic series 364. The form 昬 is a wrong one.

C 

Kuo². A development of ti (above B), the root boring in the bottom. It is phonetically contracted (— being suppressed) in

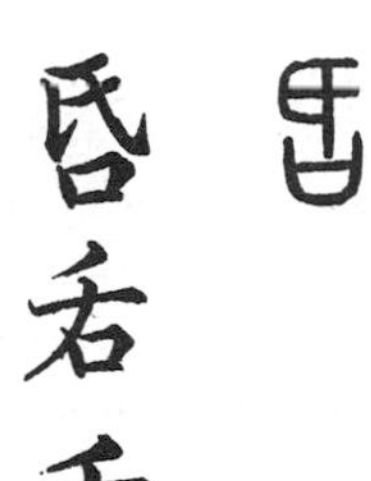

Kuo². To put or to hold in one's mouth; 从口、昏省聲。Note the modern abbreviations, specially the last one, that is written in such a way that the compounds of **kuo**² cannot be distinguished from those of **shê**². See note L. 102 C. — Phonetic series 227.

D 

Min². The people, the mass, the common multitude. Some philologists consider this character as a 毋 **mu**³ (mother, L. 67 O), with sprouts that represent the multiplication; people, the sons of women. 从毋取蕃育也。上下衆多意。指事。It is highly probable that this interpretation is erroneous. **Min**² is a primitive, a creeping plant with sprouts, that is proliferous (second ancient character, 古文像) The third ancient form, and the modern one, are arbitrary abbreviations. 民 is therefore a character resembling 氏, and not a derivative from it. — Phonetic series 137.

LESSON 115.

About the three primitives 井、幵、丹。

First series 井 **ching**³.

A 井 丼

Ching³. Primitively, it was designed to represent eight square lots of fields, divided among eight families, reserving the middle square for public use, and digging a well in it. The well is represented by a dot; 八家一井。像。Such was the custom in antiquity. See *Textes Historiques*, p. 25. The system was abolished, and the character is now used to mean, a well. — Phonetic series 49. It is phonetic in

井刂 刑 荆

Hsing[2]. Legal punishment (从刀 a sword, L. 52), which was arbitrarily written by the scribes 刑. See below B. 今課作刑。— Phonetic series 204.

Second series. 幵 ch'ien[2].

B 幵 幵 开

Ch'ien[1]. It represents two scales poised; 像。二干對構。上平也。Even, level, line, row, agreement. Note the modern arbitrary contraction which, reducing to four the six strokes of this important phonetic, is the cause, for students of Chinese, of many fruitless researches in the dictionaries. — Phonetic series 184. See 刑 above A. It forms.

幷 幷 并

Ping[1]. Two 人 men who march 幵 side by side; together, harmony, with, etc.; 相從也。从二人。从幵。會意。The remark made for the last is to be made here also, the modern contracted form counting six strokes, instead of eight. — Phonetic series 390.

C 開 開

K'ai[1]. It has nothing in common with 幵. It is a representative character. Two hands 廾 take away the 一 bar that closes a door 門; to open. It is the reverse of 閂 shuan[1], to shut, that was explained L. 1 H; 張也。从門。从廾一。會意。一者關也。

Third series. 丹 tan[1].

D 丹 丹 青 青

Tan[1]. Cinnabar. It has nothing in common with 井. The crucible or stove of the alchimists, with 丶 cinnabar in it. See L. 4 C. — Phonetic series 83. It forms

Ch'ing[1]. Light green; the colour 丹 of the 生 sprouting plants (L. 79 F); 从丹。从生。會意。木始生其色也。Note that 丹 the cinnabar is red. It seems rather curious that the two complementary colours, green and red, are here confounded (daltonism?). An author explains seriously that the green plants, when burnt, give a red fire 木生火。— It is the 174th radical. Phonetic series 337.

丹 is still found in 彤 t'ung^2, scarlet red; and in 旃 chan^1, a red banner (L. 117).

LESSON 116.

About the primitive 冄.

A 

Jan^3. The hair just growing on the body; 像形。It might be considered as 毛 inverted and doubled. See L. 100, second series. The scribes now write 冉 (nothing in common with 再 L. 35 J). — Phonetic series 128. It is phonetic in

B 

Na^4, **na**^{3}. A ancient 邑 city and State in the West, perhaps Tibet, whose inhabitants wore 冄 furs; 西夷國。今四川之西。The scribes strangely altered 冄. This character lost its primitive meaning and is now used as a demonstrative pronoun in the modern spoken language. — Phonetic series 232.

C 

So^1. Clothes 衣 made of 冄 furs or straw, against rain. It was explained, L. 16 D.

LESSON 117.

About the two primitives 方 and 㫃, that resemble each other in the modern writing, but that etymologically have nothing in common.

First series 方 fang^1.

A

Fang^1. It is supposed to represent two boats lashed together, so that they make a ferry-boat, a pontoon, a square barge; 併船也。It seems rather difficult to see this representation in the character. The ancient forms represent the four regions of the space with two dimensions, the earthly surface. By extension, square, regular, correct, a rule, etc. — It forms the 70th radical. But, with the exception of two or three of them, all the characters classified under this fictitious radical, belong to the primitive 㫃, below, B, that is unconnected with 方. — Phonetic series 56.

旁 **P'ang**². The space with three dimensions; the limits of that 方 space, indicated by 二 on the top, and two side lines. The ancient forms, as usually, are more expressive than the modern ones. By extension, border, side, lateral. — Phonetic series 556.

放 **Fang**⁴. To lead 攴, in the open space 方 (steppe, pasture-land), a drove; to feed. Compare 牧 L. 43 D. By extension, to let go, to loosen, to open out, to lay down, etc. It forms

敫 **Yao**⁴. To shine; 放 emit 白 light; 从白。从放、會意、凡光多白、故从白。— Phonetic series 766

敖 **Nao**². From 出 and 放. See L. 78 E. — Phonetic series 638.

Yen¹, has nothing in common with 方. See L. 34 K.

Second series 㫃 **yen**³.

B

㫃 **Yen**³. First, long overhanging branches. Later, the mangrove, shooting, from its branches, roots that go down and implant themselves in the ground (right side; lianæ, the jungle. Idea of a being, hanging, waving, covering, with many stalks, etc. This character is unconnected with 方. Note its successive alterations. — It forms nearly all the characters attributed to the 70th radical 方. Note the following compounds:

旋 **Hsüan**². To revolve, to move in an orbit, to do a thing in turn. Composed of 疋 foot (L. 112 C), and 㫃 motion. — Phonetic series 614.

族 **Tsu**^{2}. A bundle of arrows 矢, fifty, says the Glose; 㫃 means the numerous sticks; 从矢、从㫃、會意。By extension, a multitude of beings of the same kind, a family which traces its descent from one ancestor, kindred relatives who are like a sheaf of individuals; 父子孫人屬之正名。— Phonetic series 654.

施 **Shih**^{1}. To pour out 也 at repeated times 㫃, probably something to drink; to bestow, to diffuse, generosity; L. 107.

斿 **Yu**^{2}. Contraction of 游; the waving motions 㫃 of the swimmer 汓 (L. 94 A); to float, to swim. — Phonetic series 500.

旅 **Lü**^{3}. A campment. Men 从 encamping under the 㫃 branches of trees. By extension, men temporarily staying in a place that is not their ordinary abode, soldiers, merchants, travellers, emigrants, exiles.

C 於 **Yü**^{2}. It has certainly nothing in common with 㫃。It is probably not an arbitrary contraction of 烏 **wu**^{1} (L. 138 D) It seems to be a modern sign, invented to be used as a particle expressing the relation that exists between two terms of a proposition. It represents graphically the connection (left side) between 二 two distinct 刀 terms. — Phonetic series 419.

Sub-series 倝 **kan**^{4}. A sub-series is reserved for this derivative of 㫃, on account of its important compounds.

D 倝 **Kan**^{4}. The 日 solar rays penetrating into the 㫃 jungle, draws up the vapours of the ground which, till then, were 丂 checked (L. 1 I); 日出氣達也。The bottom of 㫃 is suppressed, to give room to 丂. Idea of evaporation, of a fog lifting up. — Phonetic series 543. It forms

乾 **Ch'ien**^{2}. A radical redundancy of the last. 乙 representing the vapours sent up. The proper room of the vapours, says the Glose, is upwards; they en-

乾 deavour 乙 to rise up; hence the meaning, cloudy firmament (and not light blue of the skies), heaven. 上出也。乙。物之達也。凡上達者。莫若氣。天爲積氣。故乾爲天。 This character is sometimes used for **kan**^{1}, dry. It is a licence. In that sense, the character 乾 is to be used, in which 旱 (L. 102) means the drying 乙 of the dampness.

榦 幹 **Kan**^{4}. A rod 木 very 𠦝 long: by extension, power, capacity. The second form is more recent, and commonly used. It is an absurd 干 phonetic redundancy, the radical 木 being suppressed; 俗作幹。

翰 **Han**^{4}. To fly 羽 very 𠦝 high. **Chia-chieh**, for [illegible] pencil, in 翰林 **Han-lin**, the Chinese Academy of old.

Note: In the three following, 人 was suppressed in the modern form.

朝 **Chao**^{1}. The rise of the sun and of the mist 𠦝 on sea, seen from a 舟 boat; dawn. By extension, the Imperial courts, so called because they were held in early morning. In this sense, they pronounced **ch'ao**^{2}. Hence, the Imperial court, a dynasty, etc. — Phonetic series 664.

韓 **Han**^{2}. A bascule 韋 (L. 31 G, to and fro) to raise 𠦝 water.

戟 **Chi**^{3}. A lance 戈 very 𠦝 long.

LESSON 118.

About the primitives 冎 and 歺
First series. 冎 kua^3.

A

冎 

Kua^3. A skeleton, skull and bones without flesh, roughly shaped. By extension, to strip the flesh off, to bone, to disarticulate, article, broken, etc. 剔人肉置其骨也。象形。 See below B, 另. It forms

Kua³. A defect in the conformation of the 冎 bones of the 口 mouth; a wry mouth with a palatal fissure. — Phonetic series 457. It forms

Kuo⁴, from 辵 (L 112 F), to go through. Phonetic series 742.

Ku². Bones 冎 with flesh 月 around. Compare 肯, whose composition is analogous, and which was explained L. 65 C. — It is the 188th radical. Phonetic series 547.

B 

Ling⁴. It is 冎 borrowed as a symbol for arithmetic. The modern sound and shape are conventional. The primive form represented a bone extracted from the skeleton, a fraction, a remainder, a surplus; 冎分也。俗字誤作另。形聲俱乖。It forms

Pieh². To divide, to distinguish, difference. Composed of 冎 and of 刀 a knife.

Second series. 歹 tai³.

C 

Tai³. A primitive; bones fallen to pieces; what remains definitively of a man's skeleton. The fourth ancient form, relatively modern, is composed of 尸 body, and of two strokes cut up by a third, to represent the disjunction of the body's elements. By extension, death, misfortune, evil, bad, to break to pieces, to shatter, to grind, fragments, dust. — It is the 78th radical. It forms

Ssŭ³. To die; 歹 dissolution of a 匕 man. See L. 26 H, and its derivative 葬 **tsang**⁴, to bury, to put a coffin into the ground, L 78 G. See also LL. 12 F and 52 D.

Ts'an². To reduce 又 into 歹 fragments, into dust.— Phonetic series 308. It forms

Ts'an⁴. Rice 米 pounded 𣦼, fine white oat-meal. By extension, a meal, a feast, whiteness, purity.

D 

Note. The two preceding 歹 and 歺, placed on the top of a compound, are written 歺 or 𣦼, and form the following compound:

Hsün⁴. A deep ravine 谷 (L. 18); 歹 represents the erosion of the rocks or of the loess by waters; 从谷. 从歹. 會意。歹殘涯意也。— Forms by substituting 目 eye (L. 158) to the 口 of 谷:

Jui⁴.Brightness and quickness of visual perception, and, by extension, of intellectual perception; shrewd, profound. The 目 eye penetrating to the very bottom of the deep hollow; 深明也。

Ho⁴. An artificial 谷 ravine, dug 歺 by men; a pit, a canal. Compare above **hsün⁴**. Now

Ho¹. A ditch, a canal; 土, L. 81, is a radical redundancy.

LESSON 119.

About the primitive 木 and its multiples.

First series. 木 **mu⁴**.

A 

Mu⁴. It represents a tree, 像. On the top, the branches; at the bottom, the roots; in the middle, the trunk. By extension, wood. It is the 75th radical of characters relating to trees. It forms

B 

K'un⁴. Weariness, exhaustion that forces to 止 stop on the way, to sleep under a 木 tree. The modern form represents the same idea, but not so clearly; 口 a camping (L. 74) under a tree 木. — Phonetic series 286

C 休 𠊳

Hsiu¹. To stop, to cease to march; 息止也。A man 人 under a 木 tree; 會意。Compare with the preceding; the idea is the same. By extension, to cease in general, in particular to cease to live with a wife, to repudiate her. — Phonetic series 205.

D 札 **Cha**^{1}. A thin wooden 木 tablet, anciently used for writing 乙, for information (L. 9 A). — **Phonetic** series 101.

E 桼 **Ch'i**^{1}. Varnish, a substance that falls in drops from the branches and the trunk of a 木 tree; **从木、像形。桼滴而下。** The drops are a primitive. — Phonetic series 598.

F 柰 奈 **Nai**^{4}. Omens 示 derived from 木 trees. Compare L. 119 M. This character lost its primitive meaning and is now used as an interjection, alas! The second modern form was invented by the scribes. See L. 99 D, the first form.

G 集 **Chi**^{2}. Three 隹 birds (a great number) roosting on 木 a tree. By extension, an assembly, a meeting, a market or fair; **羣鳥在木上也。** The scribes contracted the old character. It forms

雜 **Tsa**^{2}. Garments 衣 made 集 with variegated pieces stitched together; **从衣、从集。五采相合也。** By extension, particoloured, streaked; a mixture of colours or ingredients. The scribes placed the 木 of 集 under 衣, then contracted the two elements. Compare 卒 L. 16 M.

H 臬 **Nieh**^{4}. To shoot into the black of the target, **射準的也。** It is explained that 木 is the support, and 自 the black of the target or bull's eye; because the black is to the target what the nose (自 L. 159) is to the face, the central point. By extension, rules of shooting; *then*, rule, law, in general.

I 杏 **Hsing**^{4}. The tree 木 that produces 口 apricots; 口 represents the fruits hanging from the tree. The inverted character

J 呆 **Tai**^{1}, stupid, is modern. It is equivalent to 獃.

K 閑 **Hsien**². Threshold. From 木 wood, and 門 door; 从門中有木、會意。

染 **Jan**³. To dye, to tinge. The dipping in the 氵 infusion of 木 wood of *Gardenia tinctoria* or *Rubia cordifolia*, must be repeated 九 nine times, says the Glose; 會意。See L. 23 A.

梟 **Hsiao**¹. A bird of prey 鳥 prospecting, on the top of a tree 木; the head alone appears, the feet are not shaped. — The head of a criminal exposed on the top of a stake.

李 **Li**³. A plum-tree. The tree 木, the children 子 are fond of; 會意。Not to be confounded with 季 **chi**⁴ (L. 94 A).

枚 **Mei**². A stalk or stick 攵 in wood 木; one of, each; 會意。

沐 **Mu**⁴. To wash 氵 the hair; 木 is phonetic. To cleanse in general.

樂 **Yao**⁴, music. **Lao**⁴, joy. Here 木 represents the frame on which the instruments are hung. See L. 88 C.

Second series. Multiples of 木.

L 林 林 **Lin**². A forest, a clump of trees. Two 木 to indicate many trees together, 會意。Not to be confounded with 𣏟 **p'ai**⁴, L. 79 H. — Phonetic series 377.

M 禁 禁 **Chin**⁴. Bad 示 omens derived from 林 trees. Compare L. 119 F. By extension, to prohibit, to warn against, to forbid. — Phonetic series 727.

N 楚 楚 **Ch'u**³. A country planted with 林 trees; 疋 (L. 112 C) is phonetic. Various **chia-chieh**. — Phonetic series 730.

O 焚 **Fên**². To set a forest 林 on fire 火, in order either to drive out the wild beasts or to prepare a clearing. Hence, to burn, in general.

梵 **Fan**⁴. The soughing of the wind through 林 trees; 凡 is phonetic. In the Hindu-Chinese literature, this character is used to designate 梵王 Brahma.

婪 **Lan**². Greediness; a woman's 女 vice, says the Glose; 林 is phonetic.

棥 **Fan**². A fence. See L. 39 L.

楙 **Mao**⁴. A bushy forest. See L. 95 C.

無 **Wu**². Clearing. See L. 10 I.

森 **Shên**¹. A great number of trees, and by extension, a great number in general.

[illegible] **Yu**⁴. A park 囗 planted with 木 trees. Now 囿.

LESSON 120.

About some compounds of 木 (L. 119), that form important series.

A 本 — **Pên**³. Trunk, stump of a 木 tree, across the line 一 that denotes the earth; 木下日本。从木，一者地也。— Phonetic series 147.

B 末 — **Mo**⁴. The top, the highest 一 branches of a tree 木; end, extremity. 木上日末。从木。一在其上指事。— Phonetic series 138.

C 未 — **Wei**⁴. A tall 木 tree with its branches superposed; 从木重像。The actual meanings of this character, in the cycle and as a negation, are **chia-chieh**. — Phonetic series 167. It forms

Chih⁴. To cut a 未 big tree with a 刀 sharp instrument, an axe or an adze. The ancient form shows the notches. By extension, to work the wood, to make, to form, etc. The modern character is corrupt.

Li². A composition analogous to the preceding one. To cut down 攴 a big 未 tree; 厂 represents its falling. — Phonetic series 627.

D 朱

Chu[1]. Trees whose heart is reddish, as cedar, thuja, etc. By extension, red. A tree 木; 一 in the middle represents a cutting in the wood; 赤心木、松柏屬、从木一在其中。— Phonetic series 188.

E 耒

Lei[3]. A harrow. A 木 wood with 丰 prongs. The modern form lost one of the prongs. See L. 97 G. — It is the 127th radical

F 果

Kuo[2]. The fruit of a tree, represented by 田 on the top of 木; fruits in general. — Phonetic series 373.

G 巢

Ch'ao[2]. A nest on a tree. See L. 12 O. On the tree a nest, and on the nest, the feathers of the hatching bird. — Phonetic series 594.

H 朿

Ts'ŭ[4]. Thorns. A thorny 木 tree; 木芒也。从木、像形。— Phonetic series 243. It forms the important following compounds and multiples:

刺

Ts'ŭ[4]. Primitively, torture; 朿 thorn and 刀 knife. It is now used for 朿. Not to be confounded with 剌 la[2], below I.

責

Chai[2]. To chastise, to punish. A thorny rod 朿 and a fine in money 貝. Note the contraction of 朿 into 龶 in the modern form. — Phonetic series 590.

棘

Chi[4]. Thorny shrubs in general. The 朿 duplicated represents the great number of thorns.

棗

Tsao[3]. From thorn duplicated, referring to its abundance of thorns; the jujube tree, very common in China.

帝

Ti[4]. The Emperor, the man who rules over the Empire. The ancient character represents a man, clad in long robes (compare the ancient form of 帶 L. 24 Q) and designated by 一, an old form of 上, superior. Then the scribes added two arms. Then **Li-ssŭ** changed the bottom into 朿. Lastly the scribes contracted the character. Compare the series 君, p. 9; the evolution is the same. — Phonetic series 478. It forms

商

Ti[4]. To control 帝 one's mouth 口, to hold one's tongue. Phonetic series 650, under its modern contracted form. To be distinguished from 商 **shang**[1], L. 15 D.

I 

Shu[4]. To encompass 口 (L. 74) a tree 木, here taken to mean any object; to tie; to knot. — Phonetic series 303. It forms

Sou[4]. To cough. A 束 tight 欠 breath that becomes loose. — Phonetic series 647.

竦 **Sung**[3]. Reserve with fear. To stand 立 before a superior, as being bound 束 with fear.

敕 **Ch'ih**[4]. Government. A rod 攵 and 束 a tie, the coercitive and legislative power.

La[2]. To cut 刀 the tie that 束 binds; to cut, in general. — Phonetic series 459. It forms

Lai[4]. To solve 剌 a difficulty by 貝 giving money; to bribe in a competition, or to buy in protection. The 刀 is placed on the top of 貝 — Phonetic series 821.

Chien[3]. To partake 八 a 束 bundle, in order to pick and cull. — Phonetic series 429. It forms

Lan[2]. A bar shutting a 門 door; 柬 is phonetic. — Phonetic series 833.

This compound (case, bag), 束 increased with 口, was explained L. 75 A, with its derivatives.

K **Tung**[1]. The sun 日 appearing at the horizon. To show that it is on a level with the horizon, it is represented shining under the top of the 木 trees that are at the horizon. Compare 白 L. 88, and 且 L. 143 B; 从日在木中。By extension, the East whence light rises. — Phonetic series 405. It forms

Ts'ao[2]. Judges. There were two, in the ancient tribunals, sitting on the Eastern side (the place of honour), and deciding 曰 (L. 73 A) the cases. The modern contraction is an arbitrary one; 獄之兩曹、在廷東。从二東、治事者。从曰、按判事以言也。會意。

Chung[4]. Composed, as 壬 ting[2] (L. 81 D), of 人 man and of 土 earth; 東 contracted is phonetic. The man 人 on the top, tries to rise, from the earth 土 at the bottom, an object in the middle, which is represented by the phonetic. Hence the idea, *heavy, weight*. This interpretation is certainly erroneous. The ancient characters represent round or flat weights piled up on a kind of support. — Phonetic series 437. It forms the two following:

T'ung[2]. A slave boy; the counterpart of a slave girl 妾 (L. 102 E). Composed of 辛 a crime, 重 (contracted) grave, committed by the parents, and for which their children were reduced to slavery; 男有罪曰童。女有罪曰妾。奴婢也。Those slaves were forced to live unmarried; hence the extended meanings, a bachelor, a spinster, a virgin. — Phonetic series 716.

 **Liang**². The weight 重 (contracted), 頁 (contracted) special to some object. Weight, measure, in general. See L. 75 F.

LESSON 121.

About the primitive 禾.

A 禾 **Ho**². Grain, corn, crops. The character represents the plant (resembling 木 L. 110), ended on the top by a pendent ripe ear; 朩像其穗。Derived idea of uniformity, concord, the grains growing, waving, ripening together; 後人以意沽和也。— It is the 115th radical of characters relating to grains and their uses. — See 秀 L. 23 B; 利 L. 52 F; 科 L. 98 B etc. Note the following compounds :

B 囷 **Ch'ün**¹. A granary; the bundles of corn being enclosed; 从禾在口中,會意。— Phonetic series 351.

C 秋 **Ch'iu**¹. The season when the 禾 grain is 火 burned, i e. whitened, ripe; 禾穀熟也。The autumn. — Phonetic series 433.

D 穌 **Su**¹. To glean 禾 ears, 取禾也; 魚 is phonetic. The modern sense, to revive, to rise from the dead, is **chia-chieh**.

E 稚 **Chih**⁴. Grain 禾 still young and tender, 幼禾也。Young, delicate; 隹 is phonetic

龢 和 **Ho**². Tune 禾 of 口 mouths, formerly of 龠 musical pipes. Harmony, union; 調也。

F 委 **Wei**³. The lot of 女 woman who mast 禾 yield; 隨也,順也。By extension, to suffer, to serve. There are different derived meanings. — Phonetic series 409.

G 禿 **T'u**¹. Bald. When the head of a 儿 man is like a 禾 mowed down field.

H 年 **Nien**². The year's harvest, the 千 thousand 禾 stalks. A year (L. 24 D). The modern character is an absurd contraction.

I 

Shu[3]. The panicled millet 禾, whose 入 put in water 水 and fermented, produces spirits; 黍可爲酒、禾入水也。— It is the 202th radical. It forms

Hsiang[1]. The sweet 甘 odour of 黍 millet when it ferments. Sweet smell, or sweet to the taste. See L. 73 B. The modern character is a strange contraction. — It is the 186th radical.

秉

Ping[3]. A bundle of corn 禾 held by a 彐 hand. To uphold, to seize, to grasp in the hand. See L. 44 I. — It forms

Chien[1]. Two bundles 禾 in the 彐 hand. Union, together. See L. 44 I. — Phonetic series 519. It forms

Lien[2]. The angled 兼 joint of the 广 roof and of the walls of a house; a corner, a joint. — Phonetic series 745.

L 秝

Li[4]. Many 二 ears 禾 ripening together; crops; 从二、从禾、會意。It is phonetic in

厤

Li[4] *annual* 厂 cycle, growing and ripening of the crops. It forms

歷

Li[4]. A 止 (L. 112 A) stop in the 厤 turn, the end of a period past; to pass, a term; 从止。過也。Often contracted into 歴 by the scribes. — Phonetic series 822.

曆

Li[4]. The 日 (L. 143) solar 厤 terms, calendar, time. This character was used for the personal name of the Emperor 乾隆 **Ch'ien-lung**, and consequently was no longer employed for common use. It was superseded by 歷。

M

禾 inverted, a pendent ear, to bow the head, is found only in the following compound:

稽

Chi[1]. To bow the head in order to examine. The compound on the right side seems to be an error of the scribes for 耆 (L. 30 E) The meaning should be then, to shake the head, like old men.

LESSON 122

About the primitive 米, straight and bent down.

First series. 米 mi³ straight.

A 

Mi³. Grains of different plants. The character represents four grains, that are separated 十 by the thrashing; 粟實也。按四丶像。十其介者。彝糲一. See 彝 L. 68 D; 糲 L. 23 G, 暴 L. 78 E; 康 L. 102 B; 粟 L. 41 E; 屎 L. 32 E; 匊 L 54 D; 粥 L. 87 B; 類 L. 160 C; 毇 L. 81 A; etc.

糶 **T'iao⁴**. To sell (出 to bring out) grain 米.

糴 **Ti³**. To buy (入 to bring in) grain 米. In these two characters, 翟 L. 62 G is phonetic.

Second series. 米 mi³ bent down.

B  

Mi³. Grains. It forms

C   

胃

Wei⁴. The stomach which incloses 口 the food 米. This viscer being fleshy, later on 月 was added (L. 65); then the scribes contracted 図 into 田; 穀府也。从肉、図像形。按中𠂢米字科書之。— This series is unconnected with 鹵 L. 41 D (grains of salt, an analogous figure). — Phonetic series 胃 489.

菌 **Shih³**. Vegetables 艹 that went through the 図 stomach; excreta, dung. This character is now written 屎 (see L. 32 E).

D  

Ch'ang⁴. Grains 米 fermenting in a 凵 vase, and a 匕 spoon to take the liquor out. It was explained L. 26 C. — It is the 192th radical.

LESSON 123.

About the primitive 釆.

A 釆 **Pien**[4]. The steps of a wild beast 像. The strokes represent the print of the claws, and the points the print of the soft parts. The examination of the trail indicating the kind of animal, hence the extended meaning, to discriminate, to part, to sort out. The excreta giving the same indication, 釆 means dung in 糞 (L. 104 A). It is unconnected with 米 L. 122. — It is the 165th radical. It forms

B 悉 **Hsi**[2]. To get a perfect knowledge 心, by a thorough investigation 釆; to comprehend in all particulars.

C 关 **Chüan**[3]. To choose, to 釆 pick and cull with the 𦥑 hands. The modern character is a contraction. See L. 47 K, and below F. — Phonetic series 191.

D 番 **Fan**[1]. The tracks of a wild beast, print of the claws 釆 and the 田 sole of the foot; 獸足也。从釆。田像掌形。— Phonetic series 676. It forms

審 **Shên**[3]. To examine, to search, to get knowledge by study. To investigate 番 in one's house 宀. — Phonetic series 811.

E 釋 **Shih**[4]. To clear up 釆 by an 睪 investigation, an enquiry. (L. 102 G); 从釆。取其分别物也。By extension, to part from an accusation, to let out from confinement, etc.

F 奥 **Nao**[4]. The dark corners of a 宀 house, in which one discerns 釆 the things only by 𦥑 groping; 室中幽隱之處. By extension, mysterious, obscure. — Phonetic series 750.

粤 **Yüeh**[4]. A particle, a kind of 亐 interjection (L. 58 E), that comes before the explanation 釆 of an 宀 obscure matter. Often changed into 粵. K'ang-hsi wrongly classified it under the radical 米.

LESSON 124.

About the primitive 尗.

A 

Shu^2. Beans. The primitive is thought to represent the plant; two husks pending; 豆也像豆生之形也。It forms

B 

Shu^2. The collecting 又 of 尗 beans. This character is obsolete in that sense, and is now used **chia-chieh** to designate a father's younger brother, an uncle of the same surname (vulgo **shou^2**). — Phonetic series 393.

C 

Ch'i^1. It represents the mowing of 尗 beans, with a crooked 戉 sickle. It is now used **chia-chieh** to mean the kindred. The idea may come from the boughs of creeping plants. — Phonetic series 597.

LESSON 125.

About different forms of the primitive 水. The primitive 泉 is incidentally explained.

First series. 水 **shui^3**.

A 

Shui^3. Water. The central stroke represents a brook, a rivulet, 像形。The four small strokes represent the whirls of water. See. L. 12 A. Note the modern contracted forms. — It is the 85th radical of characters relating to water and streams. Different derivatives were already explained; e.g. 冰 L. 17 B, 沙 L. 18 M, 汙 L. 94 O, 泰 L. 47 O, 盥 L. 50 B, etc. Note the following.

沓

Ta^2. Babbling 曰 words flowing like 水 water. See L. 73 A. — Phonetic series 395.

衍

Yen^3. Water 氵 that 行 advances (L. 63 C), that spreads out; overflowing, inundation; 从水,从行,會意。It forms 愆 **ch'ien^1**, a fault, an excess, licentiousness; scandalous behaviour.

法 **Fa**[1]. Rule, law. By extension, model, pattern, means. This character is a modern one, and its explanation is too far reached: to make the morals smooth, as water 氵 is, by 去 extirpating vices; 平之如水,不直者去之。The ancient character was composed of 亼 to adapt (L. 14 A) to 正 righteousness (L. 112 I).

Second series. 雨 yü[3].

B 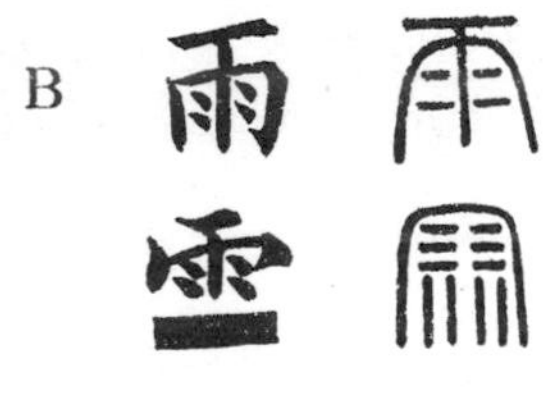

Yü[3]. Rain. According to some, the four points represent the drops, — upper line the skies, and 冂 the clouds. — Others explain as it was said in the L. 1 B. — Others still explain: — the sky, 巾 the regular falling (L 35 H) of drops (the four points are a special primitive). — An ancient form simply represented a shower of rain. — It is the 173th radical. It forms

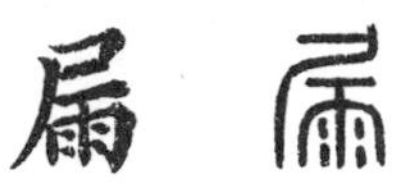

Lou[4]. Rain 雨 soaking through a 尸 roof (L. 32 G); 屋穿水下也。尸者屋省。Dropping.

Third series. 𣶒 that is 水 bent down, in

C 𣶒 

Yüan[1]. A whirlpool, a gulf, an abyss. The ancient character represented 水 water in a ◯ circle i.e. whirling. A more recent form represents the 水 water 𣶒 bouncing between two banks. Now 淵, a graphical redundancy. It forms

肅

Su[4]. Deferential fear of an official. — Modern form, 聿 to write (L. 44 D) a *report to a superior*, as if one would be on the brink of an abyss 𣶒, that is, with fear; 持事振敬也。从聿在𣶒上。會意。This idea commonly occurs in the classics; 戰戰兢兢。如臨深淵也。— An ancient form meant, to apply one's 心 heart in writing 聿 reports and in administering 卩。會意。— Phonetic series 757.

益 I[4]. It represents a 皿 vase, so full of 水 water, that it overflows. This circumstance is represented by the fact that 水 is over the vase and is bent down, thus expressing its overflowing. By extension, addition, profit, excess, overplus; 饒也、从水、从皿、會意。皿益之意也。— Phonetic series 539.

Fourth series. 永 and 𠂢.

D 永 **Yung[3].** The unceasing flow of 水 water veins in the earth, 水長也。像水巠理之長。Abstracted meaning, duration, perpetuity, but not eternity. Graphically, this character is a variant of 水; the slender threads are substituted to the whirls. — Phonetic series 173. It forms

Yang[4]. It has the same meaning as 永; 羊 is phonetic. By extension, uniformity, model, pattern, wearisomeness. See L. 103 A. — Phonetic series 659.

E 𠂢 **P'ai[4].** Graphically, it is 永 inverted. The idea is analogous; ramification of a stream; 水之别也。从反永、指事。— Phonetic series 234. It forms

衇 脈 **Mai[4].** The blood 血 running 𠂢 in the veins, the pulse. The second form, from 月 flesh and 𠂢 streams, is more recent. 血理之分行體中者、血之府也。

F 泉 **Ch'üan[2].** A spring gushing out from the ground, and flowing in rills. A special primitive. In the middle, the gush that bubbles up from the earth; on the top, the water expanding; on the sides, the flowing. The modern character is an arbitrary confection; 水 water 白 pure. 水原也。像。水流出、成川形。It forms

厡 原 **Yüan[2].** Any origin; a source. In the anciont form, there were three 泉 springs gushing out from a 厂 cliff. The scribes contracted it first, then altered this character in such a way that 水 became 小. See L. 59 C. — Phonetic series 388.

LESSON 126.

About the primitive 火.

First series. 火 **huo**^{3}.

A 火 灬

Huo^3. Fire. Ascending flames; 炎而上、像形。 — It forms the 86th radical of a large group of characters relating to heat. Note the modern contracted form 灬 that is used in combination, at the bottom of the compounds. See the compounds already explained, 然 L. 65 G, 威 L. 71 P, 秋 L. 121 C, 灰 L. 46 I, 炭 L. 59 G, 炭 L. 12 I, 焚 L. 119 O, etc. Note the following:

炙

Chih^4. To 火 roast 肉 flesh; 炮肉也。从肉在火上。會意。To cauterise, a moxa.

焦

Chiao^1. A 火 roasted 隹 bird. Singed, shrunk, dried up; melancholy, sadness. — Phonetic series 669.

煩

Fan^2. Pain in the head 頁 caused by 火 heat; 熱頭病也、从頁、从火、會意。Morally, 火 heat in the 頁 head, nervousness, disgust. See L. 160 C.

烹

P'êng^1. To roast; 亨 (L. 75 D) is phonetic.

Second series. 火 contracted in the modern writing. The ancient forms are like those of the first series. See 光 L. 24 J, 尉 L. 32 B, 票 L. 50 O, 关 L. 47 J, 丙 L. 41 A, etc. Note the following:

B 

Shên^1. The Chinese hearth, a small 穴 hole (L. 37) under the caldron, in which the hand 彐 stirs the fire 火。會意。竈也。Hence the derived meanings, deep, profound, abstruse, etc. Note 探 deep water; 深 to explore, to fathom. The scribes arbitrarily omitted the upper dot of 穴, and combined 彐 and 火 into 木。

叟

Sou^3. An old man. A man who reached the age when he must make 彐 fire 火 in his 宀 house; 从彐持火屋下。Compare it with the last character, and see how the ancient form was fancifully altered by the scribes. — Phonetic series 567.

赤 **Ch'ih**4. The 大 human 火 fire (L. 60 N), the face turning red and crimson on being angry. By extension, natural carnation, red colour, etc. — It is the 155th radical. — See 赧 nan3, L. 43 J. Note 赦 shê4, amnesty, pardon; the primitive sense was 攴 to strike the culprit and 赤 make him ashamed, *without ulterior punishment*. It forms 螫 chê1, bite or sting of venimous insects, that inflames the skin. Doubled

赫 **Ho**4. Intense blushing, shame and fear.

C **Third series.** The same dots that are used as an abbreviation of 火, are also used, specially in recent characters relating to animals, to represent:

1. The tail, e.g. 魚 fish (L. 142); 燕 swallow (L. 141).
2. The feet, e g. 馬 horse (L 137); 鳥 bird (L. 138); 爲 monkey (L. 49 H); 羔 lamb (L. 103 A), etc. See L. 136 B, C.
3. 灬 is also used as an abbreviation of more intricate forms, e.g. 無 L. 10 I; 鼎 L. 92 E; 煞 an arbitrary abbreviation of 殺 L. 45 J, etc.

Fourth series. 火 doubled, 炎 yen2,

D 

Yen2. A rising flame, fire that blazes; 火光上也、从重火、會意。— Phonetic series 416. It forms the important compounds:

Hei2 The soot let by the 炎 fire around the 囧 hole through which the smoke escapes. Black colour. See L. 40 D. — It is the 203th radical. Phonetic series 678.

Hsün1. Smoke, fumigation. A black 黑 smoke 屮 rising from the fire. See L. 40 D. — Phonetic series 781.

粦 㷠

Lin². An ignis fatuus; 炎 flames that are seen 舛 hovering. (See 舞 L. 31 E). They rise, says the Glose, on old battlefields and proceed from the blood of men and horses; 兵死及牛馬之血爲粦。粦鬼火也。从炎、从舛。會意。The scribes arbitrarily contracted 炎 into 米. — Phonetic series 696.

舜

Shun⁴. The Chinese convolvulus, that ∫ creeps and covers 土 the ground with its blooming reddish 炎 flowers. The scribes strangely altered this character. The phonetic 舛 (L. 31 E) was added later on; 舜艸也。蔓地連華、像形。Name of a famous ancient monarch who reigned about B. C. 2042. — Phonetic series 703.

E 尞

Liao³. Sacrifice offered to Heaven, on the threshing-floor, after the harvest; 古人穡精報天神。The ancient forms represent the threshing-floor, the grains, the strow The more recent form represents the straw and the grains offered as a gift 曰 (L 75 D) to be 火 burnt; burnt offering of firstlings. — Phonetic series 695.

Fifth series.

F 焱

Yen². Many lamps. Compare 炎 (above D). It forms.

熒 𤇾

Ying² The light 火 of many lamps in a 冖 room (L. 34 H) 屋下燈燭之光也。从三火、从冖、會意。This character forms a large group of compounds in which the 火 at the bottom gives room to the radical. — Phonetic series 585. Note

勞

Lao².To toil 力 at the lamp's light, during night; to fag at, to exert one's self in an extraordinary manner; to labour; 會意。— Phonetic series 694.

LESSON 127.

About the two primitives 爿 and 片, two halves of a tree (L. 119) cut in the sense of its length. It is queer enough that, in composition, 片 means, thin, feeble; while 爿 means, thick, strong.

First series. 片 p'ien^4.

A 片 **P'ien^4**. The right half of a tree, a piece of wood; bit, thin, feeble; 从半木、指事、— It is the 91th radical.

Second series. 爿 ch'iang^2.

B 爿 **Ch'iang^2**. The left half of a tree, a piece of wood; a bed, a wooden stall; thick, strong; 从半木、指事。— It is the 90th radical. Phonetic series 41. It forms

壯 **Chuang^4**. A stout 爿 man 士, or the man who feigns to be so. It forms 莊, men and things of the country. — Note the analogous characters: 妝 a woman who gives herself airs, disguise; 狀 a dog that blusters, to feign; 戕 to subduce strong enemies by arms; 臧 the humble subjection of a minister (L. 82 E). Etc. — Phonetics series 265.

Chiang^4. A strong 爿 hand 手 that rules; a general, to command.

將 **Chiang^4**. To place 寸 meat 月 upon a stall 爿. The scribes blended this character with the last. — Phonetic series 599.

These characters show the successive development of the preceding: 1. Stall and meat; 2 Stall, meat and salt; 3. Stall, meat and prine (L. 41 G)

C

Chi². To lie — on a bed 爿 (note the successive contractions). Derived meanings, to be sick, sickness; urgent, pressing, as in a grave sickness; 人有病像。The scribes arbitrarily added a dot on the top. — It is the 104th radical of a group of characters relating to diseases.

Note: Joined to 宀, 疒 forms a kind of compound radical, under which a phonetic is inserted. In the ancient forms, 疒 is complete; in the modern ones, the horizontal line was suppressed. For instance:

寤

Wu⁴. To awake; 吾 is phonetic. The sleeping man is lying 疒 in his house 宀

寢

Ch'in³. To sleep; 侵 is phonetic.

寐

Mei⁴. To sleep; 未 is phonetic.

寐

Mi³. Drowsy; 米 is phonetic. Etc.

Third series. 爿 and 片 joined.

D

A prop. It is found in

鼎

Ting³. A tripod or an urn. The third foot does not appear, on account of the perspective. 目 is not the eye (L. 158), but it represents the vase. The tripods and urns played an important part in the Chinese antiquity. See Graphies page 361. — It is the 206th radical.

LESSON 128.

About the primitve 斤.

A 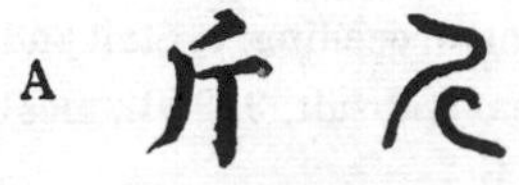

Chin¹. An axe, a hatchet; 斫木斧也。The character is supposed to represent the instrument, 像形。It means also a Chinese pound, the ancient weights having, like moneys, the form of a hatchet's iron or o a hanger. It is the 69th radical. Phonetic series 48. — Different derivatives of 斤. were already explained; e.g. 兵 L. 47 D; 匠 L. 51 A; 折 L. 48 D; 斷 L. 60 E. Add the following:

欣 **Hsin**[1]. A laughter 欠 (L.99) by jerks 斤; joy, delightness.

斬 **Chan**[3]. To cut in two, to sunder. Composed of 車 chariot, and of 斤 axe, 會意。It is a souvenir of the ancient chariots with scythes, says the Glose. More probably 車 the whirling of an 斤 axe brandished. — Phonetic series 591.

析 **Hsi**[1]. To split 斤 wood 木, to divide; 會意。— Phonetic series 357.

斯 **Ssŭ**[1]. To split 斤 wood with an axe; 其 (L. 70 C) represents, says the Glose, the basket in which the splinters are gathered. 所以盛木。會意。The modern use of this character as a demonstrative pronoun, is **chia-chieh** —. Phonetic series 704.

所 **Sho**[3]. Chopping 斤 of a door 戶 (L, 129). By extension, a place, a spot, a building; a relative pronoun.

B 斦 Two axes. This character is obsolete. It is found in

質 **Chih**[4]. To fix or settle 貝 the price of a thing. By extension, value, quality, substance, matter. — Phonetic series 799.

C 斥 **Ch'ih**[4]. To expel. It has nothing in common with 斤. It is an arbitrary abbreviation. See its etymology, L. 102 D. — Phonetic series 112.

LESSON 129.

About the primitive 戶.

First series. 戶 **hu**[4], and its compounds.

A 户 戶 **Hu**[4]. One leaf of a door, the half of the character 門 **mên**[2] (below C); a shutter; 半門曰戶、像形。 It represents the thing. By extension, house, family. — It is the 63th radical. Phonetic series 63. — See 扇 L. 62 I; 所 L. 128 A; 扁 L. 156 D; etc. It forms

戾 戾 **Li**[4]. A dog 犬 surprised, that crouches under the door to get out. By extension, wicked, to lose face; 曲也。从犬出戶、下身曲戾也、會意。— Phonetic series 375.

雇 雇 **Ku**[4]. A sort of bird 隹; 戶 is phonetic. The modern meanings, to rent, to hire, are **chia-chieh**, says the Glose. It may be that 隹 represented a sign-board placed in front of 戶 houses to let. — Phonetic series 692.

扈 扈 **Hu**[4]. Name of an ancient town 邑 and principality; 戶 is phonetic. — Phonetic series 616.

启 启 **Ch'i**[3]. To open a 戶 door, so that it is fully opened 口; to open. 開也。从口、从戶、會意。It forms

啓 啟 **Ch'i**[3]. The teaching of the master, with his 攴 rod, opens 启 the mind of the disciple. To explain, to make clear, to instruct. — Phonetic series 329, in which 口 is replaced by a radical.

戹 戹 厄 **O**[4]. Misfortune, distress. The character represents the slipping in through a narrow door; 隘也。从戶、从乙、難苦之事也。The modern form completely altered the old one, in which there is neither 厂, nor 㔾. — Phonetic series 75.

肩 **Chien**[1]. **Shoulder. It is unconnected with 戶. It is a special primitive, explained in the L. 65 F.**

B 冃 inverted is now obsolete. But in combination with the straight form, it makes the three following important series, C, D, E.

Second series. 門 **mên**².

C 門 門 **Mên**². Two leaves of a door, face to face; 从二戶相對,像形。一扇曰戶,兩扇曰門。— It is the 169th radical of characters relating to entrances. Phonetic series 381. — Note a few compounds: 悶 **mên**⁴, sad, melancholy, a heart 心 before a shut up door; 聞 **wên**², an ear at the door, to hearken; 問 **wên**⁴, a mouth at the door, to inquire of or about; 閃 **shan**³, to slip aside, in a door, to let another pass; 閂 **shuan**¹, to bar a door; 開 **k'ai**¹, to unbar a door; 閒 **hsien**², the moonlight streaming in through a chink in a door, interstice; 闖 **ch'uang**²; a horse crossing a door, impetuosity.

閔 閔 **Min**³. To condole 文 (L. 61 F) with the mourners at the 門 front door; 弔者在門也。The Chinese houses being very small, the visitors are received at the door, when there is not a 廳 **t'ing**¹, a reception hall. By extension, compassion, pity.

Third series. 丣 **mao**.

D 卯 丣 **Mao**². Two leaves of a door opened; 門兩扇開也。The modern form is a strange alteration. The compounds of this series, and those of the following and others, were all mingled. See **ch'ing**², L. 55 A. — Phonetic series 136. It forms

昴 昴 **Mao**³. The constellation of the Pleiades; 日 for 星; 丣 is phonetic.

貿 貿 **Mao**⁴. Business; 易財也。From 貝 cowries, money; 丣 is phonetic.

Note. 卿 **ch'ing**² (L. 26 M) is unconnected with 丣 **mao**³, as well as with 柳 **liu**³, (L. 129 E).

Fourth series. 丣 **yu³.**

E 丣 丣 **Yu³.** A closed door. The closing is represented by the — that joins the two leaves together (compare above D). The modern abbreviation is quite incorrect; 開戶爲卯闔戶爲丣、从卯而關其上、指事。It forms the following:

留 畱 **Liu².** To stop, to sojourn in a place 田 (L. 149): to deposit, to let; 丣 is phonetic; 止也。Phonetic series 551.

柳 桺 **Liu³.** The willow 木; 丣 is phonetic. The modern scribes write 卯, and their mistake was registrated by the 字學舉隅。

劉 鐂 **Liu²** Composed of 釗 to cut, and 丣 a phonetic. A very common family name.

LESSON 130.

About the two primitives 午 and 缶.

First series. 午 **wu³.**

A 午 **Wu³.** It represents a pestle; 像。杵形。To hit, to offend. Compare 丁 L. 57, and 干 L. 102. — Phonetic series 89. See 舂 and 秦, to pound, L. 47N. Note the following compounds:

啎 忤 **Wu³.** Stiff in holding one's opinions, obstinate; 逆也。Here 午 represents the action of offending, of shocking; 吾 is phonetic. The second form is a modern one.

B 卸 **Hsieh⁴.** To stop 止 in the exercice of an 卩 office (LL. 112 and 55), to lay down the seal, on account of a 午 fault. By extension, to lay aside, to unload, e.g. a cart. It forms

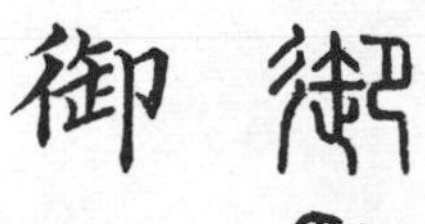

Yü⁴. The art of driving, and, by extension, of ruling over men. The modern character is an absurd phonetic compound; 彳 to march. 卸 is phonetic. The ancient character meant, to have the 又 hand over a 馬 horse; 會意。使馬也。

Second series. 缶 **fao**³.

C

缶

Fao³. Earthenware vessels in general; 瓦器也。像形。A vessel with a cover. — It is the 121th radical. It forms

匋

T'ao². A furnace 勹 for burning 缶 pottery or earthenware; 从勹、从缶。會意。瓦器竈也。— Phonetic series 396.

Yao². An earthenware vessel for cooking or keeping 月 meat. — Phonetic series 583.

D 寶 寳 宝

Pao³. Precious, valuable, noble, respected. To have jade 王, earthenware 缶, cowries 貝, in one's own house 宀; such were the precious things among the ancients, 珍也。The second and third forms are modern contractions. See page 364

E

Yü⁴. The offering 臼 of a vessel 缶 full of 鬯 fragrant wine (L. 26 C); 彡 represents the decorations of this vessel (L. 62); 冖 is probably used to keep apart the numerous elements of this compound. It forms

Yü⁴. Thicket, brushwood. The preceding is phonetic; the radical is changed, 林 (L. 119 L) instead of 臼。By extension, obstruction, hindrance. The second form is a modern arbitrary contraction.

LESSON 131.

About the primitive 矢.

A 矢

Shih3. An arrow; 弓所發矢也。像。On the top, the point; at the bottom, the feathers, 羽之形。An ancient form represents an arrow fixed in a man's body (L. 32). Abstract meaning, an action that came to its end, appointed, determined, irrevocable, as when the arrow is fixed in the target. See LL. 18 G, and 85 E. See also 矦 L. 59 H, 𥎦 L. 101 B, 短 L. 165 A. — It is the 111th radical. Note the following compounds:

B 疾

Chi2. A sudden 疒 sickness, as if one had been struck by a 矢 dart Hence the two notions, sickness, suddenness.

C 医

I4. A quiver, a case 匚 (L. 10 B) for 矢 arrows; 盛弓矢器也。會意。It forms

殹

I1. To take out an arrow from the 医 quiver, in order to 殳 shoot (L. 22 D). — Phonetic series 618. It forms

醫

I1. Medicine as it was practiced by the wizards of old. To sent arrows 殹 against the evil influences that caused the sickness 殹惡姿也, and to give to the sick 酉 elixirs to revive them, 酉所以治病也。

D 䠶 射

Shê4. To shoot an 矢 arrow against 身 somebody; 弓發於身而中也。从矢.从身、會意。In a more recent form, 寸 used for 彐 the hand, was substituted to 矢. to the detriment of the meaning. — Phonetic series 560.

E 知

Chih1. The knowledge that makes a man able to give an 口 opinion upon a subject, with the rapidity and precision of an 矢 arrow hitting the marks; 从矢、从口、會意。— Phonetic series 334.

F 規

Kui[1]. Rule, to rule, right, straight, as it ought to be. To have the eye 見 to something, in order to make it straight as an arrow 矢; 从矢、从見、會意。The great resemblance of 矢 and of 夫 in the ancient writing, gave birth to the false character 規, which became usual. — Phonetic series 624.

G 疑

I[2]. Doubt, to doubt. The modern signification is the opposite of the ancient signification of this character, which was confounded by the scribes with the next:

To miss the mark. 矢 an arrow that 匕 goes astray; hesitation, doubt, uncertainty; 未定也。从匕。从矢、會意。While 疑 primitively meant, to hit the mark; an 矢 arrow that 止 stops in the target; certitude, a settled matter. — 子 is a phonetic added later on. — The modern character is an ill-formed contraction. 定也。从矢、从止、會意。子聲。— Phonetic series 783. Note that 欸 has nothing in common with 矢. See L. 99 D.

LESSON 132.

About the primitive 牛.

A 牛

Niu[2]. An ox, a cow, a bull. The original character represents the animal seen from behind; the head, the horns, two legs and the tail; 像 etc. — It is the 93th radical of characters relating to bovine animals. — Compare 羊 the sheep, L. 103. See again 牟 to bellow, L. 85 E; 牢 a paddock for oxen, L. 17 F; 牧 to graze, L. 43 D; 牽 to drive by the halter, L. 91 C; 犀 the yak, L. 100 A; 半 an ox cut up, a half of it, L. 18 D; etc. Note the derivatives

牡 牝

Mu[3] and **P'in**[3]. A bull and a cow; 土 and 匕 are the two halves of 北 (L. 27 G). representing the pair. Now, by extension, male and female of animals in general. L. 26 I.

B 告 𠰛 **Kao⁴**. To impeach, to indict; to do, with the 口 mouth, what is done by the 牛 ox with its horns; to gore: 从牛、从口、會意. By extension, to tell of, to advise of, 教也, etc. — Phonetic series 282. It is phonetic in

造 𨓍 **Tsao⁴**. Primitive sense, 从辶, to arrive at, to reach, 至也。By extension, to construct, to build, to create; 制也。成也。

C The ox was the most valuable thing among the goods of the ancients, hence the two following characters:

物 **Wu⁴**. A thing, matter, substance; the beings, 萬物也。Because, says the Glose, the 牛 ox is the largest of things 牛爲大物; 勿 is phonetic.

件 **Chien⁴**. An, one. The idea is represented by a representative of the two nobler categories, a 亻 man and an 牛 ox; 从人、从牛、會意。

LESSON 133.

About the two primitives 不 and 至.

First series. 不 pu².

A 不 𠀚 **Pu²**. It represents a bird that rises, flapping the wings, straight towards 一 the skies; 鳥飛上也。从一、天也。像形兼指事。Compare L. 11 A, B. It is now used, **chia-chieh**, as an adverb of negation; 爲非。爲無。— Phonetic series 79. It forms

丕 𠀛 **P'ei⁴**. It represents a wast open space; a bird hovering between 一 heaven and 一 earth; 大也。从一不指形。Great, vast, unequalled. — Phonetic series 146.

否 𠀜 **Fao³**. Adverb of negation; the 口 mouth saying 不 no: 不也。不如是也。This character is a modern one, for 不 is taken in its **chia-chieh** meaning. — Phonetic series 268. It forms

杏 𠀝 音 **T'ou⁴**. To cut a speaker short by interrupting him in his speech, as a 丶 dot, a denegation 否, or that puff that is used in China to express one's contempt; 相語唾而不受也。从丶、从否、會意。Note the modern contraction, that is to be distinguished from 音 (L. 73 E). See also 卞, L. 47 H. — Phonetic series 401.

Second series. 至 chih⁴.

B 至 [seal form]

Chih⁴. It represents a bird that, bending up its wings, darts down straight towards the — earth. 鳥飛從高下至地也。像形兼指事。By extension, to go to, to arrive, to reach, etc. — It is the 133th radical. Phonetic series 186. It forms

致 [seal form]

Chih⁴. To go, to send, to make a person go or do, etc; 从至、从夂、會意。See L. 31 C. It forms 緻 **chih⁴**, fine, delicate.

到 [seal form]

Tao⁴. To arrive at, to reach; 至也。从至。刀 is phonetic. Forms 倒 **tao³**, to fall over, to prostrate; a disjunctive particle, but, on the contrary.

屋 [seal form]

Wu¹. A house, a room in a house. The place where 尸 one rests when he has 至 got to. See L. 32 G, where this character was fully explained. — Phonetic series 490.

臺 [seal form]

T'ai². A high open terrace, a turret upon which birds 至 alight. See L. 75 B. — Phonetic series 790.

室

Shih⁴. A place of rest, a house, a dwelling. Its composition is analogous to that of 屋 above; 宀 the shelter where one 至 stops and rests; 从宀。从至、會意。

C 晉 [seal form]

Chin⁴. To increase, to grow, to flourish. The 日 sun that appears on the horizon, and birds that 至 alight in order to peck. When the sun has appeared, at daylight, all go to their business, each one gains his ends, says the Book of Mutations; 進也。日出、萬物進。易曰、明出、地上晉。从日、从二至、會意。The modern form is a contraction. Do not confound another abbreviation 晋, with 普 p'u³, L. 60 L. — Phonetic series 521.

LESSON 134.

About the primitive 犬.

A 犬 犭 **Ch'üan**³. The character represents a dog; 狗也。像形。According to tradition, Confucius found the representation a very faithful one; 孔子曰。視犬之字如畫狗也。This induces to believe that the dogs, in the times of the philosopher, were strange animals. — It is the 94th radical. — See again 伏 L. 25 E; 然 L. 65 G; 突 L. 37 B; 哭 L. 72 C; 吠 L. 72 A; 莽 L. 78 G; 獸 L. 23 I. Add to these:

臭 **Ch'ou**⁴. A 犬 dog following the scent of a track with its 自 (L. 159) nose; 禽走鼻而知其迹者犬也。从犬、从自、會意。By extension, a bad smell, stench, putridity. — Phonetic series 523.

狊 **Chüeh**². A dog 犬 that stands up in the grass, to look 目 all around.

狄 **Ti**². From 犬 dog and 火 fire. Barbarians of the N. W. regions. A race of dogs, says the Glose; 本犬種。故从犬。The 火 fire indicates the havoc they wrought. — The genuine explanation is: nomads whose bivouacs (火 camp-fires), were watched by fierce 犬 dogs.

獻 **Hsien**⁴. To offer in worship to the deceased ancestors 宗廟, the cooked flesh of a fat dog; 犬肥者以獻之··从犬 dog, 从鬳 caldron, 會意。This was the utmost of filial piety, the most palatable of all offerings. General meaning, to present, to offer. Compare L. 65 G.

犮 **Pa**². A dog 犬 led in a leash, by a string 丿 tied up to a leg, according to the Chinese way; 从犬而丿之指事。曳其足也。— Phonetic series 142.

B 㹜 **Yin**². Two dogs that bite each other; 兩犬相齧也。會意。

獄 𤞷 **Yü**[4]. A litigation, a suit, 訟也。Two 犬 dogs representing the two suitors, who revile 言 each other, who accuse each other; 會意。相爭也。By extension, a tribunal, a prison, a jail.

𤞹 **Ssŭ**[1]. Judge. It represents the same idea. The 臣 judge between the two suitors.

C 尤 **Yu**[2]. A 犬 setter which sents the game, folds its ears; 像形。指事。Compare L. 134 A. By extension, amazement, surprise, singular, extraordinary, 異也。There are different **chia-chieh. K'ang-hsi** erroneously classified this character under the 43th radical 尢. — Phonetic series 95. It is found in the following (modern form; while in the ancient character, there was 犬, above A).

尨 **Mang**[2]. A 彡 shaggy 犬 dog; 犬之多毛者。从犬、从彡、會意。— Phonetic series 293.

LESSON 135.

About the primitive 虍.

A 虍 **Hu**[1]. This character represents the tiger's strips; 虎文也。像形。— It is the 141th radical. — See again 虖 L. 58 D, 豦 L. 69 D, 虛 L. 27 H, 慮 L. 40 A, etc. Note the following compounds:

B 虎 **Hu**[3]. The tiger, the king of wild beasts 山獸之君 says the Glose. It represents the tigers 虍 skin, and its hind-legs on which it stands up like a 儿 man when leaping; 會意。— Phonetic series 362. It forms 彪 **piao**[1], striped 彡 as a tiger's skin; 虎文也。See also below G.

C 虜 **Lo**[3]. To seize, to capture; 獲也。从毌 L. 153, 从力、虍聲。力而拘之。To seize 力 and to bind 毌; 虍 is phonetic.

D 盧 盧 盧 盧

Lu². It is derived from 甾 L. 150; 虍 is phonetic. A vessel. In the more recent form, 皿 vessel is a radical redundancy. There are different **chia-chieh**. — Phonetic series 823.

E 壴 壴

Hsi⁴. An ancient earthenware 豆 vase in form of a tiger; 古陶器也。从豆 L. 165 It forms 戲 **hsi**⁴, comedy, game.

F 雐 虧

K'ui¹. A bird 隹 not well determined; 虍 is phonetic. It is phonetic in

K'ui¹. To injure, to wrong, as by a pernicious 亏 breath; a grievance, a deficiency; 气損也。从亏 (L. 58 E).

G 虒 虒

Ti¹. A tiger 虎 in its 厂 cavern. Compare 厲 L. 23 H. — Phonetic series 573.

H 虐 虐

Yao. Cruel, wild. A tiger 虎 which scratches a 人 man. The tiger's feet 儿 were replaced by its 𠀀 claws. The 人 disappeared from the modern character; 虎足反爪人也。It forms 瘧 **yao**⁴, malaria, a pernicious fever.

LESSON 136.

About the two primitives 鹿 and 舄。

First series. 鹿 **lu**⁴.

A 鹿 鹿

Lu⁴. Antelope, gazelle, deer. On the top, the horns; at the bottom, the feet (L. 27 I, note 1); in the middle, the body; 山獸也。像頭角、四足之形。— It is the 198th radical. Phonetic series 633. It forms

麃 麃

Piao¹. Roe. From 鹿; 票 (L. 50 O), contracted into 灬, is phonetic. — Phonetic series 810.

慶 慶

Ch'ing⁴. To congratulate. To go 夊 (L. 31 C) and present to somebody, on a festive day, a deer's 鹿 skin with hearty 心 wishes. This fur was the gift commonly offered in ancient times; 行賀人也。从心、从夊、以鹿皮爲贄。會意。

麀 **Yu**[1]. A hind; 匕 denotes the female; compare 牝 LL. 132 A and 26 I.

麗 **Li**[4]. See L. 163.

塵 **Ch'ên**[2]. The dust 土 raised by a band of 鹿鹿鹿 stags. There is now but one 鹿 stag. Dust in general.

Second series. 舄 ssŭ[4].

B 舄  **Ssŭ**[4]. It represents an animal, either a buffalo or a yak; 像形。

C 廌 **Chai**[3]. The philologists consider this character as being composed of the two preceding primitives, A and B, contracted. The head of a lu[4], and the tail of a ssŭ[4]. Probably the elk. In the modern form, the head of the lu[4], was replaced by a small stroke, which is a common way of doing.

LESSON 137.

About the primitive 馬.

A 馬 **Ma**[3]. It represents the head, mane, legs and tail of a horse; 馬獸也。像形。— It is the 187th radical. Phonetic series 552. Different compounds of this primitive were explained elsewhere, e.g. 闖 L. 129 C; 馮 L. 17 E, etc.

LESSON 138.

About the primitive 鳥.

A 鳥 **Niao**[3]. It represents a bird with a long tail (compare 隹 L. 168); 長尾禽總名也。像形。— It is the 196th radical. — See again 梟 L. 22 B; 鳳 L. 21 C. Note 鳴 **ming**[2], 口 singing of birds 鳥. Etc.

B 烏

A contracted form of the last, without feet, in the next two:

島 **Tao**[3]. Island. The tops of mountains 山, rocks that emerge from the sea, on which the 鳥 sea-birds live. Note that 鳥 in the ancient form, is not contracted.

梟 **Hsiao**[1]. A bird of prey waiting on the top of a 木 tree. See L. 119 K. The head alone is seen; the legs are concealed in the foliages; hence the contraction.

C

Another contracted form, without head, in the following characters:

舃 **Yeh**[2]. A magpie. A special head (compare 兒 L. 29 B, 鼠 L. 139 B). It is phonetic in

寫 **Hsieh**[3]. To set in order, to arrange the objects in a 宀 house; 置物也。从宀。By extension to set one's ideas in order, by writing; to write, to compose; 書也。

焉 **Yen**[1]. The pheasant. A special head, that is not 正 (L. 112 I), Now, **chia-chieh,** an interrogative particle — Phonetic series 660.

D 烏 **Wu**[1]. A crow, a raven, black; 像形。It differs from 鳥 **niao**[3], only in this, that the stroke in the middle which represents the eyes, is omitted. Perhaps because there is no contrast, between the black eyes of the raven and its black feathers. — The second character, 於 **yü**[2], is said, by some philologists, to be an arbitrary contraction of the first. This interpretation is not well founded. **Yü**[2] is a relatively modern character, invented to be used as a particle denoting the relation that exists between the terms of a proposition; its use is a merely grammatical one. It represents graphically the connexion (left side) between 二 two distinct 刀 terms. Anyhow, 於 is unconnected with 㫃 L. 117 C. — Phonetic series 烏 582. Phonetic series 於 419.

LESSON 139.

About the primitive 臼, and incidentally about 鼠.

A  

Chiu[4]. This character represents a mortar; 像形。 The first ones, says the Glose, were holes made in the earth; hence the meanings, pit, large hole, in the compounds. Later on, the mortar was made first of wood, then later of metal. — It is the 134th radical. See 舂 L. 47 N, 臿 L. 102 A, etc. Note:

Hsien[4]. A snare, a trap. A man 人 who falls in a 臼 pit; 坎也。从人在臼上、會意。 See L. 28. B. — Phonetic series 360.

Yao[3]. To draw up with the 爫 hand, the contents of a 臼 mortar; 會意。To draw up, to empty out. — Phonetic series 584.

B  

represents the head of certain animals, e.g. 兒 L. 29 B; 舄 L. 138 C; and

Shu[3]. Rat, rodents in general; 穴蟲之總名也。像形。The head, the stiff whiskers, and the tail. The ancient character represented the animal. — It is the 208th radical. It forms 竄 **ts'uan**[4], a rat 鼠 in its 穴 hole, to hide. See L. 37 C.

Lieh[4]. It was explained L. 40 B; it is 鼠, with another head and stiffy hair.

LESSON 140.

About the primitive 龍.

A 

Lung[2]. The dragon When it ascends to heaven and flies, it rains; when it hides in the wells, there is a drought. Vapours and clouds personified. The ancient form is a representation sufficiently recognisable. The modern form is explained thus: on the right, 飛 (L. 11 A) contracted, the wings; on the left, at the bottom, 肉 (L. 65 A) the body; on the top, 立 is thonght to be 童 (L. 120 K) contracted, used as a phonetic; 从肉、从飛省、童省聲。The last derivation seems to be an artificial interpretation of a conventional abbreviation. — It is the 212th radical. Phonetic series 824. The characters of this series, the sound of which is quite different, as 襲 hsi², for instance, come from an ancient series in 龍, that was contracted by the scribes into 龍。

LESSON 141.

About the primitive 燕.

A 

Yen⁴. It represents the swallow; the head, the body, two wings expanded, the tail. 元鳥也。像形。— Phonetic series 827.

LESSON 142.

About the two primitives, 魚 and 角.

First series. 魚 yü².

A 

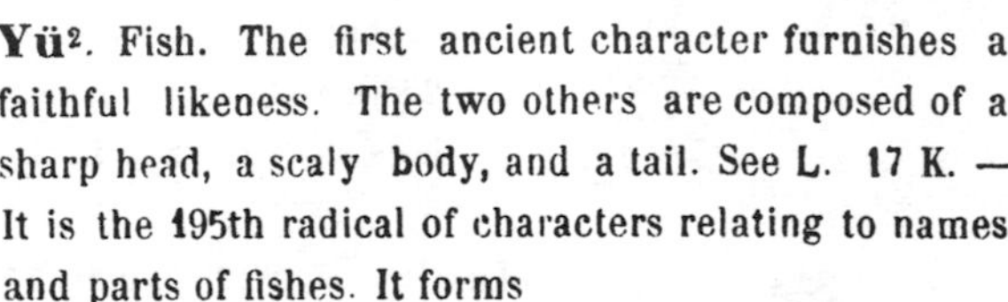

Yü². Fish. The first ancient character furnishes a faithful likeness. The two others are composed of a sharp head, a scaly body, and a tail. See L. 17 K. — It is the 195th radical of characters relating to names and parts of fishes. It forms

Lu³. Stupid, blunt; 自 (L. 159, contracted into 曰) the nose of a fish 魚, without scent, 鈍也。—Phonetic series 809.

Chi⁴. To cut open 刀 a fish 魚. It forms 薊 chi⁴, a proper name.

Yü⁴. To fish. There were, in the ancient form, two 魚 fishes denoting many, in the 氵 water.

Hsien¹. The result of a fishing, many fishes.

Second series. 角 chiao^{3}.

B 角

Chiao^{3}. Horn. It is 魚 (the second ancient form), the tail being left out, because, says the Glose, the horns have much resemblance with the lanceolated fishes. Or rather, it is simply a special primitive, that represents a striate horn. — It is the 148th radical. It forms

觜

Tsui^{3}. Egret (horn) of a heron and other birds; 頂有毛似角。从角。此聲 (the sound was changed). It is phonetic in 嘴 tsui^{3}. bill, mouth.

斛

Hu^{2}. Chinese measure, holding ten 斗 pecks (L. 98 B); 角 is phonetic (the sound being altered).

解

Chieh^{3}. To divide, to undo, to solve. A 刀 bodkin made from the horn 角 of an 牛 ox, and used to untie; 會意。散也。— Phonetic series 725.

衡

Hêng^{2}. This character is of a recent formation. A big 大 piece of wood, a yoke fixed to the horns 角 of oxen; 行 is phonetic. A transversal piece, as a beam, etc.

LESSON 143

About the primitive 日.

A 日 日

Jih^{4}. It represents the sun; 像形。— It is the 72th radical of characters relating to the sun and times. — Many compounds of this primitive were explained elsewhere. See 昌 L. 73 A, 昏 L. 114 B, 莫 L. 78 G, 昔 L. 17 J, 普 L. 60 L, 晉 L. 133 C, 㬎 L 92 E, 東 L. 120 K, 是 L. 112 I, 明 L. 42 C, 春 L. 47 P, 暴 L. 47 S, 冥 L. 34 G, etc. Note the following:

B 旦

Tan^{4}. The sun 日 above a — line, i.e. the horizon; 一地也。指事。The morning, the dawn. See L. 76 D. — Phonetic series 162.

C 杳

Yao^{3}. Darkness. The sun 日 setting below the 木 trees, 會意。

杲 **Kao**^{3}. The 日 sun shining over 木 trees, 會意。— 東 (L. 120 K) is between both. Therefore for the progressive rising of the sun, we have the fine series 白、且、杳、東、杲。Lastly

D 昦 昊 **Hao**^{4}. The 日 sun 八 pouring down its rays upon 大 men; the sun at its height 从日、从大、从八、會意。The form 昊, the sun 日 in the 天 skies, is of a relatively modern formation. Compare 皋 L. 60 F.

E 早 **Tsao**^{3}. The morning, early. Compare 杲 above C. Here the guiding-mark is 甲 (L 152, contracted into 十) a helmet, the height of a man with a helmet; 晨也。从日在甲上、會意。It is phonetic in

草 皁 皂 **Ts'ao**^{3}. Primitively a plant 艸 that was used to dye in black. In that sense, the character in now written 皁 or 皂, arbitrary forms whose actual pronunciation is **tsao**^{4}; while 草 became the generic name for herbaceous plants, as 木 is the name for ligneous plants.

F 卓 **Cho**^{1}. High, elevated. It is unconnected with the last. It represents a kind of mast surmounted with a ball and a pendant, a decoration the Chinese are very fond of. — Phonetic series 339.

G 晶 **Ching**^{1}. Luster, brightness, 光也。What is produced by the three heavenly lights, 日 月 星 sun **moon** stars; 从三日、會意。See LL. 62 C and 76 F. Note the following:

疊 叠 **Tieh**^{2}. Development of the character 宜, which was explained L 64 F. To dispose, to set 晶 objects in order. The three 日 represent three objects and are mere symbols (L. 149 F, *note*). By extension, to redouble, to pile up, to fold up. The scribes first changed 晶 into 畾, and then invented the modern character which was later on abbreviated in a strange way.

LESSON 144.

About the primitive 𠃬, which formed the character 壽.

A  **Ch'ou²**. It represents the ploughing. To trace furrows in the fields; 耕治之田也。耕屈之形。Curved lines, to lessen the figure. Now 疇. It forms.

 **Chou²**. To ask, in the Chinese way, by 𠃬 turning and returning one's 口 speach. This character is now also written 疇, which is a cause of confusion.

 **Chou²**. Another, but unauthorised, variant of the last. The modern scribes substituted 彐 to 寸. Hence the modern forms of the following.

    **Shou⁴**. Longevity, long life. On the top, 老 old, the radical contracted (L. 100 A). At the bottom, the preceding, as phonetic. The scribes altered this character in different ways. — Phonetic series 788.

LESSON 145.

About the primitive 瓦.

  **Wa³**. Tile. The Chinese roofs are made of rows alternatively convex and concave, the curved tiles covering each other at the side, and being jointed together with lime. Hence the form of the character: a tile gets hooked with another; between both, — the lime. By extension, a general name for earthenware, pottery, etc. — It is the 98th radical of a few characters relating to earthenware.

LESSON 146.

About the primitive 耳.

  **Erh³**. The ear. Intended to represent the pavilion of the ear. It forms the 128th radical of a natural group of characters relating to hearing. Phonetic series 194. — Different compounds were explained elsewhere, e.g. 聽. L. 10 O; 聖 L 81 H. Add the following:

耷 **Ta**[1]. Great 大 ears 耳 hanging like a hog's or spaniel's; hangling, dangling. This is a modern character

恥 **Ch'ih**[1]. From 耳 ear and 心 heart, because the ear reddens when a person is ashamed; to feel shame, to blush, to redden.

聞 **Wên**[2]. To learn any news by hearing 耳 at the 門 door. To hear, to learn, to smell.

耿 **Kêng**[3]. To feel 火 fire in the 耳 ears, agitation ardour, generosity. Compare 煩 L. 126 A.

B 耴 **Chê**[4]. It is supposed to represent long flapping ears, by the addition of an appendix. 耳垂也。像形。

C 咠 **Ch'i**[1]. To asperse, to blame one, which is done by 口 whispers in the 耳 ears; 从口附耳、會意。— Phonetic series 425

D 茸 **Jung**[2]. The luxuriant growth of 艸 plants. 耳 is given as an abbreviation of 聰 a phonetic.

E 耶 **Yeh**[2]. A final particle. It is said to be an arbitrary contraction of 邪 (L. 147 B). — Phonetic series 414.

F 取 **Ch'ü**[3]. To lay hold on, to take, to seize. A hand 又 that holds an 耳 ear; 从又、从耳、會意。In composition, to gather, to combine. — Phonetic series 349. It forms

聚 **Chü**[4]. To gather; 从三人、从取。It was explained L. 27 K.

叢 **Ts'ung**[1]. Collection, to join; 从丵、从取。See L. 102 I.

最 **Tsui**[4]. To scrape together; 从冃、从取、會意。See L. 34 J. — Phonetic series 711.

G 聶

Nieh^4. Composed of three 耳 ears, showing one ear coming close to two ears; to whisper, to plot, to conspire; 附耳私小語也。从三耳、會意。— Phonetic series 842.

H The following character is added as an appendix, because its modern contracted form is like 耳, though it has nothing in common with it.

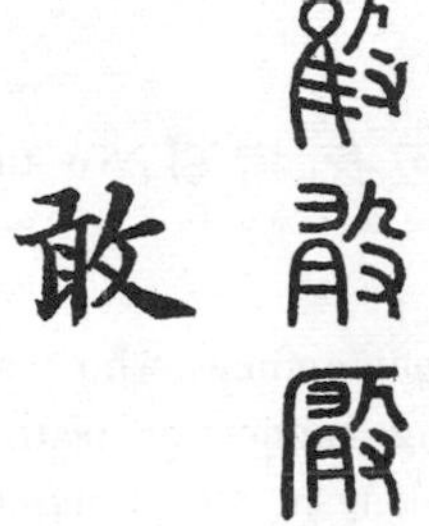

Kan^3. To dare, bold, intrepid... On the left, the bear (L. 27 J) whose paws were suppressed to give room. The modern scribes altered this primitive. On the right, a hand that whips and provokes the bear. — Phonetic series 622. It forms 㘙 **yen**^{3}, to attack a bear in its 厂 cavern, which operation does not go without 吅 cries and howlings. Hence

嚴

Yen^2. Derived meaning, a severe injunction of a superior made, in the Chinese way, with great cries. — Phonetic series 858.

LESSON 147.

About the primitive 牙.

A 牙

Ya^2. The canine teeth, hooks. The character represents their mutual jointing, 上下相錯之形。 Compare LL. 54 F and 145 A. — It is the 92th radical. Phonetic sories 91. — Different compounds of this primitive were explained elsewhere, e g. 穿 L. 37 D. Note

B 邪

Hsieh^2. Name of an ancient city 邑 lying in the East of Shantung; 牙 is phonetic. Now it means, impure, depraved, vicious (**chia-chieh** for 衺, a soiled garment). The character 耶 **yeh**^{2} (L. 146 E) used as a particle, is given as a modern difference of 邪.

LESSON 148.

About the primitive 身

A 身

Shên[1]. The primitive meaning is, conception (有身 still means, to be pregnant). The character represents a human body (L. 25), with a big belly (a partial primitive), and a leg moving forward to keep the equilibrium; 像形。By extension, the body, a person, a body's life duration. — It is the 158th radical of characters relating to the shapes of the body. Different compounds were explained; e.g. 射 L. 131 D; 躬 L. 90 F; etc.

B 㐆

I[1]. It is 身 inverted; 从反身、指事。To turn round. It forms

殷

Yin[1]. The ancient dancers and pantomimes, who made their 殳 evolutions brandishing banners or feather-brooms, and turning their 身 body in all directions; 舞之容也。殳者舞之器也。By extension, motion, activity, high spirits, zeal. In this sense, the modern compound 慇 is now commonly used.

LESSON 149.

About the primitive 田.

T'ien[2]. Field, country. It represents a furrowed field; 像形。This character being simple and easy to write, is often used, as a symbol, for any object. — It forms the 102th radical of characters relating mostly to fields and land. Phonetic series 164. — We saw the compounds 畜 L. 91 B; 當 L. 36 E; 奮 L. 60 E; 男 L.53 C; 黃 L. 171. — But 田 is substituted to another character in 畢 L. 104 A; 番 L. 123 D; 細 L. 10 A; 田 L. 150.

Miao[2] Sprouts, vegetation 艸 at the surface of the 田 fields; 艸生於田者、會意。— Phonetic series 464.

Chi[2]. A 儿 man who goes 夊 and sees his 田 fields, who works them; consequently, the growing of the plants; 治稼進也。从田儿夊、會意。It forms 稷 chi[2], corn, agriculture.

D 里 里 **Li^3**. Composed of 田 field and 土 combined; 會意。居也 The smallest hamlet, eight families cultivating a 井 **ching^3** (L. 115). By extension, the side of a **ching^3**. the Chinese mile, now usually measuring 1894 ft English, or about 600 metres. — It is the 166th radical. Phonetic series 287. It forms

廛 廛 **Ch'an^2**. The 八 distinct ground 土 on which each family in the hamlet 里 erected its 广 dwelling: — 家之居也。A shop, a stall, an estate. — Phonetic series 795.

E 畕 **Chiang^1**. Fields separated one from another. It was later on replaced by

畺 畺 **Chiang^1**. Partition represented by three lines, that divide two fields 田; a limit, a boundary; 界也。从田、从三、像形指事。— This character is now replaced by 疆, in which 土 is a redundancy, and 弓 represents the land-measuring compass. — Phonetic series 724.

F 畾 畾 **Lei^2**. The fields, the country. — Phonetic series 803. It forms

雷 靁 **Lei^2**. Rainy clouds 雨 above the fields 田 (L. 93); storm, thunder. — Phonetic series 743.

Note: 畾 is often used as a symbol, to mean a heap, an ordering of things. Compare 品 L. 72 L. For instance in

壘 **Lei^3**. To build, by 畾 piling up 土 pises.

纍 纍 累 **Lei^3**. To join in a series, to bind 糸 together many 畾 objects. The modern form 累 is a contraction. — Phonetic series 626.

疊 **Tieh^2**. To fold up. It should be written 畾. See L 143 G.

The scribes imagined, for rapidity's sake, to replace the 田 and 日 piled up, by 厶 or 叉. For instance:

LESSON 150.

About the primitive 甾

A 

Tzŭ[1]. It represents a vase, earthenware, pottery; 像形. It has nothing in common either with 田 (L 119), or with 巛 (L. 12 E) The modern character is a fanciful form invented by the scribes. Not to be confounded with 菑 **tzŭ**[1], an uncultivated field, explained L 12 I. Phonetic series 406. It occurs, as a radical, in a few compounds in which the modern scribes, and **K'ang-hsi**, always write 田. For instance:

Lu[2]. A vessel. See L. 135 D.

LESSON 151.

About the primitive 由.

A 

Yu[2]. It represents the germination of a fruit-stone, of a large grain; 田 represents the grain, on the top of which the germ is coming up; 於果中上出者芽。像形、指事。By extension, beginning, principle, origin, starting point, cause, to produce, etc. — Phonetic series 170. See its radical compounds 粤 **yu**[2] (L. 55 K), and 甹 **p'in**[2] (L. 58 C).

LESSON 152.

About the primitive 甲.

A 

Chia[3]. Primitive sense, a helmet. The character represents a helmet upon two strokes figuring a tall man, 爲一大人形. Later on, by extension, full armour; lastly, any hard coverings, as the carapace of turtles, the scales on crocodiles, etc. Different **chia-chieh**, the first of the ten stems in the cycle, etc. — Phonetic series 109. See 早, the sun risen to the height of a man wearing a helmet, L. 143 E. Compare the ancient form of 泉 L. 125 F. It forms

B 戎 戒

Jung[2]. Defensive 甲 arms and 戈 offensive weapons. See L. 71 O. — Phonetic series 217.

C 

Pi[1]. A drinking wase 甲 held with the left ⺕ hand. **Chuan-chu**, vulgar. See L. 46 E, where this character was fully explained. Here 甲 representing the vase, is properly a special primitive that happens to resemble to **chia**[3], above A. — Phonetic series 388.

LESSON 153

About the two primitives 毋 and 串.

A 

Kuan[4]. To pierce, to string, to tie together different objects. The primitive represents two objects (separated by the vertical line), two cowries strung together, says the Glose (the horizontal line); 穿物持之也。兩貝也、像形。一橫穿之、指事。It forms

Kuan[4]. Long string 毋 of cowries 貝. To pierce, to string, to tie. Hence 慣 **kuan**[4], usage, custom, experience.

Shih[2]. Primitive meaning, to have 貫 strings of cash in one's 宀 house, to be really rich, and not in appearance only. Hence the actual **chuan-chu** meaning, true, the same inside as it is outside, massive, homogeneous, etc.

虜

Lo[3]. To capture; 毋 to tie 力 strongly; 虍 represents the ferocity in capturing, and is also a phonetic. A captive. See L. 135 C. Not to be confounded with 男 L. 53 C.

B 串

Ch'uan[4]. To string. The character is like 毋, above A. Two objects (not 口 mouth) strung on a vertical rod. Compare 中 L. 109 A. It forms

患

Huan[4]. Affliction; a 心 heart 串 pierced, a series of troubles.

LESSON 154.

About the primitive 冃, written by the modern writers 同 or otherwise.

A 冃 冃

Tsêng⁴. It represents the cover of the Chinese caldron, used to stew bread etc. Now 甑。像形。It is found in

B 

Ts'uan⁴. Chinese hearth. On the top, 冃 the cover and its 臼 supports; then the masonry holding the caldron; at the bottom, the 𦥑 hands putting 林 wood in the 火 fire; 合五字。會意。It is found contracted in the following:

釁

Hsin⁴. Primitively, to sacrifice to the hearth; 祭竈也。Later on, bloody sacrifice, 血祭也。Cf. the **Li-Chi** 禮記; BK IV, Sect. VI, par 11; BK. XVIII, Sect. IV, par. 33. — On the top 爨 contracted. In the middle 酉 the offering, 所以祭也。At the bottom 分 phonetic. In order to shorten it, the scribes imagined 衅.

LESSON 155.

About the primitive 鬲.

A 

Ko². It represents a three-legged caldron 像形。See page 386. — It is the 193th radical. Phonetic series 545. — See 鬻 **li**¹, L. 87 B; 羹 **kêng**¹, L. 103 A; 獻 **hsien**⁴, L. 134 A; etc.

LESSON 156.

About the two primitives 冊 and 侖.

First series. 冊 **ch'ai**².

A 冊 冊 册

Ch'ai². It represents an ancient book, written on laths of bamboo, tied together, 竹書。The scribes imagined the modern form 册, which was wrongly classified by **K'ang-hsi** unde 冂. — Phonetic series 103. It forms

B 刪

Shan^{1}. To correct and expurge, which was done by erasing with a 刀 knife what displeased in a 冊 book; 會意。 It is from this character contracted, that are derived the compounds ended in **an**, in the series 冊.

C 典

Tien^{3}. The canonical 冊 books, Confucian Canonics. Their excellence is graphically represented by the fact that they are placed high on a 丌 stand, out of respect; 从冊在丌上。會意。 The modern scribes kept something of the ancient form. — Phonetic series 398.

D 扁

Pien^{3}. An inscription 冊 hung over a 戶 door; 从戶、从冊。會意。門戶之文也。 By extension, flat, those inscriptions being written upon a tablet. — Phonetic series 473.

E 侖

Lûn^{2}. To 亼 gather 冊 texts to develop them. See L. 14 G. — Phonetic series 380.

F 龠

Yao^{4}. A collection 亼 of pipes 冊, the holes 口 of which are put in a straight line on the top. See L. 14 H. — It is the 214th radical. Phonetic series 835.

G 嗣

Ssŭ^{4}. To assert 口 before judges 司 one's titles 冊 to a succession. To succeed, heir, etc. 會意。 The ancient character simply represented 子 son, 司 legal.

Second series 𠕁 **k'uai**^{3}.

H 𠕁

K'uai^{3}. It represents the plaiting of a mat, by interlacing the rushes. It forms

蒯

K'uai^{3}. The 又 hand plaits a 𠕁 mat with 艸 straw. A family name. The modern scribes changed 𠕁 into 朋; not to be confounded with L. 64 I.

LESSON 157

About the primitive 皿.

A 皿

Min³. It represents a vessel, porringer, plate; 飯食之用器也。像形。— It is the 108th radical of characters mostly relating to dishes. It is phonetic (**min, ming, mêng**) in the following:

B 孟

Mêng⁴. The eldest 子 son. The first. — Phonetic series 382.

C 𥁕 昷

Wên¹. To feed 皿 a prisoner 囚 (L. 25 B); benevolence, charity; 仁也。以皿食囚、會意。The scribes invented the second form. — Phonetic series 5 0. See elsewhere, 盡 L. 169 D; 盧 L 135 D; 益 L. 125 C; 盈 L 19 B; 盍 盇 L 38 G; 盥 L. 50 B; 蠱 L. 110 D, etc.

D 血

Hsüeh³. A vase 皿 full — of blood. Blood. See L. 1 J. It forms 監 L. 82 F. — It is the 143th radical of a few characters relating to blood, under which **K'ang-hsi** wrongly classified 衆 (L. 27 K). Phonetic series 208.

LESSON 158.

About the primitive 目.

A

目

Mu⁴. The human eye, 人眼像形。Firstly the socket with the two eyelids and the pupil; then the pupil was suppressed; lastly the character was placed straight in order to give room. — It is the 109th radical of characters relating to the eye and vision.

See 看 L. 48 C; 眉 L. 7 A; 冒 L. 34 J; 直 and 眞 L. 10 K. L; 睿 L. 118 D; 負 L. 37 F; 艮 L. 26 L.; etc.
See 睘 L. 16 L; 眾 L. 27 K; 悳 L. 10 O; 憲 L. 97 F; 曼 L. 34 J, etc.
See 蜀 L. 54 I, and 爵 L. 176.

First series. 目 straight.

B 相 相

Hsiang[1]. To examine, to inspect; 省視也。The primitive meaning may have been, 目 to watch from behind a tree 木, or to open the 目 eye in the woods 木, in order not to be surprised by a foe or a wild beast; 从木、从目、會意。The abstract meaning of reciprocity, that gives to this character such an extended use, is said to come from a kind of pun, the two elements 木 and 目 being both pronounced **mu**[4]. — Phonetic series 445. It forms

霜 霜 **Shuang**[1]. Hoar-frost; 从雨、相聲。— Phonetic series 834.

C 見 見

Chien[4]. To look. An 目 eye above a 儿 man; 視也。从儿、从目，會意。— It is the 147th radical of characters relating to sight. Phonetic series 259. Note the compounds:

覔 **Mi**[4]. To look for something which is not 不 seen 見. It is often contracted into 覓.

导 **Tê**[2]. To apprehend, to take 寸 something which is seen 見. Compare L. 45 E.

D 省 省 省

Hsing[3] To examine carefully, to try to understand; 省察也。Two explanations of this compound are given. — 1. In the first ancient form, 屮 is said to be the eyebrows frowning so that the 目 eye may see distinctly; in which case, 省 would be but a variant of 眉 (L. 7 A). — 2. The second ancient form gives, 少 to narrow the palpebral slit, to see 目 better. — Compare 眇, L. 18 M. — By extension **Shêng**[3], a Province, the territory supervised 目 by a governor.

E 盾 盾

Tun[4]. A shield, to shield. To cover 厂 one's self totally, the eye 目 observing the assailant through a 十 cross-shaped fissure; 所以扞身蔽目。— Phonetic series 489.

Second series. 目 bent.

F 苜

Mu⁴. The eyes 目 divergent 丫 (L. 103 G) that look in different directions; squint, confused view; 目不正也、會意。 In the following derivatives, 目 is bent in order to give room. In the whole series, the modern scribes write 艹 instead of 丫.

蔑

Mieh⁴. The 戍 guardians of the frontiers (L. 71 N) looking in all 苜 directions, so that their eyes become heavy from fatigue 勞目無精也。 Compare 幾 (L. 90 D). — Phonetic series 808.

瞢

Mêng⁴. Dimness of the view. On the top 苜, at the bottom, 旬 to rub one's eyes, 會意。 It forms the compound

Mêng⁴. The radical 夕 was substituted to the 目 of the last. Dream, to dream; the confused and dim 瞢 visions seen during 夕 night.

Third series. 目 doubled, the two eyes.

G 䀠

Chü⁴. To open large and timid eyes, to regard with reverent awe, apprehensive, fearful. Fear, circumspection. In the second form, more recent, the 心 heart was added to express the interior feelings. This character is now commonly written 懼.

瞿

Ch'ü². Vigilance 䀠 of the 隹 birds, that must always watch for their life's preservation; fear. — Phonetic series 838. It forms

矍

Kuo⁴. The vain endeavours of a bird to escape the 彐 hand by which it was seized; by extension, to snap up, to catch; 从彐、从瞿、會意。 — Phonetic series 851.

LESSON 159.

About the two primitives 自 and 者。

First series 自 tzŭ⁴.

A 

Tzŭ⁴. It is thought to resemble the nose; 鼻也。像形。— Extended meanings: 1. Self, I, my own, personally; behaviour, to act, action; the nose being the projecting part, and in some way the characteristic of the individual.. 2. Starting point, the origin, beginning, evolution; the nose being, according to the Chinese embryology, the starting point of the bodily evolution.— The successive alterations of this character are the cause why it may be confounded with the primitives 白 L. 88, 日 and 曰 LL. 143 and 73. — It is the 132th radical.

See 鼻 L. 40 C; 臭 L. 134 A; 臬 L. 119 H; 鼻 L. 34 K. See 皇 L. 83 C; 皆 L. 27 I; 魯 L. 142 A; 替 L. 60 L; etc. Add the following:

Hsi¹. To breathe. According to the Chinese theory, the 氣 ch'i⁴. of the heart 心 is breathed out, while the ch'i⁴ from outside goes to the heart, through the 自 nose; 从自、从心、會意。喘也。— Phonetic series 534.

Hsi². The first 自 (contracted) attempts to fly 羽, made by a young bird; 从羽、从自、會意. By extension, to repeat the same act, to practice. — Phonetic series 610.

Second series. 者 chê³.

B 

Che³. This character, an important grammatical particle, was invented to represent a connexion and a succession between the members of a text. It represents clearly enough what it means. On the top, two crossed branches represent the members that came first; 自 represents the point where one stands, the starting point for what follows; on the right, a descending line, the continuation of the discourse; 别事詞也。By extension, phrase, speech, document. — Compare L. 138 D. — Phonetic series 422. It forms

Chu[1]. It is used, like the primitive, to 者 separate the 言 phrases, and to express their mutual relations; 辯也。从言、从者、會意, **Chia-chieh**, all, whole, far 都

Shu[3]. To gather (网 L. 39 C, a net) documents 者; to govern; a public office. — Phonetic series 789.

Ch'ê[1]. To brag. A 大 man who spreads 者 sentences. By extension, prodigality, excess of all kind.

This is a modern character. A radical redundancy, 艸 over 者. Two sounds and two meanings. **Chu**[4], to expose, to manifest, to clear up. **Chao**[2], a particle used to indicate the moods and relations. It is often contracted into 着.

Shu[1]. To write, a writing, a book. A writing-brush 聿 that writes 者 sentences. The scribes altered 者 in a strange way.

LESSON 160.

About the primitive 首, with its developments 首、面、頁。

A **Shou**[3]. The head; 頭也。像形。 Compare with 自 the nose, ancient form, L. 159. It forms

Ka[4]. A very long 戈 spear to aim at the 首 heads of massed enemies (L. 71).

Shou[3]. The head. It is the primitive with the 巛 hair (L. 12). — It forms the 185th radical — Inverted, it becomes

Hsiao[1]. The head of a criminal, hung up. The hair is hanging down. The upper part is altered. See L. 12 N, and 縣 L. 92 B.

道

Tao[3]. To go 辵 ahead 首. A road, principle, doctrine. To lead, to go. The progress of a speech, to speak. Compare L. 169 B lü[4] and chien[4].

B 面 面

Mien[4]. The face. A primitive 口 indicating the front ot 百 the head, the face; 頭前也。从百外像人面形。The second modern form is an unauthorised abbreviation. — It forms the 176th radical. Phonetic series 466.

C 頁

Yeh[4]. A man, 百 head upon 儿 a body (L. 29). The meaning is often restricted to the head; 頭也。从百在儿上。像形。— It is the 181th radical. Different compounds were explained elsewhere, e.g. 煩 L. 126 A; 須 L. 62 B; 項 L. 82 A; etc. Note also

顛

Tien[1]. The top of the 頁 head; 頂也。It is through the fontanel, that the soul of the 眞 (L. 10 L) Taoist contemplative goes out of the body, to rove about. — Phonetic series 848.

𩓣

Yu[1]. To suffer from the 頁 head and from the 心 heart; sadness, melancholy. It is phonetic in

憂

Yu[1]. To go 夊 with 𩓣 troubles; sadness, melancholy. See how the scribes altered the bottom of 頁 — Phonetic series 816.

順

Shun[4]. To swim in a 巛 stream, the head 頁 forwards; to follow the current; docile, compliant, agreeable; 會意。

類

Lei[4]. A species, a sort, a kind; 頁 heads of 米 vegetals and 犬 animals, *capita specierum*.

D 夏

Hsia[4]. A man 頁 who walks 夊, his 臼 hands hanging down. It is the thing done by the countrymen in summer time when, the works being over, the plants grow by themselves; hence the extended meaning, *summer*. The modern character is a contraction. — This character was the first appellative of the Chinese nation. On the ancient bronzes, it is written 足 (L. 112 B) station, 亼 (L. 14 A) gathering of 㗊 (L. 40 D) huts. Sedentary state after the erratic period.

寡

Kua[3]. Separation 分 of the persons 頁 living in the same 宀 house, of married persons; a widow, a person left alone, solitary; the regal We, Ourself. By extension, partaking of goods, diminution, little.

LESSON 161

About the primitive 貝.

A 貝 — **Pei⁴**. A cowrie, a small shell used for money in China in early feudal times. They were current together with the coppers invented later on, till under the 秦 Ch'in Dynasty (3d Century B C.); then the cowries were left out; 海介蟲也。像形。古者貨貝而寶龜，周而有泉。至秦廢貝行泉. The character represents the shell, and its propulsive apparatus. — It is the 154th radical of characters relating to values and trade. Phonetic series 298. — Many compounds of this primitive were explained elsewhere. Let us recall 則 賊 L. 52 E; 貫 L. 153 A; 責 L. 120 H; 貴 L. 111 B; 寶 L. 130 D; 貪 L. 14 M; etc. Note the following:

敗 — **Pai⁴**. Ruin; to ruin; to break, to crush 攴 one's own 貝 fortune, or another's; 毀也。會意。

B 員 — **Yüan²**. A cowrie 貝 round ○; 圓貝也。Round in general. Compare 肙 L. 65 E. — Phonetic series 586.

C 賈 — **Chia³ Ku³**. To buy. To cover 襾 (L 41 C) an object with its value in 貝 cowries, 會意。

D 買 — **Mai³**. To buy. To wrap up 网 (L. 39 C) an object with its value in 貝 cowries, 會意。— Phonetic series 697.

E 負 — **Fu⁴**. The self-sufficiency of a wealthy 貝 man 人。See L. 28 C.

F 賏 — **Ying¹**. Cowries strung. A primitive form of the following:

嬰 — **Ying¹**. A necklace made with 貝 cowries, ornament of women 女 in ancient times; 頸飾也。从女，从賏，會意。賏貝連也。By extension, an infant, a babe, a suckling, still hanging to its mother's neck. — Phonetic series 836.

LESSON 162.

About the primitive 瓜.

A 

Kua¹. It represents cucurbitaceous plants as cucumber, melon, etc; 像形。The exterior strokes represent the tendrils of melons; in the middle, a fruit hanging; 按瓜縢生布於地。外像。其蔓。中像其實。— It is the 97th radical of characters relating to the parts and sorts of gourds, etc. Phonetic series.

B 

Wa¹. Hollow, to dig. From 穴 (L. 37); 瓜 is phonetic.

LESSON 163.

About the primitve 丽.

A 丽

Li⁴. A primitive, representing two pendants; hence the general notion of assortment, decoration, elegant, graceful, ornamented, etc. 兩耦也。像。相附之形。下晝𠂹者。It forms only the following compound:

B 麗

Li⁴ Antelopes, that live in droves (idea of assortment); 从鹿。从丽、鹿之性、旅行也。It is now used **chia-chieh**, instead of the primitive, to mean, elegant, graceful, bright. — Phonetic series 844.

LESSON 164.

About the two primitives 而 and 耑.

First series 而 êrh².

A 而

Erh². Two explanations of this character are given: 1. It represents the radicles of a plant spreading in 一 the ground. Compare 入 L. 15 A; 之 L. 79 B. The ground is represented by 一; 业 (之) is the part growing out of the ground; 而 is the part of the plant under the ground; 上出者曰业、下𠂹者曰而。2. It represents the beard hanging from the chin, under the 一 mouth (compare 西 L. 41 B); 毛之形。The second interpretation seems to be the true one. The first came from the fact that the old shape of 而 is like the bottom part of 耑 (below B). As to the use of 而 as a particle of transition, it is derived from the notion of *hanging from the chin*. Compare 只 L. 72 A. — It is the 126th radical. Phonetic series 193. It forms

耎 **Juan**^{3}. The beard 而 of a man 大; hair long, slender, not stiff. By extension, soft, weak. — Phonetic series 456.

耍 **Shua**^{3}. A modern character. To play, as the Chinese actors do, some with false 而 beards, others dressed like 女 women.

耐 **Nai**^{4}. To take patience, to restrain one's self, by 寸 playing with one's 而 beard. This character is relatively modern.

Second series. 耑 **chuan**^{1}.

B 耑 **Chuan**^{1}. It represents a plant that develops itself above and under the ground; 上像生形。下像其根也。按一者地也。指事。By extension, stalks and roots. See above A. — Phonetic series 434. The compounds of this series ended in **uai**, come from the following contracted:

揣 **Ch'uai**^{3} To measure with the 扌 span how high a plant grew up 耑. To feel, to estimate.

C 𢼸 **Wei**^{1}. A man 人 striking 攴 a plant 耑 (contracted into 山), to take away the fibres; to strip, to peel; fibres, thin, slender, imperceptible; 秒也。从人。攴。耑省。會意。It forms

微 **Wei**^{1}. To walk 彳 slowly 𢼸, stealthily. In composition, it is used in the sense of 𢼸. It forms

徵 **Chêng**^{1}. To explain with assurance 壬 (L. 81 D) the 𢼸 threads of an affair. To testify, to give testimony. — Phonetic series 796.

徽 **Hui**^{1}. Slender 微 thread 糸

D 段

Tuan⁴. The left part of this character is an abbreviation of 耑, the top alone 山 straightened and deformed being kept; on the right, 殳 (L. 22 D). To strike in order to reduce into fibres, as 㪔 above C; 椎也。从殳、从耑省。— Phonetic series 485.

E 需

Hsü¹. The rain 雨 necessary that the small plants strike root. Here the top 山 of 耑 was suppressed, the bottom 而 remaining. By extension, necessary, indispensable. Phonetic series 779.

LESSON 165.

About the primitives 豆 and 壴。

First series. 豆 tou⁴.

A 豆

Tou⁴ It represents a dish in which meat was served up; 古食肉器也。In the ancient form, the upper — did not exist, and a dot ⸝ indicated the contents of the vessel. — It is the 151th radical of characters relating to vessels. Phonetic series 307. — See the compounds, 豊 L. 97 B; 虘 L. 135 E, etc. — But 壹 L. 38 G, and 登 L. 112 H, have another origin. It forms

頭 **T'ou²**. The head. From 頁 L. 160 C; 豆 is phonetic.

豎 **Shu⁴**. Vertical, straight. A vase 豆 standing solidly 臤 (L. 82 E) upright.

短 **Tuan³**. Short The character was made by comparison, 喻 says the Glose. To mean *long*, the hair 長 (L. 113) was chosen as an emblem; to mean *short*, the two smallest utensils of the ancients were chosen, 矢 an arrow. and 豆 the vase tou⁴, 會意。

Second series. 壴 chou¹.

B 壴

Chou¹. A partial primitive. The bottom is not 豆, the vase above A; but it depicts the ancient drum, with its — skin, and 屮 the 彐 right hand straightened that strikes. By extension, music, feast, joy. It forms

彭 𡕥 **P'êng**[2]. The sound of the drum 壴; 彡 represents the strokes, or the isolated sounds; 鼓聲也。从壴。从彡、會意，彡擊也。— Phonetic series 799.

喜 𡗩 **Hsi**[3]. Joy; 口 singing and 壴 music. There is no feast without these; see 樂 L. 88 C. — Phonetic series 680.

嘉 **Chia**[1]. Good, excellent, delicious; 壴 a band of music; 加 is phonetic (L. 53 D).

C 鼓 𡔷 **Ku**[3]. A drum 壴 beaten by a hand 攴 holding a drumstick (L 43 D); a radical redundancy. The modern scribes often write 支 instead of 攴; 革樂也。按从壴、从攴擊之也、會意。— It is the 207th radical.

D 尌 𡔷 **Chu**[1]. A composition analogous to that of 鼓; a hand 寸 (L. 45 B) beating a 壴 drum, 會意。It is phonetic in the two following:

樹 **Shu**[4]. A tree 木.

廚 𢋰 **Ch'u**[2]. Cookery; 从广。庖屋也。— Phonetic series 800.

E 豈 𡔷 𡔷 **Ch'i**[3]. It has nothing in common wi'' 㪔 L. 164 C. Compare L. 165 B. It is another drum that made the pair, and which was beaten with the left 𠂇 hand. This meaning is now obsolete. The character is used as an interrogative particle. — Phonetic series 514. Note 獃 tai[1], stupefied, the effect of the 豈 music upon 犬 dogs.

LESSON 166.

A 豸 𧳋 **Chih**[4] A primitive. It represents a feline, a head with wiskers, paws, backbone. Feline beasts, that are characterised by their back long and supple, by their undulating gait, e g. the cat, says the Glose. Compare the characters 豕 L. 69; 馬 L. 137; 舄 L. 136. — It is the 153th radical of characters relating to feline beasts.

LESSON 167.

About the primitive 車.

A 車 車 **Ch'ê**[1]. **Chü**[1]. The ancient carriage. The character is straight, to give room; 丨 the axle; 二 the two wheels; 日 the body of the carriage; 像形，按横視之。It means in composition, to roll along, to revolve, to crush, etc. — It is the 159th radical of a large group of characters relating to vehicles. See 斬 L. 128 A; 庫 L. 59 I; 輦 L. 60 M; 轡 L. 92 D. Note the following:

B 連 連 **Lien**[2]. Carriages 車 in file 辵。Abstract notion of connexion, succession; 从辵、从車、會意。— Phonetic series 630.

C 軍 軍 **Chün**[1]. A legion 勹 of 4000 soldiers, with 車 chariots; 四千人包車爲軍。By extension, an army. See L. 54 A. — Phonetic series 438.

D 軎 軎 **Kui**[4]. The extremity of the axle, that projects outwards in all Chinese 車 chariots. This extremity was formerly provided with a stopper to hold the wheel, now replaced by a peg; 从車口像形。It forms

毄 毄 **Chi**[1]. To jostle and strike 殳 with the end of the axles, as the Chinese cars often do; 車相擊也、Phonetic series 723.

Note: In the modern writing, 口 became 凵; this wrong writing passed current.

軋 **Ya**[4]. To crush, to grind; 乚 the action of a 車 wheel (L. 9 A).

轟 **Hung**[1]. Rumbling, roaring, as the noise of many 車 chariots.

LESSON 168

About the primitive 隹

A 隹 **Chui**[1]. It represents a bird with a short tail (compare 鳥 L. 138); 鳥之短尾、像形。— It is the 172th radical. Phonetic series 344.

See 焦 L. 126 A; 奞 L. 60 E; 羅 L. 39 D; 翟 L. 62 G; 雎 L. 12 G; 雋 L. 87 C; 雟 L. 15 C; 隺 L. 34 F; 雀 L. 18 N; 雈 L. 103 C; 雚 L. 72 J; 瞿 L. 158 G; 集 L. 119 G; etc. Note the following:

B 隼 **Shun**[3]. A falcon 隹 held captive on the fist or on a 十 perch.

C 淮 **Huai**[2]. A large river in Central China, much frequented by 隹 birds of passage. — It is phonetic in

匯 **Hui**[4]. Formerly, a piece of furniture (匚 L. 51 A). Now, **chia-chieh** for 回, turning, confluence, a check, etc. It forms 攟 **k'uai**[3], to carry on the arm.

准 準 **Chun**[3]. Fixed, certain, to agree. This character is unconnected with 淮. Possibly an ancient target; 准 is a contraction.

D 唯 **Wei**[2]. To answer *yes*, to express 口 one's assent; 隹 is phonetic; 諾也。It is phonetic in

雖 **Sui**[1]. Formerly the name of an 虫 insect. Now a conjunction, 發聲之詞。Though.

E 惟 **Wei**[2]. To consider, to think on, care, sorrow; 凡思也。从心、隹聲。It is phonetic in

罹 **Li**[2]. At first it meant a net 网, a snare. It is now used to mean, care, sorrow, misfortune; while 惟 is used **chia-chieh** as an adverb, or a conjunction.

F 崔 **Ts'ui**[1]. Very high, 大高也。从山。隹聲。— Phonetic series 655.

G 隻 — **Chih⁴**. A hand 彐 holding one 隹 bird, not the pair. Hence the meaning, single, by itself; 會意. Compare L. 103 C.

雙 — **Shuang¹**. Two birds 隹 in the hand 彐 ; a couple, a pair, doubled; 會意。

H 霍 — **Ho³**. The rain 雨 surprising 隹 birds, and forcing them to seek shelter; 會意。The modern character is a contraction. — Phonetic series 819.

I 讎 讐 — **Ch'ou²**. Words 言 exchanged between two 隹 parties, altercation and its consequence, hatred. enmity. The following character was formerly composed in the same way.

售 — **Shou⁴**. To sell. Formerly 口 the mouth, and two 隹 the buyer and the seller. All know the importance of the 口 mouth in the Chinese markets. The modern character is a contraction.

J 雁 — **Yen⁴**. The wild goose; 隹 the birds dwelling on 厂 crags, and which fly in the form of 人 (a sharp angle): 雁飛、有行列似人字、故从人。Not to be confounded with

䧹 — **Ying¹**. The falcon, now 鷹 It is explained thus: the tame 广 bird 隹 that serves to 亻 men; 鷹隨人所指之、故从人。In the ancient character, there was 疒 (L. 127 C), quick, sudden. It is the general name of birds of prey, eagles, cormorans, etc. — Phonetic series 767. It forms

應 — **Ying¹. Ying⁴**. To answer, to correspond, to do what one feels 心 is right and ought to be, etc. 䧹 is phonetic; 合也。當也。

LESSON 169.

About the derivatives of 𦘒 (L. 44 D).

A 𦘒 — **Nieh⁴**. A hand 彐 writing 丨 upon a 冂 surface. See L. 44 D. It forms

B 聿

Yü^4. To trace 聿 lines 一, to write. See L. 44 D. — It is the 129th radical. It forms

筆

Pei^3. A writing-brush, whose handle is made of ⺮ bamboo.

肄

I^4 To exert one's self, to practise, as it must be done to learn how to 聿 write and how to shoot 矢 (an old form, L. 131 A).

肆

Ssŭ^4. To expound 聿 long 長, to display, indiscreet. See L. 113 B.

肁

Chao^4. To place one's self near the 戶 window in order to 聿 write. It is obsolete. It forms

肇

Chao^4. To push 攴 the window 戶 (the shutter) at dawning, in order to 聿 write. By extension, to begin, to undertake. Compare **ch'i^3**, L. 129 A.

律

Lü^4. A written regulation 聿 for the 彳 march (L 63 A); a statute, a fixed law, an ordinance, tone; 法也、常也。

建

Chien^4. The composition is like the preceding's. To write 聿 regulations for the 廴 march (L 63 D), for going on; to establish, to found, to determine, etc. — Phonetic series 430.

C 書

Shu^1. To write 聿 sentences 者; a text, a book. See L. 159 A. The modern character is a wrongly-formed contraction.

畫 畫

Hua^4. To trace with the 聿 writing-brush a 田 subject; to paint, to draw. See L. 149 A. The scribes added a 口 frame to 田, from which they first suppressed one side, then two other sides; there remains a 一 at the bottom of the modern character.

晝

Chou^4. The limits 口 of time, during which it is clear 日 enough to 聿 write; the day, the space between two nights; 日之出入、於夜爲界。 Compare the composition of the preceding.

D 𦘔 **Chin**^{1}. A writing-brush 聿 that traces 彡 lines. This character soon became obsolete, because it made a double use with 聿。It forms, contracted into 𦘔, the following phonetic compounds.

津 **Chin**^{1}. A ford, 水渡也。

Chin^{4}. Ashes that remain from a 火 fire. Hence.

盡 **Chin**^{4}. Ashes that remain in a 皿 brazier, when the fire is out; 火 contracted became 灬; 器中灰也。空也。By extension, ended, finished (the ashes being the final result of the combustion), an action that went to its term, consummation, exhaustion. — Phonetic series 774.

LESSON 170.

About the two primitives 非 and 韭.

A 非 **Fei**^{1}. A special primitive with two sides, opposite each other. Abstract notion of opposition, contradiction, negation, wrong; no, not so; 違也。相背也。指事。Compare 北 L. 27 G; and 卌 L. 127 D. — It is the 175th radical. Phonetic series 353. Note the compound

靠 **K'ao**^{4}. Primitively it meant 告 to rebuke the 非 wrongs of others; it now means, to lean against, to rely on. The meaning was changed, says the Glose; it does not say why. See L. 132 B. 从非、从告。相違也。今相依也。

B 韭 **Chiu**^{3}. It represents the famous garlic with its growing leaves; 像形。— It is the 179th radical. It is found in

韱 **Ch'ien**^{1}. Wild garlic, 山韭也。See the phonetic, L. 27 B. — Phonetic series 829.

Hsieh^{4}. Shallot, 薤菜也。From 韭; when it is 歹 pounded, it makes a precious 貝 condiment. See L. 118 C. The modern form is a contraction; 貝 was suppressed.

LESSON 171.

About the derivatives of 黃.

A 

Huang[2]. Yellow. The hue of loess. Composed of 田 (L. 149), and of an old form of 光 (L. 24 J), that are mingled together; 地之色也。从田、从古文光 See L. 24 L. — It is the 201th radical. Phonetic series 688. It forms

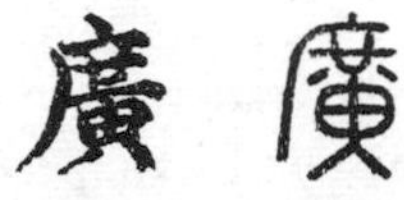

Kuang[3]. A large 广 hall; 黃 is phonetic. By extension, great, vast, wide,. 大也。— Phonetic series 802.

B 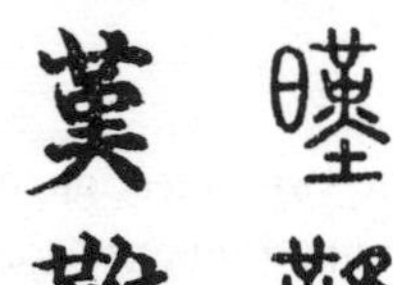

Chin[3]. Yellow 黃 (contracted) earth 土, clay potter's earth. The modern form is a contraction that passed current; 黏土也。从土、从黃省。會意。古文不省。— Phonetic series 602. It forms

Han[4]. Clay 堇 dried in the 日 sun. Contracted into 𦰩, it forms the phonetic series 609. Note the following sub-series:

Nan[2]. The state in which are the 隹 birds, when the earth is 𦰩 dried and barren; famine, misery, difficulty of living. — Phonetic series 847.

LESSON 172.

About the partial primitive 寅.

A 

Yin[2]. Behaviour, gait, ritual politeness; 居敬也。In a 宀 house, a man 工 (a special primitive, stiff bearing, on the top, a cap) pays salutations with both 臼 hands. The modern character is a contraction. — Phonetic series 661.

LESSON 173.

About the partial primitive 殸.

A 

Ch'ing[4]. On the right side, the well-known compound, 殳 to strike. On the left, 声 a primitive that represents a sonorous silex, hanging from a frame; 樂石也。See *Textes Historiques*, p. 82. Now 磬 Compare 𢏚 L. 83 B. — Phonetic series 604.

LESSON 174.

About the primitive 齊.

A 

齊

Ch'i[2]. A whole, regular and perfect, harmony. The idea comes from the even height of ears in a corn-field; 禾麥吐穗。上平也。像形。 There is, in this character, an intention of representing the perspective. The down stroke —, says the Glose, represents the fore-ground; the upper stroke — represents the back-ground. The ears are ascending when going towards the back-ground. Three ears represent a multitude. — It is the 210th radical. Phonetic series 771. Note the modern contraction. It forms

齋 **Chai**[1], abstinence; from 示 and 齊. In this character, the two horizontal strokes of 齊 are mingled together with those of 示. The meaning is, 齊 to rule one's self, so that one may be fit to receive the 示 warnings of heaven.

LESSON 175.

About the partial primitive 齒.

A 

Ch'ih[3]. The teeth. The ancient character was a mere primitive, representing the teeth appearing in an open mouth. In the more modern character, the phonetic 止 was added to the mouth with its two ranges of teeth; 像口齒之形。止聲。— It is the 211th radical.

LESSON 176.

About the partial primitive 爵.

A  

Chiao[2]. A vase for sacrifices, full of aromatic 鬯 wine (L. 26 C), held by a 彐 hand. The upper part is a cover. In the middle, the vessel, whose right descending stroke has made room for 彐。Compare L. 46 E. The modern form is an arbitrary contraction; 禮器也。中鬯酒。彐持之也。— Phonetic series 837.

LESSON 177.

About two modern primitives, invented under the 唐 T'ang Dynasty.

凸 **Ka**³. Convex. 凹 **Wa**¹. Concave.

These characters do not require any explanation.

INDEX OF ALL THE USUAL GROUPS

analysed above

arranged according to the number of strokes.

The figures given refer to the Lessons, and the letters to the paragraphs.

厶	38 H kung
厶	85 E i
厶	89 A ssŭ
㐅	39 A
乂	39 B
叉	43 B
ナ	46 B
匚	51 A
刀	52 A
刂	52 A
𠃌	52 A
力	53 A
勹	54 A
丩	54 F
卩	55 H
㔾	55 B K
马	55 K
卜	56 A
丁	57 A
丂	58 A

丂	58 I
厂	59 A
阝	86 A fu 74 C i
了	94 H

3

三	3 A
上	5 A
下	5 B
亾	10 E
亡	10 E
凢	11 B
巛	12 E
川	12 E
△	14 A
夂	17 F chung
小	18 H
凡	21 A
士	24 C
千	24 D

丈	24 E
廿	24 H
亢	26 A
兀	29 K
尸	30 A
久	31 A
夂	31 B
夊	31 C
牛	31 D
尸	32 A
毛	33 B
冃	34 I
巾	35 A chin
巾	35 H liang
宀	36 A
彐	44 A
寸	45 B
叉	45 H
廾	47 B
扌	48 A

刃	52 A
勺	54 H
勿	54 H
亏	58 E
于	58 E
丸	59 E
广	59 I
大	60 A G
矢	61 A
尢	61 C
彡	62 A
彳	63 A
亍	63 B
廴	63 D
夕	64 A
女	67 A
彐	68 A
彑	68 A
六	70 B
弋	71 A

口	72 A
口	74 A
个	77 A
屮	78 A
之	79 B
山	80 A
土	81 A
工	82 A
己	84 A chi
巳	85 A ssŭ
已	85 A i
弓	87 A
幺	90 A
子	90 A
孑	94 H
才	96 A
乞	98 A
干	102 A
丫	103 D
丬	107 A

也	107 B	殳	22 D	五	39 A	亦	52 B	曰	73 A
少	112 F	廿	24 H	爻	39 G	匀	54 E	叉	76 I
丬	125 A	卌	24 N	六	42 A	巴	55 B L	廾	78 B
豸	134 A	仁	25 G	四	42 A	艮	55 C	屯	79 A
		旡	26 D	支	43 C	㔾	55 H	巿	35 B fu
4		乍	26 E	攴	43 D	兮	58 D	市	79 B shih
不	3 D	卬	26 G	反	43 E	仈	59 E	巿	79 G fei
丏	10 G	从	27 A	父	43 G	产	59 H	币	79 C
丮	11 E	比	27 I	夬	43 O	天	60 C	𣎵	79 G
𢆶	12 I	弔	28 H	友	53 P	夫	60 J	朮	79 H
巛	13 B	允	29 E	丑	44 B	夭	61 B	壬	81 D t'ing
亼	13 D	元	29 H	尹	44 C	无	61 C	壬	82 C jên
今	14 K	化	30 D	叉	45 I	亢	61 E	王	79 D wang
內	15 C	尺	32 F	丹	47 B	文	61 F	王	83 A yü
分	18 B	切	33 B	非	48 Y	月	64 G yüeh	王	83 C wang
公	18 C	冘	34 E	卞	48 H	月	65 A ju	王	83 D chu
介	18 F	冃	34 J	手	48 A	毋	67 K	允	85 E
少	18 M	冋	34 K	爪	49 A	歺	68 A	引	87 A
勿	19 B	凶	38 D	乡	49 A	互	68 B	云	93 A
及	19 D	厷	38 H	臼	50 A	戈	71 F	去	94 E

予	95 A	丹	115 D		**5**	年	24 D	去	38 F
幻	95 B	冄	116 A			古	24 F	弘	38 H
丰	97 A	方	117 A	示	3 D	世	24 O	匆	40 E
丯	97 C	歹	118 C	乍	10 F	四	25 B	丙	41 A
气	98 A	木	119 A	匃	10 G	仙	25 I	四	42 A
斗	98 B	水	125 A	匄	10 G	尼	26 F	皮	43 H
升	98 B	火	126 A	令	14 I	北	27 G	艮	43 J
欠	99 A	灬	126 A	令	14 I	业	27 H	史	43 M
旡	99 E	片	127 A	全	15 B	丘	27 H	付	45 C
毛	100 A	爿	127 B	𥝌	16 A	产	28 E	朮	45 J
勿	101 A	斤	128 A	冬	17 F	甪	28 H	左	46 B
心	107 A	戶	129 A	半	18 D	兄	29 D	右	46 G
中	109 A	戹	129 A	㕣	18 E	宄	29 J	弁	47 H
止	112 A	午	130 A	必	18 G	司	30 C	失	48 B
辶	112 E	牛	132 A	尔	18 O	𡰥	32 B	印	49 I
乏	112 K	不	133 A	尒	18 O	尻	32 C	申	50 C
丏	112 L	犬	134 A	孕	19 C	同	34 B	召	52 C
氏	114 A	尤	134 C	処	20 B	布	35 C	加	53 D
井	115 A	日	143 A	且	20 D	穴	37 A	包	54 B
开	115 B	牙	147 A	禸	23 C	甴	38 C	句	54 F

卯 55 A ch'ing
危 55 D
犯 55 K
占 56 B
外 56 F
宁 57 B
号 58 B
乎 58 D
平 58 F
可 58 I
石 59 D
屵 59 F
屵 59 G
夲 60 F
立 60 H
央 60 K
㐱 62 C chenn
参 62 C shan
夗 64 D
奴 67 C

母 67 O
代 71 B
式 71 D
戊 71 L
戉 71 M
只 72 A
甘 73 B
囘 76 G
犮 78 A
出 78 E
匜 79 C
生 79 F
共 79 I
圣 81 A
巨 82 D
玉 83 A
主 79 D wang
主 83 D chu
目 85 B
台 85 E

弗 87 D
白 88 A
幼 90 A
玄 91 A
氶 94 B
矛 95 C
斥 102 D
羊 102 F
丫 103 C
它 108 A
㐌 108 A
丱 108 E
用 109 B
虫 111 A
疋 112 C
正 112 C
癶 112 H
正 112 I
氐 114 B
民 114 D

冉 116 A
另 118 B
歹 118 C
卢 118 D
札 119 D
本 120 A
末 120 B
未 120 C
禾 121 A
氷 125 A
永 125 D
疒 127 C
尼 129 A
卯 129 D mao
卭 129 E yu
卬 129 E yu
矢 131 A
丕 133 A
犮 134 A
旦 143 B

瓦 145 A
田 149 A
由 151 A
甲 152 A
毌 153 A
冎 154 A
冊 156 A
册 156 A
皿 157 A
目 158 A
四 158 A
瓜 162 A
聿 169 A
凸 177
凹 177

6

亘 2 E
西 10 C
巩 11 F

夙 11 G
㐱 12 F
巟 12 J
巟 12 J
州 12 L
学 12 M
合 14 B
全 15 B
衣 16 A
冰 17 B
肉 17 G 65 A
尖 18 I
朵 22 C
朶 22 C
吉 24 C
共 24 I
光 24 J
戌 25 D
伏 25 E
死 26 H

牝 26 I
旨 26 K
旨 26 K
艮 26 L
艮 26 M
爪 27 K
色 28 D
充 29 F
后 30 C
老 30 E
考 30 E
各 31 B
舛 31 E
夅 31 F
宅 33 B
同 34 I
青 34 I
再 34 J
向 36 E
宂 37 E

匈 38 D
兇 38 D
丟 38 F
网 39 C
囟 40 A
囱 40 C
四 40 D
西 41 B
襾 41 C
西 41 D
吏 43 N
叒 43 Q
伊 44 C
守 45 D
有 46 H
灰 46 I
关 47 J
类 47 K
丞 47 V
妥 49 E

印 49 I
曳 50 F
叓 50 G
匠 51 A
曲 51 B
列 52 D
劣 53 B
劦 53 E
旬 54 E
兆 56 D
夸 58 G
危 59 H
因 60 B
夷 60 D
亦 60 I
交 61 D
羽 62 E
行 63 C
名 64 B
多 64 E

肎 65 C
肎 65 D
舟 66 A
好 67 B
如 67 D
安 67 G
奻 67 I
亥 69 K
囟 70 A
式 71 C
伐 71 G
戋 71 H
成 71 M
戎 71 O
戍 71 P
吅 72 B
回 76 A
亘 76 H
竹 77 B
⺮ 77 B

艸 78 B
卉 78 F
寺 79 B
先 79 B
匡 79 D
圭 81 B
任 82 C
臣 82 E
异 85 C
牟 85 E
似 85 F
自 86 B
弜 87 B
百 88 B
𢆶 90 D
糸 92 A
在 96 D
存 96 D
邦 97 A
㓞 97 D

次 99 B
舌 102 C, 114 C
屰 102 D
辛 102 E
羊 103 A
兆 106 A
虫 110 A
曳 111 A
此 112 A
𠂹 114 C
舌 114 C
刑 115 A
幵 115 B
并 115 B
那 116 B
㫃 117 B
冎 118 A
𣦼 118 C
休 119 C
朱 120 D

耒 120 E
束 120 H
米 122 A
𠁭 122 B
赤 124 A
𠂢 125 E
缶 130 C
至 133 B
虍 135 A
乌 138 C
𠃓 138 C
臼 139 E
早 143 E
耳 146 A
邪 147 B
𠂣 148 B
血 157 D
自 159 A
而 164 A
聿 169 B

7

佞 2 C
巩 11 F
夙 11 G
攸 12 C
夌 12 F
巠 12 H
㚒 13 B shan
余 14 C
含 14 L
岑 14 Q
冏 15 C
初 16 B
冶 17 C
牢 17 F
𧮫 17 H ch'iao
谷 18 E ku
却 17 H
肖 18 J

沙 18 M
助 20 E
秀 23 B
位 25 F, 60 H
𦣞 26 L
皀 26 M
坐 27 D
巫 27 E
夾 27 F chia
坒 27 I
身 28 J, 148
皃 29 C
兑 29 D
夋 29 E
完 29 H
辰 30 B
孝 30 E
局 32 F
壳 34 I
希 35 D

侕 35 F
㒳 35 I
㒷 35 M
劫 38 F
吾 39 A
孝 39 H
囪 40 D
更 41 A
𠥔 41 D
酉 41 G
囧 42 B
君 44 C
𠬶 44 L
肘 45 G
杀 45 J
求 45 K
兵 47 D
戒 47 E
弄 47 F
折 48 D

哥 49 C
抑 49 I
臼 50 A
利 52 F
男 53 C
甬 55 K
甹 55 K
甹 58 C
吞 60 C
赤 60 N
吳 61 A
宎 64 F
冐 65 E
妥 67 F
妟 67 H
毒 67 L
每 67 P
冡 69 A
我 71 Q
言 73 C

邑 74 C
束 75 A
亨 75 D
艮 75 F
旱 75 G
克 75 K
志 79 B
㞷 79 D
狂 79 D
孛 79 G
呈 81 A
廷 81 F
呈 81 H
匠 82 G
忌 84 A
改 85 C
矣 85 E
弟 87 E
私 89 A
呂 90 F

系 92 B
孚 94 B
㐬 94 F
序 95 A
夆 97 A
夆 97 H
次 99 C
尾 100 B
尿 100 B
旱 102 A
辛 102 H
𠦒 104 A
免 106 A
卵 108 D
甫 109 D
延 112 A
足 112 B
走 112 D
辵 112 E
步 112 G

㝂 112 L
長 113 A
昏 114 C
別 118 B
奴 118 C
叔 118 D
困 119 B
杏 119 I
呆 119 I
秃 121 G
釆 123 A
壯 127 B
肩 129 A
医 131 C
告 132 B
否 133 A
狄 134 A
尨 134 C
皀 135 B
角 142 B

耴 146 B
身 149 A
里 149 D
串 153 B
删 156 B
冊 156 H
見 158 C
百 160 A
貝 161 A
豆 165 A
豸 166 A
車 167 A

8

亟 2 D
陋 10 C
直 10 K
虱 11 C
侃 12 K
來 13 C

仌仌 13 E
花 13 F
舍 14 C
侖 14 G
命 14 I
念 14 N
侌 14 P
金 14 T
表 16 K
坴 16 M
卒 16 M
卤 17 I
昔 17 J
松 18 C
宓 18 G
凭 20 C
佩 21 D
固 24 F
戔 27 B
昆 27 I

咎 28 I
兒 29 B
降 31 F
屄 32 A
居 32 C
壳 34 I
刷 35 E
兩 35 I
宗 36 B
尙 36 E
尚 36 E
屆 38 C
骨 38 D
罔 39 C
岡 39 C
肴 39 J
畀 40 C
俩 41 B
明 42 C
牧 43 D

癹 43 R
隶 44 E
疌 44 F
妻 44 G
事 44 H
秉 44 I
帚 44 K
府 45 C
㝵 45 E
卑 46 E
具 47 G
卷 47 K
奉 47 L
承 47 W
采 49 B
爭 49 D
受 49 E
奄 50 E
臾 50 G
劾 52 F

匋 54 C
匊 54 D
肥 55 E
弱 59 H
函 55 K
卦 56 E
奇 58 I
厓 59 B
忝 60 C
夜 60 I
扶 60 M
宛 64 D
宜 64 F
朋 64 I
肯 65 C
肩 65 F
肰 65 G
服 66 C
妾 67 E
毒 67 M

豖 69 G
其 70 C
或 71 J
武 71 K
戔 71 R
昌 73 A
沓 73 A
巷 74 C
京 75 C
享 75 DEH
㐭 76 B
屈 78 E
幷 78 G
旹 79 B
青 79 F
林 79 H
坴 79 K
麦 79 K
岳 80 B
垂 81 E

空 82 A
臤 82 E
臥 82 F
亞 82 H
珏 83 B
𠂤 86 A
阜 86 A
官 86 C
帛 88 A
叀 91 E
乳 94 B
育 94 E
忝 99 F
屖 100 B
忽 101 A
易 101 C
庚 102 B
幸 102 DG
㚔 102 G
羌 103 A

乖 103 C
兔 106 B
周 109 C
延 112 A
定 112 I
長 113 A
昏 114 B
并 115 B
青 115 D
放 117 A
於 117 C
奈 119 F
林 119 L
制 120 C
果 120 F
刺 120 H
東 120 K
囷 121 B
和 121 E
委 121 F

叔 124 B
法 125 A
雨 125 B
雨 125 B
炙 126 A
罙 126 B
炎 126 D
非 127 D
欣 128 A
析 128 A
所 128 A
所 128 B
戾 129 A
門 129 C
知 131 E
音 133 A
杏 133 A
到 133 B
虎 135 B
臽 139 A

杳 143 C
杲 143 C
昊 143 D
卓 143 F
耶 146 E
取 146 F
甾 150 A
典 156 C
孟 157 B
丽 163 A
隹 168 A
非 170 A

9

門 1 H
恆 2 F
眉 7 A
飛 11 A
甾 12 I
陝 13 B

𠂹	13 E	昝	26 D	畏	40 C	𢏚	55 H	某	73 B
垂	13 E	卽	26 M	便	41 A	貞	56 C	甚	73 B
乖	13 I	食	26 M	垔	41 D	矦	59 H	香	73 B
俞	14 F	皆	27 I	卣	41 E	侯	59 H	音	73 E
俞	14 F	冠	29 H	酋	41 G	昱	60 H	柬	75 A
哀	16 C	客	31 B	叚	43 I	英	60 K	亭	75 B
俎	17 G	洛	31 B	紂	45 G	並	60 L	亮	75 C
卸	17 H	韋	31 G	育	46 D	幸	60 O	亯	75 D
眇	18 M	屋	32 G	若	46 G	彥	61 F	畐	75 D
盈	19 B	冒	34 J	弇	46 I	前	66 D	郎	75 E
急	19 D	胄	34 J chou	奏	47 M	匽	67 H	厚	75 G
查	20 F	冑	65 B chou	春	47 P	姦	67 J	复	75 I
風	21 B	爯	35 K	看	48 C	帣	68 E	宣	76 H
禹	23 D	突	37 B	拜	48 E	彔	68 F	耑	78 A
禺	23 E	穿	37 D	爰	49 F	彖	69 F	奔	78 F
計	24 B	奐	37 F	臾	50 G	威	71 P	封	79 E
胡	24 F	叟	38 D	要	50 N	咸	71 P	星	79 F
度	24 M	盇	38 G	則	52 E	㗊	72 K	南	79 G
枼	24 O	思	40 A	訇	54 E	品	72 L	皇	81 A
信	25 H	𡿺	40 B	苟	54 G	咼	73 A	皇	81 A

皇 83 C
相 85 D
後 90 A
胤 90 C
幽 90 D
保 94 B
弇 94 D
柔 95 C
敄 95 C
契 97 D
昜 101 B
臿 102 A
恬 102 C
活 102 C
庴 102 D
咢 102 D
姜 103 A
美 103 A
革 105 A
皀 106 C

胥 112 C
陟 112 G
發 112 H
癸 112 H
是 112 I
施 117 B
斿 117 B
咼 118 A
柰 119 F
帝 120 H
刺 120 I
重 120 K
秋 121 C
囪 122 C
胃 122 C
衍 125 A
耑 125 C
泉 125 E
昴 129 D
柳 129 E

卸 130 B
矧 131 G
致 133 B
畀 143 D
冐 146 C
苗 149 B
扁 156 D
昷 157 C
相 158 B
省 158 D
盾 158 E
苜 158 F
者 159 B
首 160 A
県 160 A
而 160 B
頁 160 C
負 161 E
要 164 A
要 164 A

耑 164 B
段 164 D
壴 165 B
軍 167 C
律 169 B
建 169 B
隶 169 D
韭 170 B

10

眞 10 L
鬥 11 I
邕 12 G
荒 12 J
素 13 H
𠂹 13 I
脊 13 I
荅 14 B
茶 14 C
陰 14 P

衰 16 D
衰 16 D
衷 76 E
衮 16 F
袁 16 L
凋 17 D
翁 18 C
容 18 E
貨 18 K
貨 18 L
風 21 B
晃 24 K
席 25 M
閃 25 C
㘭 26 C
倉 26 M
㲋 27 I
能 27 J
辱 30 B
耆 30 E

退 31 C
桀 31 E
乘 31 E
隺 34 F
冥 34 G
散 34 I
冢 34 I
昜 34 J
窄 37 G
盍 38 G
鬼 40 C
迺 41 D
栗 41 E
桑 43 Q
兼 44 I
討 45 G
蚤 45 I
殺 45 J
差 46 C
朕 47 J

秦 47 N
泰 47 O
寒 47 T
烝 47 V
㝵 49 G
陳 50 H
昇 50 I
荔 52 G
脅 53 E
莆 54 G
庯 54 G
巽 55 H
圅 55 K
哥 58 I
原 59 C
侯 59 H
庫 59 I
皋 60 F
竝 60 L
弱 62 P

扇 62 D
屑 65 D
般 66 B
彔 68 G
彖 68 I
圂 69 B
家 69 C
冢 69 G
戚 71 P
哭 72 C
高 75 B
畗 75 D
芻 78 D
蚩 79 B
時 79 B
索 79 G
盇 79 J
垔 81 G
貢 82 A
展 82 B

珡 62 B
師 86 B
追 86 B
隽 87 C
躬 90 F
宮 90 G
畜 91 B
孫 92 B
奚 92 C
茲 92 F
害 97 E
氣 98 A
眔 100 C
唐 102 B
朔 102 D
欮 102 D
宰 102 H
亲 102 H
屖 102 H
丵 102 I

羔 103 A
冓 104 B
冤 106 B
尃 109 D
書 111 C
涉 112 G
癸 112 H
彭 113 B
旁 117 A
旅 117 B
軓 117 D
骨 118 A
臬 119 H
秝 121 L
益 125 C
叟 126 B
𤇾 126 F
留 129 E
畚 130 C
疾 131 B

射 131 D
晉 133 C
臭 134 A
虒 135 G
虐 135 H
馬 137 A
島 138 B
烏 138 D
舀 139 A
草 143 E
茸 146 D
殷 148 B
罬 149 C
鬲 155 A
盈 157 C
朋 158 G
息 159 A
書 159 B
夏 160 D
員 161 B
窯 162 B
敞 164 C
豈 165 E
軎 167 D
隻 168 G

11

匿 10 D
巢 12 O
麥 13 C
貪 14 M
會 14 O
商 15 D
衰 16 F
終 17 E
皐 18 L
雀 18 N
處 20 B
虘 20 G
离 23 E
庶 24 M
帶 24 Q
頃 26 J
既 26 M
飤 26 M
鄉 26 M
毀 26 N
從 27 A
虛 27 H
眾 27 K
寇 29 H
畧 31 B
隆 31 F
尉 32 B
㷉 32 B
曼 34 J
微 35 F
爾 35 M
堂 36 E
敎 39 H
爽 39 O
細 40 A
𡿺 40 B
恖 40 D
㝛 41 B
鹵 41 D
羞 44 B
彗 44 J
雪 44 J
婦 44 K
殺 45 J
隋 46 D
舂 47 N
異 47 R
票 50 O
罨 50 P
梁 52 B
葡 54 G
虜 58 D
雩 58 H
奞 60 E
產 61 F
參 62 C
翏 62 F
祭 65 H
婁 67 N
彖 68 H
豚 69 E
逐 69 E
隊 69 F
豙 69 H
國 71 J
區 72 L
章 73 E
竟 73 E
欶 75 A
柬 75 A
毫 75 B
孰 75 E
啚 76 F

敖 78 E
莫 78 G
莽 78 G
麻 79 H
埶 79 K
望 81 G
戜 81 H
盟 82 I
牽 91 C
率 91 D
專 91 F
紼 92 G
野 95 A
閉 96 C
逢 97 D
欵 99 D
𥏻 101 B
庸 102 B
康 102 B
執 102 G

羕 103 A
畢 104 A
兜 106 A
萈 106 D
強 110 B
徙 112 E
旋 117 B
族 117 B
乾 117 D
桼 119 E
[illegible] 120 C
責 120 H
啇 120 H
曹 120 K
悉 123 B
戚 124 C
扁 125 B
烹 126 A
將 127 B
斬 128 A

扈 129 A
啓 129 A
殹 131 C
規 131 F
造 132 B
鹿 136 A
舄 136 B
鳥 138 A
焉 138 C
魚 142 A
斛 142 B
敢 146 H
累 149 F
患 153 B
習 159 A
連 167 B
崔 168 F
晝 169 C
堇 171 B
𦰩 171 B

寅 172 A
㱿 173 A

12

喪 10 H
無 10 I
悳 10 O
猌 13 C
華 13 F
飮 14 O
喬 15 C
馮 17 E
萬 23 F
离 23 G
晉 26 D
鄉 26 M
卿 26 M
虛 27 H
殼 34 I
黹 35 G

盜 36 C
牚 36 E
敞 36 F
壺 38 G
壹 38 G
棥 39 L
黑 40 D
曾 40 D
弼 41 B
粟 41 E
奠 41 G
萌 42 C
赧 43 J
尋 45 F
陸 46 D
尊 47 C
寒 47 U
爲 49 H
絕 55 G
巽 55 H

皐 60 F
替 60 L
須 62 B
翕 62 H
飧 64 C
閒 64 H
然 65 G
猒 65 G
象 69 I
貳 71 D
戠 71 I
單 72 E
㗊 72 M
善 73 D
啇 73 E
喬 75 B
就 75 C
景 75 C
敦 75 E
量 75 F
覃 75 G
復 75 I
莽 78 G
㪔 79 H
散 79 H
堯 81 C
項 82 A
㠭 82 B
渠 82 D
惡 82 H
閏 83 C
雋 87 C
𤔔 90 B
幾 90 D
惠 91 G
緜 92 D
雲 93 B
孱 94 D
敢 94 E
棄 94 G
絜 97 D
款 99 D
毳 100 A
犀 100 B
湯 101 B
畁 102 D
厥 102 D
報 102 G
業 102 I
雈 103 C
惢 107 A
强 110 B
蚰 110 C
貴 111 B
發 112 H
登 112 H
開 115 C
朝 117 D
㕡 118 D
集 119 G
棘 120 H
棗 120 H
曾 120 H
童 120 K
黍 121 I
麻 121 L
番 123 D
焦 126 A
粦 126 D
舜 126 D
尞 126 E
焱 126 F
勞 126 F
斯 128 A
雇 129 A
閔 129 C
貿 129 D
御 130 B
舄 138 C
晶 143 G
最 146 F
貫 153 A
奢 159 B
買 161 D
揣 164 B
喜 165 B
彭 165 B
封 165 D
雁 168 K
畫 169 C
黃 171 A

13

雍 12 G
會 14 D
僉 14 E
裏 16 G
睘 16 L
[illegible] 22 B
殿 22 D

禽 23 E
萬 23 H
筮 27 E
路 31 B
當 36 E
[illegible] 39 I
盟 42 C
遣 46 D
筭 47 F
電 50 D
[illegible] 50 M
農 50 Q
賊 52 E
敬 54 G
與 54 H
蜀 54 I
詹 59 H
普 60 L
達 60 O
穌 67 P

[illegible] 68 C
豦 69 D
遂 69 F
歲 71 P
義 71 Q
喿 72 L
意 73 E
[illegible] 74 B
壺 75 A
稟 76 C
亶 76 D
嗇 76 E
賁 78 F
毀 81 A
聖 81 H
[illegible] 81 H
溼 92 E
楙 95 C
豊 97 B
款 99 D

愛 99 F
睪 102 G
辟 102 H
辠 102 H
業 102 I
黽 108 C
溥 109 D
敫 117 A
幹 117 D
過 118 A
粲 118 C
禁 119 M
楚 119 N
稚 121 E
廉 121 K
[illegible] 122 C
奧 123 F
粵 123 F
肅 125 C
煩 126 A

煞 126 C
鼎 127 D
虜 135 C
虛 135 E
鳫 136 C
鼠 139 B
觜 142 B
解 142 B
畺 149 E
雷 149 F
著 159 B
賈 161 C
微 164 C
鼓 165 C
轂 167 D
雁 168 K

14

蒜 3 E
裹 16 H
[illegible] 17 E
[illegible] 17 E
截 18 N
鳳 21 C
[illegible] 23 F
聚 27 K
舞 31 E
蒙 34 I
爾 35 L
寧 36 C
鼻 40 C
熏 40 D
算 47 G
[illegible] 49 G
翟 62 G
厭 65 G
彙 68 E
[illegible] 69 J
豪 75 B
臺 75 B

圖 76 F
葬 78 G
臧 82 E
監 82 F
㬎 92 E
兢 97 I
辡 102 H
對 102 I
蒦 103 C
遣 111 C
[illegible] 112 A
賓 112 L
賔 112 L
榦 117 D
睿 118 D
叡 118 D
巢 120 G
赫 126 B
熒 126 F
寤 127 C
疑 131 G
獄 134 B
雐 135 F
壽 144 B
壽 144 B
蒯 156 H
夢 158 F
署 159 B
寡 160 A
賏 161 F
需 164 E
嘉 165 B
肇 169 B
齊 174 A

15

德 10 O
蟲 11 C
飮 14 O
睘 16 L
厲 23 H
罾 23 I
節 26 M
罷 27 J
關 34 D
臱 34 K
臱 34 K
賞 36 E
曼 37 F
慮 40 A
鬳 47 B
暴 47 S
蔑 47 X
樊 47 Z
黎 52 F
輦 60 M
數 67 N
𩫖 75 E
履 75 J
賣 78 E mai, 75 J yu
樂 88 C
𢇍 90 E
繼 90 E
疐 91 I
繇 92 B
養 103 A
稽 121 M
審 123 D
質 128 B
劉 129 E
麃 136 A
慶 136 A
寫 138 C
魯 142 A
廛 149 D
畾 149 F
實 153 A
蔑 158 F
憂 160 C
徵 164 C
廚 165 D
盡 169 D
廣 171 A
齒 175 A

16

褱 16 J
憑 17 E
學 39 I
盥 50 B
舉 50 J
興 50 K
毀 72 H
器 72 M
轂 79 H
辥 86 K
縣 92 B
縣 92 E
憲 97 F
親 102 H

頻 112 G
賴 120 I
穌 121 D
歷 121 L
盧 135 D
龍 140 A
燕 141 A
衡 142 B
瞢 158 F
諸 159 B
霍 168 H
[illegible] 177 B

17

龠 14 H
襄 16 I
鐵 27 B
蹇 47 U
輿 50 I
舋 62 C
羲 71 Q
霝 72 K
臨 82 F
薛 86 B
營 90 G
繇 92 B
鮮 103 A
冀 104 A
[illegible] 105 B
毚 106 C
壑 118 D
霜 158 B
嬰 161 F
徽 164 C

18

雝 12 G
巂 15 C
竄 34 C
雚 72 J
歸 86 B
豐 97 B
辭 102 H
[illegible] 103 B
龜 108 B
蟲 110 D
雜 119 G
聶 146 G
瞿 158 H
雙 168 G
爵 176 A

19

邊 34 K
邊 34 K
薾 35 M
羅 39 D
彝 68 D
嚴 72 G
贊 79 B
靡 79 H
䜌 92 D
羹 103 A
類 160 C
顛 160 C
麗 163 B
難 171 B

20

黨 36 E
覺 39 I
競 73 D
寶 130 D
獻 134 A
矍 158 G

21 &

屬 54 I
竈 79 I
覽 82 F
霸 105 B
纍 149 F
[illegible] 176 A
聽 10 O
囊 72 H
[illegible] 92 D
孿 94 C
疊 143 G
羈 105 C
蠱 110 D
竊 23 G
靈 72 K
贛 73 E
廳 10 O
鬮 23 F
龗 72 E
鬱 130 E
鬱 130 E
[illegible] 194 B
夔 154 B

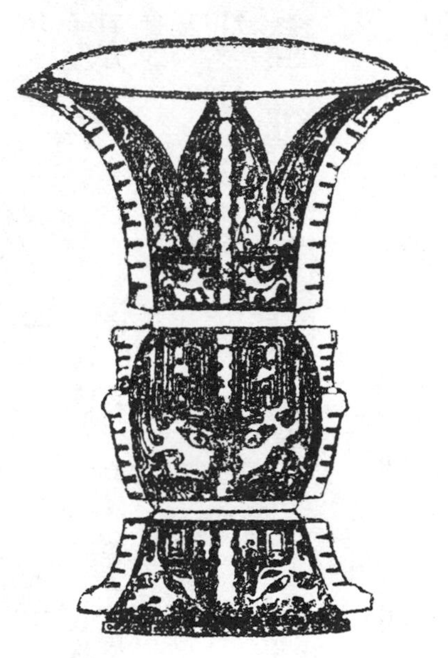

OLD GRAPHIES.

Whensoever the ancient Chinese noblemen had been favoured by their princes, or had experienced some kind of success or luck, they used to cast a bronze vase, in memoriam. Symbols and Characters relating the fact, were moulded on the *interior side* of the vase, which was placed in the ancestral temple of the family, and served henceforth as a ritual vessel, when oblations and libations were offered to the Manes. On the *exterior side* of the vase, the two eyes of the Ancestor, were figured, looking at his sons and grandsons with benevolence. We are indebted to these old bronze vases, for all the old Graphies we possess. Ancient Chinese epigraphy on stone, is non-existent. Many fac-similes of vases and inscriptions are to be found in the 4th French edition of this work, *Caractères Chinois*, pages 361-452. In this English edition, the matter has been presented in a summary way.

Now take good notice of one thing, which uses to baffle novices in Chinese epigraphy. In all modern books, the engravers have replaced the *old obsolete symbols* which are not characters, by *conventional current characters* chosen because of their form, without reference to their meaning. To translate those signs, would cause laughable blunders. For instance, instead of the symbol [illegible] offering of meat, they engrave the modern character 父 father, because the old character [illegible] father resembled the symbol [illegible] offering. — In the place of [illegible] the poured libation, they put a 己. — For the obsolete [illegible] a distaff-load of textile fibres presented to the Manes, they put a 彝. And so on. — Remember this, when reading the modern transcriptions of the following old Graphies, which have all been photographed from rare Chinese epigraphic repertories, such as 稽古齋鐘鼎彝器款識 etc.

The most frequent of all Symbols, is ⺕ a right hand offering ♦, which is neither a flame, nor incense, but the smell of the offered meat, ascending towards the Ancestors.

Almost every time, beneath this symbol of offering meat, there is 乁 a sort of tear, symbol of the poured down libation of wine. Instead of the falling wine, they sometimes figure ● the splash of the wine having fallen on naked soil. This figure is rare, because it was ritual custom to pour the libation on grass, spread out or tied into a bundle, which was burned after the ceremony was over. There are many figures of this bundle of grass, sometimes graphically reduced to a 工, or 十, or anything else.

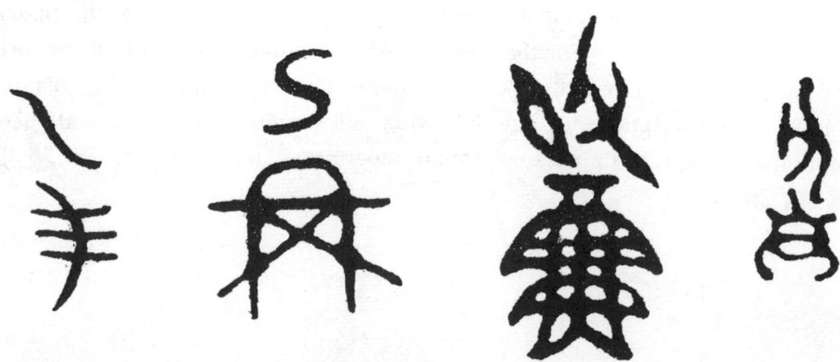

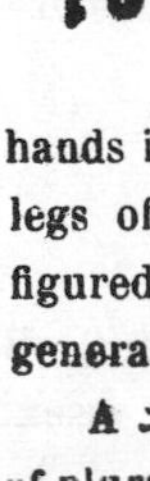

Ordinarily the son offering to his father (and ancestors) is represented in an ethereal shape, which figures his being raptured and transported mentally in the presence of his Ancestors, by his filial love and desire to please them. Sometimes arms and legs of the son are figured.

The grandsons able to stand upright, are figured beneath the son (their father) holding up their hands in prayer. — The grandsons too young to stand upright, crawl between the legs of their father, oftentimes resembling frogs. — Sometimes the grandson is figured like the son, but holding a skein of yarn, symbol of the succession of generations.

A 二 added to the figure of a son or grandson, does not mean *two*. It is a sign of plurality meaning «All of them, as many as there are».

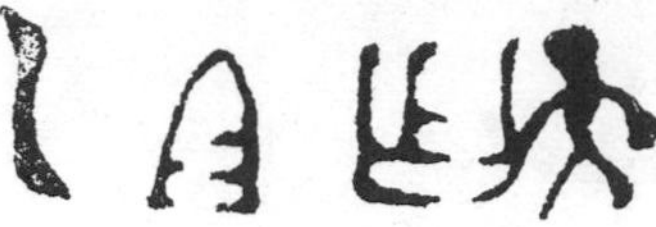

Sometimes the son does not offer the smell of the cooked meat, but the raw meat cut in slices, which are exposed on the shelves of a 且 dresser. A libation of wine is poured, as usual.

Besides the smell of meat and the libation of wine, three things are presented at almost all solemn offerings. These are .

1 寶 a box containing 玉 jade, 貝 cowries and 缶 pottery.

2 [illegible] an amphora of wine, presented by two hands, with a ladle.

3 [illegible] a distaff-load of textile fibres, with 2 or 4 hands spinning.

The idea is very clear The Ancients offered to their deceased Ancestors, all the things without which the living could not be; viz. valuables, money, vases, stuff for clothes, wine. Analyse the three figures above...

The 貝 cowries, current money of old China, are offered strung up, often in great quantities, as much as a man can carry with a pole. — In some texts, the strings of cowries are figured in a compendious conventional form.

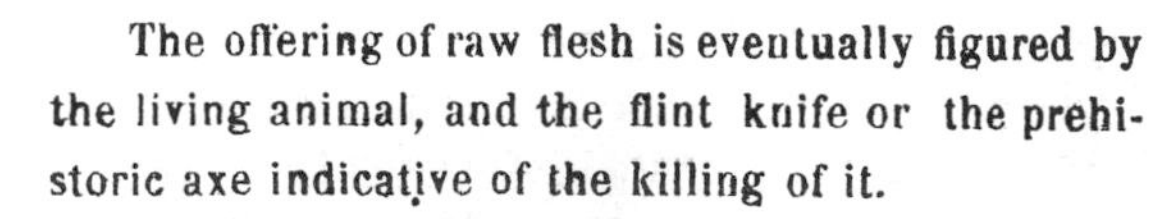

The offering of raw flesh is eventually figured by the living animal, and the flint knife or the prehistoric axe indicative of the killing of it.

When the animal is not figured, the mere knife in the hand of the son, denotes that he has killed an animal to be offered.

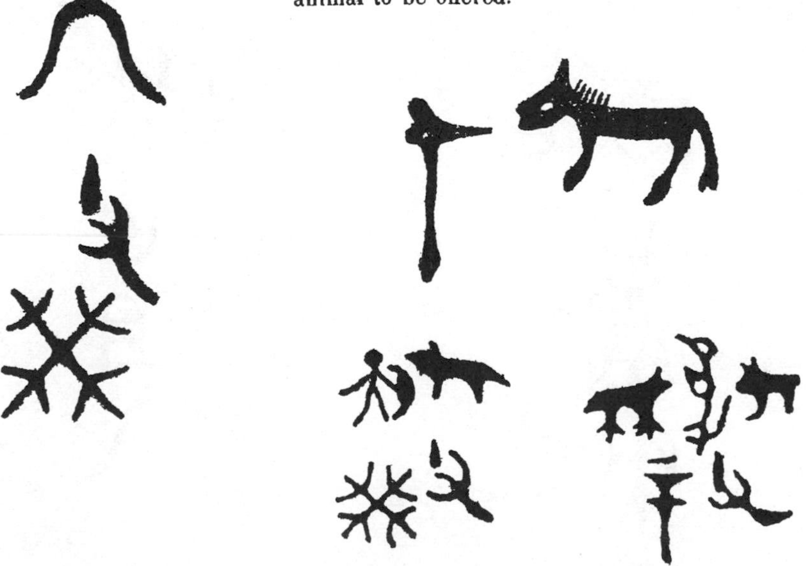

Sometimes the offering of raw meat is figured by the skinned hide of the victim fastened on a stake, accompanied by libations, etc.

The presence of the Ancestor to whom the offering is made, is ordinarily figured by 止 the heel of his foot; see Lesson 112 A. In modern Chinese, to say *in presence of*, is 在 跟 前 *before the heels of*. — Now we are able to interprete the whole of the following two inscriptions... (Left) In presence *of my Ancestors, I offer* raw meat, a libation, wine and tow... (Right) In presence *of my Ancestors*, I the son holding the flint knife, offer raw meat, libations, precious things, wine and tow.

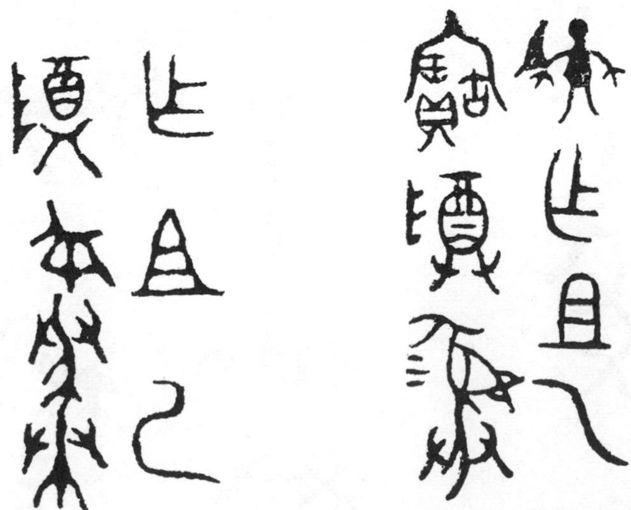

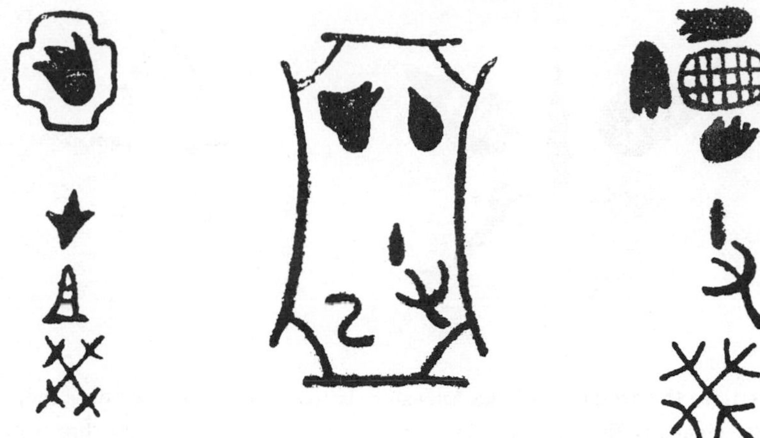

Sometimes the offering is presented to a foot-print, or to foot-prints of the deceased Ancestor. Now-a-days, as of old, the Chinese try to discern the foot-prints of the departed, on planks strewn over with sand or ashes. See above four figures showing the worship of foot-prints. In the first and second, there is one; in the third, there are two of them. In the fourth, the Ancestor has walked all around the offering, sniffing its smell. In the fifth, the legs of the Ancestor are visible. The frame which encloses three of these Graphies, will be explained on page 368.

In some very rare cases, the Ancestor is figured standing, and the offering is presented to him directly. See above.

Sometimes the presence of the Ancestor is figured by his two eyes looking with benevolence at the offerings. As has been said on page 361, the benevolent eyes of the Ancestor are figured on the outer side of all ancient sacrificial vessels, staring at the offerers. Sometimes the two eyes are replaced by one triangle, symbolising *sight* in abstracto.

The temple of the deceased Ancestor, or rather the sacred niche from whence his transcendent influence is supposed to emanate, is figured by a frame, square or rectangular, often with inward curved angles.

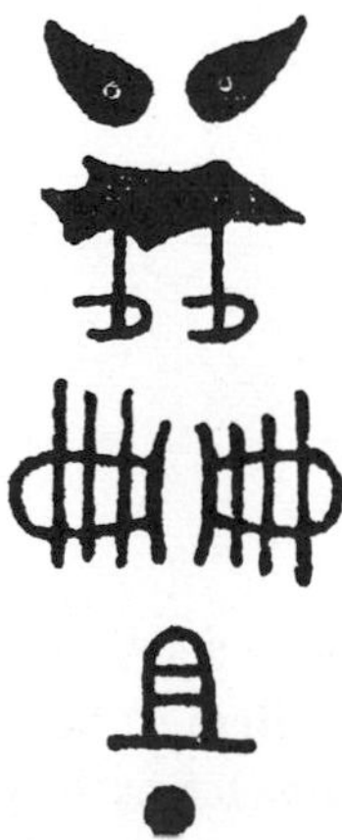

Ordinarily the temple, and the presence of the Ancestor in the temple, are figured, either by a balustrade separating the nave from the sanctuary; or by the inlet to the sanctuary, a narrow pass between two or four pillars. All the supplicants, sons and grandsons, are standing in front of this entrance, the spot where the offerings are presented. — Hereby an excellent figure of the balustrade. In the sanctuary, the eyes of the Ancestor stare at the hide of the slaughtered victim, expanded on two stakes. In front of the entrance, raw meat and libation, as usual.

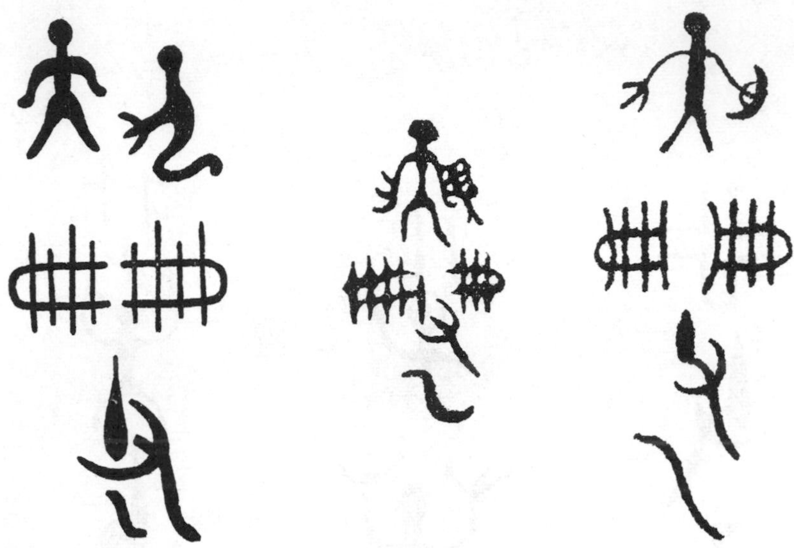

Some times, in a fit of rapture, the offering son is spiritually transported beyond the balustrade and the pillars, into the sanctuary, unto the very presence of the Ancestor. See above, on the left, the best figure Antiquity has bequeathed to us. It dates from the 2d dynasty (circa B.C. 1500), and shows a raptured son kneeling in presence of his standing father... In the two other figures, the raptured son carries cowries or meat (knife).

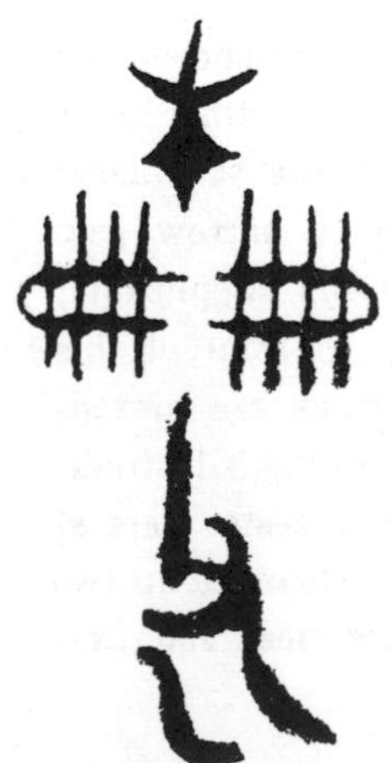

In some very rare but most precious figures, the deceased Ancestor is represented *diving*, head foremost, from heavens above, towards the hand of his offering son.

Sometimes the Ancestor is figured by a ghostlike silhouette, with a single eye, often surmounted by a triangle. I call your attention to the second line of the text reproduced beneath on the right, in which you have firstly a foot-print of the Ancestor, secondly his ghostly shade.

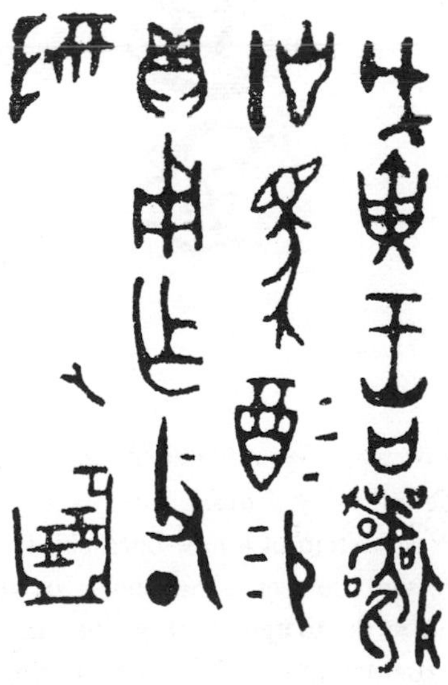

Now we are able to understand all the Graphies on top of this page, and others on the following pages...

Presentation of a new-born child, to the △ sight of his Ancestor.

Presentation of a new-born btbe, the fontanelle of whose skull is not yet closed, in the temple, with a libation

Presentation of twins, with offerings and libation.

Presentation to the Ancestor, is his temple, of a pair of twins, brother and sister, with offerings.

In the presence of the Ancestor, after libation, offering of jade wine and tow, by the son, a grandson having recently been born.

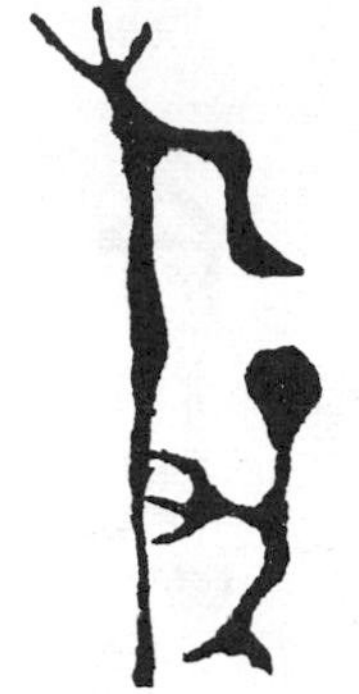

Offering of a banner. In the. second figure, the banner is offered, with a libation, to thank for the apparition of a foot-print of the Ancestor, in the temple.

Presentation of a new carriage... with offering of bleeding flesh on a stake, in the first figure.. with the ordinary offerings, in the second figure.

Bunches of wheat are offered, to thank for the harvest.

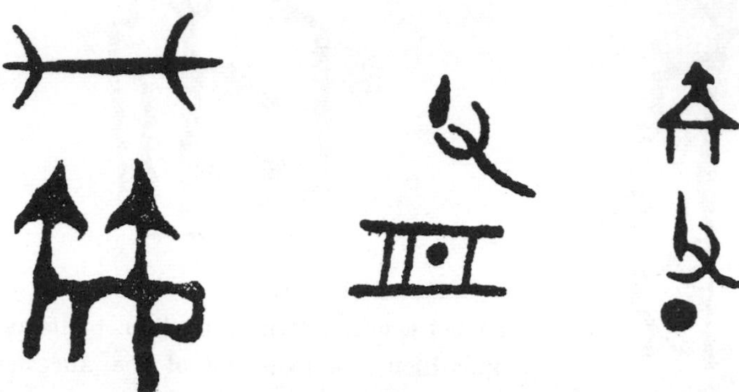

To announce to the Ancestors, the fabrication of a bow and arrows, launching of a bark, building of a dwelling-house.

Offering to the mountains... to the clouds. — Invitation to the dragon to make the clouds burst and rain pour down.

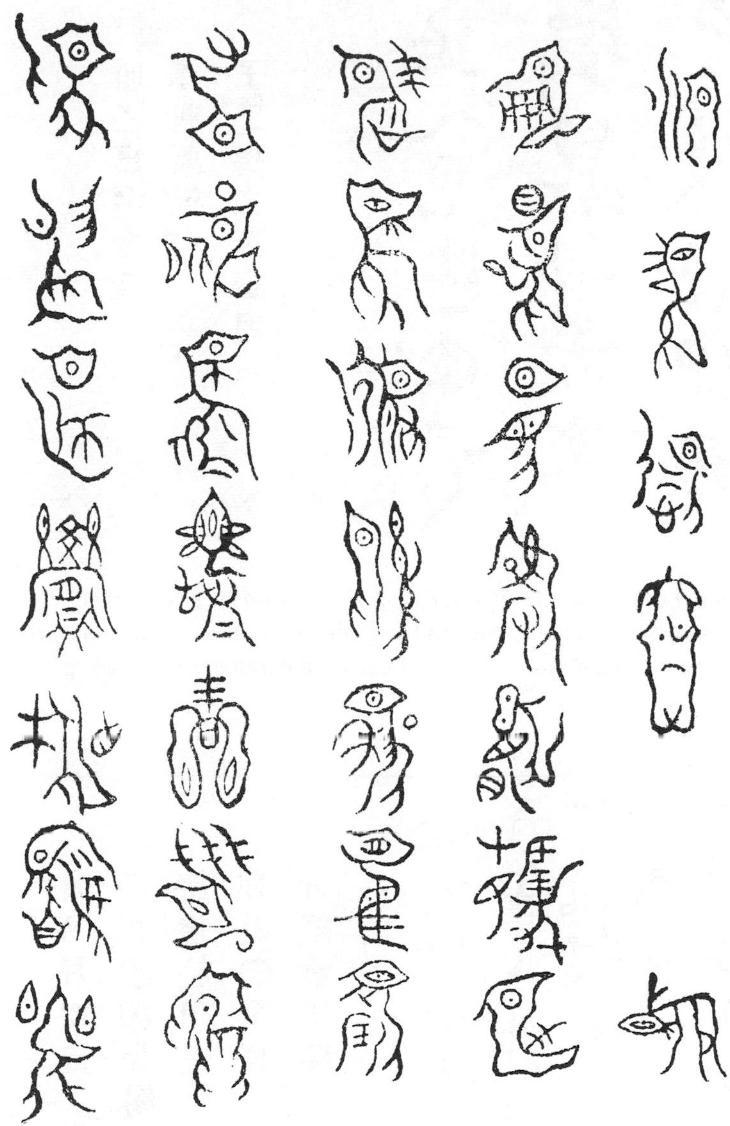

This bronze plate, dating probably from the 20th century B.C., is the oldest specimen known of Chinese writing. It is not properly a text, but the enumeration of all kinds of animals killed in a great hunting. The document reveals... 1 that the shape of the primitive characters differed greatly from that of their derivatives... 2 that the principle of composition of characters, was always the same, from the beginning.

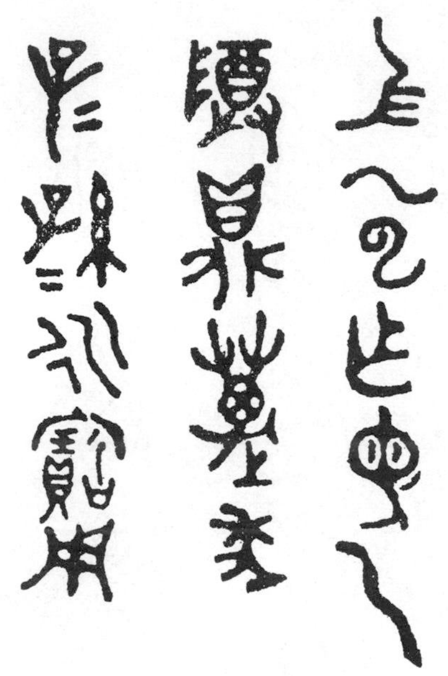

唯乙巳乍母乁
尊鼎萬年
子二孫二永寶用

On the day *i-ssu*, in presence of the deceased grandfather, the widowed grand mother (chief of the family) has offered, with wine etc., this bronze tripod, to last ten thousand years. Hoping that innumerable sons and grandsons will enjoy it for ever.

唯八月初吉
辰在乙卯公錫
旂僕旂用乍
鼎乂日乁寶
尊彝非子孫

In the eighth month, on the first auspicious day which was **i-mao**, the duke committed solemnly to the standard-bearers the new standards. This tripod was cast to commemorate the fact, and was presented before the tablet of the Ancestor of the clan, with the usual offerings... sons and grandsons worshipping in front of the sanctuary.

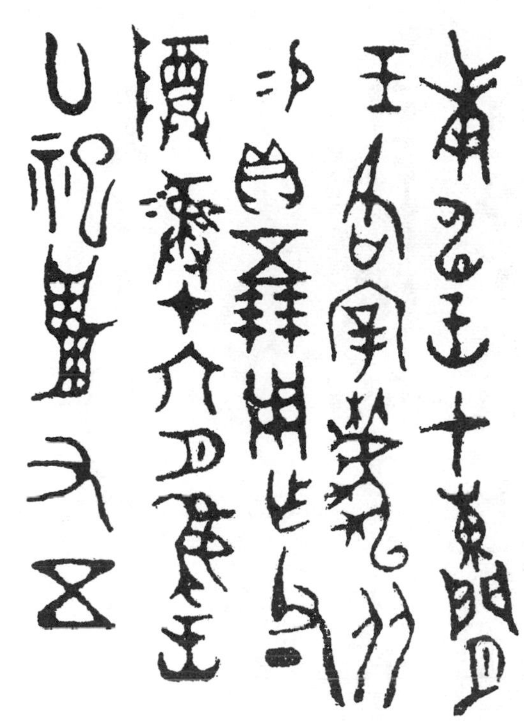

庚申王在東門夕
王格宰虎　從
錫貝五拜用乍乂●
隫齋十六月唯王
乙祀脚形手形五　鼎冊

On the day **keng-shên**, the new emperor **Wu-ting** went to the eastern gate of the city, to salute the rising sun. On the evening of the same day, he ordered minister **Hu** to deliver five man-loads of cowries, to be presented with the ordinary offerings, as a token of gratitude for the prints of feet and hands of the deceased emperor **Hsiao-i**, which had been noticed in the ancestral temple, five times, during the 16 months of mourning. This vase was cast and placed in the sanctuary, to commemorate the fact. — B.C. 1273.

王伐許侯周公
謀禽祝禽手
擊祝王錫金百鍰
禽用乍寶彝

The emperor being about to wage war against the marquis of **Hsü**, the duke of **Chou** requested me **Ch'in** (the official conjurer) to anathematise the rebels. So I **Ch'in** made with my hand the comminatory gestures, and pronounced with my mouth the imprecatory words. Therefore the emperor gave me hundred ingots of copper (of six ounces each) as a reward. I **Ch'in** have employed the imperial gift, to make this vase, which I present to my Ancestors, with the ordinary offerings, in memoriam.

In the 9th month, the moon being full, on the day **chia-hsü**, the emperor having worshipped at the ancestral temple, sat down in the hall in which the archives were kept. The Grand-Director **Nan-chuang** having introduced **U-chuan** of **Lu,** the emperor ordered first the attendant registrar to take his tablets into his hands, and then dictated his will, as follows: « **U-chuan**, I invest thee with the charge of inspector of **Hu-fang.** » — Having thus been honoured and favoured by the Son of Heaven, I, their grandson **U-chuan**, have cast this urn, to gladden my glorious Ancestors. I hope it will be the jewel of my descendants, for ever. — **9th** century B.C.

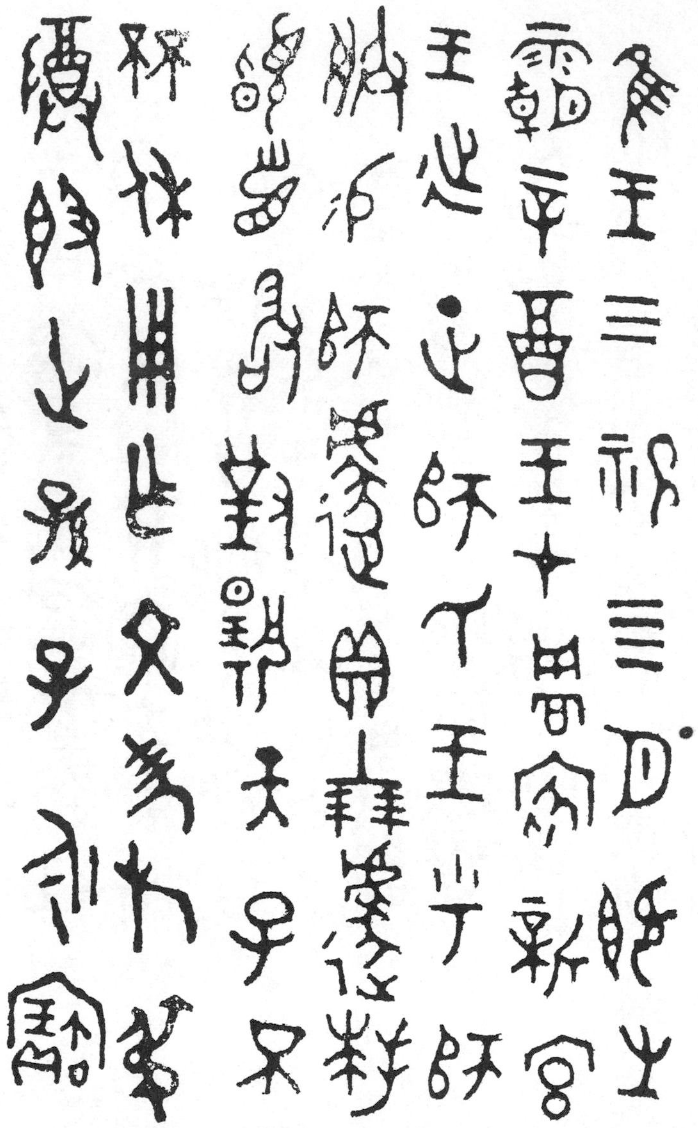

During the :th year of his reign (probably B C 768), in the 3th month, the moon beginniug to wane, on the day hsin-yu, the emperor staying at the new palace in the capital, feasted 遽 Chü, the chief of the Literati. During the banquet, as he was iu high spirits, the emperor proclaimed: «I give master Chü ten strings of cowries.». Chü fell on his knees aud thanked. — Having thus been honoured and rewarded by the Son of Heaven, I Chü offer this amphora with a basin, to the first Ancestor of my race, and place them in the aucestral temple, to be the hereditary treasure of my descendants.

唯王五月初
吉丁亥周伯邊
及仲偁父伐
南淮既俘

金用乍實
鼎其萬年
子孫永寶
用

During the fifth month (B.C. 675), on the auspicious day **ting-hai**, the emperor being at the capital **Chou**, received the spoils sent by count **Pien** and others, after having defeated the rebels south of the river **Huai**. There was some fine copper among the spoils. The emperor ordered it to be melted and cast into the form of this tripod, to be a jewel of his sons and grandsons for ever.

帝受元命天錫
帝盨用綏于神祇
罔弗各唯萬世無〇

The emperor having received the prime mandate, the great gift of Heaven (imperial rank and dignity), on ascending the throne (B.C. 571) offers this precious basin, to the Spirits of heaven and earth, hoping they will prevent internal wars... To last during ten thousands of generations, for ever — [Take notice of the fifth character in the first line, the anthropomorphic figure of Heaven.]

唯甲午八月丙寅
帝盥清廟乍禮盤

吉蠲明神神覽
是德俾帝萬年
永綏受命

In the year **chia yü** (B.C. 567), the eighth month, on the day **ping-yin**, after purification, the emperor went to the temple, performed the rites, and offered this basin to propitiate the perspicacious Spirits. May the Spirits (of heaven and earth), knowing the virtue of the emperor, give him peaceful days during ten thousand years, and conserve him his imperial mandate for ever.

I 追 **Chui** belonging to the imperial clan, remember often with veneration and compassion, my Ancestors who died in battle for the service of the emperor. The Son of Heaven having bestowed great liberalities on me, I have cast in bronze and offer now to them this vase **tun**, as a token of my filial piety. May they bestow on me long life and durable prosperity... Made by me **Chui**, after the decease of emperor **Ling** (B.C. 545), to be the jewel of my family. — [Note thrice the anthropomorphic figure of Heaven.]

This is a fragment of a long document contemporary with Confucius, which I quote to show the shape of the characters in which the Confucian Canonics were first written. After having witnessed those clumsy figures, I suppose you will be rather lenient with the blunders committed by their interpreters. [See 4th French edition, pages 442-449.]

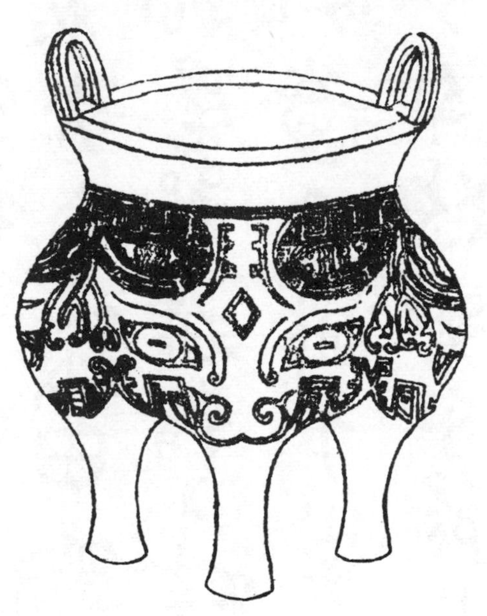

LIST OF THE 858 PHONETICS.

The following phonetic prolific elements practically used, numbered from 1 to 858, are classified according to the number of strokes, and then by alphabetical order. — The characters the romanisation of which is written in italics, are, either different writings, or wrong forms. The figures appointed to these characters, refer to the genuine form.

1

乙 1 **Ya^{2}.**

2

几 2 **Chi^{1}.**
丂 3 **Ch'iao^{3}.**
丩 4 **Chiu^{1}.**
九 5 **Chiu^{3}.**
㔾 6 **Han^{3}.**
乃 7 **Nai^{3}.**
八 8 **Pa^{1}.**
卜 9 **Pu^{3}.**
十 10 **Shih^{2}.**
丁 11 **Ting^{1}.**

3

叉 12 **Ch'a^{1}.**
丈 13 **Chang^{4}.**
己 14 **Chi^{3}.**
乞 15 **Ch'i^{4}.**
千 16 **Ch'ien^{1}.**
久 17 **Chiu^{3}.**
川 18 **Ch'uan^{1}.**
凡 19 **Fan^{2}.**
卂 20 **Hsün^{4}.**
刃 21 **Jên^{4}.**
干 22 **Kan^{1}.**
口 23 **K'ou^{3}.**
工 24 **Kung^{1}.**
山 25 **Shan^{1}.**
彡 26 **Shan^{1}.**
勺 27 **Shao^{2}.**
巳 28 **Ssŭ^{4}.**
乇 29 **T'o^{1}.**
才 30 **Ts'ai^{2}.**
寸 31 **Ts'un^{4}.**
土 32 **T'u^{3}.**
子 33 **Tzŭ^{3}.**
丸 34 **Wan^{2}.**
亾, 亡 35 **Wang^{2}.**
兀 36 **Wu^{4}.**
也 37 **Yeh^{3}.**
亏, 于 38 **Yü^{2}.**

4

爪 39 **Chao^{3}.**
及 40 **Chi^{2}.**
爿 41. **Ch'iang^{2}.**
介 42 **Chieh^{4}.**
切 43 **Ch'ieh^{1}.**
开 *184* ***Ch'ien^{1}.***
欠 44 **Ch'ien^{4}.**
支 45 **Chih^{1}.**
止 46 **Chih^{3}.**
今 47 **Chin^{1}.**
斤 48 **Chin^{1}.**
井 49 **Ching^{3}.**
丑 50. **Ch'ou^{3}.**

Character	No.	Reading
殳	51	Ch'u^2.
中	52	Chung^1.
夬	53	Chüeh^2.
乏	54	Fa^2.
反	55	Fan^3.
方	56	Fang^1.
巿	57	Fei^4.
分	58	Fên^1.
夫	59	Fu^1.
父	60	Fu^4.
心	61	Hsin^1.
凶	62	Hsiung^1.
戶	63	Hu^4.
化	64	Hua^4.
以	65	I^3.
冄	*128*	*Jan*^{3}.
壬	66	Jên^2.
亢	67	K'ang^4.
公	68	Kung^1.
厷	69	Kung^2.
毛	70	Mao^2.
丏	71	Mien^4.
𠬛	72	Mu^2.
卬	73	Nang^2.
內	74.	Nei^4.
厄	75	O^4.
巴	76	Pa^1.
比	77	Pi^3.
卞	78	Pien^4.
不	79	Pu^2.
少	80	Shao^3.
升	81	Shêng^1.
氏	82	Shih^4.
丹	83	Tan^1.
斗	84	Tou^3.
屯	85	T'un^2.
𠂔	86	Tzŭ^3.
王	87	Wang^2.
文	88	Wên^2.
午	89	Wu^4.
勿	90	Wu^4.
牙	91	Ya^2.
夭	92	Yao^1.
引	93	Yin^3.
冘	94	Yin^2.
尤	95.	Yu^2.
予	96	Yü^2.
元	97	Yüan^2.
勻	98	Yün^2.
云	99	Yün^2.
允	100	Yün^3.

5

Character	No.	Reading
札	101	Cha^1.
乍	102	Cha^4.
冊	103	Ch'ai^2.
占	104	Chan^1.
召	105	Chao^4.
㐱	106	Chên^3.
正	107	Chêng^4
加	108	Chia^1.
甲	109	Chia^3.
且	110	Ch'ieh^3.
只	111	Chih^2.
斥	112	Ch'ih^4.
丘	113	Ch'iu^1.
冋	114	Chiung^3.
主	115	Chu^3.
宁	116	Chu^4.
出	117	Ch'u^1.
句	*131*	*Chü*^{4}.
巨	118	Chü^4.
去	119	Ch'ü^4.
付	120	Fu^4.
弗	121	Fu^4.
号	122	Hao^4.
兄	123	Hsiung^1.
玄	124	Hsüan^2.
穴	125	Hsüeh^2.
囘	*241*	*Hui*^{2}.
㐌	126	I^2.
台	127	I^2.
冉, 冄	128	Jan^3.
甘	129	Kan^1.
可	130	K'o^3.
句, 勾	131	Kou^1.
古	132	Ku^3.
瓜	133	Kua^1.
立	134	Li^4.
令, 令	135	Ling^4.
卯	136	Mao^3.
民	137	Min^2.
末	138	Mo^4.
毋	139	Mu^3.
尼	140	Ni^2.
奴	141	Nu^2.
犮	142	Pa^2.
白	143	Pai^2.
半	144	Pan^4.
包	145	Pao^1.
丕	146	P'ei^1.
本	147	Pên^3.

必 148 Pi^{2}.
皮 149 P'i^{2}.
弁 *73 Pien^{4}.*
丙 150 Ping^{3}.
平 151 P'ing^{2}.
布 152 Pu^{4}.
申 153 Shên^{1}.
生 154. Shêng^{1}.
失 155 Shih^{1}.
石 156 Shih^{2}.
世 157 Shih^{4}.
朮 158 Shu^{2}.
司 159 Ssŭ^{1}.
四 160 Ssŭ^{4}.
代 161 Tai^{4}.
旦 162 Tan^{4}.
氐 163 Ti^{1}.
田 164 T'ien^{2}.
它 165 T'o^{1}.
冬 166 Tung^{1}.
未 167 Wei^{4}.
央 168 Yang^{1}.
㕣 169 Yen^{3}.
由 170 Yu^{2}.
幼 171 Yu^{4}.
右 172 Yu^{4}.
永 173 Yung^{3}.
夗 174 Yüan^{1}.
戉 175 Yüeh^{4}.

6

安 176 An^{1}.
宅 177 Chai^{2}.
兆 178 Chao^{4}.
成 179 Ch'êng^{2}.
吉 180 Chi^{2}.
㓞 181 Ch'i^{4}.
夅 182 Chiang^{4}.
交 183 Chiao^{1}.
幵 开 184 Ch'ien^{1}.
旨 185 Chih^{3}.
至 186 Chih^{4}.
州 187 Chou^{1}.
朱 188 Chu^{1}.
充 189 Ch'ung^{1}.
曲 190 Ch'ü^{1}.
龹 191 Chüan^{3}.
全 192 Ch'üan^{2}.
而 193 Erh^{2}.
耳 194 Erh^{3}.
伐 195. Fa^{1}.
伏 196 Fu^{2}.
亥 197 Hai^{4}.
合 198 Ho^{2}.
后 199 Hou^{4}.
向 200 Hsiang^{4}.
劦 201 Hsieh^{2}.
邪 *414 Hsieh^{2}.*
先 202 Hsien^{1}.
行 203 Hsing^{2}.
刑 204 Hsing^{2}.
休 205 Hsiu^{1}.
匈 206 Hsiung^{1}.
亘 207 Hsüan^{1}.
血 208 Hsüeh^{3}.
旬 209 Hsün^{2}.
巟 巟 *536 Huang^{1}.*
灰 210 Hui^{1}.
回 囘 211 Hui^{2}.
夷 212 I^{2}.
曳 213 I^{4}.
亦 214. I^{4}.
任 215 Jên^{4}.
如 216 Ju^{2}.
戎 217 Jung^{2}.
考 218. K'ao^{3}.
艮 艮 219 Kên^{4}.
各 220 Ko^{3}
夸 221 K'ua^{1}.
光 222 Kuang^{1}.
匡 223 K'uang^{1}.
圭 224 Kui^{1}.
共 225 Kung^{4}.
巩 巩 226 K'ung^{3}.
咼 227 Kuo^{2}.
列 228 Lieh^{4}.
米 229 Mi^{3}.
名 230 Ming^{2}.
牟 231 Mou^{2}.
那 232 Na^{4}.
百 233 Pai^{3}.
𠂢 234 P'ai^{4}.
邦 235 Pang^{1}.
并 *390 Ping^{4}.*
舌 *227 Shê^{2}.*
式 236 Shih^{3}.
守 237 Shou^{3}.
寺 238 Ssu^{4}.
多 239 To^{1}.

朵 朶 240 To³.
𢦏 241 Ts'ai².
𣦼 *308 Ts'an²*.
此 242 Ts'ŭ³.
朿 243 Ts'ŭ⁴.
次 244 Ts'ŭ⁴.
𠂤 245 Tui¹.
同 246 T'ung².
危 247 Wei².
羊 248 Yang².
同 249 Yin¹.
有 250 Yu³.
羽 251 Yü².

7

折 252 Chê².
岑 253 Ch'ên¹.
辰 254 Ch'ên².
呈 255 Ch'êng².
即 *424 Chi²*.
忌 256 Chi⁴.
夾 257 Chia¹.
谷 *284 Ch'iao⁴*.
戒 258 Chieh⁴.
見 259 Chien⁴.
志 260 Chih⁴.
𠬶 261 Chin⁴.
巠 262 Ching¹.
求 263 Ch'iu².
助 264 Chu⁴.
壯 265 Chuang⁴.
局 266 Chü².
君 267 Chün¹.
否 268 Fao³.
夆 269 Fêng¹.
孚 270 Fu².
甫 271 Fu³.
含 272 Han².
旱 273 Han⁴.
亨 274 Hêng¹.
希 275 Hsi¹.
孝 276 Hsiao⁴.
肖 277 Hsiao⁴.
秀 278 Hsiu⁴.
匜 279 I².
矣 280 I³.
邑 281 I⁴.
告 282 Kao⁴.
更 283 Kêng¹.
谷 284 Ku³.
狂 285 K'uang².
𠯑 *227 Kuo²*.
困 286 K'un⁴.
巩 *226 K'ung³*.
里 287 Li³.
利 𥝢 288 Li⁴.
良 289 Liang².
弄 290 Lung⁴.
呂 291 Lü³.
寽 292 Lüeh⁴.
尨 293 Mang².
每 294 Mei³.
免 295 Mien³.
圼 296 Nieh¹.
我 297 O².
貝 298 Pei⁴.
坒 299 Pi³.
甹 300 P'in².
孛 301 Po⁴.
沙 302 Sha¹.
束 303 Shu⁴.
弟 304 Ti⁴.
廷 305 T'ing².
妥 306 T'o³.
豆 307 Tou⁴.
𣦼 308 Ts'an².
坐 309 Tso⁴.
足 310 Tsu².
夋 311 Tsun¹.
㐬 312 T'u².
兌 313 Tui⁴.
完 314 Wan².
我 *297 Wo³*.
吳 315 Wu¹.
吾 316 Wu².
攸 317 Yu¹.
酉 318 Yu³.
余 319 Yü².
甬 320 Yung³.
肙 321 Yüan⁴.

8

昌 322 Ch'ang¹.
長 镸 323 Ch'ang².
爭 324 Chêng¹.
亟 325 Chi².
妻 326 Ch'i¹.
其 327 Ch'i².
奇 328 Ch'i².
啟 329 Ch'i³.
疌 330 Chieh².
妾 331 Ch'ieh⁴.

臤 332 Chien^{1}.
戔 333 Chien^{1}.
知 334 Chih^{1}.
直 335 Chih^{2}.
京 336 Ching^{1}.
青 337 Ch'ing^{1}.
咎 338 Chiu^{1}.
卓 339 Cho^{1}.
豖 340 Cho^{2}.
叕 341 Cho^{4}.
周 342 Chou^{1}.
帚 343 Chou^{3}.
隹 344 Chui^{1}.
居 345 Chü^{1}.
匊 346 Chü^{1}.
具 347 Chü^{4}.
屈 348 Ch'ü^{1}.
取 349 Ch'ü^{3}.
卷 350 Chüan^{4}.
囷 351 Ch'ün^{1}.
享 *359* *Ch'un*^{2}.

兒 352 Erh^{2}.
非 353 Fei^{1}.
奉 354 Fêng^{4}.
府 355 Fu^{3}.
函 356 Han^{2}.
析 357 Hsi^{1}.
昔 358 Hsi^{2}.
享 359 Hsiang^{3}.
臽 360 Hsien^{4}.
幸 361 Hsing^{4}.
虎 362 Hu^{3}.
昏 363 Hun^{1}
或 364 Huo^{4}.
易 365 I^{3}.
岡 366 Kang^{1}.
肯 367 K'ên^{3}.
固 368 Ku^{4}.
卦 369 Kua^{4}.
官 370 Kuan^{1}.
昆 371 K'un^{1}.
空 372 K'ung^{1}.

果 373 Kuo^{3}.
來 374 Lai^{2}.
郎 *460* *Lang*^{2}.
戾 375 Li^{4}.
兩 376 Liang^{3}.
林 377 Lin^{2}.
夌 378 Ling^{2}.
坴 379 Lu^{4}.
侖 380 Lün^{2}.
門 381 Mên^{2}.
孟 382 Mêng^{4}.
宓 383 Mi^{4}.
明 384 Ming^{2}.
念 385 Nien^{4}.
帛 386 Pai^{2}.
朋 387 P'êng^{2}.
奔 *472* *Pên*^{4}.
卑 388 Pi^{1}.
表 389 Piao^{3}.
幷 390 Ping^{4}.
尙 391 Shang^{4}.

受 392 Shou^{4}.
叔 393 Shu^{2}.
松 394 Sung^{1}.
沓 395 Ta^{2}.
匋 396 T'ao^{2}.
㝵 397 Tê^{2}.
典 398 Tien^{3}.
忝 399 T'ien^{3}.
定 400 Ting^{4}.
咅 401 T'ou^{4}.
采 402 Ts'ai^{3}.
卒 403 Tsu^{2}.
宗 404 Tsung^{1}.
東 405 Tung^{1}.
甾 406 Tzŭ^{1}.
宛 407 Wan^{3}.
罔 408 Wang^{3}.
委 409 Wei^{3}.
武 410 Wu^{3}.
亞 411 Ya^{4}.
肴 412 Yao^{2}.

厓 413 Yeh^{2}.
耶 414 Yeh^{2}.
夜 415 Yeh^{4}.
炎 416 Yen^{2}.
延 417 Yen^{2}.
奄 418 Yen^{3}.
臾 *502* *Yü*^{2}.
於 419 Yü^{2}.

9

查 420 Ch'a^{2}.
臿 421 Ch'a^{2}
者 422 Chê^{3}.
貞 423 Chêng^{1}.
卽 424 Chi^{2}.
咠 425 Ch'i^{1}.
契 426 Ch'i^{4}.
叚 427 Chia^{3}.
皆 428 Chieh^{1}.
柬 429 Chien^{3}.
建 430 Chien^{3}.

前 431 Ch'ien^{2}.
酋 432 Chiu^{1}.
秋 433 Ch'iu^{1}.
耑 434 Chuan^{1}.
垂 435 Ch'ui^{2}.
春 436 Ch'un^{1}.
重 437 Chung^{4}.
軍 438 Chün^{1}.
風 439 Fêng^{1}.
封 440 Fêng^{2}.
畐 441 Fu^{4}.
复 442 Fu^{4}.
曷 443 Ho^{2}.
矦 侯 444 Hou^{2}.
相 445 Hsiang^{1}.
咸 446 Hsien^{2}.
星 447 Hsing^{1}.
胥 448 Hsü^{1}.
宣 449 Hsüan^{1}.
胡 450 Hu^{2}.

奐 451 Huan^{4}.
皇 452 Huang^{2}.
訇 453 Hung^{1}.
若 454 Jao^{2}.
柔 455 Jou^{2}.
耎 456 Juan^{3}.
咼 457 Kua^{3}.
癸 癸 458 Kui^{3}.
剌 459 La^{2}.
郎 460 Lang^{2}.
彔 461 Lu^{4}.
冒 462 Mao^{4}.
眉 463 Mei^{2}.
苗 464 Miao^{2}.
眇 465 Miao^{1}.
面 466 Mien^{4}.
某 467 Mu^{3}.
南 468 Nan^{2}.
𡿺 469 Nao^{3}.
臬 *296 Nieh^{4}.*

咢 噩 470 O^{4}.
保 471 Pao^{3}.
奔 472 Pên^{4}.
扁 473 Pien^{3}.
便 474 Pien^{4}.
甚 475 Shên^{4}.
是 476 Shih^{4}.
思 477 Ssŭ^{1}.
帝 478 Ti^{4}.
亭 479 T'ing^{2}.
𦙃 480 To^{3}.
則 481 Tsai^{2}.
奏 482 Tsou^{4}.
㚇 483 Tsung^{1}.
度 484 Tu^{4}.
段 485 Tuan^{4}.
盾 486 Tun^{4}.
韋 487 Wei^{2}.
為 *717 Wei^{2}.*
畏 488 Wei^{4}.

胃 489 Wei^{4}.
屋 490 Wu^{1}.
敄 491 Wu^{4}.
昜 492 Yang^{2}.
要 493 Yao^{4}.
枼 494 Yeh^{4}.
匽 495 Yen^{3}.
弇 496. Yen^{3}.
彥 497 Yen^{4}.
音 498 Yin^{1}.
垔 499 Yin^{1}.
斿 500 Yu^{2}.
俞 501 Yü^{2}.
臾 502 Yü^{2}.
禺 503 Yü^{2}.
禹 504 Yü^{3}.
爰 505 Yüan^{2}.

10

差 506 Ch'a^{1}.
茶 507 Ch'a^{2}.
展 508 Chan^{3}.
眞 509 Chên^{1}.
烝 510 Chêng^{1}.
朕 511 Chêng^{4}.
乘 512 Ch'êng^{2}.
耆 513 Ch'i^{2}.
豈 514 Ch'i^{3}.
氣 515 Ch'i^{4}.
家 516 Chia^{1}.
敫 517 Ch'iao^{1}.
桀 518 Chieh^{2}.
兼 519 Chien^{1}.
蚩 520 Ch'ih^{1}.
晉 521 Chin^{4}.
秦 522 Ch'in^{2}.
臭 523 Ch'ou^{4}.
芻 524 Ch'u^{2}.
畜 525 Ch'u^{4}.
追 526 Chui^{1}.
冢 527 Chung^{3}.
尃 528 Fu^{1}.

害	529	Hai^{4}.
寒	530	Han^{2}.
函	*256*	*Han*^{2}.
隺	531	Hao^{4}.
盇 盍	532	Ho^{2}.
奚	533	Hsi^{1}.
息	534	Hsi^{1}.
巽	535	Hsüan^{4}.
荒	536	Huang^{1}.
晃	537	Huang^{3}.
圂	538	Hun^{4}.
益	539	I^{2}.
弱	540	Jao^{4}.
辱	541	Ju^{4}.
容	542	Jung^{2}.
倝	543	Kan^{4}.
高	544	Kao^{1}.
鬲	545	Ko^{2}.
冓	546	Kou^{4}.
骨	547	Ku^{3}.
鬼	548	Kui^{3}.
郭	549	Kuo^{1}.
栗	550	Li^{4}.
留	551	Liu^{2}.
馬	552	Ma^{3}.
冥	553	Ming^{2}.
能	554	Nêng^{2}.
般	555	Pan^{1}.
旁	556	P'ang^{2}.
毘	557	P'i^{2}.
桑	558	Sang^{1}.
扇	559	Shan^{4}.
射	560	Shê^{4}.
師	561	Shih^{1}.
時	562	Shih^{2}.
衰 衰	563	Shuai^{1}.
朔	564	Shuo^{4}.
索	565	So^{3}.
貨	566	So^{3}.
叟	567	Sou^{3}.
素	568	Su^{4}.
孫	569	Sun^{1}.
荅	570	Ta^{2}.
𦐇	571	T'a^{4}.
唐	572	T'ang^{2}.
虒	573	Ti^{1}.
宰	574	Tsai^{3}
倉	575	Ts'ang^{1}.
蚤	576	Tsao^{3}.
彖	577	T'uan^{3}.
退	578	T'ui^{4}.
茲	579	Tzŭ^{1}.
昷	580	Wên^{1}.
翁	581	Wêng^{1}.
烏	582	Wu^{1}.
䍃	583	Yao^{2}.
舀	584	Yao^{2}.
𤇾 熒	585	Ying^{2}
員	586	Yüan^{2}.
袁	587	Yüan$_{2}$.
原	588	Yuan^{2}.

11

虘	589	Cha^{1}.
責	590	Chai^{2}.
斬	591	Chan^{3}.
產	592	Ch'an^{3}.
章	593	Chang^{1}.
巢	594	Ch'ao^{2}.
祭	595	Chi^{4}.
既	596	Chi^{4}.
戚	597	Ch'i^{1}.
桼	598	Ch'i^{1}.
將	599	Chiang^{1}.
牽	600	Ch'ien^{1}.
執	601	Chih^{2}.
堇	602	Chin^{3}.
竟	603	Ching^{4}.
殸	60h	Ch'ing^{4}.
專	605	Chuan^{1}.
舂	606	Ch'ung^{1}.
區	607	Ch'ü^{1}.
逢	608	Fêng^{3}.
𦰩	609	Han^{4}.
習	610	Hsi^{2}.
徙	611	Hsi^{3}.
䙴	612	Hsien^{1}.
宿	613	Hsiu^{1}.
旋	614	Hsüan^{2}.
虖	615	Hu^{1}.
扈	616	Hu^{4}.
彗	617	Hui^{4}.
殹	618	I^{1}.
埶	619	I^{4}.
異	620	I^{4}.
庸	621	Jung^{1}
敢	622	Kan^{3}.
康	623	K'ang^{1}.
規	624	Kui^{1}.
國	625	Kuo^{3}.
畾	626	Lei^{3}.
𠩺	627	Li^{2}.

离 628 Li^{2}.
翏 629 Liao^{4}.
連 630 Lien^{2}
婁 631 Lou^{2}.
鹵 632 Lu^{3}.
鹿 633 Lu^{4}.
麻 634 Ma^{2}.
曼 635 Man^{2}.
㒼 636 Man^{2}.
莫 637 Mo^{4}.
敖 638 Nao^{2}.
匿 639 Ni^{4}.
畢 640 Pi^{3}.
敝 641 Pi^{4}.
票 642 Piao^{4}.
昜 643 Shang^{1}.
孰 644 Shu^{2}.
庶 645 Shu^{4}.
率 646 Shuai^{4}.
欶 647 Sou. Su.
帶 648 Tai^{4}.
堂 649 T'ang^{2}.
啇 650 Ti^{2}.
兜 651 Tou^{1}.
參 652 Ts'an^{1}.
曹 653 Ts'ao^{2}.
族 654 Tsu^{2}.
崔 655 Ts'ui^{1}.
悤 656 Ts'ung^{1}.
從 657 Ts'ung^{2}.
尉 658 Wei^{4}.
羕 659 Yang^{4}.
焉 660 Yen^{1}.
寅 661 Yin^{2}.
雩 662 Yü^{2}.

12

敞 663 Ch'ang^{3}.
朝 664 Chao^{1}.
㪿 665 Chê^{4}.
牚 666 Ch'êng^{1}.
幾 667 Chi^{1}.
强 668 Ch'iang^{2}.
焦 669 Chiao^{1}.
喬 670 Ch'iao^{2}.
戠 671 Chih^{4}.
景 672 Ching^{3}.
厥 673 Ch'üeh^{2}.
貳 674 Erh^{4}.
發 675 Fa^{1}.
番 676 Fan^{1}.
棥 677 Fan^{2}.
黑 678 Hei^{1}.
犀 679 Hsi^{1}.
喜 680 Hsi^{3}.
翕 681 Hsi^{4}.
鄉 682 Hsiang^{1}.
象 683 Hsiang^{4}.
閒 684 Hsien^{2}.
虛 685 Hsü^{1}.
尋 686 Hsün^{2}.
華 687 Hua^{2}.
黃 688 Huang^{2}.
惠 689 Hui^{4}.
壹 690 I^{1}.
然 691 Jan^{2}.
敢 *622* *Kan*^{3}.
雇 692 Ku^{4}.
貴 693 Kui^{4}.
勞 694 Lao^{2}.
尞 695 Liao^{3}.
粦 696 Lin^{2}.
買 697 Mai^{3}.
莽 698 Mang^{3}.
彭 699 P'êng^{2}.
菐 700 P'u^{2}.
散 701 San^{4}.
善 702 Shan^{4}.
舜 703 Shun^{4}.
斯 704 Ssŭ^{1}.
單 705 Tan^{1}.
覃 706 T'an^{2}.
湯 707 T'ang^{1}.
登 708 Têng^{1}.
朁 709 Tsan^{1}.
曾 710 Tsêng^{1}.
最 711 Tsui^{4}.
毳 712 Ts'ui^{4}.
尊 713 Tsun^{1}.
雋 714 Tsun^{4}.
敦 715 Tun^{1}.
童 716 T'ung^{2}.
爲 717 Wei^{2}.
無 718 Wu^{2}.
堯 719 Yao^{2}.
矞 720 Yü^{4}.

13

愛 721 Ai^{4}.
詹 722 Chan^{1}.
毄 723 Chi^{1}.
畺 724 Chiang^{1}.
解 725 Chieh^{3}.
僉 726 Ch'ien^{1}.
禁 727 Chin^{4}.

禽 728 Ch'in2.
敬 729 Ching4.
楚 730 Ch'u3.
豦 731 Chü4.
賁 732 Fên4.
𦥯 學 733 Hsiao2.
睘 734 Huan2.
毀 735 Hui3.
會 736 Hui4.
義 737 I4.
睪 738 I4.
意 739 I4.
感 740 Kan3.
貇 741 K'ên3.
過 742 Kuo4.
雷 743 Lei2.
豊 744 Li4.
廉 745 Lien2.
稟 禀 746 Lin3.
蠃 747 Lo3.
路 748 Lu4.
黽 749 Min3.
奥 750 Nao4.
農 751 Nung2.
辟 752 Pi1.
溥 753 P'u3.
普 754 P'u3.
嗇 755 Shê4.
蜀 756 Shu3.
肅 757 Su4.
遂 758 Sui2.
遀 759 Sui2.
歲 760 Sui4.
達 761 Ta2.
亶 762 T'an2.
當 763 Tang1.
喿 764 Tsao4.
萬 765 Wan4.
敫 766 Yao4.
雁 767 Ying1.
與 768 Yü3.
雍 雝 769 Yung1.

14

巢 *594 Ch'ao2.*
耤 770 Chi2.
齊 771 Ch'i2.
監 772 Chien1.
遣 773 Ch'ien3.
盡 774 Chin4.
聚 775 Chü4.
爾 776 Erh3.
豪 777 Hao2.
㬎 778 Hsien3.
需 779 Hsü1.
算 780 Hsüan4.
熏 781 Hsün1.
蒦 782 Huo1.
疑 783 I2.
歷 *822 Li4.*
蒙 784 Mêng2.
寧 甯 785 Ning2.
辡 786 Pien4.
賓 787 Pin1.
壽 788 Shou4.
署 789 Shu3.
臺 790 T'ai2.
翟 791 Ti2.
臧 792 Tsang1.
厭 793 Yen4.
㥯 704 Yin3.

15

廛 795 Ch'an2.
徵 796 Chêng1.
頡 797 Chieh2.
節 798 Chieh2.
質 799 Chih4.
廚 800 Ch'u2.
樊 801 Fan2.
廣 802 Kuang3.
畾 803 Lei2.
厲 804 Li4.
巤 805 Lieh4.
魯 806 Lu3.
慮 807 Lü4.
蔑 808 Mieh4.
暴 809 Pao4.
麃 810 Piao1.
審 811 Shên3.
數 812 Shu4.
疐 813 T'i4.
贊 賛 *849 Tsan4.*
養 814 Yang3.
樂 815 Yao4.
憂 816 Yu1.
賣 817 Yu4.

16

親 818 Ch'in1.

霍	819	Ho^3.
褱	820	Huai^2.
賴	821	Lai^4.
覽	*852*	*Lan*^{3}.
歷	822	Li^4.
盧	823	Lu^2.
龍	824	Lung^2.
頻	825	P'in^2.
騰	826	T'êng^2.
燕	827	Yen^4.

17

毚	828	Ch'an^2.
韱	829	Ch'ien^1.
羲	830	Hsi^1.
襄	831	Hsiang^1.
鮮	832	Hsien^1.
闌	833	Lan^2.
霜	834	Shuang^1.
龠	835	Yao^4.
嬰	836	Ying^1.

18

爵 / 爵	837	Chiao^2.
瞿	838	Ch'ü^2.
豐	839	Fêng^1.
巂	840	Hsi^1.
雚	841	Kuan^4.
聶	842	Nieh^4.
竄	843	Ts'uan^4.

19

麗	844	Li^4.
羅	845	Lo^2.
䜌	846	Luan^4.
難	847	Nan^2.
顛	848	Tien^1.
贊	849	Tsan^4.
贛	850	Kan^4.
矍	851	Kuo^4.
覽	852	Lan^3.
靈	853	Ling^2.

20. &

囊	854	Nang^2.
霸	855	Pa^4.
屬	856	Shu^2.
黨	857	Tang^3.
嚴	858	Yen^2.

PHONETIC SERIES.

L means Lesson and refers to tne Etymological Lesson whose number is given. — **S** means Series and refers to the Phonetic Series whose number is added, ordinarily a Sub-Series. — The figures placed behind the romanised sound, indicate the tone ot each character, as follows: 1. 上平 *shang-p'ing...* 2. 下平 *hsia-p'ing...* 3. 上聲 *shang-shêng...* 4. 去聲 *ch'ü-shêng.* — In order to facilitate the study, some important radical compounds were quoted, under the mention *It is radical in.* — The compounds in which the seeming Phonetic is an arbitrary abbreviation used by the scribes, are quoted under the mention *Abbrev. in*; and the genuine character is placed on the right side ot the abridged form.

1

乚 乙

See Lesson 9 B.

Ya 2. Swallow.

鳦 **ya 2.** Swallow.

軋 **ya 4.** To crush, to grind.

圠 **ya 4.** Fine dust; atoms.

魟 **ya 4.** A kind of sheat fish.

空 **wa 4.** A hollow, to dig, to excavate.

扎 **cha 1.** To prick, to pierce. To struggle.

札 **cha 2.** A thin wooden tablet, a missive. S 101.

鼿 **ch'iao 4.** A turned-up nose.

It is radical in

孔 **k'ung 3.** A hole. L. 94 A.

乳 **ju 3.** To suckle; milk. L. 94 B

Abbrev. in

礼 禮 **li 3.** Ceremony, rite.

糺 糾 **chiu 1.** To twist.

虬 虯 **ch'iu 2.** A dragon.

2

几 八

See Lesson 20.

Chi 1. A small table, a stool.

机 **chi 1.** A small table, a stool.

肌 **chi 1.** The flesh, meat on bones.

It is radical in

処 **ch'u 4.** Place.

凭 **p'ing 2.** To rely on.

凥 **chü 1.** Rest, repose. L. 32 C.

Abbrev. in

訉 譏 **chi 1.** To scoff.

飢 饑 **chi 1.** Dearth, to be hungry.

3

丂 丂

See Lesson 58.

Ch'iao 3. Sob, the hiccups.

巧 **ch'iao 3.** Skilful, cunning.

朽 **hsiu 3.** Decayed, worn out.

疗 **hsiu 3.** Stomach-ache.

考 攷 } **k'ao 3.** Longevity; to examine, S. 218.

It is radical in

号 **hao 4.** To sob; to cry, To call. S. 122.

兮 **hsi 1.** To sigh.

亏 **yü 2.** To stretch. S. 38.

甹 **p'in 2.** To entreat. S. 300.

4

丩 ꝏ

See Lesson 54 F.

Chiu 1. Curve, winding.

糾 **chiu 1.** To twist, to examine.

趴 **chiu 4.** An awry pace.

赳 **chiu 3.** Bravery.

虯 **ch'iu 3.** A dragon.

朻 **ch'iu 2.** Trees whose branches droop.

觓 **ch'iu 2.** Curve, bend.

收 抖 } **shou 1.** To receive, to gather, to harvest.

疛 chiao 4. Belly-ache.

叫 chiao 4. To call, to cry, to name, to cause.

[illegible] ch'iao 4. A turned-up nose.

It is radical in

句 kou 1. A hook. chü 4. A phrase.

5

See Lesson 23.

Chiu 2. Nine.

究 chiu 1. To examine into, to scrutinise.

疚 chiu 1. A chronic disease.

鳩 chiu 1. The wood-pigeon.

仇 ch'iu 2. A surname. Used as an abbreviation of *ch'ou 2*, enmity.

訄 ch'iu 1. To scoff.

朹 ch'iu 2. A kind of wild plum.

釚 ch'iu 2. Lock of a cross-bow.

肍 ch'iu 2. Dried meat.

鼽 ch'iu 2. A cold in the head.

紌 ch'iu 2. Fibrous, uncertain.

[illegible] ch'iu 2. A lance, a spear.

頄 ch'iu 2. Cheeks.

咎 ch'iu 2. A proper name.

厹 ch'iu 2. A spear whose head has three edges.

宄 kuei 3. Traitors, villains.

軌 kuei 3. The axle of a wheel; the rut, a track, a rule.

[illegible] kuei 3. To march.

氿 kuei 3. A spring issuing from the side of a hill.

[illegible] kuei 1. Tired, worn out.

馗 k'uei 2. Visage.

尻 k'ao 1. End bone of the spine. Extremity.

艽 chiao 1. Acanthus.

旭 hsü 3. Rising sun.

It is radical in

秀 hsiu 4 Prosperity, fine, elegant. S. 278.

染 jan 3. To dye. L. 119 K.

6

See Lesson 55 K.

Han 3. To bud, to grow.

犯 fan 4. To rush against, to offend against, to violate.

氾 fan 4. Water overflowing.

[illegible] fan 2. A vessel, a cup.

范 fan 4. A surname.

軓 fan 3. A transversal bar in front of the ancient carts.

範 fan 4. A law, a rule, a pattern.

It is radical in

函 han 2. To contain.

甬 yung 3. To burst forth.

[illegible] yu 2. To grow.

7

See Lesson 19.

乃 nai 3. This, here, precisely; but, then, thereupon; you, your.

疓 nai 3. Pain, sore.

鼐 nai 4. Incense tripod.

仍 jêng 1. As before, yet still.

扔 jêng 1. To throw, to throw away.

礽 jêng 2. Happiness.

艿 jêng 2. Grass, hay.

It is radical in

孕 yün 4. Pregnancy.

盈 ying 2. Full, abundance.

Abbrev. in

奶 嬭 nai 3. Breasts, milk, to suckle.

8

See Lesson 18.

八 pa 1. Eight. Division.

叭 pa 1. *La-pa* trumpet.

扒 pa 1. To pull out, to eradicate, to strip.

朳 pa 1. A harrow, a rake.

趴 p'a 1. To fall prostrate, to grovel.

It is radical in

分 fên 1. To divide, to distinguish.

公 kung 1. Common, public, just.

介 chieh 4. Limits, boundary.

小 hsiao 3. Small.

必 pi 2. Certainly.

9

See Lesson 56.

卜 pu 3. po 3. To divine, divination.

扑 p'u 1. To strike.

朴 p'o 2. Celtis sinensis. Magnolia hypoleuca.

赴 fu 4. To go to, to reach.

訃 fu 4. To announce a death.

仆 fu 4. To fall prostrate, to lie down.

It is radical in

攴 p'u 1. To strike L. 43 D.

卟 **chi** 1. To divine.

外 **wai** 4. Outside, without; beyond, foreign; to exclude.

卦 **kua** 4. The divinatory diagrams.

占 **chan** 1. Divination.

貞 **chêng** 1. Steadfastness.

兆 **chao** 4. A presage. A million.

10

See Lesson 24.

Shih 2. Ten.

十阝 **shih** 2. A District in Ssŭ-ch'uan.

汁 **chih** 1. Juice, liquor.

It is radical in

士 **shih** 4. A scholar, an officer.

什 **shih** 2. A file of ten soldiers; ten.

計 **chi** 4. To count, to calculate, to plan.

協 叶 旪 **hsieh** 2. Union, harmony; to cooperate; a regiment.

Abbrev. in

針 鍼 **chên** 1. A needle, a pin.

11

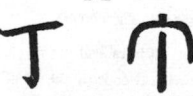

See Lesson 57.

丁 **ting** 1. A cyclical character; an adult; to mourn; a nail.

頂 **ting** 3. The vertex, crown of the head; to push against.

𩠐 **ting** 3. The vertex.

訂 **ting** 4. To decide.

釘 **ting** 1. A nail.
ting 4. To nail.

叮 **ting** 1. To enjoin; strict order.

酊 **ting** 1. Drunk.

仃 **ting** 1. Alone, lonely, forlorn.

耵 **ting** 3. Ear-wax.

飣 **ting** 4. Plates arranged for show.

虰 **ting** 1. Dragon-fly.

靪 **ting** 4. A piece; to patch.

矴 **ting** 3. Stone anchor.

玎 **ting** 1. Jingling noise.

疔 **ting** 1. Furuncle.

町 **t'ing** 3. Embankment, dike.

汀 **t'ing** 1. Low level beach.

朾 **t'ing** 1. A post.

圢 **t'ing** 3. Raised path in field.

頂 **t'ing** 2. Very, extreme.

亭 **t'ing** 2. A pavilion. S. 479.

成 **ch'êng** 2. Perfect, to accomplish. S. 179.

It is radical in

打 **ta** 3. To strike, to beat; doing in general.

12

See Lesson 45 H.

叉 **ch'a** 1. A fork; to pick up; to fold the hands.

杈 **ch'a** 4. A fork; to pitch out.

衩 **ch'a** 1. A piece. To patch.

紁 **ch'a** 1. To twist, together.

汊 **ch'a** 4. Fork of a stream.

靫 **ch'a** 1. A quiver.

釵 **ch'ai** 1. A hair pin.

13

See Lesson 43.

丈 **chang** 4. A measure (ten Chinese feet). A term of respect.

仗 **chang** 4. Weapons; to fight.

杖 **chang** 4. A staff, a stick; to beat.

14

See Lesson 84

己 **chi** 3. One's self. A cyclical character.

記 **chi** 4. To note down; history; to remember

紀 **chi** 4. Course, order; to regulate.

邔 **chi** 3. A place in Honan.

忌 **chi** 4. To fear, to avoid, to abstain from.

跽 **chi** 4. To kneel long, awe-struck.

芑 **ch'i** 3. A succory.

起 **ch'i** 3. To rise, to begin.

杞 **ch'i** 3. A willow.

玘 **ch'i** 3. A stone ornament, hung at the girdle

屺 **ch'i** 3. A bare hill.

It is radical in

妃 **fei** 1. Woman. Imperial concubine. *Hence*

配 **p'ei** 4. A mate, to pair, marriage.

圮 **p'ei** 3. Ruined, fallen.

Compare Lesson 85.

15

乞 气

See Lesson 98.

乞 **ch'i 3.** To implore, to beg.

迄 **ch'i 4.** To reach to; till; finally; at last.

訖 **ch'i 3.** To finish, ended, done, up to.

汔 **ch'i 4.** To weep.

吃 **ch'i 1.** To eat. It is used as an abbreviation for *ch'ih i*.

[日乞] **ch'i 4.** A solar halo.

犵 **ch'i 1.** Barbarians.

仡 **i 3.** Strong, tall.

屹 **i 4.** High peak; imposing, grand.

齕 **ho 4.** To bite, to gnaw.

麧 **ho 1.** Brain; oat-meal.

[足乞] **ko 1.** To jolt, to shake.

虼 **ko 1.** A flea.

忔 **ko 4.** Displeasure, disgust, angry at.

扢 **ko 3.** To rub.

紇 **ko 1.** A knot, a button.

肐 **ko 1.** Arm.

[王乞] **ko 1.** Flaw, speck.

骯 **ko 1.** Arm.

疙 **ko 1.** A boil, sore.

See Lesson 117 D, for

乾 **ch'ien 2.** Heaven.

乾 **kan 1.** Dry, clean.

16

千

See Lesson 24 D.

千 **ch'ien 1.** Thousand.

仟 **ch'ien 1,** Chiliad.

扦 **ch'ien 1.** To graft into.

杄 **ch'ien 1.** A kind of fir *abies leptolepsis.*

阡 **ch'ien 1.** A road.

迁 **ch'ien 1.** To advance, to be promoted.

芊 **ch'ien 1.** Luxuriant foliage.

It is radical in

年 **nien 2.** The year, the crops.

17

See Lesson 31 A.

久 **chiu 3.** Ancient, long since.

玖 **chiu 3.** Smoky quartz; nine.

究 **chiu 4.** Poor, sick.

灸 **chiu 3.** Moxa, to cauterise.

疚 **chiu 4.** Chronic disease.

柩 **chiu 4.** Coffin containing a corpse.

羑 **yu 3.** Name of a place.

It is perhaps found in

畝 **mu 3.** The Chinese acre.

18

See Lesson 12 E.

川 巛 } **ch'uan 1.** Stream. To flow.

甽 **ch'uan 3.** Irrigating canals.

釧 **ch'uan 4.** Bracelet.

玔 **ch'uan 4.** A jade ring.

巡 廵 } **ch'uan 2.** To go on a circuit, to patrol.

馴 **hsün 2.** Tame, docile.

紃 **hsün 2** Silk bands; law.

It is radical in

順 **shun 4.** To follow, to obey; docile, fair.

訓 **hsün 4.** To instruct to teach, to exhort.

州 **chou 1.** Fields out of water. S. 187.

巠 **ching 1.** Water veins. S. 262.

19

凡

See Lesson 21.

凡 凢 } **fan 2.** All, generality; whoever, whatever common, vulgar.

帆 **fan 1.** Sail ot a boat.

汎 **fan 4.** To overflow; immense; vague; changing.

杋 **fan 2.** A large tree.

梵 **fan 4.** Brahma, Brahmanism. Sanscrit.

芃 **p'êng 2.** Luxuriant, bushy.

風 **fêng 1.** The wind. Usage, custom.

鳳 **fêng 4.** The phœnix.

It is radical in

佩 **p'ei 4.** Pendent, to hang on the girdle.

20

See Lesson 11 B.

卂 **hsün 4.** To fly, to soar.

汛 **hsün 4.** A military post. Speedily.

迅 **hsün 4.** Speedy, sudden, quick.

訊 **hsün 4.** To interrogate, to examine judicially, to chide.

It is radical in

蝨 虱 **shih 4.** Louse. Formerly mosquitoes.

21

刃 刅

See Lesson 52 B.

刃 刄 **jên 4.** Weapon, edge.

仞 **jên 4.** Eight feet measure.

訒 **jên 4.** To speak with reserve.

紉 **jên 4.** To thread a needle.

軔 **jên 4.** Bit, curb, rein.

韌 **jên 4.** Pliant, soft.

靭 **jên 4.** Pliant, soft.

肕 **jên 4.** Strong. firm.

忍 **jên 3.** To bear patiently, to endure, patience.

認 **jên 4.** To recognise, to know, to confess.

It is radical in

办 **liang 2.** Wound. *Hence*

梁 **liang 2.** Ridge pole, beam.

粱 **liang 2.** Sorghum.

22

干 𢆉

See Lesson 102 A.

干 **kan 1.** A shield. A stem. To offend.

旰 **kan 3** To open the eyes.

骭 **kan 4.** Shin-bone.

忓 **kan 1.** To concern.

紆 **kan 4.** To smooth.

杆 **kan 1.** A stick, a post, a flag-staff; railings.

肝 **kan 1.** The liver.

秆 **kan 3.** Culm of grain, straw

玕 **kan 1.** Common jade.

旰 **kan 4.** Sunset, dusk.

皯 **kan 4.** Black spots.

赶 **kan 3.** To pursue. When.

鳱 **kan 1** The magpie.

竿 **kan 1.** Staff, cane.

刊 **k'an 1.** To carve, to cut, to engrave.

衎 **k'an 4.** A feast.

岸 **nan 4.** Bank, shore, cliff.

汗 **han 4.** Perspiration, sweat.

釬 **han 4.** To solder metals.

犴 **han.** Wild dog.

豻 **han 4.** The tapir,

鼾 **han 1.** To snore.

扞 **han 1.** To fend off, to protect.

矸 **han 4.** A rock; a mineral.

皯 **han 4.** Freckles.

邗 **han 2.** A proper name.

頇 **han 1.** Bald. Slow, apathetic.

豤 **han 4.** To flee in confusion.

閈 **han 4.** Village gate; walled village.

罕 **han 3.** Rare, scarce.

旱 **han 4.** Dry, S. 273.

軒 **hsüan 1.** A cart. A broken up road.

Abbrev. in

奸 姦 **chien 1.** Deceitful, villainous, corrupted.

It is radical in

訐 **chieh 2.** To divulge; indiscretion.

23

口 𠙵

See Lesson 72 A.

口 **k'ou 3.** The mouth, an opening.

扣 **k'ou 4.** To strike, to knock. To deduct.

犼 **k'ou 3.** Draught-horse or mule.

絇 **k'ou 4.** A knot.

釦 **k'ou 4.** A button.

叩 **k'ou 4.** To knock, to tap.

Radical 30.

24

工 工

See Lesson 82.

工 **kung 1.** Work, labour, time of work.

攻 **kung 1.** To assault, to attack.

功 **kung 1.** Merit, meritorious work.

魟 **kung 1.** Large skate.

玒 **kung 4.** To fly till.

貢 **kung 4.** Tribute, taxes.

空 **k'ung 1.** Empty, vacant. S. 372.

邛 **ch'iung 2.** Name of a place.

虹 **hung 2.** Rain-bow.

叿 **hung 1.** Din, cries.

訌 **hung 4.** Words destructive of order and peace.

烘 **hung 1.** To warm, to dry.

紅 **hung 2.** Red.

汞 **hung 3.** Mercury, quicksilver.

鴻 **hung 2.** Swan; vast.

杠 **kang 1.** A porter's pole.

缸 **kang 1.** A jar.

釭 **kang 1.** A jar.

肛 **kang 1.** The rectum, the anus.

疘 **kang 1.** Prolapse of the rectum.

槓 **kang 4.** A frame to bear a coffin; a handbarrow.

扛 **k'ang 2.** To carry on shoulders, to raise.

江 **chiang 1.** A stream.

豇 **chiang 1.** A kind of long bean.

舡 **chiang 1.** To raise.

矼 **chiang 1.** A stone foot bridge.

項 **hsiang 4.** The neck. Kind, sort. Sum, revenue.

It is radical in

式 **shih 4.** To imitate. S. 286.

左 **tso 3.** The eft; second to.

巫 **wu 1.** A witch, magic.

亞 **ya 4.** Ugly. S. 411.

25

山 山

See Lesson 80.

山 **shan 1.** Mountain, wall.

訕 **shan 4.** To vilify, to slender.

汕 **shan 4.** Port of Swatow.

疝 **shan 4.** Hernia.

仙 **hsien 1.** Genii, fairies, immortals.

秈 **hsien 1.** Kind ot rice.

籼 **hsien 1.** Rice.

Radical 46.

26

彡 彡

See Lesson 62.

彡 **shan 1.** Feathers, long hair.

杉 **shan 1.** A fir, a pole.

衫 **shan 1.** A skirt or shift.

釤 **shan 4.** Bill-hook; to cut.

雭 **shan 1.** Drizzling rain.

It is radical in

㐱 **chên 3.** Bushy hair. S. 106.

須 **hsü 1.** Beard.

Radical 59.

27

勺 勺

See Lesson 54 H.

勺 **shao 2.** Spoon.

杓 **shao 2.** Spoon.

灼 **shao 1.** To burn, to shine.

芍 **shao 2.** Peony.

酌 **chao 1.** To pour out. To consider, to deliberate.

妁 **chao 4.** A go-between.

釣 **tiao 4.** To hook, to fish.

扚 **tiao 3.** To lead, to seize.

恂 **tiao 3.** Pain, care.

訋 **tiao 4.** A proper name.

貂 **tiao 1.** The sable.

杓 **tiao 3.** The ripe ear of grain hanging down.

礿 **yao 4.** A sacrifice to the ancestors.

約 **yao 4.** To bind. A treatise, a convention. To weigh. About.

葯 **yao 4.** Medicine.

豹 **pao 4.** Leopard, panther.

趵 **pao 4.** To jump.

彴 **pao 2.** Shooting star.

罥 **ti 1.** To gather.

靮 **ti 4.** Bridle, reins.

馰 **ti 4.** Speckled horse.

玓 **ti 4.** Twinkling.

的 **ti 4.** Target, mark. A suffix.

28

巳 巳

See Lesson 85 A.

巳 **ssŭ 4.** Cyclical character

祀 **ssŭ 4.** To sacrifice.

汜 **ssŭ 4.** A river and city in Honan.

𦣝 **i 2.** The chin. *Hence*

熙 **hsi 1.** Splendor.

It is radical in

包 **pao 1.** To wrap up, to contain, gestation. S. 145.

29

See Lesson 83 B.

乇 **t'o 4.** To lean on, to trust.

託 **t'o 1.** To commission, to entrust; to feign, to allege.

托 **t'o 2.** To support; to excuse one's self, to feign, to trust.

飥 **t'o 2.** Paste. Cakes.

麪 **t'o 2.** Cakes of wheat flour.

肐 **t'o 1.** Paunch, belly.

馲 **t'o 2.** A mule.

袥 **t'o 2.** To undress.

亳 **po 4.** A city in Honan.

宅 **chai 2.** Family dwelling.

30

才

See Lesson 96.

才 **ts'ai 2.** Talent, ability.

材 **ts'ai 2.** Materials, stuff.

財 **ts'ai 2.** Riches, wealth, property, valuables, goods.

鼒 **ts'ai 2.** A small tripod.

戋 **ts'ai 2.** To wound. S. 241.

豺 豺 } **ch'ai 2.** A wolf.

在 **tsai 4.** To be, to exist, to be present, at, in.

存 **ts'un 2.** To be, to preserve, conservation.

It is radical in

閉 **pi 4.** To close, to shut.

31

寸

See Lesson 45 B.

寸 **ts'un 4.** An inch.

村 **ts'un 1.** A village.

忖 **ts'un 3.** To consider, to conjecture, to surmise, to calculate.

刌 **ts'un 4.** To cut.

It is radical in

付 **fu 4.** To give. S. 120.

守 **shou 3.** To keep. S 237.

㝵 **tê 2.** To get. 397.

討 **t'ao 3.** To repress, to punish, to provoke.

耐 **nai 4.** To suffer, to be patient.

肘 **chou 3.** The elbow. *Hence*

紂 **chou 4.** Crupper of harness An infamous king.

酎 **chou 4.** Spirits used for sacrifices.

Radical 41.

32

土

See Lesson 81 A.

土 **t'u 3.** Earth, ground, soil, dust.

吐 To spit out, to vomit.

芏 **t'u 3.** A rush, *cyperus tegetiformis.*

辻 徒 } **t'u 3.** To go on foot. A disciple, an apprentice. Temporary banishment.

塢 **t'u 3.** The cuckoo.

肚 **tu 3.** The belly; inwards; memory.

杜 **tu 4.** A wild pear-tree; to stop, to obstruct.

It is radical in

社 **shê 4.** The local Genius; its mound and sacrifice; a community.

圣 **kuai 4.** To till the ground.

塵 **ch'ên 2.** Dust; mundanity.

Radical 32.

33

See Lesson 94 A

子 **tzŭ 3.** A son; a seed; a teacher; suffix; a cyclical character.

孜 **tzŭ 1.** Zeal, care.

孖 **tzŭ 1.** Twins, two of a sort.

仔 **tzŭ 3.** To care about; sollicitude.

籽 **tzŭ 3.** Seeds of cereals.

秄 **tzŭ 3.** To hoe up earth around plants.

耔 **tzŭ 3.** To earth up.

字 **tzŭ 4.** A character, a name.

牸 **tzŭ 4.** Female.

It is radical in

孔 **k'ung 3.** A hole.

汙 **fu 2.** To swim.

孚 **fu 3.** To brood.

李 **li** 3. A plum-tiee.

季 **chi** 4. Cadet, last ; season.

孱 **ch'uan** 1. Many children, poverty.

Radical 39.

34

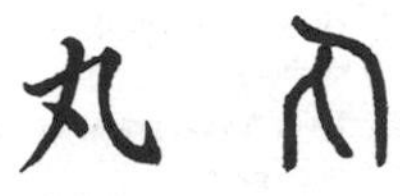

See Lesson 59 E.

丸 **wan** 2. Pill, ball.

紈 **wan** 2. White silk.

骫 **wan** 3. Sprain, luxation.

汍 **wan** 2. Tears.

芄 **wan** 2. Kind ot rush.

It is derived by inversion, from

仄 **chai** 3. Oblique, inclining.

35

See Lesson 10 E

亾 亡 } **wang** 2. To die, to cease / **wu** 2. Not, without.

忘 **wang** 2. To forget.

妄 **wang** 4. Error; falsely, wrongly.

望 **wang** 4 To look towards, to hope ; the full moon.

罔 **wang** 3. No, not. S. 408.

盲 **mang** 2. Blind.

肓 **mang** 2. Vital centre.

杗 **mang** 2. The top, the edge.

蝱 **mang** 2. Mosquitoes.

邙 **mang** 2. A place in Hunan.

氓 **mang** 2. People.

忙 **mang** 2. Busy, hurried.

甿 **mang** 2. Country people.

虻 **mang** 2. Ox-fly.

𥑅 **mang** 2. Soda.

汒 **mang** 2. Inundation ; sudden ; vast.

茫 **mang** 2. High waters ; vast and vague, chaos.

芒 **mang** 2. A beard of grain, a sharp point, a ray. *Hence*

鋩 **mang** 2. Edge, sharp.

硭 **mang** 2. Soda.

恾 **mang** 2. Stir, emotion.

It is radical in

匃 丐 } **kai** 4. To beg, mendicant.

乍 **cha** 4. At first, sudden. S. 102.

喪 **sang** 1. To die, to mourn, funeral.

無 **wu** 2. Negation. S. 718.

36

兀

See Lesson 29 K.

兀 **wu** 4. A stool.

杌 **wu** 4. Stump of a tree ; a stool.

仉 **wu** 4. Disquiet.

扤 **wu** 4. To sway.

矹 **wu** 4. Gravel.

屼 **wu** 4. Mountain.

軏 **yüeh** 4. A yoke.

37

也

See, Lesson 107 B, the note about this confused Series.

也 **yeh** 3. Also, besides, still; a final particle.

灺 **hsieh** 3. Flame.

毑 **chieh** 3. Mother, female.

施 **shih** 1. To give, to confer; to do, action *in general*.

弛 **shih** 3. To unstring, to relax.

池 **ch'ih** 2. Pool, tank, vessel.

馳 **ch'ih** 2. To pass quickly, fast.

阤 **ch'ih** 3. A hill-side, a bank ; to crumble away.

匜 **i** 2. A washing-basin, vessel.

扅 **i** 2. Bolt, barred.

扡 **i** 2. To draw, to remove.

迆 **i** 2. To go to, to advance; to turn aside, to be wrong.

貤 **i** 2. To reward, to promote ; grades, steps.

酏 **i** 2 Liquor, sweet wine.

訑 **i** 2. Arrogant, overbearing.

忚 **i** 1. Contemptuous.

地 **ti** 4. The earth, the ground, a place.

髢 t'i 4. False or unbound hair.

他 t'o 1. He, she, that, another.
柂 t'o 1. To split. A coffin.

Compare the Series 126 and 165.

38

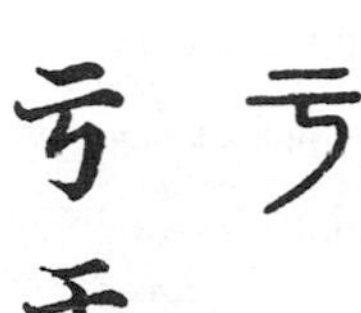

See Lesson 58 E.

亐 于 } yü 2. In, to, at, through, as to. To go.

扝 扜 } yü 1. To designate; to hold, to seize.

迂 yü 1. To go far, aberration, perversion.

紆 yü 1. A tie, to bind.

杅 yü 2. A basin, a tub.

圩 yü 2. Dike, bund.

邘 yü 2. A place in Honan.

宇 yü 3. Heaven, space; temple, a vault; the empire.

芋 yü 2. The taro, *colocasia*.

竽 yü 2. A reed organ of 36 tubes.

雩 yü 2. To pray for rain. S. 662.

盂 盂 } yü 2. A basin, a large cup.

吁 hsü 1. To sigh; an exclamation, alas.

訏 hsü 1. Vain boasting.

盱 hsü 1. Rising sun, wide.

盱 hsü 3. Eyes wide open.

冔 hsü 3. A cap or bonnet used for sacrifices.

杇 wu 1. A trowel, to roughcast.

釫 wu 1. A trowel.

圬 wu 1. To plaster.

汚 wu 1. Mud, dirt, foul, obscene, to defile, perverse.

弙 wu 1. To shoot an arrow; whizzing.

It is radical in

夸 k'ua. To boast. S. 221.

平 p'ing 2. Even, level, tranquil. S. 151.

粤 yüeh 4. To examine. Canton. Initial particle.

虧 k'uei 1. To harm, to injure; defect. L. 135 F.

39

See Lesson 49.

爪 chao 3. A claw.

笊 chao 4. A bamboo skimmer.

帊 chao 3. A turban.

抓 chua 1. To scratch, to tear, to seize.

It is radical in

采 ts'ai 3. To pluck. S. 402

爭 lüeh 4. To stretch, to draw out. S. 292.

爭 chêng 1. To wrangle, to contest. S. 324.

受 shou 4. To receive. S. 392.

Compare the Series 133.

40

See Lesson 19 D.

及 chi 2. To reach to, till.

級 chi 2. Threads, steps, grades.

汲 chi 2. Steps, degrees.

彶 chi 2. To hasten.

衱 chi 2. A robe.

伋 chi 2. The name of the grandson of Confucius.

汲 chi 1. To draw water from a well; to emulate.

芨 chi 4. Salep.

笈 chi 2. A box, a satchel.

岌 chi 4. A lofty peak; dangerous.

急 chi 2. Emotion. L. 19 D.

极 chieh 2. A pack-saddle.

吸 hsi 1. To breathe, to inhale.

歙 hsi 4. To snivel.

鈒 sa 3. To inlay, to incrust.

趿 sa 4. To drag along.

靸 sa 1. Slippers.

馺 sa 1. To run.

扱 ch'a 2. To receive, to bow, to promote.

41

爿 H

See Lesson 127 B.

爿 ch'iang 2. Wood; a bed.

戕 ch'iang 1. A spear, to wound.

斨 ch'iang 2. An ax; to hack, to chop.

狀 chuang 4. Form, appearance; to declare; an accusation.

妝 chuang 1. To adorn, to rouge, to feign.

壯 **chuang 4.** Strong. S. 265.

牀 **ch'uang 2.** A bed, a sofa.
See SS. 599 and 792.

42

See Lesson 18 F.

介 **chieh 4.** To intermeddle; a little; armour, scales.
蚧 **chieh 4.** A lizard.
衸 **chieh 4.** Facings on uniform.
砎 **chieh 4.** Hard, rocky.
价 **chieh 4.** Good, virtuous.
骱 **chieh 4.** The sole.
齘 **chieh 4.** To gnash.
玠 **chieh 4.** A small jade tablet.
[illegible] **chieh 4.** A young ox.
妎 **chieh 4.** Jealous, envious.
尬 **chieh 4.** To walk in a staggering way.
界 **chieh 4.** A boundary; limits; the world.
庎 **chieh 4.** To live alone.
疥 **chieh 4.** The itch; an itching.
芥 **chieh 4.** The mustard plant, *sinapis.*

43

切

See Lesson 33

七 **ch'i 1.** Seven.

切 **ch'ieh 1.** To cut. Eagerly. Important.

窃 **chieh 4.** To steal.

砌 **ch'i.** To lay bricks; to build.
沏 **ch'i 1.** To infuse.

44

See Lesson 99.

欠 **ch'ien 4.** To owe; deficit, debt, duty.
肷 **ch'ien 1.** The flank.
芡 **ch'ien 4.** A water plant, *euryale ferox.*

杴 **hsien 1.** A shovel.
忺 **hsien 1.** To take pleasure in; to enjoy.
掀 **hsien 1.** To lift up; to open; to turn over.

扻 **k'an 3.** To strike, to knock.
砍 **k'an 3.** To cut, to chop.
欿 **k'an 3.** Reserve, modesty.
坎 **k'an 3.** A pit, a snare.
It is radical in
吹 **ch'ui 1.** To blow upon; to chide.
炊 **ch'ui 1.** To cook.
龡 **ch'ui.** To play the flute.

㳄 **hsien 4.** Spittle, saliva; covetousness.
羡 **hsien 4.** To like, to covet; to exceed, surplus, remaining.

盜 **tao 4.** To rob, robber.
次 **ts'ŭ 4.** Succession, S. 244.
款 欵 **k'uan 3.** To long for, to like. Business. A sum, amount.

45

支

See Lesson 43 C.

支 **chih 1.** A branch, a twig; to prop; to pay, to receive.
肢 **chih 1.** The limbs.
枝 **chih 1.** A branch, a twig.
忮 **chih 1.** Aversion.

翅 **ch'ih 4.** A wing; a fin.

芰 **chi 4.** A water-caltrop, *trapa ineisa.*
庋 **chi 3.** Warehouse; to keep.
妓 **chi 4.** A courtesan.
伎 **chi 4.** Talent, cleverness.
技 **chi 4.** Dexterous, skilful.
屐 **chi 4.** Shoe.

岐 **ch'i 2.** A mountain in Shensi.
跂 **ch'i 2.** To stand on tiptoe.
歧 **ch'i 2.** Bifurcation.
蚑 **ch'i 2.** A spider.

[illegible] **kui 3.** A sacrifice to the mountains.
頍 **kui 1.** A t[illegible]p; a st[illegible]p.

攰 **k'ui 1.** Worn out

46

See Lesson 112.

止 **chih 3.** To halt, to cease from; only.

沚 **chih 3.** A small islet, a bank.

阯 **chih 3.** Base, foundation.

址 **chih 3.** Building; dwelling; address.

祉 **chih 3.** Happiness.

杫 **chih 3.** A small table.

趾 **chih 3.** The feet; to stop.

芷 **chih 3.** A fragrant plant, *Iris florentina.*

恥 **ch'ih 3** Shame, to be ashamed, to make ashamed.

扯 **ch'ê 3.** To drag, to pull apart

It is radical in

企 **ch'i 4.** On tiptoe; desire; longing for.

此 **ts'ŭ 3.** To stop. S. 243.

步 **pu 4.** A step, to walk; a pace; a measure.

正 **chêng 4.** To attain. S. 107.

47

今 今

See Lesson 14 K.

今 **chin 1.** Now, the present time.

妗 **chin 4.** Wife of a brother of my mother, etc.

衿 **chin 1.** Lapel, opening of coat.

紟 **chin 1.** A sash, a string.

坽 **ch'in.** A pit, a well.

忴 **ch'in.** Ardour.

扲 **ch'in 2.** To seize, to hold.

琴 **ch'in 2.** The Chinese lute, organ.

芩 **ch'in.** A drug, *scutellaria viscidula.*

庈 **ch'in 2.** A proper name.

衾 **ch'in 3.** A coverlet, bed-clothes.

黔 **ch'ien 1.** Brown.

鈐 **ch'ien 1.** A plough.

矜 **ching 1.** Pity, compassion.

吟 **yin 2.** To hum, to moan.

岑 **ch'ên 1.** A lone peak, lofty. S. 253.

It is radical in

含 **han 2.** To hold in the mouth. S. 272.

貪 **t'an 1.** To covet, to long for, greedy.

念 **nien 4.** To reflect, to read, to study. S. 385.

侌 陰 **yin 1.** The shadowy side; the female principle; dark, death.

蔭 **yin 4.** To overshadow, to shelter.

廕 **yin 4.** Shelter, to protect.

48

斤 斤

See Lesson 128.

斤 **chin 1.** Catty; hatchet.

近 **chin 3.** Near in time or place, intimate.

釿 **chin 1.** To chop, to chip.

靳 **chin 4.** Martingal.

芹 **ch'in 2.** Celery.

忻 **hsin 1.** Joy, delight.

炘 **hsin 1.** Great heat.

昕 **hsin 1.** Morn, dawn.

訢 **hsin 1.** To rejoice.

昕 **hsin 1.** Joyous look.

欣 **hsin 1.** Joy, to rejoice.

新 **hsin 1.** New, fresh, recently; fuel.

沂 **i 2.** A river in Shantung.

祈 **ch'i 2.** To pray.

圻 **ch'i 2** A border, Imperial lands.

肵 **ch'i 2** A sacrificial-vase; offering.

蚚 **ch'i 2.** A mantis.

旂 **ch'i 2.** A flag, a banner.

頎 **ch'i 2.** Tall, erect.

It is radical in

折 **shê 2.** To break apart.

析 **hsi 1.** To split, S. 357.

匠 **chiang 4.** Artisan

49

井 丼

See Lesson 115 A.

井 丼 **ching 3.** A well; a rood of land measuring 900 mu.

阱 **ching 3.** A pit, a trap.

穽 **ching 3.** A hole.

耕 **ching 1.** To plough, to cultivate.

荊 **ching 1.** Judas tree, *Cercis sinensis*; thorns, brambles.

50

See Lesson 44 B.

丑 **ch'ou 3.** A cyclical character; from 1 to 3 o'clock A.M.

扭 **niu 3.** To twist, to wring.

鈕 **niu 3.** A button.

紐 **niu 3.** A knot.

狃 **niu 3.** Inclined to evil; obduracy.

忸 **niu 3.** Refractory; stubborn.

衄 **niu 1.** Nose-bleed.

炄 **niu 3.** To dry.

杻 **niu 3.** A bushy tree, *Ligustrum sinense.*

It is radical in

羞 **hsiu 1.** Viands; an offering; to feel ashamed, to blush.

䐪 **hsiu 1.** Delicacies.

饈 **hsiu 1.** Sweets.

51

See Lesson 22 D.

殳 **ch'u 1.** Arm, stick, spear.

杸 **ch'u 1.** Weapon, spear.

投 **t'ou 3.** To throw at; to agree; to have recourse to; to deliver.

酘 **t'ou 2.** To distil.

It is radical in.

股 **ku 3.** The upper part of the thigh; a share.

設 **she 4.** To arrange, to set up.

殿 **tien 4.** A grand hall.

役 **i 4.** A runner, a satellite. It is phonetic contracted in

疫 **i 4.** Epidemic, pestilence.

52

See Lesson 109 A.

中 **chung 1.** Middle, within. **chung 4.** To hit, to be hit.

忠 **chung 1.** Loyal, devoted.

盅 **chung 1.** A cup, a goblet

衷 **chung 1.** Sincerity, loyalty devotedness.

仲 **chung 4.** Second.

沖 冲 **ch'ung 1.** To dash against, to rush at.

种 **ch'ung 1.** Delicate.

翀 **ch'ung 1.** To fly up.

忡 **ch'ung.** Sorrow, care.

It is radical in

用 **yung 4.** To use. *See L.109 B.*

Compare L. 153 B,

串 **ch'uan 4.** To string. *Phonetic in*

患 **huan 4.** Affliction.

53

See Lesson 43 O.

夬 **chüeh 3.** To decide, to settle, certainly, etc.

抉 **chüeh 2.** To dig.

決 决 **chüeh 2.** To settle, to decide, absolutely.

訣 **chüeh 2.** Magic formulae.

趹 **chüeh 2.** To hasten.

觖 **chüeh 2.** To be dissatisfied.

玦 **chüeh 2.** An archer's ring.

鴂 **chüeh 2.** A shrike.

芵 **chüeh 2.** A plant, *Cassia tora.*

缺 **ch'üeh 1.** A want, a deficiency, a vacancy.

駃 **k'uai 4.** A race-horse.

快 **k'uai 4.** Pleasure; cheerful; quick, sharp.

筷 **k'uai 4.** Chopsticks.

炔 **kuei 4.** A proper name.

袂 **mi.** The sleeve of a robe.

54

See Lesson 112 K.

乏 **fa 2.** Weary, tired, exhausted.

疺 **fa 2.** Weary, fatigued.

姂 **fa 2.** Handsome, elegant.

泛 **fan 4.** Great flood, immense, vague, waste.

眨 **chan 3.** Twinkling.

貶 **pien 3.** To diminish, to belittle, to censure.

砭 **pien 1.** Acupuncture with a flint needle.

窆 **pien 4.** To put a coffin into the grave.

It has nothing in common with

之 **chih 1.** Mark of the genitive; an expletive; to go.

芝 **chih 1.** Sesamum.

55

See Lesson 43 E.

反 **fan 3.** To turn back, contrary, opposite, to rebel.

坂 **fan 3.** A hill-side, a slope.

阪 **fan 3.** A bank, a mountain side.

飯 **fan 4.** Boiled grain, food in general, to eat.

返 **fan 3.** To return, to revert to.

⿰忄反 **fan 4.** To regret, to repent.

畈 **fan 4.** A plain, a field.

販 ⿰買反 } **fan 4.** To buy in order to sell, to trade, to deal in.

⿸疒反 **fan 4.** To faint.

板 **pan 3.** A board a plank, a flattened bamboo for beating.

版 **pan 3.** A board, a diploma.

昄 **pan 3.** Great, wide.

叛 **p'an 3.** To rebel.

扳 **p'an 1.** To grasp.

眅 **p'an 1.** To squint.

56

See Lesson 117 A.

方 **fang 1.** A place, a region; square, apt, regular, easy; a rule, a means; a comparison; then.

芳 **fang 1.** Fragrant, virtue, glory. *Ritual*, your.

房 **fang 2.** A house; an office. *Ritual*, the women.

髣 **fang 3.** To be like, similar, as.

妨 **fang 1.** To hinder, oppose.

防 **fang 2.** An embankment, to protect from, to avoid.

坊 **fang 1.** A district, a ward; a store, a workhouse.

彷 **fang 3.** To be like, similar, as.

紡 **fang 3.** To spin, to reel.

訪 **fang 3.** To examine, to search out, to enquire about.

枋 **fang 1.** A kind of wood, a plank.

肪 **fang 1.** Fat, grease.

魴 **fang 2.** A bream.

眆 **fang 3.** Resembling; indistinct.

昉 **fang 3.** Bright, clear.

舫 **fang 3.** A pontoon.

鈁 **fang 1.** A bell; a kettle; a coin.

瓬 **fang 2.** To mould clay, as a potter.

邡 **fang 1.** A proper name.

放 **fang 4.** To put, to depose, to let go, to issue, to set free. SS. 638 and 76C.

倣 仿 } **fang 3.** To imitate, to copy; a model.

旁 **p'ang 2.** Limits of space; side. S. 556.

57

巿

See Lesson 79 A.

巿 **fei 4.** To grow, to multiply.

芾 **fei 4.** Bushy, to overshadow.

肺 **fei 4.** The lungs.

旆 **p'ei 4.** A banner.

沛 **p'ei 4.** Name of a river in Kiangsu.

霈 **p'ei 2.** Rain falling.

It is radical in

孛 **po 4.** Procreation. S. 301.

索 **so 4.** A cord, S. 565.

南 **nan 2.** The South. S. 468.

朿 **tzŭ.** To fetter. S. 86.

It is unconnected with.

市 **shih 4.** A market. L. 34 D.

巿 **fu 4.** An apron. L. 35 B.

58

See Lesson 18 B.

分 **fên 1.** To divide, to distinguish, to discern; the tenth of a foot, of an acre; the hundredth of a ounce; a minute.
fên 4. A part, a lot, condition, duty.

芬 **fên 1.** Fragrant.

棻 **fên 2.** A kind of wood burnt for perfume.

棼 **fên 1.** Beams in the roof of a house.

氛 **fên 1.** Vapour, miasma, influx.

雰 **fên 1.** Mist, fog.

忿 **fên 4.** Anger, hatred.

翂 **fên 1.** To fly up.

坌 **fên 4.** Dust; dike.

份 **fên 4.** A part, a share, lot, function, duty.

紛 **fên 4.** Entangled, confusion, multitude.
帉 **fên 1.** A napkin, a handkerchief.
吩 **fên 1.** To command, to give orders.
汾 **fên 2.** Name of a river in Shansi.
枌 **fên 2.** A kind of elm.
衯 **fên 1.** Long flowing robes.
粉 **fên 3.** Flour, powder, plaster.
黺 **fên 3.** Embroideries, flowered silk.
鼢 **fên 3.** A kind of mole, *scaptochirus moschatus*.
坋 **fên 4.** Dust; dike.
昐 **fên 1.** Solar rays.
羒 **fên 2.** A ram.
[illegible] **fên 1,** Hair falling off; feathers moulting.

馚 **p'ên 1.** Perfume.
盆 **p'ên 2.** A basin. *Hence*
湓 **p'ên 2.** To boil.
葐 **p'ên 2.** Raspberry.

豳 **pin 2.** Name of a place in Shensi.
邠 **pin 1.** Name of a place in Shensi.

貧 **p'in 2.** Poor, poverty.

釁 **hsin 4.** To anoint with blood; a quarrel, a feud.

扮 **pan 4,** To dress up, to disguise.
朌 **pan 2.** To pay, tribute.
頒 **pan 1.** To extend, to promulgate, to bestow.
鳻 **pan 1** Wild pigeon.
攽 **pan 1,** To divide, to share.

盼 **p'an 4.** To gaze at, to long for; to expect.

It is radical in

岔 **ch'a 4.** Branching, to fork, cross-road.
寡 **kua 3.** Alone; a widow; few; I, the sovereign.

59

夫

See Lesson 60 J.

夫 **fu 1.** A husband, a man, master. *Fu-jên* dame.
fu 2. An initial particle, a demonstrative, etc.

芙 **fu 2.** The *Hibiscus mutabilis*.
扶 **fu 2.** To uphold, to assist, to aid.
枎 **fu 2.** To spread out.
蚨 **fu 2.** A butterfly, a copper cash.
趺 **fu 1** To sit cross-legged; to bow
鈇 **fu 1.** An axe.
麩 **fu 1.** Wheat bran.
衭 **fu 1.** Lapel, overall.
颫 **fu 2,** A storm, a tornado.
玞 **fu 1.** Very common jade; vulgar, bad.
砆 **fu 1.** A reddish stone.

It is radical in

替 **t'i 4.** To alternate, substitution, instead of.
輦 **nien 3.** The imperial chariot dragged by men.

60

父

See Lesson 43 C.

父 **fu 4.** Father.
斧 **fu 3.** An axe.
釜 **fu 3.** A caldron.

布 **pu 4.** Cloth. L. 35 C.

61

心

See Lesson 107 A.

心 **hsin 1.** The heart, mind, affections; centre.

沁 **ch'in 4.** To sound, to fathom.
吣 **ch'in 4.** To belch, to vomit.

伈 **shên 3.** Fear, timidity.

It is radical in

恥 **ch'ih 3.** Shame, to make ashamed of.
惢 **jui 3.** The heart of flowers.

62

See Lesson 38 D.

凶 **hsiung 1.** Unlucky, unfortunate, sad, cruel.
兇 **hsiung 1.** Violent, cruel, savage.
胷 **hsiung 1.** The breast.
匈 **hsiung 1.** The breast.

It is radical in

酗 **hsü 4.** Drunkenness.

Compare the SS. 206 and 483.

63

See Lesson 129 A.

戶 **hu 4.** Door or window; dwelling, family.

帍 **hu 4.** A handkerchief.

鳸 **hu 4.** A quail.

戽 **hu 4.** To bale out water.

扈 **hu 4.** A suite. S. 616.

妒 **tu 4.** Jealous, envious.

所 **so 3.** A place, a building; that which, who, what.

It is radical in

扇 **shan 4.** Leaves, folds. S. 559.

扁 **pien 3.** A tablet. S. 473.

戾 **li 4.** To slip in. S. 373.

戹 **nai 4. o 4.** Distress. S. 75.

64

化

See Lesson 30 D.

化 **hua 4.** To change, transformation, to convert.

花 **hua 1.** Flower, flowery; smallpox; dissipation; to spend; presbyopy.

貨 **huo 4.** Goods, merchandise; to deal.

靴 **hsüeh 1.** Boots.

吪 **o 2.** To move.

訛 **o 2.** Mistake, error; to excite, to harm.

鈋 **o 2.** To scrape, to cut.

囮 **yu 2.** To inveigle, to decoy.

65

以

See Lesson 85 B.

以 目 **i 3.** To use, with, in order to; according; a prefix connotating a relation.

苡 **i 3.** Name of a plant, *coix lachryma*.

似 **ssŭ 4.** Like, similar to, to seem.

姒 **ssŭ 4.** An elder brother's wife.

66

壬

See Lesson 82 C.

壬 **jên 2.** A cyclical character; great; bad.

妊 **jên 2.** Pregnancy.

飪 **jên 3.** To cook.

[illegible] **jên 4** Cooked, ripe.

衽 **jên 4.** The breast of a coat, buttoned under the right arm.

紝 **jên 4.** To weave.

任 **jên 4.** An employ, an office; to bear, to tolerate; confidence; to follow; any. S. 215.

67

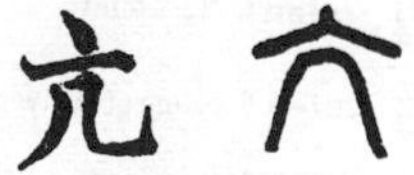

See Lesson 61 E.

亢 **k'ang 4.** Violent.

炕 **k'ang 4.** A brick bed warmed by a fire

抗 **k'ang 4.** To oppose, to resist.

忼 **k'ang 3.** Disappointment.

犺 **k'ang 4.** A fierce dog.

伉 **k'ang 4.** A companion.

砊 **k'ang 4** A shock, a clash.

匟 **k'ang 4.** The divan of a guest-chamber.

閌 **k'ang 4.** Portico; vast

杭 **hang 2.** A boat; to cross a stream.

航 **hang 2.** To navigate, to cross.

吭 **hang 3.** The throat.

沆 **hang 3.** Mist, fog.

迒 **hang 2.** Tracks, ruts.

頏 **hang 2.** To fly down.

笐 **hang 1.** Bamboo poles.

衏 **hang 2.** Musicians

骯 **ang 1.** Dirty, filthy

秔 **kêng 1.** Rice which is not glutinous.

坑 **k'êng 1** A pit, a pond, to entrap.

阬 **k'êng 1.** A pit, a trap, to ruin.

68

See Lesson 18 C.

公 **kung 1.** Common, public, official; usual, just; male; duke; sir.

蚣 **kung 1.** Centipede.

䲲 **kung 1.** Scate.

頌 **sung 4.** To praise, to celebrate, a sacrificial ode.

訟 **sung 4.** To accuse, litigation.

松 **sung 1.** Pine-tree, coniferous trees in general. S. 394.

翁 **wêng 1.** An old man, a term of respect. S. 581.

忪 **chung 1.** Agitated, emotion.

彸 **chung 1.** Restless, nervous.

衮 袞 } **kun 3.** Imperial robes, court robes.

滾 **kun 3.** To boil, to bubble, to roll.

69

厷

See Lesson 38 H.

厷 **kung 1.** Humerus, arm.

肱 **kung 1.** The arm, to help.

宏 **hung 2.** Vast, ample, spacious.

閎 **hung 2.** Vast, wide, open.

竑 **hung 2.** To measure.

耾 **hung 2.** A rumbling sound.

紘 **hung 2.** A string; to fasten.

翃 **hung 2.** To flutter.

弘 **hung 2.** Vast, large. To expand. L. 38 H.

雄 **hsiung 2.** Male, brave.

70

See Lesson 100.

毛 **mao 2.** Hair, down, feathers.

眊 **mao 4.** Muddled, confused.

牦 **mao 2.** Tibetan yak.

酕 **mao 2.** Drunk.

[illegible] **mao 2.** Flabellum.

旄 **mao 2.** Tail of a yak used as a banner

芼 **mao 4.** Vegetables.

髦 **mao 2.** Style of arranging hair.

耄 **mao 4.** A septuagenarian.

耗 **hao 4.** To use, to spend, to waste.

It is radical in

老 **lao 3.** Old, to become old.

表 **piao 3.** To manifest, clock, watch. S. 389.

尾 **wei 3.** Tail; end.

毳 **ts'ui 4.** Down, soft.

Radical 82.

71

丏

See Lesson 112 L.

丏 **mien 4.** To cover, to hide.

眄 **mien 3.** To squint.

沔 **mien 3.** Name of a river.

麪 **mien 4.** Flour; ribbon-vermicelli.

[illegible] **mien 4.** A waste of waters.

72

𠬛

See Lesson 76 I.

𠬛 **mu 2.** To plunge.

沒 **mu 2.** To plunge, to disappear, to cease; not, none.

歿 **mu 2.** To die, to perish.

73

卬

See Lesson 26 G.

卬 **nang 2.** High, noble.

枊 **nang 2.** A post.

昂 **nang 2.** To rise, lofty, high, dear.

[illegible] **nang 2.** Eaves of a Chinese roof.

仰 **yang 3.** To look up with respect.

[illegible] **yang 4.** To stop talking.

[illegible] **yang 2.** A horse running away.

迎 **ying 2.** To occur, to meet; to parry.

It is radical in

抑 **i 4.** To repress, to restrain; or, either.

To be distinguished from

印 **yin 4.** A seal, a stamp.

74

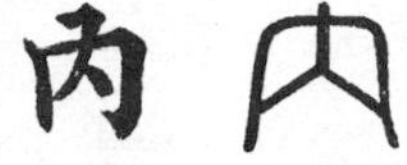

See Lesson 15 C.

内 **nei 4.** In, into, interior; near to, among.

芮 **jui 3.** Small plants budding.

汭 **jui 3.** Winding of a stream.

蚋 **jui 3.** Mosquitoes.

枘 **jui 4.** A handle, a haft.

吶 **nê 4.** Reserve, circumspection.

訥 **nê 4.** Cautious speech.

肭 **nê 4.** The new moon.

衲 **na 4.** Garments of a bonze; to patch, to line.

軜 **na 4.** Reins.

鈉 **na 4.** To sharpen.

豽 **na 4.** A seal.

魶 **na 4.** A marine animal.

納 **na 4.** To hand up, to enter, to possess, to keep.

It is radical in.

商 **shang 1.** To deliberate; a merchant.

㕯 **ne 4, na 4.** To whisper.

It is unconnected with

肉 **ju 4, jou 4.** Meat. L. 17 G

丙 **ping 3.** A fire. L. 41 A.

75

See Lesson 129 A.

厄 **o 4.** Difficulty, distress.

阨 **o 4.** A defile, a pass; distress, difficulty.

軛 **o 4.** A yoke or collar.

扼 **o 4.** To grasp, to hold.

呃 **o 4.** To belch.

鈪 **o 4.** A bracelet.

枙 **o 4.** A knot in the wood.

[illegible] **o 4.** In want of food.

Compare L. 59 H, S. 247.

76

See Lesson 55 L.

巴 **pa 1.** A proper name.

把 **pa 3.** To hold, to grasp; a handle; a handful; particle denoting the accusative.

耙 **pa 4.** A harrow.

靶 **pa 3.** A target.

吧 **pa 1.** *Ya-pa*, a dumb man.

杷 **pa 1.** A rake.

弝 **pa 4.** The part of a bow grasped.

疤 **pa 1.** Cicatrix, scar.

芭 **pa 1.** Banana-tree.

笆 **pa 1.** Hedge, fence.

琶 **pa 1.** A guitar with four strings.

爸 **pa 4.** A father, papa.

爬 **p'a 2.** To creep, to climb.

跁 **p'a 2.** To creep.

帊 **p'a 4.** A kerchief, a veil.

舥 **p'a 1.** A floating bridge.

For the following, see L. 55 B-G.

巵 **chih 1.** A cup, a siphon.

肥 **fei 2.** Fat, fleshy, fertile,

色 **shê 4.** Colour, lust.

絶 **chüeh 2.** To sever, to destroy.

See, L. 74 C, the derivatives of

邑 **i 4.** A city, a hamlet, a camp.

邕 **yung 1.** The moats of a city.

扈 **hu 4.** Name of a city.

77

比

See Lesson 27 I.

比 **pi 3.** To compare.

妣 **pi 3.** A deceased mother.

秕 **pi 3.** Empty ears without grain, *pi-la*.

鈚 **pi 3.** Sharp.

笓 **pi 4.** Fine comb.

芘 **pi 4.** A plant, *malva sylvestris*.

批 **p'i 1.** To criticise; to decide officially; wholesale.

枇 **p'i 2.** A kind of medlar, *p'i-pa*, *Eriobotrya Japonica*.

砒 **p'i 1.** Arsenic.

仳 **p'i 3.** To take leave of.

蚍 **p'i 2.** The termite.

[illegible] **p'i 2.** Limp, weak.

紕 **p'i 4.** Tassels or fringes.

毗 **p'i 2.** To aid, adjacent.

[illegible] **p'i 2.** Broken wheat.

屁 **p'i 4.** The posteriors; to break wind.

庇 **p'i 4.** To cover, to protect, to shelter.

琵 p'i 2. The Chinese guitar.
毗 p'i 2. The navel. S. 557.

It is radical in

坒 pi 3. To compare or match. S. 299.
皆 chieh 1. Cooperation S. 428.
昆 k'un 1. Multitude. S. 371.

To be distinguished from

北 pei 3. The North. L. 27 G.

78

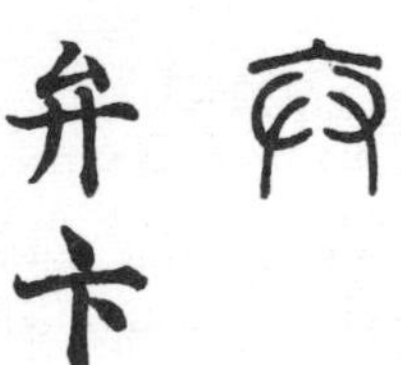

See Lesson 47 H.

One Series, double form.

卞 pien 4. A proper name.
汴 pien 4. A river in Hupeh.
忭 pien 4. Joy, delight.
抃 pien 4. To pat.

弁 pien 4. A military cap; soldier.
昪 pien 3. Joy, delight.

拚 p'in 1. To risk, to disregard.

笲 fan 2. An osier basket.

It is unconnected with

下 hsia 4. Low. L. 5 B.
卡 ch'ia 1. A guardhouse at a pass; a Customs' barrier.

79

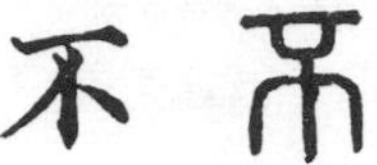

See Lessoa 133 A.

不 pu 2, pu 4. No, not.

抔 p'ou 1. A double handful.
呸 p'ou 1. To suck.

盃 杯 } pei 1. A cup, a tumbler, a glass.

罘 fu 2 A proper name.
芣 fu 2. A plant, *plantago major*.

It is radical in

丕 p'ei 1. Vast, great, unequalled. S. 146.
否 fao 3. Or not? S. 268.
杏 t'ou 4. To interrupt. S. 401.
歪 wai 1. Awry, wicked.
覔 覓 } mi 4. Invisible, to search for.

80

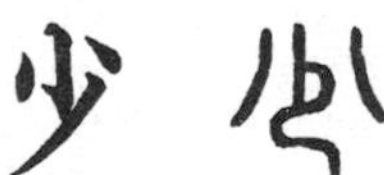

See Lesson 18 M.

少 shao 3. Few, less, to diminish, to do without.
shao 4. Young.

抄 ch'ao 1. To seize, to confiscate. To note, to copy out.
訬 ch'ao 3. To cry, to quarrel.
炒 ch'ao 3. To roast, to fry.
鈔 ch'ao 1. To hook. To copy. A receipt, money orders.
吵 ch'ao 3. An uproar; to wrangle.
眇 ch'ao 4. To harrow.
舥 ch'ao 1. A vessel rolling.
耖 ch'ao 4. A second ploughing.

眇 miao 3. One-eyed; delicate, fine. S. 465.
仯 miao 3. Small.
杪 miao 3. The tip, fine, slender, a straw.
秒 miao 3. The beard of grain; a second of time or of a degree.
妙 miao 4. Wonderful, excellent, subtle, mysterious.
玅 miao 4. Mysterious.
蚴 miao 1. A bombyx.

沙 sha 1. Sand, pebbles, dust, granulated; buddhist. S. 302.
紗 sha 1. Crape, gauze.
砂 sha 1. Different minerals; *chu-sha* cinnabar, etc.
粆 sha 1. Cassonade.
剡 sha 4. To sting, to pierce.

It is radical in

劣 lüeh 4. Weak, vicious.
省 hsing 3. To enquire.
尟 尠 } hsien 3. Small, little.
鬦 ts'ao 3. Worn out.

See Lesson 18 N.

雀 ch'iao 3. Small birds.

81

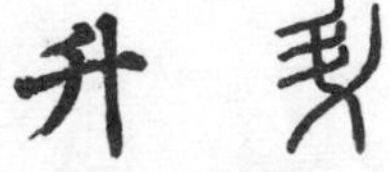

See Lesson 98 B.

升 shêng 1. The tenth part of a peck. To ascend, promotion.

昇 **shêng 1.** Rising sun, prosperity, splendour.

陞 **shêng 1.** To rise as in office, to ascend.

82

See Lesson 114 A.

氏 **shih 4.** A family, a clan, a sect.

舐 **shih 3.** To lick.

紙 **chih 3.** Paper.

扺 **chih 4.** To gesticulate.

祇 **ch'i 2.** The Genii of earth.

怟 **ch'i 2.** To venerate.

軝 **ch'i 3.** The end of the axle, outside the hub.

鴟 **ch'i 2.** A pheasant.

芪 **ch'i 2.** A plant, *ptarmica sibirica*.

Compare the Series 163.

83

See Lesson 115 D.

丹 **tan 1.** Cinnabar, red.

坍 **t'an 1.** To fall in ruins.

旃 **chan 1.** A banner, a signal flag.

栴 **chan 1.** Red sandal wood.

It is radical in

彤 **t'ung 2.** Scarlet.

青 **ch'ing 1.** Green. S. 337.

84

See Lesson 98 B.

斗 **tou 3.** A peck measure.

抖 **tou 3.** To tremble, to shake off.

枓 **tou 3.** Capital of a pillar.

蚪 **tou 3.** Tadpole.

鈄 **tou 3.** A proper name.

紏 **t'ou 3.** Raw silk.

叫 **chiao 4.** To call.

It is radical in

科 **k'o 1.** To measure, a degree, science.

料 **liao 4.** To estimate, to judge, to dispose; materials, stuff pulse for animals; coloured glass.

斜 **hsieh 2.** Oblique, wicked.

斛 **hu 2.** Ten pecks.

斝 **chia 3.** A goblet, a cup.

85

See Lesson 79 A.

屯 **t'un 2.** A camp, a village.

軘 **t'un 2.** A war-chariot.

迍 **t'un 2.** Difficulty.

豘 **t'un 2.** A sucking pig.

魨 **t'un 2.** Sea-hog.

囤 **tun 4.** A round bin.

沌 **tun 4.** The rush of water.

盹 **tun 3.** Heavy eyes; sleepiness.

鈍 **tun 4.** Dull, blunt, stupid.

砘 **tun 4.** A field roller.

飩 **tun 4.** Small meat ball coated with paste.

忳 **tun 4.** Sad, depressed.

扽 **tun 2.** To move, to shake

頓 **tun 4.** Turn, time.

醇 **ch'un 2.** Pure, exquisite.

杶 **ch'un 2.** Varnish tree, *rhus vernicifera*.

純 **ch'un 2.** Pure, unmixed, simple.

肫 **chun 1.** Flesh dried; earnest.

窀 **chun 1.** A cave; to bury.

邨 **ts'un 1.** Village.

It is radical in

春 **ch'un 1.** Spring. S. 436

86

See Lesson 79 G

𠂔 **tzŭ 3.** To stop.

姊 **tzŭ 3.** Elder sister.

秭 **tzŭ 3.** A hundred millions.

泲 **tzŭ.** To flow; a river.

胏 **tzŭ 3.** Dried meat.

笫 **tzŭ 3.** A bed mat.

Not to be confounded with

弔 **tiao 4.** To condole; to suspend. L. 28 H.

弟 **ti 4.** Younger brother S. 304.

87

王 王

See Lesson 83 G.

王 wang 2. King, prince.
wang 4. To rule, to govern.

旺 wang 4. Bright; prosperous; glorious; abundant.

枉 wang 3. Distorted; a wrong, a grievance; to no purpose.

汪 wang 1. Vast, much.

尪 wang 1. Weak, crooked.

迋 wang 4. To go; to visit.

It is radical in

皇 huang 2. Emperor. S. 458.

閏 yün 4, lün 4. Intercalary. L. 83 C.

For the following, see L. 79 D.

狂 k'uang 2. Mad. S. 285.

匡 k'uang 1. Vase. S. 223.

88

See Lesson 61 F.

文 wên 2. Strokes, lines, variegated; genteel; stylish; a classifier of cash.

紋 wên 2. Lines, traces.

蚊 wên 2. Mosquitoes, gnats.

汶 wên 2. Name of a river, in Shantung.

抆 wên 3. To rub, to wipe.

魰 wên 2. A flying fish.

雯 wên 2. Coloured clouds.

紊 wên 4. Raveled, tangled; to embroil.

吝 lin 4. Stingy, sordid.

砇 min 2. Alabaster.

旻 min 2. Pity, compassion.

忞 min 2. To try; hard.

閔 min 3. Compassion.

憫 min 3. To mourn for, to commiserate, affliction.

It is radical in

虔 ch'ien 2. Respect, veneration.

彥 yen 4. Countenance. S. 497. *Hence*

產 ch'an 3. To produce, to bear. S. 592.

Abbrev. in

斈 hsiao 2. To learn.

89

See Lesson 120 A

午 wu 3. A cyclical character; time between 11 A. M. and 1 P. M.; noon.

旿 wu 3. Noon, midday.

忤 wu 4. Disobedient, obstinate, perverse.

仵 wu 3. A coroner.

迕 wu 4. To meet; conflict.

杵 ch'u 3. A pestle.

許 hsü 3. To grant, to permit, to promise; more than.

滸 hu 3. Bank, shore.

卸 hsieh 4. To lay aside, unload.

御 yü 4. To drive; to rule; imperial; to help.

禦 yü 4. To withstand.

90

See Lesson 101 A.

勿 wu 4. No, not.

物 wu 4. A thing, a being.

㫚 wu 4. A banner.

歾 wu 4. To cease, to perish.

芴 wu 4. Manioc.

笏 hu 1. A tablet.

囫 hu 1. Whole, rough.

曶 hu 4. Bleareduess.

忽 hu 1. To neglect; suddenly; confusion.

惚 hu 1. Confusion.

揔 hu 1. To clean, to empty.

颮 hu 1. Sough of the wind.

吻 wên 3. Lips, kiss.

刎 wên 3. To cut the throat.

See the Series 492, 643, 707, 365.

91

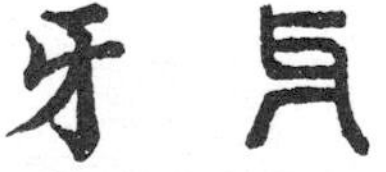

See Lesson 147.

牙 ya 2. The teeth.

齖 ya 2. Uneven teeth.

訝 ya 2. To admire, to wonder at.

迓 ya 4. To meet, to greet.

枒 ya 2. The cocoa-tree.

呀 **ya** 1. An interjection.

㤞 **ya** 2. Fear, pain.

砑 **ya** 4. To grind to polish.

鴉 **ya** 1. A raven; a crow.

雅 **ya** 3. Elegant, good.

犽 **ya** 2. The winter pear.

芽 **ya** 2. A germ; a shoot; a bud.

庌 **ya** 3. A verandah.

谺 **hsia** 1. The opening of a valley; a gorge.

颬 **hsia** 1. To breathe; to pant.

閜 **hsia** 1. To leave ajar.

衺 **hsieh** 2. Impure, lewd, bad.

邪 **hsieh** 2. Bad, perverse. S. 414.

It is radical in

穿 **ch'uan** 1. To put on or through.

92

See Lesson 61 B.

夭 **yao** 1. Delicate.

殀 **yao** 3. Untimely death.

妖 **yao** 4. Magic, phantoms.

抭 **yao** 4. To measure, to estimate.

祅 **yao** 1. Ominous influx.

窔 **yao** 3. A corner, hidden.

芺 **yao** 1. A thistle.

喬 **ch'iao** 2 Overhanging. S. 670.

笑 **hsiao** 4. To laugh.

飫 **yü** 4. Satiated, gift, favour.

沃 **wo** 4. Dew; to moisten.

It is radical in

走 **tsou** 3. To march. L. 112 D.

幸 **hsing** 4. Lucky. S. 361.

93

See Lesson 87 A.

引 **yin** 3. To draw a bow; to induce; to lead.

蚓 **yin** 3. The earthworm, *lumbricus*.

紖 **yin** 2. Leashes.

靷 **yin** 4. Harness.

矧 訠 } **shên** 3. Still more, how much more.

吲 **shên** 3. To smile.

94

See Lesson 34 E.

冘 **yin** 2. To march.

沈 **shên** 3. A surname.

忱 **shên** 2. Sincere, honest, upright.

粏 **shên** 1. Oat-meal.

枕 **chên** 3. A pillow.

酖 **chên** 4. A virulent poison.

抌 **chên** 2. To push, to knock against.

頕 **chên** 3. The occiput.

鴆 **chên** 4. Poison.

耽 **ch'ên** 2. Pleasure.

牨 **ch'ên** 2. A buffalo.

訦 **ch'ên** 2. Sincerity.

䰼 **ch'ên** 2. The roe of fish.

沈 **ch'ên** 2. To sink; heavy.

霃 **ch'ên** 2. Dull and lowering.

躭 **tan** 1. To procrastinate, to neglect.

肒 **tan** 4. Lunar twilight.

眈 **tan** 1. To procrastinate, to delay.

紞 **tan** 3. Tassels, pendents, a fringe.

髧 **tan** 3. Tresses or curls.

醓 **t'an** 3. A condiment.

䑙 **t'an** 3. Salted soy.

95

See Lesson 134 C.

尤 **yu** 2. Evils, calamities; still more; to exceed.

訧 **yu** 2. A fault or error; to accuse.

肬 **yu** 2. A tumour.

蚘 **yu** 2. The tænia.

魷 **yu** 2. The cuttle fish.

犹 **yu** 2. As though.

扰 **yu** 2. A goitre.

It is radical in

尨 **mang 2.** A shaggy dog. S. 293.

It may perhaps be found in

稽 **chi 1.** To examine.

96

See Lesson 95 A.

予 **yü 2.** I, me.

妤 **yü 2.** A housekeeper; handsome, fair.

忬 **yü 4.** Cheerful.

豫 **yü 4.** Elephant; docile; to get ready for; pleasure.

預 **yü 4.** To pre-arrange; to prepare.

垿 **hsü 4.** The side walls of an enclosure.

序 **hsü 4.** School; order, succession; preface.

芧 **hsü 4.** A species of rush.

舒 **shu 1.** To unroll; to expand; to smooth; tranquil, easy.

紓 **shu 1.** To relax; to pacify.

抒 **shu 3.** To take out.

杼 **chu 4.** A shuttle.

野 **yeh 3.** The country, a desert; savage.

墅 **shu 4.** A farm, a villa.

97

See Lesson 29 H.

元 **yüan 2.** The commencement, first cause, head, primordial.

沅 **yüan 2.** A river in Hunan.

朊 **yüan 3.** A dim moon light.

蚖 **yüan 2.** A venomous snake.

杬 **yüan 2.** A tall tree with a bitter bark

阮 **yüan 3.** Name of a place.

衏 **yüan 4.** A band of musicians.

黿 **yüan 2.** The great sea turtle.

芫 **yüan 2.** A plant, *Daphne genkwa.*

玩 **wan 4.** Trinkets or gems; to toy, to play.

忨 **wan 4.** To covet, to long for.

岏 **wan 2.** A sharp peak.

翫 **wan 4.** To practice.

刓 **wan 2.** To trim.

頑 **wan 2.** A thick-headed stupid person, obstinate.

完 **wan 2.** To end, to finish. S. 314.

It is radical in

冠 **kuan 1.** A cap, a crown, a crest.

98

匀

See Lesson 54 E.

匀 **yün 2.** Equal, uniform.

昀 **yün 2.** Plat-bands.

韵 **yün 4.** Sounds which rhyme; a harmony.

筠 **yün 2.** Bamboo splinters.

均 **chün 1.** Equal, equally.

鈞 **chün 1.** Thirty catties; great, much.

袀 **chün 1.** A plain dress.

It is phonetic contracted in

旬 **hsün 2.** A decade. S. 209.

訇 **hung 1.** Clamour. S. 45?

99

允

See Lesson 29 E.

允 **yün 3.** To permit.

狁 **yün 3.** Scythian nomads.

玧 **yün 3.** Jewels, trinkets.

沇 **yüan 3.** A river in Hunan.

夋 **tsun 1.** Dignity. S. 311.

吮 **tsun 3.** To suck, to lick.

100

云

云 **yün 2.** To speak, to say.

紜 **yün 2.** Confused, mixed up.

耘 **yün 2.** To weed.

秐 **yün 2.** To weed.

抎 **yün 3.** To lose.

䲰 **yün 4.** The secretary falcon, ***serpentarius reptilivorus.***

芸 **yün 2.** A fragrant herb, the leaves of which drive away insects; library, to weed.

雲 **yün 2.** Clouds.

侌 陰 } **yin 1.** The shady side of a hill; the inferior power.

魂 魂 } hun 2. The vital principle, soul spirit.

惃 hun 2. Melancholy.

101

札 朩乚

See Lesson 119 D.

札 cha 2. A tablet, a letter. An untimely death.

紮 cha 1. To plait, to entwine.

鳶 cha 2.

蚻 cha 1. A locust.

102

乍 乍

See Lesson 10 F.

乍 cha 4. At first; unexpectedly; hastily.

炸 cha 2. Chips, fuel.

粨 cha 4. Grits, groats.

蚱 cha 3. A locust.

拃 cha 3. A span.

詐 cha 4. To deceive, fraudulent.

咋 cha 4. A loud noise.

鮓 cha 3. A condiment of fish.

痄 cha 4. A running sore.

苲 cha 3. A water plant.

厏 ch'a 3. Not fitting.

舴 chai 4. A small boat.

窄 chai 3 Narrow, contracted.

作 tso 4. To make, to do.

怍 tso 4. Timid, shy.

酢 tso 4. To return a toast.

胙 tso 4. Sacrificial flesh; to bless, to grant.

阼 tso 4. Steps, degrees.

昨 tso 4. Yesterday; time gone.

祚 tso 4. Felicity, to confer.

柞 tso 4. Evergreen oak.

It is radical in

怎 tsen 3. How? Why?

103

冊 冊

See Lesson 156.

冊 冊 } ch'ai 2. A slip; a memorandum; a register; a book.

柵 cha 4. A fence of lats, a barrier.

刪 shan 1. To pare, to amend. This is phonetic contracted in

珊 shan 1. Coral, *shan-hu*.

跚 shan 1. To hobble, to limp

姍 shan 1. To ridicule.

It is radical in

典 tien 3. Canon, rules, records. S. 398.

侖 lün 2. To think. S. 330.

扁 pien 2. A tablet. S. 473.

嗣 ssŭ. To inherit. L. 156 G.

104

占 占

See Lesson 56 B.

占 chan 1. To divine.

苫 chan 1. To thatch.

佔 chan 4. To seize by force; to usurp.

站 chan 4. To stand up; to stop; a stage.

粘 chan 1. To paste up, to sliek up.

毡 chan 1. Rough felt.

詀 chan 1. To gabble, to joke with.

蛅 chan 2. A hairy caterpillar.

颭 chan 3. Shaken by the wind.

沾 chan 1. To moisten, to tinge; to receive benefits; infected with.

譫 chan 1. Discord; a jarring noise.

霑 chan 1. A soaking rain; to wet; to moisten; to bestow favours.

覘 ch'an 1. To spy; to glance at.

貼 ch'an 4. To spy; to look at.

閚 ch'an 4. To open a door a little; to spy.

砧 chên 1. A block, an anvil.

點 tien 3. A spot, a speck, a dot; to nod; to light; a little, a point; to set.

玷 tien 1. A flaw or stain in a gem; a defect.

踮 tien 3. To walk on tiptoe.

阽 tien 4. Bent; to fall down.

坫 tien 4. Earthen table.

痁 tien 4. The malaria.

扂 tien 3. ,To bar a gate.

店 tien 4. An inn, a shop.

惦 tien 4. To think of, to remember.

掂 tien 1. To weigh in the hand; to jolt up and down.

黏 nien 2. Glutinous.

鲇 nien 2. The mud fish.

拈 nien 2. To take up in the fingers.

帖 t'ieh 1. A billet, a note, a card.

貼 t'ieh 1. To paste up.

怗 t'ieh 1. Peacable.

It is radical in

乩 chi 1. To divine.

105

召 㕣

See Lesson 52 C.

召 chao 4. To call, to summon.

詔 chao 4. To proclaim; a proclamation, a mandate.

招 chao 1. To beckon; to invite; to confess.

昭 chao 1. Brightness; luminous.

沼 chao 3 A fish-pond; a pool

炤 chao 4. Bright.

鉊 chao 1. A scythe, to mow.

皱 chao 1. A scar.

卲 chao 4. To inquire by auguries.

照 chao 4. To enlighten, to shine on; the reflection of light; to care for; a permit; as, like.

弨 ch'ao 1. A bow unbent.

怊 ch'ao 1. To be grieved; disheartened.

超 ch'ao 1. To step over; to surpass.

貂 tiao 1. The Siberian sable, *Mustela zibelina*.

舠 tiao 1. A boat.

軺 tiao 1. A light carriage

迢 t'iao 2. Far off; remote.

齠 t'iao 2. To shed the teeth.

苕 t'iao 1. Clover.

笤 t'iao 2. A broom.

邵 shao 4. High, eminent.

邵 shao 4. A city in Shansi.

劭 shao 4. Effort, exertion.

韶 shao 2. The music of *Shun*; voices in harmony; glory, prosperity.

紹 shao 4. To connect, to hand down.

106

㐱 㐱

See Lesson 62 C.

㐱 chên 3. Bushy, thick hair.

珍 chên 1. Rare, precious.

抮 chên 3. To draw, to twist.

診 chên 1. To verify, to examine.

袗 chên 3. Plain garments.

軫 chên 3. To revolve.

眕 chên 3. Transparent; bright.

畛 chên 3. Raised paths; border.

眕 chên 3. To stare.

紾 chên 3. To bind.

疹 chên 3. Measles, scarlatina or typhus.

趁 ch'ên 4. To go to; to avail of, as an opportunity.

沴 t'ien 3. In confusion.

殄 t'ien 3. To waste.

跈 nien 3. To walk.

107

正 㱏

See Lesson 112 I.

正 chêng 4. Correct, straight; regular; to govern; the first, the principal; precisely, just.

証 chêng 4. To prove, to testify; evidence; legal testimony.

征 chêng 1. To conquer, to subjugate.

怔 chêng 1. Uneasiness.

鉦 chêng 1. Cymbals.

姃 chêng 1. A correct deportment, reserved and modest.

症 cheng 4. Disease.

整 chêng 3. To adjust; to put in order; entire; whole.

政 chêng 4. To rule; government; politics.

It is radical in

定 ting 4. Tranquil, fixed. S. 400.

是 shih 4. Is, to be, it is so. S. 476.

歪 **wai 1.** Awry.

It may be found in

罡 **kang 1.** The four stars of Ursa Major; the four guardians in Buddhist temples.

Compare S. 46.

108

See Lesson 53 D.

加 **chia 1.** To add to; to confer upon; to inflict.

枷 **chia 1.** A cangue; a flail.

珈 **chia 1.** Ornaments attached to the hairpin.

耞 **chia 1.** A flail.

迦 **chia 1.** A Sanskrit sound

跏 **chia 1.** To sit crosslegged.

[illegible] **chia 1.** To build a house.

痂 **chia 4.** The scab formed over a sore.

麚 **chia 1.** A buck, a male deer.

嘉 **chia 1.** Beautiful, good; to approve, to admire

笳 **chia 1.** A flageolet.

架 **chia 4.** A framework; a stand, a machine; to support; a quarrel.

駕 **chia 4.** A carriage; term of address, as Your Honour.

袈 **chia 1.** A dress worn by the Bonzes.

伽 **ch'ieh 2.** A Sanskrit sound.

茄 **ch'ieh 2.** Egg-plant.

瘸 **ch'üeh 2.** To be lame.

賀 **ho 4.** To congratulate.

109

See Lesson 152.

甲 **chia 3.** A scale, scaly plates, a cuirass; the finger nails; the first of the ten stems.

岬 **chia 1.** A mountain-pass, a defile.

胛 **chia 1.** The shoulder-blades.

匣 **hsia 2.** A casket.

柙 **hsia 2.** A cage, a pen.

狎 **hsia 2.** Familiarity, irreverence.

[illegible] **hsia 2.** Pleasure, delight.

[illegible] **hsia 2.** A saddle-cloth; housings.

呷 **hsia 2.** To taste.

押 **ya 1.** To compel; to arrest; to sign; to pawn.

鴨 **ya 1.** A duck.

閘 **cha 2.** A lock, a flood-gate.

110

See Lesson 20.

且 **ch'ieh 3.** And, also, moreover, further; if, should; however, absolutely.

跙 **ch'ieh 4.** A slip.

抯 **ch'ieh 3.** To extract; to draw up.

趄 **ch'ieh 4.** A slip.

姐 **chieh 3.** An elder sister.

粗 **ts'u 1.** Rough, rude, vulgar, vile.

怚 **ts'u 1.** Suspicious, to suspect.

[illegible] **ts'u 1.** The skin chapped and cracked.

麆 **ts'u 1.** A fawn.

祖 **tsu 3.** Ancestors.

阻 **tsu 3.** An obstacle; to impede.

租 **tsu 1.** Tax from fields; to lease.

徂 **tsu 3.** To go, to pass.

俎 **tsu 3.** A dresser used in sacrifices.

詛 **tsu 3.** To imprecate.

殂 **tsu 3.** To die.

組 **tsu 3.** A band, a tassel, an office.

沮 **tsu 1.** A river in Hupeh; to intimidate.

駔 **tsu 1.** A good horse.

雎 **tsu 1.** A sea-gull.

蛆 **ch'ü 1.** Maggots, worms.

咀 **chü 1.** To suck, to taste.

砠 **chü 1.** Rocky.

岨 **chü 1.** Rocky.

齟 **chü 4.** Irregular teeth; to bite.

狙 **chü 1.** A monkey; to spy.

罝 **chü 1.** A netting for hares.

苴 **chü 1.** Coarse sackcloth.

疽 **chü 1.** An ulcer.

助 **chu 4.** To help. S. 264.

查 **ch'a 2.** To examine, to inquire into. S 420.

虘 **cha 1.** A proper name. S. 580.

It is unconnected with

宜 12. Must; proper; beseeming; capable, apt; advantageous. L. 64 F.

111

See Lesson 72 A.

只 **chih 3.** Merely, only; a final particle.

枳 **chih 3.** A spinous shrub.

胑 **chih 1.** The limbs.

軹 **chih 3.** Bifurcate.

咫 **chih 3.** A foot, consisting of eight inches.

疻 **chih 3.** A bruise; a bump.

112

See Lesson 102 D.

斥 **ch'ih 4.** To blame, to scold.

拆 **ch'ai 1.** To break, to destroy.

坼 **ch'ai 4.** To split; a fissure.

訴 **su 4.** To tell, to make known; to accuse.

泝 **su 4.** To go against the stream; to meet; to remember.

柝 **t'o 4.** The watchman's clapper.

跅 **t'o 2.** To lose one's way.

113

See Lesson 27 H.

丘 **ch'iu 1.** A hillock.

邱 **ch'iu 4.** A high place; a tumulus.

坵 **ch'iu 1** A mound.

蚯 **ch'iu 1.** The common earth-worm.

齨 **ch'iu 4.** A pug nose.

It is unconnected with

兵 **ping 1.** Soldier, military arms. L. 47 D.

岳 **yao 4** A sacred mountain; a wife's parents. L. 80 B.

114

See Lesson 34 B.

冂 冋 } **chiung 3.** Space; waste land; frontiers.

坰 **chiung 3.** Desert wilds; waste lands; frontiers.

泂 **chiung 1.** Vast, extended.

駉 **chiung 1.** A good horse.

炯 **chiung 3.** Hot, bright.

詗 **chiung 3.** Tales.

絅 **chiung 3.** Unlined garment.

迥 **chiung 3.** Far apart, unlike.

扃 **chiung 1.** Bar, bolt.

115

See Lesson 83 D.

主 **chu 3.** A ruler, a lord; to govern.

炷 **chu 4.** A candle.

住 **chu 4.** To halt, to stop, to cease; to dwell; to live in.

註 **chu 4.** To explain; to comment.

拄 **chu 3** A prop; to lean on.

駐 **chu 1.** To stop, to sojourn.

柱 **chu 4.** A pillar; a support.

咮 **chu 4.** To cluck.

鞋 **chu 4.** Leathern gaiters.

黈 **chu 3.** Young.

祩 **chu 4.** A tablet.

砫 **chu 4.** A stone tablet.

鉒 **chu 4.** An ingot.

蛀 **chu 4.** Wood-worms.

注 **chu 4.** Water flowing. To give attention.

澍 **chu 4.** To soak.

麈 **chu 3.** The elk.

笙 **chu 4.** The pegs of a lute.

宔 **chu 3.** An ancestral tablet. See L. 79 D.

往 **wang 3** To go to, to start; passed; towards.

116

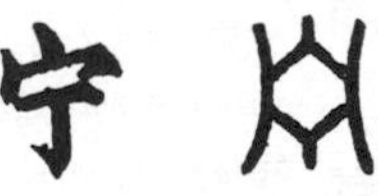

See Lesson 57 B.

宁 **chu 4.** A lobby.

佇 **chu 1.** To hope and wait.

貯 **chu 4.** To store up; to hoard.

眝 **chu 4** To stare at.

泞 **chu 4** Clear, limpid.

紵 **chu 4.** Coarse tow.

竚 **chu 4.** To hope and wait.

詝 **chu 4.** Knowledge.

羜 **chu 4.** A lamb.

苧 **chu 4.** *Urtica nivea*, China-grass.

It is unconnected with

丁 **ting 1.** A person; a nail. S. 11.

117

出

See Lesson 78 E.

出 **ch'u 4.** To go forth; to issue; to eject.

㤕 **ch'u 1.** Melancholy.

絀 **ch'u 1.** To stitch.

拙 **cho 1.** Unskillful.

䖦 **cho 1.** A spider.

䪼 **cho 4.** The cheek-bones.

茁 **cho 4.** The budding forth of plants.

黜 **ch'u 4.** To degrade, to dismiss.

柮 **tu 4.** The stump of a tree.

咄 **tu 1.** Exclamation.

䨳 **p'u 4.** Lightning.

昢 **p'u 4.** The sun rising.

It is radical in

朏 **fei 3.** The moon in a crescent form, five days old.

糶 **t'iao 4.** To sell grain.

祟 **sui 4.** Noxious influonce.

賣 **mai 4.** To sell. L. 78 E.

屈 **ch'ü 1.** Bent over, grievance. S. 348.

暴 **pao 4.** To insolate. S. 809.

敖 **nao 2.** To lounge. S. 638.

118

巨

See Lesson 82 D.

巨 **chü 4.** The chief, great, large.

拒 **chü 4.** To reject, to oppose.

矩 **chü 2.** A carpenter's square; a pattern, a rule.

距 **chü 4.** Distance, distant from.

詎 **chü 4.** How?

岠 **chü 4.** A high peak; to reach.

鉅 **chü 4.** Steel. Hard, obdurate.

炬 **chü 4.** A torch; to burn.

柜 **chü 3.** A plant from which is distilled a fragrant essence.

怇 **chü 1.** Haughty.

秬 **chü 3.** A variety of millet.

駏 **chü 4.** The offspring of a stallion and a she-ass.

粔 **chü 4.** Cakes.

苣 **chü 4.** Dandelion.

佢 **ch'ü 2.** This, that.

渠 **ch'ü 2.** A drain; he, she, it, they. *Hence*

㣄 **ch'ü 2.** That person or thing.

磲 **ch'ü 2.** Onyx.

鸈 **ch'ü 2.** Wagtail.

蕖 **ch'ü 2.** Lotus.

119

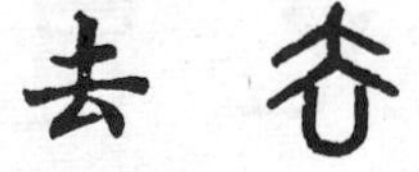

See Lesson 38 F.

去 **ch'ü 4.** To go or take away.

抾 **ch'ü 1.** To feel.

袪 **ch'ü 1.** The sleeves.

胠 **ch'ü 1.** The flank.

䮃 **ch'ü 1.** To drive away.

阹 **ch'ü 1.** A pen for cattle.

祛 **ch'ü 1.** To expel; to disperse.

呿 **ch'ü 1** To gape.

魼 **ch'ü 1.** The flounder.

弆 **ch'ü 3.** To conceal, to hide.

It is radical in

刦 **chieh 2.** To rob; to plunder.

蜐 **chieh 2.** The sea-anemone.

鉣 **chieh 2.** An iron hook.

怯 **ch'ieh 4.** Timorous, fearful, cowardly.

㾀 **ch'ieh 4.** Weakness; debility.

法 **fa 1. fa 2. fa 4.** A law, a rule; an art; to imitate. Buddhism. L. 125 A.

琺 **fa 4.** Enamel, *fa-lang*.

丟 **tiu 1.** To lose.

𧊅 **tiu 1.** A chrysalis.

𨀁 **tiu 1.** To squat down.

Abbrev. in

却 卻 **ch'iao 4.** Precisely. L. 17 H. Hence.

脚 腳 **chiao 3.** The feet.

120

付

See Lesson 45 C.

付 **fu 4.** To give, to deliver.

府 **fu 3.** A palace, a prefecture. S. 355.

符 **fu 2.** A contract cut in two pieces; to match, to agree with. A spell.

苻 **fu 2.** A herbaceous plant; buds bursting.

怤 **fu 4.** To think on with pleasure.

咐 **fu 4.** To enjoin, *chu-fu.*

弣 **fù 3.** The hold of the bow.

祔 **fu 4.** To worship ancestors.

拊 **fu 3.** To pat, to slap; to soothe.

蚹 **fu 4.** Scales of a serpent.

駙 **fu 4.** A subsidiary horse; a son-in-law of the emperor.

鮒 **fu 4.** A fish that goes in shoals; union, mutual affection.

柎 **fu 1.** Lathing.

泭 **fu 2.** A rat.

跗 **fu 1.** The ankle.

⿰禾付 **fu 1.** Bran of grain.

軵 **fu 3.** To put in the coach-house.

附 **fu 4.** To be next to; to adhere; an appendix.

⿱艹附 **fu 4.** A drug, *aconitum variegatum.*

121

See Lesson 87 D.

弗 **fu 3.** An adverb of prohibition, not; not so; do not.

怫 **fu 2.** Sorry, anxious.

彿 **fu 2.** Like, *fang-fu.*.

紼 **fu 2.** A cord, a rope.

拂 **fu 2.** To wipe off; to brush away; to oppose.

咈 **fu 4.** To resist, to refuse.

沸 **fu 4.** To boil.

⿰風弗 **fu 4.** A light breeze.

刜 **fu 4.** To chop, to cut asunder.

艴 **fu 4** To flush, anger.

茀 **fu 2.** A jungle.

髴 **fu 2.** Like, *fang-fu.*

笰 **fu 2.** A partition, a screen.

佛 **fo 2.** Buddha; Buddhist,

費 **fei 4.** To use, to spend, to lavish.

狒 **fei 4.** A kind of ape, four or five feet high.

⿰言弗 **fei 4.** Glibness of tongue; to stutter.

疿 **fei 2.** Small pimples.

122

号

See Lesson 58 B.

号 號 **hao 4.** A cry, a name, a mark, a label; to call, to summon.

枵 **hsiao 1.** Empty, hollow, vile, vain, petty.

鴞 **hsiao 1.** An owl; filial impiety.

饕 **t'ao 1.** Gluttonous, covetous.

123

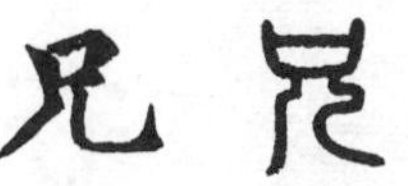

See Lesson 29 D.

兄 **huang 4,** To declaim. **hsiung 1.** An elder brother.

怳 **huang 3.** Disturbed, mad.

眖 **huang 3.** Delirium, confused.

貺 **huang 4.** To give, to bestow.

况 況 況 **k'uang 4.** Moreover, a fortiori; circumstances.

It is radical in

呪 咒 **chou 4.** To curse, to imprecate; an incantation.

詋 **chou 4.** Imprecation.

祝 **chu 4.** To pray, to wish, to bless.

兌 **yüeh 4.** To speak, to rejoice. S. 313.

124

玄

See Lesson 91 A.

玄 玄 **hsüan 2.** Black, dark, deep; abstruse, mysterious.

炫 **hsüan 4.** Brilliant, to dazzle.

眩 **hsüan 1.** Confused, dizzy, deceived.

泫 **hsüan 2.** Glistening dew drops; tears.

鉉 **hsüan 4** Tripod rings or ears.

袨 **hsüan 2.** Black clothes.

衒 **hsüan 4.** To brag, to display, to divulge.

弦 **hsien 2.** The string of a bow, the chord of an arc; a crescent; a spring.

昡 **hsien 4.** To brighten, to light up.

絃 **hsien 2.** The string of a lute; a violin.

舷 **hsien 2.** The hull of a vessel.

蚿 **hsien 2.** The milliped.

痃 **hsien 2.** Indigestion, dyspepsia.

牽 **ch'ien 1.** To pull, to haul along, to drive. S. 600.
It is radical in

率 **shuai 4.** To lead. M. 646.

畜 **ch'u 4.** Animals.
hsü 4. To feed.

125

See Lesson 37.

穴 **hsüeh 2.** A cave, a den, a cavern.

泬 **hsüeh 4.** A spring.

肸 **hsüeh 2.** To look, to spy.
Radical 116.

126

See Lesson 108 A.

虵 **i 2. t'o 1.** A cobra.

柂 **t'o 1.** To split wood; a coffin.

陁 **t'o 2.** Steep rugged path.

沲 **t'o 2.** An confluent of streams.

拖 **t'o 1.** To draw.

迤 **i 3.** To go towards, to advance.

扆 **i 1.** The bar of a gate.

About this confused Series, Cf. L. 107 B note, SS. 164 and 37.

127

See Lesson 85 E.

台 **i 2.** To speak, to express one's self.

飴 **i 2.** Sweet-meat, sugar, delicacies.

貽 **i 2.** To hand down; to leave, to neglect.

詒 **i 2.** To hand down, to leave.

怡 **i 2.** Harmonious concord; mutual pleasure.

眙 **i 2.** To gaze at fixedly.

冶 **yeh 3.** To smelt, to cast.

始 **shih 3.** Beginning; to begin; then.

治 **chih 4.** To govern, to rule, to punish, to heal.

笞 **ch'ih 1.** To flog.

台 **t'ai 2.** The Great Bear; a terrace.

抬 **t'ai 2.** To carry on a pole; to lift.

胎 **t'ai 1.** The pregnant womb; a fœtus.

鮐 **t'ai 2.** A globular fish, the *Tetraodon*.

邰 **t'ai 2.** A propre name.

炱 **t'ai 2.** Smoky soot.

苔 **t'ai 2.** Moss.

髻 **t'ai 2.** A woman's headdress of false hair.

殆 **tai 4.** Dangerous; nearly, soon.

紿 **tai 4.** Thread raveled, tangled; confusion.

迨 **tai 4.** To reach; till, to.

怠 **tai 4.** Idle, lazy.

128

See Lesson 116.

冄 冉 **jan 3.** Tender, weak; little by little.

苒 **jan 3.** Luxuriant, gradually; tender herbage.

髯 **jan 2.** The beard; the whiskers.

頾 **jan 3.** The beard; the whiskers.

袡 **jan 2.** A wrapper.

蚺 **jan 2.** A kind of boa.

枏 枬 **nan 2.** Yellowish fine wood, *Machilus*.

甜 **tan 1.** To loll the tongue.

眒 **tan 1.** A proper name.

涆 **t'an 1.** Breaking of a bank.

那 **na 4.** A demonstrative particle.
na 3. An interrogative particle. S. 282.
It is radical in

衰 **so 1.** A cloak made of straw. L. 16 D, S. 563.
It is unconnected with

再 **tsai 4.** Repetition. L. 35 J.

129

See Lesson 73 B.

甘 **kan 1.** Sweet, agreeable, voluntary.

霄 **kan 1.** Hoar-frost.

苷 **kan 1.** Liquorice.

疳 **kan 1.** Scurvy, noma.

紺 **kan 4.** A purple colour.

詌 **kan 4.** To bridle one's speech.

泔 **kan 1.** Slops.

柑 **kan 1.** An orange.

𩚵 **kan 1.** A sweet cake.

坩 **k'an 1.** A vessel which holds five pints.

甘瓦 **k'an 1.** Wine jar.

鉗 **ch'ien 2.** A pair of tweezers; pinchers.

拑 **ch'ien 2.** To pinch

箝 **ch'ien 2.** A gag, to gag.

嵌 **ch'ien 4.** To inlay, to inchase.

髟甘 **ch'ien 4.** To shear.

邯 **han 1.** A district in the south of Chihli.

欿 **han 2.** To hold in the mouth, to contain.

酣 **han 1.** Intoxicated, drunken, comatose.

蚶 魽 } **han 1.** Bivalve shells.

It is radical in

甛 **t'ien 2.** Sweet to the taste.

某 **mu 3.** A certain one; S. 467.

甚 **shên 4.** Superlative, very. S. 475.

香 **hsiang 1.** Fragrant; incense.

旨 **chih 3.** Sweet. S. 185.

130

可 可

See Lesson 58 I.

可 **k'o 3.** Convenient, proper; can, may.

齒可 **k'o 4.** To crunch with the teeth.

珂 **k'o 4.** Rock-crystal.

柯 **k'o 1.** A handle.

跒 **k'o 3.** To march.

軻 **k'o 1.** Name of Mencius.

砢 **k'o 1.** A heap of stones.

坷 **k'o 3.** Uneven, rough land; unfortunate.

㪃 **k'o 3** To knock.

欱 **k'o 2.** To cough.

岢 **k'o 1.** A hill in Shansi.

笴 **k'o 3.** The shaft of an arrow.

苛 **k'o 3** Small stalks.

疴 **k'o 4.** Pain; sickness.

閜 **k'o 3.** To open.

哿 **k'o 3.** Good, apt, possible.

嵑 **k'o 4.** To ground, to put a vessel ashore.

舸 **ko 3.** A barge.

牁 **ko 1.** A handle.

河 **ho 2.** A river; a canal.

呵 **ho 1.** To yawn, to exhale.

訶 **ho 1.** To blame, to reprove.

蚵 **ho 1.** A sort of lizard.

魺 **ho 1.** A seablubber.

何 **ho 2.** An interrogative pronoun, who, which, how?

荷 **ho 2.** Lotus, *nelumbium speciosum.*

阿 **o 1.** A hill. Used as sound before proper names. *Hence*

娿 **o 1.** Undecided, unstable.

屙 **o 1.** To ease nature.

啊 **o 1.** An interjection.

It is radical in

哥 **ko 1.** An elder brother. *Hence*

歌 **ko 1.** To sing; a song.

謌 **ko 1.** A song.

鴚 **ko 1.** A parrot.

哥戈 **ko 1.** A quay.

奇 **ch'i 2.** Strange. S. 328.

131

句 句

勾

A double series. See L. 54 F.

勾 **kou 1.** A mark, a hook, to cancel.

鈎 **kou 1.** A hook, to hook.

抅 **kou 1** To point a wall.

鉤 **kou 1.** A hook, to hook.

狗 **kou 3.** A dog.

𤱍 **kou 1.** Raised bank in a field.

坸 **kou 4.** Dirty, filthy.

怐 **kou 4.** Silly, simpleton.

岣 **kou 3.** A hill in Hunan.

枸 **kou 3.** A spinous lemon-tree.

訽 kou 4. To mock, to laugh at.

夠 够 kou 4. Much, enough, to suffice

𠛎 kou 1. A sickle or bill-hook.

苟 kou 3. Plants. Giddily. If, if so.

笱 kou 3. A trap.

耇 kou 3. Senile, decrepid.

敂 k'ou 4. To strike, to knock. To deduct

齁 hou 1. To snore.

𤙖 hou 3. To bellow

齣 ch'u 1. Act of a play, part.

句 chü 4. A phrase, a word, a line in verse.

拘 chü 1. To grasp; to hold; to restrain; to adhere to

駒 chü 1. A colt.

絇 chü 4. A shoe-string.

跔 chü 1. Feet benumbed, stiffened.

翑 chü 3. Beam-feathers.

軥 ch'ü 2. A yoke

朐 ch'ü 2. Dried meat.

泃 ch'ü 2. Name of a river in Chihli.

鴝 ch'ü 1. A thrush.

劬 ch'ü 1. Labour, toil.

痀 ch'ü 2. Hunch-back.

呴 hsü 4. Breath.

煦 hsü 4. To warm with one's breath.

昫 hsü 4. Gentleness.

煦 hsü 3. To warm, to console; kindness.

It is unconnected with

局 chü 2. To dispose. L. 32 F.

敬 ching 4. To revere. S. 729.

132

古 古

See Lesson 24 F.

古 ku 3. Ancient, old.

固 ku 4. Solid, firm. S. 368.

罟 ku 3. A net; punishment.

辜 ku 1. A fault. Ingratitude.

故 ku 4. The cause or reason of a thing; consequently; on purpose; old; to die.

鴣 ku 1. A partridge.

估 ku 1. To estimate, to set a price on.

沽 ku 1. To trade in, to buy and sell.

酤 ku 1. To deal in spirits.

跍 ku 1. To crouch down.

牯 ku 3. A bull; a male.

羖 ku 3. A ram or ewe.

軲 ku 1 A block; to revolve.

蛄 ku 1. The mole-cricket.

咕 ku 1. To mutter.

詁 ku 3. To explain; to comment.

鈷 ku 3. A smoother.

姑 ku 1. A polite term for girls; a paternal aunt; a husband's sister; a Buddhist nun.

菇 ku 1. A mush-room; a bud.

𥁕 ku 3. Earthen utensil.

盬 ku 3. Salt-works, salt, to salt.

苦 k'u 3. A bitter plant; pain, painful.

𥬠 k'u 3. A fish-trap.

枯 k'u 1. Rotten or dry wood; decayed; withered.

𣧛 k'u 1. Rotten, arid.

骷 k'u 1. The bones; a skeleton; a skull.

祜 hu 4. Protection of heaven; favour.

怙 hu 4. To rely on.

岵 hu 4. Hill with grass.

胡 hu 2. Why? What? How? Turkish tribes. S. 450.

做 作 tso 4. To do, to act.

133

瓜 瓜

See Lesson 162.

瓜 kua 1. Cucurbitaceous plants.

𠜾 kua 1. To slice.

窊 wa 1. Depression, low. *Hence*

搲 wa 3. To scoop out, to dig.

𡃐 wa 1. Infant's wail.

𨃓 wa 3, To paddle.

罛 ku 1. A large fishing-net.

笟 ku 1. A whistle.

苽 ku 1. An eatable plant.

柧 ku 1. A corner; angular.

觚 ku 1. A wine-vase; angular; vicious.

胍 ku 1. Large bellied.

蛌 ku 1. A grass-hopper.

孤 ku 1. An orphan, fatherless. *Hence*

鈲 **ku 1.** An eatable plant, *hydropyrum.*

鈲 **ku 1.** To hoop; a circlet; to draw tight.

狐 **hu 2.** The fox.

弧 **hu 2.** A bow, an arc, curved.

Radical 97. Compare S. 39.

134

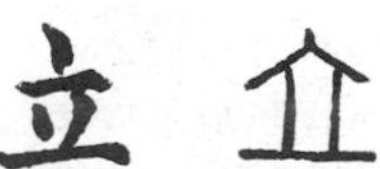

See Lesson 60 H.

立 **li 4.** To stand erect; to rear, to found; presently.

粒 **li 4.** A kernel, a grain.

砬 **li 4.** A mineral used as an antidote.

鴗 **li 4.** A green kingfisher, *alcedo bengalensis.*

颯 **li 4.** A driving blast; suddenly.

苙 **li 4.** A pen, a yard, a hemper.

笠 **li 4.** A hat of straw.

岦 **li 4.** Hilly.

[衤立] **la 2.** Rags, tatters.

拉 **la 1.** To draw, to pull.

[雨立] **la 4.** The sound of rain.

泣 **ch'i 4** To weep.

It is radical in

位 **wei 4.** Seat, dignity, condition; a person. *Hence*

涖 **li 4.** Water dripping down.

莅 蒞 } **li 4.** To exercise an office; to overlook; to govern.

昱 **yü 4.** Light, to light.

煜 **yü 4.** Flame; to shine.

竝 並 } **ping 4.** A team, and, moreover, at once. *Hence*

普 **p'u 3.** Large, universal. S. 754.

135

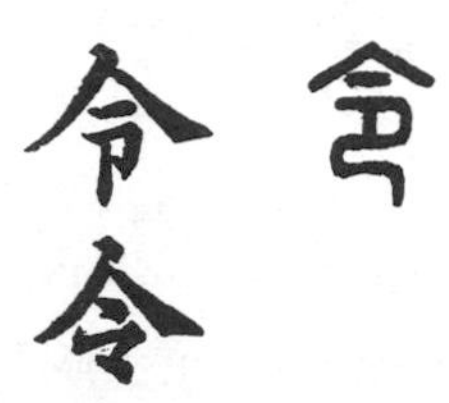

See Lesson 14 I.

令 令 } **ling 4.** An order; to command; your honoured.

囹 **ling 2.** A prison; an inclosure.

苓 **ling 2.** A sort of truffle, *pachyma cocos.*

零 **ling 2.** Small rain; a fraction, a remainder.

笭 **ling 2.** A cage.

伶 **ling 2.** Shrewd, cunning, a comedian.

袊 **ling 3.** A collar.

鈴 **ling 2.** A sleigh-bell.

聆 **ling 2.** To hear; to listen; to obey.

齡 **ling 2.** Front teeth; age.

柃 **ling 2.** A tree, the Eurya japonica.

舲 **ling 2.** A house-boat.

蛉 **ling 2.** The sand-fly, *pai-ling.*

羚 **ling 2.** The mufflon.

玲 **ling 2** To tinkle.

拎 **ling 2.** To lift.

翎 **ling 2.** A plume or tail feather.

瓴 **ling 2.** A longnecked jar.

鴒 **ling 2.** The wagtail.

領 **ling 3.** The collar; to receive.

嶺 **ling 3.** A mountain range.

冷 **lêng 3.** Cold, chilly.

命 **ming 4.** To command, a decree; fate, life.

136

See Lesson 129 D.

卯 **mao 3.** The fourth of the twelve branches; the hour from 5 to 7 A. M.; a term.

茆 **mao 3.** The mallow.

昴 **mao 3.** The Pleiades.

貿 **mao 4.** To barter, trade.

泖 **mao 3.** A river in Kiangsu.

聊 **liao 2.** To depend on; to help; a little.

窌 **chiao 4.** A cellar.

It is unconnected with

卵 **luan 3.** Eggs. L. 108 D.

卿 **ch'ing 2.** Minister. L. 55 A.

柳 **liu 3.** A willow. L. 129 E.

劉 刘 } **liu 2.** A surname. L. 129 E.

留 **liu 2.** To sojourn, to detain a guest. S 551.

Compare the Series 73.

137

See Lesson 114 D.

民 **min 2.** The people, the mass, the common multitude.

笢 min 3. A hair brush.

罠 min 2. A net to catch hares.

苠 min 2. Grass; a multitude.

⿰糸民 min 2. To fish.

抿 min 3. To smooth down; to fold.

岷 min 3. A mountain in Ssu-ch'uan.

泯 min 3. To flow over; to destroy, to perish.

怋 min 2. Emotion, trouble.

珉 min 2. Alabaster.

刡 min 3. To scrape off.

敃 min 3. To strive.

愍 min 2. Pity, compassion.

眠 mien 2. To close the eyes; to sleep.

呡 wên 3. The lips, speech.

⿰虫民 wên 2. A mosquito.

蟁 wên 2 Mosquitoes.

138

末 朩

See Lesson 120 B.

末 mo 4. The end of a branch; the end; finally; small; the meanest part of; powder; a negative.

沫 mo 4 Foam; spittle.

抹 mo 2 To wipe clean, to rub, to besmear.

袜 mo 4 A girdle.

秣 mo 4. Fodder, to feed.

靺 mo 4. Red boots.

⿰火末 mo 4. A dull fire.

麱 mo 4. Broken grain, grits.

妺 mo 4. Tricks.

帓 mo 4. A kerchief, a turban.

茉 mo 4. The jasmine.

Compare the Series 167.

139

母 𣫬

See Lesson 67 O.

母 mu 3. A mother; female; the source of; a root; a key.

姆 mu 3. An elderly matron.

拇 mu 4. The thumb.

踇 mu 3. The toes.

每 mei 3. Each, every. S. 294.

Not to be confounded with

毋 wu 2. Not, do not.

140

尼 𡰥

See Lesson 26 F.

尼 ni 2. To stop; a nun.
ni 4. Near, familiar.

苨 ni 3. B plant, *adenophora*.

妮 ni 2. A slave girl.

胒 ni 2. Fat, grease.

坭 ni 4. Mud; to coat.

䵒 ni 2. To adhere, to stick.

秜 ni 2. A kind of rice.

伲 ni 3. Thou, you.

昵 ni 4. Dawn; daily; familiar.

怩 ni 2. To blush.

⿰山尼 ni 2. A hill in Shantung.

呢 ni 1. A final particle.

柅 ni 3. Hard wood; to inquire into.

旎 ni 3. To flutter in the wind.

馜 ni 3. Very fragrant.

泥 ni 2. Mire, mud; dirt; adhesive; attached to.

埿 ni 2. Mud; to daub.

⿱艹泥 ni 2. Luxuriant.

141

奴 𡛥

See Lesson 67 C.

奴 nu 2. A slave; a term of contempt.

伮 nu 2. To strive for.

詉 nu 4. A wrangling.

努 nu 2. To exert the utmost strength; to strive.

怒 nu 4. Anger, fury.

弩 nu 3. A cross-bow.

⿱奴目 nu 4. Leucoma.

胬 nu 3. Granulations in a wound.

砮 nu 3. Sharp flint.

駑 nu 2. A weak horse.

孥 nu 2. To exterminate a family.

帑 nu 2. The children. *T'ang* 3.

怓 nao 2. To trouble, to intrigue.

呶 nao 2. Clamorous vociferations.

拏 na 2. To take, to hold.

帑 t'ang 3. The treasure.

142

See Lesson 134 A.

犮 pa 2. A dog at the leash.
拔 pa 3. To pull up; to eradicate; to draw.
菝 pa 2. A drug, *smilax china*.

泼 fa 4. To open sluices; to irrigate, to water.
髮 fa 3. The hair of the human head.

紱 fu 3. A sash; the gentry.
祓 fu 2. To remove evil, to drive off.
袚 fu 4. A knee-pad.
帗 fu 2. A wand held by dancers.
黻 fu 4. Embroidered; ornamented.
韍 fu 2. A knee-pad of leather; a cap; a strap.

妭 po 4. A wife.
跋 po 4. To trample on, to stamp.
鈸 po 4. Small cymbals.
軷 po 4. To sacrifice to the spirits of the road.
骳 po 4. The shoulderblade; a scapula.
魃 po 4. The demon of drought.
䳁 po 1. The beaver.
柭 po 4. A flail.
馛 po 4. Fragrant.
茇 po 4. A thatched cottage.
盋 po 4. A large dish.

Not to be confounded with
友 yu 3. Friend. L. 43 B.

143

See Lesson 88 A.

白 pai 2. White, pure; vain, in vain, for nothing.
伯 pai 2. A father's elder brother, a senior; an earl, a leader.
柏 pai 3. The cypress; the thuja.
舶 pai 4. A great junk.
百 pai 3. A hundred S. 233.
帛 pai 2. White silk; property, wealth. S. 386.

拍 p'ai 1. To slap; to pat.
迫 廹 } p'ai 4. To urge, to vex, to harass.
珀 p'ai 4. Amber.
粕 p'ai 4. Dregs.
魄 p'ai 4. The inferior soul; the body.

怕 p'a 4. To fear; lest.
帕 p'a 4. A kerchief, a veil.
袙 p'a 4. A turban.

箔 pao 1. A door-screen made of splints.

鉑 po 2. A thin sheet of metal.
泊 po 4. To anchor; to stop; to fasten a boat.

It is radical in
泉 ch'üan 4. A spring. Cash. L. 125 F.
原 yüan 2. A fountain, a source. S. 588.

144

半 㸚

See Lesson 18 D.

半 pan 4. To divide in two; a half.
伴 pan 4. A comrade, a fellow.
絆 pan 4. To fetter; a restraint.
拌 pan 4. To throw away, to mix.
靽 pan 4. Fetters.
姅 pan 4. A woman with catamenia.

叛 p'an 4. To rebel, to revolt.
判 p'an 4. To halve; to decide; to judge.
頖 p'an 4. To manage.
泮 p'an 4. The semicircular pool before the colleges.
冸 p'an 4. To melt as ice.
袢 p'an 4. Light clothes for summer.
畔 p'an 4. A landmark; a side or bank.
牉 p'an 4. A division, a half.

胖 p'ang 4. Corpulent, fat.

It is contracted in
衅 釁 } hsin 4. To besmear vessels with blood; a quarrel.

145

See Lesson 54 B.

包 pao 1. To wrap up, to envelop, to warrant.
郇 pao 1. A surname.

胞 pao 1. The amnion.

鉋 pao 4. A plane; to plane off.

飽 pao 3. To eat enough; satiated.

鮑 pao 4. Pickled fish; bad companies.

齙 pao 1. Projecting teeth.

抱 pao 4. To infold; to carry in the lap; to hold tight; to hide; to endure.

抱 pao 4. To incubate, to hatch.

雹 pao 2. Hail.

苞 pao 4. Reed, rush, dense, close.

袍 p'ao 3. A long robe.

跑 p'ao 3. To run, to flee.

砲 p'ao 4. A ballista.

咆 p'ao 2. To roar.

泡 p'ao 4. A bubble. To soak.

炮 p'ao 2. To roast.

匏 p'ao 2. A calabash.

骲 p'ao 2. The tip of an arrow made of bone.

鞄 p'ao 2. To work hides.

瓟 p'ao 2. A gourd.

皰 p'ao 4. A blister.

刨 p'ao 2. To dig; to extract.

炰 p'ao 2. To incinerate.

庖 p'ao 2. A kitchen.

疱 p'ao 4. A blister.

麅 p'ao 2. A buck.

颮 piao 1. A whirlwind.

罦 fu 2. A spring-net.

枹 fu 2. A drum-stick.

146

丕 丕

See Lesson 133.

丕 p'ei 1. Unequaled; great, vast; largely; everywhere.

呸 p'ei 1. To snort at.

胚 p'ei 2. An embryo; unformed, unfinished.

坯 p'ei 1. Unburnt sundried bricks.

伾 p'ei 1. Sturdy; robust.

狉 p'ei 1. A cub.

狉 p'ei 1. A cub.

怌 p'ei 1. Weak; timid. A surname.

駓 p'ei 1. To gallop.

邳 p'ei 2. A place in the north of Kiangsu.

芣 p'ei 1. Luxuriant, blooming, flowery.

髤 p'ei 1. Disheveled hair.

坯 p'i 1. Unburnt sundried bricks.

秠 p'i 1. A kind of millet.

痞 p'i 3. Dyspepsia.

Compare the SS. 79, 268 and 401.

147

本 本

See Lesson 130 A.

本 pên 3. The origin, the root; natural, original, capital; a fascicle.

体 pên 3. Rude, coarse.

体 pên 4. Stupid, dull.

笨 pên 4. Stupid, dull.

呠 p'ên 4. To spurt.

It is perhaps found in

鉢 po 1. A bowl.

148

必 必

See Lesson 18 G.

必 pi 2. Certainly, must, necessary.

祕 pi 4. Secret, mysterious.

秘 pi 4. Secret, mysterious.

泌 pi 4. A torrent.

怭 pi 4. Indecency.

珌 pi 4. Jewels.

佖 pi 4. Rude.

柲 pi 4. A handle.

拲 pi 4. To tap, to pat.

飶 pi 4. The fragrance of food.

眿 pi 4. To gaze at.

駜 pi 4. A strong horse.

韠 pi 4. A sheat for keeping two bows.

踋 pi 4. To kick, as a ball.

鮅 pi 4. A kind of bleak.

邲 pi 4. A place in Shansi.

苾 pi 4. Fragrant.

閟 pi 4. To close; to impede. Secret, hidden.

毖 pi 4. Attention, vigilance; grieve.

宓 mi 4. Retirement. S. 383.

瑟 shê 4. A lute. L. 82 B.

149

皮

See Lesson 43 H.

皮 p'i 2. Skin; leather; furs; a cover; a surface.
詖 p'i 4. To slander.
鈹 p'i 1. A large needle.
骳 p'i 4. Distorted, twisted.
怶 p'i 1. Fear.
秛 p'i 1. Rent paid on land.
㽝 p'i 1. To crack.
猈 p'i 1. To expand the wings.
旇 p'i 1. A standard.
刻 p'i 1. To peel, to cut.
疲 p'i 1. Lassitude, fatigue.

彼 pi 3. He, him, that, those.
貱 pi 4. To add, to give.
柀 pi 3. The pine, *Cunninghamia sinensis*.

披 p'ei 1. To open, to spread out.
帔 p'ei 4. A short cloak.
彼 pei 3. He, him, that, those; yonder.
被 pei 4. A coverlet; to cover; to suffer; a sign of the passive voice.
鞁 pei 4. To saddle.

破 p'o 4. To break, to destroy.
坡 p'o 1. A declivity, a slope.
跛 p'o 2. Cripple, lame.
陂 p'o 1. A declivity, a slope.
頗 p'o 1. Very, much.
波 p'o 1. A wave, a ripple.
婆 p'o 2. An old woman; a stepmother.
碆 p'o 2. Stones like flint.

玻 po 1. Vitreous, glass.
蚾 po 3. The toad.
尰 po 3. To go lame.
菠 po 1. Spinach.
簸 po 4. A winnowing basket.

li is radical in

叚 chia 3. False. S. 427.

150

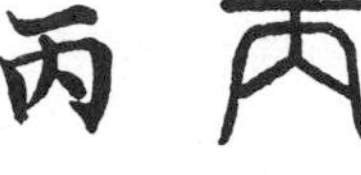

See Lesson 41 A.

丙 ping 3. The third of the ten stems.
柄 ping 3. A handle, a haft; authority.
炳 ping 3. Bright, luminous.
昞 ping 3. Bright, glorious.
蛃 ping 3. The *lepisma*.
怲 ping 1. Sad, mournful.
鮩 ping 3. A shell-fish.
邴 ping 3. A place in Kiangsu.
病 ping 4. A sickness.
寎 ping 4. To sleep.

更 kêng 1. To change. S. 283

Nothing to do with

陋 lou 4. Vile. L. 10 C.

151

平

See Lesson 58 F.

平 p'ing 2. Even equal; peaceful, quiet; scales; to weigh.
苹 p'ing 2. Sea-weed.
閛 p'ing 2. The noise of shutting a door.
坪 p'ing 2. Level land.
枰 p'ing 2. A chess-board.
評 p'ing 2. To discuss, to settle.
泙 p'ing 2. A ravine, a wady.
萍 p'ing 2. Duckweed.

砰 p'êng 1. A crashing noise.
怦 p'êng 1. Earnest, ardent.

抨 pêng 1. To seize; to accuse.
伻 pêng 1. To send, a convoy.

秤 ch'êng 4 A steelyard.

152

See Lesson 35 C.

布 pu 4. Cotton, linen; to spread out; to arrange.
怖 pu 4. To frighten; afraid; alarmed.
佈 pu 4. To extend; to diffuse.
抪 pu 4. To scatter.

153

申

See Lesson 50 C.

申 **shên 1.** A cyclic character; to extend; to report.

伸 **shên 1.** To extend; to dilate; to explain.

神 **shên 2.** Spirit, spiritual; the Genii; the natural powers; the animal spirits.

呻 **shên 1.** To groan; to mutter.

紳 **shên 1.** A large girdle; those who wear it, the gentry.

訷 **shên 1.** To tell; to believe.

柛 **shên 1.** Decayed trees.

坤 **k'un 1.** The earth; the inferior power.

It is radical in

電 **tien 4.** Lightning; electricity; telegraphy.

奄 **yen 3.** To cover. S. 418.

154

生

See Lesson 79 F.

生 **shêng 1.** To bear, to produce; to live; to come forth; unusual; unripe, unacquainted, unpolished; life.

牲 **shêng 1.** Draught animals.

甥 **shêng 1.** The children of a sister or of a daughter.

貹 **shêng 4.** Wealth.

鼪 **shêng 1.** A polecat.

甡 **shêng 1.** Numerous; a multitude.

笙 **shêng 1.** Pandean pipes.

眚 **shêng 3.** Leucoma. To obscure. Unhappy.

星 **hsing 1.** The stars. S. 447.

性 **hsing 4.** Natural disposition; temper; property.

姓 **hsing 4.** Surname.

鉎 **hsing 1.** Rust. Oxides.

旌 **ching 1.** A banner; to signal, to announce.

It is radical in

甤 **jui 3.** Prolific like swine; many.

甦 **su 1.** To revive.

青 **ch'ing 1.** Green. S. 337.

產 **ch'an 3.** To produce, to bear. S. 592.

毒 **tu 2.** Poison, virus.

隆 **lung 2.** Abundance.

155

See Lesson 48 B.

失 **shih 1.** To lose; to omit; to fail; a fault; an omission.

秩 **chih 4.** Order, degree.

帙 **chih 4.** A sheath, a wrapper.

紩 **chih 4.** To stitch; to sew.

袠 **chih 4.** A sheath.

抶 **ch'ih 4.** To flog.

迭 **tieh 2.** To alternate; to be able to.

跌 **tieh 1.** To slip and fall.

眣 **tieh 2.** The eyes unsteady.

昳 **tieh 4.** The sun beginning to decline.

詄 **tieh 2.** To forget; to neglect.

柣 **tieh 2.** Door, flight of steps, entrance.

瓞 **tieh 4.** Ranking cucumbers; posterity.

鉄 **t'ieh 3.** Iron.

蛈 **t'ieh 4.** A spider.

佚 **i 4.** Ease, negligence.

軼 **i 4.** To rush by, to rush on, to exceed.

泆 **i 4.** Licentious; to overflow.

156

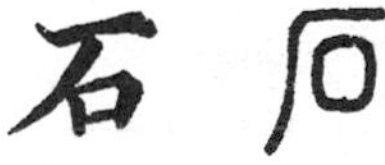

See Lesson 59 D.

石 **shih 2.** A stone; rocks, minerals. **tan 4.** A picul, 100 catties.

祏 **shih 2.** A stone shrine to keep the ancestral tablets.

鼫 **shih 4.** The marmot.

拓 **chê 2.** To gather.

柘 **chê 4.** A thorny tree, *Cudrania triloba*.

跖 **chê 2.** A proper name.

碩 **shao 2.** Abundance.

妬 **tu 4.** Jealous, envious.

蠹 **tu 4.** Worms in books or clothes.

Etc. Radical 112.

157

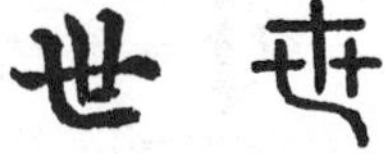

See Lesson 24 O.

世 **shih 4.** An age; a generation of thirty years; the world.

貰 **shih** 4. To buy on credit; to borrow; to pardon.

呭 **i** 4. Loquacious; garrulous.

靾 **i** 4. A saddle.

葉 **yeh** 4. Leaf, lobe, hinge S. 494.

泄 **hsieh** 4. To leak to divulge; diarrhæa.

枻 **hsieh** 4. A frame to keep a bow in good shape.

紲 **hsieh** 4. To fasten; a halter.

僁 **hsieh** 4. Reckless; extravagant.

痮 **hsieh** 4. Dysenteria.

Abbrev. in

屜 屧 **t'i** 4. A drawer.

158

See Lesson 45 J.

朮 **shu** 2. A glutinous grain, *panicum miliaceum.*

秫 **shu** 2. Sorghum stalks, *shu-chieh.*

述 **shu** 4. To follow; to narrate.

沭 **shu** 4. A river in Shantung.

術 **shu** 4. A path; an art; magical rules.

怵 **ch'u** 2. Afraid.

It is radical in

殺 **sha** 1. To kill, to decapitate.

159

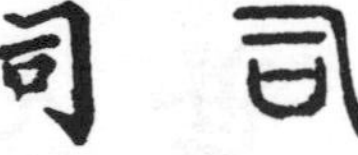

See Lesson 30 C.

司 **ssŭ** 1. To control; the officer who presides; a court; the faculties of the soul.

嗣 **ssŭ** 4. To succeed to; heirs, posterity.

飼 **ssŭ** 4. To feed.

覗 **ssŭ** 1. To peep at.

柌 **ssŭ** 4. The handle of a plough.

齝 **ssŭ** 4. To ruminate.

覗 **ssŭ** 1. To peep at.

笥 **ssŭ** 4. A hamper.

伺 **ts'ŭ** 4. To wait upon.

詞 **ts'ŭ** 2. An expression; a composition; to accuse; to request.

祠 **ts'ŭ** 2. The ancestral hall of a family; offerings.

160

See Lesson 42 A.

四 **ssŭ** 4. Four; all around.

駟 **ssŭ** 4. A team of four horses.

泗 **ssŭ** 4. A river in Shantung.

柶 **ssŭ** 1. A spoon.

161

See Lesson 71 B.

代 **tai** 4. To alter, to substitute; a generation; a series.

玳 **tai** 4. A shell.

袋 **tai** 4. A bag, a purse.

黛 **tai** 4. Indigo, black.

帒 **tai** 4. A bag, a pocket.

岱 **tai** 4. A mountain in Shantung.

貸 **tai** 4. To lend.

162

See Lesson 143 B.

旦 **tan** 4. The rising sun, the dawn; day; actors who take the parts of females.

但 **tan** 4. Only, simply.

担 **tan** 3. To dust, a duster.

胆 **tan** 3. The gall.

呾 **tan** 1. To mutter.

怛 **tan** 3. Pain, care.

靼 **tan** 2. Soft leather.

鴠 **tan** 4. A nightingale.

笪 **tan** 4. A round basket.

疸 **tan** 4. The jaundice.

坦 **t'an** 3. A plain, level place; ease.

袒 **t'an** 3. To strip, naked.

曇 **t'an** 2. Black clouds; darkness.

亶 **t'an** 2. A loft. S 762.

妲 **ta** 2. The concubine of the tyrant *Cheou-hsin.*

163

See Lesson 114 B.

氐 **ti** 3. The foundation. To reach, till.

低 **ti** 1. To bend down, low.

抵 **ti** 3. To oppose; to be equivalent; to reach.

柢 **ti** 3. The root, origin.

牴 ti 3. To gore; to strive against.

怟 ti 4. Sadness.

詆 ti 3. To vilify, to slander.

觝 ti 3. To push with the horns.

羝 ti 1. A ram or buck.

泜 ti 4. Name of a stream in Chihli.

弤 ti 3. The famous bow of the emperor *Shun*.

骶 ti 3. The os coccygis.

邸 ti 3. A hotel; a lodginghouse.

底 ti 3. Base, foundation; a suffix.

疷 ti 1. Disease.

祗 chih 3. To venerate; to cultivate; only, yet.

胝 chih 2. Thick callous skin.

秖 chih 1. Ripeness.

砥 chih 3. Whetstone.

彽 ch'ih 2 To go to and fro; irresolute.

坻 ch'ih 2. An islet; a dyke.

蚳 ch'ih 2. Larvæ of ants.

鯳 ch'ih 1. A mackerel.

鴟 ch'ih 1. An owl.

It is radical contracted in

昏 hun 1. Obscure, dark. S. 363.

Compare the Series 82 and 217.

164

See Lesson 149 A.

田 t'ien 2. A field; cultivated fields.

畋 t'ien 2. To cultivate.

佃 tien 4. To till the ground; farmers.

甸 tien 4. Government lands.

鈿 tien 4. Inlaid metal-work.

蜔 tien 4. Inlaid shell work.

It is radical in

苗 miao 2. Sprouts. S. 461.

里 li 3. Hamlet. S. 287.

It is unconnected with

思 ssŭ 1. To think L. 40 A.

細 hsi 4. Fine, thin, slender. L. 40 A.

165

See Lesson 108 A.

它 t'o 1 That, another; to charge.

佗 t'o 1. That, another; he, him.

拕 t'o 1. To pull, to drag along; to protract.

沱 t'o 2. An affluent.

鉈 t'o 2. A steelyard weight.

砣 t'o 2. A counterpoise.

陀 t'o 2. Steep and rugged paths.

紽 t'o 2. A hank of silk or floss.

柁 t'o 2. A tie-beam; to fix; solid.

詑 t'o 2. To deceive, to impose on.

粑 t'o 2. Cakes.

跎 t'o 2. To slip; a fault.

酡 t'o 2. Face flushed with drink; drunk.

骲 t'o 2. An anchylosis.

駝 t'o 2. A camel; to bear the back.

鼧 t'o 2. A beaver.

鮀 t'o 2, A snake-fish.

鴕 t'o 2. The ostrich.

鞁 t'o 2. Saddle-bags.

疕 t'o 2. Humpbacked.

舵 to 4. A rudder.

It is radical in

蛇 sha 2. A serpent. Compare the Series 126 and 37.

166

See Lesson 17 F.

冬 tung 1. Winter.

苳 tung 1. Asparagus.

佟 t'ung 2. A proper name.

炵 t'ung 2. A bright red blaze.

鼕 t'ung 1. The rattle of drums.

疼 t'êng 2. Pain, ache; to love dearly.

終 chung 1. The end; to the last.

鼨 chung 1 A rodent marked with spots.

螽 chung 1. A green grasshopper.

167

See Lesson 120 C.

未 wei 4. A cyclic character. A negation.

味 wei 4. Taste, flavour.

昧 **mei 4.** No sun; dark, obscure, hidden; to feign.
眛 **mei 4.** Dimness of vision.
妹 **mei 4.** A younger sister.
抹 **mei 4.** To feel with the hand.
韎 **mei 4.** Red boots.
袜 **mei 4.** A sleeve, a veil.
魅 **mei 4.** A demon of the woods.
沬 **mei 4.** A river in Honan.
寐 **mei 4.** To rest; to sleep.

It is radical in

制 **chih 4.** To make. L. 120 C.
𠩺 **li 2.** To fell. S. 627.

168

央

See Lesson 60 K.

央 **yang 1.** The midst; the center; to pray.
殃 **yang 1.** A misfortune; a calamity.
[illegible] **yang 1.** A calamity.
秧 **yang 1.** Shoots, young plants.
詇 **yang 4.** To speak cautiously.
[illegible] **yang 2.** The badger.
鞅 **yang 1.** A harness.
咉 **yang 1.** To vomit.
坱 **yang 2.** Fine dust; to fill.
抰 **yang 2.** To whip, to beat.
泱 **yang 1.** Wide; violent.
胦 **yang 4.** The navel.
[illegible] **yang 2.** A fish, *pseudobagrus fulvidraco.*

盎 **yang 1.** To pray, to entreat.
鴦 **yang 1.** The hen of the mandarin duck.

映 **ying 4.** To shine on, to reflect.
怏 **ying 4.** Dislike, disgust.
柍 **ying 1.** Apricot-tree.

英 **ying 1.** A flower; luster, talent, bravery. *Hence*
瑛 **ying 1.** The luster of gems.
暎 **ying 4.** To shine on, to reflect.
煐 **ying 1.** A flame; red.
鍈 **ying 1.** The sound of jingling bells.
霙 **ying 1.** Crystals of snow.

169

See Lesson 18 E.

㕣 **yen 3.** A marsh at the foot of hills.
沿 **yen 2.** Shore; along.
[illegible] **yen 2.** To go along.

鉛 **ch'ien 1.** Lead-ore.

船 **ch'uan 2.** A beat.

170

See Lesson 151.

由 **yu 2.** Cause, origin; from, by, since.
油 **yu 2.** Oil.
柚 **yu 2.** The shaddock, *citrus decumana.*
蚰 **yu 2.** A centipede.
秞 **yu 4.** Nice.
鼬 **yu 4.** A polecat.

袖 **hsiu 4.** A sleeve.
岫 **hsiu 4.** A cavernous cliff.

軸 **chou 2.** An axle, a pivot, a roller.
妯 **chou 2.** Sisters-in-law.
伷 **chou 4.** Progeny.
舳 **chou 2.** The stern of a vessel.
[illegible] **chou 4.** To bless, to pray for.
宙 **chou 4.** Earth. The universe. Always.
胄 **chou 4.** Progeny, offspring.
冑 **chou 4.** A helmet.

[illegible] **ch'ou 1.** To suck in; to smoke.
紬 **ch'ou 2.** Silk.
怞 **ch'ou 2.** Grieving; sorrowful.
抽 **ch'ou 1.** To draw out, to extract. To contract.

迪 廸 } **ti 2.** To follow; docility. To direct; to teach.
笛 **ti 2.** A fife or flute.

171

幼

See Lesson 90 A.

幼 **yu 4.** Young, immature; growing.
泑 **yu 3.** A varnish.

拗 yu 1. Sorrowful.

呦 yu 1. To bell.

黝 yu 3. Black; an ashy colour.

鰗 yu 3. A perch.

詏 yao 4. To contradict.

坳 yao 1. Hollow.

袎 yao 4. Bow.

眑 yao 3. A vacaut look.

靿 yao 4. Leg of a boot.

窈 yao 3. Obscure, deep, mysterious.

拗 niu 4. To break. Mulish, stubborn.

Not to be confounded with

幻 huan 4. A dream, unrea. L 95 B.

172

右 司

See Lesson 46 G.

右 yu 4. The right hand; on the right.

佑 yu 4. To aid, to help.

祐 yu 4. Divine care and protection; to protect.

It is radical in

若 jao 3. To gather. If. S. 454.

173

永 㳅

See Lesson 125 D.

永 yung 3. Ever-floving; perpetual.

咏 yung 3. To sing, to chant.

詠 yung 3. To recite.

泳 yung 3. To swim.

拯 yung 1. To throw.

It is radieal in

羕 yang 4. Rising. S. 659.

脉 mai 4. The pulse.

衇 mai 4. The blood vessels.

昶 ch'ang 3. A long day; lasting.

174

夗 夗

See Lesson 64 D.

夗 yüan 3. To turn in bed.

眢 yüan 1. A vacant, dull eye.

鴛 yüan 1. The drake of the mandarin duck.

怨 yüan 4. Ill treatment. to have a grudge.

苑 yüan 4. A park field.

宛 wan 2. To curve. S. 407.

盌 wan 3. A bowl, a deep dish.

腕 wan 4. The wrist.

175

戉 戉

See Lesson 71 L.

戉 yüeh 4. A halberd.

鉞 yüeh 4. A battle-ax.

哦 yüeh 1. To vomit.

狘 yüeh 4. To scamper away, to be terrified.

越 yüeh 4. To overstep; to exceed.

樾 yüeh 4. The shade of trees.

176

安 安

See Lesson 67 C.

安 an 1. Peace, rest.

按 an 4. To press down. As; accordingly.

鞍 an 1. A saddle

洝 an 4. A hot spring.

胺 an 4. Corrupted meat.

鵪 an 1. A quail.

案 an 4. A table; a tribunal; a suit.

177

宅 宅

See Lesson 33 B.

宅 chai 2. A family dwelling; to inhabit.

挓 cha 1. To open: to widen out.

烢 cha 4. A crack.

詫 ch'a 4. To talk big; to brag; to boast.

秺 ch'a 3. Four hundred sheafs.

蛇 ch'a 4. A scablubber or medusa.

侘 ch'a 4. Disappointment.

咤 ch'a 4. To chide.

姹 ch'a 3. A handsome person.

178

兆 𠂁

See Lesson 56 D.

兆 chao 4. An omen: a prognostic: a million.
垗 chao 4. Area around a grave.
狣 chao 4. A surname.
旐 chao 4. A banner with tortoises and snakes.

晁 ch'ao 2. A surname.

銚 tiao 4. A kettle.
鋚 tiao 4. A kettle.
朓 tiao 3. Planks; a bed.

挑 t'iao 1. To carry; a load; to stir up; to choose.
祧 t'iao 1. Room where the oldest ancestral tablets were kept
誂 t'iao 2. To seduce.
跳 t'iao 4. To jump.
躿 t'iao 3. A tall person.
佻 t'iao 1. Unsteady.
眺 t'iao 4. To gaze at.
恌 t'iao 1. Licentious.
朓 t'iao 4. To offer flesh in sacrifice.
脁 t'iao 4. The moon appearing before sunrise.
覜 t'iao 4. An imperial audience.
剆 t'iao 1. To cut open; to sever.
頫 t'iao 4. To salute.
庣 t'iao 1. A cavity.
窕 t'iao 3. Secret, hidden.

窕 t'iao 3. Licentiousness.

桃 t'ao 2. The peach.
洮 t'ao 1. To wash.
逃 t'ao 2. To flee; to escape.
咷 t'ao 2. To wail.
駣 t'ao 2. A colt.
鼗 t'ao 2. A small flat drum.

烑 yao 2. To shine.
姚 yao 2. Elegance.
珧 yao 2. Mother-of pearl
筄 yao 4 Laths.

179

成 㦒

See Lesson 71 M.

成 ch'êng 2. To finish; to accomplish; to become; to succeed.
誠 ch'êng 2. Guileless; sincere; to rectify; perfection.
城 ch'êng 2. A wall of a city; a city.
郕 ch'êng 2. A place in Honan.
宬 ch'êng 2. The archives.
盛 ch'êng 2. To contain.

盛 shêng 4. Abundant; flourishing.
晠 shêng 4. A bright light.

180

吉 吉

See Lesson 24 C.

吉 chi 2. Fortunate, lucky.
佶 chi 2. Robust, strong.
狤 chi 2. A monkey.
姞 chi 2. A concubine of *Huang-ti*.
劼 chi 4. Earnestly.
皵 chi 1. Black spots on the skin.

蛣 ch'i 1. The dung-beetle; a scarabee.

結 chieh 1. A knot; to tie; to contract; fixed, firm, constant.
秸 chieh 1. Thatch.
詰 chieh 4. Inquiry; to examine.
桔 chieh 4. A medicinal plant.
袺 chieh 4. To lift clothes.
硈 chieh 1. Firm; sudden.
拮 chieh 2. Labeuring hard; tenacity.
黠 chieh 1. Skill.
頡 chieh 2, hsieh 2. A proper name. S. 797.
刉 chieh 1 To flay, to scalp.
髻 chieh 1 Back hair, chignon.

壹 i 1. A vessel. One. S. 690 L. 38 G.

181

㓞 㓞

See Lesson 97 D.

㓞 ch'i 4 To cut a notch in a stick.
契 ch'i 4 A covenant. S. 426.

恝 ch'ia 4. Careless, egoistic.

齧 yeh 4. nieh 4. To bite; to eat.

挈 **hsieh** 2. To raise ; to help.

絜 **hsieh** 4. To rule; coercition.

洯 **chieh** 2. Pure, limpid.

契 **chieh** 1. To scrape ; to cleanse.

潔 **chieh** 2. Pure, to purify ; chaste, chastity.

[illegible] **lieh** 4. To praise.

[illegible] **lieh** 4 To sharpen.

182

See Lesson 31 F.

夅 **chiang** 4. To descend ; to degrade.

蜂 **chiang** 4. The rain-bow.

降 **chiang** 4. To descend ; to degrade.

䜶 **chiang** 1. A small bean.

絳 **chiang** 4 A bright red colour.

[illegible] **chiang** 4. To hate.

[illegible] **chiang** 4. Unsubmissive ; to rebel.

洚 **chiang** 4. Water overflowing.

降 **hsiang** 2. To subdue ; to yield.

[illegible] **hang** 2. A sullen dog.

䂫 **hang** 1. A ram ; to ram down the earth.

艂 **p'ang** 1. Two boats lashed together.

胮 **p'ang** 2. To swell.

逄 **p'ang** 2. A proper name.

See LL. 31 F and 79 F.

隆 **lung** 2. Abundance.

Compare. S. 269.

183

交

See Lesson 61 D.

交 **chiao** 1. To blend, to unite ; intercourse.

郊 **chiao** 1. A suburb ; imperial sacrifice.

鵁 **chiao** 1. The heron.

狡 **chiao** 3. Crafty, cunning

絞 **chiao** 3. To strangle.

較 **chiao** 4. To examine, to confront, to compare.

校 **chiao** 4. An enclosure ; a park.

餃 **chiao** 3. A meat dumpling.

跤 **chiao** 1. A slip.

鉸 **chiao** 3. To cut.

姣 **chiao** 3. Handsome.

[illegible] **chiao** 3. Leathern drawers.

蛟 **chiao** 1. A crocodile.

鮫 **chiao** 1. A shark.

佼 **chiao** 3. Graceful.

珓 **chiao** 4. Stones used for divination.

皎 **chiao** 3. Pure white ; effulgent.

咬 **yao** 3. To bark.

齩 **yao** 3. To bite.

効 **hsiao** 4. To toil ; exertion ; to imitate ; merit.

校 **hsiao** 4. A school-house.

恔 **hsiao** 4. Cheerful.

效 **hsiao** 4. To produce ; effects, results ; to imitate ; similar.

傚 **hsiao** 4. To pattern after, to imitate.

184

幵 开

See Lesson 115 B.

幵 开 } **ch'ien** 1. Even, level ; to raise in both hands.

岍 **ch'ien** 1. A hill in Shansi.

汧 **ch'ien** 1 A river in Shausi.

蚈 **ch'ien** 1. A fire-fly.

豣 **chien** 2. A full grown hog.

趼 **chien** 3 Callous hard skin.

鳽 **chien** 1. The heron.

妍 **yên** 2. Beautiful, skilled.

[illegible] **yên** 4. A big dog.

研 **yên** 2. To grind.

并 **ping** 1. Together. S. 399.

It is phon. contracted in

形 形 } **hsing** 2. Form, shape ; the body ; material ; to appear.

邢 **hsing** 2. A place in Chihli.

It is radical in

枅 **chi** 1. A tie-beam.

This is phon. contracted in

笄 **chi** 1. The hairpin, sign of nubility.

羿 **i** 4. A proper name (*form altered*).

It is unconnected with

開 k'ai 1 To open. L. 115 G.

185

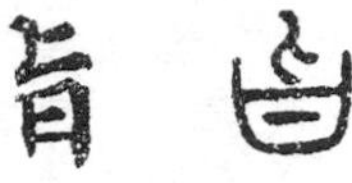

See Lesson 26 K.

旨 旨 chih 3. An Imperial Decree; purport; meaning.

指 chih 2. A finger; a toe.
chih 3. To designate; to indicate to hope.

脂 chih 1. Fat, grease; ointment; cosmetics.

詣 i 4. To visit; to go to; to reach.

耆 ch'i. A man of sixty. S. 513.

It is radical in

嘗 ch'ang 2. To taste. L. 36 E.

186

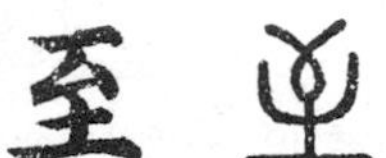

See Lesson 133 B.

至 chih 4. To go to: to reach; till; as for; utmost; solstice.

姪 chih 2. A nephew; a niece.

輊 chih 4. A chariot.

銍 chih 4. A sickle.

踁 chih 4 To go to and fro; irresolute.

侄 chih 2. Hampered.

挃 chih 1. To touch lightly, to graze.

晊 chih 1. Bright.

桎 chih 4. Manacles; fetters.

秷 chih 2. To bruise.

膣 chih 4. A gizzard.

咥 chih 4. To bite.

蛭 chih 4. A leech.

郅 chih 4. A place in Kansu; prosperity.

致 chih 4. To do, to cause, to reach.

緻 chih 4. Delicate, fine; a view.

庢 chih 1. A proper name.

荎 chih 4. A nut.

窒 chih 4. To stop up; stupid.

室 shih 4. A house; a household; a wife.

絰 tieh 2. Hempen cloth worn as mourning.

垤 tieh 2. A mound.

耋 tieh 2. Old, infirm.

187

州 巛

See Lesson 12 L.

州 chou 1. A Department.

洲 chou 1. A continent.

酬 ch'ou 2. To pledge with wine; to repay.

詶 ch'ou 3. To answer.

掫 ch'ou 3 To grasp.

188

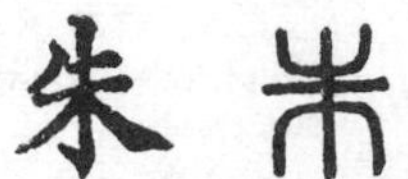

See Lesson 120 D.

朱 chu 1. Red.

珠 chu 1. A pearl; the pupil of the eye; a bead.

硃 chu 1. Vermilion; imperial.

蛛 chu 1. The spider.

誅 chu 1. To punish; to Flame; to put to death.

銖 chu 1. A light weight; a small thing; a trifle.

咮 chu 4. To peck up.

侏 chu 1. A dwarf; a pygmy.

株 chu 1. A trunk; a stump; to punish.

洙 chu 1. A river in Shantung.

袾 chu 1. Elegant garments.

脨 chu 1. The cheeks.

跦 chu 1. To hop.

邾 chu 1. A place in Shantung.

茱 chu 1. *Xanthoxylum.*

殊 ch'u 2. To differ; to kill; distinct; very.

姝 shu 1. Graceful, lovely.

189

See Lesson 29 F.

充 ch'ung 1. To fill; to satisfy; to banish.

忼 ch'ung 1. Excited, agitated.

銃 ch'ung 4. A gingal.

沇 ch'ung 1. Bubbling of water.

茺 ch'ung 1. *Lamium album.*

統 t'ung 3. The end; a whole, a system; to rule.

190

See Lesson 51 B.

曲 **ch'ü 1.** Crooked; perverse; songs.

麯 **ch'ü 1.** Leaven.

蛐 **ch'ü 1.** The common earth-worm.

筁 **ch'ü 4.** A bamboo frame, to rear silkworms.

191

See Lesson 47 K.

劵 **chüan 4** Tired, weary.

帣 **chüan 4.** A bag.

絭 **chüan 1.** A stake.

牶 **chüan 1.** The ring through an animal's nose.

眷 **chüan 4.** To love; wife and children.

卷 **chüan 3.** To roll. S. 350. **chüan 4.** A roll; a book; a section.

券 **ch'üan 4.** A deed; a diploma.

拳 **ch'üan 2.** The fist.

豢 **huan 4.** Tame animals; to feed.

Compare S. 511

192

全 仝 } **ch'üan 2.** All; the whole; complete.

詮 **ch'üan 2.** To explain; to discourse upon.

洤 **ch'üan 2.** A spring.

輇 **ch'üan 2.** A wagon.

跧 **ch'üan 2** To creep.

銓 **ch'üan 2.** To estimate.

牷 **ch'üan 2.** A fat unblemished victim.

痊 **ch'üan 2.** Cured; convalescent.

筌 **ch'üan 2.** A trap.

荃 **ch'üan 2.** A fragrant plant.

拴 **shuan 1.** To fasten; to tie up.

栓 **shuan 1.** A peg.

193

而 

See Lesson 164 A.

而 **erh 2.** A copula; a disjunctive particle.

髵 **erh 2.** The whiskers.

荋 **erh 2.** A species of mushroom.

輀 **erh 2.** A hearse or funeral carriage.

胹 **erh 1.** To boil.

栭 **erh 2.** A small column.

洏 **erh 2.** To flow.

鮞 **erh 2** The roe of fishes.

耐 **nai 4.** To endure; patient; to be able.

耏 **nai 4.** Beard; to shave.

⿸疒而 **nai 1.** Weary, sick.

Perhaps it is found in

耍 **shua 3.** To handle, to play.

Compare the SS. 434, 466, 779.

194

耳

See Lesson 146 A.

耳 **erh 3.** The ear; a handle; a final particle.

餌 **erh 3.** Bait for fish; cakes.

佴 **erh 4.** A second; an assistant.

洱 **erh 3.** A river in Honan.

珥 **erh 3.** Ear-trinkets.

咡 **erh 3.** Cheeks, face.

駬 **erh 3.** A famous steed.

衈 **erh 4.** To gash the ear of a victime.

刵 **erh 4.** To cut the ears.

毦 **erh 4.** A tuft.

It is radical in

聞 **wên 2.** To hear.

咠 **ch'i 1** To blame. S. 425.

恥 **ch'ih 1.** To be ashamed.

取 **ch'ü 3** To take. S. 349.

聶 **nieh 4.** To plot. S. 842.

Radical 128.

195

伐

See Lesson 71 G.

伐 **fa 1.** To cut down.

栰 筏 } **fa 2.** A raft.

閥 **fa 2.** A side-gate. To command.

垡 **fa 2.** To clear, to plough.

茷 **fa 2.** Leafy; luxuriant.

Not to be confounded with

代 **tai 4.** For, instead; a generation S. 161.

196

See Lesson 25 E.

伏 **fu 2** To subject; to fall prostrate; to lie in ambush; to brood; to hide; a decade in dog-days; to serve.

袱 **fu 2.** A wrapper.

洑 **fu 4** To swim

柭 **fu 2** A sheath.

茯 **fu 2.** A fungus-like substance, *pachyma cocos.*

197

See Lesson 69 K.

亥 **hai 4.** A cyclic character.

孩 **hai 2.** A child.

骸 **hai 2.** Bones, skeleton.

恢 **hai 4.** Sorrowful, depressed.

核 **hai 2.** To search, to scrutinise.

駭 **hai 4.** To frighten, fear.

咳 **hai 1.** To cough.

㤥 **hai 4** To raise up.

劾 **hai 2.** To examine, to accuse.

核 **ho 2.** A nut.

核 **hu 2.** A nut.

該 **kai 1.** Must, ought.

賅 **kai 1.** To heap up; to give; precious, rare.

峐 **kai 1.** A barren hill.

侅 **kai 1.** Extraordinary, rare.

胲 **kai 1.** The great toe.

垓 **kai 1.** Bounds, limits

陔 **kai 1.** A step; a ledge.

晐 **kai 1.** Bright light; all; thoroughly.

絯 **kai 3.** Much, many.

痎 **kai 1.** Tertian ague.

刻 **k'o 1.** To carve, to chisel; oppressive.
k'o 4. A quarter of an hour.

欬 **k'o 2** To cough.

咳 **k'o 2.** To cough.

頦 **k'o 1.** The chin.

198

See Lesson 14 B.

合 **ho 2.** To shut the mouth; to join; to unite; suitable; to match; to meet; together, with; a region.

盒 **ho 2.** A box or dish.

閤 **ho 3.** All, whole, complete.

郃 **ho 4.** Name of a place in Shensi.

頜 **ho 4.** The jaw-bone.

匌 **ho 2.** To environ; everywhere.

哈 **ha 1.** To breathe softly.

洽 **hsia 4.** To soak; to harmonise.

祫 **hsia 4.** A triennial sacrifice to the ancestors.

烚 **hsia 4.** To boil, to irritate.

峆 **ko 2.** A knoll, a mound.

蛤 **ko 2.** A clam, oyster.

鴿 **ko 1.** A domestic pigeon, a dove.

峇 **k'o 1.** A cave, a cavern.

給 **kei 3.** **chi 3.** To give; the preposition to; to suffice.

袷 **chia 2.** Lined garment.

餄 **chia 1.** Cake.

眨 **chia 1.** Eyes dim and tired.

鞈 **chia 1.** A leather jerkin.

韐 **chia 1.** A girdle worn by mourners.

恰 **ch'ia 4.** Fitting, opportune.

帢 **ch'ia 4** A scholars cap.

跲 **ch'ia 4.** To stumble.

It is radical in

荅 **ta 2.** A kind of pulse. S. 570.

弇 **yen 3.** To cover. S. 496.

拿 **na 2.** To take, to hold.

拾 **shih 2.** To gather, to collect.

199

See Lesson 30 C.

后 **hou 4.** The sovereign; an impress. After; then.

逅 **hou 4.** To meet.

郈 **hou 4.** Name of a place in Shantung.

垢 **kou 4** Dirt; sordid.

詬 **kou.** To reproach.

姤 **kou 4.** To pair, to copulate.

200

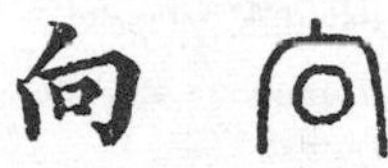

See Lesson 36 E.

向 **hsiang 4.** A window; facing, opposite to; to like; to favour.

珦 **hsiang 4.** Jewels.

餉 **hsiang 3.** Provisions; rations.

响 **hsiang 3.** A sound.

晌 **shang 3.** Noontide; midday.

扄 **shang 3.** A door knocker; a lock.

尙 **shang 4.** To esteem. S. 391.

201

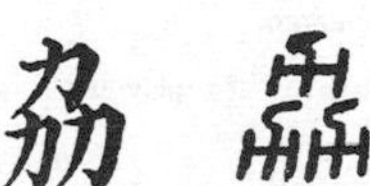

See Lesson 53 E.

協 勰 } **hsieh 2** United in agreement; concord; a regiment; to aid.

拹 **hsieh 2.** To fold; to drag.

恊 **hsieh 2.** Harmony, union.

脇 脅 } **hsieh 2.** The flanks, the sides; to intimidate.

熁 **hsieh 1.** Heat. to dry.

愶 **hsieh 2.** To intimidate.

歙 **hsieh 1.** To inhale; lean; weak

202

先

See Lesson 79 B.

先 **hsien 1.** Before.
hsien 4. To go before.

㤼 **hsien 2.** Melancholy; despondency.

侁 **hsien 1.** Multitude; concourse.

駪 **hsien 1.** In troops.

詵 **hsien 1.** The din of a multitude

銑 **hsien 2.** Polished; bright.

㧥 **hsien 3.** To take up in the fingers.

毨 **hsien 3.** To molt.

𥐨 **hsien 1.** Fine pebble.

跣 **hsién 3.** Barefooted.

𠛙 **hsien 4.** To castrate.

筅 **hsien 3.** Bamboo articles of various kinds.

洗 **hsi 3** To wash; to cleanse; to reform.

203

行

See Lesson 63 C.

行 **hsing 2.** To step; to do; elements.
hsing 4. Action, conduct.

荇 **hsing 4.** An aquatic plant.

胻 **hsing 1.** The thighbone.

行 行 } **hang 2.** A rank; a category; a profession; a corporation.

桁 **hang 2.** A row; a beam.

珩 **hang 2.** Girdle pendents.

筕 **hang 2.** A bamboo mat.

衡 **hêng 2.** A balance; to adjust.

銜 **hsien 2.** A bit; a rank, a degree.

衍 **yen 3.** To overflow; abundant; licentiousness.

𧍯 **yen 3,** A centipede.

愆 **ch'ien 1.** A fault; an error; to go beyond.

204

刑

See L. 115 A, and S. 204.

刑 **hsing 2.** Torture; to castigate.

型 **hsing 2.** A mold; an example; a statute.

侀 **hsing 2.** A figure, a form.

鉶 **hsing 2.** A sacrificial vessel.

硎 **hsing 2.** A whetstone.

205

休

See Lesson 119 C.

休 **hsiu 1.** To rest, to cease; to repudiate.

烋 **hsiu 1.** To burn; crepitation.

茠 **hsiu 1.** To cover; to weed.

庥 **hsiu 1.** Shelter; shade; protection.

咻 **hsiu 1.** To shriek.

貅 hsiu 1. A leopard.

鵂 hsiu 1. A sort of owl.

鵂 hsiu 1. A fine warsteed.

206

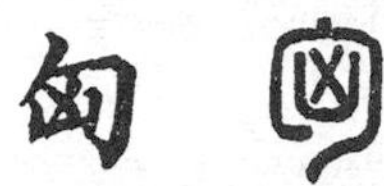

See Lesson 38 D.

匈 hsiung 1. The thorax, the breast.

胷 胸 hsiung 1. The thorax, the breast.

恟 hsiung 1. Timorous, nervous, frightened.

詾 hsiung 1. To brawl; threatenings.

洶 hsiung 1. A rush of water.

207

See Lesson 76 H.

亘 hsüan 1. To revolve.

宣 hsüan 1. A palace, to proclaim; wide. S. 449.

晅 hsüan 1. Glorious; dignified.

晅 hsüan 1. The light of the sun; to dry.

烜 hsüan 1. To smoke.

萓 huan 2. A kind of celery.

桓 huan 2. Pillars before a grave; delay.

峘 huan 2. A high hill.

狟 huan 1. A badger.

垣 yüan 2. A wall of brick.

洹 yüan 2. A river in Honan.

Abbrev. in

恒 恆 hêng 2. Constance; perseverance; stable; ordinary; commonly.

208

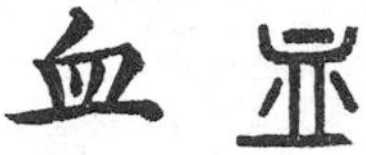

See Lesson 157 D.

血 hsüeh 3 Blood, bloody.

恤 hsü 4. Compassion, to pity; to give alms.

侐 hsü 4. Silent, still.

洫 hsü 4. A trench, a channel.

卹 hsü 4. Compassion, pity.

賉 hsi 2. Alms.

209

旬

See Lesson 54 E.

旬 hsün 2. A period of ten days; of ten years; a set time; to spread.

侚 hsün 4. To conform to.

恂 hsün 2. Sincere, true, frank.

狥 hsün 2. To follow; to accord with; comprehensive.

徇 hsün 2. To follow; according to; pervading.

栒 hsün 3. The crossbeams of a bell or drum frame.

珣 hsün 2. A branching coral.

朐 hsün 2. Larvæ.

眴 hsün 4. A look.

洵 hsün 2. Name of a river. Truly, indeed.

殉 hsün 4. To bury along with the dead; suttee.

迿 hsün 4. To begin a quarrel.

詢 hsün 2. To enquire about.

峋 hsün 2. Hills, hilly.

郇 hsün 2. A feudal state in Shansi.

荀 hsün 2. A proper name.

絢 hsüan 4. Variegated.

拘 hsüan 4. To wave the hand; to strike.

惸 ch'iung 2. Sad, forlorn.

210

See Lesson 46 I.

灰 hui 1. Ashes, embers.

黣 hui 1. An ashy colour.

盔 k'ui 1. A helmet. A porringer.

恢 k'ui 1. Great, liberal; to enlarge.

詼 k'ui 1. To play with, to jest.

211

See Lesson 76 G and A.

囘 回 囬 hui 2. To revert to, to revolve; to turn back; a time, a turn; the Moslems.

茴 hui 2. Fennel.

迴 廻 } hui 2. To come back again, to return.

徊 hui 2. Undecided; irresolute.

恛 hui 2. Disordered; indistinct.

鮰 hui 2. A salmon.

栖 hui 2. A large tree, whose fruit is red.

洄 hui 2. A whirlpool.

蛔 hui 2. The tape worm.

212

夷 𡗝

See Lesson 60 D.

夷 i 2. A barbarian; vulgar; to kill; to feel at ease.

胰 i 2. Soap.

姨 i 2. A wife's sister; a maternal aunt; a concubine.

峓 i 2. A mountain in Corea.

恞 i 2. Pleased, satisfied.

桋 i 2. A beech-tree.

洟 i 2. Snivel, mucus.

鮧 i 2. Silure, *silurus asotus*.

跠 i 2. To sit on the heels.

痍 i 2. An ulcer; a sore.

稊 t'i 2. Tires; a panic grass.

鵜 t'i 2. The pelican.

213

曳 𣌭

See Lesson 50 F.

曳 i 4. To trail, to drag after one.

袘 i 4. The train of a dress; streaming.

䄿 i 4. A kind of rice.

屜 t'i 3. A buffer, a screen, a pillow, etc.

洩 hsieh 4. To leak, to drop; to divulge.

絏 hsieh 4. To tie up, to fetter.

拽 chuai 4. To trail, to drag; to pull.

跩 chuai 4. To hobble; to swing about one's body.

輰 chuai 3. To jolt.

嗖 chuai 1 Conceited language.

214

亦 夾

See Lesson 60 I.

亦 i 4. Also, moreover.

洂 i 4. A proper name.

奕 i 4. Great, fine; to play chess.

弈 i 4. Chess.

帟 i 4. A canopy

跡 chi 4. Trace, foot marks, vestiges, results.

迹 chi 4. Trace, vestiges.

夜 yeh 4. The night. S. 415.

215

任 𠄏

See L. 82 C, and S. 66.

任 jên 4. Sincere; trusted; a duty; a burden; to bear; friendly confidence.

妊 jên 2. Pregnant.

衽 jên 4. The lappet or flap in front of a coat.

紝 jên 2. To weave; to thread.

恁 jên 3. To dwell upon; to consider.

鵀 jên 4. A head-dress of feathers.

賃 lin 4. To let.

216

如 𡛥

See Lesson 88 D.

如 ju 2. As, like; also; to go to; to desire.

洳 ju 2. Moist; to soak in.

茹 ju 2. To eat. Pain.

筎 ju 2. The skin of the bamboo.

絮 ju 4. Lint; tow.

帤 ju 2. A large napkin; a flag.

鴽 ju 2. A quail.

恕 shu 4. Benevolent; to pardon; excusing others.

絮 hsü 4 Down. Loquacity.

217

戎 𢦦

See Lesson 71 O.

戎 jung 2. Arms; soldiers; war. You, your. To assist. Barbarians.

絨 jung 2. Velvet.

毧 jung 2. Down.

狨 jung 2. A tribe of the West.

㧦 jung 2 To aid; to oppose.

㭜 jung 2. Acacia, mimosa.

駥 jung 2. A war-horse; valiant.

狨 jung 2. A gibbon; fierce.

茙 jung 2. A malvaceous plant.

娀 sung 1. A proper name.

䳒 sung 1. A kestrel.

218

See Lesson 30 E.

考 k'ao 3. Longevity; ancestors; to examine.

烤 k'ao 3 To toast; to dry.

拷 k'ao 3. To put to the question.

銬 k'ao 4. Irons, fetters.

栲 k'ao 3. Mangrove.

洘 k'ao 3. To dry up.

219

See Lesson 26 L.

艮 kên 4. Obstinate; to resist.

根 kên 1. Roots; origin, cause; a base.

跟 kên 1. The heel; to follow; to imitate.

詪 kên 3. To wrangle.

茛 kên 4. A wild plant, *ranunculus acris.*

裉 k'ên 3. A fold under the arm.

齦 k'ên 3. To gnaw.

硍 k'ên 3. Rumbling of stones.

貇 k'ên 3. To gnaw. S. 741.

哏 hên 1. Loud, angry tones.

狠 很 hên 3. Dogs quarreling; bad, cruel; very, extremely.

恨 hên 4. Hatred, resentment; sorrow.

痕 hên 4. A scar, a cicatrix.

銀 yin 2. Silver.

珢 yin 2. Stone like jade.

垠 yin 2. Beach, limit.

眼 yen 3. The eye; a hole.

限 hsien 4. A limit; a boundary; a restriction.

閬 hsien 4. The threshold.

Compare the SS. 289 and 578.

220

See Lesson 31 B.

各 ko 3. Each, every.

格 ko 2. To reach; to examine; a rule; a degree; to arrange.

胳 骼 ko 1. The armpit; the side.

蛒 ko 4. A flea.

袼 ko 4. Short sleeves.

觡 ko 2. Horns of a stag.

茖 ko 2. A wild onion.

閣 ko 2. A council-chamber; a cupboard.

擱 ko 1. To put down; to hinder; to differ; to be able; to dispute.

恪 k'o 4. Reverence.

衉 k'o 2. To vomit blood.

客 k'o 4. A guest; a dealer; a traveller. *Hence*

額 o 2. nai 2. yeh 2. The forehead.

恪 ch'iao 4. Reverent and attentive.

貉 ho 4. A badger.

垎 ho 4. To drain.

秴 ho 4. A kind of panic grass.

賂 lu 4. To give a present; to bribe.

輅 lu 4. A chariot.

路 lu 4. A road; to travel. S. 748.

駱 lo 4. A camel.

𠛋 lao 4. To lop off.

雒 lao 4. A kind of bird; fear.

酪 lao 3. Koumiss.

𣧖 lao 4. To die.

珞 lao 4. A necklace.

鵅 lao 4. A water bird, the rail.

硌 lao 4. Stones; to pile up.

絡 lao 4. Fibres.

烙 lao 4. A smoothing-iron.

詻 lao 4. To wrangle.

洛 lao 4. A river in Honan.

落 lao 4. The fall of the leaf; descend.

䀩 lliao 4. To spy, to watch.

畧 略 | liao 4. Limits, disposition, a plan: a little; to make little account of.

撂 liao 4. To lay down.

It is radical in

咎 chiu 1. A fault. S. 338.

221

夸

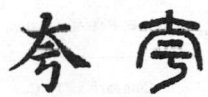

See Lesson 58 G.

夸 k'ua 1. To boast; to overpraise.

誇 k'ua 1. Landatory; conceited.

跨 k'ua 4. To straddle; to step across.

胯 k'ua 4. The thighs: to bestride

姱 k'ua 1. Pretty.

恗 k'ua 4. Self-satisfied.

骻 k'ua 3. The bones of the pelvis.

袴 k'u 4. Trowsers.

刳 k'u 1. To cut open; to rip up.

洿 wu 1. Stagnant water; foul; impure; to soil.

瓠 p'ao 2. A calabash; a gourd.

222

光

See Lesson 24 J.

光 kuang 1. Light; bright; glory; naked; only.

桄 kuang 4. Sago.

絖 kuang 4. Soft floss.

洸 kuang 1. Water sparkling

胱 kuang 1. The bladder.

觥 kung 1. A cup made of horn.

晃 huang 3. Splendour. S. 537

黃 huang 2. Yellow. L. 24. S. 688.

223

匡

See Lesson 79 D.

匡 k'uang 1. Regular.

框 k'uang 4. The frame of a thing; big branches

眶 k'uang 4 The eye-socket.

誆 k'uang 2 Wild; to deceive.

洭 k'uang 1. A river in Hunan.

恇 k'uang 1. To fear; timid.

劻 k'uang 1. Zealous; prompt.

[門匡] k'uang 4. The frame of a door.

筐 k'uang 1. A basket.

224

圭

See Lesson 81 B.

圭 kui 1. A jade sceptre; a sign of rank.

珪 kui 1. A sceptre.

桂 kui 4. The cassia or cynamon tree.

鮭 kui 1. A see-hog.

袿 kui 1. An under-petticoat.

邽 kui 1. A district in Kansu.

閨 kui 1. The gynaeceum; unmarried girls.

筀 kui 1. A kind of bamboo.

跬 k'ui 3. A stride, three cubits.

刲 k'ui 1. To cut open and clean; to stab.

奎 k'ui 2. The stride made by a man; a constellation.

恚 hui 4. Anger, rage

罣 kua 4. Obstacle; cares.

詿 kua 4. To deceive.

挂 kua 4. To suspend.

絓 kua 4. To tie.

卦 kua 4. Diagrams. S. 369.

娃 wa 2. A beautiful woman, *wa-wa*, a baby.

哇 wa 1. Wanton sounds; to retch or vomit.

蛙 wa 1 A kind of frog; wanton, obscene

鼃 wa 1. A frog; obscenities

洼 窪 | wa 1. Low ground; a puddle.

佳 chia 1. Fine, elegant.

街 chieh 1. A street.

鞋 hsieh 2. A shoe.

畦 ch'i 2. A platband.

Compare S. 440.

225

共

See Lesson 47 Q.

共 kung 4 Generally; all.

供 **kung 1.** To offer; to expose; an avowal.

拱 **kung 3.** To salute.

栱 **kung 3.** A pillar; a capital.

[忄共] **kung 3.** Disquietude.

珙 **kung 3.** A stone sceptre or official badge.

恭 **kung 1** To respect; to venerate; to revere

拲 **kung 3.** Handcuffs

龔 **kung 1.** To give, to offer.

洪 **hung 2** An inundation; immense.

哄 **hung 3.** To trick; to cheat.

[言共] **hung 3.** To trick; to cheat.

[月共] **hung 3** To roast.

烘 **hung 1.** A flame.

[音共] **hung 1.** Noise of a market-place.

衖 **hung 4.** A lane.

閧 **hung 4.** To wrangle; to fight.

226

See Lesson 11 F.

巩 **k'ung 3.** To clasp, to embrace; to beat.

恐 **k'ung 3.** To fear; to be afraid; perhaps.

鞏 **kung 3.** A proper-name.

跫 **ch'iung 2.** The tramp of men marching.

[巩木] **ch'iung 2.** To reap ripe grain

銎 **ch'iung 1.** A socket.

蛩 **ch'iung 2.** A cricket; a locust.

It is radical in

筑 **chu 2.** A lute. L. 77 B.

築 **chu 2.** To ram down; to build.

227

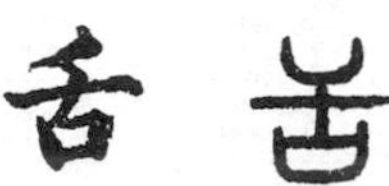

See Lesson 114 C

舌 **kuo 2.** To shut the mouth

括 **k'uo 4.** To contain; to embrace.

聒 **k'uo 4.** Noise, clamour.

佸 **k'uo 4** To meet; coöperation.

适 **k'uo 4.** To make haste; to hasten.

闊 **k'uo 4.** Large, liberal. Far, separation.

蛞 **kua 1** The mole-cricket.

䀨 **kua 4.** To glare at.

栝 **kua 3.** The *Juniperus sinensis*

颳 **kua 1.** To blow, as the wind.

刮 **kua 1** To scrape; to shave off.

鴰 **kua 1.** A crow; a raven.

筈 **kua 1.** The stem of an arrow.

話 **hua 4** A word, a sentence; language.

活 **huo 2.** To live; mobile; active.

佸 **huo 4.** To meet with; to unite; to co operate.

[舌斗] **huo 2.** To scoop up water in a basket and pour it on fields.

Compare L. 102 C.

舌 **shê 2** The tongue.

Radical in

甜 **t'ien 2.** Sweet, agreeable.

餂 **t'ien 3.** To lick, to taste; to seduce.

銛 **t'ien 1** Sharp; to cut.

栝 **t'ien 4.** A poker.

恬 **t'ien 2** Peaceful, calm.

Compare L. 14 C.

舍 **shê 4.** Dwelling.

shê 3. As the following.

捨 **shê 3.** To part with, to renounce; to give alms.

騇 **shê 4.** A mare.

228

See Lesson 52 D

列 **lieh 4.** To arrange; a series.

咧 **lieh 1.** To grimace.

冽 **lieh 4.** Cold.

洌 **lieh 4.** Pure, clear.

挒 **lieh 4** To wring, to break.

栵 **lieh 4.** A kind of chestnut.

[忄列] **lieh 4.** Unquiet.

趔 **lieh 4.** To stumble.

颲 **lieh 4.** A tempest.

茢 **lieh 4.** Sedge; rushes.

烈 **lieh 4** Burning, fiery; virtuous; glorious.

裂 **lieh 4.** To crack; to split; to rip open; a schism.

鴷 **lieh 4.** The wood pecker.

例 li 4. Rules, statute, example.

229

米 米

See Lesson 122 A.

米 mi 3. Grains of rice or millet.

眯 mi 3. Eyes blinded.

侎 mi 3. To calm, to pacify.

鮇 mi 3. Fish-spawn.

敉 mi 3. To feel; to caress; to console.

罙 mi 2. Deep.

麋 mi 2. The tailed deer; difform.

糜 mi 2. Reduced to pulp; to decompose.

迷 mi 2. To confuse; to bewitch; fascinated.

㵟 mi 2. Bewildering; illusion.

謎 mi 2. A riddle; a puzzle.

蒾 mi 2. A plant, the *viburnum dilatatum*.

230

名 名

See Lesson 64 B.

名 ming 2. A name; an appellation; fame.

銘 ming 2. To carve; to engrave.

詺 ming 4. To name.

酩 ming 2. A strong spirit; drunk.

洺 ming 2. A river in Chihli.

茗 ming 2. The teaplant.

231

牟 牟

See Lesson 85 E.

牟 mou 2. To bellow; to usurp.

眸 mou 2. The pupil of the eye.

恈 mou 2. To long for, to covet.

侔 mou 2. Alike, similar.

蛑 mou 2. A crab.

麰 mou 4. Barley.

232

那 那

See Lesson 116.

那 na 4. This, that, there.
na 3. Who? what? where?

哪 na 1. A final particle.

娜 na 2. A buddhist sound.

娜 na 2. A graceful air.

挪 no 2. To move, to remove, to displace.

跡 no 2. To slip.

233

百 百

See Lesson 88 B.

百 pai 3. A hundred; many; all.

佰 pai 3. A hundred.

栢 pai 3. A cypress, a thuja.

貊 mai 4. Wild tribes of the North.

駋 mai 4. A mule.

陌 mai 4. A raised path; a street; a road.

It is radical in

奭 shih 4. A proper name.

It is unconnected with

弼 pi 4. To assist. L. 41 B.

234

𠂢 𠂢

See Lesson 125 E.

𠂢 p'ai 4. To branch off.

派 p'ai 4. To branch, as a river; to ramify; to depute; a sect.

脈 mai 4. A contemptuous look.

脈 mai 4. The arteries; the pulse.

It is unconnected with

旅 lü 3. A troop of soldiers; to travel; exile. L. 117 B.

235

邦 邦

See Lesson 97 A.

邦 pang 1. A state; a country.

梆 pang 1. A watchman's rattle.

綁 pang 3. To tie; to bind.

挷 pang 3. To beat.

鎊 pang 1. A hoe.

幫 pang 1. To help.

236

See Lesson 71 C.

式 **shih** 4. A form, a fashion, a rule; to imitate.

拭 **shih** 4. To wipe, to dust.

試 **shih** 4. To try, to experiment, an essay.

軾 **shih** 4. A support to lean on.

弑 **shih** 4. To murder a superior.

恜 **ch'ih** 4. To fear, to regard with awe.

栻 **ch'ih** 4. A rod used in divination.

鳶 **ch'ih** 4. A crane.

237

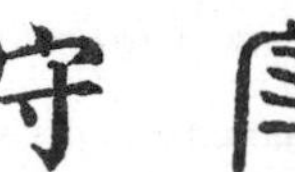

See Lesson 45 D.

守 **shou** 3. To keep; to have in custody; to ward off; to supervise.

狩 **shou** 4. A hunt; an imperial inspecting tour.

238

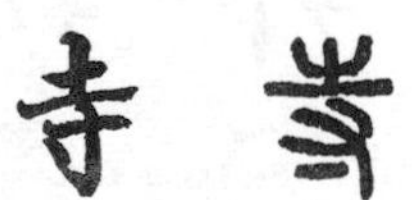

See Lessou 79 B.

寺 **ssŭ** 4. A temple; a court; a eunuch.

詩 **shih** 1. Poetry; verses.

侍 **shih** 4. To help; to wait upon.

恃 **shih** 4. To rely upon; to trust to.

洔 **shih** 3. An islet.

邿 **shih** 1. A place in Shantung.

閗 **shih** 4. A eunuch.

時 旹 } **shih** 2. Time, epoch, situation, opportunity. S. 562.

畤 **shih** 3. A sacrifical mound.

峙 **chih** 3. A hill; to pile up.

庤 **chih** 4. To keep in stock; a magazine.

痔 **chih** 4. Piles.

持 **ch'ih** 2. To seize, to grasp; to hold fast.

待 **tai** 4. To wait for; to await; to treat; as for.

特 **tê** 1. Specially; on purpose.

等 **têng** 3. To wait; a class, a rank; a sort; a sign of the plural.

239

See Lesson 64 E.

多 **to** 1. Many; much; often; too much.

陊 **to** 4. Inclined, to fall.

跢 **to** 4. Unsteady walk.

痑 **to** 3. Exhausted.

庈 **ch'ih** 3. Vast.

眵 **ch'ih** 1. Eyes dim.

誃 **ch'ih** 4. To separate; farewell.

恀 **ch'ih** 2. To cling on.

侈 **ch'ih** 1. Lavish; exaggerated.

爹 **tieh** 1. Father.

栘 **i** 2. A fruit-tree, *aronia asiatica*.

黟 **i** 1. Black; ebony.

移 **i** 2. To remove; to shift.

240

See Lesson 22 C.

朵 朶 } **to** 3. A bud; a flower; the lobe of the ear; numerative of flowers.

剁 剹 } **to** 4. To chop, to mince.

垛 垜 } **to** 3. To pile up; a battlement; a target; a buttress.

躲 **to** 3. To shun; to avoid.

跺 **to** 4. To stamp the foot.

稞 **to** 4. A stack of sheafs.

褋 **to** 3. Long sleeves.

241

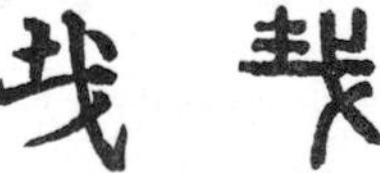

See Lesson 71 H.

𢦏 **ts'ai** 2. To wound; to attack.

裁 **ts'ai** 2. To cut out; to plan; to decide.

哉 **tsai** 1. A final particle.

栽 **tsai** 1. To plant; to transplant.

烖 **tsai 1.** A calamity.

⿺𢦏足 **tsai 1.** To stumble.

載 **tsai 4.** To contain; to load; to record, to quote.
tsai 3. A year.

胾 **tzŭ 4.** Mince-meat.

蛓 **ts'ŭ 4.** Caterpillars with stiff spiny hair.

截 **chieh 2.** To cut, to intercept; to stop.

242

此

See Lesson 112 A.

此 **ts'ŭ 3.** This; here.

玼 **ts'ŭ 2.** A flaw; a fault.

泚 **ts'ŭ 3.** The perspiration.

齜 **ts'u 1.** To gnash one's teeth.

跐 **ts'ŭ 3.** To stand on.

雌 **ts'ŭ 2.** The female of birds.

訾 **ts'ŭ 2.** To slander.

姕 **ts'ŭ 1.** A slattern.

疵 **ts'ŭ 2.** A malady; a bad habit.

骴 **tzŭ 4.** A putrid carcass.

紫 **tzŭ 3.** Purple.

貲 **tzŭ 1.** Property; wealth.

鮆 **tzŭ 1.** A mullet.

鴜 **tzŭ 1.** A cormorant.

⿱此衣 **tzŭ 4.** Clothes crumpled.

眥 **tzŭ 1.** The canthus of the eye.

茈 **tzŭ 3.** *Lithospermum.*

觜 **tsui 3.** A tuft.

嘴 **tsui 3.** The mouth; a mouthpiece; a spout.

砦 ⿰石此 } **chai 4.** A stockade; an encampment.

柴 祡 } **ch'ai 2.** To burn faggots to inform heaven; fuel.

些 **hsieh 1.** A little; few.

243

朿

See Lesson 120 H.

朿 **ts'ŭ 4.** A thorn; to prick.

茦 **ts'ŭ 4.** Thorns.

⿸疒朿 **ts'ŭ 4** The gout.

誎 **ts'ŭ 4.** To criticise; to ridicule.

捒 **ts'ŭ 4.** To help; to beat.

刺 **ts'ŭ 4.** Thorns, to prick, to stab.

蝲 **ts'ŭ 4.** The hedgehog.

莿 **ts'ŭ 4.** Thorns.

刺 **ch'i 1.** To tattoo.

策 **ch'ai 4.** A tablet; a diploma; a ferule; a stratagem.
It is radical in

棗 **tsao 3.** Jujube; the jujube tree.

棘 **chi 4.** Thorny brambles; painful.

責 **chai 2.** To reprove; to chastise, S. 590.

帝 **ti 4.** The Emperor. S. 478.

244

次

See Lesson 99 B.

次 **ts'ŭ 4.** Order, series, time; second, inferior.

佽 **ts'ŭ 4.** To be fitted for; active.

茨 **ts'ŭ 2.** Calthrop.

瓷 **ts'ŭ 2.** Crockery; porcelain.

咨 **tzŭ 1.** To consult; to plan; to propose.

趑 **tzŭ 1.** Unable to advance

粢 **tzŭ 1.** Common millet.

恣 **tzŭ 1.** Licentiousness.

姿 **tzŭ 1.** Beauty.

資 **tsŭ 1.** Property; means of living; capital.

245

𠂤

See Lesson 86 B.

𠂤 **tui 1** To heap.

⿰氵𠂤 **tui 1.** A mass of water.

⿰阝𠂤 **tui 1.** To squat.

追 **chui 1.** To follow; to go back; to revert. S. 626.

歸 **kui 1.** To return; to belong to; to give; addition.

帥 **shuai 4.** A commander, to lead.

師 **shih 1.** An army; a capital city; a teacher. S. 561.

It is radical in

埠 pu 4. A port, a mart.

246

同 同

See Lesson 34 I.

同 t'ung 2. Together; with; alike.

銅 t'ung 2. Copper; brass.

桐 t'ung 2. A varnish tree, *aleurites cordata*.

侗 t'ung 2. Ignorant; simple.

恫 t'ung 2. To be dissatisfied.

垌 t'ung 2. A surname.

挏 t'ung 2. To shake.

鮦 t'ung 2. The snakefish, ophiocephalus.

硐 t'ung 2. To polish.

詷 t'ung 2. To speak precipitately.

峒 t'ung 2. A hill in Kansu.

絧 t'ung 2. Cloth.

𦨴 t'ung 2. A long swift boat.

𧙕 t'ung 2. A coat without sleeves.

㼧 t'ung 2. The upper tiles on a roof.

衕 t'ung 2. A side-street.

筒 t'ung 2. A tube; a pipe.

茼 t'ung 2. A mugwort.

痌 t'ung 1. To moan; an ulcer.

洞 tung 4. A cavern, a hole; to comprehend; to see through.

姛 tung 4. A graceful gait.

胴 tung 4. The large intestine.

[同弋] tung 4. Boards of a boat.

247

危 危

See Lesson 59 H

危 wei 2. Perilous: precipitous.

鮠 wei 1. A kind of shad.

桅 wei 2. A mast.

洈 wei 2. A river in Hupeh.

峗 wei 2. A mountain in Kansu.

詭 kui 3. To deceive; cunning.

跪 kui 4. To kneel.

恑 kui 3. To change; a metamorphose.

垝 kui 3. In ruins.

脆 ts'ui 4. Crisp; brittle.

248

羊 羊

See Lesson 103 A.

羊 yang 2. A sheep or goat.

洋 yang 2. The ocean; vast.

烊 yang 2. To roast; to heat.

蛘 yang 2 The weevil.

徉 yang 2. To ramble; to stray.

佯 yang 2. False; deceitful.

垟 yang 2. A tutelary genius.

恙 yang 4. Illness; indisposition.

痒 yang 3. Itching.

詳 hsiang 2. To examine; to explain; minutely.

祥 hsiang 2. Felicitous; of good omen.

翔 hsiang 2. To soar; to roam about.

庠 hsiang 2. A school; an asylum for the old.

It is radical in

羴 shan 1. Rank-smelling.

羼 ch'an 3. A herd.

Radical 123.

249

See Lesson 60 B.

因 yin 1. A cause; then; because.

姻 yin 1. Marriage.

駰 yin 1. Dapple-gray.

裀 yin 1. Underclothes.

絪 yin 1. Hemp linen.

鞇 yin 1. Leather.

欭 yin 1. To lisp.

茵 yin 1 A mat.

氤 yin 1. Warm genial aura, procreation.

[鹿因] yin 1. A female deer.

烟 yen 1 Smoke.

咽 yen 4. To swallow.

胭 yen 1. Cosmetics.

恩 ên 1. Favour; grace; mercy; affection.

250

有 𠂇

See Lesson 46 H.

有 yu 3. To have, to be.

侑 yu 4. To encourage; to help.

栯 yu 4. A species of pear-tree.

蛕 yu 3. The tænia.

姷 yu 4. To assist; a pair; a couple.

囿 yu 4. To inclose; a park; a garden.

宥 yu 4. To forgive; to be lenient.

洧 wei 3. A river in Honan.

鮪 wei 3. A sturgeon.

痏 wei 3. A bruise.

賄 hui 4. Goods; to bribe; hush-money.

郁 yü 4. A place in Shansi. Elegance.

251

羽 羽

See Lesson 62 E.

羽 yü 3. Wings, feathers.

詡 hsü 3. To boast; to brag.

珝 hsü 3. A precious stone.

栩 hsü 3. A species of oak.

羿 i 4. A surname.

翌 i 4. Bright; to-morrow.

翊 i 4. To cooperate.

252

折 折

See Lesson 48 D.

折 chê 2. To snap in two; to break; to barter.

浙 chê 4. A river in *Chêkiang.*

踥 chê 4. Crippleness.

鞢 chê 4. A scabbard.

哳 } 哲 } chê 4. Light; to discern; wise.

哲 chê 4. Philosophy.

悊 chê 4. Wisdom.

蜇 chê 2. To sting; a sting.

蜇 chê 4. Infection.

碏 ch'ê 4. To stone.

誓 shih 4. To swear; to take an oath; a contract.

逝 shih 4. To pass away; to die.

253

岑 岑

See Lesson 14 Q.

岑 ch'ên 1. A lone peak; lofty; lone.

涔 ch'ên 2. A puddle; a pool.

頷 ch'ên 3. Coarse; ugly.

㑗 chên 4. Inclined, bent.

254

辰 辰

See Lesson 30 B.

辰 ch'ên 2. A cyclic character; a part of time; the heavenly bodies.

祳 ch'ên 3. A sacrifice offered in war-time.

蜃 ch'ên 3. A marine monster; mirage.

晨 ch'ên 2. Morning; dawn.

宸 ch'ên 2. The palace. Imperial.

麎 ch'ên 2. The female of the elk.

娠 chên 1. Pregnancy.

振 chên 4. To move; to shake; to stir up.

賑 chên 4. A gift; a help; alms.

桭 chên 3. A beam; a timber.

帪 chên 1. A muzzle.

侲 chên 4. A lad; a boy.

震 chên 4. To shake; to shock.

脣 } 唇 } ch'un 2. The lips.

漘 ch'un 2. Side, bank.

255

呈 呈

See Lesson 81 H.

呈 ch'êng 2. To state clearly.

程 ch'êng 2. A weight; a measure; a rule; a pattern; a degree; a period; to fix.

裎 ch'êng 2. To take off clothes; naked.
逞 ch'êng 3. Recklessness.
程 ch'êng 2. To raise.
埕 ch'êng 2. A jar.
惺 ch'êng 3. Obscure.
鋥 ch'êng 2. To polish.
徎 ch'êng 2. A by-path.
珵 ch'êng 2. A precious stone.
涅 ch'êng 2. To paste.
酲 ch'êng 2. Drunk.

桯 t'ing 1. A bed.

郢 ying 3. A place in Hupeh.

It is radical in

聖 shêng 4. Wise; holy; perfect.
鐵 t'ieh 3. Iron. L. 81 H.

256

See Lesson 84.

忌 chi 4. To avoid; to abstain.
跽 chi 4. To kneel long.
娽 chi 4. Envy, jealousy.

257

See Lesson 27 F.

夾 chia 1. To press; to squeeze; double.
袷 chia 2. A lined coat.
鋏 chia 1. Pincers.

蛺 chia 4. A butterfly.
梜 chia 4. Pincers; a box.
睞 chia 4. To twinkle.
郟 chia 4. A place in Honan.
莢 chia 4. Pods; husks.
筴 chia 1. Pincers; to pinch.

峽 hsia 2. A mountain pass.
狹 hsia 2. Narrow.
郟 hsia 3. A gorge; a defile.
浹 hsia 4. Moist; soaked. A circuit; a period.
硤 hsia 4. A place in Hupeh.
頰 hsia 4. The chia.

挾 hsieh 2. To pinch.
俠 hsieh 1. A hero.

俠 chieh 1. Brave, a hero.

愜 ch'ieh 4. Pleased; cheerful.
匧 ch'ieh 4. A trunk; a chest.
愜 ch'ieh 4. Pleased; satisfied.
篋 ch'ieh 4. A trunk; a satchel.

It is radical in

瘞 i 4. To bury.
懕 i 4. Peace; respect; retired.

It is unconnected with

陝 shên 3. Province of *Shensi*.

258

See Lesson 47 E.

戒 chieh 4. To refrain from; abstinence; to warn.

誡 chieh 4. A precept, a prohibition; to warn.
祴 chieh 4. A song.
悈 chieh 4. To enjoin on.

挭 hsieh 4. To hold; to bear.
械 hsieh 4. Weapons; arms.

259

見

See Lesson 158 C.

見 chien 4. To see; to apprehend; experience.
梘 chien 4. A wooden peg.
覷 chien 3. Soda.
筧 chien 3. A bamboo pipe.

見 hsien 4. To appear; manifest.
現 hsien 4. Present; visible; now.
峴 hsien 2. A steep hill.
睍 hsien 3. To look at with fear.
蜆 hsien 3. Mussels or clams.
俔 hsien 4. To observe; to spy.
晛 hsien 2. The sun appearing.
哯 hsien 4. To vomit.
垷 hsien 3. Mud; mire.
鋧 hsien 4. A chisel.
莧 hsien 4. Spinach.

硯 yen 4. Inkstone.

It is radical in

規 kui 1. Rule. S 624.
視 shih 4. To consider. Radical 147.

260

志

See Lesson 79 B.

志 **chih 4.** Resolution; will; fixity of purpose. Records.

誌 **chih 4.** To record; annals.

鋕 **chih 4.** To engrave.

[illegible] **chih 4.** To examine.

[illegible] **chih 4.** A plant, *polygala*, used in fevers.

261

See Lesson 44 L.

[illegible] **chin 4.** To sweep.

[illegible] **chin 4.** To seize.

浸 **chin 1.** To soak; to penetrate; gradually.

濅 **chin 1.** A marsh; gradually.

唚 **ch'in 4.** To vomit; to spit forth.

駸 **ch'in 1.** A fleet horse.

鋟 **ch'in 1.** To engrave.

綅 **ch'in 1.** Tassels; fringes.

侵 **ch'in 1.** To usurp; to encroach upon.

[illegible] **ch'in 4.** A stomp.

寑 **ch'in 4.** A proper name.

寢 **ch'in 3.** To sleep; to rest; apartments.

蓡 **shên 1.** In *hai-shên* sea-slugs; *jên-shên* ginseng.

262

巠

See Lesson 12 H.

巠 **ching 1.** Streams running under ground.

經 **ching 1.** Warp in a loom; veins or arteries; meridians of longitude; to pass through; to regulate; canonical; already.

涇 **ching 1.** A river; to flow.

桱 **ching 4.** A kind of pine.

剄 **ching 3.** To cut one's throat.

徑 **ching 4.** A diameter. Shortest way.

陘 **ching 4.** A path.

逕 **ching 4** To pass.

脛 **ching 4.** Shank; shin-bone.

[illegible] **ching 1.** A place in Shantung.

輕 **ch'ing 1.** Light; easy; frivolous.

娙 **hsing 2.** A handsome woman.

蛵 **hsing 2.** The dragon-fly.

莖 **kêng 3.** Stalks.

頸 **kêng 3.** The neck; the throat.

硜 **k'êng 1.** Clashing; obstinate.

挳 **k'êng 1.** To knock against; to attack.

牼 **k'êng 1.** A proper name.

勁 **chin 4.** Strength.

263

·求

See Lesson 45 K.

求 **ch'iu 2.** To beg; to entreat; to pray for; to aim at.

球 **ch'iu 2.** A ball; a globe.

蛷 **ch'iu 2.** The millipede.

浗 **ch'iu 2.** Chilblain.

賕 **ch'iu 2.** To bribe.

俅 **ch'iu 2.** Elegant.

銶 **ch'iu 2.** A pick.

梂 **ch'iu 2.** An acorn.

觩 **ch'iu 2.** Horns; strong; robust.

絿 **ch'iu 2.** Urgent; pressing.

[illegible] **ch'iu 2.** The *membrum virile*.

逑 **ch'iu 2.** To assemble; society.

毬 **ch'iu 2.** A ball.

莍 **ch'iu 2.** A pepper tree; *xanthoxylum*.

裘 **ch'iu 2.** Fur garments.

盚 **ch'iu 2.** A proper name.

捄 **chiu 1.** To carry ground.

救 **chiu 4.** To rescue; to save from; to help.

[illegible] **chiu 4.** Diligent; to be pleased.

264

助

See Lesson 20 E.

助 **chu 4.** To help; to succour.

筯 chu 4. Chopsticks.

鋤 ch'u 2. A hoe; to hoe.

耡 ch'u 2. To till.

勗 hsü 4 To help; to encourage.

265

壯

See Lesson 127 B.

壯 chuang 4. Strong; robust.

裝 chuang 1. To dress; to pack; to contain.

娤 chuang 1. To dress; to bedeck.

奘 chuang 4. Large; thick; stout.

莊 chuang 1. Agriculture; a farm; a village; sedate; grave.

266

See Lesson 32 F.

局 chü 2. A chess-board. A position; circumstances. An association.

鋦 chü 1. A clasp; to hook.

挶 chü 4. A handle; to hold.

侷 chü 4. Crippled.

梮 chü 2. To put spikes on.

跼 chü 4. Bent down; to salute.

267

See Lesson 44 C.

君 chün 1. Sovereign; prince; ruler; a gentleman; sir.

郡 chün 4. A city; a district.

涒 chün 1 Winding; meandering.

捃 chün 4. To sort; to arrange; to pick out.

窘 chün 3. Afflicted; in distress.

莙 chün 1. Beet.

裙 ch'ün 2. An apron.

帬 ch'ün 2. A skirt.

羣 群 ch'ün 2. A flock; a herd; a crowd.

焄 hsün 1. Fumes from sacrifices.

268

See Lesson 133 A.

否 fao 3. Not, or not.

痞 p'i 3. Obstruction.

嚭 p'i 3. Great. A surname.

咅 t'ou 4. To interrupt.

Compare the SS. 79 and 146.

269

See Lesson 97 A.

夆 fêng 1. To butt; to oppose.

峯 峰 fêng 1. The peak of a mountain.

蜂 fêng 1. A bee; a wasp; a hornet.

烽 fêng 1. A beacon fire-place.

䀱 fêng 2. Slightly open eyelids.

鋒 fêng 1. A sharp point; a vanguard.

逢 fêng 2. To meet; to happen; to incur. S. 608.

髼 p'êng 2. Tangled hair.

捀 p'êng 2. To whirl.

韸 p'êng 4. The noise of drums.

270

See Lesson 94 B.

孚 fu 2. Confidence; sympathy.

俘 fu 2. A prisoner of war; a captive.

浮 fu 2. To float; to drift; volatile; silly.

蜉 fu 2. Ant.

桴 fu 2. A raft.

烰 fu 2. To boil; to cook.

稃 fu 2. Bran of rice.

郛 fu 2. A suburb; a collection.

莩 fu 1. The epidermis of plants; intimacy.

罦 fu 2. A net; a snare.

乳 ju 2. Milk; to suckle; the breasts.

脬 p'ao 1. The bladder.

捊 p'ao 2. To seize; to hold.

殍 p'iao 3. To die of hunger.

271

See Lesson 109 D.

甫 fu 3. To begin; just now; a name.

脯 fu 3. Dried meat.

哺 fu 3. To feed.

輔 fu 3. To help: to assist; a minister.

黼 fu 3. Embroidery.

鬴 fu 3. A caldron; a measure.

魆 fu 3. Name ot a star.

尃 fu 1. To 'diffuse; ample. SS. 528, 753.

簠 簠 fu 3. A basket used at worship

捕 pu 3. To seize; to catch; the police.

賻 pu 3. To give a fee.

補 pu 3. To patch; to mend; to add on.

晡 pu 1. The time from 3 to 5 p. m.

埔 pu 3. A plain; a port.

悑 pu 4. Fear.

庯 pu 1. A roof.

鋪 p'u 1. To spread out

舖 p'u 1. A shop.

餔 p'u 4. To eat.

誧 p'u 1. To amplify.

踊 p'u 1. Track; scent.

逋 p'u 1. To flee.

鯆 p'u 1. The ray.

酺 p'u 2. A feast; to drink deep.

圃 p'u 3. A garden.

痡 p'u 1. Sickness; debility.

莆 p'u 2. Sedge-grass.

匍 p'u 2. To crawl.

葡 p'u 2. The vine.

浦 p'u 2. Shore.

蒲 p'u 3. A kind of rush; rush; mats.

牖 yu 4. A window; to teach.

272

See Lesson 14 L.

含 han 2. To hold in the mouth; to contain; to restrain; doubt.

唅 han 2. To feed by hand.

琀 han 2. Gems put into the mouth of a corpse.

谽 han 2. A cavern.

欲 han 1. To restrain.

瓴 han 2. A drain; a pipe.

頷 han 3. The chin; to bent the head.

273

See Lesson 102 A.

旱 han 4. Drought.

悍 han 4. Fierce; cruel; violent.

垾 han 4. A bank; a dyke.

捍 han 4. To ward off; to defend.

睅 han 3. Protuberant eyes.

銲 han 4. To solder.

駻 han 4. A vicious horse.

皲 han 4. Leather armlets for archers.

趕 kan 3. To pursue; quickly; when.

稈 kan 3. The stalk of millet.

桿 kan 1. A pole.

鶗 k'an 3. A nightingale. Compare the S. 22.

274

See L. 75 D, and S. 359

亨 hêng 1. To pervade; to persevere; efficacity; success.

哼 hêng 1. To moan; to hum.

脝 hêng 1. Fat; puffed up.

烹 p'êng 1. To boil; to cook.

275

See Lesson 35 D.

希 hsi 1. Few; rare; seldom; to hope.

俙 hsi 1. To appear.

唏 hsi 1. To chuckle.

悕 hsi'1. To consider; to compassionate.

晞 hsi 1. The dawn; to dry in the sun.

浠 hsi 1. A river in Hupeh.

睎 hsi 1. To long for; to gaze at.

豨 hsi 1. Swine; pigs grunting.

稀 hsi 1. Thin; scattered; separated; few; rare.

鼾 hsi 3. To snore.

欷 hsi 1. To sob; to whimper.

郗 hsi 1. Name of a city.

餙 shih 4. To adorn.

絺 ch'ih 1. Muslin.

瓻 **ch'ih 1.** An amphora.

276

See Lesson 30 E.

孝 **hsiao 4.** Filial piety; mourning.

哮 **hsiao 1.** To scream; to pant.

痚 **hsiao 1.** Asthma.

庨 **hsiao 1.** Grand; imposing.

It is unconnected with

教 **chiao 1.** To teach.
敎 **chiao 4.** Doctrines; sects; schools; to cause; to make.

酵 **chiao 4.** Leaven; to ferment.

See Lesson 39 H.

277

See Lesson 18 J.

肖 **hsiao 4.** To be like.

硝 **hsiao 1.** Saltpetre.

消 **hsiao 1.** To melt; to consume.

銷 **hsiao 1.** To melt; to consume; to expend; to cancel.

逍 **hsiao 1.** To roam; to saunter.

綃 **hsiao 1.** Raw silk.

焇 **hsiao 1.** To torrefy.

蛸 **hsiao 1.** The egg-cocoon of the mantis.

⿰麥肖 **hsiao 3.** Grits.

魈 **hsiao 1.** Mountain goblins.

鮹 **hsiao 1.** An eel.

削 **hsiao 1.** To cut; to pare; to erase.

宵 **hsiao 1.** Night; darkness.

霄 **hsiao 1.** The sky; heavens.

痟 **hsiao 1.** Headache.

俏 **ch'iao 4.** Handsome; like; elegant.

悄 **ch'iao 3.** Grief; care; silent; still.

誚 **ch'iao 4.** To ridicule.

陗 **ch'iao 4.** Steep cliffs; strict.

峭 **ch'iao 4.** Steep cliffs. Severity.

鞘 **ch'iao 4.** A sheath; a scabbard.

髾 **shao 1.** A tail; long hair.

筲 **shao 1.** A bucket.

莦 **shao 1.** Jungle grass.

哨 **shao 4.** To whistle; a patrol.

捎 **shao 1.** To carry.

䘯 **shao 1.** The lapel of a coat.

弰 **shao 1.** The ends of a bow.

艄 **shao 1.** The stern of a vessel.

颵 **shao 1.** To dry in the wind.

娋 **shao 1.** The eldest sister.

梢 **shao 1.** Twigs, small.

旓 **shao 1.** Fringes of a flag.

稍 **shao 3.** A little; a trifle.

潲 **shao 4.** Water driven by the rain.

趙 **chao 4.** A surname.

It is unconnected with

屑 **hsieh 4.** A trine.

⿰忄屑 **hsieh 4.** Sorrow.

⿰彳屑 **hsieh 4.** To shake; to float.

榍 **hsieh 4.** Chestnut tree.

⿰扌屑 **hsieh 1.** To pull out a stoper.

糏 **hsieh 4.** Grits.

See L. 65 D.

278

秀

See Lesson 23 B.

秀 **hsiu 4.** Growing grain coming into ear; luxuriant; a licentiate.

銹 **hsiu 4.** Rust of metal.

綉 **hsiu 4.** To embroider.

琇 **hsiu 4.** Coarse jade.

莠 **niu 3.** Tares. *Yu 3.*

誘 **yu 4.** To allure; to entice, to seduce.

⿰虫秀 **yu 3.** A moth.

透 **t'ou 4.** To pass through.

279

See Lesson 82 G.

𦣝 **i 2.** The chin.

⿰月𦣝 **i 2.** The fat between the viscera.

⿰魚𦣝 **i 2.** A sea-hog.

頤 **i 2.** The chin.

宧 **i 2.** A dining-hall; to feed.

280

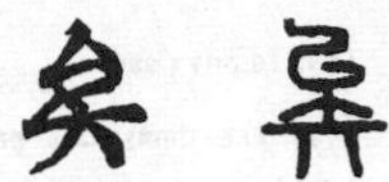

See Lesson 85 E.

矣 i 3. A final particle.

娭 hsi 1. A girl; to play.

誒 hsi 1. To giggle.

埃 yeh 2. Dust.

挨 ai 1. To suffer; to lean on; near.

唉 ai 3. To belch.

欸 ai 1. To moan.

俟 ssŭ 4. To wait upon.

涘 ssŭ 4. A river bank.

281

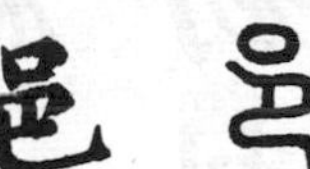

See Lesson 74 C.

邑 i 4. A walled city.

唈 i 4. Shortness of breath.

挹 i 1. To bale out; to decant.

浥 i 4. Damp; soaked.

悒 i 4. Disquiet; anxiety.

俋 i 4. Strong, robust.

[illegible] i 4. Salted fish.

裛 i 4. A bag; a sheath.

It is radical in

邕 yung 1. A moat. S. 769.

282

告

See Lesson 132 B.

告 kao 4. To tell; to announce to; to indict.

誥 kao 4. To announce to.

郜 kao 3. A place in Shantung.

酷 k'ao 4. Fierce; cruel; very; excessive.

焅 k'ao 4. Hot air; to dry.

靠 k'ao 4. To lean upon; to rely upon.

窖 chiao 4. A cellar.

硞 ch'iao 4. Stony; rocky.

浩 hao 4. A flood; vast; grand.

悎 hao 4. Fear; anxiety.

皓 hao 4. White; bright; huminous.

造 tsao 4. To make; to create; to build; parties to a suit.

慥 ts'ao 4. Sincere.

糙 ts'ao 1. Coarse paddy; inferior.

鵠 ku 3. The snow-goose; a target.

梏 ku 4. Manacles; fetters.

酷 k'u 4. Tyrannical; cruel; extremely.

嚳 k'u 1. To inform. A proper name.

283

更

See Lesson 41 A.

更 kêng 4. More; further. kêng 1. To change, to alter; a night watch.

梗 kêng 3. Thorny; stubborn; an outline.

哽 kêng 3. Choking; sobs.

埂 kêng 3. A ditch or channel.

綆 kêng 3. A well-rope.

骾 kêng 3. Hard, firm, unyielding.

鯁 kêng 3. Fish-bones.

㾘 kêng 3. Disease; sickness.

更 ching 1. Night watch.

粳 稉 } ching 1. White rice.

硬 ying 4. Hard; strong; obstinate.

It is radical in

便 pien 4. Convenient. S. 474.

甦 su 1. To revive.

284

A double Series.

谷

See Lesson 17 H.

谷 ch'iao 4. The upper lip. *It forms*

卻 ch'iao 4. To refuse; to leave; certainly; but.

脚 chiao 3. Feet; base.

⿰口卻 **ch'i 4.** To laugh boisterously.

⿰彳卻 **ch'i 4.** Labour; toil.

綌 **hsi 4.** Coarse linen.

郤 **hsi 4.** A ravine; a defect.

谷

See Lesson 18 E.

谷 **ku 4.** A valley; a ravine; the bed of a torrent.

㗇 **ku 3.** The cry of a pheasant.

裕 **yü 4.** Abundant; plenty; generous.

浴 **yü 4.** To bathe.

峪 **yü 4.** A ravine; a gully.

鋊 **yü 4.** A poker.

鵒 **yü 4.** The thrush.

欲 **yü 4.** To wish; to covet; to like.

慾 **yü 4.** Desire; lust; passion.

俗 **hsü 2.** Common; worldly; customs.

It is radical in

豁 **huo 1.** An opening; large; clear; to penetrate.

容 **jung 2.** To bear; to contain. S. 542.

睿 **hsün 4.** A ravine. L. 118 D. *Hence*

壑 **ho 4.** A ditch, a canal.

285

狂

See Lesson 79 D.

狂 **k'uang 2.** Mad; wild.

誑 **k'uang 2.** Lies; to deceive.

⿰氵狂 **k'uang 2.** Inundation.

⿰彳狂 **k'uang 2.** Abrupt; quick.

逛 **kuang 4.** To stroll; to ramble: to toss about.

286

See Lesson 119 B.

困 **k'un 4.** Fatigue; distress; poverty.

睏 **k'un 4.** To nod; sleepy.

捆 **k'un 3.** To bind; to tie up; a bunch.

綑 **k'un 3.** To bind.

稇 **k'un 3.** A sheaf.

梱 **k'un 3.** A threshold.

悃 **k'un 3.** Loyalty.

閫 **k'un 4.** Gynæceum.

287

See Lesson 149 D.

里 **li 3.** A hamlet; the third of a mile.

理 **li 3.** Veins; striæ; to rule; to manage; abstract right; the first principle.

狸 **li 2.** A fox.

娌 **li 3.** The wives of brothers; sisters-in-law

鯉 **li 3** The carp.

⿰巾里 **li 3.** A mat sail.

俚 **li 3.** Rude; rustic.

哩 **li 1.** A final particle.

梩 **li 2.** A wheel-barrow.

悝 **li 3.** To pity; sad.

厘 **li 2.** The thousandth part of a tael.

裏 裡 } **li 3.** Inside; lining; inner.

貍 **li 1.** The wild cat.

埋 **mai 2.** To bury; to conceal; to hoard.

It is radical in

廛 **ch'an 2.** A domain. S. 795.

野 **yeh 3.** Waste land; wilderness; rustic. L. 95 A. *Hence*

墅 **shu 4.** A cottage; a villa; a farm.

It is unconnected with

量 **liang 2.** To measure. L. 70 F.

288

利

See Lesson 52 F.

利 **li 4.** Sharp; interest on money; profit.

俐 **li 4.** Clever; active.

唎 **li 4.** A sound.

蜊 **li 4.** A clam.

颲 **li 4.** Driving wind and rain.

痢 **li 4.** Dysentery.

莉 **li 4.** The jasmine

棃 梨 } **li 2.** The Chinese pear.

愸 悡 li 2. To hate; hatred.

黧 li 2. Dun colour.

犂 犁 li 2. A plough; the Tibetan yak. *I-li*, Chinese Turkestan.

黎 li 2. Black.

瓈 li 1. Vitreous.

藜 li 2. A thistle.

289

See Lesson 75 F.

良 liang 2. Virtuous; good; natural gifts.

粮 liang 2. Grain, food.

晾 liang 4. To expose to the sun.

量 liang 2. To measure; to consider. L. 75 F.

狼 lang 2. The wolf.

蜋 lang 2. Different kinds of insects.

浪 lang 4. Waves; profligacy.

琅 lang 2. Enamel.

埌 lang 4. Waste land.

鋃 lang 2. A chain.

桹 lang 2. The sago-tree.

踉 lang 1. To jump.

躴 lang 2. Tall.

哴 lang 4. To wail.

烺 lang 2. Fire; blaze.

誏 lang 3. To play upon words.

稂 lang 2. Weeds.

崀 lang 2. A proper name.

㝗 lang 2. Empty, desert.

筤 lang 2. Young bamboos.

莨 lang 2. Hay.

閬 lang 4. A high door; spacious.

郎 lang 2. A gentleman; a title. S. 460.

朗 lang 3. Clear; bright.

Abbrev. in

娘 孃 niang 2. A woman; a wife; a mother.

290

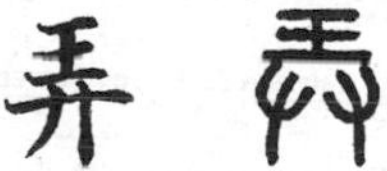

See Lesson 47 F.

弄 lung 4. To handle: to play with; to deceive.

挵 lung 4. To make a fool of.

弄 nung 4. To handle.

弄 nêng 4. To handle.

倰 nêng 4. To make a fool of.

哢 nêng 4. To chirp.

Compare S. 780.

291

See Lesson 90 F.

呂 lü 3. Vertebrae; tunes.

侶 lü 3. A comrade.

梠 lü 3. Small column; lintel.

閭 lü 2. A village; the gate of a village.

鑢 lü 4. To polish; a file.

櫚 lü 2. Cocoa-tree.

藺 lü 2. A species of *euphorbia*.

筥 chü 3. An osier basket.

莒 chü 3. A textile plant.

It is radical in

躳 躬 kung 1. To bow the body. L. 90 F. *This is phonetic contracted in*

宫 kung 1. A palace; castration; a eunuch; constellations.

292

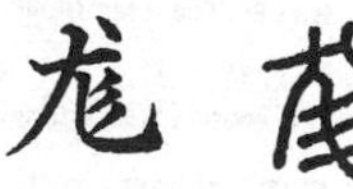

See Lesson 49 C.

寽 lüeh 4. To hold.

捋 lüeh 4. To draw through.

鋝 lüeh 4. Twenty ounces.

浖 lüeh 4. Embankment.

桴 lüeh 4. Wood for dyeing.

埒 lüeh 4. Weak.

殍 lüeh 4. Exhausted.

埓 lüeh 4. Enclosure.

捋 lo 4. To draw through.

酹 lo 4. Libation.

293

See Lesson 134 C.

尨 mang 2. A molossus.

猇 mang 2. A shaggy-haired dog.
哤 mang 2. A jargon.
牻 mang 3. A bull.
浝 mang 2. A river in Honan.
駹 mang 2. A spotted horse.
恾 mang 2. Stupid, dull.
厖 厐 mang 2. A rock; great; abundance.

294

See Lesson 67 P.

每 mei 3. Each; every.
酶 mei 2. Leaven used in fermenting.
梅 mei 2. Plums; prunes.
脢 mei 2. Breast of an animal.
鋂 mei 2. A ring, a chain.
莓 mei 2. Malt.
苺 mei 2. Strawberries.
痗 mei 4. A heart-disease.
霉 mei 2. Damp; wet.

䀀 hui 4. The three upper lines of a diagram.
誨 hui 3. To teach.
悔 hui 3. To repent; to regret.
晦 hui 4. Dark; obscure; unlucky.

海 hai 3. The sea; immensity; a crowd.

The sound was altered in

敏 min 3. Clever; witty.

It is radical in

毓 yü 4. To nurture; to rear. L. 94 F.

繁 fan 2. Luxuriant; abundant; numerous.

295

See Lesson 106 A.

免 mien 3. To avoid; to evade; to spare.
勉 mien 3. To make an effort; to excite.
俛 mien 3. To make an effort.
挽 mien 3. Parturition.
鮸 mien 3. A yellow fish.
帨 mien 4. A mourning cap.
冕 mien 3. A cap of ceremony.

悗 man 2. To err; to deceive.
鞔 man 2. A sole; to cover with leather.

晚 wan 3. The evening; late.
挽 wan 3. To lead; to drag; to draw back.
輓 wan 3. A hearse.
娩 wan 3. Complaisant.

絻 wên 4. Mourning-clothes.

The sound was altered in

浼 mei 3. To defile; to soil.

Compare L. 106 B.

兎 t'u 4. A hare. *Hence*
冤 yüan 1. Injustice.
逸 i 4. Lust.

296

See Lesson 81 A.

呈 nieh 1. To fill up.

涅 nieh 1. Slime.
埕 nieh 1. To fill up.
捏 nieh 1. To knead with the fingers.
陧 nieh 4. Disorder; danger.

Compare S. 735.

297

我 (seal form)

See Lesson 71 Q.

我 o 3. I; me; my.
俄 o 3. Sudden.
餓 o 4. Hungry.
蛾 o 2. A moth.
硪 o 2. A rocky cliff.
誐 o 2. To recite.
哦 o 2. To chant.
鵝 o 2. The domestic goose.
峩 峨 o 2. High; eminent; a mountain in Ssŭch'uan.
莪 o 2. A species of artemisia.

我 wo 3. I; me; my.
蛾 wo 2. A moth.
餓 wo 4. Hungry.
鵝 wo 2. A goose.

It is radical in

義 i 4. Justice. S. 737. *Hence*
羲 hsi 1. A proper name.

298

See Lesson 161 A.

貝 pei 4. A cowry; valuables; money.

梖 **pei 4.** The fan-palm.

[illegible] **pei 4.** A young heifer.

珼 **pei 4.** Inlaid work.

狽 **pei 4.** A gerboa; hindrance.

[illegible] **pei 4.** A liliaceous plant, *fritillaria.*

敗 **pai 4.** A defeat; to ruin; to destroy.

唄 **pai 4.** Buddhist psalmody.

299

坒

See Lesson 27 I.

坒 **pi 4.** To compare; to match; to equal.

陛 **pi 4.** Steps; the Throne.

梐 **pi 4.** A stockade.

蜌 **pi 4.** Mussels.

諀 **p'i 1.** Mistaken; wrong.

[illegible] **p'i 3.** Limp; weak.

狴 **p'i 3.** A fierce animal.

300

甹

See Lesson 58 C.

甹 **p'in 2.** To manifest one's feelings.

俜 **p'in 2.** A confident.

娉 **p'in 1.** Elegant.

聘 **p'in 4.** To enquire about; to invite by presents; to engage; to betroth.

騁 **ch'êng 3.** To run
Compare L. 65 K.

301

See Lesson 79 G.

孛 **po 4.** To beget.

餑 **po 1.** Cakes; biscuits.

脖 **po 2.** The neck.

桲 **po 4.** A flail.

[illegible] **po 4.** Dust.

浡 **po 4.** Suddenly.

[illegible] **po 4.** The chaff of rice.

鵓 **po 4.** A wood pigeon.

勃 **po 4.** Suddenly.

渤 **po 4.** Sound of waves.

挬 **p'o 4.** To pluck up.

悖 **pei 4.** Rebellious; to oppose.

誖 **pei 4.** A quarrel; a revolt.

[illegible] **pei 4.** Obscure; dark.

[illegible] **pei 4.** To resist.

荸 **pi 2.** Tulipa edulis, *pi-chi.*

302

沙

See Lesson 18 M, SS. 80 and 465.

沙 **sha 1.** Sand; gravel; pebbles.

痧 **sha 1.** The cholera.

裟 **sha 1.** A Buddhist cassock.

鯊 **sha 1.** A shark.

[illegible] **sha 1.** To bind; to tie up; to gird.

[illegible] **sha 1.** A species of *pyrus.*

[illegible] **sha 1.** Long fine hair.

桫 **so 1.** A tree, *shorea robusta.*

挱 挲 **so 1.** To feel, to palp.

莎 **so 1.** A species of sedge.

娑 **so 1.** To saunter; to meditate.

[illegible] **so 1.** Abundant vegetation.

303

束

See Lesson 120 I.

束 **shu 4.** To bind; to tie up; to restrain.

疎 **shu 1.** Distant; to separate; lax; careless.

[illegible] **shu 4.** To rinse; to suck in.

綀 **shu 1.** A sackcloth.

觫 **su 4.** To fear; to tremble

[illegible] **su 4.** To shake the head.

涑 **su 1.** A river in Shansi.

[illegible] **su 4.** A kind of birchtree.

餗 **su 4.** Boiled grain.

速 **su 4.** To urge; speedily; quickly.

[illegible] **su 4.** A cricket.

欶 **sou 4.** To cough. S. 647.

It is radical in

敕 勅 } ch'ih 4. An Imperial Edict.

剌 la 2. To cut. S. 459.

悚 sêng 3. Fear; terror.

304

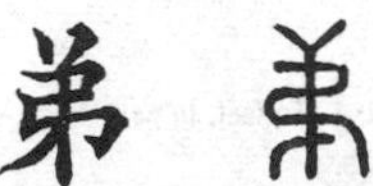

See Lesson 87 E.

弟 ti 4. A younger brother; a disciple.

悌 ti 4. To behave as a younger brother should; submission.

娣 ti 4. A young sister or sister-in-law; a girl.

睇 ti 4. To stare; to gaze.

焍 ti 4. To roast.

珶 ti 4. A girdle's clasp.

梯 t'i 1. A ladder; stairs.

涕 t'i 4. To weep.

稊 t'i 2. A panic grass.

綈 t'i 2. Coarse pongee.

䏲 t'i 1. Criple.

剃 t'i 4. To shave the head.

鵜 t'i 2. The pelican.

⿰鼻弟 t'i 4. Mucus.

罤 t'i 2. A net for catching rabbits.

It is radical in

第 ti 4. Order; series; a section; but; however.

It is unconnected with

𠂔 tzŭ 3. To stop. L. 79 G.

弔 tiao 4. To lament; to suspend; a thousand cashs. L. 28 H.

305

See Lesson 31 F.

廷 t'ing 1. The audience-chamber; the Court.

挺 t'ing 1. To erect; to stand erect, still, rigid.

梃 t'ing 3. A staff.

艇 t'ing 3. A boat.

蜓 t'ing 1. A dragon-fly.

鋌 t'ing 3. Bars; ingots.

脡 t'ing 4. Dried meat.

鞓 t'ing 1. A strap of leather.

珽 t'ing 2. A sceptre.

⿰骨廷 t'ing 1. The thigh-bone.

娗 t'ing 3. Handsome.

⿰禾廷 t'ing 3. Thatch.

莛 t'ing 2. Stalks; straw.

霆 t'ing 2. Thunder, lightning.

庭 t'ing 1. The audience-hall; a court-yard; a room; a house.

306

妥

See Lesson 67 F.

妥 t'o 3. Secure; firm; quiet; safe; prepared.

骽 t'ui 3. The legs.

⿺尢妥 t'ui 3. Lame; rheumatism.

浽 sui 2. A mist; wet.

綏 sui 1. A loop, a strap.

⿰禾妥 sui 2. Four sheafs.

桵 sui 1. The buckthorn.

荽 sui 1. Coriander.

餒 nei 3. Hungry.

鮾 nei 3. Stinking.

挼 nei 2. To rub.

307

豆

See Lesson 195 A.

豆 tou 4. A vessel.

侸 tou 1. Exhausted.

梪 tou 4. A tree.

脰 tou 4. The neck; the throat.

⿰忄豆 tou 4. To search; to spy.

逗 tou 4. To delay; to loiter.

⿱竹豆 tou 4. A sacrificial vessel.

荳 tou 4. Beans; pulse.

痘 tou 4. Smallpox.

頭 t'ou 2. The head; the top; the end; the chief; before; a suffix.

浢 t'ou 4. A river in Shansi.

It is radical in

豎 shu 4. To stand. L. 165 A.

短 tuan 2. Short. L. 165 A.

308

See Lesson 118 C.

餐 ts'an 1. To eat; a meal.

鰲 **ts'an 1.** A fish, *trichiurus armatus.*

㛑 **ts'an 4.** Elegant.

粲 **ts'an 4.** White rice; bright. *Hence*

燦 **ts'an 3.** Glittering.

璨 **ts'an 4.** Gems.

澯 **ts'an 4.** Pure, limpid.

For the following

韰 **hsieh 4.** A shalot. See L. 170 B.

309

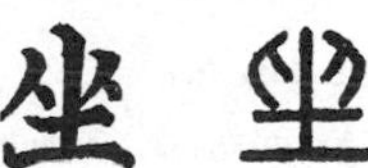

See Lesson 27 D.

坐 **tso 4.** To sit down.

䄔 **tso 4.** A clothes-bag.

𡟭 **tso 1.** Young; graceful.

𡷡 **tso 1.** A hill ready to fall.

座 **tso 4.** A seat; a divan; numerative of hills, buildings, etc.

䂳 **ts'o 3.** Stones; pebble.

矬 **ts'o 2.** Short; a dwarf.

銼 **ts'o 4.** A file.

挫 **ts'o 4.** To rub, to bruise.

脞 **ts'o 4** Minced meat.

𨁈 **ts'o 2.** To stumble.

髽 **chua 1.** To dress the hair.

310

足

See Lesson 112 B.

足 **tsu 2.** The feet; enough; to suffice.

促 **ts'u 4.** To urge; to press; constrain.

齪 **ts'u 4.** Narrow; shallow.

鋜 **cho 1.** A hoe.

捉 **cho 1.** To grasp; to seize.

浞 **cho 1.** To soak; demp.

Radical 157.

311

夋

See Lesson 29 E.

夋 **tsun 1.** To walk slowly.

俊 **tsun 4.** Elegant; refined.

浚 **tsun 4.** Deep; to dig; to enlighten.

捘 **tsun 4.** To seize; to pinch.

竣 **tsun 4.** To stop; to complete.

焌 **tsun 4.** To put out a fire.

峻 **tsun 2.** Steep; stiff; obstinate.

畯 **tsun 4.** A landlord; a bailiff.

睃 **tsun 4.** To look at.

晙 **tsun 4.** Dawn; clear.

餕 **tsun 4.** The remains; the scraps.

朘 **tsun 4.** The new moon; weak; small.

駿 **tsun 4.** A fine horse; noble; vast; to spread.

𪕗 **tsun 4.** A kind of marmot.

踆 **tsun 4.** To kick.

逡 **tsun 1.** To retire.

䜭 **ts'un 1.** To laugh at, to deride.

悛 **ts'un 1.** To correct; to amend.

皴 **ts'un 1.** Bough; to rub; to ridicule.

鋑 **chien 1.** To chisel; to cut.

痠 **suan 1.** Numbness.

狻 **suan 1.** A lion.

朘 **suan 1.** To cut; to diminish.

酸 **suan 1.** Sour; grieved; afflicted.

鵔 **hsün 4.** A phœnix; a pheasant.

梭 **so 1.** A weaver's shuttle.

唆 **so 1.** To incite; to make mischief.

㛖 **so 1.** Virtuous; maidenly.

Compare S. 100.

312

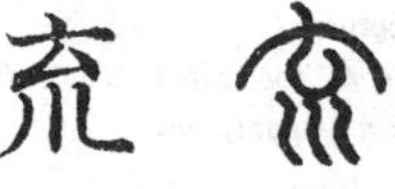

See Lesson 94 F.

㐬 **t'u 2.** Current, stream.

琉 **liu 2.** A glass-like substance; glass.

硫 **liu 2.** Sulphur.

旒 **liu 2.** Fringes; a streamer; a pennant.

流 **liu 2.** To flow; to spread abroad; exile.

鎏 **liu 2.** Pure gold.

梳 **shu 1.** A comb; to comb.

疏 **shu 1.** Distant, in relationship, time or space; lax; coarse.

蔬 **shu 1.** Coarse food.

It is radical in

毓 **yü 4.** To feed; to rear.

醯 **hsi 1.** Vinegar. L. 94 F.

313

See Lesson 29 D.

兑 **yüeh 4.** Nice words.

悅 **yüeh 4.** To be pleased; to assent.

閱 **yüeh 4.** To look at; to peruse.

兌 **tui 4.** To exchange; to barter: to pay; to deliver.

駾 **tui 4.** To gallop.

娧 **t'ui 4.** Pleasure.

脫 **t'o 1.** To take off; to escape from.

蛻 **t'o 4.** Exuviæ of insects and reptiles.

莌 **t'o 4.** The paper plant, *fatsia papyrifera.*

梲 **cho 3.** A joist; a stick.

說 **shuo 1.** To speak; to talk; to scold.

稅 **shui 4.** Duties on goods.

帨 **shui 4.** A handkerchief.

銳 **jui 4.** Pointed, acute, keen.

314

完

See Lesson 29 H.

完 **wan 2.** To finish; to complete; to settle.

睆 **wan 4.** Clear, plain.

綄 **wan 3.** To string.

垸 **wan 2.** Lacquering.

莞 **kuan 1.** Sedge, mats.

筦 **kuan 3.** A clarinet.

脘 **koan 3.** Gullet; stomach.

浣 **huan 3.** To wash.

唍 **huan 3.** To smile.

晥 **huan 3.** Bright; luminous.

皖 **huan 3.** The morning star.

捖 **huan 3.** To rub; to polish.

梡 **huan 3.** A faggot.

髖 **huan 4.** The knee-pan.

鯇 **huan 3.** A tench.

院 **yüan 4.** A court-yard; a hall. It is radical in

寇 **k'ou 4.** To rob. L. 29 H.

315

See Lesson 61 A.

吳 **wu 2.** A proper name.

蜈 **wu 2.** The centipede.

悞 **wu 4.** To neglect; to miss an opportunity.

誤 **wu 4.** A mistake; to err.

鋘 **wu 2.** A trowel.

娛 **yü 2.** To rejoice; to give pleasure.

麌 **yü 4.** A stag.

虞 **yü 2.** To foresee; to provide; to avoid. *Hence*

澞 **yü 2.** A torrent.

噳 **yü 3.** To smile.

驉 **yü 2.** Prancing.

316

See Lesson 39 A.

吾 **wu 2.** I; me.

悟 **wu 4.** To awake; to apprehend; to become conscious; intelligence.

晤 **wu 4.** To see; to meet.

鋙 **wu 2.** Fine iron.

梧 **wu 2.** *Eleococca, sterculia,* trees.

峿 **wu 2.** Rocky.

捂 **wu 4.** To oppose; to resist.

牾 **wu 4.** A wild ox; to butt, to gore.

浯 **wu 2.** Name of a river.

唔 **wu 2.** A sound.

鼯 **wu 2** Flying squirrel.

郚 **wu 2.** A place in Shantung.

寤 **wu 4.** To awake.

語 **yü 3.** Words; to discuss; to talk.

齬 **yü 3.** Irregular teeth.

敔 **yü 3.** A clapper.

圄 **yü 3.** A prison; to emprison.

衙 **ya 2.** A yamen, a tribunal.

317

See Lesson 12 C.

攸 **yu 1.** A place; that which; where.

悠 yu 1 Sadness: distance.

修 hsiu 1. To adorn; to culti-vate; to restore.

脩 hsiu 1. Dried meat; salary.

倏 倐 } shu 4. Hastily, quickly.

儵 shu 4. Deep blue.

絛 t'ao 1 A sash; a fringe.

條 t'iao 2. A twig; an article; a clause; a numerative.

蓧 t'iao 4. A basket.

鞗 t'iao 2. Reins of leather.

鯈 t'iao 2. A long narrow fish.

篠 hsiao 2. Small bamboo.

翛 hsiao 1. To flutter about.

滌 ti 2. To wash; to cleanse

318

See Lesson 41 G

酉 yu 3. A cyclic character.

莤 yu 3. A libation made on grass.

栖 yu 2. Fire-wood.

槱 yu 2. Burning wood.

酋 chiu 1. Liquor after fermen-tation. S. 432.

酒 chiu 3. Spirit, wine.

酥 su 1. Koumiss.

Radical 164.

319

See Lesson 11 C.

余 yü 2. I, me.

餘 yü 2. Remainder; surplus; excess.

鵌 yü 2. Heath-cock.

畬 yü 2 Cultivated fields.

徐 hsü Slow; sedate; dignified.

敘 敍 } hsü 4 To arrange; to state; to narrate.

斜 hsieh 1. Oblique; transverse; heterodox.

荼 t'u 2. Bitters. Affliction.

峹 t'u 2. A mountain in Anhoei.

途 t'u 2. A road; a way.

酴 t'u 2 Dregs.

鵌 t'u 2. A woodpecker.

駼 t'u 2. A hackney.

悇 t'u 2. Anxiety; care.

梌 t'u 2. A timber tree.

稌 t'u 2. A kind of rice.

涂 t'u 2. Name of a river

塗 t'u 2. Mud; to smear.

嵞 tu 2. Stupid.

蜍 ch'u 2. A toad.

除 ch'u 2. To deduct; to get rid of. *Hence*

滁 ch'u 2. A river.

蒢 ch'u 2. A legume.

茶 ch'a 2. Tea. L. 14 C. S. 507.

320

甬

See Lesson 55 K.

甬 yung 3. To burst forth.

涌 yung 3. To bubble.

踊 yung 3. To jump.

埇 yung 3. A raised path.

蛹 yung 3. A chrysalis.

俑 yung 3. Wooden figures; ef-figies.

衖 yung 3. A raised path.

勇 yung 3. Daring; brave.

恿 yung 3 To urge; to encourage.

桶 t'ung 3. A bucket; a barrel.

通 t'ung 1. To permeate; to go through; to communicate; con-tact; general; to apprehend.

捅 t'ung 3. To strike, to break.

甋 t'ung 2. The convex tiles on a roof.

筩 t'ung 2. A tube; a pipe.

痛 t'ung 4. Pain; sore.

鼟 t'ung 1. The noise of drums beating.

誦 sung 4. To hum over; to recite.

321

See Lesson 65 E.

肙 yüan 4. Larvæ, worms.

蜎 yüan 1. A small worm; a larva.

捐 **chüan 1.** To reject; to renounce, to subscribe.

悁 **chüan 4.** Anxious; angry.

琄 **chüan 1.** A scabbard; the traces of harness.

狷 **chüan 4.** Alert.

睊 **chüan 1.** To watch.

駽 **chüan 1.** A grey horse.

娟 **chüan 1.** Graceful.

鞙 **chüan 1.** A harness.

涓 **chüan 1.** Bubbling water.

䅌 **chüan 1.** Stalks of corn.

埍 **chüan 3** A police station; a postal relay.

鵑 **chüan 1.** A cuckoo.

絹 **chüan 2.** Gauze.

罥 **chüan 1.** A net, to entangle.

322

昌

See Lesson 73 A.

昌 **ch'ang 1.** The light of the sun; shining; glorious.

唱 **ch'ang 4.** To sing.

娼 **ch'ang 1.** A prostitute.

倡 **ch'ang.** To direct.

猖 **ch'ang 1.** Mad; wild.

鯧 **ch'ang 1** A conger-eel

裮 **ch'ang 1.** To throw a garment loosely over the body.

⿰龠昌 **ch'ang 4.** To sing; harmony.

菖 **ch'ang 1.** The *calamus acorus.*

閶 **ch'ang 1** The gate of heaven; the palace gates.

323

長 

镸

See Lesson 113.

長 **ch'ang 2.** Long, of time or space.

悵 **ch'ang 4.** Disappointment.

倀 **ch'ang 1.** Mad; wild.

⿰虫長 **ch'ang 2.** A scolopendra.

韔 **ch'ang 4.** A case for bows.

萇 **ch'ang 2.** A kind of fruit, *carambola.*

長 **chang 3.** To grow; senior.

脹 **chang 4.** Swelling; dropsical.

帳 **chang 4.** A curtain; a tent.

⿰目長 **chang 4.** Eyes swollen.

賬 **chang 4.** An account; a bill.

餦 **chang 1.** Cakes.

粻 **chang 1.** Provisions.

張 **chang 1.** To draw a bow; to stretch; to draw up; to display; a sheet; a numerative.

漲 **chang 4.** To over-flow; to inundate

棖 **ch'êng 2.** Door-posts.

⿰石長 **ch'êng 4.** To polish

It is radical in

套 **t'ao 4.** A case; a snare; to envelop; to include; a numerative.

肆 **ssŭ 4.** Long.

髟 **pao 1.** Hair.

324

爭 

See Lesson 49 D.

爭 **chêng 1.** To wrangle; to contest.

掙 **chêng 4.** To pierce; to earn; to make an effort.

睜 **chêng 1.** To open the eyes wide.

諍 **chêng 1.** To reprove; to remonstrate with.

錚 **chêng 1.** The clang of metal.

⿰月爭 **chêng 1.** The tendon Achilles.

猙 **chêng 1.** A fabulous griffin.

彏 **chêng 4.** To draw, to stretch.

琤 **chêng 1.** A tinkling sound.

崢 **chêng 1.** High; overtopping.

箏 **chêng 1.** A kite.

棦 **ch'êng 1.** Brambles.

竫 **ching 4.** Quiet.

淨 凈 **ching 4.** Clean; pure; net; to wash.

靜 **ching 4.** Quiet; still.

325

See Lesson 27 D.

亟 **chi 2.** Extreme.

極 **chi 2.** The maximum; very; the zenith; the pole; the first principle.

殛 **chi 2.** To kill.

326

妻

See Lesson 44 G.

妻 ch'i 1. Wife.
ch'i 4. To marry.

棲 ch'i 1. To roost; to stay.

悽 ch'i 1. Grieved; suffering.

凄 ch'i 1. Cold; freezing; miserable.

郪 ch'i 1. Name of a place.

萋 ch'i 1. Luxuriant.

霋 ch'i 1. End of the rain.

327

其

See Lesson 70 C.

其 ch'i 2. He, she, it; his, hers, its.

期 ch'i 1. A period; a limit of time; to expect; to hope.

欺 ch'i 1. To cheat; to deceive; to abuse.

僛 ch'i 1. A drunken man; unsteady.

騏 ch'i 2. A piebald horse; spotted.

祺 ch'i 2. Prosperity.

帺 ch'i 2. Cloth; band.

蜞 ch'i 2. A small crab.

[illegible] ch'i 2. A wild goose.

娸 ch'i 2. Ugly; to scoff at.

琪 ch'i 2. A gem.

粸 ch'i 2. A cake.

淇 ch'i 2. A river in Honan.

萁 ch'i 2. Stalks of pulse.

錤 ch'i 2. A hoe.

踑 ch'i 2. To cross the legs.

麒 ch'i 2. The unicorn.

魌 ch'i 1. The demon of pestilence; ugly.

旗 ch'i 2. A flag; a banner.

箕 ch'i 1. A basket for dust.

棊 棋 ch'i 2. The chess

綦 ch'i 2. A dark grey colour; very. *Hence*

[illegible] ch'i 2. Edible fern.

箕 chi 1. A proper name.

萁 chi 1. Tendrils of vines.

惎 chi 4. To fear.

朞 chi 1. A full year.

稘 chi 1. One year period.

基 chi 1. Foundation; property; the throne.

328

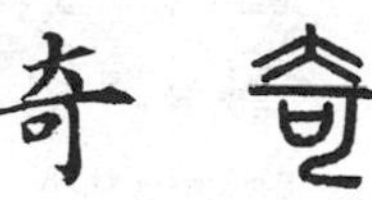

See Lesson 58 I.

奇 竒 ch'i 2. Extraordinary; strange.

騎 ch'i 2. To ride; to sit astride.

崎 ch'i 1. Precipitous; rough; irregular.

踦 ch'i 2. Lame; cripple.

齮 ch'i 1. To bite; to eat.

[illegible] ch'i 1. A spider

徛 ch'i 1. A bridge.

琦 ch'i 2. A valuable stone; a curio.

綺 ch'i 3. Variegated silk.

碕 ch'i 2. Craggy.

奇 chi 1. Odd; surplus; remainder.

畸 chi 1. Surplus; leavings.

觭 chi 1. Uneven; irregular.

剞 chi 1. A chisel.

寄 chi 4. To lodge at; to deliver; to send.

掎 chi 1. To pinch.

羇 chi 1. An inn; to lodge.

倚 i 3. To lean upon; to trust to; inclined.

椅 i 3. A chair; a seat.

掎 i 3. To drag.

陭 i 1. Projecting; steep.

錡 i 0. A pot.

輢 i 3. The sides of a chariot.

[illegible] i 3. Sweet-smelling.

旖 i 3. A waving movement; to flutter to the breeze.

欹 i 1. An exclamation.

329

啓

See Lesson 129 A.

啓 啟 ch'i 3. To open; to begin; to explain.

棨 ch'i 3. A banner; a signal flag.

綮 ch'i 3 A banner; a signal flag.

晵 ch'i 3. The sun pierciag through the clouds.

It is radical contracted in

肇 chao 4. To begin; to institute; to arrange

330

See Lesson 44 F.

疌 chieh 2. Skill; success.

捷 chieh 2. Alert; active; clever.

睫 chieh 4. The eye-lashes.

婕 chieh 2. Handsome.

箑 chieh 2. A fan; a running hand.

寁 chieh 3. Quick; to break off a friendship.

唼 ch'ieh 4. To chatter; to slander.

331

See Lesson 67 E.

妾 ch'ieh 4. A concubine.

唼 ch'ieh 4. To jabber; to speak evil.

接 chieh 1. To receive; to forward; to connect; to follow.

椄 chieh 1. To graft.

霎 sha 4. shua 4. Light; sudden; temporary.

翣 sha 4. Great feather-fans.

332

See Lesson 82 E.

臤 chien 1. Firm; solid.

掔 ch'ien 1. To hold, to grasp.

賢 hsien 2. Worthies; sages; good; virtuous.

緊 chin 3. To bind tight; urgent; important.

腎 shên 4. The kidneys; the testicles.

Sub-Series.

堅 chien 1. Firm; solid; durable. *Hence*

慳 chien 1. Stingy; to curtail expenses.

鰹 chien 1. A mullet.

硻 k'êng 1. Rumbling of stones.

摼 k'êng 1. To butt against.

鏗 k'êng 1. Jingling.

It is radical in

豎 竪 shu 4. Upright; perpendicular; to erect. L. 165 A.

333

See Lesson 71 R.

戔 chien 1. Small; narrow.

箋 chien 1. A tablet; note-paper; a letter.

牋 chien 1. A tablet; note-paper; a letter.

諓 chien 3. To flatter.

餞 chien 4. A farewell entertainment.

踐 chien 4. To tread upon; to keep one's word.

賤 chien 4. Mean; low; cheap.

濺 chien 4. Water dashing; to splash.

錢 ch'ien 2. Copper coin, or cash.

淺 ch'ien 3. Shallow; superficial; to run aground.

綫 hsien 4. Thread.

棧 chan 4. A coverep shed; a store-house; a godown.

輚 chan 4. A wagon.

羧 chan 4. A sheep-pen.

盞 chan 3. A lamp-bowl; a tea-cup.

剗 ch'an 3. To trim; to cut.

殘 ts'an 2. To ruin; to injure; mischievous; spoiled.

334

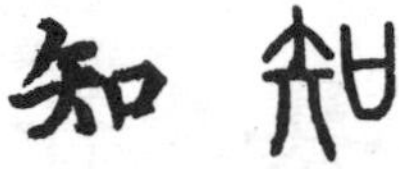

See Lesson 131 E

知 chih 1. To know.

蜘 chih 1 A spider.

智 chih 4. Wisdom; cleverness.

痴 ch'ih 1. Stupid; doting.

335

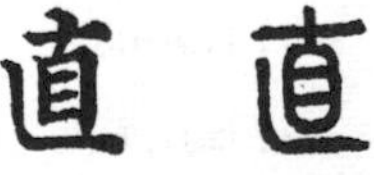

See Lesson 10 K.

直 chih 2. Straight; honest; upright.

値 chih 2. Price; value.

植 chih 3. To lean on.

稙 chih 2. Grain first sown; the first crop.

殖 chih 2 To prosper.

植 **chih 2.** To plant; a pole.

置 **chih 4.** To arrange; to govern.

Compare S. 509

336

See Lesson 75 C.

京 **ching 1.** A capital.

鯨 **ching 1.** A whale.

麖 **ching 4.** A large deer.

黥 **ch'ing 2.** To tattoo.

勍 **ch'ing 2.** Strong.

倞 **chiang 4.** To quarrel.

凉 涼 } **liang 2.** Cool; cold.

晾 **liang 4.** To dry in the sun; to aerate.

悢 **liang 2.** To grieve; melancholy.

諒 **liang 4.** To trust; to consider; to excuse.

輬 **liang 2.** A carriage.

綡 **liang 2.** Strings; bands.

椋 **liang 4.** The cornelian tree.

掠 **liao 4.** To rob; to plunder; to flog.

就 **chiu 4.** To go or come to; to follow; to make the best of; then; immediately.

It forms

[illegible] **chiu 4.** To monopolise.

僦 **chiu 4.** To hire.

鷲 **chiu 4.** A vulture.

337

See Lesson 115 D.

青 **ch'ing 1.** Green; blue; black; grey; the white of an egg.

情 **ch'ing 2.** Passions; feelings; circumstances; lust.

請 **ch'ing 3.** To beg; to request; to engage.

䝼 **ch'ing 2.** To inherit.

晴 **ch'ing 2.** Clear sky.

清 **ch'ing 1.** Pure; honest.

凊 **ch'ing 4.** To cool.

鯖 **ch'ing 1.** A mackerel.

精 **ching 1.** The essential part; essence; spirit; semen; skill.

靖 **ching 4.** Quiet; tranquil; peaceful.

睛 **ching 1.** The pupil of the eye.

蜻 **ching 1.** A dragon-fly.

靚 **ching 4.** To ornament; to paint.

鶄 **ching 1.** A heron.

菁 **ching 1.** Turnips.

圊 **ching 1.** A privy.

箐 **ch'ien 4.** Fine bamboos; a basket.

綪 **ch'ien 4.** Violet-colour.

輤 **ch'ien 4.** A pall to cover a hearse.

倩 **ch'ien 4.** Comely; pretty. *Hence*

蒨 **ch'ien 4.** Luxuriant.

猜 **ts'ai 1.** To doubt; to suspect; to guess. *The sound was altered.*

It is radical in

靝 **t'ien 1.** The blue sky.

Radical 174.

338

See Lesson 31 B.

咎 **chiu 1.** Fault; blame.

麔 **chiu 4.** The male of the elk.

[illegible] **ch'iu 2.** Hatred; to hate.

綹 **liu 3.** A skein of silk.

[illegible] **ch'i 3.** Flag; banner.

晷 **kui 3.** A sun-dial; time.

鼛 **kao 1.** A large drum.

櫜 **kao 1.** A quiver.

339

See Lesson 143 F.

卓 **cho 1.** Eminent.

倬 **cho 4.** Manifest.

棹 桌 } **cho 1.** A table.

啅 **cho 4.** Cries.

罩 [illegible] } **chao 4.** A screen. A cover.

淖 **ch'ao 4.** Drenched; wet.

綽 **ch'ao 4.** Generous; ample; liberal.

踔 **ch'ao 4.** To get ahead.

悼 **tao 4.** Affliction, to grieve for.

掉 **tiao 4.** To adjust; to move; to fall.

⿰卓攴 **t'iao 3.** To assail; to strike.

340

See Lesson **69** L.

豖 **cho 2.** A pig bound.

琢 **cho 2.** To polish stones.

啄 **cho 4.** To peck up food.

諑 **cho 2.** To accuse; to vilify.

涿 **cho 1.** To drip.

椓 **cho 4.** To strike.

冢 **chung 3.** A mound. *The sound was altered.* S. 527.

341

See Lesson 43 R.

叕 **cho 4.** To sew.

醊 **cho 2.** A libation.

餟 **cho 2.** To offer libations.

蝃 **cho 1.** A spider.

娺 **cho 1.** Quarrelling.

惙 **cho 4.** Mournful; critical.

畷 **cho 4.** Pathways betwen fields.

棳 **cho 2.** A stick.

⿰叕豕 **cho 2.** To dig.

窡 **cho 1.** To spy.

⿱窡日 **cho 1.** Gluttony.

輟 **ch o 4.** To cease.

啜 **ch'o 4.** To suck, to sip; to weep.

欼 **ch'o 4.** To suck up; to drink.

歠 **ch'o 4.** To suck up; to sip.

綴 **chui 4.** To baste; to connect; to sew.

錣 **chui 4.** To baste; to sew together.

掇 **to 4.** To pluck; to gather.

裰 **to 4.** To mend clothes.

敠 **to 4.** To weigh.

鵽 **to 4.** The turtle-dove.

剟 **to 4.** To cut; to engrave.

342

周

See Lesson **109** C.

周 **chou 1.** A dynasty; a turn.

週 **chou 1.** To revolve.

⿰足周 **chou 1.** To kick.

⿰彳周 **chou 1.** Hurried.

賙 **chou 1.** To succour; to bestow in charity.

輖 **chou 1.** A small cart.

椆 **chou 2.** An oak, *quercus glauca.*

綢 **ch'ou 2.** Silk cloth.

淍 **ch'ou 2.** To wash.

稠 **ch'ou 2.** Thick; dense.

惆 **ch'ou 2.** Disappointed.

⿰犭周 **ch'ou 3.** A gibbon.

裯 **ch'ou 2.** A coverlet; a bed-curtain.

調 **tiao 4.** Cadence; an air; to transfer.

⿰舟周 **tiao 1.** A boat.

凋 **tiao 1.** Withered.

⿰周刂 **tiao 1.** To carve; to chisel.

鵰 **tiao 1.** The fishing eagle.

雕 **tiao 1.** To carve; to engrave.

彫 **tiao 1.** To carve; to wither.

調 **t'iao 2.** To blend; to harmonise; to temper.

鯛 **t'iao 2.** The perch.

蜩 **t'iao 2.** The cicada.

倜 **t'i 1.** Free; noble.

343

帚

See Lesson **44** K.

帚 箒 } **chou 3, ch'u 2.** A broom.

⿰口帚 **sao 4.** The chirping of birds.

埽 掃 } **sao 3. sao 4.** A broom; to sweep.

It is radical in

婦 **fu 4.** A married woman.

歸 **kui 1.** To return; to belong to.

344

隹

See Lesson 168 A.

隹 **chui 1.** Short-tailed birds.

錐 **chui 1.** An awl.

騅 **chui 1.** A piebald horse.

鵻 **chui 1.** A pigeon.

鼪 **chui 1.** A rat.

萑 **chui 1.** *Leonurus sibiricus.*

椎 **ch'ui 2.** A mallet; to hammer.

碓 **tui 4.** A pestle.

推 **t'ui 1.** To push; to decline.

堆 **tsui 1.** A heap.

崔 **ts'ui 1.** High. S. 655.

奞 **sui 1.** To spread the wings; to fly.

睢 **sui 1.** To stare at.

雖 **sui 1.** Although; even if; to dismiss.

誰 **shui 2.** Who?

脽 **shui 2.** The buttocks.

匯 滙 } **hui 4.** A confluent; a bank draft. *It forms*

攉 **k'uai 3.** To carry on the arm; to scratch; to rub.

惟 **wei 2.** Only; to think of; but; and so; an initial or copulative particle.

唯 **wei 2.** Only; to consent.

帷 **wei 2.** A curtain.

維 **wei 2.** To tie; to hold fast; a rule; an initial particle.

淮 **huai 2.** A large river.

It is radical in

雀 **ch'iao 3.** A small bird. L. 18 N. *Hence*

截 **chieh 2.** To cut; to stop.

集 **chi 2.** To gather; a market. L. 119 G.

隻 **chih 4.** One by itself; single; a numerative.

雙 **shuang 1.** Double; pair; mate.

讐 **ch'ou 2.** To hate; enmity; an enemy.

Radical 172.

Perhaps it is found in

准 **chun 3.** To permit; to approve; exactly.

準 **chun 3.** A water-level; to adjust.

345

居

See Lesson 32 C.

居 **chü 1.** To inhabit; to reside in.

倨 **chü 4.** Rude; haughty.

鋸 **chü 4.** A saw; to saw.

据 **chü 1.** To seize; to gather.

琚 **chü 1.** Girdle ornaments.

裾 **chü 1.** The flap of a coat.

踞 **chü 4.** To squat.

賥 **chü 1.** To store property.

椐 **chü 1.** A hard wood.

腒 **chü 1.** Dried flesh.

崌 **chü 1.** A peak in Ssŭch'uan.

鶋 **chü 1.** The jackdaw.

346

匊 

See Lesson 54 C.

匊 **chü 2.** A handful.

掬 **chü 2.** To grasp with both hands; a handful.

椈 **chü 2.** The cypress.

鞫 **chü 2.** To investigate judicially.

踘 **chü 4.** A foot-ball.

鞠 **chü 2.** A ball; to bow; altogether.

毱 **chü 4.** A shuttlecock.

鵴 **chü 4.** The cuckoo.

菊 **chü 1.** The chrysanthemum.

麴 **ch'ü 1.** Leaven; yeast.

347

See Lesson 47 G.

具 **chü 4.** To prepare; implements; tools; to write; all, every.

俱 **chü 1.** All, every.

埧 **chü 4.** An embankment; a dyke.

踑 **chü 1.** The feet benumbed by cold.

惧 **chü 4.** To fear.

椇 **chü 3.** The fruit of the *hovenia dulcis.*

颶 **chü 4.** A typhoon.

348

See Lesson 78 E.

屈 **ch'ü 1.** A grievance; a wrong; injustice; to bend; to crouch.

猸 **ch'ü 1.** A monkey.

蛐 **ch'ü 1.** A grub.

屈 **ch'ü 1.** Worried.

堀 **k'u 1.** A hole; a den.

腒 **k'u 3.** The buttocks.

窟 **k'u 1.** A cave; a hole.

淈 **ku 1.** Turbid water.

掘 **chüeh 2.** To dig out; to excavate.

崛 **chüeh 2.** A lofty peak; eminent.

倔 **chüeh 2.** Obstinate.

㞊 **chüeh 4.** Short.

349

取 耴

See Lesson 146 F.

取 **ch'ü 3.** To take, to receive.

趣 **ch'ü 4.** To hasten to; pleasure, pleasant.

娶 **ch'ü 3.** To marry a wife.

㑒 **chü 4.** Haste; flutter.

娵 **chü 1.** A proper name.

輒 **che 4.** Sudden.

㥣 **ch'ê 4.** Emotion; vulgarity; singularity.

掫 **chou 2.** To grasp, to lift.

緅 **chou 1.** Pink silk.

陬 **chou 1.** An angle; a corner.

棷 **chou 1.** Name of a tree.

鯫 **chou 1.** Small fishes.

郰 **chou 1.** A place in Shantung.

棸 **chou 1.** A proper name.

菆 **chou 1.** Grass; weeds; a nest.

It is radical in

聚 **chü 4.** To gather. S. 775.

叢 藂 } **ts'ung 1.** A collection crowd.

See L. 102 I.

350

See Lesson 47 K.

卷 **chüan 4.** A roll of paper; to roll up; a document; a chapter.

餋 **chüan 3.** Small cakes.

錈 **chüan 3.** To bend by heating.

倦 **chüan 4.** Tired; weary.

睠 **chüan 4.** To look fondly.

埢 **chüan 4.** Enclosure.

捲 **chüan 3.** To roll up; frizzled.

圈 **chüan 4.** A piggery.

菤 **chüan 3.** *Xanthium strumarium.*

惓 **ch'üan 2.** Careful; mournful.

棬 **ch'üan 2.** A wooden bowl.

踡 **ch'üan 2.** To bent the legs.

蜷 **ch'üan 2.** The wriggling of a snake.

綣 **ch'üan 4.** Bound together; confederate.

鬈 **ch'üan 2.** Ringlets of hair.

圈 **ch'üan 1.** A circle; a ring; a dot; a snare.

弮 **ch'üan 1.** A wooden bowl.

Compare S. 191.

351

See Lesson 121 B.

囷 **ch'ün 2.** A granary.

悃 **ch'ün 1.** Weary.

箘 **ch'ün 2.** Stem of an arrow.

麕 **ch'ün 1.** A deer; a herd.

菌 **chün 3.** The mush-room.

352

See Lesson 29 D.

兒 **erh 2.** Infant; a suffix.

郳 **i 2.** A place in Shantung.

倪 **i 2.** Young; small.

睨 **i 4.** To glance at.

輗 **i 2.** A yoke.

齯 **i 2.** First dentition.

猊 **i 2.** A fabulous beast.

蜺 **i 2.** A cricket.

鶃 **i 4.** A heron.

鯢 **i 2.** A whale.

霓 **i 2.** A rainbow.

麑 **i 2.** A fawn.

鬩 **i 4.** A quarrel.

倪 **ni 2.** Young; small.

It is radical in

哾 **wa 2.** To prattle.

腉 nai 3. To suckle.

It is unconnected with

皃 mao 4. Face; form. L. 29 C.

353

非

See Lesson 170 A.

非 fei 1. Not; wrong.
緋 fei 1. Scarlet.
悱 fei 3. Eager.
誹 fei 3. To slander.
裶 fei 1. The train of a dress.
腓 fei 2. The calf of the leg.
騑 fei 1. An extra horse.
馡 fei 1. Fragrant.
剕 fei 1. To cut the feet.
蜚 fei 1. Mites; insects.
翡 fei 3. A king-fisher; blue.
斐 fei 3. Streaks; lines; graceful.
棐 fei 3. A species of yew, *torreya nucifera*.
菲 fei 3. A radish; frugal; mean.
霏 fei 1. Sleet.
厞 fei 2. A retired corner; hidden.
痱 fei 4. Swelling of the feet.
屝 fei 4. Coarse grass sandals.
扉 fei 1. A door; a leaf.
匪 fei 3. Not; without; vagabonds; rebels.

輩 pei 4. A generation; a class; a kind; a sign of plural.
悲 pei 1. To grieve; to be sad; to sympathise.

琲 p'ei 3. A string of pearls.
徘 p'ei 3. To walk to and fro; irresolute.
裴 p'ei 2. A long robe.

棑 pai 4. A raft.

排 p'ai 2. To arrange in order; to dispose.

罪 tsui 4. A crime; a wrong; a sin; punishment.

It is radical in

靠 k'ao 4. To lean on; to trust; near to. L. 170 A.

354

See Lesson 48 L.

奉 捧 } fêng 4. To receive respectfully with both hands; to pay one's respects.
俸 fêng 4. Salary; emolument.
唪 fêng 4. To chant.

⿰足奉 pêng 4. To jump; to hop; to rebound.
菶 pêng 3. Full of leaves; luxuriant.

捧 p'êng 3. To hold up in both hands; to offer; a handful.
⿰香奉 p'êng 3. Fragrant.

棒 pang 4. A club; a cudgel; stick.
⿰禾奉 pang 4. Maize.
蜯 pang 4. Shells.

355

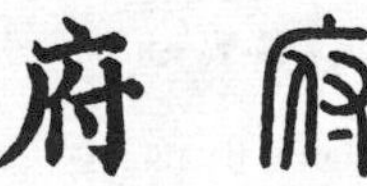

See Lesson 45 C, and S. 120.

府 fu 3. A palace; a prefecture.
俯 fu 3. To come down; to condescend.
腑 fu 3. The bowels.
捬 fu 3. To pat, to tap.
腐 fu 3. Rotten; fermented.

356

See Lesson 55 K.

圅 函 凾 } han 2. To contain; to infold; to envelop; large-minded; a letter.
菡 han 3. The bud of a lotus flower.
涵 han 2. To submerge; vast; capacious.
⿰木函 han 2. A wooden bowl.
⿰衤函 han 2. A sleeve.
⿰金函 han 2. An armour.
顄 han 2. The chin.

崡 hsien 2. A hill in Honan.

357

See Lesson 128 A.

析 hsi 1. To split; to explain.
淅 hsi 1. To wash rice.
蜥 hsi 4. A lizard.
晰 晳 } hsi 1. Clear; bright; white

惁 **hsi 1.** Sorrow; to venerate.

晳 **hsi 1.** Clear; white.

菥 **hsi 1.** *Asarum.*

358

昔

See Lesson 17 J.

昔 **hsi 2.** Old; anciently; former; the time of night.

惜 **hsi 1.** To pity; to care for; to spare.

腊 **hsi 1.** Dried meat; old; very.

耤 **chi 2.** The Emperor's field. S. 770.

踖 **chi 1.** To step; to walk slowly.

借 **chieh 4.** To borrow.

唶 **chieh 4.** To chirp.

䱜 **ch'iao 2.** A shark.

猎 **ch'iao 4.** A molossus.

碏 **ch'iao 4.** A precious stone.

鵲 **ch'iao 3.** The magpie.

皵 **ch'iao 2.** Wrinkled.

醋 **ts'u 4.** Vinegar.

錯 **ts'o 4.** To make a mistake; to be wrong; to differ.

措 **ts'o 4.** To arrange.

剒 **ts'o 4.** To carve.

厝 **ts'o 4.** A tomb.

It is radical in

䄍 **cha 4.** Imperial sacrifice made to spirits.

359

享

See Lesson 75 E.

享 **ch'un 2.** A lamb.

醇 **ch'un 2.** Pure; unmixed.

淳 **ch'un 2.** Genuine; pure; sincere.

犉 **ch'un 2.** An ox.

錞 **ch'un 2.** A pummel.

鶉 **ch'un 2.** A quail.

諄 **chun 1.** To impress upon; to reiterate; to teach.

埻 **chun 3.** A target.

啍 **t'un 1.** To bump.

焞 **t'un 1.** To roast.

惇 **tun 1.** Honest; sincere; generous.

弴 **tun 1.** Ornamented bows.

[illegible] **tun 1.** A water-bath.

敦 **tun 1.** Simple, good, honest. S. 715.

Compare S. 549.

360

臽 

See Lesson 139 A.

臽 **hsien 4.** A trap.

陷 **hsien 4.** To fall into.

餡 **hsien 4.** Hashed meat.

閻 **yen 2.** The gate to a village; the Chinese Pluto.

鵮 **ch'ien 4.** To peck, as birds.

埳 **k'an 3.** A pit; a hole.

掐 **ch'ia 1.** To pinch; to pluck.

萏 **tan 3.** To bud.

啗 **tan 4.** To eat.

窞 **t'an 3.** A cellar.

諂 **ch'an 3.** To flatter.

361

See Lesson 102 D.

幸 **hsing 4.** Fortunate; prosperous; opportune.

倖 **hsing 4.** Fortunate; lucky.

[illegible] **hsing 4.** To scold.

悻 **hsing 3.** Angry.

涬 **hsing 3.** Chaos.

For the following, see L. 102 G.

報 **pao 4.** To recompense; to requite; to report; a journal.

執 **chih 2.** To seize. S. 601.

圉 **yü 3.** A prison.

睪 **i 4.** To watch over. S. 738.

盩 **chou 1.** To whip.

[illegible] **chü 2.** To convict.

362

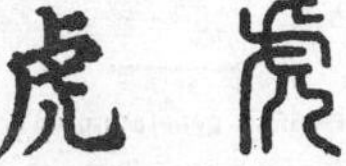

See Lesson 135 B.

虎 **hu 3.** The tiger.

唬 **hu 1**. To frighten.

諕 **hu 1**. To scare.

猇 **hu 1**. To roar.

琥 **hu 3**. Amber.

363

See Lesson 114 B.

昏 **hun 1**. Dusk; dark; confused.

閽 **hun 1**. An entrance.

婚 **hun 1**. To marry; marriage.

殙 **hun 1**. The dimness of death.

睧 **hun 1**. Dulness of vision.

涽 **hun 1**. Unstable.

惛 **hun 1**. Confused in mind; dull; stupid.

364

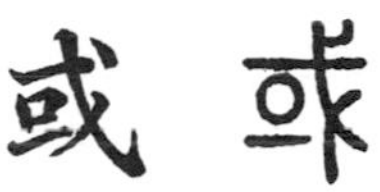

See Lesson 71 J.

或 **huo 4**. Or; either; if; supposing that; some; perhaps; doubtful.

惑 **huo 4**. Doubt; suspicion; to deceive.

魊 **huo 4**. Spell; delusion.

幗 **huo 2**. A curtain; a screen.

鰄 **huo 2**. A salamander.

域 **yü 4**. A limit; a country.

棫 **yü 4**. A kind of oak

緎 **yü 4**. A seam.

蜮 **yü 4**. A malicious fabulous creature.

淢 **yü 4**. A swift current.

閾 **yü 4**. A threshold.

罭 **yü 4**. A drag-net with fine meshes.

彧 **yü 4**. Accomplished.

It is radical in

國 **kuo 3**. A nation; a country S. 626.

365

See Lesson 101 C.

易 **i 4**. Easy; to change; to transform.

蜴 **i 4**. A chameleon.

埸 **i 4**. A boundary.

焬 **i 4**. A flame.

緆 **i 4**. Fringe.

敡 **i 4**. To change.

錫 **hsi 2**. Tin; to give; gifts.

裼 **hsi 1**. Thin clothes; to pull off one's coat.

餳 **hsi 2**. Sugar; sweetmeat.

賜 **ssŭ 4**. A gift; to give; to condescend.

踢 **t'i 1**. To kick.

惕 **t'i 4**. Fear; alarm.

掦 **t'i 1**. To pick out.

逷 **t'i 4**. To keep at a distance from; far off.

剔 **t'i 1**. To scrape off.

366

See Lesson 39 C.

岡 **kang 1**. A look-out, sentry-box.

剛 **kang 1**. Hard; unyielding. Just now.

綱 **kang 1**. Rope of a net; regulation; law.

焵 **kang 4**. To temper steel.

鋼 **kang 1**. Steel.

𦉪 **kang 1**. An earthen jar.

堈 **kang 1**. A jar.

犅 **kang 1**. A sacrificial ox.

367

See Lesson 65 C.

肯 **k'ên 3** To be willing; to assent.

啃 **k'ên 2**. To bite; to gnaw.

掯 **k'ên 3**. To annoy, to harrass.

368

See Lesson 24 F.

固 **ku 4**. Strong; firm; obstinate; assuredly.

錮 **ku 1**. To stop; to restrain.

鯝 **ku 4**. Sardine.

凅 **ku 4**. Hard frozen.

痼 **ku 4**. A chronic complaint.

箇 } 個 } **ko 2**. This one; an individual; a numerative.

涸 **k'o 4**. Dried.

369

卦

See Lesson 56 E.

卦 **kua 4.** To divine; the diagrams.

褂 **kua 4.** An outer coat.

掛 **kua 4.** To hang up; to put on.

Compare S. 224.

370

See Lesson 86 C.

官 **kuan 1.** An official, a mandarin, public, civic.

管 **kuan 3.** A clarinet; to regulate; to govern.

菅 **kuan 1.** Coarse textile fibres.

痯 **kuan 3.** Melancholy.

館 **kuan 3.** An office; a restaurant.

棺 **kuan 3.** An inner coffin.

悺 **kuan 1.** Sorrow; sadness.

琯 **kuan 3.** A jade tube.

輨 **kuan 3.** The iron band on the hub of a wheel.

[illegible] **kuan 3.** A duct in the body.

涫 **kuan 4.** To bubble.

[illegible] **kuan 3.** To lift.

[illegible] **kuan 1.** To coo as doves do.

倌 **kuan 1.** The Emperor's charioteer.

[illegible] **kuan 1.** Hair's dress.

逭 **huan 4.** To flee; to escape.

綰 **wan 3.** To bind.

371

昆

See Lesson 27 I.

昆 **k'un 1.** Afterwards; futurity an elder brother.

蜫 **k'un 1.** Insects.

錕 **k'un 1.** Steel.

琨 **k'un 1.** Mother of pearl.

鯤 **k'un 1.** A marine monster.

鵾 **k'un 1.** Heath-cock.

崑 **k'un 1.** The range of K'un-lün mountains.

棍 **kun 4.** A stick; a rowdy.

惃 **kun 4.** Confused; disturbed.

緄 **kun 3.** To embroider.

輥 **kun 3.** To turn round; to revolve.

混 **hun 4.** Chaos, confusion, to bustle.

焜 **hun 4.** Fire; flames.

餛 **hun 2.** Fritters.

372

空

See Lesson 82 A.

空 **k'ung 1.** Empty, void.
k'ung 4. A void space.

控 **k'ung 4.** To draw; to accuse.

悾 **k'ung 1.** Simple; guileless.

鞚 **k'ung 4.** A bridle; reins.

崆 **k'ung 1.** A mountain in Kansu.

倥 **k'ung 4.** Rude.

箜 **k'ung 1.** A harp.

腔 **ch'iang 1.** The throat; a tune; accent.

[illegible] **ch'iang 1.** The end bone of the spine.

[illegible] **ch'iang 1.** A melody.

椌 **ch'iang 1.** A clapper.

[illegible] **ch'iang 1.** Asthma.

啌 **chiang 1.** To cough, to spit.

373

果

See Lesson 120 F.

果 **kuo 3.** Fruit; really; effects; consequences.

菓 **kuo 3.** Fruit.

粿 **kuo 3.** Cakes.

餜 **kuo 3.** Cakes; pastry.

惈 **kuo 3.** Bravery.

輠 **kuo 3.** A grease-pot.

猓 **kuo 3.** A monkey.

蜾 **kuo 3.** The solitary wasp or *sphex.*

裹 **kuo 3.** To wrap up; to bind; to bandage.

裸 **lo 3.** Naked; to strip.

躶 **lo 3.** Naked.

倮 **lo 3.** Naked; vile.

夥 **huo 3.** Numerous; a company; colleagues.

窠 **wo 1.** A nest; a den.

踝 **huai** 3. The ankle.

祼 **kuan** 4. A libation.

課 **k'o** 4. A task.

錁 **k'o** 4. An ingot..

堁 **k'o** 4. A clod of earth.

騍 **k'o** 4. Female of horses, mules, etc.

稞 **k'o** 4. Grain.

顆 **k'o** 1. A numerative of small round things.

It is unconnected with.

彙 **hui** 4. The porcupine; a class; a collection. L. 68 E.

374

See Lesson 13 C.

來 **lai** 2. To come; in the future.

徠 **lai** 4. To induce to come; to invite.

睞 **lai** 4. To squint.

淶 **lai** 2. A river in Shantung.

鯠 **lai** 2. A kind of eel.

騋 **lai** 2. A draught horse.

崍 **lai** 2. A peak in Ssŭch'uan.

棶 **lai** 2. *Cornus macrophylla.*

郲 **lai** 2. A place in Honan.

賚 **lai** 4. To give, to bestow.

萊 **lai** 2. Weeds.

It is radical in

麥 **mai** 4. Corn.

嗇 **shê** 4. The harvest. S. 755.

憖 憗 } **yin** 2. To enquire; to ask; to force one's self.

375

See Lesson 129 A.

戾 **li** 4. A fault; tribulations.

唳 **li** 4. The cry of a heron, wild goose, etc.

悷 **li** 4. Sadness.

捩 **li** 4. To turn.

䟏 **li** 4. Slow-paced.

綟 **li** 4. A dull green.

蜧 **li** 4. A dragon-snake.

棙 **li** 4. Finger-stalls to play stringed instruments.

淚 **lei** 4. Tears.

376

See Lesson 35 I.

兩 **liang** 3. Two, both; an ounce; a tael.

掚 **liang** 3. To arrange, to dispose.

輛 **liang** 4. Numerative of chairs, carts, etc.

緉 **liang** 3. To bind; a string.

魎 **liang** 3. A sprite.

倆 **lia** 3. Two, of persons.

377

See Lesson 119 L.

林 **lin** 2. A forest; a grove; a collection.

淋 **lin** 2. To drip; to soak.

琳 **lin** 2. A precious stone.

㨆 **lin** 3. To beat, to kill.

㝝 **lin** 2. A secluded place.

菻 **lin** 2. *Incarvillea sinensis.*

痳 **lin** 2. Dysuria.

霖 **lin** 2. Refreshing rain.

彬 **pin** 1. Graceful; elegant.

霦 **pin** 1. Dew; to sparkle.

禁 **chin** 4. To prohibit. S. 727.

郴 **ch'ên** 1. A place in Hunan.

綝 **ch'ên** 1. A fringe.

惏 **lan** 2. Greedy; covetous.

婪 **lan** 2. Covetous; avaricious.

It is radical in

楚 **ch'u** 3. A woody region. S. 730.

焚 **fên** 2. To burn, to consume.

梵 **fan** 2. The soughing of wind through trees.

棥 **fan** 2. A hedge; a fence.

楙 **mao** 4. Thick forest.

378

See Lesson 97 K.

夌 **ling** 2. The top; to transgress; to offend.

陵 **ling** 2. A high mound; a tomb; to insult.

凌 **ling** 2. Ice; pure; to insult.

淩 **ling** 2. A river in Shantung.

㥄 **ling 2.** Sorrow; pity.

輘 **ling 2.** A cart-rut; the rumbling of carts.

祾 **ling 4.** A sacrifice at the Imperial tombs.

綾 **ling 2.** Damask.

掕 **ling 2.** To curb a horse.

鯪 **ling 2.** A dace.

菱 **ling 2.** The waterchestnut, *trapa.*

睖 **lêng 4.** To stare.

倰 **lêng 4.** Exhausted.

崚 **lêng 2.** Hilly country.

棱 **lêng 2.** An edge; a corner.

稜 **lêng 2.** An edge; a corner.

凌 **liang 2.** Ice.

379

坴

See Lesson 79 K.

坴 **lu 4.** A clod of earth.

陸 **lu 4.** Dry land; continuous; in succession.

蛙 **lu 4.** A small marine bivalve.

稑 **lu 4.** Grain which ripens early.

淕 **lu 4.** Sleet.

陸 **liu 4.** Six.

睦 **mu 4.** A benignant eye; harmony; concord.

逵 **ch'iu 2. k'ui 2.** A cross-road.

It is radical in

埶 **i 4.** To cultivate the ground. S. 619.

380

See Lesson 14 G.

侖 **lun 2.** To meditate.

論 **lun 4.** To discourse; with reference to.

倫 **lun 2.** Moral principles.

輪 **lun 2.** A wheel; a turn; a revolution.

淪 **lun 2.** Eddying water; engulfed; lost.

綸 **lun 2.** To wind; to regulate.

掄 **lun 1.** To wave; to brandish.

䑳 **lun 2.** The prow of a junk.

碖 **lun 2.** Rocks; reefs.

圇 **lun 2.** Complete; whole.

崙 **lun 2.** The K'un-lün mountains.

381

門

See Lesson 129 C.

門 **mên 2.** A door; a gate; a family; school; sect.

們 **mên 1.** The sign of the plural.

捫 **mên 1.** To feel for; to palp.

悶 **mên 4.** Melancholy; depressed; stupid.

閔 **min 3.** Compassion.

閩 **min 2.** The Fukien province.

問 **wên 4.** To ask; to enquire.

聞 **wên 2.** To hear; to smell; to perceive.

閿 **wên 2.** A proper name.

闅 **wên 2.** Name of a place.

閏 **yün** Intercalary.

潤 **yün 4.** To moisten.

It is radical in

間 **chien 4.** A space between; to separate. S. 684.

闖 **ch'uang 3.** To burst in; to rush violently; suddenly.

Radical 169.

382

孟 

See Lesson 157 B.

孟 **mêng 4.** Chief; head; first; eldest.

猛 **mêng 3.** Fierce; cruel.

艋 **mêng 3.** A small boat.

擝 **mêng 1.** To pull; to haul.

蜢 **mêng 3.** A locust.

383

See Lesson 18 G.

宓 **mi 4.** Still; silent.

蜜 **mi 4.** Honey.

密 **mi 4.** Intimate; secret; dense; thick.

榓 **mi 4.** The eagle-wood tree, *aloexylon.*

[illegible] **mi 4.** Strong; brave.

㨸 **mi 4.** To strike.

蔤 **mi 4.** The roots of the lotus.

Compare S. 148.

384

明

See Lesson 42 C.

明 **ming 2.** Bright; light; clear; to explain; intelligent.

鵬 **ming 2.** A kind of pheasant.

盟 **mêng 2.** A covenant.

萌 **mêng 2.** A germ; a shoot; to thrive.

385

See Lesson 14 N.

念 **nien 4.** To think; to ponder on; to study; to read.

捻 **nien 3.** To nip with the fingers.

埝 **nien 4.** To sink; to gather.

[illegible] **nien 1.** To stop; silent.

[illegible] **nien 3.** To pursue.

錜 **nien 4.** A hair-pin.

艌 **nien 4.** A hawser.

惗 **nien 1.** To like.

淰 **nien 3,** Muddy.

[illegible] **nien 4.** A tow-rope.

敜 **nien 1.** To fill.

騐 **yen 4.** To inspect; to verify: evidence.

諗 **shên 3.** To reflect on; to reprove.

稔 **jên 3.** Pipe grain; a harvest.

棯 **jên 3.** A jujube.

腍 **jên 3.** Cooked food.

386

帛

See Lesson 88 A.

帛 **pai 2.** Silk; wealth.

It is radical in

緜 **mien 2.** Soft; down. *This is phonetic contracted in.*

棉 **mien 2.** The cotton tree; cotton.

綿 **mien 2.** Soft; downy; floss silk.

Radical in

錦 **chin 3.** Embroidered.

387

朋

See Lesson 64 I.

朋 **p'êng 2.** A friend; to associate; to match.

淜 **p'êng 1.** Noise of dashing water.

棚 **p'êng 1.** A mat-shed.

硼 **p'êng 2.** Borax.

鵬 **p'êng 2.** The rukh, a fabulous eagle.

堋 **pêng 4.** To cover with earth.

弸 **pêng 1.** A stiff bow; strong.

綳 **pêng 1.** Swaddling-clothes.

痭 **pêng 1.** Menorrhagia.

崩 **pêng 1.** To collapse; the Emperor's death; a flux.

It is unconnected with

蒯 **k'uai 3.** Rush. L. 156 H.

388

卑 

See Lesson 46 E.

卑 **pi 1.** Low; base; applied conventionally to one's self.

裨 **pi 4.** To aid; to benefit.

婢 **pi 4.** A slave-girl.

睥 **pi 4.** To glance around; to spy.

髀 **pi 4.** The pelvis.

俾 **pi 4.** To cause; to enable.

椑 **pi 1.** A wine vessel.

鞞 **pi 3.** A scabbard.

痺 **pi 4.** Rheumatism; numbness.

萆 **pi 1.** Castor-oil plant.

脾 **p'i 2.** The spleen.

埤 **p'i 3.** A low wall.

崥 **p'i 2.** Hilly.

陴 **p'i 2.** A parapet; a battlement.

郫 **p'i 2.** A place in Ssŭch'uan.

[illegible] **p'i 1.** To peel; to trim.

鵯 **p'i 1.** The jackdaw.

鼙 **p'i 1.** A war-drum.

卑 **pei 1.** Low base.

婢 **pei 4.** A slave-girl.

碑 **pei 1.** A stone tablet; a tombstone.

箄 **pei 1.** A basket-trap for catching fish.

稗 **pai 4.** Weeds; tares; a panic grass.

粺 **pai 4.** White rice.

牌 **p'ai 2.** A tablet; a signboard; a warrant; a token; cards.

捭 **p'ai 2.** To strike.

簰 **p'ai 2.** A raft.

389

See Lesson 16 K.

表 **piao 3.** Outside; external; to make known; to manifest; a watch.

婊 **piao 3.** A prostitute.

裱 **piao 3.** To paste.

捸 **piao 4.** To bind; to tie up.

俵 **piao 3.** To distribute.

390

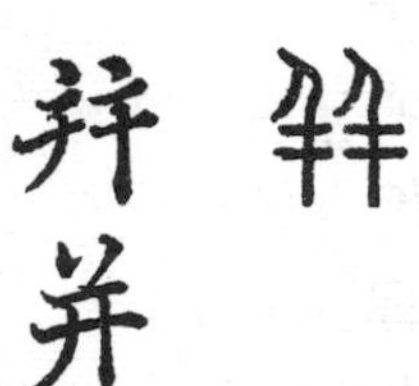

See Lesson 115 B.

幷 幵 } **ping 4.** United; together; moreover; also.

併 **ping 4.** On a level with; even; together.

鉼 **ping 3.** A plate of metal.

餅 **ping 3.** Cakes; pastry.

駢 **ping 4.** A couple; a pair; a band.

栟 **ping 1.** The sago-palm.

屏 **ping 3.** A screen; to screen.

缾 **p'ing 2.** A bottle.

拼 **p'ing 1.** To attack.

軿 **p'ing 2.** A cart with screens.

姘 **p'ing 1.** Misconduct; bad behaviour.

洴 **p'ing 2.** Noise of water.

瓶 **p'ing 2.** A bottle.

郱 **p'ing 2.** A place in Shantung.

荓 **p'ing 1.** To stimulate; to prick.

屏 **p'ing 2.** A screen; to cover.

胼 **p'ien 1.** Callous; rough.

弸 **pêng 1.** To pull a bow to the full; a swindler.

絣 **pêng 1.** To join; to connect.

迸 **pêng 4.** To bound.

It is phonetic contracted in

形 **hsing 2.** Substance, appearance. See S. 204.

邢 **hsing 2.** A place in Chihli.

Compare S. 204.

See L. 60 L for the following.

竝 **ping 4.** Together.

並 **ping 4.** Together; moreover.

傡 **ping 4.** Together.

碰 **p'êng 4.** To bump; to collide with.

掽 **p'êng 4.** To run against; to clash.

391

尚

See Lesson 36 E.

尙 **shang 4.** To wish; to esteem; if; still.

賞 **shang 3.** To bestow; to reward.

裳 **shang 1.** The clothes on the lower half of the body.

掌 **chang 3.** The palm; a sole; a paw; to rule; to control.

鞝 **chang 3.** Horse-shoe.

惝 **ch'ang 3.** Agitated; alarmed.

徜 **ch'ang 2.** Inconstant; to loiter.

敞 **ch'ang 3.** High level land; open. S. 663.

常 **ch'ang 2.** Constant; ordinary; frequent.

嘗 **ch'ang 2.** To taste; to try; ordinary.

償 **ch'ang 2.** To pay back; to indemnify.

牚 **ch'êng 1.** To resist. S. 666.

倘 **t'ang 3.** If; supposing that.

𨋍 **t'ang 4.** A time; a turn.

淌 **t'ang 3.** To flow; not lasting.

躺 **t'ang 3.** To lie down.

棠 **t'ang 2.** Sorb-tree.

堂 **t'ang 2.** A hall; a court; a church; a residence. S. 649.

當 **tang 1.** Ought; suitable to act as.
tang 4. To pawn; a trap.

黨 **tang 3.** A party; a club; a gang.

瓽 **tang 4.** A large earthenware tub.

党 **tang 3.** A proper name.

392

See Lesson 49 E.

受 **shou 4.** To be a recipient of; to suffer; to bear.

授 **shou 4.** To give; to transmit.

綬 **shou 4.** A ribbon; a band; a seal.

393

See Lesson 124 B.

叔 **shu 2.** A father's younger brother.

淑 **shu 4.** Clear; pure; virtuous.

俶 **shu 4.** To begin; a beginning.

婌 **shu 1.** The governess of the women in palace.

菽 **shu 4.** Pulse; coarse food.

督 **tu 1.** To inspect; to watch over; to rule.

裻 **tu 4.** A suture; a seam.

踧 **tsu 4.** To walk with respect.

寂 **chi 2** Silent; quiet.

椒 **chiao 1.** Pepper; *piper, capsicum*, etc.

394

松

See Lesson 18 C.

松 **sung 1.** Coniferous trees.

淞 **sung 1.** Name of a place, Woosung.

凇 **sung 1.** Icicles.

崧 **sung 1.** A mountain in Honan.

菘 **sung 1.** Turnips.

鬆 **sung 1.** Dishevelled; loose; to untie, to relax.

鶱 **sung 1.** The kestrel.

395

See Lesson 73 A.

沓 **ta 4.** A babble of words.

嵱 **ta 2.** A knoll; a mound.

鞜 **ta 2.** A thimble.

鞜 **ta 2.** A timbrel.

偺 **t'a 4.** To idle.

塔 **t'a 4.** To pile up.

幍 **t'a 4.** Tester of a bed.

碏 **t'a 4.** A mortar.

榙 **t'a 4.** A capital.

錔 **t'a 4.** Ironclad.

踏 **cha 4, ch'a 1.** To trample on.

396

See Lesson 54 C.

匋 **t'ao 2.** A kiln.

陶 **t'ao 2.** A kiln for making pottery; to mould.

掏 **t'ao 1.** To take out.

淘 **t'ao 2.** To clean out.

裪 **t'ao 2.** Sleeves.

綯 **t'ao 2.** A cord; to tie.

啕 **t'ao 2.** To chatter; to prattle.

祹 **t'ao 2.** Happiness; success.

錭 **t'ao 2.** Blunt.

醄 **t'ao 2.** Drunk.

萄 **t'ao 2.** The grape.

397

See Lesson 45 E.

㝵 **tê 2.** To get.

得 **tê 2.** To get; to effect.
tei 3. Must, ought.
to 2. To suffice.

㝵 **tê 2.** To beat.

淂 **tê 2.** Watery.

㝵 **t'ê 2.** Success; satisfaction.

398

See Lesson 156 C.

典 **tien 3.** A law; a rule; a canon; to govern.

㙉 **tien 1.** To offer.

㥏 **t'ien 3.** Bashful; timid.

琠 **t'ien 4.** Ear-rings.

淟 **t ien 3.** Dirty; defiled.

腆 **t'ien 3.** To prosper; abundance.

399

See Lesson 60 C.

忝 **t'ien 3.** To disgrace.

添 **t'ien 1.** To add to; to increase.

舔 **t'ien 3.** To lick.

掭 **t'ien 4.** To dip the writing-brush.

[illegible] **t'ien 3.** To await in a respectful attitude.

[illegible] **t'ien 4.** To stammer.

菾 **t'ien 2.** The beet.

400

See Lesson 112 I.

定 **ting 4.** To fix; to settle; to decide; certain; a settled mind.

錠 **ting 4.** An ingot.

碇 **ting 4.** A large stone used as an anchor.

淀 **tien 4.** A marsh.

靛 **tien 4.** Indigo.

綻 [illegible] } **chan 4.** An opened seam in a garment; to rip; cracked.

401

See Lesson 133 A.

咅 **t'ou 4.** To interrupt.

敨 **t'ou 3.** To explain.

剖 **p'ou 1.** To split.

瓿 **p'ou 3** A jar.

菩 **p'u 2** The *ficus religiosa*. *P'u-sa*.

涪 **pu 2.** Name of a river.

部 **pu 4.** A class; a category; a Board.

培 **p'ei 4.** To bank up with earth; to strengthen.

賠 **p'ei 2.** To make good; to indemnify; to lose.

掊 **p'ei 3.** To take; to rob

醅 **p'ei 1.** Must.

毰 **p'ei 2.** To spread the wings.

陪 **p'ei 2.** To bear one company; to aid; to match.

[illegible] **pei 1.** A tablet.

棓 **pei 1.** Chinese galls.

焙 **pei 4.** To dry over a fire.

涪 **pei 4.** Thick fog; dark.

倍 **pei 4.** Double; to double; to multiply.

402

See Lesson 49 B.

采 **ts'ai 3.** Variegated; objects.

彩 **ts'ai 3.** Gay-coloured; elegant; lucky.

採 **ts'ai 3.** To pick; to gather; to collect; to make enquiries.

綵 **ts'ai 3.** Coloured.

睬 **ts'ai 3.** To take notice.

埰 **ts'ai 4.** Allotments to feudal nobles.

棌 **ts'ai 3.** A species of oak.

菜 **ts'ai 4.** Culinary vegetables; food.

403

See Lesson 16 M.

卒 [illegible] } **tsu 2.** Servants; to conclude; to end; to die.

[illegible] **tsu 2.** To die.

椊 **tsu 1.** To put a handle in a socket.

捽 **tsu 4.** To grasp.

猝 **ts'u 4.** To rush out; precipitate; suddenly.

踤 **ts'u 4.** To run against.

崒 **ts'u 4.** The summit of a peak.

醉 **tsui 4.** Drunk; unconscious.

稡 **tsui 4.** To gather; to collect.

啐 **ts'ui 4.** To spit.

粹 **ts'ui 4.** Unmixed; pure.

悴 **ts'ui 4.** Grieved; downcast.

倅 **ts'ui 4.** An assistant.

淬 **ts'ui 2.** To dye.

焠 **ts'ui 4.** To burn.

萃 **ts'ui 1.** A jungle; a bundle; a collection.

瘁 **ts'ui 4.** Worn out.

翠 **ts'ui 4.** A kingfisher.

碎 **sui 4.** Fragments; small pieces; bits.

誶 **sui 4.** To abuse; to rail at.

睟 **sui 4.** Clear; net.

晬 **sui 4.** A year elapsed.

404

See Lesson 36 B.

宗 **tsung 1.** Ancestors; clans; family; kind; class; to follow; to honour.

踪 **tsung 1.** A footstep; a trace.

綜 **tsung 4.** The threads of a texture: to arrange; to gather up.

騌 **tsung 1.** A horse's mane.

棕 **tsung 1.** The coir-palm.

粽 **tsung 4.** Dumplings.

賨 **tsung 1.** A tribute.

猣 **tsung 1.** A pig.

琮 **ts'ung 1.** Badges of rank made of jade.

悰 **ts'ung 2.** Joy; enjoyment.

淙 **ts'ung 2.** Rushing water.

𨛬 **ch'ung 2.** A feudal state in Shansi.

崇 **ch'ung 2.** Lofty; eminent; to reverence; to adore.

405

東

See Lesson 120 K.

東 **tung 1.** The East; the place of honour.

凍 **tung 4.** To freeze.

棟 **tung 4.** Beams in a roof; a prop.

㥈 **tung 1.** Stupid; dull.

蝀 **tung 1.** A rainbow.

涷 **tung 1.** Heavy rain, to soak.

倲 **tung 1.** Weak, sickly.

It is unconnected with

陳 **ch'ên 3.** Old. To arrange. See L. 50 H.

406

甾

See Lesson 12 I.

甾 **tzŭ 1.** Waste land.

𦓡 **tzŭ 1.** To plough.

緇 **tzŭ 1.** Dark colour.

鯔 **tzŭ 1.** A mackerel.

輜 **tzŭ 1.** Baggage waggons.

淄 **tzŭ 1.** A river in Shantung.

錙 **tzŭ 1.** The fourth part of a tael; petty.

Compare L. 40 B, S. 469.

407

宛

See Lesson 64 D.

宛 **wan 3.** To give way; to yield, courtesy.

腕 **wan 4.** The wrist; a flexible joint.

婉 **wan 3.** Complaisant; obliging.

帵 **wan 1.** Remnants; snips

琬 **wan 3.** A sceptre.

晼 **wan 3.** The declining sun.

豌 **wan 1.** The garden pea.

捥 **wan 4.** To bend the wrist.

𩩲 **wan 4.** The knee-joint.

畹 **wan 3.** A field.

惋 **wan 3.** Painful.

碗 **wan 3.** A bowl.

涴 **wan 3.** To whirl.

剜 **wan 1.** To cut; to pick out.

菀 **wan 3.** To grow luxuriantly.

𣨐 **yüan 3.** Inert.

蜿 **yüan 1.** To move sinuously.

鵷 **yüan 1.** The argus pheasant.

It is radical in

黦 **yeh 4.** To fade; discoloured.

Compare S. 174.

408

See Lesson 39 C.

罔 **wang 3.** A net; not; without.

網 **wang 3.** A net; a web.

惘 **wang 3.** To lose one's self-possession.

誷 **wang 3.** To slander.

魍 **wang 3.** A sprite.

輞 **wang 3.** The felly of a wheel.

Compare S. 366.

409

See Lesson 121 F.

委 **wei 3.** To give up; to throw away; to send; to depute; a wrong; a grievance.

萎 **wei 1** To wither; to decay.

痿 **wei 3.** Paralysis; weakness.

餧 **wei 4.** To feed.

緌 **wei 1.** A bridle; a string.

䅗 **wei 2.** Four sheafs.

蜲 **wei 3.** A wood-louse.

䴧 **wei 1.** The best cut of venison.

諉 **wei 3.** To shirk; to evade.

痿 **wei 3.** Diseased; weak.

逶 **wei 1.** To swagger.

魏 **wei 4.** A proper name; lofty; eminent. *Hence*

[illegible] **wei 2.** Asa fœtida.

蘶 **wei 4.** Sprouts.

巍 **wei 1.** Rocky; precipitous.

倭 **wo 1.** A Japanese, a dwarf.

踒 **wo 1.** To sprain.

矮 躷 } **yeh 3.** Low; dwarf.

捼 **nei 2.** To rub; to caress; to polish.

410

武

See Lesson 71 K.

武 **wu 3.** Warlike; weapons.

珷 **wu 3.** An inferior kind of jade.

碔 **wu 3.** The common jade.

鵡 **wu 3.** A cockatoo.

賦 **fu 4.** To give; to levy; rhytmic prose; natural.

411

亞 亞

See Lesson 82 H.

亞 **ya 4.** Secondary; similar.

啞 **ya 3.** Dumb, *ya-pa.*

稏 **ya 4.** A kind of rice.

椏 **ya 1.** A fork.

㤷 **ya 4.** Sorrow.

𥓏 **ya 1.** Rough; uneven.

婭 **ya 4.** A brother-in-law.

掗 **ya 4.** To shake.

𠛮 **ya 1.** To pierce through.

𣢇 **ya 4.** Hiccough.

瘂 **ya 3.** Hoarse.

𥥩 **ya 1.** Crooked; awry.

It is radical in

惡 o 4. Evil; wrong.
wu 4. To hate.

412

See Lesson 39 J.

肴 **yao 2.** Sacrificial meats; exquisite viands.

餚 **yao 4.** Food; viands.

崤 **yao 2.** Mountains in Honan.

淆 **yao 2.** Mixed; confused.

殽 **yao 3.** To eat; viands.

413

厓 厓

See Lesson 59 B.

厓 **yeh 2. yai 2.** A bank; a shore; a limit.

涯 **yai 2.** A bank; a shore; a limit.

睚 **yai 2.** To stare.

捱 **yai 2.** To endure; to delay.

㤜 **yai 4.** To hate

崖 **yai 2.** A steep bank; a cliff; a precipice.

𤸷 **yai 2.** Stupid; doltish.

414

邪 耶

See LL. 146 E 147 B.

耶 **yeh 2.** A final particle.

椰 **yeh 2** The cocoa-nut tree.

揶 **yeh 1.** To gesticulate; to posture.

瑘 **yeh 2.** Name of part of Shantung.

鎁 **yeh 1.** The name of a famous sword.

爺 **yeh 2.** A grandfather; a term of respect; a gentleman.

梛 **yeh 2.** The cocoa-nut tree.

挪 **yeh 1.** To gesticulate; to ridicule.

琊 **yeh 2.** Name of a place in Shantung.

鋣 **yeh 1.** A sword.

415

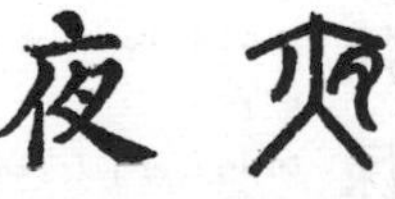

See Lesson 60 I.

夜 **yeh 4.** Night; darkness.

掖 **yeh 4.** To support; to uphold.

液 **yeh 4.** Spittle; sweat; juice; secretion.

腋 **yeh 4.** The arm-pit.

腋 **yeh 4.** The arm-pit.

[illegible] **yeh 4.** Flame; blaze.

416

炎

See Lesson 126 D.

炎 **yen 2.** To flame; to blaze; very hot.

掞 **yen 2.** To spread over; to cover.

琰 **yen 2.** The lustre of gems.

[illegible] **yen 3.** Agreeable; sweet.

燄 **yen 4.** Fire; flames.

剡 **yen 3.** Sharp; to sharpen.

扊 **yen 3.** The bar of a door.

淡 **tan 4.** Insipid; tasteless; colourless.

談 **t'an 2.** To talk; to chat.

毯 **t'an 3.** Rugs; carpets.

賧 **t'an 4.** To redeem oneself from punishment.

惔 **t'an 3.** Consumed with grief.

錟 **t'an 2.** A long spear.

餤 **t'an 2.** Aliments.

郯 **t'an 2.** Name of a place.

痰 **t'an 2.** Phlegm.

菼 **t'an 3.** A kind of rush.

睒 **shan 3.** To glance at.

晱 **shan 3.** Bright.

It is radical in

黑 **hei 1.** Soot; black. S. 678.

熏 **hsün 1.** To smoke. S. 781.

粦 **lin 2.** Ignis fatuus. S. 696.

417

延

See Lesson 112 A.

延 **yen 2.** To drag out; to protract; delay; to invite; to engage.

埏 **yen 2.** A boundary; a limit.

綖 **yen 2.** Strings or tassels.

蜒 **yen 2.** Scolopendra.

梴 **yen 2.** A long piece of timber; long.

郔 **yen 2.** The name of a place.

莚 **yen 2.** Climbing plants.

筵 **yen 2.** A bamboo mat; a feast; a banquet.

涎 **hsien 2.** Spittle; saliva; to covet.

誕 **tan 4.** To boast; to bear children; birth.

418

奄

See Lesson 50 E.

奄 **yen 3.** To extend, to spread.

掩 **yen 3.** To cover; to conceal.

淹 **yen 1.** To soak; to steep.

[illegible] **yen 1.** To cover the fire.

埯 **yen 3.** To cover with earth.

晻 **yen 3.** Obscured; hidden.

崦 **yen 1.** A mountain in the West.

腌 **yen 1.** Pickled meat.

醃 **yen 1.** To salt; to pickle.

剦 **yen 1.** To castrate; a eunuch.

閹 **yen 1.** A eunuch of the palace.

唵 **nan 1.** To snap up.

俺 **nan 1.** I, me.

鵪 **nan 1.** A quail.

庵, 菴 **nan 1.** A hut; a cottage; a Buddhist monastery.

419

於

See Lesson 138 D.

於 **yü 2.** In; at; on; among; to; for; than.

淤 **yü 1.** To silt up; alluvion.

棜 **yü 4.** A tray with long handles.

閼 **yü 4.** To close; to shut up.

瘀 **yü 1.** Extravasated blood.

菸 **yen 1.** Tobacco.

Compare S. 582.

420

See Lesson 20 F.

查 **ch'a 2.** To examine into; to investigate.

碴 **ch'a 4.** A potsherd.

蹅 **ch'a 1.** To flounder about.

喳 **ch'a 1.** To twitter.

[illegible] **ch'a 1.** Leather.

楂 **cha 1.** Azerole-tree.

⿰火查 **cha 2.** To fry.

揸 **cha 1.** To seize; a handful.

渣 **cha 1.** Dregs; residue.

421

See Lesson 102 A.

臿 **ch'a 2.** To pound in a mortar.

插 **ch'a 1.** To insert; to stick in; a bolt.

⿰言臿 **ch'a 4.** To talk much; to interfere.

鍤 **ch'a 2.** A cymbal.

⿰衤臿 **ch'a 1.** Border; fringe.

⿰糹臿 **ch'a 1.** To sew and hem.

喢 **ch'a 4.** To prattle.

歃 **ch'a 4.** To anoint one's lips with blood; an oath.

牐 **cha 2.** A shop front.

422

See Lesson 159 B.

者 **chê 3.** A final particle; a suffix.

赭 **chê 3.** The colour of ochre.

奢 **ch'ê 1.** Prodigal; dissipated.

撦 **ch'ê 3.** To tear.

著 **chao 2.** To actuate, to determine.

著 **chu 4.** To make manifest.

箸 **chu 4.** Chopsticks.

煮 **chu 4.** To boil; to decoct.

翥 **chu 2.** To fly up; to soar.

渚 **chu 3.** An islet.

陼 **chu 3.** A bank.

豬 **chu 1.** The pig.

諸 **chu 1.** All; every; a final particle; at; in.

櫧 **chu 1.** An evergreen oak.

藷 **chu 1.** The sugar-cane.

褚 **ch'u 3.** A sheath, a satchel.

蝫 **ch'u 2.** A toad.

楮 **ch'u 3.** The paper-mulberry *Broussonetia papyrifera*; paper money; a letter.

躇 **ch'u 2.** Undecided; irresolute.

儲 **ch'u 2.** To collect; to store up.

瀦 **ch'u 2.** Name of a river.

蠩 **ch'u 1.** A toad.

覩 **tu 3.** To gaze at; to observe.

睹 **tu 3.** To gaze at; to observe.

暏 **tu 3.** Morning; dawn.

堵 **tu 3.** To block up; to stop.

賭 **tu 3.** To gamble; to bet.

都 **tu 1.** The capital. All.

嘟 **tu 1.** To grumble.

瘏 **t'u 2.** To be exhausted.

屠 **t'u 2.** To kill; to butcher.

⿱艹都 **t'ou 2.** A bud.

暑 **shu 3.** Summer's heat; heat of the sun.

署 **shu 3.** A public court; a tribunal; to appoint temporary; to write. S. 789.

緒 **hsü 4.** Succession, connexion.

423

貞 

See Lesson 56 C.

貞 **chêng 1.** Chaste; pure; virtuous.

楨 **chêng 1.** A common evergreen, *ligustrum lucidum*.

禎 **chêng 1.** Lucky; propitious.

幀 **chêng 4.** Flowered silken-curtain.

湞 **chêng 1.** Name of a river.

赬 **chêng 1.** Purple.

偵 **ch'êng 1.** To spy; to explore.

424

See Lesson 26 M.

卽 即 即 } **chi 2.** Now; immediately; near. **chi 4.** Then; consequently.

蝍 **chi 2.** A cicada.

喞 **chi 1.** The hum of insects; chirping.

楖 **chi 2.** A tree allied to the ash.

鯽 **chi 4.** The bastard carp.

堲 **chi 4.** To brick a grave.

節 **chieh 2.** An article; a period; temperance. S 798.

Compare S. 596.

425

See Lesson 146 C.

咠 **ch'i 1.** To whisper in the ear; to blame.

緝 ch'i 1. To twist; to join; to pursue.

葺 ch'i 1. To repair; to put in order.

楫 chi 4. An oar; to row.

輯 chi 4. To arrange; order; collection; agreeable.

戢 chi 4. To cease to fight, to abscond.

揖 i 1. Reverence; to salute.

426

契 契

See Lesson 97 D.

契 ch'i 4. To notch; a covenant; a deed; adopted; dedicated to.

鍥 ch'i 4. A chisel.

葜 ch'ia 1. A felicitous plant.

猰 ch'ien 2. A leopard.

褉 hsieh 4. A short garment.

楔 hsieh 1. A peg.

揳 hsieh 4. To feel, to estimate.

喫 ch'ih 1. To eat; to absorb; to suffer.

Compare S. 181.

427

叚 叚

See Lesson 43 I.

叚 chia 3. False; borrowed.

假 chia 3. False.
chia 1. A leave.

徦 chia 3. To reach.

嘏 chia 3. Felicity; prosperity; strong.

豭 chia 1. A boar.

葭 chia 3 Reed; relationship.

椵 chia 1. A kind of lemon-tree.

瘕 chia 2. Constipation.

麚 chia 1. Antlers.

霞 hsia 2. Clouds tinged red; vapour.

暇 hsia 2. Leisure.

蝦 hsia 1. Batrachians.

鰕 hsia 1. Shrimps; prawns.

瑕 hsia 1. A flaw; a blemish.

騢 hsia 2. A spotted horse.

瞎 hsia 4. To gaze at; to watch.

軀 hsia 1. Hunchbacked.

遐 hsia 2. Long; far; old; an interrogative particle.

蕸 hsia 2. Water-rushes.

蝦 ho 2. A frog, *ho-ma*.

428

皆 皆

See Lesson 27 I.

皆 chieh 1. All; every; together.

階 chieh 1. A flight of steps; a degree; a rank.

堦 chieh 2. A degree; a rank.

稭 chieh 1. Stalks.

鶛 chieh 1. A quail.

鍇 chieh 3. Fine iron.

湝 chieh 1. The rippling of water.

喈 chieh 1. Music; melody.

揩 ch'ieh 1. To rub; to strike.

偕 hsieh 2. Together; with.

諧 }
龤 } hsieh 2. To accord; to agree; to harmonise.

楷 k'ai 3. A model; a pattern; the modern style of writing.

429

柬 柬

See Lesson 120 I.

柬 chien 3. A slip of paper; to abridge; to select.

諫 chien 4. To warn; to reprove.

揀 chien 3. To select; to choose.

暕 chien 3. To shine; to light.

練 lien 4. To boil raw silk to soften it; to drill in; to practice.

鍊 lien 4. To smelt ores; to refine.

煉 lien 4. To separate dross by fire, to test.

湅 lien 4 To whiten.

楝 lien 4. The *Melia azedarach*, bearing lilac flowers.

揀 lien 4. To hammer out; to beat.

闌 lan 2. A screen; to separate. S. 833.

430

建 建

See Lesson 169 B.

建 chien 4. To found; to establish.

揵 chien 4. To bear; to raise; to fix.

健 **chien 4.** Strong; constant.

楗 **chien 4.** Fence, enclosure.

犍 **chien 1.** A gelded bull.

鞬 **chien 1.** A bow-case.

鍵 **chien 4.** A bolt, a spring.

踺 **chien 1.** To kick.

腱 **chien 4.** The tendon.

毽 **chien 4.** A shuttle-cock.

431

See Lesson 66 D.

前 **ch'ien 2.** Before, in time or in place.

媊 **ch'ien 2.** The morning star, Venus.

湔 **chien 1.** To wash; to water; to sprinkle.

揃 **chien 3.** To tie; to strike.

箭 **chien 4.** An arrow.

鬋 **chien 1.** Locks of hair.

煎 **chien 1.** To fry; to decoct

剪 **chien 3.** To cut; scissors.

翦 **chien 3.** To cut; scissors.

432

See Lesson 41 G.

酋 **chiu 1.** Liquor after fermentation; perfect.

湭 **chiu 1.** To float.

䰫 **chiu 1.** The hair done up in a knot.

煪 **ch'iu 1.** To scorch; to dry.

鰌 **ch'iu 1.** The loach, *cobitis*.

遒 **ch'iu 1.** To urge on.

蝤 **ch'iu 2.** A crab.

緧 **ch'iu 1.** A crupper.

猷 **yu 2.** To plan; to deliberate.

猶 **yu 2.** As; like; similar.

楢 **yu 2.** Fellies.

輶 **yu 2.** A light carriage; light.

It is radical in

尊 **tsun 1.** Noble. S. 713.

And in

奠奠 **tien 4.** To pour a libation; to present. *Hence*

鄭 **chêng 4.** A feudal state, now in Honan.

擲 **chih 4.** To throw; to fling away.

Compare S. 318.

433

秋

See Lesson 121 C.

秋 **ch'iu 1.** Autumn; harvest.

楸 **ch'iu 1.** The catalpa.

[illegible] **ch'iu 1.** The spokes of a wheel.

鞦 **ch'iu 1.** A crupper.

鰍 **ch'iu 1.** The loach, *cobitis*.

偢 **ch'iu 1.** To look at.

萩 **ch'iu 1.** A plant like the may-weed, *antennaria*.

[illegible] **ch'iu 1.** A chicken.

甃 **ch'iu 4.** To brick a well.

鶖 **ch'iu 1** A stork.

揪 **chiu 1.** To grasp.

啾 **chiu 1.** Onomatopœia.

湫 **chiu 4.** To shrivel.

煍 **ch'iao 3.** To smoke, to blacken.

愀 **ch'iao 3.** To blush.

[illegible] **ch'iao 1.** A kind of turban worn as mourning; to hem.

鍫 **ch'iao 1.** A hoe; to hoe.

愁 **ch'ou 3** Melancholy; sad; fearful.

瞅 **ch'ou 3.** To look at; to gaze.

僽 **ch'ou 4.** A quarrel; to insult.

434

耑

See Lesson 164 B.

耑 **chuan 1.** Roots, to develop.

顓 **chuan 1.** Respect, dignified.

喘 **ch'uan 3.** To pant; to breathe quick and short.

諯 **ch'uan 1.** To number; to reckon.

遄 **ch'uan 1.** To hurry.

端 **tuan 1.** Correct, regular, article, end; to serve a meal.

剬 **tuan 1.** To chisel.

湍 **t'uan 2.** Rapid current; boisterous.

煓 **t'uan 2.** Fire, red.

揣 **ch'uai 3.** To feel for; to estimate.

It is phonetic contracted in

惴 **ch'uai 4.** Mournful.

踹 **ch'uai 4.** To stamp on.

椯 **chui 3.** A rod.

瑞 **jui 4.** Precious; auspicious.

435

See Lesson 13 E.

𠂹 垂 **ch'ui 2.** To hang down; to let fall; to condescend.

棰 **ch'ui 2.** A bat.

捶 **ch'ui 2** To beat, to flog.

陲 **ch'ui 2.** A frontier; a boundary.

錘 **ch'ui 2.** A counter-poise.

倕 **ch'ui 2.** A proper name.

腄 **ch'ui 2.** The buttocks.

[illegible] **ch'ui 2.** To bend to the wind.

箠 **ch'ui 2.** A rod.

鬌 **ch'ui 2.** The front tresses of a girl.

硾 **chui 4.** To weight; to press things down.

睡 **shui 4.** To sleep.

唾 **t'o 4.** To spit; saliva. *T'u 4.*

埵 **to 3.** A mound.

郵 **yu 2.** A post house; a courier.

436

See Lesson 47 P.

春 **ch'un 1.** Spring; pleasant; wanton.

椿 **ch'un 1.** *Cedrela, ailantus.*

偆 **ch'un 3.** Rich, liberal.

鰆 **ch'un 1.** A mullet.

[illegible] **ch'un 3.** Corpulent; fat.

踳 **ch'un 3.** Obstinate.

蠢 **ch'un 3.** Stupid; doltish.

437

See Lesson 120 K.

重 **chung 4.** Heavy; important, severe.

種 **chung 3.** A seed.
chung 4. To sow.

鍾 **chung 1.** A measure.

腫 **chung 3.** To swell.

偅 **chung 3.** Heedless.

[illegible] **chung 4.** Pregnancy.

諥 **chung 4.** To offend.

踵 **chung 3.** The heel; to follow.

煄 **chung 3.** To kindle.

瘇 **chung 3.** Dropsy.

重 **ch'ung 2.** Repetition; again.

揰 **ch'ung 4.** To push into; to stir out.

衝 **ch'ung 1.** To rush towards, or against.

動 **tung 4.** To move; to displace; to shake.

董 **tung 3.** To regulate, trustees

懂 **tung 3.** To understand.

畽 **t'ung 4.** A thrashing-floor.

慟 **t'ung 4.** Moved; affected; grieved.

438

軍

See Lesson 167 C.

軍 **chün 1.** A legion of 12 500 men; military.

皸 **chün 1** A chap; a crack.

運 **yün 4.** To turn round; a revolution; a circuit; fate.

惲 **yün 3.** To plan.

韗 **yün 4.** A drum.

鄆 **yün 4.** Nime of a place in Shantung.

暈 **yün 4.** To be giddy. A halo.

渾 **hun 3.** A torrent; turbid; chaotic; the whole.

諢 **hun 4.** A joke.

琿 **hun 4.** A gem.

餫 **hun 4** Small fritters.

鼲 **hun 2.** A sort of marmot.

[illegible] **hun 2.** An appellation of women.

葷 **hun 1** Sapid meat forbidden to those who fast.

褌 **k'un 1.** Loose trowsers.

輝 **hui 1.** Bright; splendid.

暉 **hui 1.** Bright.

揮 **hui 1.** To move; to shake; to give a signal.

楎 **hui 1.** A peg to hang clothes on a wall.

煇 **hui 1.** The glare of fire.

翬 **hui 1.** A pheasant, to fly.

439

See Lesson 21 E.

風 **fêng 1.** The wind; custom; rumour; reputation.

瘋 **fêng 1.** Nervous affections; paralysis; madness.

葻 **fêng 1.** Sough of the wind, psalmody.

楓 **fêng 1.** The maple; *liquidambar*.

渢 **fêng 2.** The rippling of waves along a shore.

諷 **fêng 3.** To chant; to ridicule.

440

封

See Lesson 79 E.

封 **fêng 1.** A fief; to appoint; to seal up.

葑 **fêng 1.** Turnips, coarse food.

崶 **fêng 1.** A hill; difficulty.

犎 **fêng 1.** An ox with a hump, the zebu.

幫 幇 } **pang 1.** To help.

[封手] **pang 1.** To resist.

441

畐

See Lesson 75 n.

畐 **fu 4.** To be full.

福 **fu 4.** Happiness; luck; blessings.

匐 **fu 4.** To crawl; to creep.

富 **fu 2.** Wealth.

蝠 **fu 2.** The bat.

幅 **fu 2.** A strip of cloth; a roll of paper; a hem.

輻 **fu 2.** The spokes of a wheel; a centre.

副 **fu 4.** To aid; to assist; a second; to assort.

逼 **pi 4.** To press; to compel.

愊 **pi 4.** Pain, sorrow.

偪 **pi 4.** To compel.

蔔 **pai 4.** Carrot; turnip.

442

复

See Lesson 75 I.

复 **fu 2** To go back.

蝮 **fu 2.** A venomous snake, cobra.

腹 **fu 4.** The belly.

複 **fu 4.** Double or lined garments.

[土复] **fu 2.** A cave.

輹 **fu 2.** Pegs of a cart.

鰒 **fu 2.** Ear-shell, *haliotis*.

馥 **fu 4** A fragrant smell.

復 **fu 4.** To come or go back; again; to reply; to restore.

覆 **fu 3.** The reverse; to overthrow; to defeat.

It is radical in

愎 **pi 4.** Perverse, obstinate.

It is unconnected with

履 **li 3.** Shoes, to walk. L. 75 J.

443

曷

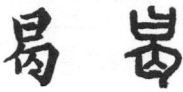

See Lesson 73 A.

曷 **ho 2.** How? Why? Where? What? When?

喝 **ho 1.** To shout out; to drink.

褐 **ho 2.** Coarse woollen stuff. Poor, low.

蝎 **ho 1.** A worm; a grub.

鞨 **ho 2.** Half-boot.

鶡 **ho 4.** A pheasant, *syrmaticus Reevesii*.

[曷力] **ho 2.** To shake.

猲 **hsieh 4.** A fierce dog.

歇 **hsieh 1.** To stop, to rest.

蠍 **hsieh 1.** A scorpion.

謁 **yeh 4.** To visit; to receive a visit.

暍 **yeh 4.** Sunstroke.

竭 **chieh 2.** To exhaust; the utmost.

揭 **chieh 1.** To lift up; to solve; to borrow.

碣 **chieh 2.** A stone; a tablet; a pillar.

愒 **chieh 3.** To rest; to desire.

朅 **chieh 2.** Bravery.

楬 **chieh 2.** A board.

羯 **chieh 2.** A gelded ram; deer's skin.

葛 **ko 2.** A textile bean, *pueraria phaseoloides*.

渴 **k'o 3.** Thirsty.

遏 o 4. To stop; to check.

堨 o 4. A crack in a wall.

藹 o 3. A park; a crowd.

靄 o 3. Cloudy.

餲 nai 4. Spoiled food.

444

矦 侯

See Lesson 59 H.

矦 侯 } hou 2. Nobles; a marquis; a target; a particle.

候 hou 4. To await; to expect the arrival of; time.

喉 hou 2. The throat.

堠 hou 4. Mounds for fire-signals.

[illegible] hou 2. Wanton; lewd.

睺 hou 2. A constellation, regarded as unlucky.

猴 hou 2. A monkey.

餱 hou 2. Dry provisions.

睺 hou 2. Dim of sight; a Buddhist syllable.

褔 hou 2. To pray for blessings.

鍭 hou 2. The metal head of an arrow.

鯸 hou 1. A poisonous fish.

鄇 hou 2. Name of a place.

瘊 hou 2. Warts; pimples.

篌 hou 2. A large lute.

緱 kou 1. A sword-knot.

445

相 相

See Lesson 158 B.

相 hsiang 1. Mutual; to help. hsiang 4. To look at.

湘 hsiang 1. To boil.

緗 hsiang 1. A light yellow colour.

箱 hsiang 1. A box; a chest.

廂 hsiang 1. Side rooms.

想 hsiang 3. To think about; to reflect; to hope; to earn.

霜 shuang 1. Hoar-frost. S. 834.

446

咸 咸

See Lesson 71 I.

咸 hsien 2. Entirely; all.

鹹 hsien 2. Salted.

諴 hsien 2. Harmony.

麙 hsien 4. A roebuck.

蝛 hsien 1. A mussel.

羬 hsien 2. The nylgau.

減 减 } chien 3. To lessen; to diminish.

椷 chien 3. A casket.

[illegible] ch'ien 2. Uneasy in mind.

喊 han 3. To cry; to call.

感 kan 3. To influence; affected by; moved. S. 740.

鍼 chên 1. A needle; a pin.

葴 chên 1. A proper name.

箴 chên 1. A needle; to prick.

鱵 chên 1. A kind of white-bait, *hemiramphus*.

It is radical in

觱 pieh 3. Musical horn.

447

星 星

See Lesson 79 F.

星 hsing 1. A star; a spark; a spot.

腥 hsing 1. Rank strong smelling.

醒 hsing 3. To become sober; to wake up; to startle.

煋 hsing 1. A spark.

猩 hsing 1. The orang-outang.

鍟 hsing 1. Rust on iron.

箵 hsing 1. A screen.

戥 têng 3. A small steelyard for weighing money.

448

See Lesson 112 C.

胥 hsü 1. Mutually; together.

壻 hsü 2. A son-in-law.

婿 hsü 4. A son-in-law.

醑 hsü 3. To strain spirits.

稰 hsü 3. Ripe grain.

湑 **hsü 3.** Clear, limpid.

糈 **hsü 1.** Income.

諝 **hsü 3.** Prudence; ability.

449

See L. 76 H, and S. 207

宣 **hsüan 1.** To proclaim; to display.

揎 **hsüan 1** To pull up.

愃 **hsüan 1.** Joy; enthusiasm.

瑄 **hsüan 1.** A jasper discus.

喧 **hsüan 1.** Clamour; hubbub.

諠 **hsüan 1.** Clamour.

楦 **hsüan 4.** A last.

暄 **hsüan 1.** Genial; pleasant.

萱 **hsüan 1.** A day-lily, *hemerocallis.*

450

胡

See Lesson 24 F.

胡 **hu 2.** A dewlap; Mongols; how? why?

箶 **hu 2.** A quiver.

葫 **hu 2.** The bottle-gourd.

鬍 **hu 2.** The beard.

蝴 **hu 2.** A butterfly.

糊 **hu 3.** Paste; to paste; foolish; muddled.

𩋶 **hu 2.** A quiver.

煳 **hu 2.** To singe.

湖 **hu 2.** A lake.

猢 **hu 2.** A monkey.

楜 **hu 2.** Pepper-plant; pepper.

瑚 **hu 2.** A red coral.

餬 **hu 1.** Congee; food; to feed.

醐 **hu 2** Oil of butter.

衚 **hu 2.** A lane.

鶘 **hu 2.** The pelican.
Compare SS. 132 and 368.

451

奐

See Lesson 37 F.

奐 **huan 4.** Elegant.

換 **huan 4.** To change; to exchange.

喚 **huan 4.** To call out.

煥 **huan 4.** A flame; brightness.

渙 **huan 4.** High-water.

㛂 **huan 4.** Variegated.

瘓 **huan 4.** Sick; ill.

452

皇

See Lesson 83 C.

皇 **huang 2.** The Emperor; august.

徨 **huang 2.** Vacillating; irresolute.

惶 **huang 2.** Afraid; nervous; doubtful.

隍 **huang 2.** A moat; the tutelar deity of a city.

蝗 **huang 2.** The locust.

餭 **huang 2.** Pastry; cakes.

遑 **huang 2.** Leisure; careless.

湟 **huang 2** Name of a river.

鰉 **huang 2.** The sturgeon.

煌 **huang 2.** Blazing; bright.

鍠 **huang 2.** Clanging; jiggling.

艎 **huang 2.** A ferry-boat.

凰 **huang 2.** The female phœnix.

453

訇

See Lesson 54 E.

訇 **hung 1.** A crashing noise.

渹 **hung 1.** The roar of water.

𥕢 **hung 1.** A crash.

鍧 **hung 2.** A noise.

It is radical in

鞫 **chü 2.** To investigate judicially. L. 102 G.

454

若

See Lesson 46 G.

若 **jo 4.** To be as; if; as to; to follow; much.

鄀 **jo 1.** A place in Hupeh.

楉 **jo 4.** A kind of pomegranate-tree.

箬 **jo 4.** A variety of bamboo.

惹 **jê 3.** To provoke; to rouse; to incite.

偌 **jê 4.** An interjection; indeed; what!

婼 **jê 2.** Unsubdued.

蠚 **chê 1.** A dart; to prick.

喏 nê 3. To assent.

諾 nê 3. To assent.

踏 nê 4. To tread upon.

It is radical in

匿 ni 4. To conceal. L. 10 D. S. 659.

455

See Lesson 95 C.

柔 jou 2. Soft; yielding; pliant.

揉 jou 2. To bend; to twist; to subdue.

楺 jou 3. To bend.

煣 jou 3. To bend by fire or steam.

糅 jou 4. Mixed together.

鞣 jou 2. Soft leather.

腬 jou 2. Fat; juicy.

輮 jou 2. The fellies of a wheel.

蹂 jou 2. To tread out; to trample.

456

See Lesson 164 E.

耎 juan 3. Soft; weak.

輭 juan 3. Soft; yielding; pliable.

揬 juan 1. To dip; to soak.

楩 juan 3. A name for *diospyros lotus*.

愞 juan 4. Timid; nervous.

瑌 juan 3. A whitish quartz.

堧 juan 2. The vacant space outside a city wall.

鍱 juan 4. Soft, ductile.

腝 juan 2. Debility.

暝 juan 2. A vacant field.

蝡 juan 3. To squirm, to wriggle.

煗 } nuan 3. Warm; mild.
暖

渜 nuan 3. Lukewarm.

The sound is altered in

陾 jêng 2. A crowd.

457

See Lesson 118 A.

咼 kua 3. A wry mouth.

剮 kua 3. To cut a criminal in pieces.

蝸 kua 1. A snail.

喎 kua 3. Distorted.

腡 kua 1. The lines of the hand.

騧 kua 1. A cream-coloured horse.

篙 kua 3. The reel.

媧 wa 1. The sister of Fuhsi.

渦 wo 1. A whirlpool.

窩 wo 1. A nest; a den.

萵 wo 1. Dandelion.

禍 ho 4. Calamity, adversity.

鍋 kuo 1. A boiler, a caldron.

堝 kuo 1. A crucible.

過 kuo 4. To pass; to go by; to exceed; to transgress. S. 742.

458

See Lesson 112 H.

癸 kuei 3. A cyclic character.

鄈 k'uei 2. Name of different places.

戣 k'uei 2. A lance.

暌 k'uei 2. Opposition of stars; separated; distant.

睽 k'uei 2. To squint.

悷 k'uei 2. Anxiety.

楑 k'uei 2. A mallet.

揆 k'uei 2. To consider; to judge.

葵 k'uei 2. The mallow.

459

See Lesson 120 I.

剌 la 2. To cut; to slash.

揦 la 1. To clutch; to pull.

喇 la 3. To chatter; a final particle.

瘌 la 2. Poisonous; fatal.

It is phonetic contracted in

辣 la 4. Acrid, biting.

賴 } lai 4. To rely upon; to trust to; to accuse. S. 821.
頼

460

郎

See Lesson 75 F.

郎 lang 2. A term of respect; a gentleman

瑯 lang 2. Enamel.

榔 lang 2. The arec-palm.

螂 lang 2. Various insects.

廊 lang 2. A verandah; a corridor.

Compare S. 289.

461

See Lesson 68 F.

彔 lu 4. To carve wood.

盝 lu 4. A wooden bowl.

祿 lu 4. Happiness; prosperity; salary.

碌 lu 4. Green jasper; rough; coarse.

⿰𧾷彔 lu 4. To walk.

逯 lu 4. To advance with caution.

醁 lu 4. A liquor made in Hunan.

騄 lu 4. Name of one of Mu Wang's steeds.

淥 lu 4. To strain.

娽 lu 4. A proper name.

⿰彔皮 lu 4. Shrivelled; wrinkled.

錄 lu 4. To record; to write down; to choose; an index.

籙 lu 4. A map; a list.

綠 lü 4. Green.

菉 lü 4 A kind of lentiles.

It is radical in

剝 po 1. pao 1. To flay; to peel; to extort.

Compare S. 577.

462

See Lesson 54 J.

冒 mao 4. To presume; to brave out; rash.

帽 mao 4, A cap or head covering of any kind.

媢 mao 4. Ill-will and jealousy.

⿰氵冒 mao 4. To rise and overflow.

⿰忄冒 mao 4. Covetous.

⿰木冒 mao 4. A lintel.

瑁 mao 4. Tortoise shell.

曼 man 2. Long. S. 635.

Perhaps it is found in

賵 lêng 4. To give aid in preparing for a funeral.

463

See Lesson 7 A.

眉 mei 2. The eyebrows.

媚 mei 4. To love; to coax; to flatter.

湄 mei 2. The edge of the water.

嵋 mei 2. A mountain in Ssŭ-ch'uan.

楣 mei 2. Lintel of a door or window.

郿 mei 2. A district in Shensi.

464

See Lesson 149 B.

苗 miao 2. Sprouts; shoots; name of wild tribes.

緢 miao 2. A fringe.

描 miao 2. To delineate; to draw; to sketch; to depict.

媌 miao 2. Elegant, delicate.

喵 miao 1. To mew.

錨 mao 2. An anchor.

貓 mao 2. A cat.

465

See Lesson 18 M.

眇 miao 3. A one-eyed man; to glance at.

渺 miao 3. Vast; boundless; vague.

緲 miao 3. Minute; subtle; indistinct.

Compare SS. 80 and 302.

466

See Lesson 160 B.

面 mien 4. The face; the front; the surface; to meet; turn; time.

偭 mien 3. To look towards; to urge.

愐 mien 3. Timidity, bashfumess.

湎 **mien** 3. To flush with drink; drunk.

麵 **mien** 3. Wheat-flour; vermicelli.

緬 **mien** 3. Fine silk thread. Burma.

⿰巾面 **mien** 3. A screen.

It is radical in

靦 **t'ien** 3. To face; to front.

467

See Lesson 73 B.

某 **mu** 3. A certain one.

煤 **mei** 2. Coal.

媒 **mei** 2. A go-between.

禖 **mei** 2. A sacrifice offered to obtain the birth of a son.

腜 **mei** 2. Premature birth.

謀 **mo** 2. To plot; to scheme.

468

See Lesson 79 G.

南 **nan** 2. The South.

楠 **nan** 2. A cedar, *machilus nanmu*.

喃 **nan** 2. To chatter.

諵 **nan** 2. Chattering.

腩 **nan** 3. To boil meat.

揇 **nan** 3. To grasp with the hand.

蝻 **nan** 2. Immature locusts.

罱 **lan** 3. A fishing net.

Abbrev. in

献 獻 **hsien** 4. To present, to offer.

469

See Lesson 40 B.

匘 **nao** 3. The brain.

It is phon. contracted in

腦 **nao** 3. The brain.

惱 **nao** 3. Irritation; anger.

瑙 **nao** 3. Cornelian; agate.

Compare SS. 406 and 805.

470

See Lesson 72 F.

咢 **o** 4. To accuse.

崿 **o** 4. A cliff; a precipice.

諤 **o** 4. Honest; sincere.

鰐 **o** 4. The crocodile.

腭 **o** 4. The roof of the mouth.

愕 **o** 4. Fear; to be frightened.

鍔 **o** 4. A sharp point.

遌 **o** 4. To encounter; to meet with.

鶚 **o** 4. The osprey or fish-eagle.

鄂 **o** 4. Name of different places.

蕚 **o** 4. The calyx of a flower.

噩 **o** 4. Startling; sad; unlucky.

鱷 **o** 4. The crocodile.

讍 **o** 4. Honest; sincere.

471

保

See Lesson 94 B.

保 **pao** 3. To guarantee; to protect; to keep safe.

緥 **pao** 3. Swaddling-clothes.

褓 **pao** 3. Swaddling-clothes.

煲 **pao** 1. To heat; to boil.

葆 **pao** 3. Luxuriant foliage; to cover.

褒 **pao** 1. State-robes, favour; to criticise.

堡 **pu** 3. A rampart; a redoubt; a village; a station.

472

See Lesson 78 F.

奔 **pên** 1. To run, to rush.

逩 **pên** 4. To run quickly.

⿰馬奔 **pên** 1. To gallop.

錛 **pên** 1. An adze.

捹 **pên** 4. To mix up; to throw into confusion.

473

See Lesson 41 A.

扁 **pien** 3. A tablet; a sign-board; flat.

徧 **pien** 4. Everywhere; all round; one time.

編 **pien** 1. To arrange in order; to compose.

遍 **pien** 4. Everywhere; to make a round; a whole.
蝙 **pien** 1. The bat.
褊 **pien** 3. Narrow; mean.
揙 **pien** 3. To pound.
瑂 **pien** 1. Agate.
稨 **pien** 3. A trailing bean, *dolichos lablab.*
碥 **pien** 2. A pebble.
糄 **pien** 3. Parched grain.
艑 **pien** 4. A lighter.
鯿 **pien** 1. The bream.
惼 **pien** 3. Irritable; hasty-tempered.
腷 **pien** 4. A muscle.
匾 **pien** 3. Horizontal tablets.
萹 **pien** 1. Knotgrass, *polygonum aviculare.*

偏 **p'ien** 1. Inclined; leaning; partial.
騙 **p'ien** 4. To mount a horse.
諞 **p'ien** 3. Deceitfulness.
蹁 **p'ien** 1. To walk lame.
楄 **p'ien** 1. *Sapindus mukorossi.*
犏 **p'ien** 1. The domestic yak.
副 **p'ien** 4. To cut into slices.
翩 **p'ien** 1. To flutter.
篇 **p'ien** 1. A leaf of a book; an essay.
瘺 **p'ien** 1. Paralysis.

474

便 㪻

See Lesson 156 D.

便 **pien** 4. Easy; to relieve nature; then; even if.
緶 **pien** 3. To hem.
鞭 **pien** 1. A whip.
箯 **pien** 1. A bamboo sledge.

便 **p'ien** 2. Advantageous cheap; to profit.
楩 **p'ien** 2. A kind of laurel, *lindera.*
蝙 **p'ien** 2. The red sand tick.

475

甚 㞾

See Lesson 73 B.

甚 **shên** 4. What? very; any.
葚 椹 **shên** 2. The fruit of the mulberry-tree.
愖 **shên** 2. Sincere; upright.
煁 **shên** 2. A brazier.
諶 **shên** 2. Sincere. Commonly *ch'ên* 2.

斟 **chên** 1. To pour out; to deliberate.
戡 **chên** 1. To beat; to tread upon.
碪 **chên** 1. A block to beat clothes on when washing them; an anvil.
揕 **chên** 4. To strike or stab.
黮 **chên** 4. Black; to smut.

諶 **ch'ên** 2. Sincere; upright; to trust to.

湛 **chan** 4. To soak.

堪 **k'an** 1. To bear; to sustain; to be capable; fit.
嵁 **k'an** 1. Rocky.
歁 **k'an** 3. Dissatisfied.
戡 **k'an** 1. To subdue; to kill.
勘 **k'an** 4. To investigate.

It is radical in

尠 **hsien** 3. Very little.

476

是 㫑

See Lesson 112 I.

是 **shih** 4. To be; is; right; positive; absolute.
湜 **shih** 4. Clear water; true; sincere.
褆 **shih** 4. Handsomely dressed.
諟 **shih** 4. To judge; to consider.
匙 **shih** 2. A spoon; a key.
寔 **shih** 2. Solid; real; true.

隄 **ti** 1. A dyke; a bank; to guard against.
堤 **ti** 1. An embankment.
睼 **ti** 4. To stare; to gaze.
鞮 **ti** 1. Leather shoes

提 **t'i** 2. To pull up; to lift; to bring forward; to mention.
鯷 **t'i** 2. The pike fish.
禔 **t'i** 2. Luck.
蝭 **t'i** 2. A cicada.
媞 **t'i** 2. Pretty; fascinating.
踶 **t'i** 2. To kick.
醍 **t'i** 2. A liquor.
題 **t'i** 2. A heading; a theme; a subject; to discuss.
鶗 **t'i** 2. The sparrow-hawk.

It is radical in

尟 **hsien** 3. A little.

477

See Lesson 40 A.

思 ssŭ 1. To think; to reflect.
緦 ssŭ 1. Coarse cloth for mourning.
偲 ssŭ 1. To warn.
楒 ssŭ 1. A tree, *abrus precatoria*.
颸 ssŭ 1. A cool breeze.
[illegible] ssŭ 1 A thick beard.
罳 ssŭ 1. A screen.

葸 hsi 3. Timid; timorous; hesitating.

顋 sai 1. The jaws.
愢 sai 1. Modesty.
揌 sai 1. To shake.
腮 sai 1. The jaws.
鰓 sai 1. The gills of a fish.

It is radical in

慮 lü 4. To consider. S. 807.

478

See Lesson 120 H.

帝 ti 4. The Emperor; the Sovereign.
諦 ti 4. To investigate; to make researches.
渧 ti 4. To drop; a drop.
禘 ti 4. Offerings to the remotest ancestors.
締 ti 4. A knot; a close connection.
蔕 ti 4. A stem; a peduncle.
啼 t'i 2. To wail.
蹄 t'i 2. The hoof of a horse, to kick.
鯑 t'i 2. A salamander.
啻 商 } t'i 4. Only; otherwise. S. 647.

479

See Lesson 75 B.

亭 t'ing 2. A pavilion.
停 t'ing 2. To stop; to cease; to delay; settled.
渟 t'ing 2. Stagnant water.
婷 t'ing 2. Ladylike.
楟 t'ing 2. A wild peartree.
葶 t'ing 2. Peduncle.

Compare SS. 11 and 179.

480

See Lesson 46 D.

[illegible] to 4. Mince-meat. sui 2. A proper name.
惰 to 4. Lazy; careless.
[illegible] to 4. A long robe.
隋 to 4. Mince-meat. *Sui 2.*
墮 to 4. To be ruined.
嶞 to 4. A mountain peak.

毻 t'o 1. To shed feathers.
碢 t'o 2. A heavy weight.
媠 t'o 2. Not properly dressed.
堶 t'o 2. The game of throwing quoits.
楕 t'o 3 Slender.

隋 sui 2. A proper name.
[illegible] sui 2 Cakes; biscuits.
遀 sui 2. To follow. S. 759.

隳 hui 1. To destroy.

481

則

See Lesson 52 E.

則 tsai 2, tsê 2. Then; and so; a rule.
鰂 tsê 2. The cuttlefish.
崱 tsê 2. A chain of mountains.

側 chai 1. The side; inclining to one side; low; mean.

側 ch'ai 2. Oblique.
測 ch'ai 4. To fathom; to sound; to estimate.
惻 ch'ai 4. To pity.
[illegible] ch'ai 2. To beat.

廁 厠 } ssŭ 4. A privy.

Compare

賊 tsei 2. A thief. L. 52 E.

482

See Lesson 47 M.

奏 tsou 4. To report to the Throne; to advance; to play on instruments.

湊 湊 } ts'ou 4. To collect; to bring together; to meet.

腠 ts'ou 4. Between the skin and the flesh; the pores.

輳 ts'ou 4. The hub of a wheel.

楱 ts'ou 4. A lemon-tree.

483

See Lesson 38 D.

㚇 𡕥 } tsung 1. To gather the feet. A proper name.

騣 tsung 1. A horse's mane.

糉 tsung 4. Dumplings.

稯 tsung 1. A sheaf of grain.

[耒㚇] tsung 1. To sow seed without first ploughing the ground.

艐 tsung 1. To run aground.

鯼 tsung 1. A shark.

鬷 tsung 1. A caldron.

椶 tsung 1. The coir palm.

朡 tsung 1. An ancient kingdom.

猣 tsung 1. To flutter.

葼 tsung 1. Soft twigs.

It is radical in

傻 sha 3. Foolish, simple.

484

度

See Lesson 24 M.

度 tu 4. A measure; a limit; a degree; a rule; to cross over.

渡 tu 4. A ferry; to ford; to cross.

[土度] tu 3. To stop up; to stuff.

鍍 tu 4. To gild; to plate.

踱 tu 4. To go to and fro.

[度鳥] tu 4. A moor-hen.

[忄度] to 4. To calculate, to estimate.

喥 to 4. To chatter.

[言度] to 4. To cheat.

485

段

See Lesson 164 D.

段 tuan 4. A piece; a section; skill; prosperity.

緞 tuan 4. Satin.

碫 tuan 4. A whetstone.

腶 tuan 4. Meat spiced and dried.

鍛 tuan 4. To forge metal.

椴 tuan 4. The lime-tree, *tilia*.

葮 tuan 4. The *hibiscus syriacus*.

Not to be confounded with the Series 427.

486

盾

See Lessos 158 E.

盾 tun 4 A shield.

腯 tun 4. Fat; stout.

楯 tun 3. A barrier; to guard.

遁 tun 4. To hide away; to wanish.

輴 ch'un 1. A hearse; a mud sledge.

循 hsün 2. To follow; to acquiesce in; docility.

揗 hsün 2. To encourage; to sympathise with; to excite.

487

韋

See Lesson 31 G.

韋 wei 2. Soft leather; pliant; flexible.

偉 wei 3. Great; noble.

緯 wei 3. The woof of a web; latitude; fringe; tassels.

違 wei 2. To oppose; to disobey; rebellion.

褘 wei 2. The robes of an empress; beauty; virtue.

瑋 wei 3. A kind of jade or jasper.

幃 wei 2. A curtain; women's apartments.

[虫韋] wei 4. Wingless insects.

颹 wei 3. A storm.

暐 wei 3. Bright sunlight.

煒 wei 3. A fire; blazing; glowing.

湋 wei 2. To flow back.

圍 wei 2. To surround; to besiege; circumference.

葦 wei 3. The common reed.

闈 wei 2. Lateral doors.

衛 衞 } wei 4. To escort; to guard; Tientsin.

躗 wei 4. To exaggerate.

[衛心] wei 4. To dream.

諱 hui 4. To shun; a taboo.

禕 i 1. Excellent; precious.

488

畏

See Lesson 40 C.

畏 **wei 4.** To fear; to dread.

餵 **wei 4.** To feed animals.

喂 **wei 4.** To feed animals.

㱬 **wei 3.** Unfit; unable to.

猥 **wei 3.** To bark; a crowd.

偎 **wei 1.** To fondle.

煨 **wei 1.** Glowing embers.

椳 **wei 2.** A lintel.

隈 **wei 1.** A bend in a coastline; a bay.

489

胃 

See Lesson 122 C.

胃 **wei 2.** The stomach.

謂 **wei 4.** To speak; to say; to be.

渭 **wei 4.** Name of a river.

媦 **wei 3.** A younger sister.

㥜 **wei 4.** Anxiety; fear.

䮹 **wei 4.** An ass.

蝟 **wei 1.** The hedgehog.

喟 **k'ui 1.** To breathe heavily.

It is radical in

膚 **fu 1.** The skin.

490

屋 

See Lesson 32 G.

屋 **wu 1.** A room, a house.

渥 **wu 1.** To soak; to steep.

偓 **wu 4.** To restrain.

喔 **wu 4.** The cackling of fowls.

幄 **wu 4.** A tent.

剭 **wu 4.** To put to death.

握 **wo 4.** To grasp; to hold tight.

齷 **wo 4.** Paltry; mean.

𨂊 **wo 4.** Cripple.

491

See Lesson 95 C.

敄 **wu 4.** Strong; valiant.

騖 **wu 4.** To gallop.

婺 **wu 4.** Name of a star.

鶩 **wu 4.** A duck.

務 **wu 4.** To attend to earnestly; business.

霚 **wu 4.** Fog; mist.

瞀 **mou 4.** Dull; blind.

鍪 **mou 3.** A caldron; a helmet.

愗 **mou 4.** Stupid.

蓩 **mao 2.** The amaryllis.

蝥 **mao 3.** The Spanish fly.

楘 **mao 4.** Carriage-pole.

492

昜 

See Lesson 101 B.

昜 **yang 2.** Activity of the sun.

陽 **yang 2.** The south of a hill; the male or positive principle; light; life.

禓 **yang 2.** Offerings to wayside deities.

揚 **yang 2.** To raise; to extend; to winnow.

楊 **yang 2.** The poplar.

煬 **yang 2.** To heat.

颺 **yang 2.** To fly.

暘 **yang 2.** Sunshine; fair weather.

崵 **yang 2.** A mountain in Honan.

鍚 **yang 2.** Bells on a horse's collar.

瘍 **yang 2.** An ulcer.

婸 **tang 4.** Dissolute; wanton.

碭 **tang 4.** To exceed; to overpass.

湯 **t'ang 1.** Hot water; soup; to scald. S. 707.

餳 **t'ang 2.** Sugar; delicacies.

逿 **t'ang 4.** To pass by; a time; a turn.

趟 **t'ang 1.** To go through water; to wade.

蝪 **t'ang 1.** A species of spider.

愓 **t'ang 3.** Dissolute; profligate.

暢 **ch'ang 4.** Joyous; to spread; prosperous.

畼 **ch'ang 4.** Waste fields.

腸 **ch'ang** 3. The intestines; the feelings.

場 **ch'ang** 3. An area of level ground; a time, a turn.

𥏼 **shang** 1. To wound. S. 643.

493

See Lesson 50 N.

要 **yao** 4. To want; to need; to be about to; necessary; essential; if.

偠 **yao** 3. Delicate; slim.

腰 **yao** 1. The loins; the waist.

褄 **yao** 1. A fold; a plait.

喓 **yao** 1. Chirping.

494

業

See Lesson 24 O.

枼 **yeh** 4. A leaf; a plate.

偞 **yeh** 4. Gay; alert.

韘 **yeh** 4. A bowman's finger-stall.

殜 **yeh** 4. Thin; weak.

楪 **yeh** 4. A window.

鍱 **yeh** 4. A thin plate of metal.

葉 **yeh** 4. A leaf; a plate.

媟 **hsieh** 4. To outrage.

緤 **hsieh** 4. To fasten.

屧 **hsieh** 4. Shoes; sandals.

碟 **tieh** 4. A plate; a small dish.

惵 **tieh** 4. Timid; nervous.

揲 **tieh** 2. To fold.

喋 **tieh** 2. To chatter.

渫 **tieh** 4. Waves.

㷸 **tieh** 4. Frozen hard.

煠 **tieh** 2 To fry.

諜 **tieh** 2. To play the traitor.

艓 **tieh** 2. A small boat.

牒 **tieh** 2. Mince-meat.

堞 **tieh** 4. Battlements; crenelated walls.

牒 **tieh** 2. Tablets; documents; records.

𤗉 **tieh** 2. A bed.

鰈 **tieh** 2. A sole.

蝶 **tieh** 3. A butterfly.
Compare S. 157.

495

匽

See Lesson 67 H.

匽 **yen** 3. To hide away; to repress.

堰 **yen** 4. A dike; a bund.

偃 **yen** 3. To cease; to recline.

褗 **yen** 3. A collar.

蝘 **yen** 3. A lizard.

鼴 **yen** 3. The tapir.

鰋 **yen** 3. A pike.

鶠 **yen** 3. The phœnix.

郾 **yen** 3. A place in Honan.

揠 **ya** 4. To pull up; to eradicate.

496

See Lesson 47 I.

弇 **yen** 3. To cover over; to hide; narrow.

揜 **yen** 3. To cover.

渰 **yen** 1. To overflow, to submerge.

黭 **yen** 3. Black.

497

See Lesson 61 F.

彥 **yen** 4. Elegant.

諺 **yen** 4. A common saying; a proverb.

喭 **yen** 4. To condole with.

顏 **yen** 2. Colour; the countenance.

498

See Lesson 73 E.

音 **yin** 1. Sound; a musical note; tone.

醅 **yin** 1. Drunk.

愔 **yin** 1. Quiet; peaceful.

喑 **yin** 1. To be dumb.

窨 **yin** 3. A cellar; weaver's work-room.

瘖 **yin** 1. Dumb.

歆 **hsin** 1. To taste; to agree.

暗 **an 4.** Obscure; gloomy; stealthily.

諳 **an 1.** Skilled in.

堷 **an 1.** A burying-place for free interment.

婄 **an 1.** Impure, dirty.

腤 **an 1.** To boil flesh; broth.

隌 **an 4.** Hidden.

揞 **an 3.** To hide; to press on.

䬓 **an 4.** A squall.

闇 **an 4.** To shut the door; dark; dim.

It is radical in.

章 **chang 1.** A section; a period. S. 593.

499

See Lesson 41 D.

垔 **yin 1.** To stop up, as water.

堙 **yin 1.** To bar, to dam in.

湮 **yin 1.** To soak, to spread.

禋 **yin 1.** A sacrifice.

諲 **yin 1.** To respect; to reverence.

闉 **yin 1.** The wall which protects a city gate.

煙 **yen 1.** Smoke; opium; tobacco.

鄄 **chüan 4.** A place in Shantung.

甄 **chên 1.** To mould; to fashion.

500

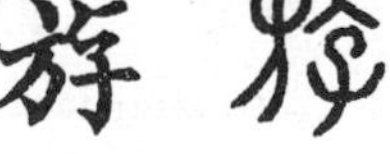

See Lesson 117 B.

斿 **yu 3.** The dog-tooth bordering to a flag.

游 **yu 2.** To wander about; to ramble; to float.

遊 **yu 2.** To ramble.

蝣 **yu 2.** Water-flies.

501

See Lesson 14 F.

俞 兪 } **yü 2** To say *yes*; to agree.

喻 **yü 4.** To instruct; a similitude.

諭 **yü 4.** To issue orders; an edict; to notify.

榆 **yü 2** The elm.

瑜 **yü 2.** Precious stones; lustre; glory.

踰 **yü 2.** To cross over; to exceed; to transgress.

愉 **yü 2.** To enjoy; pleasure.

堬 **yü 2.** A grave-mound.

蝓 **yü 2.** A snail.

逾 **yü 2.** To cross over; to pass; to exceed.

颵 **yü 2.** A hurricane.

貐 **yü 2.** A porcupine.

愈 **yü 2.** More; further; to recover.

瘉 **yü 4.** To be cured; convalescent.

萮 **yü 2.** A wild plant, *eutrema washabi.*

闟 **yü 2.** To spy; to peep.

窬 **yü 2.** A small window.

輸 **shu 1.** To overturn; to lose.

毹 **shu 1.** Felt; coarse woollen cloth.

偷 **t'ou 1.** To steal; fraudulent; clandestine.

502

See Lesson 50 G.

臾 **yü 2.** A moment; a little while.

諛 **yü 2.** To flatter.

腴 **yü 2.** Fat; fertile.

㥚 **yü 2.** Sorrowful; grieved.

楰 **yü 2.** A sort of *catalpa.*

萸 **yü 2.** A kind of pepper-tree, the *xanthoxylum.*

瘐 **yü 3.** Sick; weak.

庾 **yü 3.** A stack; a measure; a granary.

Compare S. 213.

503

See Lesson 23 E.

禺 **yü 2.** A monkey.

隅 **yü 2.** A corner; an angle.

䗂 **yü 2.** A water-beetle, *dytiscus.*

鍝 **yü 4.** An awl.

髃 **yü 2.** The clavicle.

嵎 **yü 2.** A mountain in Shantung.

喁 **yü 1.** To gape; to stand openmouthed.

齵 **yü 2.** Uneven teeth; discord.

遇 **yü 4.** To meet; to fall in with; to occur.

愚 **yü 2.** Simple; stupid; rude.

寓 **yü 4.** To dwell; to reside; to sojourn.

庽 yü 4. An hospital.

偶 ou 3. An image; an idol; to mate; suddenly

耦 ou 3. Two furrows; a pair; a mate.

藕 ou 3. The root-stock of the lotus.

The sound is altered in

顒 yung 2. Bearing; dignity.

Compare SS. 628 and 728

504

See Lesson 23 D.

禹 yü 3. A proper name.

瑀 yü 3. Agate stone.

楀 yü 3. Name of a tree.

鄅 yü 3 A place in Shantung.

萭 yü 3. Grass; plants.

齲 chü 3. A spoiled tooth.

踽 chü 3. To walk alone.

505

See Lesson 49 F.

爰 yüan 2. Thereupon; a particle.

援 yüan 2. To seize, to hold fast; to rescue; to quote.

湲 yüan 2. Current of water.

瑗 yüan 4. A large ring of jade.

猨 yüan 2. The gibbon ape.

褑 yüan 4. Girdle-ornaments.

鶢 yüan 2. Sea-mew.

諼 hsüan 1. To deceive.

楥 hsüan 4. A last.

愋 hsüan 1. To hate.

緩 huan 3. Slow; tardy; to delay.

鍰 huan 2. Six ounces.

鰀 huan 3. A tench.

煖 nuan 3. nang 3. Warm; mild.

暖 nuan 3. nang 3. Warm; mild.

506

See Lesson 46 C.

差 ch'a 1. To mistake.
ch'ai 1. To send.
ts'ŭ 1. An accident.

䐤 ch'a 1. Dried meat.

槎 ch'a 1. To fell trees; a raft

艖 ch'a 1. A skiff.

[illegible] ch'a 1. To prick.

[illegible] ch'a 2. A basket.

溠 cha 4. The name of a river.

嗟 chüeh 1. To sigh; alas.

[illegible] chüeh 1. To complain.

搓 ts'o 1. To rub; to scrub.

磋 ts'o. To rub and polish.

蹉 ts'o 1. To miss; to err.

[illegible] ts'o 1. Bones.

瑳 ts'o 3. Scintillating, fascinating.

嵯 ts'o 1. Hilly.

鹺 ts'o 1. Briny; salt.

瘥 ts'o 2. A disease.

507

See Lesson 14 C.

茶 ch'a 2. The tea.

[illegible] ch'a 2. The tea.

搽 ch'a 2. To anoint; to paint; to smear.

嗏 ch'a 1. Onomatopœia.

508

See Lesson 82 B.

展 chan 3. To open out; to unroll; to explain.

輾 chan 3. To roll over; to revolve.

驏 chan 4. A horse rolling himself in the dust.

搌 chan 3. To wipe away, as tears.

[illegible] chan 3. To gaze at stupidly.

囅 chan 3. A horse-laugh.

碾 nien 3. A roller.

509

See Lesson 10 L.

眞 chên 1. True; truly; genuine.

鎭 chên 4. To keep: to protect; a market-town; a brigade.

禛 **chên 1.** Blessed; auspicious; good omen.

縝 **chên 3.** Thin cloth.

黰 **chên 3.** Black; to blacken.

衠 **chên 1.** Pure; genuine.

鬒 **chên 3.** Bushy hair.

瞋 **ch'ên 1.** An angry look.

䐜 **ch'ên 1.** A swelling.

嗔 **ch'ên 1.** To be angry at; to rail at.

慎 **shên 4.** To act carefully; cautious; considerate.

蹎 **tien 1.** To run.

[illegible] **tien 1.** To amble.

滇 **tien 1.** A lake south of Yunnanfu.

搷 **tien 1.** To beat.

槙 **tien 1.** A fallen tree.

齻 **tien 1.** To get one's wisdom teeth.

[illegible] **tien 1.** A horse with spots.

瘨 **tien 1.** Mad, insane.

顛 **tien 1.** The top; the apex; the summit; to upset; to overthrow; to be ruined. S. 848.

填 **t'ien 2.** To fill up; to stuff; to complete.

瑱 **t'ien 4.** Ear-rings.

磌 **t'ien 2.** The base of a pillar.

[illegible] **t'ien 2.** The sound of drums.

鷏 **t'ien 2.** A wader.

闐 **t'ien 2.** The noise of a multitude.

Compare S. 335.

510

See Lesson 47 V.

烝 **chêng 1.** Steam; to steam.

[illegible] **chêng 1.** Withered; lean.

蒸 **chêng 1.** To steam; vapour; all; many.

Note

丞 **ch'êng 2.** To help; to second.

拯 **ch'êng 3.** To raise; to help; to rescue.

承 **ch'êng 2.** To offer; to receive; to enjoy; to undertake.

511

朕

See Lesson 47 J.

朕 **chêng 4.** A joint.
chên 4. I the Emperor.

塍 **ch'êng 2.** A jetty; a raised path.

勝 **shêng 4.** To conquer; to outdo.

賸 **shêng 4.** Overplus; residue.

騰 **t'êng 2.** To leap on; to mount; to move. S. 826.

謄 **t'êng 2.** To copy; to transcribe.

縢 **t'êng 2.** To bind, a band.

螣 **t'êng 2.** A serpent or dragon.

鰧 **t'êng 2.** A gurnard.

滕 **t'êng 2.** An proper name.

藤 **t'êng 2.** Lianas; the rattan.

媵 **ying 4.** An escort of maid-servants to a bride; concubines.

512

乘

See Lesson 31 E.

乘 **shêng 4.** A war-chariot.

剩 **shêng 4.** An overplus; leavings.

乘 **ch'êng 2.** To ride; to mount; a classifier of sedans; to take advantage of; to multiply. The Buddhist means of salvation.

騬 **ch'êng 2.** To geld.

嵊 **ch'êng 4.** A district in Chêkiang.

513

耆

See Lesson 30 E.

耆 **ch'i 2.** A man of sixty.

鰭 **ch'i 2.** Dorsal fin of fish.

愭 **ch'i 2.** Respect; care.

鬐 **ch'i 2.** A horse's mane.

嗜 **shih 4.** To love; to desire; to covet; to be addicted to.

蓍 **shih 1.** The *Achillea sibirica*, which is used for divination.

搘 **chih 1.** To set up; to prop; to raise; to support.

榰 **chih 1.** A base.

514

豈

See Lesson 165 E.

豈 **ch'i 3.** How? why?

榿 **ch'i 1.** The alder-tree.

覬 **chi 4.** To aim at.

螘 **i 3.** The ant.

愷 **k'ai 3.** Good; brave; joyous.
塏 **k'ai 3.** A terrace; a dwelling.
體 **k'ai 3.** Slender.
鎧 **k'ai 3.** An armour; a cuirass.
剴 **k'ai 3.** A scythe; to mow down.
凱 **k'ai 3.** A victory; the triumphant return of an army.
顗 **k'ai 3.** Joy; happiness.
颽 **k'ai 3.** A genial breeze.
闓 **k'ai 3.** To open, to begin; to desire.

皚 **nai 2.** White.
敳 **nai 2.** To govern; to settle.

獃 **tai 1.** Stupid; to stand open-mouthed; idle.

515

See Lesson 98 A.

氣 **ch'i 4.** Air; ether; vapour; spirit; temper; feelings; the fate.
愾 **ch'i 4.** To sigh; to moan.

餼 **hsi 4.** Offering of meat; a banquet; provisions.
愾 **hsi 4.** To sigh; to groan.
犔 **hsi 4.** Epizooty.
霼 **hsi 4.** Cloudy.

516

See Lesson 69 C.

家 **chia 1.** A household; a family; a profession or class; a suffix.
傢 **chia 1.** Tools; furniture; family things.
嫁 **chia 4.** To marry a husband; to give one's daughter in marriage.
稼 **chia 4.** Harvest.
榢 **chia 4.** A stand; a frame-work.

517

See Lesson 34 I.

㱿 殼 } **ch'iao 4.** A shell; a scale.
愨 **ch'iao 4.** Uprightness.
㲉 **ch'iao 1.** An egg's shell.

彀 **kou 4.** To draw a bow to its full stretch; enough; adequate.

鷇 **k'ou 4.** The young of birds.

㱿 **ku 2.** The top of the foot.
穀 **ku 3.** A paper mulberry.
穀 **ku 3.** Millet; corn.
轂 **ku 3.** The nave or hub of a wheel.

518

See Lesson 31 E.

桀 **chieh 2.** To quarter; a perch,
傑 **chieh 2.** A hero.
榤 **chieh 2.** A hen-roost.
搩 **chieh 2.** A span; to measure.

519

See Lesson 44 I.

兼 兼 } **chien 1.** To comprehend in; together with; equally.
鹻 **chien 3.** Soda.
縑 **chien 1.** Taffety.
鰜 **chien 1.** A sole.
蹇 **chien 1.** To walk lame.
歉 **chien 4.** Scanty; deficient.
鶼 **chien 1.** The spoonbill, *platalea major.*
瀸 **chien 1.** A quinsy.

謙 **ch'ien 1.** Respectful; yielding; modest; to revere.
慊 **ch'ien 3.** Unsatisfied; hungry.
鼸 **ch'ien 3.** A hamster.
鶼 **ch'ien 4.** To peck; to pick up.

嫌 **hsien 2.** To disdain, to depreciate; to have an aversion to.
隒 **hsien 3.** A steep path.

臁 **lien 3.** The calf of the leg.
幨 **lien 2.** A door-screen.
稴 **lien 2.** Green grain.
磏 **lien 3.** Coarse sandstone.
溓 **lien 3.** A thin sheet of ice.
濂 **lien 2.** A waterfall.

熑 **lien 2.** To bend in the fire.
鎌 **lien 2.** A sickle; a reaping-hook.
蠊 **lien 2.** A stinking insect.
廉 **lien 2.** A corner; angular; incorrupt; to search out. S. 745.

賺 **chuan 4.** To earn.
謙 **tsuan 4.** To deceive.

慊 **ch'ieh 4.** Pleasure; joy.

520

蚩 

See Lesson 79 B.

蚩 **ch'ih 1.** A worm; ignorant; rustic.
嗤 **ch'ih 1.** To laugh at.
媸 **ch'ih 1.** An ugly woman.
⿰犭蚩 **ch'ih 1.** A kind of long-haired dog.
⿰蚩欠 **ch'ih 1.** To hoot.

⿰扌蚩 **ch'ên 1.** To draw; to extend.
⿰金蚩 **ch'ên 1.** A cuirass.

521

晉 

See Lesson 133 C.

晉, 晋 **chin 4.** To increase; to grow; a proper name.
搢 **chin 4.** To stick into; to insert.
瑨 **chin 4.** A precious stone.
縉 **chin 4.** Rosy, pink.

鄑 **chin 4.** A place in Shantung.

榗 **chien 4.** A hard wood.
戩 **chien 3.** To exhaust; to destroy; to kill.

522

秦 

See Lesson 47 N.

秦 **ch'in 2.** A kind of rice; a proper name.
螓 **ch'in 2.** A small cicada.
⿰牛秦 **ch'in 2.** An ox.

搸 **chên 1.** To gather; a multitude.
榛 **chên 1.** The hazel-tree.
溱 **chên 1.** Name of a river.
臻 **chên 1.** To spread; to reach to; abundance.
蓁 **chên 1.** Bushy; spreading.

523

臭 

See Lesson 134 A.

臭 **hsiu 4.** To smell; to scent. *Ch'ou 4.*
糗 **hsiu 3.** Grains; food.
⿰食臭 **hsiu 3.** Spoiled food.
嗅, 齅 **hsiu 4.** To smell; to scent out.

闃 **ch'iu 4.** Confined.

臭 **ch'ou 4.** To smell; to stink. *Hsiu 4.*
殠 **ch'ou 4.** Stench.

溴 **ch'ou 4.** The name of a river.
⿺走臭 **ch'ou 4.** To go as if weary.

524

See Lesson 78 D.

芻 **ch'u 2.** Grass; hay; vulgar; worthless.
⿰禾芻 **ch'u 2.** Stalk; straw.
⿰火芻 **ch'u 3.** To roast.
媰 **ch'u 2.** A widow; a pregnant woman.
鶵 **ch'u 2.** To rear a brood.
雛 **ch'u 2.** Chicken.
蒭 **ch'u 2.** Straw.

搊 **chou 1.** To hold, to lift.
謅 **chou 1.** To recriminate.
⿰亻芻 **chou 4.** To hire one's self.
⿰革芻 **chou 3.** A leather-strap.
騶 **chou 1.** Swift.
⿰衤芻 **chou 4.** Wrinkles; folds.
縐 **chou 4.** A crape; wrinkled.
皺 **chou 4.** Wrinkled; creased.
鄒 **chou 1.** A place in Shantung.

⿰目芻 **ch'ou 3.** To spy; to observe.

篘 **ch'ih 1.** A basket to strain liquors.

⿰石芻 **ch'ü 1.** The bite of a serpent.
趨, 趋 **ch'ü 1.** To run to; aim; towards.

525

See Lesson 91 B.

畜 ch'u 4. Animals.
hsü 4. To rear.

慉 ch'u 1. To nourish; to foster; to support.

滀 ch'u 1. Water flowing; to flush.

鄐 ch'u 4. A proper name.

搐 ch'ou 1. To draw; to shake; spasm.

526

See Lesson 86 B.

追 chui 1. To pursue; retrospective.

糙 chui 1. To stick; to adhere.

腿 chui 4. A swelling of the foot.

縋 chui 4. To suspend.

磓 chui 1. To pile up stones.

饋 chui 1. Steamed loaves.

搥 ch'ui 2. To beat; to strike; to throw away.

槌 ch'ui 2. A wooden mallet.

鎚 ch'ui 2. A hammer.

髓 ch'ui 2. The vertebræ.

煺 t'ui 1. To scald.

527

See Lesson 69 G.

冢 chung 3. A tumulus; a mound.

塚 chung 3. A tomb.

崍 chung 3. A small hill.

528

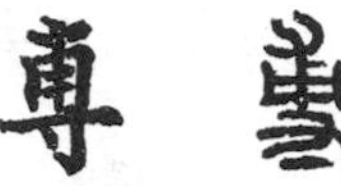

See Lesson 109 D.

尃 fu 1. To spread.

縛 fu 2. To bind; to tie up.

傅 fu 4. To superintend; to teach; to anoint.

賻 fu 4. To give toward defraying funeral expenses.

敷 fu 1. To spread out; to diffuse; to promulge.

膊 髆 } po 2. The arm.

搏 po 2. To seize; to strike.

煿 po 4. To crackle; to burst from heat.

鎛 po 2. A large bell.

博 博 } po 2. Ample; spacious; universal learning.

簙 po 2. An ancient game.

溥 p'u 3. Inundation. Large; extensive. S. 753.

膊 髆 } p'ai 2. The arm.

Compare SS. 271 and 753.
See L. 91 F, S. 605.

529

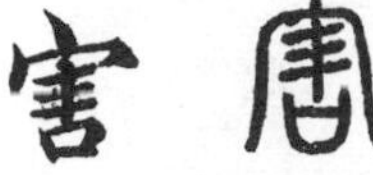

See Lesson 97 E.

害 hai 4. To injure; to hurt; a damage.

嗐 hai 1. An exclamation.

骸 hai 4. Bones.

瞎 hsia 1. Blind; blindly.

轄 hsia 2. The bolt of a wheel; to govern; to regulate.

豁 ho 1. A pass; open; spacious; clear; generous; to understand.

割 ko 1. To cut.

犗 chieh 4. A gelded bull.

Compare L. 97 F.

憲 hsien 4. An example, rule, law, constitution.

蕙 hsien 1. Hemerocallis.

幰 hsien 3. The curtain in front of a carriage.

530

See Lesson 47 T.

寒 sai 1. To stop up.

賽 sai 4. To contest; competition.

蹇 sai 4. Simplicity.

塞 sai 1. To obstruct, to stop.

僿 sai 1. A trifle.

簺 sai 1. To bar.

寨 chai 4. A stockade; an encampment.

See Lesson 47 U.

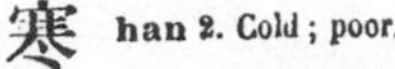

寒 han 2. Cold; poor.

It is phonetic contracted in the following.

鶱 **hsien 1.** To soar high.

騫 **ch'ien 1.** Glanders of horses.

搴 **ch'ien 1.** To pluck up.

謇 **ch'ien 3.** Frank; open.

[illegible] **ch'ien 3.** A kettledrum.

褰 **ch'ien 1.** To raise the skirt.

蹇 **ch'ien 3.** To go lame; misfortune; arrogance.

531

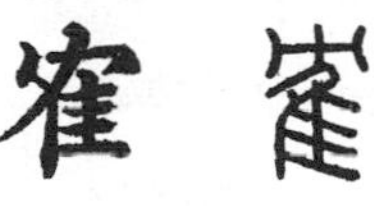

See Lesson 34 F.

隺 **hao 4.** To rise; to soar.

鶴 **hao 2.** A crane.

榷 **chiao 1.** A foot-bridge; a toll-gate.

傕 **chiao 4.** A proper name.

搉 **ch'iao 4.** To strike.

確 **ch'iao 4.** True; positive; certainly.

532

See Lesson 38 G.

盇 盍 } **ho 2.** Why not?

欱 **ho 1.** To drink; to suck in.

嗑 **ho 1.** The noise of voices; to sip.

闔 **ho 2.** A two leaved door; a family; the whole.

磕 **k'o 1.** To tap, to knock.

榼 **k'o 2.** A wooden cup to hold spirits.

溘 **k'o 2.** To ground. Failure.

瞌 **k'o 2.** Sleepy; dozing.

[illegible] **o 4.** Coiffure.

饁 **yeh 4.** To supply with food.

[illegible] **shê 4.** The genius of pleasant dreams.

It-forms

[illegible] 蓋 } **kai 4.** A covering; a roof. For, since.

[illegible] **kai 4.** Outer garments.

壒 **ai 3.** Dust rising, defilement.

533

See Lesson 92 C.

奚 **hsi 1.** An interrogative particle, why? how? what?

傒 **hsi 2.** A waiter; a boy.

㜎 **hsi 2.** A waiting-maid.

徯 **hsi 1.** To wait for; to expect; to hope.

溪 **hsi 1.** A current.

螇 **hsi 2.** A grasshopper.

[illegible] **hsi 1.** Side slits in a gown.

蹊 **hsi 1.** A footpath.

鞵 **hsi 2.** A shoe.

鼷 **hsi 2.** A mouse.

嵠 谿 } **hsi 1.** A mountain gorge; to disagree; discord.

嗘 **chi 1.** To cackle.

雞 鷄 } **chi 1.** Gallinaceous birds; cock; hen.

534

See Lesson 159 A.

息 **hsi 1.** To breathe, a respiration. To produce; interest. To stop; repose.

熄 **hsi 1.** To put out a fire.

媳 **hsi 1.** A wife; a daughter-in-law.

[illegible] **hsi 2.** To breathe, to swallow.

鄎 **hsi 1.** A place in Honan.

瘜 **hsi 1.** A polypus.

535

See Lesson 55 H

巽 **hsüan 4.** To select, to chose out; quiet; to yield.

選 **hsüan 3.** To select; to choose out; to elect.

[illegible] **hsüan 3.** Pleasure; effeminacy.

簨 **hsüan 3.** A support.

[illegible] **hsüan 3.** A snare..

噀 **hsün 4.** To spit.

潠 **hsün 4.** To besprinkle.

膞 **hsün** 3. To hash; to mince.

僎 **chuan** 4. A proper name.
譔 **chuan** 4. To praise.
瑑 **chuan** 4. Precious; gems.
饌 **chuan** 4. Food; provisions.
撰 **chuan** 4. To collect; a note; a composition.

536

See Lesson 12 J.

㠵 } **huang** 1. A watery waste; to
巟 } reach.
荒 **huang** 1. Jungle; wild; unproductive. *Hence*
慌 **huang** 1. Nervous; affected.
謊 **huang** 3. To lie; a lie.
朚 **huang** 3. Obscure.
晃 **huang** 3. Hot and dry.
穅 **huang** 1. Grain not ripening.
㡆 **huang** 1. To boil silk.

537

See Lesson 24 K.

晃 **huang** 3. The full brightness of the sun; to dazzle; a flash.
幌 **huang** 3. A curtain; a shop-sign; a screen.
愰 **huang** 3. Uncertain; disturbed; at times.
熀 **huang** 3. The blaze of fire.
榥 **huang** 3. A partition.

鎤 **huang** 3. The sound of bells. Compare S. 222.

538

See Lesson 69 B.

圂 **hun** 4. A piggery; a privy.
溷 **hun** 4. Confused; dirty; unclean; a privy.
掍 **hun** 4. To take up with tongs.
慁 **hun** 4. To disturb; to disgrace; to disobey.

539

See Lesson 125 C.

益 **i** 4. A dish filling with water; to increase; to benefit; more and more.
嗌 **i** 4. The throat; to hiccough.
縊 **i** 4. To hang; to strangle.
溢 **i** 4. A vessel full to the brim; to overflow.
鎰 **i** 4. A weight.
齸 **i** 4. To chew.
艗 **i** 4. The bow of a junk.
鷁 **i** 4. A vulture.

隘 **yeh** 4. A pass; narrow; trouble; difficulty.

搤 **o** 4. To seize.

It is radical in

蠲 **chüan** 1. To purify; to dispense with; to condone.

Abbrev. in

謚 諡 **shih** 4. The posthumous title; the epitaph name.

540

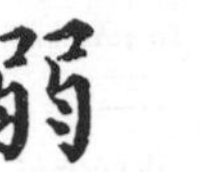

See Lesson 32 D.

弱 **jao** 2. Weak; feeble; to grow weak.
蒻 **jao** 4. A rush.

嫋 **niao** 3. Delicate; slender.

溺 **ni** 4. To sink; to be drowned; greedy; doting on.
愵 **ni** 4. Greedy; blindly doting on.
搦 **ni** 4. To catch hold.

541

See Lesson 30 B.

辱 **ju** 4. To insult; to disgrace.
嗕 **ju** 4. Slow; negligent.
褥 **ju** 4. A stuffed mat; a mattress.
溽 **ju** 4. Damp; muggy.
縟 **ju** 4. Adorned; gay; elegant.
蓐 **ju** 4. Shoots; sprouts; a cushion of grass.

耨 **nou** 4. A hoe; to weed.

542

See Lesson 18 E.

容 **jung** 2. **yung** 2. To receive; to contain; to endure; to bear with; the air; the countenance; the face.

鎔 **jung 2.** To smelt; to cast.

瑢 **jung 2.** Trinkets.

鰫 **jung 2.** A tench.

榕 **jung 2.** The *ficus indica.*

嗒 **jung 3.** To gasp.

溶 **jung 2.** To dissolve.

傛 **jung 2.** Leading man.

蓉 **jung 2.** The *hibiscus mutabilis.*

543

See Lesson 117 D.

倝 **kan 4.** The dawn.

幹 **kan 4.** A stem; affairs; to manage; capacity.

乾 **ch'ien 2.** Heaven; male; father; constant.

斡 **kuan 3.** To turn; a handle by which to turn a machine.

韓 **han 2.** A fence.

翰 **han 4.** A pencil; the Academy of old.

It is radical in

朝 **chao 1.** The dawn. S. 664. **ch'ao 2.** A court.

戟 **chi 3.** A halberd.

544

See Lesson 75 B.

高 髙 **kao 1.** High; lofty; noble; eminent; your, in direct address.

膏 **kao 1.** Fat; grease; ointment, fertilising; a favour; to enrich.

槀 槁 **kao 3.** Decayed wood; withered.

稾 稿 **kao 3.** Straw; a draft, a sketch.

藁 **kao 3.** Straw; a first draft.

縞 **kao 3.** Plain white.

瘍 **kao 3.** The itch.

暠 **kao 3.** Clear; bright.

篙 **kao 1.** A pole.

熇 **k'ao 3.** Hot; to warm.

犒 **k'ao 4.** To reward, to regale.

敲 毃 **ch'iao 1.** To tap, to knock.

謞 **hao 4.** To criticise; to disparage.

滈 **hao 4.** The bubbling of water.

鰝 **hao 4.** A craw-fish.

鎬 **hao 4.** An old town.

皜 **hao 3.** Luminous; bright.

鄗 **hao 4.** The name of a place.

蒿 **hao 1.** Aromatic plants, like the *artemisia.*

豪 **hao 2.** The porcupine. S. 777.

毫 **hao 2.** Down, pubescence. The thousandth part of a ounce; a trifle; an atom.

歊 **hsiao 1.** Vapour; to fume.

It is radical in

嵩 **sêng 1.** A mountain in Honan.

亳 **po 4.** A city in Honan.

亭 **t'ing 2.** A pavilion. S. 479.

喬 **ch'iao 2.** To overhang. S. 670.

臺 **t'ai 2.** A stage. S. 790.

545

See Lesson 155.

鬲 **ko 2.** A tripod pot.

隔 **ko 2.** A partition; to separate; to intercept; next to. *Chieh* **4.**

槅 **ko 2.** A screen.

膈 **ko 2.** The diaphragm; to hiccough, to belch.

嗝 **ko 2.** To belch.

翮 **ko 4.** A quill.

鷊 **i 4.** A pheasant with a collar, tragopan.

It is radical in

融 **jung 2. yung 2.** Vapour; melting; harmonising; combining; specie, cash.

546

See Lesson 104 B.

冓 **kou 4.** A frame-work.

褠 **kou 1.** A garment with narrow sleeves.

構 **kou 4.** To construct; to unite; sexual intercourse.

媾 **kou 4.** Relationship; fondness; sexual intercourse.

遘 **kou 4.** To meet; to happen.

搆 **kou 4.** To reach up to.

溝 **kou 1.** A drain; a ditch.

購 **kou 4.** To buy.

韝 鞲 **kou 4.** A leathern vambrace used by archers.

覯 **kou 4.** To see or meet one suddenly; to occur; accidentally.

篝 **kou 1.** A bamboo frame; a cage.

The sound was altered in

講 **chiang 3.** To explain.

耩 **chiang 3.** To sow.

547

See Lesson 118 A.

骨 **ku 2.** A bone.

搰 **ku 4.** To dig.

愲 **ku 3.** Perturbed; distressed.

縎 **ku 2.** Tangled; knotted.

榾 **ku 3.** Ivory-nut.

滑 **hua 2.** Slippery; comical, farcical.

猾 **hua 2.** Treacherous.

磆 **hua 2.** Soapstone.

鰨 **hua 2.** An otter.

It is radical in

骰 **shai 3.** Dices.

548

See Lesson 40 C.

鬼 **kuei 3.** Ghosts; devils.

瑰 **kuei 4.** The rose.

魁 **k'uei 2.** A giant; eminent; monstrous.

愧 **k'uei 4.** Ashamed; repentant.

餽 **k'uei 4.** A present of food.

傀 **k'uei 3.** A doll.

磈 **k'uei 4.** Rocky.

膭 **hui 4.** A swelling.

殨 **hui 4.** Stupid.

隗 **wei 3.** Lofty; eminent.

嵬 **wei 2.** Lofty; eminent.

魏 **wei 4.** Asafœtida.

巍 **wei 1.** Lofty; eminent.

塊 **k'uai 4.** A clod; a lump.

褢 **huai 2.** To carry in the bosom; to conceal.

槐 **huai 2.** A tree, *sophora japonica.*

蒐 **sou 1.** *Rubia cordifolia.* To hunt.

醜 **ch'ou 3.** Ugly; hideous; shameful; evil.

549

See Lesson 75 H.

享 **kuo 1.** A wall.

崞 **kuo 4.** A mountain in Shansi.

郭 **kuo 1.** An outer wall of fortification.

椁 槨 **kuo 3.** An outer coffin.

鞹 **k'uo 4.** Leather.

漷 **k'uo 4.** A proper name.

廓 **k'uo 2.** Great; to enlarge.

霩 **k'uo 4.** The clouds dispersing.

崞 **k'uo 4.** A ravine; a gorge.

Compare S. 359.

550

See Lesson 41 E.

栗 **li 4.** The chestnut-tree. Care; reverence.

傈 **li 4.** Ancestral tablets.

慄 **li 4.** Fear; to tremble.

摽 **li 4.** To smooth; to draw through the hands.

溧 **li 4.** Name of a river.

凓 **li 4.** Cold; chilly.

篥 **li 4.** A kind of bamboo.

551

See Lesson 129 E.

畱 留 **liu 2.** To leave, to cease, to sojourn, hospitality.

榴 **liu 2.** The pomegranate.

溜 **liu 4.** A current; a flow.

瑠 **liu 2.** A glass-like substance.

塯 **liu 4.** A beggar's alms-bowl.

餾 **liu 4.** To steam rice.

遛 **liu 2.** To linger; to saunter.

飀 **liu 2.** The sighing of wind.

騮 **liu 2.** A bay horse.

獵 **liu 2.** The seal.

鼦 **liu 2.** The fieldmouse.

鶹 **liu 2.** The large horned owl.

瘤 **liu 2.** A goiter, a tumour.

廇 **liu 4.** A ball.

罶 **liu 3.** A fish-trap.

霤 **liu 4.** Atrium open to the sky.

552

馬 

See Lesson 137.

馬 **ma 3.** A horse.

螞 **ma 3.** An ant *ma-i*; a locust *ma-cha.*

榪 **ma 4.** A peg.

禡 **ma 4.** A sacrifice offered for the army.

瑪 **ma 3.** Agate; cornelian.

媽 **ma 1.** A nurse; a procuress.

嗎 **ma 1.** An interrogative particle.

碼 **ma 3.** Weights; numerals; a stone-anchor.

獁 **ma 4.** A monkey.

鰢 **ma 3.** Prawns.

傌 **ma 4.** A knight in chess.

[illegible] **ma 4.** To pile up.

䣕 **ma 3.** A proper name.

罵 **ma 4.** To curse; to revile.

553

See Lesson 34 G.

冥 **ming 2.** Dark; obscure.

暝 **ming 3.** Dark; obscure.

瞑 **ming 3.** To close the eyes.

螟 **ming 2.** A weevil.

溟 **ming 3.** Ocean. Drizzle; mist.

嫇 **ming 2.** A young wife.

慏 **ming 3.** Reticent.

幎 **ming 2.** A veil; to veil.

覭 **ming 2.** To examine closely.

蓂 **ming 2.** An auspicious plant.

It is radical in

塓 **mi 4.** To plaster walls; to whitewash.

554

能 

See Lesson 27 J.

能 **nai 4.** A brown bear.
nêng 2. To be able to; talent.

褦 **nai 1.** Stupid.

It is radical in

熊 **hsiung 2.** Black bear.

態 **t'ai 4.** Behaviour; bearing; attitude.

罷 **pa 4.** To stop; to finish; to dismiss; an imperative particle.

擺 **pai 3.** To spread out; to arrange; to wave; a ferry.

羆 **p'i 2.** The bear.

555

See Lesson 66 B.

般 **pan 1.** Manner; sort; fashion; kind.

搬 **pan 1.** To remove; to transport; a thumb-ring.

瘢 **pan 1.** Marks on the skin; moles.

螌 **pan 1** Cantharides.

盤 **p'an 2.** A dish; a plate; to coil up; to examine; expenses.

槃 **p'an 2.** A tray.

媻 **p'an 2.** An old woman.

幋 **p'an 2.** A large veil.

磐 **p'an 2.** A huge stone; a base.

[illegible] **p'an 2.** Cross-legged.

鞶 **p'an 2.** A leather strap.

556

See Lesson 117 A.

旁 / [illegible] } **p'ang 2.** Side; beside; near.

傍 **p'ang 2.** The side.

螃 **p'ang 3.** A crab.

鎊 **p'ang 2.** To hoe.

膀 **p'ang 2.** The bladder.

嗙 **p'ang 3.** To boast; to brag.

㥬 **p'ang 2.** Timid; fearful.

徬 **p'ang 2.** Indecision.

磅 **p'ang 1.** To pound.

[illegible] **p'ang 2.** To trample.

滂 **p'ang 2.** Heavy rain.

霶 **p'ang 1.** A heavy fall.

傍 **pang 4.** Near; the side; imminent.

榜 **pang 3.** A placard; a notice.

牓 **pang 3.** A tablet; a pattern.

謗 **pang 4.** To slander.

髈 **pang 3.** The shoulder.

綁 **pang 3.** To bind.

搒 **pang 3.** To beat; to propel a boat.

艕 **pang 4.** Two boats fastened side by side.

557

See Lesson 40 A.

毘 **p'i 2.** The navel.

砒 **p'i 1.** An ore of arsenic.

膍 **p'i 2.** The stomach of an animal.

⿰扌毘 **p'i 1.** To criticise.

媲 **p'i 4.** To pair; to match.

鎞 **p'i 2.** A needle.

貔 **p'i 2.** A leopard.

螕 **p'i 2.** A cattle-tick.

篦 **pi 4.** A comb; to comb.

558

See Lesson 43 B.

桑 **sang 1.** The mulberry-tree, *morus alba.*

搡 **sang 3.** To shake.

嗓 **sang 3.** The throat; the voice.

磉 **sang 3.** The stone base of a pillar.

顙 **sang 3.** The forehead.

⿸疒桑 **sang 3.** The glanders in horses.

559

See Lesson 62 I.

扇 **shan 4.** A folded fan; the leaf of a door; a screen.

搧 **shan 1.** To fan; to shake; to strike.

煽 **shan 1.** To excite; to inflame.

謆 **shan 4.** To wheedle; to seduce.

騸 **shan 4.** To geld.

560

See Lesson 131 D.

射 **shê 4. shih 2.** To shoot out; to dart.

麝 **shê 4.** The musk deer.

謝 **hsieh 4.** To thank; to cease; to resign; to confess.

榭 **hsieh 4.** A terrace; a tribune.

561

See Lesson 86 B.

師 **shih 1.** A sage; a master; a legion; a metropolis.

獅 **shih 1.** The lion.

溮 **shih 1.** An affluent of the Hwai.

螄 **shih 1.** A spiral shell; a screw.

蒒 **shih 1.** A floating marine plant.

篩 **shai 1.** A sieve; to sieve.

562

時 

See Lesson 79 B.

時 **shih 2.** Time; a season; a period.

塒 **shih 2.** A henroost.

溡 **shih 2.** A small stream in Shantung.

榯 **shih 2.** Erect; lofty; to set up.

鰣 **shih 2.** The shad, *alosa Reevesii.*

蒔 **shih 2.** To plant; to set up. Compare S. 338.

563

See Lesson 16 D.

衰 **shuai 1. suo 1.** Wearing away; fading; ruin.

蓑 **suo 1.** Grass rain cloak.

縗 **ts'ui 1.** Mourning dress.

榱 **ts'ui 1.** Small rafters projecting from the eaves.

564

See Lesson 102 D.

朔 **shuo 4.** The first day of the moon.

搠 **shuo 4.** To smear; to daub.

嗍 **shuo 4.** To suck in.

槊 **shuo 4.** A long spear.

溯 **su 4.** To trace up to the source; to remember.

遡 **su 4.** To trace up to the origin; to remember.

愬 **su 4.** To tell; to make known; to inform; to state plainly.

塑 **su 4.** To model in clay; to mold into shape.

565

See Lesson 79 G.

索 **so 3.** Strings; a cord; reins; to search into.

⿰扌索 **so 4.** To feel; to rub.

綤 **so 3.** A cord; to tie up.

鎍 **so 3.** A wire.

溹 **so 4.** The name of a river.

566

See Lesson 18 K.

𧴪 **so 3.** A cowrie; small things.

鎖 **so 3.** A lock; chains; to lock; to fetter.

瑣 **so 3.** Fragments; minute; petty.

567

See Lesson 126 B.

叟 **sou 3.** An old man; venerable.

傁 **sou 3.** An old man; venerable.

搜 **sou 1.** To search; to investigate; to enquire.

瞍 **sou 3.** Blind.

謏 **sou 3.** To scold; to censure.

溲 **sou 3.** To soak in water.

餿 **sou 1.** Spoilt; sour.

嗖 **sou 1.** A cry.

艘 **sou 1.** A boat; a junk.

鎪 **sou 1.** To engrave on metal.

颼 **sou 1.** A cold blast.

廋 **sou 1.** Secret; to search for.

嫂 **sao 3.** An elder brother's wife.

鄋 **sao 1.** Name of a place.

瘦 **shou 4.** Thin; lean; poor; valueless.

568

See Lesson 13 H.

素 **su 4.** Pure white silk; simple; coarse; common; lean.

嗉 **su 4.** The gizzard of a bird.

⿰食素 **su 4.** Abstinence; to eat vegetables.

愫 **su 4.** Sincere; one's real intentions.

⿰言素 **su 4.** To thoroughly comprehend.

膆 **su 4.** The crop of a bird.

傃 **su 4.** Towards; facing.

塐 **su 4.** To model things in clay; to mould.

⿰扌素 **su 4.** To steal.

569

孫 

See Lesson 92 B.

孫 **sun 1.** A grandson; a grandchild.

猻 **sun 1.** A monkey.

蓀 **sun 1.** A fragrant orchid.

遜 **hsün 4.** Complaisant; docile; modest; humble.

It is phon. contracted in

鯀 **kun 3.** A great fish.

570

See Lesson 14 B.

荅 **ta 2.** A species of pulse; to get entangled; to join; to answer.

搭 **ta 1.** To pile up; to join; to add to; to suspend; to lean against.

繨 **ta 2.** A knot.

褡 **ta 1.** A wrapper; a girdle.

嗒 **ta 1.** Absent; melancholy.

⿰足荅 **ta 1.** To jump.

劄 **ta 2.** A hook; curled; a quire.

匒 **ta 1.** Piled on each other.

瘩 **ta 2.** A sore; a boil.

塔 **t'a 3.** A pagoda, Buddhist tower.

鞳 **t'a 3.** A leather cuirass.

Modern form

答 **ta 2.** To answer. *Hence*

箚 **cha 2.** To prick; to puncture; to stitch in.

571

See Lesson 34 J.

𦐇 **t'a 4.** A flight of birds.

榻 **t'a 4.** A long bed; a couch.

塌 **t'a 1.** To fall down.

搨 **t'a 4.** To rub over; a fac-simile; an impression.

禢 **t'a 4.** Rakish.

遢 **t'a 4.** Hurried; careless.

䑜 **t'a 4.** To drink; to lap up.

𩋗 **t'a 4.** A leather tunic.

𥔲 **t'a 4.** A mortar.

𢡐 **t'a 1.** Depressed; in despair.

鰨 **t'a 4.** The dugong.

蹋 **t'a 1.** To stamp.

毾 **t'a 4.** A coarse woolen cloth.

闒 **t'a 4.** A window in a loft.

溻 **t'a 1.** To dampen; to soak through.

572

唐

See Lesson 102 B.

唐 **t'ang 2.** Uncivil; a proper name.

搪 **t'ang 2.** To waid off; to guard against.

糖 **t'ang 2.** Sugar.

煻 **t'ang 2.** To warm.

磄 **t'ang 2.** A bund; a dike.

溏 **t'ang 2.** Mud.

螗 **t'ang 2.** A mantis.

塘 **t'ang 2.** A pool; a pond; a post-station.

鄌 **t'ang 2.** A place in Shansi.

573

虒

See Lesson 135 G.

虒 **ti 1.** A fabulous tiger.

遞 **ti 4.** To transmit; to convey from hand to hand; to succeed.

榹 **ti 1.** A wild plum-tree.

鷉 **t'i 1.** A species of grebe.

𨧫 **tiao 2.** An alembic.

搋 **ch'uai 1.** To put in the bosom; to knead.

褫 **ch'ih 3.** To undress.

螔 **i 2.** A slug.

574

宰 

See Lesson 102 H.

宰 **tsai 3.** To govern; to preside; to slaughter.

縡 **tsai 3.** An affair; a business.

𣫂 **tsai 3.** To slaughter.

滓 **tzŭ 3.** Sediment, dregs.

575

See Lesson 26 M.

倉 **ts'ang 1.** A granary; a storehouse.

艙 **ts'ang 1.** The hold of a ship.

螥 **ts'ang 1.** The house fly.

傖 **ts'ang 1.** A worthless fellow.

滄 **ts'ang 1.** Vast.

瑲 **ts'ang 1.** The tinkle of stones and bells.

䲔 **ts'ang 1.** The conger.

鶬 **ts'ang 1.** A kind of crane.

蒼 **ts'ang 1.** Green; azure.

搶 **ch'iang 3.** To take by force; to ravish; to oppose; ahead.

槍 **ch'iang 1.** A spear; a lance; a swindler.

鎗 **ch'iang 1.** A gun; an opium pipe.

嗆 **ch'iang 4.** Hooping-cough.

謒 **ch'iang 1.** To oppose; to contradict; to scold.

蹌 **ch'iang 1.** To skip about.

戧 **ch'iang 4.** To prop; to etch on lacker-ware.

創 **ch'uang 1.** A wound.

愴 **ch'uang 4.** Sad; to pity.

瘡 **ch'uang 1.** Ulcer, abscess.

576

See Lesson 45 I.

蚤 / 𧕐 } **tsao 3.** A flea; to scratch.

騷 sao 1. Disquiet; grief.

慅 sao 1. Troubled; distressed.

搔 sao 1. To scratch.

膰 sao 1. Rank; fetid.

溞 sao 1. Rippling.

鰠 sao 3. A bream.

颾 sao 1. The sound of the wind.

瘙 sao 1. A sore; to itch.

577

See Lesson 68 I.

彖 t'uan 4. A hog; an interpretation.

褖 t'uan 4. Robes worn by the Empress.

瑑 chuan 4. To engrave, to inlay.

墢 chuan 4. To plough.

篆 chuan 4. The ancient Chinese characters.

椽 ch'uan 2. A rafter; the lathing.

猭 ch'uan 4. A hare.

鶨 ch'uan 4. A penguin.

殎 chüan 4. Exhaustion.

掾 yüan 4. Substitute of an officer.

蝝 yüan 2. The young of locusts before their wings have grown.

緣 yüan 2. A cause, a motive.

For the following, See L. 68 H.

蠡 li 4. wood-borer.

喙 hui 4. The mouth; to breathe. Compare S. 461.

578

See Lesson 31 C.

退 t'ui 4. To retreat; to draw back; to refuse.

腿 t'ui 3. The thigh; the leg.

It is radical in

褪 t'un 4. To pull the hands within the sleeves; to put off clothes.

579

See Lesson 92 F.

茲 兹 tzŭ 1. This, this one; now.

滋 tzŭ 1. Sap; juice; taste.

嗞 tzŭ 1. To propose; to deliberate.

黰 tzŭ 1. Black.

鎡 tzŭ 1. A hoe.

嵫 tzŭ 1. A hill in Shantung.

孳 tzŭ 1. To bear; to produce and suckle.

磁 ts'ŭ 2. Crockery; porcelain.

螆 ts'ŭ 4. Hairy caterpillars.

鷀 ts'ŭ 2. The fishing cormorant.

慈 ts'ŭ 2. Maternal affection; mercy.

580

See Lesson 157 C.

昷 wên 1. Benevolence.

溫 wên 1. To warm; tepid; mild.

殟 wên 1. Miscarriage.

榲 wên 1. The quince.

媼 wên 2. A matron.

瘟 wên 1. Pestilence; epidemic.

搵 en 4. To press down.

氳 yün 1. The aura; the generative influences of heaven and earth.

慍 yün 4. To be grieved; sad.

熅 yün 4. To smooth; to iron.

蝹 yün 1. To wriggle, as a snake.

韞 yün 4. To conceal.

醞 yün 4. Fermented liquor; wine.

縕 yün 4. Coarse cloth.

蘊 yün 4. To collect; to bring together.

The sound is altered in

膃 wu 4. Fat; obese.

嗢 wu 4. To laugh; to hem.

581

See Lesson 18 C.

翁 wêng 1. An old man; a venerable sir.

嗡 wêng 1. The lowing of cattle; the hum of insects.

塕 wêng 3. A gust of wind, dust.

螉 wêng 1. A wasp.

鞥 wêng 1. The uppers of a boot

膐 wêng 1. Stinking.

滃 **wêng 3.** Cloudy; foggy;

[翁頁] **wêng 1.** The neck feathers of a bird.

蓊 **wêng 3.** Luxuriant.

582

See Lesson 138 D.

烏 **wu 1.** Crows; black; an interrogative particle.

槝 **wu 1.** Ebony.

摀 **wu 3.** To cover; to stop up.

嗚 **wu 1.** An exclamation of regret; alas!

熓 **wu 3.** To bank a fire.

隖 **wu 3.** A walled village.

㡔 **wu 3.** A turban.

塢 **wu 3.** An entrenchment.

鄔 **wu 4.** A district in Chèkiang.

583

See Lesson 130 C.

䍃 **yao 2.** A jar.

搖 **yao 2.** To shake; to move.

謠 **yao 2.** A rumour.

媱 **yao 2.** Handsome.

愮 **yao 2.** Troubled; distressed.

徭 **yao 2.** Duty; forced labour; *corvees.*

瑤 **yao 2.** Green jasper.

鰩 **yao 2.** The flying-fish.

熎 **yao 4.** Dead coal.

猺 **yao 2.** A jackal.

[車䍃] **yao 2.** A light cart.

[足䍃] **yao 2.** To leap.

遙 **yao 2.** Distant; remote.

鷂 **yao 4.** A falcon; a paper kite.

颻 **yao 2.** Fluttering.

窰 **yao 2.** A kiln; a furnace.

繇 **yu 2.** Cause; means; consequently.

See L. 92 B.

584

See Lesson 139 A.

舀 **yao 3.** To bale out; to ladle out.

蹈 **tao 4.** To tread on.

稻 **tao 4.** Rice growing in the field.

慆 **t'ao 1.** License.

搯 **t'ao 1.** To take out; to bale out.

韜 **t'ao 1.** A scabbard; military tactics.

謟 **t'ao 1.** To doubt; to suspect.

縚 **t'ao 1.** A band; a sash.

槄 **t'ao 2.** A kind of catalpa.

滔 **t'ao 1.** Rushing water; to overflow.

幍 **t'ao 1.** The cap of literati.

Compare S. 860.

585

See Lesson 168 F.

熒 **ying 2.** To shine; bright; twinkling.

鶯 **ying 1.** The oriole.

瑩 **ying 2.** Bright; lustrous.

塋 **ying 2.** A grave; a burying-place.

罃 **ying 1.** An earthenware jare.

嫈 **ying 1.** A modest demeanour.

螢 **ying 2.** A glow-worm.

營 **ying 2.** An encampment; an army corps; to manage; business.

醟 **yung 4.** Drunkness.

禜 **jung 2.** A sacrifice to avert a national calamity.

縈 **jung 2.** To bind round; a circuit.

滎 **jung 2.** A rivulet.

榮 **jung 2.** Honour; glory.

煢 **ch'iung 2.** Alone; forlorn.

檾 **ch'ing 3.** A plant from the fibres of which cords are made, *sida tiliæfolia.*

It is radical in

勞 **lao 2.** To work. S. 694.

586

See Lesson 161 B.

員 **yüan 2.** An official; officers.

圓 **yüan 2.** Round; circular; complete; a dollar.

塤 **hsüan 1.** The Chinese ocarina.

溳 **yün 2.** Name of a river.

殞 **yün 3.** To die; to perish.

愪 **yün 2.** Grieved; sad.

隕 **yün 3.** To fall; to let fall; to perish.

䢵 **yün 2.** To weed.

磒 **yün 3.** An aërolite.

韻 **yün 4.** Harmony of sound; rhyme.

鄖 **yün 2.** A place in Hupeh.

䚋 **yün 3.** A proper name.

篔 **yün 2.** A large variety of bamboo.

損 **hsün 3.** To harm; to injure; chastisement.

587

See Lesson 16 L

袁 **yüan 2.** A long robe. A surname.

轅 **yüan 2.** The shafts of a cart.

榬 **yüan 2.** A reel.

猿 **yüan 2.** The gibbon.

遠 **yüan 3.** Far off; distant; to remove.

園 **yüan 2.** An enclosure; a garden.

睘 **huan 2.** To look at with respect. S 734.

588

See Lesson 59 C.

原 **yüan 2.** A high level; origin; principle.

源 **yüan 2.** A spring of water.

嫄 **yüan 2.** The mother of *Hou Chi*, her full name being *Chiang Yüan*.

傆 **yüan 4.** Unprincipled; cunning.

騵 **yüan 2.** A bay horse.

螈 **yüan 2.** A silk worm.

豲 **yüan 2.** The porcupine.

願 **yüan 4.** To wish; to be willing; to desire; a vow.

愿 **yüan 4.** Honest; respect.

589

See Lesson 20 G.

虘 **cha 1.** A proper name.

樝 **cha 1.** The azerole.

摣 **cha 1.** To seize; to hold fast.

謯 **cha 1.** To hum or sing.

䅊 **cha 1.** A kind of rice.

齇 **cha 1.** Irregular teeth.

𤺺 **cha 1.** A crust.

𢋈 **cha 1.** Ruins.

𧍧 **ch'ü 1.** Vermin.

覰 **ch'ü 4.** To spy; to peep.

590

See Lesson 120 H.

責 **chai 2.** To reprove; to punish; to require from; duty.

債 **chai 4.** To be in debt.

嘖 **chai 4.** To acclaim.

醋 **chai 1.** A press used in making spirits.

幘 **chai 1.** A conical cap; a turban.

簀 **chai 4.** A mat; fibres.

漬 **tzü 4.** To soak; to steep.

蹟 **chi 1.** Foot prints; traces; vestiges; results.

積 **chi 1.** To gather; to store up.

績 **chi 1.** To spin; to twist; meritorious deeds.

磧 **chi 2.** A rocky desert.

襀 **chi 1.** A plait.

591

斬 斬

See Lesson 123 A.

斬 **chan 3.** To decapitate; to sever.

暫 **chan 4.** A short time; temporarily; in the interim; meanwhile; briefly; suddenly.

磛 **ch'an 3.** A cliff.

獑 **ch'an 2.** A kind of monkey.

嶄 **ch'an 2.** A high peak.

鏨 **tsan 4.** To chisel; to cut out.

慙 慚 **ts'an 2.** Mortified; ashamed.

漸 **chien 4.** To gradually soak; to advance by degrees.

聻 魙 **chien 4.** Death of a man's ghost.

塹 **ch'ien 4.** A ditch; a kennel.

槧 **ch'ien 4.** Boards; tablets.

592

See Lesson 79 F.

產 **ch'an 3.** To produce; to bear; productions of a country.

樺 **ch'an 3.** A kind of peach-tree.

犍 **ch'an 3.** To breed domestic animals.

滻 **ch'an 3.** Name of a river.

嵼 **ch'an 3.** A winding mountain path.

鏟 **ch'an 3.** A spade; to dig.

剷 **ch'an 3.** A paring-knife.

薩 **sa 4.** *P'u-sa*, i.e. bodhisattva.

593

See Lesson 73 E.

章 **chang 1.** A section; a document, an essay; elegant; rule; law.

障 **chang 4.** An embankment; to separate; to screen.

熚 **chang 4.** To crackle; a cracker.

樟 **chang 1.** The camphor tree, *laurus camphora*.

璋 **chang 1.** A sceptre; a cup.

嫜 **chang 1.** A husband's father.

嶂 **chang 4.** A range of mountains.

瞕 **chang 4.** A cataract.

漳 **chang 1.** Name of a river.

慞 **chang 1.** Terrified.

韞 **chang 1.** Flap of a saddle.

鄣 **chang 1.** A place in Shantung.

彰 **chang 1.** Beautiful; to exhibit; to manifest.

鷾 **chang 1.** The moor-hen.

麞 **chang 1.** The musk-deer.

瘴 **chang 4.** Malaria.

594

See Lesson 12 O.

巢 **ch'ao 2.** A nest; a haunt; a den.

樔 **ch'ao 2.** A hut built on piles.

轈 **ch'ao 2.** A look-out on a war chariot.

僺 **ch'ao 3.** Tall.

漅 **ch'ao 2.** A lake in Anhui.

璅 **ch'ao 2.** Tinkling.

勦 **ch'ao 2.** To grieve; to molest.

繅 **sao 1.** To reel silk from cocoons.

595

See Lesson 38 G.

祭 **chi 4.** To sacrifice.

際 **chi 4.** An angle; a limit; a juncture; an occasion; a time; relations.

漈 **chi 4.** Side; bank.

穄 **chi 4.** A panicled millet, *panicum miliaceum*.

瘵 **chi 4.** Consumption.

察 **ch'a 2.** To examine; to find out; enquiries.

魔 **ch'a 2.** Demons which bring pestilence.

擦 **ts'a 1.** To rub; to wipe.

縩 **ts'ai 4.** New clothes; the rustle of garments.

蔡 **ts'ai 4.** Grass; hay.

596

See Lesson 26 M.

旣 既 既 } **chi 4.** Since; when; to finish; all.

塈 **chi 4.** To plaster a wall; to gather; to rest.

暨 **chi 4.** The sun peeping out; and; with.

蔇 **chi 4.** Grass.

穊 **chi 4.** Plants growing thickly.

漑 **chi 4.** To wash.

槩 概 } **kai 4.** To level; to adjust; altogether; generally.

慨 **k'ai 4.** Generous; noble-minded.

廏 廐 } **chiu 4.** A stable. L. 26 N.

Compare S. 424.

597

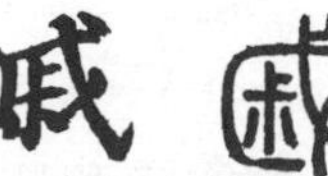

See Lesson 124 C.

戚 **ch'i 4.** A battle-axe; related to; kin; sorrow; to pity; to distress.

嘁 **ch'i 1.** To whisper.

慽 **ch'i 1.** Grief; sorrow.

鏚 **ch'i 1.** A battle-axe.

墄 **ch'i 1.** The steps of a stairway.

慼 **ch'i 1.** Grief; sorrow.

顣 **ts'u 4.** To frown.

槭 **tsu 1.** The *acer palmatum*.

蹙 **tiu 1.** To squat.

摵 **shê 1.** The fall of the leaves; elegiac.

598

See Lesson 119 E.

桼 **ch'i 1.** The varnish.

㯃 **ch'i 1.** The varnish tree, *rhus vernicifera*.

漆 **ch'i 1.** Varnish; lacquer.

膝 **ch'i 2.** The knees.

599

See Lesson 127 B.

將 **chiang 1.** To take in the hand; to act; future; about to; to receive; to give.
chiang 4. A commander.

蹡 **chiang 4.** To walk quickly.

摪 **chiang 1.** To lead.

蔣 **chiang 3.** *Hydropyrum latifolium.*

䉃 **chiang 3.** Splinters; fibres.

醬 **chiang 1.** Soy; sauce.

糨 **chiang 1.** Starch.

漿 **chiang 1.** Broth; congee.

槳 **chiang 3.** An oar.

獎 **chiang 3.** To praise; to encourage.

螿 **chiang 1.** A cricket.

600

See Lesson 91 C.

牽 **ch'ien 1.** To pull; to haul; to connect.

撁 **ch'ien 1.** To pull; to lead; to drag.

縴 **ch'ien 4.** A tow-rope.

𣛮 **ch'ien 4.** A board.

601

See Lesson 102 G.

執 **chih 2.** To grasp; to hold; to manage.

摯 **chih 4.** To grasp; to hold; to offer up.

慹 **chih 4.** To lose heart.

贄 **chih 4.** A present; offerings; gifts.

縶 **chih 4.** To tie up.

騺 **chih 4.** A packhorse.

鷙 **chih 4.** Birds of prey.

蟄 **chê 2.** To hibernate; to become torpid.

熱 **jê 4.** Hot; to heat; feverish.

褻 **hsieh 4.** Underwear; dirty; irreverence.

It is radical in

墊 **tien 4.** To fill up; to steady; to pay.

602

See Lesson 71 E.

堇 **chin 3.** Clay; to plaster.

墐 **chin 3.** To stop with mud.

謹 **chin 3.** Cautious; vigilant.

僅 **chin 3.** Only; hardly; scarcely.

漌 **chin 3.** Pure; limpid.

瑾 **chin 3.** The lustre of gems.

殣 **chin 3.** To die of starvation.

饉 **chin 3.** A dearth.

槿 **chin 3.** The *hibiscus syriacus*.

覲 **chin 3.** To have an audience with the Emperor.

靳 **chin 4.** Firmness; avarice.

廑 **chin 3.** A hut; narrow.

䈽 **chin 1.** A large variety of bamboo.

蓳 **chin 3.** Aconit; poison.

慬 **ch'in 2.** Compassion.

勤 **ch'in 2.** Diligence; zeal; to toil; to work.

鄞 **yin 2.** A place in Chêkiang. Compare S. 609.

603

See Lesson 73 E.

竟 **ching 4.** To search; to finish; after all; finally.

境 **ching** 4. Frontier; boundary; a region; a district; circumstances.

鏡 **ching** 4. A mirror; a looking-glass.

獍 **ching** 4. A panther.

璄 **ching** 3. The lustre of gems.

糡 **chiang** 4. Starch.

604

See Lesson 173 A.

声 **ch'ing** 4. Sonorous stones.

殸 **ch'ing** 4. To beat.

磬 **ch'ing** 4. Sonorous stones.

罄 **ch'ing** 4. Empty; exhausted; entirely.

漀 **ch'ing** 4. A torrent.

[illegible] **ch'ing** 4. Very hot.

聲 **shêng** 1. Sound; tone; accent; fame.

馨 **hsin** 1. To smell sweetly.

605

See Lesson 91 F.

專 **chuan** 4. Single; particular; to specially care.

傳 **chuan** 4. A commentary.

磚 **chuan** 1. A brick, a flag.

轉 **chuan** 4. To turn round; to revolve.

縳 **chuan** 4. To tie; to enwrap.

嫥 **chuan** 1. Gentle.

鱄 **chuan** 1. A salmon.

甎 **chuan** 1. A brick, a flag.

鄟 **chuan** 1. Name of a place in Honan.

傳 **ch'uan** 2. To transmit; to hand down; to propagate.

蓴 **ch'un** 2. Gentian.

摶 **t'uan** 2. To roll round.

䊜 **t'uan** 2. Dumplings.

漙 **t'uan** 2. Name of a river.

慱 **t'uan** 2. Grieved.

團 **t'uan** 2. A ball; a sphere; a fump.

606

See Lesson 47 N.

舂 **ch'ung** 1. To pound grain; to hull.

惷 **ch'ung** 1. Simple; doltish.

摏 **ch'ung** 1. To pound; to run against.

[illegible] **ch'uang** 1. Grain half withered.

[illegible] **ch'uang** 1. To see indistinctly.

[illegible] **ch'uang** 4. A stake.

椿 **chuang** 1. A post; an affair; a kind.

[illegible] **chuang** 1. Short dress.

踳 **chuang** 1. To tread on.

[illegible] **chuang** 1. A cuckoo.

607

區 

See Lesson 72 L.

區 **ch'ü** 1. A place; a district.

軀 **ch'ü** 1. The body; one's own self.

驅 **ch'ü** 1. A fore-runner. To expel.

嶇 **ch'ü** 1. A steep mountain.

貙 **ch'ü** 4. A lynx.

[illegible] **ch'ü** 1. A moth.

傴 **ch'ü** 3. A hunch-back.

嫗 **yü** 4. A matron.

饇 **yü** 4. Glutted; satisfied.

摳 **k'ou** 1. To raise.

瞘 **k'ou** 1. Deep sunken eyes.

彄 **k'ou** 1. The horn at the end of a bow.

剾 **k'ou** 1. To cut out; to dig out.

熰 **ou** [illegible]. To smoke.

漚 **ou** 4. To soak; to steep.

嘔 **ou** 1. To vomit; to spit.

謳 **ou** 1. Ballads; to sing.

慪 **ou** 4. To excite; to irritate.

塸 **ou** 3. A tumulus; a tomb.

毆 **ou** 1. To beat; to strike.

歐 **ou** 1. To womit; to retch.

甌 **ou** 1. A bowl.

鷗 **ou** 1. A sea-gull.

樞 **shu** 1. A pivot; an axis; cardinal.

It is radical in
奩 lien 2. A lady's dressing-case; a bridal *trousseau*.

608

See Lesson 97 A.

逢 fêng 2. To meet; to happen; an accident.
縫 fêng 3. To sew.
fêng 4. A split.
漨 fêng 2. A pool; a marsh.
蠭 fêng 1. A bee; a wasp.

摓 p'êng 2. To whirl.
憉 p'êng 4. Satisfaction; to please.
蓬 p'êng 2. A plant whose seeds are winged; to flutter about.
篷 p'êng 2. A sail.

Compare S. 269.

609

See Lesson 171 B.

暵 han 2. Hot; parched; dry. Is phonetic contracted in the following
漢 han 4. Name of a dynasty; hence, China, Chinese.
熯 han 4. To roast; to dry.
暵 han 4. Arable land.

難 nan 2. Difficult; to distress. S. 847.

歎 t'an 4. To sigh.
嘆 t'an 4. To sigh.

艱 chien 1. Labour; difficulty.

Compare S. 602.

610

See Lesson 159 A.

習 hsi 2. To practise; a custom; a usage.
槢 hsi 2. Hard wood.
熠 hsi 4. To sparkle.
霫 hsi 2. Heavy rain.
嶍 hsi 2. A mountain in Yunnan.

褶 tieh 2. A lined garment.

歙 chê 2. Bad humour.
磖 chê 1. Stony.
摺 chê 2. To ford; a digest; a memorial.

611

See Lesson 112 E.

徙 hsi 3. To change house.
蹝 hsi 3. Sandals.
縰 hsi 3. A hair-net.
蓰 hsi 3. A plant; fivefold.
屣 hsi 3. Straw sandals.

篩 shai 1. A sieve; to sift.

612

See Lesson 50 P.

 ch'ien 1. To climb.

躚 hsien 1. To saunter.
僊 hsien 1. Genii.

613

See Lesson 41 B.

宿 hsü 1. A constellation.
滀 hsü 1. To soak in.
蓿 hsü 4. Lucern.

宿 hsiu 3. Night; to lodge for the night.
鏥 hsiu 4. Rust; oxides.

縮 so 1. To draw back; to shorten.
蹜 so 1. To drag one's feet.

614

旋

See Lesson 117 B.

旋 hsüan 2. To turn round; to revolve; consequently; then.
璇 hsüan 2. An armillary sphere.
漩 hsüan 1. Whirling water.
鏇 hsüan 4. A turning-lathe; a pulley.
蜁 hsüan 3. A kind of snail.
縼 hsüan 4. A tether.
颴 hsüan 4. A whirlwind; a typhoon.

615

See Lesson 58 D.

虖 hu 1. An exclamation.

歑 **hu 1.** To breathe on.

嘑 **hu 1.** To cry.

謼 **hu 1.** To call out.

[忄虖] **hu 1.** To boast; to exaggerate.

滹 **hu 1.** Name of a river.

嫭 **hu 4.** Graceful.

[石虖] **hsia 4.** A split.

罅 } **hsia 4.** A crevice; a leak; a crack.
[阝虖] }

616

See Lesson 129 A.

扈 **hu 4.** Name of a city.

滬 **hu 4.** Shanghai.

[扌扈] **hu 4.** To distribute.

[山扈] **hu 4.** A ridge.

簄 **hu 4.** Fishing-stakes.

617

彗 彗

See Lesson 44 J.

彗 **hui 4.** A broom.

槥 **hui 4.** A coffin.

[扌彗] **hui 1.** To break; to destroy.

嘒 **hui 4.** Jingling.

[目彗] **hui 4.** Fine; minute.

篲 **hui 4.** A broom.

慧 **hui 4.** Intelligent; quick; wise; virtuous.

It is radical in

雪 **hsüeh 3.** Snow.

618

See Lesson 131 C.

医 **i 1.** A quiver.

殹 **i 1.** To draw; to strike.

醫 **i 4.** To heal; to cure; a doctor.

瞖 **i 4.** A film in the eye.

[殹土] **i 1.** Dust; dirt.

嫛 **i 1.** A lying-in woman.

鷖 **i 1.** The widgeon.

[殹石] **i 1.** Jet.

翳 **i 1.** To screen; a film.

蠮 **i 4.** The solitary wasp or sphex.

619

See Lesson 79 K.

埶 **i 4.** Skill; handicraft; art.

槷 **i 4.** A limit; to plant.

褹 **i 4.** The sleeves of a robe.

槸 **i 4.** The rubbing together of branches in a wind.

蓺 } **i 4.** To cultivate; agriculture; a law; a rule; art.
藝 }

囈 **i 4.** To mutter.

熱 **jê 4.** Warm; to warm.

勢 **shih 4.** Power; authority; influence; circumstances.

Compare S. 379.

620

See Lesson 47 R.

異 **i 4.** Different; foreign; strange; heterodox.

[匚異] **i 4.** A censer.

廙 **i 4.** A shop.

翼 **i 4.** The wings of a bird; to shelter; to assist.

潩 **i 4.** Name of a river.

冀 **chi 4.** To hope; to wish. *It forms*

[示冀] **chi 4.** The duration of a reign or a dynasty.

懻 **chi 4.** Violent; proud; overbearing.

驥 **chi 4.** A thorough-bred horse.

戴 **tai 4.** To wear on the head; to sustain; to uphold; to obey.

It is unconnected with

糞 **fên 4.** Ordure. L. 104 A.

621

See Lesson 102 B.

庸 **jung 1.** Common.

傭 **jung 1.** To engage for hire.

庸 **yung 1.** Common; ordinary.

傭 **yung 1.** To engage for hire.

墉 **yung 1.** A wall.

鏞 **yung 3.** A large bell.

慵 **yung 2.** Idle; sluggish.

鱅 **yung 2.** A tench.

鄘 **yung 1.** A place in Honan.

622

敢

See Lesson 146 H.

敢 **kan 3**. To dare; to venture.

澉 **kan 3**. To wash.

橄 **kan 3**. The olive.

闞 **k'an 4**. To spy; to watch.

矙 **k'an 3**. To spy; to watch.

憨 㦑 } **han 1**. Foolish, silly.

鬫 **han 3**. To quarrell.

It is radical in

嚴 **yen 2**. Severe. S. 858.

623

康

See Lesson 102 B.

康 **k'ang 1**. Peace; repose; prosperity.

慷 **k'ang 3**. Generous; magnanimous.

躿 **k'ang 1**. Tall; long.

糠 穅 } **k'ang 1**. Chaff; husks of grain; refuse; useless.

嵻 **k'ang 3**. A cave; hollow.

㝩 **k'ang 1**. Empty; deserted.

624

規

See Lesson 131 F.

規 **kuei 1**. A pair of compasses; a rule.

槻 **kuei 1**. The bark of a tree.

摫 **kuei 1**. To cut cloth for clothes.

[illegible] **kuei 1**. The sea-hog.

嫢 **kuei 1**. A graceful woman.

闚 **k'uei 2**. To spy.

窺 **k'uei 2**. To peep; to watch.

625

國

See Lesson 71 J.

國 **kuo 3**. A nation; a country; a State.

幗 **kuo 1**. A turban.

嘓 **kuo 4**. To chatter.

摑 **kuai 1**. To slap.

蟈 **kuai 1**. A cricket.

膕 **kuai 1**. The calf of the leg.

聝 **kuo 4**. To cut off the ears of the slain.

馘 **kuo 4**. To cut off the head of the slain.

Compare S. 364.

626

纍

See Lesson 149 F.

累 **lei 3**. To tie; to bind.
lei 4. To embarrass.

縲 **lei 3**. To bind.

[illegible] **lei 2**. Fat; big.

樏 **lei 3**. A box with partitions.

漯 **lei 3**. Glittering of water.

[illegible] **lei 3**. A squirrel.

瘰 **lei 3**. Scrofula.

蘽 **lei 3**. A small tree.

騾 **lo 2**. A mule.

摞 **lo 2**. To pile up.

螺 **lo 2**. A conch; a screw.

627

𠩺 

See Lesson 129 C.

𠩺 **li 2**. To fell.

釐 **li 2**. To regulate; the thousandth part of a tael; minute.

嫠 **li 2**. A widow.

犛 **li 2**. The yak of Tibet.

氂 **li 2**. Tail of a yak.

漦 **li 2**. Mucus.

628

离 

See Lesson 23 E.

离 **li 2**. The unicorn.

摛 **li 2**. To stretch.

醨 **li 2**. Dregs.

褵 **li 2**. A sash.

謧 **li 2**. To jest.

璃 **li 1**. A vitreous translucent substance.

[illegible] **li 2**. Shavings.

[illegible] **li 2**. Good omens.

樆 **li 2**. Wild pears.

漓 li 2. Water dripping.
糲 li 2. Slimy; sticky.
篱 li 2. A ladle.
離 li 2. To separate; to leave; distance.
羅 li 2. A wrapper.
籬 li 2. A fence.

瞝 ch'ih 1. To scrutinise.
黐 ch'ih 1. To stick.
螭 ch'ih 1. A dragon.
魑 ch'ih 1. A mountain elf. Compare S. 728.

629

翏 翏

See Lesson 62 F.

翏 liao 4. To fly.
蟉 liao 4. A cicada.
蹘 liao 2. To run away.
瞭 liao 2. To burn the grass on a field.
憀 liao 2. To trust to.
鏐 liao 3. Darkened gold.
飂 liao 2. A constant wind.
熮 liao 2. To toast.
漻 liao 2. Clear water.
鷚 liao 4. A lark.
鄝 liao 3. A place in Honan.
寥 liao 2. Waste; vast.
廖 liao 3. A proper name.
蓼 liao 3. A bitter drug.

醪 lao 2. The lees of spirits.
嫪 lao 4. Libertinism.

戮 lu 4. To kill.
穋 lu 4. Precocious.
僇 lu 4. To scorn.

磟 liu 4. A stone roller.
漻 liu 2. Frost-bitten.

繆 niu 4. To bind; a mixture.
謬 niu 4. Falsehood; error.
璆 niu 4. Jasper.

樛 chiu 1. Hanging or weeping branches.

轇 chiao 1. Confusion.
摎 chiao 1. To shrivel up.
膠 chiao 1. Glue; gum.

嘐 hsiao 1. Boasting; bragging.

繆 miao 4. A proper name.

瘳 ch'ou 1. To cure.

630

連 連

See Lesson 167 B.

連 lien 2. To connect; to join; to continue.
摙 lien 3. To lift; to remove.
漣 lien 2. To weep.
褳 lien 2. A pouch; a pocket.
蓮 lien 2. To crawl.
僆 lien 3. A series.
鏈 lien 2. A chain.
麰 lien 3. Oats.
槤 lien 2. An orange-tree.
鰱 lien 3. A tench.
璉 lien 2. A vessel.
蓮 lien 2. The lotus, *nelumbium speciosum*.

631

婁 婁

See Lesson 67 N.

婁 娄 } lou 2. To trail along; to wear.
摟 lou 3. To embrace.
螻 lou 2. Ants.
樓 lou 2. An upper-storey; a terrace.
耬 lou 3. Chinese sowing-machine.
髏 lou 2. A skull-bone.
嶁 lou 3. A mountain in Hunan.
慺 lou 2. Contented; diligent.
謱 lou 2. To chatter.
塿 lou 2. A mound over a grave.
鏤 lou 4. To carve, to engrave.
嘍 lou 2. Chattering; prattle.
遱 lou 2. Unbroken; continuous.
䅹 lou 2. A sow.
艛 lou 3. A war-junk with a high poop.
數 lou 3. To plunder.
劃 lou 4. To carve; to hollow out.
甊 lou 3. A bottle.
瘻 lou 4. A fistula.

簍 lou 3. A basket.

蔞 lou 2. Parsley.

僂 lü 2. Hunchbacked.

褸 lü 3. Rags.

縷 lü 3. To spin; to state in detail.

騪 lü 2. A donkey.

漊 lü 3. Drizzling.

屢 lü 3. Many times; repeatedly.

窶 lü 3. Poor; rustic.

屨 chü 3. Sandals; straw shoes.

數 shu 3. To count. S. 812.
shu 4. A number.

632

See Lesson 41 D.

鹵 lu 3. Potash. Rude; incivil.

滷 lu 3. Lye.

磠 lu 3. Gravel.

擄 lu 3. To wipe; to shake.

憦 lu 3. Abashed.

㯭 lu 3. A long oar.

It is radical in

鹻 chien 3. Soda.

鹹 hsien 2. Salt.

鹽 yen 2. Salt.

633

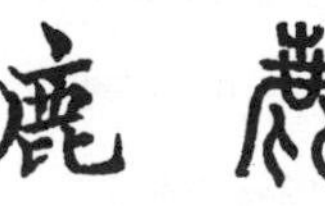

See Lesson 136 A.

鹿 lu 4. A stag; a deer.

轆 lu 4. A pulley.

樚 lu 4. A pulley; a windlass.

摝 lu 4. To roll; to rock.

㦝 lu 4. Careless.

漉 lu 4. To filter.

螰 lu 4. A cicada.

簏 lu 4. A basket.

麓 lu 4. Wooded hills.

鏖 lu 4. A proper name.

It is radical in

麤 ts'u 1. Deer-herd.

塵 ch'ên 2. Dust.

麃 piao 1. A roebuck. S. 817.

慶 ch'ing 4. To congratulate. L. 136 A.

634

See Lesson 79 H.

麻 ma 2. Textile fibres.

嘛 ma 1. Lama, a Tibetan bonze.

䲨 ma 2. A wild goose.

䁡 ma 2. To see indistinctly.

犘 ma 2. The tibetan yak.

蔴 ma 2. Sesam.

痳 ma 2. Numbness.

麽 mo 1. An interrogative particle.

䭥 mo 2. Steamed bread.

魔 mo 2. A devil; a demon.

磨 mo 2. To rub, to polish.
mo 4. To grind; a mill.

摩 mo 2. To feel with the hand; to caress.

蘑 mo 2. The mushroom.

穈 mei 2. A kind of millet.

塺 mei 4. Dust.

縻 mei 2. To bind; to tie.

靡 mei 2. No, not; malice; defeat; loss.

麾 hui 1. A signal flag.

635

See Lesson 34 J.

曼 man 2. Wide; long.

慢 man 4. Slow; remiss; neglectful; rude.

漫 man 4. Water over-flowing; spreading.

謾 man 2. To recriminate.

襔 man 2. Large clothes.

饅 man 2. Bread.

墁 man 4. To plaster; to pave.

僈 man 4. Negligent; remiss.

幔 man 4. A curtain; a screen.

鰻 man 2. The eel.

鏝 man 2. A trowel.

縵 man 4. Plain; simple.

鄤 man 4. Name of a place.

蔓 man 2. A kind of turnip.

鬘 man 2. A head-dress.
Compare S. 463.

636

See Lesson 35 M.

㒼 man 2. Equilibrium.
顢 man 1. A large round face.
瞞 man 2. To deceive.
蹣 man 2. To jump over; to limp.
樠 man 2. Pine; resine.
⿺毛㒼 man 2. A red carpet.
璊 man 2. Cornelian.
⿰土㒼 man 2. To plaster.
⿰米㒼 man 2. Pap.
滿 man 3. Full; complete; Manchu.
懣 man 3. Melancholy.

637

See Lesson 78 G.

莫 mo 4. Not; is it not?
糢 mo 1. Confused.
謨 mo 2. A scheme; a plan; to meditate.
漠 mo 4. A sandy desert; the Gobi.
慔 mo 4. Effort; diligence.
貘 mo 4. The Malacca tapir.
瞙 mo 4. Leucoma.
暯 mo 4. Dark; obscure.
鏌 mo 4. A famous sword.
膜 mo 4. The skin.
塻 mo 4. Dust.
嗼 mo 4. Silent.
鄚 mo 1. A proper name.
摹 摸 mo 1. To feel for; to get; to succeed. *Mao* 1.
寞 mo 4. Silent; solitary.
瘼 mo 4. Sickness; distress.

莫 mu 4. Not. *Mo* 4.
模 mu 2. A pattern; a model; a mould.
嫫 mu 2. A proper name.
⿺毛莫 mu 4. Woollens.
慕 mu 4. To love.
墓 mu 4. A grave.
募 mu 4. To summon; to enlist.
暮 mu 4. Evening; sunset.
驀 mu 4. To jump over.
幕 幙 mu 4. A tent; a curtain; a screen.
冪 mu 4. A veil; to cover.

糢 ma 1. Confused.
蟆 ma 1. A frog.

⿱莫夕 mei 4. Silent; still.

638

See Lesson 78 E.

敖 nao 2. ao 2. Tall; proud.

傲 ao 4. Proud; arrogant.
嗷 ao 1. Clamours.
璈 ao 2. Sonorous stones.
磝 ao 2. A stony surface.
遨 ao 2. To ramble.
熬 ao 2. To boil; to decoct.
聱 ao 2. Refusing to hear; a bad character.
驁 ao 2. A vicious horse; stubborn.
鏊 ao 4. A round iron cooking kettle.
鷔 ao 2. A bird of ill omen.
鼇 ao 2. A huge turtle.
鰲 ao 2. A sea monster.
獒 ao 2. A fierce dog.
摮 ao 2. To shake.
⿱敖廾 ao 2. The stem of a vessel.
螯 ao 2. A large shell.
廒 ao 2. A granary.

It is radical in

贅 chui 4. Overplus, appendix; a pledge; an adoption.

639

See Lesson 46 G.

匿 ni 4. To hide; to abscond.
⿰忄匿 ni 3. Ashamed; mortified.
暱 ni 4. Morning; to visit.
⿰目匿 ni 4. To blink.
⿰木匿 ni 4. A fabulous tree.
⿰齒匿 ni 4. Rotten teeth.
⿱匿虫 ni 4. Gnats.

慝 t'ê 4. Evil; wicked.
Compare S. 454.

640

畢

See Lesson 104 A.

畢 pi 2. To finish; ended; all; together.

⿰冫畢 pi 4. A cold wind.

滭 pi 4. Bubbling water.

縪 pi 4. Fringe.

⿰木畢 pi 4. Box-wood.

韠 pi 4. A knee-pad.

彃 pi 2. The cord of a bow.

篳 pi 4. A fence.

蓽 pi 2. Pepper.

641

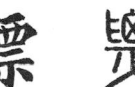

敝

See Lesson 35 F.

敝 pi 4. Worn out; vile.

獘 弊 pi 4. Abuses; corrupt practices; evil.

幣 pi 4. Silk; presents; wealth.

蔽 pi 4. To conceal; to shade; to darken.

徶 pieh 1. Flowing robes.

⿰忄敝 憋 pieh 1. To forbear.

斃 獘 pieh 4. To die; to perish.

鼈 鱉 pieh 1. A turtle.

蹩 pieh 1. To limp; to tread upon.

鷩 pieh 4. The golden pheasant.

鄨 pieh 1. A town in Hupeh.

癟 pieh 1. An ulcer.

潎 p'ieh 1. Rippling.

撇 撆 p'ieh 1. To skim off; to reject.

⿱敝刀 p'ieh 1. To cut through.

嫳 p'ieh 1. Nervous; inconstant.

642

See Lesson 50 O.

票 p'iao 4. A slip of paper; a warrant; a bank note; a ticket.

漂 p'iao 1. To float; to drift.

嫖 p'iao 2. Lewdness.

瞟 p'iao 3. To spy.

⿰日票 p'iao 4. To dry in the sun.

僄 p'iao 1. Light.

縹 p'iao 3. Azure.

鏢 p'iao 1. A weapon.

慓 p'iao 1. High spirits.

驃 p'iao 4. Nimble; brisk.

嘌 p'iao 1. Out of breath.

螵 p'iao 1. Eggs of mantis.

膘 p'iao 3. The flanks of an animal.

醥 p'iao 3. Clear spirits.

魒 p'iao 1. The Genius of the Great Bear.

勡 p'iao 4. To seize by force.

彯 p'iao 4. Ornamented with fringe.

瓢 p'iao 2. A gourd; a calabash.

剽 p'iao 4. To pierce.

⿰票鳥 p'iao 1. A sea-gull.

飄 p'iao 1. To be blown about.

標 piao 1. A signal; a flag; notice; a warrant.

摽 piao 1. To give a signal.

鰾 piao 4. Fish-glue.

⿰山票 piao 3. A high peak.

幖 piao 1. A streamer.

⿰票見 piao 3. To look at carefully.

643

𥏻 

See Lesson 101 B.

𥏻 shang 1. To wound.

傷 shang 1. To wound; to injure; distress.

殤 shang 1. To die prematurely.

觴 shang 1. A goblet.
Compare SS. 365, 492, 707.

644

See Lesson 76 E.

孰 shu 2. Who? which? what?

熟 shu 2. Ripe; cooked; mature; versed in; common. *Shou* 2.

塾 shu 2. A school-room.
Cf. SS. 359, 549, 716.

645

See Lesson 50 O.

庶 **shu 4.** All; a multitude, in abundance; a concubine; so that, about; nearly.

遮 **chê 1.** To cover; to screen; to intercept.
摭 **chê 1.** To gather.
謶 **chê 1.** To deceive.
嗻 **chê 1.** Loquacity.
儦 **chê 1.** Fierce; brutal.
樜 **chê 1.** The sugar-cane.
蟅 **chê 4.** A cokroach.
蹠 **chê 2.** A proper name.
鷓 **chê 2.** The partridge.
蔗 **chê 1.** The sugar-cane.

墌 **chih 1.** Foundations. A proper name.

646

See Lesson 91 D.

率 **shuai 4.** To lead; to follow; rule; usually.
摔 **shuai 3.** To fall down; to throw down.
蟀 **shuai 4.** A cricket.

繂 **lü 4.** A rope.
膟 **lü 4.** Flesh offered in sacrifice.
悸 **lü 4.** Sadness.
蓚 **lü 4.** Seeds beginning to sprout.

647

See Lesson 120 L

欶 **su 4.** To suck.
sou 4. To cough.

樕 **su 4.** A species of oak.
簌 **su 4.** A fine sieve.
蔌 **su 4.** Culinary vegetables.

嗽 **sou 4.** To rinse out.
漱 **sou 4.** To rinse out.
瘶 **sou 4.** To cough.

Compare S. 308.

648

See Lesson 24 Q.

帶 **tai 4.** A girdle; a sash; a zone; to take with one; to lead; together with.
懘 **tai 4.** Disturbed in mind.
縹 **tai 4.** A ribbon, a girdle.
瘭 **tai 4.** Flux; leucorrhœa.

艜 **t'ai 4.** A junk.

螮 **ti 4.** The rainbow.
遰 **ti 4.** To go away; hidden.
蹛 **ti 4.** High; exalted.
蔕 **ti 4.** A peduncle.

滯 **chih 4.** Coagulation; obstruction; opposition.

649

See Lesson 36 E.

堂 **t'ang 2.** A hall; a court; a church.
膛 **t'ang 2.** The thorax. The roof of the mouth.
摚 **t'ang 2.** To resist; to ward off.
螳 **t'ang 2.** A mantis.
鏜 **t'ang 2.** Noise of drums, etc.
瞠 **t'ang 2.** To gaze at.

650

See Lesson 120 H.

啇 **ti 2.** Stem; base; origin.
嫡 **ti 2.** The legal wife.
樀 **ti 2.** Short rafters
滴 **ti 1.** To drop; to leak.
鏑 **ti 2.** The point of an arrow.
蹢 **ti 2.** To walk.
豴 **ti 2.** The hoof of a pig.
敵 **ti 2.** An enemy; to oppose.

摘 **chai 1.** To pick; to take off; to deprive of.
謫 **chai 4.** To reproach; to blame.

適 **shih 4.** To go to; to reach; to suit; suddenly.

651

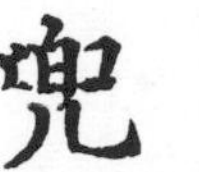 

See Lesson 106 A.

兜 **tou 1.** A sack; a bag.

篼 **tou 1.** A basket.

⿰扌兜 **tou 1.** To grasp.

652

See Lesson 62 C.

參 **ts'an 1.** To counsel; to consult. Orion. *Shên* 1.

慘 **ts'an 3.** Grieved; sad; miserable; cruel.

傪 **ts'an 1.** Handsome; fine-looking.

摻 **ts'an 1.** To hold; to mix.

驂 **ts'an 1.** The two outside horses of a team of four.

穇 **ts'an 1.** A kind of millet.

⿺走參 **ts'an 1.** To hurry;.a runner; a van-guard.

謲 **ts'an 4.** To rail at; to irritate.

黲 **ts'an 3.** Speckled; black and white.

[illegible] **ts'an 4.** A hair-pin.

糝 **san 3.** Porridge.

毿 **san 1.** Long feathers.

鬖 **san 1.** Dishevelled hair.

蔘 **shên 1.** In *Hai shên*, sea-slugs; *Sên-shên*, ginseng. *Ts'an* 1.

⿱木參 **shên 1.** Thick branches. It is sometimes used for the preceding.

滲 **shên 4.** To absorb; to infiltrate; to soak.

槮 **shên 4.** A fish-trap.

墋 **ch'ên 3.** Dirty.

磣 **ch'ên 3.** Sand; grit.

醦 **ch'ên 3.** Vinegar.

嵾 **ch'ên 1.** Uneven; irregular.

653

See Lesson 120 K.

曹 **ts'ao 2.** A company; a class; officials; the plural.

槽 **ts'ao 3.** A trough; a manger; a distillery.

漕 **ts'ao 2.** To transport by water.

螬 **ts'ao 2.** Maggots in fruit.

嘈 **ts'ao 2.** Noise; hubbub.

艚 **ts'ao 2.** A sea-going junk.

⿰扌曹 **ts'ao 4.** To stir.

䐬 **ts'ao 2.** Crisp; friable.

⿰曹少 **ts'ao 2.** Worn-out; decayed.

遭 **tsao 1.** To meet with; to experience; a turn; a time.

糟 **tsao 1.** Sediment; dregs; spoilt; rotten.

⿰歹曹 **tsao 1.** Spoilt; rotten.

蹧 **tsao 1.** To tramp on; to ill-treat; to abuse.

醩 **tsao 1.** Sediment; dregs.

褿 **tsao 1.** A short tunic.

慒 **tsao 1.** In confusion.

鰽 **tsao 2.** A herring.

654

族 𬩽

See Lesson 117 B.

族 **tsu 2.** To collect together; a tribe; a clan; a family; relatives.

鷟 **tsu 2.** A kind of duck.

蔟 **ts'u 4.** A nest; a crowd.

簇 **ts'u 4.** A frame.

嗾 **sou 2.** To excite; to tease.

655

See Lesson 168 F.

崔 **ts'ui 1.** Rocky; precipitous.

墔 **ts'ui 1** A heap; a lot.

催 **ts'ui 1.** To urge; to press.

摧 **ts'ui 1.** To break.

磪 **ts'ui 1.** High; precipitous.

膗 **ts'ui 1.** Fat; corpulent.

凗 **ts'ui 1.** Snow; snowy.

璀 **ts'ui 4.** The lustre of gems; brilliant.

漼 **ts'ui 4.** Clear and deep.

656

See Lesson 40 D.

悤 **ts'ung 1.** Hurried; excited.

聰 **ts'ung 1.** Quick of apprehension; clever.

驄 **ts'ung 1.** A piebald.

璁 **ts'ung 1.** A precious stone.

總 **tsung 3.** To unite; to sum up; to comprise.

傯 **tsung 3.** Wearied; worn-out.

憁 **tsung 3.** Disappointment; deception.

摠 **tsung 3.** To tie; to gather.

稯 tsung 3. A sheaf of grain.

Abbreviated (L. 40 D, 3)

匆 ts'ung 1. In hurry.
怱 ts'ung 1. Hastily. *Hence*
聰 ts'ung 1. Quick; clever.
驄 ts'ung 1. A piebald.
楤 ts'ung 1. *Aralia spinosa.*
葱 ts'ung 1. The onion.
𢈢 ts'ung 1. A flight of steps.

總 tsung 1. Dark green.
傯 tsung 3. Wearied; worn-out.

657

從

See Lesson 27 A.

從 ts'ung 2. To follow; to pursue; to comply with; from; by; since.
瑽 ts'ung 1. The tinkling of pendent gems.
鏦 ts'ung 1. A javelin.
樅 ts'ung 1. A drum-stick; to beat.
蝬 ts'ung 1. A kind of gadfly.
蓯 ts'ung 1. Grassy.

縱 tsung 4. To be lax; to yield to; to let go; to rumple; although; even if.
蹤 tsung 1. A footstep; a track; a trace.
𡐓 tsung 1 A kind of mushroom.
豵 tsung 1. A pig.
瘲 ʻtsung 4. Crippleness.
慫 tsung 3. To alarm.

聳 sung 3. Deafness. To raise; to excite; lofty; high.

658

尉

See Lesson 32 B.

尉 尉 } wei 4. To iron. yü 4. A name.

熨 wei 4. To iron; to soothe.
慰 wei 4. To comfort; to pacify; kindness.
螱 wei 4. The white ant.
蔚 wei 4. Luxuriant; prosperous.
霨 wei 4. Clouds.
罻 wei 4. A net to catch birds.

659

羕

See Lesson 103 A.

羕 yang 4. Flowing of water.
漾 yang 4. Name of a river.
樣 yang 4. A pattern; a kind; a style.
懩 yang 4. Displeasure; disgust.
𠐊 yang 4. To sway.

660

焉

See Lesson 138 C

焉 yen 1. How? why? where?
撝 yen 4. To trim; to measure.
傿 yen 4. A broker.
嫣 yen 1. Charming.
鄢 yen 1. A place in Honan.

蔫 nien 1. Withered; faded.

661

寅

See Lesson 172 A.

ʻ寅 yiu 2. A cyclic character.
縯 yin 4. To sew; to stitch.
螾 yin 3. The earthworm.
戭 yin 3. A long spear.
夤 yin 2. To respect; to advance; distant places.

演 yen 3. Wide; to practise; to drill; to perform.

662

雩

See Lesson 53 H.

雩 yü 2. A ceremony to get rain.

嫮 hu 4. Handsome.
鄠 hu 3. A place in Shansi.

樗 ch'u 1. *Ailantus glandulosa*; a useless stuff.
摴 ch'u 1. To spread; dice; pantomim; mimic.
𤩝 ch'u 1. A precious stone.

嶀 t'u 2. A mountain in Chekiang.

663

敞

See Lesson 36 E.

敞 **ch'ang 3.** A plateau; open; high.

廠 **ch'ang 3.** A shed; a workshop.

鷩 **ch'ang 3.** Down, feathers.

惝 **ch'ang 3.** Alarmed.

664

朝

See Lesson 117 D.

朝 **ch'ao 2.** The Court; audiences given in the early morning; a dynasty; towards; facing. *Chao* **1.**

潮 **ch'ao 2.** The tide; moist; damp.

朝 **ch'ao 2.** A proper name.

朝 **chao 1.** The morning. *Ch'ao* **2.**

嘲 **chao 1.** To jest at.

It is radical in

廟 **miao 4.** A temple; a fair.

665

敎

See Lesson 94 E.

敎 **chê 4.** Education.

轍 **chê 2.** A rut; the track of a wheel.

撤 **ch'ê 4.** To tear; to pull apart.

徹 **ch'ê 4.** To penetrate; to understand; all; entire; general.

澈 **ch'ê 4.** Clear water; to the bottom.

666

掌

See Lesson 36 E.

牚 堂 **ch'êng 1.** A prop.

橕 **ch'êng 1.** A prop, to support.

饓 **ch'êng 1.** To eat too much.

撐 撐 **ch'êng 1.** To prop up; to assist.

667

幾

See Lesson 90 D.

幾 **chi 1.** To be near; to approximate; almost; minute.

饑 **chi 1.** Dearth; famine.

譏 **chi 1.** To rail at; to jeer.

璣 **chi 1.** A pearl.

機 **chi 1.** A moving power; a machine; opportune; motive.

禨 **chi 1.** An omen; opportune.

蟣 **chi 3.** Nits.

磯 **chi 1.** A jetty; an eddy.

鐖 **chi 1.** A hook.

檵 **chi 4.** The *loropetalum sinense.*

魕 **chi 1.** Devilish; magic.

鞿 **chi 1.** The bit on a bridle.

畿 **chi 1.** Imperial lands.

668

強

强

See Lesson 110 B.

强 **ch'iang 2.** Strong; good.

勥 **ch'iang 4.** To exert one's strength.

襁 **chiang 3.** Swaddling-clothes.

鏹 **chiang 3.** To string up cash.

膙 **chiang 3.** Callosities; corns.

糨 **chiang 4.** Starch.

蔃 **chiang 3.** Small roots.

669

焦

See Lesson 126 A.

焦 **chiao 1.** Scorched; dried up; care; a surname.

燋 **chiao 1.** To char; to scorch.

醮 **chiao 1.** A sacrifice; a festival.

膲 **chiao 1.** Stomach.

鐎 **chiao 1.** A brass kettle.

趭 **chiao 4.** To run; to flee.

噍 **chiao 4.** To eat.

僬 **chiao 1.** Clever; to understand.

潐 **chiao 3.** To filter.

礁 **chiao 1** A reef of rocks.

顦 **chiao 1.** Wrinkled; faded.

䌭 **chiao 1.** Tow.

鷦 chiao 1. The wren.
𤢚 chiao 1. Thin; lean.
蕉 chiao 1. Banana.

瞧 ch'iao 2. To look on.
憔 ch'iao 2. Distressed.
譙 ch'iao 4. To blame; to ridicule.
樵 ch'iao 2. Fuel.
嶕 ch'iao 2. Rocky.
劁 ch'iao 4. To cut; to castrate.

670

See Lesson 75 B.

喬 ch'iao 2. Lofty; high; proud.
橋 ch'iao 2. A bridge.
蹻 ch'iao 1. To stand.
鞽 ch'iao 1. Boots.
燆 ch'iao 1. Flames.
僑 ch'iao 2. A guest; to sojourn.
趫 ch'iao 2. Agile; to run.
翹 ch'iao 2. To fly downwards.
蕎 ch'iao 2. Buck-wheat.

驕 chiao 1. Proud; haughty.
嬌 chiao 1. Delicate; to pet.
轎 chiao 4. A sedan; a cabin.
觰 chiao 3. To cock horns.
矯 chiao 3. To falsify; to feign; false.
譑 chiao 3. To divulge.
蟜 chiao 3. To wriggle.

穚 chiao 1. The blooming of corn.
嶠 chiao 4. A ridge.
鱎 chiao 3. The culter, a fish peculiar to China.
鷮 chiao 1. A pheasant.
敿 chiao 3. To roll up; to tie up.
鷮 chiao 1. A large harpsichord.

671

See Lesson 71 I.

戠 chih 1. A sword; to gather; potter's clay.
識 chih 4. To remember; a note; a document; a memorandum. *Shih 2.*
職 chih 2. A charge, an office.
織 chih 1. To weave.
膱 chih 1 Dried meat.
軄 chih 2. An official position.
熾 chih 4. To burn; a blaze of fire
擿 chih 4. To try.
樴 chih 4. A post.

幟 ch'ih 4. A pennon.
旘 ch'ih 4. A pennon.

識 shih 2. To know; experience. *Chih 4.*

672

See Lesson 75 C.

景 ching 3. Bright; scenery; a view; circumstances.

憬 ching 2. To excite; to perceive; to feel.

擤 hsing 4. To feel; to estimate.

影 ying 3. A shadow; an image; a vestige.
璟 ying 3. The lustre of gems.

673

See Lesson 102 D.

厥 chüeh 2. He; him; this. *Ch'üeh 2.*
噘 chüeh 1. To pout.
撅 chüeh 1. To break, to pluck.
鐝 chüeh 2. A pick; a hoe.
蹶 chüeh 2. To stumble.
獗 chüeh 2. Insolent; unruly.
蟨 chüeh 2. A gerboa.
鱖 chüeh 4. A perch.
橛 chüeh 2. The end of the backbone.
蕨 chüeh 2. Bracken.
勪 chüeh 4. To compel; to urge.
橜 chüeh 2. A peg.

厥 ch'üeh 2. He; him; this; *Chüeh 2.*
闕 ch'üeh 4. A fault; wanting.

674

See Lesson 71 D.

貳 erh 4. To be double; two; second.

樲 **erh 4.** Thorny shrubs.

膩 **ni 4.** Grease; fat.

[忄貳] **ni 4.** Ardor, zeal.

[虫貳] **ni 4.** Plant-louse.

675

See Lesson 112 H.

發 **fa 1.** To send forth; to issue; to dismiss; to utter; to produce; to rise; to be manifest; to act.

[竹發] **fei 4.** A rush mat.

廢 **fei 4.** Ruined; useless; to abandon; to destroy.

癈 **fei 4.** Incurably diseased.

橃 **fei 1.** An orange-tree.

撥 **po 1.** To spread; to open out; to distribute.

襏 **po 4.** A rain-coat.

潑 **p'o 1.** To sprinkle.

鏺 **p'o 1.** A scyth; to mow.

醱 **p'o 1.** Must.

676

See Lesson 123 D.

番 **fan 4.** A time; a turn; barbarians.

蕃 **fan 2.** Luxuriant; increasing; plenty; Tibet.

幡 旛 } **fan 1.** The banner carried before a corpse.

繙 **fan 1.** To translate; to interpret.

璠 **fan 2.** A precious stone.

墦 **fan 2.** A grave.

燔 **fan 2.** To roast; to burn.

膰 **fan 2.** Meats used in sacrifices.

蹯 **fan 2.** An animal's paw.

轓 **fan 1.** A screen for a cart.

翻 **fan 1.** To come back; to turn over; alternatives.

藩 **fan 2.** A fence; a frontier.

籓 **fan 2.** A sieve; a basket.

潘 **p'an 1.** Name of a river.

蟠 **p'an 2.** To coil up; to curl round.

磻 **p'an 2.** A silex.

[疒番] **p'an 1.** A falling womb.

播 **po 3.** To sow; to publish; to winnow; to cast aside.

嶓 **po 1.** A mountain in Shensi.

皤 **po 1.** White; clear.

鄱 **p'o 2.** A place in Kiangsi.

It is radical in

審 **shên 3.** To scrutinise S. 811.

667

See Lesson 39 L.

棥 **fan 2.** A hedge; a fence. *It forms*

樊 **fan 2.** A hedge. S. 801.

678

黑

See Lesson 40 D.

黑 **hei 1.** Black; dark; evil.

默 **mei 4.** Dark; retired; secret, silent.

嘿 **mei 4.** Silent.

[禾黑] **mei 3.** Mildewed grain.

墨 **mei 4.** Ink; black.

纆 **mei 4.** A cord.

It is radical in

熏 **hsün 1.** To smoke. S. 781.

黨 **tang 3.** To blacken.

679

See Lesson 100 B.

犀 **hsi 1.** A yak.

樨 **hsi 1.** *Olea fragrans.*

稺 **chih 4.** Recent; delicate.

遲 **ch'ih 2.** Slow; to defer; a delay; late.

墀 **ch'ih 2.** A court-yard.

[犀刂] **ch'ih 2.** To dismember.

680

喜

See Lesson 165 B.

喜 **hsi 3.** Joy; gladness; to delight in.

僖 **hsi 1.** Cautious.

嘻 **hsi 1.** An interjection.

嬉 **hsi 1.** To play; to amuse one's self.

熺 **hsi 1.** To roast.

禧 **hsi 1.** Blessings; good luck.

蟢 **hsi 3.** A spider of good omen.

譆 **hsi 1.** To grieve; to lament.

熹 **hsi 1.** To warm; heat; glory; prosperity.

憙 **hsi 3.** To delight in.

681

See Lesson 62 H.

 **hsi 4.** Harmonious; to unite; together; all.

 **hsi 1.** To inhale.

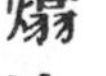 **hsi 4.** To roast; to burn.

 **hsi 1.** Noise of flowing water.

 **hsi 4.** To join; to shut up.

 **hsi 4.** To close; to rest.

682

鄉 𨞰

See Lesson 26 M.

鄉 **hsiang 1.** A village; country; a suburban district.

 **hsiang 3.** Sound; echo.

 **hsiang 3.** Offerings; a feast; to relish.

 **hsiang 4.** Towards; facing; encouraging; to favour.

 **hsiang 3.** Insects.

 **hsiang 4.** Formerly.

To be distinguished from

卿 **ch'ing 2.** Minister. L. 26 M.

683

See Lesson 69 L.

 **hsiang 4.** The elephant; ivory; an image; the elements of the Diagrams.

像 **hsiang 4.** An image; to resemble.

橡 **hsiang 4.** The oak.

潒 **hsiang 3.** A torrent.

⿰飠象 **hsiang 3.** A meal.

⿰象鳥 **hsiang 4.** The hornbill.

684

See Lesson 64 H.

閒 間 } **hsien 2.** Leisure; quiet; idle.

僩 **hsien 3.** Courageous; martial.

嫺 **hsien 2.** Graceful; refined; accomplished.

憪 **hsien 3.** Pleasure; peace; happiness.

撊 **hsien 3.** Brave; wrathful.

瞯 **hsien 4.** To watch; to peep at.

癇 **hsien 2.** Convulsions; fits.

閒 間 } **chien 4.** A crevice; a space between.

簡 **chien 3.** A slip of bamboo; a tablet; documents; records; to abridge.

襇 **chien 3.** Embroidered plaits on a robe.

澗 **chien 4.** Mountain streams.

⿰木間 **chien 4.** Buildings.

鐧 **chien 4.** The iron inside the hub.

覵 **chien 4.** To spy into; to mix up.

685

See Lesson 27 H.

虛 虗 } **h'sü 1.** Empty; vacant; vain; false; weak; useless.

噓 **hsü 1.** To blow; to breathe; to suck up.

㦽 **hsü 1.** Humble; modest.

墟 **hsü 1.** Waste, wild land; a market.

歔 **hsü 1.** To snort; to sigh; to breathe hard.

⿰山虛 **ch'ü 1.** Steep rocks.

覷 **ch'ü 4.** To peep at.

686

See Lesson 45 F.

尋 **hsün 2.** To search for; to seek common.

撏 **hsün 2.** To elect; to seize.

鱘 **hsün 2.** The sturgeon.

蟳 **hsün 2.** A hairy sea-crab.

⿰月尋 **hsün 2.** A proper name.

潯 **hsün 2.** A steep bank.

鄩 **hsün 2.** A place in Shantung

蕁 **hsün 2.** *Anemarrhena asphodeloides.*

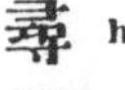 **hsin 2.** To marry. *Hsün 2.*

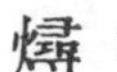 **hsin 2.** To scald.

 **t'an 3.** Timidity.

687

See Lesson 13 F.

華 **hua 2.** Flowers; flowery; China.

華 **hua 4.** A mountain in Shansi.

嘩 **hua 2.** Cries.

譁 **hua 4.** Clamour; noise.

鏵 **hua 2.** A plough-share.

樺 **hua 4.** A kind of birch.

曄 **hua 4.** Glim; lightning.

鞾 **hsüeh 1.** Boots.

燁 **yeh 2.** Fire; glory; prosperity.

688

See Lesson 171 A.

黃 **huang 2.** Yellow.

磺 **huang 2.** Sulphur.

璜 **huang 2.** A jade gem.

潢 **huang 2.** A pool.

獚 **huang 2.** A dog; barbarians.

鱑 **huang 2.** The sturgeon.

纊 **huang 4.** A rope.

蟥 **huang 2.** A leech.

簧 **huang 2.** A reed; a spring.

癀 **huang 2.** Jaundice.

黌 **huang 2.** The yolk of an egg.

廣 **kuang 3.** Wide; broad. S. 802.

觵 **kuang 1.** A cup of horn.

黌 **hung 2.** An academy.

橫 **hêng 4.** Cross-wise; perverse; obstinate.

It is radical in

堇 **chin 3.** Loess. S. 602.

689

See Lesson 91 G.

惠 **hui 4.** Kind; gracious; to obey; to be docile.

蕙 **hui 4.** An orchid.

譓 **hui 4.** Sagacious.

蟪 **hui 4.** A cicada.

憓 **hui 4.** Compliant; obedient; docile.

穗 **sui 4.** An ear; a spike.

繐 **sui 1.** Tassels, fringes.

690

See Lesson 48 E.

壹 **i 1.** One.

饐 **i 4.** Spoilt food.

膉 **i 4.** Lean.

曀 **i 1.** Cloudy.

殪 **i 4.** To kill.

墤 **i 4.** Dust.

鷧 **i 4.** The fishing cormorant.

懿 **i 4.** Admirable; suitable; excellent.

噎 **yeh 1.** To choke; the throat obstructed.

691

然

See Lesson 65 G.

肰 **jan 2.** Dog's meat.

然 **jan 2.** Thus; so; however; but.

燃 **jan 2.** To light a fire.

獄 **jan 2.** A monkey.

撚 **nien 3.** To roll in the fingers.

蹨 **nien 3.** Afoot.

Compare S. 793.

692

雇

See Lesson 129 A.

雇 **ku 4.** To hire; to borrow.

僱 **ku 4.** To hire; to borrow.

顧 **ku 4.** To look after; to regard; to consider.

693

See Lesson 111 B.

貴 **kuei 4.** Esteemed; prized; dear.

鐀 **kuei 4.** A box.

憒 **kuei 4.** Troubled.

⿰犭貴 **kuei 4.** A weasel.

櫃 **kuei 2.** A press; a trunk.

饋 **k'uei 4.** Provisions; food.

樻 **k'uei 4.** A small knotty tree.

墤 **k'uei 4.** A heap; a bit.

⿰扌貴 **k'uei 4.** To draw; to monopolise; to take.

聵 **k'uei 4.** Deaf.

瞶 **k'uei 4.** Dimmed sight; blurred vision.

⿰禾貴 **k'uei 4.** A ribbon; to tie up.

簣 **k'uei 4.** A basket.

蕢 **k'uei 4.** A basket.

⿱髟貴 **k'uei 4.** A ribbon for tying the hair in a knot.

匱 **k'uei 4.** Wearied; exhausted.

⿸疒貴 **t'ui 2.** Worn out.

隤 **t'ui 2.** Ruined; lost

潰 **hui 4.** To flood.

繢 **hui 4.** Embroidery.

嬇 **hui 4.** A proper name.

殨 **hui 4.** A sore.

⿰酉貴 **hui 4.** To wash the face.

闠 **hui 4.** A gate.

It is radical in

遺 **i 2.** To let; to transmit; to bequeath.

694

See Lesson **126** F.

勞 **lao 2.** To toil, to labour; trouble.

撈 **lao 2.** To fish up; to drag out of water.

蟧 **lao 2.** A cicada.

嘮 **lao 2.** To chatter.

澇 **lao 4.** A flood.

憦 **lao 2.** Sorry; wearied.

⿱艹勞 **lao 2.** *Rhynchosia volubilis.*

癆 **lao 2.** Phthisis.

695

See Lesson **126** E.

尞 **liao 3.** A holocaust.

撩 **liao 1.** To grasp; to raise.

憭 **liao 3.** Intelligent; cheerful.

⿰言尞 **liao 2.** Cunning of speech.

蟟 **liao 2.** The cicada.

繚 **liao 2.** To bind; to wrap; a turn.

燎 **liao 2.** A signal-light, a beacon.

獠 **liao 2.** To hunt at night with torches.

⿰土尞 **liao 4.** A surrounding wall.

暸 **liao 3.** Bright; shining.

橑 **liao 2.** A rafter.

僚 **liao 2.** A companion; a colleague.

膫 **liao 2.** Fat; grease.

嫽 **liao 2.** To sport with.

鐐 **liao 4.** Fetters.

瞭 **liao 3.** A clear eye.

寮 **liao 2.** A window; a companion.

簝 **liao 3.** A bamboo tray.

療 **liao 2.** To cure; to heal.

遼 **liao 2.** Distant; a river; *Liao-tung* Manchuria.

潦 **lao 4.** A flood; to overflow.

696

See Lesson **126** D.

粦, ⿱炎舛 } **lin 2.** A flitting light.

燐 **lin 2.** The ghost-lights; phosphorus.

潾 **lin 2.** Mountain streams.

嶙 **lin 2.** Rugged; precipitous.

橉 **lin 4.** A tinctorial wood.

獜 **lin 2.** A pangolin.

磷 **lin 4.** To polish.

遴 **lin 2.** To select.

疄 **lin 2.** A raised path.

鱗 **lin 2.** The scales of a fish.

璘 **lin 2.** Veined, as marble.

麟 **lin 2.** The female of the unicorn.

⿰虫粦 **lin 2.** A firefly.

鄰 **lin 2.** Near; contiguous; neighbour.

憐 **lien 2.** To pity; to desire; to covet.

697

 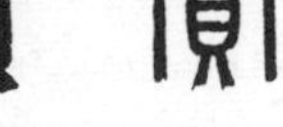

See Lesson **161** D.

買 **mai 3.** To buy; to purchase.

賣 **mai 4.** To sell. L. 78 E.

賣 mai 3. Chicory.

瀆 mai 3. The name of a river.

嘪 mai 3. To bleat.
Compare L. 79 J. S. 817.

698

See Lesson 78 C.

莽 mang 3. Jungle; undergrowth; rustic.

蟒 mang 3. A boa constrictor.

㟌 mang 3. Disturbed in mind; agitated.

漭 mang 2. Vast; a waste.

曭 mang 3. The sun obscured.

699

彭 彭

See Lesson 165 C.

彭 p'êng 2. A surname. To beat drum.

碰 p'êng 4. To hit against.

膨 p'êng 2. Swollen, flatulence.

澎 p'êng 1. Noise of dashing waters.

憉 p'êng 2. To strive.

髼 p'êng 2. A pitcher.

蟚 p'êng 2. A land crab.

700

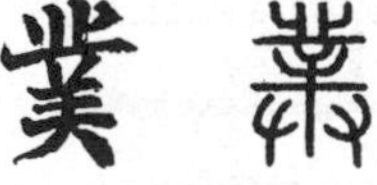

See Lesson 102 I.

菐 p'u 2. To gather.

僕 p'u 2. A servant; a subject.

撲 p'u 1. To strike.

璞 p'u 4. An unpolished gem; simple; rude.

幞 p'u 4. A turban.

鏷 p'u 4. A dart.

轐 p'u 4. The pieces of a cart which hold the axle firm.

蹼 p'u 4. Fin-toed; webbed.

醭 pu 2. The mother of vinegar.

樸 p'o 2. A natural substance, plain; simple; sincere.

墣 p'o 4. A clod of earth.

瞨 p'o 4. Near sight.

Compare

業 yeh 4. Property. L. 102 I.

701

See Lesson 79 H.

散 san 4. To scatter; to disperse; to separate.

饊 san 3. Fried cakes.

繖 san 3. A parasol; an umbrella.

霰 hsien 4. Sleet.

𨯔 hsien 4. To castrate.

撒 sa 1. To loose.
sa 3. To scatter.

𥊛 sa 2. To glance at.

702

See Lesson 73 D.

善 shan 4. Good; clever; virtuous; to approve; to love.

繕 shan 4. To write out; to copy.

膳 } shan 4. Delicacies; food; viands.
饍 }

蟮 shan 4. The earthworm.

僐 shan 4. Elegant.

墡 shan 4. Fine plastic clay.

磰 shan 4. White clay used for porcelain.

鱔 shan 4. The eel.

703

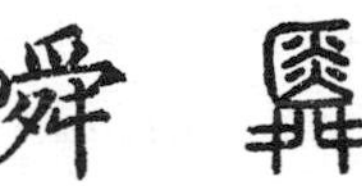

See Lesson 126 D.

舜 shun 4. Name of an ancient monarch.

瞬 shun 4. To blink; to glance.

僢 shun 4. Melancholy.

橓 shun 4. *Hibiscus syriacus.*

蕣 shun 4. *Hibiscus mutabilis*; fugacious; transitory.

704

See Lesson 128 A.

斯 ssŭ 1. This; he; they; a final particle; then.

撕 ssŭ 1. To rend; to tear.

傂 ssŭ 1. A servant.

凘 ssŭ 1. To thaw; to melt.

澌 ssŭ 1. To exhaust.

燍 ssŭ 1. To burn.

廝 } ssŭ 1. A menial; a servant; to serve.
厮 }

[illegible] **hsi 1.** Fear; dread.

[illegible] **shai 1.** A sieve; to sift; to strain.

705

See Lesson 72 E.

單 **tan 1.** Single; alone; unlined. *Shan* 4.

撣 **tan 3.** To dust.

彈 **tan 4.** A crossbow; a bullet. *T'an* 2.

殫 **tan 1.** To exhaust; utterly.

襌 **tan 1.** Unlined garment.

憚 **tan 4.** To dread; to shrink from.

磾 **tan 1.** Sulphate of iron.

鄲 **tan 1.** A place in Shantung.

簞 **tan 1.** A basket for holding steamed rice.

癉 **tan 1.** Blight.

匰 **tan 1.** The shrine for tablets in the ancestral hall.

潬 **t'an 1.** A sandbank.

彈 **t'an 2.** To play on stringed instruments; to rebound; to press down; to accuse. *Tan* 4.

單 **shan 4.** A proper name. *Tan* 1.

燀 **shan 4.** To poke a fire.

墠 **shan 4.** Smooth; level; a thrashing-floor.

禪 **shan 4.** To abdicate.

鱓 **shan 4.** The eel.

戰 **chan 4.** To fight; to fear; to tremble

闡 **ch'an 4.** To explain; to enlarge.

蟬 **ch'an 2.** The cicada.

嬋 **ch'an 1.** Graceful.

禪 **ch'an 2.** Contemplation.

The sound is altered in

觶 **chih 4.** A goblet made of horn.

706

See Lesson 75 G.

覃 **t'an 2.** Coarse taste.

罈 **t'an 2.** An earthenware jar.

墰 **t'an 2.** A jar; a jug.

憛 **t'an 4.** Solicitude.

驔 **t'an 3.** A dark horse.

橝 **t'an 2.** A tinctorial wood.

禫 **t'an 3.** The sacrifice offered at the expiration of the mourning.

鐔 **t'an 2.** A handle.

醰 **t'an 2.** Bitter wine.

撢 **t'an 4.** To play on.

燂 **t'an 2.** To heat; to dry.

譚 **t'an 2.** To boast.

[illegible] **t'an 2.** To run.

潭 **t'an 2.** Deep water; to sound.

[illegible] **t'an 2.** A place in Shantung.

蕈 **t'an 4.** A mushroom.

簟 **tien 4.** A fine bamboo mat.

蟫 **yin 2.** An insect, *lepisma*.

707

See Lesson 101 B.

湯 **t'ang 2.** Infusion; soup; to scald.

鐋 **t'ang 4.** A plane; to polish.

燙 **t'ang 4.** To heat by placing in hot water.

[illegible] **t'ang 1.** To oppose.

盪 **tang 4.** A bath.

簜 **tang 4.** A large kind of bamboo.

蕩 **tang 4.** Large; vast; dissolute; reckless.

Compare SS. 492 and 648.

708

See Lesson 112 H.

登 **têng 1.** To ascend; to record; to complete.

燈 **têng 1.** A lamp; a lantern.

澄 **têng 4.** To filter; to clarify.

蹬 **têng 4.** To bump.

僜 **têng 4.** Weak; exhausted; incapable.

磴 **têng 4.** Stone steps.

墱 **têng 4.** A ledge; steps.

瞪 **têng 4.** To stare at; to gaze.

鐙 **têng 4.** A stirrup.

[illegible] **têng 4.** Exhausted.

[illegible] **têng 1.** An offering of food.

橙 **têng 1.** An orange-tree.

嶝 **têng 4.** A cliff.

[illegible] **têng 1** A heron.

[illegible] **têng 1.** A light tissue.

鄧 **têng 4.** A place in Honan.

簦 **têng 1.** An umbrella.

[illegible] **têng 4.** To wake from sleep.

霯 **têng 4.** Heavy rain.

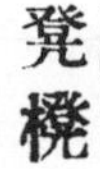 têng 4. A stool; a bench.

鼟 t'êng 1. The roll of drums.

證 chêng 4. To testify; to bear witness; a proof.

⿰黑登 chêng 4. To become black.

⿰巾登 chêng 4. To unroll.

憕 ch'êng 2. Peace.

709

See Lesson 26 D.

朁 tsan 1. To murmur; if; however.

簪 tsan 1. A hair-pin.

蠶 ts'an 2. A silk worm.

僭 chien 4. To arrogate to one's-self.

潛 ch'ien 2. To plunge; to abscond; secrete.

譖 chên 3. To slander.

It is contracted in

昝 偺 tsan 2. I, we. L. 26 D.

喒 tsan 2. A final particle.

710

See Lesson 40 D.

曾 tsêng 1. To add to; to increase. *Ts'êng* 2.

增 tsêng 1. To add to; to increase; supernumerary.

贈 tsêng 4. To give a present; to offer; a title.

譄 tsêng 1. To add; to state further.

憎 tsêng 1. To hate; to abhor.

⿰目曾 tsêng 1. Dimness of sight.

鏳 tsêng 1. The ring of metal when struck.

繒 tsêng 1. Silken fabrics.

磳 tsêng 3. Rocky; stony.

矰 tsêng 1. A dart.

⿰衤曾 tsêng 4. A handkerchief.

橧 tsêng 1. A hut.

⿰黑曾 tsêng 4. A black face.

⿰曾戈 tsêng 1. A captive arrow.

甑 tsêng 4. A boiler to stew food.

鄫 tsêng 1. Name of a place.

罾 tsêng 1. A large fishing-net.

曾 ts'êng 2. Past; done; finished.

蹭 ts'êng 4. To slip; to graze.

噌 ts'êng 1. Noise; clamour.

嶒 ts'êng 2. Tiers of hills.

竲 ts'êng 2. Lofty; high.

⿰曾刂 ts'êng 4. To cut or wound.

層 ts'êng 2. A layer; a stratum.

⿱宀曾 ts'êng 2. A building.

It is a radical in

會 hui 4. A meeting. S. 736.

711

See Lesson 146 F.

最 tsui 4. Very; most; extreme; to gather.

⿱竹最 ts'ui 4. A broom.

嘬 tso 1. To suck; to lap up.

繓 tso 3. A hank of thread.

蕞 tso 4. A few; small; a gathering; a hamlet.

撮 ts'o 4. To pinch up; to gather up.

The sound is altered in

⿰火最 tsuan 4. A proper name.

712

See Lesson 100 A.

毳 ts'ui 4. Down; fur; soft; fragile.

膬 ts'ui 4. Tender; delicate; crisp.

竁 ts'ui 4. To dig.

橇 yao 4. ch'iao 4. To force up by leverage; to prise open.

713

尊 tsun 1. Noble; venerable; numerative of cannons.

遵 tsun 1. To follow; to conform to; to obey.

繜 tsun 1. Drawers.

譐 tsun 3. To talk together; conversation.

樽 tsun 1. A goblet; a cup.

撙 tsun 1. To adjust; to regulate; economical.

墫 tsun 1. A wine-jar.

鐏 tsun 1. A spear.

鐏 **tsun 1.** A vessel.

嶟 **tsun 1.** A peak; lofty.

鱒 **tsun 4.** A gurnard.

蹲 **tun 1.** To squat down; to rest.

714

雋 

See Lesson 87 C.

雋 **tsun 4.** Savoury.

儁 **tsun 4.** Valiant.

懏 **tsun 4.** Perspicacity.

臇 **tsuan 3.** Hashed meat.

鐫 **chien 1.** To cut; to chisel; to damage.

715

See Lesson 75 E.

敦 **tun 1.** Honest; sincere; true; to perform.

噋 **tun 1.** To gobble up.

燉 **tun 4.** To stew.

鐓 **tun 1.** A knob.

橔 **tun 1.** A wooden cover.

驐 **tun 1.** To castrate

蜳 **tun 1.** A water-beetle.

墪 墩 } **tun 1.** A mound; a beacon. A tun.

撉 **tun 1.** To pound.

暾 **t'un 1.** The sun just above the horizon.

朜 **t'un 1.** Moon-light.

譈 **tui 4.** To provoke; to instigate.

憝 **tui 4.** To hate; to detest.

716

童 

See Lesson 120 K.

童 **t'ung 2.** A boy under 15 years and unmarried; a virgin.

僮 **t'ung 2.** A slave boy.

瞳 **t'ung 2.** The pupil of the eye.

曈 **t'ung 2.** Dim light; confused.

朣 **t'ung 2.** The moon just rising.

犝 **t'ung 2.** A young calf.

橦 **t'ung 2** A cotton-tree.

獞 **t'ung 2.** Savage tribes of the south.

疃 **t'ung 3.** A thrashing-floor.

䍶 **t'ung 2.** A young ram.

潼 **t'ung 2.** Name of a river.

穜 **t'ung 2.** Grain which is gathered last.

艟 **t'ung 2.** Cabin-boys.

鶇 **t'ung 2.** The hornbill.

鄣 **t'ung 2.** A proper name.

蕫 **t'ung 2.** An edible plant.

罿 **t'ung 2.** A fowler's trap.

鐘 **chung 1.** A bell; a clock.

蹱 **chung 1.** To stagger.

憧 **ch'ung 1.** Irresolute.

衝 **ch'ung 1.** Towards; facing; to rush; to collide with.

撞 **chuang 4.** To strike; to run against.

䡴 **chuang 4.** A war-chariot.

𩞯 **ch'uang 2.** To eat immoderately.

𦔣 **ch'uang 2.** To sow.

幢 **ch'uang 2.** A curtain for a carriage.

717

See Lesson 49 H.

爲 **wei 2.** To be; to make. **wei 4.** For; because; on account of; in order to.

僞 **wei 3.** Counterfeit; false.

蔿 **wei 3.** Grass; weed.

闟 **wei 3.** A half-open door.

撝 **hui 1.** To split.

嬀 **hui 1.** A river in Shansi.

譌 **o 2.** To deceive.

718

See Lesson 10 I.

無 **wu 2.** Not; nothing; without.

憮 **wu 2.** To love; to cherish.

潕 **wu 3.** A river in Hunan.

嫵 **wu 3.** To flatter; to seduce.

蕪 **wu 2.** Full of weeds; poor; vulgar

廡 **wu 3.** A verandah.

橆 **wu 2.** A forest; luxuriant; thick.

舞 **wu 3.** To make postures; to dance. L. 31 E.

撫 **hu 3.** To caress. *Fu* 3.

幠 **hu 1.** A veil; a screen; to cover.

膴 **hu 1.** Dried meat.

⿰火無 **hu 2.** To scorch.

撫 **fu 3.** To caress. *Hu* 3.

蟱 **mu 2.** A spider.

719

See Lesson 81 C.

堯 **yao 1.** Eminent; name of an Emperor.

嶢 **yao 1.** Towering; lofty.

繞 **jao 3.** To wind round; to surround; to avoid..

遶 **jao 3.** To round; to involve; to be entangled in.

饒 **jao 2.** Plenty; abundance; to pardon.

嬈 **jao 2.** Graceful.

襓 **jao 2.** A sheath.

蟯 **jao 2.** Worms in the bowels.

燒 **shao 1.** To burn; to roast; feverish.

撓 **nao 2.** To vex; to scratch; to trouble.

譊 **nao 2.** A noisy dispute.

鐃 **nao 3.** Cymbals.

橈 **nao 2.** An oar.

蕘 **nao 1.** Straw; fuel; vile; valueless.

嘵 **hsiao 1.** To cry; to quarrel.

驍 **hsiao 1.** A fine horse; brave.

曉 **hsiao 3.** Dawn; light; to understand; to know.

膮 **hsiao 1.** Savoury.

澆 **chiao 1.** To water.

僥 **chiao 3.** Happy; fortunate.

蹺 **ch'iao 1.** To raise; curious; stilts.

磽 **ch'iao 1.** Stony soil.

墝 **ch'iao 1.** Barren soil.

翹 **ch'iao 2.** The long tail-feathers; to raise; to long for.

⿰堯堯 **ch'iao 4.** Turned up at the ends.

720

See Lesson 15 E.

矞 **yü 4.** To bore through.

繘 **yü 4.** A well-rope.

驈 **yü 4.** A piebald.

噊 **yü 4.** To alarm.

鱊 **yü 4.** A bleak.

遹 **yü 4.** Succession; to transmit.

鷸 **yü 4.** A lark.

霱 **yü 4.** Coloured clouds.

橘 **chü 2.** An orange-tree; an orange.

獝 **chü 2.** To fear; to flee.

鐍 **chü 2.** A brooch.

蹫 **chü 4.** Lame.

潏 **chü 2.** A delta.

譎 **chüeh 2.** To feign; to delude.

憰 **chüeh 2.** Hypocrisy.

劀 **kua 1.** To cut away.

It may be found in

氄 **jung 2.** Down.

721

See Lesson 99 F.

愛 **ai 4.** To love; to like.

僾 **ai 4.** Like; similar.

曖 **ai 4.** Dull; obscure.

靉 **ai 4.** Cloudy; obscure.

薆 **ai 4.** Luxuriant; thick; to conceal.

噯 **ai 1.** An exclamation.

722

See Lesson 59 H.

詹 **chan 1.** To chatter.

瞻 **chan 1.** To look up to; to venerate.

譫 **chan 1.** Wild delirious talking.

襜 **chan 1.** A skirt.

幨 **ch'an 1.** A screen; a curtain.

蟾 **ch'an 2.** A toad; the moon.

膽 **ch'an 4.** Rafters.

⿰足詹 **ch'an 4.** To gallop.

韂 **ch'an 4.** A saddle flap.

贍 **shan 4.** To give; to supply; to aid.

擔 **tan 1.** To carry on a pole; to sustain.
tan 4. A load.

膽 **tan 3.** Gall bladder; courage.

儋 **tan 4.** Load that a man can carry.

憺 **tan 4.** Tranquil; easy.

澹 **tan 4.** Flat; dull.

⿰石詹 **tan 3.** Vitriol.

甔 **t'an 2.** A jar.

⿰舌詹 **t'an 1.** To lisp.

簷 **yen 2.** Edge of the roof.

檐 **yen 2.** End of the rafters.

723

毄 毄

See Lesson 167 D.

毄 **chi 1.** To hit against; to strike.

擊 **chi 1.** To hit against; to strike; to attack.

⿱毄心 **chi 4.** Sorrow.

墼 **chi 2.** Unburnt bricks.

罊 **ch'i 4.** An empty vessel.

繫 **hsi 4.** To fasten; to tie, to remember.

檕 **hsi 4.** A kind of plum-tree.

724

畺 畺

See Lesson 3 C.

畺 **chiang 1.** A boundary.

薑 **chiang 1.** Ginger.

⿰氵畺 **chiang 1.** Congealed; coagulated.

橿 **chiang 1.** A handle.

⿰虫畺 **chiang 1.** Silkworms chrysalis.

礓 **chiang 1.** Gravel; small stones.

僵 **chiang 1.** Catalepsy; a vampire.

疆 **chiang 1.** A boundary; a frontier.

韁 繮 } **kang 1.** A halter.

725

解 解

See Lesson 142 B.

解 **chieh 3.** To loosen; to undo; to explain; convoy.

廨 **chieh 4.** A palace; a court.

懈 **hsieh 4.** Idle; remiss.

澥 **hsieh 4.** A rivulet.

嶰 **hsieh 4.** A valley.

邂 **hsieh 4.** To meet unexpectedly.

獬 **hsieh 4.** A fabulous animal.

蟹 **hsieh 4.** A crab.

726

僉 僉

See Lesson 14 E.

僉 **ch'ien 1.** All; unanimous.

簽 **ch'ien 1.** Labels; to subscribe.

儉 **chien 3.** Frugal; economical.

撿 **chien 3.** To tie; to restrain; to revise; to gather.

檢 **chien 3.** To examine; to forbid; rule.

鹼 **chien 3.** Soda.

羷 **chien 3.** A goat.

劍 劒 } **chien 4.** A two edged sword.

歛 **hsien 4.** To long for; to pray earnestly.

險 **hsien 3.** Dangerous; hazardous.

獫 **hsien 3.** A fierce dog; Barbarians.

驗 **yen 4.** To verify; evidence; fulfilment; effect; proof.

臉 **lien 3.** Face; honour.

殮 **lien 4.** To shroud a corpse.

襝 **lien 3.** Clothes set in order.

澰 **lien 3.** Rising of waters.

斂 **lien 4** To collect; to gather; to concentrate.

蘞 **lien 3.** Wild vine.

匳 **lien 2.** A dressing case.

727

禁 禁

See Lesson 119 M.

禁 **chin 4.** To forbid; to prohibit; to retrain.

噤 **chin 4.** Lockjaw.

⿰忄禁 **chin 4.** Determined; resolute.

襟 **chin 1.** The overlap of a robe.

凚 **chin 4.** Cold; chilled.

僸 **chin 4.** To look up at.

728

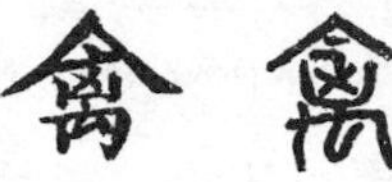

See Lesson 23 E.

禽 ch'in 2. Birds.

噙 ch'in 2. To hold in the mouth; to restrain.

擒 ch'in 2. To seize, to clutch.

蠄 ch'in 2. A long-legged spider.

檎 ch'in 2. Apple-tree.

729

See Lesson 54 G.

敬 ching 4. To revere; reverence.

儆 ching 3. To warn; to caution; to take care.

憼 ching 3. To take care.

璥 ching 3. A precious stone.

警 ching 3 To warn; to caution; police; constables.

驚 ching 1. Frightened; to frighten.

擎 ch'ing 2. To lift up; to uphold.

檠 ch'ing 2. A stand; a prop.

檠 ch'ing 2. A frame for a bow.

730

楚

See Lesson 119 N.

楚 ch'u 3. Woody; pain; to settle.

噓 ch'u 1. To scold.

憷 ch'u 3. Grief; pain.

濋 ch'u 3. Small rivulet.

礎 ch'u 3. Pedestal.

齼 ch'u 3. The teeth set on edge.

731

See Lesson 69 D.

豦 chü 4. A wild boar; to fight; to struggle.

據 chü 4. To take in the hand; to rely upon; a legal instrument; evidence; according to.

璩 chü 4. Earrings.

懅 chü 4. Ashamed; bashful.

㩀 chü 4. A big fire.

臄 chü 4. The snout.

鐻 chü 4. A hammer.

遽 chü 4. To send; a messenger; hurried; suddenly.

劇 chü 4. A tragedy; a stage play; much.

籧 ch'ü 2. Coarse bamboo matting.

蘧 ch'ü 1. A kind of mushroom; pleasure.

732

See Lesson 78 F.

賁 fên 4. Ornaments.

墳 fên 2 A grave; a mound.

噴 fên 4. To sneeze.

幩 fên 2. the ornaments on a bridle.

濆 fên 2. A river in Honan.

鱝 fên 4. A skate.

憤 fên 4. Zeal; energy; to exert one's self.

饙 fên 1. To steam rice.

癀 fên 2. Fever boils.

蕡 fên 2. Luxuriant; abundant.

噴 p'ên 1. To spirt out of the mouth; to sprinkle.

歕 p'ên 1. To exhale; fragrance.

733

See Lesson 39 I.

學 𦥯 hsiao 2. To learn; to study.

嶨 hsiao 2. Basement.

澩 hsiao 2. A torrent.

鷽 hsiao 2. A blue jay, *urocissa sinensis*.

覺 chiao 3. To feel; to awake; to perceive.
chiao 4. To sleep.

攪 chiao 1. To stir up; to mix; to excite.

鱟 hou 4. The king-crab, *limulus polyphemus*.

734

See Lesson 16 L.

睘 huan 2. Timid looks.

寰 **huan** 2. Imperial domains a closure; the universe.

鬟 **huan** 2. A slave-girl's hair done up.

闤 **huan** 2. A walled city.

繯 **huan** 2. A lace.

擐 **huan** 4. To tuck up.

懁 **huan** 4. Cares; anger.

蠉 **huan** 1. To crawl.

轘 **huan** 4. To quarter.

儇 **huan** 2. Ingenious.

環 **huan** 2. To surround; an enclosure; a ring.

鐶 **huan** 2. A metal ring.

還 **huan** 2. To go back; to return; to repay; to compensate; still; further.

翾 **huan** 1. To flutter.

圜 **huan** 2. To surround.

嬛 **hsüan** 1. Solitary; alone.

735

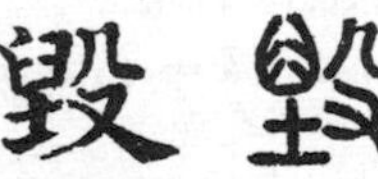

SI

See Lesson 31 A.

毀 **hui** 3. To injure; to spoil.

燬 **hui** 3. To burn down.

譭 **hui** 3. To slander; to vilify.

736

See Lesson 14 D.

會 **hui** 4. To meet together; to collect; to unite, a guild; a society; to know.
hui 3. An instant.

薈 **hui** 4. A bundle; in abundance.

繪 **hui** 4. To draw; to sketch; to embroider; to adorn.

懀 **wei** 4. To abhor.

劊 **kuei** 4. An executioner.

禬 **kuei** 4. To pray.

檜 **kuei** 4. Juniper.

癐 **kuei** 4. A disease.

鄶 **kuai** 4. A place in Honan.

澮 **k'uai** 4. A drain; a canal.

獪 **k'uai** 4. Crafty; mischievous.

襘 **k'uai** 4. A large girdle.

膾 **k'uai** 4. Minced meat.

噲 **k'uai** 4. To gulp down; greedy.

儈 **k'uai** 4. A broker.

鱠 **k'uai** 4. Stewed fish.

It is radical in

僧 **sêng** 1. A Buddhist priest.

737

See Lesson 71 Q.

義 **i** 4. Duty; right; loyal; idea; meaning; purport; common; free; adopted.

儀 **i** 2. Rites; observances; manners.

議 **i** 4. To consider; to deliberate upon; to discuss.

蟻 **i** 4. Ants.

檥 **i** 3. A post; a signal.

嶬 **i** 4. Steep peaks.

艤 **i** 3. To run ashore.

鸃 **i** 2. A pheasant.

羲 **hsi** 1. A proper name. S. 830.

738

睪 

See Lesson 102 G.

睪 **i** 4. Vigilance.

驛 **i** 4. The government postal service; a courier.

繹 **i** 4. To unravel; to unfold; to explain; continuous; unceasing.

譯 **i** 2. To explain; to interpret.

懌 **i** 4. Joy; pleasure.

嶧 **i** 4. A hill in Kiangsu.

檡 **i** 4. Wild jujube.

釋 **shih** 4. To loosen; to set free; to explain; the Buddhism. S. 123 E.

擇 **chai** 2. To choose; to setect.

澤 **chai** 2. A marsh; moist; slippery; to soak; to enrich; favour; kindness.

襗 **chai** 4. Underclothes.

鸅 **chai** 2. The white pelican.

鐸 **to** 2. A small bell.

739

See Lesson 73 E.

意 **i** 4. A thought; an idea; a sentiment; an intention; meaning; wish; purpose.

億 **i** 4. A hundred thousand; numberless.

噫 **i** 1. An interjection; to sigh; alas.

譩 i 1. To sigh; to moan.

憶 i 4. To reflect; to call to mind; to remember.

臆 i 4. The breast; the feelings; opinions.

醷 i 4. Liquor.

繶 i 4. A silk string.

檍 i 4. *Lindera glauca.*

薏 i 4. The seeds of lotus.

740

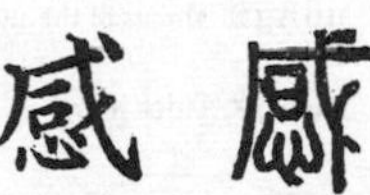

See Lesson 71 P.

感 kan 3. To influence; to be moved; to excite.

鰔 kan 3. A mullet.

埳 k'an 3. Hindered; unlucky.

轗 k'an 3. To jolt, to bump; unlucky.

憾 han 4. Regret; displeasure.

撼 han 4. To shake; to excite.

741

See L. 26 L, L. 116.

豤 k'ên 3. To gnaw.

墾 k'ên 3. To break new soil.

懇 k'ên 3. To beg; to implore.

Compare S. 219.

742

See Lesson 118 A.

過 kuo 4. To pass by; past; transgression; fault.

喎 kuo 4. To prattle.

薖 k'uo 1. Herbs; vast.

撾 chua 1. To beat; to strike.

膼 chua 1. The thigh.

簻 chua 1. A whip.

Compare S. 457.

743

See Lesson 149 F.

雷 lei 2. Thunder.

擂 lei 2. To pound; to beat.

蠕 lei 2. An edible clam.

鐳 lei 2. Bronzes; old vases.

癗 lei 3. Pimples; blisters.

蕾 lei 3. The bud of a flower.

744

See Lesson 97 B.

豊 li 3. A vessel used in sacrificing.

澧 li 3 A river in Hunan.

醴 li 3. Must.

鱧 li 3. A mullet.

禮 li 3. Ceremony; etiquette; presents; worship.

體 t'i 3. The limbs; the trunk; the body; substance; style; manner; to conform; respectable.

745

See Lesson 121 K.

廉 lien 2. A corner.

螊 lien 2. A door-screen.

濂 lien 2. A waterfall; a cascade.

鐮 lien 2. A sickle; a reaping-kook.

臁 lien 2. the leg.

鰜 lien 2. A kind of shad.

簾 lien 2. A door-screen.

Compare S. 519.

746

See Lesson 76 C.

稟 lin 3. A granary; a grant from the public funds.

壈 lin 3. To be deceived; unlucky.

檁 lin 3. Cross-beams; rafters.

凜 lin 3. To shiver with cold or fear.

燣 lin 3. To toast; to torrefy.

懍 lin 3. To fear.

廩 lin 3. A government granary.

稟 ling 3. To warn; to announce; to receive; natural gifrs.

747

See Lesson 74 B.

羸 lo 3. Fattening of animals.

蠃 lo 4. The solitary wasp, *sphex.*

驘 lo 2. A mule.

鸁 lo 3. The grebe.

It is radical in.

羸 lei 2. Lean; thin; emaciated; sick.

𣩡 lei 4. A plague among the animals.

and in

贏 ying 2. A profit; to gain; to win, *Hence (contr. phon.)*

嬴 ying 2. To fill up.

瀛 ying 2. The ocean.

籯 ying 2. A basket.

748

See Lesson 31 B.

路 lu 4 Road; way.

鏴 lu 4. To solder.

璐 lu 4. Girdle gems.

潞 lu 4. Name of a river.

鷺 lu 4. A heron.

露 lu 4. Dew. *Lou* 4.

露 lou 4. To be exposed, disclosed. *Lu 4.*

749

See Lesson 108 C.

黽 min 3. Toads; obscenities.

僶 min 3. To make an effort.

鄳 min 2. A place in Honan.

蠅 ying 2. A house fly.

繩 shêng 2. A cord; a string; a rope; a line; to tie; to restrain.

憴 shêng 2. To be careful.

澠 shêng 2. Name of a river. *Mien* 3.

It is radical in

鼉 t'o 2. An iguana.

鼂 ch'ao 2. A siren.

竈 tsao 4. A cooking-stove.

Radical 205.

750

See Lesson 123 F.

奧 nao 4. ao 4. The corner where the *lares* were placed; secret; mysterious.

襖 ao 3. An outer garment; a coat.

懊 ao 4. Vexed; angry.

澳 ao 4. Macao.

噢 ao 3. To moan.

㜵 ao 4. Jealous.

隩 ao 4. A shore; a bank; a bay.

㬈 ao 4. Warmth; warm sun.

鱜 ao 4. A large kind of perch.

擙 ao 4. To grind.

䐿 ao 4. A gizzard.

燠 ao 4. Heat; a hot fire.

墺 ao 4. An open flat; a plain.

𨞾 yü 4. A proper name.

薁 yü 4 A wild vine.

751

See Lesson 50 Q.

農 nung 2. To cultivate; agriculture, farmer.

膿 nung 2. Pus, matter.

噥 nung 1. To mutter.

濃 nung 2. Thick; sticky.

襛 nung 2. Thick clothes.

穠 nung 2. Blooming; dense.

醲 nung 2. Strong wine.

𩟗 nung 2. To stuff with food.

憹 nung 2. Satisfied.

齈 nung 2. Mucus of the nose.

鬞 nung 2. Thick hair.

噥 ang 3. An interrogative particle.

752

辟

See Lesson 102 H.

辟 pi 4. Prince; law; to rule. *P'i* 4.

避 pi 4. To flee from; to avoid; to yield.

鐴 pi 4. To sharpen; edge.

繴 pi 4. A string, a twist.

臂 pi 4. The arm.

壁 pi 4. A wall. *Pei* 4.

璧 pi 4. A gem; a cameo.

躄 pi 4. Lame.

嬖 pi 4. A favourite.

甓 pi 4. Glazed tiles.

薜 pi 4. Smallage; celery.

辟 p'i 4. To punish; penalty; perverse, mean, oblique; to open, to spread. *Pi* 4.

僻 p'i 4. Singular; mean; perverse.

擗 **p'i 3.** To cleave; to open.

劈 **p'i 3.** To cleave; kindlings.

鸊 **p'i 4.** A grebe.

譬 **p'i 4.** To compare; if; an example.

檗 **p'i 4.** Wood for dyeing.

闢 **p'i 4.** To burst forth; to open up.

霹 **p'i 1.** Thunder; to thunder-strike.

癖 **p'i 3.** Dyspeptic; greediness; passion.

廦 **p'i 4.** Oblique.

壁 **pei 4** A wall. *Pi* 4.

擘 **pai 1.** To break apart with the hand; to destroy.

753

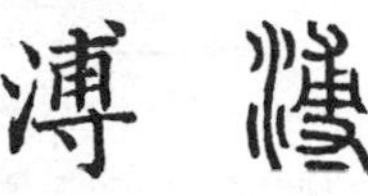

See Lesson 109 D.

溥 **p'u 3.** Vast; pervading.

簿 **pu 4.** A register; a tablet; a record.

薄 **po 2.** Mint. *Pao* 2.

薄 **pao 2.** Thin, shabby; insignificant. *Po* 2.

Compare S. 528.

754

See Lesson 60 L.

普 **p'u 3.** Large; universal.

氆 **p'u 3.** Yak's hair.

譜 **p'u 3.** Chronicle; register; catalogue. *Pu* 3.

譜 **pu 3.** Register. *P'u* 3.

755

See Lesson 76 E.

嗇 **shê 4.** The harvest; stingy.

穡 **shê 4.** The harvest; to reap.

[亻嗇] **shê 4.** To harvest.

懎 **shê 4.** To hate.

濇 **shih 4.** Astringent.

Perhaps it is found in

牆 **ch'iang 2.** A wall.

Phon. contr. in

檣 **ch'iang 2.** A main-mast.

墻 **ch'iang 2.** A wall.

艢 **ch'iang 2.** A gaff.

嬙 **ch'iang 2.** Female palace officials.

薔 **ch'iang 2.** A red rose.

756

See Lesson 54 I.

蜀 **shu 3.** A caterpillar; a name of Ssŭch'uan.

蠋 **shu 3.** A caterpillar; a larva.

鸀 **shu 4.** A kind of jay.

屬 **shu 2.** To be of; to depend on; to belong to; connected with; sort; kind; class; kindred.

獨 **tu 2.** Solitary; single; only.

髑 **tu 2.** A skull.

韣 **tu 2.** A case or covering.

燭 **chu 4.** A candle; a light; to illumine.

觸 **chu 4.** To butt; to strike against; to offend.

躅 **chu 4.** Footsteps.

歜 **ch'u 4.** Anger; wrath.

斣 **ch'u 4.** To measure; to quarrel.

濁 **cho 2.** Muddy; foul.

鐲 **cho 2.** A bracelet.

噣 **cho 2.** Beak; to peck.

[忄蜀] **cho 4.** Anxiety.

擉 **ch'o 1.** To pierce.

It is radical in

蠲 **kuan 1.** Pure; to purify; to exempt; to pardon.

757

See Lesson 125 C.

肅 **su 4.** Circumspection; respect; diligence.

鷫 **su 4.** Turquoise kingfisher.

鏽 **hsiu 4.** Rust; oxides.

繡 **hsiu 4.** To embroider.

嘯 **hsiao 4.** To whistle; to scream.

蠨 **hsiao 1.** A spider.

彇 **hsiao 1.** The extremity of a bow.

橚 **hsiao 1.** Foliage; leaves.

䐑 **hsiao 4.** Mince-meat.

歗 **hsiao 4.** To lament; to sigh.

簫 **hsiao 1.** Pandean pipes.

蕭 **hsiao 1.** An artemisia; a surname; reverence; poor, destitute.

758

See Lesson 69 F.

遂 **sui 2.** To accord with; to succeed; consequently.

繸 **sui 4.** Girdle-string; tassel.

墜 **sui 4.** A path to a tomb; a path.

穟 **sui 4.** Ripening grain.

檖 **sui 4.** Wild pear.

襚 **sui 4.** The clothes of the deceased.

燧 **sui 4.** To get fire by friction.

隧 **sui 4.** Way to a tomb.

澻 **sui 4.** A ditch; a canal.

璲 **sui 4.** A precious stone.

邃 **sui 4.** A deep apartment; concealed.

759

遀 

See Lesson 46 D.

遀 **sui 2.** To follow.

髓 **sui 3.** Marrow.

隨 **sui 2.** To follow, to comply with; consequently.

Compare S. 480.

760

See Lesson 71 P.

歲 **sui 4.** The planet Jupiter; year; harvest.

穢 **hui 4.** Unclean; to defile.

濊 **hui 4.** Muddy.

噦 **hui 4.** Rumbling.

譿 **hui 4.** To hum.

761

達

See Lesson 60 O.

達 **ta 2.** To reach, to attain.

韃 **ta 2.** Tartars.

繨 **ta 2.** A knot.

薘 **ta 2.** Beet-root.

撻 **t'a 4.** To chastise.

躂 **t'a 4.** To maltreat.

闥 **t'a 4.** Inner door; screen; palace; dwellings.

澾 **ts'a 1.** To slip; slippery.

762

See Lesson 76 D.

亶 **t'an 2.** A granary filled with grain; to trust; sincerely.

癉 **t'an 2.** Rheumatism; pain; sorrow.

壇 **t'an 2.** A platform; an altar; an arena.

檀 **t'an 2.** Sandal-wood.

繵 **t'an 2.** A ribbon; violet.

襢 **t'an 3.** To strip; bared.

膻 **t'an 3.** The thorax.

䆄 **chan 4.** A sheaf.

邅 **chan 1.** To turn around.

軇 **chan 3.** To strip; bared.

儃 **chan 1.** To go over; to advance.

旜 **chan 1.** Thick rich congee.

饘 **chan 1.** A banner.

驙 **chan 1.** A pack-horse.

鱣 **chan 1.** A sturgeon.

顫 **chan 4.** To shake; to tremble.

氈 **chan 1.** A rough felt.

鸇 **chan 1.** A sparrow-hawk.

皽 **chan 4.** To tear off; to peel off.

𦒄 **chan 1.** To flutter about.

嬗 **ch'an 1.** Beautiful; graceful.

擅 **shan 4.** To assume; to usurp.

禪 **shan 4.** To sacrifice to heaven. Imperial dignity.

羶 **shan 1.** Rank; stinking.

澶 **shan 2.** Still water.

763

See Lesson 36 E.

當 **tang 1.** Ought; to bear; to match; to resist.
tang 4. To pawn.

擋 **tang 3.** To obstruct; to withstand.

檔 **tang 4.** A joist.

鐺 **tang 1.** A bell.

璫 **tang 1.** Pendents; jingles.

𦗲 **tang 1.** Long pendent ears.

䡴 tang 1. The tail of a cart.

襠 tang 1. Crutch of trowsers.

簹 tang 1. A kind of knotted bamboo.

闣 tang 3. To close; filled.

劏 t'ang 1. To split; to kill.

鼞 t'ang 1. The roll of drums.

764

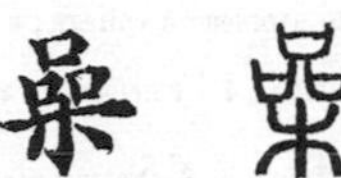

See Lesson 72 L.

喿 tsao 4. Twittering.

噪 tsao 4. To twitter.

懆 tsao 4. Sad, troubled.

燥 tsao 4. Dry; parched.

躁 tsao 4. Hasty; irascible..

繰 tsao 3. Violaceous.

璪 tsao 3. Pendents hung around a coronet.

澡 tsao 3. To bathe.

藻 tsao 3. An aquatic grass; graceful.

操 ts'ao 1. To manage; to drill; rule; method.

鄵 ts'ao 4. A proper name.

譟 sao 4. Voice; murmur.

臊 sao 4. Shame.
sao 4. Rancid.

鐰 sao 4. Fine steel.

765

See Lesson 23 H.

萬 wan 4. Ten thousand; an indefinite number; wholly.

蠆 ch'ai 4. A scorpion.

邁 mai 4. To walk; to advance; old.

⿰言萬 mai 4. To speak angrily.

勱 mai 4. To exert one's strength.

厲 li 4. A whetstone; sharp; severe. S. 804.

躉 tun 3. Wholesale; in the lump.

766

See Lesson 117 A.

敫 yao 4. To shine; to light.

邀 yao 1. To invite; to engage; to seek.

繳 chiao 3. To hand over; to surrender.

儌 chiao 3. Lucky, fortunate.

徼 chiao 4. To go around; to search.

噭 chiao 1. To wail.

皦 chiao 3. Clear; bright.

⿰巾敫 chiao 3. Strips.

竅 ch'iao 4. A hole; an orifice.

激 chi 1. Noise of waters; to excite.

檄 chi 1. A decree; a missive.

覈 ho 4. hai 4. To pare; to examine thoroughly; to question by torture.

767

See Lesson 168 K.

䧹 ying 1. Accipitrine birds, as the eagle, hawk, etc.

應 ying 1. Ought to be; suitable; necessary.
ying 4. An answer; to respond; correspondent; proportionate.

鷹 ying 1. An eagle.

膺 ying 1. The breast; self; office; to oppose.

Compare

雁 yen 4. A wild goose. L. 168 K.

贗 yen 4. False, counterfeit.

768

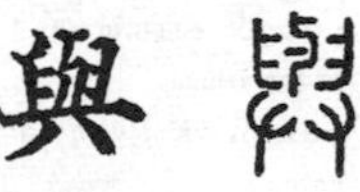

See Lesson 50 J.

與 yü 3. To give; to share; with; together.

⿰禾與 yü 1. A good harvest.

璵 yü 2. A striped stone.

鱮 yü 3. A tench.

旟 yü 2. A flag.

歟 yü 2. A final particle.

藇 yü 4. Yam.

礜 yü 4. Arsenic.

譽 yü 2. To eulogise.

⿱與心 yü 3. Haste; hurry.

鸒 yü 2. A crow.

嶼 hsü 3. An islet.

⿰酉與 hsü 3. Wine agreeable to the taste.

舉 chü 3. To raise, to lift up; to begin, to promote; actions, manners; all, whole.

Compare

輿 yü 2. Carriage; earth. L. 50 I.

興 hsing 1. Agreement; fashion; flourishing. L. 50 K.

769

雝 雝

雍

See Lesson 12 G.

雝 } **yung 1.** Wagtail. Harmony;
雍 } union.

擁 **yung3.** To embrace; to carry in the arms.

澭 **yung1.** A sluice; a water-gate.

臃 **yung3.** To swell.

[illegible] **yung 1.** Surly.

[illegible] **yung 1.** The leg of a boot.

噰 **yung 1.** Singing of birds; spasm.

壅 **yung 3.** To dam; to hinder; to stop up.

饔 **yung 1.** Meats.

甕 **wêng 4.** An earthern jar.

灉 **yung 1.** A canal; a ditch.

癰 **yung 1.** A malignant ulcer.

770

耤 耤

See Lesson 17 J.

耤 **chi 2** The Emperor's field.

籍 **chi 2.** A list; a register.

藉 **chieh 4.** A mat; to lean on for aid; to help; to avail of, in order that.

771

齊 

See Lesson 174.

齊 **ch'i 2.** Even; harmony; order; perfect.

臍 **ch'i 2.** The navel.

[illegible] **ch'i 3.** The peg for resting the scull on.

鱭 **ch'i 4.** A mullet.

蠐 **ch'i 2.** A maggot.

濟 **chi 4.** To cross over; to aid; to releave.

擠 **chi 3.** To press; to milk.

隮 **chi 1.** To scale.

穧 **chi 4.** A kind of millet.

嚌 **chi .** To taste; to sip.

懠 **chi 4.** Angry; suspicious.

櫅 **chi 3.** A variety of jujube.

[illegible] **chi 1.** To bite, a mouthful

躋 **chi 1.** To ascend.

劑 **chi 4.** To adjust; to trim; a dosee.

薺 **chi 4.** *Tulipa edulis*

霽 **chi 4.** The clouds clearing away.

癠 **chi 4.** Sick; diseased.

[illegible] **chi 3.** To squeeze out.

齎 **chi 1.** To offer to; to give.

齏 **chi 1.** A leek.

齍 **tzŭ 1.** A ritual offering.

齌 **tzŭ 1.** Hem.

齋 **chai 1.** To respect; to abstain from; abstinence; a study; a retiring room.

[illegible] **chai 1.** A hut, a dwelling of thatch.

儕 **ch'ai 1.** A class; a company; a sign of the plural.

772

監 監

See Lesson 82 F.

監 **chien 1.** To examine carefully; to oversee; a college; a jail.

檻 **chien 4.** Enclosure; a cage.

轞 **chien 3.** A shut up car.

艦 **chien 4.** A'war vessel.

[illegible] **chien 4.** A tub.

鑒 } **chien 4.** A mirror; an example; historic events; do-
鑑 } cuments; rule; to survey, to audit.

鹽 **yen 2.** Salt.

襤 **lan 2.** Ragged garments.

爁 **lan 2.** To scorch.

[illegible] **lan 4.** Greedy, covetous.

濫 **lan 4.** To overflow, profuse; lawless.

籃 **lan 2.** A basket.

藍 **lan 2.** Indigo; blue.

[illegible] **lan 2.** Rocks; deep cave.

[illegible] **lan 2.** Dishevelled hair.

擥 **lan 3.** To grasp; to interfere with.

覽 **lan 3.** To inspect; to behold; to understand. S. 853.

773

遣 

See Lesson 111 C.

遣 **ch'ien 3.** To commission; to send off.

譴 ch'ien 3. To reprimand; to scold; to chastise.

繾 ch'ien 3. Closely joined; attached to.

韆 ch'ien 4. A belt.

774

See Lesson 169 D.

盡 chin 4. To exhaust; to indulge; to end; to achieve; the last.

燼 chin 4. Ashes; a residuum; the remains of.

儘 chin 3. Entirely; completely; all; the utmost.

贐 chin 4. Parting gifts.

濜 chin 4. Name of a river.

藎 chin 4. A dyeing plant.

It is radical in

𢷾 nai 1. A son born when the father is old.

775

See Lesson 27 K.

聚 chü 4. To meet; to gather; collection.

驟 chou 4. Swift; intense.

鄹 chou 1. A place of Shantung.

㔌 ch'ung 1. Intrusion; an intruder.

776

See Lesson 35 L.

爾 erh 3. Thou, you; if; so, just so; an expletive final.

邇 erh 3. Near; close, proximate.

禰 ni 3. Ancestral tablets.

濔 ni 3. Many; overflow.

懦 ni 3. Weak; timid.

嬭 nai 3. Breasts; to suckle; milk.

籋 mi 2. Splinters; fibres.

彌 mi 2. To fill up; full; very, much.

瀰 mi 2. A vast expanse of waters; wild; much.

璽 hsi 3. The great seal.

Sound altered in

獮 hsien 3. Imperial hunt.

777

See Lesson 75 B.

豪 hao 2. A boar; brave.

嚎 hao 2. To roar.

壕 hao 2. A ditch; a canal.

擤 hao 2. To pull out; to estimate.

蠔 hao 2. An oyster.

778

See Lesson 92 E.

㬎 hsien 3. Fibres; minute.

顯 hsien 3. Light; apparent; clear; glorious.

讘 nan 1. Jokes.

㒖 nan 1. Stupid.

It is radical in

濕 溼 shih 1. Wet; damp; low-lying grounds. L. 92 E.

779

See Lesson 164 E.

需 hsü 1. Necessity.

繻 hsü 1. Fringe.

鑐 hsü 1. A bolt.

儒 ju 2. Chinese literati; the Confuciauists.

孺 ju 3. A suckling; a child; wives of officials.

濡 ju 2. To immerse; to moisten; thick; mild.

醹 ju 2. Generous spirit.

鞾 ju 3. Shoes.

擩 ju 4. To stain; to dye; to rub.

嚅 ju 2. Chattering.

嬬 ju 2. A concubine; delicate.

襦 ju 2. A jacket.

薷 ju 2. A fungus.

䨲 nou 2. A leveret.

懦 no 4. Weakness, incapacity.

檽 no 4. A kind of pine.

臑 no 4. The fore-arm.

穤 no 4. Glutinous rice.

獳 no 4. A mongrel.

糯 no 4. Pap; sticky.

壖 **juan 2.** The ground near the walls of a city.

瓀 **juan 1.** A reddish stone.

蠕 **juan 3.** Squirming; wriggling.

780

See Lesson 47 G.

算 **hsüan 4.** To cypher; to estimate; to be regarded as; to be.

匴 **hsüan 4.** A box.

篹 **hsüan 4.** To cypher.

灢 **shuan 4.** To scrub a horse.

纂 **tsuan 3.** Back-hair; a compilation.

籑 **chuan 4.** Victuals.

篡 **ch'uan 4.** A rebellion; an usurpation.

劄 鍘 } **cha 2.** A grass-cutter; to cut.

781

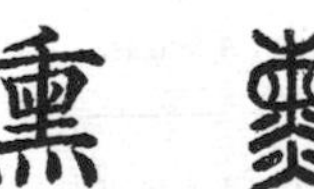

See Lesson 40 D.

熏 **hsün 1.** Smoke; to fumigate.

勳 **hsün 1.** Meritorious deeds; effort; merit.

燻 **hsün 1.** To fumigate.

醺 **hsün 1.** Drunkness.

曛 **hsün 1.** Twilight; sunset; evening.

纁 **hsün 1.** Light scarlet colour.

櫄 **hsün 1.** The wild varnish tree.

獯 **hsün 1.** The Huns.

薰 **hsün 1.** Fragrant; to perfume.

782

See Lesson 103 C.

蒦 **huo 1.** To catch.

剨 **huo 1.** To split open; to risk; to expose. *Ho* 1.

獲 **huo 2.** To take in hunting; to catch; to obtain. *Huai* 2.

擭 **huo 4.** A snare.

檴 **huo 4.** A sort of birch.

㦜 **huo 4.** Dread.

濩 **huo 4.** Rain.

臒 **huo 4.** Strength; violence.

嚄 **huo 4.** To bawl after.

䨼 **huo 4.** Unsavoury; insipid.

穫 **huo 1.** To reap the crops; harvest.

矱 **huo 4.** A measure; a marking line.

雘 **huo 4.** A kind of vermilion.

鑊 **huo 4.** A caldron.

蠖 **huo 4.** Caterpillar.

鸌 **huo 4.** A rail, crake.

鱯 **huo 4.** A silure.

護 **hu 4.** To protect, to guard.

783

See Lesson 131 G.

疑 **i 2.** To doubt; to suspect; to suppose.

擬 **i 3.** To compare; similar.

儗 **i 3.** To deliberate.

嶷 **i 2.** A mountain in Shansi.

薿 **i 3.** Flourishing, vigorous plants.

礙 **ai 4.** To hinder, to oppose; obstacle.

癡 **ch'ih 1.** Stupid; stupidity.

凝 **ning 2.** To freeze, to congeal.

784

See Lesson 34 I.

蒙 **mêng 2.** To cover; to conceal; ignorant; to receive; Mongol.

矇 **mêng 2.** Dimsighted; blind; ignorant.

曚 **mêng 2.** Early dawn.

朦 **mêng 2.** Obscure, confused; to deceive.

蠓 **mêng 3.** A gnat.

礞 **mêng 2.** The mica.

獴 **mêng 2.** A weasel.

艨 **mêng 2.** A war-junk; a cruiser.

𦆌 **mêng 2.** Tangled.

朦 **mêng 2.** Corpulent, fat.

檬 **mêng 2.** A kind of *sophora.*

饛 **mêng 2.** Abundance.

懞 **mêng 3.** Stupid.

濛 **mêng 2** Small, drizzling rain.

幪 **mêng 2.** A screen; to protect.

鸏 **mêng 2.** A toucan.

785

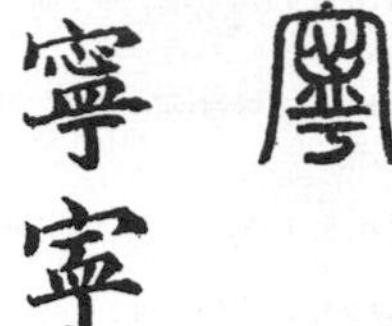

See Lesson 36 C.

寧 寍 } **ning 2.** Rest; repose; rather, better; why, how?

嚀 **ning 2.** To enjoin upon.

擰 **ning 2.** To wring.

檸 **ning 2.** The lemon.

[illegible] **ning 3.** To take one's fill.

聹 **ning 2.** Ear wax.

薴 **ning 2.** Thick plants, jungle.

濘 **nêng 4.** Muddy.

獰 **nêng 2.** Brutal, fierce.

786

See Lesson 102 H.

辡 **pien 4.** To accuse each other.

辦 **pien 4.** To cut asunder; to distinguish.

辮 **pien 4.** To plait; to braid; a cue.

辯 **pien 4.** To quarrel about; to debate.

辦 **pan 4.** To act; to execute.

瓣 **pan 4.** A slice, as of a melon; petals; a lobe.

辯 **pan 4.** To contradict. *Pien* 4.

787

See Lesson 112 L.

賓 **pin 1.** A guest; to entertain; to acknowledge; to trust in.

儐 **pin 4.** To receive and entertain a guest.

擯 **pin 4.** To expel; to reject.

嬪 **pin 1.** Imperial concubines. To wed.

殯 **pin 4.** A funeral.

蠙 **pin 1.** The pearl oyster.

繽 **pin 1.** Confused, blending.

髕 **pin 4.** The patella.

濱 **pin 1.** Beach, shore.

鑌 **pin 1.** A fine steel.

獱 **pin 1.** An otter.

鬢 **pin 4.** The hair on the temples.

[illegible] **p'in 2.** Worn out.

檳 **ping 1.** The areca-palm.

788

See Lesson 144 B.

壽 **shou 4.** Longevity; age.

儔 **ch'ou 2.** A comrade, a partner; who?

疇 **ch'ou 2.** Cultivated field; a species; who?

醻 **ch'ou 2.** To pledge a guest; to toast him; to repay.

譸 **ch'ou 2.** To impose upon, to deceive.

躊 **ch'ou 2.** Irresolute, wavering.

籌 **ch'ou 2.** To calculate; a lot; a ticket.

鑄 **chu 4.** To cast; to fuse metals.

禱 **tao 3.** To pray; to request.

擣 **tao 3.** To pound or grind fine.

懤 **tao 3.** Grief, sorrow.

壔 **tao 3.** A tumulus.

幬 **tao 5.** A canopy; a curtain; to cover.

燾 **tao 4.** A proper name.

濤 **t'ao 1.** Great waves.

檮 **t'ao 2.** A block of wood; stupid.

789

See Lesson 159 B.

署 **shu 3.** A public court; an office; acting; temporary.

薯 **shu 3.** The yam, sweet potatoe.

曙 **shu 3.** Dawn; clear.

Compare S. 422.

790

See Lesson 75 B.

臺 **t'ai 2.** A terrace. A title of respect

檯 **t'ai 2.** A table; a stage.

擡 **t'ai 2.** To carry on a pole; to raise; to elevate.

[illegible] **t'ai 4.** To laugh; to mock.

儓 **t'ai 2.** A charioteer.

薹 **t'ai 2.** A grass, *scirpus maritimus.*

懛 **tai 1.** Frightened; disheartened

791

See Lesson 62 G.

翟 **ti 2.** The pheasant.

鸐 **ti 2.** The pheasant.

糴 **ti 2.** To buy grain.

籊 **ti 4.** Long tapering bamboos.

嬥 **tiao 3.** Beautiful; upright.

糶 **t'iao 4.** To sell grain.

耀 **yao 4.** Bright; honour; glorious.

曜 **yao 4.** Light; glory; to dazzle.

燿 **yao 4.** To illumine.

躍 **yao 4.** To jump; to dance.

櫂 **chao 4** An oar; to row.

擢 **cho 2.** To select; to employ.

[犭翟] **cho 4.** A monkey.

濯 **cho 2.** To rinse; clean.

戳 **ch'o 1.** To stamp; to stab; a seal.

792

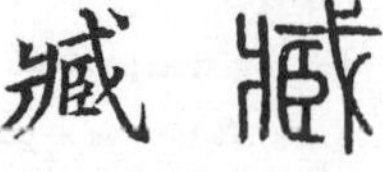

See Lesson 82 E.

臧 **tsang 1.** Complacency.

[氵臧] **tsang 1.** Muddy; dirty.

藏 **tsang 4.** Thibet. *Ts'ang* 2.

臟 **tsang 4.** The parenchymatous viscera.

贓 **tsang 1.** Booty; stolen goods; bribes.

藏 **ts'ang 2.** To hide away; to store up. *Tsang* 4.

793

See Lesson 65 G.

猒 **yen 4.** Filled; satiated.

[礻厭] **yen 3.** To pray for.

饜 **yen 4.** Filled; satiated.

懕 **yen 1.** Satisfied.

嬮 **yen 1.** Amiable.

檿 **yen 3.** A wild mulberry.

魘 **yen 3.** Nightmare.

[厭皮] **yen 3.** A scar.

黶 **yen 3.** Black; a spot.

[厭甲] **yen 3.** A breast-plate.

靨 **yen 3.** A pock-mark.

壓 **ya 1.** To press down; to subject; to crush.

擪 **yeh 4.** To put into the bosom.

794

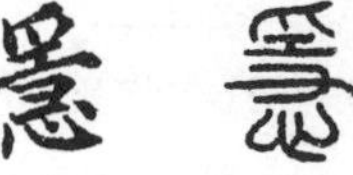

See Lesson 49 G.

㥯 **yin 3.** Solicitude; care.

[車㥯] **yin 3.** The rattling of carts.

[糸㥯] **yin 4.** To sew and stitch.

[扌㥯] **yin 4.** To dispose; to share; to measure.

檼 **yin 3.** The ridge-pool of a roof.

嶾 **yin 3.** Lofty and montainous

隱 **yin 3.** Retired; small; screened, in private life.

癮 **yin 3.** A vice; bound by a bad habit.

穩 **wên 3.** Firm; safe stable; grave.

795

See Lesson 149 D.

廛 **ch'an 2.** A market-place.

壥 **ch'an 2.** A market-place; a shop.

纏 **ch'an 2.** To bind up; to wrap; to entwine.

躔 **ch'an 2.** To revolve; a course.

[貝廛] **ch'an 4.** To try to buy up.

瀍 **ch'an 2.** Name of a river.

796

See Lesson 164 C.

徵 **chêng 1.** A sign; a proof; an effect; to testify.

癥 **chêng 1.** Calculi.

懲 **ch'êng 2.** To repress; to correct; to restrain.

澂 **ch'êng 2.** Pure water; clear; limpid.

797

頡

See Lesson 24 C.

頡 **chieh** 2. To raise the head. *Hsieh* 4.

襭 **chieh** 3. To hold up the skirt; the lapel; the breast.

纈 **chieh** 3. A knot.

擷 **chieh** 3. To pick up; to gather.

798

See Lesson 26 M.

節 **chieh** 2. An article; a joint; a time; a term; temperance.

櫛 **chieh** 2. A comb.

幯 **chieh** 2. To wipe.

癤 **chieh** 1. An ulcer.

Compare S. 424.

799

See Lesson 128 B.

質 **chih** 4. The substance; matter; a pledge.

櫍 **chih** 4. A note.

懫 **chih** 4. Displeasure.

躓 **chih** 4. To stumble.

鑕 **chih** 4. An anvil.

劕 **chih** 4. A deed; a ticket; a token.

800

See Lesson 165 D.

廚 **ch'u** 2. A kitchen.

幮 **ch'u** 2. A screen; a partition.

蹰 **ch'u** 2. Puzzled; incertain what to do.

801

See Lesson 47 Z.

樊 **fan** 2. Hedge; fence.

礬 **fan** 2. Sulphates; alum, etc.

蠜 **fan** 2. A grasshopper.

攀 **p'an** 1. To grasp; to climb; to exert one's self.

襻 **p'an** 4. A loop; a sash; a belt.

Compare S 677.

802

See Lesson 171 A.

廣 **kuang** 3. Broad; large; liberal.

纊 **kuang** 4. Fine floss.

瀇 **kuang** 3. To splash.

鄺 **kuang** 3. A proper name.

𠠎 **kuang** 3. To spread.

曠 **k'uang** 4. A vacant waste; empty; spacious.

壙 **k'uang** 4. A grave; a desert.

懭 **k'uang** 4. Deception.

鑛 **kung** 3. A mine.

礦 **kung** 3. A mine.

獷 **kung** 3. Fierce; rude.

穬 **kung** 3. The awn of barley, etc.

𦢊 **kuo** 4. The pavilion of the ear.

擴 **k'ou** 4. To stretch; to expend.

彍 **k'ou** 4. To bend a bow.

Compare S. 688.

803

畾

See Lesson 149 F.

畾 **lei** 2. Fields parted by dikes.

攂 **lei** 4. To pound.

儡 **lei** 3. Puppets.

𤢺 **lei** 3. A squirrel, *Pteromys*.

礧 **lei** 2. Heap of stones.

𦢖 **lei** 3. To swell.

壘 **lei** 3. Mason's work.

罍 **lei** 2. A wine jar.

藟 **lei** 3. A creeper.

纍 **lei** 2. To creep; to cling to.

儽 **lei** 3. Tired out; exhausted.

虆 **lei** 3. A basket.

It is found in

疊 **tieh** 2. To fold; to reiterate; still; again. *Hence*

㩸 **tieh** 2. To pile on; to fold over.

氎 **tieh** 2. Cashmere.

804

See Lesson 23 H.

厲 li 4. A whetstone; bad, malignant.

礪 li 4. A whetstone.

糲 li 4. Husks; void.

⿰忄厲 li 4. To fear.

濿 li 4. A ford; to ford.

蠣 li 4. Rock oysters.

勵 li 4. To stimulate; to exert one's self.

癘 li 4. A pestilential disease; virulent.

Compare S. 765.

805

See Lesson 40 B.

巤 lieh 4. Stiff hair; bristles.

鬣 lieh 4. Stiff hair.

擸 lieh 4. To draw; to tear.

儠 lieh 4. Strong; robust.

獵 lieh 4. To hunt; the chase,

躐 lieh 4. To skip over.

鱲 lieh 4. Perch.

⿰皮巤 la 2. Rough skin.

蠟 la 4. Wax; a candle.

⿰禾巤 la 1. Empty; sterile.

⿰米巤 la 1. Coarse; vile.

鑞 la 4. Tin.

⿰衤巤 la 4. Mean apparel.

邋 la 4. To omit.
la 2. Neglected, dirty.

⿰土巤 la 1. A cold.

臘 la 4. The winter solstice sacrifice; the 12th moon.

806

See Lesson 142 A.

魯 lu 3. Stupid; coarse.

嚕 lu 3. To spit.

艣 lu 3. A poop.

櫓 lu 3. A tower; an oar.

氌 luo 3. A yak's hair cloth.

807

See Lesson 40 A.

慮 lü 4. To think; to meditate.

⿰亻慮 lü 3. Indifferent; easy going.

櫖 lü 2. Liana.

⿰言慮 lü 4. To deceive.

鑢 lü 4. A file; to polish.

濾 lü 4. To filter; to strain.

勴 lü 4. To help; to encourage.

藘 lü 3. Madder.

攄 ch'u 1. To extend; to scatter.

808

See Lesson 158 F.

蔑 mieh 4. Minute, worthless. Without, not.

衊 mieh 4. To stain with blood; to defile.

蠛 mieh 4. Sand flies.

⿰扌蔑 mieh 4. To heat.

礣 mieh 4. Pebbles.

幭 mieh 4. A cart screen.

篾 mieh 4. Splints.

襪 } wa 4. Stockings; socks.
韈 }

809

See Lesson 475.

暴 pao 4. A scorching heat; violent; to illtreat.

曝 pao 4. To dry in the sun.

襮 pao 4. An embroidered collar.

⿰言暴 pao 4. Passionate speech.

瀑 pao 4. A water-fall.

㦒 pao 4. Sadness.

⿰暴皮 pao 4. Wrinkled; creviced.

爆 p'ao 4. Crackling; crackers.

810

See Lesson 136 A.

麃 piao 1. A spotted deer.

臕 piao 1. Fat.

穮 piao 1. To weed.

儦 piao 1. Crowds.

爊 piao 1. To bake.

皫 **piao 1.** White; pale.

鑣 **piao 1.** Bridle and bit.

瀌 **piao 1.** A heavy rain.

藨 **piao 1.** A rapsberry bush.

811

See Lesson 123 D

審 **shen 3.** To investigate; to inquire.

嬸 **shên 3.** Sisters-in-law.

瀋 **shên 3.** Gravy; sap.

Compare S. 676.

812

See Lesson 67 N.

數 **shu 3.** To count; to enumerate; to blame.
shu 4. A number.

藪 **sou 4.** A marsh.

籔 **sou 2.** A basket.

擻 **so 2.** To shake; to tremble.

Compare S. 631.

813

See Lesson 91 I.

疐 **t'i 4.** To trammel.

嚏 𪖐 **t'i 4.** To sneeze.

懥 **chih 4.** Resentment; hatred.

814

See Lesson 103 A.

養 **yang 3.** To nourish; to rear.

瀁 **yang 4.** Waves.

癢 懩 **yang 3.** To itch; to scratch; to long for.

815

See Lesson 88 C.

樂 **yao 4.** Music. *Lao* 4.

藥 **yao 4.** A medicine; a drug.

樂 **lao 4.** Pleasure; to like to. *Yao* 4.

濼 **lao 4.** Name of river.

爍 **shao 4.** To light; to shine.

鑠 **shao 4.** To polish; to shine.

礫 **li 4.** Gravel.

躒 **li 4.** A step, a pace.

轢 **li 4.** The rut of a wheel; to crush.

瓅 **li 4.** The luster of gems.

皪 **li 4.** Brightness.

櫟 **li 4.** A scrubby oak, *quercus serrata.*

擽 **li 4.** To select; to exclude.

816

See Lesson 160 C.

憂 **yu 1.** Grieved; in mourning, melancholy.

懮 **yu 3.** Sorrow; cares.

優 **yu 1.** Abundant! favour; actor; mimes.

耰 **yu 1.** A harrow; to cover in seed.

嚘 **yu 1.** To stammer.

鄾 **yu 1.** A place in Hupeh.

擾 **jao 3.** To trouble; to disturb; to tame.

犪 **jao 3.** Docile, well-trained ox.

817

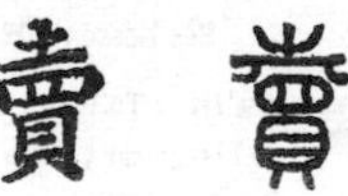

See Lesson 79 J.

賣 **yu 4.** To hawk about.

贖 **shu 2. ch'u 2.** To purchase; to redeem; to pay; a pledge; a ransom; a compensation.

瀆 瀆 **tu 4.** A ditch; an outlet; foul; filthy; to annoy.

讀 **tu 2.** To read carefully; to study.

櫝 **tu 4.** A case; a sheath.

牘 **tu 2.** Tablets; documents; archives; a note; a letter.

嬻 **tu 4.** To defile; to disgrace.

殰 **tu 4.** An abortion.

犢 **tu 2.** A calf.

𥢶 **tu 2.** A sheath.

瓄 **tu 2.** The onyx.

黷 **tu 4.** To blacken; to soil.

匵 **tu 4.** A case for books.

讟 **tu 2.** To murmur; to rail at; seditious.

竇 tou 4. A hole; a drain; deep.

覿 ti 2. To visit; to see face to face.

續 hsü 4. To join on; to add; to succeed to.

價 yü 4. To sell.

Compare *mai* 4, L. 78 E.

818

See Lesson 102 H.

親 ch'in 1. To love; to approach; to kiss; near; one's self, own.
ch'in 4. Kindred; affinity.

襯 ch'ên 4. Inner garments.

賵 ch'ên 4. To donate; alms.

櫬 ch'ên 2. The inner coffin.

819

See Lesson 168 H.

霍 huo 3. A sudden rain.

藿 huo 3. Peas, vetches.

癨 huo 3. The cholera.

攉 huo 3. To knead; to mix up.

臛 huo 4. A broth.

820

See Lesson 16 J.

褱 huai 2. To hide in one's bosom.

壞 huai 4. To spoil; to ruin; to destroy; vicious; depraved.

懷 huai 2. The bosom; to cherish kindly; to put in the bosom; to conceal; to think of.

821

See Lesson 120 I.

賴 lai 4. To depend on; to rely; to get advantage; to squeeze; to deny.

攋 lai 3. To draw.

瀨 lai 4. Name of a river.

鯻 lai 4. The *trypauchen vagina*.

癩 lai 4. Leprosy.

籟 lai 4. A musical pipe.

藾 lai 4. Legumes.

懶 lan 3. Lazy, remiss.

禶 lan 3. Impious.

嬾 lan 3. Idle.

獺 t'a 3. An otter.

822

歷 歷

See Lesson 121 L.

歷 歷 li 4. Idea of duration of succession; to pass through; to experience.

瀝 li 4. A drop; to drip.

嚦 li 4. A noise of splitting.

櫪 li 4. The oak.

羷 li 4. Black sheeps.

轣 li 4. A carriage rut.

劚 li 4. To cut up or open.

靂 li 4. A clap of thunder.

藶 li 4. Mustard.

癧 li 4. Scrofulous swellings.

See, L. 121 L.

曆 歷 li 4. Astronomy; a calendar.

823

盧 盧

See Lesson 135 D.

廬 lu 4. A hut.

爐 lu 2. A stove.

鑪 lu 2. A brazier

臚 lu 2. The skin.

轤 lu 2. A pulley.

罏 lu 2. A wine jar.

髗 lu 2. A skull.

嚧 lu 3. Onomatopœia.

攎 lu 2. To pick up.

纑 lu 2. Hempen thread.

鱸 lu 2. A perch.

壚 lu 2. Clods.

獹 lu 2. A large dog.

艫 lu 2. A square boat.

瓐 lu 2. A blue gem.

瀘 lu 2. Name of a river.

矑 lu 2 To look at.

櫨 lu 2. Sumac.

瓟 lu 2. A gourd.

鸕 lu 2 The fishing cormorant.

籚 lu 2. A large basket.
蘆 lu 2. Water rushes.
廬 lu 2. A thatched hovel.
瀘 lu 2. Tuberculosis.

驢 lü 2. A donkey.

824

龍 龖

See Lesson 140 A.

龍 lung 2. A dragon; imperial; glorious.
櫳 lung 2 A pen; a cage.
隴 lung 3. A dike.
攏 lung 3. To grasp; to collect; a comb.
嚨 lung 2. The throat.
曨 lung 2. The rising sun.
朧 lung 2. The rising moon; dim.
瓏 lung 2. Tinkling.
爖 lung 2. To kindle a fire.
徿 lung 3. To walk straight ahead.
襱 lung 2. The leggings worn in winter.
躘 lung 1. To totter; to stagger.
礲 lung 2. To reap grain.
儱 lung 2. Rude, unpolished.
瀧 lung 2. Dew; to bedew.
韄 lung 2. A halter.
籠 lung 2. A cage.
竉 lung 3. A hole; a cave
巃 lung 2. A peak.
聾 lung 2. Deaf.
礱 lung 2 To sharpen; to grind.
蠪 lung 2 An insect on the olive.
壟 lung 3. A grave; a mound.
甕 lung 2. Tiles.
龔 lung 2. A screen.

寵 ch'ung 3. Kindness, grace, favours.

龐 p'ang 2. A great house; a palace.

It is contracted in

襲 hsi 2. An overcoat. Hereditary, to inherit. L. 140

It is radical in

龕 k'an 1. A shrine for an idol; a niche.

825

頻 顭

See Lesson 112 C.

頻 p'in 2. Often.
櫇 p'in 2. The apple-tree.
嚬 p'in 2. To knit the brows.
蘋 p'in 2. *Marsilea quadrifolia.*

瀕 pin 1. A bank; a shore.

826

朕

騰 t'êng 2. To mount, contracted as above, forms
黱 t'êng 2. Black; obscure.
儯 t'êng 2. Long; to differ. See S. 191. and L. 47 K.

827

燕 燕

See Lesson 141.

燕 yen 4. A swallow.
嚥 yen 4. To swallow.
嬿 yen 4. Graceful.
讌 yen 4. A feast; merriment; to talk.
曣 yen 4. A serene morning.
臙 yen 1 Cosmetics.

828

毚 毚

See Lesson 106 C.

毚 ch'an 2. A hare.
儳 ch'an 1. Disorder.
攙 ch'an 1. To lift; to support; to mix.
饞 ch'an 3. Greedy; gluttonous.
巉 ch'an 2. A high peak.
欃 ch'an 1. A magnolia.
瀺 ch'an 2. Rippling of water.
鑱 ch'an 1. A chisel; to cut off.
獑 ch'an. A hare.
韂 ch'an 2. Paddings.
壥 ch'an 4. The border which defines the limit of a grave.
甗 ch'an 4. An earthen pitcher.

讒 ts'an 2. To detract.

纔 ts'ai 2. An adverb of time, near, at hand, presently.

829

See Lesson 27 B.

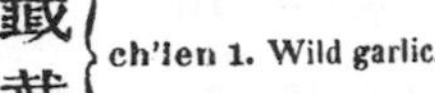

韱 [韭戈] } **ch'ien 1.** Wild garlic.

[巾韱] **ch'ien 1.** To record; a slip; a label.

[韱刂] **ch'ien 1.** To pierce.

籤 **ch'ien 1.** A slip; a warrant; a ticket; a peg.

殲 **chien 1.** To destroy; to exterminate.

瀸 **chien 1.** To soak; to imbue.

櫼 **chien 1.** A threshold.

鑯 **chien 1.** A sharp point.

襳 **hsien 1.** Under-clothes.

纖 **hsien 1.** Fine, delicate; small.

讖 **ch'an 4.** To divine; to augur.

懺 **ch'an 4.** To regret; to repent; expiatory formulae.

830

See Lesson 71 Q.

羲 **hsi 1.** The Emperor *Fu-hsi.*

犧 **hsi 1.** Victims fit to be offered in sacrifice.

曦 **hsi 1.** The light of day.

831

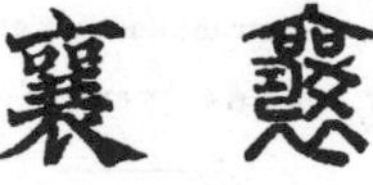

See Lesson 16 I.

襄 **hsiang 1.** To act; to assist.

鑲 **hsiang 1.** To inlay; to inchase.

[月襄] **hsiang 3.** The fat of hogs.

纕 **hsiang 1.** To hold up the sleeves.

欀 **hsiang 1.** A species of sago-palm.

瓖 **hsiang 1.** Jewels.

儴 **hsiang 1.** To stroll about; to ramble.

饟 **hsiang 3.** To take food to labourers.

驤 **hsiang 1.** To prance.

孃 **niang 2.** A woman; a mother.

讓 **jang 4.** To cede, to yield; to give way to; to forgive.

嚷 **jang 3.** To cry out; to scold.

攘 **jang 3.** To seize.

釀 **jang 4.** To ferment, to cause confusion or woes.

穰 **jang 2.** Abundant; prosperous.

[弓襄] **jang 3.** A bow bent.

瀼 **jang 2.** Dew.

壤 **jang 3.** Humus, soil; a region.

懹 **jang 4.** To lose heart; to fall back.

禳 **jang 2.** To fast and pray in order to deprecate evil.

[米襄] **jang 4.** To mix; to blend.

瓤 **jang 2.** Pulp; flesh.

[毛襄] **jang 2.** Wadding; cotton.

勷 **jang 2.** Urgent; zeal.

蘘 **jang 2.** *Lilium giganteum.*

鬤 **jang 2.** The hair dishevelled and uncombed.

832

See Lesson 103 B.

鮮 **hsien 1.** Fresh fish; fresh; new. **hsien 3.** Few; rare.

廯 **hsien 3.** A granary.

蘚 **hsien 3.** Mosses.

833

See Lesson 120 I.

闌 **lan 2.** A screen; to close.

爛 **lan 4.** To cook thoroughly; worn out.

攔 **lan 2.** To hinder; to obstruct.

欄 **lan 2.** A railing; a balustrade.

襴 **lan 2.** A sort of doctor's robe.

躝 **lan 2.** To overpass.

糷 **lan 4.** Thick gruel.

瀾 **lan 2.** Billows; waves.

鑭 **lan 4.** Luster; brilliant.

讕 **lan 2.** To defame; to calumniate.

[歹闌] **lan 4.** Corrupted.

孄 **lan 2.** Striped.

瓓 **lan 4.** The lustre of gems.

蘭 **lan 2.** Orchideous plants.

籣 **lan 2.** A quiver.

Compare S. 429.

834

See Lesson 158 B.

霜 **shuang 1.** Frozen dew, hoar frost; efflorescence; crystallised.

孀 **shuang 1.** A widow.

礵 **shuang 1.** Arsenic, *p'i-shuang.*

驦 **shuang 1.** A famous Bucephalus.

鷞 **shuang 1.** A hawk.

835

See Lesson 14 H.

龠 **yao 4.** Pandean pipes.

鑰 **yao 4.** The bolt of a lock; a key.

爚 **yao 4** Fiery; hot; bright.

禴 **yao 4.** A sacrifice in the ancestral temple.

瀹 **yao 4.** To wash.

籥 **yao 4.** Pan's-pipes.

龥 **yü 4.** To cry; to invoke; to implore.

籲 **yü 4.** Music; to invoke; to implore.

836

See Lesson 161 F.

嬰 **ying 1.** An infant, a babe.

纓 **ying 1.** Tassels.

攖 **ying 1.** To run against; to assail.

嚶 **ying 1.** Sound of birds calling.

孾 **ying 1.** Infants; babies.

瓔 **ying 1.** Precious stones.

櫻 **ying 1.** The cherry.

鸚 **ying 1.** A parrot.

癭 **ying 1.** A goitre.

蘡 **ying 1.** Wild vine.

837

See Lesson 176 A

爵 **chiao 2.** A cup; a degree of nobility; dignities.

嚼 **chiao 2.** To chew; to bite; to ruminate; the bit of a bridle.

穱 **chiao 2.** Early ripe.

釂 **chiao 2.** To drain a goblet.

𥌓 **chiao 4.** To close the eyes; to sleep.

皭 **chiao 3.** A pure white.

爝 **chiao 2.** A torch.

838

瞿

See Lesson 158 G.

瞿 **ch'ü 2.** The timid look of a bird; alarmed; vigilant.

欋 **ch'ü 2.** Roots; relations.

臞 **ch'ü 1.** Emaciated; thin

戵 **ch'ü 2.** A long spear.

氍 **ch'ü 2.** A square mat; a carpet.

鸜 **ch'ü 1.** A thrush.

斸 **ch'ü 1** To chop.

衢 **ch'ü 1.** A road; a path.

癯 **ch'ü 1.** Emaciated; thin.

懼 **chü 2.** To fear; to tremble from awe.

玃 **chü 1.** Orang-outang.

839

See Lesson 97 B.

豐 **fêng 1.** Abundant; plenty; copious.

僼 **fêng 1** Fairies, genii.

灃 **fêng 1.** Name of a river.

酆 **fêng 1.** A district in Ssŭ-ch'uan; a term for hell, *fêng-tu*.

It is radical in

豔 豓 艷 **yen 4.** Beautiful; winsome; wanton; dissipated; to admire and desire.

灩 **yen 4.** Bubbling waters.

840

See Lesson 15 C.

巂 **hsi 1.** A swallow.

觿 **hsi 1.** A horn stiletto.

蠵 **hsi 2.** A land tortoise.

鑴 **hsi 2.** A tripod or boiler.

酅 **hsi 2.** Name of a place.

攜 **hsieh 2.** To lead by the hand; to carry.

841

See Lesson 72 J.

 **kuan 4.** A heron.

觀 **kuan 1.** To consider; to examine; to see.
kuan 4. A Taoist convent.

鸛 **kuan 4.** A heron.

灌 **kuan 4.** To water; to pour; to force one to drink.

瓘 **kuan 4.** A variety of jade.

爟 **kuan 4.** To light a fire or beacon.

罐 **kuan 4.** A jar; a mug.

鑵 **kuan 4.** A mug.

懽 **kuan 4.** Cares; pain.

歡 **huan 1.** To rejoice; merry; to like.

讙 **huan 1.** To vociferate.

驩 **huan 1.** Frolicksome.

貛 } **huan 1.** The badger.
獾 }

權 **ch'üan 2.** A weight; rights; power, authority.

勸 **ch'üan 4.** To exhort; to admonish.

顴 **ch'üan 2.** The cheekbones.

842

聶

See Lesson 146 G.

聶 **nieh 4.** To whisper; to plot.

攝 **nieh 4.** To help. *Shê* 4.

鑷 **nieh 1.** Pincers.

讘 **nieh 4.** Garrulous.

躡 **nieh 4.** To tread or step on; to advance.

[illegible] } **nieh 4.** Warm; genial.
[illegible] }

[illegible] **nieh 4.** A fleet horse.

攝 **shê 4.** To help; interim; to govern. *Nieh* 4.

灄 **shê 4.** A river in Hupeh.

欇 **chê 4.** Trailing.

懾 **chê 4.** To seduce.

843

竄

See Lesson 37 G.

竄 **ts'uan 4.** To hide.

攛 **ts'uan 1.** To instigate; to rouse; to entice.

[illegible] **ts'uan 4.** To jump; to prance.

844

麗

See Lesson 163 B.

麗 **li 4.** Antelopes; elegant; graceful; glorious.

儷 **li 4.** A companion; a mate.

邐 **li 3.** advance; snccessively.

矖 **li 2.** To look at angrily.

攦 **li 4.** To break; to split.

穲 **li 2.** A good harvest.

纚 **li 2** A rope; a cable.

欐 **li 2.** Top; roof.

孋 **li 2.** A proper name.

鱺 **li 2.** A frosh waier eel.

[illegible] **li 2.** A milleped.

驪 **li 2.** A fleet horse.

鸝 **li 2.** The oriole.

酈 **li 4.** A place in Shantung.

躧 **hsi 3.** Straw sandals.

釃 **shai 1.** To warm wine.

曬 **shai 4.** To dry in the sun; to cure in the sunshine.

灑 **sha 3.** To sprinkle; to scatter.

845

羅

See Lesson 39 D.

羅 **lo 2.** A spring-net; a sieve; to spread out; humpbacked.

鑼 **lo 2.** A gong.

攞 **lo 3.** To rend.

儸 **lo 2.** Clever.

欏 **lo 2.** *Æsculus sinensis*, a chestnut-tree.

[illegible] **lo 2.** Embarrassed; to walk slowly.

饠 **lo 2.** A baked wheaten cake.

[illegible] **lo 2.** Name of a river.

囉 **lo 2.** To prattle; annoying.

邏 **lo 2.** To patrol; to spy.

籮 **lo 2.** Deep and open baskets.

蘿 **lo 2.** Carrot; beet.

846

See Lesson 92 D.

䜌 **luan 4.** Wrangling.

圝 **luan 2.** Spherical; round.

羉 **luan 2.** A net for catching animals.

孿 luan 2. Twins.

䜌 luan 2. A cord of silk.

巒 luan 2. The peaks of a hill.

鑾 luan 2. Little bells; imperial cars; a term of respect.

鸞 luan 2. Argus pheasant.

欒 lüan 2. A proper name.

孌 lüan 3. Nice; amiable.

攣 攣 } lüan 2. To bind or tie.

臠 lüan 3. Minced meat.

癵 lüan 2. Contraction of the hands and feet.

戀 lüan 3. Ardent love; to long after; to dot on.

䜌 lüan 4. Thick congee.

變 pien 4. To transform; to metamorphose.

蠻 man 2. Barbarous tribes in the south of China.

彎 wan 1. To draw a bow; to bend; arched; crooked.

灣 wan 1. A cove; a bay; to moor.

847

難 𪆧

See Lesson 171 B.

難 nan 2 Difficult; hard; irksome; to distress; trouble; is it not?

戁 nan 3. To be in awe of.

䕼 nan 4. Gnats.

灘 t'an 1. A flat.

攤 t'an 1. To open and spread out; to share.

癱 t'an 1. Paralysis.

儺 no 2. To exorcise the demons which cause pestilence.

臡 ni 2. Meat pickled.

848

顛 𩕊

See Lesson 160 C.

顛 tien 1. The top, the apex; to upset; to fall over; to amble along.

傎 tien 1. To turn over or upside down.

巔 tien 1. The peak or apex of a hill.

癲 tien 1. Crazed; deranged; mad.

𩕲 tien 1. High; far off.

849

贊 贊

See Lesson 79 B.

贊 tsan 4. To assist, to second; to praise.

儹 tsan 3. To gather; to hoard up.

讚 tsan 4. To commend; to laud, to praise.

瓚 tsan 4. A sceptre.

巑 tsan 2. Lofty mountains.

臢 tsan 1. Unclean.

禶 tsan 4. To implore.

濽 tsan 4. To splash.

欑 tsan 2. A shed.

趲 tsan 3. To hasten, to urge.

酇 tsan 4. A place in Hupeh.

纘 tsuan 3. To tie together, to connect.

儹 tsuan 2. To lose one's way.

躦 tsuan 1. To jump.

攢 tsuan 4. To seize; to catch.

鑽 tsuan 3. To bore; to pierce; to penetrate.

鬢 tsuan 3. Knotted hair; a chignon.

穳 ts'uan 2. To stack.

850

贛 𧶜

See Lesson 73 E.

贛 kan 4. Name of a place.

灨 kan 4. Name of a river.

匱 kan 3. A box or trunk.

鼜 k'an 4. To beat the drum.

戇 chuang 4. Honest; simple; stupid.

851

矍 矍

See Lesson 158 G.

矍 kuo 4. To look here and there; to seize.

攫 kuo 4. To seize; to capture.

戄 kuo 4. Frightened; surprised.

钁 kuo 4. A large hoe or pick.

籰 kuo 4. A reel.

躩 ch'iao 4. To walk cautiously.

852

 覽 覽

See Lesson 82 F.

 覽 **lan 3.** To inspect; to behold.

 攬 **lan 3.** To interfere with; to monopolise; to clutch.

 纜 **lan 3.** A rope, a hawser, a cable.

 欖 **lan 3.** The olive.

 爦 **lan 3.** To scorch.

853

  靈 靈

See Lessou 71 K.

靈 **ling 2.** A subtle substance; the spirit or energy of a being, soul; spiritual; a transcendent power.

 醽 **ling 4.** A rich kind of liquor, from Hunan.

 櫺 **ling 2.** A trellis.

 灵 **ling 2.** A bank.

 酃 **ling 2** A city in Hunan.

 麢 **ling 2.** The antelope.

854

  囊 囊

See Lesson 72 H.

囊 **nang 2.** A bag; a sack; a purse.

嚷 **nang 1.** To mutter.

 齉 **nang 4.** To snuffle.

 攮 **nang 3.** To stab.

 饢 **nang 4.** Mouldy; spoiled.

 灢 **nang 1.** Muddy; dirty.

 壤 **nang 4.** Dust, dirt; a cave.

曩 **nang 3.** In former times; previously; passed by.

855

  霸 霸

See Lesson 105 B.

 霸 **pa 4.** To govern; a sovereign; to incroach on; a tyrant.

灞 **pa 4.** A small river in Shensi.

 壩 **pa 4.** A dike.

856

  屬 屬

See Lesson 51 I.

屬 **shu 2.** Belonging to.

囑 **chu 3.** To enjoin upon.

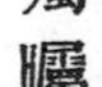 燭 **chu 3.** To illuminate.

 钃 **chu 3.** A pick-axe.

 孎 **chu 1.** Modesty.

 矚 **chu 3.** To look earnestly.

蠋 **chu 1.** A spider.

 斸 **chu 3.** To dig.

857

  黨 黨

See Lesson 36 E.

 黨 **tang 3.** A club, a party, a cabal.

 攩 **tang 3.** To impede.

 欓 **tang 4.** A cross-piece.

 曭 **tang 3.** Dull, cloudy.

讜 **tang 3.** Right words; persuasive speech.

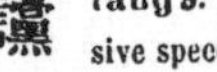

 儻 **t'ang 3.** If; suppose; an unforeseen thing.

858

  嚴 嚴

See Lesson 146 H.

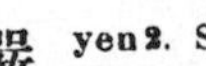

嚴 **yen 2.** Severe; stern; rigid; solemn; very; a night-watch.

 儼 **yen 3.** Grave; as if.

釅 **yen 2.** Strong, concentrated.

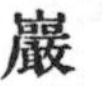 巖 **yen 2.** A rocky cliff; steep; dangerous.

 玁 **hsien 3.** Barbarians.

LEXICON BY ORDER OF SOUNDS

THE WADE SYSTEM.

阿 A
爱 Ai
安 An
昂 Ang
傲 Ao

乍 Cha
茶 Ch'a
窄 Chai
柴 Ch'ai
斬 Chan
產 Ch'an
章 Chang
唱 Ch'ang
兆 Chao
吵 Ch'ao

這 Chê
車 Ch'ê
眞 Chên
臣 Ch'ên
正 Chêng
成 Ch'êng
吉 Chi
奇 Ch'i
家 Chia
恰 Ch'ia
江 Chiang
搶 Ch'iang
交 Chiao
巧 Ch'iao
街 Chieh
且 Ch'ieh
見 Chien
欠 Ch'ien
知 Chih
尺 Ch'ih
斤 Chin
親 Ch'in
井 Ching
輕 Ch'ing
角 Chio
卻 Ch'io
酒 Chiu
秋 Ch'iu
窘 Chiung
窮 Ch'iung
卓 Cho
輟 Ch'o
晝 Chou
抽 Ch'ou
句 Chü
取 Ch'ü
捐 Chüan
全 Ch'üan
絕 Chüeh
缺 Ch'üeh
君 Chün
羣 Ch'ün
主 Chu
出 Ch'u
抓 Chua
拽 Chuai
揣 Ch'uai
專 Chuan
穿 Ch'uan
壯 Chuang
牀 Ch'uang
追 Chui
吹 Ch'ui
准 Chun
春 Ch'un
中 Chung
充 Ch'ung

恩 En
兒 Erh

法 Fa
反 Fan
方 Fang
否 Fao
非 Fei
分 Fên
風 Fêng
佛 Fo
夫 Fu

哈 Ha
害 Hai
寒 Han
砊 Hang
好 Hao
黑 Hei
很 Hên
恆 Hêng
河 Ho
後 Hou
戶 Hu
花 Hua
壞 Huai
換 Huan
黃 Huang
回 Hui
混 Hun
紅 Hung
火 Huo

西 Hsi
夏 Hsia
向 Hsiang
小 Hsiao
些 Hsieh
先 Hsien
心 Hsin
性 Hsing
修 Hsiu
兄 Hsiung
須 Hsü
喧 Hsüan
雪 Hsüeh
巡 Hsün

衣 I

染 Jan
嚷 Jang
繞 Jao
熱 Jê
人 Jên
扔 Jêng
日 Jih
若 Jo
肉 Jou
如 Ju
軟 Juan
瑞 Jui
潤 Jun
絨 Jung

嘎 Ka
改 Kai
開 K'ai
甘 Kan
看 K'an
剛 Kang
炕 K'ang
告 Kao
老 K'ao
給 Kei
刻 K'ei. K'o
根 Kên
肯 K'ên
更 Kêng

坑 K'êng
各 Ko
可 K'o
狗 Kou
口 K'ou
古 Ku
苦 K'u
瓜 Kua
跨 K'ua
怪 Kuai
快 K'uai
官 Kuan
寬 K'uan
光 Kuang
況 K'uang
規 Kuei
愧 K'uei
棍 Kun
困 K'un
工 Kung
孔 K'ung
果 Kuo
闊 K'uo

拉 La
來 Lai
懶 Lan
浪 Lang
老 Lao
累 Lei
冷 Lêng
立 Li
倆 Lia
兩 Liang
了 Liao
裂 Lieh
連 Lien
林 Lin
另 Ling
略 Liao
留 Liu

駱 Lo
陋 Lou
律 Lü
戀 Lüan
略 Lüeh
掄 Lün
路 Lu
亂 Luan
論 Lun
龍 Lung

馬 Ma
買 Mai
慢 Man
忙 Mang
毛 Mao
美 Mei
門 Mên
夢 Mêng
米 Mi
苗 Miao
滅 Mieh
面 Mien
民 Min
名 Ming
末 Mo
牟 Mou
木 Mu

那 Na
奶 Nai
男 Nan
囊 Nang
鬧 Nao
內 Nei
嫩 Nên
能 Nêng
你 Ni
娘 Niang
鳥 Niao
揑 Nieh
念 Nien
您 Nin
寧 Ning
牛 Niu
挪 No
耨 Nou
女 Nü
奴 Nu
暖 Nuan
濃 Nung

訛 O
偶 Ou

罷 Pa
怕 P'a
拜 Pai
派 P'ai
半 Pan
盼 P'an
幫 Pang
旁 P'ang
包 Pao
跑 P'ao
北 Pei
陪 P'ei
本 Pên
盆 P'ên
迸 Pêng
朋 P'êng
必 Pi
皮 P'i
表 Piao
票 P'iao
別 Pieh
撇 P'ieh
扁 Pien
片 P'ien
賓 Pin
貧 P'in
兵 Ping
憑 P'ing
波 Po
破 P'o
剖 P'ou
不 Pu
普 P'u

撒 Sa
賽 Sai
散 San
桑 Sang
掃 Sao
僧 Sêng
索 So
搜 Sou
素 Su
算 Suan
碎 Sui
孫 Sun
送 Sung

殺 Sha
曬 Shai
山 Shan
賞 Shang
少 Shao
舌 Shê
身 Shên
生 Shêng
事 Shih
手 Shou
書 Shu
刷 Shua
衰 Shuai
拴 Shuan
雙 Shuang
水 Shui
順 Shun
說 Shuo

絲 Ssŭ

大 Ta
他 T'a
歹 Tai
太 T'ai
單 Tan
炭 T'an
當 Tang
湯 T'ang
道 Tao
逃 T'ao
得 Tê
特 T'ê
等 Têng
疼 T'êng
的 Ti
替 T'i
弔 Tiao
挑 T'iao
疊 Tieh
貼 T'ieh
店 Tien
天 T'ien
定 Ting
聽 T'ing
丢 Tiu
多 To
妥 T'o
豆 Tou
頭 T'ou
妒 Tu
土 T'u
短 Tuan
團 T'uan
對 Tui
退 T'ui
敦 Tun
呑 T'un
冬 Tung
同 T'ung

雜 Tsa
擦 Ts'a
在 Tsai
才 Ts'ai
贊 Tsan
慚 Ts'an
葬 Tsang
倉 Ts'ang
早 Tsao
草 Ts'ao
則 Tsê
策 Ts'ê
賊 Tsei

怎 Tsên
参 Ts'ên
增 Tsêng
層 Ts'êng
作 Tso
錯 Ts'o
走 Tsou
湊 Ts'ou
祖 Tsu
粗 Ts'u
攢 Tsuan
竄 Ts'uan
嘴 Tsui

催 Ts'ui
尊 Tsun
寸 Ts'un
宗 Tsung
蔥 Ts'ung

子 Tzŭ
次 Tz'ŭ, Ts'ŭ

瓦 Wa
外 Wai
完 Wan
往 Wang

爲 Wei
文 Wên
翁 Wêng
我 Wo
武 Wu

牙 Ya
涯 Yai
羊 Yang
要 Yao
夜 Yeh
言 Yen
益 Yi cf I

音 Yin
迎 Ying
約 Yao
魚 Yü
原 Yüan
月 Yüeh
雲 Yün
有 Yu
用 Yung

A

啊 呀 **a 1.** An exclamation; a final particle.

AI (nai)

厄 **ai 4.** Distress.
阨 **ai 4.** A defile; distress.
軛 **ai 4.** A yoke.

艾 **ai 4.** Artemisia.
哎 **ai 4.** Aiya, alas!

挨 **ai 1.** To suffer; near.
唉 **ai 3.** To belch.

愛 **ai 4.** To love; to like.
噯 **ai 1.** An exclamation.

礙 碍 **ai 4.** To hinder, to oppose; obstacle.

哀 **ai 1.** To grieve for; sorrow; sad.

餲 **ai 4.** Spoiled food.

AN (nan)

安 **an 1.** Rest; peace; to lay down; how?
按 **an 4.** To press down; as; accordingly.
鞍 **an 1.** A saddle.
案 **an 4.** A table; a tribunal; a suit; law.

暗 **an 4.** Dark; secretly.
諳 **an 1.** Skilled in; fully acquainted with.
闇 **an 4.** To shut the door; dark; secrete.

ANG (nang)

嚷 **ang 3.** An interrogative particle.
骯 **ang 1.** Filthy. *Na* 1.
卬 **ang 2.** High, noble.
昂 **ang 2.** To rise, lofty, high, imposing.

AO (nao)

敖 **ao 2.** Pride, arrogance.
傲 **ao 4.** Proud; arrogant.
遨 **ao 2.** To ramble.
熬 **ao 2.** To boil; to decoct; to endure.
聱 **ao 2.** Refusing to hear; a bad character.
驁 **ao 2.** A vicious horse; stubborn.
鏊 **ao 4.** A round iron cooking utensil.
廒 **ao 2.** A granary.

奧 **ao 4.** The corner where the *Lares* were placed; mysterious; secret.
襖 **ao 3.** An outer garment; a coat.
懊 **ao 4.** Vexed; angry; to regret.
澳 **ao 4.** Macao.

鬧 **ao 4.** Noise; bustle, tumult; to scold.
奡 **ao 4.** A proper name.

CHA

扎 **cha 1.** To prick; to pierce.
札 **cha 2.** A tablet, a letter, an untimely death.
紮 **cha 1.** To tie together, to tress.
蚻 **cha 2.** A locust.

煠 **cha 2.** To fry.
揸 **cha 1.** To seize; a handful; to squeeze.
渣 **cha 1.** Dregs; residue.

樝 **cha 1.** A species of hawthorn, azerole.
摣 **cha 1.** To seize; to hold; a handful.
皻 **cha 1.** A crust, a scab.

挓 **cha 1.** To open; to expand.
吒 **cha 4.** A crack; report of a gun.

乍 **cha 4.** At first; unexpectedly.
炸 **cha 2.** Shavings.
蚱 **cha 3.** A locust.
拃 **cha 3.** A span.
詐 **cha 4.** To deceive, fraudulent.
咋 **cha 4.** A noise.
鮓 **cha 3.** A condiment, a sauce.

鍘 鍘 **cha 2.** A grass-cutter.
劄 **cha 2.** To prick; to puncture.
柵 **cha 4.** A fence of lats; a barrier.
眨 **cha 3.** Twinkling. *Chan* 3.
踏 **cha 4.** To trample on.
閘 **cha 2.** A lock, a flood-gate.
羨 **cha 3.** Stone-coal.

CH'A

插 **ch'a 1.** To insert; to stick in.
詬 **ch'a 4.** To talk muck; to interfere.
鍤 **ch'a 2.** A hair-pin.

㴙 ch'a 4. Freezing.

喢 ch'a 4. To prattle.

歃 ch'a 4. To anoint one's lips with blood; an oath.

查 ch'a 2. To examine, to investigate.

餷 ch'a 4. A postherd

蹅 ch'a 1. To paddle, to flounder.

叉 ch'a 1. A fork.

杈 ch'a 4. A fork; to pitch out.

衩 ch'a 1. A wallet.

茶 ch'a 2. The tea.

搽 ch'a 2. To anoint; to besmear.

察 ch'a 2, To examine; enquiries.

詫 ch'a 4. To brag; to wonder at.

差 ch'a 1. To err, to differ. *Ch'ai* 1.

岔 ch'a 4. Branching, to fork, cross-road.

刹 ch'a 4. A temple; a Buddhist monastery.

CHAI

責 chai 2. To reprove; to punish; to require from; duty.

債 chai 4. A debt.

幘 chai 4. A turban.

擇 chai 2. To choose; to select.

澤 chai 2. A marsh; to soak; kindness; favour.

齋 chai 1. Abstinence. A retired studious life.

窄 chai 3. Narrow, contracted.

仄 chai 3. Oblique, inclining.

宅 chai 2. Family dwelling.

寨 chai 4. A stockade; encampment.

砦 chai 4. A wall; a camp.

側 chai 1. The side; inclining to one side; low; mean.

摘 chai 1. To pluck; to take off; to deprive of.

翟 chai 2. A proper name.

CH'AI

測 ch'ai 4. To sound; to estimate.

惻 ch'ai 4. To pity; to sympathise with.

柴 ch'ai 2. To burn faggots to heaven; fuel.

策 ch'ai 4. A tablet; a diploma; a ferule; a stratagem.

豺 犲 ch'ai 2. A wolf.

冊 ch'ai 2. A memorandum; a fascicle.

拆 ch'ai 1. To break up, to demolish.

差 ch'ai 1. To send; a legate. *Ch'a* 1.

儕 ch'ai 1. A class; a company; a sign of the plural.

蠆 ch'ai 4. A scorpion.

釵 ch'ai 1. A bodkin.

CHAN

顫 chan 4. To shake; to tremble.

氈 chan 1. A rough felt.

鸇 chan 1 A sparrow-hawk.

展 chan 3. To open out; to unroll and inspect; to explain.

輾 chan 3. To roll over; to revolve.

搌 chan 3. To clean.

棧 chan 4. A covered shed; a store-house; a godown.

盞 chan 3. A shallow cup; a lamp.

瞻 chan 1. To look up to; to revere.

襜 chan 1. Lap of a coat.

斬 chan 3. To cut in two; to decapitate; to sever.

暫 chan 4. A short time; temporarily; in the interim; meanwhile; briefly; suddenly.

占 chan 1. To divine.

苫 chan 1. To thatch.

佔 chan 4. To seize by force; to usurp.

站 chan 4. To stand up; to stop; a stage.

粘 chan 1. To paste up; to stick.

毡 chan 1. Rough felt.

沾 chan 1. To moisten, to tinge; to receive benefits; to be soiled.

戰 chan 4. To fight; to fear; to tremble.

旃 chan 1. A banner, a signal flag; this, that.

綻 chan 4. An opened seam in a garment; to rip; cracked.

蘸 chan 4. To dip; to soak.

湛 chan 4. To soak in. Very. Many.

眨 chan 5 Twinkling. *Cha* 3.

CH'AN

儳 ch'an 1. Disorder; ill-assorted.

攙 ch'an 1. To lift, to support; to mix.

饞 ch'an 2. To love good eating; greedy; gluttonous.

產 ch'an 3. To produce; to bear; productions of a country.

鏟 剗 **ch'an 3.** A paring-knife; to trim.

廛 **ch'an 2.** A market-place.

纏 **ch'an 2.** To bind up; to wrap; to entwine.

躔 **ch'an 2.** To revolve; a course.

讖 **ch'an 4.** To divine; to augur.

懺 **ch'an 4.** To regret; to repent; expiatory formulae.

蟬 **ch'an 2.** The cicada.

禪 **ch'an 2.** Contemplation. *Shan* 4.

闡 **ch'an 3.** To explain, to develop.

蟾 **ch'an 2.** A toad; the moon.

韂 **ch'an 4.** A saddle.

剗 **ch'an 3.** To trim; to cut; to pare.

諂 **ch'an 3.** To flatter, to fawn.

覘 **ch'an 1.** To spy

CHANG

長 **chang 3.** To increase; to grow; senior chief. *Ch'ang* 2.

脹 **chang 4.** Swelling; dropsical.

帳 **chang 4.** A curtain; a tent.

賬 **chang 4.** An account; a bill.

張 **chang 1.** To draw a bow; to display; a sheet; a numerative.

漲 **chang 4.** To overflow; to inundate

章 **chang 1.** A section; a document; an essay; elegant; rule; law; to manifest.

障 **chang 4.** An embankment; to protect.

[illegible] **chang 4** To crackle; crackers.

樟 **chang 1.** The camphor tree.

璋 **chang 1.** A sceptre.

漳 **chang 1.** Name of a river.

彰 **chang 1.** Beautiful; to exhibit; to manifest.

麞 **chang 1.** The river-deer, musc.

瘴 **chang 4.** Malaria; miasma.

丈 **chang 4.** A measure (ten Chinese feet). A term of respect.

仗 **chang 4.** Weapons; to fight.

杖 **chang 4.** A staff.

掌 **chang 3.** The palm; the sole. To control, to manage.

CH'ANG

長 **ch'ang 2.** Long, of time or space. *Chang* 3.

悵 **ch'ang 4.** Depressed; disappointed; vexed.

萇 **ch'ang 2.** A proper name.

暢 **ch'ang 4.** Joyous; clear; to spread; perspicuous; long.

腸 **ch'ang 2.** The intestines; the feelings.

場 塲 **ch'ang 2.** An area of level ground; a thrashing-floor.

昌 **ch'ang 1.** The light of the sun; shining; glorious.

唱 **ch'ang 4.** To sing.

娼 **ch'ang 1.** A prostitute.

倡 **ch'ang 1.** To direct.

猖 **ch'ang 1.** Mad; wild.

菖 **ch'ang 1.** The *Calamus*.

閶 **ch'ang 1.** The gate of heaven; the palace gates.

敞 **ch'ang 3.** A plateau; high; open.

廠 **ch'ang 3.** A shed; a workshop.

常 **ch'ang 2.** Constant, regular; frequent; a rule; a principle.

嘗 **ch'ang 1.** To taste; to try; ordinarily.

償 **ch'ang 2.** To pay back; to indemnify.

鬯 **ch'ang 4.** A sacrificial wine.

昶 **ch'ang 3.** A long day; long, remote.

CHAO

召 **chao 4.** To call; to summon.

詔 **chao 4.** To announce; to instruct by decree or order, proclamation, a mandate.

招 **chao 1.** To beckon; to invite; to provoke; to confess.

沼 **chao 3.** A fish-pond.

鉊 **chao 1.** To mow down.

昭 **chao 1.** Brightness; luminous; to display.

照 **chao 4.** To enlighten, to shine on; the reflection of light; as.

兆 **chao 4.** An omen; a prognostic; a million.

垗 **chao 4.** A bank around a grave.

爪 **chao 3.** A claw. *Chua* 3.

笊 **chao 4.** A bamboo skimmer.

酌 **chao 1.** To pour out, to feast, to deliberato.

妁 **chao 4.** A go-between.

朝 **chao 1.** The dawn; the morning. *Ch'ao* 2.

著 着 **chao 2.** To cause; to send; to put on; a preposition; a suffix; etc. *Chu* 2.

罩篧 chao 4. A fish-trap; a cover; a screen.

肇 chao 4. To begin; to institute; to arrange.

找 chao 3. To seek; to look for.

斫 chao 4. To cut; to chop.

趙 chao 4. To hasten to; a surname.

櫂 chao 4 An oar; to row.

釗 chao 1. A proper name.

CH'AO

抄 ch'ao 1. To seize, to confiscate, to note, to copy out.

吵訬 ch'ao 3. To cry, to quarrel.

炒 ch'ao 3. To roast as coffee, to fry.

鈔 ch'ao 1. To hook; to copy; money orders.

巢 ch'ao 2. A nest.

轈 ch'ao 2. A look-out place on a war chariot.

勦 ch'ao 2. To grieve; to molest.

剿 ch'ao 3. To attack; to destroy.

朝 ch'ao 2. The Court; audiences given in the early morning; a dynasty; towards; facing.

潮 ch'ao 2. The tide; moist; damp.

晁 ch'ao 2. A surname.

超 ch'ao 1. To step over; to surpass.

綽 ch'ao 4. Ample, liberal, generous.

CHÊ

遮 chê 1. To screen; to intercept; to hide.

蟅 chê 2. A proper name.

蔗 chê 1. The sugar-cane.

折 chê 2. To sunder; to deduct; discount. *Shê* 2.

浙 chê 4. River from which the province of Chêkiang derives its name.

晰晢 chê 4. To light; to know; wise; discerning.

哲 chê 4. Philosophy.

輒輙 chê 4. Abruptly; suddenly.

懾 chê 4. To influence; afraid; timid.

跖 chê 2. A proper name.

者 chê 3. A final particle; a suffix.

摺 chê 2. To fold; to bend, a digest; a memorial.

蟄 chê 2. To hibernate; to become torpid.

螫 chê 1. To sting; a sting.

轍 chê 2. A rut; the track of a wheel.

這这 chê 4. This; here; now.

CH'Ê

車 ch'ê 1. A cart, barrow, coach. *Chü* 1.

奢 ch'ê 1. Prodigal; dissipated.

扯 ch'ê 3. To haul, to drag.

撤 ch'ê 4. To tear; to pull apart.

徹 ch'ê 4. To penetrate; to understand; all; general.

澈 ch'ê 4. Clear water; exhausted; run off.

CHÊN

珍 chên 1. Precious, rare, delicate.

診 chên 1. To examine, to verify.

袗 chên 3. Clothes of one thickness.

紾 chên 3. To twist.

疹 chên 3. Pustules; scarlatina or typhus; measles.

娠 chên 1. Pregnancy.

振 chên 4. To move; to shake; to stir up.

賑 chên 4. A gift; a help; alms.

震 chên 4. To shake; to shock.

眞 chên 1. True; truly; genuine.

鎭 chên 4. To keep; to protect; a market-town.

榛 chên 1. The hazel-tree.

溱 chên 1. Name of a river.

臻 chên 1. To spread; to reach; abundance.

蓁 chên 1. Bushy; thick.

鍼針 chên 1. A needle; a pin.

箴 chên 1. A needle; to excite.

枕 chên 3. A pillow.

酖 chên 4. A virulent poison; deadly.

斟 chên 1. To pour out; to deliberate.

碪 chên 1. A stone to beat clothes on when washing them.

鍖 chên 1. An anvil.

陣 chên 4. To set in order; an army; a battle; a gust; a shower.

砧 chên 1. A block.
譖 chên 4. To sneer at; to slander.
甄 chên 1. To mould.
朕 chên 4. I; myself.

CH'ÊN

辰 ch'ên 2. A part of time; the heavenly bodies.
蜃 ch'ên 3. A marine monster; mirage.
晨 ch'ên 2. Morning; dawn.
宸 ch'ên 2. The private apartments of the Emperor; Imperial.

耽 ch'ên 2. Pleasure, ease.
沈 沉 } ch'ên 2. Heavy; to sink; to indulge.

襯 ch'ên 4. Inner garments.
櫬 ch'ên 4. Inner coffin.

墋 ch'ên 3. Dirty; filthy.
磣 ch'ên 3. Sand; grit.

瞋 ch'ên 1. An angry look.
嗔 ch'ên 1. To scold.

岑 ch'ên 1. A lone peak.
搵 ch'ên 3. To extend.
陳 ch'ên 2. Ancient. To arrange; old, a long time.
塵 ch'ên 2. Dust; vice; worldly.
臣 ch'ên 2. A minister, a subject.
齔 ch'ên 4. To shed milk teeth.
諶 ch'ên 2. Sincere; upright; to trust to. *Shên 2.*
趁 趂 } ch'ên 4. To go to; to avail of as an opportunity

稱 ch'ên 4. Fit; suitable. *Ch'êng 1.*

CHÊNG

爭 chêng 1. To wrangle; to contest.
掙 chêng 4. To make an effort; to earn.
睜 chêng 1. To open the eyes wide.
諍 chêng 1. To remonstrate.
箏 chêng 1. A kite.

正 chêng 4. Correct, straight, regular; to govern; the first, the principal; just, precisely.
証 chêng 4. To prove, to testify; evidence; legal testimony.
征 chêng 1. To proceed; a war; to subjugate; to levy taxes.
怔 chêng 1. Restless; afraid.
鉦 chêng 1. Cymbals.
症 chêng 4. Disease; a chronic malady.
整 chêng 3. To adjust; to put in order; entire; whole.
政 chêng 4. To rule; government; politics.

貞 chêng 1. Chaste; pure; virtuous.
楨 chêng 1. A common evergreen.
禎 chêng 1. Luck; propitious.

拯 chêng 3. To raise; to help; to rescue.
烝 蒸 } chêng 1. Steam; to steam.
證 chêng 4. To testify; a proof.
徵 chêng 1. A sign; a proof; to make clear; to testify; to levy; to enlist.
鄭 chêng 4. A feudal State, now in Honan.

CH'ÊNG

承 ch'êng 2. To offer; to receive; to enjoy, to undertake; to flatter.
丞 ch'êng 2. To help, to second.

呈 ch'êng 2. To state clearly; to file a plaint.
程 ch'êng 2. A measure; a weight; a rule; a pattern; a limit; a period; to fix.
裎 ch'êng 2. To take off clothes; naked.
逞 ch'êng 3. Presumptuous; reckless; to follow; to obey.

稱 ch'êng 1. To style, to designate. *Chên 4.*
ch'êng 4. To weigh; to buy.
乘 ch'êng 2. To ascend, to mount on; to avail one's self; to multiply; a numerative. *Shêng 4.*

成 ch'êng 2. To finish; to accomplish; to become; to succeed.
誠 ch'êng 2. Guileless; sincere; to rectify; perfection.
城 ch'êng 2. A wall of a city; a city.
盛 ch'êng 2. To contain. *Shêng 4.*
晟 ch'êng 2. A proper name.

饓 ch'êng 1. To eat too much.
撐 撑 } ch'êng 1. To prop up; to assist; to punt.

懲 ch'êng 2. To repress; to correct; to restrain.
棖 ch'êng 1. A post; door-posts.
秤 ch'êng 4. A steelyard, to weigh
偵 ch'êng 1. To spy; to explore.

CHI (Tsi)

几 chi 1. A stand; a small table.

机 **chi 1.** A small table, a stool.

肌 **chi 1.** The flesh; meat on bones.

訉 **chi 1.** To scoff.

飢 **chi 1.** Dearth, hungry.

幾 **chi 1.** To be near; to approximate; almost; minute.

饑 **chi 1.** Dearth; famine.

譏 **chi 1.** To slander; to rail at; to jeer; to blame.

璣 **chi 1.** A sphere.

機 **chi 1.** A machine; a moving power; opportune; motive.

蟣 **chi 3.** Nits.

磯 **chi 1.** A rock; an obstruction.

畿 **chi 1.** Imperial lands.

吉 **chi 2.** Fortunate, lucky.

佶 **chi 2.** Robust, strong.

姞 **chi 2.** A proper name.

箕 **chi 1.** A proper name. *Ch'i* 2.

朞 **chi 1.** A full year; an anniversary.

基 **chi 1.** A foundation; land; property; the throne.

己 **chi 3.** One's self. A cyclical character.

記 **chi 4.** To note down; to mark; to remember; history.

紀 **chi 4.** Course, order.

忌 **chi 4.** To fear, to avoid, to abstain from.

跽 **chi 3.** To kneel long.

及 **chi 2.** To reach to; till.

級 **chi 2.** Threads, steps, grades.

伋 **chi 2.** Name of the grandson of Confucius.

汲 **chi 1.** To draw water from a well; to emulate.

芨 **chi 4.** An orchidaceous plant, salep.

岌 **chi 4.** A lofty peak; dangerous.

芰 **chi 4.** Water-chestnut, trapa.

妓 **chi 4.** A courtesan.

伎 技 } **chi 4.** Talent, cleverness, skilful.

奇 **chi 1.** Odd; surplus; fraction *Ch'i* 2.

畸 **chi 1.** Surplus; leavings.

觭 **chi 1.** Uneven; irregular.

寄 **chi 4.** To lodge at; to deliver over; to send.

亟 **chi 2.** Haste; speed; urgent; often; a crisis.

極 **chi 2.** The extreme limit; very; the zenith; the first principle.

殛 **chi 2.** To kill; to imprison for life.

既 旣 既 } **chi 4.** Since; when; to finish; all.

暨 **chi 4.** The sun peeping out. And; with.

激 **chi 4.** Rush of waters; to hit; to excite.

檄 **chi 1.** A decree; a missive.

繼 **chi 4.** To continue; to succeed; adoption.

笄 **chi 1.** A hairpin; to do up the hair; marriageable.

急 **chi 2.** Emotion; passion; haste.

擊 **chi 1.** To strike, to hit against, to whip.

季 **chi 4.** The least, the last. A season.

冀 **chi 4.** To hope, to wish.

戟 **chi 3.** A halberd.

稽 **chi 1.** To bow the head, to examine.

薊 **chi 4.** Thistles.

羈 **chi 1.** A halter, to restrain.

棘 **chi 4.** Thorns, brambles.

罽 **chi 4.** A fishing-net.

雞 鷄 } **chi 1.** Gallinaceous birds; cock; hen.

計 **chi 4.** To count, to calculate, to plan.

給 **chi 3.** To give; the preposition to; to suffice. *Kei* 3.

姬 **chi 1.** A proper name.

乩 **chi 1.** To divine by the pencil.

卟 **chi 1.** To consult a diviner.

覡 **chi 1.** A diviner, a witch.

祭 **chi 4.** To sacrifice; to worship.

際 **chi 4.** An angle; a limit; a juncture; an occasion; a time.

瘵 **chi 4.** Consumption.

濟 **chi 4.** To cross over; to aid, to releave.

擠 **chi 3.** To crowd; to press; to milk.

躋 **chi 1.** To rise, to ascend.

劑 **chi 4.** To adjust; to trim; a dose.

齏 **chi 4.** *Tulipa edulis.*

霽 **chi 4.** The clouds clearing away; serene.

齎 **chi 1.** To offer to; to give; to send.

蹟 **chi 1.** Foot-prints; traces; vestiges; results.

積 **chi 1.** To gather; to store up.

績 chi 1. To spin; to twist; meritorious service.

楫 chi 4. An oar; to row.
輯 chi 4. To arrange; order; collection.
戢 chi 4. To cease war; to join; to collect.

卽 卽 即 chi 2. Immediately. chi 4. Consequently.
蝍 chi 2. A cicada.
喞 chi 1. The hum of insects.
鯽 chi 4. The bastard carp.

脊 chi 2. The spine; the back; a ridge.
瘠 chi 2. Emaciated; lean; barren.

疾 chi 2. Sickness; urgent; hasty; to hate.
嫉 chi 4. Jealousy; envy; to dislike.
蒺 chi 2. Caltrops.

蹐 chi 1. To step; to walk slowly.
側 chi 2. The Emperor s field.
籍 chi 2. A list; a register; one's original family seat.

跡 迹 chi 4. Trace, foot marks, vestiges, results.

集 亼 chi 2. To flock together; a market; a meeting.

寂 chi 2. Silent; quiet.
稷 chi 2. Crops, agriculture.

CH'I (Ts'i)

齊 ch'i 2. Even; harmony; order; to equalise.

臍 ch'i 2. The navel.

妻 ch'i 1. Wife. ch'i 4. To marry.
棲 ch'i 1. To roost; to stay.
悽 ch'i 1. Grieved; suffering.
淒 ch'i 1. Cold; misery.

戚 ch'i 4. A battle-axe; related to; kin; sorrow.
嘁 ch'i 1. To whisper.
慽 ch'i 1. Grief; sorrow.

㯃 ch'i 1. The varnish tree.
漆 ch'i 1. Varnish; lacker.
膝 ch'i 2. The knees.

咠 ch'i 4. To whisper in the ear; to blame.
緝 ch'i 1. To sew; to join.
葺 ch'i 1. To repair; to put in order.

七 ch'i 1. Seven.
柒 ch'i 1. The number seven.

沏 ch'i 1. To infuse, to draw.

砌 ch'i 4. To build, to pave.

刺 ch'i 1. To tattoo. *Tz'ŭ* 4.

其 ch'i 2. He, she, it.
期 ch'i 1. A period; a limit of time; to hope.
欺 ch'i 1. To cheat; to deceive; to insult.
祺 ch'i 3. Prosperity.

淇 ch'i 2. A river in Honan.
麒 ch'i 2. The unicorn.
魌 ch'i 1. The demon of pestilence.
旗 ch'i 2. A flag; a banner.
箕 ch'i 2. A basket for dust. *Chi* 1.
棊 棋 ch'i 2. The chess.
綦 ch'i 2. A dark colour; very.

奇 ch'i 2. Extraordinary; marvellous; rare. *Chi* 1.
騎 ch'i 2. To ride; to sit astride.
崎 ch'i 1. Precipitous; dangerous.
踦 ch'i 2. Lame; cripple.
琦 ch'i 2. A precious stone; a curio.
綺 ch'i 3. Variegated silk.

起 ch'i 3. To rise, to begin.
杞 ch'i 3. A willow.
玘 ch'i 3. Stone ornaments hung at the girdle.
屺 ch'i 3. A bare hill.

乞 ch'i 3. To implore, to beg.
迄 ch'i 4. To reach to; till; finally; at last.
訖 ch'i 4. To finish, ended, done, up to.
汔 ch'i 4. To weep; perhaps; nearly; dried.
吃 ch'i 1. To eat. It is used for *ch'ih* 1.

气 氣 ch'i 4. Air; ether; vapour; spirit; temper; feelings; the two principles; the fate.
啓 啟 ch'i 3. To open; to begin; to explain.
契 ch'i 4. To notch; a covenant; a deed.

祇 ch'i 2. The spirits of the earth.

祈 ch'i 2. To pray.

耆 ch'i 2. A man of sixty; old; aged.

豈 ch'i 3. How? why?

祁 ch'i 2. Great, vast, much.

嵠 ch'i 1. A valley with a stream in it.

棄 ch'i 4. To reject; to throw off; to forget.

畦 ch'i 2. A field, a garden, a plathand.

企 ch'i 4. On tip toe; to desire; longing for.

泣 ch'i 4. To weep.

器 噐 ch'i 4. Vessels, utensils.

炁 ch'i 4. Influences.

蘄 ch'i 2. The *Aralia*.

岐 ch'i 2. A proper name.

憩 憇 ch'i 4. To rest.

CHIA

假 chia 3. False.
chia 4. Leave.

嘏 chia 3. Felicity; prosperity; strong.

葭 chia 1. Reeds; rushes; kindred.

夾 chia 1. To press; to squeeze; double; to help.

裌 chia 2. A lined coat.

挾 chia 1. To pinch. *Hsieh 2.*

俠 chia 1. Generous, bold. *Hsia 2.*

郟 chia 4. A place in Honan.

莢 chia 4. Pods; seeds; a felicitous plant.

加 chia 1. To add to; to confer upon; to inflict.

枷 chia 1. A cangue.

迦 chia 1 Sound used for the Sanscrit *ka* or *kia*.

痂 chia 1. The scab which grows over a sore. *Ka 1.*

嘉 chia 1. Beautiful, good; to approve, to admire.

架 chia 4. A stand; a case; a framework; a quarrel; a classifier.

駕 chia 4. A horse in the harness; to harness; to drive; Your Honour.

袈 chia 1. A dress worn by the Bonzes.

家 chia 1. A household; a family; a profession or class; a suffix.

傢 chia 1. Tools; furniture; family things.

嫁 chia 4. To marry a husband; to give one's daughter in marriage.

稼 chia 1. Crops, *chuang-chia*.

賈 chia 3. A surname. *Ku 3.*

價 chia 4. The value of a thing; the price.

檟 chia 3. Catalpa; a stick.

袷 chia 2. Lined garments.

甲 chia 3. Hard coverings, scaly plates, a cuirass; the finger nails; the first of the Ten Stems.

佳 chia 1. Fine, elegant.

斝 chia 3. A hanap.

CH'IA

恰 ch'ia 4. Fitting, opportune.

跲 ch'ia 4. To stumble.

㓞 ch'ia 4. Careless, egoistic.

掐 ch'ia 1. To pinch; to pluck.

卡 ch'ia 1. A guard-house at a pass; a Custom's barrier.

CHIANG (Tsiang)

蜂 chiang 4. The rainbow.

降 chiang 4. To descend; to come into the world; to subject. *Hiang 2.*

絳 chiang 4. Pink colour.

悻 chiang 4. To dislike; a bad temper.

倴 chiang 4. Unsubmissive; to rebel.

洚 chiang 4. Water overflowing; an inundation.

薑 chiang 1. Ginger.

澢 chiang 1. Congealed; coagulated.

礓 chiang 1. Gravel; pebbles.

殭 chiang 1. Stiff; numb; impassive.

僵 chiang 1. A stiff corpse.

疆 chiang 1. A limit, a border; a boundary.

江 chiang 1. A river.

豇 chiang 1. A kind of bean, *chiang-tou*.

姜 chiang 1. A proper name.

葁 chiang 1. Ginger.

繈 chiang 3. Swaddling-clothes.

膙 chiang 3. Callosities; corns.

講 chiang 3. To explain.

耩 chiang 3. To plough; to cultivate the soil.

糨 chiang 4. Starch; paste.

港 chiang 3. Streams diverging; a reach; a channel.

倞 chiang 4. To quarrel.

將 chiang 1. To take in the hand; to act; future; about to; to receive; to give; the side.
chiang 4. To command.

蔣 chiang 3. A proper name.

醬 chiang 4. A soy; sauce.

漿 chiang 1. Broth; congee; sauce.

槳 chiang 3. An oar.

獎 chiang 3. To praise; to encourage.

匠 chiang 4. Artisan, workman.

CH'IANG (Ts'iang)

搶 ch'iang 3. To take by force; to ravish; to oppose; ahead.

槍 ch'iang 1. A lance.

鎗 ch'iang 1. A gun; an opium pipe.

嗆 ch'iang 4. Hiccup.

謒 ch'iang 1. To blame, to scold.

蹌 ch'iang 1. To walk rapidly; to skip about.

戧 ch'iang 4. To prop; to etch.

戕 ch'iang 1. A spear, to wound, to kill.

牆 墻 } ch'iang 2. A wall.

檣 ch'iang 2. A mast.

薔 ch'iang 2. A red rose.

羗 羌 } ch'iang 1. Shepherd nomads on the West of China.

蜣 ch'iang 1. The tumble-dung.

腔 ch'iang 1. The throat; a tune; accent.

䗵 ch'iang 1. A tune; a melody.

彊 強 强 } ch'iang 2 Strong; good.
ch'iang 3. To force; to compel.

CHIAO (Tsiao)

交 chiao 1. To unite; intercourse.

郊 chiao 1. An open common beyond the city; imperial sacrifice.

鵁 chiao 1. The egret; the heron.

狡 chiao 3 Crafty; cunning.

絞 chiao 3. To strangle.

較 chiao 4. To examine, to confront, to compare; evidence.

校 chiao 4. An enclosure; a park; a school. *Hsiao* 4.

餃 chiao 3. A meat dumpling.

跤 chiao 1. A slip.

鉸 chiao 3. To cut, to clip.

姣 chiao 3. Handsome.

蛟 chiao 1. A crocodile.

鮫 chiao 1. A shark.

皎 chiao 3. Pure white; immaculate.

繳 chiao 3. Thread; to tie; to hand over.

徼 chiao 3. Lucky; prosperous.

皦 chiao 3. Clear; bright.

驕 chiao 1. Haughty; proud.

嬌 chiao 1. Delicate; to pet.

轎 chiao 4. A sedan.

矯 chiao 3. False, to feign; to correct; to rise.

撟 chiao 3. To lift up; to grasp; to twist; to bend.

嶠 chiao 4. A ridge.

叫 呌 } chiao 4. To call to or upon, to cry out; to name; to induce, to cause.

覺 chiao 3. To feel; to awake; to perceive.
chiao 4. To sleep.

攪 chiao 3. To stir up; to mix; to excite.

敎 教 } chiao 1. To teach.
chiao 4. Doctrines; sects; schools; to cause; to make.

酵 chiao 4. Leaven; to ferment.

澆 chiao 1. To irrigate; to water.

僥 chiao 3. Happy; fortunate.

窖 chiao 4. A hole.

窌 chiao 4. A cellar.

膠 chiao 4. Glue; sticky.

角 chiao 3. A horn.

榷 chiao 1. A foot-bridge; a tax.

脚 腳 } chiao 3. The feet.

焦 chiao 1. To scorch; dried up; care; a surname.

醮 chiao 1. A festival; a feast.

蕉 chiao 1. Banana.

爵 chiao 2. A cup; a degree of nobility; dignities.

嚼 chiao 2. To chew; to bite; to ruminate.

椒 chiao 1. Spice-plants; peppery; pepper.

CHIAO (Ts'iao)

俏 ch'iao 4. Handsome; elegant.

悄 ch'iao 3. Grief; care; silent; still.

誚 ch'iao 4. To scold; to ridicule.

鞘 ch'iao 4. A sheath; a scabbard.

瞧 ch'iao 2. To look on; to consider.

憔 ch'iao 2. Distressed, decaying.

譙 ch'iao 4. To blame; to scold; to ridicule.

樵 ch'iao 2. Fuel.

劁 ch'iao 4. To cut; to castrate; to reap.

幧 ch'iao 1. A kind of turban worn as mourning; to hem.

鍫 ch'iao 1. A hoe; to hoe.

雀 ch'iao 3. Small birds in general.

鵲 ch'iao 3. The magpie.

喬 ch'iao 2. Lofty; high; eminent; proud.

橋 ch'iao 2. A bridge.

僑 ch'iao 2. To sojourn, a guest.

趫 ch'iao 2. Agile.

蕎 ch'iao 2. Buck-wheat.

蹺 ch'iao 1. To stand up; curious; bizarre; stilts.

磽 ch'iao 1. Stony soil.

翹 ch'iao 2. Tail-feathers; to raise; high.

轎 ch'iao 4. Curved; turned up at the ends.

殼 殼 ch'iao 1. Husk; scale; shell; hard covering.

竅 ch'iao 4. A hole; an orifice.

確 ch'iao 4. True; positive; certainly.

巧 ch'iao 3. Skilful, cunning, artful.

撬 ch'iao 4. To prise open; to force up by leverage. *Yao* 4.

卻 却 ch'iao 4. To refuse; to leave; certainly, but.

敲 ch'iao 1. To knock; to tap.

碻 ch'iao 4. Stony; rocky.

蹻 ch'iao 4. To walk cautiously.

恪 ch'iao 4. Reverent and attentive. *K'o* 4.

CHIEH (Tsieh)

介 chieh 4. Difference; an assistant; great; a little; scales; to patronise.

蚧 chieh 4. A lizard.

价 chieh 4. Good, virtuous.

玠 chieh 4. A jade tablet.

界 chieh 4. A boundary; the world.

疥 chieh 4. The itch; an itching.

芥 chieh 4. The mustard plant.

桀 chieh 2. To quarter. A hen-roost.

傑 chieh 2. A hero.

皆 chieh 1. All; every; together.

階 chieh 1. A flight of steps; degrees; a rank.

堦 chieh 1 A degree.

稭 chieh 1. Stalks; straw.

喈 chieh 1. Music; melody.

戒 chieh 4. Precautions; to refrain from; abstinence; a rule.

誡 chieh 4. Rules of conduct; to prohibit; to warn.

解 chieh 3. To loosen; to undo; to explain, to get rid of.
chieh 4. To convoy.

繲 chieh 4. Worn-out cloth.

廨 chieh 4. A palace; a court.

結 chieh 1. A knot; to tie; fixed, firm, constant.

詰 chieh 4. Inquiry; to examine.

拮 chieh 2. Labouring hard.

髻 chieh 1. Back-hair, chignon.

黠 chieh 1. Black.

頡 chieh 2. To raise the head. *Hsieh* 2.

竭 chieh 2. To exhaust; the utmost; finished.

揭 chieh 1. To lift up; to pull apart; to solve; to borrow.

碣 chieh 2. A stone-tablet.

揭 chieh 2. Martial-looking.

偈 chieh 2. Martial; brave.

潔 chieh 2. Pure, chaste.

街 chieh 1. A street.

隔 chieh 4. Partition, to separate. *Ko* 2.

俠 chieh 1. Brave; a hero.

屆 chieh 4. To reach to; to arrive at; a limit.

杰 chieh 2. A proper name.

訐 chieh 2. To divulge; indiscretion.

孑 **chieh 4.** Maimed; alone.

接 **chieh 1.** To receive; to forward; to connect; to follow.
椄 **chieh 1.** To graft.

捷 **chieh 2.** Alert; active; clever.
箑 **chieh 2.** A fan.

節 **chieh 2.** An article; a joint; a time; a term; temperance.
癤 **chieh 1.** A sore, an ulcer.

借 **chieh 4.** To borrow.
藉 **chieh 4.** A mat; to lean on for aid; to help; to avail of; in order that.

劫 刧 **chieh 2.** To plunder; to rob openly.
截 **chieh 2.** To cut; to stop.
姐 **chieh 3.** An elder sister.

CH'IEH (Ts'ieh)

怯 **ch'ieh 4.** Timorous, fearful, cowardly.
茄 **ch'ieh 2.** Egg-plant.
篋 **ch'ieh 4.** A casket.
慊 **ch'ieh 4.** Pleasure; joy.
客 **ch ieh 4.** A guest. *K'o* 4.

且 **ch'ieh 3.** And, also, moreover, further; if, should; however, absolutely.
趄 **ch'ieh 4.** To slip.

切 **ch'ieh 1.** To cut; important; earnestly; to spell.

竊 **ch'ieh 4.** To steal, to pilfer; clandestine; I, my.
妾 **ch'ieh 4.** A concubine.

CHIEN (Tsien)

箋 **chien 1.** A tablet; a note-paper; a letter.
牋 **chien 1.** A tablet; a deed.
餞 **chien 4.** A farewell entertainment.
踐 **chien 4.** To tread upon; to keep one's word.
賤 **chien 4.** Cheap; mean; low.
濺 **chien 4.** To splash.

箭 **chien 4.** An arrow.
煎 **chien 1.** To fry; to decoct.
剪 翦 **chien 3.** To cut with scissors.

薦 **chien 4.** Pasture grounds; to introduce; to patronise.
荐 **chien 4.** To repeat; again.
殲 **chien 1.** To destroy; to exterminate.
漸 **chien 4.** To soak; gradually; by degrees.
戩 **chien 3.** To kill; to destroy.
尖 **chien 1.** Tapering; pointed.
僭 **chien 4.** To arrogate to one's-self.
鐫 **chien 1.** To cut; to chisel; to damage.

見 **chien 4.** To see; to visit; to appear. *Hsien* 4.
梘 **chien 4.** A wooden peg.
筧 **chien 3.** A bamboo pipe.

間 閒 **chien 4.** A crevice; a space between; during. *Hsien* 2.

簡 **chien 3.** A lath of bamboo; documents; records; to abridge.
澗 **chien 4.** Mountain streams.
鐧 **chien 4.** Iron protecting a wooden axle.
覸 **chien 4.** To spy into.

柬 **chien 3.** To select.
諫 **chien 4.** To reprove.
揀 **chien 3.** To select; to choose.

減 **chien 3.** To diminish; to decrease; to abbreviate.
緘 **chien 1.** To bind up; to close.
椷 **chien 3.** A casket.

兼 兼 **chien 1.** To comprehend in; together with; equally.
鹻 **chien 3.** Soda.
縑 **chien 1.** Taffeta.
歉 **chien 4.** Scanty; deficient.
蒹 **chien 1.** Reed, reedy.

建 **chien 4.** To establish; to found.
揵 **chien 4.** To fix; to raise.
健 **chien 4.** Strong; vigorous.
犍 **chien 1.** A gelded bull.
毽 **chien 4.** A shuttle-cock

儉 **chien 3.** Frugal; economical.
撿 **chien 3.** To tie; to gather.
檢 **chien 3.** Envelop; to label; to examine; to forbid; a rule.
劍 劒 **chien 4.** A two edged sword.

堅 **chien 1.** Firm; solid; durable.
慳 **chien 1.** Stingy; economical; to curtail expenses.

監 **chien 1.** To examine carefully; to oversee, a college; a jail.

檻 **chien 4.** Enclosure; a cage.

轞 **chien 3.** A shut up car.

艦 **chien 4.** A war vessel; a cruiser.

鑒鑑 **chien 4.** A mirror; an example; historic events; documents; to survey.

肩 **chien 1.** The shoulder; to take upon.

件 **chien 4.** An article, a subject, affair.

艱 **chien 1.** Labour; difficulty; care; suffering.

錽 **chien 3.** To plate.

姦奸 **chien 1.** Illicit intercourse; adultery; to ravish; wicked; a villain.

蠒 **chien 3.** The cocoon of the silkworm.

CH'IEN (Ts'ien)

褰 **ch'ien 1.** To tuck up; to raise the skirt.

蹇 **ch'ien 3.** Misfortune; limping; restive.

騫 **ch'ien 1.** To stumble; to fail; to be disgraced.

謙 **ch'ien 1.** Respectful; yielding; modest; humble.

嗛 **ch'ien 4.** To peck

鼸 **ch'ien 3.** A hamster.

牽 **ch'ien 1.** To pull; to haul; to connect.

撁 **ch'ien 1.** To lead; to drag.

縴 **ch'ien 4.** A tow-rope.

遣 **ch'ien 3.** To commission; to send off.

譴 **ch'ien 3.** To reprimand; to chastise.

欠 **ch'ien 4.** To owe; to be wanting in; duty.

芡 **ch'ien 4.** A water plant, *Euryale ferox.*

虔虔 **ch'ien 2.** Respect, veneration.

鉗 **ch'ien 2.** A pair of tweezers; pinchers, tongs.

箝 **ch'ien 2.** A gag; to gag.

嵌 **ch'ien 4.** To inchase; to inlay.

乾 **ch'ien 2.** Heaven; male; constant.

黔 **ch'ien 1.** Black.

鉛 **ch'ien 1.** Lead-ore.

愆 **ch'ien 1.** A fault; an error; a mistake; to go beyond.

[illegible] **ch'ien 4.** To peck, as birds.

錢 **ch'ien 2.** Copper coin, cash; a mace; wealth.

淺 **ch'ien 3.** Shallow; superficial; to run aground.

僉 **ch'ien 1.** Unanimous; all.

簽 **ch'ien 1.** Slips; to subscribe.

遷 **ch'ien 1.** To remove; to ascend; to be promoted; to change; henceforth.

韆 **ch'ien 1.** A swing.

千 **ch'ien 1.** Thousand; very many.

仟 **ch'ien 1** A thousand.

潛 **ch'ien 2.** Secrete; to abscond; hidden.

前 **ch'ien 2.** Before, in time or place.

籤 **ch'ien 1.** A slip, a ticket, a fish, a counter.

倩 **ch'ien 4.** Comely, pretty.

CHIH

只 **chih 3.** Merely, only.

枳 **chih 3.** Spinous shrub.

咫 **chih 3.** A measure of eight inches.

止 **chih 3.** To halt, to cease from, to be still; an object; only.

沚 **chih 3.** A bank.

阯 **chih 3.** Base, foundation.

址 **chih 3.** A place; dwelling.

祉 **chih 3.** Happiness; satisfaction.

趾 **chih 3.** The toes.

芷 **chih 3.** *Iris florentina.*

至 **chih 4.** To go to; to reach; till; as for; utmost; best; solstice.

姪 **chih 2.** A nephew; a niece.

輊 **chih 4.** A war-chariot low in front.

銍 **chih 4.** A sickle.

晊 **chih 1.** Bright; splendid.

桎 **chih 4.** Manacles; fetters.

蛭 **chih 4.** A leech.

致 **chih 4.** To offer; to resign; to bring about, to cause; to reach; the end.

緻 **chih 4.** Delicate, fine; a view.

咥 **chih 4.** To bite.

窒 **chih 4.** To stop up; to obstruct; stupid.

志 **chih 4.** Will; resolution; fixity of purpose; annals.

誌 **chih 4.** To remember; to record; annals.

痣 **chih 4.** A spot, a mark.

知 **chih 1.** To know; to be aware of; to govern; intimate.

蜘 chih 1. A spider.

智 chih 4. Wisdom; cleverness.

旨 台 chih 3. An Imperial Decree; purport; meaning.

指 chih 2. A finger; a toe. chih 3. To designate; to indicate; to hope; to confide in.

脂 chih 1. Grease; ointment; cosmetics.

識 chih 4. To remember; a deed. *Shih* 4.

職 chih 2. The duties of office; a tribute.

織 chih 1. To weave.

熾 chih 4. To burn; a blaze of fire.

擿 chih 4. To try; to ascertain.

樴 chih 4. A post.

峙 chih 3. A peak; to store up.

痔 chih 4. Piles.

紙 chih 3. Paper.

扺 chih 4. To move, to gesticulate.

祇 chih 3. To venerate; only, yet.

砥 chih 3. Whetstone, to polish.

執 chih 2. To hold; to grasp; to manage.

摯 chih 4. To offer up.

贄 chih 4. A present; offerings.

支 chih 1. A branch, a twig, to prop; to pay.

肢 chih 1. The limbs.

枝 chih 1. A branch, a twig; a classifier of slender things.

忮 chih 4. Aversion.

吱 chih 1. To growl.

制 chih 4. To cut and pare; to regulate; to make; a rule; a system.

製 chih 4. To invent; to manufacture.

卮 chih 1. A rhyton.

梔 chih 1. The *Gardenia tinctoria*.

直 chih 2. Straight; honest; upright.

值 値 chih 2. Price; value, to cost.

搘 chih 3. To lean on; to hold.

穉 chih 2. Grain first sown.

殖 chih 2. To fatten; to prosper.

植 chih 2. To plant; to stick; a pole.

置 chih 4. To get rid of; to arrange; to govern.

擲 chih 4. To throw; to fling away.

躑 chih 4. Irresolute, unquiet.

之 chih 1. Mark of the genitive; an expletive; to go.

芝 chih 1. Sesamum.

質 chih 4. The substance, matter, or nature of.

櫍 chih 4. A block.

劕 chih 4. A deed; a token; a pledge.

秩 chih 4. Order, degree.

紩 chih 4. To stitch; to sew.

陟 chih 4. To ascend; to mount; promotion.

騭 chih 1. Merit; promotion.

雉 chih 4. A pheasant.

稚 chih 4. Young, recent, delicate.

汁 chih 4. Juice, liquor.

豸 chih 4. Felines.

炙 chih 4. To warm; to burn; moxa; to cauterise.

隻 chih 4. One by itself; single; a numerative.

黹 chih 3. Embroidery.

治 chih 4. To govern, to rule; to punish, to heal.

彘 chih 4. A hog.

滯 chih 4. Coagulation; obstruction; opposition.

搘 chih 1. To raise, to prop, to support.

懥 chih 4. Resentment, hatred.

寘 chih 4. To order; to lay out.

CH'IH

蚩 ch'ih 1. A beetle. Stupid.

嗤 ch'ih 1. To laugh at.

眵 ch'ih 1. Eyes dim.

拸 ch'ih 3. To seize; to beat; to break.

侈 ch'ih 1. Lavish; exaggerated.

遲 ch'ih 2. Slow; to defer; a delay, late.

剻 ch'ih 2. To cut open; to dismember.

池 ch'ih 2. Pool, tank, vessel.

馳 ch'ih 2. Fast, to pass quickly.

彽 ch'ih 2. To go to and fro; irresolute.

坻 ch'ih 2. A dyke; an embankment.

蚳 ch'ih 2. Eggs or larvæ of ants.

鯴 ch'ih 1. The mackerel.

齒 **ch'ih 3.** The front teeth; the mouth; age.

赤 **ch'ih 4.** Flesh colour; naked; sincere.

翅 **ch'ih 4.** A wing; a fin.

幟 **ch'ih 4.** A pennon.

絺 **ch'ih 1.** Fine linen.

褫 **ch'ih 3.** To undress; to degrade.

尺 **ch'ih 3.** The Chinese foot.

痴 **ch'ih 1.** Stupid; doting.

勅 敕 勑 **ch'ih 4.** An imperial edict.

飭 **ch'ih 4.** To direct; to adjust; order; edict.

治 **ch'ih 2.** To govern. *Chih4.*

笞 **ch'ih 1.** To flog.

恥 耻 **ch'ih 3.** Shame, to be ashamed, to make ashamed of.

斥 席 **ch'ih 4.** To expel, to scold.

掣 **ch'ih 4.** To select; to obstruct; to hinder.

叱 **ch'ih 4.** To scold to drive out.

喫 吃 **ch'ih 1** To eat; to swallow; to suffer.

癡 **ch'ih 1.** Stupid; doting on.

持 **ch'ih 2.** To grasp; to hold; to manage.

CHIN (Tsin)

盡 尽 **chin 4.** To exhaust; to indulge, to end; to achieve; the last.

燼 **chin 4.** Ashes; the remains of.

儘 **chin 3.** Entirely; all; the utmost.

贐 **chin 4.** Partiag gifts.

進 **chin 4.** To advance; to enter; to bring in; a promotion, to make progress.

津 **chin 1.** A ford. Saliva; to moisten.

浸 **chin 1.** To float, to soak.

晉 晋 **chin 4.** To increase; to grow; a proper name.

搢 **chin 4.** To stick into.

縉 **chin 4.** Carnation silk.

-◇- -◇-

今 **chin 1.** Now, the present time.

妗 **chin 4.** A wife's sister.

衿 **chin 1.** Lapel of coat.

墐 **chin 3.** To plaster; to cover; to stop with mud.

謹 **chin 3.** Cautious; vigilant; respectful.

僅 **chin 3.** Only; hardly; scarcely.

瑾 **chin 3.** The lustre of gems; brilliant.

饉 **chin 3.** A dearth.

槿 **chin 3.** The *Hibiscus syriacus.*

覲 **chin 3.** To have an audience with the Emperor.

靳 **chin 4.** Firmness; avarice.

廑 **chin 3.** A hut.

禁 **chin 4.** To forbid; to prohibit; to restrain; to keep off.

噤 **chin 4.** Lockjaw, silent from grief.

憷 **chin 4.** Determined; resolute.

襟 **chin 1.** The overlap of a robe.

斤 **chin 1.** Catty; axe, hatchet.

近 **chin 4.** Near in time or place.

靳 **chin 4.** Ornaments of a harness.

筋 **chin 1.** The sinews; strenth, strong.

觔 **chin 1.** A pound.

勁 **chin 4.** Strength.

巾 **chin 1.** A kerchief; a bonnet.

金 **chin 1.** Gold.

錦 **chin 3.** Embroidered.

緊 **chin 3.** To bind tight; urgent; important.

巹 蒷 **chin 3.** The nuptial wine cup.

CH'IN (Ts'in)

琴 **ch'in 2.** The Chinese lute, organ.

芩 **ch'in 2.** A medicinal root.

衾 **ch'in 2.** A coverlet, blankets.

禽 **ch'in 2.** Wild birds.

噙 **ch'in 2.** To hold in the mouth; to restrain.

擒 **ch'in 2.** To seize.

勤 **ch'in 2.** Diligent; attentive; to toil; to work.

懃 **ch'in 2.** Zealous.

欽 **ch'in 1.** To revere; to venerate.

芹 **ch'in 2.** Cress.

-◇- -◇-

唚 **ch'in 4.** To vomit; to spit forth.

鋟 **ch'in 1.** To engrave, to cut.

綅 **ch'in 1.** Tassels, fringes.
侵 **ch'in 1.** To usurp; to encroach upon.
寢 **ch'in 3.** To sleep ; to rest ; to stop; apartments.

沁 **ch'in 4.** Name of a river.
秦 **ch'in 2.** A proper name.
親 **ch'in 1.** To love; to approach ; to kiss; one's self, own.
ch'in 4. Kindred; affinity.

CHING (Tsing)

經 **ching 1.** Warp in a loom ; veins or arteries ; meridians of longitude ; to pass through ; to regulate, canonical ; already.
剄 **ching 3.** To cut one's throat.
徑 **ching 4.** A diameter ; shortest way.
逕 **ching 4.** To pass.
脛 **ching 4** Shank ; shin-bone.
郅 **ching 1.** A place in Shantung.

敬 **ching 4.** To show respect to ; to venerate.
儆 **ching 3.** To warn , to be cautious.
憼 **ching 3.** To warn; to caution, to take care.
警 **ching 3.** To warn; to stimulate; police.
驚 **ching 1.** Frightened, terrified.

竟 **ching 4.** To search ; after all ; finally.
境 **ching 4.** Frontier; boundary ; a region; a district, circumstances.
鏡 **ching 1.** A mirror; a looking-glass; spectacles.

京 **ching 1.** A height ; a capital.
鯨 **ching 1.** A whale.

景 **ching 3.** Bright, beautiful ; scenery; a view, prospects, circumstances.

耕 **ching 1.** To plough, to cultivate.
荊 **ching 1.** Judas-tree, *Cercis sinensis*, Thorn , brambles.

更 **ching 1.** Night watch. *Kêng* 1.
粳 稉 **ching 1.** Rice which is not glutinous.

矜 **ching 1.** Pity, compassion ; reserve.
競 **ching 4** To struggle , to quarrel.
兢 **ching 4.** To fear; to be anxious.

井 **ching 3.** A well ; a rood of land, measuring 900 *mu*.
穽 **ching 3.** A pit-fall, a hole.

精 **ching 1.** The essential part; essence; spirit; semen; skill.
靖 **ching 4.** Order ; peace, quiet.
睛 **ching 1.** The iris of the eye ; the pupil.
菁 **ching 1.** Turnips.
淨 **ching 4.** Pure, spotless; clean; to wash; only.
靜 **ching 4.** Quiet; still; repose.

晶 **ching 1.** Lustre; clear; crystal.
旌 **ching 1.** A banner ; a standard; to make signals ; to make manifest; to honour.

CH'ING (Ts'ing)

青 **ch'ing 1.** Green; blue; black ; grey, the white of an egg.
情 **ch'ing 2.** Passions; emotions ; feelings, circumstances, nature, facts.

請 **ch'ing 3.** To beg; to request; please; to engage.
賙 **ch'ing 2.** To inherit.
晴 **ch'ing 2.** A clear sky.
淸 **ch'ing 1.** Pure; honest; clear; distinct.
凊 **ch'ing 4.** Cool.

磬 **ch'ing 4.** Sonorous stones.
罄 **ch'ing 4.** Empty ; exhausted ; all ; everything.

擎 **ch'ing 2.** To lift up; to uphold.
黥 剠 **ch'ing 2.** To tattoo the face.
頃 **ch'ing 3.** A hundred *mu*. *K'êng* 3.
輕 **ch'ing 1.** Light ; frivolous , easy.
檾 **ch'ing 3.** The *Sida tiliæfolia*.
慶 **ch'ing 4.** Good luck ; to congratulate.
卿 卿 **ch'ing 2.** Minister.

CHIU (Tsiu)

久 **chiu 3.** Ancient, long since.
玖 **chiu 3.** Smoky quartz ; nine.
灸 **chiu 3.** Moxa, to cauterise.
疚 **chiu 4.** Chronic disease, vice, ennui.
柩 **chiu 4.** A corpse in coffin.

九 **chiu 3.** Nine.
鳩 **chiu 1.** The pigeon.
究 **chiu 1.** To examine into, to search out.

臼 chiu 4. A mortar.

桕 chiu 4. The tallow tree, *Stillingia sebifera*.

舅 chiu 4. A mother's elder brother; a wife's brother.

舊 chiu 4. Old; formerly.

糾 糺 chiu 1. To twist, to involve.

咎 chiu 1. Fault, blame, calamity.

救 chiu 4. To rescue, to save from.

廐 chiu 4. A stable.

韭 韮 chiu 3. Leeks.

鬮 鬮 chiu 1. A lot; to draw, as lots.

酒 chiu 3. Spirits distilled from grain.

酒 chiu 1. To swim.

揪 chiu 1. To grasp with the hand.

瘷 chiu 4. To shrink; contraction.

就 chiu 4. To go or come to; to follow; to make the best of; then; immediately.

僦 chiu 4. To rent; to hire.

鷲 chiu 4. A vulture.

CH'IU (Ts'iu)

求 ch'iu 2. To beg; to pray for; to aim at.

球 ch'iu 2. A ball; a globe.

俅 ch'iu 2. Elegant.

銶 ch'iu 2. A chisel.

逑 ch'iu 2. To collect; to assemble; society.

毬 ch'iu 2. A ball.

裘 ch'iu 2. Fur garments.

丘 ch'iu 1. A natural hillock. Mou 3.

邱 ch'iu 1. To heap up; a tumulus.

坵 ch'iu 1. A natural hillock; a mound.

蚯 ch'iu 1. The common auth-worm.

仇 ch'iu 2. A surname. Used as an abbreviation of *ch'ou* 2, enmity.

惎 ch'iu 2. Hatred, to hate.

秋 ch'iu 1 Autumn; harvest.

楸 ch'iu 1. The catalpa.

鞦 ch'iu 1. A crupper.

鰍 ch'iu 1. The loach, *Cobitis*.

偢 ch'iu 1. To spy.

甃 ch'iu 4. To brick a well.

鶖 ch'iu 1. A crane.

囚 ch'iu 2. To imprison; to confine.

遒 ch'iu 1. To urge; to end.

CHIUNG

冋 chiung 3. Waste land.

坰 chiung 3. Pesert, waste lands; wilds.

迥 chiung 3. Far apart, unlike.

冏 chiung 3, A small window.

烱 chiung 3. Bright, hot.

CH'IUNG

芎 ch'iung 1. A depurative drug.

穹 ch'iung 2. A vault; the sky.

窮 ch'iung 2. Exhausted; the end; limits; poor.

蛩 ch'iung 2. A cricket; a locust.

瓊 ch'iung 2. Brilliant, precious.

煢 ch'iung 2. Alone; forlorn.

CHO

琢 cho 2. To cut; to polish stones.

啄 cho 4. To peck up food.

涿 cho 1. To drop; to fall drop by drop.

濁 cho 2. Muddy; foul.

鐲 cho 2. A bracelet.

鋜 cho 1. A hoe.

捉 cho 1. To grasp; to seize.

浞 cho 1. To soak; demp.

卓 cho 1. Eminent.

棹 cho 1. A table.

桌 cho 1. A table.

斲 斵 cho 2. To chop; to hash.

斸 cho 2. An adze; to cut.

擢 cho 2. To choose.

濯 cho 2. To rinse; clean.

棁 cho 2. A joist.

拙 cho 1. Unskillness, stupid.

CH'O

輟 ch'o 4. To cease; to finish.

啜 ch'o 4. To suck up; to sip.

歠 ch'o 4. To suck up; to sip.

戳 ch'o 1. To stamp; to stab; a seal.

黜 ch'o 4. To degrade, to dismiss.

CHOU

舟 chou 1. A vessel; a boat.

州 chou 1. A political district.

洲 chou 1. A continent.

軸 chou 2. An axle, a pivot, a roller.

妯 chou 2. Sisters-in-law, *chou-li*.

宙 chou 4. Earth, time; the universe; always.

胄 chou 4. Progeny; offspring.

冑 chou 4. A helmet.

周 chou 1. A dynasty; a bend; to surround; complete.

週 chou 1. To revolve.

賙 chou 1. To kick.

掤 chou 1. To heap.

賙 chou 1. To succour; to bestow in charity.

椆 chou 2. An oak.

謅 chou 1. To rail.

鞠 chou 3. A strap; to tie up.

縐 chou 4. Clothes creased.

縐 chou 4. A crape; wrinkled.

皺 chou 4. Wrinkled; creased.

鄒 chou 1. A place in Shantung.

肘 chou 3. The elbow, a cubit.

酎 chou 4. Spirits used for sacrifices.

紂 chou 4. An infamous king.

鞦 chou 4. A crupper.

掫 chou 2. To lift, to raise.

緅 chou 1. Purple silk.

驟 chou 4. Swift; intense.

鄹, 郰 chou 1. A place in Shantung. *Tsou* 1.

呪, 咒 chou 4. To curse, to imprecate; an incantation.

詋 chou 4. Imprecations.

晝 chou 4. Daytime.

粥 chou 1. Gruel, congee, porridge.

帚, 箒 chou 3. A broom.

籒, 籀 chou 4. A proper name.

CH'OU

綢 ch'ou 2. Silk cloth.

淍 ch'ou 2. To wash.

稠 ch'ou 2. Thick; close; dense.

惆 ch'ou 2. Vexed; disappointed.

呥 ch'ou 1. To suck in; to smoke.

紬 ch'ou 2. Silk cloth.

抽 ch'ou 1. To draw out, to extract; to contract; to decrease.

儔 ch'ou 2. A comrade, a partner; who?

疇 ch'ou 2. Cultivated field; a species; who?

躊 ch'ou 2. Irresolute, wavering, timid.

籌 ch'ou 2. To calculate; a lot; a ticket.

酬, 醻 ch'ou 2. To pledge with wine; to entertain; to repay.

詶 ch'ou 2. To answer.

愁 ch'ou 2. Melancholy; sad; fearful.

瞅 ch'ou 3. To look at; to gaze.

臭 ch'ou 4. To smell; to stink. *Hsiu* 4.

讎, 讐, 仇 ch'ou 2. To hate; to revenge; an enmity.

丑 ch'ou 3. A cyclical character; the second hour of the day, from 1 to 3 o'clock A. M.

醜 ch'ou 3. Ugly; hideous; evil.

搐 ch'ou 1. Spasm; contractions.

瘳 ch'ou 1. To cure, to be healed.

CHÜ (Tsü)

巨 chü 4. Great, large, very.

拒 chü 4. To reject, to oppose.

矩 chü 3. A carpenter's square; a rule.

距 chü 4. To go to, to reach; distant from, different.

詎 chü 4. How? in what manner?

苣 chü 4. The dandelion.

居 chü 1. To inhabit; to occupy; to be in.

倨 **chü 4.** Haughty.

鋸 **chü 4.** A saw, to saw.

据 **chü 1.** To seize.

踞 **chü 4.** To squat.

局 **chü 2.** A game of chess; position; circumstances, a board; an association.

鋦 **chü 1.** A clasp; to hook.

具 **chü 4.** To prepare; implements; tools; to write; all, every.

俱 **chü 1.** All, every.

颶 **chü 4.** A typhoon.

句 **chü 4.** A phrase; a word.

拘 **chü 1.** To grasp; to hold; to restrain.

駒 **chü 1.** A colt.

掬 **chü 2.** To grasp with both hands; a handful.

踘 **chü 4.** A football.

鞠 **chü 4.** A feather-ball.

毱 **chü 4.** A ball.

菊 **chü 1.** The chrysanthemum.

橘 **chü 2.** An orange-tree; an orange.

蹫 **chü 4.** Lame.

據 **chü 4.** To take in the hand; to rely upon; a legal instrument; evidence; according to.

璩 **chü 4.** Ear-rings.

懅 **chü 4.** Ashamed, bashful.

[illegible] **chü 4.** A big fire.

遽 **chü 4.** To send a messenger; hurried; suddenly.

劇 **chü 4.** Cares, misery; game; comedy, much, to add.

舉 **chü 3.** To raise, to lift up; to begin, to promote; actions, manners; all, whole a promoted man.

懼 **chü 2.** To fear; to tremble from awe.

屨 **chü 3.** Sandals; straw shoes.

莒 **chü 3.** A textile plant.

踽 **chü 3.** To walk alone; independent.

車 **chü 1.** A cart. *Ch'ê* 4.

鞫 **chü 2.** To investigate judicially.

足 **chü 2.** Enough; to suffice. *Tsu* 2.

聚 **chü 4.** To meet; to gather; collection.

咀 **chü 3.** To suck, to taste.

苴 **chü 1.** Hemp; sackcloth, coarse.

疽 **chü 1.** A deep-seated ulcer.

CH'Ü (Ts'ü)

取 **ch'ü 3.** To take hold of.

趣 **ch'ü 4.** To hasten to, pleasant.

娶 **ch'ü 3** To marry a wife.

[illegible] **ch'ü 1.** The bite of a serpent.

趨趋 **ch'ü 1.** To run to; to hasten; aim; towards.

蛆 **ch'ü 1.** Maggots, vermin.

去 **ch'ü 4.** To go, to leave, past, gone.

駈 **ch'ü 1.** To drive away.

祛 **ch'ü 1.** To avert; to exorcise.

曲 **ch'ü 1.** Crooked; perverse, songs.

麯 **ch'ü 1.** Leaven.

蛐 **ch'ü 1.** The common earthworm.

區 **ch'ü 1.** A place; a district.

軀 **ch'ü 1.** The body; one's own self.

驅 **ch'ü 1.** To drive away; vanguard, precursor.

嶇 **ch'ü 1.** A steep mountain.

傴 **ch'ü 3.** A hunchback.

敺 **ch'ü 1.** To expel; to drive away.

渠 **ch'ü 2.** A drain; a gutter; he, she, it, they.

蕖 **ch'ü 2.** The waterlily.

[illegible] **ch'ü 2.** A plant resembling basil.

蘧 **ch'ü 1.** A mushroom; pleasure.

泃 **ch'ü 2.** Name of a river.

劬 **ch'ü 1.** Labour, distress, severe toil.

瞿 **ch'ü 2.** The timid look of a bird; vigilant; alarmed.

衢 **ch'ü 1.** A road; a path

癯 **ch'ü 1.** Emaciated; thin; phthisis.

屈 **ch'ü 1.** A grievance; a wrong, injustice; te bend; to crouch.

[illegible] **ch'ü 1.** A monkey.

[illegible] **ch'ü 1.** Horripilation.

麴 **ch'ü 1.** Leaven; yeast.

CHÜAN

劵 **chüan 4.** Tired, weary.

帣 **chüan 4.** A bag.

眷 **chüan 4.** To love; to be fond of; family, relatives.

卷 **chüan 3.** To roll.
chüan 4. A roll; a book; a section.

餋 **chüan 3,** Cakes.

倦 **chüan 4.** Tired; weary.

捲 **chüan 3.** To roll up, to curl.

圈 **chüan 4.** A pen; a piggery. *Ch'üan* 1.

捐 **chüan 1.** To reject; to renounce; to subscribe; to purchase.

悁 **chüan 4.** Anxious; distressed.

狷 **chüan 4.** Alert, quick.

睊 **chüan 1.** To glare at.

娟 **chüan 1.** Graceful; elegant.

鞙 **chuan 1.** The traces of harness.

涓 **chüan 1.** Bubbling water.

鵑 **chüan 1.** A cuckoo.

絹 **chüan 4.** Gauze.

鄄 **chüan 4.** A place in Shantung.

蠲 **chüan 1.** Pure; to purify; to dispense with; to condone.

CH'ÜAN (Ts'üan)

券 **ch'üan 4.** A deed; an instrument in writing, cut in two.

拳 **ch'üan 2.** The fist.

惓 **ch'üan 2.** Careful; mournful.

棬 **ch'üan 2.** A wooden bowl.

圈 **ch'üan 1.** A circle; a ring; a dot; a snare. *Chüan* 4.

犬 **ch'üan 3.** A dog.

甽 **ch'üan 3.** Small drains between fields.

權 **ch'üan 2.** A weight; power, authority; to judge; circumstances.

勸 劝 **ch'üan 4.** To exhort; to admonish.

顴 **ch'üan 2.** The cheekbones.

全 仝 **ch'üan 2.** All; the whole; complete.

詮 **ch'üan 2.** To explain; to discourse upon.

痊 **ch'üan 2.** Cured; convalescent.

筌 **ch'üan 2.** A bamboo trap.

泉 **ch'üan 2.** A spring; money.

CHÜEH (Tsüeh)

絶 **chüeh 2.** To sever, to destroy, very.

嗟 **chüeh 1.** To sigh; alas.

決 决 **chüeh 2.** To decide; to settle; firm; absolutely.

訣 **chüeh 2.** A magic formula, mantra.

昳 **chüeh 2.** Penumbra.

鴃 **chüeh 2.** A shrike.

芵 **chüeh 2.** A plant, *Cassia tora*.

厥 **chüeh 2** He, him, this. *Ch'üeh* 2.

噘 **chüeh 1.** To pout.

撅 **chüeh 2.** To break, to pluck.

钁 **chüeh 2.** A hoe.

蹶 **chüeh 3.** To stumble.

蕨 **chüeh 2.** Bracken, *Pteris aquilina.*

橜 **chüeh 2.** A wooden peg.

掘 **chüeh 2.** To dig out; to excavate.

倔 **chüeh 2.** Crabbed; boorish.

崛 **chüeh 2.** A lofty peak; eminent.

譎 **chüeh 2.** To feign; to delude; hypocrisy.

CH'ÜEH

缺 **ch'üeh 1.** Broken, defective, a want, a vacancy.

厥 **ch'üeh 2.** He, him, this. *Chüeh 2.*

闕 **ch'üeh 4.** A deficiency, a *fault.*

瘸 **ch'üeh 2.** To be lame.

CHÜN

君 **chün 1.** Sovereign; price; ruler, a gentleman, sir.

郡 **chün 4.** A city, a district.

窘 **chün 3.** Afflicted, in distress.

軍 **chün 1.** An army, military, a camp.

均 **chün 1.** Equal, equally, all, impartiality, harmony.

鈞 **chün 1.** Thirty catties, great, much.

袀 **chün 1.** A plain dress.

菌 **chün 3.** Microbes.

CH'ÜN

裙 ch'ün 2. The skirt of a woman's dress, an apron.

羣 群 ch'ün 2. A flock, a herd, a crowd, a company.

CHU

朱 chu 1. Red.

珠 chu 1. A pearl, a bead, the eye-ball.

硃 chu 1. Vermilion, imperial.

蛛 chu 1. The spider.

誅 chu 1. To blame, to punish, to put to death.

銖 chu 1. A light weight, a small thing, a trifle.

株 chu 1. A trunk, numerative of trees, etc.

邾 chu 1. Name of a place.

主 chu 3. A ruler, a lord, to govern.

炷 chu 4. A candle; a stick of incense.

住 chu 4. To halt, to stop, to cease; to dwell; to live in.

註 chu 4. To explain; to comment.

拄 chu 3. A prop; to lean on.

駐 chu 4. To rest one's horse; to stop, to sojourn.

柱 chu 4. A pillar; a support.

咮 chu 4. A chuck for fowls.

鞋 chu 4. Leathern gaiters.

砫 chu 4. A stone tablet.

蛀 chu 4. Moths; worm-eaten.

注 chu 4. Water flowing; to soak; to record; to fix mind or eyes on.

助 chu 4. To help; to succour.

筯 chu 4. Chopsticks.

宁 chu 4. Waiting-room.

佇 竚 chu 4. To hope and wait.

貯 chu 4. To store up; to hoard; to engross.

紵 chu 4. Coarse linen.

詝 chu 4. Knowledge.

苧 chu 4. *Urtica nivea*, China-grass.

煮 chu 3. To boil; to decoct.

翥 chu 3. To fly up to soar.

著 chu 4. To make manifest, to publish. *Chao* 2.

箸 chu 4. Chopsticks.

渚 chu 3. An islet.

豬 chu 1. The pig.

諸 chu 1. All; every; a final particle; at; on, about.

燭 chu 2. A candle, a light, to illumine.

觸 chu 4. To butt, to strike against, to offend.

囑 嚼 chu 3. To bid, to order.

逐 chu 2. To drive or push out, to exorcise, successively.

祝 chu 4. To pray, to supplicate, to celebrate.

築 chu 2. To beat down, to ram down, to build.

竺 chu 4. The common name of India.

竹 chu 2. Bamboo.

丶 chu 3. A point, a dot.

鑄 chu 4. To cast, to fuse metals.

磚 chu 4. A stone roller.

杼 chu 4. A shuttle.

CH'U

芻 ch'u 2. Grass, hay, vulgar, worthless.

雛 ch'u 2. Chicks, to rear a brood.

蒭 ch'u 2. Straw.

畜 ch'u 4. Animals, brutes. *Hsü* 4.

楚 ch'u 3. Woody, thick, pain, order, to settle.

除 ch'u 2. To deduct, to take away, the end.

楮 ch'u 2. A mulberry, *Broussonetia papyrifera*, paper money, a letter.

褚 ch'u 3. A bag.

躇 ch'u 2. Undecided, perplexity.

儲 ch'u 2. To collect, to store up, savings.

出 ch'u 1. To go forth, to issue, to beget, to eject.

怡 ch'u 1. Melancholy, despondency.

樗 ch'u 1. *Ailantus glandulosa*, a useless stuff.

摴 ch'u 1. Pantomim, mimic.

廚 ch'u 2. A kitchen.

躕 ch'u 2. Puzzled; incertain what to do.

處 処 ch'u 3. To stop; to stay; to rest; to dwell; to judge; to decide; to punish.
ch'u 4. A place; a condition; a matter.

初 ch'u 1. To begin; beginning.

怵 ch'u 4. Afraid, timorous.

殊 ch'u 4. To differ; distinct; very; to kill.

輸 **ch'u 1.** To pay; to lose. *Shu1.*

杵 **ch'u 3.** A pestle.

贖 **ch'u 2.** To redeem; to ransom. *Shu 2.*

帚 箒 } **ch'u 2.** A broom. *Chou 3.*

攄 **ch'u 1.** Pleased; to explain.

齣 **ch'u 1.** Act of a play, a part.

鋤 **ch'u 2.** A hoe; to hoe.

殳 **ch'u 1.** Stick, spear, a weapon.

CHUA

爪 **chua 3.** Claws of animals. *Chao 3.*

抓 **chua 1.** To scratch, to tear, to seize.

撾 **chua 1.** To beat a drum or bell; to strike.

髽 **chua 1.** Girls head-dress, *chua-chieh.*

CHUAI

拽 **chuai 4.** To trail, to drag.

跩 **chuai 4.** To hobble.

[illegible] **chuai 3** To jolt.

㖨 **chuai 1.** Conceited language.

CH'UAI

揣 **ch'uai 4.** To feel for; to think over; to estimate.

惴 **ch'uai 4.** Mournful; in grief.

踹 **ch'uai 4.** To stamp on; to trample.

搋 **ch'uai 1.** To put in the bosom; to knead.

CHUAN

專 **chuan 4.** Single; particular; to specially care.

傳 **chuan 4.** A commentary. *Ch'uan 2.*

甎 **chuan 1.** A brick; a tile for paving.

轉 **chuan 4.** To turn round; to revolve; change of front; to transmit; to negotiate for.

鄟 **chuan 1.** Name of a place.

僎 **chuan 4.** To prepare; preparation.

譔 **chuan 4.** To praise; to extol.

饌 **chuan 4.** Food; provisions.

撰 **chuan 4.** To collect; to dispose.

瑑 **chuan 4.** To engrave on precious stones.

篆 **chuan 4.** The ancient seal-characters.

賺 賺 } **chuan 4.** To gain, to earn.

顓 **chuan 1.** To carry the head erect; dignified.

CH'UAN

喘 **ch'uan 3.** To pant; to breathe quick and short.

諯 **ch'uan 1.** To number; to reckon.

遄 **ch'uan 1.** To hurry.

川 巛 } **ch'uan 1.** River, to flow, flood, stream.

甽 **ch'uan 3.** Irrigating canals.

釧 **ch'uan 4.** Bracelet.

椽 **ch'uan 2.** A rafter; the lathing.

猭 **ch'uan 4.** A hare.

鶨 **ch'uan 4.** A penguin.

舛 **ch'uan 3.** Error; mistake; discord.

篡 **ch'uan 4.** To rebel; an usurpation.

傳 传 } **ch'uan 2.** To transmit; to hand down; to interpret. *Chuan 4.*

串 **ch'uan 4.** To string.

穿 **ch'uan 1.** To put on; to slip in.

船 **ch'uan 2.** A boat.

孱 **ch'uan 1.** Poor, unfit for.

CHUANG

庄 **chuang 1.** A village; a hamlet; a farm.

粧 **chuang 1.** To adorn; to disguise; to feign.

壯 **chuang 4.** Strong; robust.

裝 **chuang 1.** To pack; to contain.

莊 **chuang 1.** Agriculture; a farm; a village.

狀 **chuang 4.** Form, appearance; to declare in writing; an accusation.

妝 **chuang 1.** To adorn the head and paint the eyes; to rouge, to feign.

樁 **chuang 1.** A post; an affair; a kind.

撞 **chuang 4.** To strike; to run up against.

戇 **chuang 4.** Honest, simple, stupid.

CH'UANG

床 **ch'uang 2.** A bed; a sofa; a sled.

牀 **ch'uang 2.** A bed, a sofa.

饞 **ch'uang 2.** To eat immoderately.
幢 **ch'uang 2.** A curtain; a pennant.

窗 牕 } **ch'uang 1.** A window

創 **ch'uang 1.** To cut; to begin; origin.
愴 **ch'uang 4.** Sad; to pity.
瘡 **ch'uang 1.** Boil; abscess.

闖 **ch'uang 3.** To burst in; to rash violently; suddenly.

CHUI

錐 **chui 1.** An awl.
追 **chui 1.** To follow; to pursue; to go back; revert.
綴 **chui 4.** To baste; to connect; to sew.
贅 **chui 4.** To repeat, useless, an excrescence; an adoption.
墜 **chui 4.** To sink, to fall.

CH'UI

垂 **ch'ui 2.** To hang down; to droop; to let fall; to condescend; to become.
捶 **ch'ui 2.** To beat.
錘 **ch'ui 2.** A counterpoise.

搥 **ch'ui 2.** To beat; to strike.
槌 **ch'ui 2.** A wooden mallet.
鎚 **ch'ui 2.** A hammer.

吹 **ch'ui 1.** To blow upon; to chide.
炊 **ch'ui 1.** To cook.

CHUN

准 **chun 3.** To permit; to approve. to grant.
準 **chun 3.** To equalise; to level; a rule; just; exactly; certain.

諄 **chun 1.** To impress upon; to teach.

肫 **chun 1.** Dried flesh, very.
窀 **chun 1.** A cave; to inter; to bury.

CH'UN

春 **ch'un 1.** Spring; pleasant; wanton.
椿 **ch'un 1.** A tree, *Ailantus.*
蠢 **ch'un 3.** To wriggle; stupid; doltish.

醇 醕 } **ch'un 2.** Pure; generous; unmixed.
淳 湻 } **ch'un 2.** Pure; genuine; unmixed.
鶉 **ch'un 2.** A quail.

醇 **ch'un 2.** Pure, exquisite.
純 **ch'un 2.** Pure, unmixed, simple.

脣 唇 } **ch'un 2.** The lips.

CHUNG

中 **chung 1.** Middle, within.
chung 4. To accomplish, to hit.
忠 **chung 1.** Loyal, faithful, devoted, sincere, honest, right.
盅 **chung 1.** A cup, a goblet.

衷 **chung 1.** Rectitude, sincerity, loyalty, uprightness.
仲 **chung 4.** Second.

重 **chung 4.** Heavy; weighty; important; severe.
種 **chung 3.** A seed.
chung 4. To sow.
鍾 **chung 1.** A cup; a measure; natural gifts.
腫 **chung 3.** To swell.
踵 **chung 3.** The heel; to follow; to reach; often.

終 **chung 1.** The end; the termination, to the last; the utmost.
螽 **chung 1.** A green grasshopper.

冢 塚 } **chung 3.** A tumulus, a tomb.
鐘 **chung 1.** A bell; a clock.
衆 眾 } **chung 4.** All; multitude; many; numerous.

CH'UNG

重 **ch'ung 2.** A fold; a layer; a repetition.
衝 **ch'ung 1.** To rush towards or against; to break through.

沖 **ch'ung 1.** To dash against, to rush at.
忡 **ch'ung 1.** Sorrow, care.

虫 蟲 } **ch'ung 2.** Insects, etc.

充 **ch'ung 1.** To fill; to satisfy; to stuff up; to banish.
銃 **ch'ung 4.** A gingal.

崇 **ch'ung 2.** Lofty ; eminent ; to reverence; to adore.

寵 **ch'ung 3.** Kindness, grace, favours.

EN (nên)

恩 **en 1.** Favour ; grace ; mercy ; affection.

搵 **en 4.** To press down.

嫩 **en 4.** Delicate, tender.

ERH

爾 尔 **erh 3.** Thou, you ; if ; so just so ; an expletive final.

邇 迩 **erh 3.** Near; close.

兒 **erh 2.** Infant; boy; son ; a suffix.

二 弍 **erh 4.** Two.

貳 **erh 4.** Two; second.

樲 **erh 4.** Wild jujube, thorny shrubs.

而 **erh 2.** A copula, and, also, together; a disjunctive conjunction, still, yet.

輀 **erh 2.** A hearse or funeral carriage.

胹 **erh 1.** To boil.

耳 **erh 3.** The ear ; a handle ; a side; a final particle.

餌 **erh 3.** Bait for fish ; a temptation; cakes.

佴 **erh 4.** A second ; an assistant.

洱 **erh 3.** A river in Honan.

珥 **erh 3.** Ear-trinkets.

衈 **erh 4.** To slice the ear of a victim.

刵 **erh 4.** To cut the ears.

毦 **erh 4.** Feathers, hairs.

FA

伐 **fa 1.** To cut down ; to chastise, to destroy.

筏 **fa 2.** A bamboo raft.

閥 **fa 2.** Military hierarchy; ranks.

垡 **fa 2.** To clear, to plough.

法 **fa 1. fa 2. fa 4.** A law, a rule; an art ; to imitate. Buddhism, Buddhist.

珐 **fa 4.** Enamel, *fa-lang*.

乏 **fa 2.** Weary, fatigued; to be in want, poor.

髮 **fa 3.** The hair of the human head.

發 **fa 1** To send forth ; to issue, to dismiss ; to utter; to produce ; to rise ; to be manifest ; to act.

罰 **fa 2.** A fault; a crime; to punish.

FAN

番 **fan 1.** A time; a turn; aborigenes ; savages.

蕃 **fan 2.** Luxuriant vegetation; increasing.; Tibet,

幡 旛 **fan 1.** The banner carried before a corpse.

繙 **fan 1.** To interpret, to translate.

璠 **fan 2.** A precious stone.

墦 **fan 2.** A grave.

燔 **fan 2.** To roast ; to burn.

膰 **fan 2.** Meats used in sacrifices.

蹯 **fan 2.** An animal's paw.

羳 **fan 2.** A small-sized deer.

轓 **fan 1.** A screen for a cart.

翻 **fan 1.** To turn over ; action and reaction ; alternatives.

藩 **fan 2.** A fence ; a frontier.

籓 **fan 2** A sieve ; a basket.

反 **fan 3.** To turn back ; contrary, opposite ; to rebel.

坂 **fan 3.** A hill-side, a slope.

阪 **fan 3.** A bank.

飯 **fan 4.** Boiled grain ; food in general ; a meal, to eat.

返 **fan 3.** To return, to revert to, to come back.

販 **fan 4.** To buy in order to sell.

𤵸 **fan 4.** To faint.

凡 凢 **fan 2.** All, whoever, whatever, common, vulgar.

帆 **fan 1.** A sail.

汎 **fan 4.** To overflow ; immense ; vague ; changing.

梵 **fan 4** Brahma, Brahmanism. Sanskrit.

犯 **fan 4.** To rush against, to offend against, to violate.

氾 **fan.** To float ; universal ; purposeless.

范 **fan 4.** A surname.

範 **fan 4.** A law, a rule, a pattern.

棥 樊 **fan 2.** A hedge ; a fence.

礬 **fan 2.** Sulphates ; alum, etc.

繁 **fan 2.** Luxuriant ; abundant ; numerous.

蘩 **fan 2.** A species of *Artemisia*.

煩 **fan 2.** Heat and pain in the head; trouble; disgust.
泛 **fan 4.** To float, to drift; excessive; careless.

FANG

方 **fang 1.** A place, a region; square, regular, apt, easy; a rule, a prescription, a means; a comparison; then, actually.
芳 **fang 1.** Fragrant, virtue, glory. *Ritual*, your.
房 **fang 2.** A house; the registry office of a tribunal; a constellation; a wife or a concubine.
髣 彷 **fang 3.** To be like, similar, as.
妨 **fang 1.** To hinder, to oppose.
坊 **fang 1.** A ward; a store; a workhouse.
防 **fang 2.** An embankment, to protect from, to guard against; to avoid, to defend.
紡 **fang 3.** To spin.
訪 **fang 3.** To search out; to inquire into.
舫 **fang 3.** A large boat, a galley.
瓬 **fang 3.** To mould clay, as a potter.
放 **fang 4.** To put, to let go, to loosen, to issue; disorderly; to feed; to set free.
倣 **fang 3.** To imitate, to copy, a model.

FAO

缶 缻 **fao 3.** Earthenware vessels.
否 **fao 3.** Not, or not.

FEI

飛 **fei 1.** To fly; swift.
妃 **fei 1.** Imperial concubine.
朏 **fei 3.** The moon five days old.
吠 **fei 4.** To bark.
肥 **fei 2.** Fat, fleshy, fertile.

芾 **fei 4.** Umbrageous, to overshadow.
肺 **fei 4.** The lungs.

費 **fei 4.** To use, to spend, to lavish.
疿 **fei 2.** Small pimples on the skin.

非 **fei 1.** Wrong; not.
緋 **fei 1.** Scarlet.
悱 **fei 3.** Eager; to exert one's self.
誹 **fei 3.** To slander; to calumniate.
剕 **fei 1.** To maim a criminal.
翡 **fei 3.** A king-fisher; blue.
斐 **fei 3.** Streaks; lines; graceful.
棐 **fei 3.** A species of yew.
菲 **fei 3.** A radish; frugal; mean.
霏 **fei 1.** Sleet.
痱 **fei 4.** Swelling.
扉 **fei 1.** A door; a leaf.
匪 **fei 3.** Not; without; vagabonds; rebels.

廢 **fei 4.** Ruined; useless; to abandon; to dismiss.
癈 **fei 4.** Incurably diseased.

FEN

分 **fên 1.** To divide, to distinguish, to discern; the tenth of a *mu*; the hundreth of a foot, of a tael; a minute.
fên 4. A part, a lot, a share, function, duty.
芬 **fên 1.** Fragrant.
氛 **fên 1.** Vapour, miasma, meteor, omen, influx.
忿 **fên 4.** Anger, hatred, spite.
份 **fên 4.** A part, a share, lot, function, duty.
紛 **fên 1.** Disorder, confusion.
吩 **fên 1.** To command, to give orders.
汾 **fên 2.** Name of a river in Shansi.
粉 **fên 3.** Flour, plaster, powder, face-powder.

墳 坟 **fên 2.** A grave, a burial-ground.
噴 **fên 4.** To puff out. *P'ên 2.*
幩 **fên 2.** Ornaments on a bridle.
憤 **fên 4.** Ardor; to exert one's strength.

焚 **fên 2.** To burn; to consume.
糞 **fên 4.** Ordure, filth.
奮 **fên 4.** To arouse; impetuous action; to strive.

FÊNG

風 **fêng 1.** The wind; custom; habit; rumour; reputation.
瘋 **fêng 1.** Paralysis; insanity; madness.
諷 **fêng 3.** To recite; to criticise.

封 **fêng 1.** A fief; a territory; to appoint to office; to seal up; to blockade.

葑 **fêng 1.** Coarse legumes.

豐 **fêng 1.** Abundant; copious.

僼 **fêng 1.** Fairies, genii.

酆 **fêng 1.** A district in Ssŭ-ch'uan; a term for hell.

峯 峰 **fêng 1.** The peak of a hill.

蜂 **fêng 1.** A bee; a wasp; a hornet.

烽 **fêng 1.** A beacon fire-place.

鋒 **fêng 1.** A sharp point, vanguard.

逢 **fêng 2.** To meet, to happen, to incur, an accident.

縫 **fêng 2.** To sew, to stitch.
fêng 4. A crack, a split.

奉 捧 **fêng 4.** To receive respectfully with both hands, to pay one's respects, to flatter.

俸 **fêng 4.** Salary, emolument, *fêng-lu*.

馮 **fêng 2.** A proper name.

鳳 **fêng 4.** The phœnix.

賵 **fêng 4** To give aid in preparing for a funeral.

FO

佛 **fo 2.** Buddha, Buddhist.

FU

夫 **fu 1.** A husband, a man, master.
fu 2. Initial and final particle.

芙 **fu 2.** The *Hibiscus* flower.

扶 **fu 2.** To uphold, to assist.

蚨 **fu 2.** A butterfly; a copper cash.

趺 **fu 1.** To sit cross-legged.

鈇 **fu 1.** An axe.

麩 **fu 1.** Wheat bran.

颫 **fu 2.** A tempest, whirl-wind.

付 **fu 4.** To give, to deliver, to hand over.

符 **fu 2.** A deed in two pieces, to match, to agree with, a spell.

咐 **fu 4.** To enjoin, to command.

拊 **fu 3.** To pat, to tap, to soothe.

蚹 **fu 4.** Scales of serpents.

駙 **fu 4.** A subsidiary horse, a son-in-law of the emperor.

鮒 **fu 4.** A fish that goes in shoals, union, mutual affection.

附 **fu 4.** To be next to, to lean on, an appendix.

蔀 **fu 4.** A drug *Aconitum variegatum*.

府 **fu 3.** A palace, a department or bureau, prefecture.

俯 **fu 3.** To stoop, to condescend,

腑 **fu 3.** The bowels.

腐 **fu 3.** Rotten, putrid.

孚 **fu 2.** To brood on, to rely on, confidence.

俘 **fu 2.** A prisoner of war, a captive.

浮 **fu 2.** To float, to swim, volatile, fleeting, silly.

桴 **fu 2.** A raft.

郛 **fu 2.** Suburbs.

莩 **fu 2.** The epidermis of plants, related, friendly.

弗 **fu 2.** An adverb of prohibition, not, not so, do not, will not, can not.

髴 佛 **fu 2.** Like, as if, *fang-fu*.

紼 **fu 2.** A cord, a rope.

拂 **fu 4.** To oppose. To wipe.

咈 **fu 4.** To contradict, to refuse.

沸 **fu 4.** To boil, to bubble.

甫 **fu 3.** To begin, great, large, just now, a name.

脯 **fu 3.** Dried meat.

哺 **fu 3.** To feed.

輔 **fu 3.** To help, to assist, a minister.

黼 **fu 3** Embroidery.

鬴 **fu 3.** A caldron, a measure.

尃 **fu 1.** To diffuse.

縛 **fu 2.** To bind, to tie up.

傅 **fu 4.** To superintend, to teach, to anoint.

賻 **fu 4.** To give toward defraying funeral expenses.

榑 **fu 2.** The mangrove-tree.

敷 **fu 1.** To spread out, to diffuse, to promulge, extensively.

紱 **fu 2.** A special sash, the gentry.

祓 **fu 2.** To remove evil.

袚 **fu 4.** Knee-pads.

黻 **fu 4.** Embroidered, ornamented.

伏 **fu 2.** To subject; to lie or fall prostrate; to humble; to lie in ambush; to brood; to hide; to serve; a decade in dog-days.

袱 **fu 2.** A strong cloth used for wrapping.

茯 **fu 2.** A truffle-like drug, *Pachyma coces*.

畐 **fu 4.** To be full.

富 **fu 4.** Rich; abundant; wealth.

匐 fu 4. To crawl; to creep.
福 fu 2. Happiness; luck; blessings.
蝠 fu 2. The bat.
幅 fu 2. A strip of cloth; a roll of paper; a hem; an edge.
副 fu 4. To aid; an assistant, a second.

复 fu 2. To go back.
蝮 fu 2. A venomous snake.
腹 fu 4. The belly.
複 fu 4. Double or lined garments.
鰒 fu 2 Ear-shell, *Haliotis*.
馥 fu 4. A fragrant smell.
復 fu 4. To come or go back; again; to reply; to restore.
覆 fu 2. The reverse; to overthrow; to cover.

父 fu 4. Father.
斧 fu 3. An axe.
釜 fu 3. A caldron, a boiler.

赴 fu 4. To go to, to reach.
訃 fu 4. To announce a death.
仆 fu 4. To fall prostrate, to lie down.

負 fu 4. To carry on the back; to bear; to disregard; to turn the back on, ungrateful, rebellion.
偩 fu 4. Resembling.

阜 } 阝 } fu 4. A mound, a place, prosperity, abundance.
枹 fu 2. A drum-stick.
罘 fu 2. A net.
膚 fu 1. The skin, surface.
服 fu 2. Clothes, mourning, to think, to undergo, accustomed to, to subject, office, affair.

撫 fu 3. To caress, to pat. *Hu* 3.
鳧 fu 4. Wild duck.
賦 fu 4. To give, a rhytmic prose, natural.
婦 fu 4. A married woman.

HA

哈 } 呵 } ha 1. An exclamation. To laugh. To exhale gently.

HAI

亥 hai 4. A cyclic character.
孩 hai 2. A child.
骸 hai 2. Bones, skeleton.
核 hai 2. To search, to accuse. *Ho* 2. *Hu* 2.
駭 hai 4. Fear, dreadful, to frighten. *Hsieh* 2.
咳 hai 2. To cough. *K'o* 2.
劾 hai 2. To examine, to scrutinise, to accuse. *Ho* 2.

盍 hai 3. A jar.
榼 hai 3. A wooden tub.
醢 hai 3. To preserve.

害 hai 4. To injure, to hurt, to offend, to damage.
嗐 hai 1. An exclamation.

海 hai 3. The sea, the ocean, immensity.
覈 hai 4. To examine, to scrutinise. *Ho* 4.

HAN

邯 han 1. A district in the south of Chihli.

酣 han 1. Exhilarated, as from drink; jolly, tipsy.

憨 } 懺 } han 1. Foolish, silly.

汗 han 4. Sweat.
釬 han 4. To solder metals.
豻 han 4. The tapir.
鼾 han 1. To snore.
扞 han 4. To fend off.
頇 han 1. Slow, apathetic.
閈 han 4. Village gate, walled village.
罕 han 3. Rare, scarce, unfrequent.
旱 han 4. Dry, want of rain. *Hence*
悍 han 4. Fierce, violent.

凾 } 函 } han 2. To contain, to envelop, large-minded, a letter, armour.
菡 han 3. The bud of a lotus flower.
涵 han 2. To swamp, to submerge, vast; capacious.

含 han 2. To hold in the mouth, to contain, to restrain, doubt.
琀 han 2. Gems put into the mouth of a corpse.
頷 han 3. The chin, to shake the head.

韓 han 2. A proper name.
翰 han 4. A pencil, brush.
瀚 han 4. The northern sea, a desert.

喊 han 3. To cry, to call.
憾 han 4. Regret, remorse.
撼 han 4. To move, to shake, to excite.

漢 han 4. A proper name. Of or belonging to China.

暵 han 2. Hot, dry, parched.

寒 han 2. Cold, shivering, poor, a depreciating term for my.

HANG

硂 夯 hang 1. To pound, to ram down the earth, a rammer.

杭 hang 2. A boat. *Hang-chou.*

航 hang 2. A vessel, to sail, to navigate.

衖 hang 2. A band of musicians.

行 行 hang 2. A rank, a category, a profession, a corporation.

HAO

蒿 hao 1. Aromatic plants, like the *Artemisia.*

鎬 hao 4. The name of a place.

皜 hao 3. The light of heaven, luminous, bright. *Kao* 1.

毫 hao 2. Down, pubescence, the thousandth part of a tael, an atom.

豪 hao 2. A boar, brave.

嚎 hao 2. To roar.

壕 hao 2. A ditch, a moat.

濠 hao 2. A moat, a ditch.

浩 hao 4. Overwhelming, as a flood; vast, grand.

皓 hao 4. White, bright, luminous, splendid.

皞 皡 hao 4. White, effulgent.

昊 hao 4. The bright sky, august, heaven.

郝 hao 3. A proper name.

號 号 hao 4. A mark, a designation, a label, a name, a style, a signal; an order, to cry, to call.

好 hao 3. Good, right, very.
hao 4. To love.

耗 hao 4. To spend, to waste.

鶴 hao 2. A crane. *Ho* 2.

貉 hao 4. A badger.

HEI

黑 hei 1. Black, dark, evil.

HÊN

哏 hên 1. Loud, angry tones, *hên-tu.*

狠 很 hên 3. Bad, cruel, extremely, very.

恨 hên 4. Hatred, spite, resentment.

痕 hên 2. A scar, a cicatrix, a stain.

HÊNG

亨 hêng 1. To pervade; efficacity; success.

哼 hêng 1. To moan; to hum.

衡 hêng 2. A balance; to adjust.

橫 hêng 2. Cross-wise; horizontal.

恆 恒 hêng 2. Constance; perseverance; stable.

HO

See Huo.

曷 ho 2. Which, what, how, why, when, where?

喝 ho 1. To shout.

褐 ho 2. Coarse stuff; a poor man.

毼 ho 2 Coarse woollen cloth.

勂 ho 2. To shake.

河 ho 2. A river; a canal.

呵 ho 1. To laugh. *Ha* 1.

訶 ho 1. To blame; to reprove; to scold.

何 ho 2. An interrogative pronoun, who, which, what, where, how?

荷 ho 2 Water-lily. *Nelumbium speciosum;* to bear; to be obliged for, indebted to.

合 ho 2. To shut the mouth; to join; to unite; suitable; to match; to meet; together with; a region.

哈 ho 1. To laugh; to exhale gently. *Ha* 1.

郃 ho 4. Name of a place in Shênsi.

頜 ho 4. Inferior maxillary bone.

盒 ho 2. A box or dish.

閤 ho 2. Side-doors.

盇 盍 ho 2. Why not?

歃 嗑 ho 1. To drink.

闔 ho 2 The whole family; all, complete.

貉 ho 4. A badger. *Hao* 4.

齕 ho 4. To gnaw; to peculate.

劾 核 ho 2. To examine; to scrutinise; to accuse. *Hai* 2.

覈 ho 4. To examine thoroughly; to question by torture. *Hai* 4.

豁 ho 1. A pass; open; spacious; clear; generous; to understand; to penetrate.

赫 ho 4. Bright; glorious; to frighten.

壑 ho 4. A ditch.

蝦 ho 2. Frog. *Hsia* 1.

賀 ho 4. To congratulate; to send presents.

鶴 ho 4. A crane. *Hao* 4.

HOU

矦 侯 hou 2. The second title of nobility; a marquis; a target.

候 hou 4. To await, to expect the arrival of; time.

喉 hou 2. The throat.

猴 hou 2. A monkey.

餱 hou 2. Dry provisions.

鍭 hou 2. The metal head of an arrow.

齁 hou 1. To snore; very.

吼 hou 3. To roar.

后 hou 4. A ruler; the sovereign; an empress; after; then.

後 hou 4. After; behind; then; to postpone; posterity.

厚 hou 4. Thick; large; generous; very, rich.

鱟 hou 4. The king-crab.

HSI (Si)

希 hsi 1. Few; rare; seldom; to hope.

欷 hsi 1. To sob, to whimper.

郗 hsi 4. Name of a place.

奚 hsi 1. An interrogative particle, why? how? what?

徯 hsi 1. To wait for, to expect; to hope.

溪 hsi 1. A current.

蹊 hsi 1. A footpath; a narrow way.

鞵 hsi 2. A shoe, the sole.

嵠 谿 hsi 1. A valley with a stream in it, a ravine, discord.

喜 hsi 3. Joy, gladness, to delight in.

嘻 hsi 1. An interjection.

嬉 hsi 1. To play, to sport, to flirt.

禧 hsi 1. Blessing, good luck.

熹 hsi 1. Heat, glory, prosperity.

饎 hsi 1. Food, victuals.

系 hsi 1. Connection, succession, relation. A system.

係 hsi 1. To connect, to be.

兮 hsi 1. A prosodial expletive.

盻 hsi 4. To look at in anger.

羲 hsi 1. A proper name.

犧 hsi 1 Victims fit to be offered in sacrifice.

戲 戱 hsi 4. To play, to joke, a comedy, to make fun of.

繫 hsi 4. To tie, to fasten, to remember.

吸 hsi 1. To inhale, to breathe.

餼 hsi 4. Provisions; food.

翕 hsi 4. Harmonious, to unite, together, all.

隙 hsi 4. A fissure, a crack, a gap, leisure time, discord.

肸 hsi 4. Music.

醯 hsi 1. Vinegar.

熙 hsi 1. Splendor.

昔 hsi 2. Old, anciently, former, the time of night.

惜 hsi 1. To pity, to care for, to spare.

腊 hsi 1. Dried meat.

息 hsi 2. A full breath, a respiration, to produce, interest, to stop, repose, quiet.

熄 hsi 1. To put out a fire.

媳 hsi 1. A daughter-in-law, a wife.

悉 hsi 2. All, fully, very, to investigate, to know.

蟋 hsi 4. A cricket.

徙 hsi 3. To change one's residence.

蓰 hsi 3. To increase fivefold.

屣 hsi 3. Straw sandals.

析 hsi 1. To split; to explain.

淅 hsi 1. To wash rice.

晰 晳 hsi 1. Clear; bright; white.

西 hsi 1. West.

恓 hsi 1. Vexed; grieved.

錫 hsi 2. Tin. To give; gifts.

裼 hsi 1. A single garment; to pull off one's coat.

夕 hsi 4. Evening; end.

汐 **hsi 4.** The evening tide.

洗 **hsi 3.** To wash; to cleanse; to reform.

襲 **hsi 2.** Overcoat. United; attached. To inherit.

璽 **hsi 3.** The Imperial seal.

細 **hsi 4.** Fine, thin, slender.

席 蓆 } **hsi 2.** A mat; a table; a repast; rest.

葸 **hsi 3.** Timorous, meticulous.

習 **hsi 2.** To practise; custom, usage.

犀 **hsi 1.** Yak. Rhinoceros.

HSIA

暇 **hsia 2.** Leisure.

蝦 **hsia 1.** Batrachia. *Ho* 2.

鰕 **hsia 1.** Crustacea; shrimps etc.

瑕 **hsia 1.** A flaw; a blemish.

騢 **hsia 2.** A spotted horse.

遐 **hsia 2.** Long; far; old; to abandon; an interrogative particle.

霞 **hsia 2.** Clouds tinged red.

瞎 **hsia 1.** Blind; heedless; blindly.

轄 **hsia 2.** Linch-pins; to regulate.

匣 **hsia 2.** A box, a casket.

柙 **hsia 2.** A pen; a cage.

狎 **hsia 2.** A pet dog; too familiar; irreverent.

俠 **hsia 2.** Brave. *Chia* 1.

峽 **hsia 2.** A gorge; a mountain pass; a defile.

狹 **hsia 2.** Narrow.

頰 **hsia 4.** The chin.

洽 **hsia 4.** To harmonise with; just, exactly.

祫 **hsia 4.** Triennial oblation to the ancestors.

下 **hsia 4.** Low; below; down; underneath; to go down; inferior.

苄 **hsia 4.** The *Rehmannia chinensis.*

罅 **hsia 4.** A fissure, a chink; a crack, a split.

夏 **hsia 4.** Summer; the first Dynasty; Chinese.

嚇 **hsia 4.** To frighten.

HSIANG (Siang)

鄉 **hsiang 1.** A village; country; suburban district.

響 **hsiang 3.** Noise; sound; echo; clear.

饗 **hsiang 3.** Offerings; a feast; to relish; to agree.

嚮 **hsiang 4.** Towards; facing; to favour.

曏 **hsiang 4.** Formerly; past time.

向 **hsiang 4.** A window; facing; to favour.

餉 **hsiang 3.** Provisions; rations; taxes.

响 **hsiang S.** An echo; a noise; sounding.

香 **hsiang 1.** Fragrance; perfumes.

巷 **hsiang 4.** A side street; a lane.

降 **hsiang 2.** To submit; to surrender. *Chiang* 4.

享 **hsiang 3.** To offer up; to accept; to enjoy.

項 **hsiang 4.** The neck; a sort; a sum, a revenue.

相 **hsiang 1.** Mutual; to help.
hsiang 4. To look at.

湘 **hsiang 1.** Name of a river.

箱 **hsiang 1.** A box; a chest.

廂 **hsiang 1.** Side rooms: suburbs.

想 **hsiang 3.** To think about; to reflect; to hope; to earn.

象 **hsiang 4.** Elephant. A figure; an image. Elements of the Diagrams.

像 **hsiang 4.** An image; to resemble.

橡 **hsiang 4.** The oak.

[illegible] **hsiang 4.** The horn-bill of Siam.

襄 **hsiang 1.** To effect; to assist.

鑲 **hsiang 1.** To inlay, to inchase, to insert.

欀 **hsiang 1.** A sago-palm.

驤 **hsiang 1.** A spirited horse.

詳 **hsiang 2.** To examine, to report; minutely.

祥 **hsiang 2.** Felicitous, of good omen.

翔 **hsiang 2.** To hover; to roam.

庠 **hsiang 2.** A school, an asylum.

HSIAO (Siao)

小 **hsiao 3.** Small.

肖 **hsiao 4.** To be like.

硝 **hsiao 1.** Saltpetre.

消 **hsiao 1.** To dissolve, to consume; to expend.

銷 **hsiao 1.** To melt, to consume, to cancel, to annul.

逍 **hsiao 1.** To roam, to saunter.

焇 **hsiao 1.** To torrefy.

魈 **hsiao 1.** Mountain sprites.

削 **hsiao 1.** To cut, to pare, to erase.

宵 **hsiao 1.** Night, darkness.

霄 **hsiao 1.** The sky.

嘯 **hsiao 4.** To whistle, to scream.

彇 **hsiao 1.** The extremity of a bow.

橚 **hsiao 1.** Foliage, leaves.

歗 **hsiao 4** To lament, to cry, to sigh.

簫 **hsiao 1.** Pandean pipes.

蕭 **hsiao 1.** An artemisia, reverence, poor; destitute.

笑 **hsiao 4.** To laugh, to ridicule.

⟡ ⟡

孝 **hsiao 4.** Filial piety, mourning.

哮 **hsiao 1.** To scream, to pant, to gasp, asthma.

枵 **hsiao 1.** Empty, hollow, vile, *hsiao-pao.*

鴞 **hsiao 1.** An owl, filial impiety.

學 **hsiao 2** To learn, to study.

壆 **hsiao 2.** Basement.

鷽 **hsiao 2.** The *Urocissa sinensis.*

礐 **hsiao 2.** Rocks.

嘵 **hsiao 1.** To cry, to quarrel.

驍 **hsiao 1.** A fine horse.

曉 **hsiao 3.** Dawn, light, to understand, to know.

効 **hsiao 4.** To toil, exertion, to imitate, merit.

校 **hsiao 4.** A building for a school. *Chiao 4.*

恔 **hsiao 4.** Cheerful, satisfied.

效 **hsiao 4.** To produce, effects, results, to imitate, similar.

囂 **hsiao 1.** To cry, clamour, noise.

嘐 **hsiao 1.** Boasting, bragging.

梟 **hsiao 1.** To expose the head of a criminal.

HSIEH (Sieh)

泄 **hsieh 4.** To leak, to ooze out, to divulge, diarrhœa.

洩 **hsieh 4.** To leak, to drop, to divulge.

紲 **hsieh 4.** To tie, to fetter.

屑 **hsieh 4.** A fragment, to condescend, lightly, triflingly.

燮 **hsieh 4.** To blend, to harmonise.

邪 **hsieh 2.** Bad, perverse.

褻 **hsieh 4.** Underclothes, dirty, filthy.

謝 **hsieh 4.** To thank, to cease, to resign, to confess.

楔 **hsieh 1.** A wedge, a peg.

寫 寫 寫 } **hsieh 3.** To write, to sketch. To leak.

瀉 **hsieh 4.** To flow off, diarrhœa.

些 **hsieh 1.** A little, few, some.

斜 **hsieh 2.** Transverse, oblique, opposite, heterodox.

卸 **hsieh 4.** To lay aside, to unload.

⟡ ⟡

猲 **hsieh 4.** A fierce dog.

歇 **hsieh 1.** To rest, to stop, to leave off.

蠍 **hsieh 1.** A scorpion.

挈 **hsieh 2.** To raise, to help.

絜 **hsieh 4.** To rule, to settle.

解 **hsieh 4.** A proper name. *Chieh 3.*

懈 **hsieh 4.** Idle, remiss.

澥 **hsieh 4.** A creek, a rivulet, watery.

嶰 **hsieh 4.** A valley.

蟹 **hsieh 4.** A crab, *P'ang-hsieh.*

協 勰 叶 } **hsieh 2.** United in, agreement, concord; a regiment, to aid.

愶 **hsieh 1** To intimidate.

脅 **hsieh 2.** The flanks, the sides, to intimidate.

薤 **hsieh 4.** The shallot, *Allium ascalonicum.*

蟹 **hsieh 4.** Bravery, courageous.

偕 **hsieh 2.** Together, with.

諧 龤 } **hsieh 2.** To accord, to agree, to harmonise.

械 **hsieh 4.** Arms, weapons.

挾 **hsieh 2.** To pinch, to oppress. *Chia 1.*

鞋 **hsieh 2.** A shoe.

攜 攜 } **hsieh 2.** To lead by the hand, to carry off.

HSIEN (Sien)

閒 **hsien 2.** Repose, leasure, at ease, idle, vacant.

嫺 **hsien 2.** Graceful, refined, accomplished.

憪 **hsien 3.** Pleasure, happiness.

癇 **hsien 2.** Convulsions, fits.

閑 **hsien 2.** A bar, a fence, to close, to forbid.

鷴 **hsien 2.** The silver pheasant.

險 **hsien 3.** Dangerous, hasardous.

玁 獫 **hsien 3.** Barbarians, Huns.

嶮 **hsien 3.** Height, precipitous.

嫌 **hsien 2.** To loath, to depreciate, to have an aversion to.

隒 **hsien 3.** A narrow or steep path.

弦 **hsien 2.** The string of a bow, the chord of an arc, a crescent, a spring.

絃 **hsien 2.** The strings of a lute.

見 **hsien 4.** To appear, manifest. *Chien 4.*

現 **hsien 4.** The glitter of gems, visible, now, at present.

峴 **hsien 3.** A steep hill.

咸 **hsien 2.** All, entirely, to unite.

鹹 **hsien 2.** Salt, bitter, brackish.

諴 **hsien 2.** Sincerity, harmony.

羬 **hsien 2.** The nylgau.

憲 **hsien 4.** An example, law, constitution.

幰 **hsien 3.** The curtain in front of a carriage.

顯 **hsien 3.** Apparent, clear, illustrious, glorious.

賢 **hsien 2.** Worthies, good, virtuous.

陷 **hsien 4.** To fall down, to sink.

限 **hsien 4.** A limit, a boundary, a restriction.

閾 **hsien 4.** A threshold.

獻 献 **hsien 4.** To offer, to give, to hand up to.

掀 **hsien 1.** To lift up, to open.

縣 **hsien 4.** A prefecture, a district.

銜 **hsien 2.** A bit, affected, indignant, a rank, a degree.

祆 **hsien 1.** Fire-worship of the Persians.

啣 **hsien 2.** To hold in the mouth.

杴 **hsien 1.** A shovel.

先 **hsien 1.** Before, former, to precede

恍 **hsien 2.** Melancholy, despondency.

銑 **hsien 3.** Polished, bright.

挑 **hsien 3.** To pull, to tear.

跣 **hsien 3.** Barefooted.

刎 **hsien 4.** To castrate.

仙 **hsien 1.** Genii, fairies, immortals.

秈 **hsien 1.** Common rice.

鮮 **hsien 1.** Fresh fish, fresh, new, few, rare.

纖 **hsien 1.** Fine, delicate, small, atomlike.

僊 **hsien 1.** Genii.

羨 **hsien 4.** To like, to covet, to exceed, surplus.

綫 線 **hsien 4.** Thread.

涎 **hsien 2.** Spittle, saliva, to covet.

暹 **hsien 1.** The increasing light of the sun. Siam.

HSIN (Sin)

忻 **hsin 1.** Joy, delight, elation.

昕 **hsin 1.** Morn, dawn.

訢 **hsin 1.** Affable, gracious.

欣 **hsin 1.** Joy, to rejoice.

歆 **hsin 1.** To taste, to agree.

馨 **hsin 1.** To smell sweetly.

釁 衅 **hsin 4.** To anoint with blood. A quarrel, a feud.

辛 **hsin 1.** Bitter, toilsome, the eighth of the ten stems.

莘 **hsin 1.** A marshy plant.

新 **hsin 1.** New, fresh, recent.

薪 **hsin 1.** Fuel.

心 **hsin 1.** The heart, mind, motives, intentions, affections, centre.

尋 **hsin 2.** To search for, to marry. *Hsün.*

信 **hsin 4.** Faith, sincerity, to believe in, a message.

HSING (Sing)

性 **hsing 4.** Natural disposition, temper, property, innate.

姓 **hsing 4.** Surname.

星 **hsing 1.** A star, a spark, a spot.

腥 **hsing 1.** Rank, strong smelling.

醒 **hsing 3.** To become sober, to wake up.

惺 **hsing 1.** To perceive.

猩 **hsing 1.** The orang-outang.

省 **hsing 3.** To enquire, to examine, to perceive. *Shêng* 3.

擤 **hsing 2.** To blow the nose.

-◇-◇-

幸 **hsing 4.** Fortunate, prosperous, lucky, opportune.

倖 **hsing 4.** Fortunate, lucky.

諱 **hsing 4.** To scold.

悻 **hsing 3.** Angry, enraged.

形 形 形 } **hsing 2.** Form, shape, the body, material, manner, visage, air, to appear, to show.

邢 **hsing 2.** A place in Chihli.

刑 **hsing 2.** Torture, to castigate.

型 **hsing 2.** A mould, an example.

行 **hsing 2.** To step, to go, natural powers, perhaps.
hsing 4. Action, conduct.

杏 **hsing 4.** Apricot-tree.

興 **hsing 1.** To rise, fashion, flourishing, high spirits.

HSIU (Siu)

臭 **hsiu 4.** To smell, to scent out. *Ch'ou* 4.

糗 **hsiu 3.** Grains, food.

嗅 **hsiu 4.** To scent out.

休 **hsiu 1.** To rest, to cease, to spare, to repudiate, stop, don't, to deal gently.

烋 **hsiu 1.** To burn, crepitation.

咻 **hsiu 1.** To call out clamorously, a shriek.

朽 殀 } **hsiu 3.** Rotten, decayed, putrid.

-◇-◇-

秀 **hsiu 4.** Growing grain coming into ear, luxuriant, a licentiate.

銹 **hsiu 4.** Rust of metal.

綉 **hsiu 4.** To embroider.

羞 **hsiu 1.** Viands, delicacies, an offering, to bring forward, to feel ashamed, to blush.

饈 **hsiu 1.** Savoury food.

饈 **hsiu 1.** Delicacies, sweets.

修 **hsiu 1.** To adorn, to mend, to cultivate.

脩 **hsiu 1.** Dried meat, salary, to prepare, to regulate.

鏽 **hsiu 4.** Rust, oxides.

繡 **hsiu 4.** To embroider.

袖 **hsiu 4.** Sleeves.

宿 宿 } **hsiu 3.** Night, to lodge for the night. *Hsü* 1.

HSIUNG

凶 **hsiung 1.** Unlucky, unfortunate, sad.

兇 **hsiung 1.** Violent, cruel, savage.

匈 **hsiung 1.** The breast, the thorax.

胷 胸 } **hsiung 1.** The thorax.

洶 **hsiung 1.** A tumultuous rush.

兄 **hsiung 1.** Elder brother.

雄 **hsiung 2.** Male, brave.

熊 **hsiung 2.** Black bear.

HSÜ (Sü)

虛 虛 } **hsü 1.** Empty; vacant; vain; false; weak; useless.

噓 **hsü 1.** To exhale.

墟 **hsü 1.** Waste, wild land.

歔 **hsü 1.** To sigh.

吁 **hsü 1.** To sigh; an exclamation, alas.

盱 **hsü 1.** Rising sun.

冔 **hsü 3.** A cap used for sacrifices.

姁 **hsü 1.** Handsom, graceful.

煦 **hsü 4.** To blow; breath.

煦 **hsü 3.** To heat; to console; warm; kind.

畜 **hsü 4.** To feed; domestic animals. *Ch'u* 4.

蓄 **hsü 4.** To gather.

詡 **hsü 3.** To boast; to brag; to display.

旭 **hsü 3.** Rising sun.

許 **hsü 3.** To grant, to allow, to permit, to promise; a few.

酗 **hsü 4.** Drunkenness.

頊 **hsü 3.** Careful, attentive.

勗 **hsü 4.** To help; to encourage.

-◇-◇-

胥 **hsü 1.** Mutually; together. Constables; clerks.

壻 婿 } **hsü 2.** A son-in-law.

恤 卹 } **hsü 4.** Compassion, to pity; to give, alms.

洫 hsü 4. A trench, a channel.

序 hsü 4. A school; order, succession; preface.
戌 hsü 1. A cyclical character.
需 hsü 1. Duty, obligation, necessity.

須 hsü 1. Ought; must; necessary; to wait for; an instant.
鬚 hsü 1. Beard.

宿 hsü 1. Constellations. *Hsiu* 3.
蓿 hsü 4. Lucern.

敘 敍 } hsü 4. To arrange; in detail; to state; to narrate; to chat; preface.
徐 hsü 2. Sedate; dignified.

俗 hsü 2. Common; worldly; customs.
絮 hsü 4. Coarse silk or cotton; fleecy; garrulity.
緒 hsü 4. To connect; a conclusion; the end.
夙 hsü 4. Early, dawn. Formerly.
續 hsü 4. To continue; to succeed to.

HSÜAN (Süan)

玄 玄 } hsüan 2. Dark, profonnd, deep; abstruse, mysterious.
炫 hsüan 4. Bright, luminous.
眩 hsüan 1. Confused, dull.
泫 hsüan 2. Glistening dew drops; tears.
怰 hsüan 2. Fun, funny.
衒 hsüan 4. To brag, to display; to let out.

喧 諠 } hsüan 1. Clamour; hubbub.

楦 hsüan 4 A last.
暄 hsüan 1. Genial; pleasant.
塇 hsüan 4. Spongious.
萱 hsüan 1. *Hemerocallis.*

諼 hsüan 1. To forget; to err; to deceive.
愋 hsüan 1. Harsh, crabbed.

絢 hsüan 4. Coloured; variegated.
懸 hsüan 2. To suspend; to hang; in suspense; anxious; unlike.
軒 hsüan 1. A cart.
塤 hsüan 1. The Chinese ocarina.

-◇-◇-

宣 hsüan 1. A palace; to proclaim; to display, wide.
揎 hsüan 1. To pull up.

痠 hsüan 1. Benumbedness.
酸 hsüan 1. Vinegar, sour. Pain.

旋 hsüan 2. To turn round, to revolve; consequently, then.
璇 hsüan 2. An armillary sphere.
鏇 hsüan 4. A turning-lathe.
蜁 hsüan 3. A spiral conch.
颷 hsüan 4. A typhoon; a whirlwind.

選 hsüan 3. To select; to choose out; to elect.
筭 算 } hsüan 4. To reckon; to calculate; to estimate.
蒜 hsüan 4. Alliaceous plants.
癬 hsüan 3. Ringworm.

HSÜEH (Süeh)

血 hsüeh 3. Blood, bloody.
穴 hsüeh 2. A cave, a den, a cavern.
鞾 靴 } hsüeh 1. Boots.

-◇-◇-

薛 hsüeh 1. A proper name.
雪 hsüeh 3. Snow

HSÜN (Sün)

熏 hsün 1. Smoke; steam; to smoke; to fumigate.
勳 hsün 1. Meritorious deeds.
醺 hsün 1. Drunkness.
纁 hsün 1. Light scarlet colour.
獯 hsün 1. The Huns.
薰 hsün 1. Fragrant; to perfume.

訓 hsün 4. To instruct, to teach, te exhort, to persuade.

-◇-◇-

旬 hsün 2. A period of ten days; of ten years.
侚 hsün 4. To desire; to conform.
恂 hsün 2. Sincere, true, frank.
狥 hsün 2. To follow; to accord with.
徇 hsün 2. To follow; according to; pervading.
洵 hsün 2. Name of a river; truly, indeed.
殉 hsün 4. Suttee to bury along with the dead.
詢 hsün 2. To enquire about.
荀 hsün 2. A proper name.

尋 hsün 2. To search for; to seek; to think of; common, usual. *Hsin* 2.
循 hsün 2. To follow, to acquiesce; docile.
遜 hsün 4. Complaisant, docile; modest, humble.

汛 hsün 4. A military post, a guard house; speedily.
迅 hsün 4. Speedy, sudden, quick.
訊 hsün 4. To interrogate, to examine judicially, to chide.

巡 廵 hsün 2. To go on a circuit, to patrol.
馴 hsün 2 Tame, docile.

隼 hsün 3. A dressed falcon.
損 hsün 3. To harm; to injure.

HU

虎 hu 3. The tiger; cruelty, bravery.
唬 hu 1. To frighten.
諕 hu 1. To scare.
琥 hu 3. Amber.

乎 hu 1. hu 2. A particle of varied uses, interrogative, comparative, expletive.
呼 hu 1. To breathe out; to address, to invoke.

歔 hu 1. To breathe out.
嘑 hu 1. To roar; to howl.
滹 hu 1. Name of a river in Chihli.

撫 hu 3. To caress. *Fu* 3.
幠 hu 1. A veil, a screen, to cover.

互 hu 4. Interlocking, reciprocal, mutual.

祜 hu 4. Protection of heaven, favour.
怙 hu 4. To rely on, to presume on.
胡 hu 2. Why? what? how? Mongols.
葫 hu 2. The bottle-gourd.
鬍 hu 2. The beard.
蝴 hu 2. A butterfly.
糊 hu 2. Paste, to paste, foolish, muddled.
鞠 hu 2. A quiver.
煳 hu 2 To roast, to singe.
湖 hu 2. A lake.
猢 hu 2. A monkey.
椒 hu 2. Pepper-plant, pepper.
瑚 hu 2. Coral.
餬 hu 1. Congee, food, to feed.
衚 hu 2. A smaller street, lane.

笏 hu 1. A tablet.
囫 hu 1. Whole, entire.
曶 hu 4. Bleareduess.
忽 hu 1. To disregard, confusion, suddenly.
惚 hu 1. Confusion, distraction.
颮 hu 1. Sough of the wind.

戶 hu 4. Door or window, dwelling, family.
扈 hu 4. Retinue.
滬 hu 4 To stake. A name for Shanghai.

斛 hu 2. The Chinese bushel, holding ten pecks.
觳 hu 1. A goblet, to tremble.
狐 hu 2. The fox.

護 hu 4. To protect, to gaard.
滸 hu 3. Bank, shore.
核 hu 2. The stone or kernel of fruits *Hai* 2.
壺 hu 3. A jug, a pot.

HUA

華 hua 2. Flowers, flowery, variegated, China.
嘩 譁 hua 2. Clamour, noise.
鏵 hua 2 A plough-share.
曄 hua 4. Glim, lightning.

化 hua 4. To change, transformation, to convert.
花 hua 1. Flower, flowery, debauchery, long sightedness.

滑 hua 2. Smooth, slippery, cunning, artful.
猾 hua 2. Treacherous.
磆 hua 2. Soapstone.

話 hua 4. A word, a sentence, language.
划 hua 2. A boat, a scow.
畫 hua 4. A picture, a drawing.

HUAI

壞 huai 4. To spoil; to ruin, to destroy; vicious, depraved.
懷 huai 2. The bosom, to cherish kindly, to put in the bosom, to conceal, to think of.

槐 huai 2. A large tree, *Sophora japonica.*
踝 huai 3. The ankle.
淮 huai 2. A stream in Honan and Anhui.
獲 huai 2. To take in hunting, to catch, to obtain. *Huo* 2.

HUAN

寰 **huan 2.** Imperial domains, a closure, the universe.
鬟 **huan 2.** A slavegirl's hair done up.
繯 **huan 2.** Fine silk, to gird, to tie round.
蠉 **huan 1.** To crawl.
環 **huan 2.** A ring; a bracelet; to surround.
還 还 **huan 2.** To go back; to return, to repay; to compensate; still, further.

歡 **huan 1.** To rejoice; jolly; merry, to like.
讙 **huan 1.** To vociferate; to rouse.
驩 **huan 1.** A gentle, tractable horse; gleeful, frolicksome; to play.
貛 獾 **huan 1.** A badger.

換 **huan 4.** To remove; to change; to exchange.
喚 **huan 4.** To call out to summon; to name.
煥 **huan 4.** A flame; brightness.
瘓 **huan 4.** Sick; ill; paresis.

浣 **huan 3.** To wash; a period of ten days.
患 **huan 4.** Affliction, sorrow.
緩 **huan 3.** Slow, tardy lax, to delay.
桓 **huan 2** Pillars or stone tablets before a grave, to delay.
宦 **huan 4** A dignitary
幻 **huan 4.** Illusion, unreal, false.
豢 **huan 4** Domestic animals, to rean
逭 **huan 4.** To flee, te escape.

HUANG

皇 **huang 2.** The Emperor, imperial.
惶 **huang 2.** Afraid, nervous.
隍 **huang 2.** The moat around a city, the tutelar deity of a city.
蝗 **huang 2.** The locust.
遑 **huang 2.** Leisure, careless.
鰉 **huang 2.** The sturgeon.
煌 **huang 2.** Blazing, bright.
凰 **huang 2.** The female phœnix.

晃 **huang 3.** The full brightness of the sun, to dazzle.
愰 **huang 3** Uncertain, agitated.
幌 **huang 3.** A curtain, a screen.
熀 **huang 3.** The blaze of fire, effulgent.
鎤 **huang 3.** The sound of bells.
旗 **huang 3.** A shop-sign.

怳 **huang 3.** Disturbed, sorrowful.
眖 **huang 3.** Delirium, confused.
貺 **huang 4.** To give, to bestow, to confer on.

黃 **huang 2.** Yellow, imperial, a surname.
磺 **huang 2.** Brimstone.
璜 **huang 2.** Jade, gems.
簧 **huang 2.** A reed, a spring, to catch.
癀 **huang 2.** Jaundice.

荒 **huang 1.** Wild, unproductive, empty, blasted, a jungle, a famine.
慌 **huang 1.** Apprehensive, nervous, obscure.
謊 **huang 3.** To lie, to mislead.

HUI

囘 回 **hui 2.** To revert to, to turn back, a time, a turn, a revolution, the Moslems.
茴 **hui 2.** Fennel or caraway.
迴 廻 **hui 2.** To return, to double.
徊 **hui 2.** Undecided, irresolute.
蛔 **hui 2.** The tape-worm.

彗 **hui 4.** A broom.
慧 **hui 4.** Intelligent, quick, wise, virtuous.

穢 **hui 4.** Unclean, to defile.
濊 **hui 4.** Muddy.
譿 **hui 4.** Rumbling, to hum.

惠 **hui 4.** Kind, gracious, to be docile.
蕙 **hui 4.** A marshy orchid.
蟪 **hui 4.** A kind of cicada.

潰 **hui 4.** To rush, to flee, angry.
殨 **hui 4.** A sore, to suppurate.

卦 **hui 4.** The three upper lines of a diagram.
誨 **hui 3.** To teach, to advise.
悔 **hui 3.** To repent, to regret.
晦 **hui 4** Dark, obscure, unlucky.

會 会 **hui 4.** To meet together, to collect, to unite, a guild, a society, to know.
薈 **hui 4.** A bundle, in abundance.
繪 **hui 4.** To draw, to sketch, to embroider, to adorn.

毀 **hui 3.** To break, to injure, to spoil, to slander.

燬 **hui 3.** To burn down.

譭 **hui 3.** To slander, to defame.

輝 **hui 1.** Bright, glistering.

揮 **hui 1.** To move, to shake, to rouse, to brush away.

匯 滙 } **hui 4.** A confluence, to deposit, a check, a draft.

徽 **hui 1.** Excellent, beautiful, Nganhui.

虫 **hui 1.** A cobra.

灰 **hui 1.** Ashes, embers.

卉 **hui 4.** Plants, herbs.

隳 **hui 1.** To destroy.

麾 **hui 1.** A signal flag.

彙 **hui 4.** A porcupine, a class, a series, to classify.

賄 **hui 4.** Goods, to bribe, to hush money.

恚 **hui 4.** Anger, rage.

諱 **hui 4.** To conceal, to shun, a taboo.

HUN

昏 **hun 1.** Dusk, dark, confused.

閽 **hun 1.** An entrance.

婚 **hun 1.** To marry, marriage.

殙 **hun 1.** The dimness of death.

睧 **hun 1.** Dulness of vision.

惛 **hun 1.** Confused in mind, dull, stupid.

渾 **hun 2.** Turbid, chaotic, the whole, the mass.

腪 **hun 1.** Meat which must not be eaten on fast days.

琿 **hun 2.** A fine stone, a gem.

鼲 **hun 2.** A sort of marmot.

葷 **hun 1.** Strong smelling vegetables, forbidden to those who fast.

圂 **hun 4.** A piggery, a privy.

溷 **hun 4.** Confused, dirty, unclean, a privy.

混 **hun 1.** Confused, turbid, stupid.

餛 **hun 2.** Fritters.

䰟 魂 } **hun 2.** The soul, the manes, the vital principle.

HUNG

宏 **hung 2.** Vast, ample, spacious.

閎 **hung 2.** Vast, wide, open.

弘 **hung 2.** Large, vast, expanded, to make great, to magnify

泓 **hung 2.** Deep, mysterious.

吰 **hung 2.** To bellow.

洪 **hung 2.** An inundation, vast, immense.

哄 訌 } **hung 3.** Noise, to trick, to cheat.

衖 **hung 4.** A lane.

鬨 **hung 4.** The din of battle, to fight.

虹 **hung 2.** Rain bow.

訌 **hung 4.** Words destructive of order and peace.

紅 **hung 2.** Red.

汞 **hung 3.** Mercury, quick-silver.

哢 **hung 3.** Sound of birds.

鴻 **hung 2.** Swan, vast.

薨 **hung 1.** To die, suddenly.

轟 **hung 1.** The rumbling of carriages.

黌 **hung 2.** A school, an academy.

HUO

See Ho.

或 **huo 4.** Or, either, if, supposing that, perhaps.

惑 **huo 4.** Doubt, suspicion, unbelief, to deceive.

魊 **huo 4.** Spell, delusion.

劐 **huo 1.** To split open, to risk, to expose.

獲 **huo 2.** To catch, to get, to obtain. *Huai 2.*

擭 **huo 4.** A snare.

穫 **huo 1.** To reap the crops, harvest.

霍 **huo 3.** A sudden rain.

癨 **huo 3.** The cholera.

擢 **huo 4.** To knead, to mix up.

活 **huo 3.** To live, mobile, active, versatile.

佸 **huo 4.** To meet with, to unite. *K'uo 4.*

火 灬 } **huo 3.** Fire, flame, to burn, fever.

伙 **huo 3.** Furniture, gear.

禾 **ho 2.** Grain.

和 **ho 1.** Agreement, concord, to gather, with.

龢 **ho 2.** Harmony.

夥 **huo 3.** Numerous, a band, colleagues.

禍 **huo 4.** Misfortune, calamity.

貨 huo 4. Goods, merchandise, to deal.

豁 huo 1. Open, spacious, clear.

I

夷 i 2. A foreigner or barbarian, distant, vulgar, to kill, to feel at ease.

胰 i 2. Soap.

姨 i 2. A wife's sister, maternal aunt, a concubine.

峓 i 2. A noted hill in Corea.

恞 i 2. Pleased, well satisfied.

洟 i 2. Snivel, mucus.

倪 i 2. Young, delicate. *Ni* 2.

睨 i 4. To glance at, to spy.

輗 i 2. A yoke.

霓 i 2. A rainbow.

麑 i 2. A roe.

鬩 i 4. A quarrel.

弋 i 4. A dart, to aim at.

弌 i 1. One.

黓 i 4. Black.

驛 i 4. The government postal service, a courier.

繹 i 4. To unravel; to unfold; to explain; continuous; unceasing.

譯 i 4. To translate; to interpret.

懌 i 4. Joy; pleasure.

斁 i 4 Wearied; worn out. *Tu* 4.

倚 i 3. To lean upon; to trust to; inclined.

椅 i 3. A chair; a seat.

錡 i 3. A caldron.

欹 i 1. An exclamation.

壹 i 1. A vessel; one.

饐 i 4. Spoilt food.

懿 i 4. Admirable; suitable, excellent.

義 i 4. Duty, right, loyal, idea, meaning, purport, common, free, adopted, justice.

儀 i 2. Usages, observances, manners.

議 i 4. To consider, to deliberate upon, to discuss.

蟻 i 4. Ants.

意 i 4. A thought; an idea, a sentiment; an intention, meaning; wish, purpose.

億 i 4. A hundred thousand; numberless.

噫 i 1. An interjection; to sigh; to moan.

憶 i 4. To reflect; to call to mind, to remember.

臆 i 4. The breast, the heart; the feelings.

益 i 4. A dish filling with water; to increase; to benefit; more and more.

縊 i 4. To hang, to strangle.

溢 i 4. To overflow.

鎰 i 4. A piece of gold, a weight.

衣 i 1. Clothes.
i 4. To dress, to wear.

依 i 1. To rely on, to trust to, to conform to, to accede; according to.

裔 i 4. The train of a robe, a border, a frontier; posterity.

已 i 3. To cease, to finish, to decline; already, excess.

异 i 4. An interjection, to stop.

栘 i 2. A fruit-tree, *Aronia asiatica*.

移 i 2. To remove, to shift; to influence; to announce.

飴 i 2. Sweet cakes, sugar, a delicacy; joy.

貽 i 2. To hand down, to leave, to induce.

怡 i 2. Harmonious concord, mutual pleasure.

邑 i 4. A city.

挹 i 4. To bale out, to decant, to press.

疑 i 2. To doubt, to suspect; to fear, to dislike, similar, suppose.

擬 i 3. To compare; similar; to guess; to decide, to intend.

肄 i 4. To practise; to learn, toil, pain, sprouts.

醫 i 1. To heal, to cure; a doctor.

翳 i 1. To screen, leucoma in the eyes.

蠮 i 4. The solitary wasp or sphex.

異 i 4. Different; foreign, strange, heterodox.

翼 i 4. The wings of a bird, to shelter, te assist.

遺 i 2. To let to transmit, to bequeath.

贐 i 2. To send presents.

埶 i 4. Skill, handicraft, trade, art, to plant.

蓺 藝 i 4. To cultivate; agriculture; handicraft; trade; a law; a rule; art.

易 i 4. Easy; to be at ease to change; to transform.

蜴 i 4. A chameleon.

胰 i 2. The fat around the viscera.

鮧 i 2. A porpoise.

頤 i 2. The chin; the jaws.

佚 i 4. Ease, luxury, negligence.

軼 i 4. To rush by, to rush on, to exceed.

泆 i 4. To overflow; licentious.

亦 i 4. Also, moreover.

奕 i 4. Great, fine; to play chess.

弈 i 4. Chess.

羿 i 4. A proper name.

翌 i 4. Bright; to morrow.

翊 i 4. To assist; ready to fly.

伊 i 1. He, him, this. *I-li.* Turkestan.

洢 i 1. A river in Honan.

貤 i 2. To reward, to promote; grades, steps.

酏 i 2. Liquor, sweet wine.

訑 i 2. Arrogant, overbearing.

恞 i 1. Contemptuous.

迆 迤 i 3. To go to, to advance; to turn aside, to be wrong.

疫 i 4. Epidemic, pestilence.

役 i 4. A petty official; a satellite.

毅 i 4. Firm; intrepid; fortitude.

曳 i 4. To trail; to drag.

裔 i 4. The train of a dress.

宜 宐 i 2. Fit and right; proper; ought; should; must.

誼 i 2. Suitable; right; proper; relations.

以 i 3. To use, with, in order to; according; a prefix connotating a relation.

苡 i 3. Name of a plant; *Coix lachryma.*

乙 i 1. A cyclic character. To mark.

一 i 1. One; alike; to unite; the whole of; as soon as.

尾 i 3. A tail. *Wei* 3.

抑 i 4. To repress, to restrain, to curb; an initial particle; or, either.

彝 i 2. Offerings; rule; principle; law.

佾 i 4. A band of eight dancers.

沂 i 2. A river in Shantung.

逸 i 4. To exceed; to let loose; lust.

詣 i 4. To visit; to go to; to reach.

揖 i 1. Reverence; to bow.

矣 i 3. A final particle.

射 i 4. To dislike.

逆 i 4. To encounter, to oppose; rebellious; to conjecture.

瘞 i 4. To bury.

JAN

冉 jan 3. Tender, weak; little by little.

苒 jan 3. Tender herbage.

髯 jan 2. The beard; the whiskers.

然 jan 2. To light; thus; so; however; but.

燃 jan 2. To light a fire, to burn.

染 jan 3. To dye; to impregnate; to soil.

JANG

讓 jang 4. To cede, to yield, to give way to, to scold.

嚷 jang 3. To cry out, to scold.

攘 jang 3. To seize, to reject.

釀 jang 4. To ferment, to cause confusion or woes.

穰 jang 2. The culm of grain, abundant, prosperous.

壤 jang 3. Mould, humus, soil, a region.

禳 jang 3. To fast and pray in order to deprecate evil.

瓤 jang 2. Pulp, flesh.

㲽 jang ?. Wadding, cotton.

蘘 jang 2. *Lilium giganteum.*

JAO (Jo)

繞 jao 3. To wind round, to surround, to avoid.

遶 jao 3. To wind round, to involve, to be entangled in.

饒 jao 2. Plenty, abundance, liberal, to pardon.

弱 jao 4. Weak, feeble.

擾 jao 3. To trouble, to disturb, to tame animals.

若 jao 4. If. *Jo* 4.

JÊ (Jo)

熱 爇 jê 4. Warm, to warm.

JÊN

仁 jên 2. Humanity, benevolence, perfection.

人 jên 2. A man.

魜 jên 2. A seal.

刃 刄 jên 4. Edge blade

仞 jên 4. A measure of eight feet.

紉 jên 4. To thread (a needle).

訒 jên 4. To speak cautiously.

軔 jên 4. Bit, curb, rein.

牣 jên 4. To stuff, to fill.

靭 jên 4. Pliant, soft.

忍 jên 3. To bear patiently, to endure, fortitude, patience.

認 jên 4. To recognize, to know, to consider, to confess.

壬 jên 2. A cyclical character.

妊 jên 2. Pregnancy.

飪 jên 3. To cook.

衽 jên 4. The breast of a coat, buttoned under the right arm.

任 jên 4. An employ, an office, to bear, to tolerate, confidence, to follow, any.

姙 jên 2. Pregnancy.

袵 jên 4. The flap in front of a coat.

荏 jên 3. Creepers (plants).

恁 jên 3. To dwell upon, then.

稔 jên 3. Ripe grain, a harvest.

腍 jên 3. Well cooked food.

JÊNG

仍 jêng 2. As before, yet, still.

扔 jêng 1. To throw, to fling away.

JIH

日 jih 4. Sun, day.

JO (Jao. Jê)

若 jo 4. To be as; if, as to, to follow, to be in sympathy with, much.

惹 jo 3. To provoke, to rouse, to incite.

鄀 jo 4. Name of a place.

楉 jo 4. A kind of plum.

箬 jo 4. A variety of bamboo.

JOU

肉 jou 4. Flesh, meat, corporeal. *Ju* 4.

柔 jou 2. Soft, yielding, pliant.

揉 jou 2. To bend, to twist, to subdue.

煣 jou 3. To bend by fire or steam.

糅 jou 4. Mixed together, pap.

鞣 jou 2. Soft leather.

腬 jou 2. Tender meat.

蹂 jou 2. To trample.

JU

入 ju 4. To enter.

肉 ju 4. Flesh, meat, corporeal. *Jou* 4.

乳 ju 2. Milk, to suckle, the breasts.

女 ju 3. Thou, you. *Nü* 3.

汝 ju 3. Thou, you, your.

如 ju 2. As, like also, to go to, to desire.

茹 ju 2. Roots, to examine, to eat, to toil.

辱 ju 4. To insult; to dishonour, to defile, to humble one's self.

褥 ju 4. A thick stuffed mat, a mattress.

儒 ju 2. The literati, Confucianists.

孺 ju 2. A child, wives of officials.

濡 ju 2. To immerse, to moisten.

JUAN

輭 軟 juan 3. Soft, yielding, pliable.

梗 juan 3. The *Diospyros lotus*.

愞 juan 4. Timid, nervous.

鑂 juan 4. Ductil metal.

蝡 蠕 juan 3. To wriggle.

JUI

芮 jui 3. Plants budding, springing.

汭 jui 3. Junction of two rivers.

蜹 jui 3. Gnats.

枘 jui 4. A handle, a haft.

蕊 蕋 蘂 jui 3 Central organs of a flower.

睿 jui 4. Perspicacious, clever, shrewd.

銳 jui 4. Pointed, acute, keen.

瑞 jui 4. Precious; auspicious.

JUNG

螢 jung 2. A fire-fly. *Ying* 2.

縈 jung 2. To bind round, to reel, a circuit.

榮 jung 2. Honour, glory.

容 **jung 2.** To receive, to contain, to endure, to bear with, the air, the countenance, the face. *Yung* 2

鎔 **jung 2.** A mould; to smelt, to cast.

瑢 **jung 2.** Trinkets.

榕 **jung 2.** The banian, *Ficus indica.*

蓉 **jung 2.** The *Hibiscus mutabilis.*

庸 **jung 1.** To use, to employ, to display, to make, merit, ordinary, how? *Yung* 1.

傭 **jung 1.** A hireling, to hire, just, impartial. *Yung* 1.

慵 **jung 2.** Indolent, easy-going.

戎 **jung 2.** Weapons, arms; soldiers. You, your. To assist. Barbarians.

絨 **jung 2.** Velvet.

毧 **jung 2.** Down. Fur.

宂 冗 **jung 3.** Affairs, duties, extra, supernumerary.

融 **jung 2.** To melt, to alloy, cash. *Yung* 2.

氄 **jung 3.** Down.

茸 **jung 2.** Thick, dense, luxuriant.

KA

戞 **ka 1.** A lance. A scamp.

嘎 **ka 1.** Laughing, cackling.

蛤 **ka 2.** A clam. *Ko* 2.

峆 **ka 2.** A mound. *Ko* 2.

凸 **ka 3.** Convex.

紇 **ka 1.** A knot.

疙 **ka 1.** A tumour.

痂 **ka 1.** A scab. *Chia* 1.

KAI

蓋 葢 盖 **kai 4.** To cover, a covering, a roof, to build; for, since.

顡 **kai 4.** The vertex.

襶 **kai 4.** A cloak.

該 **kai 1.** Must, ought.

賅 **kai 1.** To give; supplies.

垓 **kai 1.** Bounds, limits.

槩 概 **kai 4.** To level, to adjust, altogether, generally.

漑 **kai 4.** To wash, to water.

匄 丐 **kai 4.** To ask alms, to beg, a mendicant.

改 **kai 3.** To change, to alter, another.

K'AI

愷 **k'ai 3.** Good, brave, zealous.

鎧 **k'ai 3.** An armour.

剴 **k'ai 3.** A scythe, to mow down.

凱 **k'ai 3.** A victory, the triumphant return of an army, joy, a minister.

慨 **k'ai 4.** Generous, loyal, noble-minded, worried.

開 **k'ai 1.** To open, to begin, to write out, boiling.

楷 **k'ai 3.** A model, a pattern, the classic style of Chinese characters.

KAN

甘 **kan 1.** Sweet, agreeable, winsome, voluntary.

苷 **kan 1.** Liquorice.

疳 **kan 1.** Gingivitis.

紺 **kan 4.** A purple colour.

泔 **kan 1.** Slops.

柑 **kan 1.** An orange.

𩚵 **kan 1.** Sweets.

干 **kan 1.** A shield, a trunk, a stem, to offend.

忓 **kan 1.** Concerned, anxious.

衦 **kan 4.** To smooth down.

杆 **kan 1.** A stick, a post, railings.

肝 **kan 1.** The liver.

旰 **kan 4.** Sunset, dusk.

竿 **kan 1.** A bamboo stake.

趕 赶 **kan 3.** To pursue, to follow after; to eject, quickly, when.

稈 **kan 3.** The stalk of millet, hay.

桿 **kan 1.** A pole, a handle.

幹 **kan 4.** The trunk of a tree, a tree, a stem; affairs, skilful, capable.

乾 **kan 1.** Dry, clean.

敢 **kan 3.** To dare, to venture, presumptuous.

澉 **kan 3.** To wash.

橄 **kan 3.** The Olive.

感 **kan 3.** To influence, to be affected by, to be moved, to excite.

灨 **kan 4.** A river in Kiangsi.

K'AN

堪 **k'an 1.** To bear, to sustain, to be capable, fit.

勘 **k'an 4.** To investigate, to examine.

砍 **k'an 3.** To cut, to chop.

欿 **k'an 3.** Reserve, modesty.

坎 **k'an 3.** A pit, a hole, a snare, a pun.

闞 / 矙 **k'an 3.** To spy, to watch.

看 **k'an 4.** To look at, to examine, to watch.

龕 **k'an 1.** A niche for an idol.

侃 **k'an 3.** Grave, dignified.

衎 **k'an 4** A feast, pleased, contented.

刊 **k'an 1.** To carve, to cut, to engrave.

KANG

岡 / 崗 **kang 1.** A mound. A sentry-box.

剛 **kang 1.** Hard, unyielding, just now, recently.

綱 **kang 1.** Rope of a net, regulation, law.

鋼 **kang 1.** Steel, hard.

⿰缶岡 **kang 1.** An earthen jar.

杠 **kang 1.** A porter's pole.

缸 **kang 1.** A jar with wide mouth.

肛 **kang 1.** The rectum.

槓 **kang 4.** A frame to bear a coffin.

罡 **kang 1.** The four stars of the Dipper, ; the four guardians of Buddhist temples.

繮 / 韁 **kang 1.** A tether.

K'ANG

亢 **k'ang 4.** Violent, excessive.

炕 **k'ang 4.** A brick bed warmed by a stove.

抗 **k'ang 4.** To oppose, to resist.

忼 **k'ang 3.** Deceived, annoyed, disappointed.

伉 **k'ang 4.** To match, a companion.

匟 **k'ang 4.** The divan of a guest-chamber.

康 **k'ang 1.** Peace, repose, prosperity.

慷 **k'ang 3.** Generous, magnanimous.

糠 / 穅 **k'ang 1.** Chaff, husks of grain.

扛 **k'ang 2.** To carry on shoulders. To bear.

KAO

告 **kao 4.** To tell, to announce to, to indict.

誥 **kao 4.** To announce to, an edict.

郜 **kao 3.** Name of a place.

高 / 髙 **kao 1.** High, lofty, noble, eminent, your, in direct address.

膏 **kao 1.** Fat, ointment, a plaster.

槀 / 槁 **kao 3.** Decayed wood, dry, rotten, withered.

稾 / 稿 **kao 3.** Straw, a sketch, a draft.

藁 **kao 3.** Straw, a rough draft.

皜 **kao 3.** Whiteness, brightness. *Hao* 3.

縞 **kao 3.** Plain white, undyed, simple.

篙 **kao 1.** A boat-hook.

羔 **kao 1.** A lamb, a kid.

餻 **kao 1.** Cakes.

糕 **kao 1.** Sweets.

皋 臯 皐 **kao 1.** High, eminent.
kao 1. High, eminent. A proper name.

K'AO

考 / 攷 **k'ao 3.** Aged, longevity, ancestors, to examine.

烤 **k'ao 3.** To toast, to heat.

拷 **k'ao 3.** To put to the question, to torture.

銬 **k'ao 4.** Irons, fetters.

酷 **k'ao 4.** Cruelty, very, extremely. *K'u* 4.

焅 **k'ao 4.** Hot air, to dry.

靠 **k'ao 4.** To lean on, to trust, near to.

熇 **k'ao 3.** Hot, to warm.

犒 **k'ao 4.** Bounty money, to feast, to regale.

K'Ê

刻 **k'ê 1.** To carve, to chisel. *K'o.*

克 **k'ê 1.** To bear. *K'o* 1.

KÊN

亙亘 kên 4. A border, a limit, since, till.

艮 kên 4. To resist, obstinate.

根 kên 1. Roots, origin, cause, a base.

跟 kên 1. The heel, to follow, with, to.

K'ÊN

齦 k'ên 3. To gnaw.

狠 k'ên 3. To gnaw. *Hence.*

懇 k'ên 3. To beg, to supplicate.

墾 k'ên 3. To open new land, to plough.

肯 k'ên 3. To be willing, to assent.

掯 k'ên 3. To annoy, to worry.

KÊNG

更㪅 kêng 4. More, further.
kêng 1. To change, to alter.
kêng 1. A night watch. *Ching* 1

梗 kêng 3. Thorns, opposition, a whole, an outline.

哽 kêng 3. Choking, sobbing.

埂 kêng 3. A ditch or channel.

綆 kêng 3. A well-rope.

耿 kêng 3. Constant, virtuous.

羹 kêng 1. A ragout.

庚 kêng 1. A cyclical character, age.

莖 kêng. Stalks.

頸 kêng 3. The nape of the neck.

K'ÊNG

頃 k'êng 3. A moment. *Ch'ing* 3.

傾 k'êng 1. Aslant, inclined, to overturn, to pour out.

坑 k'êng 1. A pond, a pool.

阬 k'êng 1. A pit, a hole, to entrap, to ruin.

樫 k'êng 1. A proper name. Obstinate.

硜 k'êng 1. The tinkling of gems.

鏗 k'êng 1. The jingling of metals.

KO

各 ko 3. Each, every.

格 ko 2. To reach, to examine, a rule, a pattern.

胳骼 ko 1. The arm.

蛒 ko 4. Dung-beetle

閣 ko 2. A council-chamber, the court, a cupboard.

擱 ko 1. To put down, to differ, to support, to dispute.

跎 ko 1. To jolt; to bump.

虼 ko 4. A flea.

忔 ko 4 Displeasure, disgust.

紇 ko 1. A knot.

玫 ko 1. A flaw.

疙 ko 1. A boil, sore.

峆 ko 2. A knoll. *Ka* 2.

蛤 ko 2. A clam. *Ka* 2.

鴿 ko 1. A domestic pigeon, a dove.

隔 ko 2. A partition, a shelf, to interpose, next to. *Chieh* 4.

槅 ko 2. A screen.

膈 ko 2. The diaphragm.

嗝 ko 2. Spasm, to hiccough.

哥 ko 1. An elder brother.

歌謌 ko 1. To sing, a song.

鴚 ko 1. A parrot.

哿 ko 1. A quay.

革 ko 2. Raw hide, to flay, to degrade.

個箇个 ko 2. An individual or thing, a classifier, this, this one.

戈 ko 1. A spear. *Kuo* 1.

割 ko 1. To cut.

槨 ko 3. The outer coffin.

葛 ko 3. *Pueraria phaseoloides,* a textile.

K'O

可 k'o 2. Convenient, proper, can, may, to permit.

齣 k'o 4. To crunch with the teeth.

珂 k'o 4. Quartz gem.

軻 k'o 1. Name of Mencius.

砢 k'o 1. A heap of stones.

坷 k'o 3. Uneven, rough, unfortunate.

敂 k'o 3. To knock, to beat, to thump.

苛 k'o 3. Small plants, petty, trifle.

疴 k'o 4. Pain, sickness.

柯 k'o 1. A proper name.

課 k'o 4. A task.

稞 k'o 4, Grain.

錁 k'o 4. An ingot.

堁 k'o 4. A clod ot clay.

騍 k'o 4. Female of horses, mules, etc.

棵 k'o 4. Numerative of trees.

顆 k'o 1. Numerative of small round things.

括 k'o 4. To envelop; to embrace; to include. *K'uo* 4.

适 k'o 4. To make haste. *K'uo* 4.

佸 k'o 4. To cooperate. *K'uo* 4.

闊 k'o 4. Large, vast, liberal. *K'uo* 4.

科 k'o 1. To measure, a degree. Science.

蝌 k'o 1. A tadpole.

刻 k'o 1. To earve.
k'o 4. A quarter of an hour.

欬 咳 k'o 2. To cough. *Hai* 4.

頦 k'o 1. The chin.

恪 k'o 4. Reverent. *Ch'iao* 4.

客 k'o 4. A guest; a dealer; a stranger. *Ch'ieh* 4.

克 k'o 4. Can, able; to be fit for; to sustain; to subdue, to repress. *K'ê* 1.

剋 尅 k'o 1. To subdue to overcome. *K'ê* 1.

磕 k'o 1 To knock.

榼 k'o 2. A wooden cup to hold spirits.

渴 k'o 3. Thirsty, parched.

涸 k'o 4. Dried.

KOU

勾 kou 1. A mark, to hook on.

抅 kou 1. To point a wall.

鈎 鉤 kou 1. A hook; to hook; to detain.

狗 kou 3. A dog.

枸 kou 3. A spinous lemon-tree.

够 kou 4. To suffice, enough.

苟 kou 3. Grass; if, if so; impromptu; carelessly.

垢 kou 4. Dirty; sordid, immorality.

姤 kou 4. To pair, to copulate.

構 kou 4. To construct; to unite; to copulate.

媾 kou 4. Love; sexual intercourse.

遘 kou 4. To meet with; to happen.

搆 kou 4. To reach up to.

溝 kou 1. A drain; a ditch; a moat.

購 kou 4. To buy.

覯 kou 4. To meet one suddenly; to occur.

篝 kou 1. A bamboo frame.

彀 kou 4. To draw a bow to its full stretch; enough; adequate.

K'OU

口 k'ou 3. The mouth. Numerative of persons, etc.

扣 k'ou 4. To strike, to knock; to fix, to close, to cover; to seize; to deduct.

犳 k'ou 3. Domestic animal.

絇 k'ou 4. A knot.

鈕 k'ou 4. A button.

叩 k'ou 4. To knock; to tap.

摳 k'ou 1. To raise; to feel for; to dig.

瞘 k'ou 1. Deep sunken eyes.

寇 寇 k'ou 4. To rob; brigandage.

蔻 k'ou 4. The seeds of cardamoms.

KU

古 ku 3. Ancient, old.

罟 ku 3. A net, involved.

辜 ku 1. A fault; to hinder others; ungrateful.

故 ku 4. The cause or reason of a thing; consequently; on purpose; old; to die.

估 ku 1. To estimate, to reckon; to set a price on, second-hand.

沽 ku 1. To trade in, to buy and sell.

酤 ku 1. To deal in spirits.

跍 ku 1. To squat.

牯 ku 3. A bull.

羖 ku 3. A ram or ewe.

軲 ku 1. A wheel; to revolve.

蛄 ku 1. The mole-cricket.

咕 ku 1. To gurgle.

姑 ku 1. A polite term for females, a young lady, a paternal aunt, husband s sister, Buddhist nun, to tolerate. *Hence.*

菇 ku 1. A mush-room, a bud

固 ku 4. Strong, firm, lasting. *Hence.*

錮 ku 4. To stop, to restrain.

涸 ku 4. Hard frozen.

痼 ku 4. A chronic disease.

盬 ku 3. Salt pond; to care for

觚 ku 1. A wine-vase; angular, vicious.

孤 ku 1. Fatherless; no protector; solitary.

菰 ku 1. The eatable *Hydropyrum*.

箍 ku 1. To hoop, to draw tight.

骨 ku 2. Bones.

搰 ku 4. To trouble, to try, to dig.

穀 ku 3. A sort of paper mulberry.

穀 ku 3. Millet grain; corn.

轂 ku 3. The nave or hub of a wheel.

雇 ku 4. To hire, to borrow.

僱 ku 4. To hire, to borrow.

顧 ku 4. To look after, to regard, to consider.

鼓 皷 ku 3. A drum, drumshaped, bulging, to excite.

臌 ku 3. Dropsical.

瞽 ku 3. Blind.

鵠 ku 3. The snow-goose, a target.

梏 ku 4. Manacles, fetters.

谷 ku 3. A valley, a ravine.

股 ku 3. The upper part of the thigh, a slice, a share.

賈 ku 3. A shopman, to traffic. *Chia* 3.

蠱 ku 3. Worms. A slow poison. Dropsy.

箍 ku 1. A circlet, to hoop.

K'U

苦 k'u 1. Sow-thistle, bitter, painful, afflictions.

枯 k'u 1. Dry wood, decayed, withered.

骷 k'u 1. A skeleton, a skull.

酷 k'u 4. Tyrannical, cruel, very, extremely. *K'ao* 4.

嚳 k'u 1. A proper name.

庫 k'u 4. A storehouse; a shop.

褲 k'u 4. Trowsers; pantaloons.

哭 k'u 1. To weep bitterly

窟 k'u 1. A cave, a hole.

KUA

瓜 kua 1. Cucurbitaceous plants.

刮 kua 1. To slice.

颳 kua 1. To blow, as the wind.

刮 kua 1. To scrape, to shave off.

鴰 kua 1. A crow, a rook.

剮 kua 3. To cut a criminal in pieces.

蝸 kua 1. A garden slug, a snail.

喎 kua 3. Awry, distorted.

卦 kua 4 To divine, the diagrams.

褂 kua 4. An outer coat.

掛 kua 4. To hang up, in suspense; a numerative.

寡 kua 3. Alone, forlorn, a widow, few, seldom; I, the sovereign.

K'UA

誇 k'ua 1. To boast, conceited.

跨 k'ua 4. To straddle, to step across.

胯 k'ua 4. The thighs; to bestride.

姱 k'ua 1. Pretty; vain.

KUAI

拐 kuai 3. To deceive, to seduce, a kidnapper, to limp.

柺 kuai 3. A staff.

摑 kuai 1. To slap.

蟈 kuai 1. A green cricket.

膕 kuai 1. The calf of the leg.

虢 kuai 2. A proper name.

怪 恠 kuai 4. Strange, monstrous, to dislike, to blame.

乖 kuai 1. Strange, odd.

鄶 kuai 4. Name of a place.

K'UAI

澮 k'uai 4. A drain, a trench.

獪 k'uai 4. Crafty, mischievous.

膾 k'uai 4. Minced meat.

噲 k'uai 4. To gulp down, greedy.

快 k'uai 4. Pleasure, cheerful, quick, speedy, sharp, keen.

筷 k'uai 4. Chopsticks.

塊 k'uai 4. A clod, a lump.

擓 k'uai 3. To rub, to smooth, to carry.

蒯 k'uai 3. Rush.

KUAN

官 **kuan 1.** An official, a mandarin, public.

管 **kuan 3.** A tube, a clarinet, to regulate, to govern.

菅 **kuan 1.** Coarse textile fibres.

錧 **kuan 3.** An office, a hall, a school.

館 **kuan 3.** A restaurant, a club-house, a school-room, etc.

棺 **kuan 1.** An inner coffin.

脘 **kuan 3.** A duct in the body, œsophagus.

倌 **kuan 1** The Emperor's charioteer.

悺 **kuan 3.** Sorrow, sadness.

觀 观 } **kuan 1.** To consider, to examine. **kuan 4.** An observatory, a Taoist convent.

鸛 **kuan 4.** A heron.

灌 **kuan 4.** To water, to pour, to force one to drink.

罐 **kuan 4.** A jar, a mug.

鑵 **kuan 4.** A box.

懽 **kuan 4.** Cares, pain.

貫 **kuan 4.** To traverse, to go through, a string, a series, habitual.

慣 **kuan 4.** Habitual, addicted to.

莞 **kuan 1.** Rush, reed.

筦 **kuan 3.** A flute.

關 關 関 } **kuan 1.** To bar the door, a barrier; a custom-house, to bear upon, involving, results, connected. *Kuan-ti* the Chinese god of war.

鰥 **kuan 1.** A huge fish. A bachelor, a widower.

冠 **kuan 1.** A cap, a crown, a crest.

盥 **kuan 4.** To wash the hands.

祼 **kuan 4.** A libation.

斡 **kuan 3.** To turn, a handle by which to turn a machine.

K'UAN

款 欵 } **k'uan 2.** Sincere, true, liberal, to treat well, an article, a sum.

寬 **k'uan 1.** Large, indulgent; to forbear.

KUANG

光 **kuang 1.** Light, bright, glory, naked, only.

洸 **kuang 1.** Water sparkling in the sun.

胱 **kuang 1.** The bladder.

廣 **kuang 3.** Broad; large, liberal.

逛 **kuang 4.** To stroll, to ramble.

K'UANG

狂 **k'uang 2.** Mad, wild.

誑 **k'uang 2.** Lies, to deceive.

匡 **k'uang 1.** Regular, to rule, to help.

框 **k'uang 4.** Big branches, the frame of a thing.

眶 **k'uang 4.** The eye-socket.

誆 **k'uang 2.** To deceive.

筐 **k'uang 1.** A basket.

曠 **k'uang 4.** A vacant waste, empty, spacious, lazy, to waste.

壙 **k'uang 4.** A vault; a grave. A desert.

懬 **k'uang 4.** Deception.

兄 况 } **k'uang 4.** Moreover, a fortiori; circumstances.

KUEI (KUI)

圭 **kuei 1.** Jade sceptre, insignia of rank.

珪 **kuei 1.** A sceptre.

桂 **kuei 4.** The cinnamon tree.

邽 **kuei 1.** Name of a place.

閨 **kuei 1.** The door to the women's apartments; girls.

宄 **kuei 3.** Traitors, villains.

軌 **kuei 3.** The axle of a wheel, the rut, a track, a routine.

劊 **kuei 4.** To behead; an executioner.

禬 **kuei 4.** To pray.

檜 **kuei 4.** Chinese juniper.

貴 **kuei 4.** Honourable; esteemed; prized; dear.

憒 **kuei 4.** Troubled; anxious.

櫃 **kuei 2.** A press; a box.

詭 **kuei 3.** To deceive; to pretend.

跪 **kuei 4.** To kneel.

鬼 **kuei 3.** Spirits; a ghost; devils.

瑰 **kuei 4.** The rose.

規 **kuei 1.** A pair of compasses, a rule, custom.

晷 **kuei 3.** A sundial; time.

歸 帰 归 } **kuei 1.** To return; to send back; to restore; to belong to; addition.

龜 **kuei 1.** A tortoise.

癸 **kuei 3.** A cyclical character.

K'UEI

郰 k'uei 2. Name of different places.

暌 k'uei 2. In opposition; separated; distant.

睽 k'uei 2. To squint.

揆 k'uei 2. To consider; to calculate.

葵 k'uei 2. The mallow.

魁 k'uei 2. A giant; chief; eminent, great.

餽 k'uei 4. A present of victuals.

愧 k'uei 4. Ashamed, bashful.

饋 k'uei 4. Provisions, victuals.

墤 k'uei 4. A heap.

撌 k'uei 4. To draw.

簣 蕢 k'uei 4. A basket.

匱 k'uei 4. Wearied, exhausted.

奎 k'uei 2. The stride made by a man, a constellation.

闚 窺 k'uei 2. To peep, to watch, to spy.

盔 k'uei 1. A helmet, a porringer.

夔 k'uei 2. A mountain goblin. A proper name.

虧 k'uei 1. To harm, to injure, wanting, defect.

喟 k'uei 4. To breathe heavily, to sigh.

逵 k'uei 2. Cross-roads, a thoroughfare.

KUN

棍 kun 4. A stick, a rowdy.

輥 kun 3. To turn round, to revolve.

袞 袞 kun 3. Imperial robe, court robes.

滾 kun 3. To boil; to roll, to move back.

鯀 kun 3. A great fish; a proper name.

K'UN

困 k'un 4. Distress, poverty, disconcerted.

綑 k'un 3. To bind, to tie.

捆 k'un 3. To tie up, a bunch.

稛 k'un 3. A sheaf.

梱 k'un 3. The threshold.

悃 k'un 3. Sincere, loyal, true.

閫 k'un 4. Women's apartments.

昆 k'un 1. Elder brothers.

崑 k'un 1. The range of K'unlün mountains, between the desert of Gobi and Thibet.

坤 k'un 1. What is inferior, the earth, the moon, the wife, the minister, compliant.

壼 k'un 3. Corridors, gynæceum.

髡 k'un 1. To shave the head.

KUNG

共 kung 4. Generally, all, in common.

供 kung 1. To offer, to expose, a testimony, an avowal.

拱 kung 3. To bow, with the hands before the breast, an arch, a vault.

栱 kung 3. A pillar.

珙 kung 3. An official sceptre.

恭 kung 1. To respect, to venerate, to revere.

龔 kung 1. To offer; a cult.

工 kung 1. Work, labour, time of work.

攻 kung 1. To assault, to attack.

功 kung 1. Merit, meritorious service.

汞 kung 3. Quick-silver.

貢 kung 4. Tribute, taxes. *Hence*

蟥 kung 3. To burrow as a mole; to stir up.

公 kung 1. Common, public, official, usual, just, male, duke, sir.

蚣 kung 1. Scolopendra.

弓 kung 1. A bow, a measure of five or six cubits.

躬 kung 1. Body, person, to bow.

宮 kung 1. A palace, castration, a eunuch, constellations.

腔 kung 1. Castration.

鑛 礦 kung 3. A mine, mineralogy.

肱 kung 1. The humerus, to help.

鞏 kung 3. A proper name.

觥 kung 1. A cup made of horn.

K'UNG

空 k'ung 1. Empty, void.
k'ung 4. A space, blank.

控 k'ung 4. To draw, to rein in, to accuse.

悾 k'ung 1. Simple, guileless.

恐 k'ung 3. To fear, to be afraid, perhaps.

孔 k'ung 3. The surname of Confucius.

KUO

果 **kuo 3.** Fruit, really, effects, consequences.

菓 **kuo 3.** Fruit, cakes.

裹 **kuo 3.** To wrap up, to bind, bandage.

鍋 **kuo 1.** A pot, a boiler.

過 过 **kuo 4.** To pass by, past, transgression, fault.

攫 **kuo 4.** To seize, to capture.

戄 **kuo 4.** Frightened, surprised.

籰 **kuo 4.** A reel.

郭 **kuo 4.** An outer wall of fortification.

椁 槨 **kuo 3.** An outer coffin.

戈 **kuo 1.** A lance, a spear. *Ko* **1.**

國 国 **kuo 3.** A nation, a country, a State.

K'UO

鞹 **k'uo 4.** Curried leather.

廓 **k'uo 4.** To cut off, great, to enlarge.

崞 **k'uo 4.** A ravine, a gorge.

擴 **k'uo 4.** To stretch, to expand.

聒 **k'uo 4.** Noise of talking, clamour.

佸 **k'uo 4.** To cooperate, to meet. *K'o* **4.**

括 **k'uo 4.** To envelop, to embrace, ro include. *K'o* **4.**

适 **k'uo 4.** To hasten. *K'o* **4.**

闊 **k'uo 4.** Large, liberal. *K'o* **4.**

LA

蠟 **la 4.** Wax, a candle.

𥢊 **la 1.** Empty, sterile.

䊕 **la 1.** Coarse, vile.

鑞 **la 4.** Tin.

䙉 **la 4.** Mean apparel.

邋 **la 4.** To omit, neglected, dirty.

臘 **la 4.** The winter solstice sacrifice, the 12th moon.

剌 **la 2.** To cut.

喇 **la 3.** A sound.

瘌 **la 2.** A scar.

拉 **la 1.** To draw, to pull, etc.

辣 **la 4.** Acrid, biting.

LAI

來 **lai 2.** To come, the future.

賚 **lai 4.** To give, to bestow.

萊 **lai 2.** Weed.

箂 **lai 2.** A variety of bamboo.

賴 **lai 4.** To rely upon, to trust to, to accuse, to repudiate.

癩 **lai 4.** Leprosy.

LAN

爛 **lan 4.** Cooked thoroughly, worn out, disaggregated.

攔 **lan 2.** To hinder; to embarrass, to obstruct.

欄 **lan 2.** A railing; a balustrade.

瀾 **lan 2.** Billows; waves.

瓓 **lan 4.** The lustre of a gem.

蘭 **lan 2.** Orchideous plants.

襤 **lan 2.** Ragged garments, *lan-lü.*

㦨 **lan 4.** Greedy, covetous.

濫 **lan 4.** To overflow, profuse, lawless.

籃 **lan 2.** A basket.

藍 **lan 2.** Blue, indigo.

𩯭 **lan 2.** Dishevelled hair.

覽 **lan 3.** To inspect; to behold. *Hence*

攬 **lan 3.** To grasp; o interfere with; to monopolise.

纜 **lan 3.** A rope, a hawser.

欖 **lan 3.** The olive.

懶 **lan 3.** Lazy; remiss; idleness.

婪 **lan 2.** Covetous, avaricious.

嵐 **lan 2.** Mist; fog.

LANG

狼 **lang 2.** The wolf.

蜋 **lang 2.** Different kinds of insects.

浪 **lang 4.** Profligate waves.

琅 **lang 2.** White cornelian.

踉 **lang 1.** To jump.

朗 **lang 3.** Clear, bright.

郎 **lang 2.** A gentleman; a term of respect. *Hence*

瑯 **lang 2.** Enamel, *fa-lang.*

榔 **lang 2.** Arec-palm, *ping-lang.*

螂 **lang 2.** A dung-beetle, a mantis.

廊 **lang 2.** A verandah; a corridor.

LAO

老 lao 3. Old, to become old.
姥 lao 3. The mother of my mother.
狫 lao 3. Inhabitants of the Laos.
荖 lao 3. Betel.

雒 lao 4. Name of a place.
酪 lao 3. Koumiss.
絡 lao 4. Silk not yet reeled; fibres.
烙 lao 4. A branding-iron; to burn in.
洛 lao 4. Name of a river.
落 lao 4. The fall of the leaf; to obtain; an abode.

勞 lao 2. To toil; labour; trouble.
撈 lao 2. To fish up; to drag out of water.
嘮 lao 2. To chatter.
癆 lao 2. Wasting away from toil or anxiety; phthisis.

牢 lao 2. A stable for cattle; a jail; firm; strong.
哰 lao 2. To scold.

潦 lao 4. A flood, to overflow.
樂 lao 4. Joy, to rejoice. *Yao* 4.

LEI

耒 lei 3. A harrow.
誄 lei 3. To eulogise the dead; prayers.

雷 lei 2. Thunder.
擂 lei 2. To pound; to beat.
蠕 lei 2. An edible clam.
鐳 lei 2. Bronzes; copper coins.
瘤 lei 3. Pimples.

累 lei 3. To tie; to bind, to implicate in, to harass.
縲 lei 3. To bind with ropes.
瘰 lei 3. Scrofulous glands.

擂 lei 4. To pound, to crush.
儡 lei 3. Puppets.
壘 lei 3. A wall, masonry.
罍 lei 2. A wine jar.
纍 lei 2. To creep, to cling to. *Hence.*
儽 lei 2. Tired out, exhausted.
虆 lei 3. A basket.

類 lei 4. A species; a kind, a class.
肋 lei 4. The ribs, the side of a body.
羸 lei 2. Lean, thin, emaciated; to destroy.
勒 lei 1. A bridle, the reins; to restrain.
淚 lei 4. Tears.
磊 lei 3. A heap of stones.

LENG

睖 lêng 4. To look fixedly.
棱 稜 } lêng 2. An edge, a corner.

楞 lêng 2. A sharp edge, a crest.
冷 lêng 3. Cold, chilly.

LI

摛 li 2. To stretch, to spread.
醨 li 2. Dregs.
褵 li 2. A sash.
璃 li 1. A vitreous substance.
禠 li 2. Good omens.
漓 li 2. Water dripping.
糐 li 2. Slimy, sticky.
離 li 2. To separate, to leave, distance, distinction. *Hence*
籬 li 2. A ladle.

麗 li 4. Antelopes; elegant, graceful.
儷 li 4. A companion, a mate.
邐 li 3. To advance, successively.
纚 li 2. A rope, a cable.
蠡 li 2. A milliped.
驪 li 2. A fleet horse.
鸝 li 2. The oriole.
酈 li 4. A place in Shantung.

栗 li 4. The chestnut-tree; care, dignified.
慄 li 4. Fear, terror, to tremble.
搮 li 4. To smooth.

澧 li 3. A river in Hunan.
醴 li 3. Must, newly distilled spirits.
鱧 li 3. A mullet.
禮 礼 } li 3. Ceremony; etiquette; presents, worship.

戾 li 4. To transgress, to come to; to stop.
唳 li 4. The cry of a heron, wild goose, etc.
悷 li 4. Sadness.

礫 li 4. Small stones, gravel.

瓅 li 4. The lustre of gems.

櫟 li 4. A scrubby oak, *Quercus serrata.*

曆 歷 li 4. Astronomy, calendar.

歷 歴 li 4. Idea of duration, of succession, to array in order, to experience.

瀝 li 4. A drop, to drip.

力 li 4. Strength; energy.

荔 栛 li 4. The *Nephelium lichih.*

立 li 4. To stand erect; to rear, to found; presently.

粒 li 4. A kernel, a grain.

苙 li 4. A pen, a yard.

笠 li 4. A conical hat of straw.

泣 li 4. Rain-water.

莅 蒞 li 4. To overlook, to exercise an office, to govern.

厲 li 4. A whetstone, bad, cruel.

礪 li 4. A whetstone.

糲 li 4. Coarse, husks.

濿 li 4. A ford, to ford.

蠣 li 4. Rock oyster.

勵 li 4. To stimulate, to incite.

利 li 4. Sharp; witty; profit; interest on money.

俐 li 4. Clever; active.

唎 li 4. A sound.

痢 li 4. Dysentery.

莉 li 4. The white jasmine.

棃 梨 li 2. A pear-tree.

黧 li 2. A dark dun colour.

犂 犁 li 2. A plough; the Thibetan yak. *I-li.*

黎 li 2. Black. *Hence*

藜 li 2. Thistles.

里 li 3. A hamlet; the third of a mile.

理 li 3. Veins; striæ; to rule; to manage; abstract right.

狸 li 2. The fox.

貍 li 2. The wild cat.

娌 li 2. The wives of brothers; sisters-in-law.

鯉 li 3. The carp.

哩 li 1. A final sound.

裏 裡 li 3. Inside; lining; inner.

釐 厘 兀 li 2. To regulate; to give; the thousandth part of a tael.

嫠 li 2. A widow.

氂 li 2. The yak of Thibet.

氂 li 2. Tail of a yak.

例 li 4. Rule, example.

履 li 3. Shoes; to walk.

李 li 3. A plum-tree.

吏 li 4. Magistrates, officers.

詈 li 4. To scold about; to rail at.

罹 li 2. Sorrow, grief; to suffer; to incur.

蠡 li 4. A wood-borer.

隸 隷 隸 li 4. Attached to; belonging; underlings; government; administration; the square style.

LIA

倆 lia 3. Two, of persons.

LIANG

兩 両 两 liang 3. Two, both, an ounce; a tael.

輛 liang 4. Numerative of chairs, carts, etc.

魎 liang 3. A sprite.

良 liang 2. Good; virtuous; natural gifts.

粮 liang 2. Grain, food.

量 liang 2. To measure, to consider.

糧 liang 2. Rations; food; grain.

粱 liang 2. Sorghum.

梁 liang 2. Ridge pole, beam.

涼 凉 liang 2. Freshness; to cool.

晾 liang 4. To dry in the sun; to aerate.

悢 liang 2. To grieve; melancholy.

諒 liang 4. Faithful; to trust; to consider; to excuse.

輬 liang 2. A hearse.

亮 liang 4. Clear, luminous; bright.

凌 liang 2. Ice. *Ling* 2.

LIAO

撩 liao 1. To grasp; to raise; to stir up.

憭 liao 3. Cheerful.

譤 liao 2. Cunning of speech.

蟟 liao 2. The cicada.

繚 liao 2. To bind, to wrap, a turn.

燎 liao 2. Fire, to burn, a signal-light.

獠 liao 2. To hunt at night with torches.

墝 liao 4. A surrounding wall.

瞭 liao 3. Bright, shining.

橑 liao 2. A rafter.

僚 liao 2. A companion, a colleague.

鐐 liao 4. Fetters.

瞭 liao 3. A clear eye, clear.

寮 liao 2. A companion, a petty official, a window.

屪 liao 2. The penis.

療 liao 2. To cure, to heal.

遼 liao 2. Distant, a river in Manchuria.

畧 略 liao 4. Limits, disposition, a plan, a little, to make little account of.

掔 liao 4. To lay down, to let, to take.

漻 liao 2. Deep and clear.

鄝 liao 3. Name of a place.

寥 liao 2. Waste, wast.

廖 liao 4. A proper name.

蓼 liao 3. Waterpepper, bitter experience.

了 liao 3. Fixed, concluded, done.

聊 liao 2. To depend on, to help, a little.

料 liao 4. To estimate, to judge, to reckon, to dispose, materials. stuff, pulse for animals, colored glass.

掠 liao 4. To rob, to plunder, to flog.

LIEH

擸 lieh 4. To draw.

儠 lieh 4. Strong, robust.

獵 lieh 4. To hunt, the chase.

躐 lieh 4. To skip over.

列 lieh 4. To arrange, a series.

咧 lieh 1. To grimace.

悧 lieh 4. Anxious.

趔 lieh 4. To stumble.

烈 lieh 4. Burning, fiery, virtuous, glorious.

裂 lieh 4. To crack, to split, a schism.

LIEN

連 lien 3. To connect, to continue.

摙 lien 3. To take, to remove.

漣 lien 2. To weep.

褳 lien 2. A pouch.

鏈 lien 2. A chain.

璉 lien 2. A vessel, a cup.

蓮 lien 2. The lotus, *Nelumbium speciosum*.

練 lien 4. To boil raw silk to soften it, to drill in, to practise.

鍊 lien 4. To smelt ores, to refine.

煉 lien 4. To separate dross by fire, to purify.

楝 lien 4. The *Melia azedarach*.

臉 lien 3. Face, honour.

殮 lien 4. To shroud a corpse.

斂 lien 3. To collect, to gather, to concentrate.

蘞 lien 3. A wild vine berry.

匳 lien 2. A lady's dressing-case, a bridal *trousseau*.

廉 lien 2. A corner, angular, incorrupt, to search out.

幨 lien 2. A door-screen of cloth.

濂 lien 2. A waterfall, a cascade.

鐮 lien 2. A sickle, a reaping-hook.

臁 lien 2. The leg.

簾 lien 2. A bamboo blind.

聯 lien 2. Connected, united, to combine with, to assemble.

憐 lien 2. To pity; to desire, to covet.

帘 lien 2. A sign showing where wine is sold.

奩 lien 2. A dressing case, the bridal outfit.

LIN

燐 lin 2. The ghost lights, phosphorus.

隣 鄰 lin 2. Neighbouring, near, contiguous.

嶙 lin 2. Rugged, precipitous.

獜 lin 2. A pangolin.

磷 lin 4. To grind, to abrade.

遴 lin 2. To select.

麟 lin 2. The female of the unicorn.

鱗 lin 2. The scales of a fish.

璘 lin 2. Veined, as marble.

蟒 lin 2. A firefly.

稟 lin 3. A granary, a grant from the public funds, salary.

凜 lin 3. To shiver with cold or fear.

燷 lin 2. To toast, to torrefy.

懍 lin 3. To fear, to tremble.

廩 lin 3. A government granary. *Ling* 3.

檁 lin 3. Cross-beams, rafters.

林 lin 2. A forest, a grove, a collection.

淋 lin 2. To drip, to soak.

琳 lin 2. A precious stone.

痳 lin 2. Diseases of the bladder, dysuria.

霖 lin 2. Refreshing rain.

吝 lin 4. Avarice, stinginess.

藺 lin 4. A rush.

臨 lin 2. To condescend, about, temporary.

賃 lin 4. To let.

LING

陵 ling 2. A mound, a tomb, to desecrate, to insult.

凌 ling 2. Ice, pure, to insult. *Liang* 2.

綾 ling 2. Silk cloth, damask.

菱 ling 2. The waterchestnut, *Trapa*.

令 } ling 4. A law, an order, to
令 } command. Your honoured.

伶 ling 2 Alone. A mime. Shrewd, cunning.

衿 ling 3. A collar.

鈴 ling 2. A sleigh-bell.

聆 ling 2. To hear, to listen, to obey.

齡 ling 2. Front teeth ; age.

蛉 ling 2. The venimous sand-fly.

玲 ling 2. To tinkle.

翎 ling 2. Plume, feathers.

領 ling 3. The throat, a collar, to manage, to receive.

嶺 ling 3. A mountain range.

囹 ling 2. A prison, an enclosure.

苓 ling 2. A huge truffle, *Pachyma cocos.*

零 ling 2. Small rain, a fraction, a residue, a remainder.

靈 ling 2. A subtle substance, the spirit or energy of a being, soul, spiritual, transcendent power.

欞 ling . A trellis.

另 ling 4. Apart, separate, besides, furthermore.

LIU

留 liu 2. To keep, to stop, hospitality.

榴 liu 2. The pome-granate.

溜 liu 4. A current, a stream.

鎦 liu 2. A ring.

遛 liu 3. To linger ; to saunter.

瘤 liu 2. A tumour, a wen.

琉 liu 2. A glass-like substance.

硫 liu 2. Sulphur.

旒 liu 2. Fringes of pearls; A streamer; a pennant; fringes.

流 liu 2. To flow; to spread abroad; to circulate.

磟 liu 4. A stone roller.

劉 } liu 2. A proper name.
刘 }

六 } liu 4. Six. *Lu* 4.
陸 }

綹 liu 3. A skein of thread.

栁 liu 3. A willow; debauchery.

LO

羅 lo 2. A spring net ; a sieve ; to spread out; humpbacked.

鑼 lo 2. A gong.

攞 lo 3. To rend.

儸 lo 2. Clever, lively.

囉 lo 2. To prattle, to annoy.

邏 lo 2. To cruise about; to patrol; to explore.

籮 lo 2. Deep and open baskets.

蘿 lo 2. Wisteria. Carrot, turnips.

裸 lo 3. Naked; to strip.

騾 lo 2. A mule.

摞 lo 4. To pile up.

螺 lo 2. A conch; a spiral; a screw.

虜 } lo 3. To seize; to capture ; pri-
擄 } soners.

捋 lo 4. To stretch ; to draw. *Lüeh* 4.

酹 lo 4. Libation.

駱 lo 4. A camel.

LOU

婁 lou 2. To trail along.

摟 lou 3. To embrace.

螻 lou 2. Ants.

樓 lou 2. An upperstorey; a tower.

耬 lou 3. A sowing-machine.

髏 lou 2. A skull.

鏤 lou 4. To carve; to engrave.

僂 lou 2. Misshapen, hunchbacked. *Lü* 2.

簍 lou 3. A basket.

屚 lou 4. To trickle, to drop.

瘺 lou 4. Piles.

陋 lou 4. Vile.

露 lou 4. To expose; to disclose; to appear. *Lu* 4.

LÜ

呂 lü 3. Vertebrae. Musical tunes.

侶 lü 3. A comrade.

梠 lü 3. Small column.

閭 lü 2. The gate of a village.

慮 lü 4. To think, to meditate; to care for.

驢 lü 2. An ass; a donkey.

僂 lü 2. Hunchbacked; misshapen. *Lou* 2.

褸 lü 3. Torn clothes, ragged, *lan-lü*.

縷 lü 3. A thread; to state in detail.

屢 lü 3. Many times; repeatedly.

旅 lü 3. A body of 500 soldiers, to travel, exile.

膂 lü 2. The backbone, strength.

律 lü 4. Musical notes, law, right.

綠 lü 4. Green.

LÜAN

欒 lüan 2. A proper name.

攣 lüan 2. To bind or tie, to bend, to crook, to contract.

臠 lüan 3. Flesh cut into slices.

戀 lüan 4. Ardently loving, to dot on, to lust after.

LÜEH

劣 lüeh 4. Weak, feeble, vicious.

捋 lüeh 4. To draw out between two fingers.

LU

盧 lu 2. A hut.

爐 lu 2. A stove.

鑪 lu 2. A brazier.

臚 lu 2. The skin, to state.

轤 lu 2. A windlass, a pulley.

罏 lu 2. A wine jar.

顱 lu 2. A skull.

嚧 lu 3. Gurgling.

纑 lu 2. Hempen thread.

[illegible] lu 2. A gourd.

鸕 lu 2. A cormorant.

蘆 lu 2. Water rushes.

廬 lu 2. A thatched hovel.

鹿 lu 4. A stag; a deer.

轆 lu 4. A block.

簏 lu 4. A basket.

麓 lu 4. A wooded mountain.

盝 lu 4. A box, a case.

祿 lu 4. [illegible] salary.

碌 lu 4. Green jasper, rough, laborious.

逯 lu 4. To advance; to proceed.

淥 lu 4. To drip; to leak, to strain.

[illegible] lu 4. The skin shrivelled, wrinkled.

錄 lu 4. To record, to write down, an index.

魯 lu 3. Stupid, coarse.

嚕 lu 3. To growl.

櫓 lu 3. A tower. An oar.

[illegible] lu 3. A grape.

鹵 lu 3. Natural salt; rude; incivil.

滷 lu 3. Potash.

磠 lu 3. Gravel, pebbles.

陸 lu 4. Dry land, a continent. Used for the numeral *liu* six

稑 lu 4. Grain which ripens early, precocious.

戮 lu 4. To kill, to slaughter.

僇 lu 4. To scorn.

賂 lu 4. To give a present, to bribe.

輅 lu 4. A chariot.

路 lu 4. Road, way, path. *Hence*

鷺 lu 4. A heron.

露 lu 4. Dew. *Lou* 4.

LUAN

圞 luan 2. Spherical, round.

孿 luan 2. Twins.

鑾 luan 2. Little bells, imperial cars.

鸞 luan 2. Argus pheasant, small bells; imperial.
灤 luan 2. A river in the north-east of Chihli.

卵 luan 3. Eggs, testicles.
亂 乱 luan 4. Trouble, disorder, discord, anarchy.

LUN (Lün)

論 lun 4. To discourse, logic, with reference to.
倫 lun 2. Constant, regular, morals.
輪 lun 2. A wheel, a disk, a turn, to revolve.
淪 lun 2. Eddying water, engulfed, lost.
綸 lun 2. To wind, to regulate, to classify.
掄 lun 2. To choose, to select. To wave, to brandish.
圇 lun 2. Complete, whole.
崙 lun 2. The K'unlün mountains.

閏 lun 4. The intercalary moon, extra.
潤 lun 4. To moisten.

LUNG

龍 lung 2. A dragon, imperial, glorious.
櫳 lung 2. A pen, a cage.
隴 lung 3. A dike.
攏 lung 3. To grasp, to collect. A comb.
嚨 lung 2. The throat.
曨 lung 2. Dull, dim, obscure.
瓏 lung 2. Tinkling.
朧 lung 2. Fleshy.
爖 lung 2. To kindle a fire.
韝 lung 2. A halter.
籠 lung 2. A cage, to monopolise.
竉 lung 3. A hole, a cave.
聾 lung 2. Deaf, deafness.
壟 lung 3 A barrow, a grave.

隆 lung 2. Abundant.
窿 lung 2. The vault of heaven, a cavity, a hole.

弄 lung 4. To handle, to play with, to deceive. *Nung, neng.*

MA

馬 ma 3. A horse.
螞 ma 3. Locusts, ants, etc.
榪 ma 4. A graft.
禡 ma 4. A military sacrifice.
瑪 ma 3. Agate, cornelian.
媽 ma 1. A nurse.
嗎 ma 1. An interrogative particle.
碼 ma 3. Weights, numerals.
傌 ma 4. A knight in chess.
隲 ma 3. To pile up.
罵 ma 4. To curse, to revile.

麻 ma 2. Hemp, textile fibres.
嘛 ma 1. Lama, a tibetan bonze.
麽 ma 1. An interrogative particle. *Mo* 1.
䁖 ma 2. To see indistinctly.
痲 ma 2. Numbness, pock-marks.

糢 ma 1. Confused. *Mo* 1.
蟆 ma 1. A frog.

MAI

麥 mai 4. Corn.

買 mai 3. To buy, to purchase.
賣 mai 4. To sell.

邁 mai 4. To step, to go.
譪 mai 4. To brag.
勱 mai 4. To exert one's strength.

埋 mai 2. To bury, to conceal, to hoard.

貊 mai 4. Wild tribes of the North.
陌 mai 4. A raised path, a street, to walk.

衇 脈 mai 4. The veins or arteries, the pulse.

MAN

曼 man 2. Wide, long.
慢 man 4. Slow, remiss, neglectful, rude.
漫 man 4. Water overflowing, wild, reckless.
謾 man 2. To recriminate.
饅 man 2. Steamed dumplings.
墁 man 4 To plaster, to lay, to pave.
幔 man 4. A curtain, a screen.
鏝 man 2. A trowel.
縵 man 4. Plain, simple.
蔓 man 2. A kind of turnip.

顢 man 1. Brazenfaced.
瞞 man 2. To deceive, to blind, to conceal.
蹣 man 2. To limp.

滿 **man 3.** Full, complete, Manchu.

鞔 **man 2.** To cover with leather.

蠻 **man 2.** Barbarous tribes in the South of China.

MANG

盲 **mang 2.** Blind.

肓 **mang 2.** Cardiac region.

氓 **mang 2.** People.

甿 **mang 2.** Country people.

忙 **mang 2.** Busy, hurried, fluttered.

芒 **mang 2.** A beard of grain, a sharp point, a ray. *Hence*

茫 **mang 2.** High waters, vast and vague, chaos.

硭 **mang 2.** Alkalines.

莽 **mang 3.** Jungle, undergrowth, rustic.

蟒 **mang 3.** A kind of boa.

MAO

冒 **mao 4.** A covering for the head, to rush on, rash.

帽 **mao 4.** A cap or head covering of any kind.

媢 **mao 4.** Ill-will and jealousy.

瑁 **mao 4.** A tortoise-shell.

皃 **mao 4.** The outward mien.

貌 **mao 4.** The outward mien, aspect, manner, gait.

矛 **mao 2.** A lance.

茅 **mao 2.** Reed used for thatching, a hut, a privy.

楙 **mao 4.** Abundance, energy. *Mou 4.*

蝥 **mao 3.** Cantharides.

錨 **mao 2.** An anchor.

貓 **mao 2.** A cat.

毛 **mao 2.** Hair, down, feathers, delicate.

眊 **mao 4.** Muddled, confused.

旄 **mao 2.** Tail of a yak used as a banner.

芼 **mao 4.** Vegetables.

耄 **mao 4.** A man of seventy.

卯 **mao 3.** A cyclic character, a term, a mortise.

茆 **mao 3.** The mallow.

昴 **mao 3.** The Pleiades.

貿 **mao 4.** To barter, trade.

茂 **mao 4.** Exuberant, flourishing.

摹 摸 **mao 1.** To feel for, to palp. *Mo 1.*

MEI

每 **mei 3.** Each, every.

梅 **mei 2.** Plums, prunes.

眉 **mei 2.** The eyebrows.

媚 **mei 4.** To love, to coax, to flatter.

嵋 **mei 2.** A mountain in Ssŭ-ch'uan.

楣 **mei 2.** Lintel of a door or window.

昧 **mei 4.** No sun, dark, hidden, to conceal.

眛 **mei 4.** Dimness of vision.

妹 **mei 4.** A younger sister.

魅 **mei 4.** Hamadryads.

寐 **mei 4.** To rest, to sleep.

玫 **mei 2.** Rosy jade, a rose.

枚 **mei 2.** A stalk, a stick, a gag, a numerative.

糜 **mei 2.** A kind of millet.

縻 **mei 2.** To bind, to tie.

醾 **mei 2.** Arrack.

靡 **mei 2.** No, not, malice, defeat, loss.

默 嘿 **mei 4.** Dark, retired, secret, silent.

墨 **mei 4.** Ink, black.

煤 **mei 2.** Coal.

媒 **mei 2.** A go-between.

黴 **mei 2.** Microbes.

美 **mei 3.** Delicious, beautiful, well.

彪 **mei 4.** Dryads.

浼 **mei 3.** To defile, to foul.

密 **mei 4.** Thick, close. *Mi 4.*

MÊN

門 **mên 2.** A door, a gate, a family, a school, a sect.

們 **mên 1.** The sign of the plural.

捫 **mên 1.** To feel for, to press.

悶 **mên 4.** Depressed, melancholy, stupid.

MÊNG

蒙 **mêng 2.** To cover, to conceal, ignorant, to receive, Mongol.

矇 **mêng 2.** Dimsighted, ignorant.

朦 mêng 2. Obscure, confused, to deceive, to mislead.
蠓 mêng 3. Gnats.
艨 mêng 2. A cruiser.
濛 meng 2. Drizzling rain, mist.

孟 mêng 4. Chief, head, first.
猛 mêng 3. Fierce, savage, cruel.

盟 mêng 2. A covenant.
萌 mêng 2. A germ, a shoot, to thrive.

夢 mêng 4. A dream, to dream.
懞 mêng 3. Stunned, stupid.

MI

米 mi 3. Grains of rice or millet, etc.
眯 mi 3. Photophobia.
麋 mi 2. The elk, difform.
糜 mi 2. Reduced to pulp, rice gruel.
迷 mi 2. To confuse, to bewitch, fascinated.
謎 mi 2. A riddle, a puzzle.

宓 mi 4. Still, silent.
蜜 mi 4. Honey.
密 }
峹 } mi 4. Close, intimate, secret. *Mei* 4.

彌 mi 2. To complete, full, very, much.
瀰 mi 2. To inundate, vast, much.

弭 mi 3. Ends of a bow, to stop, to keep down.
袂 mi 4. Sleeves of a robe.

覔 }
覓 } mi 4. Invisible, to search for.
秘 mi 4. Secret, mysterious.

MIAO

苗 miao 2. The tender blades of grass; sprouts; aborigines.
描 miao 2. To delineate; to sketch; to depict.

杪 miao 3. The tip, a straw, trifling.
秒 miao 3. A second of time or of a degree.
妙 miao 4. Wonderful, excellent, subtle, mysterious.
眇 miao 3. A one-eyed man. *Hence*
渺 miao 3. Vast; boundless; vague.

藐 miao 3. To despise, to insult.
杳 miao 3. Obscure; mysterious. *Yao* 3.
廟 }
庿 } miao 4. A temple. A fair.
繆 miao 4. A proper name *Niu* 4.

MIEH

滅 mieh 4. To put out; to extinguish; to destroy.

蔑 mieh 4. Minute, worthless; not, without.
篾 mieh 4. Splints.

MIEN

免 mien 3. To avoid, to evade; to spare.
勉 mien 3. To make an effort; to excite; to constrain.
俛 mien 3. To incline, to bow.

娩 }
娩 } mien 3. Parturition.
帨 mien 4. A mourning cap.
冕 mien 3. A cap of ceremony.

沔 mien 3. Name of river.
麪 mien 4. Flour; nouilles.

面 mien 4. The face; the front; the surface; to visit; to meet; turn; time.
愐 mien 3. Modesty, timidity.
麵 mien 3. Wheat-flour; vermicelli.

棉 mien 2. The cotton-plant; cotton.
綿 mien 2. Soft; downy; floss silk; continuous.

眠 mien 2. To close the eyes; to sleep.

MIN

民 min 2. The people, the common multitude.
緡 min 2. To angle.
抿 min 3. To smooth down; to handle gently.
岷 min 2. A mountain in the Ssŭ-ch'uan.
泯 min 3. To inundate; destruction.
珉 min 2. Alabaster.
敃 min 3. Strong. *Hence*
愍 min 3. Pity, compassion.
暋 min 3. Strong, brave.
旻 min 2. Pity, compassion, sympathy.
閔 }
憫 } min 3. Pity, compassion, sympathy.

敏 min 3. Quick of perception; clever; witty.

黽 min 3. Turtle; tadpoles.

皿 min 3. Pottery, vases.

閩 min 2. The Fukien province.

MING

冥 ming 2. Dark, obscure.

暝 ming 3. Obscurity.

瞑 ming 3. To close the eyes.

溟 ming 2. Ocean, mist.

慏 ming 3. Reticent.

幎 ming 2. A veil.

名 ming 2. A name, an appellation, fame.

銘 ming 2. To carve, to engrave.

酩 ming 2. A strong spirit, drunk.

洺 ming 2. A river in Chihli.

茗 ming 2. The tea-plant.

明 ming 2. Bright, light, clear, to explain, intelligent.

命 ming 4. To command, a decree, fate, life.

鳴 ming 2. The cry of a bird, to sound.

MO

魔 mo 2. A devil, a demon.

麽 mo 1. An interrogative particle. *Ma* 1.

𥂕 mo 2. A basin.

磨 mo 2. To rub, to polish. A mill, to grint.

饝 mo 2, Steamed bread in small loaves.

摩 mo 2. To feel with the hand, to palp, to caress. *Hence*

蘑 mo 2. Mushrooms.

莫 mo 4. A negative, an interrogative, is it, is it not? *Mu* 4.

謨 mo 2. A plan, a scheme, to mediate.

糢 mo 1. Confused. *Ma* 1.

漠 mo 4. A sandy desert, the Gobi.

瞙 mo 4. A thickening of the cornea.

膜 mo 4. The skin, to caress.

塻 mo 4. Dust.

摹 摸 mo 1. To feel, to palp, to succeed. *Mao* 1.

寞 mo 4. Silent, solitary.

末 mo 4. The end of a branch, the end, finally, accessory, powder, a negative.

沫 mo 4. Foam, scum, saliva.

抹 mo 3. To wipe clean, to rub out, to anoint to cut.

秣 mo 4. Fodder, straw.

茉 mo 4. Jasmine.

謀 mo 2. To plot, to scheme, strategy.

沒 mo 2. To plunge, to disappear. *Mu* 2.

MOU

牟 mou 2. To bellow.

眸 mou 2. The pupil of the eye.

麰 mou 2. Barley.

丘 mou 3. The personal name of Confucius *ch'iu* 1, being respectfully pronounced *mou* 3.

瞀 mou 4. Dull, blind.

懋 mou 4. To exert one's energy, prosperity. *Mao* 4.

MU

莫 mu 4. Not, is it not? *Mo* 4.

模 mu 2. A pattern, a model, a fashion, a mould.

慕 mu 4. To love, to long for.

墓 mu 4. A grave, a tomb.

募 mu 4. To collect alms, to invite, to enlist.

暮 mu 4. Evening, sunset.

驀 mu 4. To bestride.

幕 mu 4. A curtain, a screen.

目 mu 4. The eye, an index, to look.

苜 mu 4. Lucern.

母 mu 3. A mother, that which produces, the source of, the root, the key.

姆 mu 3. An elderly matron.

拇 mu 3. The thumb.

踇 mu 3. The toes.

木 mu 4. Wood, a tree.

沐 mu 4. To wash, to give, to receive.

沒 mu 2. To plunge, to disappear, to cease, not, none. *Mo* 2.

歿 mu 2. To die, to perish.

牧 mu 4. To pasture, a shepherd, to superintend, a ruler, a teacher.

牡 mu 3. The male of quadrupeds, a bull. The peony.

某 mu 3. A certain one.

穆 mu 4. Majestic, to revere.

睦 mu 4. A benignant eye, harmony, concord.

畝 畆 mu 3. The Chinese acre.

NA

那 **na 4.** This, there.
na 3. Who? what? where.

哪 **na 1.** A final particle.

㑚 **na 2.** A buddhist sound.

衲 **na 4.** Robe of a bonze, to patch.

豽 **na 4.** A seal.

納 **na 4.** To hand up, to pay, to keep.

拿 挐 **na 3.** To take, to hold, etc.

骯 **na 1.** Filthy. *Ang* 1.

NAI (AI)

耐 **nai 4.** To endure, to bear; to be able.

乃 廼 **nai 3.** This; here; precisely; then; thereupon.

嬭 奶 **nai 3.** Breasts; to suckle; milk.

奈 柰 **nai 4.** Means; resource; to endure.

額 **nai 2.** The forehead.

NAN (AN)

俺 **nan 1.** I, me.

鵪 **nan 1.** A quail.

庵 菴 **nan 1.** A hut; a Buddhist monastery.

南 **nan 2.** The south.

楠 **nan 2.** A kind of cedar.

喃 **nan 2.** To recite.

難 难 **nan 2.** Difficult, hard; is it not?

男 **nan 2.** The male of the human species; a man.

赧 **nan 3.** To blush, shame.

岸 **nan 4.** Bank, shore.

柟 枏 **nan 2.** An even grained reddish wood.

NANG

囊 **nang 3** A bag; a sack.

囔 **nang 1.** To mutter.

齉 **nang 4.** To snuffle.

攮 **nang 3.** To stab.

饢 **nang 4.** Mouldy; spoiled.

灢 **nang 1.** Muddy.

壤 **nang 4.** Dust.

曩 **nang 3.** In former times; previously.

煖 暖 **nang 3.** Warm, mild. *Nuan* 3.

NAO (AO)

腦 **nao 3.** The brain.

惱 **nao 3.** Vexation; irritation; anger.

瑙 **nao 3.** Cornelian; agate.

撓 **nao 2.** To scratch, to vex, to trouble.

鐃 **nao 2.** Cymbals.

橈 **nao 2.** Curved; weak.

蕘 **nao 1.** Straw; fuel; vile.

硇 **nao 2.** Impure ammoniacal salt.

NEI (Nê)

內 **nei 4.** In, into, interior; near to, among.

[illegible] **nei 4.** Sadness.

吶 訥 **nei 4.** To speak cautiously. *Nê* 4.

喏 諾 **nei 3.** To assent. *Nê* 3.

餒 **nei 3.** Hunger.

挼 捼 **nei 2.** To rub; to polish. *Nê* 2.

NÊNG

能 **nêng 4.** A bear, able to, ability, power.

濘 **nêng 4.** Muddy.

弄 **nêng 4.** To handle. *Lung* 4.

NI

尼 **ni 2.** To stop; a nun.

妮 **ni 2.** A slave girl.

泥 坭 **ni 2.** Mud, miry, to adhere, to stick.

怩 **ni 2.** To blush.

屔 **ni 2.** A hill in Shantung.

呢 **ni 1.** A final sound.

匿 **ni 4.** To hide, to abscond.

慝 ni 3. Ashamed, mortified.

禰 ni 3. Ancestral tablets.

瀰 ni 3. Overflow.

溺 ni 4. To sink, to be drowned, doting on.

搦 ni 4. To grasp, to catch hold.

膩 ni 4. Grease, fat.

你 伱 } ni 3. The second personal pronoun, thou, you.

倪 ni 2. Young, small, delicate. I 2.

逆 ni 4. Revolt. I 4.

NIANG

孃 娘 } niang 2. A mother; a lady.

NIAO

鳥 niao 3. Birds.

虐 niao 4. Cruel. Yao 4.

尿 niao 4. Urine. Sui 1.

NIEH

聶 nieh 4. To whisper, to plot.

鑷 nieh 4. Pincers, to pinch.

孼 孽 } nieh 4. A son of a concubine, evils of sin, sorrow, retribution. Yeh 4.

涅 湼 } nieh 1. Mud, slime.

揑 捏 } nieh 1. To knead with the fingers, to fabricate, to trump up.

齧 嚙 } nieh 4. To gnaw, to eat. Yeh 4.

苶 nieh 1. Worn out, weary.

臬 nieh 4. A target, a judge.

NIEN

念 nien 4. To think, to ponder on, to study, to recite.

捻 nien 3. To nip with the fingers, to twist.

埝 nien 4. A dike.

艌 nien 4. To calk.

縴 nien 4. A tow-rope.

黏 nien 2. Glutinous, to stick up.

鮎 nien 2. The mud fish.

拈 nien 2. To take up in the fingers, to pick out.

輦 nien 3. Imperial vehicle.

攆 nien 3. To expel, to dismiss.

撚 nien 3. To roll in the fingers, to twist.

蹨 nien 3. To go afoot.

年 nien 2. The year, the crops.

碾 nien 3. A roller.

廿 廿 } nien 4. Twenty.

蔫 nien 1. Withered, faded.

NIN

您 nin 2. Your honour, you, sir.

NING

甯 寧 寍 } ning 2. Rest, repose, serenity, peace, to prefer, how, why?

嚀 ning 2. To enjoin upon, to charge straitly.

擰 ning 3. To wring.

佞 ning 4. Persuasive, insinuating, flattering.

凝 ning 2. To freeze, to congeal.

NIU

牛 niu 2. An ox, a bull, a cow, cattle.

扭 niu 3. To twist, to wring, to turn.

鈕 niu 3. A button.

紐 niu 3. A knot.

狃 niu 3. Inclined to evil.

忸 niu 3. Morose, stubborn.

衄 niu 4. Nose-bleed, fright, defeat, rout.

妞 niu 1. A lass.

繆 niu 4. Connexion, union, mixture. Miao 4.

謬 niu 4. Mistaken, fallacious, error.

莠 niu 3. Tares. Yu 3.

拗 niu 4. To clutch, stubborn.

NO

挪 no 2. To shift, to remove.

NOU (Ou)

耨 nou 4. A hoe, to weed.
偶 nou 3. A mate. *Ou* 3.
毆 nou 1. To beat *Ou* 1.

NÜ

女 nü 3. Women, a girl. *Ju* 3.

NU

奴 nu 2. A slave, a term of contempt.
努 nu 3. To exert the utmost strength, to strive.
怒 nu 4. Anger, fury.
弩 nu 3. A cross bow.
胬 nu 3. Granulations.
孥 nu 2. Children weak and tender, to exterminate a family.
帑 nu 2. Children. See *T'ang* 3.

NUAN

暖 暎 } nuan 3. Mild. *Nang* 3.
煖 煗 } nuan 3. Lukewarm. *Nang* 3.

NUNG

農 nung 2. To cultivate, agriculture, a farmer.
膿 nung 2. Pus, matter.
噥 nung 1. To mutter.
濃 nung 2. Sticky.
齉 nung 2. Mucus of the nose.

弄 nung 4. To handle. *Lung* 4. *Nêng* 4.

O (No)

我 o 3. I, me, my. *Wo* 3.
俄 o 2. Sudden.
娥 o 2. Good, beautiful.
餓 o 4. Hungry. *Wo* 4.
哦 o 2. To hum.
蛾 o 2. A moth. *Wo* 2.
鵝 o 2. The domestic goose. *Wo* 2.
峩 o 2. A mountain in Ssŭch'uan.

崿 o 4. A precipice.
諤 o 4. Honest, sincere.
鰐 o 4. The crocodile.
愕 o 4. To be frightened.
鍔 o 4. A sharp point.
鶚 o 4. The osprey or fish-eagle.
鄂 o 4. Name of different places.

鱷 o 4. The crocodile.
惡 o 4. Evil, wrong. *Wu* 4.
懦 o 4. Weakness, incapacity.
遏 o 4. To stop, to check.
訛 o 2. To deceive, to harm.
阿 啊 } o 1. Used as sounds. *A*.
儺 o 2. To exorcise the demons which cause pestilence.

厄 o 4. Difficulty, distress.
阨 o 4. A defile, a pass, difficulty.
軛 o 4. A yoke or collar.

額 o 2. The forehead. *Nai* 2.
臥 o 4. To rest, to lie down. *Wo* 4.

OU

熰 ou 3. To heat, to smoke.
漚 ou 4. To soak, to steep.
嘔 ou 1. To vomit, to spit.
謳 ou 1. To recite.
慪 ou 4. To excite, to irritate.
塸 ou 3. A tumulus, a tomb.
毆 ou 1. To beat, to strike, to fight.
歐 ou 1. To vomit, to retch.
甌 ou 1. A bowl, a cup.
鷗 ou 1. A sea gull.

偶 ou 3. An image, an idol, to mate, suddenly.
耦 ou 3. Two furrows, a pair, a mate.
藕 ou 3. The root-stock of the lotus.

PA

巴 pa 1. A proper name, sign of the optative.
把 pa 3. To hold, to grasp, to seize, a bundle, a particle denoting the accusative, a specificative, to lease.
pa 4. A handle.
耙 pa 4. A harrow.
靶 pa 3. A target.
吧 pa 1. A dumb man, *ya-pa*.
杷 pa 1. A rake.
弝 pa 4. The part of a bow grasped.
疤 pa 1. Cicatrix, scar.

芭 pa 1. A banana-tree.

笆 pa 1. A hedge, *li-pa*.

琶 pa 1. A guitar.

爸 pa 4. A father, papa.

霸 pa 4. To govern, to incroach on, a tyrant.

壩 pa 4. A dike.

八 pa 1. Eight.

叭 pa 1. Trumpet, *la-pa*.

扒 pa 1. To strip.

捌 pa 1. Eight.

拔 pa 2. To draw, to eradicate, to extirpate.

罷 pa 4. To stop, to finish, to resign, an imperative particle.

P'A

爬 跁 } p'a 2. To grovel, to oreep, to climb, to fall prostrate.

怕 p'a 4. To fear; to apprehend; lest.

帕 p'a 4. A kerchief, a veil.

袙 p'a 4. A turban.

啪 p'a 4. Onomatopœia.

PAI

白 pai 2. White, clear, pure vain, in vain, for nothing.

伯 pai 2. A father's elder brother; a senior; an earl; a leader.

柏 pai 3. A thuja.

帛 pai 2. Silk; wealth, property.

百 佰 } pai 3. A hundred; many; all.

稗 pai 4. Weeds tares.

敗 pai 4. A defeat; to ruin; to destroy.

擺 pai 3. To unfold, to expand, to expose. A ferry.

憊 pai 4. Exhausted; worn out.

拜 pai 4. To salute; to reverence.

擘 pai 1. To break.

蔔 pai 1. Carrot; turnip.

P'AI

派 p'ai 4. To branch, as a river; to ramify, to deputo; to appoiut to a post. A school, a sect.

⿰木𠂢 p'ai 4. Textile fibres.

拍 p'ai 1. To pat; to slap.

迫 廹 } p'ai 4. To urge, to insist upon; to vex, to harass.

珀 p'ai 4. Amber.

魄 p'ai 4. The inferior soul; figure, body.

牌 p'ai 2 A token, a card, a medal; an arch; a shield.

排 p'ai 2. To arrange; to dispose; to discard, to expel.

膊 髆 } p'ai 2. The arm

PAN

半 pan 4. To divide in two; a half.

伴 pan 4. A comrade, a fellow.

絆 pan 4. To fetter; to embarrass.

拌 pan 4. To mix.

板 pan 3. A board, a plank, a flattened bamboo for beating.

版 pan 3. A board, a plank, a diploma.

扮 pan 4. To dress up, to disguise, style of dress.

頒 pan 1. To extend, to expend, to promulgate, to bestow.

般 pan 1. Manner; fashion; sort; kind.

搬 pan 1. To remove; to transport.

瘢 pan 1. Marks on the skin; moles.

螌 pan 1. Cantharides

班 pan 1. To dispose; a series; a rank a troop.

斑 pan 1. Variegated.

辦 办 } pan 4. To manage, to act; to execute.

瓣 pan 4. A slice; a lobe; a petal.

辯 pan 4. To reply. *Pien* 4.

P'AN

盤 p'an 2. A dish; a plate, to coil up; to examine; expenses.

磐 p'an 2 A huge stone, a basis.

⿱般足 p'an 2. Cross-legged.

攀 p'an 1. To grasp; to drag down or towards one; to implicate; to climb.

襻 p'an 4. A loop.

叛 p'an 4. To rebel, to revolt.

判 p'an 4. To halve; to decide; to judge.

泮 p'an 4. The semicircular pool before the provincial collegos of old; a college; a graduate.

畔 p'an 4 A landmark; a side or bank.

潘 p'an 1. A proper name.
盼 p'an 4. To gaze at, to long for; to expect.
拚 p'au 4. To risk, *P'in* 4.

PANG

傍 pang 4. Near, imminent. p'ang 2 The sice.
榜 膀 pang 3. A board, a notice a model, a pattern.
謗 pang 4. To slander.
髈 pang 3. The shoulder.
綁 pang 3. To bind, to tie.
搒 pang 3. To beat, to propel a boat.
艕 pang 4, Two boats fastened side by side, a lighter.

牪 pang 1. Uncouth, rude.
蚌 pang 4. Mussels.

邦 pang 1. A state, a country.
梆 pang 1. A watchman's rattle.
綁 pang 2. To tie, to bind.
梆 pang 3. To beat.
幇 pang 1. To help.

幫 幚 pang 1. To help.
拲 pang 1. To resist.
棒 pang 4. A club, a cudgel, a stick.
稖 pang 4. Maize.
蚌 pang 4. Shells.

P'ANG

旁 方 p'ang 2. The limits, the sides, near to.

螃 p'ang 2. A crab.
鎊 p'ang 2. To hoe.
膀 p'ang 2. The blatter.
嗙 p'ang 3. To boast, to brag.
㥬 p'ang 2. Timid, fearful.
逄 p'ang 2. Heavy rain.

龐 p'ang 2. A palace.
胖 p'ang 1. Fat, corpulent.

PAO

包 pao 1. To wrap up, to envelop, to warrant.
胞 pao 1 The uterus.
鉋 pao 4 A plane, to plane off.
飽 pao 3. To eat enough, satiated, satiety.
鮑 pao 4. Pickled fish, bad companies.
抱 pao 4 To infold, to carly in the lap, to hold tight, to conceal, to endure.
雹 pao 2. Hail.
苞 pao 1. Reeds, thick, dense.

暴 pao 4. A great heat, violent, to illtreat, to abuse.
曝 pao 4. A fierce heat, to scorch, to dry.
瀑 pao 4. A water-fall.
爆 pao 4. Passionate.

保 pao 3. To guarantee, to protect, to keep safe.
褓 pao 3. Swaddling-clothes.
葆 pao 3. Luxuriant foliage, to cover.
褒 pao 1. Official dress, favour, to censure.

寶 寳 宝 pao 3. Precious things, valuable, honourable.

報 pao 4 To recompense, to requite, to report, a journal.
襃 pao 1. Court robes.
箔 pao 4. A mat made of reed.
鴇 pao 3. A bustard.
豹 pao 4. Leopard, panther.
薄 pao 2. Thin. *Po* 2.
剝 pao 1. To peal *Po* 1.

P'AO

袍 p'ao 2. A long robe.
跑 p'ao 3. To run, to flee.
砲 p'ao 4. A ballista, a cannon.
咆 p'ao 2. To roar.
泡 p'ao 4. A bubble, to soak, to macerate.
炮 p'ao 2. To roast.
匏 p'ao 2. A calabash, a gourd.
刨 p'ao 2. To dig, to extract.
庖 p'ao 2. A kitchen.
疱 p'ao 4. A blister.
麃 p'ao 2. the follow-deer.

爆 p'ao 4. Crackers, to crackle.
脬 p'ao 1. The bladder.
瓟 p'ao 2. Calabash, gourd.
拋 p'ao 1. To fling, to cast off, to deduct. *P'ou* 1.
礮 p'ao 4 A cannon, guns.

PEI

貝 pei 4. Cowries; money; valuables.

狽 pei 4. A gerboa; hindrance.

北 pei 3. The North.

背 pei 4. The back; behind, rear; to turn the back on; to carry; rebellion; to apostatise; to recite; secretly; deaf.

輩 pei 4. A generation; a class; a kind; sign of plural.

悲 pei 1. To grieve; to be sad; to sympathise.

棓 pei 1. Chinese galls.

焙 pei 4. To dry over a fire.

倍 pei 4. Double; to double; to multiply.

悖 pei 4. To rebel against; perverse; evil.

誖 pei 4. Contradiction, to oppose.

彼 pei 3. Other, another. He, him, that, those. *Pi* 3.

被 pei 4. A coverlet; to cover; to suffer; a sign of the passive voice.

鞁 pei 4. To saddle.

卑 pei 1. Vile, vulgar. *Pi* 1.

婢 pei 4. A slave-girl; a maid-servant. *Pi* 1.

碑 pei 1 A stone tablet; a stele.

筆 pei 3. A pencil.

備 俻 } pei 4. To prepare; complete; perfect. *Pi* 4.

盃 杯 } pei 1. A cup, a tumbler, a glass.

壁 pei 4. A wall. *Pi* 4.

P'EI

丕 p'ei 1. Great, vast, largely.

呸 p'ei 1. To snort at.

胚 p'ei 1. An embryo; an unformed thing; unfinished.

坯 p'ei 1. Pisé. *P'i* 1.

徘 p'ei 3. To stroll to and fro; irresolute.

裴 p'ei 2. A proper name.

培 p'ei 4. To bank up with earth; to strengthen.

賠 p'ei 2. To make good; to indemnify; to lose.

棓 p'ei 3. To take; to rob.

陪 p'ei 2. To bear one company.

披 p'ei 1. To open; to spread; to carry on one.

帔 p'ei 4. A mantle.

旆 p'ei 4. A banner, to weave. To travel.

沛 p'ei 4. Name of a river. Flowing, copious.

佩 p'ei 4. Pendent, to hang on the girdle.

珮 p'ei 4. Girdle ornaments; tinkling things.

配 p'ei 4. A mate, to pair, marriage.

圮 p'ei 3. Ruined, fallen.

轡 p'ei 4. The reins of a bridle.

PÊN

本 pên 3. The origin, the root; natural, original, native; capital; a book, documents.

体 pên 3. Coarse. *T'i* 3.

笨 怽 } pên 4. Stupid, dull of apprehension.

奔 } pên 1. To rush.

逩 } pên 4. To run quickly.

驞 pên 1. To gallop.

錛 pên 1. An adze.

㖹 pên 4. To pick up.

P'ÊN

盆 p'ên 2. A basin.

馚 p'ên 1. Fragrance; to exhale.

噴 p'ên 1. To spirt out of the mouth. *Fen* 4.

馩 p'ên 1. Fragrance; to exhale.

PÊNG

堋 pêng 4. To cover with earth.

弸 pêng 1. A stiff bow, strong, perfect.

綳 pêng 1. To bandage.

㿶 pêng 1. Menorrhagia.

崩 pêng 1. To collapse, the Emperor's death.

絣 pêng 1. To band a bow, a swindler.

迸 pêng 4. To bounce, to rebound.

浜 pêng 1. A wet dock, a side-creek or canal, canal, a creek.

P'ÊNG

朋 p'êng 2. A friend, to associate, to match.

淜 p'êng 1. Dashing water.

棚 p'êng 1. A mat awning, a shed.

硼 p'êng 2. Borax.

鵬 p'êng 2. The rukh, a fabulous eagle.

彭 p'êng 2. A surname, drumming.

膨 p'êng 2 Distension, swelling.

捧 p'êng 3. To hold up in both hands, to offer, a handful.

蓬 p'êng 2. A plant whose seeds are winged; to flutter about.

篷 p'êng 2. Chinese mat sail of a vessel.

碰 掽 } p'êng 4. To run against, to collide with, to bump.

烹 p'êng 1. To boil, to cook.

Pi

卑 pi 1. Low, mean, applied conventionally to one's self. *Pei* 1.

裨 pi 4. To aid, to give, to benefit.

婢 pi 4. A slave girl. *Pei* 4.

俾 pi 4. To cause, to enable.

庳 pi 4. Vulgar, mediocre.

痺 pi 4. Rheumatism, numbness.

辟 pi . Prince, law, to rule. *P'i*4.

避 pi 4. To flee from, to avoid, to retire.

臂 pi 4. The arm.

壁 pi 4. A wall. *Pei* 4.

璧 pi 4. A gem, a cameo.

躄 pi 4. Lame.

嬖 pi 4. A favorite.

甓 pi 4. Glazed tiles.

必 pi 2. Certainly, must, determined on, necessary.

祕 pi 4. Secret, abstruse, mysterious.

泌 pi 4. A torrent.

閟 pi 4. To close, to impede, secret, hidden.

苾 pi 4. Fragrant.

毖 pi 4. Attention, vigilance.

敝 pi 4. Worn out, vile.

弊 獘 } pi 4. Abuses, frauds, evil.

幣 pi 4. Silk, presents, wealth.

蔽 pi 4 To shade, to conceal.

彼 pi 3. He, him. *Pei*3.

柀 pi 3. The pine, *Cunninghamia sinensis*.

比 pi 3. To compare.
pi 4. To join.

妣 pi 3. A deceased mother.

秕 pi 3. Ears void of grain.

陛 pi 4. Steps, the Throne.

篦 pi 4. A comb, to comb.

畀 pi 4. To give, to grant.

畢 pi 2. To finish, ended, all, together.

逼 偪 } pi 4. To press, to compel.

備 僃 } pi 4. To prepare, to achieve, complete, perfect. *Pei* 4.

鼻 pi 2. The nose.

閉 pi 4. To close, to shut.

弼 pi 4. To assist, a minister.

鄙 pi 3. Vulgar, vile.

碧 pi 4. Green jade stone.

屄 pi 4. The vagina.

荸 pi 2. Tulipa edulis.

P'i

皮 p'i 2. The skin, leather, furs, a cover, a wrapper, a surface.

詖 p'i 4. To slander.

疲 p'i 2. Lassitude, fatigue.

批 p'i 1. To criticise, to reply officially.

砒 p'i 1. Arsenic.

屁 p'i 4. The posteriors, to break wind.

庇 p'i 4. To cover, to shelter, to protect.

琵 p'i 2. The Chinese guitar.

坯 坏 } p'i 1. Unburnt sundried tiles or pottery.

痞 痦 } p'i 3. Constipation.

辟 p'i 4. To rend or split open, bad, false, to repress. *Pi*4.

僻 p'i 4. Private, singular, mean.

擗 p'i 3 To cleave, to open.

劈 p'i 3. To cleave kindlings.

譬 p'i 4. To compare, an example, if.

闢 p'i 4. To open up.

霹 p'i 1. Thunder, to thunder-strike, a clash.

癖 p'i 3. Dyspeptic, greediness, passion.

脾 p'i 2. The spleen.

匹 p'i 3. Individual, single, a fellow, vulgar.

疋 p'i 3. A roll of cloth.

羆 p'i 2. A species of bear, high and strong.

PIAO

彪 piao 1. A tiger; striped like a tiger; streaks; ornate.

臕 piao 1. Fat; very corpulent.

皫 piao 3. White; pale; to grow pale.

鑣 piao 1. Bridle and bit.

表 piao 3. Outside; to make known; external; to manifest; a watch.

婊 piao 3. A prostitute.

裱 piao 3. To paste.

摽 piao 4. To bind; to tie up.

標 piao 1. A signal; a flag; a warrant; graceful.

摽 piao 1. To give a signal.

鰾 piao 4. Fish-glue.

P'IAO

票 p'iao 4. A slip of paper; a warrant; a bank note; a ticket.

漂 p'iao 1. To float; to drift; to bleach.

嫖 p'iao 2. Lewdness; fornication.

鏢 p'iao 1. A weapon; the point of a sword.

慓 p'iao 1. High spirits.

瓢 p'iao 2. A gourd; a calabash.

飄 p'iao 1. To whirl; to be blown about.

殍 p'iao 3. To die of hunger.

PIEH

憋 懋 pieh 1. Nervous; to forbear; to be suffocated.

斃 獘 pieh 4. To die; to perish.

鼈 鱉 pieh 1. A turtle.

蹩 pieh 1. To limp.

癟 pieh 1. An ulcer.

別 pieh 2. To separate; to part; to recede from; another; not, do not.

癟 pieh 3. Distorted.

觱 pieh 3. Musical horn.

P'IEH

潎 p'ieh 1. Rippling; dancing, as waves.

撇 擎 p'ieh 1. To skim off; to reject; to abandon.

嘝 p'ieh 1. To grimace.

丿 p'ieh 1. A stroke to the left in penmanship.

PIEN

扁 pien 3. A horizontal tablet; flat.

編 pien 1. To arrange in order; to compose.

遍 徧 pien 4. Everywhere; to make a round; a whole.

蝙 pien 1. The bat.

褊 pien 3. Narrow.

匾 pien 3. Horizontal tablets.

便 pien 4. Convenient; handy; to relieve nature; then; even if. *P'ien* 2.

煡 pien 3. A string of crackers.

鞭 pien 1. A whip.

邊 边 pien 1. A bank; an edge; on the border; the frontier.

籩 pien 1. A flat basket.

辨 pien 4. To cut asunder; to distinguish; to separate.

辮 pien 4. To plait, to braid; Tartar cue.

辯 pien 4. To quarrel about, to debate.

貶 pien 3. To diminish, to belittle, to censure, to cashier.

砭 pien 1. Acupuncture.

窆 pien 4. To put a coffin into the grave.

卞 pien 4. A proper name.

汴 pien 4. A river in Hupeh.

弁 pien 4. A military cap, soldier.

變 变 pien 4. To transform, to metamorphose.

P'IEN

偏 p'ien 1. Inclined, leaning, partial.

騙 p'ien 4. To bestride a horse, to swindle, to dupe.

諞 p'ien 3. Deceitful, to defraud.

副 p'ien 4. To cut into slices.

篇 p'ien 1. A slip of bamboo, a leaf of a book, an essay.

便 p'ien 2. Advantageous, profitable. *Pien*.

片 p'ien 4. A card, a piece, a section, a moment.

胼 p'ien 1. Hard, callous.

PIN

賓賔 pin 1. A guest, a visitor, to entertain, to acknowledge, to trust in.

擯擯 pin 4. To find fault with, to reject.

嬪 pin 1. Imperial concubines, a wife, to wed.

殯 pin 4. A funeral, to carry out, to burial.

蠙 pin 1. The pearl oyster.

髕 pin 4. The patella.

濱 pin 1. Beach, shore.

鬢 pin 4 The hair on the temples.

彬 pin 1. Graceful, elegant.

豳邠 pin 1 A place in Shênsi.

斌 pin 1. Elegant, graceful.

P'IN

聘 p'in 4. To enquire about, to invite by presents, to engage, to betroth.

娉 p'in 1. Elegance.

頻 p'in 2. Sorrow, duration.

櫇 p'in 2. An apple-tree.

蘋 p'in 2. *Marsilea quadrifolia.*

品 p'in 3. A kind, series, rank, order.

貧 p'in 2. Poor, impoverished.

牝 p'in 3. The female of beasts, a cow.

拚 p'in 1. To risk, to disregard, to neglect. *P'an* 4.

PING

丙 ping 3 A cyclical character.

柄 ping 3. A handle, a haft, authority.

炳 ping 3. Bright, luminous.

怲 ping 3. Sad, mournful.

邴 ping 3 Name of a place.

病 ping 4 Sickness.

幷并 ping 4. United, together, moreover, also, really, all.

併 ping 4. On a level with, together with, unitedly.

餅 ping 3. Cakes, pastry.

屏 ping 3 To set aside, to refect. *P'ing* 2.

竝並 ping 4. Together, united, moreover, even, all.

兵 ping 1. Soldier, military, arms.

梹 ping 1. The areca-palm and nut.

秉 ping 3. A sheaf, to seize, to hold, to maintain.

冰氷 ping 1. Ice.

稟 ping 3. To warn, to announce, to receive, natural gifts.

檳 ping 1. The areca-palm and nut.

P'ING

平 p'ing 2. Even, equal, peaceful, quiet, to adjust, to harmonise, to weigh in scales.

評 p'ing 2. To discuss, to settle, to arrange.

苹 p'ing 2. Duck weed, *lemna.*

缾瓶 p'ing 2. A bottle, a flagon.

郱 p'ing 2. Name of a place.

屛 p'ing 2. A screen, to cover, protection. *Ping* 3.

凴憑凭 p'ing 2. A stand, to lean upon, to trust to, proof evidence, according to.

PO

玻 po 1. Vitreous, glass.

菠 po 1. Spinach.

簸 po 4. A winnowing-basket, to winnow.

妭 po 4 A name for a wife.

跋 po 4. To stamp.

鈸 po 4. Small cymbals.

魃 po 4. The demon of drought.

餑 po 1. Bread.

脖 po 2. The neck.

桲 po 4. A flail.

浡 po 4. Suddenly.

勃 po 4. Suddenly.

播 po 3. To sow, to winnow, to spread abroad, to publish.

皤 po 1. White, clear.

撥 po 1. To spread, to open, to distribute.

襏 po 1. A rain-coat.

鉑 po 4. A thin sheet of metal.

泊 po 2. To fasten a boat, to stop, to rest.

髆 髉 po 2. The arm. *P'ai* 2.

搏 po 2. To seize, to strike.

煿 po 4. To crackle, to burst from heat.

愽 博 po 2. Ample, spacious, universal knowledge.

薄 po 2. Thin, shabby. Peppermint. *Pao* 2.

卜 po 3. Divination.

剝 po 1. To flay, to peel, *Pao* 1.

亳 po 4. A city in Honan.

鉢 po 1. A bowl.

駁 駮 po 2. A piebald horse, mixed, to dispute, to refute.

P'O

叵 叵 p'o 3. Do not, ought not, incapacity.

破 p'o 4. To break, to ruin, to defeat.

坡 p'o 1. A declivity, a slope.

跛 p'o 3. Cripple, lame.

陂 p'o 1. A bank, a talus.

頗 p'o 1. An excess, very, much, plentiful.

波 p'o 1. A wave, a ripple, wave-like.

婆 p'o 2. An aged woman, a stepmother.

樸 p'o 2. A natural substance, plain; simple, sincere.

潑 p'o 1. To sprinkle, to gush out.

朴 p'o 4. *Magnolia hypoleuca.*

鄱 p'o 2. Name of a place.

P'OU

剖 p'ou 1. To cut up, dissection, anatomy.

抛 p'ou 1. To throw away. *P'ao* 1.

PU

布 pu 4. Cloth, linen, to spread out, to publish.

佈 pu 4. To extend, to diffuse, spreading everywhere.

怖 pu 4. To frighten, alarmed

捗 pu 4. To scatter.

捕 pu 3. To seize, to catch, the police.

補 pu 3. To patch, to mend, to add on; to make up.

晡 pu 1. The time from 3 to 5 p. m.

簿 pu 4. A register, a tablet, a record.

部 pu 4. A class, a genus, a category, a Board.

卜 pu 3. To conjecture, to divine. *Po* 3.

不 pu 2. No, not. *Pu* 4.

步 pu 4. A step, to walk, footmen, a pace.

譜 pu 3. Chronicle, catalogue, album. *P'u* 3.

堡 pu 3. A rampart, a redoubt, a station.

醭 pu 2. The mother of vinegar.

埠 pu 4. A port, a mart.

P'U

鋪 pu 1. To spread out, a bed.

舖 pu 1. A shop.

餔 pu 4. To eat.

誧 p'u 1. To amplify.

踊 p'u 1. A track.

逋 p'u 1. To flee, a debt, to refuse payment.

圃 p'u 3. A garden, an orchard.

匍 p'u 2. To fall prostrate, to crawl. *Hence*

葡 p'u 2. The vine.

浦 p'u 2. Shore of a river. *Hence*

蒲 p'u 3. Reed, rush.

溥 p'u 3. Large, universal.

僕 p'u 2. A servant.

撲 p'u 1. To strike, to assault.

璞 p'u 4. An unpolished gem, simple, rude.

幞 p'u 4. A turban.

鏷 p'u 4. A dart.

普 普 p'u 3. Large, universal.

氆 p'u 3. Coarse cloth made of yak's hair.

譜 p'u 3. An album. *Pu* 3.

扑 p'u 1. To strike, to flog.

菩 p'u 2. A Buddhist sound. *P'u-sa.*

SA

撒 sa 1. To let go, to scatter.

𥊬 sa 2. To glance at.

薩 sa 4. A Buddhist sound. *P'u-sa. Bodhisattva.*

SAI

顋 腮 sai 1. The cheeks.

鰓 **sai 1**. The gills of a fish.

揌 **sai 1**. To shake.

賽 **sai 4**. To contest, rivality, a match.

塞 㩙 **sai 1**. To cork, To stop, to obstruct.

SAN

三 叄 **san 1**. Three.

散 **san 4**. To scatter, to disperse, to separate, to dismiss.
san 3. Powder.

饊 **san 3**. Porridge.

傘 **san 3**. A parasol, an umbrella.

SANG

喪 **sang 1**. To die, to mourn, funeral.
sang 4. To lose, to ruin, to destroy.

桑 **sang 1**. The mulberry-tree.

搡 **sang 3**. To push over, to push back.

嗓 **sang 3**. The throat, the voice.

顙 **sang 3**. The forehead.

SAO

譟 **sao 4**. Voice; murmur; humming.

臊 **sao 4**. Shame. Rancid.

騷 **sao 1**. To rub down a horse; disquiet; to annoy.

搔 **sao 1**, To scratch.

颾 **sao 1**. The sound of the wind.

[illegible] **sao 4**. The chirping of birds.

埽 掃 **sao 3**. To sweep.
sao 4. A broom.

嫂 **sao 3**. An elder brother's wife; a matron.

繅 **sao 1**. To reel silk from cocoons.

SÊNG

僧 **sêng 1**. A Buddhist priest.

SHA

沙 **sha 1**. Sand, granulated; Buddhist.

紗 **sha 1**. Crape, gauze.

砂 **sha 1**. Gravel, sand. Different minerals.

粆 **sha 1**. Cassonade.

[illegible] **sha 4**. To pierce, a small hole.

痧 **sha 1**. The malaria.

裟 **sha 1**. A Buddhist cassock.

鯊 **sha 1**. A shark.

桬 **sha 1**. A species of pyrus.

[illegible] **sha 1**. To tie, to gird.

殺 **sha 1**. To slay, to kill, to decapitate.

[illegible] **sha 4** To hem. A seam.

鎩 **sha 1** A long spear.

廈 **sha 4**. A great building.

嗄 **sha 4**. A hoarse voice.

霎 **sha 4**. Sudden. *Shua* 4.

翣 **sha 4**. A flabellum.

蛇 **sha 2**. A serpent.

傻 **sha 3**. Silly; foolish; simple.

杉 **sha 1** A pine; a pole.

煞 **sha 4**. To kill, to murder; to end; very.

灑 洒 **sha 3**. To sprinkle.

SHAI

篩 簁 簛 **shai 1**. A sieve; to sieve; to strain.

釃 **shai 1**. To warm wine.

曬 晒 **shai 4**. To dry in the sun.

骰 **shai 3**. Dices.

[illegible] **shai 1** To beat a gong.

SHAN

山 **shan 1**, Mountain; wall.

訕 **shan 4**. To slender.

汕 **shan 4**. Port of Swatow.

疝 **shan 4**. Hernia.

衫 **shan 1**. A skirt or shift.

釤 **shan 4**. Bill-hook; to cut.

[illegible] **shan 1** Drizzling rain.

扇 **shan 4**. A fan; a screen.

搧 **shan 1**. To fan; to strike.

煽 **shan 1**. To excite; to inflame.

諞 **shan 4**. To wheedle; to seduce.

騸 **shan 4**. To geld a horse.

珊 **shan 1**. Coral.

刪 **shan 1**. To pare, to amend.

跚 **shan 1**. To hobble, to limp.

善 **shan 4**. Good; virtuous; to know; to approve.

繕 **shan 4**. To write out; to copy.

膳 饍 } **shan 4**. Viands; to eat.

蟮 **shan 4**. The earthworm.

僐 **shan 4**. Elegant; refined.

單 **shan 4**. A proper name. *San* 1.

禪 **shan 4**. Offerings; to abdicate. *Ch'an* 2.

鱓 **shan 4**. The eel.

闡 **shan 3**. To explain; to enlarge; to open. *Ch'an* 3.

擅 **shan 4**. To assume; to usurp; to dare.

禮 **shan 4**. A sacrifice to heaven.

羶 **shan 1**. Rank; stinking.

贍 **shan 4**. To give; to supply; to aid.

閃 **shan 2**. To slip aside, to shun; a flash.

芟 剣 } **shan 1**. To mow.

潸 **shan 3**. To weep.

羴 **shan 1**. Rank-smelling, stinking.

SHANG

上 **shang 4**. Up, upwards, over; above; high; superior; before.

尙 **shang 4**. If. To wish; to esteem; to add.

晌 **shang 3**. Noontide; midday.

扄 **shang 3**. A door knocker; a lock.

啇 **shang 1**. Trade A merchant. To deliberate.

謪 **shang 1**. To consult, to deliberate.

賞 **shang 3**. To bestow; to reward.

裳 **shang 1**. The clothes on the lower half of the body.

傷 **shang 1**. To wound; to injure; to distress.

殤 **shang 1**. To die prematurely.

觴 **shang 1**. A great cup made of horn.

SHAO

少 **shao 3**. Few, to lessen.
shao 4. Young.

勺 杓 } **shao 2**. A spoon.

灼 **shao 2**. To burn; brightness, luminous.

芍 **shao 2**. Peony.

筲 **shao 1**. A bucket.

莦 **shao 1**. Jungle grass.

哨 **shao 4**. To whistle; a patrol.

捎 **shao 1**. To carry.

艄 **shao 1**. The stern of a vessel.

颵 **shao 1**. To dry in the wind.

旓 **shao 1**. Fringes of a flag.

梢 **shao 1**. A twig; small.

稍 **shao 3**. A little.

潲 **shao 4**. Water driven by the rain.

邵 **shao 4**. A proper name.

劭 **shao 4**. Effort, exertion.

韶 **shao 2**. The music of *Shun*; harmony; glory.

紹 **shao 4**. To connect, to hand down, to continue.

爍 **shao 4**. To light, to shine.

鑠 **shao 4**. To polish.

燒 **shao 1**. To burn; to roast; feverish.

碩 **shao 2**. Abundance.

SHÊ

色 **shê 4**. Colour; air; manner, lust.

舌 **shê 2**. The tongue.

舍 **shê 4**. A cottage, a dwelling.

捨 **shê 3**. To part with, to renounce; to give gratis.

射 **shê 4**. To shoot. *Shih* 4.

麝 **shê 4**. The musk deer.

嗇 **shê 4**. The harvest. Saving, stingy.

穡 **shê 4**. The harvest; to harvest.

懎 **shê 4**. To hate.

攝 **shê 4**. To help; plurality of offices; interim. *Nieh* 4.

設 **shê 4**. To found, to establish.

賒 **shê 1**. To buy or sell on credit; to defer.

折 **shê 2**. To break. *Chê* 2

厙 **shê 4**. A proper name.

瑟 shê 4. A lute.

赦 shê 4. To remit punishment; amnesty.

涉 shê 4, To ford; to concern; relations.

社 shê 4. The local Genius. A society.

SHÊN

申 shên 1. A cyclic character. The ninth of. To extend.

伸 shên 1. To extend to report.

神 shên 2. Soul, spirit, genius, manes, transcendent.

呻 shên 1, To recite, to mutter.

紳 shên 1. The large girdle worn by the gentry.

甚 shên 4. Superlative, very, what?

椹 shên 2. The mulberry-tree.

諶 shên 2. Sincere. *Ch'en* 2.

審 shên 3. To inquire, to investigate.

嬸 shên 3. A father's younger brother's wife, sisters-in-law.

瀋 shên 3. Gravy, sap, to leak out.

沈 shên 2. A proper name. *Ch'en* 2.

糂 shên 1. Oat-meal.

參 蔘 shên 1, in *hai-shên* holothuria, in *jên-shên* ginseng.

槮 shên 1. Thick branches.

滲 shên 4. To absorb, to infiltrate, to soak.

矧 訠 shên 3. Still more, how much more.

哂 哂 shên 3. To smile.

身 shên 1. The body, the trunk, one's self, personal.

娠 shên 1. Pregnancy.

森 shên 1. A forest, thick, somber, abundance.

慎 shên 4. To act carefully, cautious, attentive.

腎 shên 4. The kidneys, the testicles.

諗 shên 3. To reflect on, to reprove.

深 shên 1. Deep, abstruse, intense.

陝 shên 3. Province of *Shênsi*.

SHÊNG

生 shêng 1. To bear, to produce, to come forth, to live, life, unripe, unpolished, unacquainted.

牲 shêng 1. Draught animals.

甥 shêng 1. The sons of a sister or of a daughter.

笙 shêng 1. A Pandean pipe.

眚 shêng 3. Leucoma.

升 shêng 1. A pint, the tenth part of a peck, to ascend, promotion.

昇 shêng 1. Rising sun, prosperity, splendour.

陞 shêng 1. To rise in office, to ascend.

乘 shêng 4. A chariot, a Buddhist term for the means of salvation. *Ch'êng* 2.

剩 賸 shêng 4. An overplus, fragments, leavings, to retain.

勝 shêng 4. To sustain, to conquer, to outdo.

省 shêng 3. A province, to spare. *Hsing* 3.

聖 圣 shêng 4. Wise.

聲 声 shêng 1. Sound, music, accent, tone, to declare, fame.

盛 shêng 1. Abundant, flourishing. *Ch'êng* 2.

繩 shêng 2. A cord, a string, to tie, to restrain.

SHIH

尸 shih 1. A corpse. A child personating the Ancestor.

屍 shih 1. A corpse.

屎 shih 3. Excreta, dung.

鳲 shih 1. The turtle dove.

十 shih 2. Ten.

什 shih 2. A file of ten soldiers, ten.

士 shih 4. An officer, a scholar.

仕 shih 4. A public officer,

史 shih 3. An annalist, history.

駛 shih 3. To gallop, post-haste.

使 shih 3. To order, to send, a messenger.

師 shih 1. A sage, a master, a model, a leader, the people, a legion, troops, a metropolis.

獅 shih 1. The lion.

螄 shih 1. A spiral shell, a screw.

詩 shih 1. Poetry, verses, poems.

侍 shih 4. To help, to wait upon.

恃 shih 4. To rely upon, to trust to.

郝 shih 1. Name of a place.

閹 shih 4. A eunuch.

時 旹 shih 2. Time, epoch, situation, opportunity.

式 shih 4. A form, a fashion, a rule.

拭 shih 4. To wipe, to rub and dust.

試 shih 4. To try, to experiment.

軾 shih 4. A fulcrum in a carriage, to lean on.

弒 shih 4. To murder a superior.

是 shih 4. To be, is, positive, absolute.

諟 shih 4. To judge, to consider.

匙 shih 2. A spoon, a key.

寔 shih 2. Solid, real, true.

氏 shih 4. A clan, a family, a sect.

舐 shih 3. To lick.

市 shih 4. A market.

柹 shih 4. The *Diospyros kaki*.

筮 shih 4. To divine with stems of the milfoil, *Achillea*.

噬 shih 1. To gnaw, to eat.

示 shih 4. To reveal, to teach.

視 shih 4. To consider, to perceive.

嗜 shih 4. To love, to be addicted to.

蓍 shih 4. The *Achillea sibirica*, which is used for divination.

誓 shih 4. To swear, imprecations.

逝 shih 4. To pass away, to depart, to die.

食 shih 2. To eat, food. *Ssŭ*.

飾 shih 4. Jewels, to adorn.

蝕 shih 2. An eclipse.

世 丗 shih 4. An age, a generation of thirty years, the world.

貰 shih 4. To borrow, to pardon.

石 shih 2. Stone, rocks. *Tan* 4.

祏 shih 2. A stone shrine to keep the ancestral tablet.

蝨 虱 shih 1. A louse.

施 shih 1. To give, to confer, to do.

拾 shih 2. To gather, to collect, ten.

矢 shih 3. A dart, to shoot.

失 shih 1. To lose, to omit, to fail.

豕 shih 3. A pig.

始 shih 3. Beginning, to begin, then.

事 shih 4. An affair, business, a service.

實 shih 2. Real, solid, fruit of plants.

射 shih 2. To shoot. *Shê* 4.

室 shih 4. A house, a home, a household.

溼 濕 shih 1. Wet, damp.

澀 澁 濇 shih 4. Rough, astringent.

適 shih 4. To go to, to reach, to suit, suddenly, pleasure.

勢 shih 4 Power, authority, influence, circumstances

釋 shih 4. To loosen, to set free, to cease, to explain, the Buddhism.

識 shih 2. To know, experience. *Chih* 4.

謚 諡 shih 4. The posthumous title, the epitaph name.

奭 shih 4. A proper name.

弛 shih 3. To unstring, to relax, loose, dissolute.

SHOU

手 shou 3. The hand, a workman.

首 shou 3. The head, a chief, foremost, stanzas

收 収 shou 1. To receive, to gather, to earn.

售 shou 4. To sell.

瘦 shou 4. Thin, lean.

獸 shou 4. Wild animals.

壽 夀 shou 4. Longevity, age.

守 shou 3. To keep, to ward off.

狩 shou 4. A hunt, an imperial inspecting tour.

受 shou 4. To suffer, to bear.

綬 shou 4. A band, a seal.

授 shou 4. To give, to transmit.

SHU

梳 shu 1. A comb, to comb.

疏 疎 shu 1. Distant, in time, space, or relationship. Lax, remiss. To report.

蔬 shu 1. Coarse vegetable food.

束 **shu 4.** To bind, to tie up, to restrain.

[illegible] **shu 4.** To rinse.

綀 **shu 1.** Sack-cloth.

朮 **shu 2.** *Panicum miliaceum.*

秫 **shu 2.** Sorghum stalks.

述 **shu 4.** To narrate, to publish.

術 **shu 4.** A path, an art, magical tricks.

孰 **shu 2.** Who? which? what?

熟 **shu 2.** Ripe, cooked, mature, versed in. *Shou* 2.

塾 **shu 2.** A school-room.

叔 **shu 2.** A father's younger brother. *Shou* 2.

淑 **shu 4.** Clear, pure, virtuous.

俶 **shu 4.** To begin, a beginning.

婌 **shu 1.** The governess of the women in palace.

菽 **shu 4.** Leguminous plants, pulse.

蜀 **shu 3.** The Ssŭch'uan.

屬 属 } **shu 2.** To depend on, to belong to, connected with, sort, kind, class.

暑 **shu 3.** Summer's heat of the sun.

署 **shu 3.** A public court, a tribunal, interim, to write.

薯 **shu 3.** The Chinese yam, sweet potatoes.

曙 **shu 3.** Dawn, clear.

舒 **shu 1.** To unroll, to expand, to smooth, tranquil, easy, good humour.

紓 **shu 1.** To relax, to pacify.

抒 **shu 1.** To pour out, to state freely.

樞 **shu 1.** A pivot, hinge, an axis.

鼠 **shu 3.** The rodents.

輸 **shu 1.** To overturn, to pay, to lose, to confess. *Ch'u* 1.

倏 倐 } **shu 4.** Hastily, quickly. *Shua* 4.

戍 **shu 4.** To guard the frontiers.

樹 **shu 4.** Tree, to plant, to establish.

墅 **shu 4.** A villa, a farm.

書 **shu 1.** To write, a book.

姝 **shu 1.** Lovely.

贖 **shu 2.** To redeem, to compensate. *Ch'u* 2.

黍 **shu 3.** The panicled millet.

數 **shu 3.** To count.
shu 4. A number.

恕 **shu 4.** Benevolent, merciful, to pardon.

庶 **shu 4.** All, the multitude, nearly, about.

豎 竪 } **shu 4.** Upright, perpendicular, to erect.

SHUA

刷 **shua 1.** A brush, to brush.

涮 **shua 4.** To wash, to rinse. *Shuan* 4.

耍 **shua 3.** To play with, to handle.

霎 **shua 4.** Suddenly. *Sha* 4.

倏 倐 } **shua 4.** Suddenly, rapidly. *Shu* 4.

SHUAI

率 **shuai 4.** To lead, to follow, to obey, rule, usually, universally.

摔 **shuai 3.** To fall down, to throw down, to spread, to sprinkle.

蟀 **shuai 4.** A cricket.

帥 **shuai 4.** A leader, a commander.

衰 **shuai 1.** Wearing away, fading, ruin.

SHUAN

拴 **shuan 1.** To fasten; to tie up.

栓 **shuan 1.** A peg; a pencil.

閂 **shuan 1.** To bolt a door.

[illegible] **shuan 4.** To scrub a horse.

涮 **shuan 4.** To rinse. *Shua* 4.

SHUANG

雙 双 } **shuang 1.** Double; pair, mate.

霜 **shuang 1.** Frozen dew, hoar frost; efflorescence; crystallised.

孀 **shuang 1.** A widow.

礵 **shuang 1.** Arsenic shale.

爽 **shuang 3.** Sunny; cheering; alert.

SHUI

水 **shui 3.** Water; a fluid.

誰 **shui 2.** Who? who; any one.

睡 **shui 4.** To sleep.

稅 **shui 4.** Duty on merchandise; taxes.

帨 **shui 4.** A handkerchief.

SHUN

順 **shun 4.** To follow, to obey; pliant, docile, easy, graceful, fair.

舜 shun 4. Name of an ancient Emperor.

瞬 shun 4. To blind; to glance.

憣 shun 4. Melancholic; sad.

橓 shun 4. *Hibiscus syriacus.*

蕣 shun 4. *Hibiscus mutabilis* ; fugacious; transitory.

SHUO

朔 shuo 4. The first day of the moon.

搠 shuo 4. To roughcast.

嗍 shuo 4. To suck in ; to inhale.

槊 shuo 4. A loug spear.

說 shuo 1. To speak ; to talk ; to scold.

所 shuo 3. Relative pronoun. *So* 3.

縮 shuo 1. To draw back. *So* 1.

SO

索 so 3. Strings; a cord; to search into.

摍 so 4. To feel one's way.

抄 挲 } so 1. To feel, to palp, to rub.

娑 so 1. To saunter.

鎖 so 3. A lock; chains; to lock.

瑣 so 3. Fragments; fine; minute; petty.

梭 so 1. A weaver's shutle.

唆 so 1. To incite ; to make mischief.

蓑 so 1. A rain-coat of grass.

擻 so 2. To tremble.

縮 so 1. To draw back; to shorten. *Shuo* 1.

所 so 3. A place, a building ; a relative pronoun, that which, who, what. *Shuo* 3.

SOU

叟 sou 3. An old man; venerable.

搜 sou 1. To search ; to investigate ; to enquire.

瞍 sou 3. Blind.

謏 sou 3. To censure.

餿 sou 1. Spoilt; sour.

艘 sou 1. A junk.

颼 sou 1. A cold blast.

廋 sou 1. Secret ; hidden ; to search for.

嗽 sou 4. To cough.

漱 sou 4. To rinse out.

藪 sou 4. A marsh ; a gathering place.

籔 sou 2. A flat basket.

嗾 sou 2. To excite; to tease.

SU

肅 su 4. Circumspection ; respect ; diligence.

潚 su 4. A proper name.

穌 蘇 } su 1. To revive.

攄 su 1. To rub with the hand.

蘇 su 1. Numbness.

素 su 4. Pure, simple, common.

嗉 su 4. The gizzard of a bird.

餗 su 4. To fast, to eat vegetables.

愫 su 4. Sincere, one's real intentions.

速 su 4. To invite, to urge on, speedily, quickly.

蟀 su 4. A cricket.

觫 su 4. To fear, to tremble.

欶 su 4. To suck.

簌 su 4. A fine sieve.

蔌 su 4. Culinary vegetables.

溯 遡 } su 4. To trace up to the source, to remember.

愬 su 4. To tell, to inform.

塑 su 4. To model in clay, to mould into shape.

訴 su 4. To tell, to make known, to accuse.

酥 su 1. Koumiss.

甦 su 1. To revive.

粟 su 4. Grain, food.

SUAN (Hsüan)

痠 suan 1. Aching of the limbs, muscular pains.

酸 suan 1. Sour, grieved, afflicted.

算 suan 4. To estimate, to plan, to calculate, to reckon.

宣 suan 1. To proclaim.

旋 suan 2. To revolve.

選 suan 3. To elect.

蒜 suan 4. Garlick.

SUI

碎 sui 4. Fragments, small pieces, bits.

誶 **sui 4.** To abuse, to rail at.
睟 **sui 4.** Clear, not.

綏 **sui 1.** A loop, settled, quiet.
荽 **sui 1.** The parsley.

隋 **sui 2.** A proper name. *To* 4.
饍 **sui 3** Cakes, biscuits.
髓 **sui 3.** Marrow.
隨 **sui 2.** To follow, to imitate, to comply with.

遂 **sui 2.** To accord with, to succeed, entirely, consequently.
繸 **sui 4.** Tassels, fringes.
墜 **sui 4.** Tunnel to a tomb.
襚 **sui 4.** The clothes of the deceased.
燧 **sui 4.** To get fire by friction.
隧 **sui 4.** Avenue to a tomb.
澻 **sui 4.** A ditch, a canal.

穗 **sui 4.** A head of grain, an ear, a spike.
繐 **sui 4.** Tassels.

睢 **sui 1.** To gaze at.
雖 **sui 1.** Although, even if, to dismiss.

尿 **sui 1.** Urine. *Niao* 4.
祟 **sui 4.** Noxious spirits, haunted.
歲 歳 **sui 4.** The planet Jupiter year, harvest.

SUN

筍 笋 **sun 3.** Bamboo sprouts.
飧 **sun 1.** An evening meal.

孫 **sun 1.** A grandson, a grandchild.
搎 **sun 1.** To feel or rub.
猻 **sun 1.** A monkey.

SUNG

頌 **sung 4.** To praise, to celebrate, a sacrificial ode.
訟 **sung 3.** To accuse, litigation.
松 **sung 4.** Pine-tree, coniferous trees in general.
淞 **sung 1.** Name of a river, Woosung.
鬆 **sung 1.** Dishevelled, loose, lax, to untie.

竦 **sung 3.** Fear, terror.
宋 **sung 4.** A proper name.
送 **sung 4.** To send, to convoy.
誦 **sung 4.** To recite.
聳 **sung 3.** Deaf, lofty, high, ambitious.
嵩 **sung 1.** A mountain in Honan.

SSŬ

四 **ssŭ 4.** Four.
駟 **ssŭ 4.** A team of four horses.
泗 **ssŭ 1.** A river in Shantung.

司 **ssŭ 1.** To control, the officer who presides, a court, the faculties of the soul.
嗣 **ssŭ 4.** To connect, to adopt, heirs, posterity, hereafter.
飼 **ssŭ 4.** To feed.
笥 **ssŭ 4.** A hamper.

思 **ssŭ 1.** To think, to reflect.
緦 **ssŭ 1.** Coarse cotton cloth, mourning.
偲 **ssŭ 1.** To warn.

斯 **ssŭ 1.** This, he, they, a final particle, then.
撕 **ssŭ 1.** To rend, to tear.
廝 **ssŭ 1.** A servant.
厮 **ssŭ 1.** Servants. Offices.

俟 **ssŭ 4.** To wait upon.
涘 **ssŭ 4.** River bank.

巳 **ssŭ 4.** A cyclical character.
祀 **ssŭ 4.** To sacrifice. A year.
汜 **ssŭ 4.** A river in Honan.

絲 絲 **ssŭ 1.** Silk, thread.
鷥 **ssŭ 1.** The white crane.
蕬 **ssŭ 1.** The dodder, *Cuscuta.*

私 **ssŭ 1.** Private, personal, selfish, partial.

似 **ssŭ 4.** Like, similar to, to seem.
姒 **ssŭ 4.** An elder brother's wife.

相 耜 **ssŭ 4.** A plough-share.
肆 **ssŭ 4.** To expand, to expose, four, reckless.
廁 **ssŭ 4.** A privy.
寺 **ssŭ 4.** A palace, a temple, a court, a eunuch.
賜 **ssŭ 4.** A gift, to give, to condescend.
死 **ssŭ 3.** Death, to die, firm, obstinate.
兕 **ssŭ 4.** A yak, a rhinoceros.

TA

答 **ta 2.** To answer.

荅 **ta 2.** Vetch, entangled, to answer.

搭 **ta 1.** To add to, to arrange.

繨 **ta 2.** A knot.

褡 **ta 1.** A wrapper, a wallet.

瘩 **ta 2.** A sore, a boil.

達 **ta 2.** To open, to see through, a way, to succeede.

韃 **ta 2.** Tartars.

[山沓] **ta 2.** A knoll.

大 **ta 4.** Great, noble, highly, very. *Tai* 4.

耷 **ta 1.** Hanging ears, dragging.

打 **ta 3.** To strike, to beat, doing in general, from.

T'A

塔 **t'a 3.** A Buddhist pagoda or tower.

撻 **t'a 4.** To chastise, to flog.

躂 **t'a 4.** To maltreat, to defame.

榻 **t'a 4.** A long bed, a couch.

塌 **t'a 1.** To fall down.

搨 **t'a 4.** To rub over, a fac-simile, an impression.

溻 **t'a 1.** To dampen, to soak through.

遢 **t'a 4.** Hurried, careless.

蹋 **t'a 1.** To stamp, to kick.

他 **t'a 1.** He, him. *T'o* 1.

獺 **t'a 3.** An otter.

TAI

代 **tai 4.** To alter, to substitute, a generation, a series.

玳 **tai 4.** A shell.

袋 **tai 4.** A bag, a pocket, a purse.

黛 **tai 4** Indigo.

岱 **tai 4.** A sacred mountain in Shantung.

貸 **tai 4.** To lend, to borrow.

帶 **tai 4.** Ribbons, a belt, a zone, take with one, together with.

[疒帶] **tai 4.** Leucorrhœa, a flux.

殆 **tai 4.** Dangerous, perilous, approaching, nearly, soon.

迨 **tai 4.** To reach, till, to.

怠 **tai 4.** Idle, lazy, to treat harshly.

大 **tai 4.** Great. *Ta* 4.

歹 **tai 4.** Bad; evil.

待 **tai 4.** To wait for; to await; to treat, as for.

獃 呆 } **tai 1.** Stupid, to stand open-mouthed, idle.

戴 **tai 4.** To wear on the head, to sustain, to obey.

逮 **tai 4.** To reach, to capture. Till, to, when

T'AI

臺 **t'ai 2.** A terrace, a stage, a title of respect.

擡 **t'ai 2.** To carry on a pole, to raise, to elevate.

台 **t'ai.** The Great Bear. A terrace.

抬 **t'ai 2.** To carry, to lift.

胎 **t'ai 1.** The pregnant womb, to commence.

邰 **t'ai 2.** A proper name.

苔 **t'ai 2.** Moss.

太 **t'ai 4.** Excessive, very, supreme, an epithet of distinguished persons.

汰 **t'ai 4.** To wash, to correct.

泰 **t'ai 4.** Large, extensive, liberal, extreme.

態 **t'ai 4.** Attitude, bearing, manner, mien.

TAN

單 **tan 1.** Single, alone, unlined. *Shan* 4.

撣 **tan 3.** To dust.

彈 **tan 4.** A bullet, a shot, a shell, a pill. *T'an* 2.

殫 **tan 4.** Exhausted, worn-out.

襌 **tan 1** Unlined garment.

憚 **tan 4.** To dread, to shrink from.

鄲 **tan 1.** Name of a place.

簞 **tan 1.** A basket.

癉 **tan 1.** Mildew.

旦 **tan 4.** The rising sun, the dawn, actors who take the parts of females.

但 **tan 4.** Only, simply.

担 **tan 3.** To dust, a duster.

胆 **tan 3** The gall.

妲 **tan 2.** An ill-famed woman.

擔 **tan 1.** To carry a burden on a pole, to sustain.
tan 4. A load.

膽 **tan 3.** Gall, courage.

躭 **tan 1.** To procrastinate, neglectful.

誕 **tan 4.** To boast, to beget, birth.

丹 **tan 1.** Cinnabar, red.

耼 **tan 1.** A proper name.

淡 **tan 4.** Insipid, tasteless, flat.

石 [illegible] } **tan 2.** A picul. *Shih* 2.

蛋 **tan 4.** Eggs.

T'AN

談 **t'an 2.** To talk, to chat.

毯 **t'an 3.** Rugs, carpets.

痰 **t'an 2.** Phlegm.

壇 坛 } **t'an 2.** A platform, an altar, an arena.

檀 **t'an 2.** Sandal wood, Buddhistic.

鐔 **t'an 2.** An earthenware jar.

憛 **t'an 4.** Solicitude.

燂 **t'an 2.** To heat, to dry.

譚 **t'an 2.** To talk much, to boast.

潭 **t'an 2.** Deep water, a pool.

彈 **t'an 2.** To play on stringed instruments, to rebound. *Tan* 4.

嘽 **t'an 1.** To snort.

歎 嘆 } **t'an 4.** To sigh.

灘 **t'an 1.** A sand-bank.

攤 **t'an 1.** To open and spread out, to dub, to share.

癱 **t'an 1.** Paralysis, palsy.

坦 **t'an 3.** A plain, level place.

袒 **t'an 3.** To strip, naked.

坍 **t'an 1.** To fall in ruins.

醓 **t'an 3.** A condiment.

忐 **t'an 3.** Timorous.

炭 **t'an 4.** Charcoal.

貪 **t'an 1.** To covet, to long for, greedy.

探 **t'an 1.** To feel for, to explore, to try, to sound.

TANG

黨 **tang 3.** To club together, a cabal.

攩 **tang 3.** To impede.

曭 **tang 3.** Dull, cloudy.

當 当 } **tang 1.** Ought, it must, suitable, to act as, to bear. **tang 1.** To pawn, a snare.

擋 **tang 3.** To withstand.

檔 **tang 4.** A cross-piece.

鐺 **tang 1.** A bell.

璫 **tang 1.** Jingles.

盪 **tang 4.** A bath-tub; to move.

蕩 **tang 4.** Large, vast, dissolute, reckless, agitation.

T'ANG

唐 **t'ang 2.** A proper name.

搪 **t'ang 2.** To ward off, to guard against.

糖 **t'ang 2.** Sugar.

煻 **t'ang 2** To warm.

塘 **t'ang 2.** A dike, a bath, a post-station.

磄 **t'ang 2.** A stone embankment.

倘 **t'ang 3.** If, supposing that.

[illegible] **t'ang 4.** A time, a turn.

淌 **t'ang 3.** To flow, not lasting.

躺 **t'ang 3.** To lie down.

棠 **t'ang 2.** Pear, sorb, etc.

堂 **t'ang 2.** A hall, a court, a church, a residence, a title. *Hence*

膛 **t'ang 2.** The thorax, the roof of the mouth.

螳 **t'ang 2.** A mantis.

鏜 **t'ang 2.** Noise of drums, etc.

逿 **t'ang 4.** To pass a time, a turn.

趟 **t'ang 1.** To go through water, to wade.

踼 **t'ang 3.** To slip down.

湯 **t'ang 1.** Hot water, soup, to scald.

燙 **t'ang 4.** To heat by placing in hot water, to scald.

儻 **t'ang 3.** If, suppose.

帑 **t'ang 3.** A treasury. *Nu* 2.

TAO

刀 **tao 1** A knife.

島 **tao 3.** An island.

搗 **tao 3.** To pound.

禱 **tao 3.** To pray.

擣 **tao 3.** To pound.

幬 **tao 4.** A canopy, to cover, the sky.

燾 **tao 4.** To light, to do good.

到 **tao 4.** To arrive at, to attain, to go to, up to.

倒 tao 3. To fall over.
tao 4. To pour out, on the contrary.

道 tao 4. A road, a way, a doctrine, to talk.

導 tao 4. To lead, to conduct, to direct.

蹈 tao 4. To trample on.

稻 tao 4. The rice-plant.

盜 tao 4. To rob, robber.

悼 tao 4. To be afflicted, to grieve for.

T'AO

桃 t'ao 2. The peach.

洮 t'ao 1. To wash.

逃 t'ao 2. To flee, to escape.

咷 t'ao 2. To wail.

鼗 t'ao 2. A small flat drum.

濤 t'ao 1. Great waves.

檮 t'ao 2. A block of wood; stupid.

陶 t'ao 2. A kiln for making pottery.

掏 t'ao 1. To draw out.

淘 t'ao 3. To scour, to clean out.

綯 t'ao 2. A cord, to tie.

啕 t'ao 2. To prattle.

祹 t'ao 2. Happiness, success.

萄 t'ao 2. The grape.

搯 t'ao 1. To draw, to bale out.

韜 t'ao 1. A scabbard, military tactics.

縚 t'ao 1. A cord, a loop.

滔 t'ao 1. Rushing water, to overflow

套 t'ao 4. A case; a snare; to envelop; to harness.

討 t'ao 3. To punish; to search; to discuss; to beg; to provoke.

叨 t'ao 1. To chat, *la-t'ao*.

饕 t'ao 1. Gluttonous, covetous.

絛 t'ao 1. A tress.

TÊ

德 tê 2. Moral excellence; goodness; power; quality; virtue.

得 tê 2. To get; to effect.
tei 3. Must, ought.

特 tê 4. Specially; on purpose. *T'ê 4.*

T'Ê

忑 t'ê 4. Timorous.

忒 t'ê 4. An excess; too, very.

慝 t'ê 4. Evil; wicked.

頺 t'ê 2. Bald. Inaction. Gradually.

特 t'ê 4. Specially, deliberately. *Tê 4.*

TÊNG

登 têng 1. To mount; to ascend; to record; to complete.

燈 灯 têng 1. A lamp; a lantern.

澄 têng 4. To filter.

蹬 têng 4. To step; to bump.

磴 têng 4. A ledge; stone steps.

瞪 têng 4. To stare at; to gaze in a supercilious way.

鐙 têng 4. A stirrup.

橙 têng 1. An orange-tree.

鄧 têng 4. A proper name.

凳 櫈 têng 4. A stool; a bench.

等 têng 3. To wait; a class; a rank; a sort; a sign of the plural.

戥 têng 3. A small steelyard for weighing money.

T'ÊNG

謄 t'êng 2. To copy; to transcribe.

縢 t'êng 2. To bind; to fasten; a band; a cord.

螣 t'êng 2. A serpent or dragon.

滕 t'êng 2. A proper name.

籐 藤 t'êng 2. Lianas; the rattan.

騰 t'êng 2. To leap on; to mount; to move out; to differ.

儯 t'êng 2. A dawdler.

疼 t'êng 2. Pain, ache, to love dearly.

TI

低 ti 1. To bend down, to incline; low.

抵 ti 3. To oppose; to be equivalent; to reach.

柢 ti 3. The root, origin, foundation.

牴 觝 ti 3. To gore; to push with the horns; to strive against.

怟 ti 4. Sadness.

詆 ti 3. To vilify, to slander.

羝 ti 1. A ram or buck.

弤 ti 3. The famous bow of the emperor *Shun*.

邸 ti 3. A hotel ; a lodging-house ; the Peking gazette.

底 ti 3. Base, bottom ; to settle ; but.

帝 ti 4. The supreme ruler ; the sovereign.

諦 ti 4. To investigate, to meditate.

渧 ti 4. To drop; a drop.

禘 ti 4. The great sacrifice to the remotest ancestor.

締 ti 4. A knot; a close connection.

蔕 ti 4. A stem; a peduncle.

弟 ti 4. A younger brother, a disciple.

第 ti 4. Order ; series ; a section ; but.

苐 ti 4. Panic grass ; order ; but.

悌 ti 4. To behave as a younger brother should ; submission.

娣 ti 4. A young sister or sister-in-law ; a girl.

睇 ti 4. To gaze ; to piep ; to spy.

翟 鸐 ti 2. The Tartar pheasant.

糴 ti 2. To buy grain.

遞 ti 4. To transmit ; to convey from hand to hand ; to exchange ; to succeed.

榹 ti 1. A wild plum-tree.

啇 ti 2. The peduncle ; the stem ; the origin.

嫡 ti 2. The legal wife.

滴 ti 1. To drop.

鏑 ti 2. A point.

敵 ti 2. An enemy ; a competitor ; to oppose.

的 ti 4. Target, mark ; clear, true ; a suffix.

地 ti 4. The earth, the ground ; a place.

隄 堤 ti 1. An embankment, a dyke, to guard against.

狄 ti 2. Nomadic tribes of the NW.

迪 廸 ti 2. To follow ; docile ; to lead ; to teach ; to intimate to.

笛 ti 2. A flute.

篴 ti 2. A flute.

覿 ti 2. To visit ; to see face to face.

棣 ti 4. A sort of plum ; fraternal love.

滌 ti 2. To wash ; to cleanse.

T'I

嗁 t'i 2. To cry, to wail.

蹄 t'i 2. The hoof of a horse, ox, pig, etc.

啻 t'i 4. Only ; to stop ; otherwise.

梯 t'i 1. A ladder ; stairs.

涕 t'i 4. To weep.

剃 t'i 4. To shave the head.

鵜 t'i 2. The pelican.

鼻+弟 t'i 4. To snivel ; mucus.

提 t'i 2. To pull up ; to lift to bring forward ; to mention ; to submit ; to govern.

題 t'i 2. The forehead ; a heading ; a theme ; a subject ; to propose.

踢 t'i 1. To kick.

惕 t'i 4. Trouble ; fear ; alarm.

剔 t'i 1. To scrape off ; to pick out.

嚏 嚔 t'i 4. To sneeze.

替 t'i 4. To substitute ; to supersede ; instead of.

體 体 t'i 3. The body ; substance ; style ; manner, to conform ; respectable.

薙 t'i 4. To root up grass, to weed out.

屜 屉 t'i 4. A drawer ; a screen, pillow, etc.

荑 t'i 2. A grassy plant, *panicum*.

TIAO

吊 tiao 4. To condole, to suspend ; to hang ; a thousand cash.

弔 tiao 4. To condole ; to wail ; to hang.

釣 tiao 4. To hook, to fish.

㣿 tiao 3. Pain, care.

刁 tiao 1. Bad ; wicked.

叼 tiao 1. To hold in the mouth.

凋 tiao 1. Exhausted ; faded ; withered.

琱 tiao 1. To carve ; to chisel.

鵰 tiao 1. The fish-eagle.

雕 tiao 1. To carve ; to engrave.

彫 tiao 1. To carve ; to wither.

調 tiao 4. To transfer. *Tiao* 2.

銚 銚 tiao 4. A boiler.

貂 tiao 1. The Siberian sable. *Mustela zibelina*.

窵 tiao 4. Deep, secret.

掉 tiao 4. To move, to fall.

T'IAO

挑 t'iao 1. To carry, a load, to stir up, to choose.

祧 **t'iao 1** An ancestral shrine.

跳 **t'iao 4.** To jump, to skip, to dance.

佻 **t'iao 1.** Weak, unsteady.

朓 **t'iao 1.** To offer flesh to the manes.

覜 **t'iao 4.** An imperial audience.

[illegible] **t'iao 1.** To cut open, to sever.

窕 **t'iao 3.** Deep, hidden.

迢 **t'iao 2.** Remote, far off.

齠 **t'iao 2.** To shed the teeth.

苕 **t'iao 1.** Clover.

笤 **t'iao 2.** A broom.

條 **t'iao 2.** A twig, a classifier, a bill, an article.

蓧 **t'iao 4.** A basket.

窱 **t'iao 4.** Deep, profound.

調 **t'iao 2.** To blend, to harmonise, to adjust, to temper. *Tiao* 4.

糶 **t'iao 4.** To sell grain.

TIEH

迭 **tieh 2.** To alternate, to change, to be able to.

跌 **tieh 1.** To slip and fall.

碟 **tieh 2.** A plate, a small dish.

惵 **tieh 4.** Timid, nervous.

喋 **tieh 2.** To chatter.

蝶 **tieh 3.** Butterfly.

諜 **tieh 2.** To spy.

堞 **tieh 4.** Battlements, crenelated walls.

牒 **tieh 2.** Tablets, documents, records.

絰 **tieh 2.** Hempen cloth worn as mourning.

垤 **tieh 2.** A mound.

耋 **tieh 2.** Old, infirm.

疊, 叠 **tieh 2.** To pile up, to fold, to reiterate, still, again.

爹 **tieh 1.** Father.

褶 **tieh 2.** A lined garment.

T'IEH

帖 **t'ieh 1.** A billet; a visiting-card.

貼 **t'ieh 1.** To paste up.

鐵, 鉄 **t'ieh 3.** Iron, firm.

餮 **t'ieh 4.** Gluttonous.

蝶 **t'ieh 2.** A butterfly.

TIEN

點 **tien 3.** A spot, a speck, a dot; to nod; to light; a little, a point.

玷 **tien 4.** A flaw or stain; a defect.

坫 **tien 4.** Earthen ledge or table.

点 **tien 3.** To light.

店 **tien 4.** A tavern, an inn, a shop. *Hence*

惦 **tien 4.** To think of, to remember.

掂 **tien 1.** To weigh in the hand.

佃 **tien 1.** To till the ground; farmers.

鈿 **tien 4.** Inlaid work; jewels.

甸 **tien 4.** A royal domain.

淀 **tien 4.** A marsh.

靛 **tien 4.** Indigo.

蹎 **tien 1.** To run.

[illegible] **tien 1.** To jolt, to bump.

滇 **tien 1.** A lake south of Yünnanfu.

搷 **tien 1.** To beat, to knock.

瘨 **tien 1** Crazed, deranged, mad, wild.

顛 **tien 1.** The top, the apex, the summit, to upset, to overthrow, to be ruined, to amble.

殿 **tien 4.** A grand hall, a palace.

典 **tien 3.** A code, a canon, to rule.

奠 **tien 4.** To pour a libation.

電 **tien 4.** Lightning, electricity, telegraphy.

墊 **tien 4.** To fill up, to wedge up.

T'IEN

天 **t'ien 1.** Heaven, the sky, a day, weather, celestial.

忝 **t'ien 3.** To disgrace.

添 **t'ien 1** To add to, to increase.

舔 **t'ien 3.** To lick.

掭 **t'ien 4.** To dip the writing-brush.

甜 **t'ien 2.** Sweet to the taste.

餂 **t'ien 3.** To lick, to taste, to seduce.

恬 **t'ien 2.** Peaceful, calm.

田 **t'ien 2.** A field, cultivated fields.

畋 **t'ien 2.** To cultivate.

㥏 **t'ien 3.** Bashful, timidity.

腆 **t'ien 3.** Prosperous, plenty, many.

填 **t'ien 2.** To fill up, to stuff, to complete.
磌 **t'ien 2.** The base of a pillar.
闐 **t'ien 2.** The noise of a multitude.

殄 **t'ien 3.** To extirpate, to waste.
藭 **t'ien 1.** The blue sky.

TING

丁 **ting 1.** A cyclical character, an adult, to mourn.
頂 **ting 3.** The top, to push with the head, to oppose. *T'ing 2.*
釘 **ting 1.** A nail.
ting 4. To nail.
訂 **ting 4.** To examine, to decide, to subscribe.
叮 **ting 1.** To enjoin.
酊 **ting 1.** Drunk.
仃 **ting 1.** Alone, lonely, forlorn.
虰 **ting 1.** Dragon-fly.
靪 **ting 4.** A piece, to patch.
疔 **ting 1.** Furuncle, pustula maligna.

定 **ting 4.** To fix, to settle to decide, certain.
碇 **ting 4.** A large stone used as an anchor.
錠 **ting 4.** An ingot.

鼎 **ting 3.** A tripod.

T'ING

頂 **t'ing 2.** Extremely. *Ting 3.*

亭 **t'ing 2.** A pavilion.
停 **t'ing 2.** To stop, to cease, to delay, settled.

廷 **t'ing 1.** The court the audience-chamber.
挺 **t'ing 1.** To stand up, stiff, rigid.
梃 **t'ing 3.** A staff.
艇 **t'ing 3.** A boat.
莛 **t'ing 2.** Stalks, to mince.
霆 **t'ing 2.** Lightning.
庭 **t'ing 1.** The audience-hall.

聽 听 } **t'ing 1.** To hear, to listen.
廳 **t'ing 1.** A court, a tribunal.

TIU

丟 **tiu 1.** To cast away, to lose.
蛁 **tiu 1.** A chrysalis.
跮 **tiu 1.** To squat down.

蹵 **tiu 1.** To squat.

TO

朵 朶 } **to 3.** A bud, a flower, the lobe of the ear, numerative of flowers.
剁 刴 } **to 4.** To chop, to mince.
垛 埵 } **to 3.** To pile up, a battlement, a buttress.
躲 **to 3.** To shun, to avoid.
跺 **to 4.** To stamp the foot.
稞 **to 4.** A stack, a heap.

惰 **to 4.** Lazy, careless, indifferent.
隋 **to 4.** Mince-meat. *Sui 2.*
墮 **to 4.** To fall, to sink, to be ruined.

掇 **to 4.** To gather up, to arrange.
多 **to 1.** Many, much, mostly, often, too much.
度 **to 1.** To calculate. *Tu 4.*
鐸 **to 2.** A small bell, a clapper.
奪 **to 2.** To take by force, to carry off, to strive.
馱 **to 4.** A load.
舵 **to 4.** A rudder.
抖 **to 3.** To tremble. *Tou 3*

T'O

脫 **t'o 1.** To take off, to doff, to strip; to escape from.
蛻 **t'o 4.** Exuviæ of insects and reptiles.

柝 **t'o 4.** A watchman's clapper.

他 她 牠 } **t'o 1.** He, she, that, another. *T'a.*
託 **t'o 1.** To commission, to entrust, to allege.
托 **t'o 2.** To support on the hand.
飥 **t'o 2.** Paste, pulp.

佗 **t'o 1.** He. Another.
鉈 **t'o 2.** The weight on a steelyard.
陀 **t'o 2.** A steep path.
詑 **t'o 2.** To deceive, to impose on.
酡 **t'o 2.** Drunk, nonsense.
駝 **t'o 2.** A camel, to bear as a pack.
鮀 **t'o 2.** A mud-fish.
拕 **t'o 1.** To pull, to drag, to impli ate, to protract.

鴕 t'o 2. The ostrich.

鼉 t'o 2. An iguana.

橐 t'o 2. A sack.

妥 t'o 3. Secure, firm, quiet, safe.

唾 t'o 1. Spittle, saliva.

TOU

斗 tou 3. A peck measure.

抖 tou 3. To tremble. *To* 3.

枓 tou 3. Capital of a pillar.

蚪 tou 3. Tadpole.

鈄 tou 3. A surname.

豆 tou 4. A vessel. Beans, pulse.

荳 tou 4. Beans, pulse.

痘 tou 4. Small pox.

逗 tou 4. To delay, to loiter.

兜 tou 1. A cowl, a bag.

鬥 鬭 鬪 } tou 4. To quarrel.

陡 tou 3. Steep.

竇 tou 4. A hole.

T'OU

頭 t'ou 2. The head, the top, the end, the chief, before, a suffix.

投 t'ou 2. To throw, to join, to agree, to have recourse to.

紏 t'ou 3. Yellow silk.

偷 t'ou 1. To steal, fraudulent, clandestine.

透 t'ou 4. To penetrate.

蔀 t'ou 2. A bud.

TSA

帀 tsa 1. To go round, a circuit, a revolution.

砸 tsa 2. To crush.

咂 tsa 1. To suck in, to taste.

雜 tsa 2. Variegated, mixed, mingled.

紮 tsa 1. To trellis. *Cha* 1.

髒 tsa 1. Filthy. *Tsang* 1.

TS'A

擦 ts'a 1. To rub, to wipe.

澾 ts'a 1. To slip, slippery.

TSAI

哉 tsai 1. A final particle.

栽 tsai 1. To plant, to transplant.

烖 tsai 1. A calamity.

㦲 tsai 1. To stumble.

載 tsai 4. To carry, a load, to record.
tsai 3. A year.

宰 tsai 3. To govern, a minister, to slaughter.

則 tsai 2. Then, and so, in accordance with, a rule, principles.

在 tsai 4. To be, to exist, to be present, alive, to depend from.

再 tsai 4. Repetition.

災 灾 } tsai 1. Fire, misfortune.

崽 tsai 3. Young of animals, a term of abuse.

TS'AI

采 tsai 3. Variegated, objects.

彩 ts'ai 3. Gay-coloured, ornamented, elegant, lucky, clouds.

採 ts'ai 3. To pick, to gather, to collect, to make enquiries.

綵 ts'ai 3. Coloured.

菜 ts'ai 4. Culinary vegetables, meat.

才 ts'ai 2. Talent, ability, strength, endowments.

材 ts'ai 2. Materials, stuff.

財 ts'ai 2. Riches, wealth, property, valuables, goods.

裁 ts'ai 2. To cut out, to plan, to decide.

蔡 ts'ai 4. Grass, hay. A proper name.

纔 ts'ai 2. Near, at hand, presently.

猜 ts'ai 1. To doubt, to suspect, to guess.

TSAN

贊 tsan 4. To assist, to advise.

讚 tsan 4. To commend, to laud, to praise.

儹 tsan 3. To gather, to hoard up.

趲 tsan 3. To hasten, to urge.

酇 tsan 4. Name of a place.

昝 偺 } tsan 2. A personal pronoun. I, me, we.

喒 tsan 2. Then, when, a final particle.

簪 鐕 } tsan 1. A hair-pin.

桚 tsan 3. To torture by finger sticks.

鏨 tsan 4. To chisel.

TS'AN

粲 ts'an 4. White rice, food.

燦 ts'an 3. Bright, glittering.

餐 湌 ts'an 1. To eat, a meal.

參 叅 ts'an 1. To counsel, to advise, to consult. *Shên* 1.

慘 ts'an 3. Grieved, sad.

謲 ts'an 4. To rail at, to chide.

蠶 ts'an 2. Silk worms.

殘 ts'an 2. To injure, mischievous, spoiled, maimed, leavings, cruelty.

讒 ts'an 2. To detract, to disparage.

慙 慚 ts'an 2. Mortified, ashamed.

TSANG

臧 tsang 1. Good, kind, to approve.

臟 tsang 4. The parenchymatous viscera.

贓 賍 tsang 1. Booty, bribes, stolen, goods, to bribe.

藏 tsang 4. Tibet. *Ts'ang* 2.

葬 塟 tsang 4. To bury, to inter a coffin.

髒 tsang 1. Filthy, dirty. *Tsa* 1.

TS'ANG

倉 仓 ts'ang 1. A granary, a storehouse.

艙 ts'ang 1. The hold of a ship.

滄 ts'ang 1. Vast.

蒼 ts'ang 1. Green, azure.

藏 ts'ang 2. To hide. *Ts'ang* 4.

TSAO

噪 tsao 4. Twittering, cries.

懆 tsao 4. Sad, troubled, anxious.

燥 tsao 4. Dry, parched.

躁 tsao 4. Hasty, irascible.

澡 tsao 3. To bathe, to cleanse.

藻 tsao 3. Sea-weed, graceful.

遭 tsao 1. To meet with, to experience, a turn, a time.

糟 tsao 1. Sediment, dregs, spoilt, rotten.

殨 tsao 1. Spoilt, rotten.

蹧 tsao 1. To tramp on, to ill-treat, to abuse.

醩 tsao 1. Sediment, dregs.

皁 皂 tsao 3. Black, lictors.

早 tsao 3. Morning, soon, formerly.

蚤 tsao 3. A flea.

棗 tsao 3. Jujube.

造 tsao 4. To make, to create, to build, parties to a suit.

竈 灶 tsao 4. A cooking-stove, a furnace.

鑿 tsao 2. A chisel, to cut into, a mortise.

TS'AO

曹 ts'ao 2. A company; a class, officials, the plural.

槽 ts'ao 2. A trough, a manger, a distillery.

漕 ts'ao 2. To transport by water.

嘈 ts'ao 2. Noise, hubbub.

髒 ts'ao 2. Crisp, friable.

䴛 ts'ao 2. Worn out, decayed.

草 ts'ao 3. Plants with herbaceous stems, grass, the running hand, a rough copy.

騲 ts'ao 3. A mare.

慥 ts'ao 4. Plainness.

糙 ts'ao 1. Coarse paddy.

操 ts'ao 1. To practise; to drill; exercise.

TSÊ (tsei)

賊 tsê 2. A thief, to ruin, to chastise.

蠈 tsê 2. A worm which eats the joints of rice.

鰂 tsê 2. The cuttle fish. *Sepia*.

TSÊN

怎 tsên 3. How? why?

TSÊNG

曾 tsêng 1. A proper name. *Ts'êng* 2.

增 tsêng 1. To add to; to increase.

贈 tsêng 4. To give a present; a title.

譄 tsêng 1. To add; to state further.

憎 tsêng 1. To hate; to abhor.

甑 tsêng 4. A boiler, to steam.

鄫 tsêng 1. Name of a place.

TS'ÊNG

曾 ts'êng 2. Past, done, yet, but, still. *Tsêng* 1.

蹭 ts'êng 4. To graze.

層 ts'êng 2. A layer; a stratum; a story.

TSO

坐 tso 4. To sit down; to reign.

座 tso 4. A seat; a divan; numerative of hills, etc.

作 tso 4. To make, to work.

怍 tso 4. Modesty.

胙 tso 4. Sacrificial flesh, to bless, to grant.

阼 tso 4. Steps, degrees.

昨 tso 2. Yesterday.

柞 tso 4. Evergreen oak.

左 tso 3. The left, second to, bad.

佐 tso 3. To second, an assistant.

嘬 tso 1. To suck, to lap up.

蕞 tso 4. A few, small, a gathering, a hamlet.

做 tso 4. To do, to act.

TS'O

硶 ts'o 3. Stones, rubble.

矬 ts'o 2. Short, a dwarf.

銼 ts'o 4. A file.

挫 ts'o 4. To shock, to break.

錯 ts'o 4. To make a mistake, to err, to be wrong, to differ.

措 ts'o 4. To arrange, to collect, to publish.

搓 ts'o 1. To rub, to scrub.

磋 ts'o 1. To work on, to rub and polish.

蹉 ts'o 1. To slip.

撮 ts'o 4. To pinch up, to gather up, sum up.

TSOU

走 tsou 3. To walk, to march.

奏 tsou 4. To report to the Throne, to advance, to play on instruments.

鄹 郰 } tsou 1. A place in Shantung. *Chou* 1.

鄒 tsou 1. A proper name.

TS'OU

湊 凑 } ts'ou 4. Confluence; to collect, to gather, a reunion, a subscription.

輳 ts'ou 4. The hub of a wheel.

TSU

祖 tsu 3. Ancestors; to begin; a model.

阻 tsu 3. An obstacle; to impede.

租 tsu 1. Tax from fields; to lease.

徂 tsu 3. To advance.

俎 tsu 3. A dresser used in sacrifices.

殂 tsu 3. To die.

組 tsu 3. A band; a girdle; an office.

沮 tsu 1. A river in Hupeh; to intimidate.

卒 卆 } tsu 2. Servants; to conclude; to finish; to die.

族 tsu 2. To collect together; a tribe; a clan; a family; relatives, to destroy.

足 tsu 2. The feet; enough; sufficient; to be satisfied with. *Chü* 2.

TS'U

粗 ts'u 1. Coarse, rude, vulgar, vile.

猝 ts'u 4. To rush out; abrupt; precipitate.

促 ts'u 4. To urge; to press; to constrain.

簇 ts'u 4. A frame; a crowd.

醋 ts'u 4. Vinegar.

麤 ts'u 1. A herd of antelopes; coarse.

蹴 踧 } ts'u 4. To walk slowly; reverence.

顣 ts'u 4 To frown.

TSUAN

謙 tsuan 4. To deceive, to hoax, to mystify.

纘 tsuan 3. To tie things together.

攢 tsuan 4. To catch, to clutch, to hold.

躦 tsuan 1. To jump.

鑽 tsuan 3. To bore, to pierce; to penetrate.

鬗 tsuan 3. Knotted hair; a chignon.

纂 tsuan 3. A compilation; to gather; to order.

TS'UAN

竄 ts'uan 4. To hide, to skulk; exile.

攛 ts'uan 1. To rouse; to inveigle; to entice.

蹿 ts'uan 4. To leap, to jump.

爨 ts'uan 4. A hearth.

TSUI

最 **tsui 4.** Very; most; extreme; to gather.

醉 **tsui 4.** Drunk; unconscious.

嘴 **tsui 3.** The mouth; a mouthpiece.

罪 辠 **tsui 4.** A crime; a wrong; a sin; punishment.

堆 **tsui 1.** A heap; a pile.

TS'UI

啐 **ts'ui 4.** To spit out.

粹 **ts'ui 4.** Pure, unmixed.

悴 **ts'ui 4.** Grieved; downcast.

萃 **ts'ui 1.** A bundle; to collect.

瘁 **ts'ui 4.** Worn out.

翠 **ts'ui 4.** The king-fisher; blue.

崔 **ts'ui 1.** Rocky; precipitous.

催 **ts'ui 1.** To urge; to press; to importune.

摧 **ts'ui 1.** To break; to destroy.

縗 **ts'ui 1.** Mourning dress.

榱 **ts'ui 1.** Small rafters.

脆 **ts'ui 4.** Crisp, brittle.

篲 **ts'ui 4.** A broom.

TSUN

俊 **tsun 4.** Elegant, refined.

浚 **tsun 4.** Deep, to dig, to enlighten.

竣 **tsun 4.** To complete, to stop.

峻 **tsun 2.** Steep, obstinate, stiff.

駿 **tsun 4.** A fine horse, noble, vast, to spread.

尊 **tsun 1.** Noble, venerable, numerative of cannons etc.

遵 **tsun 1.** To follow, to conform to, to obey.

樽 **tsun 1.** A cup.

撙 **tsun 4.** To adjust, to regulate, economical.

濬 **tsun 4.** Deep, abstruse.

TS'UN

諓 **ts'un 1.** To laugh at, to deride.

悛 **ts'un 1.** To correct, to amend.

皴 **ts'un 1.** Rough, to rub, to ridicule.

存 **ts'un 2.** To be, to exist, to preserve, to continue.

寸 **ts'un 4.** An inch.

村 **ts'un 1.** A village.

忖 **ts'un 3.** To consider, to surmise, to calculate.

邨 **ts'un 1.** Village.

TSUNG

宗 **tsung 1.** Ancestors, kind, to follow, to venerate, religious.

踪 **tsung 1.** A footstep, a trace.

綜 **tsung 1.** The throads of a texture, synthesis.

騌 **tsung 1.** A horse's mane.

粽 **tsung 4.** Dumplings.

總 **tsung 3.** To unite, to sum up, to comprise.

摠 **tsung 3.** To tie, to gather, to sum up.

騣 **tsung 1.** A horse's mane.

糉 **tsung 4.** Dumplings.

椶 **tsung 1.** The coir palm.

鏓 **tsung 1.** Ornaments on a harness.

縱 **tsung 4.** A warp. To be lax, to yield to, to let go. Although, even if.

蹤 **tsung 1.** A footstep, a track, a trace.

TS'UNG

从 從 **ts'ung 2.** To follow, to pursue, to comply with, from, by, since.

聰 **ts'ung 1.** Quick of apprehension, clever.

怱 **ts'ung 1.** Hurried, excited.

葱 **ts'ung 1.** The onion.

叢 **ts'ung 1.** A bushy place, crowded, assembled, a collection.

TU

杜 **tu 4.** A wild pear-tree, to stop, to fill up.

肚 **tu 3.** The belly, inwards, memory.

瀆 **tu 4.** A ditch, foul, to defile.

讀 **tu 2.** To read carefully, to study.

鑟 **tu 1.** An amphora.

櫝 **tu 4.** A case, a sheath.

牘 **tu 2.** Tablets, documents, a note, a letter.

嬻 **tu 4.** To defile, to disgrace.

犢 **tu 2.** A calf.

瓄 **tu 2.** The onyx.

匵 **tu 4.** A drawer, a case.

讟 **tu 2.** To murmur, to rail at, seditious.

蘐 tu 1. A grape.

覩睹 } tu 1. To gaze at, to observe.

堵 tu 3. To block up, to stop, to guard.

賭 tu 3. To gamble, to bet.

都 tu 1. The capital, all, full.

嘟 tu 1. To grumble.

度 tu 4. A measure, a limit, a degree, a rule, to cross over.

渡 tu 4. A ferry, to ford, to cross.

塿 tu 3. To stop up.

鍍 tu 4. To gild, to plate.

獨 tu 2. Solitary, single, only.

髑 tu 2. A skull.

韣 tu 2. A case or covering.

毒 tu 2. Poison, virus, violent, to hate.

督 tu 1. To inspect, to watch over, to rule.

篤 tu 3. A sure horse, constant, firm, to augment.

启 tu 2. The anus. Sting of wasps.

妬妒 } tu 4. Jealous, envious.

蠹 tu 4. Worms in books or clothes.

塗 tu 3. Stupid. *T'u 2.*

T'U

土 t'u 3. Earth, ground, soil, dust, aborigines, local.

吐 t'u 3. To spit out, to vomit, to reject, to bud.

徒 t'u 2. To go on foot, foot-soldier, a disciple, an apprentice, a companion, only, banishment, emprisonment.

途 t'u 2. A road, a path, a journey, future.

塗 t'u 2. Mud, mire, to besmear. *Tu 2.*

屠 t'u 2. To kill, to butcher.

唾 t'u 4. To spit, saliva.

兔兎 } t'u 4. A hare.

突 t'u 4. Impetuous, sudden.

禿 t'u 1. A scald head.

圖 t'u 2. A plan, to sketch, to scheme, to calculate, to try for.

TUAN

端 tuan 1. A beginning, an end, correct, proper, to serve a meal.

段 tuan 4. A piece, a section, skill, prosperity.

緞 tuan 4. Satin.

鍛 tuan 4. To forge. Asceticism.

斷 tuan 4. To cut asunder, to stop, to cease, to settle, to judge, certainly, decidedly.

短 tuan 3. Short.

T'UAN

湍 t'uan 2. Rapid current, boisterous.

摶 t'uan 2. To roll round.

糰 t'uan 2. Dumplings.

慱 t'uan 2. Grieved, deeply moved.

團 t'uan 2. A ball, a sphere, lump, to collect. to coil.

TUI

兌 tui 4. To exchange, to barter, to pay, to deliver.

譈 tui 4. To provoke, to instigate.

憝 tui 4. To hate, to detest.

對对 } tui 4. To correspond to, to suit, to answer, parallel sentences on scrolls, opposite.

懟 tui 4. To hate.

隊 tui 4. A squad, a company.

碓 tui 4. A pestle, to pound.

T'UI

忒 t'ui 4. Too, excessive, a mistake. *T'ê 4.*

推 t'ui 1. To push, to decline, to reckon, to reason.

魋 t'ui 3. A were-wolf.

退 t'ui 4. To retreat, to draw back, to refuse.

腿 t'ui 3. The thigh, the leg.

骽 t'ui 3. The thigh, the leg.

煺 t'ui 1. To scald.

TUN

囤 tun 4. A round bin.

沌 tun 4. The rush of a torrent, confusion, chaos.

盹 tun 3. Heavy eyes, half asleep.

鈍 tun 4. Dull, blunt, stupid.

砘 tun 4. A roller.

飩 tun 4. Meat ball rolled in flour.

頓 tun 4. To bow the head, to salute, to spoil.

顚 tun 4 A ton.

惇 tun 1. Honest, sincere.

敦 tun 1. Honest, true, to perform, great.

燉 tun 4. To stew, to heat.

墩 墪 } tun 1. A mound, a tumulus, a block.

撴 撉 } tun 1. To strike, with the fist, to pound with a rammer.

盾 tun 4. A shield.

遁 tun 4. To hide away, to vanish.

蹲 tun 1. To squat down.

遯 tun 4. To flee, to hide away.

躉 tun 3. To store, wholesale.

T'UN

屯 t'un 2. To collect together, a village, a camp.

吞 t'un 1. To swallow up, to engulf.

褪 t'un 4. To pull the arm within the sleeve, to put off clothes.

豚 t'un 2. A sucking pig.

TUNG

東 tung 1. The east, the place of the master.

凍 tung 4. To freeze.

棟 tung 4. Beams in a roof.

動 tung 4. To move, to shake, to stir, to displace.

董 tung 3. To regulate. *Hence*

懂 tung 3. To understand.

洞 tung 4. A cavern, a hole, to comprehend, to penetrate.

冬 tung 1. Winter.

T'UNG

童 t'ung 2. A boy under 15 years and unmarried.

僮 t'ung 2. A slave boy, a waiting-boy.

瞳 t'ung 2. The pupil of the eye.

犝 t'ung 2. A young calf.

羶 t'ung 2. A young ram.

艟 t'ung 2. Cabin-boys.

同 t'ung 2. Together, with, alike.

銅 t'ung 2. Copper, brass.

桐 t'ung 2. A varnish tree, *aleurites cordata.*

侗 t'ung 2. Simple, ignorant.

衕 t'ung 2. A side-street, a lane.

筒 t'ung 2. A tube, a pipe.

桶 t'ung 3. A bucket, a barrel.

通 t'ung 1. To go through, to communicate, to touch, contact, general.

痛 t'ung 4. Pain.

烔 t'ung 2. A bright red blaze.

鼕 t'ung 1. The rattle of drums.

統 t'ung 3. The end, a system, a whole, all, collectively, to rule.

彤 t'ung 2. Red, purple.

慟 t'ung 4. To be moved, affected.

TZŬ (Tsŭ)

茲 玆 } tzŭ 1. This, this one, now, here.

滋 tzŭ 1. To soak, humid, juicy, taste.

鎡 tzŭ 1. A hoe.

孳 tzŭ 1. To bear, to produce and suckle.

紫 tzŭ 3. Purple, violet.

鯔 tzŭ 1. A mullet.

鷀 tzŭ 1. A cormorant.

貲 tzŭ 1. A fine, property, wealth.

子 tzŭ 3. Boy, son, sir; seed; a suffix, a cyclical character.

孜 tzŭ 1. Zeal, solicitude, effort, care.

仔 tzŭ 3. To care about, exactly.

字 tzŭ 4. Characters. A name.

粢 tzŭ 1. Grain.

恣 tzŭ 1. Licentiousness, lust.

姿 tzŭ 1. Mien, beauty, demeanour.

資 tzŭ 1. Property, valuables, means of living.

咨 tzŭ 1. To consult, to plan, to propose.

緇 tzŭ 1. Black, dark.

輜 tzŭ 1. Baggage, waggons.

淄 tzŭ 1. A river in Shantung.

菑 tzŭ 1. An uncultivated field, waste.

漬 tzŭ 4. To soak to steep.

梓 tzŭ 3. The *Rottlera japonica*, plank, wood, fellow citizen.

滓 tzŭ 3. Sediment, dregs.

姊 tzŭ 3. Elder sister.

自 tzŭ 4. From, since; self. "I; my own; spontaneously.

TZ'Ŭ (Ts'ŭ)

伺 **tz'ŭ 4.** To wait upon, to attend.

詞 **tz'ŭ 2.** An expression, a composition, to accuse, to request.

祠 **tz'ŭ 2.** The ancestral hall of a family, offerings.

次 **tz'ŭ 4.** Order, series, time, second, inferior, stay.

茨 **tz'ŭ 2.** Thorns.

磁 **tz'ŭ 2.** Crockery; porcelain.

慈 **tz'ŭ 2.** Maternal affection; love; mercy.

茦 **tz'ŭ 4.** A thorn; to prick.

[illegible] **tz'ŭ 4.** The gout.

誎 **tz'ŭ 4.** To criticise.

刺 **tz'ŭ 4.** To prick, to tattoo, to stab.

蝲 **tz'ŭ 4.** The hedge-hog.

莿 **tz'ŭ 4.** Brambles.

此 **tz'ŭ 3.** This; this one.

泚 **tz'ŭ 3.** Sweat; cool.

雌 **tz'ŭ 2.** The female of birds.

疵 **tz'ŭ 2.** A malady; a vice.

齜 **tz'ŭ 1.** To gnash one's teeth.

跐 **tz'ŭ 3.** To tread; to stand on.

訾 **tz'ŭ 2.** To slander.

姕 **tz'ŭ 1.** A slattern.

辭 **tz'ŭ 2.** To decline; to refuse; to resign; an expression; a plea; an apology.

WA

穵 **wa 1.** A hollow.

挖 **wa 1.** To scoop out; to dig out; to criticise.

娃 **wa 2.** A beautiful woman; a baby.

哇 **wa 1.** Wanton sounds; retching, vomiting.

蛙 **wa 1.** A frog; wanton, talk; obscenities.

窪 **wa 1.** Low ground; a puddle; the fields.

瓦 **wa 3.** Tiles, pottery.

[illegible] **wa 4.** To cover with tiles.

襪 韤 } **wa 4.** Socks; stockings.

凹 **wa 1.** Concave, hollow.

媧 **wa 1.** The sister of *Fu-hsi.*

WAI

外 **wai 4.** Outside, without; beyond, foreign; to exclude.

歪 **wai 1.** Awry; bad, wicked, insolent.

WAN

晚 **wan 3.** The evening; late.

挽 **wan 3.** To bend; to knot.

娩 **wan 3.** Docility. *Mien* 3.

玩 **wan 4.** Trinkets; to toy, to play; to enjoy.

翫 **wan 4.** To practise.

刓 **wan 2.** To trim.

頑 **wan 2.** A thick-headed stupid person.

完 **wan 2.** To finish; to complete; to settle.

盌 **wan 3.** A bowl.

宛 **wan 3.** Of course; to give way; to yield.

腕 **wan 4.** The wrist; a flexible joint.

婉 **wan 3.** Complaisant; obliging.

琬 **wan 3.** A sceptre.

捥 **wan 4.** To bend.

碗 **wan 3.** A bowl.

涴 **wan 3.** To whirl.

剜 **wan 1.** To pick out.

彎 **wan 1.** To bend; arched; crooked.

灣 **wan 1.** A winding bank; a cove; a bay, to moor.

萬 万 卍 } **wan 4.** Ten thousand, an indefinite number; wholly.

綰 **wan 3.** To bind.

丸 **wan 2.** A pill. A steamer, *maru.*

WANG

王 **wang 2.** King, prince.
wang 4. To rule.

旺 **wang 4.** Prosperous; glorious; abundant; much.

枉 **wang 3.** Distorted, crooked. A wrong, a grievance. Needlessly; to no purpose.

汪 **wang 1.** Vast and still, much; abundant; immense.

罔 **wang 3.** No, not.

網 **wang 3.** A net; a web.

惘 **wang 3.** Grieved; irresolute disconcerted.

魍 **wang 3.** A sprite.

亾 亡 } **wang 2.** To die, to cease.
wu 2. Not, without.

忘 wang 2. To forget.

妄 wang 4. Error; disorder; falsely, wrongly, incoherent, irregular.

望 wang 4. To look towards, to hope, the full moon.

往 徃 } wang 3. To go to, to start; passed; frequently.

WEI

胃 wei 4. The stomach.

謂 wei 4. To speak, to say; to be.

渭 wei 4. Name of a river.

蝟 wei 1. The hedgehog.

爲 為 } wei 2. To be; to do. wei 4. For; because; on account of; in order to.

僞 wei 3. False.

委 wei 3. To give up; to throw away; to send; to depute, a wrong, a grievance.

萎 wei 1. To wither; to decay.

痿 wei 3. Weakness; paraplegia.

餧 wei 4. To feed.

諉 wei 3. To retract, to recant.

逶 wei 1. To walk crookedly; to swagger.

魏 wei 4. A proper name; lofty, eminent; asafœtida.

巍 wei 1. Lofty; eminent; precipitous.

危 wei 2. Lofty, perilous.

桅 wei 2. A mast.

韋 wei 2. Soft leather; pliant; flexible.

偉 wei 3. Great; brave; a hero.

緯 wei 3. The woof of a web; latitude; fringe, tassels.

違 wei 2. To oppose; to disobey; rebellion.

瑋 wei 3. A kind of jade.

幃 wei 2. A curtain; women's apartments.

韙 wei 3. Good, right; natural gifts.

圍 wei 2. To surround; to besiege; circumference.

葦 wei 3. The common reed.

闈 wei 2. An examination-hall.

衛 衞 } wei 4. To escort; to guard; Tientsin.

尉 wei 4. To soothe. *Yü* 4.

熨 wei 4. To iron.

慰 wei 4. To comfort, to pacify, kindness.

蔚 wei 4. Luxuriant, fine, prosperous.

威 wei 1. Majesty, imposing, imperious, to overawe.

葳 wei 1. Flourishing, luxuriant.

未 wei 4. A cyclical character, a negation.

味 wei 4. Taste, flavour.

畏 wei 4. To fear, to dread.

餵 喂 } wei 4. To feed animals.

煨 wei 1. To roast, to bake.

惟 wei 2. Only, but, and so, an initial or copulative particle.

唯 wei 2. Only, to consent.

帷 wei 2. A curtain.

維 wei 2. To tie, to hold fast, a rule, a law, an initial particle.

微 wei 1. Small, trifling, minute, hidden, to fade, to diminish; not.

薇 wei 2. Ferns.

囗 wei 2. An inclosure.

尾 wei 3. Tail, end. *13*.

洧 wei 3. A river in Honan.

亹 wei 3. Indefatigable, resolved, tenacity.

位 wei 4. Seat, throne, dignity, condition, a person.

隗 wei 3 A proper name.

WÊN

文 wên 2. Strokes, lines, variegated, genteel, stylish, scholarly, a classifier of cash.

紋 wên 2. A mark, line, or trace.

蚊 wên 2. Musquitoes.

汶 wên 2. Name of a river.

紊 wên 4. Raveled, tangled, to embroil.

温 溫 } wên 1. Lukewarm, to warm, genial, mild.

媪 wên 2. An old matron.

瘟 wên 1. Pestilence, epidemic, typhus.

吻 wên 3. Corners of the mouth. A kiss, to kiss.

刎 wên 3. To cut one's throat.

問 wên 4. To ask, to enquire.

聞 wên 2. To hear, to smell, news.

穩 wên 3. Firm, stable, grave, reserved.

WÊNG

翁 wêng An old man, venerable sir.

嗡 wêng 1. The lowing of cattle, the hum of insects.

甕 wêng 4. An earthern jar.

WO

窩 wo 1. A nest, a hole.
萵 wo 1. Dandelion.
渦 wo 1. A whirlpool.

倭 wo 1. A dwarf.
踒 wo 1. To sprain an articulation.

握 wo 4. To grasp, to shake. *Wu* 3.
齷 wo 4. Crumpled, rumpled.

窠 wo 1. A nest, a den.
臥 wo 4. To lie down.
沃 wo 4. Dew, to wet, to wash.

我 wo 3 and his series, see *O* 3.

WU

五 wu 3. Five.
伍 wu 3. Five, men arranged by fives, a squad.
吾 wu 2. I, me. *Hence*
悟 wu 4. To awake, to apprehend, to become conscious, intelligence.
晤 wu 4. To see, to meet.
梧 wu 2. *Eleococca, Sterculia,* trees.
牾 wu 4. To butt, to gore.
寤 wu 4. To awake.

無 wu 2. Not, nothing, without.
憮 wu 3. To love, to cherish.
嫵 wu 3. To flatter, to seduce.
蕪 wu 2. Full of weeds, poor, vulgar.
舞 wu 3. To make postures, to dance, mimic.

吳 wu 2. To brag. A proper name.
蜈 wu 2. Scolopendra.
悞 wu 4. To neglect, to delay, to miss an opportunity.
誤 wu 4. A mistake, an error.

勿 wu 4. No, not.
物 wu 4. A thing, an article, a being.

午 wu 3. A cyclic character, noon.
忤 wu 4. Disobedient, obstinate.
仵 wu 3. A coroner.

兀 wu 4. A stool.
杌 wu 4. Stump of a tree, a stool.

屋 wu 1. A room, a house.
渥 wu 1. To soak, to steep.
武 wu 3. Military, war, weapons.
鵡 wu 3. A cockatoo.

巫 wu 1. A sorceress, a witch, magic.
誣 wu 1. To slander, to calumniate.

毋 wu 2. Not, do not.

侮 }
侮 } wu 3. To insult.

杇 }
釫 } wu 1. A trowel, to rougheast.

汚 }
洿 } wu 1. Mud, dirt, foul, unclean, to defile.

務 wu 4. To attend to earnestly, to be necessary, business.
霧 wu 4. Fog, mist.
騖 wu 4. To gallop, boisterous.
婺 wu 4. Name of a star.

烏 wu 1. Crows, black, an interrogative particle.
槝 wu 1. Ebony.
摀 wu 3. To cover, to stop up.
嗚 wu 1. An exclamation of grief, alas!
幠 wu 3. A turban.
隖 wu 3. A wall round a village.

亡 wu 2. Not, without. *Wang* 2.
无 wu 2. Negation, not.
戊 wu 4. A cyclical character.
惡 wu 4. To hate, to dislike. *O* 4. wu 1. How? where?

YA

亞 ya 4. Secondary, alike.
啞 ya 3. Dumb, stammerer, *ya-pa.*
瘂 ya 3. Hoarse.

牙 ya 2. The teeth.
呀 ya 1. An interjection.
芽 ya 2. To bud, to sprout, shoots.
訝 ya 2. To admire, to wonder at, to exclaim.
迓 ya 4. To meet, to greet.
鴉 ya 1. A raven, a crow. Opium.
雅 ya 3. Elegant, genteel.

軋 ya 4. To crush, to grind.

圠 ya 4. Fine dust, atoms.

鴨 ya 1. A duck.

押 ya 1. To compel, to keep in custody, to sign, to pawn.

丫 ya 1. A fork. *Ya-t'ou*, a young slave girl.

衙 ya 2. A *ya-men*, a tribunal.

壓 ya 1 To press down, to subject, to crush.

揠 ya 4. To pull up, to eradicate.

YAI

崖 yai 2. A steep bank, a cliff, a precipice.

㥌 yai 4. To hate.

捱 yai 2. To repulse, to delay.

涯 yai 2. A bank, a shore, a limit.

YANG

羊 yang 2. A sheep or goat.

洋 yang 2. The ocean.

徉 yang 2. To ramble, to stray.

佯 yang 2. False, deceitful.

恙 yang 4. Low-spirited, sickness.

痒 yang 3. Itching.

養 yang 3. To nourish, to rear, to feed. *Hence*

癢 yang 3. To itch, to long for.

懩 yang 4. Displeasure, disgust.

様 yang 4. A pattern, a kind, a style.

漾 yang 4. Waves, flood, tide.

央 yang 1. The midst, the centre, to press earnestly, urgently, to the utmost.

殃 yang 1. A misfortune, a calamity.

秧 yang 1. Shoots, cuttings to plant.

詇 yang 4. To know, to teach.

盎 yang 1. Abundance.

鴦 yang 1. The hen of the mandarin duck.

仰 yang 3. To look up with respect and hope.

陽 阳 yang 2. The sunny side, the male or positive principle, light, life.

揚 yang 2. To raise, to hold up, to extend.

楊 yang 2. The poplar.

颺 yang 2. To flutter.

暘 yang 2. Sunshine, fair weather.

瘍 yang 2. An ulcer.

YAO

搖 yao 2. To shake, to move.

謠 yao 2. A false report, a rumour.

媱 yao 2. A prostitute.

徭 yao 2. Duty, forced labour, *corvées*.

瑤 yao 2. Green jasper.

遙 yao 2. Distant, remote.

鷂 yao 4. A kite, a paper kite.

颻 yao 2. Fluttering.

窰 yao 2. A kiln, a furnace.

爻 yao 2. Action and reaction, the lines of a diagram.

肴 餚 yao 2. Sacrificial meats, food, viands.

淆 yao 2. Mixed, confused.

要 yao 4. To seek for, to want, to intend, necessary, a sign of the future, if.

腰 yao 3. The loins, the waist.

夭 yao 3. An untimely death.

殀 yao 3. Misfortune, to perish.

妖 yao 1. Bewitching, a phantom, noxious spectres.

窔 yao 3. Hidden, secret.

約 yao 4. To bind, to agree, a treatise, a convention, to weigh, about.

葯 yao 4. Medicine.

喲 yao 1 An interjection.

幺 么 yao 1. Small, tender. The ace.

吆 yao 1. The bawling of peddlers.

窈 yao 3. Obscure, deep, retired, mysterious.

耀 yao 4. To illumine, bright, glorious, honour.

躍 yao 4. To jump, to dance.

鑰 yao 4. The key of a lock.

瀹 yao 4. To soak, to wash.

籥 yao 4. Pandean pipes.

樂 yao 4. Music. lao 4. Pleasure, to rejoice in, to like to.

藥 yao 4. A medicine, a drug.

虐 yao 4. Brutish, tyrannical, fierce, cruel. *Niao 4.*

瘧 yao 4. Fever, malaria.

邀 yao 1. To invite, to engage, to seek.

姚 **yao 2.** Handsome, elegant.

堯 **yao 1.** An ancient Emperor.

嶽 **yao 4.** The five sacred mountains.

咬 **yao 3** To bark.

齩 **yao 3.** To bite.

岳 **yao 4.** A sacred mountain, a wife's parents.

舀 **yao 3.** To bale out, to ladle out.

窅 **yao 3.** Hollow, obscure.

撬 **yao 4.** To force up by leverage, to prise open. *Ch'iao* 4.

YEH

夜 **yeh 4.** The night.

掖 **Yeh 4.** To uphold.

液 **yeh 4.** Spittle, sweat, juice, secretion.

腋 **yeh 4.** The arm-pits.

業 **yeh 4.** Patrimony, trade, office, business, merit, past.

鄴 **yeh 4.** Name of a place.

鸈 **yeh 4.** A magpie.

耶 **yeh 2.** A final particle.

爺 **yeh 2.** Grandfather. Gentleman.

嚙 齧 } **yeh 4.** To bite, to gnaw, to eat. *Nieh* 4.

謁 **yeh 4.** To visit, to receive a visit.

埃 **yeh 2.** Dust. *Ai* 1.

頁 **yeh 4.** The head, a page, beginning.

野 **yeh 3.** A waste, a desert, savage.

葉 **yeh 4.** A leaf, a slip, a plate.

額 **yeh 2.** The forehead.

隘 **yeh 4.** A pass, narrow trouble, difficulty.

噎 **yeh 1.** To choke, the throat obstructed.

冶 **yeh 3.** To smelt, to fuse.

擪 **yeh 4.** To put into the bosom.

矮 躷 } **yeh 3.** Low, dwarfish.

也 **yeh 3.** Also, besides, still, a final particle.

琊 **yeh 2.** Name of a place.

YEN

奄 **yen 3.** To propagate, to spread, forthwith.

掩 **yen 3.** To cover, to conceal, to close, to seize.

淹 **yen 1,** To inundate, to drown.

裺 **yen 3.** A hem, to hem.

㷈 **yen 1.** To cover a fire.

晻 **yen 3.** Obscured, to screen.

醃 **yen 1.** To pickle.

剦 **yen 1.** To castrate.

閹 **yen 1.** Eunuchs.

弇 **yen 3.** To cover over.

揜 **yen 3.** To cover, to shut.

渰 **yen 1.** To overflow, to drown.

烟 **yen 1.** Smoke.

咽 **yen 4.** To swallow, to gulp down.

胭 **yen 1.** Cosmetics.

晏 **yen 4.** Evening, peace, repose, late.

宴 **yen 4.** A feast, a banquet, rest, repose.

匽 **yen 3.** To enclose.

堰 **yen 4.** A dam, a barrage.

偃 **yen 3.** To recline, to sleep.

嚴 **yen 2.** Severe, stern, rigid, solemn, very, a night-watch.

儼 **yen 3.** Grave, as if.

釅 **yen 4.** Strong spirits, concentrated.

巖 **yen 2.** A rocky cliff, steep, dangerous.

檐 **yen 2.** Eaves, end of the eaves.

簷 **yen 2.** Border of a roof.

焉 **yen 1.** How? why?

鄢 **yen 1.** Name of a place.

彥 **yen 4.** Elegant, refined.

諺 **yen 4.** A common saying, a proverb.

唁 **yen 4.** To condole with.

顏 **yen 2.** Colour, the countenance.

延 **yen 2.** To protract, to delay, to invite, to engage.

埏 **yen 2.** A boundary, a limit.

綖 **yen 2.** Fringe.

蜒 **yen 2.** A kind of centipede.

筵 **yen 2.** A bamboo mat, a feast, a banquet.

厭 **yen 4.** Satiated.

饜 **yen 4.** Satiated.

懕 **yen 1.** Satisfied.

魘 **yen 3.** Indigestion, nightmare.

讞 **yen 4.** To decide on a judicial case, to pronounce judgment.

巘 **yen 3.** The top of a mountain.

燕 yen 4. A swallow, a feast, black, Peking.
嚥 yen 4. To swallow.

炎 yen 2. To flame, to blaze, hot.
掞 yen 2. To spread over, to cover.
琰 yen 2. The lustre of gems.
餤 yen 4. Fire, flames.

姸 yen 2. Elegant, skilled.
硏 yen 2. To grind, to rub fine.

衍 yen 3. To overflow, abundant, much, to relax.
驗 騐 yen 4. To inspect, to verify, evidence, fulfilment, effect, proof.
言 yen 2. Words, to speak, to tell.
煙 yen 1. Smoke, opium.
豔 豓 艷 yen 4. Beautiful, bright, winsome, dissipated, to desire.
沿 㳂 yen 2. Shore, along, to go along.
閻 閆 yen 2. The gate of a village, the king of hell.
雁 鴈 yen 4. A wild goose.
眼 yen 3. The eye, a hole.
緣 yen 2. To bind, to harmonise, the cause, the motive, fortune, favour. *Yüan* 2.
菸 yen 1. Tobacco.
演 yen 3. To practise, to drill, to perform.
兗 yen 3. A prefecture in Shantung.
硯 yen 4. Inkstone.
鹽 yen 2. Salt.

YIN

堙 yin 1. To stop up, to dam in.
湮 yin 1. To soak, to spread.
禋 yin 1. To sacrifice devoutly.

因 yin 1. A cause, because, then, to follow, to rely on.
姻 yin 1. A bride, marriage.
氤 yin 1. Warm genial aura, fecundation.

隱 yin 3. Retired, screened, in private life, enigma, affection, compassion.
癮 yin 3. A vice, bound by a bad habit

吟 yin 2. To hum, to moan.
陰 隂 yin 1. The shadowy side, the female principle, dark, secret, death.
蔭 yin 4. To overshadow, to shelter, to protect.
廕 yin 4. Shade, shadow, to shelter, to protect.

引 yin 3. To draw a bow, to seduce, to lead, a bait, a lure.
蚓 yin 3. The earthworm, *Lumbricus*.

銀 yin 2. Silver.
垠 yin 2. Beach, limit.

音 yin 1. Sound, a musical note, tone, pronunciation.
喑 瘖 yin 1. To be dumb.
窨 yin 3. A cellar.

寅 yin 2. To revere, a cyclic character.
縯 yin 4. To sew, to stitch.

殷 yin 1. Very, much, prosperity, great, intense, zeal, ardor.
慇 yin 1. Sadness, anxiety.

胤 yin 4. Offspring, to succeed, to inherit, to follow.
酳 yin 4. To rince the mouth with spirits.

淫 婬 yin 2. The rising of waters, licentiousness, lewd.
霪 yin 2. A continued rain.

誾 yin 2. To speak gently, courteous.
尹 yin 3. To rule, a chief, an officer.
印 yin 4. A seal, a stamp.
飲 yin 3. To drink.
yin 4. To give to drink.
婣 yin 1. A wedding.
憖 yin 4. To ask, to be satisfied, to force one's self.

YING

映 ying 4. To shine on, to reflect.
怏 ying 4. Dislike, disgust.
英 ying 1. A flower, brave, superior. *Hence*
瑛 ying 1. The lustre of gems.
鍈 ying 1. The sound of jingling bells.

盈 ying 2. Full, excess, overplus.
楹 ying 2. A column, a pillar.

贏 ying 2 A gain; profit; to win.
籯 ying 2. A strong-box; a safe.
嬴 ying 2. Full; abundance. *Hence*
瀛 ying 2. The ocean.

嬰 **ying 1.** An infant, a babe.

纓 **ying 1.** Tassels, tufts.

攖 **ying 1.** To run against; to assail; to injure.

孾 **ying 1.** An infant; a suckling.

櫻 **ying 1.** The cherry.

鸚 **ying 1.** A parrot.

癭 **ying 3.** A wen; a goitre.

雁 **ying 1.** An eagle.

應 **ying 1.** Ought to be; suitable; necessary.
ying 4. An answer; to respond; correspondent; proportionate; to bear; to nndertake; to fulfil, to come up to expectation.

鷹 **ying 1.** An eagle.

膺 **ying 1.** The breast, to oppose.

熒 **ying 2.** To shine; bright; twinkling.

鶯 **ying 1.** The oriole.

瑩 **ying 2.** Bright; lustre.

塋 **ying 2.** A grave; a burying-place.

罃 **ying 1.** An earthen-ware jar.

營 **ying 2.** An encampment; a battalion; to regulate; to manage; a living; business.

螢 **ying 2.** A fire-fly. *Jung* 2.

硬 **ying 4.** Hard; obstinate.

影 **ying 3.** A shadow, an image; a vestige.

迎 **ying 2.** To occur, to meet; to parc.

蠅 **ying 2.** A house fly.

郢 **ying 3.** Name of a place.

YÜ

于 亏 } **yü 2.** In, to, at, through, as to. To go.

迂 **yü 1.** To go astray, aberration, perversion.

宇 **yü 3.** Heaven, space; a temple; the universe; to cover.

芋 **yü 2.** The taro, and other edible uoers.

竽 **yü 2.** Pandean pipes.

雩 **yü 2.** To pray for rain.

盂 盂 盂 } **yü 2.** A basin; a large bowl.

予 **yü 2.** I, me.

豫 **yü 4.** Elephant; docile; cheerfulness.

預 **yü 4.** To prepare; in advance.

余 **yü 2.** I, me.

餘 **yü 2.** Remainder; surplus; excess.

於 **yü 2.** In; at; on; among; for; through; than.

淤 **yü 1.** To silt up; to be blocked; mud.

瘀 **yü 1.** Extravasated blood.

御 **yü 4.** To drive; to manage, to rule; imperial; to wait on, to help, to offer.

禦 **yü 4.** To withstand, to oppose.

育 **yü 4.** To bear and bring up to rear; education.

蜟 **yü 4.** Larva of the cicada.

隅 **yü 2.** A corner; an angle.

蝺 **yü 2.** A water-beetle.

鍝 **yü 4.** An awl.

髃 **yü 2.** The clavicle.

嵎 **yü 2.** A mountain in Shantung.

遇 **yü 4.** To meet; to occur.

愚 **yü 2.** Simple; rude; stupid.

寓 **yü 4.** To dwell; to reside; to sojourn; allegory; to receive.

臾 **yü 2.** A moment; a little while.

諛 **yü 2.** To flatter.

腴 **yü 2.** Fat; fertile.

㥚 **yü 2.** Grieved, sorrowful.

瘐 **yü 3.** Sick; weak.

庾 **yü 3.** A stack of grain; granaries.

魚 **yü 2.** A fish, a letter.

漁 **yü 2.** To fish.

繘 **yü 4.** A well-rope.

遹 **yü 4.** Succession; to transmit.

鷸 **yü 4.** A woodpecker.

俞 俞 } **yü 2.** Yes, to reply; to agree.

喻 **yü 4.** To instruct; to understand; a metaphor.

諭 **yü 4.** To issue orders; an edict; to notify.

楡 **yü 2.** The elm.

瑜 **yü 2.** Lustre; glory.

踰 **yü 2.** To cross over; to exceed.

愉 **yü 2.** To enjoy; to be happy.

逾 **yü 2.** To cross over; to pass; to exceed.

愈 **yü 4.** More; further; to exceed; to be better; to rejoice.

瘉 **yü 4.** To be cured; convalescent.

窬 **yü 2.** A dormer-window.

域 **yü 4.** A frontier; a limit; a country.

緎 **yü 4.** A seam.

蜮 **yü 4.** A malicious goblin.

閾 yü 4. A door-sill; a threshold.

舁 yü 2. To raise a thing; to lift it for presentation.

輿 yü 2. Carriage; earth.

與 yü 2. To give; to share; together, union; to resemble; to compare; fit for. *Hence*

歟 yü 2. A final particle of surprise or doubt.

譽 yü 2. To eulogise; to extol; fame.

禹 yü 3. The founder of the first Dynasty.

偊 yü 3. Alone; solitary.

娛 yü 2. To rejoice; pleasure; to amuse ones-self.

虞 yü 2. To foresee; to provide; to be anxious; to avoid.

澞 yü 2. A torrent between two high banks.

裕 yü 4. Abundance; plenty; generous.

浴 yü 4. To bathe.

欲 yü 4. To wish; to like.

慾 yü 4. Desire; lust; passion.

語 yü 3. Words; to talk.

圄 yü 3. A prison; to imprison.

玉 yü 4. A gem; white jade.

嫗 yü 4. A matron.

昱 yü 4. Light, to light.

籲 yü 4. Music; to invoke; to implore.

雨 yü 3. Rain.

羽 yü 3. Wings, feathers.

聿 yü 4. A pencil; a pen; and, then.

獄 yü 4. A prison; a litigation.

尉 yü 4. A proper name; a military officer. *Wei* 4.

郁 yü 4. A place in Shansi. Elegant.

飫 yü 4. Satiated, glutted with; gift, favour.

圉 yü 3. Marches, banishment.

鬱 }
欝 } yü 4. Bushy; dense; obstruction.

鬻 yü 1. Food; to sell.

毓 yü 4. To feed; to raise.

YÜAN

袁 yüan 2 A surname.

轅 yüan 2. The shafts of a cart.

猿 yüan 2. The gibbon.

遠 yüan 3. Distant.
yüan 4. To remove.

園 yüan 2. A garden, an orchard.

爰 yüan 2. Thereupon, a particle.

援 yüan 2. To hold fast, to pull out, to rescue, to quote.

瑗 yüan 4. A large ring of jade.

元 yüan 2. The commencement, the first cause, origin, principle.

阮 yüan 3. Name of a place.

衏 yüan 4. A band of musicians.

黿 yüan 2. The great sea turtle.

院 yüan 4. A court-yard.

鴛 yüan 1. The drake of the mandarin duck.

怨 yüan 4. Ill treatment, to have a grudge.

苑 yüan 4. A park.

原 yüan 2. A high level, a plain, origin, source, beginning.

源 yüan 2. A spring of water.

嫄 yüan 2. A proper name, *Chiang Yüan*.

羱 yüan 2. The wild sheep or argali.

豲 yüan 2. The porcupine.

願 yüan 4. To wish, to be willing, to desire, a vow.

愿 yüan 4. Honesty, respect, diligence.

掾 yüan 4. A substitute.

緣 yüan 2. Cause. *Yen* 2.

員 yüan 2. An official, member of a partnership.

圓 yüan 2 Round, circular, complete, a dollar.

垣 yüan 2. A wall.

淵 yüan 1. Abyss, deep.

冤 }
寃 } yüan 1. To injure, to oppress, wrong, to have a grudge.

鳶 yüan 2. The kite, *Milvus*. A paperkite.

YÜEH

戉 yüeh 4. A halberd.

鉞 yüeh 4. A battle-ax.

哕 yüeh 1. To vomit.

越 yüeh 4. To overstep, to exceed, moreover.

月 yüeh 4. The moon, a lunar month.

刖 yüeh 4. To maim.

悅 yüeh 4. To be pleased, gratified.

閱 yüeh 4. To look at, to peruse, merits.

粵 yüeh 4. Canton. An initial.

軏 yüeh 4. A yoke.

曰 yüeh 4. To speak, to say.

YÜN

云 yün 2. To speak, to say, etc.

紜 yün 2. Confused, mixed up.

耘 yün 2. To weed.

芸 yün 2. A fragrant herb, the leaves of which drive away insects, library, to weed.

雲 yün 2. Clouds.

殞 yün 3, To die, to perish.

隕 yün 3. To fall, to perish.

韻 yün 4. Harmony of sound, rhyme.

磒 yün 3. An aërolite.

氳 yün 1. Aura, Procreation, destiny.

蝹 yün 1. To wriggle.

慍 yün 4. To be grieved.

熅 yün 4. To iron, to smooth.

韞 yün 4. To enclose, to conceal.

緼 yün 4. Coarse cloth. *Hence*

蘊 yün 4. To collect, to bring together.

運 yün 4. To turn round, to revolve, a revolution, a circuit.

惲 yün 3. Sincere.

暈 yün 4. To be giddy, a halo, vapour.

鄆 yün 4. Name of a place.

閏 yün 4. Intercalary *Lün* 4.

潤 yün 4. To moisten. *Lun* 4.

勻 yün 2. Equal, uniform.

允 yün 3. To permit, promised, true, loyal.

孕 yün 4. To conceive, to be pregnant.

YU

酉 yu 3. A cyclic character.

猷 yu 2. To plan, to take counsel, to deliberate.

猶 yu 2. Still, yet, as, like, similar.

輶 yu 2. A light carriage, light.

由 yu 2. Cause, origin, from, after, by.

油 yu 2. Oil, to anoint.

柚 yu 2. The shaddock, *Citrus decumana.*

蚰 yu 2. A scolopender.

鼬 yu 4. A polecat.

幼 yu 4. Young, immature.

泑 yu 3. A varnish.

黝 yu 3. Black, an ashy colour.

憂 yu 1. Grieved, anxious, in mourning, melancholy.

優 yu 1 Abundant, excessive, a mime.

耰 yu 1. A harrow, to cover in seed.

有 yu 3. To have, to be.

囿 yu 4. To inclose, a park, a garden to limit.

宥 yu 4. To forgive, to be lenient.

蛕 yu 2. A tænia.

繇 yu 2. Cause, means, consequently.

蘨 yu 2. Luxuriant vegetation.

游 yu 2. To float, to ramble.

遊 yu 2. To ramble, to travel.

蝣 yu 2. Ephemera.

誘 yu 4. To lead on, to allure, to entice, to seduce.

莠 yu 3. Darnel, tares, false. *Niu* 3.

攸 yu 1. A place, that which, whereby, some.

悠 yu 1. Sadness, distant, far-reaching.

右 yu 4. The right hand, on the right, to honour, to support.

佑 yu 4. To aid, to help.

祐 yu 4. To protect, divine care and protection.

尤 yu 2. Evils, calamities, error, to blame, to murmur, more, still more, to exceed, to surpass.

疣 yu 2. A swelling, a wen.

又 yu 4. And, also, still again.

友 yu 3. Friend.

臾 yu 2. A moment, a little while, to draw.

幽 yu 1. Darkish, secret, hidden, prison, hades.

郵 yu 2. A post-house, a lodge.

莠 yu 3. Name of a place.

牖 yu 4. A window, to teach.

褎 yu 4. Elegantly dressed.

麀 yu 1. The female of the stag, a doe.

YUNG

用 yung 4. To use, to employ, so as to, thereby, thereon.

甬 yung 3. To burst forth. *Hence*

涌 yung 3. To gush, to bubble.

踊 **yung 3.** To jump, to skip.

蛹 **yung 3.** A chrysalis.

俑 **yung 3.** Wooden figures, effigies.

衕 **yung 3.** A paved alley.

恿 **yung 3.** To urge, to encourage.

勇 **yung 3.** Brave, daring. *Hence*

湧 **yung 3.** To bubble and run off, rushing.

永 **yung 3.** Ever-flowing, perpetual.

詠 **yung 3.** To recite.

邕 **yung 1.** A four square city with a moat around it, concord, harmony.

雝 **yung 1.** A wag-tail, concord, harmony.

癰 **yung 1.** A malignant ulcer, carbuncle.

雍 **yung 1.** Harmony, union.

擁 **yung 1.** To embrace, to carry in the arms, to push.

噰 **yung 1.** Singing of birds.

壅 **yung 3.** To dam, to hinder.

饔 **yung 1.** Meats, food.

庸 **yung 1.** To use, ordinary, simple. *Jung* **1.**

傭 **yung 1.** To engage for hire, *Jung* 1.

融 **yung 3.** To melt, bullion, cash, harmony. *Jung* **2.**

容 **yung 2.** To bear, air, demeanour. *Jung* **2.**

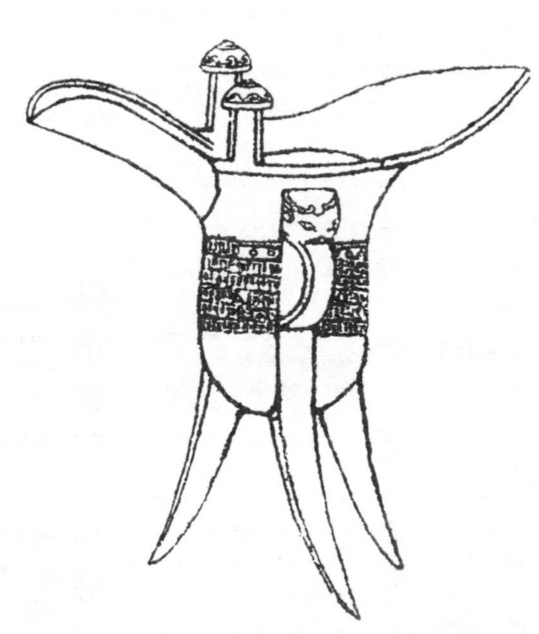

LEXICON BY ORDER OF RADICALS.

THE KEYS OF 康熙 K'ANG-HSI.

1	**2**	冂 13	勹 20	厂 27	士 33	宀 40
一 1	二 7	冖 14	匕 21	厶 28	夂 34	寸 41
丨 2	亠 8	冫 15	匚 22	又 29	夊 35	小 42
丶 3	人 9	几 16	匸 23	**3**	夕 36	尢 43
丿 4	儿 10	凵 17	十 24	口 30	大 37	尸 44
乙 5	入 11	刀 18	卜 25	囗 31	女 38	屮 45
亅 6	八 12	力 19	卩 26	土 32	子 39	山 46

巛 47
工 48
己 49
巾 50
干 51
幺 52
广 53
廴 54
廾 55
弋 56
弓 57
彐 58
彡 59

彳 60

4

心 61
戈 62
戶 63
手 64
支 65
攴 66
文 67
斗 68
斤 69
方 70
无 71

日 72
曰 73
月 74
木 75
欠 76
止 77
歹 78
殳 79
毋 80
比 81
毛 82
氏 83
气 84

水 85
火 86
爪 87
父 88
爻 89
爿 90
片 91
牙 92
牛 93
犬 94

5

玉 95
玄 96

瓜 97
瓦 98
甘 99
生 100
用 101
田 102
疋 103
疒 104
癶 105
白 106
皮 107
皿 108
目 109

矛 110
矢 111
石 112
示 113
禸 114
禾 115
穴 116
立 117

6

竹 118
米 119
糸 120
缶 121

网 122
羊 123
羽 124
老 125
而 126
耒 127
耳 128
聿 129
肉 130
臣 131
自 132
至 133
臼 134

舌 135
舛 136
舟 137
艮 138
色 139
艸 140
虍 141
虫 142
血 143
行 144
衣 145
襾 146

7

見 147
角 148
言 149
谷 150
豆 151
豕 152
豸 153
貝 154
赤 155
走 156
足 157
身 158
車 159
辛 160
辰 161
辵 162
邑 163
酉 164
釆 165
里 166

8

金 167
長 168
門 169
阜 170
隶 171
隹 172
雨 173
青 174
非 175

9

面 176
革 177
韋 178
韭 179
音 180
頁 181
風 182
飛 183
食 184
首 185
香 186

10

馬 187
骨 188
高 189
髟 190
鬥 191
鬯 192
鬲 193
鬼 194

11

魚 195
鳥 196
鹵 197
鹿 198
麥 199
麻 200

12

黃 201
黍 202
黑 203
黹 204

13

黽 205
鼎 206
鼓 207
鼠 208

14

鼻 209
齊 210

15

齒 211

16

龍 212
龜 213

17

龠 214

The figures appointed to these characters refer to the figures in the preceding Table. The dark lines indicate the position of the phonetic.

乚 5	彐 58	日 72	辶 162	糸 120
亻 9	忄 61	灬 86	歹 78	⺷ 123
刂 18	扌 64	爫 87	氺 85	𧾷 157
㔾 26	氵 85	王 94	目 109	長 168
阝 163	犭 94	玄 96	穴 116	雨 173
阝 170	尣 43	礻 113	罒 122	青 174
土 32	彑 58	罒 122	罓 122	面 176
大 37	⺗ 61	月 130	衤 145	食 184
川 47	旡 71	艹 140	⺮ 118	

Rad. 1

See Lesson 1 A.

一 弌 } **i 1.** One; alike; to unite; the whole of; as soon as.

万 **wan 4.** Ten thousand.

丁 **ting 1.** A cyclical character; an adult; to mourn.

七 **ch'i 1.** Seven.

丈 **chang 4.** A measure (ten Chinese feet). A term of respect.

三 **san 1, sa 1.** Three.

上 **shang 4.** Up, upwards, over; above. to go up; superior, before.

下 **hsia 4.** Low; below; down; underneath; to go down; inferior; following.

不 **pu 2, pu 4.** No, not.

丕 **p'ei 1, p'i 1.** Great, vast; largily.

丐 **kai 4.** To ask alms, to beg; a mendicant.

卄 廿 } **nien 4.** Twenty.

卅 **san-shih.** Thirty.

丗 世 } **shih 4.** An age; a generation of thirty years; the world.

兝 **li 2.** The thousandth part of a tael, of a *li*.

丑 **ch'ou 3.** A cyclical character.

丘 **ch'iu 1.** A hillock. **mou 3.** The book name of Confucius.

丙 **ping 3.** A cyclical character.

両 两 } **liang 3.** Two; a pair; , a tael; a ounce.

且 **ch'ieh 3.** And, also, moreover, further; if, however, absolutely.

丞 **ch'êng 2.** To help; to second.

丟 **tiu 1.** To lose, to abandon.

並 **ping 4.** Together; united; moreover; really.

Rad. 2

See Lesson 6 A.

丨 **kun 3.** A vertical line; to thread.

丩 **chiu 1. chiao 1.** To catch hold and join things.

个 **ko 4.** An individual or thing; a classifier.

丫 **ya 1.** *Ya-t'ou*, a young slave girl.

中 **chung 1.** Middle, within. **chung 4.** To hit; to be hit.

丰 **fêng 1.** Luxuriant, graceful; prosperous.

㠯 **i 3.** To use; by means of, etc.

串 **ch'uan 4.** To string to connect; to slip in.

Rad. 3

See Lesson 4 A.

丶 **chu 3.** A point, a dot.

丸 **wan 2.** Pill, ball. A steamer *maru*.

丹 **tan 1.** Cinnabar, red.

主 **chu 3.** A ruler, a lord, the head, to direct.

Rad. 4

See Lesson 7 A.

丿 **p'ieh 1.** A stroke to the left in penmanship.

乂 **i 4.** To mew grass.

乃 **nai 3.** This, here, precisely, but, then, thereupon, you, your.

乇 **t'o 4.** To lean on, to trust.

久 **chiu 2** Ancient, long since.

乍 **cha 4.** At first, unexpectedly, hastily.

之 **chih 1.** Mark of the genitive, an expletive, to go, to proceed.

乏 **fa 2.** Weary, fatigued, to be in want, poor.

乎 **hu 1. hu 2.** A particle of varied uses, interrogative, comparative, expletive.

乖 **kuai 1.** Strange, odd, perverse.

乘 **shêng 4.** A chariot. **ch'êng 2.** To ride, to mount, a classifier of vehicles or sedans, to take advantage of, to sum up, to multiply, Buddhist means of salvation.

Rad 5

See Lesson 9 A

乙 **i 1.** A cyclical character, to mark.

九 **chiu 3.** Nine.

乞 **ch'i 3.** To implore, to beg.

也 **yeh 3.** Also, besides, still, a final particle.

乩 **chi 1.** To divine by the pencil.

乳 **ju 2.** Milk, to suckle, the breasts.

乾 **ch'ien 2.** Heaven, male, constant.

乾 **kan 1.** Dry, clean.

亂 乱 } **luan 4.** Trouble, disorder, discord.

Rad. 6

See Lesson 6 B.

亅 **chüeh** 2. To mark.

了 **liao** 3. Fixed, concluded.

予 **yü** 2. I, me.

事 **shih** 4. An affair, business, to serve.

Rad. 7

See Lesson 2 A.

二弍 **erh** 4. Two.

于亐 **yü** 2. In, to, at, through, as to.

云 **yün** 2. To speak, to say, etc.

互 **hu** 4. Interlocking, reciprocal, mutual.

井 **ching** 3. A well, a rood of land measuring 900 *mu*.

五 **wu** 3. Five.

亙 **kên** 4. Borders, limits, till.

亘 **hsüan** 1. To revolve, to go through.

些 **hsieh** 1. A little, few.

况 **k'uang** 4. Moreover, a fortiori, circumstances.

亞 **ya** 4. Secondary, inferior.

亟 **chi** 2. Haste, speed, urgent, a crisis.

Rad. 8

See Lesson 4 D.

亡 **wang** 2. To die, to cease. **wu** 2. Not, without.

亢 **kang** 1. Violent, excessive. *K'ang* 4.

亥 **hai** 4. A cyclical character.

交 **chiao** 1. To blend, to unite, intercourse.

亦 **i** 4. Also, moreover.

亨 **hêng** 1. To pervade, efficacity, success.

享 **hsing** 3. To offer, to enjoy.

京 **chiang** 1. A capital.

亮 **liang** 4. Clear, luminous, bright, to light.

亭 **t'ing** 2. A pavilion.

亳 **po** 4. A city in Honan.

亶 **t'an** 3. A granary filled with grain.

亹 **wei** 3. Indefatigable, tenacious.

Rad 9

See Lesson 25 A.

It is often written as a contraction of Rad. 60.

人亻 **jên** 2. A man

个 **ko** 4. An individual or thing, a classifier.

仆 **fu** 4. To fall prostrate, to lie down.

仁 **jên** 2 Humanity, benevolence.

仍 **jêng** 2. As before, yet, still.

什 **shih** 2. A file of ten soldiers, ten.

仇 **ch'iu** 2. A surname. **ch'ou** 2. Enmity.

仉 **chang** 3. The family name of Mencius mother.

仃 **ting** 1 Alone, forlorn.

化 **hua** 4. To transform

从 **ts'ung** 2. To follow, from.

以 **i** 3. To use, with, in order to, according, a prefix connotating a relation.

仄 **chai** 3. Oblique, inclining.

介 **chieh** 4. Difference, a servant, an assistant, great, a little, scales, to patronise.

今 **chin** 1. Now, the present time.

3

他 **t'o** 1. He, she, that, another. *T'a* 1.

付 **fu** 4. To give, to deliver, to hand over, to engage.

仗 **chang** 4. Weapons, to fight, *Ta-chang*.

代 **tai** 4 To alter, to substitute, a generation, a series.

仙 **hsien** 1 Genii, fairies, immortals.

仕 **shih** 4. To fill an office, a public officer.

仔 **tzü** 3. To care about, exactly.

仟 **ch'ien** 1. A thousand.

仞 **jên** 4. Eight feet measure.

令令 **ling** 4. An order, to command, to make, your honoured.

仝 **t'ung** 2. With.

4

伏 **fu** 2. To subject, to lie or fall prostrate, to humble, to lie in ambush, to brood, to hide, to serve, a decade in dog-days.

休 **hsiu** 1. To rest, to cease, to repudiate, stop, don't.

任 **jên** 4. An employ, an office, to bear, to tolerate, confidence, to follow, any.

似 **ssŭ** 4. Like, similar to, to seem.

件 **chien** 4. A classifier, an article, an affair.

伍 **wu** 3. Five; men arranged by fives, a file.

仰 **yang** 3. To look up with respect.

伐 **fa** 1. To cut down, to chastise, to destroy, to brag, meritorious deeds.

仲 **chung** 4. Second.

侮 **wu** 3. To outrage.

伊 **i** 1. He, him, this, *I-li*, Turkestan.

伙 **ho** 3. Utensils, *chia-ho*.

仵 **wu** 3. A coroner, *wu-tso*.

伎 **chi** 4. Talent, cleverness.

伋 **chi** 2. The name of the grandson of Confucius.

份 **fên** 1. A part, a share, lot, function, duty.

伉 **k'ang** 4. A companion.

价 **chieh** 4 Good, virtuous.

企 **ch'i** 4. On tip toe, desire, longing for.

会 **hui** 4. Gathering, meeting.

5

住 **chu** 4. To halt, to stop, to cease, to dwell, to live in.

低 **ti** 1. To bend down, to incline.

作 **tso** 4. To make, to work.

位 **wei** 4. Seat, throne, dignity, condition, a person.

伸 **shên** 1. To extend, to dilate, to explain, to redress.

伴 **pan** 4. A comrade, a fellow.

何 **ho** 2. An interrogative pronoun, who, which, what, where, how?

估 **ku** 1. To estimate, to set a price on.

伶 **ling** 2. Alone, a mime, shrewd, cunning.

佔 **chan** 4. To seize by force, to usurp.

佛 **fo** 2. Buddha, Buddhist.

你 伱 伲 **ni** 3. The second personal pronoun, thou, you.

体 **pên** 3. Rude, coarse.
t'i 3. Body, susbtance.

伯 **pai** 2. A father's elder brother, a senior, an earl, a leader.

佈 **pu** 4. To extend, to diffuse, spreading everywhere.

伺 **ts'ŭ** 4. To wait upon, to attend.

但 **tan** 4. Only, simply.

佃 **tien** 4. To till the ground, farmers.

佐 **tso** 3. To second, an assistant, a deputy.

佞 **ning** 4. Insinuating, flattering.

佇 **chu** 4. To hope and wait.

伽 **ch'ieh** 2. The Sanskrit sounds *ga* and *ka*.

佢 **ch'ü** 2. This, that.

佗 **t'o** 1. That, another. He, him.

佚 **i** 4. Ease, negligence.

佑 **yu** 4 To aid, to help.

余 **yü** 2. I, me.

6

使 **shih** 3. To order; to command, to send, a messenger.

依 **i** 1. To rely on, to trust to, to conform to, to accede, according to.

佳 **chia** 1. Fine, elegant.

供 **kung** 1. To offer, to expose, a testimony, an avowal.

例 **li** 4. Rules, statute.

佩 **p'ei** 4. Pendent, to hang on the girdle.

侍 **shih** 4. To help, to wait upon.

侈 **ch'ih** 1. Lavish, prodigality.

佾 **i** 4 A band of eight dancers.

佰 **pai** 3. A hundred.

佭 **chiang** 4. Unsubmissive, to rebel.

佸 **k'o** 4. To co-operate, *K'uo* 4.

侇 **i** 2. A class, sign of the plural.

㑷 **jung** 2. A tribe of the West.

侃 **k'an** 3. Grave, dignified, plain spoken.

併 **ping** 4. On a level with even, together.

佴 **erh** 4. A second, an assistant.

㑚 **na** 2, **no** 2. A buddhist sound.

侁 **hsien** 1. Multitude, concourse.

侐 **hsü** 4. Silent, still.

佻 **t'iao** 1 Weak, unsteady.

侗 **t'ung** 2. Ignorant, simple.

佯 **yang** 2. False, deceitful.

來 **lai** 2. To come; in the future. 5

命 **ming** 4. To order, fate, life, etc.

7

便 **pien** 4. Convenient; handy; to relieve nature; then; even if.
p'ien 2. Advantageous; cheap; to profit.

保 **pao** 3. To guarantee, to protect; to keep safe.

信 **hsin** 4. Faith; sincerity; to believe in; a message; arsenic.

俗 **hsü** 2. Common; worldly; customs.

俟 **ssŭ** 4. To wait upon; until.

俊 **tsun** 4. Elegant; refined.

俏 **ch'iao** 4. Like; handsome; elegant.

侵 **ch'in 1.** To usurp; to encroach upon

侮 **wu 3.** To insult. *See above* 4.

俐 **li 4.** Clever; active sharp.

俄 **o 2.** Sudden. Russia.

侯 **hou 2.** A marquis; feudal princes.

係 **hsi 1.** To connect with; a system; to be.

侶 **lü 3.** A comrade.

俑 **yung 3.** Wooden figures; effigies.

俘 **fu 2.** A prisoner of war; a captive.

俠 **chieh 1.** Brave; a hero.

倂 **nêng 4** To deceive; to make a fool of.

俛 **mien 3.** To incline, to nod.

促 **ts'u 4.** To urge; to press; to constrain.

修 **hsiu 1.** To cultivate.

俎 **tsu 4.** A dresser used in sacrifices.

8

俯 **fu 2.** To incline; to condescend.

俸 **fêng 4.** Salary; emolument.

倆 **lia 3.** Two, of persons.

們 **mên 1.** A sign of the plural.

倫 **lun 2.** Constant; regular; principles of right conduct; morals.

俾 **pi 4.** To cause.

倍 **pei 4.** Double, to multiply.

併 **ping 4.** Together; unitedly.

倒 **tao 3.** To fall over.
tao 4. To pour out; on the contrary.

借 **chieh 4.** To lend; to borrow.

倘 **t'ang 2** If; supposing that.

值 値 **chih 2.** Price; value.

倣 **fang 3.** To imitate; like.

倡 **ch'ang 1.** A prostitute.

個 **ko 4.** This; this one; an individual; a numerative.

倞 **chiang 4.** To quarrel.

俱 **chü 1.** All, every.

倦 **chüan 4.** Tired; weary.

倰 **lêng 4.** Fatigued.

俶 **shu 4.** To begin; to act.

俺 **nan 1.** I, me.

倖 **hsing 4.** Fortunate; lucky.

候 **hou 4.** To await; to expect the arrival of; time.

倪 **ni 2. i 2.** Young; small.

倨 **chü 4.** Haughty.

倩 **ch'ien 4.** Comely; pretty.

倀 **ch'ang 1.** Mad; bewildered; slave.

倚 **i 3.** To lean upon; to trust to; inclined.

倔 **chüeh 2.** Crabbed.

倌 **kuan 1.** The Emperor's charioteer.

脩 **hsiu 1.** To adorn; to mend; to cultivate.

倓 **t'an 2.** Quiet; peaceful.

倜 **t'i 1.** Free; noble; energetic.

倅 **ts'ui 4.** An assistant.

倭 **wo 1.** A dwarf.

倉 **ts'ang 1.** A granary; a storehouse.

9

假 **chia 3.** False.
chia 4. Leave of absence.

偕 **hsieh 2.** Together; with.

偶 **ou 3.** An image; an idol; to mate; suddenly

偏 **p'ien 1.** Inclined; leaning; partial.

偋 **ping 4.** Together; all; united; even.

偷 **t'ou 4.** To steal; fraudulent; clandestine.

停 **t'ing 2.** To stop, to cease; to delay; settled.

偺 **tsan 2.** I, we.

側 **chai 1.** Inclining to one side, low; mean.

做 **tso 4.** To do, to act.

傻 **sha 3.** Foolish, simple.

偵 **ch'êng 1.** To spy; to explore.

偩 **fu 4.** To protest.

偟 **huang 2.** Agitated; in consternation.

偌 **jê 4.** An interjection.

偈 **chieh 2.** Martial; brave.

健 **chien 4.** Strong; vigorous; healthy.

偪 **pi 4.** To press, to compel.

偲 **ssŭ 1.** To warn.

偠 **t'u 4.** Hurried, headlong.

偢 **ch'iu 1.** A spy.

偉 **wei 3.** Great, talented, brave.

偃 **yen 3.** To cease, to sleep, to recline.

偐 **yen 4.** False, counterfeit, spurious.

倏 儵 **shua 4. shu 4.** Suddenly, rapidly.

條 **t'iao 2.** A twig, etc.

脩 **hsiu 1.** Dried meat, wages.

10

傍 **pang 4** Near, imminent.
p'ang 2. The side.

備 俻 **pei 4. pi 4.** To prepare, complete, perfect.

傅 **fu 4.** A master, to teach, to anoint.
傢 **chia 1.** Tools, furniture, family things.
傑 **chieh 2.** A hero.
傚 **hsiao 4.** To pattern after, to imitate.
傁 **sou 3.** An old man, venerable.
傓 **shan 4.** To excite, to inflame, a blaze.
傖 **ts'ang 1.** A worthless fellow.
傒 **hsi 1.** A waiter, a boy, to serve.
傔 **ch'ien 4.** A file, a series, to follow.
傀 **k'uei 3.** Great, gigantic.
傈 **li 4.** Ancestral tablets.
傌 **ma 4.** A knight in chess.
傏 **t'ang 2.** Wayward, brutish.
傘 **san 3.** A parasol, an umbrella.

11

債 **chai 4.** To be in debt.
傳 **ch'uan 2.** To transmit, to hand down, to propagate.
chuan 4. A commentary.
僅 **chin 3.** Only, hardly, scarcely.
傾 **k'êng 1.** Aslant, inclined, to overturn, to exhaust.
傕 **chiao 4.** A proper name.
傲 **ao 4.** Proud, arrogant.
傷 **shang 1.** To wound, to injure, to distress.
催 **ts'ui 1.** To urge, to press, to importune.
傭 **jung 1.** To engage labour, just, impartial. *Yung* 1.
傽 **chang 1.** To be afraid.
僂 **lü 2.** Hunchbacked, misshapen.
傴 **ch'ü 3.** A hunchback.
僇 **lu 4.** To scorn.
⿰亻密 **mi 4.** Strong, brave.
僈 **man 4** Negligent.
僄 **p'iao 1.** Light, airy.
僊 **hsieh 1.** Genii, to hop about.
僋 **t'an 4.** Silly, stupid.
傮 **tsao 1.** A turn, time.
翛 **hsiao 1.** The rapid flight of birds.
絛 **t'an.** A band, a tress.
僉 **ch'ien 1.** Unanimous, all.

12

僱 **ku 4.** To hire, to borrow.
僕 **p'u 2.** A servant, a subject.
僧 **sêng 1.** A Buddhist priest.
像 **hsiang 4.** An image; to resemble.
僮 **t'ung 2.** A slave boy, a waiting-boy.
僞 **wei 3.** False, counterfeit.
僚 **liao 2.** A companion, a colleague.
⿰亻斯 **ssŭ 1.** A servant.
僦 **chiu 4.** To rent, to hire.
僭 **chien 4.** To arrogate to one's-self.
僎 **chuan 4.** To prepare, preparation.
僑 **ch'iao 2.** To sojourn temporarily.
⿰亻渠 **ch'ü 2.** That person or thing.
僯 **lin 3.** Ashamed.
僐 **shan 4.** Elegant, refined.
僬 **chiao 1.** To understand, clever.
僥 **chiao 3.** Happy, fortunate.
傻 **sha 3.** Silly, foolish.

13

儀 **i 2.** Rites, observances, manners.
價 **chia 4.** The value of a thing, the price.
儉 **chien 3.** Frugal, economical.
儆 **ching 3.** To warn, to caution.
僻 **p'i 4.** Singular, mean, perverse.
億 **i 4.** A hundred thousand, numberless.
僨 **fên 4.** To ruin.
儊 **ch'u 4.** Rough, rugose.
僵 **chiang 1.** To overthrow, to fall, stiff body.
儌 **chiao 3.** Lucky, prosperous.
僸 **chin 4.** To look up at.
儈 **k'uai 4** A broker.
僶 **min 3.** To make an effort.
僿 **sa 1.** Inattentive, disrespectful.
儃 **shan 4.** Manner, air.
儋 **tan 1.** A man-load.
⿰亻愁 **chou 4.** To quarrel.
僷 **yeh 4.** Gay, jolly, light-hearted.

14

儕 **ch'ai 1.** A class, a sign of the plural.
儔 **ch'ou 2.** A comrade, a partner, who?
儒 **ju 2.** Literati, Confucianists.
儘 **chin 3.** Entirely, completely, to the utmost.
儐 **pin 4.** To receive and entertain a guest.
儓 **t'ai 2.** A satellite.
⿰亻㥯 **wên 3.** Firm, secure.

儛 **wu** 3. To skip about, to dance, postures.

儜 **ning** 2. Weariness, discouragement.

15

償 **ch'ang** 3. To pay back, to indemnify.

儡 **lei** 3. Puppets.

儠 **lieh** 4. Strong, robust.

儢 **lü** 3. Indifferent, easy going.

儤 **pao** 4. A soldier.

儦 **piao** 1. Crowds, a company.

儁 **tsun** 4. Valiant, brave.

優 **yu** 1. Abundant, excessive, overmuch, a mime.

儥 **yü** 4. To sell.

16 &

儲 **ch'u** 2. To collect, to store up.

儭 **ch'ên** 4. Inner garments.

儱 **lung** 2. Rude, unpolished.

㒟 **niao** 3. Gracious, alert.

儯 **t'êng** 2. Long, idle.

儴 **jang** 2. Because, for.

㒨 **ch'ien** 3. Lofty, proud.

儳 **ch'an** 1. Disorder, ill-assorted.

儵 **shua** 4. **shu** 4. A dark colour.

僼 **fêng** 1. Fairies, genii.

儷 **li** 4. A companion, a mate.

儸 **lo** 2. Clever, lively.

儺 **no** 2. To exercise the demons which cause pestilence.

傎 **tien** 1. To turn over or upside down.

儹 **tsan** 3. To gather, to hoard up.

儼 **yen** 3. Grave, as if.

儻 **t'ang** 3. If, suppose.

儽 **lei** 4. Tired out, exhausted.

Rad. 10

儿

See Lesson 29 A.

兀 **wu** 4. A stool.

兝 **li** 2. The thousandth part of a tael.

元 **yüan** 2. The commencement, the first cause, origin, principle.

允 **yün** 3. To permit, to promise, true, loyal.

充 克 } **ch'ung** 1. To fill, to satisfy, to stuff up, to banish.

兄 **hsiung** 1. An elder brother.

兆 **chao** 4. An omen, a prognostic, a million.

兇 **hsiung** 1. Violent, cruel, savage.

光 **kuang** 1. Light, bright, glory, naked, only.

先 **hsien** 1. Before, former. **hsien** 4. To go before, to put first.

克 **k'o** 4. **k'êi** 4. Can, able, to be fit for, to sustain, to subdue, to repress.

免 **mien** 3. To avoid, to evade, to spare.

兌 **tui** 4. To exchange, to barter, to pay, to deliver.

兒 **erh** 2. Infant, boy, son, a suffix.

兕 **ssŭ** 4. Rhinoceros, yak.

兔 兎 } **t'u** 4. A hare.

兗 **yen** 3. A prefecture in Shantung.

党 **tang** 3. A proper name.

兜 **tou** 1. A cowl, a sack.

兢 **ching** 1. To fear.

Rad. 11

入 

See Lesson 15 A.

入 **ju** 4. To enter.

亾 **wang** 2. To die.

內 **nei** 4. In, into, interior, near to, among.

全 仝 } **ch'üan** 2. All, the whole, complete.

兩 **liang** 3. Two, both, an ounce, a tael.

兪 俞 } **yü** 2. To say yes, to agree.

Rad. 12

See Lesson 18 A.

八 **pa** 1. Eight. Division.

兮 **hsi** 1. To sigh, an expletive used in poetry.

公 **kung** 1. Common, public, official, usual, just, male, duke, sir.

六 **liu** 4. Six.

共 **kung** 4. Generally, all, in fine.

兵 **ping** 1. Soldier, military, arms

其 **ch'i 2.** He, she, it, his, hers, its.

具 **chü 4.** To prepare, implements, tools, to write, all, every.

典 **tien 3.** A law, a rule, a canon, to govern.

兼 兼 } **chien 1.** To comprehend in, together with, equally.

冀 **chi 4.** To hope, to wish.

Rad. 13

See Lesson 34 A.

冂 冋 } **chiung 3.** Waste lands, frontiers, wilds.

冄 冉 } **jan 3.** Tender, weak, little by little.

囘 **hui 2.** To revert to, to turn back, a time, a turn.

册 冊 } **ch'ai 2.** A fascicle, a memorandum, a register, a census.

再 **tsai 4.** Repetition.

冏 **chiung 3.** A small window.

冑 **chou 4.** A helmet.

冒 冐 } **mao 4.** A covering for the head, to rush on, to presume, to brave out, rash.

冔 **hsü 3.** A cap used for sacrifices.

冕 **mien 3.** A cap of ceremony.

冓 **kou 4.** A frame-work.

Rad. 14

See Lesson 34 H.

冘 **yu 2.** Doubtful, hesitating.

冗 **jung 3.** Affairs; duties; supernumerary; scattered.

尔 **erh 3.** Thou. A final particle.

冠 **kuan 1.** A cap, a crown, a crest; to excel.

軍 **chün 1.** An army.

冥 **ming 2.** Dark, obscure.

冤 **yüan 1.** Injustice, wrong.

冢 **chung 3.** A tumulus; eminent, honorable.

冡 **mêng 2.** To receive, to cover.

寫 **hsieh 3.** To write.

冪 **mu 4.** To cover; to veil.

寵 **ch'ung 3.** Kindness; grace.

Rad. 15

See Lesson 17 A.

It is often written as a contraction of Rad. 85.

冬 **tung 1.** Winter; the end.

冰 **ping 1.** Ice.

冲 **ch'ung 1.** To rush against.

决 **chüeh 2.** To decide.

冱 **hu 4.** Congealed.

况 **k'uang 4.** How much more.

冹 **fu 2.** Cold.

冷 **lêng 3.** Cold, chilly.

冸 **p'an 4.** To melt as ice.

冶 **yeh 3.** To smelt, to fuse.

冽 **lieh 4.** Cold raw air.

洛 **lao 4.** Frozen.

凂 **mei 3.** To defile.

浹 **hsieh 2.** Frozen.

求 **ch'iu 2.** Chilblain.

准 **chun 3.** To permit; to approve.

凅 **ku 4.** Hard frozen.

凉 **liang 2.** Cool.

凌 **ling 2. liang 2.** Ice; coldness; to illtreat; to insult.

淕 **lu 4.** Hoarfrost.

凇 **sung 1.** Icicles.

凋 **tiao 1.** Withered.

净 **ching 1.** Clean; pure.

凄 **ch'i 1.** Cold; miserable.

凊 **ch'ing 4.** To cool

凍 **tung 4.** To freeze.

减 **chien 3.** To diminish.

渫 **tieh 4.** Frozen hard.

凑 **ts'ou 4.** To collect.

飡 **ts'an 1.** A meal.

凭 **p'ing 2.** To trust to.

凒 **i 2.** Hoarfrost.

溓 **lien 3.** A thin sheet of ice.

凓 **li 4.** Cold; chilly.

漻 **liu 2.** Chilled; frostbitten.

滭 **pi 4.** A cold wind.

潅 **ts'iu 2.** Chilblain.

澌 ssŭ 1. To thaw; to melt.

凚 chin 4. Cold; chilled.

凜 lin 3. To shiver with cold or fear.

凷 chiang 1. Congealed; coagulated.

凙 to 4. An icicle.

凝 ning 2. To freeze, to coagulate, to crystallise.

凟 tu 4. To defile.

Rad. 16

几 八

See Lesson 20 A.

几 chi 1. A small table.

凡 凢 fan 2. All, commonly; whoever, whatever; common, vulgar.

処 ch'u 4. Place.

凨 fêng 1. Wind.

凭 p'ing 2. To rely on.

凫 fo 4. A duck.

凰 huang 2. The female phœnix.

凱 k'ai 3. A victory; joy; a minister.

凳 têng 4 A stool; a bench.

凴 p'ing 2. To lean on.

Rad 17

凵 凵

See Lesson 38 B.

凶 hsiung 1. Unlucky, unfortunate, sad, cruel.

凸 ka 3. Protuberant; convex.

凹 wa 1. Hollow; concave.

出 ch'u 1. To go forth; to issue; to beget; to eject.

函 凾 han 2. To contain; to envelop; to endure; a letter; armour.

Rad. 18

刀 刂

See Leson 52 A.

刀 刂 tao 1. A knife; a lot.

刁 tiao 1. Bad, wicked.

刃 刄 jên 1. Weapon, edge.

办 ch'uang 1. To wound.

分 fên 3. To divide, to distinguish, to discern; the tenth of a *mu*; the hundreth of a foot, of a tael; a minute.
fên 4. A part, a lot, a share; function, duty.

切 ch'ieh 1. To cut, to carve; important; earnestly; absolutely; to spell.

刈 i 4. To mow; to destroy.

刊 k'an 1. To carve, to cut, to engrave.

刘 liu 2. To kill; an axe; a surname.

刌 ts'un 4. To cut fine, to divide.

4

刑 hsing 2. Torture; punishment; criminal jurisprudence.

列 lieh 4. To arrange, a series. 4

刎 wên 3. To cut one's throat.

刹 sha 4. To pierce, to stab, a small hole.

划 hua 2. A boat; a scow.

刪 shan 1. To mow.

刓 wan 2. To trim.

刖 yüeh 4. To maim.

刧 ch'i 4. To cut a notch in a stick.

5

刪 shan 1. To erase, to revise, to amend.

判 p'an 4. To halve; to decide; to judge.

別 pieh 2. To separate, to part, to recede from, another, not, do not.

刦 刼 chieh 2. To plunder, to rob openly, looting.

刨 p'ao 2. To dig, to deduct from, to extract.

初 ch'u 1. To begin, beginning.

利 lu 4. Sharp, profit, interest on money.

刻 p'i 1. To peel, to flay.

刡 min 3. To scrape off.

刮 tien 3. A nick in a blade.

刵 kou 1. A sickle or bill-hook.

6

剁 剁 to 4. To chop, to mince.

刮 kua 1. To scrape, to shave off.

到 tao 4. To arrive at, to attain, to go to, up to.

制 chih 4. To cut and pare, to regulate, to make, a rule, a system.

刷 shua 1. A brush, to brush.

刺 ts'ŭ 4. A thorn, to prick, to tattoo, to blame.
剎 ch'a 4. A pagoda.
刻 k'ê 1. k'o 1. To carve, to chisel, oppressive.
k'o 4. A quarter of an hour.
刮 chieh 1. To flag, to scalp.
刳 k'u 1. To cut open, to rip up.
劳 lao 4. To lop off.
刵 erh 4. To cut the ears.
刐 hsien 4. To castrate.
刔 t'iao 1. To cut open, to split.
券 ch'üan 4. A deed, an instrument in writing, cut in two.

7

剄 ching 3. To cut one's throat.
削 hsiao 1. To cut, to pare, to erase.
剃 t'i 4. To shave the head.
剌 la 2. To cut.
剋 k'o 1. k'ê 1. To subdue, to overcome.
則 tsai 2. Then; and so, in accordance with, a principle.
剉 ts'o 4. To file, to trim.
前 ch'ien 2. Before, in time or in place.

8

凋 tiao 1. To carve, to chisel.
剖 p'ou 1. To cut open, anatomy.
剔 t'i 1. To scrape off.
剛 kang 1. Hard, unyielding, constant, just now, recently.
剜 wan 1. To cut, to pick out.
剗 ch'an 3. To level down, to trim.
剕 fei 1. To cut the feet.
剳 ch'ia 1. To pinch, to pluck.
剠 ch'ing 2. To tattoo.
剞 chi 1. A chisel.
剟 to 4. To cut, to engrave.
剒 ts'o 4. To carve.
剚 tzŭ 4. To stick into.
剦 yen 1. To castrate, a eunuch.
剡 yen 3. Sharp, to sharpen.
契 chieh 1. To notch.

9

剝 po 1. pao 1. To flay, to peel, to extort.
剮 kua 3. To cut a criminal in pieces.
副 p'ien 4. To cut into slices.
副 fu 3. To aid, an assistant, a deputy, a second, a duplicate, a numerative.
剫 to 4. To cut, to hew.
剬 tuan 1. To chisel.
剪 chien 3. Scissors, to cut.

10

剩 shêng 4. An overplus, fragments, leavings, to retain.
割 ko 1. To cut.
創 ch'uang 1. To wound, gashed, to found, to create.
剴 k'ai 3. A scythe, to mow down.
剳 ta 2. A hook.
剔 t'a 1. A clash.
剭 wu 1. A chaff-cutter.
劇 chien 1. To castrate.

11

剿 勦 ch'ao 3. To attack, to destroy.
斲 cho 2. A cooper's adze, to cut.
剷 ch'an 3. To level down, to spade.
剙 ch'uang 4. To wound slightly.
圓 k'ou 1. To cut out
劃 lou 4. To carve, to hollow out.
剽 p'iao 4. To cut, to stab, violent.
剸 chuan 1. To mutilate.
彗 hsüeh 1. To sweep away.
嫳 p'ieh 1. To cut through.

12

剻 ch'ih 2. To cut in pieces.
劃 hua 4. To split, to rend, to mark.
劂 chüeh 2. A gouge.
劇 shan 3. To work on, to cut out.
劊 ts'êng 4. A sudden cut or stroke.
劀 kua 1. To cut out an ulcer.
粼 lin 2. To pare or peel.
剽 su 4. To mince.
劁 ch'iao 4. To cut, to castrate, to reap.

13

劉 liu 2. An axe, to kill. A surname.
劊 kuei 4. An executioner.
劍 chien 4. A two edged sword.

劇 **chu 4.** A stage play, tragic, calamity.

劈 **p'i 3.** To split, kindlings.

14

劑 **chi 4.** To adjust, to trim, a dose.

劄 **cha 2.** To cut, a grass cutter.

劐 **huo 1.** To split open, to risk, to expose. *Ho 1.*

[illegible] **ts'ou 4.** To mince, to cut into small pieces.

劓 **i 4.** To cut off the nose.

劒 **chien 4.** A sword.

15 &

劕 **chih 4.** A deed, a ticket, a token.

劙 **li 2.** To rive.

劖 **ch'an 1.** To cut off.

[illegible] **ch'ien 1.** To stick in.

劘 **mei 2.** To cut.

Rad. 19

力

See Lesson 53 A.

力 **li 4.** Strength, energy.

办 **pan 4.** To do.

劝 **ch'üan 4.** To exhort, to press.

功 **kung 1.** Merit, meritorious service, work.

幼 **yu 4.** Young.

加 **chia 1.** To add to, to confer upon, to inflict.

劤 **chin 4.** Strength.

劣 **lüeh 4.** Weak, feeble, vicious.

5

劫 **chieh 2.** To rob, to plunder.

劬 **ch'ü 1.** Labour, distress, severe toil.

助 **chu 4.** To help, to succour.

劭 **shao 4.** Effort, exertion, beauty.

努 **nu 3.** To exert the utmost strength, to strive.

男 **nan 2.** Male.

6

効 **hsiao 4.** To imitate.

劼 **chi 4.** Earnestly.

劾 **hai 2.** To examine, to scrutinise, to accuse. *Ho 2.*

劻 **k'uang 1.** Zealous, prompt.

劵 **chüan 4.** Tired, weary.

7

勁 **chin 4.** Strength. Taste.

勅 **ch'ih 4.** An imperial edict.

勃 **po 4.** Suddenly.

勉 **mien 3.** To make an effort, to excite, to urge.

勄 **min 3.** Active, clever, witty.

觔 **chin 1.** A pound.

勇 **yung 3.** Brave, daring.

8

勑 **ch'ih 4.** An imperial edict.

勍 **ch'ing 2.** Strong, violent.

9

勘 **k'an 4.** To investigate, to examine.

勒 **lei 1.** A bridle, the reins, to restrain, to vex.

動 **tung 4.** To move, to displace, to shake, to stir.

勖 **hsü 4.** To encourage.

務 **wu 4.** To attend to earnestly; to be necessary, business.

10

勛 **hsün 1.** Loyal merit.

勝 **shêng 4.** To conquer, to outdo, to sustain.

劳 **lao 2.** To toil, to labour, reward.

11

勤 **ch'in 2.** Diligence, to toil, to work.

勢 勢 **shih 4.** Power, authority, influence. Circumstances.

勣 **chi 1.** Meritorious deeds, merit.

勦 **ch'ao 2.** To grieve, to molest.

勡 **p'iao 4.** To seize by force.

勠 **lu 4.** To join, to combine forces.

[illegible] **ao 2.** Strong, brave.

募 **mu 4.** To summon, to collect subscriptions.

勥 **ch'iang 4.** To exert one's strength.

12 &

勩 **i 4.** Cares, toil.

[illegible] **chüeh 4.** To compel.

[illegible] **chüeh 2.** To break.

勰 **hsieh 2.** Harmony.

勱 **mai 4.** To exert one's strength.

勳 **hsün 1.** Meritorious effort, loyal merit.

勵 **li 4**. To stimulate.

勴 **lü 4**. To encourage.

勷 **jang 2**. Urgent, zeal.

勸 **ch'üan 4**. To exhort, to admonish.

Rad. 20

See Lesson **54 A**.

勺 **shao 2**. Spoon.

匀 **yün 2**. Equal, uniform.

勾 **kou 1**. A mark, to entice, to hook on.

勼 **chiu 1**. The turtle dove.

勿 **wu 4**. No, not.

包 **pao 1**. To wrap up, to envelop, to hold, to warrant, gestation.

句 **chü 4**. A phrase, a word.

匃 **kai 4**. To beg, mendicant.

匆 **ts'ung 1**. In a hurry.

旬 **hsün 2**. A decade, a whole.

匈 **hsiung 1**. The breast, the thorax.

甸 **tien 4**. A domain, to administer.

匌 **ho 2**. To environ, everywhere.

匊 **chü 2**. A handful.

匋 **t'ao 2**. A kiln.

匍 **p'u 2**. To fall prostrate, to crawl.

芻 **ch'u 2**. Hay, dried grass, valueless.

匏 **p'ao 2**. A calabash, a gourd.

匐 **fu 4**. To crawl, to creep.

Rad. 21

See Lesson **26 B**.

匕 **pi 3**. A spoon.

化 **hua 4**. To change, transformation, to convert.

北 **pei 3**. The North.

匙 **shih 2**. A key.

Rad. 22

See Lesson **54 A**.

匚 **fang 1**. A chest.

匜 **i 2**. A washing-basin.

匝 **tsa 1**. To go round, a circuit, a revolution.

叵 **p'o 3**. No, not.

匠 **chiang 4**. Artisan.

匡 **k'uang 1**. Regular, to rule.

匟 **k'ang 4**. The divan of a guest-chamber, to seat, two.

匣 **hsia 2**. A casket.

匧 **ch'ieh 4**. A trunk, a chest.

匪 **fei 3**. Not, without, vagabonds, rebels.

匬 **yü 4**. A granary.

匯 **hui 4**. Confluent, a bank draft.

[illegible] **i 4**. A censer.

匱 **k'uei 4**. Wearied, to exhaust.

匰 **tan 1**. The shrine for tablets in the ancestral hall.

匲 匳 **lien 2**. A lady's dressing-case, a bridal *trousseau*.

匴 **hsüan 4**. A box.

匵 **tu 4**. A case, a receptacle for books.

[illegible] **kan 3**. A trunk.

Rad 23

See Lesson **10 B**.

匸 **hsi 3**. To conceal.

匹 **p'i 3**. A single fellow; vulgar.

㔷 **lou 4**. To retire into obscurity.

医 **i 1**. A quiver.

匽 **yen 3**. To hide away.

匾 **pien 3**. Horizontal tablets.

匿 **ni 4**. To hide; to abscond.

區 **ch'ü 1**. A district; to store away; to discriminate between.

Rad. 24

See Lesson **24 A**.

十 **shih 2**. Ten; perfect.

千 **ch'ien 1**. Thousand; very many.

升 **shêng 1**. A pint, the tenth part of a peck. To ascend, promotion.

午 **wu 3**. A cyclical character; noon.

卉 **hui 4**. Plants, herbs.

半 **pan 4.** To divide in two; a half.

卍 **wan 4.** 10.000; the symbol of Buddha's heart, the Indian *swastika*.

卓 **cho 1.** Eminent; to surpass; to establish.

協 **hsieh 2.** United in; agreement; concord; a regiment; to aid.

卑 **pi 1. pei 1.** Low; base; applied conventionally to one's self.

卒 **tsu 2.** Servants; to conclude; to finish; to die.

南 **nan 2.** The South.

卙 **shih 4.** Full; abundant; to assemble.

博 **po 2.** Ample; spacious; universal science.

準 **chun 3.** Exactly, certain.

Rad. 25

See Lesson 56 A.

卜 **pu 3. po 3.** To divine.

卞 **pien 4.** A proper name.

占 **chan 1.** To divine.

卟 **chi 1.** To consult a diviner.

卡 **ch'ia 1.** A guard-house at a pass; a Customs' barrier.

[illegible] **chao 4.** To inquire by auguries.

卣 **yu 3.** A sacrificial vase.

[illegible] **chao 4.** An omen; a prognostic.

卦 **kua 4.** The divinatory diagrams.

[illegible] **hui 4.** To repent; the three upper lines of a diagram.

Rad. 26

See Lesson 56 B.

卩 **chieh 2.** A badge; authority.

卬 **nang 2. ang 2.** High, noble, used as the pronoun *I*.

卯 **mao 3.** A cyclical character; a term; a mortise.

卮 **chih 3.** A rhyton.

印 **yin 4.** A seal, a stamp.

危 **wei 2.** Perilous; precipitous.

却 **ch'iao 1.** Precisely; to reject.

卵 **luan 3.** Eggs; testicles.

卲 **shao 4.** Eminent.

卷 **chüan 3.** To roll. **chüan 4.** A roll; section of a book.

卺 **chin 3.** The nuptial wine cup.

卸 **hsieh 4.** To lay aside, to unload.

卹 **hsü 4.** To feel for; pity.

卻 **ch'iao 4.** Certainly; but; to reject.

卽 即 即 } **chi 2.** Immediately. **chi 4.** Consequently.

卿 卿 } **ch'ing 2.** Minister.

Rad. 27

See Lesson 59 A.

It is often written as a contraction of R. 53.

厂 **han 4.** A cliff.

仄 **chai 3.** Oblique.

厄 **o 4.** Difficulty, distress.

厓 **yeh 2. yai 2.** A bank; a shore; a limit.

厚 **hou 4.** Thick; large; generous.

厘 **li 2.** The thousandth part of a tael.

厖 **mang 2.** A rock.

厙 **shê 4.** A proper name.

厞 **fei 2.** The south corner of a room; hidden.

厝 **ts'o 4.** To bury; a tombstone.

厜 **ch'ui 2.** A cliff.

原 **yüan 2.** A high level; a plain; origin; source; beginning.

厠 **ssŭ 4.** A privy.

雁 **yen 4.** A wild goose.

厥 **ch'üeh 2.** He; him; this. *Chüeh* 2.

厦 **sha 4.** Penthouse.

厩 **chiu 4.** A stable.

厪 **chin 3.** A hut; narrow, anxious.

厰 **ch'ang 3.** A shed; a storehouse.

厨 厨 } **ch'u 2.** A kitchen.

厬 **kui 3.** Dried.

厮 **ssŭ 1.** Servants.

厭 **yen 4.** Filled; satiated.

鴈 **yen 4.** A wild goose.

[illegible] **p'i 4.** Steep.

厲 **li 4.** A whetstone. Evil, bad, noxious.

Rad. 28

See Lesson 89 A.

厶 **ssŭ 1.** Private.

么 **yao 1.** Young. An ace.

厷 **kung 1.** Humerus, arm.

厹 **ch'iu 2.** A trident.

去 **ch'ü 4.** To go; to leave; past, gone.

叁 **san 1.** Three.

參 **ts'an 1.** To counsel; to consult; to visit.
shên 1. In *hai-shên*, seaslugs; *jênn-shên*, ginseng.

Rad 29

See Lesson 43 B.

又 **yu 4.** The right hand; and, also, still again; more.

叉 **ch'a 1.** A fork; to pick up, to fold the hands.

収 **shou 1.** To receive, to gather.

反 **fan 3.** To turn back, contrary, opposite, to rebel.

及 **chi 2.** To reach to, till.

双 **shuang 1.** Double.

𠬛 **mu 4.** To disappear.

友 **yu 3.** Friend.

圣 **shêng 4.** Holy.

变 **pien 4.** To change.

受 **shou 4.** To be a recipient of, to suffer, to bear.

叔 **shu 2.** A father's younger brother. *Shou* 2.

㕞 **shua 1.** To brush.

取 **ch'ü 3.** To take hold of, to take a wife.

叚 **chia 3.** False, unreal.

叛 **p'an 4.** To rebel, to revolt.

叙 **hsü 4.** To arrange in order, to talk together.

叟 叜 **sou 3.** An old man, venerable.

叠 **tieh 2.** To redouble, to fold.

叡 **jui 4.** Perspicacious, shrewd.

叢 **ts'ung 1.** Bushy, a crowd, collection.

Rad. 30

See Lesson 72 A.

口 **k'ou 3.** The mouth. Numerative of persons, etc.

兄 **hsiung 1.** Elder brother.

另 **ling 4.** Apart, separate, besides, furthermore.

只 **chih 3.** Merely, only, a final particle.

号 **hao 4.** To cry, to call.

召 **chao 4.** To call by words, to summon.

古 **ku 3.** Ancient, old.

右 **yu 4.** The right hand, on the right, to honour, to support.

台 **t'ai 2.** The Great Bear, a terrace.

叴 **ch'iu 2.** A proper name.

可 **k'o 3.** Convenient, proper, can, may, to permit.

司 **ssŭ 1.** To control, the officer who presides, a court, the faculties of the soul.

句 **chü 4.** A sentence, a word.

叵 **p'o 3.** Do not, ought not.

史 **shih 3.** An annalist, a history, a register.

叫 **chiao 4.** To cry, to call, to name, to cause.

叱 **ch'ih 4.** To scold.

叮 **ting 1.** To enjoin.

叩 **k'ou 4.** To knock.

叼 **tiao 1.** To hold in the mouth.

叨 **t'ao 1.** To talk, to chat.

叭 **pa 1.** Trumpet, *la-pa*.

叶 **hsieh 2.** Concord, harmony.

3

吊 **tiao 4.** To condole, to suspend, to hang, a thousand cash.

吉 **chi 2.** Fortunate, lucky.

舌 **shê 2.** Tongue.

各 **ko 3.** Each, every, all.

名 **ming 2.** A name, an appellation, fame.

后 **hou 4.** The sovereign, an empress, after, then.

合 **ho 2.** To shut the mouth, to join, to unite, suitable, to match, to meet, together, with, a region.

向 **hsiang 4.** A window, facing, opposite to, like, to favour.

同 **t'ung 2.** Together, with, alike.

吏 **li 4.** Officers, petty magistrates.

吐 **t'u 3.** To spit out, to vomit, to reject, to bud.

吆 **yao 1.** The bawling of peddlers.

吃 **ch'i 1.** To eat. It is used as an abbreviation for *ch'ih* 1.

吸 **hsi 1.** To inhale, to suck up.

吁 **hsü 1.** To sigh, alas.

吒 **ch'a 4.** To vociferate.

叿 **hung 1.** Din of workers.

4

呆 **tai 1.** Silly, stupid.

呈 **ch'êng 2.** To state clearly, to file a plaint.

吳 **wu 2.** To brag, a proper name.

呂 lü 3. Vertebrae, musical tunes

吝 lin 4. Stingy, sordid.

含 han 2. To hold in the mouth, to contain, to restrain, doubt.

君 chün 1. Sovereign, prince, ruler, a gentleman, sir.

呑 t'un 1. To swallow, to engulf.

告 kao 4. To tell, to announce to, to indict.

否 fao 3. Not, or not. An interrogative particle.

吾 wu 2. I, me.

叫 chiao 4. To call.

吟 yin 2. To hum, to moan.

吠 fei 4. To bark.

吩 fen 1. To command.

吧 pa 1. A dumb man, *ya-pa*.

听 t'ing 1. To hear, to listen to.

吵 ch'ao 3. A clamour, uproar, to wrangle.

吹 ch'ui 1. To blow, to chide.

吲 shên 3. To smile.

吻 wên 3. The lips, to kiss, a kiss.

吮 tsun 3. To suck, to lick.

吣 ch'in 4. To vomit.

吚 i 1. Yes.

吽 hung 1. To bellow.

咂 tsa 1. To suck, to lick.

呀 ya 1. An interjection.

呐 nê 4. Reserve, circumspection, taciturnity.

呃 o 4. To belch.

吼 hou 3. To roar.

吱 chih 1. To growl.

㕮 fu 3. To chew, to ruminate.

5

咎 chiu 1. Fault, blame, calamity.

周 chou 1. A dynasty, a bend, to surround, complete.

尚 shang 4. Still. To like, to esteem.

命 ming 4. To command, a decree, fate, life.

呥 ch'ou 1. To suck in, to smoke.

呢 ni 1. A final particle.

味 wei 4. Taste, flavour.

呸 p'ei 1. To snort at.

呪 呪 } chou 4. To curse, to imprecate, an incantation.

咂 tsa 1. To suck in, to taste, to lick.

咐 fu 4. To enjoin.

呻 shên 1. To recite, to mutter, to hum, to groan.

呼 hu 1. To breathe out, to address, to invoke.

呵 ho 1, ha 1. To scold, to laugh.

咏 yung 3. To sing, to chant.

呦 yu 1. To bell.

咎 chiu 1. Fault, blame.

咕 ku 1. Sound of gurgling, etc.

咆 p'ao 2. To roar.

咙 yüeh 1. To vomit.

咋 cha 4. Chirping.

咮 chu 4. To chuck.

咈 fu 4. To contradict, to resist, to refuse.

哓 hsiao 1. To cry.

哄 hung 2. To bellow.

呭 i 4. Loquacious, garrulous.

呿 ch'ü 1. To gape.

呠 p'ên 4. To spurt.

咀 chü 3. To suck, to taste.

呱 wa 1. The wailing of an infant.

和 ho 2. Harmony, concord, agreement, with, together, to.

6

品 p'in 3. A kind, series, rank, order, a rule.

咠 ch'i 4. To whisper in the ear, to slander.

哀 ai 1. To grieve for, sorrow, sad.

咨 tzŭ 1. To consult, to plan, to propose.

哉 tsai 1. A final particle.

咸 hsien 2. All, entirely, to unite.

咳 hai 2. An interjection. k'o 2. To cough.

响 hsiang 3. An echo, a noise, sounding.

咬 yao 3. To bite.

咱 tsan 2, tsa 2. We, our.

咽 yen 4. To swallow, to gulp down.

哄 hung 3. Noise, to trick, to cheat.

哂 shên 3. To smile.

咻 hsiu 1. To clamour, a shriek.

咧 lieh 1. To grimace, to sob.

哈 ha 1. To exhale. The sound of laughter.

哪 na 1. A final particle.

咯 lao 4. A final particle.

哎 ai 4. Aiya, alas!

哇 wa 1. To retch or vomit, wanton sounds.

咮 chu 4. To peck up.

咙 hsü 4 To whistle.

哏 hên 1. Loud angry tones. To scold.

咥 **chih 4.** To bite.

咵 **k'ua 3.** To boast.

咩 **mieh 1.** The bleating of sheep.

咷 **t'ao 2.** To wail.

咫 **chih 3.** A foot of eight inches.

7

員 **yüan 2.** An official, officers.

唇 **ch'un 2.** The lips.

哲 **chê 4.** Wise, philosophy.

唐 **t'ang 2.** Boasting. A proper name.

哭 **k'u 1.** To weep bitterly, to scream.

哿 **k'o 3.** Good, apt, possible.

哥 **ko.** An elder brother.

哸 **shu 4.** To rinse.

哦 **o 2.** To chant, to hum.

唚 **ch'in 4.** To vomit.

哨 **shao 4.** To whistle, to patrol, an outpost.

哧 **ch'ih 1.** To frighten.

哺 **fu 3.** To feed.

哩 **li 1.** A final particle.

哼 **hêng 1.** An interjection, *hm!*

哮 **hsiao 1.** To roar.

哽 **kêng 3.** Choking, sobbing

唆 **so 1.** To incite, to make mischief.

唉 **ai 3.** To belch.

啊 **o 1. a 1.** An interjection.

唏 **hsi 1.** To grieve.

哯 **hsien 4.** To vomit.

唠 **lao 2.** To gabble, loquacity.

唎 **li 4.** A final sound.

哴 **lang 4.** The inarticulate crying of infants.

唈 **i 4.** Panting.

哤 **mang 2.** A jargon.

哶 **mieh 1.** To bleat.

唄 **pai 4.** To chant, as in Buddhist temples.

8

售 **shou 4.** To sell.

啓 啟 **ch'i 3.** To open, to begin, to explain.

問 **wên 4.** To ask, to enquire.

商 **shang 1.** To consult, a merchant, a proper name.

啇 **ti 2.** The peduncle, stalk, origin.

唬 **hu 1.** To frighten.

唯 **wei 2.** Only, to consent.

唱 **ch'ang 4** To sing.

啣 **hsien 2.** To hold in the mouth.

啐 **ts'ui 4.** To spit.

啞 **ya 3.** Dumb.

啜 **ch'o 4.** To suck up, to sip, to weep.

啄 **cho 4.** To peck up food.

唳 **li 4.** The cry of a heron, wild goose, etc.

啉 **lan 2.** Greedy, covetous.

唼 **ch'ieh 4.** To jabber.

唲 **wa 2.** To prattle.

唵 **yeh 4.** The cry of birds at night.

唪 **fêng 3.** To intone, to chant.

啃 **k'ên 3.** To bite, to gnaw.

唴 **ch'iang 1.** The wailing of infants.

啌 **kuan 1.** To coo to each other, as doves do.

唵 **nan 1.** To gobble up with the mouth.

啸 **sao 1.** To chirp, to hum.

唰 **shua 1.** To preen feathers.

啖 **tan 4.** To chew; to eat.

啕 **t'ao 2** To cry.

9

善 **shan 4.** Good; virtuous; to know apt at; to approve.

喜 **hsi 3.** Joy; gladness; to delight in.

啻 **t'i 4.** Only.

喬 **ch'iao 2.** Lofty; proud.

單 **tan 1.** Single.
shan 4. A name.

喪 **sang 1.** A funeral; to mourn; to lose to ruin.

喫 **ch'ih 1.** To eat; to suffer.

喣 **hsü 4.** To blow; breath, spittle, smile.

唾 **t'u 4, t'o 4.** To spit; saliva.

喳 **ch'a 1.** To twitter; to whisper.

喘 **ch'uan 3.** To pant.

喊 **han 3.** To cry.

喉 **hou 2.** The throat; the oesophagus.

喝 **ho 1.** To drink. To cry.

喧 **hsüan 1.** Clamour; hubbub.

喚 **huan 4.** To call out; to summon; to name.

喤 **huang 2.** Jingling of bells.

喏 **nê 4. jê 3.** To assent; to salute.

喈 **chieh 1.** Music; melody.

喇 **la 3.** A final sound.

喨 **liang 4.** Children wailing.

喃 **nan 2.** To whisper.

嵘 jou 4. Bad words.

唽 ch'a 4. To prattle..

嗿 tai 4. To prattle.

啼 t'i 2. To weep.

喋 tieh 2. To chatter.

喥 to 4. To chatter.

喟 k'oei 4. To sigh.

喒 tsan 2. Then, when; a final particle.

喞 chi 1. The hum of insects.

啾 chiu 1. Onomatopœia.

喎 kua 3. Awry distorted.

喂 wei 4. To feed animals.

喔 wu 4. The cackling of fowls.

喓 yao 1. The chirping of grass-hoppers.

喭 yen 4. To condole with.

喑 yin 1. To be dumb.

喻 yü 4. To instruct; to understand, metaphor, example.

喁 yü 1. To gape; to stand open-mouthed.

喵 miao 1. To mew.

喲 yao 1. An interjection.

10

嗇 shê 4. The harvest; stingy; parsimony.

喿 tsao 4. The twittering of birds; noise.

嗣 ssŭ 4. To connect; to adopt; heirs, posterity; hereafter.

嗏 ch'a 1. Onomatopœia.

嗔 ch'ên 1. To be angry at; to rail at.

嗹 chan 3. To gaze at stupidly.

嗤 ch'ih. To laugh at.

嗐 hai 1. An exclamation of regret or surprise.

嗅 hsiu 4. To smell; to scent out.

嗑 ho 1. To drink.

嗊 hung 3. To sing.

嗕 ju 4. To pity.

嗘 chi 1. To whisper.

嗛 ch'ien 4. To peck.

嗝 ko 2. Spasm; the hiccups.

嗎 ma 1. An interrogative particle, etc.

嗙 p'ang 3. To boast, to brag.

嗓 sang 3. The throat, the voice.

嗄 sha 4. A hoarse voice.

嗖 sou 1. A sound.

嗜 shih 4. To love; to desire; to covet; to be addicted to.

嗍 shuo 3. To suck in; to smoke; to inhale.

嗉 su 4. The gizzard of a bird; a jug.

嗒 ta 1. Melancholy; absent; abstracted.

嗁 t'i 2. To bewail.

嗆 ch'iang 1. Spasm of the glottis.

嗟 chüeh 1. To sigh; alas.

嗞 tzŭ 1. To propose; to deliberate.

嗡 wêng 1. The hum of insects.

嗢 wa 1. Infant's wail.

嗚 wu 1. An exclamation; alas.

嗌 i 4. The throat; to swallow.

嗢 wu 4. To clear the throat.

嗂 yao 2 Joyful; merry.

嗈 yung 1. Singing of birds.

嗏 ch'ai 2. To bark.

喙 hui 4. Mouth; beak; to pant.

嗕 jung 3. yung 3. To retch; to choke.

11

嘗 ch'ang 2. To taste; to try; formerly; continually.

嘉 chia 1. Beautiful, good; to approve.

嘏 chia 3. Felicity; prosperity; strong.

嗻 chê 1. Loquacity.

嘑 hu 1. o howl at.

嘒 hui 4. Jingling.

嘎 ka 1. Loud laughing.

嘐 hsiao 1. Boasting, bragging.

嘓 kuo 4. To chatter.

嘮 lao 2. A great noise.

嘍 lou 2. Chattering; prattling.

嘆 mo 4. Silent; peaceful.

嗷 ao 1. Buzz of voices; clamours.

嘔 ou 1. To vomit.

嘌 p'iao 1. Cries of charioteers.

嗺 tsui 1. To kiss.

嗽 sou 4. To cough.

嗾 sou 2. To excite; to tease.

嗦 so 4. To sip.

嘼 hsi 2 To shiver with cold.

嘾 t'an 3. The noise of eating.

嘆 t'an 4. To sigh; to moan.

嘈 ts'ao 2. Noise, hubbub.

嘖 chai 4. To bawl.

嘁 ch'i 1. To whisper.

嘟 tu 1. To grumble.

鳴 **ming 2.** Cry ; sound ; to resound.

嘛 **ma 1.** Lama, a tibetan bonze.

嚀 **ning 2.** To enjoin.

12

嘼 **hsiu 4.** Animals pasturing.

噐 **ch'i 4.** A vessel, a tool, a utensil, ability.

嘘 **hsü 1.** To blow, to breathe, to suck up.

嘲 **chao 1.** To jeer at.

嘬 **tso 1.** To suck, to lap up.

嘷 **hao 2.** To howl.

嘻 **hsi 1.** An interjection

噏 **hsi 1.** To inhale.

嘩 **hua 2.** Clamour, noise.

嚍 **hua 4.** To cry.

嘵 **hsiao 1.** To quarrel.

噙 **ch'in 2.** To hold in the mouth, to restrain.

噘 **chüeh 1.** To pout.

嘹 **liao 2.** A sound.

嘪 **mai 3.** To bleat.

嘿 **mei 4.** Retired, secret, silent.

噃 **p'an 1.** To insult, to provoke.

嘶 **hsi 1.** To neigh.

噀 **hsün 4.** To spit, to besprinkle.

嘽 **t'an 1.** To pant.

噋 **tun 1.** To swallow down, to gobble up.

噌 **ts'êng 1.** Noise.

噂 **tsun 3.** To talk, fair words.

噎 **yeh 1.** To choke, the throat obstructed.

嘮 **lao 2.** To chatter.

噍 **chiao 4.** To masticate.

13

器 **k'i 4.** A vessel, a tool, a utensil ability, useful.

噩 **o 4.** Startling, sad, unlucky.

嘯 **hsiao 4.** To whistle, to scream.

嘴 **tsui 3.** The mouth, a mouthpiece, a spout.

噬 **ch'u 1.** To scold, to abuse.

噫 **i 1.** An interjection.

噭 **chiao 1.** To neigh.

噤 **chin 4.** Lockjaw.

噱 **chü 4.** To talk, to laugh.

噲 **k'uai 4.** Greedy, cheerful.

噜 **lu 3.** To call pigs.

噯 **ai 1.** An exclamation.

噥 **nung 1. ang 3.** To grumble. An interrogation.

噴 **p'ên 1.** To spirt out, to puff out, to exhale.
fên 1. To sneeze.

噪 **tsao 4.** To twitter.

噬 **shih 1.** To bite, to eat, an initial particle.

噞 **yen 1.** To gape.

噳 **yü 3.** To smile.

噰 **yung 1.** Singing of birds.

14

嚎 **hao 2.** To roar, to howl.

嚂 **hsien 2.** To hold in the mouth.

嚇 **hsia 4.** To frighten, to awe, afraid.

嚄 **huo 4.** To bawl.

嚅 **ju 2.** To stammer.

嚀 **ning 2.** To enjoin, to charge straightly.

嚞 **t'ai 2.** To mock.

嚌 **chi 4.** To taste, to sip

15

嚚 **yin 2.** Knavery.

嚮 **hsiang 4.** Towards, facing, to favour.

嚜 **mei 4.** To speak erroneously.

嚏 **t'i 4.** To sneeze.

嚙 **yeh 4. nieh 4.** To bite, to gnaw, to eat.

16

嚫 **ch'ên 4.** To help a Buddhist mendicant by alms.

嚦 **li 4.** A noise of splitting.

嚨 **lung 2.** The throat

嚬 **p'in 2.** To smirk.

嚥 **yen 4.** To swallow.

嚕 **lu 3.** To pout.

嚴 **yen 2.** Severe, stern, rigid, solemn, very, a night-watch.

17

嚳 **k'u 1.** A proper name.

嚷 **jang 3.** To cry, to scold.

嚶 **ying 1.** Birds calling.

嚵 **ch'an 2.** Gluttonous, greedy.

18 &

囂 **hsiao 1.** To bark, to cry, vile, contemptible.

嚼 **chiao 2.** To chew, to ruminate.

囊 **nang 2.** A bag, a sack.

囈 **i 4.** To talk in one's sleep.

囉 **lo 2.** To annoy.

囋 **tsan 4.** To laugh at.

轡 **p'ei 4.** Bridle, reins.

囑 **chu 3.** To bid, to order, to enjoin upon.

囔 **nang 1.** To grumble, to speak through one's nose.

讎 **ch'ou 2.** The altercations of birds, enmity.

鼉 **t'o 2.** A crocodile.

Rad 31

See Lesson 74 A.

囗 **wei 2.** An inclosure.

囚 **ch'iu 2.** To imprison, to confine.

四 **ssŭ 4.** Four, all around.

回 囘 } **hui 2.** To revert to, to turn back, a time, a turn, the Moslems.

囝 **chien 3.** A slave-boy.

囡 **nieh 1.** A slave-girl.

因 **yin 1.** A cause, because, then, to follow, to rely on.

囫 **hu 1.** Whole, rough.

困 **k'un 4.** Distress, poverty, to surround, to wrap.

囤 **tun 4.** A round bin.

园 **wan 2.** To clip and round.

囮 **yu 2.** To decoy.

囱 **ch'uang 1.** A window.

囷 **ch'ün 2.** A granary.

固 **ku 4.** Strong, firm, secure, obstinate.

囹 **ling 3.** A prison.

囿 **yu 4.** To inclose, a park, a garden.

圂 **hun 4.** A piggery, a privy.

圃 **p'u 3.** An orchard, to cultivate.

圄 **yü 3.** A prison, to imprison.

圈 **ch'üan 1.** A circle, a ring.
chüan 4. A piggery.

國 国 } **kuo 3.** A nation, a country, a State.

圇 **lun 2.** Complete, whole.

圊 **ching 1.** A privy.

圉 **yü 3.** A prison.
yü 4. To guard.

圍 **wei 2.** To surround, to besiege, circumference.

圓 **yüan 2.** Round, circular, complete, to change, a dollar.

園 **yüan 2.** A garden.

圖 **t'u 2.** A plan, a drawing, to sketch, to scheme, to estimate, to calculate, to try for.

團 **t'uan 2.** A ball, a sphere, a lump, to collect, to coil.

[illegible] **yu 2.** A decoy-bird, to inveigle, to seduce.

圜 **huan 2.** To surround.

圞 **luan 2.** Spherical.

Rad. 32

See Lesson 81 A.

土 **t'u 3.** Earth, ground, soil, dust, aborigines, local.

𡈼 **t'ing 3.** To defend one's rights.

圠 **ya 4.** Fine dust, atoms.

圢 **t'ing 3.** Raised path.

圣 **kuai 4.** To till the ground.

圭 **kui 2.** A jade sceptre, sign of rank.

在 **tsai 4.** Te be, to exist, to be present, alive, to depend from, at, in.

圯 **i 2.** A bank.

圮 **p'ei 3.** Ruined.

地 **ti 4.** The earth, the ground, a place.

圬 **wu 1.** To plaster.

圩 **yü 2.** Dike, bund.

4

坌 坋 } **fên 4.** Dust.

圼 **nieh 1.** Clay.

坒 **pi 4.** To compare, to match.

坐 **tso 4.** To sit down, to rest, to reign.

址 **chih 3.** Foundation, dwelling-place, address.

坂 **fan 3.** A hill-side, a slope.

坊 **fang 1.** A district, a ward, a workhouse.

坎 **k'an 3.** A pit, a hole, a snare, a quibble.

坑 **k'êng 1.** A pond, a trap, to entrap, to ruin.

圻 **ch'i 2.** Border-land.

均 **chün 1.** Equal, equally, impartially.

坏 **p'i 1, p'ei 1.** Unburnt bricks.

[illegible] **hsü 4.** The side walls of an enclosure.

坍 **t'an 1.** To fall in ruins.

坉 **t'un 2.** A village.

坛 **t'an 2.** An altar.

5

坴 **lu 4.** A clod of earth.

垢 **kou 4.** Dirty, filthy.
坻 **ch'ih 2.** A dyke, an embankment.
坵 **ch'iu 1.** A natural hillock, a mound.
坰 **chiung 3.** Waste lands, wilds, desert.
坷 **k'o 3.** Uneven, rough.
坤 **k'un 1.** What is inferior, the earth, the moon, the wife, the minister, compliant.
坭 **ni 2.** Mud, to coat.
ni 4. To dote.
坯 **p'i 1.** Unburnt bricks.
坪 **p'ing 2.** A flat, level place; a plateau.
坡 **p'o 1.** A declivity, a slope.
坦 **t'an 3.** A plain, level place, contented, quiet.
坫 **tien 4.** Earthen ledge or table.
坼 **ch'ai 4.** A crevice.
坱 **yang 1.** Fine dust, to fill, infinite.

6

垂 **ch'ui 2.** To hang down, to droop, to let fall, to condescend, to become.
垈 **fa 4.** To clear and plough land.
型 **hsing 2.** A mould, an example.
垔 **yin 1.** To construct mith mud.
城 **ch'êng 2.** A wall of a city, a city.
垗 **chao 4.** Area around a grave.
垎 **ho 4,** Water drying off.
垓 **kai 1.** Bounds, limits.
垢 **kou 4.** Dirty, sordid, immorality.
垝 **kui 3.** In ruins.
垤 **tieh 2.** A mound.
垌 **t'ung 3.** A surname.

垛 垜 **to 3.** To add up, to pile up, a battlement, a target, a buttress.
垟 **yang 2.** A sprite.
垠 **yin 2.** Beach, limit.
垣 **yüan 2.** A wall of brick.

7

埕 **ch'êng 2.** A jar.
垾 **han 4.** A dyke.
埂 **kêng 3.** A ditch or channel.
埍 **chüan 3.** A police station; a post-relay.
埌 **lang 4.** A wild; waste land.
埒 **lüeh 4.** Enclosure.
埋 **mai 2.** To bury; to conceal.
埃 **yeh 2. ai 1.** Dust.
埕 **nieh 1.** To fill up.
埔 **pu 3.** A port.
埻 **po 4.** Dust in clouds.
埇 **yung 3.** A path, an alley.

8

基 **chi 1.** The foundation of a wall; land; property; the throne.
堅 **chien 1.** Firm; solid.
聚 **ch'ü 4.** To heap up earth.
堂 **t'ang 2.** A hall; a court; a church; a residence; an official title.
埜 **yeh 3.** A waste, a wild, etc.
堇 **chien 3.** Yellow loam or loess; clay; to daub.
執 **chih 2.** To hold; to grasp; to seize, to attend to, to manage.
埶 **i 4.** Skill; handicraft; trade; art; to plant.

埠 **pu 4.** A port, a mart.
埏 **yen 2.** A boundary; a limit.
埧 **chü 4.** An embankment.
埻 **chun 3.** A target.
堈 **kang 1.** A jar.
堁 **k'o 4.** A clod of earth.
堀 **k'u 1.** A hole; a den.
堋 **pêng 4.** To cover with earth.
培 **p'ei 2.** To bank up with earth; to assist; rear.
埤 **p'i 2.** A low wall; a parapet.
埽 **sao 3.** To weep.
sao 4. A broom.
埭 **tai 4.** A jetty; a wharf.
埝 **tien 4.** A dyke.
堆 **tsui 1.** A heap; a pile.
埰 **ts'ai 4.** Allotments to feudal nobles.
埯 **yen 3.** To cover with earth.
埸 **i 4.** A boundary.
淤 **yü 1.** To silt up; muddy.
域 **yü 4.** A frontier; a limit; a country.

9

堡 **pu 3. p'u 3. pao 3.** A rampart; a station; a village.
堲 **chi 4.** To brick a grave.
報 **pao 4.** To recompense; to requite; to report; a journal.
堯 **yao 1.** Eminent; name of an Emperor.
埵 **to 3.** A mound
場 **ch'ang 2.** An area of level ground; a threshing-floor.
塍 **ch'êng 2.** A ridge between fields.
堍 **tu 2.** A cave; a cavern.

堠 **hou 4.** Mounds for fire-signals.

堭 **huang 2.** The moat outside a city wall.

堧 **juan 2.** The vacant space inside a city wall.

堪 **k'an 1.** To bear; to sustain; to be capable; fit.

堩 **kêng 4.** The path leading up to a sepulchre.

堦 **chieh 1.** Steps; a degree; a rank.

堝 **kuo 1.** A crucible.

堷 **an 1.** A burying-place for free interment.

堨 **o 4.** A crack in a wall.

堤 **ti 1.** An embankment; to prevent.

堞 **tieh 4.** Battlements.

堵, ⿰土度 **tu 3.** To block up; to stop.

堫 **tsung 1.** To sow.

堰 **yen 4.** A barrage, a dam.

堙 **yin 1.** To stop ut; to dam in.

堬 **yü 2.** A grave-mound.

10

塞 **sai 1.** To cork.
sai 4. To vie with.

塑 **su 4.** To model in clay; to mould into shape.

塗 **tu 2.** Stupid.
t'u 2. To besmear.

⿱棍土 **tun 1.** A tumulus.

塟 **tsang 4.** To bury with decorum.

塋 **ying 2.** A grave; a burying-place.

塍 **ch'êng 2.** A raised path.

⿰土彖 **chuan 4.** To plough.

塚 **chung 3.** A tumulus, a tomb.

塤 **hsüan 1.** The Chinese ocarina.

塏 **k'ai 3.** A terrace.

塊 **k'uai 4.** A clod; a lump; together.

塯 **liu 4.** An alms-bowl.

塓 **mi 4.** To whitewash.

塒 **shih 2.** A hen-roost.

塐 **su 4.** To mould.

塌 **t'a 1.** To fall down; to crumble.

塔 **t'a 3.** A pagoda, Buddhist tower.

塘 **t'ang 2.** A bath-house; a post-station.

塡 **t'ien 2.** To fill up; to stuff.

塕 **wêng 3.** Dust.

塢 **wu 3.** A bank; a wall, an entrenchment.

塳 **p'êng 3.** Whirling dust.

11

塵 **ch'ên 2.** Dust; carnal; dissipation, pleasure; wordly.

⿱殹土 **i 1.** Dust.

墍 **chi 4.** To plaster a wall.

塺 **mei 4.** Dust.

墓 **mu 4.** A grave, a tomb.

墅 **shu 4.** A farm, a villa.

塾 **shu 2.** A school-room.

墊 **tien 4.** To fill up, to make good; to advance money.

塹 **ch'ien 4.** A ditch; a kennel.

墜 **chui 4.** To settle down, to slide; to sink. Ear-rings.

⿱敝土 **pieh 1.** A town in Hupeh.

墋 **ch'ên 3.** Dirty.

墇 **chang 4.** An embankment; to separate by a bank.

場 **ch'ang 2.** An area of level ground; a thrashing-floor.

墐 **chin 3.** To plaster; to cover; to stop with mud.

境 **ching 4.** Frontier, boundary, a region, a district, circumstances.

⿰土袞 **k'un 3.** To spatter.

塿 **lou 2.** A mound over a grave.

墁 **man 4.** To plaster, to lay, to pave.

塻 **mo 4.** Dust.

墄 **ch'i 1.** The steps of a stairway.

墉 **yung 1.** A fortified wall.

⿰土㒼 **man 2.** To cover over.

⿰土虖 **hsia 4.** A fissure, a chink.

塸 **ou 3** A tomb.

墔 **ts'ui 1.** Heap, pile.

12

墨 **mei 4.** Ink, black.

墮 **to 4.** To fall, to sink, to be ruined.

墩, ⿱敦土 **tun 1.** A mound, a tumulus, a beacon mound, a ton.

墦 **fan 2.** A grave.

⿰土复 **fu 2.** A cave, a grotto.

⿰土壹 **i 4.** Dust, dark.

墀 **ch'ih 2.** A court-yard.

墝 **ch'iao 1.** Stony soil.

墟 **hsü 1.** Waste, wild land, a cemetery.

⿰土尞 **liao 4.** A surrounding wall.

墣 **p'o 4.** A clod of earth.

墠 **shan 4.** Smooth, level.

墡 **shan 3.** Fine white clay.

墰 **t'an 2.** A jar, a jug.

墱 **têng 4.** Steps.

墤 **k'uai 4.** A heap, a bit.

增 **tsêng 1.** To add to, to increase, supernumerary.

墫 **tsun 1.** A wine-jar.

隧 **sui 4.** A tunnel to a tomb, a passage.

13

壆 **hsiao 2.** Basement.

墾 **k'ên 3.** To open new land, to plough.

墼 **chi 2.** Unburnt bricks.

壁 **pi 4. pei 4.** A wall.

壅 **yung 3.** To dam, to hinder.

壂 **tien 4.** A place, a hall.

墳 **fên 2.** A grave, a mound, a cemetery.

環 **huan 2.** An enclosing wall.

墈 **k'an 3.** Hindered, unlucky.

壇 **t'an 2.** A platform, an altar, an arena.

墻 **ch'iang 2.** A wall.

14

壍 **ch'ien 4.** The moat round a city.

壑 **ho 4.** A wady, a pool.

壐 **hsi 3.** The Imperial great seal.

壓 **ya 1** To press down, to subject, to crush.

壒 **ai 3.** Dust rising in the air.

墀 **ch'ih 4.** Ground dried by the sun.

壕 **hao 2.** A ditch, a canal.

壎 **hsüan 1.** The ocarina.

壖 **juan 2.** The ground near the walls of a city.

壔 **tao 3.** A tumulus.

15 &

壘 **lei 3.** A rampart, a pile, to wall.

壥 **ch'an 2.** A market-place.

壙 **k'uang 4.** A vault, a grave, desert.

壝 **wei 3.** A low terrace wall.

壞 **huai 4.** To spoil, to ruin, to destroy, vicious, depraved.

壚 **lu 2.** Clods, a cottage.

壜 **t'an 2.** Earthenware jars.

壠 **lung 3.** A grave, a pile of earth.

壤 **jang 3.** Mold, humus, soil, a place, a region.

壥 **ch'an 4.** The border which defines the limit of a grave.

壅 **yung 3.** To stop with earth.

墽 **ch'iao 4.** Curved, turned up at the ends.

壩 **pa 4.** A dike, a breakwater.

𡓾 **nang 4.** A cave.

Rad. 33

士 士

See Lesson 24 C.

士 **shih 4.** A learned man, a scholar, an officer.

壬 **jên 2.** A cyclical character.

声 **shêng 1.** A sound.

声 **ch'ing 4.** A harpsichord of sonorous stones.

壮 **chuang 4.** Strong, robust.

壳 **ch'iao 1. k'o 1.** Shell, hard covering.

壺 **hu 2.** A jug, a pot.

壼 **k'un 3.** Paths and corridors, gynæceum.

壹 **i 1.** A vessel. One.

壽 壽 **shou 4.** Longevity, age.

壻 **hsü 4.** A son-in-law.

Rad. 34

See Lesson 31 B.

夂 **chih 3.** To march, to progress.

夅 **chiang 4.** To descend, to fall, to subject, to degrade.

夆 **fêng 2.** To butt, to oppose.

Rad. 35

See Lesson 31 C.

夊 **sui 1.** To walk slowly.

夋 **tsun 1.** To walk with dignity.

夌 **ling 2.** To transgress, to offend.

复 **fu 2.** To go back.

㚇 㚇 **tsung 1.** To gather the feet under the body.

夏 **hsia 4.** Summer, the first Dynasty, China.

夐 **ch'iung 3.** To aim at, to scheme.

夔 夔 **k'ui 2.** A mountain goblin. A proper name.

Rad. 36

夕

See Lesson 64 A.

夕 **hsi 4.** Evening, end.

外 **wai 4.** Outside, without, beyond, foreign, to exclude.

夗 **yüan 3.** o turn in bed, a curling motion.

夙 **hsü 4.** Early, dawn, formerly, long since.

多 **to 1.** Many, much, mostly, often, too much.

夜 **yeh 4.** The night.

夠 够 **kou 4.** Much, to suffice, enough.

夥 **hou 3.** Numerous, a band, a company, a colleague.

夢 梦 **mêng 4.** A dream, to dream.

𡖖 **mei 4.** Silent, still.

夤 **yin 2.** To respect, to advance, distant places.

Rad. 37

大

See Lesson 60 A.

大 **ta 4.** Great, noble, chief, highly, very. *Tai4.*

夫 **fu 1.** A husband, a man, master. A lady.
fu 2. An initial and final particle, a demonstrative, etc.

夬 **chüeh 3.** To cut off, to decide, certainly.

太 **t'ai 4.** Excessive, very, too, grand, enormous, an epithet of a distinguished person.

天 **t'ien 1.** Heaven, the sky, a day, weather, celestial, the emperor, great, immense.

夭 **yao 3.** An untimely death.

夯 **hang 1.** To strain, to pound, a beater.

夰 **kao 3.** To let go.

夲 **t'ao 1.** To advance.

失 **shih 1.** To lose, to omit, to fail, an omission, a fault.

央 **yang 1.** The midst, the center, to press earnestly, urgently, to the utmost.

尖 **chien 1.** A point.

夷 **i 2.** A barbarian, vulgar, to squat, to kill, to feel at ease.

夸 **k'ua 1.** To boast, to over-praise.

夾 **chia 1.** To press, to double, to help.

奉 **fêng 4.** To receive or present with both hands, to serve, to flatter.

奇 **ch'i 2.** Extraordinary, marvellous, rare.
chi 1. Odd surplus, remainder.

奈 **nai 4.** Means, resource, unfortunately, to endure.

奄 **yen 1.** Ere long, anon.
yen 3. To propagate, to spread, to cover.

奓 **cha 1.** To open out, to stretch open.

奐 **huan 4.** Lively, gay.

契 **ch'i 4.** To notch, a covenant, a deed.

奎 **k'ui 2.** The stride made by a man, a constellation.

耷 **ta 1.** Hanging ears, dragging.

奔 **pên 1.** To rush, to be in a hurry.

奏 **tsou 4.** To report, to advance, to play on instruments.

奕 **i 2.** Great, fine, to play chess.

奘 **chuang 4.** Large, stout.

奚 **hsi 1.** An interrogative particle, why? how? what?

套 **t'ao 4.** A case, a snare, to envelop, to include, to harness.

奣 **huang 3.** The morn.

奞 **sui 1.** To spread the wings, to fly.

奡 **ao 4.** Haughty, lofty.

奢 **ch'ê 1.** Prodigal, dissipated.

喫 **ch'ih 1.** To eat.

奠 **tien 4.** To pour a libation, to fix, to settle.

奧 **nao 4. ao 4.** The corner where the *Lares* were placed, secret, mysterious.

奩 **lien 2.** A dressing-case, the bridal outfit.

奪 **to 2.** To take by force, to carry off, to strive.

奬 **chiang 3.** To praise, to encourage.

奫 **yün 1.** An abyss.

獘 **pi 4.** Abuses, fraud.

樊 **fan 2.** Hedge, fence.

奭 **shih 4.** A proper name, red, anger.

奮 **fên 4.** To fly, to arouse, impetuous action, to strive, to propagate.

Rad. 38

See Lesson 67 A.

女 **nü 3.** Women, a girl.

奶 **nai 3.** Breasts, milk, to suckle.

奴 **nu.** A slave, a term of contempt.

妁 **chao 4.** A go-between.

妃 **fei 1.** Imperial concubine.

好 **hao 3.** Good, right.
hao 4. To love.

如 ju 2. As, like, also, to go to, to desire.

奸 chien 1. Deceitful, villainous, corrupted.

妄 wang 4. Error, disorder, falsely, wrongly

4

妥 t'o 3. Secure, firm, quiet, safe, prepared.

妨 fang 1. To hinder, to oppose.

妎 chieh 4. Jealousy.

妊 jên 2. Pregnancy.

妓 chi 4. A courtesan.

妞 niu 1. A lass.

妗 chin 4. A wife's sister.

妙 miao 4. Wonderful, subtle, mysterious.

妠 na 4. To take a wife.

妣 pi 3. A deceased mother.

妒 tu 4. Jealous, envious.

姘 ching 4. Female virtue.

妧 wan 4. A handsome woman.

妖 yao 1. Bewitching, strange, a phantom, malignant.

妤 yü 2. A house-keeper.

妜 chüeh 1. Nice, elegant.

姊 tzŭ 3. Elder sister.

妋 fa 2. Ladylike.

姒 ssŭ 4 An elder brother's wife.

妝 chuang 1. To adorn the head and paint the eyes, to rouge, to feign, disguise.

5

妻 ch'i 1. Wife.
ch'i 4. To give in marriage.

妾 ch'ieh 4. A concubine.

委 wei 3. To send, to depute, a wrong, a grievance.

姃 chêng 1. Correct deportment, reserved and modest.

妯 chou 2. Sisters-in-law.

姁 hsü 1. Handsome, graceful.

姑 ku 1. A polite term for females, a young lady, a paternal aunt, husband's sister. Buddhist nun.

妹 mei 4. A younger sister.

妺 mo 4. Tricks.

姆 mu 3. An elderly widow, a matron.

妮 ni 2. A slave girl.

姅 pan 4. Catamenia.

妭 po 4. A wife.

姍 shan 1. To criticise.

始 shih 3. Beginning, to begin, then.

妬 tu 4. Jealous, envious.

姐 chieh 3. An elder sister.

姓 hsing 4. Surname.

妲 ta 2. The concubine of the tyrant *Cheou-hsin*.

6

姦 chien 1. Illicit intercourse, adultery, to ravish, wicked.

姜 chiang 1. A proper name.

姕 ts'ŭ 1 A slattern.

姿 tzŭ 1. Mien, carriage, beauty.

要 shua 3. To play with.

姹 ch'a 3. A handsome young lady.

姪 chih 2. A nephew, a niece.

姝 chu 1. Lovely.

姨 i 2. A wife's sister, maternal aunt, a concubine.

姙 jên 2. Pregnancy.

姸 yên 2. Skilled.

姤 kou 4. To pair, to copulate.

姬 chi 1. The name of *Huang-ti's* family.

姞 chi 2. A concubine of *Huang-ti*.

姱 k'ua 1. Vain, pretty.

姥 lao 3. An elderly widow, maternal grandmother.

姺 hsien 3. Name of a place.

娃 wa 2. A beautiful woman; *wa-wa*, a baby.

姚 yao 2. Handsome, elegant.

姻 yin 1. A bride, marriage.

姷 yu 4. A couple.

娜 na 2. A graceful air.

威 wei 1. Majesty, imposing, to overawe.

7

娑 so 1. To saunter.

娿 o 1. Unstable.

妝 chuang 1. To dress, to bedeck.

娡 chi 4. Envy, hatred.

娟 chüan 1. Graceful.

娌 li 3. Sisters-in-law.

娥 o 2. Good, pretty.

娘 niang 2. A woman, a wife, a mother.

娉 p'in 1. Elegance.

娠 } chên 1. Pregnancy.
娠 }

娋 shao 1. The eldest sister.

娞 so 1. Maidenly.

娣 ti 4. A young sister or sister-in-law, a girl.

娩 **wan 3.** Docility.
mien 3. Parturition.

娛 **yü 2.** To rejoice, pleasure,

㛮 **sao 3.** An elder brother's wife, sister-in-law.

8

婓 **fei 2.** A nymph.

婪 **lan 2.** Greediness.

婁 **lou 2.** To trail along.

婆 **p'o 2.** An old woman, a step-mother.

娶 **ch'ü 3.** To marry a wife.

娼 **ch'ang 1.** A prostitute.

婦 **fu 4.** A married woman.

婚 **hun 1.** To marry, marriage.

娸 **ch'i 2.** Ugly.

婩 **an 4.** Elegance.

姘 **p'ing 1.** Bad behaviour.

婢 **pei 4.** **pi 4.** A slave-girl, a maid-servant.

婊 **piao 3.** A prostitute.

婕 **chieh 2.** Handsome.

娵 **chü 1.** A constellation.

婐 **wo 3.** A waiting-maid.

婭 **ya 4.** A brother-in-law.

婉 **wan 3.** Complaisant, lovely.

婞 **hsing 3.** Angry.

娺 **cho 1.** Quarrelling.

婥 **ch'ao 4.** Pretty.

婬 **yin 2** Lewd, obscene, impurity,

婧 **ching 4.** Modesty, chasteness.

婌 **shu 1.** The governess of the women in palace.

9

婺 **wu 4.** Name of a star.

婿 **hsü 4.** A son-in-law.

婣 **yin 1.** A bride, a wedding.

婼 **jê 2.** Unsubdued.

𡟖 **hou 2.** Wanton, lewd.

媧 **wa 1.** The sister of *Fu-hsi*.

媢 **mao 4** Ill-will.

媒 **mei 2.** A go-between.

媚 **mei 4.** To love, to coax, to flatter.

媌 **miao 2.** Elegance.

𡟫 **an 1.** Impureness.

媆 **nên 4.** Delicate, soft.

媟 **hsieh 4.** To insult women, to outrage.

媞 **t'i 2.** Lovely.

婸 **tang 4.** Dissolute, wanton.

婷 **t'ing 2.** Ladylike.

婧 **t'o 2.** Not properly dressed, indecency.

媊 **ch'ien 2.** The morning star, Venus.

媦 **wei 4.** A younger sister.

婹 **yao 3.** Slender.

媛 **yüan 4.** A beautiful person

10

媻 **p'an 2.** An old woman.

嫈 **ying 1.** A careful demeanour.

媸 **ch'ih 1.** A worthless woman.

媰 **ch'u 2.** A widow.

嫨 **hsi 2.** A waiting-maid.

嫌 **hsien 2.** To suspect, to loath, to depreciate, to have an aversion to.

媾 **kou 4.** Fondness, sexual intercourse.

嫁 **chia 4.** To marry a husband, to give one's daughter in marriage.

媿 **k'uei 4.** Ashamed, conscience-stricken.

媽 **ma 1.** A nurse, a procuress.

嫐 **nao 3.** Lewd sports.

嫂 **sao 3.** An elder brother's wife, a matron.

媳 **hsi 1.** A daughter-in-law, a wife.

嫉 **chi 4.** Jealousy, envy, to dislike.

媼 **wên 2.** An old woman.

媱 **yao 2.** Prostitutes.

嫄 **yüan 2.** The mother of *Hou Chi*, *Chiang Yüan*.

媷 **ju 4.** Lax, lazy.

媵 **ying 4.** An escort of maid-servants to a bride, concubines.

11

嫠 **li 2.** A widow.

嫳 **p'ieh 1.** Irritable, hasty, nervous, inconstant.

嫜 **chang 1.** A husband's father.

嫥 **ch an 1.** Gentle.

嫭 **hu 4.** Graceful.

嫪 **lao 4** To dote on, lustful.

嫚 **man 4.** To despise.

嫫 **mu 2.** A proper name.

嫩 **nên 4.** Tender, delicate, soft, fresh.

嫖 **p'iao 2.** Levity, lewdness, fornication.

嫦 **ch'ang 2.** Name of a goddess.

嫡 **ti 2.** The legal wife.

嫣 **yen 1.** Charming.

嫗 **yü 4.** A mother, a matron.

12

嬉 **hsi 1.** To play, to sport.

嫺 嫻 **hsien 2.** Graceful, refined, accomplished.

嬇 **hui 4.** A proper name.

嬈 **jao 2.** Graceful, charming.

嬌 **chiao 1.** Delicate, to pet.

嬀 **hui 1.** A river in Shansi.

嫽 **liao 2.** To sport with.

嬋 **ch'an 1.** Graceful.

嫵 **wu 3.** To seduce.

13

嬖 **pi 4.** A favorite, lecherous.

嬴 **ying 2.** Full, a surplus, to fill up.

嬗 **ch'an 1.** Graceful.

嬙 **ch'iang 2.** Female court officials.

[女奧] **ao 4.** Jealous.

14 &

嬰 **ying 1.** An infant, a babe.

嬮 **yen 1.** Amiable.

嬲 **nao 3.** Lewd sports.

嬤 **ma 2.** A mother.

嬭 **nai 3.** Breasts; to suckle, milk.

嬪 **pin 1.** Imperial concubines, a wife, to wed.

嬬 **ju 2.** A lady.

嬸 **shên 3.** A father's younger brother's wife, sisters-in-law.

嬻 **tu 4.** To defile; to disgrace.

嬿 **yen 4.** Graceful.

嬾 **lan 3.** Idle.

孃 **niang 2.** A young lady, a mother.

孅 **hsien 1.** Small, fine, delicate, trifling.

孀 **shuang 1.** A widow.

孋 **li 2.** Pretty.

[女贊] **tsan 4.** Fair, handsome.

孌 **lüan 3.** Lovely.

孎 **chu 1.** Modesty, reserve, respect.

Rad. 39

See Lesson 94 A.

子 **tzŭ 3.** Boy, son; sir, seed; a suffix, a cyclical character.

孑 **chieh 4.** Maimed, alone; a remnant.

孔 **k'ung 3.** A hole. The surname of Confucius.

孕 **yün 4.** To conceive, to be pregnant.

存 **ts'un 2.** To be, to exist, to preserve, to continue.

字 **tzŭ 4.** A character, a name, a letter

孖 **tzŭ 1.** Twins.

孚 **fu 1.** To brood on, to rely on, confidence.

孝 **hsiao 4.** Filial piety, mourning.

孛 **po 4.** To beget. **pei 4.** Rebellion.

孜 **tzŭ 1.** Zeal, sollicitude.

季 **chi 4.** A cadet, season.

孥 **nu 2.** A child, weak and tender, to exterminate a family.

孟 **mêng 4.** Chief, head, first, eldest.

孤 **ku 1.** Fatherless, destitute, orphan.

孩 **hai 2.** A child.

㝃 **mien 3.** Parturition.

孫 **sun 1.** A grandson, a grandchild.

孬 **wai 1.** Bad, wicked.

孰 **shu 2.** Who? which? what?

孱 **ch'uan 1.** Poor; weak, unfit, for.

孳 **tzŭ 1.** To bear, to rear.

學 **hsiao 2.** To learn, to study.

孺 **ju 2.** A suckling, a child, wives of officials.

孻 **nai 1.** The last son born to an old man.

孽 孼 **nieh 4. yeh 4.** A son of a concubine; evils of sin.

孾 **ying 1.** An infant; a suckling.

孿 **luan 2.** Twins.

Rad. 40

See Lesson 36 A.

宀 **mien 2.** A roof.

宁 **chu 4.** Space for attendants.

宂 **jung 3.** Scattered; affairs.

宄 **kuei 3.** Traitors, villains.

它 **t'o 1.** That, another; to charge.

[宀久] **chiu 4.** A long stay.

安 **an 1.** Still; rest; peace; to place; to lay down; how?

守 **shou 3** To keep; to attend to; a charge; a prefect.

宅 **chai 2.** Family dwelling.

宇 **yü 3.** Heaven, space; temple; the roof; to cover, to protect; the empire.

字 **tzŭ 4.** Characters.

宏 **hung 2.** Vast, ample, spacious.

宋 **sung 4.** A feudal state; a Chinese Dynasty.

完 **wan 2.** To finish; to complete; to settle.

宐 **i 2.** Fit and right; proper; ought; should; must.

灾 **tsai 1.** Misfortune.

牢 **lao 2.** A prison; firm.

㝑 **p'ang 2.** Side.

5

宙 **chou 4.** Earth, time, the universe; always.

宔 **chu 3.** An ancestral tablet.

宜 **i 2.** Must; proper; beseeming; capable; apt; advantageous.

官 **kuan 1.** An official; a mandarin; public; civic.

宓 **mi 4.** Still; silent; quiet.

宕 **tang 4.** A grotto.

定 **ting 4.** To fix; to settle; to decide; certain.

宗 **tsung 1.** Ancestors; kind; class; to follow; to honour; to worship; religion.

[illegible] **wa 4.** To cover with tiles.

宛 **wan 3.** As if, of course; to yield.

宝 **pao 3** Precious; valuable things.

6

宦 **huan 4.** Officials.

宧 **i 2.** A dining-hall.

客 **k'o 4. ch'ieh 4.** A guest; a dealer; a stranger; a traveller.

室 **shih 4.** A house; a home; a household; a wife.

宣 **hsüan 1.** Chancellory; to promulgate.

宗 **chi 2.** Quiet; peaceful.

宥 **yu 4.** To forgive; to be lenient.

宨 **t'iao 3.** Mean; volatile.

宬 **ch'êng 2.** The archives.

7

宸 **ch'ên 2.** The private apartments of the Emperor; Imperial.

害 **hai 4.** To injure; to hurt; to offend; to damage; to suffer.

家 **chia 1.** A household; a family; a profession or class, a suffix.

宮 **kung 1.** A palace; castration; a eunuch; constellations.

宺 **lang 2.** Empty, deserted.

宵 **hsiao 1.** Night; darkness.

宰 **tsai 3.** To govern; to slaughter; a minister.

宴 **yen 4.** A feast, a banquet; rest, repose.

容 **jung 2. yung 2.** To receive; to contain; to endure; to bear with; the air; the countenance; the face.

宾 **pin 1.** A guest.

宼 **k'ou 4.** To rob; a robber or pirate.

案 **an 4.** A table; a suit.

8

寄 **chi 4.** To lodge at; to deliver over, to send.

寇 寇 **k'ou 4.** To rob; a robber or pirate.

㝒 **chü 1.** To dwell.

密 **mi 4.** Close; thick; intimate; secret.
宻 **mei 4.** Dense; thick.

寕 **ning 2.** Rest, repose; rather, better; why, how?

宿 **hsiu 3.** Night; to lodge for the night.
㝛 **hsü 1.** The constellations.

寂 **chi 2.** Silent; quiet.

寅 **yin 2.** To revere; to show respect; a cyclical character.

寃 **yüan 1.** To injure; to oppress; wrong; to have a grudge; revenge.

㝝 **lin 2.** A secluded place.

9

富 **fu 4.** Rich; affluent; abundant; wealth.

寒 **han 2.** Cold, shivering; poor; a depreciating term for my.

寐 **mei 4.** To rest; to sleep.

寎 **ping 2.** To sleep; drowsy.

寍 **ning 2.** Peace.

寔 **shih 2.** Solid, real, true.

寓 **yü 4.** To dwell, to reside, to sojourn, allegory.

甯 **ning 2.** Peace.

寫 **hsieh 3.** To write.

10

寘 **chih 4.** To order, to dispose.

寗 **ning 2.** Peace.

塞 **sai 1.** To cork, to stop up.

11

察 **ch'a 2.** To examine, to find out, enquiries.

寨 **chai 4.** A stockade, a palisade, encampment.

㝩 **k'ang 1.** Empty, deserted.

寠 **lü 3.** Poor, rustic.

寡 **kua 3.** A lone. A widow, I the sovereign. Few, seldom.

寥 **liao 2.** Waste, vast.

寞 **mo 4.** Silent, solitary.

寧 **ning 2.** Rest, repose, serenity, peace, to prefer, how, why?

實 **shih 2.** Real, solid, compact, hard, fruit of plants, to fill.

寢 **ch'in 3.** To sleep, to rest, to stop, apartments.

寤 **wu 4.** To awake.

賓 賔 } **pin 1.** A visitor, a guest To submit.

蜜 **mi 4.** Honey.

12 &

寬 **k'uan 1.** Large, ample, gentle, indulgent, to forbear.

寮 **liao 2.** A companion, a petty official, a window, a hut.

審 **shên 3.** To inquire, to investigate, to discriminate.

寫 **hsieh 3.** To write, to sketch, to leak.

寪 **wei 3.** Ill at ease, bored.

[illegible] **ts'êng 2.** A storied building.

寰 **huan 2.** Imperial domains, a closure, the universe.

憲 **hsien 4.** Rule, law, constitution, officials.

賽 **sai 4.** To vie with.

蹇 **ch'ien 3.** Lame. Misfortune.

寵 **ch'ung 3.** Kindness, grace, favours.

寶 寳 } **pao 3.** A gem, a coin, precious, valuable, term of compliment, as honourable; a mode of gambling.

顛 **tien 1.** Far off, high.

Rad. 41

See Lesson 45 B.

寸 **ts'un 4.** An inch. A little.

寺 **ssŭ 4.** A palace, a temple, a court, a eunuch.

守 **shou 3.** To keep, to have in custody, to ward off, to supervise.

寽 **lüeh 4.** To clutch, to rub.

尀 **p'o 3.** An *adverb*, do not, may or can not.

封 **fêng 1.** A fief, a territory, to appoint to office, to seal up, to blockade.

辱 **ju 4** To insult.

尃 **fu 1.** To diffuse, ample.

尅 **k'o 1. k'ê 1.** To subdue, to overcome, to dominate.

射 **shê 4. shih 4.** To shoot out, to dart.

專 **chuan 4.** Single, particular, to specially care.

將 **chiang 1.** To act, future, about to; accusative case; to be satisfied with.
chiang 4. A commander.

尉 **wei 4.** To soothe.
yü 4. An officer.

尋 **hsün 2.** To search for, to seek, common, usual.
hsin 2. To marry.

尊 **tsun 1.** Noble, venerable, numerative of cannons.

對 对 } **tui 4.** To correspond to, to suit, to answer, parallel sentences on scrolls, opposite, objective.

導 **tao 4.** To lead, to conduct.

Rad. 42

See Lesson 18 H.

小 **hsiao 3.** Small. I.

少 **shao 3.** Few, less, slightly, to diminish, te be without.
shao 4. Young.

尔 尒 } **erh 3.** Thou, a final particle.

尖 **chien 1.** A point, pointed.

尚 **shang 4.** To wish, to esteem, still, if.

[illegible] **hsi 4.** A fissure.

尞 **liao 3.** Fuel used in sacrifices.

尟 尠 } **hsien 3.** Small, few, rarely, exhausted.

[illegible] **ts'ao 2.** Worn out, decayed.

Rad. 43

See Lesson 61 C.

尢 尣 } **wang 1.** Lame.

尤 **yu 2.** Evils, calamities, error, to blame, to murmur, more, still more, to exceed.

尥 **p'ao 2.** To toddle along.

尬 **chieh 4.** To stagger.

尪 **wang 1.** Weak, lame, exhausted.

[illegible] **po 3.** To go lame.

尵 **t'ui 3.** Rheumatic.

[illegible] **ch'ao 4.** To limp.

就 **chiu 4.** To follow, to make the best of, then, immediately, to achieve.

尰 **chung 3.** Swollen feet.

尲 **chien 1.** To stumble.

Rad. 44

See Lesson 32 A.

尸 **shih 1.** A corpse, the impersonator of an ancestor.

尺 **ch'ih 3.** The Chinese foot.

尽 **chin 4.** To exhaust, to end.

尻 **k'ao 1.** End bone of the spine, extremity.

凥 **chü 1.** Rest, repose, to dwell.

尼 **ni 2** A nun

启 **tu 2.** The anus, the end of.

屐 **chi 4.** Shoes.

局 **chü 2.** A chess-board, position, circumstances, an association.

尿 **niao 4. sui 1.** Urine.

尾 **wei 3. i 3.** Tail, end.

屁 **p'i 4.** The posteriors.

屆 届 } **chieh 4.** To reach to, to arrive at, a limit, set time.

𡰯 **shih 3.** Excretions.

屈 **ch'ü 1.** A grievance, a wrong, injustice, to crouch.

屄 **pi 4.** The vagina.

屉 **t'i 4.** A drawer.

屍 **shih 1.** A corpse.

居 㞐 } **chü 1.** To inhabit, to reside in, to occupy, to be in.

屎 **shih 2.** Filth, excretions.

屌 **tiao 3.** The penis.

屋 **wu 1** A room, a house.

展 **chan 3.** To open out, to unroll, to explain.

屐 **chi 4.** Shoes.

屑 **hsieh 4.** A fragment, to condescend, lightly, triflingly.

屙 **o 1.** To ease nature.

屚 **lou 4.** To trickle; to drop.

屝 **fei 4.** Coarse grass sandals.

屏 **p'ing 2.** A screen.
ping 3. To keep away.

屜 **t'i 4.** A buffer, a screen, a pillow, etc.

屟 **hsieh 4** Sandals.

屠 **t'u 2.** To kill; to butcher.

犀 **hsi 1.** A yak.

孱 **ch'uan 1.** Poor, unfit for.

屢 **lü 3.** Many times; repeatedly.

屣 **hsi 3.** Straw sandals.

履 **li 3.** Shoes; to walk.

層 **ts'êng 2.** A layer; a stratum.

屧 **hsieh 4.** Shoes.

屨 **chü 3.** Sandals.

屪 **liao 2.** The penis.

屩 **chiao 1.** Wooden-shoes.

屬 属 㞕 } **shu 2.** To be of, to depend on; to belong to; connected with; sort; kind; class; kindred.

屭 **hsi 4.** The Chinese Hercules, *Pi-hsi*.

Rad. 45

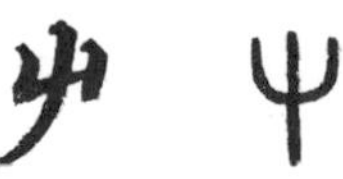

See Lesson 73 A.

屮 **ch'ê 4.** A sprout.

屯 **t'un 2.** To collect together; to amass; a camp; a village.

屰 **i 4. ni 4.** Rebellious.

旹 **shih 2.** Time.

Rad. 46

See Lesson 80 A.

山 **shan 1.** Mountain; heights; wall.

岌 **chi 4.** A lofty peak; dangerous.

屺 **ch'i 3.** A bare hill.

屼 **wu 4.** Mountain.

屹 **i 4.** High peak; imposing, grand.

岑 **ch'ên 1.** A lone peak; lofty; lone.

岔 **ch'a 4.** Branching, to fork, cross-road.

岐 **ch'i 2.** A mountain in Shensi. *Ch'i-pai*, the physician of *Huang-ti*. *Ch'i-huang*, the physicians.

岏 **wan 2** A sharp summit.

5

岸 **nan 4.** Bank, shore, cliff.

岩 **yen 2.** A rocky cliff.

岡 **kang 1.** A mound. A watch-box.

岱 **tai 4.** A sacred mountain in Shantung.

岳 **yao 4.** Sacred mountains, a wife's parents.

岵 **hu 4.** Hill with trees and grass.

岷 **min 2.** A mountain in the Ssŭ-ch'uan.

屔 **ni 2.** A hill in Shantung.

6

幽 **yu 1.** Dark; a prison.

旹 **shih 2.** Time.

峇 **k'o 2.** A cavern.

炭 **t'an 4.** Charcoal.

耑 **chuan 1.** The cause or origin of anything.

峙 **chih 3.** A peak; to pile up; to store up.

峓 **i 2.** A noted hill in Corea.

峐 **kai 1.** A barren hill.

峆 **ka 2. ko 2.** A knoll.

島 **tao 3.** An island.

峹 **t'u 2.** A mountain in Nganhoei.

峯 峰 } **fêng 1.** The peak of a mountain.

豈 **ch'i 3.** How?

峩 峨 } **o 2.** A sacred mountain in Ssŭch'uan.

峽 **hsia 4.** A gorge; a mountain pass.

峻 **tsun 2.** Steep; obstinate; stiff.

㟇 **tso 4.** A crumbling hill.

峪 **yü 4.** A ravine; a gully.

峴 **hsien 3.** A proper name.

8

崇 **ch'ung 2.** Lofty; eminent; to reverence; to adore.

華 **hua 4.** A sacred mountain in Shansi.

崑 **k'un 1.** The range of K'unlün mountains between the desert of Gobi and Thibet.

崙 **lun 2** The K'unlün ridge.

崩 **pêng 1.** To collapse; the Emperor's death.

崧 **sung 1.** A mountain in Honan.

崔 **ts'ui 1.** Rocky; precipitous.

崖 **yai 2.** A steep bank; a cliff; a precipice.

豳 **pin 2.** Name of a place in Shensi.

崢 **chêng 1.** High; overtopping; excelling.

崎 **ch'i 1.** Precipitous; dangerous.

崛 **chüeh 2.** A lofty peak; eminent.

崚 **lêng 2.** Hilly; uneven country.

崦 **yen 1.** A mountain in the west, sunset.

崉 **ta 2.** A knoll.

9

嵌 **ch'ien 4.** To inchase, to inlay.

嵐 **lan 2.** Mist, fog.

崽 **tsai 3.** To bring forth, said of animals.

嵆 嵇 } **hsi 1.** A mountain in Nganhoei.

嵒 **yen 2.** Rocky.

嵋 **mei 2.** A mountain in Ssŭch'uan.

崿 **o 4.** A precipice.

嵎 **yü 2.** A mountain in Shantung.

10

嵩 **sung 1.** A sacred mountain in Honan, eminent, lofty.

嵗 **sui 4.** A year.

崞 **k'uo 4.** A ravine, a gorge.

嵞 **t'u 2.** A mountain in Nganhoei.

𡼖 **chung 3.** A tumulus, a small hill.

嵠 **ch'i 1.** A valley with a stream in it, a gorge and a rivulet.

11

嶇 **ch'ü 1.** A rugged, steep mountain.

嶁 **lou 3.** A mountain in Hunan.

𡾰 **piao 3.** A high peak.

𡾐 **hu 4.** A ridge.

嶀 **t'u 2.** A mountain in Chêkiang.

嶞 **to 4.** A mountain peak.

12

嶔 **ch'in 1.** Steep peaks.

嶠 **chiao 4.** A mountain path.

𡾊 **ch'ü 1.** Steep rocks.

嶙 **lin 2.** Rugged, precipitous.

嶓 **po 1.** A mountain in Shensi.

嶕 **ch'iao 2.** Mountainous peaks, rocky.

嶟 **tsun 1.** A peak.

嶢 **yao 1.** Covering, lofty.

13 &

嶨 **hsiao 2.** Rocks.

嶼 **hsü 3.** An islet.

嶮 **hsien 3.** Height, danger.

嶺 **ling 3.** A mountain range.

嶽 **yao 4.** The five sacred mountains.

巂 **hsi 1.** Salangane.

巃 **lung 2.** A cloudy peak.

巍 **wei 4.** Lofty, eminent, rocky, precipitous.

巔 **tien 1.** The apex of a hill.

巖 **yen 2.** A high bank, a rocky cliff, steep, dangerous.

巒 **luan 2.** The peaks of a ridge.

巇 **hsi 1.** A crack, a crevice.

Rad. 47

巛 川

See Lesson 12 E.

巛 川 **ch'uan 1.** River, to flow, flood, stream.

州 **chou 1.** Fields out of water, a political district.

巟 巟 **huang 1.** A watery waste.

巡 巡 **hsün 2.** To go on a circuit, to patrol.

巠 **ching 1.** Water running underground.

巤 **lieh 4.** Foams.

甾 **tzŭ 1.** Pottery. *L. 150.*

邕 **yung 1.** A moat.

巢 **ch'ao 2.** A nest.

巤 **lieh 4.** Bristles.

巛 **tsai 1.** Calamity.

甾 **tzŭ 1.** An uncultivated field. *L. 12. I.*

Rad. 48

工 工

See Lesson 82 A.

工 **kung 1.** Work, labour, time of work.

左 **tso 3.** The left, second to, bad.

功 **kung 1.** Merits.

巧 **ch'iao 3.** Skilful, cunning, artful.

巨 **chü 4.** Great, large, very.

攻 **kung 1.** To attack.

巩 **k'ung 3.** To clasp, to beat.

汞 **kung 3.** Quick-silver.

巫 **wu 1.** A witch, magic.

差 **ch'a 1.** To mistake, to differ. **ch'ai 1.** To send, a legate.

貢 **kung 4.** Taxes, tribute.

項 **hsiang 4.** A sort, class, thing.

Rad. 49

己 己

See Lesson 84 A.

己 **chi 3.** One's self. A cyclical character.

已 **i 3.** To cease, to finish, already, excess.

巳 **ssŭ 4.** A cyclical character.

巴 **pa 1.** A proper name, a clap of the hand, a sign of the optative.

㠯 **i 3.** According to, to use, with, for.

卮 **chih 1.** A syphon.

巷 **hsiang 4.** A lane.

巽 **hsüan 4.** To select.

Rad. 50

巾 巾

See Lesson 35 A.

巾 **chin 1.** A kerchief, a bonnet.

帀 **tsa 2.** To go round, circuit, pervading.

巿 **fei 4.** Prolific, vegetation.

市 **shih 4.** A market, to buy, goods.

布 **pu 4.** Cotton, linen, to spread out, to publish.

吊 **tiao 4.** A thousand cash, to suspend, condolence.

帆 **fan 2.** A sail.

希 **hsi 1.** Few, rare, seldom, to hope.

帍 **hu 4.** A fine napkin.

5

帚 **chou 3. ch'u 2.** A duster, broom.

帘 **lien 2.** Sigh of a tavern.

帛 **pai 2.** Silk, taffety, wealth, property.

帒 **tai 4.** A bag, a pocket.

帑 **nu 2.** The children. **t'ang 3.** A treasure.

帙 **chih 4.** A wrapper.

帕 **p'a 4.** A kerchief, a veil.

帔 **p'ei 4.** A coil, a mantle.

帖 **t'ieh 1.** Written scrolls, documents, a billet, a visiting-card.

6

帤 **ju 2.** A large napkin.

帝 **ti 4.** The supreme ruler, the sovereign.

帮 **pang 1.** To help.

帨 **shih 4.** To dust and wipe.

帥 **shuai 4.** A leader, a commander.

7

帬 **ch'ün 2.** An apron.

席 **hsi 2.** A mat, a repast, a feast.
帨 **shui 4.** A handkerchief.
帨 **mien 4.** A mourning cap.
師 **shih 1.** A sage, a master, a model, a leader, the people, a legion, troops, a metropolis.

8

常 **ch'ang 2.** Constant, regular, frequent, a rule, a principle.
帶 **tai 4.** A girdle, a sash, a belt, a zone; to take with one, to lead, together, with.
帳 **chang 4.** A curtain, a tent.
帽 **ch'ang 1.** To throw a garment loosely over the body.
幍 **t'a 4.** The tester of a bed.
帷 **wei 2.** A curtain.

9

幂 **mi 4.** To cover, to veil.
幇 **pang 1.** To help.
幓 **ch'iao 1.** To hem.
幅 **fu 2.** A strip of cloth, a roll of paper, a hem, an edge.
帽 **mao 4.** A head covering of any kind.
幃 **wei 2.** A curtain, women's apartments.
幄 **wu 4.** A tent.

10

幏 **p'au 2.** A large veil.
幌 **huang 3.** A curtain, a shop-sign, a screen.
幍 **wu 3.** A black turban.
幐 **lien 2.** A door-screen.
幍 **t'ao 1.** The cap of literati.

11

幣 **pi 4.** Silk, presents, wealth.
幕 **mu 4.** A curtain, a tent, intimacy.
幗 **kuo 1.** A turban.
幔 **man 4.** A curtain, a screen.
幖 **piao 1.** A streamer, a pennon.
幘 **chai 4.** A conical cap.

12

幝 **tan 3.** Worn out.
幟 **chih 4.** A pennon.
幢 **ch'uang 2.** A curtain for a carriage.
幡 **fan 1.** A pennant.
幠 **hu 1.** A veil, a screen, to cover.
幞 **p'u 4.** A turban, a cap.

13 &

幦 **pi 4.** A curtain.
幂 **mi 4.** A veil.
幩 **fên 2.** Ornaments on a bridle.
幨 **lien 2.** A door-screen.
幫 **pang 1.** To help.
幪 **mêng 2** To screen.
幬 **tao 4.** A canopy.
幯 **p'in 2.** Worn out.
幭 **mieh 4.** Cover for a cart.
幰 **hsien 3.** Curtain in a carriage or sedan.
襴 **lan 2.** The robe of the literati.
幱 **ch'ien 1.** A slip, a label.
幓 **luan 2.** A cord of silk.

Rad 51

干 干

See Lesson 102 A.

干 **kan 1.** A shield, a stem, much, concern, offense, etc.
平 **p'ing 2.** Even, equal; quiet, to harmonise, to weigh in scales.
年 **nien 2.** The year, the crops.
幵 开 **ch'ien 1.** Even, level, to raise in both hands.
幷 并 **ping 4.** United, together, moreover, also, really, all.
幸 **hsing 4.** Fortunate, prosperous, lucky, opportune.
幹 **kan 4.** The trunk of a tree, a stem, affairs, skilful, capable.

Rad. 52

幺 幺

See Lesson 90 A.

幺 么 **yao 1.** Small, tender, the ace.
幻 **huan 4.** A dream, unreal.
幼 **yu 4.** Young, immature, growing.
玆 **tzŭ 1.** Herbs and grass, this, this one, now, for.
幽 **yu 1.** Dark, secret; hidden, prison, hades.
𢆶 **kuan 1.** To run the threads through the webs.
幾 **chi 1.** To be near, to approximate, almost, minute.
chi 3. How many.

㡭 **chi 4.** To continue.

𢇍 **chüeh 2.** To cease.

Rad. 53

See Lesson 59 I.

广 **yen 3.** A covering.

庄 **chuang 1.** A store; a village.

⿸广下 **hsia 4.** Rooms.

床 **ch'uang 2.** A bed, a sofa, a sled.

庋 **chi 3.** Warehouse.

庇 **p'i 4.** To cover, to protect, to shelter.

序 **hsü 4.** The east and west walls of a room; school, order, succession; preface.

庌 **ya 3.** A verandah.

庎 **chieh 4.** To live alone.

5

府 **fu 3.** A palace; a department or bureau; a prefecture, a storehouse, a collection.

庚 **kêng 1.** A cyclical character, age.

庙 **miao 4.** A temple.

庖 **p'ao 2.** A kitchen; offices.

底 **ti 3.** Base, foundation; low, to settle, a conjunction.

店 **tien 4.** An inn, a shop.

6

庤 **chih 4.** To keep in stock.

庍 **ch'ih 4.** To scold, to expel.

庥 **hsiu 1.** Shade, protection.

庠 **hsiang 2.** A school, an asylum for the old.

庣 **t'iao 1.** A cavity.

度 **tu 4.** A measure, a limit, a degree; a rule, to cross over.

⿸广多 **ch'ih 3.** Vast.

7

席 **hsi 2.** A mat, a feast.

庨 **hsiao 1** Grand, imposing.

庫 **k'u 4.** A storehouse.

庭 **t'ing 1.** The audience-hall.

座 **tso 4** A seat; a divan. Numerative of buildings, etc.

8

⿸广朋 **pêng 1.** To collapse.

⿸广雨 **lou 4.** To drop.

康 **k'ang 1.** Peace, repose, prosperity.

庵 **nan 1.** A hut, a cottage, a Buddhist monastery.

庳 **pi 4.** Low, vulgar.

庶 / 庻 **shu 4.** All, so that, a multitude, nearly, in abundance, about, a concubine.

庸 **jung 1. yung 1.** To use, to employ, to display, to make, merit, ordinary, how?

麻 **ma 2.** Hemp.

9

庾 **yü 3.** A stack, a granary.

廂 **hsiang 1.** Side rooms.

廁 **ssŭ 4.** A privy.

廊 **lang 2.** A verandah.

10

廈 **hsia 4. sha 4.** A building.

廅 **k'o 2.** A cave or grot.

廉 **lien 2** A corner, angular, incorrupt, to search out.

廋 **sou 1.** Secret, to search for.

廓 **k'uo 4.** Great, to enlarge.

廕 **yin 4.** Shade, shadow, to shelter, to protect.

䧹 **ying 1.** An eagle.

11

⿸广差 **ch'a 2.** Ruins.

廑 **chin 3.** A hut; a lodge.

廄 / 廐 **chiu 4.** A stable.

廖 **liao 4.** A proper name.

廒 **ao 2.** A granary.

腐 **fu 3.** To ferment, to rot.

廙 **i 4.** A shop, an inn.

12

廠 **ch'ang 3.** A workshop.

廛 **ch'an 2.** A market-place.

廚 **ch'u 2.** A kitchen.

廢 **fei 4.** Ruined, useless, to abandon, to dismiss.

廣 **kuang 3.** Broad, large, liberal.

廟 **miao 4.** A temple, a fair.

廝 **ssŭ 1.** A menial, servants, together.

廡 **wu 2.** A verandah.

⿸广屠 **t'u 2.** A butchery.

13

廨 **chieh 4.** A palace, a court.

廥 **kuei 4.** A barn.

廩 **lin 3. ling 3.** A government granary.

應 **ying 1.** That which is right and should be, suitable.
ying 4. To answer.

膺 **ying 1.** The breast, to oppose.

廬 **lu 2.** A thatched hovel.

龐 **p'ang 2.** A great house.

[illegible] **su 1.** A hut, a cabin.

廯 **hsien 3.** A granary.

廱 **yung 1.** A moat, harmony.

鷹 **ying 1.** An eagle.

廳 **ting 1.** A hall, a saloon, a court.

Rad. 54

See Lesson 63 D.

廴 **yin 3.** To move on.

廵 **hsün 2.** To go about, to go on a circuit, to cruise.

廷 **t'ing 1.** The court, the audience-chamber.

延 **yen 2.** To drag out, to protract, delay, to invite, to engage.

廹 **p'i 4.** To urge, to vex, to harass.

廸 **ti 2.** To follow, docile, to direct, to intimate.

廻 **hui 2.** To return.

建 **chien 4.** To establish, to found.

廼 **nai 3.** This, here, precisely, then.

Rad. 55

See Lesson 47 B.

廾 **kung 3.** The hands folded.

廿 **nien 4.** Twenty.

弁 **pien 4.** A military cap, soldier, officer.

彝 **i 1.** Offerings, nature, dispositions.

[illegible] **p'ing 2.** To rely on.

弄 **lung 4. nung 4. nêng 4.** To handle, to make, to play with, to deceive.

弃 **ch'i 4.** To throw away.

弇 **yen 3.** To cover over, to hide.

弈 **i 4.** Chess.

弊 **pi 4.** Abuses, corrupt practices, evil.

奬 **ching 3.** To exhort, to encourage.

Rad. 56

See Lesson 71 A.

弋 **i 4.** A dart.

弌 **i 1.** One.

弍 **erh 4.** Two.

式 **shih 4.** A form, a fashion, a rule, to imitate.

忒 **t'ê 4.** Too, very.

[illegible] **tsang 1.** A quay.

武 **wu 3.** Military.

[illegible] **tung 4.** Boards of a boat.

貳 **erh 4.** Two.

弒 **shih 4.** To murder a superior.

[illegible] **ko 1.** A quay.

鳶 **yüan 2.** A kite.

[illegible] **tsêng 1.** An arrow.

Rad. 57

See Lesson 87 A.

弓 **kung 1.** A bow, a measure of five or six cubits.

弔 **tiao 4.** To condole, to hang, a thousand cash.

引 **yin 3.** To draw a bow, to tempt, to induce, to lead.

弗 **fu 4.** An adverb of prohibition, not, not so, do not, will not, can not.

弘 **hung 2.** Large, vast, expanded, to magnify.

弛 **shih 3.** To unstring, to relax.; loose, dissolute.

弡 **chüeh 2.** An archer's ring.

弝 **pa 4.** The part of a bow grasped.

弟 **ti 4.** A younger brother, a disciple.

5

弨 **ch'ao 1.** A bow unbent.

弣 **fu 3.** Two halves of a bow.

弦 **hsien 2.** The string of a bow, the chord of an arc, a crescent, a guitar.

弧 **hu 2.** A bow, an arc, curved.

弢 **t'ao 1.** A bow-case, military strategy.

弤 **ti 3.** The famous bow of the emperor *Shun*.

弩 **nu 3.** A cross bow.

6-8

弭 **mi 3.** Ends of a bow. To stop, to keep down.

弱 **jao 4.** Weak, feeble.

張 **chang 4.** To draw a bow, to stretch, to draw up, to display, a sheet, a numerative.

⿰弓爭 **chêng 4.** To draw a bow.

彊 強 强 **ch'iang 2.** Strong; firm; violent; to force, to compel.

弸 **pêng 1.** A stiff bow; strong; perfect.

⿰弓并 **pêng 1.** To swindle, a swindler.

9 &

粥 **chou 1.** Gruel, congee, porridge.

弲 **yüan 2.** The curvature of a bow.

弼 **pi 4.** To help, to assist; a minister; double.

弽 **yeh 4.** A bowman's finger-stall.

彀 **kou 4.** To draw a bow to its full stretch; enough; adequate.

彈 **tan 4.** A bullet; a shot; a shell; a pill.
t'an 2. To play on stringed instruments; to rebound; to press down.

彇 **hsiao 1.** The extremity of a bow.

彌 **mi 2.** To shoot an arrow; to complete; full; very; much.

疆 **chiang 1.** A boundary, a frontier.

彎 **wan 1.** To draw a bow; to bend; arched; crooked.

Rad. 58

See Lesson 68 A.

彐 ⺕ 彑 **chi 4.** A hog's head.

归 **kui 1.** To return; to belong to.

当 **tang 1.** It must; necessary.

彔 **lu 4.** To carve wood.

彖 **t'un 4.** A hog; a glose.

彗 **hui 4.** A broom.

雪 **hsüeh 3.** Snow.

彘 **chih 4.** A hog.

彙 **hui 4.** A porcupine; a class; a collection.

彝 **i 2.** Offerings to the Manes.

Rad. 59

See Lesson 62 A.

彡 **shan 1.** Feathers, hairs.

彤 **t'ung 2.** Red, purple.

形 形 形 **hsing 2.** Form, shape; the body; material, manner, visage, air; to appear; to show.

彥 **yen 4.** Elegant; refined; accomplished.

彧 **yü 4.** Accomplished; elegant.

彬 **pin 1.** Graceful, elegant; simple.

參 **ts'an 1.** To advice; to consult.

翏 **liao 2.** To dart.

彪 **piao 1.** A tiger; striped like a tiger; streaks; ornate.

彫 **tiao 1.** To carve. To wither.

彩 **ts'ai 3.** Gay-coloured; ornamented; clouds.

彭 **p'êng 2.** The sound of drums, a proper name.

彯 **p'iao 4.** Ornamented with fringe.

彰 **chang 1.** Beautiful; to exhibit; to manifest.

影 **ying 3.** A shadow; an image; a vestige.

Rad. 60

See Lesson 63 A.

彳 **ch'ih 4.** A step, to walk.

行 **ting 1.** To walk alone.

彴 **shao 4.** A foot-bridge.

彶 **chi 2.** To hasten.

彷 **fang 3.** To be like; as.

役 **i 4.** A petty official; a satellite; to serve.

彽 **ch'ih 2.** To go to and fro, irresolute.

征 **chêng 1.** To proceed, to get on, to subjugate; to levy taxes.

彿 **fu 4.** Like, as if.

彼 **pei 3. pi 3.** A distributive pronoun, he, him, that, those.

徂 **tsu 3.** To go to.

往 **wang 3.** To go to; passed; frequently.

6

很 **hên 3.** Very.

後 **hou 4.** After; behind; then; to postpone; posterity.

徊 **hui 2.** Undecided; irresolute.

律 **lü 4.** The sharped musical notes; law; regulation; to adjust.

徇 **hsün 2.** To pervade.

待 **tai 4.** To wait for; to await; to treat; as for.

徉 **yang 2.** To ramble; to stray.

7

徑 **ching 1.** The diameter; straight way.

徐 **hsü 2.** Slow; sedate; dignified.

徒 **t'u 2.** To go on foot; foot-soldier; a disciple, an apprentice, a companion: only, futile; to banish.

8

徟 **chou 1.** Hurried; flustered.

徛 **ch'i 1.** A foot-bridge.

徠 **lai 4.** To invite.

徘 **p'ei 2.** Irresolute.

徜 **ch'ang 2.** Inconstant; fickle; to loiter.

徙 **hsi 3.** To change place; to be moved.

得 **tê 2.** To get; to effect.
tei 3. Must, ought.

從 **ts'ung 2.** To follow; to pursue; to comply with; from; by; since.

御 **yü 4.** To drive; to manage, to rule; imperial; to wait on, to help.

9

復 **fu 4.** To come or go back; again; to reply; to restore.

徨 **huang 2.** Irresolute.

徧 **pien 4.** Everywhere; all round; one time.

循 **hsün 2.** To follow; to acquiesce in; docile.

10 &

徯 **hsi 1.** To wait for; to expect; to hope.

徭 **yao 2.** Duty; forced labour; *corvées*.

微 **wei 1.** Small, trifling, minute, hidden, to fade, to diminish, not.

徫 **chang 1.** To walk fast.

徹 **ch'ê 4.** To penetrate, to understand, all, entire, general.

徵 **chêng 1.** A sign, a proof, an effect, to make clear, to testify, to levy, to enlist.

德 **tê 2.** Moral excellence, goodness, virtue, quality.

徼 **chiao 3.** Lucky, fortunate.

徼 **chiao 4.** Frontiers, to inspect.

儃 **shan 4.** To quicken one's step.

徻 **hui 1.** Excellent, beautiful, Nganhui.

徿 **lung 3.** To walk straight ahead.

忀 **hsiang 1.** To stroll about, to ramble.

儹 **tsuan 2.** To lose one's way.

Rad. 61

心 

See Lesson 107 A.

心 忄 㣺 **hsin 1.** The heart, mind, motives, intention, affections, centre.

必 **pi 2.** Certainly, must, determined on, necessary.

忉 **tao 1.** Care, grief.

3

志 **chih 4.** Will, resolution, fixity of purpose, ambition, desires, annals.

忒 **t'ê 4.** An excess, too, very.

忌 **chi 4.** To fear, to avoid, to dread, to abstain from.

忐 **t'an 3.** Hearty.

忑 **t'ê 4.** Heartless.

忘 **wang 2.** To forget.

忍 **jên 3.** To bear patiently, to endure, fortitude, patience.

忚 **i 1.** Contemptuous.

忓 **kan 1.** Concerned, anxious.

忔 **ko 4.** Displeasure, disgust, angry et.

忙 **mang 2.** Busy, hurried, fluttered, occupation.

忉 **tiao 3.** Pain, care.

忖 **ts'un 3.** To consider, to conjecture, to surmise, to calculate.

4

忠 **chung 1.** Loyal, faithful, devoted, sincere, honest, right.

忿 **fên 4.** Anger, hatred.

忽 **hu 1.** To disregard, suddenly, a trifle.

念 **nien 4.** To think, to ponder on, to study, to repeat.

忥 **hsi 4.** Joy, peace.

忝 **t'ien 3.** To disgrace.

㤕 忱 **shên 2.** Sincere, honest, upright. *Ch'ên* 2.

忡 **ch'ung 1.** Sorrow, care.

忮 **chih 4.** Stubborn.

忪 **chung 1.** Agitated, emotion.

㤆 **fan 4.** To regret, to repent.

忺 **hsien 1.** To take pleasure in, to enjoy.

忻 **hsin 1.** Joy, delight, elation.

忶 **hun 2.** Melancholy.

忼 **k'ang 3.** Deceived, annoyed, disappointed.

忯 **ch'i 2.** To venerate.

㤉 **ya 2.** Fear, pain.

快 **k'uai 4.** Pleasure, cheerful, quick, speedy, sharp, keen.

忸 **niu 3.** Refractory, annoyed, stubborn.

㤌 **pang 1.** Harsh, cross.

忲 t'ai 4. Extravagant.

忳 tun 4. Sad, sorrowful, depressed.

忨 wan 4. To covet, to long for.

忤 wu 4. Disobedient, obstinate.

忬 yü 4. Cheerful.

忴 ch'in 2. Strength, energy.

怲 nê 4. Sadness.

5

怤 fu 1. To think on with pleasure, pleased with.

急 chi 2. Emotion, passion, haste, impatience.

怒 nu 4. Anger, fury.

思 ssŭ 1. To think, to reflect, to consider, a particle.

怠 tai 4. Idle, lazy.

怎 tsên 3. How? Why?

怱 ts'ung 1. Hurried, excited.

怨 yüan 4. Illtreatment, to have a grudge.

怊 ch'ao 1. To be grieved, disheartened.

怔 chêng 1. Restless, afraid.

怞 ch'u 1. Melancholy, despondency.

怵 ch'u 4. Afraid, timorous.

怫 fu 4. Anxiety.

怞 hsia 2. Pleasure, delight.

怙 hu 4. To rely on, to presume on.

怳 huang 3. Wild, mad, disturbed, sorrowful.

怡 i 2. Harmonious concord, mutual pleasure.

怐 kou 4. Silly, simpleton.

怯 ch'ieh 4. Timorous, fearful, cowardly.

怚 chü 1. Haughty, disrespectful.

怪 kuai 4. Strange, monstrous, to dislike, to blame, to deem strange, very.

怩 ni 2. To blush.

怕 p'a 4. To fear, to apprehend, lest.

怶 pên 4. Stupid, dull.

怦 p'êng 1. Earnest, ardent.

怌 p'ei 1. Weak, idle.

怭 pi 4. Dignified, grave.

怲 ping 3. Sad, mournful.

怖 pu 4. Afraid, to frighten, alarmed.

性 hsing 4. Natural disposition, temper, innate.

怛 tan 3. Pain, care.

怗 t'ieh 1. Peacable, quiet, resigned.

怍 tso 4. Modesty.

怚 ts'u 1. Suspicious, to suspect.

怏 ying 4. Dislike, disgust.

怮 yu 1. Timidity.

怋 min 2. Emotion, trouble.

怟 ti 4. Sadness.

怶 p'i 1. Shivering.

6

恚 hui 4. Anger, rage.

恁 jên 3. To dwell upon, to consider.

恝 ch'ia 4. Careless, egoistic.

恐 恐 k'ung 3. To fear, to be afraid, in fear of, perhaps.

恩 en 1. Favour, grace, mercy, affection.

恕 shu 4. Benevolent, tender, merciful, to pardon.

息 hsi 1. A full breath, a gasp, a respiration, to produce, interest, to stop, repose, quiet.

恣 tzŭ 1. Licentiousness, lust.

恙 yang 4. Indisposition, illness.

恭 kung 1. To respect, to venerate, to revere.

恥 ch'ih 3. Shame, to make ashamed of.

恍 hsien 2. Melancholy, stupidity, despondency.

恀 ch'ih 2. To cling on, to rely on.

恜 ch'ih 4. To fear, to regard with awe.

恱 ch'ung 1. Excited, agitated.

恞 hai 4. Sorrowful, depressed.

恨 hên 4. Hatred, spite, resentment.

恆 恒 hêng 2. Constance, perseverance, stable, ordinary, commonly.

恔 hsiao 4. Cheerful, elated, hilarity.

恊 hsieh 2. Harmony, union.

恟 hsiung 1. Timorous, nervous, frightened.

恍 huang 3. Wild, mad, disturbed.

恛 hui 2. Disordered.

恞 i 2. Pleased, well satisfied.

恰 ch'ia 4. Fitting, opportune.

恾 chiang 4. A bad temper.

恪 ch'iao 4. k'o 4. Reverent and attentive.

恤 hsü 2. Violence.

恭 kung 3. To fear and tremble.

恗 k'ua 4. Satisfied, self-complacent.

恠 kuai 4. Strange.

恇 k'uang 1. To fear

恑 kui 3. To change, a metamorphose.

恢 k'ui 1. Great, liberal, to enlarge.

恅 **lao** 3. Confused.
恃 **shih** 4. To rely upon, to trust to.
恓 **hsi** 1. Troubled, vexed, grieved.
恂 **hsün** 2. Sincere, true, frank.
恤 **hsü** 4. Compassion, to pity, to give, alms.
恌 **t'iao** 1. Mean, volatile.
恬 **t'ien** 2. Peaceful, calm.
恫 **t'ung** 2. To be dissatisfied.
忡 **ch'ung** 2. Remorse.
恈 **mou** 2. To long for.
㤠 **lieh** 4. Unquiet.

7

悊 **chê** 4. Wise.
患 **huan** 4. Affliction, sorrow.
您 **nin** 2. Your honour, you, sir.
悉 **hsi** 2. All, fully, very, to investigate throughout.
悐 **t'i** 4. To fear.
悤 **ts'ung** 1. Hurried, excited.
慈 **tzŭ** 2. Goodness.
悠 **yu** 1. Sadness, distant, far-reaching.
恿 **yung** 3. To urge, to encourage.
𢗰 **kuang** 4. Lies, to deceive.
悡 **li** 2. To hate, hatred.
㤅 **ai** 4. To love.
悜 **ch'êng** 3. Dubious.
悍 **han** 4. Fierce, cruel.
悎 **hao** 4. Fear, anxiety.
悕 **hsi** 1. To consider, to reflect, to compassionate.
悔 **hui** 3. To repent, to regret.
悈 **chieh** 4. To enjoin on, to charge.
悁 **chüan** 4. Anxious, distressed.
悃 **k'un** 3. Sincere, loyal, true.
悋 **lin** 4. Stingy.
悖 **pei** 4. To rebel against, perverse, evil.
悚 **sung** 3. Fear, terror.
悌 **ti** 4. To behave as a younger brother should, submission.
悇 **t'u** 2. Anxiety, care.
悄 **ch'iao** 3. Grief, care, silent, still.
悛 **ts'un** 1. To correct, to amend.
悟 **wu** 4. To awake, to apprehend, to become conscious, intelligence.
悮 **wu** 4. To neglect, to delay, to miss an opportunity.
悒 **i** 4. Disquiet, anxiety.
悅 **yüeh** 4. To be pleased, gratified, to assent, to please.
悏 **ch'ieh** 4. Cheerful.
悑 **pu** 4. Fear.
悓 **hsien** 4. To observe, to spy.
㤶 **mang** 2. Disturbed in mind, stupid.
悙 **hêng** 1. Presumption.
㤡 **lüeh** 4. Weak.
悢 **liang** 4. Pity.
㤗 **tou** 4. To search.

8

惉 **chan** 1. Illwill.
惩 **ch'êng** 2. To repress, to punish.
惑 **huo** 4. Doubt, suspicion, unbelief, to deceive.
惠 **hui** 4. Kind, gracious, to obey, to be docile.
惎 **chi** 4. Injurious, fatal.
㥢 **ch'iu** 2. Hatred, to hate.
悶 **mên** 4. Depressed, melancholy, to stupify.
悲 **pei** 1. To grieve, to be sad, to sympathise.
惁 **hsi** 1. To venerate.
惡 **o** 4. Evil, wrong.
wu 1. How?
wu 4. To hate.
惌 **yüan** 4. A grudge.
惢 **jui** 3. Stamens, pistils, heart of a flower.
惝 **ch'ang** 3. Agitated, alarmed.
悵 **ch'ang** 4. Depressed, disappointed.
惆 **ch'ou** 2. Vexed, disappointed.
悱 **fei** 3. Eager, to exert one's self.
悻 **hsing** 3. Angry, enraged.
惚 **hu** 1. Confusion, distraction.
惛 **hun** 1. Confused in mind, dull, stupid.
悸 **chi** 4. Troubled.
惧 **chü** 4. Alone, unfriended.
惓 **ch'üan** 2. Careful, mournful.
悾 **k'ung** 1. Ignorant, simple, guileless.
悺 **kuan** 3. Sorrow, sadness.
惈 **kuo** 3. Courageous.
惃 **kun** 4. Confused, disturbed.
惏 **lan** 2. Greedy, covetous.
悷 **li** 4. Sadness.
惊 **liang** 2. Melancholy.
㦖 **mên** 4. Depressed, melancholic.
惜 **hsi** 1. To pity; to care for; to spare.
惔 **t'an** 3. To burn; consumed with grief.

悼 **tao 4.** To be afflicted, to grieve for.

惦 **tien 4.** To think of, to remember.

㥏 **t'ien 3.** Bashful; to be ashamed.

惕 **t'i 4.** Trouble; fear; alarm.

惇 **tun 1.** Honest; sincere; generous.

[illegible] **tung 1.** Stupid; doll.

悽 **ch'i 1.** Grieved; suffering.

情 **ch'ing 2.** Passions; emotions; feelings; circumstances; lust; nature; facts.

悰 **ts'ung 2.** Joy.

悴 **ts'ui 4.** Grief.

惘 **wang 3.** To lose one's self-possession.

惟 **wei 2.** Only; to think of; but; and, so; an initial or copulative particle.

[illegible] **yen 1.** Pleased.

[illegible] **t'ê 2.** To success; satisfaction.

[illegible] **yai 4.** To hate.

[illegible] **hu 4.** To lean on.

[illegible] **ch'ê 4.** Emotion; vulgarity; singularity.

惞 **hsin 1.** Joy; pleasure.

[illegible] **ya 4.** Sorrow.

[illegible] **ch'ün 1.** Weary.

[illegible] **ling 2.** Sorrow; pity.

9

[illegible] **hsiang 4.** Haughty; hard; angry.

意 **i 4.** A thought; an idea; a sentiment; an intention; meaning; wish; purpose.

惹 **jo 3.** To provoke; to rouse; to incite.

感 **kan 3.** To influence; to be affected by; to be moved; to excite.

愆 **ch'ien 1.** A fault; an error; a mistake; to go beyond.

愍 **min 3.** Pity compassion.

想 **hsiang 3.** To think about; to reflect; to hope; to earn.

愁 **ch'ou 2.** Melancholy; sad; fearful.

愚 **yü 2.** Simple; stupid; rude.

愈 **yü 4.** More; further; to exceed; to be better; to rejoice.

惷 **ch'un 3.** Stupid; dolt.

[illegible] **pei 4.** To resist.

愗 **mou 4.** Stupid.

愛 **ai 4.** To love; to like.

惴 **ch'uai 4.** Mournful.

愋 **hsüan 1.** Unsocial.

惶 **huang 2.** Afraid; nervous; doubtful.

惛 **hun 1.** Stupid; dull; troubled.

[illegible] **yü 2.** Grieved.

愞 **juan 4.** Timid; nervous.

愜 **ch'ieh 4.** Pleased; satisfied.

[illegible] **ch'ien 2.** Uneasy in mind.

[illegible] **ch'iao 4.** Tired, exhausted.

惸 **ch'iung 2.** Sad, forlorn.

[illegible] **k'ui 2.** Anxiety; agitation of mind.

[illegible] **mao 4.** Rashness.

愐 **mien 3.** Timidity.

惱 **nao 3.** Vexation; irritation, anger.

愕 **o 4.** To be moved, affected.

愊 **pi 4** To be oppressed.

愎 **pi 4.** Self-willed; resisting; reproof.

愖 **shên 2.** Sincere; upright.

惺 **hsing 1.** Intelligent.

愓 **t'ang 3.** Profligate.

惵 **tieh 4.** Timid; nervous.

惰 **to 4.** Lazy; careless; indifferent.

[illegible] **to 4.** To estimate; to calculate.

惻 **ch'ai 4.** To pity; to sympathise with.

[illegible] **wu 3.** To love; to fondle.

愔 **yin 1.** Quiet; peaceful.

惲 **yüan 3.** To deliberate; to plan.

愃 **hsüan 1.** Joy; enthusiasm.

10

慁 **hun 4.** To dishonour; to disgrace.

愳 **chü 4.** Fear.

愬 **su 4.** To tell to inform.

愻 **hsün 4.** Complaisant; docile; modest, humble.

態 **t'ai 4.** Behaviour; bearing; manner; attitude.

慈 **tz'ü 2.** Maternal affection; a mother; love; mercy.

慇 **yin 1.** Sadness; anxiety.

[illegible] **yin 3.** Solicitude; care.

愿 **yüan 4.** Honest; respect; diligence.

慂 **yung 3.** To urge; to encourage.

[illegible] **i 4.** Peace; respect; retired.

[illegible] **kêng 3.** Sad; anxious.

[illegible] **sai 4.** Simplicity; peace.

慍 **yün 4.** To be grieved; sad.

慉 **hsü 3.** To nourish; to foster.

愴 **ch'uang 4.** Sad; to pity.

愾 **ch'i 4.** To sigh; to groan.

慌 **huang 1.** Apprehensive; nervous, obscure; grieved.

愰 **huang** 3. Uncertain; disturbed; agitated; at times.

愷 **k'ai** 3. Good; brave; joyous.

慊 **ch'ieh** 4. Pleasure; joy.

愲 **ku** 3. Perturbed; distressed.

愧 **k'uei** 4. Ashamed; bashful.

慄 **li** 4. Fear; terror; to tremble.

㥬 **p'ang** 2. Timid.

愽 **po** 2. Vast, etc.

慅 **sao** 1. Distressed.

慎 **shên** 4. To act carefully; cautious; attentive; still, considerate.

愫 **su** 4. Sincere; one's real intentions.

愓 **t'a** 1. Depressed; in despair.

㥭 **t'ai** 4. Prodigal; extravagant.

慆 **t'ao** 1. Insolent.

愮 **yao** 2. Troubled, distressed.

愪 **yün** 2. Grieved; sad.

憊 **pai** 4. Wearied; disheartened.

㤳 **hai** 4. Gay; sprightly.

愵 **ni** 4. Greedy; blindly doating on.

慒 **ts'ao** 3. Trouble.

㣯 **hsieh** 4. Sorrow,

㦏 **mi** 2. Illusion.

愱 **chi** 4. Envy.

愭 **ch'i** 2. Respect, care.

11

慸 **chih** 4. To lose heart.

惷 **ch'ung** 1. Simple, doltish.

慧 **hui** 4. Intelligent, quick, wis', virtuous.

憇 **ch'i** 4. To rest.

慦 **chiu** 4. To be pleased, diligent.

慝 **t'ê** 4. **t'o** 4. Evil, wicked.

㦗 **ti** 4. High, exalted.

慙 **ts'an** 2. Mortified, ashamed

慼 慽 **ch'i** 1. Grief, sorrow.

慫 **ts'ung** 3. To alarm, to rouse.

慰 **wei** 4. To comfort, to pacify, kindness.

慾 **yü** 4. Desire, lust, passion.

憨 **han** 1. Foolish, silly.

憋 㦐 **pieh** 4. Irritable, nervous, hasty.

慩 **lien** 2. Pity; constance.

慜 **min** 3. Quick-witted, sharp.

㦴 **an** 3. To blush.

慠 **ao** 2. Pride.

憑 **p'ing** 2. A proof, etc.

㦒 **ch'iao** 4. Uprightness.

慮 **lü** 4. To think, to meditate, to care for.

慕 **mu** 4. To love, to long for.

慶 **ch'ing** 4. Good luck, to congratulate.

憂 **yu** 1. Grieved, anxious, in mourning, melancholy.

㦃 **ch'an** 4. Complete virtue.

慞 **chang** 1. Terrified.

慣 **kuan** 4. Habitual, addicted to, to spoil.

慵 **yung** 2. Idle, sluggish.

慨 **k'ai** 4. Generous, loyal, noble-minded.

慷 **k'ang** 3. Generous, magnanimous.

慳 **chien** 1. Stingy, economical, to curtail expenses.

慬 **ch'in** 2. Intrepid, brave, compassionate, cautious.

慺 **lou** 2. Contented, diligent.

憀 **liao** 2. To trust to, to take counsel with.

慢 **man** 4. Slow, remiss, neglectful, rude.

㟿 **mang** 3. Disturbed in mind, agitated.

慪 **ou** 4. To excite.

㦊 **hu** 1. To boast, to exaggerate.

㥾 **ni** 3. Ashamed, mortified.

㦹 **yang** 4. Displeasure, disgust.

㦅 **tai** 4. Disturbed in mind.

慟 **t'ung** 4. Moved, affected, excited.

慱 **t'uan** 2. Grieved, deeply moved.

慚 **ts'an** 2. Shame, confusion.

慘 **ts'an** 3. Grieved, sad, miserable.

慒 **tsao** 1. In confusion.

慥 **ts'ao** 4. Sincere.

憁 **tsung** 3. Disappointment, deception.

慯 **shang** 4. Grief, pity.

慡 **shuang** 3. Shrewdness.

慻 **kuan** 4. To love.

㦘 **lu** 3. Abashed, sottish.

㦇 **lu** 4. Careless.

慓 **p'iao** 1. High spirits.

㦀 **p'êng** 2. Satisfaction, to please.

㥲 **chai** 2. To grumble, to chide.

12

憲 **hsien** 4. An example, constitution, law, pattern; a rule. To follow. Officials.

憑 **p'ing 2.** A stand, to lean upon; to trust to, proof, evidence, according to.

憝 **tui 4.** To hate, to detest.

憖 **yin 4.** To enquire, to ask.

憊 **pai 4.** Exhausted, worn out.

憩 **ch'i 4.** To rest.

憣 **fan 1.** Inconstancy.

㥡 **hsi 4.** Union.

惝 **ch'ang 3.** Alarmed.

憧 **ch'ung 1.** Irresolute, hesitating.

憪 **hsien 3.** Pleasure, peace, happiness.

憓 **hui 4.** Compliant, obedient, docile.

憍 **chiao 1.** Vain, proud.

憰 **chüeh 2.** To feign.

憢 **hsiao 1.** Fear.

㥧 **shun 4.** Melancholy.

憘 **hsi 3.** Pleasure.

憬 **ching 3.** To perceive, to feel.

憒 **kuei 4.** Troubled, anxious.

憦 **lao 2.** Sorry, wearied.

憭 **liao 3.** Intelligent, cheerful, to sympathise with.

憐 **lien 2.** To pity, to desire, to covet.

憫 **min 3.** To mourn for, to commiserate, affliction.

𢢼 **hsi 1.** Fear, dread.

憟 **su 4.** To flatter.

㦏 **hsüan 3.** Effeminacy.

憚 **tan 4.** To dread, to shrink from.

憛 **t'an 4.** Solicitude.

憯 **ts'an 3.** Grief.

憎 **tsêng 1.** To hate, to abhor.

憔 **ch'iao 2.** Distressed and pining.

憮 **wu 3.** To love, to cherish.

𢥔 **tsun 4.** Perspicacity.

㦛 **hsü 1.** Humble, modesty.

憉 **p'êng 2.** To strive, to try.

憏 **ch'ai 4.** Pain.

憕 **ch'êng 2.** Peace.

13

懇 **k'ên 3.** To beg, to ask earnestly, to supplicate.

懃 **ch'iu 2.** Zealous, particular about.

懋 **mou 4.** To exert one's mind, efforts, great.

應 **ying 1.** Ought to be, suitable, necessary.

ying 4. An answer, to respond, correspondent, proportionate, to bear, to undertake, to fulfil, to come up to expectation.

憼 **ching 3.** To warn, to caution, to take care.

𢤏 **chi 4.** Exhaustion, sorrow.

憤 **fên 4.** Impatient zeal, ardor, to exert one's strength.

憷 **ch'u 3** Grief, pain.

懈 **hsieh 4.** Idle, remiss.

憾 **han 4.** Regret, remorse, vexation.

憿 **chan 1.** Lucky, prosperous.

㦗 **chin 4.** Determined, resolute.

懅 **chü 4.** Ashamed; bashful.

懁 **huan 4.** Cares, anger.

懍 **lin 3.** To fear, to tremble at.

憹 **nung 2.** Satisfied.

懊 **ao 4.** Vexed, to regret.

懎 **shê 4.** To hate.

憴 **shêng 2.** To be careful.

憸 **hsien 1.** Skilled in arguments, a fawner, quarrelsome.

憺 **tan 4.** Tranquil; easy.

懂 **tung 3.** To understand; troubled.

懆 **tsao 4.** Sad; troubled; anxious.

憶 **i 4.** To reflect; to call to mind; to remember.

懌 **i 4.** Joy; pleasure.

㦣 **yeh 4.** To fear; danger.

㦴 **cho 4.** Anxiety.

懀 **wei 4.** To abhor.

14

懯 **fu 1.** Hasty; urgent; irascible.

懣 **man 3.** Melancholy; care.

懟 **tui 4.** To abhor; to hate.

懕 **yen 1.** Satisfied; satiated.

懘 **ch'ih 4.** A dissonance.

𢤻 **mao 4.** Beautiful; good; to praise.

𢥉 **shê 1.** Sparing; stingy.

愧 **hun 2.** Melancholy.

懢 **lan 4.** Greedy, covetous.

懜 懵 懞 } **mêng 3.** Giddy-pate; blockhead.

懦 **no 4.** Weakness, incapacity.

懛 **tai 1.** Alarmed; frightened; disheartened.

懤 **tao 3.** Grief, sorrow.

懠 **chi 4.** Angry; suspicious.

㦾 **ying 4.** Displeasure; deception.

㦐 **ni** 3. Weak; timid.

懗 **hsia** 4. To deceive.

㦜 **huo** 4. Dread.

懝 **ai** 4. Fear stupor.

15 &

懲 **ch'êng** 2. To repress; to correct; to restrain.

𢣷 **wei** 4. To talk in one's sleep.

懸 **hsüan** 2. To suspend; to hang; in suspense; anxious; unlike.

戀 **lüan** 4. Ardently loving; to dot on; to lust after.

戁 **nan** 3. To venerate; to be in awe of.

戇 **chuang** 4. Honest; simple; stupid.

懿 **i** 4. Admirable; suitable; excellent.

懥 懫 } **chih** 4. Resentment; hatred; displeasure.

懭 **k'uang** 4. Waste; empty; deception.

㦭 **li** 4. To fear.

懩 **yang** 3. To itch; to scratch; to long for.

懮 **yu** 3. Sorrow; grief; cares.

懪 **pao** 4. Sad.

懷 **huai** 2. The bosom; to cherish kindly; to put in the bosom; to conceal; to think of.

懶 **lan** 3. Lazy; remiss; sleepy.

㺀 **nao** 2. Weak; delicate.

懻 **chi** 4. Violent; proud; overbearing.

懹 **jang** 4. To lose heart; to fall back.

懺 **ch'an** 4. To regret; to repent; ritualistic works.

懾 **chê** 4. To subdue; to influence; afraid; timid.

懼 **chü** 2. To tear; to tremble from awe.

懽 **kuan** 4. Cares; pain; joy; pleasure.

㦼 **sêng** 3. Fear; terror.

㦪 **hsieh** 4. Disquiet; inconstant.

戄 **kou** 4. Frightened; surprised.

Rad. 62

戈 戈

See Lesson 71 F.

戈 **ko** 1. A spear.

戊 **wu** 4. A cyclical character.

戉 **yüeh** 4. A halberd.

成 **ch'êng** 2. To finish; to accomplish; to become; to succeed. 7

戎 **jung** 2. A weapon, arms; soldiers; war; violent; you, your; to assist; barbarian.

戍 **shu** 4. To guard the frontiers.

戌 **hsü**. A wound; a cyclical character.

𢦔 **chiu** 2. A lance, a spear.

𢦏 **ts'ai** 2. To wound; to attack.

戒 **chieh** 4. Precautions; to refrain from; abstinence; to warn; a limit; rule.

我 **o** 3. I; my. *Wo* 3.

或 **huo** 4. Or; either; if; supposing that; perhaps; some; doubtful.

戕 **ch'iang** 1. A spear, to wound, to kill.

戔 **chien** 1. Small; narrow.

咸 **hsien** 2. All; whole.

威 **wei** 1. Majesty.

哉 **tsai** 1. A final particle.

戙 **tung** 4. Planks; boards of a boat.

栽 **tsai** 1. To set out; to plant.

烖 **tsai** 1. Misfortune.

𢦶 **kan** 1. A shield.

戛 **ka** 1. A lance.

戚 **ch'i** 4. A battle-axe; related to; kin; sorrow; to pity; to distress.

惑 **huo** 4. To suspect, etc.

戟 **chi** 3. A halberd.

裁 **ts'ai** 2. To cut out.

戡 **k'an** 1. To subdue; to stab; to kill.

戣 **k'ui** 2. A lance.

戠 **chih** 1. A sword; to gather; potter's clay.

戥 **têng** 3. A small steelyard for weighing money.

戢 **chi** 4. To put away weapons; to collect; to fold up.

感 **kan** 3. To move.

載 **tsai** 4. To contain; to carry; to bear; to sustain.
tsai 3. A year.

截 **chieh** 2. To cut; to stop.

臧 **tsang** 1. Good.

戧 **ch'iang** 4. To prop; to etch on lacker-ware.

戩 **chien** 3. To exhaust; to destroy; to kill; to clip.

𢧐 **ch'uang** 4. A stake.

戮 **lu** 4. To kill; to slaughter.

戭 **yin** 3. A long spear.

戰 **chan** 4. To fight; to fear; to tremble.

𢨋 **tsêng** 1. An arrow.

戯 戲 } **hsi** 4. To play, to joke; a comedy, to make fun of.

戴 **tai** 4. To wear on the head; to sustain; to uphold; to obey.

戳 **ch'o** 1. To stamp; to stab; a seal.

戵 **ch'ü** 2. A long spear.

Rad. 63

See Lesson 129 A.

戶 **hu 4.** Door or window; dwelling, family; a man; treasury.

戹 **nai 4.** Distress.

𢨤 **i 2.** Bolt, barred.

戺 **shih 3.** The pivot in a Chinese door.

帍 **hu 4.** A fine napkin.

房 **fang 2.** A house, the registry office of a tribunal; a constellation; a wife or a concubine.

戽 **hu 4** To bale out water.

戻 **ch'ien 3.** A small door.

戾 **li 4.** Tribulations; calamity; to transgress.

肩 **chien 1.** Shoulder.

所 **so 3.** A place, a building; a relative pronoun, that which, who, what.

扃 **chiung 1.** Bar, bolt, gate.

扁 **pien 3.** A tablet, a sign-board, flat.

扂 **tien 3.** To bar a gate.

𢩐 **i 2.** The bar of a gate.

𢩌 **hsien 4.** The threshold.

扅 **i 2.** Poverty.

扆 **i 3.** A curtain.

扄 **shang 3.** A door knocker, a lock.

扇 **shan 4.** Leaves, folds, a fan, a screen.

扈 **hu 4.** Gate of a city, a proper name.

雇 **ku 4.** To hire, to borrow.

扉 **fei 1.** A door, a leaf.

扊 **yen 3.** The bar of a door.

𢩢 **k'o 2.** To shut a door.

𢩫 **shuan 1.** To bar the door.

Rad. 64

See Lesson 48 A.

手 **shou 3.** The hand, handy, a workman, skill.

才 **ts'ai 2.** Talent, ability, strength, endowments.

扎 **cha 1** To pull up, to prick, to pierce.

扔 **jêng 1.** To throw, to throw away.

抖 **shou 1.** To receive, to gather.

扒 **pa 1.** To strip, to eradicate, to split.

扑 **p'u 1.** To strike, to flog.

打 **ta 3.** To strike, to beat, doing in general, from.

3

扠 **ch'a 1.** To fork up, to seize, to pitch out.

扞 **han 4.** To fend off, to guard.

扦 **ch'ien 1.** To graft into, to put in.

扣 **k'ou 4.** To knock. To fix, to close, to cover. To seize. To deduct.

扢 **ko 3.** To rub.

扚 **tiao 3.** To seize.

托 **t'o 2** To support, to excuse one's self, to feign, to trust.

扛 **k'ang 2.** To carry as on shoulders.

扤 **wu 4.** To stuff in.

扜 扝 } **yü 1.** To seize, to hold.

4

扶 **fu 2.** To uphold, to assist, to protect.

扻 **k'an 3.** To strike, to knock.

抗 **k'ang 4.** To set up, to oppose to resist.

抅 **kou 1.** To hook, to point a wall.

技 **chi 4.** Dexterous, skilful.

抓 **chua 1.** To scratch, to tear, to seize.

找 **chao 3.** To seek, to look for, to exchange, to make up.

抄 **ch'ao 1.** To search, to seize, to confiscate, to copy out.

折 **shê 2.** To break apart, to snap in two.
chê 2. To diminish, to barter.

扯 **ch'ê 3.** To haul.

抉 **chüeh 2.** To dig, to draw.

抐 **na 4.** To dip, to stain.

扼 **o 4.** To grasp, to seize, to hold.

扭 **niu 3.** To twist, to wring.

把 **pa 3.** To grasp, to hold, a particle denoting the accusative.
pa 4 Handle.

扮 **pan 4.** To dress up, style of dress.

扳 **p'an 1.** To drag down.

抨 **p'êng 3.** To scoop up in both hands.

抔 **p'ou 1.** A double handful.

抃 **pien 4.** To clap the hands.

批 **p'i 1.** To peel, to criticise, to reply officially; wholesale.

抒 **shu 1.** To pour out, to state freely.

抩 **t'an 1.** To carry a thing in both hands.

抖 **tou 3.** To tremble, to shake. *To 3.*

投 **t'ou 2.** To throw at, to agree on, to have recourse to, to deliver.

拂 **tiao 4.** To carry.

扽 **tun** 4. To shake.

抆 **wên** 3. To rub.

扰 **chên** 4. To push, to knock against.

抑 **i** 4. To repress, to restrain, an initial particle, or, either.

抈 **yüeh** 4. To bend.

抎 **yün** 3. To lose, to fall.

抭 **yao** 4. To measure, to estimate.

抵 **chih** 3. To move, to gesticulate.

抏 **wan** 2. To rub, corruption.

承 **ch'êng** 2. To offer, to receive, to enjoy, to undertake, to flatter, to avow.

5

抛 **p'ao** 1. To fling, to throw, to reject, to cast off.

招 **chao** 1. To beckon, to let people know, to invite, to provoke, to confess.

抽 **ch'ou** 1. To draw out, to extract, to contract, to decrease.

抶 **ch'ih** 4. To flog.

拙 **cho** 1. Stupid, unskillful.

拄 **chu** 3. A prop, to lean on.

拊 **fu** 3. To pat, to slap, to soothe.

拂 **fu** 4. To shake off; to brush, to oppose.

拑 **ch'ien** 2. To pinch.

拘 **chü** 1. To hook, to grasp, to restrain, to adhere to, whose ever. *Kou* 1.

拃 **cha** 3. A span.

拒 **chü** 4. To oppose, to withstand.

抾 **ch'ü** 1. To lift.

抓 **kua** 1. To clutch.

拐 **kuai** 3. To deceive, to seduce, a kidnapper, to twist, to turn, lame.

拉 **la** 1. To draw, to pull.

拎 **ling** 2. To dangle a thing.

抑 **liu** 3. To feel with the hand.

抹 **mo** 3. To wipe, to rub, to besmear, to cut.

抺 **mei** 4. To feel with the hand.

拇 **mu** 3. The thumb.

抿 **min** 3. To smooth down, to handle gently.

拌 **pan** 4. To throw, to mix.

拈 **nien** 3. To knead with the fingers.

拔 **pa** 2. To draw out, to eradicate, to extirpate.

拚 **p'in** 4. To risk, to disregard, to expose.

抯 **ch'ieh** 3. To extract.

抮 **chên** 3. To draw.

抱 **pao** 4. To infold, to carry in the arms, the bosom, the lap, to hold tight, to hide, to feel, to endure.

披 **p'ê** 1. To open, to spread out, to throw on.

拯 **pi** 4. To strike playfully.

拍 **p'ai** 1. To pat, to slap, to beat.

抪 **pu** 4. To open out, to disperse, to scatter.

抬 **t'ai** 2. To carry on a pole, to lift.

抵 **ti** 3. To oppose, to be equivalent, to atone for, to reach.

担 **tan** 3. To dust, a duster.

拕 拖 **t'o** 1. To pull, to drag along, to protract.

拆 **ch'ai** 1. To break, to destroy.

押 **ya** 1. To compel, to control, to keep in custody, to pawn. **ya** 2. To sign, signature.

抰 **yang** 3. To whip, to beat.

拗 **niu** 4. Mulish, stubborn.

拏 **na** 2. To take, to hold.

拜 **pai** 4. To salute, reverence, to appoint to an office.

6

挓 **cha** 1. To open, to widen out.

拫 **ch'ên** 2. To adjust.

挒 **ch'ou** 3. To grasp.

指 **chih** 2. A finger, a toe. **chih** 3. To designate, to indicate, to hope, to confide in.

持 **ch'ih** 2. To seize in the hand, to hold, to maintain.

挃 **chih** 1. To touch.

拯 **chêng** 3. To raise, to help, to rescue.

挄 **ch'ung** 4. To leap, to skip.

拽 **chuai** 4. To trail, to drag.

挪 **yeh** 1. To gesticulate, to ridicule.

拷 **k'ao** 3. To put to the question, torture.

拮 **chieh** 2. To press after, to pursue.

挌 **ko** 2. To fend off.

拱 **kung** 3. To bow, with the hands before the breast. An arch, a vault.

挂 **kua** 4. To suspend.

括 **k'uo** 4. **ko** 4. To envelop, to embrace, to include. A notch.

按 **an** 4. To press down, to stop, to prevent, to examine, as, accordingly.

拾 **shih** 2. To gather, to collect, ten.

拭 **shih** 4. To wipe, to rub and dust.

拴 **shuan** 1. To fasten, to tie up.

挄 **hsien** 3. To tear away.

挑 **t'iao** 1. To carry, a load, to stir up, to choose, to seduce.

挅 **to** 4. To consider, to estimate.

挏 t'ung 2. To draw off.

挖 wa 1. To scoop out, to dig out, to criticise.

挪 no 2. To move, to remove.

挋 jên 3. To seize, to shake.

挒 lieh 4. To wring, to break.

挌 ch'ih 3. To seize, to beat, to break, ample.

拵 ts'un 2. To pierce.

挷 pang 3. To propel a boat, to beat.

訾 tzŭ 4. To gather, to seize.

挈 hsieh 2. To raise, to help.

拳 ch'üan 2. The fist.

拿 挐 na 2. To take, to hold.

7

捏 nieh 1. To knead with the fingers, to fabricate, to trump up.

拶 tsan 3. To torture by finger sticks.

挨 ai 1. To suffer, to belay, to lean on, near.

振 chên 4. To move, to shake, to stir up.

捉 cho 1. To grasp, to seize.

捍 han 4. To ward off, to defend.

挾 hsieh 4. To hold, to bear.

捖 huan 3. To rub, to polish.

挭 kêng 3. To stir up.

挾 hsieh 1. To pinch, to contain.

捃 chün 4. To sort, to pick out.

捐 chüan 1. To subscribe, to purchase, to collect.

挶 chü 4. A handle.

捆 k'un 3. To plait, to bind, to tie up, a bunch.

捋 lo 4. lüeh 4. To tuck up, to draw between the fingers.

挼 nei 2. To rub, to caress.

捌 pa 1. Eight.

捊 p'ao 2. To seize, to hold.

捊 p'o 4. To pluck up.

捕 pu 3. To seize, to catch, the police.

捎 shao 1. To carry.

捒 shu 4. To bind tight.

挺 t'ing 3. Stiff, rigid, to stand up, to support.

捅 t'ung 3. To break through.

挫 ts'o 4. To maltreat, to wrong.

捘 tsun 4. To seize.

挽 wan 3. To hold, to bend.

捂 wu 4. To oppose, to resist.

挹 i 4. To pour out, to repress.

捀 fêng 1. To offer.

挳 k'êng 1. To knock against.

程 ch'êng 2. To raise.

捜 chin 4. To seize.

拼 p'in 4. To risk, to expose, etc.

抄 挲 so 1. To palp, to feel.

8

捵 tien 1. To offer.

掙 chêng 4. To make an effort, to earn.

捝 cho 1. To grasp.

掾 shan 1. To entice, to seduce.

捬 fu 3. To rub, to caress.

掀 hsien 1. To lift up, to open, to peruse.

捧 p'êng 3. To hold up in both hands, to offer, a handful.

捴 hu 1. To empty.

掍 hun 4. To inlay.

掯 k'ên 3. To annoy, to vex.

掐 ch'ia 1. To pluck.

据 chü 1. To seize.

掘 chüeh 2. To dig out, to excavate.

捲 chüan 3. To roll up, frizzled.

掬 chü 2. To grasp, a handful.

控 k'ung 4. To accuse.

掛 kua 4. To hang up, in suspense, anxious, a numerative.

掂 kuai 1. A slap.

掠 liao 4. To rob, to flog.

掄 lun 2. To choose.
lun 1. To brandish.

捫 mên 1. To feel for, to compress.

掹 mêng 1. To haul.

捺 na 4. To press.

捻 nien 3. To nip with the fingers, to twist.

捼 nei 2. To rub, to polish.

排 p'ai 2. To arrange in order, to dispose, to eliminate.

捹 pên 4. To mix up, to throw into confusion.

掊 p'ei 3. To take, to rob.

拼 p'ing 1. To drive away, to expel.

掃 sao 3. To sweep.
sao 4. A broom.

捨 shê 3. To part with, to renounce, to give alms.

授 shou 4. To give, to transmit, to teach.

探 t'an 1. To feel for, to explore, to try, to sound.

掏 t'ao 1. To extract.

掉 tiao 4. To move, to fall.

掂 tien 1. To weigh in the hand, to appraise.

掭 t'ien 4. To dip the writing-brush.

掇 to 4. To pluck, to gather, to arrange.

推 t'ui 1. To push, to decline, to shirk, to reason.

採 ts'ai 3. To pick, to gather, to collect, to make enquiries.

掫 chou 2. To lift.

接 chieh 1. To receive, to forward, to connect, to follow.

捷 chieh 2. To succeed, alert, active, clever.

措 ts'o 4. To arrange, to place, to publish.

捽 tsu 4. To clutch.

捥 wan 4. To bend the wrist.

捱 yai 2. To delay, to refuse.

掞 yen 2. To cover.

掩 yen 3. To cover, to conceal, to close, to surprise, to seize.

掖 yeh 4. To support, to uphold.

摽 piao 4. To bind, to tie up.

揶 yeh 1. To gesticulate.

掌 chang 3. The palm, a sole, a paw, to rule, to control.

掣 ch'ih 4. To draw, to hold.

掔 ch'ien 1. To ravel up.

9

捶 ch'ui 2. To beat.

揑 nieh 1. To knead with the fingers, to fabricate.

揸 cha 1. To seize, to hold fast, a handful.

插 ch'a 1. To insert, to stick in, to meddle.

揕 chên 4. To strike or stab.

揰 ch'ung 4. To push into to stir out.

揣 ch'uai 3. To feel for, to estimate.

換 huan 4. To change, to exchange.

揮 hui 1. To move, to shake, to signal, to direct.

揉 jou 2. To bend, to twist, to subdue.

揭 chieh 1. To lift up, to solve, to borrow.

揀 chien 3 To select, to choose.

揆 k'ui 2. To consider, to calculate.

描 miao 2. To delineate, to draw, to sketch, to depict.

揞 min 3. To feel and smooth down, to fold.

揞 an 3. To cover, to hide.

掽 p'êng 4. To run against, to bump.

揣 to 3. To slip, to fall.

揌 sai 1. To shake.

揗 hsün 2. To encourage; to excite.

揎 hsüan 1. To pull up.

提 t'i 2. To pull up; to lift; to help; to bring forward; to mention; to propose; to govern.

揙 pien 3. To pound.

揪 chiu 1. To grasp, to clutch, to drag.

揝 tsuan 4. To seize.

握 wo 4. To grasp; to hold tight.

揠 ya 4. To pull up; to eradicate.

揚 yang 2. To raise; to hold up; to extend; to winnow.

揜 yen 3. To cover; to shut.

揖 i 1. Reverence; to bow.

揄 yü 2. To draw out; to extol.

援 yüan 2. To lay hold on; to hold fast; to pull out; to rescue; to quote.

揻 han 4. To shake.

楹 ying 2. To carry on the shoulders.

揸 ch'ê 3. To draw.

揍 ts'ou 4. To expect.

10

搽 ch'a 2. To anoint; to paint; to smear.

搌 chan 3. To wipe away.

搷 ch'ên 3. To extend.

掾 yüan 4. An officer, a substitute.

搘 chih 1. To raise; to support; to prop.

搋 chih 4. To stab, to pierce.

搐 ch'ou 1. Spasm; contractions.

搥 ch'ui 2. To beat; to strike.

搋 ch'uai 1. To put in the bosom; to pocket; to knead.

携 hsieh 2. To lead by the hand.

搧 shan 1. To fan; to excite; to slap.

搜 sou 1. To search; to investigate; to enquire.

搠 shuo 4. To smear; to daub.

搳 hsia 2. To scrape.

搖 yao 2. To shake; to move; to sway.

搆 kou 4. To pull; to connect; to reach up to.

搬 pan 1. To remove; to transport; a thumb-ring.

搡 sang 3. To shake, to push over.

搔 sao 1. To scratch.

搭 ta 1. To pile up; to join; to add to.

搪 t'ang 2. To ward off; to guard against; to shun.

搯 t'ao 1. To take out; to bale out.

搶 ch'iang 3. To take by force; to ravish; to oppose; ahead.

搓 ts'o 1. To twist; to rub; to scrub.

搵 en 1. To press down.

搗 wu 3. To cover; to stop up.

搵 hun 4. To take up with tongs.

揖 jung 3. To pound.
搩 chieh 2. A span; to measure.
搛 chien 1. To grasp with the chopsticks.
搕 k'o 1. To knock.
摞 li 4. To smooth t to draw through the hands.
搣 mieh 4. To pluck up.
搙 nou 4. To manipulate.
搦 ni 4. To catch hold.
搒 pang 3. To beat; to propel a boat.
搏 po 2. To seize to strike.
搮 so 4. To feel; to grope for.
揗 hsieh 1. To pull out a stopper.
損 hsün 3. To harm; to injure; chastisement.
搨 t'a 4. To rub over; a facsimile; an impression.
搗 tao 3. To pound.
搷 tien 1. To knock a thing to pieces.
搊 chou 1. To hold in the fingers.
搢 chin 4. To stick into; to insert.
搲 wa 3. To scoop out.
揗 hsün 2. To resist.
摉 su 4. To steal.
搴 ch'ien 1. To pluck up; to take out, to extirpate.

11

摣 cha 1. To seize; to hold fast; a handful.
摺 chê 2. To fold; a memorandum book.
摭 chê 1. To gather.
摴 ch'u 1. Pantomim; mimic.
摚 lêng 2. To sew.
摼 k'êng 1. To thump; to butt against.
摳 k'ou 1. To raise; to lift.
掎 chi 1. To take up with pincers.
摎 chiao 1. Twisted; confused; to unravel.
摑 kuai 1. To slap.
摟 lou 3. To embrace.
摛 li 2. To display.
摙 lien 3. To arrange.
摞 lo 4. To pile up.
擄 lu 3. To rub; to wipe; to strip off; violence.
摝 lu 4. To roll; to rock.
摇 mi 3. To strike.
摽 piao 1. To give a signal.
摵 shê 1. The fall of the leaf, elegy; elegiac.
摼 ch'ien 1. To pull; to lead; to drag.
摏 ch'ung 1. To pound.
摔 shuai 3. To fall down, to throw down.
摢 hu 1. To break, to destroy.
摥 t'ang 4. To separate, to sunder.
摫 tou 1. To split, to open.
摶 t'uan 2. Round, to roll round.
摲 chan 4. To mow.
摷 ts'ao 4. To stir.
摘 chai 1. To pluck, to pick, to take off.
摪 chiang 1. To lead.
摧 ts'ui 1. To press, to urge.
摠 tsung 3. To gather, to sum up.
摄 yang 4. A pattern.
摀 yen 4. To pare, to trim.
撇 p'ieh 1. To skim off, to reject, to abandon.
摜 kun 4 To roll.
摚 t'ang 2. To resist, to push back.
摗 tsu 2. To gather.
擊 p'ieh 1. To skim off, to reject, to abandon.
摯 chih 4. To grasp, to offer up.
撆 liao 4. To lay down, to let.
摩 mo 2. To feel with the hand, to rub, to caress.
摹 摸 mo 1. mao 1. To feel for, to get, to succeed.

12

撫 fu 3. hu 3. To caress, to pat.
撐 撑 ch'êng 1. To prop up, to assist; to punt.
撦 ch'ê 3. To tear, to pull apart, to haul up.
撤 ch'ê 4. To tear, to pull apart, to pull.
撖 chih 4. To try, to ascertain, to compare.
摜 kuan 4. To be familiar with, to lift, to let drop.
撁 ch'ien 1. To graft into, to stick in.
撞 chuang 4. To strike, to run up against.
撰 chuan 4. To collect, to edict, a note, a composition.
夯 hang 1. To pound earth, a beater, to ram.
撊 hsien 3. Brave, wrathful.
撝 hui 1. To split.
撋 juan 2. To rumple.
撟 chiao 3. To lift up the hand, to grasp, to bend.
撬 yao 4. ch'iao 4. To force up by leverage, to prise open.
撅 chüeh 2. To pluck, to break.

撈 **lao 2.** To fish up; to drag out of water.
撩 **liao 1.** To grasp, to raise, to stir up.
撓 **nao 2.** To scratch, to trouble.
撚 **nien 3.** To roll in the fingers.
⿰扌景 **hsing 4.** To feel; to estimate.
播 **po 3.** To sow, to publish, to winnow, to cast aside.
撥 **po 1.** To spread, to open out, to expel, to distribute, to send away.
撲 **p'u 1.** To strike; to assault.
撒 **sa 1.** To loose.
sa 3. To scatter.
摠 **shai 1.** To beat the gongs.
撏 **hsün 2.** To elect, to seize.
撕 **ssŭ 1.** To rend; to tear.
撣 **tan 3.** To dust.
撢 **t'an 4.** To grasp, to play on.
撮 **ts'o 4.** To pinch up, to choose, to make, to gather.
撙 **tsun 4.** To adjust; to regulate, economy.
撌 **k'uei 4.** To take, to monopolise.
⿰扌就 **chiu 4.** To engross.
⿱敦手 **tun 1.** To strike with the fist.

13

⿰扌肅 **su 4.** To pound.
擉 **ch'o 1.** To pierce.
撾 **chua 1.** To beat, to strike.
撼 **han 4.** To move; to shake, to excite.
擀 **kan 3.** A rolling pin, to laminate.
撿 **chien 3.** To revise, to gather.
擒 **ch'in 2.** To seize, to clutch.
擖 **ko 4.** To scrape.

據 **chü 4.** To take in the hand, to rely upon, a legal instrument, evidence, according to.
⿰扌匯 **k'uai 3.** To rub, to smooth, to carry.
擂 **lei 2.** To pound, to beat.
擄 **lo 3.** To capture prisoners; prisoners.
⿰扌奧 **ao 4.** To grind.
擗 **p'i 3.** To cleave, to open.
⿰扌塞 **sai 1.** To stop, to obstruct.
擅 **shan 4.** To assume; to usurp.
撻 **t'a 4.** To chastise, to beat.
擔 **tan 1.** To carry a burden, to sustain.
tan 4. A load.
擋 **tang 3.** To withstand.
操 **ts'ao 1.** To practise, to drill, rule, method.
擇 **chai 2.** To choose, to select.
擁 **yung 3.** To embrace, to carry in the arms; to press, a crowd.
攜 **hsieh 2.** To hold, to carry.
擊 **chi 1.** To hit against, to attack.
擎 **ch'ing 2.** To lift up, to uphold.
擘 **pai 1. po 4.** To break apart with the hand.

14

擢 **chê 2.** To select, to employ.
⿰扌豪 **hao 2.** To compare and estimate.
擤 **hsing 2.** To blow the nose with the fingers.
擭 **huo 4.** A snare, a trap.
擰 **ning 3.** To wring.
擬 **i 3.** To compare, similar, to guess, to decide, to intend.
擩 **ju 4.** To stain, to dye, to dib, to rub.
擱 **ko 1.** To lay on; to put down, to hinder, to differ, to support, to be able, to dispute.

擯 擯 } **pin 4.** To receive a guest, to expel; to find fault with, to reject.
擡 **t'ai 2.** To carry on a pole, to raise, to elevate.
擣 **tao 3.** To pound or grind fine.
擠 **chi 3.** To crowd; to upset; to press; to milk.
擲 **chih 4.** To throw; to fling away.
擦 **ts'a 1.** To rub; to wipe.
⿰扌蒙 **mêng 2.** To cover.
擥 **lan 3.** To grasp; to interfere with.
擪 **yeh 4.** To put into the bosom; to tuck up.

15

攄 **ch'u 1.** To scatter; to ramble.
擷 **chieh 3.** To pick up; to gather.
擾 **jao 3.** To trouble, to disturb; to tame animals, mild.
擴 **k'uo 4.** To stretch; to expand.
擸 **lieh 4.** To draw; to tear.
⿰扌畾 **lei 4.** To pound; to triturate.
擽 **li 4.** To choose; to allow; to exclude.
擮 **mieh 4.** To beat.
攆 **nien 3.** To expel; to dismiss.
擺 **pai 3.** To spread out; to arrange; to wave; a ferry.
擿 **t'i 1.** To break.
攀 **p'an 1.** To grasp; to pull down or towards one; to implicate; to mount.

16-17

攉 **huo 4.** To knead; to mix up.
攏 **lung 3.** To grasp; to collect; a comb.

[手+圜] **huan 3**. A cage; to shut in.
攘 **jang 3**. To seize; to reject; to embroil.
攔 **lan 2**. To hinder; to embarrass; to obstruct.
攖 **ying 1**. To run against; to assail; to injure.
[手+糞] **fên 4**. To remove dirt.
攙 **ch'an 1**. To mix; to support; to lift.

18 &

攜 **hsieh 2**. To lead by the hand; to go with; to carry off.
攝 **shê 4**. **nieh 4**. To help; plurality (of offices); interim; to raise; peace, order.
攛 **ts'uan 1**. To rouse; to inveigle; to entice.
攤 **t'an 1**. To open and spread out; to rate; to share; to pay instalments.
攞 **lo 3**. To rend.
攢 **tsoan 4**. To gather; to hoard up.
攦 **li 4**. To split.
攪 **chiao 3**. To stir up; to mix; to excite; to interrupt.
攫 **kuo 4**. To seize; to capture.
攩 **tang 3**. To impede.
攬 **lan 3**. To grasp; to interfere with; to monopolise.
攮 **nang 3**. To stab.
[手+疊] **tieh 2**. To fold over, to pile up.
攣 **lüan 2**. To bind or tie; to bend; to crook; to contract.

Rad. 65

See Lesson 43 C.

支 **chih 1**. A branch, a twig; to prop; to pay wages.
[多+支] **chih 4**. Many, numerous.
[尗+支] **shih 4**. Salt peas.
攲 **ch'i 1**. Leaning; inclined.

Rad. 66

See Lesson 43 D.

攴 攵 } **p'u 1**. To tap.
攷 **k'ao 3**. Aged; to examine.
收 **shou 1**. To receive, to gather, to harvest.
改 **kai 3**. To change; to alter; another.
攻 **kung 1**. To assault, to attack.
攸 **yu 1**. A place; that which; whereby; some.
孜 **tzŭ 1**. Zeal, care.
放 **fang 4**. To put, to let go, to loosen, to issue; disorderly; to feed; to set free.
攽 **pan 1**. To divide, to share.
[今+攵] **ch'in 2**. To seize, to hold.

5-6

政 **chêng 4**. To rule; government; laws politics.
敂 **k'ou 4**. To strike, to knock against; to deduct.
[可+攴] **k'o 3**. To knock, to beat, to thump.
故 **ku 4**. The cause or reason of a thing; consequently; on purpose; old; to die.
敃 **min 3**. Strong, robust; to strive.
效 **hsiao 4**. To produce; effects, results; to imitate; similar.
敉 **mi 3**. To caress; to console; to encourage.

7-8

敕 **ch'ih 4**. An Imperial Edict.
敎 教 } **chiao 1**. To teach. **chiao 4**. Doctrines; sects; schools; to cause; to make.
救 **chiu 4**. To rescue; to save from; to help.
敏 **min 3**. Quick of perception; clever; sharp; witty.
敖 **nao 3**. To ramble; tall; proud.
敗 **pai 4**. A defeat; to ruin; to destroy.
敘 **hsü 4**. To arrange; in detail; to state; to narrate; to chat; a preface.
敔 **yü 3**. To stop, to cease.
敢 **kan 3**. To dare; to venture; presumptuous.
敝 **pi 4**. Worn out; vile; humble.
赦 **shê 4**. To forgive; to pardon.
啟 **ch'i 3** To open; to begin; to explain.
敞 **ch'ang 3**. A plateau; high; open.
[谷+攴] **ch'ien 4**. To peck.
散 **san 4**. To scatter, to disperse, to separate, to dismiss.
san 3. Powder.
敦 **tun 1**. Honest, sincere, true, to perform.

9-10

敬 **ching 4**. To revere, to show respect to, to venerate.
敫 **yao 4**. To shine, to light.
[柬+攴] **lien 4**. To hammer out.
[甚+攴] **chên 1**. To beat.
敳 **nai 2**. To govern, to settle.
敲 **ch'iao 1**. To knock, to tap.
[兼+攴] **ch'ien 4**. To peck, to pick up.

11-12

敷 fu 1. To spread out, to diffuse, to promulge, to equal, extensively.

敺 ch'ü 1. To expel, to drive away.

數 shu 3. To count, to enumerate, to blame.

shu 4. A number, a bill, several, an art, a rule.

敵 ti 2. An enemy, a competitor, to oppose.

整 chêng 3. To adjust, to put in order, entire, whole.

13 &

鼖 fên 2. A large bass drum.

斂 lien 4. To collect, to gather, to concentrate.

斁 14. tu 4. Wearied, worn out, to break, to ruin.

斀 cho 2. To castrate.

斣 ch'o 1. To pierce, a darting pain.

斁 ch'ung 1. Intrusion, an intruder.

斆 hsiao 4. To teach.

斃 pieh 4. To die, to kill.

變 pien 4. To change, to transform.

Rad. 67

See Lesson 61 F.

文 wên 2. Strokes, lines, ripples, variegated, genteel, stylish, scholarly, a classifier of cash.

吝 lin 4. Avarice.

斐 fei 3. Streaks, lines, graceful.

斌 pin 1. Elegant, graceful.

斒 pien 1. Veined.

斕 lan 2. Ornamented with bands.

斑 pan 1. Variegated, striped, mottled.

Rad. 68

See Lesson 98 B.

斗 tou 3. A peck measure, a vessel.

斛 huo 2. To scoop up water in a bucket and pour it on fields.

料 liao 4. To estimate, to judge, to reckon, to dispose, materials, stuff, pulse for animals, colored glass.

斛 hu 2. The Chinese bushel.

斜 hsieh 2. Transverse, oblique, opposite, heterodox.

斝 chia 3. A hanap.

斞 yü 4. A stack of grains.

斟 chên 1. To pour out, to deliberate.

斡 kuan 3. To turn, a handle by which to turn a machine.

魁 k'ui 2. The head, the chief, gigantic.

斢 tou 3. To plunder.

Rad. 69

══ See Lesson 128 A.

斤 chin 1. Catty, hatchet.

斥 ch'ih 4. To expel, to scold.

劤 chin 4. Strength.

斧 fu 3. An axe.

所 sho 3. A place, a relative pronoun.

欣 hsin 1. To rejoice.

斫 chao 4. To cut, to chop.

斬 chan 3. To cut in two, to decapitate, to sever.

斯 ssŭ 1. This, he, they, a final particle, then, immediately.

新 hsin 1. New, fresh, recently, fuel.

斲 斵 } cho 2. To chop, to hash.

斷 tuan 4. To cut asunder, to stop, to cease, to settle, to judge, certainly, decidedly.

斸 ch'ü 1. To chop.

斸 chu 3. To dig.

Rad. 70

See Lesson 117 A.

方 fang 1. A place, a region, square, regular, apt, easy, a rule, a prescription, a means, a comparison, then, actually.

斻 hang 2. A pontoon, a ferry-boat.

於 yü 2. In, at, on, among, for, through, than.

放 fang 4. To let go, to loosen, etc.

施 shih 1. To expand, to exhibit, to use, to give, to confer, to do, to set, action in general.

斿 yu 2. The dog-tooth bordering to a flag.

6-7

旃 chan 1. A flag, a signal, this, that.

旂 **ch'i 2.** A flag.

旅 **lü 3.** A body of 500 men, to travel, exile.

旄 **mao 2.** A tail of a yak used as a banner.

旆 **p'ei 4.** A banner, to travel.

旀 **wu 4.** A streamer.

旁 **p'ang 2.** The limits, the sides, by the sides, near to.

旊 **fang 3.** To mould clay, as a potter.

旋 **hsüan 2.** To turn round, to revolve, consequently, then.
hsüan 4. A whirlwind.

族 **tsu 2.** To collect together, a tribe, a clan, a family, relatives, to destroy.

旌 **ching 1.** A banner, a standard, to make signals, to make manifest, to honour.

8 &

旐 **chao 4.** A banner with tortoises and snakes.

旒 **liu 2.** Fringes, a streamer, a pennant.

旓 **shao 1** Fringes of a flag.

旖 **i 3.** A waving movement, to flutter to the breeze.

旗 **ch'i 2.** A flag, a banner.

旘 **ch'ih 4.** A pennon.

[illegible] **huang 2.** A sign denoting a tavern, a sign.

旛 **fan 1.** The banner carried before a corpse.

Rad. 71

无 兂

See Lesson 61 C.

无 **wu 2.** Negation, not.

[illegible] **chi 4.** The hiccups, a sob.

既 旣 既 既 **chi 4.** Since, when, to finish, all.

Rad. 72

日 ⊖

See Lesson 143 A.

日 **jih 4.** Sun, day.

旦 **tan 4.** The rising sun, the dawn, actors who take the parts of females.

旪 **hsieh 2.** Concord, harmony.

旭 **hsü 3.** Rising sun.

阳 **yang 2.** The superior of the dual powers in Chinese philosophy.

早 **tsao 3.** Morning, soon, formerly.

旨 旨 **chih 3.** An Imperial Decree, purport, meaning, fine, excellent.

旬 **hsün 2.** A period of ten days, of ten years, a set time, to spread.

亘 **hsüan 1.** To revolve.

旰 **kan 4.** Sunset, dusk.

[illegible] **ch'i 4.** A solar halo.

旱 **han 4.** Dry, want of rain.

4

明 **ming 2.** Bright, light, clear, to explain, intelligent.

旺 **wang 4.** Bright, prosperous, glorious, abundant, much.

旿 **wu 3. ho 3.** Midday, noontide.

昐 **fên 1.** Solar rays.

[illegible] **chüeh 2.** Penumbra.

昉 **fang 3** Bright, lucid, to occur.

昕 **hsin 1.** Morn, dawn.

昄 **pan 3.** Great, wide.

昂 **nang 2.** To rise, lofty, imposing, high price, dear.

昌 **ch'ang 1.** The light of the sun, shining, glorious.

易 **i 4.** Easy, to be at ease, to change, to transform.

昆 **k'un 1.** Together, futurity, an elder brother.

旻 **min 3.** Pity, compassion, sympathy.

昇 **shêng 1.** Rising sun, prosperity, splendour.

昃 **chai 4.** Declining sun, afternoon.

昊 **hao 4.** The bright sky, august, heaven.

昏 **hün 1.** Dusk, dark, confused.

昔 **hsi 2.** Old, anciently, former, the time of night.

旹 **shih 2.** Time, epoch, situation, opportunity.

5

昡 **hsien 4.** To brighten, to light up.

昫 **hsü 4.** Warm, kind, pleasant.

昣 **chên 3.** Transparent.

昭 **chao 1.** Brightness, luminous, to display.

昧 **mei 4.** No sun, dark, obscure, hidden.

昵 **ni 4.** The sun drawing near, familiar, favorites.

昳 **tieh 4.** The sun beginning to decline.

昨 **tso 2.** Yesterday, time gone.

映 **ying 4.** To shine on, to reflect, to favour.

昞 **ping 3.** Bright, glorious.

昶 **ch'ang 3.** A long day, remote, long, filled.

昴 mao 3. The Pleiades.
是 shih 4. To be, is, right, positive, absolute.
星 hsing 1. A star, a spark, a spot.
昜 yang 2. To expand, glorious.
昱 yü 4. Light, to light.
曷 ho 2. Why? how? which? where?
冐 mao 4. Rashness.
春 ch'un 1. Spring, pleasant, wanton or lewd.
昝 tsan 2. A personal pronoun, I, me.
者 chê 4. A suffix.

6

晠 shêng 4. Daylight.
晌 shang 3. Noontide, midday.
時 shih 2. Time, a season, a period.
晊 chih 1. Bright, splendid.
晅 hsüan 1. The light of the sun.
晒 shai 4. To dry in the sun.
晁 ch'ao 2. A surname.
晃 huang 3. To dazzle, a flash.
晏 yen 4. Evening, peace, repose, late.
晉 晋 } chin 4. To increase, to grow, a proper name.
耆 ch'i 2. A sexagenarian.
書 shu 4. A book, to write.

7

晣 晢 } chê 4. To light, to know intuitively, wise, discerning.
晞 hsi 1. The dawn.

晛 hsien 4. The sun appearing.
晥 huan 3. Bright, luminous.
晦 hui 4. Dark, obscure, unlucky.
脖 pei 4. Obscure, dark.
晡 pu 1. The time from 3 to 5 p. m.
晙 tsun 4. Dawn, bright, clear.
晧 hao 4. Day, light.
晤 wu 4. To see, to meet.
晚 wan 3. The evening, late.
晡 pieh 3. To dry in the sun.
晨 ch'ên 2. Morning, dawn.
曹 ts'ao 2. A company or class.
晝 chou 4. Daytime.

8

晾 liang 4. To dry in the sun, to spread out to air.
晬 sui 4 A year of a person's life.
晴 ch'ing 2. A clear sky.
晼 wan 3. The declining sun.
睒 shan 3. Bright, to glitter.
晻 yen 3. Obscured, hidden, to screen.
晣 晢 } hsi 1. Clear, bright, white.
智 chih 4. To know, to be aware of, to feel, to inform, wisdom, cleverness.
替 t'i 4. To abolish, to substitute, to supersede, instead of.
曾 tsêng 1, ts'êng 2. Past, done, how? etc.
景 ching 3. Bright, beautiful, scenery, a view, prospects, circumstances.
晷 kui 3. Shadow, the gnomon of a sun-dial, time.

最 tsui 4. Very.
量 liang 2. To measure.
冕 mien 3. A crown, a coronet, kind of cap.
晶 ching 1. Luster, clear, crystal.

9

睺 hou 2. A constellation, regarded as unlucky.
暇 hsia 2. Leisure.
暄 hsüan 1. Genial, pleasant.
暉 hui 1. Bright, splendid.
暌 k'ui 2. In opposition, separated, distant.
暗 an 4. Obscured, dark, gloomy, invisible.
暖 暵 } nuan 3. nang 3. Warm, mild.
暕 chien 3. To shine, to light.
睹 tu 3. Morning, dawn.
暐 wei 3. Bright, sun-light.
暘 yang 2. Sunshine, fair weather.
暎 ying 4. To shine on, to reflect, to favour.
暋 min 3. Strong, brave.
普 普 } p'u 3. Large, universal.
最 cheng 3. The sun rising.
暑 shu 3. Summer's heat, heat of the sun.
暈 yün 4. To be giddy, a halo, vapour.

10-11

暝 ming 3 To close the eyes.
曂 huang 3. Dry and hot.

暢 **ch'ang** 4. Joyous, pleasant, clear, to spread, perspicuous.

暠 **kao** 3. Clear, white.

嘗 **ch'ang** 2. To taste, to try, ordinarily.

暵 **han** 2. Hot, dry, parched.

㬓 **p'iao** 4. To dry in the sun.

暮 **mu** 4. Evening, sunset.

暫 **chan** 4. A short time, temporarily, in the interim, meanwhile, briefly, suddenly.

暴 **pao** 4. A scorching heat, stormy, cruel, violent, to strike, to waste, to oppress

12-13

[illegible] **mang** 3. The sun obscured.

曉 **hsiao** 3. Dawn, light, to know, to understand.

曀 **i** 1. Cloudy.

曢 **liao** 3. Bright, shining.

曄 **hua** 4. Bright.

曏 **hsiang** 4. A little while, formerly.

曇 **t'an** 2. Black clouds, darkness.

暹 **hsien** 1. The increasing light of the sun, to advance. Siam.

曆 **li** 4. Astronomy, calendar.

暨 **chi**. The sun peeping out, the end, to reach, and, with.

[illegible] **ao** 4. Warm sun.

14 &

曤 **huo** 4. Strength, violence.

曛 **hsün** 1. Twilight, sunset, evening.

曚 **mêng** 2. Early dawn.

曙 **shu** 3. Bright, dawn, clear.

曜 **yao** 4. Light, brightness, glory, to dazzle

曠 **k'uang** 4. A vacant waste, empty, spacious, lazy, to waste; olden.

曝 **pao** 4. A fierce heat, to burn, to dry.

曣 **yen** 4. A serene morning.

曨 **lung** 2. The sun obscured.

曦 **hsi** 1. The light of day.

[illegible] **nieh** 4. A little warm, genial.

曬 **shai** 4. To dry in the sun, to cure in the sunshine.

曭 **tang** 3. Dull, cloudy.

曯 **chu** 3. To light up, to illuminate.

曩 **nang** 3. In former times, previously, passed by.

Rad. 73

See Lesson 73 A.

曰 **yüeh** 4. To speak, an expletive particle.

曲 **ch'ü** 1. Crooked, perverse, songs.

曳 **i** 4. To trail, to pull.

臾 **yü** 2. To trail.

更 **kêng** 4. More.
kêng 1. To change.
ching 1. A night watch.

曷 **ho** 2. Which, what, how, why, when, where?

書 **shu** 1. To write, a record, a letter, a book.

曼 **man** 2. Wide, long.

曹 **ts'ao** 2. A company, a class, officials, the plural.

替 暜 } **t'i** 4. To substitute, instead of.

朁 **tsan** 1. To murmur, if, however.

曾 **tsêng** 1. To add to.
ts'êng 2. Past, done, finished, but, still.

最 **tsui** 4. Very, most, extreme, to gather.

會 **hui** 4. To meet together, to collect, to unite, a guild, a society, to know.
hui 3. An instant.

朅 **chieh** 2. Martial-looking.

Rad 74

See Lesson 44 G.

月 **yüeh** 4. The moon, a lunar month, monthly.

有 **yu** 3. To have, to be.

阴 **yin** 1. The inferior power in Chinese philosophy

朊 **yüan** 3. A dim moon light.

服 **fu** 2. Clothes, mourning, to think, to undergo, accustomed to, to subject, office, affair.

朒 **nê** 4. The new moon.

朋 **p'êng** 2. A friend, to associate, to match.

朏 **fei** 3. The moon five days old.

朔 **shuo** 4. The first day of the moon.

朕 **chên** 4. I, the Emperor.

朓 **t'ao** 4. The moon appearing before sunrise.

[illegible] **hung** 3. The moon rising.

朘 **tsun** 4. The new moon, feeble, small.

望 朢 } **wang** 4. To look towards, to hope, to expect, towards, the full moon.

朖 **lang** 3. Clear, bright.

朙 **ming** 2. Clear.

朝 **chao 1.** The dawn.
ch'ao 2. The Court, audiences given in the early morning; a dynasty, towards; facing.

期 **ch'i 1.** A period, a limit of time, to expect, to hope.

朞 **chi 1.** A full year, an anniversary.

朡 **tsung 1.** An ancient kingdom.

㬻 **huang 3.** Obscure.

朣 **t'ung 2.** Dim light, obscure, confused.

朦 **mêng 2.** Obscure, confused, to deceive.

朧 **lung 2.** The rising moon, dim, obscure.

曦 **hsi 1.** The moon-light.

曭 **t'ang 3.** Obscure.

Rad 75

See Lesson 119 A.

木 **mu 4.** Wood, a tree.

末 **mo 4.** The end of a branch, the end, finally, small, the meanest part of, powder, a negative.

未 **wei 4.** A cyclical character, a negation.

本 **pên 3.** The origin, the root, natural, original, native, the capital, book, documents.

朮 **shu 2.** A glutinous grain, *Panicum miliaceum.*

札 **cha 2.** A tablet, a letter, untimely death.

2

朱 **chu 1.** Red, vermilion.

朵 朶 **to 3.** A bud, a flower, the lobe of the ear, numerative of flowers.

朿 **tz'ŭ 4.** A thorn, to prick.

朴 **p'o 4.** *Magnolia hypoleuca.*

朽 **hsiu 3.** Decayed, worn out.

朲 **jên 2.** A rafter.

机 **chi 1.** A small table.

朻 **ch'iu 2.** Trees whose branches droop like the weeping willow.

朳 **pa 1.** A handle, a rake.

朾 **t'ing 1.** A post.

3

李 **li 3.** A plum-tree.

杏 **hsing 4.** Apricot-tree.

呆 **tai 1.** Foolish, silly.

束 **shu 4.** To bind, to tie up, to restrain, to keep in order.

杈 **ch'a 4.** A fork, to pitch.

杖 **chang 4.** A staff, a club, to fight.

杓 **shao 2.** Spoon.

杋 **fan 2.** A large tree.

杆 **kan 1.** A stick, a post, a flag-staff, railings.

杠 **kang 1.** A porter's pole, to carry.

杞 **ch'i 3.** A willow.

杉 **sha 1. shan 1.** A pine, a pole.

杜 **tu 4.** A wild pear-tree, to stop, to fill up.

材 **ts'ai 2.** Materials, stuff.

杄 **ch'ien 1.** *Abies leptolepsis.*

村 **ts'un 1.** A village.

杇 **wu 1.** A trowel, to roughcast.

杌 **wu 4.** Stump of a tree, stunted, a stool.

4

杲 **kao 3.** The rising sun, clear.

果 **kuo 3.** Fruit, really, effects, consequences.

東 **tung 1.** The east, the place of honour.

杳 **miao 3. yao 3.** Obscure, mysterious, dark.

杰 **chieh 2.** A proper name.

枊 **nang 2.** A horse post.

枕 **chên 3.** A pillow.

枝 **chih 1.** A branch, a twig, a classifier of slender things.

杼 **chu 4.** A shuttle.

杵 **ch'u 3.** A pestle, a beater.

杶 **ch'un 1.** *Rhus vernicifera.*

枌 **fên 2.** A kind of elm.

枋 **fang 1.** A plank.

杭 **hang 2.** A boat to cross a stream.

杴 **hsien 1.** A shovel.

枘 **jui 4.** A handle.

林 **lin 2.** A forest, a grove, a collection.

枚 **mei 2.** A shrub, a cane, a gag, a classifier.

杪 **miao 3.** The tip, slender, delicate.

枏 **nan 2.** A yellowish fine wood.

杻 **niu 3.** *Ligustrum sinense.*

杷 **pa 1.** A rake.

板 **pan 3.** A board, a plank, a flattened bamboo for beating.

枇 **p'i 2.** *Eriobotrya japonica.*

杯 **pei 1.** A cup, a tumbler, a glass.

柿 **shih 4.** *Diospyrus kaki.*

析 **hsi 1.** To split, to explain.

松 **sung 1.** Pine-tree, coniferous trees in general.

枓 **tou 3.** Capital of a pillar.

枉 **wang 3.** Distorted, crooked, a wrong, a grievance, needlessly, to no purpose.

枒 **ya 2.** The cocoa-nut.

5

查 ch'a 2. To examine into, to investigate.

柰 nai 4. A kind of plum, a remedy, a resource, Buddhist.

枼 yeh 4. A leaf, a slip, a plate.

某 mu 3. A certain one, I.

染 jan 3. To dye.

柔 jou 2. Soft; yielding; pliant.

架 chia 4. A stand; a case; a framework; a quarrel; a classifier.

枲 hsi 3. The china-grass; its fibres.

柒 ch'i 1. The number seven.

柬 chien 3. A slip of paper; to abridge; to select.

柙 hsia 2. A pen; a lock-up, to cage.

枵 hsiao 1 Empty, hollow, vile, vain.

柑 kan 1. An orange.

柶 ssŭ 4. A spoon.

枸 kou 3. A spinous lemon-tree.

枷 chia 1. A cangue; a flail.

柩 chiu 4. A corpse in coffin.

柯 k'o 1. A handle.

柧 ku 1. A corner; angular.

枯 k'u 1. Rotten or dry wood; decayed, arid, withered.

柺 kuan 3. A staff.

柃 ling 2. *Eurya japonica*.

liu 3. The willow; lewdness.

柀 pi 3. *Cunninghamia sinensis*.

柄 ping 3. A handle, a haft; authority.

枰 p'ing 2. A chess-board.

柏 pai 3. The thuja; durable.

相 hsiang 1. Mutual, etc.

梠 ssŭ 4. A plough.

柢 ti 3. The root, origin, foundation.

柝 t'o 4. The watchman's clapper.

柞 tso 4. Evergreen oak.

柚 yu 2. *Citrus decumana*.

柂 t'o 1. To split wood; a coffin.

柘 chê 4. A thorny tree, *Cudrania triloba*.

柵 cha 4. A fence of lats, a barrier.

枳 chih 3. A hedge-thorn or spinous shrub.

柱 chu 4. A pillar; a support.

柎 fu 1. Lathing.

枹 fu 2. A drum-stick.

6

柴 ch'ai 2. To burn faggots to advertise heaven; fuel.

桌 chọ 1. A table.

桀 chieh 2. To quarter; a perch; bravery.

案 an 4. A tribunal; a suit; order; law.

桑 sang 1. The mulberry-tree.

栗 li 4. The chestnut-tree; care; reverence.

栽 tsai 1. To plant; to transplant.

栴 chan 1. Red sandal wood.

桎 chih 4. Manacles; fetters.

㭘 hsia 2. A case.

株 chu 1. A trunk; a stump; numerative of posts, etc; to punish.

栰 fa 2. A raft.

桁 hang 2. A row.

㭜 jung 2. Acacia.

栩 hsü 3. A species of oak; to flutter about.

核 hai 2. ho 2. To search; to accuse.
hu 2. A nut.

桓 huan 2. Pillars before a grave; delay.

栘 i 2. A fruit-tree, *Arona asiatica*.

桋 i 2. A tall timber tree.

根 kên 1. Roots; origin, cause; a base.

栲 k'ao 3. Mangrove.

校 chiao 4. hsiao 4. An enclosure; a park; a school; to examine; to compare.

桔 chieh 4. A medicinal plant.

桕 chiu 4. The tallow tree, *Stillingia sebifera*.

格 ko 2. To reach; to examine; a rule; a frame; to move; obstinate; to fight.

栝 kua 3. *Juniperus sinensis*.

框 k'uang 4. Big branches; the frame of a thing.

桂 kui 4. The cinnamon tree.

栳 lao 3. A basket made of osiers.

栛 li 4. A medlar-tree, *Nephelium lichih*.

栵 lieh 4. The sweet chestnut.

梆 pang 1. A watchman's rattle.

㭛 p'ai 4. Textile fibres.

栟 ping 1. The coir palm.

栢 pai 3. A thuja.

栭 erh 2. A small column.

栓 shuan 1. A peg; a pencil.

栖 ch'i 1. To roost; to sojourn.

栒 hsün 3. The cross-beams of a bell or drum frame.

桃 t'ao 2. The peach.

椰 yeh 2. The cocoa-nut tree.

桐 t'ung 2. A varnish tree. *Aleurites cordata*.

桅 wei 2. A mast.

7

梟 hsiao 1. A species of owl; wicked; to expose the head of a criminal.

梨 li 2. The Chinese pear.

梁 liang 2. Ridge pole, beam.

桬 sha 1. A species of pyrus.

桼 ch'i 1. The varnish tree, *Rhus vernicifera.*

梵 fan 4. The soughing of wind through trees; stillness; Brahma, Brahmanism, Sanskrit.

梗 kêng 3. Thorny; to prick; stubborn; an outline.

梜 chia 4. Pincers.

桱 ching 4. A kind of haad timber.

梘 chien 4. A trough, a tray.

桷 chiao 4. The ends of beams.

梡 ch'iao 1. Skins of a *citrus*; a medicine.

梏 ku 4. Manacles, fetters.

梱 k'un 3. The threshold.

桹 lang 2. A species of palm, *Caryota ochlandra.*

桻 fêng 1. Branches.

梩 li 2. A dorsel.

梒 han 2. A cherry-tree.

桸 hsi 1. A ladle.

梠 lü 3. Small column, lintel.

梅 mei 2. Plums, prunes.

梍 tsao 4. A kind of oak.

桮 pei 1. A cup, a tumbler.

梐 pi 4. A palisade, a stockade.

梖 pei 4. A palm-tree.

桲 po 4. A flail.

梹 ping 1. The areca-palm.

梫 shên 1. The cinnamon-tree.

梢 shao 1. The tip of a branch, a twig.

梳 shu 1. A comb, to comb.

桫 so 1. The name of a tree, *Shorca robusta.*

梭 so 1. A weaver's shuttle.

梀 su 4. A kind of birchtree.

梯 t'i 1. A ladder, steps, stairs.

桯 t'ing 1. A bed.

梃 t'ing 3. A staff, a cudgel.

桶 t'ung 3. A bucket, a barrel.

桚 tsan 3. To torture by finger sticks.

桴 fu 2. A raft.

械 hsieh 4. Weapons, arms.

條 t'iao 2. A twig, a classifier, a bill, an article, a manner.

桿 kan 1. A pole, a handle.

梔 chih 1. The *Gardenia tinctoria*, used to dye yellow.

梲 cho 2. A joist, a stick.

桭 chên 3. A timber.

梓 tzŭ 3. The *Rottlera japonica*, plank, wood, one's native village or country.

梧 wu 2. *Eleococca, Sterculia*; trees.

8

棃 li 2. A pear-tree.

渠 ch'ü 2. A drain, he, she, it, they.

棐 fei 3. A species of yew, *Torreya nucifera.*

棊 ch'i 2. The chess.

綦 ch'i 3. A banner, a signal flag.

棠 t'ang 2. Various species of *pyrus.*

棸 tsou 1. A proper name.

棗 tsao 3. The jujube tree.

棘 chi 4. Thorny brambles; pain.

棥 fan 2. A hedge, a fence.

棼 fên 1. Beams in the roof of a house.

焚 fên 2. To burn.

森 shên 1. A forest, thick, somber.

棹 cho 1. A table.

椆 chou 2. An oak, *Quercus glauca.*

植 chih 2. To plant, to stick, a pole.

椈 chü 2. The cypress.

椎 ch'ui 2. A mallet, a beetle, a rammer.

棿 i 2. The cross-bar at the end of a carriage-pole.

梴 yen 2. A long piece of timber, long.

椅 i 3. A chair, a seat.

棉 nang 2. Eaves of a roof.

棋 ch'i 2. The game of chess.

棖 ch'êng 1. A thorn.

椌 ch'iang 1. A wooden clapper.

棖 ch'êng 2. To prop, door-posts.

極 chi 2. The txtreme limit, very, the zenith, the first principle.

椐 chü 1. A knotty tree.

椇 chü 3. The edible fruit of the *Hovenia dulcis.*

棧 chan 4. A covered shed, a store-house, a godown.

棬 ch üan 2. A wooden bowl.

棺 kuan 1. An inner coffin.

椁 kuo 2. An outer coffin.

棍 kun 1. A stick, a rowdy.

棶 lai 2. *Cormus macrophylla.*

棱 lêng 2. An edge, a corner.

棙 li 4. Finger-stalls to play stringed instruments.
棉 mien 2. The cotton plant, cotton.
棒 pang 4. A club, a cudgel.
棚 p'êng 2. A mat awing, a shed.
椑 pi 1. A wine-cup.
棓 pei 1. Chinese galls.
栟 ping 1. The sago-palm.
棅 ping 4. Handle, authority.
棲 ch'i 1. To roost, to settle, to stay.
榙 t'a 4. A capital.
棣 ti 4. A sort of plum, fraternal love.
棟 tung 4. Beams in a roof, a prop.
棌 ts'ai 3. A species of oak.
棷 tsou 1. Name of a tree, a rattle.
椒 chiao 1. Spice-plants, peppery, pepper.
椄 chieh 1. To graft.
棤 tso 4. Bark.
椊 tsu 1. To put a handle in a socket.
棕 tsung 1. The coir palm.
樬 ts'ung 1. The *Aralia spinosa*.
椀 wan 3. A bowl.
棫 yü 4. A kind of oak.

9

喿 tsao 4. Twittering, noise, hum.
楘 mao 4. Carriage-pole.
業 yeh 4. Patrimony, trade, employment, office, merit, past.
棄 ch'i 4. To reject, to throw off, to forget
楙 mao 4. Thick forest.

楚 ch'u 3. Woody, thick, pain, order, to settle.
禁 chin 4. To prohibit, to forbid, to bear.
楓 fêng 1. *Liquidambar*.
楜 hu 2. Pepper-plant, pepper.
楦 hsüan 4. A last.
楎 hui 1. A peg to hang clothes on a wall.
楺 jou 3. To bend by fire or steam.
楉 jo 4. A kind of plum.
楰 juan 3. A name for *Diospyros lotus*.
榫 kau 1. A slender stick.
椵 chia 3. A kind of lemon-tree.
楷 k'ai 3. A model, a pattern; the elegant style of Chinese characters.
楬 chieh 2. A board; a ticket or slip.
椷 chien 3. A casket; a box.
楇 kuo 3. A grease-pot.
楑 k'ui 2. A mallet.
楞 lêng 2. Turned up corner, edge, crest.
楝 lien 4 The *Melia azedarach*.
楣 mei 2. The lintel of a door or window.
棰 ch'ui 2. A bat.
楠 nan 2. The *Machilus nanmu*.
楄 p'ien 1 *Sapindus mukorossi*.
楩 p'ien 2. A kind of laurel, *Lindera*.
楯 tun 3. A barrier; to guard.
楔 hsieh 1. A wedge, a peg.
楒 ssŭ 1. *Abrus precatorius*.
楫 chi 4. An oar; to row.
楱 ts'ou 4. A lemon-tree.

榔 lang 2. The arec-palm.
楸 ch'in 1. The catalpa.
椶 tsung 1. The coir palm.
楤 ts'ung 1. *Aralia spinosa*.
椳 wei 2. A lintel.
楊 yang 2. The poplar.
楪 yeh 4. A window.
榆 yü 2. The elm.
楹 ying 2. A column; a pillar.
楂 cha 1. Edible hawtree, azerole.
椹 shên 2. The fruit of the mulberry-tree.
chêng 1. A block; an anvil.
楨 chêng 1. *Ligustrum lucidum*.
楮 ch'u 3. *Broussonetia papyrifera*; paper money; a letter.
椿 ch'un 1. *Ailantus*.

10

槊 shuo 4. A great spear.
槃 p'an 2. A tray; a hut.
榮 jung 2. Honour; glory.
槀 kao 3. Decayed wood; withered, a draft.
榦 kan 4. A beam.
榖 ku 3. Paper mulberry.
榝 sha 4. All-spice.
榨 cha 4. A press; to squeeze.
槎 ch'a 1. To fell trees; a raft
榛 chên 1. The hazel-tree
榰 chih 1. A base; to uphold; to prop
槌 ch'ui 2. A wooden mallet; a club.
榧 fei 3. Hazel-tree.
榹 ti 1. A wild plum-tree.

榼 **hai 3.** A wooden tub.

椷 **han 2.** A wooden bowl; a casket.

槐 **huai 2.** A large tree, *Sophora japonica.*

榥 **huang 3.** A screen.

椽 **ch'uan 2.** A lathing, rafters.

槨 **ko 3.** The outer coffin.

槁 **kao 3.** Dry, rotten, as wood.

構 **kou 4.** The truss of a roof; to construct; to unite; copulate.

榿 **ch'i 1.** A species of the willow.

榢 **chia 4.** A stand; a framework.

榎 **hsia 3.** *Catalpa Bungei.*

榤 **chieh 2.** A hen-roost.

榷 **chiao 1.** A foot bridge; a tax.

槅 **ko 2.** A screen.

榼 **k'o 2.** A wooden cup to hold spirits.

榊 **hu 3.** The ivory-nut.

榴 **liu 2.** The pome-granate.

槓 **kang 4.** A frame to bear a coffin.

榪 **ma 4.** A peg, a dovetail.

榓 **mi 4.** The eagle-wood.

槈 **nou 4.** To weed.

榜 **pang 3.** A placard; a notice; a model.

榯 **shih 2.** Erect; lofty; to set up.

榍 **hsieh 4.** Chestnut tree.

榭 **hsieh 4.** A terrace; a tribune.

榫 **hsün 3.** **hsun 3.** A tenon.

榻 **t'a 4.** A long bed; a couch.

榣 **t'ao 2.** A kind of catalpa.

槙 **tien 1.** A fallen tree.

榋 **ts'ou 1.** The stick in a bullock's nose.

槍 **ch'iang 1.** A spear; a lance; a swindler.

榱 **ts'ui 1.** Small rafters projecting from the eaves.

槝 **wu 1.** Ebony.

榕 **jung 2.** The bastard banian, *Ficus indica.*

11

槩 **kai 4.** To level; to adjust; altogether; generally.

樂 **yao 4.** Music.
lao 4. Pleasure.

槳 **chiang 3.** An oar.

槧 **ch'ieh 4.** Logs.

槷 **i 4.** A limit; a boundary; a fence.

樊 **fan 2.** A hedge; a cage.

樝 **cha 1.** A species of hawthorn, azerole.

樟 **chang 1.** The camphor tree, *Laurus camphora.*

樔 **ch'ao 2.** A raised lodge in a marsh.

樜 **chê 1.** The sugar-cane.

樞 **shu 1.** A pivot; an axis; the central point; cardinal; fundamental.

樗 **ch'u 1.** *Ailantus glandulosa*; a useless stuff.

樁 **chuang 1.** A hitching post; an affair, a kind.

槺 **k'ang 1.** A hollow trunk.

槲 **hu 1.** An oak, *Quercus aliena.*

槵 **huan 1.** A species of *Sapindus.*

槪 **kai 4.** To level to even, a rule, a summing up.

槣 **chi 1.** Inclined.

槿 **chin 3.** The *Hibiscus syriacus.*

樛 **chiu 1.** Hanging or weeping branches.

槻 **kuei 1.** A bark of which they made ink.

槫 **t'uan 2.** A car.

樏 **lei 3.** A box with partitions.

樓 **lou 2.** An upper-storey, a tower, a terrace.

槤 **lien 2.** An orange-tree.

樐 **lu 3.** A turret.

樚 **lu 4.** A pulley, a windlass.

槾 **man 2.** A trowel.

樠 **man 2.** Pine, resine.

樒 **mi 4.** The eagle-wood tree, *Aloexylon.*

模 **mu 2.** A pattern, a model, a fashion, a mould.

標 **piao 1.** A signal, a flag, a notice, a warrant, a body of troops, graceful.

樨 **pi 4.** A yellow wood.

槮 **shên 1.** Without leaves.

橄 **kan 3.** The Chinese olive.

槢 **hsi 2.** A kind of hard wood.

樕 **su 4.** A species of oak.

槥 **hui 4.** A chest, a coffin.

樀 **ti 2.** Short rafters.

槽 **ts'ao 2.** A trough, a manger, a distillery.

桼 **ch'i 1.** The varnish tree.

槭 **tsu 1.** Maple, *Acer palmatum.*

樣 **yang 4.** A pattern.

槱 **yu 2.** Fire-wood for sacrifice.

12

橜 **chüeh 2.** A peg.

橐 **t'o 2.** A sack, a bag.

叢 **ts'ung 1.** A bushy place.

橆 **wu 2.** A forest, luxuriant, thick.

機 chi 1. A moving power, a machine, opportune, motive.
橋 ch'iao 2. A bridge.
橺 chien 4. Rooms, houses, buildings.
橘 chü 2. An orange-tree, green orange.
樻 k'uei 4. A knotty tree.
橑 liao 3. A rafter.
橉 lin 4. A bark used as a dye.
樸 p'o 2. A natural substance, plain, simple, sincere.
樲 erh 4. Wild jujube-tree.
樹 shu 4. Tree, to plant, to establish.
橓 shun 4. *Hibiscus syriacus.*
橡 hsiang 4. The oak.
橝 t'an 2. A wood used in dyeing.
橔 tun 1. A wooden cover.
樵 ch'iao 2. Fuel, fagots.
樽 tsun 1. A cup.
樴 chih 4. A post.
橕 ch'êng 1. A prop.
橙 têng 1. An orange-tree, yellow orange.
樨 hsi 1. Olea fragrans.
樿 chan 4. Hard wood.
橫 hêng 2. Cross-wise, horizontal.
hêng 4. Arrogant, obstinate.
樺 hua 4. A kind of birch.
橈 nao 2. Curved, perverted, weak, an oar.

13

繫 hsi 4. An axis, a pivot.
檠 ch'ing 2. A fram, a stand.
檗 p'i 4. Wood for dyeing.
檒 fêng 1. The wind swaying the tops of the trees, psalmody.
橿 chiang 1. The handle of a hoe, vigorous.
檢 chien 3. Envelop, a label, to examine, to forbid, rule.
檎 ch'in 2. A species of *Pyrus*.
檜 kuei 4. Chinese juniper.
檁 lin 3. Rafters.
檖 sui 4 Wild pear.
檀 t'an 2. Sandal wood, Buddhistic.
檔 tang 4. A cross-piece, a prop.
檣 ch'iang 2. A mast.
檐 yen 2. Eaves, end of the eaves.
檍 i 4. *Lindera glauca.*
檉 ch'êng 1. The tamarix.
橚 hsiao 1. Foliage.
檄 chi 1. A decree, a missive.
檟 chia 3. Catalpa; a rod.

14

檿 yen 3. Wild mulberry.
檾 ch'ing 3. A plant from the fibres of which they make cords, *Sida tiliæfolia.*
檞 shê 4. The genius of dreams.
櫃 kuei 4. A press, a box.
檬 mêng 2. A kind of *Sophora*.
檳 ping 1. The areca-palm.
檼 yin 3. The ridge-pole of a roof.
檯 t'ai 2. A table, a theatre, a stage.
櫈 têng 4. A long bench.
檮 t'ao 2. A block of wood, stupid.
櫂 chao 4. An oar, to row.
檫 hsün 1. Wild varnish tree.
檻 chien 4. Enclosure, a cage.
檵 chi 4. The *Loropetalum sinense.*

15 &

櫜 kao 1. A quiver, a case for bows.
龒 lung 2. A pen, a cage.
櫱 nieh 4. A stump, suckers.
檃 yin 3. A square.
欒 lüan 2. A proper name.
鬱 yü 4. Thick, dense, obstruction.
櫁 shên 3. Wine palm-tree.
櫟 li 4. A scrubby oak, *Quercus serrata*; unworthy.
櫓 lu 3. A tower, an oar.
櫚 lü 2. A species of palm.
櫖 lü 2. Liana.
櫝 tu 4. A case, a receptacle.
櫛 chieh 2. A comb.
櫍 chih 4. A block.
櫌 yu 1. A harrow, to cover in seed.
櫩 yen 2. A verandah.
櫬 ch'ên 4. The inner coffin.
櫧 chu 1. An evergreen oak.
櫨 lu 2. The Chinese medlar.
櫳 lung 2. A pen, a cage.
櫇 p'in 2. An apple-tree.
櫯 su 1. *Cæsalpinia sappan.*
櫸 chü 3. A species of willow.
欄 lan 2. A railing, a balustrade.
櫺 ling 2. A trellis-work.

櫦 shuan 1. To bar the door.

欀 hsiang 1. A sago-palm.

櫼 chien 1. A threshold.

櫻 ying 1. The cherry.

欃 ch'an 1. A kind of magnolia.

欋 ch'ü 2. Roots, relations.

權 ch'üan 2. A weight, power, authority, to judge; circumstances.

欏 lo 2. *Aesculus sinensis.*

欐 li 2. Top, roof.

欑 tsan 2. A shed.

欓 tang 4. A bench, a cross-piece, etc.

欖 lan 3. The Chinese olive.

欛 pa 4. A handle; authority.

欞 ling 2. A trellis.

Rad. 76

欠

See Lesson 99 A.

欠 ch'ien 4. To owe, to be wanting in.

次 tz'ŭ 4. Order, series, second, inferior.

吹 ch'ui 1. To blow.

欣 hsin 1. Joy, to rejoice.

㰹 han 2. To hold in the mouth, to contain.

欨 hsü 2. To blow gently, to exhale.

㰤 k'o 2. To cough.

欯 hsi 2. To laugh.

欭 yin 1. To lisp.

欬 k'o 2. To cough.

欮 chüeh 1. To choke.

欦 han 1. To restrain.

欷 hsi 1. To whimper.

欵 k'uan 3. To long for, to like, to love, business, occupation.

欸 ai 1. To moan.

欶 su 4. To suck.
sou 4. To cough.

欲 yü 4. To whish, to cover, to like.

欼 ch'o 4. To suck up, to drink.

欻 hu 1. Agitation.

欹 i 1. An exclamation.

欿 k'an 3. Reserve, modesty, discontented.

欺 ch'i 1. To cheat, to deceive, to insult, to ridicule.

欽 ch'in 1. To revere, to venerate, imperial,

款 k'uan 3. Sincere, true, liberal, to treat well; a kind, an article, pain, delay.

歇 hsieh 1. To rest, to stop, to leave off.

歂 ch'uan 3. To pant.

歆 hsin 1. To rejoice.

歁 k'an 3. To eat and not be satisfied.

歃 ch'a 4. To anoint one s lips with blood, an oath.

歉 chien 4. Scanty, deficient, dissatisfied.

歌 ko 1. To sing, a song.

欱 ho 1. To drink, to suck in.

歑 hu 1. To breathe on.

𣤌 chê 2. Bad humour.

歐 ou 1. To vomit, to retch.

歎 t'an 4. To sign, to moan, to approve, to repeat.

𣤎 chai 1. To talk and laugh.

歒 ti 2. To laugh.

歖 hsi 1. Joy, pleasure.

歙 hsi 4. To join, to shut up.

歔 hsu 1. To snort.

歕 p'ên 4. To blow out, to puff out.

歗 hsiao 4. To lament, to cry, to sigh.

歜 ch'u 4. Anger, wrath.

歛 lien 4. To gather, to collect.

歟 yü 2. A final particle of irony or surprise.

歠 ch'o 4. To suck up, to sip.

歡 huan 1. To rejoice, jolly, merry.

Rad. 77

止

See Lesson 112 A.

止 chih 3. To halt, to cease from, to be still, an object, only.

正 chêng 4. Correct, straight, regular, to govern, the first, the principal, just, precisely.

此 tz'ŭ 2. This, subjective.

步 pu 3. A step, to walk, footmen, a pace, a course.

歧 ch'i 2. Forked, different.

武 wu 3. Military, warlike.

歪 wai 1. Awry, astant, wicked, insolent.

歬 ch'ien 2. Before.

𣥺 ch'êng 1. To resist, to sustain.

歱 chung 3. To visit, to follow, to imitate.

歰 shih 4. Rough, hard to turn round, astringent.

歳 sui 4. The planet Jupiter, year, harvest. 7

𣦌 chai 2. Just, proper.

歷 歴 li 4. Idea of duration, of succession, to array in order, to pass through, to exhaust, to experience.

歸 帰 kui 1. To return, to send back, to restore, to belong to, to give, to divide.

Rad. 78

See Lesson 118 C.

歹 tai 3. Bad, evil.

歺 cha 2. An untimely death.

死 ssŭ 3. Death, to die; firm, fixed, obstinate.

歽 hsiu 3. Rotten decayed, putrid.

列 lieh 4. To separate, to set out.

歿 mu 2. To die, to perish.

殀 yao 3. To measure, to estimate.

殆 k'u 1. Dead, rotten, decayed.

殆 tai 4. Dangerous, perilous, approaching, nearly, soon.

殄 t'ien 3. To extirpate, to waste.

殂 tsu 3. To pass away, to die.

殃 yang 1. A misfortune, a calamity, to punish.

殊 ch'u 4. To differ, distinct, very, to kill.

殦 lao 4. To die.

殉 hsün 4. To bury along with the dead, suttee.

殍 p'iao 3. To die of hunger.

殖 chih 2. To fatten, to get rich, to prosper.

殙 hun 1. The dimness of death.

殑 lêng 4. Exhausted.

殘 ts'an 2. To ruin, to injure, mischievous, spoiled, withered, leavings.

殚 tsu 2. To die, to end.

殜 yüan 3. Inert.

殛 chi 2. To kill, to imprison for life

飧 sun 1. An evening meal, supper.

殜 yeh 4. Thin, weak.

殠 ch'ou 4. Stench.

殞 yün 3. To die, to perish.

殣 chin 3. To die of starvation.

殨 tsao 1. Spoilt, rotten.

殤 shang 1. To die young, to die prematurely.

殦 liao 4. Defeated, bad, evil.

殫 tan 1. To exhaust, utterly, deeply.

殪 têng 4. Exhausted, ready to perish.

殭 chiang 1. Stiff, impassive.

殮 lien 4. To shroud a corpse.

殯 fên 4. Bad, rotten.

殤 p'êng 2. Swollen.

殬 i 4. To lose, to perish.

殯 pin 4. A funeral, to carry out to burial.

殰 tu 4. An abortion.

殱 lan 4. Corrupted.

殲 chien 1. To destroy, to exterminate.

殧 lei 4. A plague among the animals.

Rad. 79

See Lesson 22 D.

殳 ch'u 1. Arm, stick, spear.

段 tuan 4. A piece, a section, skill; prosperity.

殷 yin 1. Very, much, prosperity, great, intense, zeal, ardor.

殺 sha 1. To slay, to kill; to decapitate.

殽 yao 2. Mixed, to eat, viands.

殼 ch'iao 1. Scale, a shell.

毀 hui 3. To break, to injure, to spoil, to slander.

毄 chi 1. To hit against.

殿 tien 4. A grand hall, a palace.

彀 kou 4. To draw a bow to its full stretch, full, enough.

毃 ch'iao 1. To strike, to tap.

毅 tsai 3. To slaughter, skin and dress animals.

榖 ku 3. The paper-mulberry.

毅 i 4. Firm, intrepid, patient, fortitude.

穀 ku 3. Cereals, corn.

毆 ou 1. To beat, to strike, to fight.

轂 ku 3. The nave or hub of a wheel.

觳 hu 1. A goblet, trembling.

㲉 ch'iao 1. An egg's shell.

鼜 k'an 4. To beat the drum.

Rad. 80

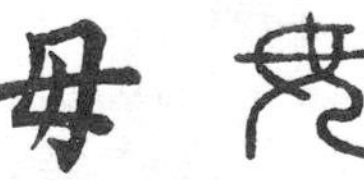

See Lesson 67 K.

毋 wu 2. Not, do not.

母 mu 3. A mother, that which produces, the source of, the root; the key.

毑 chieh 3. Mother, female.

毒 tu 2. Poison, virus, to hate.

每 **mei** 3. Each, every, always. *Hence.*

毓 **yü** 4. To feed, to raise.

Rad. 81

比

See Lesson 27 I.

比 **pi** 3. To compare, to examine, to judge.
pi 4. To join, to be near to, to harmonise, according to, regular.

毖 **pi** 4. Attention, vigilance, to prevent, to grieve.

毗 **p'i** 2. To aid, adjacent.

毘 **p'i** 2. The navel.

㲋 **ch'ao** 4. Gerboa. *Hence*

毚 **ch'an** 2. Rodents.

Rad. 82

See Lesson 100 A.

毛 **mao** 2. Hair, down, feathers, young, delicate.

毥 **chih** 1. Light down, plush.

毟 **fên** 1 Hair falling off, feathers moulting.

毡 **chan** 1. Rough felt.

毦 **pao** 4. To incubate, to hatch.

毧 **jung** 2. Soft fur.

毦 **erh** 4. A feather-duster.

毤 **t'o** 1. To moult.

耄 **mao** 4. A septuagenarian.

毫 **hao** 2. The down or pubescence on plants, a soft hair, the thousandth part of a tael, a straw, an atom.

毬 **ch'iu** 2. A feather ball.

毨 **hsien** 3. To moult.

毟 **sha** 1. Outer robe of a Buddhist monk.

麾 **chü** 1 Distressed.

毱 **chü** 1. A ball.

毰 **p'ei** 2. To spread open the wings.

毯 **t'an** 3. Rugs; carpets.

毴 **tsu** 4. Short hair.

毳 **ts'ui** 4. Down; fur; soft; fragile.

毼 **ho** 2. Coarse woollen cloth.

毽 **chien** 4. A shuttlecock.

毸 **shuai** 1. Long hair.

毦 **jung** 2. Plume of feathers.

毾 **t'a** 4. A kind of felt.

氂 **li** 2. Tail of a yak.

氀 **lü** 2. Torn; ragged.

氈 **man** 2. A carpet.

氁 **mu** 4. A woollen tissue.

氅 **ch'ang** 3. Down.

氄 **jung** 3. Down.

氆 **p'u** 3. Yak's hair.

氋 **nung** 2. Thick hair.

氈 **chan** 1. A rough felt

氌 **lu** 3. Yak's hair cloth.

氇 **jang** 2. Wadding; cotton.

氎 **tieh** 2. Cashmere.

Rad. 83

氏

See Lesson 124 A.

氏 **shih** 4. A family, a clan, a sect.

氐 **ti** 2. The foundation, the radical; to reach, till.

民 **min** 2. The people, the mass, the common multitude.

氓 **mang** 2. People.

Rad. 84

See Lesson 98 A.

气 **ch'i** 4. Cloudy vapour, aura, etc.

氛 **fên** 1. Vapour, miasma, meteor, omen, influx.

氜 **yang** 2. The male principle.

氞 **yin** 1. The female principle.

氣 **ch'i** 4. Air; ether; vapour; spirit; temper; feelings; the two principles; the fate.

氤 **yin** 1. Warm genial aura, fecundating influence.

氳 **yün** 1. The aura; the generative influences of heaven and earth.

Rad. 85

See Lesson 125 A.

水 **shui** 3. Water; a fluid. 11

冰 **ping 1.** Ice.

永 **yung 3.** Ever-flowing; perpetual eternal.

求 **ch'iu 2.** To beg, to entreat; to pray for; to aim at.

汁 **chih 1.** Juice, liquor.

氿 **chi 1.** Bank; side.

氿 **kuei 1.** A spring.

氾 **pan 4.** Water overflowing; immense, confused.

汀 **t'ing 1.** Low level beach.

3

汞 **hung 3.** Mercury, quick-silver.

池 **ch'ih 2.** Pool, tank, vessel.

汎 **fan 4.** To overflow, to float; immense; vague; changing.

汗 **han 4.** Sweat.

汔 **ch'i 4.** To weep. Perhaps; nearly; dried.

汊 **ch'a 4.** Fork of a stream.

汝 **ju 3.** Thou; you; your.

江 **chiang 1.** A great streem.

汒 **mang 2.** Inundation.

汕 **shan 4.** Port of Swatow.

汐 **hsi 4.** The evening tide.

汛 **hsün 4.** A military post; speedily.

汜 **ssŭ 4.** A river in Honan.

汋 **shao 2.** A clepsydra.

污 汙 **wu 1.** Mud, dirt, foul, unclean, obscene, to defile.

4

沓 **ta 2.** A babble of words.

沈 沉 **ch'ên 2.** To sink, heavy.

沚 **chih 3.** A bank.

沖 **ch'ung 1.** To dash against, to rush at young; to infuse.

汾 **fên 2.** A river in Shansi.

沆 **hang 4.** Mist, fog; a waste.

沂 **i 2.** A river in Shantung.

汭 **jui 3.** Junction of two rivers; winding of a stream.

汲 **chi 1.** To draw water from a well, to emulate.

決 **chüeh 2.** To settle, to decide, absolutely.

汩 **ku 3.** The noise of waves.

沔 **mien 3.** Name of a river.

沒 **mu 2.** To plunge, to disappear, to cease; not, none.

沐 **mu 4.** To wash; to give; to receive.

汴 **pien 4.** A river in Hupeh.

沛 **p'ei 4.** A river in Kiangsu; flowing, copious, vehement.

沙 **sha 1.** Sand, pebbles, dust, granulated; Buddhist.

泲 **tzŭ 3.** To flow.

汰 **t'ai 4.** Slippery; to clean; to correct.

沌 **tun 4.** The rush of a torrent; confusion, chaos.

沞 **tsa 2.** Bubbling up.

沏 **ch'i 1.** To infuse, to draw.

㳄 **hsien 4.** Spittle, saliva; covetousness.

沁 **ch'in 4.** To sound, to fathom.

汪 **wang 1.** Vast ant still; much; abundant; immense.

汶 **wên 4.** A river in Shantung.

沃 **wo 4.** Dew; to wet; fertile.

沕 **wu 4.** Abstruse, hidden.

5

泰 **t'ai 4.** Large; extensive, liberal, extreme.

泉 **ch'üan 2.** A spring; money, cash.

沼 **chao 3.** A fish-pond; a pool.

沾 **chan 1.** To moisten, to tinge; to receive benefits; infected with.

治 **chih 4.** To govern, to rule, to punish, to heal.

注 **chu 4.** Water flowing off in streamlets; to soak; to record; to fix mind or eyes on.

泞 **chu 4.** Clear, limpid.

法 **fa 1, fa 2, fa 4.** A law, a rule; an art; to imitate. Buddhism, Buddhist. Weight.

泛 **fan 4.** To float, to drift, to sail; immense, excessive; unguided, careless, reckless.

沸 **fu 4.** To boil.

河 **ho 2.** A river; a canal.

泫 **hsüan 2.** Glistening dew drops; tears.

泓 **hung 2.** Deep; mysterious.

況 **k'uang 4.** Moreover, circumstances.

泄 **hsieh 4.** To leak, to ooze out, to divulge; diarrhœa.

泔 **kan 1.** Slops.

泣 **ch'i 4.** To weep, to lament.

沽 **ku 1.** To trade in, to buy and sell.

泃 **ch'ü 2.** A river in Chihli.

泪 **lei 4.** Tears; to weep.

泠 **ling 2.** The name of different rivers.

泖 **mao 3.** A river in Kiangsu.

沫 **mo 4.** Foam; froth at the mouth; to perspire; to finish.

泯 **min 3.** To flow off; drained; destroyed.

沬 **mei 4.** A river in Honan.

泥 **ni 2.** Mire, mud; dirt; adhesive, attached to, doting on.

泮 **p'an 4.** The semicircular pool before the provincial colleges; a college; a graduate.

泡 **p'ao 4.** A bubble; to soak,

泌 pi 4. A torrent.

波 p'o 1. A wave, a ripple; vast, wave-like.

泊 po 3. To stop; to fasten a boat.

沭 shu 4. A river in Shantung.

泅 ch'iu 2. To swim; to float.

泝 su 4. To go against the stream; to revert to.

泗 ssŭ 4. A river in Shantung.

沴 t'ien 3. In confusion.

沺 t'ien 2. Inundation.

沲 沱 t'o 2. An affluent; a heavy rain; falling tears.

沰 to 4. To let down; to immerge.

沮 tsu 1. A river in Hupeh; to intimidate.

沿 沿 yen 2. Shore; along.

泱 yang 1. Moving; impetuous, violent.

泆 i 4. To overflow; licentious.

泑 yu 3. The glassy coating upon pottery.

油 yu 2. Oil, to paint.

泳 yung 3. To swim.

6

洯 chieh 2. Pure, limpid.

洲 chou 1. A continent; an island.

洙 chu 1. A river in Shantung.

沖 ch'ung 1. Bubbling of water.

洑 fu 4. To swim.

洽 hsia 4. To soak; to instil; to harmonise with; just, exactly.

洪 hung 2. An inundation; vast, immense.

活 huo 2. To live; mobile; active; versatile.

洄 hui 2. A whirlpool.

洢 i 1. A river in Honan.

洟 i 2. Snivel, mucus.

洶 hsiung 1. A tumultuous rush.

洚 chiang 4. An inundation.

汧 ch'ien 1. A river in Shansi

洸 kuang 1. Water glistening and sparkling in the sun.

洭 k'uang 1. A river in Hunan.

洌 lieh 4. Pure, clear.

洛 lao 4. A river in Honan.

洺 ming 2. A river in Chihli.

洝 an 4. A hot spring..

派 p'ai. To branch, as a river; to ramify; to depute; to appoint to a post.

洴 p'ing 2. Noise of water.

洏 erh 2. To flow.

洱 erh 3. A river in Honan.

洒 sha 3. To besprinkle.

洔 shih 4. An islet.

洗 hsi 3. To wash; to cleanse; to reform.

洩 hsieh 4. To leak, to drop; to divulge.

洵 hsün 2. Name of a river; truly, indeed.

洫 hsü 4. A trench, a channel.

洮 t'ao 1. To wash.

洞 tung 4. A cavern, a hole; to comprehend, to see through.

津 chin 1. A ford a ferry; a secretion; saliva; to moisten.

洤 ch'üan 2. A spring.

洼 wa 1. Low ground, a puddle.

洈 wei 2. A river in Hupeh.

洧 wei 3. A river in Honan.

洿 wu 1. Stagnant water; foul, impure; to defile.

洋 yang 2. The ocean; vast.

洹 yüan 2. A river in Honan.

7

浙 chê 4. The river from which the province of Chêkiang derives its name.

浞 cho t. To soak; damp.

浛 han 4. Soaked ground.

浫 han 1. To hesitate; perhaps.

浮 fu 2. To float; to drift; volatile; fleeting; silly.

海 hai 3. The sea; the ocean; immensity; a crowd.

浩 hao 4. Overwhelming, as a flood, vast; grand.

浠 hsi 1. A river in Hupeh.

浹 hsia 4. Moist; soaked; a circuit a period.

浣 huan 3. To wash; a period of ten days.

浥 i 4. Pamp; soaked.

浖 ching 1. A river; to flow.

涔 ch'ên 2. A puddle; a pool.

涓 chüan 1. A brook.

浬 li 3. Nautical mile.

涒 chün 1. Winding, meandering.

浪 lang 4. Profligate, waves.

涖 li 4. Water dripping down.

流 liu 2. To flow, to spread abroad, to circulate.

浝 manu 2. A river in Honan.

涯 k'uang 2. Inundation.

浼 mei 3. To defile, to foul; in polite language, to annoy.

涅 nieh 1. Black mud, slime.

浜 pêng 1. A side-creek or canal.

浦 p'u 2. Shore, bank.
浡 po 4. Suddenly.
涉 shê 4. To ford, to wade, to concern, relations.
消 hsiao 1. To melt, to consume, to disperse.
浚 tsun 4. Deep, to dig, to scrutinise.
涘 ssŭ 4. A river bank.
浢 t'ou 4. A river in Shansi.
涕 t'i 4. To weep.
涂 t'u 2. Name of a river.
渗 tsan 2. To bespatter.
酒 chiu 3. Wine, distilled liquor.
浸 chin 1. To flood, to soak, to penetrate, gradually.
浯 wu 2. Name of a river.
浴 yü 4. To bathe.
涌 yung 3. To gush.

8

淼 miao 3. Ocean, immense.
淌 t'ang 3. To flow, a passenger, not lasting.
涿 cho 1. To drop, to fall drop by drop.
淍 ch'ou 2. To wash.
淝 fei 2. Name of a river.
涪 pei 4. Thick fog, dark.
涎 hsien 2. Spittle, saliva, to covet.
涵 han 2. To swamp, to submerge, vast, capacious.
淆 yao 2 Mixed, confused.
涬 hsing 3. A watery expanse, chaos.
涸 k'o 4. Dried.
淴 hu 4 To hale out water a baling ladle.
淈 ku 1. Turbid water.
淮 huai 2. A large river in Honan and Anhui.
混 } hun 4. Confused, turbid, to loaf, to work.
溷
淦 kan 4. Water leaking into a boat, to sink.
涫 kuan 4. To bubble.
淇 ch'i 2. A river in Honan.
港 chiang 3. Streams diverging, a reach, a channel.
淶 lai 2. A river in Shantung.
淚 lei 4, Tears.
涼 liang 2. Refreshing, cool.
淋 lin 2. To drip, to soak.
淩 ling 2. A river in Shantung.
淪 lun 2. Eddying water, engulfed, lost.
淖 ch'ao 4. Drenched, wet.
淰 nieu 3. Muddy.
淜 p'êng 1. Noise of dashing water.
深 shên 1. Deep, abstruse, ardent, intense, deep-tinted.
淑 shu 4. Clear, pure, virtuous.
淳 ch'un 2. Pure, genuine, sincere.
涮 shua 4. shuan 4. To wash, to rinse.
淅 hsi 1. To wash rice.
淞 sung 1. Name of a river, Woosung.
淡 tan 4. Insipid, tasteless.
淘 t'ao 2. To scour, to clean out.
淂 tê 2. Watery.
淀 tien 4. Shallow water.
添 t'ien 1. To add to, to increase.
淟 t'ien 3. Dirty, defiled.
涷 tung 1. Heavy rain or dew.
淒 ch'i 1. Cold, freezing, miserable.
淺 ch'ien 2. Shallow, superficial, to run aground.
淨 ching 4. Pure, spotless, clean, to wash, only.
清 ch'ing 1. Pure, honest, clear, to clear off.
淬 ts'ui 4. To temper.
淙 ts'ung 2. Rushing water.
淄 tzŭ 1. A river in Shantung.
涴 wan 3. To whirl.
涯 yai 2. A bank, a shore, a limit.
淹 yen 1. To soak, to steep.
液 yeh 4. Spittle, sweat, juice, secretion.
淫 yin 2. The rising of waters, licentiousness, lewd, excessive, to become addicted.
淤 yü 1. To sit up, to be blocked, mud.
淯 yü 4. Name of a river.

9

渠 ch'ü 2. A drain, a gutter.
渣 cha 1. Dregs, residue.
湛 chan 4. Deep, placid, to sink, to soak in.
湞 chêng 1. Name of a river.
渚 chu 3. A sand-bank.
渢 fêng 2. The rippling of water.
淵 yüan 1. Abyss, vast, deep.
湁 chi 2. Dashing water.
涶 t'u 4. To spit, saliva.
湖 hu 2. A lake.
渹 hung 1. The roar of water.
湲 yüan 2. Murmur of water.
渙 huan 4. Broad, swelling, scattered.
湟 huang 2. A river in Kansu.

渾 **hun 2.** A roaring torrent, vast, turbid, chaotic, the whole, the mass.

減 **chien 3.** To diminish, to decrease, to abbreviate, to lighten.

渴 **k'o 3.** Thirsty, dry, parched.

湅 **lien 4.** To boil raw silk, to whiten.

湄 **mao 4.** To rise and overflow.

湄 **mei 2.** The edge of the water.

湎 **mien 3.** To flush with drink, drunk.

渺 **miao 3.** Vast, boundless, vague.

湎 **mien 4.** A waste of waters.

湣 **hun 1.** Confused, troubled.

湼 **nieh 1.** Mud, dirty.

渜 **nuan 3.** Lukewarm.

湢 **pi 4.** A public bathhouse.

渤 **po 4.** An arm of the sea.

湜 **shih 4.** Clear water, true, sincere.

湒 **ch'ou 2.** Pure, unmixed.

湘 **hsiang 1.** To heat, to boil.

溯 **su 4.** To trace up to a source, to go against a stream.

湏 **hsü 1.** Ought, must, necessary, to wait for, a short time.

湑 **hsü 3.** Clear, bright, abundant.

湯 **t'ang 1.** Hot water, soup, to scald.

渧 **ti 4.** To drop, a drop.

渫 **t'ieh 4** Waves.

渟 **t'ing 2.** Stagnant water.

渡 **tu 4.** A ferry, to ford, to cross.

湍 **t'uan 2.** Rapid current, boisterous.

測 **ch'ai 4. ts'ê 4.** To fathom, to sound, to estimate.

湊 **ts'ou 4.** Confluence, to collect, to gather, a reunion, a subscription.

湔 **chien 1.** To sprinkle.

湫 **chiu 1.** A pool, mournful.

湭 **chiu 1.** To swim.

温 **wên 1.** Lukewarm, to warm.

渨 **wei 4.** A bay, a cove.

湋 **wei 2.** To flow back.

渭 **wei 4.** Name of a river.

渦 **wo 1.** A whirlpool.

渥 **wu 4.** To soak, to steep.

渷 **yen 1.** To soak, to overflow.

湮 **yin 1.** To sink in water, to soak, to spread.

游 **yu 2.** To wander about, to ramble, to travel, to float.

渝 **yü 2.** Name of a river.

湧 **yung 3.** To bubble and run off; rushing on.

滁 **ch'u 2** A river.

10

滎 **jung 2.** Streams of water.

滕 **t'êng 2.** A proper name.

準 **chun 3.** To equalise, to level, just, exactly, certain, to grant.

潠 **hsün 4.** To besprinkle.

滀 **ch'u 1.** Water flowing, to flush.

溱 **chên 1.** Name of a river.

滈 **hao 4.** The bubbling of water.

滆 **ho 1.** Name of a lake in Kiangsu.

滑 **hua 2.** Smooth, slippery, cunning, artful.

滉 **kuang 4.** A bright expense of water.

滙 **hui 4.** A confluence, to deposit; a check, a draft.

溷 **hun 4.** Dirty, unclean, a privy.

溠 **cha 4.** The name of a river.

溰 **i 2.** Reflecting water.

溽 **ju 4.** Damp, muggy, steaming.

溶 **jung 2.** A deep and slow current, leisure.

溳 **kan 4.** Name of a river.

溝 **kou 1.** A drain, a ditch, an aqueduct, a moat.

溪 **hsi 1.** A current.

溢 **i 4.** A vessel full to the brim, to overflow, abundant.

溘 **k'o 2.** To get to suddenly, to ground, to lean against, to reach.

溓 **lien 2.** To stick, to adhere.

溧 **li 4.** A small stream, in Kiangsu.

溜 **liu 4.** A current, a stream.

滅 **mieh 4.** Destroyed by fire, to cut off, to destroy.

溟 **ming 2.** Ocean, mist, drizzle.

溺 **ni 4.** To sink, to be drowned, greedy, doting on.

滂 **p'ang 2.** Heavy rain.

溥 **p'u 3.** Large, universal, extensive, to smear.

溞 **sao 1.** A rinsing sound.

潸 **shan 3.** Water rippling and glinting.

溲 **sou 3.** To soak meal in water.

溮 **shih 1.** An affluent of the Hwai.

溡 **shih 2.** A small stream in Shantung.

溼 **shih 1.** Wet, damp, low-lying grounds, dejected.

溫 **wên 1.** Warm, genial, tepid, mild, to warm, to revive.

溯 **su 4.** To trace up to the source, to remember.

溹 **so 4.** The name of a river.

溻 **ta 1.** To dampen, to soak through.

滔 **t'ao 1.** Rushing water, to overflow.

溏 **t'ang 2.** Mud.

滇 tien 1. A lake south of Yün-nanfu.

滄 ts'ang 1. Vast, cold.

滋 tzŭ 1. Name of several rivers, humid, juicy, many, taste.

滓 szŭ 3. Sediment, dregs.

滃 wêng 3. Cloudy, foggy, to float.

溦 wei 1. A slight shover of rain.

溔 yao 3. Boundless.

源 yüan 2. A spring of water.

溳 yün 2. A small river in Hupeh.

11

漀 ch'ing 4. A spring.

漦 li 2. Spittle, mucus.

漿 chiang 1. Broth, congee, starch.

潁 ying 3. A proper name.

滴 shang 1. Name of a river.

漳 chang 1. A river in Honan and Chihli.

漲 chang 4. To overflow, to inundate.

漅 ch'ao 2. A lake in Anhui.

滯 chih 4. Coagulation, obstruction, opposition.

滸 fu 2. To cross a stream on floats.

漨 fêng 2. A pool, a marsh, anxious.

漺 shuang 3. Pure, to purify.

漢 han 4. The Milky Way, name of a river, a famous dynasty; *hence* of or belonging to China.

滹 hu 1. Name of a river in Chihli.

滸 hu 3. Bank, shore.

滬 hu 4. To stake, a name for Shanghai.

澉 kan 3. To wash, insipid.

漷 k'uo 4. A proper name.

溉 chi 4. To wash, since.

漌 chin 3. Pure, limpid.

湛 ch'ên 2 To founder, to go down.

滾 kun 3. To boil, water rashing along, to roll, to return.

漤 lan 3. To pickle fruits in brine.

漏 lou 4. To drop.

漓 li 2. Water dripping.

漻 liao 2. Deep and clear.

漣 lien 2. Water flowing, to weep.

滷 lu 3. Salt, bitter.

漊 lü 3. Drizzling, as rain.

漉 lu 4. To drip, to leak.

滿 man 3. Full, complete, Manchu.

漫 man 4. Water overflowing, spreading, wild, reckless.

漠 mo 4. A sandy desert, careless.

漚 ou 4. To soak, to steep.

漰 p'êng 1. Dashing water.

滮 piao 1 Name of a lake.

漂 p'iao 1. To float, to drift, to be tossed about, to bleach.

潎 pi 4. Bubbling water.

潎 p'ieh 1. Dancing, as waves.

滲 shên 4. To absorb, to infiltrate, to soak, to flow.

漱 sou 4. To rinse out.

滀 hsü 1 To soak in.

溡 shih 4. A small islet.

滃 t'an 1. To sink.

漘 ch'un 2. Side, bank.

滫 hsiu 3. Rice-gruel.

滌 ti 2. To wash, to cleanse.

漩 hsüan 2. Circling water.

漯 lei 3. Glittering of water.

滴 ti 1. To drop, to leak.

滻 ch'an 3. A stream in Shensi.

漙 t'uan 2. A heavy fall of dew.

漕 ts'ao 2. To transport by water.

漬 tzŭ 4. o soak, to steep.

漸 chien 4. To gradually melt, to advance by degrees.

漈 chi 1. Side, bank.

漆 ch'i 1. Varnish, lacker.

漼 ts'ui 4. Clear and deep.

漁 yü 2. To fish.

漥 wa 1. A puddle, a hollow, a swamp.

漾 yang 4. Waves, rapids.

演 yen 3. Wide, to practise, to drill, to perform.

滺 yu 1. Water flowing.

12

潮 ch'ao 2. The tide, moist, damp.

澈 ch'ê 4. Clear water, exhausted, run off.

澄 têng 4. To filter, to clarify.

澂 ch'êng 2. Pure water, clear, limpid.

潴 chu 1. A pool, a puddle.

澍 chu 4. Moistened, well watered.

潪 chih 4. Soaked ground.

潺 ch'uan 1. The sound of water.

濆 fei 4. To bubble up.

潝 hsi 1. Noise of flowing water.

澒 hung 3 Flood, chaos, confusion.

潢 huang 2. A pool, a dyke, to glitter.

潰 **hui** 4. To rush, to flee, routed, angry.

漭 **mang** 3. Vast, a waste.

澆 **chiao** 1. To irrigate, to water.

潔 **chieh** 2. Pure, to purify, chaste, chastity.

澗 **chien** 4. Mountain streams.

潤 **yün** 4. To moisten. *Lun* 4.

潏 **chü** 2. A delta.

潦 **lao** 4. A flood, to overflow.

澇 **lao** 4. A torrent, a flood.

潾 **lin** 2. Mountain streams.

[illegible] **mai** 3. The name of a river.

潣 **min** 3. Water flowing.

潘 **p'an** 1. Name of a river.

濘 **nêng** 4. Muddy.

澎 **p'êng** 1. Noise of dashing waters.

潷 **pei** 4. To drain, to filter.

潑 **p'o** 1. To throw out, to sprinkle.

澁 **shih** 4. Rough, uneven, astringent.

潸 **shan** 3. To weep, to lament.

潲 **shao** 4. Water driven by the rain.

潟 **hsieh** 1. Land overflowed and thus become salt.

潯 **hsün** 2. A steep bank.

澌 **ssŭ** 1. To exhaust, to run dry.

潬 **t'an** 1. A sandbank, a rapid.

潭 **t'an** 2. Deep water, to sound, to penetrate, a pool.

潒 **hsiang** 3. A stream.

潼 **t'ung** 2. A tributary of the Yellow River.

潐 **chiao** 3. To filter.

潛 濳 **ch'ien** 2. Secrete, to abscond, reserved, careful.

潗 **chi** 2. To bubble up.

潨 **chung** 1. The place where the waters meet.

潕 **wu** 3. A river in Hunan.

澐 **yün** 2. The waves rising high.

13

澩 **hsiao** 2. A stream, trouble, disorder.

濋 **ch'u** 3. Small rivulet.

澥 **hsieh** 4. A creek, a cove, a rivulet, watery.

濁 **cho** 3. Muddy, foul.

澣 **huan** 3. To wash and cleanse, a decade.

[illegible] **i** 4. Water raised high, billows.

激 **chi** 1. Noise of waters, to hit, to excite, to try, to fetter, to lower, low.

[illegible] **k'u** 1. Gulf, abyss.

澮 **k'uai** 4. A drain, a water-tank.

濆 **fên** 2. A river in Honan.

澧 **li** 3. A river in Hunan.

澰 **lien** 3. Rising of waters.

濂 **lien** 2. A waterfall, a cascade.

潞 **lu** 4. A river in Shensi.

潚 **su** 4. A proper name.

溦 **wei** 2. A drizzling rain.

澳 **ao** 4. Macao.

濃 **nung** 2. Sticky, rich, thick, strong.

澼 **p'i** 4. To wash, to purify.

濇 **shih** 4. Astringent, acrid.

澨 **shih** 4. Name of a river in Hupeh, a quay.

澶 **shan** 2. Still water.

澠 **shêng** 2. A river in Shantung. **mien** 3. A city in Honan.

澻 **sui** 4. A ditch, a canal

澾 **ts'a** 1. To slip, slippery.

澹 **tan** 4. Fresh, weak, flat, dull.

濎 **ting** 3. A rivulet or brook.

[illegible] **tung** 3. To splash

澡 **tsao** 3. To bathe, to cleanse.

澤 **chai** 2. A marsh; to enrich, moist, slippery, to soak, kindness, favour.

濈 **chi** 4. Friendly, to flow, harmonious.

澯 **ts'an** 4. Pure, limpid.

濊 **hui** 4. Muddy, unclean.

澞 **yü** 2. A torrent between two high banks.

澦 **yü** 4. A river in Ssŭch'uan.

澭 **yung** 1. A sluice, a watergate.

14

濯 **cho** 2. To rinse, clean.

濠 **hao** 2. A moat, a ditch.

濩 **huo** 4. To rain profusely.

濡 **ju** 2. To immerse, to moisten, thick, mild.

濫 **lan** 4. To overflow, profuse, lawless, irregular.

濛 **mêng** 2. Drizzling rain, mist.

濔 **ni** 3. Many, overflow.

[illegible] **tsang** 1. Muddy, dirty.

濘 **nêng** 4. Muddy.

澀 **shih** 4. Rough, uneven, astringent.

濱 **pin** 1. Beach, shore, near.

濮 **p'u** 2. Name of a river.

濕 **shih** 1. Wet, moist.

濬 **tsun** 4. Deep, serious, abstruse, shrewd.

濤 **t'ao** 2. Great waves.

濟 **chi** 4. To cross over, to aid, to releave.
濜 **chin** 4. Name of a river.
濰 **wei** 2. Name of a river in Shantung.
潕 **wu** 3. Name of a river in Hunan.
濥 **yin** 3. Water-courses running underground.
濴 **ying** 2. To revolve, a whirlpool

15

瀍 **ch'an** 2. A river in Hupeh.
瀇 **kuang** 3. Deep water.
漻 **chiao** 1. Name of a river, a vast prospect.
濿 **li** 4. A ford, to ford.
瀏 **liu** 2. Deep water.
濼 **lao** 4. A river in Shantung
濾 **lü** 4. To filter, to strain.
瀌 **piao** 1. A heavy rain.
瀑 **pao** 4. A water-fall.
瀋 **shên** 3. Gravy, sap, to leak out.
瀉 **hsieh** 4. To flow off, to leak, diarrhœia.
瀡 **sui** 3. Slippery, smooth.
瀆 **tu** 4. A ditch, an outlet, foul, muddy, to annoy.
濺 **chien** 4. Water dashing along, to splash.
瀁 **yang** 4. Waves, rapids.

16

瀦 **ch'u** 2. A river in the north of Shansi.
瀚 **han** 4. The northern sea, a desert.
瀣 **hsieh** 4. Mist, dew.
瀨 **lai** 4. Name of a river.
瀝 **li** 4. A drop, to drip.
瀘 **lu** 2. Name of a river in Kiangsi.
瀧 **lung** 2. Name of a river, dew, to bedew.
瀕 **pin** 1. A bank, a shore.
瀟 **hsiao** 1. Big rain, a river in Yünnan.
潠 **ch'uan** 4. To drink.
瀛 **ying** 2 The ocean, a lake, to fill up.
瀜 **yung** 3. Vast, deep.

17 &

瀿 **fan** 2. To water plants.
瀵 **fên** 4. A stream in Shansi.
瀼 **jang** 2. Dew, muddy water.
瀾 **lan** 2. Billows, waves.
瀲 **lien** 4. Water overflowing.
瀰 **mi** 2. A vast expanse of waters, wild, much.
澄 **têng** 4. To drain off.
瀺 **ch'an** 2. Rippling sound of water.
瀸 **chien** 1. To moisten, to soak, to imbue.
瀷 **i** 4. Name of a river.
瀯 **ying** 2. A brook, a rivulet.
瀹 **yao** 4. To boil, to cook with water.
灋 **fa** 1. Rule.
灃 **fêng** 1. A stream in Shensi.
灌 **kuan** 4. To run or flow together, to water, to pour, to force one to drink.
灄 **shê** 1. A river in Hupeh.
灊 **ch'ien** 2. A river in Ssŭch'uan.
灂 **chiao** 2. The rippling rush of ater caused by stones, the noise of waves.
灉 **yung** 1. A canal, a ditch
⿰氵羅 **lo** 2. Name of a river.
灑 **sha** 3. To sprinkle, to scatter.
灘 **t'an** 1. Rapids, a flat.
灒 **tsan** 4. o stir up water, to soil.
灝 **hao** 4. Vast.
灞 **pa** 4. A small river in Shensi.
灢 **nang** 1. Muddy, dirty.
灣 **wan** 1. A winding bank, a cove, a bay, to moor.
灤 **luan** 2. A river in the north-east of Chihli.
瀳 **shuan** 4. To scrub a horse.
⿰氵靈 **ling** 2. A winding reach in a river, a bank.
灨 **kan** 4. A river in Kiangsi.
灩 **yen** 4. Bubbling waters.

Rad 86

火 灬

See Lesson 126 A.

火 灬 **huo** 3. Fire, flame, to burn, exciting humors, fever.
⿰火乚 **cha** 2. To fry.
灰 **hui** 1. Ashes, embers.
灯 **têng** 1. A lamp.
灹 **cha** 4. Crepitation.
灸 **chiu** 3. Moxa, to cauterise.
災 灾 **tsai** 1. Fire, misfortune.
灼 **shao** 2. To burn, to roast, brightness, luminous.

灯 **hung 1.** To heat.

灶 **tsao 4.** A furnace, a kitchen-range.

4

炎 **yen 2.** To flame, to blaze, very hot.

炙 **chih 4.** To burn, moxa, to cauterise.

炁 **ch'i 4.** Influences.

杰 **chieh 2.** A proper name.

炒 **ch'ao 3.** To roast as coffee, to fry.

炄 **niu 3.** To dry.

炊 **ch'ui 1.** To cook.

炕 **k'ang 4.** A brick bed warmed by a fire.

炉 **lu 2.** A furnace.

5

炱 **t'ai 2.** Smoky soot.

炭 **t'an 4.** Charcoal.

炰 炮 **p'ao 2.** To roast.

点 **tien 3.** To light, a dot.

炤 **chao 4.** Bright.

炷 **chu 4.** A candle, a stick of incense.

炬 **chü 4.** A torch, to burn.

[illegible] **mo 4.** A dull fire.

炸 **cha 2.** Shavings.

炳 **ping 2.** Bright, luminous.

炵 **t'ung 2.** A bright red blaze.

6

烝 **chêng 1.** Steam, to steam.

烋 **hsiu 1.** To burn, crepitation.

烈 **lieh 4.** Burning, fiery, virtuous, majestic, glorious.

烏 **wu 1.** Crows, black, an interrogative particle.

烖 **tsai 1.** A calamity.

烕 **mieh 4.** To put out, to extinguish.

烜 **hsüan 1.** To smoke.

烘 **hung 1.** To heat.

烤 **k'ao 3.** To toast, to warm.

烙 **lao 1.** A branding-iron, to burn in.

烚 **hsia 4.** To cook.

炫 **hsüan 4.** Brilliant, to dazzle.

烊 **yang 2.** To roast.

烟 **yen 1.** Smoke.

烑 **yao 2.** To shine.

烛 **chu 2.** A fire-fly.

7

焄 **hsün 1.** Fumes from sacrifices.

烹 **p'êng 1.** To boil, to cook.

焉 **yen 1.** How ? why ? where ?

烰 **fu 2.** To boil, to cook.

烽 **fêng 1.** A beacon fire-place.

焇 **hsiao 1.** To torrefy.

焀 **hu 1.** Flames.

焅 **k'ao 4.** Hot air, to dry.

烱 **chiung 3.** Hot, burning.

焍 **ti 4.** To roast.

烺 **lang 2.** Fire, blaze.

焌 **tsun 2.** To put out a fire.

8

焱 **yen 4.** Fire; flames.

焚 **fên 2.** To burn; to consume.

[illegible] **hsü 4.** Warm breath ; to blow gently; to smile.

然 **jan 2.** To light ; thus ; so ; however, but.

焦 **chiao 1.** Scorched ; dried up ; care.

無 **wu 3.** Not; nothing; without.

尉 **wei 4.** A flat-iron ; to smooth.

焬 **i 4.** Flame.

焵 **kang 4.** To temper steel.

焙 **pei 4.** To dry over a fire.

焞 **t'un 1.** To stew.

焯 **ch'ao 4.** Light; bright.

焠 **ts'ui 4.** To burn.

[illegible] **yen 1.** To cover a fire.

9

煞 **sha 4.** To strike dead, as by the sun; to murder; to end.

煎 **chien 1.** To fry; to decoct.

照 **chao 4.** To enlighten, to shine on ; the reflection of light ; to care for ; a permit ; as, like.

煦 **hsü 3.** To heat; to mature ; to console, warm; kind.

煲 **pao 1.** To heat.

煮 **chu 3.** To boil.

焭 **ch'iung 2.** Alone; forlorn

煄 **chung 3.** To kindle.

煩 **fan 2.** Heat and pain in the head; trouble ; perplexity ; disgust.

煆 **hsia 1.** Fire blazing up.

煳 **hu 2.** To singe.

煥 huan 4. A flame; brightness.
煌 huang 2. Blazing; bright.
煇 hui 1. Brilliant; lustrous.
煣 jou 3. To bend by fire.
煖 nuan 3. nang 3. Warm; mild.
煉 lien 4. To separate dross by fire; to test.
煤 mei 2. Coal.
煏 p'i 4. To dry by the fire.
煁 shên 2. A brazier.
煋 hsing 1. A fire; a spark.
煠 cha 2. To fry.
煓 t'uan 2. Fire; red.
煠 tieh 2. To fry.
煪 ch'iu 1. To scorch; to roast; to dry.
煨 wei 1. To bake.
煒 wei 3. Blazing; glowing.
煬 yang 2. To heat.
煙 yen 1. Smoke; opium; tobacco.
煐 ying 1. A flame; red.
煜 yü 4. Flame; to shine.

10

熏 hsün 1. Smoke; steam; to smoke; to fumigate.
熙 hsi 1. Splendor.
熊 hsiung 2. Black bear.
熒 ying 3. To shine; bright; twinkling; to doubt.
燐 lin 2. A flitting light.
熑 lien 2. To bend in the fire.
熇 k'ao 3. To warm.
熀 huang 3. The blaze of fire; effulgent.
煿 po 4. To crackle; to burst from heat.
煽 shan 1. To excite; to inflame.
熌 shan 4. To scintillate.
熄 hsi 1. To put out a fire.
煻 t'ang 2. To warm.
熠 ch'u 3. To roast.
熥 t'ui 1. To scald.
熓 wu 3. To bank a fire.
熎 yao 4. Dead coal.
熅 yün 4. To iron, to smooth.

11

熲 ch'ing 4. Hot; scorching.
熨 wei 4. To iron; to smooth.
熟 shu 2. shou 2. Ripe; cooked, mature; versed in; common.
熱 熱 jê 4. Warm; to warm.
熬 ao 2. To boil; to decoct; to distil; to endure.
熪 yu 2. A fire to notify heaven.
熯 han 4. To roast; to dry; wearied.
熮 liao 2. To toast.
熠 hsi 4. To sparkle; to glitter.
熰 ou 3. Heat; drought.
熚 pi 4. Fiery; blazing; scorching.
熗 chang 4. To crackle; a cracker.

12

燙 t'ang 2. To heat by placing in hot water.
熹 hsi 1. To warm; heat; glory; prosperity.
燕 yen 4. A swallow; a feast; easy; black.
燄 yen 4. Fire, flames.
燌 chih 4. To burn; a blaze of fire; illustrious.
燋 chao 2. To set fire to.
燔 fan 2. To roast; to burn.
燆 ch'iao 1. Flames.
燁 yeh 2. Glory; prosperity
熺 hsi 1. Lucky stars shining.
爨 tsuan 4. A proper name.
熻 hsi 4. To roast; to burn.
無 hu 2. To scorch; to blacken.
燃 jan 2. To light a fire; to burn.
燎 liao 2. Fire; to burn; s signal-light.
燐 lin 2. The ghostlights; phosphorus.
燒 shao 1. To burn; to roast; feverish.
燀 shan 4. To make a fire; to boil.
燖 hsin 2. To scald.
燍 ssŭ 1. To burn; to redden.
燂 t'an 2. To heat; to dry.
燈 têng 1. A lamp, a lantern.
燉 tun 4. To stew.
燋 chiao 1. To char; to scorch.
燂 ch'ien 2. To quench.

13

營 ying 2. An encampment; an army corps; to regulate; to manage; a living; business.
燮 hsieh 4. To blend; to harmonise; to mature.
燬 hui 3. To burn down.
爈 chü 4. A big fire.
燩 ch'iao 4. To dry up.

燣 lin 2. To torrefy.
燥 tsao 4. Dry; parched.
燭 chu 2. A candle
燧 sui 4. To get fire by friction.
燦 ts'an 3. Bright; glittering.
燠 ao 4. Warm.

14

燹 hsien 3. To set fire to brushwood.
燾 tao 4. To cover over; to light; to do good.
爁 lan 3. A raging fire; to scorch.
燻 hsün 1. To fumigate.
燼 chin 4. Ashes; a residuum; the relics; the remains of.
燿 yao 4. To illumine; bright.

15 &

爇 jê 4. Warm; to burn.
羆 p'i 2. A bear.
熛 piao 1. To stew.
爆 p'ao 4. Crackling; crackers.
爍 shao 4. To light; to shine.
爖 lung 2. To kindle a fire.
爦 lan 3. A hot raging fire.
爥 yeu 4. Fire covered.
爐 lu 2. A stove.
爓 yen 4. Fire.
爛 lan 4. Thoroughly cooked; disaggregated; ragged.
熽 hsiao 1. To burn.
爚 yao 4. Fiery; bright.
爟 kuan 4. To light a fire or beacon.

㸎 nieh 4. Warm; genial.
爝 chiao 2. A torch.
爨 ts'uan 4. A furnace for cooking.

Rad. 87

爪 爪

See Lesson 49 A.

爪 chao 3. chua 3. A claw.
爬 p'a 2. To scratch, to creep, to climb.
受 shou 4. To receive; to endure.
爭 chêng 1. To wrangle, to contest; how?
爰 yüan 3. To lead on to; thereupon; a particle.
奚 hsi 1. How?
舀 yao 3. To bale out water.
爲 wei 2. To be; to make.
wei 4. For; because; on account of; in order to.
舜 shun 4. Name of an ancient monarch.
愛 ai 4. To love.
爵 chiao 2. A cyathus; a cup; a degree of nobility; dignities.

Rad. 88

父 父

See Lesson 43 G.

父 fu 4. Father.
爸 pa 4. A father, papa.
爹 tieh 1. Father.
爺 yeh 2. A father; a term of respect; a gentleman.

Rad. 89

爻 爻

See Lesson 39 G.

爻 yao 2. Lines of the diagrams.
爽 shuang 3. Sunny; cheering; to teach; healthy; appetite; a defect; to miss.
爾 erh 3. Thou, you; if; so, just so; an expletive final.

Rad. 90

爿 爿

See Lesson 127 B.

爿 ch'iang 2. Wood; a bed.
壯 chuang 4. Healthy; strong.
妝 chuang 1. To adorn; to rouge, to feign, to gloss.
牀 ch'uang 2. A bed, a sofa.
戕 ch'iang 1. A spear.; to kill.
狀 chuang 4. Form; to appear; to accuse; to state.
牂 ching 1. A pen.
將 chiang 1. A general; a sign of the future; to receive; t give, etc.
牄 ch'iang 1. A granary.
牆 ch'iang 2. A wall.
[illegible] yeu 2. End of the eaves

Rad. 91

片 片

See Lesson 127 A.

片 p'ien 4. A leaf; a strip; a bit; a section; a moment.

版 **pan** 3. A board, a plank, a diploma.

牉 **p'an** 4. A division, a half.

牌 **p'ai** 2. A tablet; a board, a notice; a warrant; a token; cards.

牋 **chien** 1. A bamboo tablet; a note-paper; a letter.

⿰片咅 **pei** 1. A tablet.

牐 **cha** 2. A shop front.

牒 **tieh** 2. Tablets; documents; records.

牏 **t'ou** 2. A privy.

牓 **pang** 3. A tablet; a register; a model; a pattern.

牕 **ch'uang** 1. A window.

牖 **yu** 4. A window; to teach.

⿰片离 **li** 2. Shavings.

⿰片詹 **ch'an** 4. Rafters.

牘 **tu** 2. Tablets; documents; archives; a note; a letter.

Rad. 92

See Lesson 147 A.

牙 **ya** 2. The teeth.

邪 **hsieh** 2. Bad, perverse.

犽 **ya** 2. The winter pear, *Pekingèse.*

⿰牙艮 **k'ên** 3. To gnaw.

⿰牙奇 **ch'i** 1. Good teeth.

牚 **ch'êng** 1. A prop, a shore.

Rad. 93

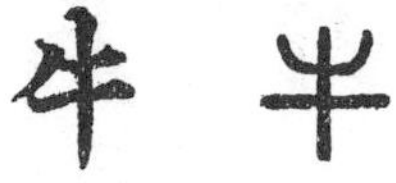

See Lesson 132 A.

牛 **niu** 2. An ox; a bull; a cow; cattle.

牟 **mou** 2. To bellow; to usurp.

牝 **p'in** 3. The female of beasts; a cow.

牣 **jên** 4. To stuff, to fill.

⿰牛卩 **k'ou** 3. Domestic animals.

牢 **lao** 2. A stable for cattle; a jail; firm, strong.

牡 **mu** 3. The male of quadrupeds. The peony.

牦 **mao** 2. The wild yak.

牧 **mu** 4. To pasture; a shepherd; to superintend; a ruler; a teacher.

物 **wu** 4. A thing; an article; a being.

⿰牛介 **chieh** 4. A young ox.

牲 **shêng** 1. Draught animals.

牴 **ti** 3. To gore; to push with the horns; to strive against.

⿱龹牛 **chüan** 1. The ring through the nose of an ox.

⿰牛兆 **chao** 4. A surname.

特 **tê** 4. **t'ê** 4. A bull. **tê** 4. Specially, on purpose.

牷 **ch'uan** 2. A fat unblemished victim.

牸 **tzŭ** 4. Female.

牼 **k'êng** 1. A proper name.

牽 **ch'ien** 1. To pull, to haul, connexion.

牿 **ku** 4. A shed or pen for cattle.

犂 犁 } **li** 2. A plough, the Thibetan yak. *I-li*, Chinese Turkestan.

牻 **mang** 2. An ox.

⿰牛貝 **pei** 4. A young heifer.

⿱沙牛 **sha** 1. A buffalo.

犀 **hsi** 1. A yak, a rhinoceros.

牾 **wu** 4. To but.

犇 **pên** 1. A paddock. To run away.

犉 **chun** 2. A full-grown ox.

犎 **fêng** 1. An ox with a hump.

犍 **chien** 1. A gelded bull.

犏 **p'ien** 1. The domestic yak.

⿰牛氣 **hsi** 4. Cattle starving, epizooty.

犒 **k'ao** 4. Bounty money, to reward.

犗 **chien** 4. To geld a bull.

犝 **t'ung** 2. A calf without horns.

犪 **jao** 3. A docile, well-trained ox.

犢 **tu** 2. A calf.

犧 **hsi** 1. Victims fit to be offered in sacrifice.

Rad. 94

See Lesson 134 A.

犬 **ch'üan** 3. A dog.

犯 **fan** 4. To rush against, to offend against, to violate.

犲 **ch'ai** 2. A wolf.

狀 **chuang** 4. Form, appearance, to accuse in writing.

狂 **k'uang** 2. Mad, wild, raging, ambitious.

狃 **niu** 3. Inclined to evil, doing repeatedly.

狄 **ti** 2. Ancient tribes of the N.W.

狁 **yün** 3. The Huns.

狒 **fei** 4. A kind of ape.

狎 **hsia** 2. A pet dog, familiar, irreverent.

狐 **hu** 2. The fox.

狗 **kou** 3. A dog.

狉 p'ei 1. A cub.

狙 chü 1. A monkey.

狠 hên 3. Dogs quarreling, very, intense.

6-7

狨 jung 2. A gibbon.

狡 chiao 3. Crafty, cunning.

狤 chi 2. A monkey.

狫 lao 3. The Laos and its inhabitants.

狩 shou 4. A hunt, an imperial inspecting tour.

狥 hsün 2. To follow, to go over, comprehensive.

狹 hsia 2. Narrow.

狷 chüan 4. Cautious.

狼 lang 2. The wolf, cruel.

狸 li 2. The fox, *hu-li*.

狵 mang 2. A shaggy-haired dog.

狽 pei 4. A gerboa, hindrance.

狴 p'i 3. A fierce animal.

狻 suan 1. A lion from Thibet.

8-9

猖 ch'ang 1. Mad, wild, seditious.

猙 chêng 1. A fabulous griffin.

猇 hu 1. To roar.

猗 i 1. An interjection, a final particle.

猊 i 2. A fabulous monster.

猛 mêng 3. Fierce, savage, biting.

猜 ts'ai 1. To doubt, to suspect, to guess.

猎 ch'iao 4. A bull-dog.

猝 ts'u 4. To rush out, abrupt, precipitate.

猪 chu 1. A hog.

猴 hou 2. A macaque.

猲 hsieh 4. A fierce dog.

猢 hu 2. A monkey.

猰 ch'ieh 2. A leopard.

猫 mao 2. A cat.

猩 hsing 1. The orang-outang.

猥 wei 3. To bark.

猬 wei 1. The hedgehog.

猨 yüan 2. The gibbon.

猶 yu 2. Still, yet, as, like, similar.

猷 yu 2. To plan, to deliberate.

献 hsien 4. To present, to offer.

10-11

獃 tai 1. Stupid, to stand openmouthed, idle.

猾 hua 2. Treacherous.

獂 liu 2. The sea-otter.

豩 ch'uan 4. A hare.

獅 shih 1. The lion.

猻 sun 1. A monkey.

猺 yao 2. A jackal; aborigenes of the S W.

猿 yüan 2. The gibbon.

獄 yü 4. A prison, a litigation.

獍 ching 4. A panther.

獂 lei 3. The flying squirrel, pteromys.

獏 mo 4. The Malacca tapir.

獘 pieh 4. To perish.

獒 ao 2. A large dog.

12-13

獞 t'ung 2. Dwarf tribes of the South.

獚 huang 2. Barbarians.

獛 jan 2. A kind of monkey.

獗 chüeh 2. Insolent, unruly.

獠 liao 2. To hunt at night with torches.

獜 lin 2. A pangolin.

獬 hsieh 4. A fabulous animal.

獫 hsien 3. Barbarians.

獪 k'uai 4. Crafty, mischievous.

斁 i 4. To ruin, to destroy.

獨 tu 2. Solitary, single, only.

14 &

獯 hsün 1. The Huns.

獲 huai 2. huo 2. To take in hunting, to catch, to obtain.

獰 nêng 2. Brutal, fierce.

獴 mêng 2. A weasel.

獮 hsien 3. Imperial hunt.

獷 kung 3. Fierce, rude.

獵 lieh 4. To hunt, the chase.

獸 shou 4. Wild animals.

獻 hsien 4. To offer, to give, to hand up to.

獺 t'a 3. An otter.

獑 ch'an 2. A hare.

獾 huan 1. A badger.

玁 hsien 3. Dogs. Barbarians. Huns.

玃 chü 1. A species of large ape.

Rad. 95

玉 王

See Lesson 83 A.

玉 **yü 4.** A gem, white jade.

王 **wang 2.** King, prince.
wang 4. To govern.

玎 **ting 1.** Jingling noise

玘 **ch'i 3.** Stone ornaments hung at the girdle.

玖 **chiu 3.** Smoky quartz, nine.

玠 **chieh 4** A jade tablet.

玦 **chüeh 2.** An archer's ring.

玫 **mei 2.** A red gem, a rose.

玩 **wan 4.** Trinkets, to toy, to play.

珍 **chên 1.** Noble, precious, rare, delicate.

珏 **chüeh 4.** Two assorted gems.

珂 **k'o 1.** Quartz gem.

玲 **ling 2.** To tinkle.

珉 **min 2.** Alabaster.

玻 **po 1.** Vitreous, glass.

珀 **p'ai 4.** Amber.

珊 **shan 1.** Precious coral.

玷 **tien 4.** A flaw or stain in a gem, a defect.

6

玼 **ts'ü 2** A flaw, a fault.

珠 **chu 1.** A pearl, a bead, the pupil of the eye.

珙 **kung 3.** A [illegible] sceptre or [illegible].

珪 **kui 1.** A sceptre.

珞 **[illegible] 4.** A [illegible].

班 **pan 1.** To confer rewards and places, a series a rank, order, grade, a troop.

珮 **p'ei 4.** Girdle ornaments.

珥 **erh 3.** Ear-trinkets.

珣 **hsün 2.** A branching coral.

珧 **yao 2.** Mother-of-pearl.

琊 **yeh 2.** A place in Shantung.

7

琀 **han 4.** Gems put into the mouth of a corpse.

現 **hsien 4.** The glitter of gems, visible, now, at present.

球 **ch'iu 2.** A ball, a globe.

琅 **lang 2.** A kind of white cornelian.

理 **li 3.** Veins, striæ, to rule, to manage, abstract right, the first principles.

琉 **liu 2.** A glass-like substance.

珼 **pei 4.** Tortoise-shell ornament.

8

琴 **ch'in 2.** The Chinese lute, organ.

琶 **pa 1.** A guitar.

琵 **p'i 2.** The Chinese guitar.

斑 **pan 1.** Variegated, striped, streaked.

琖 **chan 3.** A precious cup.

琢 **cho 2.** To cut, to polish stones.

琺 **fa 4.** The enameled ware of the Chinese.

琥 **hu 3.** Amber.

琦 **ch'i 2.** A valuable stone, a cure.

琚 **chü 1.** Trinkets.

琯 **kuan 3.** A jade tube.

琨 **k'un 1.** Mother of pearl.

瑯 **lang 2.** Enamel.

琳 **lin 2.** A precious jade.

琱 **tiao 3.** To cut gems, to engrave.

琠 **t'ien 4.** An ear-plug.

琮 **ts'ung 1.** Badges of rank made of jade.

琰 **yen 2.** The lustre of gems.

琬 **wan 3.** A sceptre.

9

瑟 **shê 4.** A lute.

瑕 **hsia 1.** A flaw, a blemish.

瑚 **hu 2.** A red coral.

瑁 **mao 4.** A tortoise-shell.

瑙 **nao 3.** Agate.

瑞 **jui 4.** Precious, auspicious.

瑋 **wei 3.** A kind of jasper.

瑛 **ying 1.** The lustre of gems.

瑜 **yü 2.** Lustre, glory.

瑗 **yüan 4.** A large ring of jade.

10

瑩 **ying 2.** Bright, lustrous.

瑰 **kuei 4.** The rose.

瑠 **liu 2.** A glass-like substance.

瑪 **ma 3.** Agate.

瑣 **so 3.** Fragments, fine, minute, petty.

瑲 **ts'ang 1.** The tinkle of stones.

瑤 **yao 2.** Green jasper.

11

璋 **chang 1.** A sceptre, cup.

瑾 chin 3. The lustre of gems, brilliant.
璆 niu 4. Jasper.
璃 li 1. A vitreous substance.
璉 lien 2. A vessel.
璊 man 2. Cornelian.
璇 hsüan 2. An armillary sphere.
璀 ts'ui 4 Brilliant.
瑽 ts'ung 1. Tinkling.

12-13

璠 fan 2. A precious stone.
璜 huang 2. A semi-circular jade gem
璣 chi 1. A pearl.
璘 lin 2. Veined, as marble.
璞 p'u 4. An unpolished gem; simple, rude.
璧 pi 4. A cameo.
環 huan 2. A ring, a bracelet, to surround.
璥 ching 3. A precious stone.
璩 chü 4. Ear-rings.
璫 tang 1. Jingling, tinkling.
璨 ts'an 4. The lustre of gems.
璪 tsao 3. Pendents hung around a coronet.

14 &

璽 hsi 3. The Royal signet, the great seal.
璿 hsüan 2. A planetarium.
璺 wei 4. A cracked porcelain, a flaw.
璵 yü 2. A striped stone.
瓏 ch'iung 2. Brilliant, precious.
璨 li 1. Vitreous.
瓅 li 4. The lustre of a pearl.
璶 tu 2. The onyx.
瓐 lu 3. A gem like the topaz.
瓏 lung 2. Tinkling.
瓓 lan 4. Brilliant.
瓚 tsan 4. A kind of sceptre.
瓛 hsien 4. A sceptre.

Rad. 96

玄 㝎

See Lesson 91 A.

玄 玄 } hsüan 2. Dark, profound, deep; abstruse, mysterious. 1
玅 miao 4. Wonderful, admirable, mysterious.
玆 tzŭ 1. Dark, obscure.
率 shuai 4. To lead, to follow, to obey, rule, usually, universally.
玈 lü 2. Black.

Rad. 97

瓜 𤓯

See Lesson 162 A.

瓜 kua 1. Cucurbitaceous plants.
瓟 p'ao 2. A gourd.
瓝 p'ao 2. Calabash.
瓢 p'iao 2. A gourd a calabash.
瓣 pan 4. A slice, as of a melon, a slip, a petal.
瓐 lu 2. A pumpkin.
瓤 jang 2. Pulp, fleshy kernel.

Rad. 98

瓦 㼾

See Lesson 145 A.

瓦 wa 3. Tiles, glazed bricks, pottery, a roof.
瓬 fang 3. To mould, to work clay into shape.
瓪 fan 3. A concave tile.
瓮 wêng 4. A jar.
瓴 ling 2. A long necked jar.
瓶 p'ing 2. A jug, a bottle.
㼧 t'ung 2. A convex tile.
瓷 tz'ŭ 2. Crockery, porcelain.
甋 t'ung 2. The upper tiles on a roof.
瓿 p'ou 3. A jar, a pot.
甇 tang 4. A large earthenware bowl.
甄 chên 1. To mould, to fashion.
甃 ch'iu 4. To brick a well.
甌 ou 1. A bowl, a cup.
甊 lou 3. A long-necked jar.
甍 mêng 2. Roof-tiles.
甎 chuan 1. A brick.
甓 p'ieh 4. A large bottle.
甑 tsêng 4. A boiler, a caldron.
甓 pi 4. Glazed tiles.
甔 t'an 2. A jar, an amphora.
甕 wêng 4. A large jar.

[illegible] **chin 4.** A tub.

甖 **ying 1.** A pitcher.

甗 **hsien 3.** An earthen vessel without a bottom, used in steaming.

Rad. 99

甘 𠃛

See Lesson 73 B.

甘 **kan 1.** Sweet, agreeable, winsome, voluntary.

甚 **shên 4.** Superlative, very, what?

[illegible] **k'an 1.** Wine jar.

甜 **t'ien 2.** Sweet to the taste.

[illegible] **yen 3.** Agreeable, sweet.

甞 **ch'ang 2.** To taste, to essay, usually.

[illegible] **hsien 1.** Sweet, pleasant.

Rad. 100

生 生

See Lesson 79 F.

生 **shêng 1.** To bear, to produce, to come forth, to live, life, unripe, unpolished, unacquainted, unusual.

甡 **shêng 1.** A multitude, numerous.

產 **ch'an 3.** To produce, to bear, productions of a country.

甤 **jui 3.** Prolific, luxuriant.

甥 **shêng 1.** The sons of a sister or of a daughter.

甦 **su 1.** To revive.

Rad. 101

用 用

See Lesson 109 B.

用 **yung 4.** To use, to employ, so as to, thereby, thereon.

甫 **fu 3.** To begin, great, large, just now, a name.

甬 **yung 3.** To burst forth.

𤰈 **pei 4.** **pi 4.** To prepare.

甯 **ning 2.** A surname, rather, it is better.

Rad. 102

田 田

See Lesson 149 A.

田 **t'ien 2.** A field, cultivated fields.

由 **yu 2.** Cause, origin, from, after, by, to permit.

甲 **chia 3.** A cyclical character. Hard coverings, scaly plates, a cuirass, the finger nails.

申 **shên 1.** A cyclical character. To extend, to increase, to state, to report.

甴 **fu 4.** A devil's head.

男 **nan 2.** The male of the human species, a man, a son.

甸 **tien 4.** Government lands.

町 **t'ing 3.** Embankment, dike.

甽 **ch'uan 3.** Drains, irrigation.

甿 **mang 2.** Country people, fugitives.

畀 **pi 4.** To give, to grant.

甾 **tzŭ 1.** Fields, to till.

𤱈 **ch'ao 4.** To harrow.

畈 **fan 4.** A plain, a field.

畐 **fu 4.** To be full, a roll of cloth.

畊 **ching 1.** To plough.

界 **chieh 4.** A boundary, the world.

畎 **ch'üan 3.** Drains, watering.

畆 **mu 3.** A Chinese acre.

畋 **t'ien 2.** To cultivate.

思 **ssŭ 1.** To think.

畏 **wei 4.** To fear.

胃 **wei 4.** The stomach.

畇 **yün 2.** Platbands.

5

畛 **chên 3.** Raised paths.

畜 **ch'u 4.** Animals.
hsü 4. To feed, to rear.

畂 **kou 1.** Raised bank.

留 **liu 2.** To keep, to detain, to leave behind, hospitality.

畝 **mu 3.** The Chinese acre.

畔 **p'an 4.** A landmark.

畚 **pên 3.** A hod.

畟 **chi 2.** A plough.

6

畤 **shih 3.** Name of a place.

畦 **ch'i 2.** A garden, a platband.

異 **i 4.** Different, foreign, strange, heterodox.

畧 略 **liao 4.** Limits, disposition, a plan, a little, to make little account of.

畢 **pi 2.** To finish, ended, all, together.

7-8

番 **fan 1.** A time, a turn, aborigenes, savages.

畫 **hua 4.** A picture, a drawing, a mark, to map.

畱 **liu 2.** To detain, to keep back.

畬 **yü 2.** Cultivated fields.

畸 **chi 1.** Surplus, leavings.

畺 **chiang 1.** A boundary.

當 **tang 1.** Ought, suitable, to act as, to meet, to bear.
tang 4. To pawn, to pledge. A snare.

㽣 **yü 4.** A frontier, a country.

9 &

畼 **ch'ang 4.** Waste fields.

㽭 **juan 2.** A vacant space.

畻 **ch'êng 1.** Raised paths in a field.

畿 **chi 1.** Imperial lands.

畾 **lei 2.** Field parted by dikes.

暵 **han 4.** Arable land.

疄 **lin 2.** A raised path.

疃 **t'ung 3.** A thrashing-floor.

疇 **ch'ou 2.** Cultivated field, a species, who?

疆 **chiang 1.** A limit, a border, a boundary.

疊 **tieh 2.** To pile up, to fold, to reiterate, still, again.

Rad. 103

See Lesson 112 C.

疋 **p'i 3.** A roll of cloth.

疎 疏 **shu 1.** Distant, in time, space, or relationship; to separate, lax, remiss, a report.

疐 **chih 4.** To trammel, to impede.

疑 **i 2.** To doubt, to suspect, to fear, to dislike, similar, suppose.

楚 **ch'u 3.** A wooded region.

Rad. 104

See Lesson 127 D.

疒 **ni 1. chi 1.** Disease.

㽱 **chiao 3.** Belly-ache.

疓 **nai 3.** Pain, sore.

疔 **ting 1.** Pimple, furuncle, ulcer, anthrax.

𤴮 **hsia 4.** Diarrhœa.

疚 **chiu 4.** Chronic disease, vice, ennui.

疙 **ko 1.** A boil, sore.

疘 **kang 1.** Prolapsus of the rectum.

疝 **shan 4.** Hernia.

疺 **fa 4.** Weary, exhausted.

疢 **ch'ên 4.** A febrile feeling.

𤵜 **fan 4.** To faint.

疥 **chieh 4.** The itch; an itching.

疤 **pa 1.** Cicatrix, scar.

疫 **i 4.** Epidemic, pestilence.

疣 **yu 2.** A swelling, a wen.

疪 **pi 4.** Numbness.

5

痄 **cha 4.** A sudden disease.

疹 **chên 3.** An exanthema; scarlatina, typhus, measles, etc.

疻 **chih 3.** A bruise.

症 **chêng 4.** Disease; malady.

疿 **fei 2.** Small pimples; prickly heat.

痃 **hsien 2.** Vertigo.

疳 **kan 1.** Gingivitis.

痂 **chia.** The scab over a sore. *Ka* **1.**

㽷 **ch'ieh 4.** Debility.

痼 **ku 4.** A chronic complaint.

疴 **k'o 4.** Sickness.

疱 **p'ao 4.** A blister.

痞 **p'i 3.** Dyspepsia.

疲 **p'i 2.** Lassitude, fatigue.

病 **ping 4.** Sickness.

疶 **hsieh 4.** Dysenteria.

疸 **tan 4.** The jaundice.

疼 **t'êng 2.** Pain, ache; to love dearly.

疷 **ti 1.** Disease, weakness.

痁 **tien 4.** Malaria, ague.

𤵥 **t'o 2.** Humpbacked.

疾 **chi 2.** Sickness; urgent; hasty.

疽 **chü 1.** A deep-seated ulcer.

6

疵 **tz'ŭ 2.** A malady; a bad habit.

痔 **chih 4.** Piles.

痕 **hên 2.** A scar, a cicatrix, a stain.

痐 **hui 2.** The tape-worm.

痍 **i 2.** An ulcer; a sore.

痓 **tz'ŭ 4.** The gout.

痊 **ch'üan 2.** Cured ; convalescent.

痒 **yang 2.** Prurigo, itching.

7

痣 **ch'ih 4.** A mark; a mole.

痚 **hsiao 1.** Asthma.

㾘 **kêng 3.** Sickness.

痢 **li 4.** Dysentery.

痞 **p'i 3.** Constipation.

痡 **p'u 1.** Debility.

痧 **sha 1.** Malaria.

痠 **suan 1.** Aching of the limbs ; muscular pains.

痘 **tou 4.** Smallpox.

痜 **t'u 1.** The scald head.

痛 **t'ung 4.** Pain; sore.

8

痮 **chang 4.** Swelling; dropsical; dilatation.

痴 **ch'ih 1.** Stupid; doting.

痱 **fei 4.** Swelling of the feet.

痼 **ku 4.** A chronic disease.

痯 **kuan 3.** Worn out, ill.

痳 **lin 2.** Diseases of the bladder , gravel; dysuria.

痲 **ma 2.** Numbness; pock-marks.

痭 **pêng 1.** Menorrhagia.

痺 **pi 4.** Rheumatism; numbness.

痰 **t'an 2.** Phlegm.

瘁 **ts'ui 4.** Distressed; worn out.

痿 **wei 3.** Paralysis ; paraplegia.

瘂 **ya 3.** Dumb; hoarse.

瘀 **yü 1.** Extravasated blood.

9

瘇 **chung 3.** Swelling of the legs, dropsy.

瘋 **fêng 1.** Leprosy ; paralysis ; insanity; madness; etc.

瘊 **hou 2.** Warts; pimples.

瘓 **huan 4.** Sick; ill.

瘌 **la 2.** A scar.

⿸疒扁 **p'ien 1.** Hemiplegia.

瘏 **t'u 2.** To be ill.

⿸疒秋 **chiu 4.** To contract, shrivelled.

瘖 **yin 1.** Dumb.

瘉 **yü 4.** To be convalescent, healed.

10

瘡 **ch'uang 1.** Ulcer, abscess.

瘞 **i 4.** To bury.

瘚 **chüeh 2.** The hiccough ; convulsions, fits.

瘤 **liu 2.** A tumour ; a wen.

瘧 **yao 4.** Fever; ague.

瘢 **pan 1.** Marks on the skin ; moles; scars.

⿸疒桑 **sang 3.** The glanders in horses.

瘦 **shou 4.** Thin; lean.

瘩 **ta 2.** A sore ; a boil.

瘨 **tien 1.** Crazed ; deranged ; mad , wild.

瘠 **chi 2.** Emaciated ; lean ; barren.

癊 **yin 4.** A disease of the heart.

瘟 **wên 1.** Pestilence ; epidemic.

11

⿸疒虘 **cha 1.** A scab, a scar.

瘵 **chi 2.** Consumption.

瘬 **chang 4.** A swelled belly; dropsical.

瘴 **chang 1.** Malaria ; miasma.

瘳 **ch'ou 1.** To be healed, cured, convalescent.

瘸 **ch'üeh 2.** To be lame.

瘺 **lou 4.** Fistula.

瘰 **lei 3.** Scrofulous glands.

⿸疒敝 **pieh 1.** An ulcer.

瘷 **sou 4.** To cough.

⿸疒帶 **tai 4.** Flux , leucorrhœa.

12

癈 **fei 4.** Incurably diseased.

癇 **hsien 2.** Convulsions ; fits.

癀 **huang 2.** Jaundice.

癆 **lao 2.** Wasting away from toi or anxiety ; catarrh.

療 **liao 2.** To cure : to heal.

癉 **tan 1.** Blight ; worn out.

癄 **chiao 1.** Thin ; emaciated.

13

癐 **kuei 4.** A disease.

癗 **lei 3.** Pimples ; blisters.

癘 **li 4.** A virulent disease.

癖 **p'i 3.** Dyspeptic ; greediness ; passion.

癙 **shu 3.** Sick from grief ; melancholy.

14 &

癡 **ch'ih 1.** Stupid ; doting on.

癟 **pieh 3.** Deformation, atrophy.

癥 **chêng 1.** Calculi.

癤 **chieh 1.** A sore, an ulcer.

癢 **yang 3.** To itch; to scratch; to long for.

癨 **huo 3.** The cholera.

癩 **lai 4.** Leprosy.

[illegible] **su 1.** Anaesthesia.

癮 **yin 3.** A vice; bound by an evil habit.

癬 **hsüan 3.** Ringworm.

癭 **ying 1.** A wen; a goitre.

癯 **ch'ü 1.** Emaciated; thin; ghastly.

癰 **yung 1.** A malignant ulcer, carbuncle.

癱 **t'an 1.** Paralysis, palsy.

癵 **lüan 2.** Contraction of the hands and feet.

癲 **tien 1.** Crazed, deranged; mad.

Rad. 105

See Lesson 112 H.

癶 **po 1.** Back, to back.

癸 **kuei 3.** A cyclical character.

登 **têng 1.** To mount; to ascend; to record; to complete.

發 **fa 1.** To send forth; to issue; to dismiss; to utter; to produce; to rise; to be manifest; to act.

Rad. 106

See Lesson 88 A.

白 **pai 2.** White, clear, pure; vain, in vain, for nothing.

百 **pai 3.** A hundred; many; all.

皃 **mao 4.** The outward mien; gait, manner; the face.

皁 皂 **tsao 3.** Black; lictors.

帛 **pai 2.** Plain white silk; wealth.

的 **ti 4.** Target, mark; clear, true; sign of the possessive.

皇 **huang 2.** The Emperor; imperial.

泉 **ch'üan 2.** A spring; money.

皆 **chieh 1.** All; every; together; cooperation.

皈 **kui 1.** To conform to law (a Buddhist term).

皋 **kao 1.** High, eminent.

皎 **chiao 3.** Pure white; effulgent.

皓 **hao 4.** White, bright; luminous; splendour.

皖 **huan 3.** Luminous; the morning star.

皙 **hsi 1.** White; clear.

皞 **hao 4.** White, effulgent.

皜 **hao 3. kao 3.** The light of heaven; luminous; bright.

魄 **p'ai 4.** The inferior soul. Body; matter.

皤 **po 1.** White; clear.

皦 **chiao 3.** Clear; bright.

皪 **li 4.** Brightness.

皫 **piao 3.** Pale; to grow pale.

皭 **chiao 3.** A pure white.

[illegible] **t'ang 3.** Whiteness.

Rad. 107

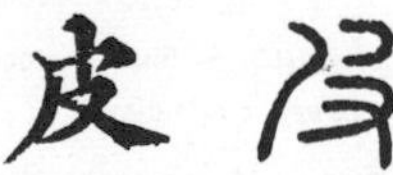

See Lesson 43 H.

皮 **p'i 2.** The skin; leather; furs; a cover; a wrapper; a surface.

𤿍 **p'i 1.** To crack; to chap; crevices.

[illegible] **chao 1.** A scar.

皰 **p'ao 4.** A blister.

皯 **ch'a 1.** Wrinkles.

[illegible] **ts'u 1.** The skin chapped and cracked.

𤿋 **han 4.** Leather armlets for archers.

皴 **ts'un 1.** Rough.

皵 **ch'iao 2.** Wrinkled; rough.

皷 **ku 3.** A drum.

皺 **chou 4.** Wrinkled; creased.

皻 **cha 1.** Cracks of the skin.

皽 **chan 4.** To tear off, to peel off.

𥀬 **chien 3.** Callosity, corn.

Rad. 108

See Lesson 157 A.

皿 **min 3.** A dish.

盂 盓 **yü 2.** A basin, a large cup.

盅 **chung 1.** A cup, a mug, a goblet.

盆 **p'ên 2** A basin.

盃 **pei 1.** A cup, a tumbler.

盈 **ying 2.** Full, excess, overplus 3

盎 **yang 1.** Abundance. Centre. To pray.

盍 盇 **ho 2.** To cover, why not?

盉 **ho 2.** A vase, concave.

盌 wan 3. A bowl, a deep dish.
𥁕 wên 1. Benevolent, kind, compassionate.
益 i 4. A dish filling with water, to increase, to benefit, more and more.
盒 ho 2. A box or dish.
盖 kai 4. To cover, etc.
盔 k'ui 1. A helmet, a porringer.
盚 ch'iu 2. A proper name.
盛 shêng 4. Abundance.
ch'êng 2. To contain.
盙 fu 3. A basket used at worship.
盖 kai 4. A cover, to build, for.
盜 tao 4. To rob, robber.
盞 chan 3. A shallow cup, a lamp.
盝 lu 4. A box, a case.
盟 mêng 3. A covenant.
監 chien 1. To examine carefully, to oversee, a college, a jail.
盡 chin 4. To exhaust, to indulge, to end, to achieve, the last.
盤 p'an 2 A dish, a plate, to coil up, to examine, expenses.
盥 kuan 4. To wash the hands.
盧 lu 2. A pan to hold fire.
盩 chou 1. To strike.
盪 tang 4. A bath, to move.
盬 ku 3. Salt pond, temporary, to care for.
鹽 yen 2. Salt.

Rad 109

See Lesson 158 A.

目 mu 4. The eye, an index, a look, to designate.
直 chih 2. Straight, honest, upright, only.
盲 mang 2. Blind.
盱 hsü 2. Eyes wide open, to hope for.
旰 kan 3. To open the eyes.

4

𥄂 hu 4. To see obscurely.
看 k'an 4. To look at, to examine, to practise.
省 hsing 3. To enquire, to examine, to perceive.
shêng 3. A province, to spare.
眉 mei 2. The eyebrows.
苜 mu 4. Lucern.
盾 tun 4. A shield.
相 hsiang 1. Mutual.
hsiang 4. To look at.
眆 fang 3. Resembling.
盻 hsi 4. To look at in anger.
眇 miao 3. A one-eyed man, to glance at, to take aim.
眄 mien 3. To ogle.
盼 p'an 4. To gaze at, to long for, to expect.
眂 shih 4. To inspect, to observe.
盹 tun 3. Heavy eyes, half asleep.
眨 cha 3. chan 3. Twinkling.
眊 mao 4 Muddled, confused.

5

眞 chên 1. True, truly, genuine.
眚 shêng 3. A film, a cloud, to obscure, a calamity.
眢 yüan 1. A vacant, dull eye
眲 nu 4. Leucoma.
眛 mei 4. Indistinct sight.
眝 chu 4. To stare at.
眑 hsüeh 2. To spy about.
眩 hsüan 1. Confused, troubled, deceived, dizzy.
眙 i 2. To gaze at fixedly.
眠 mien 2. To close the eyes, to sleep.
眮 ssŭ 1. To peep at.
眣 tieh 2. The eyes unsteady.

6

衆 chung 4. All, multitude, many, numerous.
眥 tzŭ 1. The canthus of the eye.
眷 chüan 4. To love, to be fond of, family, relatives.
眵 ch'ih 1. Eyes dim.
眶 k'uang 4. The eye-socket.
眸 mou 2. The pupil of the eye.
眯 mi 3. Eyes blinded.
眼 yen 3. The eye, a hole.

7

晢 chê 4. To see, discern.
睎 hsi 1. To long for, to gaze at.
睏 k'un 4. To nod, sleepy.
睊 chüan 1. To spy.
睇 ti 4. To stare, to gaze.
睞 chia 4. Eyelashes, to twinkle.
睃 tsun 4. To look at.

8

睪 i 4. To watch over.
睘 huan 2. To look at with respect.

瞢 **mêng** 2. To dream.

督 **tu** 1. To inspect, to watch over; to rule.

睧 **hun** 1. Dulness of vision.

睨 **i** 4. To glance at, to look askance.

睖 **lêng** 4. To stare at.

睦 **mu** 4. A benignant eye, harmony, concord.

睟 **sui** 4. Clear, net.

睜 **chêng** 1. To open the eyes, wide.

睬 **ts'ai** 3. To take notice of.

睫 **chieh** 4. The eyelashes.

睛 **ching** 1. The iris of the eye, the pupil.

9

睿 **jui** 4. Perspicacious, clever, shrewd.

瞀 **mou** 4. Dull, blind.

睡 **shui** 4. To sleep.

睽 **k'ui** 2. To squint.

睺 **hou** 2. Dim of sight, a Buddhist sound.

睹 **tu** 3. To gaze at, to observe.

10

瞎 **hsia** 1. Blind, benighted, heedless, to do things blindly.

瞋 **ch'ên** 1. An angry look.

瞌 **k'o** 2. Sleepy, dozing.

瞑 **ming** 3. To close the eyes.

瞍 **sou** 3. Blind.

瞅 **ch'ou** 3. To spy, to observe.

11

瞐 **ma** 2 To see indistinctly.

瞖 **i** 4. A film in the eye, leucoma.

瞥 **p'ieh** 1. To glance at.

瞕 **chang** 4. A cataract.

瞞 **man** 2. To deceive, to hide.

瞘 **k'ou** 1. Deep sunken eyes.

12

瞯 **hsien** 3. To watch, to peep at.

瞶 **k'uei** 4. Dimmed sight, blurred vision.

瞭 **liao** 3. A clear eye.

瞰 **sa** 2. To glance at.

瞬 **shun** 4. To blink, to glance.

瞪 **têng** 4. To stare at.

瞳 **t'ung** 2. The pupil of the eye.

瞧 **ch'iao** 2. To look on, to consider.

13 &

瞽 **ku** 3. Blind.

瞿 **ch'ü** 2. The timid look of a bird, alarmed, vigilant.

瞻 **chan** 1. To look up to, to respect.

矁 **ch'ou** 3. To look at, to gaze.

矇 **mêng** 2. Dimsighted, blind, ignorant.

矍 **kuo** 4. To look here and there, to seize.

矐 **chiao** 4. To sleep

矗 **ch'u** 2. Rising above others, lofty, straight.

矖 **li** 2. To look at angrily.

矙 **k'an** 3. To spy, to watch.

矚 **chu** 3. To look earnestly.

Rad. 110

矛 矛

See Lesson 95 C.

矛 **mao** 2. A halberd.

矜 **ching** 1. Pity, compassion, to venerate, reserve.

矟 **shao** 2. A kind of harpoon.

矞 **yü** 4. To bore through.

Rad. 111

矢 矢

See Lesson 131 A.

矢 **shih** 3 A dart, swift, to shot, to resolve, to swear.

矣 **i** 3. A final particle.

知 **chih** 1. To know, to be aware of, to govern, intimate.

矦 **hou** 2. A target, a title.

矧 **shên** 3. Still more, how much more.

矩 **chü** 3. A carpenter's square, a rule, a pattern.

短 **tuan** 3. Short.

矬 **ts'o** 2. Short, a dwarf.

矮 **yeh** 3. Low, dwarf.

雉 **chih** 4. A pheasant.

矲 **chüeh** 4. Short, scanty.

矯 **chiao** 3. To feign, to correct, to rise.

矰 **tsêng** 1. A dart.

矱 **huo** 4. A measure, a marking line.

Rad. 112

石 厂

See Lesson 59 D.

石 **shih** 2. A stone, rocks.

石 **tan** 4. A picul, 100 catties.

矴 **ting** 4. Stone anchor.

矸 **han** 4. A rock, a mineral.

硭 **mang** 2 Soda-ash.

4

砆 **fu** 1. A reddish stone.

砍 **k'an** 3. To cut, to chop.

砊 **k'ang** 4. Shock, clash.

砎 **chieh** 4. Hard.

砇 **min** 2. Alabaster.

砭 **pien** 1. A flint needle, acupuncture.

砒 **p'i** 1. Arsenic.

砂 **sha** 1. Gravel, sand. Different minerals.

砌 **ch'i** 4. To lay bricks, to pave.

砑 **ya** 4. To grind, to polish.

5

砧 **chên** 1. A block, an anvil.

砥 **chih** 3. Whetstone, to polish.

砫 **chu** 4. A stone tablet.

砰 **p'êng** 1. Crashing noise.

砲 **p'ao** 4. A ballista, a cannon.

砯 **p'êng** 1. Sound of billows rushing against a cliff.

破 **p'o** 4. To break, to ruin. to defeat, to solve, to detect.

砣 **t'o** 2. The weight on a steelyard.

砸 **tsa** 2. To pound.

6

砦 **chai** 4. A stockade for defence, an encampment.

硃 **chu** 1. Vermilion, imperial.

硦 **hang** 1. To ram, a rammer.

硌 **lao** 4. Stones, to pile up.

硉 **lü** 4. Gravel.

硇 **nao** 2. Ammoniacal salt.

硐 **t'ung** 2. To plane.

研 **yen** 2. To grind, to rub fine.

7

硜 **k'êng** 1. To butt.

硫 **liu** 2. Sulphur.

硭 **mang** 2. Crude soda.

硪 **o** 2. A rocky cliff.

硝 **hsiao** 1. Saltpetre.

硯 **yen** 4. Inkstone.

硬 **ying** 4. Hard, obstinate.

8

碕 **ch'i** 2. A craggy.

碌 **lu** 4. Green jasper, rough, laborious.

碍 **nai** 4. To hinder, to impede.

硼 **p'êng** 2. Borax.

碑 **pei** 1. A stone tablet, a stele.

碎 **sui** 4. Fragments, small pieces, bits.

碴 **t'a** 4. A mortar.

碇 **ting** 4. A large stone used as an anchor.

碓 **tui** 4. A pestle.

碗 **wan** 3. A bowl.

9

碧 **pi** 4. Green jade stone.

嵒 **yen** 2. Rocks.

碪 **chên** 1. A block to beat clothes on, when washing them.

碣 **chieh** 2. A stone, a tablet.

碯 **nao** 3 Agate.

碰 **p'êng** 4. To bump, to collide with.

硾 **chui** 1. To weight, to press things down.

碩 **shao** 2. Abundance.

碟 **tieh** 2. A plate, a small dish.

礴 **chu** 4 A stone roller.

10

磊 **lei** 3. A heap of stones.

磐 **p'an** 2. A huge stone, a base, firm.

磆 **hua** 2. Soapstone.

確 **ch'iao** 4. True, positive, certainly.

磕 **k'o** 1. To knock.

碼 **ma** 3. Weights, numerals.

碾 **nien** 3. A roller, a mill.

磇 **p'i** 1. An ore of arsenic.

磅 **p'ang** 1. Noise of stones crashing.

磄 **t'ang** 2. A bund, a dike.

磌 **t'ien** 2. The base of a pillar.

磓 **chui** 1. To pile up stones.

磋 **ts'o** 1. To rub and polish.

磁 **tz'ŭ 2.** Crockery, porcelain.

磒 **yün 3.** An aërolite.

11

磛 **ch'an 2.** A cliff, a steep ascent.

磬 **ch'ing 4.** Sonorous stones. *See page 569.*

磨 **mo 2.** To rub, to polish, to grind, a mill.

磢 **shuang 1.** Arsenic shale.

磚 **chuan 1.** A brick, a tile for paving.

磍 **hsia 4.** Cracked, a crevice, a split.

硜 **k'êng 1.** Rumbling noise.

磠 **lu 3.** Gravel, pebbles.

磟 **liu 4.** A stone roller.

磣 **ch'ên 3.** Sand, grit.

磧 **chi 2.** Rocky; desert.

磪 **ch'ui 1.** High, precipitous

12

磺 **huang 2.** Brimstone.

磯 **chi 1.** A rock.

磽 **ch'iao 1.** Stony soil.

磷 **lin 4.** To grind, to abrade.

磰 **shan 3.** White clay, used for porcelain.

磴 **têng 4.** A ledge, stone steps.

磾 **tan 1.** Sulphate of iron.

13 &

礐 **hsiao 2.** Rocks, hill.

礜 **yü 4.** A white ore of arsenic.

礎 **ch'u 3.** Pedestal.

礓 **chiang 1.** Gravel, small stones.

礞 **mêng 2.** The mica.

礙 **ai 4.** To hinder, to oppose, obstacle.

礮 **p'ao 4.** A cannon, great guns.

礬 **fan 2.** Sulphates, alum, etc.

礥 **hsien 2.** Difficult, hard.

礦 **kung 3.** A mine.

礪 **li 4.** A whetstone.

礱 **lung 2.** To sharpen, to grind.

礵 **chuang 1.** The arsenic shale.

礶 **kuan 4.** A jar, a mug.

Rad. 113

示 礻

See Lesson 3 D.

示 **shih 4.** To reveal, to teach.

礼 **li 3.** Ceremony, rite, courtesy, offerings.

礽 **jêng 2.** Happiness.

祁 **ch'i 2.** Great, vast, much, many.

社 **shê 4.** A local Genius, its mound, a community.

祀 **ssŭ 4** To sacrifice.

礿 **yao 4.** A sacrifice to the ancestors.

祉 **chih 3.** Happiness.

祅 **yao 1.** Supernatural sights and ominous prodigies.

祇 **ch'i 2.** The Genii of earth.

祈 **ch'i 2.** To pray.

5

祟 **sui 4.** Influence of malignous spirits, haunted.

祗 **chih 3.** To venerate, to cultivate, only, yet.

祩 **chu 4.** A stone tablet.

祝 **chu 4.** To pray, to supplicate, to celebrate.

祓 **fu 2.** To remove evil, to deprecate sickness.

祜 **hu 4.** Protection of heaven, favour.

祛 **ch'ü 1.** To expel, to avert, to disperse.

祕 **pi 4.** Secret, abstruse, mysterious.

神 **shên 2.** Soul, spirit, spiritual, manes, genii, natural powers, animal spirits, very.

祏 **shih 2.** A stone shrine to keep the ancestral tablet.

祖 **tsu 3.** Ancestors, the first, to begin, a model.

祚 **tso 4.** Felicity, favour.

祠 **tz'ŭ 2.** The ancestral hall of a family.

䄃 **yang 1.** A misfortune, a calamity.

祐 **yu 4.** Divine care and protection.

6

祡 **ch'ai 2.** Fagots burned to advertise heaven.

票 **p'iao 4.** A slip of paper, a warrant, a bank note, a ticket.

祭 **chi 4.** To sacrifice, to worship.

祣 **lü 3.** Sacrifice to heaven.

祥 **hsiang 2.** Felicitous, of good omen.

祧 **t'iao 1.** The ancestral shrine.

祫 **hsia 4.** A triennal sacrifice to the ancestors.

7-8

視 **shih 4.** To consider.

祳 **ch'ên 3.** Offering of raw meat.

禁 **chin 4** To forbid, to prohibit, to restrain, to keep off.

禬 **chà 4.** Sacrifice made to earth for the crops.
祺 **ch'i 2.** Prosperity.
祼 **kuan 4.** A libation.
祾 **ling 2.** A sacrifice at the Imperial tombs.

9

稟 **ping 3.** To warn, to announce, to receive, natural gifts.
祿 **lu 4.** Happiness, salary.
禂 **t'ao 2.** Luck, success.
禎 **chêng 1.** Lucky, propitious.
福 **fu 2.** Happiness, luck, blessings.
禊 **hsi 4.** A sacrifice offered to avert evils.
禍 **ho 4.** Calamity, adversity.
禖 **mei 2.** Sacrifice offered to obtain the birth of a son.
禘 **ti 4.** The great sacrifice to the remotest ancestor.
禓 **yang 2.** Wayside Genii.
禋 **yin 1.** To sacrifice devoutly.

10-11

禜 **jung 2.** Sacrifice in times of national calamity.
禡 **ma 4.** Sacrifice offered to obtain victory.
禛 **chêng 1.** Blessed, auspicious, good omen.
禦 **yü 4.** To withstand, to oppose.
禠 **li 2.** Good omens.

12 &

禧 **hsi 3.** Blessings, good luck.
禪 禫 **shan 4.** To sacrifice to the hills and fountains; to abdicate.
ch'an 2. Contemplation; meditation.

禬 **kuei 4.** To pray.
禮 **li 3.** Ceremony; etiquette; presents; worship.
禪 **shan 4.** To sacrifice to heaven. Imperial dignity.
禰 **ni 3.** Ancestral tablets.
禱 **tao 3.** To pray; to request.
禳 **jang 3.** To fast and pray in order to deprecate evil.
禶 **tsan 4.** To implore.

Rad. 114

内 禸

See Lesson 23 C.

内 **jou 2.** A footprint; a step.
禹 **yü 3.** The founder of the first Dynasty.
禺 **yü 2.** Spider-monkey.
离 **li 2.** A bogy; bright.
禽 **ch'in 2.** Birds.
禼 **lei 4.** A kind of ape, four to five feet high.

Rad. 115

禾 禾

See Lesson 121 A.

禾 **ho 2.** Grain.
秃 **l u 1.** A scald head.
秀 **hsiu 4.** Growing grain coming into ear; luxuriant; a licentiate.
私 **ssŭ 1.** Private; selfish; personal; partial.
利 **li 4.** The edge of a knife; sharp; happy; gains.
秉 **ping 3.** A handful of grain; to seize; to maintain.

委 **wei 3.** To send off; to reject; to delegate; a grievance.
季 **chi 4.** The youngest of brothers; tender, little; the least; a season.
和 **ho 2.** Harmony, concord; to unite; with.
秆 **kan 3.** The stalk of grain; straw.
秈 **hsien 1.** Common rice growing.
杓 **tiao 3.** The ripe ear of grain hanging down.
秄 **tzŭ 3.** To hoe up earth around plants.

4

香 **hsiang 1.** Fragrance.
秔 **kêng 1.** Rice which is not glutinous.
科 **k'o 1.** To measure, a degree, science.
秒 **miao 3.** The beard of grain; a second of time or of a degree.
秕 **pi 3.** Blasted or withered or unformed grain.
秋 **ch'iu 1.** Autumn; harvest. 6
秐 **yün 2.** To weed.

5

秦 **ch'in 2.** A fine kind of rice; a proper name.
秩 **chih 4.** Order, degree.
秤 **ch'êng 4.** To weigh.
柎 **fu 1.** Bran of rice.
秣 **mo 4.** Straw; fodder.
秘 **mi 4.** Secret, mysterious, divine.
秛 **p'i 1.** The rent on land paid by dividing the crop with the landlord.
秫 **shu 2.** Sorghum stalks, *shu-chieh*.
租 **tsu 1.** Tax in kind from fields; to lease.
秧 **yang 1.** Shoots, young plants.

6

移 i 2. To remove; to shift; to influence. to announce; a letter.

秸 chieh 1. Thatch.

稅 to 4. A stack; a heap.

7

程 ch'êng 2. A measure; a weight; a rule; a pattern; a limit; a period; to fix.

稀 hsi 1. Thin, scattered; separated; few; rare.

稈 kan 3. The stalk of millet; hay.

粳 ching 1. White rice.

稍 shao 3. A little; to diminish; slightly.

稅 shui 4. Duty on merchandise; taxes.

嵇 hsi 1. A mountain in Nganhui.

稊 t'i 2. Tares.

8

稟 lin 3. A granary; a grant from the public funds salary.

稇 k'un 3. Bundle of corn; sheaf.

稚 chih 4. Young, recent, delicate.

稙 chih 2. Grain first sown; the first crop.

稕 chun 4. A truss of hay or straw.

稔 jên 3. Ripe grain; a harvest; versed in.

稞 k'o 4. Grain.

稜 lêng 2. An edge a corner.

稠 ch'ou 2. Thick; dense.

稗 pai 4. Weeds, tares.

稡 tsui 4. To gather, to collect.

9

稱 ch'êng 1. To style.
ch'êng 4. To weigh.
ch'ên 4. To fit.

種 chung 3. A seed.
chung 4. To sow.

稭 chieh 1. Stalks; straw.

稯 tsung 1. A sheaf of grain; to collect.

10

稾 稿 kao 3. Straw; a sketch.

穀 ku 3. Millet.

稺 ch'u 2. Stalk; straw.

穅 huang 1. Grain not ripening.

稺 chih 4. Recent, delicate.

稽 chi 1. To examine; to bow the head.

稼 chia 1. Farming, *chuang-chia*.

稻 tao 4. Rice growing in the field.

稷 chi 2. Agriculture, crops.

11

穈 mei 2. A kind of millet.

穎 ying 3. A proper name.

穌 su 1. To revive.

穅 k'ang 1. Chaff; husks of grain.

穋 lu 4 Precious.

穆 mu 4. Imposing; to revere.

積 chi 1. To gather; to store up.

穗 tsung 3. A sheaf of grain.

12

穲 mei 3. Mildewed grain.

穉 chih 4. Young, delicate.

穗 sui 4. A head of grain; an ear; a spike.

穜 t'ung 2. Grain which is gathered last.

穚 chiao 1. The blooming of corn.

13

穡 shê 4. The harvest; to reap.

穟 sui 4. Ripening grain.

穥 yü 1. A good harvest.

穠 chan 4. A sheaf.

穦 tzŭ 1. Grain piled up.

穢 hui 4. Unclean; to defile.

14 &

穫 huo 1. To reap the crops, harvest.

穩 wên 3. Firm; safe; stable; grave, reserved.

穲 la 1. Empty; sterile.

穮 piao 1. To hoe fields.

穠 lung 2. To reap grain.

穰 jang 2. The culm of grain; abundant; prosperous.

穲 li 2. A good harvest.

穳 ts'uan 2. To stack.

Rad. 116

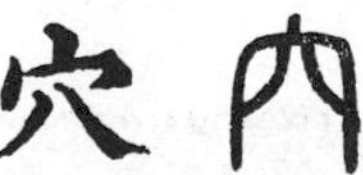

See Lesson 37 A.

穴 hsüeh 2. A cave, a den, a cavern.

穵 wa 1. To dig, to excavate.

究 **chiu 1.** To examine into, to search out.
穹 **ch'iung 2.** Lofty; high and vast as the sky; a vault.
帘 **lien 2.** A flag or sign.
空 **k'ung 1.** Empty, void.
k'ung 4. A space; blank.
穸 **hsi 4.** Death; burial.

4

窀 **chun 1.** A cave; to bury.
穿 **ch'uan 1.** To put on or through.
宏 **hung 2.** A vast hall, a mansion.
突 **t'u 4** Impetuous; sudden.
窃 **ch'ieh 4.** To steal.
窆 **pien 4.** To put a coffin into the grave.
穽 **ching 3.** A pit-fall; a hole.

5-6

窌 **chiao 4.** A cellar, a pit
窄 **chai 3.** Narrow, contracted.
窊 **wa 1.** Depression, low.
窈 **yao 3.** Obscure, deep, retired, tranquil, composed.
窅 **yao 3.** Hollow; obscure.
窒 **chih 4.** To stop up; to obstruct; stupid.
窓 **ch'uang 1.** A window.
窕 **t'iao 3.** Hidden, secret.

7-8

窗 **ch'uang 1.** A window.
窖 **chiao 4.** A cellar.
窘 **chün 3.** Afflicted; in distress.
窠 **wo 1.** A nest; a den.
窟 **k'u 1.** A cave; a hole.

9-10

窩 **wo 1.** A nest; a hole.
窨 **yin 3.** A vault.
窬 **yü 2.** A hole in a wall.
窪 **wa 1.** Low ground; a puddle; the fields.
窮 **ch'iung 2.** Exhausted: the end, limits, poor.
窯 **yao 2.** A kiln; a furnace.

11-12

窺 **k'uei 2.** To peep; to watch.
窿 **lung 2.** The vault of heaven; a hole.
窻 **ch'uang 1.** A window.
窵 **tiao 4.** Deep; cavernous.
窾 **k'uan 3.** Hollow, a joint.

13 &

竅 **ch'iao 4.** A hole; an orifice.
邃 **sui 4.** A deep apartment, concealed.
竄 **ts'uan 4.** To hide, to skulk, exile.
竆 **ch'iung 2.** Poor.
竇 **tou 4.** A hole, a drain, deep.
竉 **lung 3.** A hole, a cave.
竈 **tsao 4.** A cooking-stove, a furnace.
竊 **ch'ieh 4.** To steal, to pilfer, clandestine, I, my.

Rad. 117

See Lesson 60 H.

立 **li 4.** To stand erect, to found, presently.

妾 **ch'ieh 4.** A concubine.
竑 **hung 2.** To measure, to estimate.
音 **yin 1.** A sound.
奇 **ch'i 2.** Extraordinary, new, strange.
站 **chan 4.** To stand up, to stop, a stage.
竚 **chu 4.** To hope and wait.
竜 **lung 2.** A dragon, to issue forth.
竝 **ping 4.** Together.
章 **chang 1.** A section, a document, an essay, elegant, rule, law, to manifest.
竟 **ching 4.** To search, to finish, after all, finally.
翊 **i 4.** To help.
竦 **sung 3.** Fear, terror.
竢 **ssŭ 4.** To wait upon, until.
童 **t'ung 2.** A boy under 15 years and unmarried, a bachelor, virginity.
竣 **tsun 4.** To stop, to complete.
意 **i 4.** A thought, inclination, sentiment.
竪 **shu 4.** Upright, perpendicular, to erect
靖 **ching 4.** Order, peace, quiet.
竭 **chieh 2.** To exhaust, the utmost, finished.
端 **tuan 1.** A beginning, an end, correct, proper; to serve a meal.
競 **ching 4.** Strong, envious, to struggle, to be quarrelsome.

Rad. 118

See Lesson 77 B

竹 **chu 2.** Bamboo.

竺 **chu 4.** The common name of India.

竿 **kan 1.** Staff, cane, pole, handle.

竽 **yü 2.** A reed organ of 36 tubes.

4

笊 **chao 4.** A bamboo skimmer.

笐 **hang 1.** Bamboo poles.

笏 **hu 1.** A tablet.

笄 **chi 1.** A hairpin, marriageable.

笈 **chi 2.** A box, a satchel.

笆 **pa 1.** Hedge, a fence.

笓 **pi 4.** Fine comb.

笑 **hsiao 4.** To laugh, to be pleased, to ridicule.

笋 **sun 3.** Bamboo sprouts.

笹 **tun 4.** A round bin.

5

笞 **ch'ih 1.** To flog.

笁 **chu 4.** The nuts or pegs of a lute.

符 **fu 2.** A deed in two pieces, to match, to agree with, a spell.

笰 **fu 2.** A bamboo screen..

笱 **kou 3.** A trap.

笳 **chia 1.** A whistle.

笴 **k'o 3.** The shaft of an arrow.

笻 **ch'iung 2.** A kind of crooked dulcimer.

笘 **k'u 3.** A trap for catching fish.

笠 **li 4.** A hat of straw.

笭 **ling 2.** A bamboo tray.

笢 **min 3.** A hair brush.

笨 **pên 4.** Stupid, dull of apprehension.

笙 **shêng 1.** A Pandean pipe, composed of 13 dissimilar reeds.

笥 **ssŭ 4.** A hamper.

笪 **tan 4.** A round basket.

第 **ti 4.** Order, series, a section, but, however.

笤 **t'iao 2.** A broom.

笛 **ti 2.** A flute.

笮 **chai 3.** Narrow.

6

筑 **chu 2.** A kind of zither.

筏 **fa 2.** A bamboo raft.

筓 **chi 1.** A hairpin, to do up the hair, marriageable.

筊 **chiao 3.** A rope made of bamboo splints.

筋 **chin 1.** The tendons, strong.

筁 **ch'ü. 4** A bamboo frame, to rear silkworms.

筐 **k'uang 1.** A basket.

筆 **pei 3.** A pencil.

筍 **sun 3.** Edible bamboo sprouts.

答 **ta 2** To answer.

等 **têng 3.** To wait, a class, a rank, a sort, a sign of the plural.

筒 **t'ung 2.** A tube, a pipe.

策 **ch'ai 4** A tablet, a diploma, a ferule, a stratagem.

筌 **ch'üan 2.** A bamboo trap.

筄 **yao 4.** Bamboo laths.

7

筯 **chu 4.** Chopsticks.

筧 **chien 5.** A bamboo pipe.

筥 **chü 3.** A basket.

筦 **kuan 3.** A clarinet.

筤 **lang 2.** Young bamboos.

筢 **p'a 2.** Flower, to flourish.

筲 **shao 1.** A bucket.

筮 **shih 4.** To divine with stems of the millfoil.

筭 **suan 4.** To estimate, to plan, to calculate.

筩 **t'ung 3.** A tube, a pipe.

筴 **chia 1.** Pincers, to pinch.

筷 **k'uai 4.** Chopsticks.

筠 **yün 2.** Bamboo skin.

8

箚 **cha 2.** To prick, to puncture, to stitch in.

箏 **chêng 1.** A paper kite.

䈇 **chao 4.** A cover.

箒 **chou 3. ch'u 4** A broom.

箙 **fu 2.** A quiver.

筕 **hang 4.** Bamboo poles on which clothes are hung.

箕 **chi 1.** A proper name. **ch'i 2.** A winnowing basket, a basket for refuse.

箝 **ch'ien 2.** Tweezers, a gag.

箇 **ko 4.** The culm of the bamboo, a classifier, an individual

箍 **ku 1.** A circlet, to hoop, to draw tight

管 **kuan 3.** A reed, a tube, a flute, to regulate, to govern.

箄 **pei 1.** A fish-trap.

箔 **pao 4.** A coarse mat.

節 **chieh 2.** An article, a joint, a time, a term, temperance.

箑 **chieh 2.** A fan, a running hand,

算 **süan 4.** To cypher, to estimate, to be regarded as, to be.

箋 **chien 1.** A bamboo tablet, note-paper, a letter.

筵 **yen 2** A bamboo mat, a feast, a banquet.

箐 **ch'ien 4.** Fine bamboos, a basket.

9

箴 **chên 1.** A needle, to probe, to warn.

箸 **chu 4.** Chopsticks.

箠 **ch'ui 2.** A rod, to beat.

範 **fan 4.** A law, a rule, a pattern.

箶 **hu 2.** A quiver.

篁 **huang 2.** A hard bamboo.

篛 **jo 4.** A variety of bamboo.

篋 **ch'ieh 4.** A casket.

箯 **pien 1.** A bamboo sledge.

篇 **p'ien 1.** A slip of bamboo, a leaf of a book, an essay.

箱 **hsiang 1.** A box, a chest.

箭 **chien 4.** An arrow.

[illegible] **ch'in 4.** An instrument used to draw lines.

10

篡 **ch'uan 4.** Rebellion, an usurpation.

篚 **fei 3.** A bamboo basket.

篧 **ho 4.** A weir.

篙 **kao 1.** A pole, a rod.

篝 **kou 1.** A bamboo frame.

篦 **pi 4.** A comb, to comb.

篩 **shai 1.** A sieve, to sieve, to strain.

篆 **chuan 4.** The ancient Chinese characters.

築 **chu 2.** To beat down, to ram down, to build.

[illegible] **t'a 4.** A window, one sash.

篤 **tu 3.** A sure horse, sincere, honest, firm, generous; to augment.

11

[illegible] **chin 1.** A large variety of bamboo.

簋 **kui 3.** A basket.

簍 **lou 3.** A basket.

篱 **li 2.** A ladle.

簏 **lu 4.** A basket.

篾 **mieh 4.** Splints.

篷 **p'êng 2.** A sail.

篳 **pi 4.** A fence.

箳 **p'ing 2.** A bamboo screen.

簁 **shai 1.** A sieve, a riddle, to sift.

篠 **hsiao 3.** Small bamboos.

簌 **su 4.** A fine sieve.

篲 **hui 4.** A broom.

篴 **ti 2.** A flute.

篼 **tou 1.** A muzzle.

簀 **chai 4.** A mat, fibres.

[illegible] **chiang 3.** Splinters, fibres.

簇 **ts'u 4.** A frame, a crowd.

12

簠 **fu 3.** A sort of basket.

簧 **huang 2.** A reed, a spring.

簡 **chien 3.** A slip of bamboo, a tablet, documents, records, to arrange, to abridge, rude.

簣 **k'uei 4.** A basket.

簝 **liao 2.** A bamboo tray.

簛 **shai 1.** A sieve, to sift, to strain.

簨 **hsüan 3.** A prop.

簞 **tan 1.** A basket.

簜 **tang 4.** A large kind of bamboo.

簦 **têng 1.** An umbrella.

簪 **tsan 1.** A hair-pin.

[illegible] **ts'ui 4.** A broom.

13

簾 **lien 2.** A door-screen, a blind.

簸 **po 4.** A winnowing-fan, to shake grain.

簿 **pu 4.** A register, a tablet, a record.

簫 **hsiao 1.** A flageolet.

簺 **sai 1.** A barrage.

簹 **tang 1.** A kind of knotted bamboo.

簽 **ch'ien 1.** Slips, to subscribe.

簷 **yen 2.** End of the eaves.

14

籌 **ch'ou 2.** To calculate, a lot, a ticket.

籄 **k'uei 4.** A basket.

籃 **lan 2.** A basket.

籋 **mi 2.** Splinters, fibres.

籕 **chou 4.** A proper name. Ancient characters.

籍 **chi 2.** A list, a register, one's original family seat.

纂 **tsuan 3.** A compilation, to arrange.

15 &

籀 **chou 4.** Ancient characters.

籐 **t'êng 2.** Lianas, the rattan.

籚 **lu 2.** A large basket.

籙 **lu 4.** A map, a chart, a list.

籠 **lung 2.** A cage. To monopolise.

籞 **yü 4.** Pisciculture.
籧 **ch'ü 2.** Coarse bamboo matting.
籤 **ch'ien 1.** A slip, a warrant, a fish, a peg.
籥 **yao 4.** A flute.
籩 **pien 1.** A flat basket.
籬 **li 2.** A hedge.
籮 **lo 2.** Deep baskets.
籪 **tuan 4.** A weir.
籰 **kuo 4.** A reel.
籢 **yen 2.** A fence.
籯 **ying 2.** A strong-box, a safe.
籲 **yü 4.** Music, to invoke, to implore.

Rad. 119

米 米

See Lesson 122 A.

米 **mi 3.** Grains of rice or millet.
籽 **tzŭ 3.** Seeds of cereals.

4-5

粃 **shên 1.** Gruel.
粉 **fên 3.** Powder, face powder, plaster.
粃 **pi 3.** Ears void of grain.
粆 **sha 4.** Cassonade.
料 **liao 4.** To consider, to calculate, matter, grain, glass.
敉 **mi 3** To caress, to console.
粒 **li 4.** A grain, a kernel.
粘 **chan 1.** To paste up.
粗 **ts'u 1.** Rough, rude, vulgar, vile.

6-7

粥 **chou 1.** Gruel, congee, porridge.
粧 **chuang 1.** To adorn, to rouge, to feign, to gloss.
粦 **lin 2.** Ignis fatuus.
粟 **su 4.** Grain, food.
粢 **tzŭ 1.** Common millet.
粵 **yüeh 4.** To examine, initial particle. Canton.
粳 **ching 1.** Rice which is not glutinous.
粮 **liang 2.** Grain, food.
粖 **mei 2.** Leaven, ferments.
粰 **po 4.** The chaff of rice.
粱 **liang 2.** Sorghum.
粲 **ts'an 4.** White rice; aliments, food.

8

粸 **ch'i 2.** Sweet cakes.
粿 **kuo 3.** Rice cakes.
粹 **ts'ui 4.** Pure, unmixed.
粷 **ch'i 4.** Flour made from rice.
精 **ching 1.** The essential part, essence, spirit, semen, skill.
粽 **tsung 4.** Dumplings.

9-10

糇 **hou 2.** Dry provisions.
糊 **hu 2.** Paste, to paste, foolish, muddled.
糅 **jou 4.** Mixed together.
糉 **tsung 4.** Dumplings made with rice.
穀 **ku 3.** Grain, corn.
糗 **hsiu 3.** Grains, food.

糙 **chui 1.** To stick, to adhere.
糒 **pi 4.** Dried rations.
糕 **kao 1.** Cakes, pastry.
糖 **t'ang 2.** Sugar.

11

糲 **li 2.** Slimy, sticky.
糙 **ts'ao 1.** Coarse paddy, inferior.
糠 **k'ang 1.** Chaff or skin of grain.
糨 **chiang 4.** Starch, paste.
糢 **ma 1. mo 1.** Confused.
糝 **san 3.** Rice and meat porridge, to mix.
糰 **t'uan 2.** Paste.
糟 **tsao 1.** Sediment, dregs, spoilt, rotten.
糞 **fên 4.** Ordure.
糜 **mi 2.** Reduced to pulp, to decompose.
漿 **chiang 1.** Broth, congee

12 &

糦 **hsi 1.** Food, victuals.
糧 **liang 2.** Rations, food, grain.
糤 **san 3.** Biscuits.
糰 **t'uan 2.** Dumplings.
糲 **li 4.** Coarse, husks.
糷 **la 1.** Coarse, vile.
纕 **jang 4.** To mix.
䊵 **lüan 4.** Thick congee.
糴 **ti 2.** To buy grain.
糶 **t'iao 4.** To sell grain.

Rad. 120

See Lesson 92 A.

糸 **ssŭ 1.** Threads, floss.

系 **hsi 1.** Connection, party, system, succession, related to.

糾 糺 **chiu 1.** To twist, to involve.

紂 **chou 4.** Crupper of harness. An infamous king.

紇 **ko 1.** A knot.

紅 **hung 2.** Red.

紉 **jên 4.** To thread (a needle).

紆 **kan 4.** To smooth down.

𥾛 **k'ou 4.** A knot.

紀 **chi 4.** Course, order, to regulate, to arrange, to note down.

約 **yao 4.** To bind, to compel, to be agreed about, a treatise, a convention, to weigh, poverty, about.

紆 **yü 1** A tie, to bind.

4

紊 **wên 4.** Raveled, tangled, to embroil.

索 **so 3.** Strings, a cord, reins, to search into.

素 **su 4.** Pure white silk, simple, coarse, common, lean.

紛 **fên 1.** Disorder, confusion, multitude, ill-assorted.

紡 **fang 3.** To spin, to reel, to twist.

級 **chi 2.** Threads, steps, grades.

納 **na 4.** To hand up, to enter, to collect, to possess, to keep.

紐 **niu 3.** A knot, to tie.

紗 **sha 1.** Crape, gauze.

紓 **shu 1.** Remiss, to relax.

純 **ch'un 2.** Pure, unmixed, simple.

紙 **chih 3.** Paper.

紖 **yin 3.** Leashes, traces.

紞 **tan 3.** Tassels, pendents.

紏 **t'ou 3.** Yellow silk.

紋 **wên 2.** Lines, traces.

紜 **yün 2.** Confused, mixed up.

5

累 **lei 3.** To tie, to bind.
lei 4. To implicate in, to embarrass.

紮 **cha 1.** To bind up, to tie together, a frame.

紾 **chên 3.** To twist, to bind.

紬 **ch'ou 2.** Pongee.

紵 **chu 4.** China-grass.

絀 **ch'u 1.** To stitch coarsely, to baste.

終 **chung 1.** The end, the termination, to the last, the utmost.

紱 **fu 3.** A sash.

絃 **hsien 2.** Strings of a lute.

紺 **kan 4.** A purple colour.

絇 **chü 4.** A shoe-string.

緡 **min 2.** To fish.

絆 **pan 4.** To fetter, to trip, a restraint.

紳 **shên 1.** A large girdle, those who wear it, the gentry.

紹 **shao 4.** To join, to tie together, relation, succession.

絁 **shih 1.** Coarse thread for weaving.

細 **hsi 4.** Fine, thin, slender.

紲 **hsieh 4.** To fasten, a halter.

紽 **t'o 2.** A hank of silk.

組 **tsu 3.** A band, an office.

6

紫 **tzŭ 3.** Purple, a dark red brown.

絜 **hsieh 2.** To rule, to settle, coercition.

絮 **hsü 4.** Floss, cotton, fleecy, to drivel, garrulity.

絍 **jên 4.** To thread (a needle).

絨 **jung 2.** Velvet.

絳 **chiang 4.** Bright red colour, scarlet.

絞 **chiao 3.** To strangle.

結 **chieh 1.** A knot, to tie, fixed, firm, constant.

給 **chi 3.** To give, the preposition to, to suffice.
kei 3. To give.

絙 **hêng 2.** A rope.

絖 **kuang 4.** Floss not spun.

絡 **lao 4.** Thread, fibres.

絥 **fu 2.** A curtain-band.

綁 **pang 3.** To tie, to bind.

絏 **hsieh 4.** To tie up.

絢 **hsüan 4.** Variegated.

絲 **ssŭ 1.** Silk, gloss, thread.

絰 **tieh 2.** Hempen cloth worn as mourning.

統 **t'ung 3.** The end, a beginning, all, collectively, to rule, a system.

絶 **chüeh 2.** To sever, to destroy, very.

7

絛 **t'ao 1.** Loop, fringes.

絺 **ch'ih 1.** Fine linen.

綆 **kêng 3.** A well-rope.

絺 **hsi** 4. Thin linen.

經 **ching** 1. Warp in a loom, veins or arteries, meridians of longitude, to pass through, to regulate, canonical, already.

絿 **ch'iu** 2. Urgent, pressing.

絹 **chüan** 4. Silk-gauze.

綑 **k'un** 3. To band.

綀 **shu** 1. Sackcloth.

絲 **ssŭ** 1. Silk. Floss.

綃 **hsiao** 1. Raw silk.

綉 **hsiu** 4. To embroider.

綏 **sui** 1. A loop.

8

緊 **chin** 4. To bind tight, urgent, important.

綮 **ch'i** 3. A banner, a signal flag.

綦 **ch'i** 2. A dark colour; very.

綢 **ch'ou** 2. Silk cloth.

綽 **ch'ou** 4. Gentle; ample; liberal, generous.

綴 **chui** 4. To baste, to sew.

緋 **fei** 1. Dark red.

綱 **kang** 1. Rope of a net; regulation; law.

綖 **yen** 2. Fringes.

綻 **chan** 4. An opened seam in a garment; cracked; to rip.

綺 **ch'i** 3. Variegated silk.

綶 **kuo** 3. To bandage.

綟 **li** 4. A dark dull green.

綡 **liang** 2. Strings, bands.

綾 **ling** 2 Figured silk cloth. Damask.

綹 **liu** 3. A skein of silk.

綸 **lun** 2. To wind; to adjust; to classify.

綿 **mien** 2. Soft; downy; cotton; continuous.

綛 **nien** 4. A tow-rope.

綳 **pêng** 1. To bind.

絣 **pêng** 1. To join; to connect.

綬 **shou** 4. Band of a seal; an office.

綫 **hsien** 4 Thread.

緆 **i** 4. Fringe.

綯 **t'ao** 2. A cord; a band; to tie.

綵 **ts'ai** 3. Coloured, variegated.

緅 **chou** 1. Pink colour.

緀 **ch'i** 1. Ornamented; elegant.

緁 **chieh** 1. To join; to braid.

綜 **tsung** 4. The threads of a texture; to arrange in order; to gather up.

緇 **tzŭ** 1. Black silk; dark.

綰 **wan** 3. To bind.

網 **wang** 3. A net; a web.

維 **wei** 2. To tie; to hold fast; a rule; a law; an initial particle.

緎 **yü** 4. A seam.

9

緜 **mien** 2. Soft; floss; cotton.

緩 **huan** 3. Slow; tardy; lax; gradually; to delay.

緱 **kou** 1. A sword-knot.

緘 **chien** 1. To bind up; to close.

練 **lien** 4. To boil raw silk to soften it; to drill in; to select.

綠 **lü** 4. Green.

緲 **miao** 3. Minute; subtle, indistinct.

緥 **pao** 3. Swaddling-clothes.

編 **pien** 1. To tress, to dispose, to compose.

緶 **pien** 3. To hem.

緗 **hsiang** 1 A light yellow colour.

緤 **hsieh** 4. To fasten with cords.

線 **hsien** 4. Thread.

緧 **ch'iu** 1. A crupper.

緒 **hsü** 4 A skein of thread; continuation; connection; the clue.

緦 **ssŭ** 1. Coarse cotton cloth for mourning.

緧 **ch'a** 1. To sew and hem.

締 **ti** 4. A knot; close; connection.

緻 **chih** 4. To mend garments; delicate, fine; a view.

緞 **tuan** 4. Satin.

緝 **ch'i** 1. To twist; to join; to pursue; to catch.

緯 **wei** 3. The woof of a web; latitude; tassels.

10

縈 **jung** 2. To bind round; to reel; a circuit.

縢 **t'êng** 2. To bind; to fasten; a band; a cord.

縣 **hsien** 4. A prefecture; district.

縛 **fu** 2. To tie up.

縊 **i** 4. To hang; to strangle.

縟 **ju** 4. Adorned, gay; elegant.

縞 **kao** 3. Plain undyed silk; simple.

縑 **chien** 1. Taffeta.

縎 **ku** 2. Tangled; knotted.

縍 **pang** 3 To bind.

緣 **yen** 2. **yüan** 2. To bind; to harmonise; the cause; the motive; fortune.

縒 **ta** 2 A knot.

縚 **t'ao** 1. A cord; a band.

縐 **chou 4.** Crape; wrinkled.
縉 **chin 4.** A light red, carnation colour.
縗 **ts'ui 1.** Mourning dress
縓 **ts'uan 1.** Reddish yellow, orange colour.
縕 **yün 4.** Tow; very; a coarse cloth.

11

繁 **fan 2.** Luxuriant; abundant; numerous.
縻 **mei 2.** To bind; to tie.
繇 **yu 2.** Cause; means; consequently.
縫 **fêng 2.** To sew; to stitch.
fêng 4. A crack, a split.
縳 **chuan 4.** To bundle; to enwrap.
繈 **chiang 3.** Swaddling-clothes.
縴 **ch'ien 4.** A tow-rope.
縲 **lei 3.** To bind with ropes.
縭 **li 2.** A sash; a girdle.
縷 **lü 3.** Tow, to spin; to state in detail.
繆 **miao 4.** A proper name.
niu 4. To bind; to join.
繅 **sao 1.** To reel silk from cocoons.
縮 **so 1.** To draw back; to shorten; to contract.
緉 **shuang 3** Straps which ties the shoes.
縰 **hsi 3.** A hair-net.
繀 **sui 4.** A spinning-wheel.
縪 **tai 4.** A waistband.
績 **chi 1.** To spin; to act; meritorious service; an affair.
縱 **tsung 4.** A warp; to be lax; to yield to; to let go; although, even if.
總 **tsung 3.** To unite; to sum up to comprise; to manage.
縯 **yin 4.** To sew.

12

織 **chih 1.** To weave.
繙 **fan 1** To display; to interpret.
繞 **jao 3.** To wind round; to surround; to avoid.
繎 **jan 2.** Red silk.
繚 **liao 2.** To bind; to wrap.
繖 **san 3.** A parasol; an umbrella.
繕 **shan 4.** To write out; to copy.
繡 **hsiu 4.** To embroider.
繐 **sui 4.** Fine cloth; tassels, fringes.
繒 **tsêng 1** Silken fabrics.
繑 **chiao 1.** Hempen tow.
繘 **yü 4.** A well-rope.

13

繫 **hsi 4.** To tie to fasten; connexion, relation.
繴 **pi 4.** A fowler's snares.
繭 **chien 3.** The cocoon of the silkworm.
繨 **ta 2.** A knot.
繯 **huan 2.** Silk-cord, a noose; to hang.
繪 **hui 4.** To draw; to sketch; to embroider; to adorn.
繳 **chiao 3.** A thread tied to an arrow; to hand over; to surrender.
繮 **kang 1.** A tether.
繩 **shêng 2.** A cord; a line; to tie; to restrain.
繸 **sui 4.** Tassels, tufts.
繹 **i 4.** To unravel; to reel; to develop; continuous; unceasing.

14 &

纂 **tsuan 3.** To collect; to compile; a digest.
辮 **pien 4.** To plait, to braid; a cue.
纆 **mêng 2.** Tangled, mixed.
繼 **chi 4.** To continue; to succeed; adoption.
纍 **lei 2.** To creep; to cling to.
纏 **ch'an 2.** To bind up; to wrap; to bandage.
續 **hsü 4.** To join on; to add; to succeed to.
纑 **lu 2** Hempen thread.
罽 **chi 4.** A persian carpet.
纖 **hsien 1.** Fine, delicate; small; atom-like.
纔 **ts'ai 2.** A adverb of time, near, at hand, presently.
纓 **ying 1** Tassels, tufts or fringes.
纚 **li 2.** A rope; a cable.
纘 **tsuan 2.** To tie things together; to carry on.
纜 **lan 3.** A rope, a hawser.
纛 **tu 1.** A banner.

Rad. 121

缶 

See Lesson 130 C.

缶 **fao 3.** Earthenware vessels; vases.
缸 **kang 1.** A jar with bulging sides and wide mouth.
缻 **fao 3.** Earthenware vessels.
缺 **ch'üeh 1.** Broken, defective, a want, a deficiency; an official vacancy.
缾 **p'ing 2.** A bottle.

銚 **tiao 3.** A boiler.

缸 **kang 1.** An earthen jar.

𦉜 **ch'a 3.** A postherd.

罃 **ying 1.** An earthen-ware jar.

罅 **hsia 4.** A crevice; a leak; a crack.

罄 **ch'ing 4.** Empty; exhausted; all; everything.

罈 **t'an 2.** An earthen-ware jar with narrow mouth.

罇 **tsun 1.** A vase.

罋 **wêng 4.** A large earthern jar.

罍 **lei 2.** A sacrificial vessel.

罏 **lu 2.** A wine jar.

罐 **kuan 4.** A mug.

Rad. 122

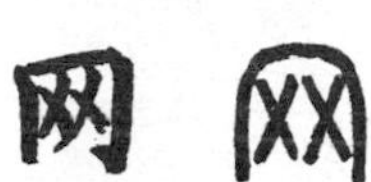

See Lesson 39 C.

网 **wang 3.** A net; to entrap.

罕 **han 3.** Rare, scarce, unfrequent.

罔 **wang 3.** A net; not; without.

罘 **fu 2.** A net.

罡 **kang 1.** The four stars which form the bowl of the Dipper; the four guardians in Buddhist temples.

罟 **ku 3.** A net; a drag-net; involved.

罣 **kua 4.** Obstacle; cares.

眾 **chung 4.** All.

罦 **fu 2.** A net; a snare.

詈 **li 4.** To scold about; to rail at.

罥 **chüan 1.** A net.

買 **mai 3.** To buy.

罤 **t'i 2.** A net for catching rabbits.

罩 **chao 4.** A basket for snaring fish; to catch; to cover.

置 **chih 4.** To arrange; to lay out; to govern.

罧 **shên 1.** A net to catch wild animals.

蜀 **shu 3.** Ssŭch'uan.

罪 **tsui 4.** A crime; a sin; punishment.

罭 **yü 4.** A drag-net with a fine mesh.

罰 **fa 2.** A fault; a crime; a fine; to punish.

署 **shu 3.** A public court; a tribunal; to appoint to an office; temporary; to write.

罶 **liu 3.** A fish-trap.

罵 **ma 4.** To curse, to revile.

罷 **pa 4.** To stop, to finish, to resign, a final or imperative particle, be off.

罹 **li 2.** Sorrow, grief, to suffer, to incur.

䍡 **lu 4.** A net to catch deer.

罿 **t'ung 2.** Snares to catch birds.

罽 **chi 4.** A fishing-net.

罾 **tsêng 1.** A drag-net.

羂 **chüan 4.** To entangle, to catch.

羅 **lo 2.** A spring-net, a sieve, to spread out, to bolt, to bestow, humpbacked.

羆 **p'i 2.** A species of bear, high and strong.

䍤 **chi 3.** To squeeze out, to strain out.

羇 **chi 1.** An inn, to lodge.

羈 **chi 1.** Trammels, to trammel.

䍦 **li 2.** A veil.

羉 **luan 2.** A net for catching small animals.

Rad. 123

羊 羊

See Lesson 103 A.

羊 **yang 2.** A sheep or goat.

羋 **mei 2.** The bleating of a sheep.

羌 羗 **ch'iang 1.** Shepherd nomads of the West.

姜 **chiang 1.** A proper name.

美 **mei 3.** Delicious, beautiful, well, to commend.

羑 **yu 3.** Name of a place.

差 **ch'a 1.** To err, to miss the mark, a fault.
ch'ai 1. To commission, a delegate.

羒 **fên 2.** A ram.

羔 **kao 1.** A lamb, a kid.

恙 **yang 4.** Low-spirited, sickness.

羖 **ku 3.** A ram er ewe.

羕 **yang 4.** A rising of water.

盖 **kai 4.** To cover, etc.

羜 **chu 4.** A lamb.

𦍩 **ku 3.** An ewe.

羚 **ling 2.** A mufflon.

羞 **hsiu 1.** Viands, delicacies, an offering, to bring forward, to feel ashamed, to blush.

羝 **ti 1.** A ram or buck.

着 **chao 2.** To cause, to send, to put on, a preposition, a suffix.

善 **shan 4.** Good, to agree.

翔 **hsiang 2.** To soar, to flutter about.

義 **i 4.** Duty, right, loyal, idea, meaning, purport, common, free, adopted, justice.

羣 群 **ch'ün 2.** A flock, a herd, a crowd, a company.

羨 **hsien 4.** To like, to covet, to exceed, surplus, remaining.

⿰羊戔 **chan 4.** A sheep-pen.

羹 **kêng 1.** A thick broth.

養 **yang 3.** To feed, to rear.

羯 **chieh 2.** A gelded ram.

羬 **hsien 2.** The nylgau.

羱 **yüan 2.** The argali.

羲 **hsi 1.** A proper name.

羵 **fên 2.** The Genius of pastures.

⿰羊韋 羶 **shan 1.** Rank-smelling, stinking:

⿰羊童 **t'ung 2.** A young ram.

⿰羊僉 **chien 3.** A goat.

羸 **lei 2** Lean, thin, emaciated, to upset.

羼 **ch'an 3.** A herd, a multitude, a rout.

Rad. 124

羽

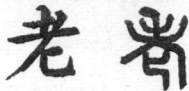

See Lesson 62 E.

羽 **yü 3.** Wings, feathers.

羿 **i 4.** A proper name.

羾 **kung 4.** To fly till, to attain.

翅 翍 **ch'ih 4.** A wing, a fin.

翀 **ch'ung 1,** To fly up, to mount up.

翂 **fên 1.** To start flying.

翃 **hung 2.** To swarm around.

⿱日羽 **t'a 4,** Wandering birds flying together.

翁 **wêng 1.** An old man, venerable sir.

翑 **chü 3.** Crooked plumes.

翏 **liao 4.** Flying high, soaring.

翎 **ling 2.** Long tail feathers.

習 **hsi 2.** To practise, a custom, a usage.

翌 **i 4.** To-morrow.

翊 **i 4.** To assist.

翕 **hsi 4.** To unite, together, all.

翔 **hsiang 2.** To hover over, to roam, to flutter.

翡 **fei 3.** A kingfisher; blue.

翣 **sha 4.** A flabellum.

翟 **ti 2.** The Tartar pheasant.

翠 **ts'ui 4.** The kingfisher; blue.

翥 **chu 3.** To fly up.

翬 **hui 1.** To fly, as a pheasant does.

翦 **chien 3.** To cut, scissors.

翪 **tsung 1.** Uneven flight.

翫 **wan 4.** To practise, drilling.

翰 **han 4.** A pencil, the academy of old.

翯 **hao 4.** White plumage.

翮 **ko 4.** A quill.

翳 **i 1.** To screen, leucoma.

翼 **i 4.** The wings of a bird, to join, to aid.

翻 **fan 1.** To come back, to turn over, to modify, action and reaction, alternatives.

翹 **ch'iao 2.** Tail-feathers, to raise, to desire.

⿰喬羽 **ch'iao 2.** To fly downwards.

耀 **yao 4.** To illumine, bright, glorious, honour.

Rad. 125

老

See Lesson 30 E.

老 **lao 3.** Old, to become old.

考 **k'ao 3.** Aged, longevity, ancestors, to examine, to build, to make.

者 **chê 3.** A final particle, a suffix.

耆 **ch'i 2.** A man of sixty, aged.

耄 **mao 4.** A man of seventy.

耇 **kou 3.** Senile, decrepit, drivelling.

耋 **tieh 2.** Old, infirm.

Rad. 126

而

See Lesson 164 A.

而 **erh 2.** The whiskers, a copula, and, also, together, disjunctive conjunction, still, yet, an initial or final particle.

耐 **nai 4.** To endure, to suffer, patient, to be able.

耏 **nai 4.** Beard, to shave.

耎 **juan 3.** Soft, weak, pliable.

耍 **shua 3.** To handle, to play.

耑 **chuan 1.** Rootlets, the spring or cause of anything.

Rad. 127

See Lesson 120 E.

耒 **lei 3.** A harrow.

耖 ch'ao 4. To harrow after ploughing.

耗 hao 4. To use, to spend, to waste.

耕 ching 1. To cultivate, plough and harrow.

耙 pa 4. To harrow.

耘 yün 2. To weed.

耞 chia 1. A flail.

耜 ssŭ 4. A spade.

耡 ch'u 2. To till.

耤 chi 2. The Emperor's field.

⿰耒甾 tzŭ 1. To plough.

耦 ou 3. Two furrows, a pair, a mate.

⿰耒㚇 tsung 1. To sow seed without first ploughing the ground.

耩 chiang 3. To sow.

耨 nou 4. A hoe, to hoe.

⿰耒員 yün 2. To weed.

耬 lou 3. A sowing-machine.

耰 yu 1. To cover in seed.

Rad. 128

耳

See Lesson 145 A.

耳 erh 3. The ear, a handle, a final particle.

耴 chê 4. Hanging ears.

取 ch'ü 3. To seize.

刵 erh 4. To cut the ears.

耵 ting 3. Ear-wax.

耶 yeh 2. A final particle.

耷 ta 1. Great ears, hanging, trailing.

咠 ch'i 1. To blame.

茸 jung 2. Thick, dense.

恥 耻 ch'ih 3. Shame, to be ashamed, to make ashamed of.

耾 hung 2. A rumbling sound.

毦 erh 4. Tufts.

耿 kêng 3. Bright, constant, virtuous.

耽 ch'ên 2, Pleasure.

聃 tan 1. The name of *Lao-tzŭ*.

聊 liao 2. To depend on, inclined to, to help, a little.

聆 ling 2. To hear, to listen, to obey.

聒 k'uo 4. Noise of talking, clamour, hubbub.

聘 p'in 4. To enquire about, to invite by presents, to engage, to betroth.

聖 shêng 4. Wise, perfect, holy.

聝 kuo 4. To cut off the ears of slain foes.

聚 chü 4. To meet, to gather, collection.

聞 wên 2. To hear, to smell, to state.

⿰耳秋 chiu 1. A singing in the ears.

聯 lien 2. Connected, united, to combine with, to assemble.

聱 ao 2. Refusing to hear, a bad character

聲 shêng 1. Sound'music, voice, accent, tone, to declare, fame.

聳 sung 3. To raise, to excite, lofty, high.

聰 ts'ung 1. Quick of apprehension ; clever.

職 chih 2. The duties of office, a tribute, principally.

聶 nieh 4. To whisper, to plot.

聵 k'uei 4. Deaf.

⿰耳當 tang 1. Long pendent ears.

聻 chien 4. Death of a man's ghost.

⿰耳廓 kuo 4. The rim of the ear.

聾 lung 2. Deaf.

聽 t'ing 1. To hear, to listen, to understand ; to let.

Rad. 129

聿

See Lesson 169 B.

聿 yü 4. A pencil, a pen, forthwith, and, then.

肂 ssŭ 4. To dig a grave.

肄 i 4. To practise, to toil, pain, sprouts.

肅 su 4. Circumspection, respect, diligence.

肆 ssŭ 4 To expend, to expose, four, excessive, reckless, now.

肇 chao 4. To begin, to institute, to arrange.

Rad. 130

肉

See Lesson 65 A.

Compare Rad. 74.

肉 月 jou 4. ju 4. Flesh, meat, fat ; corporeal.

肌 chi 1. The flesh, meat on bones.

肋 lei 4. The ribs, the side of a body.

刖 yüeh 4. To cut of the feet.

3

肓 mang 2. The cardiac region.

肖 hsiao 4. To be like, to reproduce.

肙 yüan 4. Worms.
肐 ko 1. A defect.
肕 jên 4. Cartilage.
肝 kan 1. The liver.
肛 kang 1. The rectum.
肚 tu 3. The belly, the entrails, inwards, memory.
肘 chou 3. The elbow, a cubit.
肜 yung 1, Repeated offerings.

4

肴 yao 2. Sacrificial meats, exquisite viands.
肯 k'ên 3. To be willing, to assent.
肩 chien 1. The shoulder, the scapula, to take upon.
育 yü 4. To bear and bring up, education.
肺 fei 4. The lungs.
肥 fei 2. Flesh, fat, fertile.
服 fu 2. To use, to wait on, clothes, mourning.
肸 hsi 4. Music.
肰 jan 2. Dog's meat.
肚 jên 3. Cooked, ripe.
股 ku 3. The upper part of the thigh, a part, a share.
肱 kung 1. The upper part of the arm.
肦 pan 2. To bestow.
胖 p'ang 4. Fat, obese.
肧 p'ei 1. An embryo, a fœtus, an unformed thing.
朋 p'êng 2. Friend.
肢 chih 1. The limbs.
肳 wên 3. Lips.
肫 chun 1. Flesh dried, earnest.
肬 yu 2 A swelling, a wen.

5

胃 wei 1. The stomach.
胄 chou 4. Progeny, offspring. A helmet.
胥 hsü 1. Mutually, to gather, constables, clerks.
腕 wan 4. The wrist, a flexible joint, to twist.
背 pei 4. The back, behind, rear, to turn the back on, to carry, rebellion, to apostatise, to recite, secret, deaf.
胬 nu 3. Granulations.
胤 yin 4. Offspring, to succeed, to inherit, to follow.
胡 hu 2. A dewlap. Why? what? how? Turkic tribes.
脉 mai 4. The pulse, blood or water running.
胒 ni 2. Fat, grease.
胖 p'ang 4. Fat, corpulent.
胞 pao 1. The amnion, uterine.
胚 p'ei 1. Embryo, embryonal.
胗 chên 3. Pustules, eruption.
胝 chih 2. Thick callous skin.
胦 yang 4. The navel.
胎 t'ai 1 The pregnant womb, to commence.
胆 tan 3. The gall.
胙 tso 4. Sacrificial flesh, to bless, to grant.
胏 tzŭ 3. Dried meat.

6

胔 tzŭ 4 A putrid carcass.
胹 chêng 1. Cooked meat.
脅 脇 } hsieh 2. The flanks, the sides, the ribs, to press, to compel.
胷 胸 } hsiung 1. The thorax, the breast.
脊 chi 2. Vertebrae, the spine, the back, a ridge.
胾 tzŭ 4. Mince-meat.
能 nai 4. A brown bear. nêng 2. To be able to, talent.
胰 i 2. Soap.
朐 hsün 2. Larvæ.
胳 ko 1. The arm.
胯 k'ua 4. The thighs, to bestride.
胱 kuang 1. The bladder.
脈 mai 4. The veins or arteries, the pulse.
胹 erh 1. To boil, to cook.
脁 t'iao 1. To offer flesh.
胴 tung 4. The large intestine.
朕 chên 4. I, myself.
脂 chih 1. The fat of animals, grease, ointment, cosmetics.
脆 脃 } ts'ui 4. Crisp, brittle, delicate.
胵 chih 4. A crop, a gizzard.
胭 yen 1. Cosmetics.

7

脣 ch'un 2. The lips.
脩 hsiu 1. Dried meat, salary.
脯 fu 3. Dried meat.
脝 hêng 1. Puffed up.
脛 ching 4. Shank, shin-bone.
脚 chiao 3. The feet, base of a hill, etc.
脘 kuan 3 Œsophagus.
脬 p'ao 1. The bladder.

脖 po 2. The neck.
脫 t'o 1. To take off, to strip, to escape from.
豚 t'un 2 A hog.

8

腎 shên 4. The kidneys, the testicles.
腐 fu 3. Rotten, putrid, cheese.
勝 shêng 4. To overcome, to defeat.
腓 fei 2. The calf of the leg.
腑 fu 3. Viscera, the bowels.
腍 jên 3. Good, ripe, well cooked.
脫 nai 3. Breasts, to suckle.
腔 ch'iang 1. The throat, tune, accent, to retort.
腒 k'u 3. The coccyx.
脘 kuan 3. A duct in the body, œsophagus.
脾 p'i 2. The spleen, the stomach.
脹 chang 4. Swelling, dropsical.
胼 p'ien 1. Hard, callous.
腊 hsi 1. Dried meat.
腆 t'ien 3. Prosperous, abundance.
腁 chêng 1. The tendon Achilles, the heel.
腕 wan 4. The wrist, a flexible joint.
腌 yen 1. Pickled meat.
腋 yeh 4. The arm-pits.

9

羸 lo 3. Fattening of animals.
腴 yü 2. Fat, fertile.
腸 ch'ang 2. The intestines, the feelings.
腄 ch'ui 2. The buttocks.
腫 chung 3. To swell.
腹 fu 4. The belly, interior.
腪 hun 1. Meat which must not be eaten on buddhist fast days.
腬 jou 2. Soft juicy meat.
腝 juan 3. Numbness of the feet.
腳 chiao 3. The feet, a base.
腦 nao 3. The brain.
腭 o 4. The roof of the mouth.
腷 pien 4. A muscle, a tendon.
腮 sai 1. The cheeks, the gills of a fish.
腥 hsing 1. Rank, strong smelling.
腺 ch'üan 2. Secreting glands.
腶 tuan 4. Meat spiced and dried.
腰 yao 3. The loins, the waist.

10

膏 kao 1. Fat, ointment, greasy, rich.
膋 liao 2. Tallow.
膂 lü 3. The backbone, strength, basis.
膈 ko 2. The diaphragm, to hiccough.
腔 kung 1. Castration.
膀 p'ang 2. The bladder.
膍 p'i 2. The stomach of an animal.
膊 po 4. p'ai 2. The shoulder-blade, the arm.
膰 sao 1. Rank, strong, fetid.
膆 su 4. The crop or gizzard of a bird.
腿 t'ui 3. The thigh, the leg.

11

膚 fu 1. The skin, surface.
膠 chiao 1. Glue, gum, sticky.
膗 ts'ui 1. Fat, corpulent.
膙 chiang 3. Callosities, corns.
膜 mo 4. The skin, a membrane, diaphragm.
膝 t'êng 2. A proper name
膝 ch'i 2. The knees.
膛 t'ang 2. The thorax, the roof of the mouth.

12

膱 chih 1. Pieces of dried or pickled meat.
膉 i 4. Lean, cadaverous.
膰 fan 2. Meats used in sacrifices.
膩 ni 4. Grease, fat.
膨 p'êng 2. Distended, swelled.
縢 t'êng 2. To tie.
膳 shan 4. Food, viands, delicacies.

13

臂 pi 4. The arm.
臀 t'un 2. The seat, the buttocks.
膺 ying 1. The breast, self, office, to oppose.
臌 ku 3. Dropsical.
膾 k'uai 4. Minced meat.
臁 lien 2. The leg.
臉 lien 3. Face, honour.
膿 nung 2. Pus, matter.
賸 shêng 4. Remainder, rest.
謄 t'êng 2. To copy.

臊 **sao 4.** Shame.
sao 1. Rancid.

膽 **tan 3.** Gall, courage.

臆 **i 4.** The interior, feelings, opinions.

14 &

臏 **pin 4.** The patella.

臍 **ch'i 2.** The navel.

臘 **la 4.** The winter solstice sacrifice, the 12th moon.

臕 **piao 1.** Fat, very corpulent.

[illegible] **tu 2.** An abortion.

騰 **t'êng 2.** To ascend.

臚 **lu 2.** The skin, to state, to intimate.

臙 **yen 1.** Cosmetics.

臝 **lo 3.** Naked.

臞 **ch'ü 1.** Emaciated; thin, ghastly.

臟 **tsang 4.** The parenchymatous viscera.

臠 **lüan 3.** Flesh cut into slices.

Rad. 131

臣

See Lesson 82 E.

臣 **ch'ên 1.** A vassal; a minister; a subject; a statesman; I.

𦣞 **i 2.** The chin.

臤 **chien 1.** Firm; solid.

臥 **o 4.** To rest; to cease; to lie down.

臧 **tsang 1.** Good; to commend; to approve.

臨 **lin 2.** To condescend; to look down sympathisingly; about; during; like.

Rad. 132

自

See Lesson 159 A.

自 **tzŭ 4.** From, commencing at; self, I; my own; spontaneously.

𦣻 **shou 3.** The head.

臬 **nieh 4.** A target; a mark; a rule; a judge.

臭 **ch'ou 4, hsiu 4.** To smell, to stink.

臯 皐 **kao 1.** High, eminent; to announce; a proper name.

Rad. 133

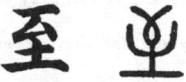

至

See Lesson 133 B.

至 **chih 4.** To go to; to reach; till; as for; utmost; best; solstice.

致 **chih 4.** To offer, to give up; to resign; to bring about, to cause; to call; to reach; the end.

臺 **t'ai 2.** A terrace, a turret, a stage; a title of respect.

臻 **chên 1.** To spread; to reach to; abundance.

Rad. 134

臼

See Lesson 139 E.

臼 **chiu 4.** A mortar.

臽 **hsien 4.** A pitfall; a trap.

臾 **yü 2.** A moment; a little while, to bind; to draw.

臿 **ch'a 2.** To pound in a beetle.

舁 **yü 2.** To raise a thing; to lift it for presentation.

[illegible] **lei 4.** To hull rice.

舀 **yao 3.** To bale out; to ladle out.

舂 **ch'ung 1.** To pound grain; to hull.

舃 **ch'iao 3.** A magpie.

舅 **chiu 4.** A mother's elder brother; a wife's brother.

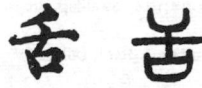

與 **yü 3.** To give: to share, together· union; to resemble, to co fit for.
yü 2. A final particle.

興 **hsing 1.** Agreement; fashion; flourishing.

舉 **chü 3.** To raise, to lift up; to begin, to promote; actions, manners; all, whole; a promoted man.

舊 **chiu 4.** Old; formerly.

Rad. 135

舌

See Lesson 102 C.

舌 **shê 2.** The tongue.

舍 **shê 4.** A shed, a cottage.
shê 3. To do without.

舓 **shih 3.** To lick.

[illegible] **chin 4.** To be silent.

舐 **shih 3.** To lick.

甜 **t'ien 2.** Sweet, agreeable.

舑 **tan 1.** To loll the tongue.

舒 **shu 1.** To unroll; to expand; to smooth; tranquil, easy, good humour.

舔 **t'ien 3.** To lick.

舖 **p'u 1.** A shop.

館 **kuan 3.** A residence ; a lodging-house ; a school ; a restaurant.

Rad. 136

舛 

See Lesson 31 E.

舛 **ch'uan 3.** Error ; mistake ; discord.

舜 **shun 4.** Name of an ancient monarch.

舞 **wu 3.** To make postures ; to dance.

Rad. 137

舟 

See Lesson 66 A.

舟 **chou 1.** A boat.

舠 **tao 1.** A long narrow canoe.

舢 **ch'ao 1.** A vessel pitching and rolling.

舫 **fang 1.** A large open boat ; a lighter.

航 **hang 2.** A large vessel ; to sail, to navigate.

舥 **p'a 1.** A floating bridge.

般 **pan 1.** Manner ; fashion ; sort ; kind.

舳 **chou 2.** The stern of a vessel.

船 **ch'uan.** A boat.

舷 **hsien 2.** The gunwale of a vessel ; the bulwarks.

舸 **ko 3.** A large galley.

舲 **ling 2.** A boat with windows.

艄 **shao 1.** The stern of a vessel.

艇 **t'ing 3.** A barge.

艑 **lün 2** The prow of a junk.

艌 **nien 4.** A tow-rope ; a hawser.

艎 **huang 2.** A ferry-boat.

艑 **pien 4.** A raft.

艏 **shou 3.** The bow of a vessel.

艓 **tieh 2.** A small boat.

艐 **tsung 1.** To run aground ; to land.

艖 **ch'a 1.** A skiff ; a scow.

艕 **pang 1.** Boats fastened side by side.

艘 **sou 1.** A junk.

艙 **ts'ang 1.** The hold of a ship, cabins.

艛 **lou 2.** A war-junk with turrets.

䑱 **ao 2.** The stem of a vessel ; the keel.

艜 **t'ai 4.** A long narrow boat.

艚 **ts'ao 2.** A sea-going junk.

艞 **chang 3.** An oar.

艟 **t'ung 2.** Cabin-boys.

艂 **p'êng 2.** Mat sail of a vessel.

艢 **ch'iang 2.** A gaff.

艥 **chi 4** An oar.

艦 **chien 4.** A war vessel.

艨 **mêng 2.** A war junk.

艩 **ch'i 3.** The peg for resting the scull on.

艪 **lu 3.** A turret.

艫 **lu 2.** The bow of a boat.

Rad. 138

艮 

See Lesson 26 L.

艮 **kên 4.** Perverse, obstinate ; to resist.

良 **liang 2.** Good ; virtuous ; natural gifts ; freeborn ; docile ; very.

限 **hsien 4.** A term ; a limit ; an obstacle.

眼 **yen 3.** The eye.

銀 **yin 2.** Silver.

艱 **chien 1.** Labour ; difficulty ; care ; suffering.

Rad. 139

色 

See Lesson 28 D.

色 **shê 4.** Colour ; air ; manner ; lust ; a Buddhist term for the material world and body.

艴 **fu 4.** To turn pale.

艷 **yen 4.** Beautiful ; winsome ; wanton.

Rad. 140

艸 

See Lesson 78 B.

艸 **ts'ao 3.** Plants ; herbs ; grass.

艿 **jêng 2.** Grass, hay.

艽 **chiao 1.** Acanthus.

艾 ai 4. Mugwort; artemisia.

芀 tiao 1. Clover.

芐 hsia 4. The *Rehmannia chinensis.*

芄 wan 2. A kind of sedge.

芑 ch'i 3. A succory.

芎 ch'iung 1. A sort of *Angelica.*

芒 mang 2. Beard of grain, a sharp point, a ray.

芃 p'êng 2. Luxuriant, bushy.

芍 shao 2. The herbaceous peony.

芏 t'u 3. A rush.

芊 ch'ien 1. Luxuriant foliage.

芋 yü 2. The taro, *colocasia*, and other edible tubers.

芝 chih 1. Sesamum.

4

芷 chih 3. The fragrant *Iris florentina.*

芻 ch'u 2. Grass; hay; vulgar; worthless.

芝 fan 4. Sea-weed.

芬 fên 1. Fragrant.

芳 fang 1. Fragrance, virtue, glory; your.

芾 fei 4. Umbrageous, to overshadow.

芣 fu 2. The *Plantago major.*

芙 fu 2. The *Hibiscus mutabilis*

花 hua 1. Flower, flowery; dissipation, pleasure; to spend; indistinct vision.

芮 jui 3. Plants budding; springing.

芥 chieh 4. The mustard plant.

芡 ch'ien 4. A water plant, *Euryale ferox.*

芰 chi 4. An orchidaceous plant, salep.

芩 ch'in 2. A medicinal root, *Scutellaria viscidula.*

芹 ch'in 2. Cress.

芵 chüeh 2. The *Cassia tora.*

芉 niu 2. *Achyranthes aspera.*

芭 pa 1. The banana-tree.

芘 pi 4. The thorny *Malva sylvestris.*

芟 shan 1. To mow.

芧 hsü 4. A species of sedge.

芴 wu 4. Manioc.

芽 ya 2. A germ, a shoot; to bud.

芫 yüan 2. The *Daphne genkwa.*

芸 yün 2. A fragrant herb which drives away insects; a library; to weed.

5

苲 cha 3. A water plant.

茁 cho 4. Grass starting.

苧 chu 4. *Urtica nivea.* China-grass.

范 fan 4. Plants, grass. A surname.

巷 hsiang 4. An alley; passage.

苻 fu 2 Buds bursting.

茀 fu 2. A veil, a screen.

苛 k'o 3. Small plants; petty; trifling.

苡 i 3. The *Coix lachryma.*

苒 jan 3. Luxuriant.

若 jo 4. To be as; if; as to; to follow; to be in sympathy with; much.

苷 kan 1. Liquorice.

苟 kou 3. Plants, herbage; wayward; if, if so; impromptu; carelessly; but, nevertheless.

茄 ch'ieh 2. Egg-plant.

苺 mei 2. A general name for berries.

苦 k'u 3. Sow-thistle; bitter; painful; to mortify; afflictions.

苣 chü. The dandelion.

苙 li 4. A pen, a yard.

苓 ling 4. A sort of truffle, *Pachyma cocos.*

茅 mao 2. A grass used for thatching; a hut; a privy.

茆 mao 3. The mallow.

茂 mao 4. Exuberant; flourishing; to exert; strong.

苗 miao 2. The tender blade of herbs and grass; sprouts; the issues of; wild tribes.

苠 min 2. The skin of bamboo.

苜 mo 4. The lucern.

茉 mu 4. Jasmine.

苨 ni 3. A medicinal plant, *Adenophora.*

苶 nieh 1. Worn out; weary.

苞 pao 1. Reed, rush; thick, dense.

苤 p'ei 1. Blooming.

苾 pi 4. Fragrant.

苹 p'ing 2. Duck-weed.

茇 po 4. Stubble.

苫 chan 1. To thatch, straw.

苔 t'ai 2. Moss.

苐 ti 4. Panic grass, order, sequence.

苕 t'iao 1. Clover.

苳 tung 1. A thistle.

苴 chü 1. A textile, sackcloth, coarse.

英 ying 1. A flower, luxuriant, brave, superior.

苑 yüan 4. A park field, to rear animals.

6

茶 ch'a 2. The tea.

茥 **chih** 4. A nut.

茱 **chu** 1. The *Evodia rutæcarpa*.

茺 **ch'ung** 1. A labiate, *Lamium album*.

茷 **ia** 2. Leafy, to mow.

茯 **iu** 2. A sort of truffle, *Pachyma cocos*.

茠 **hsiu** 1. To weed.

荇 **hsing** 4. An aquatic plant.

荁 **huan** 2. A kind of celery

荒 **huang** 2. Empty; unproductive, desert, famine.

茴 **hui** 2. Fennel or caraway.

荏 **jên** 3. Flexible, gentle.

茹 **ju** 2. Roots, to examine, to eat.

茸 **jung** 2. Thick, dense.

茛 **kên** 4. The *Ranunculus acris*.

茭 **chiao** 1. Dried grass

荊 **ching** 1. The *Cercis sinensis*.

茖 **ko** 2. A wild onion.

[illegible] **ch ü** 1. A coarse tray for silkworms.

荖 **lao** 3. Betel.

荔 茘 } **li** 4. The *Nephelium lichih*.

茢 **lieh** 4. Sedge, rushes.

茫 **mang** 2. High waters, vast and vague, chaos.

茗 **ming** 2. The tea-plant.

荀 **hsün** 2 A proper name.

荅 **ta** 2. Vetch, to join, to get entangled, to answer.

荑 **t'i** 2. Name of a grassy plant, *Panicum*.

茼 **t'ung** 2. A mugwort.

草 **ts'ao** 3. Plants with herbaceous stems, grass, the running hand, a rough copy.

茦 **tz'ŭ** 4. A thorn, thorns, brambles.

荐 **chien** 4. To continue, to repeat, again.

茜 **ch'ien** 4. *Rubia cordifolia*, used to dye.

荃 **ch'üan** 2. A fragrant plant.

茲 **tzŭ** 1. Grass growing thickly, this, this one, now, still, for.

茨 **tz'ŭ** 2. Cithrop.

7

[illegible] **chih** 4. A *Polygala*, used in fevers.

莊 **chuang** 1. Agriculture, a farm, a village, sedate, grave.

莖 **kêng** 3. Stalks.

莧 **hsien** 4. Spinach.

荷 **ho** 2. The Lotus, *Nelumbium speciosum*; to bear, to be obliged for.

莢 **chia** 4. A felicitous plant.

莍 **ch'iu** 2. A spice tree, *Xanthoxylum*.

莒 **chü** 3. A textile plant.

莞 **kuan** 1. Sedge. A mat.

莨 **lang** 2. Reed or marsh grass.

莉 **li** 4. The white jasmine.

莅 **li** 4. Water rushes, to overlook, to govern.

莓 **mei** 2. Edible berries.

莫 **mu** 4 **mo** 4. Not, is it not? to settle.

莔 **mêng** 2. *Fritillaria*.

[illegible] **lu** 4. *Aconitum variegatum*.

[illegible] **shê** 2. A proper name.

莪 **o** 2. A species of artemisia.

[illegible] **pei** 4 *Fritillaria*.

莩 **lu** 2. The pellicle of plants, related, intimacy.

荸 **pi** 2. *Tulipa edulis*.

莘 **hsin** 1. A marshy plant.

莦 **shao** 4. Jungle grass.

莎 **so** 1. Rush.

荽 **sui** 1. The coriander.

荳 **tou** 4. Beans, pulse.

莛 **t'ing** 2. Stalks, straw.

莌 **t'o** 4. The *Fatsia papyrifera*.

荼 **t'u** 2. Bitters, anxious, careworn.

莝 **ts'o** 4. To chop straw.

莤 **yu** 3. To strain wine.

莠 **yu** 3. **niu** 3. Tares, false.

8

莚 **yen** 2. Climbing plants.

菖 **ch'ang** 1. The sweet flag *Calamus*.

萇 **ch'ang** 2. *Carambola*. A proper name.

菗 **ch'ou** 2. *Hedysarum*.

[illegible] **chih** 1. *Anemarrhena asphodeloides*.

[illegible] **ssŭ** 4. Vegetable gums.

菲 **fei** 3. Turnips, poor, mean, frugality.

菡 **han** 3. The bud of a flower.

華 **hua** 2. Flowers, flowery, variegated, China

萑 **chui** 1. *Leonurus sibiricus*.

[illegible] **kang** 1. A trailing plant, *Vitis labrusca*.

萁 **chi** 1. Tendrils of vines.

菅 **kuan** 1. Textile fibres.

堇 **chin** 3. Clay, to plaster.

菤 **chüan** 3. *Xanthium strumarium*.

菌 **chün** 3 Mouldiness, microbes.

菰 **ku** 1. The edible *Hydropyrum*.

菇 ku 1. A mush-room, o bud.

菊 chü 1. The chrysanthemum.

菓 kuo 3. Fruit.

萊 lai 2. Goosefoot.

莨 li 4. A kind of stiff grass.

菻 lin 2. *Incarvillea sinensis.*

菱 ling 2. The water-chestnut, *Trapa.*

莽 mang 3. Jungle, undergrowth; rustic.

萌 mêng 2. A germ, a shoot, to thrive.

菴 an 1. A thatched cottage, a Buddhist convent.

菶 pêng 3. Full of leaves, luxuriant.

萆 pi 2. The castor-oil plant.

萍 p'ing 2. Duck-weed.

菠 po 1. Spinach.

菩 p'u 2. A character used by the Buddhists. *Ficus religiosa. The bodhi.*

菽 shu 4. Leguminous plants, pulse.

菼 t'an 3. Rush or sedge.

菪 tang 4. *Hyoscyamous niger.*

萄 t'ao 2. The grape.

菟 t'u 4. The *Cuscuta.*

菜 ts'ai 4. Culinary vegetables, food.

菆 tsou 1. A nest.

菁 ching 1. Turnips.

萃 ts'ui 1. A jungle, thick, to collect.

莿 tz'ŭ 4. A thorn.

菑 tzŭ 1. An uncultivated field, waste.

菋 mei 4. *Schizandra sinensis.*

萎 wei 1. To wither, to decay.

菸 yen 1. Tobacco.

9

菉 lü 4. Lentiles.

著 chu 4. To make manifest, to set forth.
chao 2. To make manifest, to place, to put on, an imperative, to endorse, to determine, to burn.

葑 fêng 1. Coarse vegetables.

葫 hu 2. The bottle-gourd.

萱 hsüan 1. A day-lily. *Hemerocallis.*

葷 hun 1. Strong smelling vegetables, forbidden to the Buddhists who fast.

葢 kai 4. A coarse grass used for thatching, a covering, a roof, to build, for, since.

葭 chia 3. Reeds, rushes, matrimonial alliance.

惹 jê 3. To provoke, to excite.

韭 chiu 3. Leek.

薑 chiang 1. Ginger.

葛 ko 2. A textile, *Pueraria phaseoloides.*

葵 k'ui 2. The mallow.

落 lao 4. The fall of the leaf, to tumble in, to descend, an abode.

葎 lü 4. The wild hop, *Humulus japonicus.*

茅 mao 2. The amaryllis.

募 mu 4. To collect alms, to invite, to enlist.

萼 o 4. The stem and calyx of a flower.

葐 p'ên 2. A kind of raspberry.

葆 pao 3. Luxuriant foliage, to cover.

萹 pien 1. *Polygonum aviculare.*

蔀 pu 4. To cover, a shed.

葡 p'u 2. The vine.

葠 shên 1. In *hai-shên*, sea-slugs; *jên-shên*, ginseng.

葚 shên 2. The berries of the mulberry.

葸 hsi 3. Timid, timorous, hesitating.

葙 hsiang 1. *Celosia argentea.*

蒂 ti 4. A stem, a peduncle.

董 tung 3. To direct, to regulate, trustees.

葮 tuan 4. The *Hibiscus syriacus.*

葬 tsang 4. To bury, to inter a coffin.

葺 ch'i 1. To repair, to put in order, to cover.

萩 ch'iu 1. *Antennaria.*

葼 tsung 1. A soft twig

葱 ts'ung 1. The onion.

葘 tzŭ 1. An uncultivated field, waste.

萬 wan 4. Ten thousand, an indefinite number, wholly.

葦 wei 3. The common reed.

萵 wo 1. Lettuce.

葽 yao 1. *Polygala tenuifolia.*

葉 yeh 4. A leaf, a slip, a plate, a period.

葯 yao 4. A medicine.

萸 yü 2. The *Xanthoxylum*, a spice.

萮 yü 2. *Eutrema Washabi.*

10

蓁 chên 1. Rushy, dense.

蒸 chêng 1. To steam, vapour, all.

蒭 ch'u 2. Straw.

蒃 ch'ai 2. A sudorific medicine.

蓄 hsü 4. To feed, to rear.

蒿 hao 1. Fragrant or aromatic plants, like the *Artemisia.*

蒻 jao 4. A rush.

蓐 ju 4. Suckers, shoots, sprouts, a cushion of grass.

蓋 kai 4. To cover, a cover, to build, for.

莄 **kêng** 3. Stalks, culm.
蒹 **chien** 1. Rattan.
蒟 **chü** 3. The betel pepper.
蒯 **k'uai** 3. Rush.
蒞 **li** 4. To govern, to administer, functionaries.
蓏 **lo** 3. Fruit which ripens on the ground, as melons, etc.
蒾 **mi** 2. *Viburnum dilatatum.*
蓂 **ming** 2. An auspicious plant.
夢 **mêng** 4. A dream, to dream.
蒙 **mêng** 2 A creeper, to cover, to conceal, ignorant, to receive; Mongol.
蒳 **na** 4. Fan palm.
蒡 **p'ang** 2. *Arctium lappa.*
蒲 **p'u** 2. Rush, rush mats.
蒐 **sou** 1. Herbs; to hunt.
蓍 **shih** 1. The *Achillea sibirica*, which is used for divination.
蒔 **shih** 2. To plant, to cultivate.
蒓 **ch'un** 2. A species of gentian.
蓆 **hsi** 2. A mat, a feast.
蓑 **suo** 1. Grass rain cloak.
蓌 **so** 1. Abundant vegetation.
蓀 **sun** 1. A fragrant purple orchid.
蒜 **hsüan** 4. Alliaceous plants.
蒼 **ts'ang** 1. Green, azure.
蒨 **ch'ien** 4. Luxuriant herbage, fine grain, prosperous.
蒺 **chi** 2. Caltrops.
蔭 **yin** 4. To overshadow, to shelter, to protect.
蓊 **wêng** 3. Luxuriant.
墓 **mu** 4 A tomb.
幕 **mu** 4. A tent, intimacy.
蓉 **jung** 2. A flower, the *Hibiscus mutabilis.*

11

蔗 **chê** 1. The sugar-cane.
慕 **mu** 4. To love.
暮 **mu** 4. Evening.
摹 **mo** 1. To feel.
蓺 **i** 4. To cultivate, agriculture, handicraft, trade.
蔻 **k'ou** 4. The seeds of cardamoms.
菫 **chin** 3. Aconite.
蘔 **ch'ing** 3. The *Sida tiliæfolia.*
蓼 **liao** 3. Smartweed, bitter experience.
蓮 **lien** 2. The lotus, *Nelumbium speciosum.*
蔴 **ma** 2. Hemp, *Cannabis.* Plants furnishing textile fibres.
蔑 **mieh** 4. Minute, worthless, not, without.
蔦 **niao** 3. A climbing wild vine.
蓬 **p'êng** 2. A plant whose seeds are winged, to flutter about, inconstant.
蔽 **pi** 4. To conceal, to shade, to darken.
蔔 **pai** 4 Carrot, turnip.
蔘 **shên** 1. Bushy, dense.
蔏 **shang** 1. *Phytolacca.*
蓴 **ch'un** 2. Gentian.
蓰 **hsi** 3. A plant, to increase fivefold.
蔌 **su** 4. Culinary vegetables.
蓿 **hsü** 4. Lucern.
蔸 **t'ou** 2. A bud.
蔕 **ti** 4. A stalk.
蓧 **t'iao** 4. A basket.
蓷 **t'ui** 1. *Leonurus sibiricus.*
蓪 **t'ung** 1. *Aralia papyrifera.*

蔡 **ts'ai** 4. Grass, hay.
蔣 **chiang** 3. *Hydropyrum latifolium.*
蔟 **ts'u** 4. A nest.
蓯 **ts'ung** 1. Grassy.
蔓 **man** 2. Turnips, *man-ching.*
蔚 **wei** 4. Luxuriant, fine, elegant.
蔫 **nien** 1 Withered, faded.

12

蔬 **shu** 1. Vegetable food.
瞢 **mêng** 4. To-dream obscure.
蕃 **fan** 2. Luxuriant vegetation, increasing, to breed, Tibet.
蕡 **fên** 2. Luxuriant, abundant
蕌 **lu** 4 Herbs.
蕙 **hui** 4. A marshy orchid.
蕘 **jao** 2. Straw, fuel, vile, valueless.
蕊 } 蕋 } **jui** 3. The heart of a flower.
蕤 **jui** 1. Pendent twigs.
蕎 **ch'iao** 2. Buck-wheat.
𦿃 **k'u** 4. The stalk and flower of the onion.
蕖 **ch'ü** 2. The waterlily.
蕨 **chüeh** 2 Bracken, *Pteris aquilina.*
蕢 **k'uei** 4. A straw basket.
䕩 **lao** 2. *Rhyncosia volubilis.*
蕒 **mai** 3. Chicory.
蓃 **sao** 1. *Stellaria aquatica.*
蕣 **shun** 4. *Hibiscus mutabilis*, fugacious, transitory.
蕭 **hsiao** 1. An artemisia, a surname, reverence; poor, destitute.

蕮 **hsieh** 4. *Portulaca.*

蕈 **t'an** 4. A mushroom.

蕬 **ssŭ** 1. The dodder, *Cuscuta.*

蕁 **hsün** 3. *Anemarrhena asphodeloides.*

⿱艹登 **têng** 1. A kind of tea.

蕩 **tang** 4. Large, vast, dissolute, to subvert, reckless.

蕉 **chiao** 1. Banana-tree.

蕝 **chüeh** 2. A bundle of grass, used to strain spirits.

蕞 **tso** 4. A few, small, a gathering, a hamlet.

蔿 **wei** 3. Grass.

蕪 **wu** 2. Full of weeds, vague, poor, vulgar.

13

⿱艹稚 **chih** 4. Tender, delicate.

薠 **fan** 2. A sedge.

薅 **hao** 1. To clear, to weed.

蕸 **hsia** 2. Water-rushes.

薤 **hsieh** 4. The shallot, *Allium ascalonicum.*

獲 **huai** 2. To seize.

薨 **hung** 1. To die, suddenly.

薏 **i** 4. The seeds of a water-plant.

薊 **chi** 4. Thistles.

薑 **chiang** 1. Ginger.

薖 **k'uo** 1. Herbs, vast.

薐 **lêng** 2. Spinach

薟 **lien** 3. A wild vine berry.

蕾 **lei** 3 The but of a flower.

薜 **pi** 1. Smallage celery.

薄 **po** 2. Peppermint.
pao 2 Thin, shabby, insignificant.

薩 **sa** 4. Buddha. *P'u-sa.*

薛 **hsüeh** 1. A proper name.

薪 **hsin** 1. Fuel.

薝 **tan** 3. A fragrant white flower.

薙 **t'i** 4. To root up grass, to weed out.

薡 **ting** 3. A textile plant.

薔 **ch'iang** 2. A red rose.

薦 **chien** 4. Pasture grounds, to introduce, to recommend.

薇 **wei** 2. Ferns.

薈 **hui** 1. A bundle, in abundance.

蕷 **yü** 4. An edible tuber, the Chinese yam.

薀 **yün** 4. To gather.

薁 **yü** 4. A wild grape-vine.

蕹 **yung** 1. *Ipomea aquatica.*

14

⿱艹甄 **chên** 1. A bright blue orchid.

薰 **hsün** 1 Fragrant, to perfume.

薿 **i** 3. Flourishing, vigorous plants.

薷 **ju** 2. A kind of fungus.

藁 **kao** 3. Straw, a first draft.

藄 **ch'i** 2. Edible fern.

藒 **chieh** 1. A fragrant plant.

舊 **chiu** 4. Old.

藍 **lan** 2. Blue, indigo.

薶 **mai** 2 To bury, to hoard.

藐 **miao** 3. Petty, to despise, to insult.

薴 **ning** 2. Thick plants, jungle.

薸 **p'iao** 2. Duckweed, *Lemna minor.*

藊 **pien** 3. A trailing bean, *dolichos lablab.*

薯 **shu** 3. Plants with tubers, the Chinese yam, sweet potatoes.

蕷 **yü** 4. Yam.

薹 **t'ai** 2. *Scirpus maritimus.*

薱 **tui** 4. Abundant vegetation.

藏 **ts'ang** 2. To hide away, to store up. 6
tsang 4. Tibet, booty.

薺 **chi** 4. *Tulipa edulis.*

藉 **chieh** 4. A mat, to lean on for aid, to help, to avail of, in order that.

藎 **chin** 4. A dyeing plant, attached to, sincere.

15

⿱艹遮 **chê** 1. The sugar cane.

⿱艹齒 **ch'ih** 3. The purslane.

藩 **fan** 2. A fence, a frontier, a wall.

⿱艹膚 **lu** 1 *Kochia scoparia.*

藝 **i** 4. To cultivate, agriculture, aptitude, a craft, a law, a rule.

繭 **chien** 3. A cocoon.

藭 **ch'iung** 2. Smyrnium, a medicine.

爇 **jê** 4. Warm.

藟 **lei** 3. A creeper, a vine-branch.

藜 **li** 2. A kind of bramble.

⿱艹閭 **lü** 2. A species of *Euphorbia.*

藘 **lü** 3. Madder.

藦 **mo** 2 The mushroom.

藕 **ou** 3. The edible root-stock of the lotus

藨 **piao** 1. A rapsberry bush.

藪 **sou** 4. A marsh, a gathering place.

⿱艹膝 **hsi** 2. *Aehyranthes aspera.*

藚 **su** 4. Alisma.

藫 t'an 2. Moss.

藤 t'êng 2. The rattan, lianas.

藬 t'ui 1. *Rumex crispus.*

藥 yao 4. A medicine, a drug.

16

藹 o 3. A park, a crowd.

蘅 hêng 2. The *Asarum.*

藼 hsien 1 *Hemerocallis.*

藿 huo 3. Peas, vetches.

蘂 jui 3. The heart of a flower.

蘄 ch'i 2. The *Aralia*; to seek for.

藾 lai 4. Legumes, umbrageous.

藶 li 4. Mustard.

藺 lin 4. A rush.

蘆 lu 2. Water rushes.

蘋 p'in 2. *Marsilea quadrifolia.*

藷 chu 1. The sugar-cane.

蘇 su 1. A species of thyme; to revive, to cheer up.

蕁 t'an 2. Sea weeds.

蘈 t'ui 2. *Leonurus.*

藻 tsao 3. Algæ, graceful.

蘢 lung 2. A water weed, to collect.

蘊 yün 4. To collect, to bring together, to conceal, sadness.

17

蘩 fan 2. A species of *Artemisia.*

蘙 i 1. Plants, vegetation.

蘘 jang 2. *Lilium giganteum.*

蘧 ch'ü 1. A kind of mushroom, pleasure.

蘭 lan 2. Orchideous plants.

蘗 pi 4. Box-wood.

蘚 hsien 3. Mosses.

蘖 nieh 4. The stump of a tree, sprouts, shoots.

蘡 ying 1. A vine like the grape.

蘨 yu 2. Luxuriant vegetation.

18 &

[illegible] chieh 1. Stalks.

[illegible] tsa 2 *Scirpus sinensis.*

蘶 wei 4. Sprouts.

蘸 chan 4. To dip, to soak.

蘺 li 2. A hedge.

蘿 lo 2. Wisteria, carrot, beet.

藟 lei 3. A creeper.

蘪 mei 2. The asparagus.

[illegible] têng 4. To wake from sleep.

虉 i 2. An herb of various hues.

虆 lei 3. A basket.

虀 chi 1. A leek.

Rad. 141

See Lesson 135 A.

虍 hu 3. A tiger.

虎 hu 3. The tiger; cruelty; bravery.

虐 yao 4. niao 4. Brutish; tyrannical; fierce; cruel.

虒 ti 1. A fabulous tiger.

虓 hsiu 1. Roaring of the tiger.

虔 䖍 ch'ien 2. Respect, veneration.

處 䖏 ch'u 3. To stop; to stay; to rest; to dwell; to judge; to decide; to punish.
ch'u 4 A place; a condition; a matter.

虖 hu 1. To cry; an exclamation.

虚 虛 hsü 1. Empty; vacant; vain; false; weak; useless.

虜 lo 3. To seize; to capture; a prisoner.

號 hao 4. A mark, a designation; a label, a name; a style; a signal; an order; to cry, to summon.

䖒 hsi 4. An ancient vase used in sacrifices.

虞 yü 2. To foresee; to provide; to reckon; to be anxious; to avoid.

虢 kuai 2. A proper name.

虦 chan 4. A striped wild cat.

虣 pao 4. Violent; cruel.

慮 lü 4. To meditate.

膚 fu 1. The skin.

盧 lo 2. A hut.

虧 k'uei 1. To harm, to injure; wanting, defect.

虩 hsi 4. Frightened; alarmed.

Rad. 142

See Lesson 110 A.

虫 ch'ung 2. Insects.

虱 shih 1. Louce.

虬 ch'iu 2. A young dragon.

虰 **ting 1.** Dragon-fly.

虹 **hung 2.** Rain-bow.

虼 **ko 4.** A flea.

虻 **mang 2.** Mosquito.

虺 **hui 1.** A venimous serpent, cobra.

4

蚩 **ch'ih 1.** Insects; stupid; a proper name.

蚤 **tsao 3.** A flea.

蚨 **fu 2.** A butterfly; a copper cash.

蚘 **yu 2.** The tape-worm.

蚋 **jui 3.** Gnats.

蚑 **ch'i 2.** A spider.

蚚 **ch'i 2.** A mantis.

蚧 **chieh 4.** A lizard.

蚣 **kung 1.** Scolopendra.

蚌 **miao 2.** Silkworms just hatched.

蚆 **pa 1.** A species of cowry, used for money.

蚌 **pang 4.** Large and thick marine shells.

蚍 **p'i 2.** The moth in furs.

蚪 **tou 3.** Tadpole.

蚇 **ch'ih 4.** Caterpillars.

蚺 **jan 2.** A sort of boa.

蚤 **tsao 3.** A sand flea, chigo.

蚝 **tz'ŭ 4.** Caterpillars which have stiff hairs.

蚊 **wên 2.** Mosquitoes.

蚓 **yin 3.** The earthworm, *Lumbricus.*

蚖 **yüan 2.** A venomous snake.

5

蚻 **cha 2.** A locust.

蛋 **tan 4.** Eggs.

蚳 **ch'ih 2.** Larvæ of ants.

蚰 **cho 1.** A spider.

蛀 **chu 4.** Worm-eaten

蚹 **fu 4.** Scales of a serpent.

蚶 **han 1.** Bivalve shells.

蛔 **hui 2.** A long intestinal worm.

蚿 **hsien 2.** The milleped.

蚵 **ho 1** A sort of lizard.

蚺 **jan 2.** A large serpent.

蛅 **chan 2.** A venomous caterpillar.

蛣 **chieh 2.** The sea-anemone.

蚯 **ch'iu 1.** The common earthworm, the *Lumbricus.*

蛄 **ku 1.** The mole-cricket.

蛉 **ling 2.** The venimous sand-fly.

蛃 **ping 2.** The *Lepisma.*

蚾 **po 3.** The toad.

蛇 **sha 2. shê 2.** A serpent; serpentine.

蛈 **t'ieh 4.** A spider.

蚱 **cha 3.** A locust.

蛆 **ch'ü 1.** Maggots, worm.

蚰 **yu 2** A scolopendra.

6

蛩 **ch'iung 2.** Crickets.

蛓 **tz'ŭ 4.** Caterpillars with stiff spiny hair.

蛛 **chu 1.** The spider.

蛕 **yu 2.** The tænia.

蛜 **i 1.** The sow-bug.

蜂 **chiang 4.** The rain-bow.

蛟 **chiao 1.** A crocodile.

蛢 **ch'ien 1.** A fire-fly.

蛣 **ch'i 1.** Scarabs.

蛒 **ko 4.** Dung-beetle.

蛤 **ka 2. ko 2.** A clam, oyster, mussel.

蛐 **ch'ü 1.** The common earthworm.

蛞 **kua 1.** The spawn of frogs.

蛑 **mou 2.** A crab.

蛇 **ch'a 4.** A sea-blubber, *Medusa.*

蛭 **chih 4** A leech.

蛙 **wa 1.** A green frog; wanton, obscene.

蛘 **yang 2.** The mantis.

7

蜀 **shu 3.** A caterpillar; a name of Ssŭch'uan.

蜃 **ch'ên 3.** A marine monster; mirage.

蜇 **chê 2.** To sting; a sting.

蜍 **ch'u 2.** A kind of toad.

蜉 **fu 2.** Ants.

蜂 **fêng 1.** A bee; a wasp; a hornet.

蜆 **hsien 3.** Mussels or clams.

蛵 **hsing 2.** The dragon-fly.

蜘 **chih 2.** The sea-anemone.

蛺 **chia 4.** A butterfly.

蛷 **ch'iu 2.** A milleped.

蜎 **yüan 1.** Worms, larvæ.

蜋 lang 2. Different kinds of insects.
蜊 li 2 A species of clam.
蛾 o 2. wo 2. A moth.
蜌 pi 4. A mussel.
蛸 hsiao 1. The egg-cocoon of the mantis.
蜔 t'ien 4. Inlaid shellwork.
蜓 t'ing 1. A dragon-fly.
蛻 t'o 4. Slough or exuviæ of insects and reptiles.
蜈 wu 2. Scolopendra.
蝆 mi 3. A weevil.
蜏 yu 3. A moth.
蛹 yung 3. The chrysalis of the silkworm.

8

蜜 mi 4. Honey.
蜚 fei 1. Mites.
蜡 la 4. Wax
蜋 ch'ang 2. A kind of centiped.
蜘 chih 1. A spider.
蜻 ch'i 1. A spider.
蜞 ch'i 2. A small land crab.
蜣 ch'iang 1. The tumble-dung.
蜷 ch'üan 2. The wriggling of a snake.
蝺 ch'ü 1. A grub ; a woodlouse.
蜾 kuo 3. The solitary wasp or *Sphex*.
蜫 k'un 1. Insects.
蜧 li 4. A dragon-snake.
蜦 lu 4. A small marine bivalve.
蜦 lun 2. To crawl ; to wriggle.
蜢 mêng 2. A locust.

蜒 yen 2. A scolopendra.
蜥 hsi 4. A lizard.
蝃 cho 1. A spider.
蜩 t'iao 2. The cicada.
蜻 ching 1. A dragon-fly.
蝲 tz'ŭ. A hedge-hog
蜲 wei 3. A wood-louse.
蜴 i 4. A chameleon.
蜿 yüan 1. Tortuous; stealthy.
蜮 yü 4. A malicious fabulous creature.
蜟 yü 4. Larva of the cicada.

9

蝥 mao 1. The Spanish fly, cantharides.
蝨 shih 1. A louse.
蝱 mang 2. Ox-fly.
蝕 shih 2. To eat away; an eclipse.
蝮 fu 2. A venomous snake.
蝦 hsia 4. ho 2. Batrachia. A frog.
蝛 hsien 2. A flat bivalve.
蝎 ho 1. A grub.
蝴 hu 2. A butterfly.
蝗 huang 2. The locust.
蝡 juan 3. To squirm, to wriggle.
蝌 k'o 1. A tadpole.
蝸 kua 1. A garden slug ; a snail.
蝍 lang 2. Different insects.
蝻 nan 2. Immature locusts.
蝙 pien 1. The bat.
蝡 p'ien. The red sand tick.

蝠 fu 2. The bat.
蝪 t'ang 4. A species of spider.
蝭 t'i 2. A cicada.
蝶 t'ieh 3. A butterfly.
蝍 chi 2. A centiped.
蝤 ch'iu 2. A crab.
蝛 wei 1. The sow bug.
蝟 wei 4. The hedgehog.
蝰 wei 4. Wingless insects.
蝘 yen 3. A lizard.
蝺 yü 2. A water-beetle.
蝓 yü 2 A snail.
蝯 yüan 2. The gibbon ape.
蝫 ch'u 2. A toad.
蝹 yün 1. To wriggle, as a snake.
蛹 yung 3. Chrysalis.
蝣 yu 2. Water-flies.

10

螢 jung 2. ying 2. A glow worm.
螌 pan 1. Cantharides.
蠹 tu 4. Grubs in wood.
螘 i 3. The ant.
螼 kung 3. To squirm as a worm.
螞 ma 3. A leech; a locust; an ant.
螟 ming 2. A caterpillar.
螃 p'ang 2. A crab.
螕 p'i 2. A cattle-tick.
螄 shih 1. A spiral shell; a screw.
螇 hsi 2. A green grasshopper.
螗 t'ang 2. A mantis.

螔 i 2. A slug.

螥 ts'ang 1. The house fly.

螓 ch'in 2. A small cicada.

螆 tz'ŭ 4. Hairy and poisonous caterpillars.

螉 wêng 1. A kind of gadfly.

螈 yüan 2. A silkworm.

蝝 yüan 2. The young of locusts before their wings have grown.

融 jung 2. yung 2. To melt; bullion, cash; harmony.

螣 t'êng 2. A serpent or dragon.

11

蟅 chê 4. A cockroach.

螯 ao 2. A large crab.

蟄 chê 2. To hibernate; to become torpid.

螫 chê 1. To sting, a sting; to poison.

蟞 p'ieh 4. A large ant.

螽 chung 1. A longheaded green grasshopper.

蟊 mao 3. A grub which eats grain.

蟁 wên 2. Mosquitoes.

蟈 kuai 1 A green cricket.

蟉 liao 4. A cicada.

螻 lou 2 Ants.

蠊 lien 2. A species of snake.

螺 lo 2. A spiral univalve shell; a conch; a screw.

螰 lu 4. A cicada.

蟆 ma 1 A frog.

螶 ch'ü 2 A moth.

螵 p'iao 1. A chrysalis.

蜁 hsüan 3. A spiral univalve.

蟋 hsi 4. A cricket.

蟀 shuai 4. A cricket.

螳 t'ang 2. A mantis.

螬 t'ao 2. Maggots in fruit.

12

蟲 ch'ung 2. Insects; reptiles.

蟚 p'êng 2. A land crab.

蠁 hsiang 3. Larvæ of insects.

蟩 chüeh 2. A gerboa.

蟢 hsi 3. A spider of good omen.

蟥 huang 2. A leech.

蟪 hui 2. A cicada.

蟣 chi 3. Nits.

蟒 mang 3. A kind of boa.

蟧 lao 2. A shell-fish.

蟟 liao 2. The cicada.

䗲 lin 2. A fire-fly.

蟦 ni 4. Aphides.

蟠 p'an 2. To coil up to curl round.

蟬 ch'an 2. The cicada.

蟮 shan 4. The earthworm.

蠴 shu 3. The slater.

蟫 yin 2. *Lepisma*

蟳 hsün 2. A hairy sea-crab.

蜄 chin 4. The shell *Pinna*.

13

蠃 lo 3. The solitary wasp.

蠈 tsei 2. The *thief-worm* which eats the joints of rice.

蟹 hsieh 4. A crab.

蠆 ch'ai 4. A scorpion

蟶 ch'êng 1. An oyster.

蠍 hsieh 1. A scorpion.

蠉 huan 1. To crawl.

蟻 i 4. Ants.

蠄 ch'iu 2 A long-legged spider.

蠝 lei 2 An edible clam.

蟕 tsui 1. A species of tortoise.

蟾 ch'an 2. A toad, the moon.

蟺 shan 4. The earthworm.

蠋 shu 4. A caterpillar.

蟰 hsiao 1. A spider.

蠅 ying 2. A house fly

14

蠡 lu 4. Crickets.

蠔 hao 2. An oyster.

蠕 juan 3. Squirming, wriggling

蠓 mêng 3. Gnats.

蠙 pin 1. The pearl oyster.

蠐 ch'i 2. Maggots.

蠖 huo 4. To creep.

蠑 jung 2. A lizard.

蟙 chih 1. A big caterpillar.

15-&

蠢 ch'un 3. To wriggle, stupid, doltish.

蠜 fan 2. A small grasshopper.

蠟 la 4. Wax, a candle.

蠡 **li 4.** Wood-borers.

蠣 **li 4.** Rock oysters.

蠛 **mieh 4.** Ephemera.

蠩 **ch'u 1.** A toad.

蠹 **tu 4.** Grubs in wood, worms in books or clothes.

蠭 **fêng 1.** Bees, wasps.

蠮 **i 4.** The solitary wasp or *sphex*.

蠨 **hsiao 1.** A long legged spider.

蠱 **ku 3.** Worms in the belly; a slow poison, dropsy.

蠲 **chüan 1.** Pure, to purify, to dispense with, to condone.

螱 **wei 4.** An ant with wings, white ants.

蠵 **hsi 2,** A land tortoise.

蠶 **ts'an 2.** A silk worm.

蠻 **man 2.** Barbarous tribes in the South of China.

[illegible] **nan 4.** Gnats.

[illegible] **li 2.** A milliped.

蠾 **chu 1.** A short legged spider.

Rad. 143

血

See Lesson 157 D.

血 **hsüeh 3.** Blood, bloody.

衁 **huang 1.** Hemorrhage.

衄 **niu 4.** Nose-bleed from fright, defeat.

衃 **fu 2.** Clot of blood.

衅 **hsin 4.** To besmear with blood.

衇 **mai 4.** The pulse, the blood vessels.

衉 **k'o 2.** To vomit blood.

衈 **erh 4.** To incise the ears of a victim.

衊 **mieh 4.** To stain with blood, to defile.

Rad. 144

行

See Lesson 63 C.

行 **hsing 2.** To step, to send off, natural powers, suitable, perhaps.
hsing 4. Action, conduct.

行 **hang 2.** A rank, a category, a profession, a corporation, a firm.

衎 **k'an 4.** A feast, pleased, contented.

衍 **yen 3.** To overflow, abundant, much, licentiousness.

衏 **hang. 2** Musicians.

衒 **hsüan 4.** To brag, to display, to let out.

術 **shu 4.** A path, an art, a plan, a precept, magical rules.

衖 **hung 4.** A road, a lane.

街 **chieh 1.** A street.

[illegible] **ch'iao 4.** Weary, exhausted.

衕 **t'ung 2.** A side-street.

衙 **ya 2.** A yamen, a tribunal.

[illegible] **yung 3.** A raised path.

衘 **hsien 2.** A bit, affected, indignant, a rank, a degree.

衝 **ch'ung 1.** To rush towards or against, to attack.

衚 **hu 2.** A smaller street or lane.

衛 衞 **wei 4.** To escort, to guard, Tientsin.

衠 **chên 1.** Pure, genuine.

衡 **hêng 2.** A balance, to adjust.

衢 **ch'ü 1.** A road, a path.

Rad. 145

衣

See Lesson 16 A.

衣 **i 1.** Clothes.
i 4. To dress, to wear.

卒 **tsu 2.** Servants, soldiers.

初 **ch'u 1.** Beginning.

表 **piao 3.** Outside, to make known, external, to manifest, a watch.

哀 **ai 1.** To moan, pity.

衩 **ch'a 1.** Outside half pants, *ch'a-k'u.* To insert a piece.

衫 **shan 1.** A skirt or shift.

[illegible] **t'o 2.** To undress.

4

衷 **chung 1.** Rectitude, sincerity, loyalty, uprightness.

衰 **shuai 1.** Wearing away, fading, decadency.

衮 **kun 2.** Imperial robes, court robes.

衺 **hsieh 2.** Impure, lewd, bad.

衾 **ch'in 2.** A coverlet, bed-clothes.

袁 **yüan 2.** A long robe. A surname.

衽 **jên 4.** The breast of a coat, buttoned under the right arm.

衱 **chi 2.** The hinder skirt of a robe.

衿 **chin 1.** Lapel opening of coat.

衯 **fên 1.** Long flowing robes.

袂 **chün 1.** A plain dress.

袧 **mi 4.** The sleeves of a robe.

衲 **na 4.** The robe of a bonze, to patch.

科 **tou 3.** D.ess sleeves.

5

袞 kun 3. Imperial robes, court robes.

衮 mao 2. A long gown.

袈 chia 1. The Buddhist cope.

袋 tai 4. A bag, a pocket, a purse.

袗 chên 3. A loose overcoat.

袚 fu 4. Knee-pads.

袨 hsüan 2. Dark clothes.

袪 ch'ü 1. Sleeves.

袔 la 2. Mean apparel, poor garments.

袜 mo 4. A hem.

袊 ling 3. A collar

袂 mei 4. A veil.

袙 p'a 4. A turban.

袢 p'an 4. Light clothes for summer.

袍 p'ao 2. A long robe.

被 pei 4. A coverlet, to cover, to suffer, a sign of the passive voice.

袖 hsiu 4. A sleeve, to sleeve.

袒 t'an 3. To strip, naked.

6

裂 lieh 4. To crack, to split, to rip open, a schism.

袈 ju 4. Poor, worn-out garments.

裁 ts'ai 2. To cut out, to plan, to deceive.

裒 p'ou 1. To collect, to diminish.

袾 chu 1. Red garments, elegance.

袱 fu 2. A strong cloth used for wrapping.

袲 i 4. The train of a dress.

袵 jên 4. The lappel or flap in front of a coat.

袷 chia 2. Lined garment.

袎 chiao 3. Drawers.

袼 ko 4. Short sleeves.

袴 k'u 4. Trowsers.

袿 kui 1. The upper gown of women.

袳 to 3 Long sleeves.

裀 t'ung 2. A close coat.

裀 yin 1. A mattress.

7

裔 i 4. The train of a robe, a border, posterity.

裝 chuang 1. To pack, to contain.

裟 sha 1. A Buddhist cope.

裘 ch'iu 2. Fur garments.

裏 裡 li 3. Inside, lining, inner.

裌 chia 3. A lined coat.

裙 ch'ün 2. A petticoat, an apron.

裢 tso 4. A clothes-bag.

補 pu 3. To patch, to mend, to add on, to make up.

裕 yü 4. Abundant, plenty, generous.

裑 shao 1. The lapel of a coat.

裎 ch'êng 2. To take off clothes, naked.

8

製 chih 4. To cut out, to invent, to manufacture.

裴 p'ei 2. A long robe.

裰 tu 4. A fringe.

裳 shang 1. The clothes on the lover half of the body.

裹 kuo 3. To wrap up, to bind, bandage.

裮 ch'ang 1. To throw a garment loosely over the body.

裶 fei 2. The train of a dress.

裾 chü 1. The flap of a coat.

褂 kua 4. A coat; robe, skir.

裸 lo 3. Naked, to strip.

裨 pi 4. To add, to aid, to benefit.

裱 piao 3. To paste.

裼 hsi 1. Thin clothes, to pull off one's coat.

綻 chan 4. A seam which has opened, to rip, split.

裺 yen 3. The selvage of cloth.

9

褎 yu 4. Elegantly dressed, easy, plenty, to enjoy.

褒 pao 1. State robes, to praise, to criticise.

褔 ch'a 1. Tassels, fringe.

褚 ch'u 3. A satchel.

複 fu 4. Double or lined garments.

福 fu 2. Clothes.

褉 hsieh 4. A short garment.

褐 ho 2. Coarse woollen stuff.

褑 juan 1. Seam, border, selvedge.

褌 k'un 1. Loose trowsers.

褓 pao 3. Swaddling-clothes.

褙 pei 4. To paste papers.

褊 pien 3. Narrow, tight.

褆 shih 4. Handsomely dressed.

褙 to 4. A long robe.

褘 wei 2. A queen's garment, virtue.

襖 yao 1. A fold.

褗 yen 3. A collar.

10

褰 ch'ien 1. To tuck up, to raise the skirt.

褑 ch'i 1. The side slits in a gown or robe.

褟 t'a 4. Pakish.

褡 ta 1. A wrapper, a girdle.

褥 ju 4. A mattress.

褠 kou 1. Single garments with narrow sleeves.

褪 t'un 4. To pull the hands within the sleeves.

縐 chou 4. Clothes creased, wrinkles, folds.

褲 k'u 4. Trowsers, pantaloons.

褫 ch'ih 3. To strip, to take away official insignia.

褯 chieh 4. Children's clothes.

11

襄 hsiang 1. To effect, to assist.

褻 hsieh 4. Undress, under-clothes, filthy, indecent familiarity.

褒 pao 1. Court robes, to censure.

褵 li 2. An ornamented sash.

褳 lien 2. A pouch, a pocket.

褸 lü 3. Torn, dirty clothes.

縵 man 2. Large clothes.

褶 tieh 2. A lined garment, to fold.

褿 tsao 1. A short tunic.

積 chi 1. A plait.

12

襀 k'uei 4. The loop for fastening a coat.

襆 p'u 4. A turban.

襌 tan 1. Unlined garment.

禫 t'an 3. To change clothes at the expiration of the mourning.

襁 chiang 3. Swaddling-clothes.

襍 tsa 2. Variegated, a mixture.

襘 tsêng 4. A handkerchief.

13

襞 pi 4. A long robe.

襛 nung 2. Coarse clothes.

襟 chin 1. The overlap of a robe.

襘 k'uai 4. A loose girdle.

襖 ao 3. An outer garment, a coat, quilted or furred.

襜 chan 1. An apron, a screen.

襹 sa 1. Tattered, disordered.

襚 sui 4. Clothes of the deceased.

襢 t'an 3. To strip, bared.

襠 tang 1. Crutch of trowsers.

襗 chai 4. Underclothes.

14 &

襦 ju 2. A jacket.

襶 kai 4. Outer garments.

襤 lan 2. Ragged garments.

齌 tzŭ 1. To hem.

襭 chieh 2. To hold up the skirt.

襴 la 4. Mean apparel.

襮 pao 4. An embroidered collar.

襡 tu 2. A drawer, a sheath.

襪 wa 4. Stockings, hose, socks.

襯 ch'ên 4. Inner garment, ornamental.

襱 lung 2. The leggings worn in winter.

襲 hsi 2. A cloak, to add, to repeat, attached, to inherit.

襴 lan 2. A sort of doctor's robe.

襳 hsien 1. Small underclothes.

襵 chê 4. A fold, a tuck.

襻 p'an 4. A loop, a sash, a belt.

Rad. 146

西 覀

See Lesson 41 C.

襾 hsia 4. A cover.

西 hsi 1. The west.

要 yao 4. To want, to intend, necessary, a sign of the future, if.

覂 ta 2. Exhausted.

栗 li 4. Chestnut-tree.

覃 ch'ien 1. To climb.

票 p'iao 4. A warrant, a bill.

覃 t'an 2. Wide, extensive, enduring.

粟 su 4. Rice in the husk, grains.

賈 ku 3. A shopman, to traffic. chia 3. A proper name.

覆 fu 2. The reverse, to overthrow, to ruin.

覈 ho 4, hai 4. To examine thoroughly, to pare, to question by torture.

覊 chi 1. To bridle, to restrain.

Rad. 147

見

See Lesson 158 C.

見 **chien 4.** To see, to apprehend, to visit, to appear, to estimate, experience.
hsien 4. To appear, manifest.

規 **kuei 1.** A pair of compasses, a rule, a custom, a fee.

覔覓 **mi 4.** Invisible, to search for.

覘 **ch'an 1.** To spy, to glance at.

視 **shih 4.** To consider, to perceive, to compare, to imitate.

覗 **ssŭ 1.** To peep, to steal a glance at.

覜 **t'iao 4.** An imperial audience.

覟 **chih 4.** To examine.

覡 **chi 1.** A witch.

覥 **t'ien 3.** To be timid, timidity.

覩 **tu 3.** To gaze at, to observe.

親 **ch'in 1.** To love, to approach, to kiss, near, one's self, own.
ch'in 4. Kindred, affinity.

覬 **chi 4.** To aim at.

覯 **kou 4.** To see or meet one suddenly, to occur, accidentally.

覭 **ming 2.** To examine closely.

覲 **chin 3.** To have an audience with the Emperor.

䚋 **piao 3.** To look at carefully.

覰覷 **ch'ü 4.** To spy, to peep.

覵 **chien 4.** To spy into, to mix up.

覺覐 **chiao 3.** To feel, to awake, to perceive, to instruct.
chiao 4. To sleep.

覽 **lan 3.** To inspect, to behold, to understand.

覿 **ti 2.** To visit, to see face to face.

觀観观 **kuan 1.** To consider, to examine, to gaze on, to see.
kuan 4. To show, an observatory, a Taoist convent.

Rad. 148

角

See Lesson 142 B.

角 **chiao 3.** A horn.

觔 **chin 1.** The Chinese pound, strength, the tendons.

斛 **hu 2.** The Chinese bushel, holding ten pecks.

觖 **chüeh 2.** To be dissatisfied.

觚 **ku 1.** A vase, angular, vicious.

觝 **ti 3.** To push with the horns, to strive against.

觜 **tsui 3.** A constellation.

解觧 **chieh 3.** To loosen, to undo, to explain.
chieh 4. To send, to convoy.
hsieh 4. To understand.

觡 **ko 2.** Antlers.

觥 **kung 1.** A cup made of a horn.

觫 **su 4.** To start, to fear, to tremble.

觭 **chi 1.** Uneven, irregular.

觱 **pieh 3** Musical horn.

觳 **hu 1** To tremble.

觴 **shang 1.** A big cup.

觼 **chiao 3.** To cock horns.

觸 **chu 4.** To butt, to strike against, to offend.

Rad. 149

言

See Lesson 73 C.

言 **yen 2.** Words, to speak, to tell.

訇 **hung 1.** Noise of voices.

訃 **fu 4.** To announce a death.

計 **chi 4.** To count, to calculate, to plan.

訆 **chiao 4.** To call, to name.

訉 **chi 1.** To scoff.

訂 **ting 4.** To decide, to subscribe.

訏 **hsü 1.** Vain boasting.

訓 **hsün 4.** To instruct, to teach, to exhort, to persuade.

訌 **hung 4.** Words destructive of order and peace.

訋 **tiao 4.** A proper name.

訑 **i 2.** Arrogant, overbearing.

訒 **jên 4.** To speak with reserve, to be cautious.

記 **chi 4.** To note down, history, mark, to remember.

訐 **chieh 2.** To accuse, to divulge, indiscretion.

訖 **ch'i 4.** To finish, ended, done, up to.

訕 **shan 4.** To vilify, to slender.

訊 **hsün 4.** To interrogate, to examine judicially, to chide.

討 **t'ao 3.** To repress, to punish, to search, to ask for, to beg, to provoke.

託 **t'o 1.** To commission, to entrust, to engage; for; to feign, to allege.

4

訬 **ch'ao 3.** To cry, to annoy, to quarrel.

訨 chih 3. To reprove, to impeach.
訪 fang 3. To search out, to inquire into.
訩 hsiung 1. To litigate.
訢 hsin 1. Affable, gracious.
許 hsü 3. To grant, to allow, to permit, to promise, more than, an excess, very.
訣 chüeh 2. Magic formulae, parting or dying words.
訛 o 2. Mistake, error, to harm.
訥 nê 4. To be cautious, or low of speech.
訠 shên 3. Still more, how much more.
設 shê 4. To arrange, to set up.
訟 sung 4. To accuse, litigation.
訝 ya 2. To admire, to wonder at, to exclaim.
訒 yang 4. To stop talking.

5

詈 li 4. To scold about, to rail at.
詐 cha 4. To deceive, to feign, artful, fraudulent.
診 chên 1. To verify, to examine, diagnosis.
詔 chao 4. To announce, to instruct by decree or order, proclamation, a mandate.
詋 chou 4. To imprecate, a spell.
証 chêng 4. To prove, to testify, evidence, legal testimony.
詛 tsu 3. To imprecate.
註 chu 4. To comment, to annotate.
詝 chu 4. Knowledge.
誁 fei 4. To stutter.
訶 ho 1. To blame, to reprove, to ridicule.
詒 i 2. To hand down, to leave.
詁 ku 3. To explain, to comment.

詎 chü 4. How? in what manner?
詖 p'i 4. To slander. To deceive.
評 p'ing 2. To discuss, to criticise.
訴 su 4. To tell, to make known, to accuse.
詆 ti 3. To vilify, to slander.
詄 tieh 2. To forget, to neglect.
詑 t'o 2. To deceive, to impose on.
詇 yang 4. To speak cautiously, to know, to teach.
詞 tz'ŭ 2. An expression, a composition, to accuse, to request.
詏 yao 4. To contradict.
詠 yung 3. To compose, to recite, to sing.

6

訾 tz'ŭ 2. To slander.
詶 ch'ou 2. To answer.
誃 ch'ih 3. To separate; farewell.
誅 chu 1. To blame, to punish; to put to death.
詨 hsiao 4. To hail.
詾 hsiung 1. To brawl; threatenings.
詡 hsü 3. To boast; to brag; to display.
話 hua 4. A word, a sentence; language; speak; to tell.
訌 hung 3. To trick; to cheat.
詣 i 4. To visit; to go to; to reach.
該 kai 1. Must, ought.
詪 kên 3. To wrangle.
詬 kou 4. To reproach.
詰 chieh 4. Inquiry; to examine.
誇 k'ua 1. To praise; boast.
誆 k'uang 2. To lie; to deceive.

詭 kui 3. To deceive; maliciousness.
誄 lei 3. To eulogise the dead; prayers.
詫 ch'a 4. To brag; to boast oneself. To wonder at.
詺 ming 4. To name.
詻 lao 4. To wrangle.
詵 hsien 1. The din of a multitude.
詩 shih 1. Poetry; verses; poems.
試 shih 4. To try, to experiment; to use; to examine; a trial, an examination.
詳 hsiang 2. Details; minutely; to examine; to report.
詢 hsün 2. To enquire about.
誠 ch'êng 2. Quileless; sincere; to rectify; perfection.
誂 t'iao 2. To seduce.
詷 t'ung 2. To speak precipitately.
詮 ch'üan 2. To explain; to discourse upon.
誎 tz'ŭ 4. To criticise; to ridicule.

7

誓 shih 4. To swear; to take an oath; a contract.
誌 chih 4. To remember; to record; annals.
誜 ts'un 1. To laugh at, to deride.
誒 hsi 1. To laugh at.
誨 hui 3. To teach; to advise.
認 jên 4. To recognise, to know, to consider, to confess; to mistake.
誥 kao 4. To announce to; to order; to grant; an edict.
誡 chieh 4. Rules of conduct; to prohibit; to warn.
誑 k'uang 2. Lies, to deceive.
誏 lang 3. To play upon words.
誐 o 2. To hum.
諀 p'i 1. Erroneous; wrong; mistaken.

誧 p'u 1. To amplify.

誖 pei 4. A quarrel; a revolt.

說 shou 1. To speak; to talk; to scold.

誦 sung 4. To recite; to intone.

誘 p'u 1. Sly, cunning.

誚 ch'iao 4. To ridicule.

誣 wu 1. To calumniate.

誤 wu 4. A mistake; to neglect.

誘 yu 4. To lead on; to allure; to entice; to seduce.

語 yü 3. Words; to discuss; to talk.

8

誾 yin 2. To speak gently, courteously.

諍 chêng 1. To remonstrate with.

諂 ch'an 3. To flatter; to fawn.

諄 chun 1. To impress upon; to teach.

誹 fei 3. To slander; to criticise.

謔 hu 1. To frighten.

誼 i 2. Suitable; right; proper; relations.

諉 wei 3. To shirk; to evade.

誕 tan 4. To brag; to boast; to bear children; birth.

課 k'o 4. An example; a task; to experiment.

諒 liang 4. Sincere; to trust; to consider; to excuse.

論 lün 4. To discourse; to discuss; with reference to.

諗 shên 3. To reflect on; to reprove.

誰 shui 2. shei 2. Who? who; any one.

誶 sui 4. To abuse; to rail at.

談 t'an 2. To talk; to chat.

調 t'iao 2. To blend; to harmonise; to adjust; to temper. 8

tiao 4. Removal or permutation of officials.

請 ch'ing 3. To beg; to request; please; to engage.

9

諛 yü 2. To flatter.

諿 ch'a 4. To talk much; to interfere.

諸 chu 1. All; every; a final particle; at; on; about.

諥 chung 4. To offend.

諯 ch'uan 1. To reckon.

諷 fêng 3. To chant; to scoff at.

諧 hsieh 2. To accord; to agree; to harmonise.

諴 hsien 2. Sincerity; harmony.

諠 hsüan 1. Clamour; hubbub.

諼 hsüan 1. To forget; to err; to deceive.

諻 hui 3. To slander; to vilify.

諱 hui 4. To conceal; to shun; a taboo.

諫 chien 4. To warn; to reprove.

謀 mo 2. To plot; to scheme.

諳 an 1. Skilled in; fully acquainted with.

諾 nê 3. To assent.

諞 p'ien 3. Deceitful; to deceive.

諶 ch'ên 2. Sincere; upright; to trust to. *Shên* 2.

諟 shih 4. To judge; to consider.

諡 shih 4. The posthumous title; the epitaph name.

諝 hsü 3. Knowledge; prudence; ability.

諦 ti 4. To investigate; to make researches.

諜 tieh 2. To spy; to play the traitor.

謂 wei 4. To speak; to say; to be.

謁 yeh 4. To visit; to receive a visit.

諺 yen 4. A common saying; a proverb.

諲 yin 1. To respect; to reverence.

諭 yü 4. To issue orders; an edict; to notify.

10

謇 ch'ien 3. Frank; open.

謄 t'êng 2. To copy; to transcribe.

謑 hsia 4. A lie.

謔 yao 4. niao 4. To ridicule.

謞 hao 4. To criticise; to disparage.

謊 huang 3. To lie; to mislead.

講 chiang 3. To develop; to explain, to esteem.

謙 ch'ien 1. Respectful; yielding; modest; humble.

謌 ko 1. A song.

謎 mi 2. A riddle; a puzzle.

謗 pang 4. To slander.

謏 sou 3. To censure.

謆 shan 4. To wheedle; to seduce by fair speeches.

謚 shih 4. The epitaph name; the posthumous title.

謝 hsieh 4. To thank; to cease; to resign; to confess.

謟 t'ao 1. To doubt; to suspect.

謅 chou 1. To jest; to rail.

謒 ch'iang 1. To contradict; to oppose.

謠 yao 2. False reports, rumours.

11

謶 chê 1. To deceive.

謼 hu 1. To call; to invoke.

謹 chin 3. Cautious; respectful.

謴 **kuan** 4. To play tricks.

謱 **lou** 2. To chatter.

謧 **li** 2. To jest; to ridicule.

謾 **man** 2. To deceive; to insult.

謬 **niu** 4. Falsehood; error.

謨 **mo** 2. A plan; a scheme; to meditate.

謳 **ou** 1. Ballads; to sing.

謪 **shang** 1. To consult, to deliberate.

謲 **ts'an** 4. To rail at; to scold.

⿰言曹 **ts'ao** 2. Noise; hubbub.

謫 **chai** 4. To reproach; to blame.

12

譂 **ch'an** 3. Incoherent talk.

證 **chêng** 4. To testify; to bear witness; a proof.

譖 **chên** 4. To slander

譁 **hua** 2. Clamour; noise.

譓 **hui** 4. Sagacious.

譏 **chi** 1. To rail at; to jeer.

譑 **chiao** 3. To tattle.

譎 **chüeh** 2 To feign; hypocrisy.

⿰言尞 **liao** 2. Cunning of speech.

譒 **po** 4. To promulgate; to spread abroad.

識 **shih** 2. To know; experience. **chih** 4. To remember; a note; a document; a memorandum.

譚 **t'an** 2. To talk much; to boast.

譈 **tui** 4. To provoke; to instigate.

譄 **tsêng** 1. To add; to state further.

譙 **ch'iao** 4. To rail at, to ridicule.

譐 **tsun** 3. Dignified conversation.

13

警 **ching** 3. To warn; to caution; to stimulate; the police.

譬 **p'i** 4. To compare; an example; for instance.

譍 **ying** 4. To answer verbally.

譽 **yü** 2. To eulogise; to extol; fame.

譭 **hui** 3. To slander, to defame.

譩 **i** 1. An interjection; to sigh; to moan.

議 **i** 4. To consider; to deliberate upon; to discuss.

譫 **chan** 1. Wild delirious talking.

⿰言萬 **mai** 4. To brag; to speak angrily.

譜 **pu** 3. **p'u** 3. Chronicle; register; catalogue.

譟 **sao** 4. Voice; murmur.

譧 **tsuan** 4. To deceive, to hoax, to mystify.

譯 **i** 4. To interpret, to translate.

14

譸 **chou** 4. To impose upon, to deceive.

譹 **hao** 2. To cry out.

護 **hu** 4. To protect, to guard.

譴 **ch'ien** 3. To reprimand; to scold; to chastise.

15 &

⿰言暴 **pao** 4. Passionate violent speech.

讀 **tu** 2. To read carefully; to study.

讎 讐 **ch'ou** 2. To hate; to revenge; enmity.

變 **pien** 4. To transform; to metamorphose.

讌 **yen** 4. To talk; merriment.

讓 **jang** 4. To cede, to yield; to give way to; to forgive.

讕 **lan** 2. To defame.

讖 **ch'an** 4. To divine; to augur.

讙 **huan** 1. To vociferate; to rouse.

讒 **ts'an** 2. To detract; to disparage.

讘 **nieh** 4. Garrulous.

讛 **i** 4. To talk in one's sleep.

讚 **tsan** 4. To commend; to laud; to praise.

讜 **tang** 3. Persuasive speech.

讞 **yen** 4. To decide on judicial cases; to pronounce judgment.

讟 **tu** 2. To murmur; seditious.

Rad. 150

谷

See Lesson 18 E.

谷 **ku** 3. A valley; a ravine.

谺 **hsia** 1. A valley; a gorge.

谽 **han** 1. A gorge, a defile.

豁 **ho** 1. A pass; open; spacious; clear; generous; to understand; to penetrate.

谿 **hsi** 1. Discord.

Rad. 151

豆

See Lesson 165 A.

豆 **tou** 4. A vessel, a peck, beans, pulse.

豈 **ch'i** 3. How? why?

豇 **chiang 1.** A kind of long bean.

豉 **ch'ih 3.** To gather in beans.

䜶 **chiang 1.** A small kidney bean.

豊 **li 3.** A vessel used in sacrificing.

豋 **t'êng 1.** Sacrificial platters.

[illegible] **ch'i 2.** Stalks of pulse.

豎 **shu 4.** To stand erect.

豌 **wan 1.** The garden pea.

[illegible] **chin 3.** The nuptial wine cup.

豐 **fêng 1.** Abundant, plenty, copious. *Hence*

豔 豓 艷 } **yen 4.** Beautiful, to covet, licentiousness.

Rad. 152

豕 豕

See Lesson 69 A.

豕 **shih 3.** A pig.

豖 **cho 2.** A shackled pig.

[illegible] **han 4.** To flee in confusion.

豗 **hui 1.** The grunting sound of pigs.

豝 **pa 1.** A saw.

豚 豘 } **t'un 2.** A sucking pig.

[illegible] **jui 3.** To swarm.

象 **hsiang 4.** Elephant; a figure, an image, the elements of the Diagrams.

豢 **huan 4.** Domestic animals, to feed, to allure.

豜 **chien 2.** A full grown hog.

豦 **chü 4.** A wild boar, to fight, to struggle.

豪 **hao 2.** A boar, a porcupine, brave, excellent.

豨 **hsi 1.** Pigs grunting.

豩 **cho 2.** To dig, as pigs do.

[illegible] **tsung 1.** A little pig.

豬 **chu 1.** The pig.

豭 **chia 1.** A boar.

豫 **yü 4.** Elephant; docile, indulgent, to get ready for, pleasure, satisfaction.

豳 **pin 1.** A place in Shênsi.

豲 **yüan 2.** The porcupine.

[illegible] **lou 2.** An old sow, a lewd woman.

豴 **ti 2.** The hoof of a pig.

豵 **tsung 1.** A pig.

Rad. 153

豸 豸

See Lesson 166 A.

豸 **chih 4.** Reptiles.

豺 **ch'ai 2.** A wolf.

豻 **han 4.** Wild dog.

豹 **pao 4.** Leopard, panther.

豽 **na 4.** A striped seal.

貂 **tiao 1.** The Siberian sable, *Mustela zibelina.*

貅 **hsiu 1.** A bear.

貉 **hao 4.** The badger.

貆 **huan 1.** A badger.

貇 **k'ên 3.** To gnaw.

貊 **mai 4.** Wild tribes of the North.

貍 **li 1.** Wild cat, a serval.

貌 **mao 4.** The outward mien, manner, gait, the visage, the aspect, like.

[illegible] **suan 1.** A lion from Tibet.

貓 **mao 2.** A cat.

貒 **tuan 1.** A small badger.

貔 **p'i 2.** A bear.

貙 **ch'ü 4.** A lynx.

貘 **mo 4.** The Malacca tapir.

[illegible] **liao 2.** To hunt at night with torches.

貛 **huan 1.** A badger.

Rad. 154

貝 貝

See Lesson 161 A.

貝 **pei 4** A cowry, a shell, money, valuables.

貞 **chêng 1.** Continence, persevering.

負 **fu 4.** To carry on the back, to bear, to disregard, to slight, to refuse, to fail, to turn the back on, ungrateful, rebellion, apostasy.

則 **tsai 2.** Rule, then.

貢 **kung 4.** Tribute, taxes.

貤 **i 2.** To reward, to promote, grades, steps.

財 **ts'ai 2.** Riches, wealth, property, valuables, goods.

責 **chai 2.** To reprove, to punish, to require from, duty.

貨 **huo 4.** Goods, merchandise, to deal.

貧 **p'in 2.** Poor, impoverished.

貪 **t'an 1.** To covet, to long for, greedy.

貶 **pien 3.** To diminish, to belittle, to censure, to cashier.

販 **fan 4.** To buy in order to sell, to trade, to deal in.

敗 **pai 4.** Ruin, defeat.

5

貫 **kuan 4.** A string of a thousand cash, to traverse, to go through, a series, habitual.

費 **fei 4.** To use, to spend, to lavish.

賀 **ho 4.** To congratulate, to send presents.

貸 **tai 4.** To lend, to confer.

貰 **shih 4.** To buy on credit, to borrow, to pardon.

貴 **kuei 4** Honourable, esteemed, prized, dear.

買 **mai 3.** To buy, to purchase.

貿 **mao 4.** To barter, trade.

貳 **erh 4.** To be double, two, second, to divide.

貯 **chu 4.** To store up, to hoard, a treasure.

貺 **huang 4.** To give, to bestow, to confer on.

貽 **i 2.** To hand down, to leave, to induce.

貼 **t'ieh 1.** To leave in pledge, to lean on, adjacent; to paste up.

6

貲 **tzŭ 1.** A fine. Property, wealth.

資 **tzŭ 1.** Property, valuables, means of living.

賃 **lin 4.** To let.

賁 **fên 4.** Embellishments.

賈 **ku 3.** A shopman, to sell, to traffic.
chia 3. A surname.

賂 **lu 4.** To give a present, to bribe.

賍 **tsang 1.** To receive bribes, booty, loot.

賄 **hui 4.** Goods, to bribe, to hush money.

賉 **hsi 2.** Alms.

賊 **tsei 2.** A thief, to ruin, to chastise.

賅 **kai 1.** To heap up.

7

賓 賔 **pin 1.** A guest, a visitor, to entertain, to acknowledge, to trust in.

賕 **ch'iu 2.** To bribe.

賻 **pu 3.** To give a fee.

賑 **chên 4.** A gift, a help, alms.

賖 **shê 1.** To buy or sell on credit, to defer, to put off.

8

質 **chih 4.** The substance, matter or grosser nature of, to cross-examine, a pledge, a hostage.

賢 **hsien 2.** Worthies, good, virtuous.

賣 **mai 4.** To sell.

賞 **shang 3.** To bestow, to reward, to take pleasure in.

賚 **lai 4.** To give, to bestow.

賬 **chang 4.** An account, a bill.

賙 **chou 1.** To succour, to bestow in charity.

賝 **ch'ên 1.** Precious, rare.

賦 **fu 4.** To give, to spread, to levy, a taxation, a rhytmic prose, natural.

䝼 **chü 1.** To store property.

賠 **p'ei 2.** To make good, to indemnify, to lose.

賜 **ssŭ 4.** A gift, to give, to condescend.

賤 **chien 4.** Mean, low, cheap.

賩 **ch'ing 2.** To receive, to come into possession of.

9

販 **fan 4.** To traffic.

賵 **fêng 4.** To give aid in preparing a funeral.

賴 頼 **lai 4.** To rely upon, to trust to; to accuse, to repudiate.

賭 **tu 3.** To gamble, to bet.

10 &

賺 **chuan 4.** To gain.

賻 **fu 4.** To give toward defraying funeral expenses.

購 **kou 4.** To buy, to hire, to induce.

賽 **sai 4.** To contest, a rival, concurrence.

賸 **shêng 4.** Overplus, residue, to retain.

贄 **chih 4.** A present, offerings, gifts of ceremony.

贅 贅 **chui 4.** To repeat, to connect; useless, an excrescence, a pledge, an adoption.

贊 **tsan 4.** To assist, to second, to clear up, to praise.

贈 **tsêng 4.** To give a present, to offer, a title.

贋 **yen 4.** False, counterfeit.

贃 **chuan 4.** To gain.

贍 **shan 4.** To give, to supply, to aid.

贏 **ying 2.** A surplus, gain, profit, to win.

贉 **ch'an 4.** To try, to buy up.

贔 **pi 4.** Great strength.

贐 **chin 4.** Parting gifts.

贖 **shu 2, ch'u 2.** To purchase, to redeem, to pay, a pledge, a ransom, a compensation.

贗 **yen 4.** Counterfeit, spurious.

䞋 **ch'ên 4.** To donate, alms.

贛 **kan 4.** Name of a place.

贜 **tsang 1.** Booty, bribes, to suborn, stolen goods.

Rad. 155

赤 赤

See Lesson 60 N.

赤 ch'ih 4. Flesh colour, carnation, naked, sincere.

赦 shê 4. To remit punishment, to forgive, amnesty.

赧 nan 3. To blush, to turn red, shame.

䞓 chêng 1. Purple.

赫 ho 4. Bright, gleaming, glorious, to frighten.

赭 chê 3. The colour of ochre.

赬 chêng 1. Purple.

Rad. 156

走 走

See Lesson 112 D.

Compare Rads 157 and 162.

走 tsou 3. To walk, to march.

赴 fu 4. To go to, to reach.

赳 chiu 3. A martial gait.

起 ch'i 3. To rise, to begin.

趁 趂 } ch'ên 4. To follow, to go to, to avail of, as an opportunity.

超 ch'ao 1. To step over, to surpass.

趄 ch'ieh 4. To slip.

越 yüeh 4. To overstep, to exceed, moreover.

趍 ch'ih 2. To move rapidly.

趔 lieh 4. To stumble.

趒 t'ao 2. To flee, to escape.

趙 chao 4. To hasten to, a surname.

趕 赶 } kan 3. To pursue, to follow after, to eject, quickly, when.

趝 nien 3. To pursue.

趣 ch'ü 4. To hasten to, to incline towards, bias, pleasant, elegant.

趟 t'ang 1. To go through water, to wade.

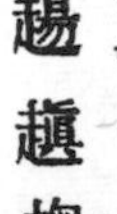 tien 1. To jolt, to bump.

趨 趋 } ch'ü 1. To run to, to hasten, towards.

趲 ts'an 1. To hurry, to run, a runner, a vanguard.

趪 huang 2. To exert one's self.

趫 ch'iao 2. Agile, vigourous.

Rad. 157

足 足

See Lesson 112 B.

Compare Rads. 156 and 162.

足 tsu 2. chü 2. The feet, enough, sufficient, to be satisfied with.

趷 ko 1. To jolt, to shake.

趵 pao 4. To jump.

趾 chih 3. The toes, the foot, to stop, a domicile.

趺 fu 1. To sit cross-legged.

跁 趴 } p'a 2. To creep, to grovel, to fall prostrate.

5

跖 chê 2. A proper name.

跗 fu 1. The top of the foot.

跏 chia 1. To sit crosslegged.

跒 k'o 3. To march.

跍 ku 1. To squat.

跔 chü 1. Feet benumbed, stiffened.

距 chü 4. A spur, to go to, to reach, distant from, to oppose.

踇 mu 3. The toes.

跈 nien 3. To tread to powder.

跑 p'ao 3. To run, to flee.

跛 p'o 3. Cripple, lame.

跋 po 4. To trample.

跚 shan 1. To hobble, to limp.

跌 tieh 1. To slip and fall.

跕 tien 3. To walk on tiptoe.

跎 t'o 3. To slip, to miss, a mistake.

跙 ch'ieh 4. To slip.

6

跫 ch'iung 2. The tramp of men marching.

䟴 tsai 1. To stumble.

跐 跴 } ts'ü 3. To stand upon, to trample.

跮 chih 4. To go to and fro, irresolute.

跤 chiao 1. A slip.

跠 i 2. To sit on the heels.

跟 kên 1. The heel, to follow, presence, with.

跲 ch'ie 4. To stumble.

趼 chien 3. Callous skin.

跩 chuai 4. To hobble.

跨 k'ua 4. To straddle, to step across.

跪 kui 4. To kneel.

路 lu 4. Road, way, path.

跣 hsien 3. Barefooted.

跳 t'iao 4. To jump, to skip.

跺 to 4. To stamp the foot.

跡 chi 4. Trace, foot marks, vestiges, results.

7

踅 chê 4. Contracted.

跽 chi 4. To kneel long, awestruck.

跼 chü 4. Bent down, cramped.

踉 lang 1. To jump.

踆 tsun 4. To stop.

踊 yung 3. To jump, to skip.

8

踔 ch'ao 4. To get ahead, to excel.

踟 ch'ih 2. Undecided, embarrassed.

踝 huai 3. The ankle.

踦 ch'i 2. Crippled.

踞 chü 4. To squat.

踘 chü 4. A leather-ball.

踃 chou 1. To kick.

踏 cha 4 ch'a 4. To trample on.

踧 ts'u 4. To walk slowly and carefully.

踢 t'i 1. To kick.

踐 chien 4. To tread upon, to keep one's word.

踖 chi 1. To walk slowly.

踤 ts'u 4. To butt, to run against.

踪 tsung 1. A footstep, a trace.

踒 wo 1. To sprain.

9

踷 ch'a 1. To paddle.

踹 ch'uai 4. To trample.

踵 chung 3. The heel, to follow, often.

蹂 jou 2. To trample.

踽 chü 3. To walk one, independent.

蹁 p'ien 1. To walk ame, to contort the body.

踼 t'ang 3. To lay down.

蹄 t'i 2. The hoof of a hor ox, pig, etc.

蹀 tieh 2. To step.

踴 yung 3. To bound.

踰 yü 2. To cross over, to exce d, to transgress.

10

蹇 ch'ien 3. To go lame, misfortune, arrogance.

蹒 p'an 2. Cross-legged.

蹩 p'ang 4. To hurry on, to rush on.

蹹 ta 1. To jump.

蹋 t'a 1. To tread heavily, to stamp, to kick.

蹈 tao 4. To trample on, to violate.

蹏 t'i 2. A hoof.

蹎 tien 1. To run.

蹊 hsi 1. A footpath, a narrow way.

蹌 ch'iang 1. To walk rapidly, to skip about.

蹉 ts'o 1. To slip, to miss, to err.

踩 wa 3. To paddle.

11

蹙 tiu 1. To press upon, to contract, careworn.

蹩 pieh 1. To limp.

蹘 liao 2. To run away, to escape

蹣 man 2. To jump, to limp.

蹜 so 1. To drag one's feet.

蹝 hsi 3. Sandals.

蹮 hsien 1. To whirl.

蹧 tsao 1. To tramp on, to illtreat, to abuse, to spoil.

蹟 chi 1. Foot-prints, traces, vestiges, results.

蹠 chê 2. A proper name.

蹤 tsung 1. A track, a trace.

12

蹯 fan 2. An animal's paw.

蹺 ch'iao 1. To raise, curious, stilts.

蹶 chüeh 3. To stumble, to fall.

蹨 nien 3. To walk afoot.

蹼 p'u 4. Fin-toed, webbed.

蹬 teng 4. To jolt.

蹭 ts'êng 4. To graze.

蹴 ts'u 4. To walk reverently.

蹲 tun 1. To squat down. To stop, to rest.

13

躔 ch'an 4. Rapid canter.

躇 ch'u 2. Undecided, at a loss, perplexity.

躄 pi 4. Lame.

躂 t'a 4. To maltreat.

躉 tun 3. Wholesale. To store.

躁 tsao 4. Hasty, irascible.

14 &

躊 ch'ou 2. Irresolute, wavering, timid.
躋 chi 1. To ascend, to scale, to rise.
躍 yao 4. To jump, to dance, glee.
躔 ch'an 2. To tread in, to revolve.
躑 chih 4. Irresolute, unquiet.
躕 ch'u 2. Incertain what to do.
躐 lieh 4. To skip over.
躘 lung 1. To totter, to stagger.
躝 lo 2. Embarrassed.
躧 hsi 3. Sandals or slippers.
躦 tsuan 1. To jump.
躩 ch'iao 4. To walk cautiously.
躪 lin 4. A trodden path.

Rad. 158

See Lesson 148 A.

身 shên 1. The body, one's self, personal, pregnant.
躬 kung 1. Body, person. To bow.
射 shê 4. To shoot.
躭 tan 1. To procrastinate, neglectful.
䠷 t'iao 3 A giant.
躲 to 3. To shun, to avoid
躴 lang 2. Tall, strong.
躳 kung 1. The body, to bow.
躷 p'i 2. Limp ; weak.
躷 yeh 3. Low of stature.
躶 lo 3. Naked.
躲 ni 4. To abscond.
躺 t'ang 3. To lie down.
軀 chung 4. Pregnancy.
軀 ch'ü 1. The body, one's own self.
軃 chan 3. To strip, bared.
軆 yü 4. Virility, vitality.

Rad. 159

See Lesson 167 A.

車 ch'ê 1. chü 1. A cart, barrow, coach, revolving engine.
軋 ya 4. To crush, to grind.
軍 chün 1. An army, military, martial, a camp.
軌 kuei 3. The axle of a wheel, the rut, a track, rails, a rule.
軒 hsüan 1. A proper name.
軔 jên 4. Bit, rein.
軏 yüeh 4. A yoke.
軟 juan 3. Muffled wheels, soft.
軝 ch'i 2. The end of the axle, outside the hub.
軜 na 4. Reins.
軛 o 4. A yoke or collar.
斬 chan 3. To behead.
軐 hsin 1. The hub of a wheel.

5

輩 pei 4. A line of chariots, a generation, etc.
軸 chou 2. An axle, a pivot, a roller.
軵 lu 3. To put in the coachhouse.
軥 ch'ü 2. The ends of the yoke.
軻 k'o 1. Name of Mencius.
軲 ku 1. A block, to revolve.
軺 liu 3. A hurdle.
軷 po 4. A sacrifice to the spirits of the road.
軫 chên 3. A carriage.
軺 tiao 1. A light carriage.
軼 i 4. To rush by, to exceed.

6

載 tsai 4. To contain, to load, to complete, to record.
tsai 3. A year.
輊 chih 4. A war-chariot.
較 chiao 4. To examine, to confront, to compare, evidence.
輐 chuai 3. To jolt.
輅 lu 4. A coach.
輀 erh 2. A hearse.
軾 shih 4. A stretcher before a carriage, or in a sedan, to lean on when bowing.
輇 ch'üan 2. A wagon.

7

輒 chê 4. The sides of a chariot, abruptly, suddenly.
輔 fu 3. To help to assist, a minister.
輕 ch'ing 1. Light, frivolous, easy, to esteem lightly.

8

輦 nien 3. An imperial vehicle

輩 **pei 4.** A generation; a class; a kind; the sign of plural.

輝 **hui 1.** Bright; splendid; glistering.

輈 **chou 1.** A heavily laden cart; heavy.

輟 **ch'o 4.** To cease; to finish.

輗 **i 2.** The cross-bar at the end of a carriage-pole.

輢 **i 3.** The sides of a war-chariot.

輨 **kuan 3.** The iron band in the hub of a wheel.

輠 **kuo 3.** A grease-pot.

輥 **kun 3.** To turn round; to revolve.

輛 **liang 4.** Numerative of chairs, carts, etc.

輬 **liang 2.** A wagon.

輒 **chê 4.** Suddeh.

輘 **ling 2.** A cart-rut.

輪 **lun 2.** A wheel; a disk; a revolution; a turn.

輚 **chan 4.** A war-chariot.

輧 **p'ing 2.** A cart with screens.

輖 **t'ang 4.** A time; a turn.

輤 **ch'ien 4.** A pall to cover a hearse.

輜 **tzŭ 1.** Baggage waggons.

9

輻 **fu 2.** The spokes of a wheel.

輭 **juan 3.** Soft; yielding; pliable.

輸 **shu 1. ch'u 1.** To overturn; to report; to pay; to lose; to confess.

輳 **ts'ou 4.** The hub of a wheel.

輯 **chi 4.** To arrange; order; collection; agreeable.

輶 **ch'iu 1.** The spokes of a wheel.

輶 **yu 2.** A light carriage; light.

10

輿 **yü 2.** A carriage; the earth; basis.

轂 **ku 3.** The nave of a wheel.

轄 **hsia 2.** Linchpins.

輾 **chan 3.** To roll over; to revolve.

轅 **yüan 2.** The shafts of a cart.

11 &

轈 **ch'ao 2.** A look-out place on a war-chariot.

轉 **chuan 4.** To turn round; to revolve; to transmit.

轆 **lu 4.** A pulley; a block.

轍 **chê 2.** A rut; the track of a wheel.

轓 **fan 1.** A screen for a cart.

轎 **chiao 4.** A sedan; a mule litter; a cabin.

轐 **p'u 4.** The pieces which hold the car on the axle.

轘 **huan 4.** To quarter.

轞 **chien 3.** A shut up car; rolling.

轟 **hung 1.** The rumbling of carriages; any stunning noise.

轡 **p'ei 4.** The reins of a bridle.

轤 **lu 2.** A windlass; a pulley.

Rad. 160

辛

See Lesson 102 H.

辛 **hsin 1.** Bitter; toilsome; a cyclical character.

辜 **ku 1.** A fault; ungrateful; to squeeze.

辟 **pi 4.** Prince; to rule.
p'i 4. To punish; penalty; perverse, mean, oblique; to open, to spread, to scatter.

辠 **tsui 4.** Crime, sin.

辥 **pien 4.** To accuse each other.

辣 **la 4.** Acrid, biting.

辦 **pan 4.** To act; to execute.

辪 **nieh 4.** Sin, crime.

辨 **pien 4.** To cut asunder; to distinguish.

辧 **pan 4.** A slice, as of a melon, carpels; petals; lobe.

辭 辞 } **tz'ŭ 2.** To decline; to refuse; to resign; an expression; a plea; an apology.

辮 **pien 4.** To plait, to braid; a cue.

辯 **pien 4.** To debate.
pan 4. To contradict.

Rad. 161

辰

See Lesson 30 B.

辰 **ch'ên 2.** A part of time; a cyclical character; the heavenly bodies, stars. 4

辱 **ju 4.** To insult; to dishonour; to defile; to disgrace one's self, a polite term.

農 **nung 2.** To cultivate; agriculture, farmer.

Rad 162

辵

See Lesson 112 E.

Compare Rads. 156 and 157.

辵 辶 } **cho 4.** Going and pausing.

边 **pien 1.** An edge; a boundary.

迄 ch'i 4. To reach to; till; finally; at last.

迆 i 3. To go to, to advance.

迅 hsün 4. Speedy, sudden, quick.

巡 hsün 2. To go on a circuit; to patrol.

过 kuo 4. To pass by; to exceed.

迖 t'u 2. To go afoot.

迁 ch'ien 1. To advance, to be promoted.

迂 yü 1. To go far, aberration, perversion.

迍 t'un 2. Difficulty.

返 fan 3. To return, to revert to, to come back.

这 chê 4. To meet; this; now.

迒 hang 2. Tracks, ruts.

还 huan 2. To return; to repay.

近 chin 4. Near in time or place, intimate.

迊 tsa 1. To go round; a revolution.

迋 wang 4. To go; to visit.

迕 wu 4. To meet; opposition, conflict, contrary.

迓 ya 4. To meet; to greet; to provide.

迎 ying 2. To occur, to meet. To ward off.

远 yüan 3. Distant, remote.

5

迤 i 3. To go to; to advance.

迩 erh 3. Near; close.

迦 chia 1. A sound, the Sanscrit *ka* or *kia*.

迥 chiung 3. Far apart, unlike.

迫 p'ai 4. To urge; to vex; distress.

述 shu 4. To follow; to narrate, to publish.

迨 tai 4. To reach; till, to; ween.

迢 t'iao 2. Remote; far off.

迭 tieh 2. To alternate; to change, to be able to.

迪 ti 2. To follow; docile; to bring forward; to lead; to teach; to intimate to.

沿 yen 2. To go along; to sail along.

6

追 chui 1. To follow; to press out; to go back; to revert.

逅 hou 4. To meet.

迴 hui 2. To return.

迻 i 2. To remove.

适 k'uo 4. ko 4. To hasten.

迷 mi 2. To confuse; to bewitch; fascinated.

迺 nai 3. This; here; then; if; also; but.

逆 i 4. ni 4. To encounter, to oppose; rebellious; to reckon on; to conjecture.

迸 pêng 4. To rebound.

逄 p'ang 2. A proper name.

迿 hsün 4. To begin a quarrel.

送 sung 4. To accompany; to convoy; to see a guest out.

逃 t'ao 2. To flee; to escape.

退 t'ui 4. To retreat; to draw back; to refuse; to abate; to break.

迹 chi 4. Trace, vestiges.

7

這 chê 4. This; here; now.

逞 ch'êng 3. To act with effrontery; presumptuous; reckless; to follow; to obey.

逐 chu 2. To drive or push out; to exorcise; to press; successively.

逢 fêng 2. To meet; to happen; to incur; an accident.

逕 ching 4. To pass, direct way.

逑 ch'iu. To collect; to unite; a society.

逛 kuang 4. To stroll; to ramble; to toss about.

連 lien 2. To connect; to continue.

逋 p'u 1. To flee; a debt; to refuse payment.

逝 shih 2. To pass away; to depart; to die.

逍 hsiao 1. To roam; to saunter.

速 su 4. To invite; to urge on; speedily; quickly.

逗 tou 4. To delay; to loiter.

透 t'ou 4. To pass through; thoroughly.

逖 t'i 4. Far away; remote.

途 t'u 2. A road; a path; a journey.

通 t'ung 1. To go through; to communicate; to touch; contact; general; to apprehend.

造 tsao 4. To make; to create; to build; parties to a suit.

逡 tsun 1. To retire; to shrink.

8

逈 chou 1. To revolve.

逭 huan 4. To flee; to escape.

逵 k'ui 2. Cross-road.

逮 tai 4. Till, to; when; to reach; to capture.

迸 pêng 4. To rebound.

進 chin 4. To advance; to enter, to bring in; a promotion, to make progress; to prefer.

逶 wei 1. To walk crookedly; to swagger.

逸 i 4. Lust.

9

遄 ch'uan 2. To hurry.

遐 hsia 2. Long; far; old; to abandon.
遑 huang 2. Leisure.
過 kuo 4. To pass by; past; transgression; fault.
遏 o 4. To stop; to check.
逩 pên 4. To run quickly.
遍 pien 4. Everywhere; to make a round; a whole.
逼 pi 4. To press; to compel.
遂 sui 2. To follow; to advance, to succeed; entirely; consequently.
逿 t'ang 4. A time; a turn.
達 ta 2. To penetrate, to reach, to succeed; Tartar.
道 tao 4. A road, path, or way; a doctrine; to lead; to talk.
遁 tun 4. To hide away, to vanish.
逯 lu 4. To advance; to proceed.
違 wei 1. To oppose; to disobey; rebellion.
遊 yu 2. To ramble, to travel.
逾 yü 2. To cross over; to pass; to exceed.
遇 yü 4. To meet; to fall in with; to occur.
運 yün 4. To turn round; to revolve; a revolution; a circuit.

10

遘 kou 4. To meet with; to happen.
遣 ch'ien 3 To commission; to send off.
遛 liu 3. To linger; to saunter.
遡 su 4. To trace up to the source; to remember.
遜 hsün 4. Complaisant; docile; modest; humble.
遝 t'a 4. Confusion.
遢 t'a 4. Hurried; careless.
遞 ti 4. To transmit; to convey from hand to hand; to exchange; to succeed.

遙 yao 2. Distant; remote.
遠 yüan 3. Far off; distant.
yüan 4. To remove; to thrust aside.

11

遮 chê 1. To cover; to hide; to screen; to intercept.
遱 lou 2. Unbroken; continuous.
遨 ao 2. To ramble; to sport.
適 shih 4. To go to; to reach; a plan; to happen; to suit; suddenly; pleasure.
遯 tun 4. To flee; to hide away.
遭 tsao 1. To meet with; to experience; a turn; a time.
遷 ch'ien 1. To remove; to ascend; to be promoted; to change; henceforth.

12

遴 lin 2. To select.
遺 i 2. To let; to transmit; to bequeath.
遶 jao 3. To wind round; to involve; to be entangled in.
遼 liao 2. Distant; name of a stream.
選 hsüan 3. To select, to elect.
暹 hsien 1. Siam.
遲 ch'ih 2. Slow, to defer, a delay, late.
遵 tsun 1. To follow, to conform to, to obey.
遹 yü 4. Succession, to transmit.

13 &

邅 chan 1. To turn around, to remove.
邂 hsieh 4. To meet unexpectedly.
還 huan 2. To go back, to return, to repay, to compensate, still, further.

遽 chü 4. To send, a messenger, hurried, suddenly.
邁 mai 4. To walk, to advance, senile, old.
避 pi 4. To flee from, to avoid, to yield.
邀 yao 1. To invite, to engage, to seek.
邈 miao 3. Small, hidden.
邃 sui 4. Retired, hidden.
邇 erh 3. Near, close, recent.
邋 la 4. To pass by, to neglect.
la 2. Neglected, dirty.
邊 pien 1. A bank, an edge, on the border, the frontier.
邐 li 3. To walk slowly, step by step.
邏 lo 2. To explore, to patrol, to spy.

Rad. 163

邑 阝

See Lesson 74 C.

邑 阝 i 4. A walled city.

邡 shih 2. A place in Ssŭ-ch'uan.
邕 yung 1. A four square city with a moat around it; concord, harmony.
邔 chi 3. A place in Honan.
邛 ch'iung 2. Name of a place.
邙 mang 2. A place in Hunan.
邘 yü 2. A place in Honan.
邗 han 2. A proper name.

4

邡 fang 1. A place in Chêkiang.
邢 hsing 2. A place in Chihli.

那 na 4. This, that, there.
na 3. Who? what? where ?

邦 pang 1. A state, a country.

邠 pin 1. A place in Shènsi.

邪 hsieh 2. Bad, perverse.

邨 ts'un 1. Village.

5

邯 han 1. A place in Chihli.

[illegible] pao 1. A surname.

祁 ch'i 2. Full, large.

邱 ch'iu 1. A tumulus.

邳 p'ei 2. A place in Kiangsu.

[illegible] fu 1. A proper name.

邶 pei 4. A place in Honan.

邲 pi 4. A place in Shansi.

邴 ping 3. A place in Kiangsu.

邵 shao 4. Name of several places.

邰 t'ai 2. An ancient city in Shên-si.

邸 ti 3. A residence, a lodging-house, the Peking gazette.

6

郅 chih 4. A place in Kansu, flourishing, very.

邾 chu 1. An old place in Shantung.

耶 yeh 2. A final particle.

郃 ho 4. A place in Shênsi.

郊 chiao 1. The suburbs of a city; imperial sacrifice.

郄 hsi 4. Name of a place.

邽 kui 1. A place in Kansu.

郇 hsün 2. An old place in Shansi.

郱 p'ing 2. A place in Shantung.

邿 shih 1. A place in Shantung.

郁 yü 4. A place in Shansi. Elegant.

郕 ch'êng 2. A place in Honan.

7

郛 fu 2. Suburbs, glacis.

郗 hsi 1. Name of a city.

郝 hao 3. A place in Shansi.

郜 kao 3. A fief in Shantung.

郟 chia 4. A place in Honan.

郤 hsi 4. A ravine, a crack, dissension.

[illegible] k'uai 4. A proper name.

[illegible] ching 1. A place in Shantung.

郡 chün 4. A city, a district.

郎 lang 2. A gentleman, a secretary, a term of respect.

郚 wu 2. A town in Shantung.

郢 ying 3. A place in Hupeh.

8

[illegible] p'ei 2. A proper name.

郴 ch'ên 1. A place in Hunan.

[illegible] ch'ung 2. A feudal State in Shansi.

郳 i 2. A place in Shantung.

郭 kuo 1. An outer wall of fortification.

郲 lai 2. An ancient city in Honan.

郫 p'i 2. A place in Ssŭch'uan.

[illegible] p'ing 2. A place in Shantung

部 pu 4. A class, a genus, a category, a Board.

郯 t'an 2. Name of an old place in Shantung.

郰 tsou 1. The town where Confucius was born.

郪 ch'i 1. Name of an old town.

9

郵 yu 2. A post-house, a lodge.

鄇 hou 4. Name of a place.

鄀 jo 4. A feudal State in Hupeh.

鄈 k'uei 2. Name of different places.

郿 mei 2. A district in Shênsi.

鄂 o 4. Name of different places.

鄃 shu 1. A place in Shantung.

都 tu 1. The capital, a large city, all, full, elegant, refined.

郾 yen 3. A place in Honan.

鄅 yü 3. A place in Shantung.

鄆 yün 4. An ancient city in Shantung.

10

鄗 hao 4. A place in Chihli.

鄉 hsiang 1. A village, country, a suburban district.

鄋 sao 1. Name of a place.

鄎 hsi 1. A place in Honan.

鄌 t'ang 2. A place in Shansi.

鄒 chou 1. A place in Shantung.

鄑 chin 4. A town formerly in Chihli.

鄔 wu 4. A place in Chêkiang.

鄖 yün 2. A place in Hupeh.

11

鄣 chang 1. A place in Shantung.

鄟 chuan 1 Name of a place in Honan.

鄠 hu 3. A place in Shansi.

鄝 liao 3. A feudal State in Honan.

鄙 pi 3. Vulgar, vile, to scorn.
鄤 man 4. Name of a place.
鄢 yen 1. A place in Honan.
鄞 yin 2. A place in Chêkiang.
鄘 yung 1. A small feudal State in Honan.

12

鄭 chêng 4. A feudal State, now in Honan.
鄰 lin 2. Near, contiguous, neighbour.
鄯 shan 4. A district in the West.
鄮 mao 4. A place in Chêkiang.
鄷 fêng 2. An old fief.
鄱 p'o 2 A place in Kiangsi.
鄩 hsün 2. A place in Shantung.
鄲 tan 1. A place in Chihli.
鄿 t'an 2. A place in Shantung.
鄧 têng 4. A place in Honan.
鄫 tsêng 1. Name of a place in Shantung.

13 &

鄶 kuai 4. A place in Honan.
鄳 min 2. Honan.
鄵 ts'ao 4. A proper name.
鄴 yeh 4. A place in Honan.
鄹 chou 1. A place in Shantung.
鄾 yu 1. A place in Hupeh.
酆 fêng 1. A district in Ssŭ-ch'uan, a term for hell.
酅 hsi 3. Name of a place.
酈 li 4. A place in Shantung.
酇 tsan 4. A place in Hupeh.
酃 ling 2. A city in Hunan.

Rad. 164

See Lesson 41 G.

酉 yu 3. A cyclical character. Amphora. Liquor.
酋 chiu 1. Liquor after fermentation, perfect, to end.
酊 ting 1. Drunk.
酎 chou 4. Spirits used for sacrifices in the ancestral temple.
酌 chao 1. To pour out, to feast, to consider, to deliberate.
酏 i 2. Liquor, sweet wine.
配 p'ei 4. A mate, to pair, marriage.
酒 chiu 3. Spirit, as distilled from grain; wine.

4-5

酗 hsü 4. Drunkenness.
酕 mao 2. Drunk.
酖 chên 4. A poisonous bird, a virulent poison, deadly.
醇 ch'un 2. Pure, exquisite, liberal.
酘 t'ou 2. To distil.
酣 han 1. Exhilarated, as from drink; jolly, tipsy; deep, as sleep.
酤 ku 1. To deal in spirits.
酥 su 1. Curd, cheese, koumiss, crisp.
酡 t'o 2. Face flushed with drink, drunk.
酢 tso 4. To return a health.

6-7

酬 酧 ch'ou 2. To pledge with wine, to entertain, to repay.
酪 lao 3. Koumiss.
酩 ming 2. A strong spirit, drunk.
酲 ch'êng 2. Stupid from drink.
酵 chiao 4. Leaven, to ferment.
酷 k'u 4. k'ao 4. Cruel, tyrannical, very, extremely.
酹 lo 4. Libation.
酶 mei 2. Leaven used in fermenting.
酺 p'u 2. A feast, to drink deep.
酸 suan 1. Sour, grieved, afflicted.
酴 t'u 2. Unstrained spirits.
酳 yin 4. To rince the mouth with spirits.

8-9

醆 chan 3. Thick muddy wine, a goblet.
醊 cho 2. A libation.
醅 p'ei 1. Unstrained spirits.
醇 ch'un 2. Pure, generous, rich, unmixed.
醄 t'ao 2. Drunk.
醋 ts'u 4. Vinegar.
醉 tsui 4. Drunk, unconscious.
醃 yen 1. To salt, to pickle.
醁 lu 4. A kind of wine, made in Hunan.
醐 hu 2. Oil of butter.
醑 hsü 3. To strain spirits.
醒 hsing 3. To become sober, to wake up, to startle.
醓 t'an 3. A condiment.

醍 t'i 2. A liquor; oil.
醕 ch'un 2. Pure.
醅 yin 1. Drunk.
醖 yün 4. Fermented liquor, wine.

10-11

醡 cha 3. A wine-press.
醜 ch'ou 3. Ugly, hideous, shameful, evil, sorts, kinds, to compare, a crowd.
醫 i 4. To heal, to cure, a doctor.
醬 chiang 4. A soy, sauce, pickled food.
醦 ch'ên 3. Vinegar, sour.
醪 lao 2. The lees of spirits.
醨 li 2. Poor wine.
醥 p'iao 3. Clear spirits.
醩 tsao 1. Sediment, dregs.

12 &

醯 hsi 1. Vinegar.
醱 p'o 1. Must.
醭 pu 2. The mother of vinegar.
醮 chiao 4. A sacrifice, a festival, a wedding-feast.
醷 i 4. Liqueur.
醴 li 3. Newly-distilled spirits.
醲 nung 2. Strong wine, thick, rich.
醻 ch'ou 2. To pledge a guest, to toast him, to repay.
醺 hsün 1. Drunkness.
醹 ju 2. Generous spirit.
醼 hsü 3. Wine agreeable to the taste.
醿 mei 2. Arrack.
釀 jang 4. To ferment, to cause confusion or woes.
釁 hsin 4. To anoint with blood, to cement, quarrel, a feud.
釂 chiao 4. To drain a goblet.
釃 shai 1. To warm wine.
釅 yen 4. Concentrated liquors.
醽 ling 2. A rich kind of liquor, from Hunan.

Rad. 165

采 釆

See Lesson 123 A.

釆 pien 4. To sort, to separate.
采 ts'ai 3. Variegated, to gather, objects.
釉 yu 4. Nice, glossy.
釋 shih 4. To loosen, to set free, to open out, to cease, to explain, the Buddhism.

Rad. 166

里 里

See Lesson 149 D.

里 li 3. A village, the third of a mile.
重 chung 4. Heavy, weighty, important, severe.
ch'ung 2. Repetition, again.
野 yeh 3. A waste, a desert, savage.
量 liang 2. To measure, to consider.
釐 厘 } li 2. To regulate, to give, the thousandth part of a tael, minute.

Rad. 167

See Lesson 14 T.

金 chin 1. Metal. Gold. 11
釜 fu 3. A caldron, a boiler
針 chên 1. A needle, a pin.
釗 chao 1. To pare.
釘 ting 1. A nail.
ting 4. To nail.
釵 ch'ai 1. A hair pin.
釧 ch'uan 4. Bracelet.
釬 han 4. To solder metals.
釫 wu 1. A trowel, to roughcast.
釭 kang 1. A globular jar.
釦 k'ou 4. A button.
釤 shan 4. Bill-hook, to cut.
釣 tiao 4. To hook, to fish.
釴 i 4. The ears of a tripod.

4

鈔 ch'ao 1. To hook, to get hold of, to copy, a document, a receipt, money orders.
鈁 fang 1. A bell, a coin, a kettle.
鈇 fu 1. An axe.
鈎 kou 1. A hook, to hook, to detain.
鈐 ch'ien 1. A seal, to seal.
釿 chin 1. To chop, to chip.
欽 ch'in 1. To revere.
鈞 chün 1. Thirty catties, great, much.
鈉 na 4. To sharpen.

鈋 o 2. To scrape.

鈄 tou 3. A surname.

鈪 o 4. A bracelet.

鈕 niu 3. A knob, a button, a hilt or handle.

鈀 pa 4. A rake.

鈚 pi 2. Point of an arrow.

鈒 sa 3. To inlay, to incrust.

鈍 tun 4. Dull, blunt, stupid.

5

鉊 chao 1. A scythe, to mow.

鉦 chêng 1. Cymbals or small gongs.

鉒 chu 4. To inter valuables with the dead.

鉏 ch'u 2. A hoe.

鉉 hsüan 4. Tripod ears or rings.

鉤 kou 1. A hook, to hook, to detain.

鉗 ch'ien 2. A pair of tweezers, pinchers, tongs.

鈷 ku 3. A short javelin.

鉅 chü 4. Hard, as iron ; fierce, obdurate.

鈴 ling 2. A sleigh-bell.

鉋 pao 4. A plane, to plane off.

鈹 p'i 1. A stiletto, a bodkin.

鉑 po 4. A thin sheet of metal.

鉢 po 1. A bowl

鈸 po 4. Small cymbals.

鉎 hsing 1. Rust, verdigris.

鈶 ssŭ 1. A plough-share.

鉄 t'ieh 3. Iron, firm.

鈿 tien 4. Inlaid work.

鉈 t'o 2. A steelyard weight.

鉞 yüeh 4. A battle-ax.

鉛 ch'ien 1. Lead-ore.

6

銜 hsien 2. A bit, affected by, rank.

銃 ch'ung 4. Fire-arms.

銍 chih 4. A sickle.

銬 k'ao 4. Irons, fetters.

鉸 chiao 3. To cut, to clip.

銘 ming 2. To carve, to engrave.

鉼 ping 3. A plate of metal.

銖 chu 1. A light weight, a small thing, a trifle.

銛 t'ien 1. Sharp, to cut.

銑 hsien 3. Polished, bright.

銕 t'ien 3. Iron.

銚 tiao 4. A boiler.

銅 t'ung 2. Copper, brass.

銓 ch'üan 2. To estimate, to choose.

銀 yin 2. Silver.

7

鋈 wu 4. To plate.

銡 chih 4. To engrave.

鋜 cho 1. A hoe.

鋤 ch'u 2. A hoe, to hoe.

鋒 fêng 1. A sharp point, a spear head, weapons.

銲 han 4. To solder.

鋧 hsien 4. A chisel.

鋘 wu 2. A trowel, to parget.

銳 jui 4. Pointed, acute, keen, shrewd.

鋏 chia 1. Pincers.

錽 chien 3. To plate.

銶 ch'iu 2. A pick, a stone chisel.

鋦 chü 1. A clasp, to hook.

鋃 lang 2. A collar.

鋝 lieh 4. Twenty ounces.

鋩 mang 2. Edge, sharp.

鋂 mei 2. A large lock, a ring.

鋣 pang 1. A hoe.

鋪 p'u 1. To spread out, a bed.

銷 hsiao 1. To fuse, to melt, to consume, to cancel.

銹 hsiu 4. Rust of metal.

鋌 t'ing 3. Bars ; ingots.

鋟 ch'in 1. To slaughter.

銼 ts'o 4. A file.

鋙 wu 2. Fine iron.

鋥 ch'êng 4. To polish.

鋊 yü 4. A poker.

8

錚 chêng 1. The clang of metal.

錣 chui 4. To sew together, to baste.

錐 chui 1. An awl, the tip, trip, a trifle.

錎 han 2. An armour.

錡 i 3. A pan.

鋼 kang 1. Steel, hard.

錤 ch'i 2. A hoe.

錦 chin 3. Embroidered.

錮 ku 4. To stop, to caulk, to restrain.

鋸 chü 4. A saw, to saw.

錈 chüan 3. To bend iron.

銙 **k'o 4.** An ingot.

錕 **k'un 1.** Steel.

錜 **nien 4.** A hairpin, a nail.

錫 **hsi 2.** Tin. To give, gifts.

鉼 **ping 3.** Thin plates of gold or silver.

錔 **t'a 4.** Ironclad.

錭 **t'ao 2.** Blunt.

錟 **t'an 2.** A long spear.

錠 **ting 4.** An ingot, a slab, an anchor.

錞 **ch'un 2.** A pummel.

錢 **ch'ien 2.** Copper coin, cash, a mace, wealth.

錯 **ts'o 4.** To make a mistake, to err, to be wrong, to differ, to polish, to set up.

9

鍫 **ch'iao 1.** A hoe, to hoe.

鍪 **mou 2.** A helmet.

鍼 **chên 1.** A needle, a pin.

鍾 **chung 1.** A cup, a measure, to gather, natural gifts.

鍧 **hung 2.** A noise.

鍭 **hou 2.** The metal head of an arrow.

錘 **ch'ui 2.** A counterpoise.

鍰 **huan 2.** A ring.

鍠 **huang 2.** Clanging, jiggling.

鍥 **juan 4.** Soft, ductile metal.

鍇 **chieh 3.** A fine iron.

鍥 **ch'i 4.** A chisel.

鍵 **chien 4.** The bolt of a Chinese lock, a spring.

鍋 **kuo 1.** A caldron.

鍊 **lien 4.** To smelt ores, to refine, to discipline.

錄 **lu 4.** To record, to write down, to choose, an index.

鍔 **o 4.** A sharp point.

錛 **pên 1.** An adze.

鍉 **shih 2.** A key.

鍟 **hsing 1.** Rust on iron.

鍍 **tu 4.** To gild, to plate.

鍛 **tuan 4.** To forge, to harden.

鍤 **ch'a 2.** A hee.

鍐 **tsung 1.** Metal ornament.

錨 **mao 2.** An anchor.

鍚 **yang 2.** Small bells on a horse's bridle.

鍱 **yeh 4.** A thin plate of metal.

鍈 **ying 1.** The sound of jingling bells.

鍝 **yü 4.** An awl.

10

鎏 **liu 2.** Pure gold.

鎮 **chên 4.** To keep, to protect, a market-town, a brigade.

鎭 **ch'ên 1.** To extend, to pull.

鎚 **ch'ui 2.** A hammer.

鎬 **hao 4.** A stove. The capital of *Wu wang* of *Chou*.

鎋 **hsia 2.** A linch-pin. To govern, to rule.

鎤 **huang 3.** The sound of bells.

鎧 **k'ai 3.** An armour, a cuirass.

鎌 **lien 2.** A sickle, a reaping-hook.

鏟 **ch'an 3.** A plane, to cut and pare.

鎒 **nou 1.** A hoe, to weed.

鎊 **p'ang 2.** To hoe.

鎞 **p'i 2.** A spindle.

鎛 **po 2.** A large bell.

鎪 **sou 1.** To engrave on metal.

鎩 **sha 1.** A long spear.

鎙 **sho 4.** A long spear.

鎍 **so 3.** A wire.

鎖 **so 3.** A lock, chains, to lock, to fetter.

鎥 **tiao 2.** An alembic.

鎗 **ch'iang 1.** A gun, an opium pipe.

鎡 **tzŭ 1.** A mattock.

鎰 **i 4.** A piece of gold, a weight.

鎔 **jung 2.** A mould in which to pour castings, to smelt, to cast.

11

鏨 **tsan 4.** To chisel, to cut out.

鏊 **ao 1.** A round iron cooking utensil.

鏖 **lu 4.** A proper name.

鐩 **sui 4.** A burning mirror.

鏆 **kuan ?.** A finger-ring.

鏗 **k'êng 1.** Jingling.

鏡 **ching 4.** A mirror. Spectacles.

鏤 **lou 4.** To carve, to engrave.

鏈 **lien 2.** A chain.

鏐 **liao 3.** Darkened gold.

鏝 **man 2.** A trowel.

鏌 **mo 4.** The name of a famous sword.

鏢 **p'iao 1.** A weapon, the point of a sword.

鏥 **hsiu 4.** Rust, oxyde.

鏑 **ti 2.** The point of an arrow.

鏇 **hsüan 4.** A pulley, a windlass.

鏜 **t'ang 2.** Noise of drums, etc.

鏟 **ch'an 1.** A spade, a shovel, to dig.

鏘 **ch'iang 1.** Peal.

鏚 **ch'i 1.** A battle-axe.

鏃 **tsu 2.** The point of an arrow.

鏞 **yung 3.** A large bell.

12

鐘 **chung 1.** A bell, a clock.

鏵 **hua 2.** A spade, a shovel.

鐖 **chi 1.** A barb on a hook.

鐗 **chien 4.** Iron protecting an axle.

鐝 **chüeh 2.** A pick, a mattock.

鐍 **chü 2.** A brooch.

鑇 **k'uan 4.** A branding-iron.

鐀 **kuei 4.** A wardrobe.

鐐 **liao 4.** Fetters, a chain.

鐃 **nao 2.** Cymbals.

鏺 **p'o 1.** A scythe, to mow.

鏷 **p'u 4.** A dart.

鏾 **hsien 4.** To castrate.

鐔 **t'an 2.** A handle.

鏽 **hsiu 4.** Rust; oxides.

鐋 **t'ang 4.** A file; a plane; to poligh.

鐙 **têng 4.** A stirrup.

鐓 **tun 1.** A weapon flail-shaped.

鐕 **tsan 1.** A hair-pin.

鏳 **tsêng 1.** The ring of metal when struck.

鐎 **chiao 1.** A brass kettle.

鐫 **chien 1.** To cut; to chisel.

鐏 **tsun 1.** The butt-end of a spear.

13-14

鐲 **cho 2.** A bracelet.

鐶 **huan 2.** A metal ring.

鐳 **lei 2.** Bronzes; small copper coins.

鐮 **lien 2.** A sickle; a reaping-hook.

鐴 **pi 4.** To sharpen; edge.

鐰 **sao 4.** Fine steel.

鐺 **tang 1.** A bell.

鐵 **t'ieh 2.** Iron.

鐸 **to 2.** A clapper.

鑒 鑑 **chien 4.** A mirror; an example; historic events; documents; rule; to survey, to audit.

鑄 **chu 4.** To cast metals.

鑊 **huo 4.** A caldron.

鑌 **pin 1.** A fine steel.

鑐 **hsü 1.** A bolt.

15 &

鑕 **chih 4.** An anvil.

鑛 **kung 3.** A mine; an ore.

鑞 **la 4.** Tin.

鑢 **lü 4.** A rasp.

[illegible] **lü 4.** To polish; a file.

鑣 **piao 1.** Bridle and bit.

鑠 **shao 4.** To polish; to be resplendent.

[illegible] **cha 2.** A grass-cutter.

鑪 **lu 2.** A stove, a brazier.

鑲 **hsiang 1.** To inlay; to inchase; to insert or set.

鑯 **chien 1.** An iron instrument, sharpened like an awl.

鑰 **yao 4.** The bolt of lock; a key.

鑴 **hsi 2.** A tripod or boiler.

鑵 **kuan 4.** A metal pot.

鑷 **nieh 4.** Pincers.

鑼 **lo 2.** A gong.

鑾 **luan 2.** Little bells; imperial cars; a term of respect.

鑿 **tsao 2.** A chisel; to cut into; to open out.

鑽 **tsuan 3.** To bore; to pierce; to penetrate.

Rad. 168

長

See Lesson 113 A.

長 **chang 3.** To increase; to grow; to excel; senior.
ch'ang 2. Long, of time or space.

套 **t'ao 4.** Large; to enwrap; a harness.

镽 **liao 4.** Long; tall.

Rad. 169

門

See Lesson 129 C.

門 **mên 2.** A door; a gate; a family; a school; a sect.

閂 **shuan 1.** The bolt used to bar doors; to bolt a door.

閃 **shan 3.** To cross a door-way; to shun; to slip aside; a flash.

閈 **han 4.** Village gate; walled village.

閉 **pi 4.** To close, to shut, to stop up.

問 **wên 4.** To ask.

閆 **yen 2.** The gate in the village; the king of bell.

4-5

閜 **hsia** 1 To leave ajar.

閑 **hsien** 2. A threshold; to close; to forbid; to be trained.

閒 } **chien** 4. A space between; during; a numerative.
間 } **hsien** 2. Leisure; quiet; idte; light.

閎 **hung** 2. Vast, wide, open.

閏 **yün** 4. **lün** 4. Intercalary. 7

開 **k'ai** 1. To open; to begin, to write out; boiling.

閌 **k'ang** 4. Portico.

悶 **mên** 4. Melancholy.

閔 **min** 3. To feel for.

閘 **cha** 3. A lock, a flood-gate.

鬧 **ao** 4. Wrangling.

閟 **pi** 4. To close; to impede; secret, hidden.

閛 **p'ing** 2. The noise of shutting or opening a door.

6-7

閥 **fa** 2. The left side of a gate; rank, degree.

[門艮] **hsien** 4. A threshold.

閧 **hung** 4. A road; a lane.

閣 **ko** 2. A vestibule; a council-chamber; the court.

閤 **ho** 2. All, whole, complete.

[門匡] **k'uang** 4. The frame of a door.

関 **kuan** 1. A barrier, custom-house.

閨 **kui** 1. The door to the inner apartments; the women's apartments; unmarried girls.

閩 **min** 2. The Fukien province.

閡 **hai** 4. To shut a door; to prevent; to hinder.

[門寺] **shih** 4. A eunuch.

聞 **wên** 2. To hear, news.

閫 **k'un** 4. Women's apartments.

閬 **lang** 4. A high door; waste.

閭 **lü** 2. A village; the gate of a village.

閱 **yüeh** 4. To look at; to peruse; to inspect; merits.

誾 **yin** 2. Nice words.

8-9

閶 **ch'ang** 1. The gate of heaven; the palace gates.

闀 **hsiang** 4. A path.

閽 **hun** 1. An entrance.

閼 **yü** 4. To close; to shut up.

闅 **wên** 2. To look closely at.

閹 **yen** 1. Eunuchs; to geld.

閻 **yen** 2. The gate to a village; the Chinese Pluto.

閾 **yü** 4. A door-sill; a threshold.

闊 **k'uo** 1. **k'o** 4. Large, liberal; far, separation.

闌 **lan** 2. A screen; to close.

闇 **an** 4. To shut the door; dark, dim.

闈 **wei** 2. Examination-hall.

闉 **yin** 1. The circular wall which incloses the gates of cities.

[門俞] **yü** 2. To spy; to peep.

10 &

闖 **ch'uang** 3. To burst in; to rush violently; suddenly.

闔 **ho** 2. A family; the whole.

闓 **k'ai** 3. To open.

闕 **ch'üeh** 4. A void space; wanting; to eliminate.

關 **kuan** 1. A barrier.

闒 **t'a** 4. A window in a loft.

闐 **t'ien** 2. The noise of a multitude.

闑 **nieh** 4. The threshold.

關 **kuan** 1. To bar the door; a barrier; a custom-house; to bear upon; involving; results; connected. *Kuan-ti*, the Chinese god of war.

闚 **k'uei** 2. To look at, to spy.

闡 **ch'an** 3. To explain; to enlarge, develop.

闟 **hsi** 4. To fold; to unite.

闠 **hui** 4. A gate.

闞 **k'an** 1. To spy; to watch.

[門爲] **wei** 3. A half-open door.

闤 **huan** 2. A wall around a city.

闢 **p'i** 4. To burst forth; to open up.

Rad. 170

See Lesson 86 A.

阜 } **fu** 4. A mound; prosperity;
阝 } abundance.

阤 **ch'ih** 3. A slide on a hill-side.

阡 **ch'ien** 1. A road.

阯 **chih** 3. Base, foundation.

阪 **fan** 3. A slope.

防 **fang** 2. An embankment, to protect from, to guard against; to avoid, to defend.

阬 **k'êng** 1. A pit; to ruin.

[阝及] **chi** 2. Steps, degrees.

阨 **o** 4. A defile, a pass; distress, difficulty.

阱 **ching** 3. A pit-fall.

阳 **yang** 2. The active principle.

阴 **yin** 1. The passive principle.

阮 **yüan** 3. Name of a pass.

5

阻 **tsu** 3. An obstacle; to impede.

附 **fu** 4. To be next to; near; an appendix.

阿 **o** 1. A hill; used as sound before proper names.

阨 **ai** 4. A defile; distress.

陂 **p'o** 1. Uneven, inclined, a declivity.

陀 **t'o** 2. Steep and rugged path.

阼 **tso** 4. Steps, degrees.

6

限 **hsien** 4. A limit; a boundary; a restriction.

降 **chiang** 4. To descend; to degrade.
hsiang 2. To submit; to yield.

陋 **lou** 4. Vile.

陌 **mai** 4. A raised path; to go.

7

陣 **chên** 4. To dispose; an army, a battle; a gust; a shower.

陟 **chih** 4. To ascend; to mount; promoted; to proceed.

除 **ch'u** 2. To deduct; to take away; to get rid of; to pass away; the end.

陘 **ching** 4. A path.

陛 **pi** 4. The steps of the Throne.

陜 **hsia** 2. A file; a gorge.

陝 **shên** 3. Province of *Shênsi*.

陞 **shêng** 1. To rise, as in office; to ascend.

陡 **tou** 3. The slope of a hill; suddenly.

院 **yüan** 4. A court-yard; atrium.

8

陳 **ch'ên** 2. To arrange; to state; a long time; old.

陷 **hsieu** 4. To fall down; to sink.

陭 **i** 1. Steep.

陵 **ling** 2. A mound; a tomb; to desecrate; to insult.

陸 **lu** 4. Dry land; continuous; in succession; used for the numeral *liu* six.

陪 **p'ei** 2. To bear one company; to aid; to match.

陶 **t'ao** 2. A kiln for making pottery; to mould.

陬 **tsou** 1. A corner.

陰
隂 } **yin** 1. The shady side of a hill; the inferior power; night; death.

9

陼 **chu** 3. An islet; a bank.

陲 **ch'ui** 2. A frontier; a boundary.

隊 **tui** 4. A squad, a company.

隍 **huang** 2. A moat; a ditch; a city; the Genius of a city.

階 **chieh** 1. A flight of steps; degree; rank.

隆 **lung** 2. Abundant.

隌 **an** 4. Invisible; hidden; opaque.

陧 **nieh** 4. Wrathful; to rail at.

隋 **to** 4. Mince-meat.
sui 2. A proper name.

隄 **ti** 1. A dyke; a bank; to guard against.

隈 **wei** 1. A bend in a coastline; a bay.

陽 **yang** 2. The south of a hill; superior power; light; life. 8

陻 **yin** 1. To stop up, to dam in.

隅 **yü** 2. A corner, an angle.

10

隘 **yeh** 4. A pass, narrow, trouble, difficulty.

隒 **ch'ien** 3. A summit.

隙 **hsi** 4. A fissure, a crack, a gap, leisure time, discord

隔 **ko** 2. **chieh** 4. A partition, a shelf, to interpose, next, to.

⿰阝馬 **ma** 3. To pile up.

隗 **wei** 3. Lofty, eminent.

隖 **wu** 3. A wall round a village.

隕 **yün** 3. To fall, to let fall, to perish.

障 **chang** 4. An embankment, to screen, to protect.

⿰阝虖 **hsia** 4. A crack, a fissure.

際 **chi** 4. An angle, a limit, a juncture, an occasion, a time, a chance.

隣 **lin** 2. Neighbouring, near.

險 **hsien** 3. Dangerous, hazardous.

隩 **ao** 4. A shore, a bank, a bay.

隨 **sui** 2. To follow, to imitate, to comply with, presently.

隧 **sui** 4. A path to a tomb, way.

⿰阝頓 **tuu** 4. A ton.

隰 **shih** 1. Low, marshy land, wet.

隮 **chi** 1. To go up, to scale, to rise.

隱 **yin** 3. Retired, screened, in private life, enigma, affection, compassion.

隳 **hui** 1. To destroy.

隴 **lung** 3. A dike.

隲 **chih** 1. Merit, promotion.

Rad. 171

隶 隶

See Lesson 44 E.

隶 **tai 4.** To reach to.

肆 **ssŭ 4.** To expand, etc.

隸 隷 隸 **li 4.** Attached to, belonging, underlings, government, administration; the square plain style.

Rad. 172

隹 隹

See Lesson 168 A.

隹 **chui 1.** Short-tailed birds.

隻 **chih 4.** One by itself, single, a numerative.

隺 **hao 4.** To rise, to soar.

隼 **hsün 3.** A falcon.

难 **nan 2.** Difficult, hard.

售 **shou 4.** To sell.

焦 **chiao 1.** Scorched, dried up.

雀 **ch'iao 3.** Small birds in general, especially the sparrow.

雄 **hsiung 2.** Male, brave.

雇 **ku 4.** To hire, to borrow.

雋 **tsun 4.** Fat, savoury.

集 **chi 2.** To flock together, a market.

雅 **ya 3.** Elegant, genteel, polished, often, your.

雁 **yen 4.** A wild goose.

雉 **chih 4.** A pheasant.

雎 **tsu 1.** A sea-gull.

雍 **yung 1.** Harmony, union.

雒 **lao 4.** A kind of bird, fear.

雌 **tz'ŭ 2.** The female of birds.

雕 **tiao 1.** The fish-eagle, to carve, to engrave.

雖 **sui 1.** Although, even if; to dismiss.

雛 **ch'u 2.** A chicken.

雞 **chi 1.** Gallinaceous birds, a cock, a hen.

雙 **shuang 1.** Double, pair, mate.

雜 **tsa 2.** Variegated, mixed, mingled, a mixture.

雝 **yung 1.** A wag-tail, singing, concord.

離 **li 2.** To separate, to leave, distance, distinction.

難 **nan 2.** Difficult, hard, irksome, to distress, trouble, is it not?

讐 讎 **ch'ou 2.** Ta hate, a foe, enmity.

Rad. 173

雨 雨

See Lesson 125 B.

雨 **yü 3.** Rain.

[illegible] **shan 1.** Drizzling rain.

雪 **hsüeh 3.** Snow.

雩 **yü 2.** To pray for rain.

雰 **fên 1.** Misty, foggy.

雱 **p'ang 1.** An abundant fall of snow or sleet.

雯 **wên 2.** Coloured clouds.

雲 **yün 2.** Clouds, a fog.

5-6

[illegible] **kau 1.** Hoar frost, rain.

雷 **lei 2.** Thunder.

零 **ling 2.** Small rain, a fraction, a residue, a remainder.

雹 **pao 2.** Hail.

電 **tien 4.** Lightning, electricity, to telegraph.

需 **hsü 1.** Needful, bent on doing.

[illegible] **t'i 2.** To clear up.

7-8

震 **chên 4.** To shake, to shock.

霃 **ch'ên 2.** Dull and lowering.

霉 **mei 2.** Damp, mildew.

霂 **mu 4.** Fine rain.

霈 **p'ei 4.** Rain falling.

霄 **hsiao 1.** Heaven, the sky.

霆 **t'ing 2.** The noise of thunder.

霑 **chan 1.** A soaking rain, to moisten, to wet, to bestow favours.

霔 **chu 4.** A seasonable rain.

霏 **fei 1.** Sleet.

霓 **i 2.** A rainbow.

霍 **huo 3.** A sudden rain.

[illegible] **la 4.** The sound of rain.

霖 **lin 2.** Refreshing rain.

霎 **sha 4. shua 4.** Sudden, temporary, light.

9-10

霞 **hsia 2.** Clouds tinged red; vapour.

霝 **ling 2.** Drops of rain.

霡霂 mai 4. A fine rain.

霒 yin 1. Cloudy.

霜 shuang 1. Frozen dew, hoar frost, efflorescence, crystallised.

霙 ying 1. Crystallised snow.

霩 k'uo 4. The clouds dispersing.

霤 liu 4. To drip.

11-12

霨 wei 4. Clouds rising.

霧 wu 4. Fog, mist.

霖 lan 3. A long continued rain.

霦 pin 1. Dew, to sparkle.

霫 hsi 2. Heavy rain.

霪 yin 2. A continued rain.

霰 hsien 4. Sleet, snow.

霯 têng 4. Heavy rain.

13 &

露 lou 4. To expose, to disclose, naked.
lu 4. Dew.

[illegible] nung 2. Mud, slimy.

霸 pa 4. To govern, a sovereign, to incroach on, a tyrant.

霶 p'ang 1. A heavy fall, a driving gale.

霹 p'i 1. Thunder, to thunderstrike, a clash.

霵 chi 4. A driving rain.

霼 hsi 4. Cloudy.

霾 mai 2. A sand-storm.

霿 mêng 2. Fog, mist.

[illegible] suan 2. A slight shower.

霽 chi 4. The clouds clearing away, serene.

靄 o 3. Cloudy.

靂 li 4. A clap of thunder.

靈 ling 2. A subtle substance, the spirit or energy of a being, soul, spiritual, a marvellous power.

靆 tai 4. Cloudy.

[illegible] cho 2. Rain pouring down.

靐 p'ing 2. The sound of thunder, a cannonading.

Rad. 174

青

See Lesson 79 F.

青 ch'ing 1. Green, blue, black, grey, the white of an egg, a tablet.

靖 ching 4. Quiet, tranquil, peaceful.

靘 ch'ing 1. Blue, azure.

靚 ching 4. To ornament, to paint the face.

靛 tien 4. Indigo.

靜 ching 4. Quiet, still, repose.

靝 t'ien 1. The blue sky.

Rad. 175

非

See Lesson 170 A.

非 fei 1. Wrong, not.

靠 k'ao 4. To lean on, to trust, near to.

靡 mei 2. No, not; malice, defeat, loss.

Rad. 176

面 

See Lesson 160 B.

面 mien 4. The face, the front, the surface, to visit, to meet, turn, time.

䩄 han 4. Freckles.

靦 t'ien 3. To feel ashamed, timid.

靧 hui 4. To wash the face.

𩈾 chiao 1. Wrinkled, faded.

靨 yen 3. A pock-marked face.

Rad. 177

革

See Lesson 105 A.

革 ko 2. Raw hide, to change, to degrade.

靪 ting 4. A piece, to patch.

勒 lei 1. To bridle.

靫 ch'a 1. A quiver.

靭 jên 4. Pliant, soft.

靮 ti 4. Bridle, reins.

靴 hsüeh 1. Boots.

靶 pa 3. A target.

靷 yin 4. A horse collar, a harness.

5-6

鞇 i 4. A saddle.

靺 mo 4. Red socks.

靽 pan 4. Trammels.

鞁 pei 4. To saddle.

鞄 p'ao 2. To work and soften hides.

靼 tan 2. Soft leather.

鞅 yang 1. A martingale.

靿 yao 4. The leg of a boot.

鞋 hsieh 2. A shoe.

鞈 chia 1. A leather jerkin.

鞏 kung 3. A proper name.

鞍 an 1. A saddle.

鞉 t'ao 2. A small flat drum with a handle.

鞇 yin 1. A cushion.

7-8

鞙 chüan 1. The traces of harness.

鞔 man 2. A sole, to cover with leather.

鞘 ch'iao 4. A sheath, a scabbard.

鞗 t'iao 2. The reins of a bridle.

鞓 t'ing 1. A strap of leather.

鞕 ying 4. Hard, obstinate.

鞝 chang 3. A sole, a flap.

鞠 chü 2. A ball, to nourish, to bow, to exhaust.

9-10

鞧 chou 4. A crupper.

鞨 ho 2. A stocking.

[illegible] hu 2. A quiver.

鞣 jou 2. Well-dressed leather, soft.

鞫 chü 2. To investigate judicially.

鞭 pien 1. A whip.

[illegible] shih 4. A leather sheath for a sword.

鞮 ti 1. Leather shoes.

鞦 ch'iu 1. A crupper.

[illegible] yün 4. A worker in leather.

鞲 kou 4. A leathern vanbrace used by archers.

鞹 k'uo 4. Curried leather.

[illegible] t'a 4. A leather tunic.

鞳 t'a 4. A leather cuirass.

[illegible] chou 3. A strap.

[illegible] wêng 1. The uppers of a boot.

11 &

[illegible] chang 1. Flap of a saddle.

鞾 hsüeh 1. Boots.

鞽 ch'iao 1. A hurdle.

韂 ch'an 4. A saddle flap.

韁 kang 1. A tether.

[illegible] pang 1. The vamp of a shoe.

韃 ta 2. Tartars.

韆 ch'ien 1. A swing.

韈 wa 4. Socks, stockings.

[illegible] lung 2. A halter.

[illegible] ch'an 2. Paddings.

Rad. 178

See Lesson 31 G.

韋 wei 2. Soft leather, pliant, flexible.

韌 jen 1. Pliant, soft.

靯 chu 4. Leathern gaiters.

韍 fu 2. A knee-pad of leather, a cap, a strap.

韎 mei 4. Leather buskin of soldiers.

[illegible] pi 4. A frame for keeping bows.

韐 chia 1. A girdle worn by mourners.

韒 ch'iao 4. A sheath, a scabbard.

韔 ch'ang 4. A case for a bow.

韓 han 2. A fence or wall around a lot, a proper name.

韘 tieh 4. An archer's finger-stall.

韚 tuan 4. An over-leather.

韙 wei 2. The right, natural gifts.

韗 yün 4. A worker in leather.

韛 pai 4. A leather tube appended to bellows.

韜 t'ao 1. A scabbard, military tactics.

韠 pi 4. A knee-pad.

Rad. 179

See Lesson 170 B.

韭 chiu 3. Leeks.

韮 chiu 3. Leeks.

韰 hsieh 4. A shalot, courageous, bold.

韱 ch'ien 1. Wild garlic.

Rad. 180

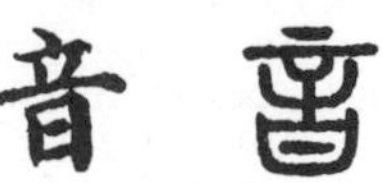

See Lesson 73 E.

音 yin 1. Sound, a musical note, tone, pronunciation.

韵 **yün 4.** A harmony.
韶 **shao 2.** The music of Shun, harmony, glory.
䪦 **hung 1.** Noise, clamour.
韸 **p'êng 2.** The noise of drums.
䪨 **ch'iang 1.** A tone, melody.
䪵 **nie 1.** To stop, silent.
韻 **yün 4.** Harmony of sound, rhyme.
響 **hsiang 3.** Noise, sound, echo, clear.

Rad. 181

See Lesson 160 C.

頁 **yeh 4.** The head, a page, beginning.
頃 **ch'ing 3.** A hundred *mu*.
k'êng 3. An instant.
頂 **ting 3.** The top, to touch with the head, to lean against, to contradict, to argue.
t'ing 2. Very, extremely.
頇 **han 1.** Bald, slow, apathetic.
項 **hsiang 4.** The neck, kind, sort, sum, revenue.
順 **shun 4.** To follow, to obey, pliant, docile, easy, graceful, fair.
須 **hsü 1.** Beard, ought, must, necessary, to wait for, an instant.
頒 **pan 1.** To extend, to expend, to promulgate, to bestow.
頊 **hsü 3.** Confiding, careful.
頌 **sung 4.** To praise, to extol, to celebrate, a sacrificial ode.
頓 **tun 4.** To bow the head, to salute, to rest, to injure.
頑 **wan 2.** A thickheaded stupid person.
預 **yü 4.** To pre-arrange, to prepare.

5-6

䪼 **cho 4.** The cheekbones.
䫇 **jan 3.** The beard, the whiskers.
領 **ling 3.** The throat, the collar, to manage, to receive.
頗 **p'o 1.** Very, much.
頦 **k'o 1.** The chin.
頡 **chieh 2. hsieh 2.** To raise the head.
頜 **ho 4.** Inferior maxillary bone.
熲 **kung 3.** To light.
潁 **ying 3.** A river.
頤 **i 2.** The chin.
額 頟 } **o 2. ai 2. yeh 2.** The forehead, a fixed number.
顖 **hsin 4.** The fontanel.
頫 **t'iao 4.** To salute, an audienee.

7-8

䫖 **ch'ên 3.** Coarse, ugly.
頷 **han 3.** The chin, to bend the head.
顐 **hun 1.** A ringing in the head.
頰 **hsia 4.** The chin.
頸 **kêng 3.** The neck, the throat.
賴 **lai 4.** To lean on.
頻 **p'in 2.** Urgent, incessant, sorrow.
頭 **t'ou 2.** The head, the top, the end, the chief, before, a suffix.
頹 **t'ê 2.** Bald, a gust of wind, to fall, gradually.
頴 **ying 3.** A sharp point, a fine critical taste.
顄 **han 2.** The chin.
顆 **k'o 1.** A numerative of small round things.
顇 **ts'ui 4.** Worn out, downcast.

9-10

顓 **chuan 1.** To carry the head high, dignified, sedate.
額 **o 2. ai 2. yeh 2.** The forehead.
顋 **sai 1.** The cheeks.
題 **t'i 2.** The forehead, a heading, a theme, a subject.
顏 **yen 2.** Colour, the countenance.
顒 **yung 2.** Bearing, dignity.
顗 **k'ai 3.** Joy, happiness.
類 **lei 4.** A species; a kind; a class; to assimilate.
顙 **sang 3.** The forehead.
顖 **hsin 4.** The fontanels.
顛 **tien 1.** The top; the apex; the summit; to upset; to overthrow; to be ruined; to amble.
願 **yüan 4.** To wish; to be willing; to desire; a vow.

11 &

䫺 **ma 2.** Stammering; hesitating.
顢 **man 1.** A large round face.
顣 **ts'u 4.** To frown.
䫲 **tsan 3.** To bend the head.
顥 **hao 4.** Bright.
顧 **ku 4.** To look after; to regard; to consider.
顦 **ch'iao 2.** Grieving; depressed.
顫 **chan 4.** To shake, unsteady.
䫴 **chin 4.** To gnash the teeth; exhausted.
顯 **hsien 3.** Light; apparent; clear; illustrious; glorious.
䫦 **kai 4.** The vertex.
𩕢 **ning 3.** The top of the head.
纇 **lei 4.** Knots in silk thread.

顰 **p'in 3.** To knit the brows.

顱 **lu 2.** A skull.

顳 **nieh 4.** Temporal bone.

顴 **ch'üan 2.** The cheekbones.

Rad 182

See Lesson 21 B.

風 **fêng 1.** The wind; custom; habit; rumour; reputation; example; lust.

颩 **tiu 1.** To fan.

颫 **fu 2.** A storm.

颬 **hsia 1.** To pant.

颭 **chan 3.** Shaken by the wind.

颰 **fu 4.** A light breeze.

颮 **piao 1.** A strong whirlwind.

颯 **li 4.** A gust; suddenly.

颳 **kua 1.** To blow, as the wind.

颲 **lieh 4.** A violent gust.

[illegible] **li 4.** Driving wind and rain.

颵 **shao 1.** To dry in the wind.

颴 **hsüan 4.** A whirlwind.

[illegible] **fêng 1.** The wind swaying the trees; the Buddhist psalmody.

[illegible] **hu 1.** Sough of the wind.

颶 **chü 4.** A typhoon.

[illegible] **liang 2.** A cold north wind.

[illegible] **ch'ui 2.** To bend to the wind.

[illegible] **an 4.** A hurricane.

颸 **ssŭ 1.** A cool breeze.

颹 **wei 3.** A fresh breeze.

颺 **yang 2.** To be tossed about, as by wind; to fly.

䬝 **yü 2.** A hurricane.

颽 **k'ai 3.** The genial south wind.

颾 **sao 1.** The sound of the wind.

颼 **sou 1** A cold blast.

颻 **yao 2.** Floating; roaming.

飂 **liao 2.** A constant wind.

飄 **p'iao 1** To whirl, to be blown about; floating.

Rad. 183

飛

See Lesson 11 A.

飛 **fei 1.** To fly; swift.

翥 **chu 4.** To fly up; to soar.

Rad. 184

食

See Lesson 26 M.

食 **shih 2.** To eat; food.
ssŭ 4. To feed; to rear.

飢 **chi 1.** Dearth, hungry.

飡 **ts'au 1.** A meal.

飧 **sun 1.** An evening meal.

飥 **t'o 2** Paste, bread.

飭 **ch'ih 4.** To direct; to adjust, to prepare; order; edict.

飯 **fan 4.** Boiled grain; food in general; a meal, to eat.

飪 **jên 3** To cook,

飩 **tun 4.** Meat ball rolled in flour.

飲 **yin 3.** To drink.
yin 4. To give to drink.

飫 **yü 4.** Satiated, glutted with; gift, favour.

5-6

飴 **i 2.** Sweet cakes, sugar; a delicacy; joy.

飽 **pao 3.** To eat enough; satiated; happy

飶 **pi 4.** The fragrance of food.

飾 **shih 4.** An ornament; to paint.

飼 **ssŭ 4.** To feed.

蝕 **shih 2.** To eat away; an eclipse.

餉 **hsiang 3.** Provisions; rations; taxes.

餃 **chiao 3.** A meat dumpling.

餀 **ai 4. nai 4.** Spoiled food.

餅 **ping 3.** Cakes; pastry.

餌 **erh 3.** Bait for fish; a temptation; cakes.

養 **yang 3.** To nourish; to rear; to take care of.

7-8

餐 **ts'an 1** To eat; a meal.

餒 **nei 3.** Hungry.

餓 **o 1. wo 4.** Hungry.

餑 **po 1.** Cakes; biscuits.

餔 **p'u 4.** To eat.

餙 **shih 4.** To adorn; to deceive.

餗 **su 4.** Boiled rice.

餕 **tsun 4.** The remain; the scraps.

餘 **yü 2.** Remainder; surplus; excess. 7

餦 **chang 1.** Cakes made of flour.

餟 **cho 2.** Offerings.

餚 **yao** 4. Food; viands.

餡 **hsien** 4. Dumplings.

餛 **hun** 2. Fritters.

餋 **chüan** 3. Thin dry wafer cakes.

餜 **kuo** 3. Cakes; pastry.

館 **kuan** 3. An inn; a hall; a club-house; an office; a school-room.

餅 **ping** 3. A cake, pastry.

餤 **t'an** 2. To increase; a cake.

餞 **chien** 4. A farewell entertainment.

餧 **wei** 4. To feed.

9-10

餲 **ai** 4. **nai** 4. Spoiled food.

餴 **fên** 1. To steam rice.

餱 **hou** 2. Dry prevision.

餬 **hu** 1. Congee, rice gruel, food.

餭 **huang** 2. Pastry, cakes.

餫 **hun** 2. Provisions, rations.

餪 **nuan** 3. A present of food.

餳 **t'ang** 2. Sugar, delicacies.

[illegible] **sui** 3. Cakes, biscuits.

餵 **wei** 4. To feed animals.

餮 **t'ieh** 4. Gluttonous.

餻 **kao** 1. Cakes.

[illegible] **hsiu** 3. Spoiled food.

餽 **k'ui** 4. Presentation of food to the Manes.

[illegible] **ch'ien** 3. Hungry; unsatisfied.

餿 **sou** 1. Spoilt, sour.

[illegible] **hsi** 2. To suck up.

[illegible] **su** 4. Vegetarian diet.

餹 **t'ang** 2. Sugar, honey, candy.

[illegible] **chui** 1. Steamed loaves.

11-12

饉 **chin** 3. A dearth.

饅 **man** 2. Steamed dumplings.

[illegible] **mo** 2. Steamed bread in small loaves.

饆 **pi** 4. A dumpling with meat inside.

饈 **hsiu** 1. Delicacies, sweets.

饇 **yü** 4. Glutted, satisfied.

[illegible] **ch'êng** 1. To eat much.

饎 **hsi** 1. Food, victuals, an offering.

[illegible] **ch'uang** 2. To eat immoderately.

饌 **chuan** 4. Food, provision, a delicacy.

饐 **i** 4. Spoilt food, sour.

饒 **jao** 2. Plenty, abundance, liberal, to pardon.

饑 **chi** 1. Dearth, famine.

饋 **k'uei** 4. Provisions, food.

饊 **san** 3. Fried cakes.

饍 **shan** 4. Viands, delicacies.

13 &

饘 **chan** 1. Thick congee.

饗 **hsiang** 3. Offerings, a feast, to relish, to agree.

[illegible] **nung** 2. To stuff one's self with food.

饕 **t'ao** 1. Gluttonous, covetous.

饔 **yung** 1. Breakfast, meats.

饛 **mêng** 2. A plentiful table, abundance.

[illegible] **ning** 2. To take one's fill.

饜 **yen** 4. Filled, satiated, disgust.

饝 **mo** 2. **mei** 3. To feed an infant, congee.

饟 **hsiang** 3. To carry victuals.

饞 **ch'an** 2. To love good eating, greedy, gluttonous.

饠 **lo** 2. A baked wheaten cake.

Rad. 185

See Lesson 160 A.

首 **shou** 3. The head, a chief, foremost, the origin, sorts, stanzas.

馗 **k'uei** 4. A proper name.

䭫 **ting** 3. The apex.

道 **tao** 4. Way, road.

馘 **kuo** 4. To cut off the head o the slain.

Rad. 186

See Lesson 73 B.

香 **hsiang** 1. Fragrant, incense.

馚 **p'ên** 1. Pragrant, to exhale.

馜 **ni** 3. Very fragrant.

馞 **po** 4. Fragrant.

馡 **fei** 1. Fragrant.

[illegible] **i** 3. Sweet-smelling.

[illegible] **p'êng** 3. Fragrant.

馥 **fu** 4. A fragrant smell.

馨 hsin 1. To smell sweetly.

馩 p'ên 1. To exhale, fragrant.

馫 wei 2. Asafœtida.

Rad. 187

馬 𢒠

See Lesson 137 A.

馬 ma 3. A horse.

馮 p'ing 2. A timid horse.
fêng 2. A proper name.

馭 yü 4. To drive, to oversee.

馳 ch'ih 2. Fast, to pass quickly.

馴 hsün 2. Tame, docile.

馯 han 4. A vicious horse.

馰 ti 4. Speckled horse.

4-5

馹 jih 4. A post-horse, a courier.

馽 chih 4. To trammel a horse.

馿 lü 2. An ass, a donkey.

髦 mao 2. Hair from the tail of horses.

駁 po 2. A piebald horse, mixed, to dispute, contradictory, to cavil at.

馱 to 4. A load.

駐 chu 4. To rest one's horse, to stop, to sojourn.

駙 fu 4. A subsidiary horse, a son-in-law of the emperor.

駕 chia 4. A horse in the harness, to harness, to yoke, to drive, to ride, term of address, Your Honour.

駒 chü 1. A colt under two years.

駏 chü 4. The offspring of a stallion and a she-ass.

駈 ch'ü 1. To drive away, to expel.

駓 p'ei 1. To run, to gallop.

駛 shih 3. A horse running swiftly, to hasten.

駟 ssŭ 4. A team of four horses.

駘 t'ai 2. A wearied or worn-out hack.

駝 t'o 2. A camel. To bear as a pack.

6-7

駭 hai 4. Fear, dreadful, to frighten.

駥 jang 2. A war-horse, valiant.

駱 lo 4. A camel.

駼 lü 2. A post-house.

駬 mai 4. A mule.

駪 hsien 1. In troops.

駦 t'êng 2. To mount, to run.

駣 t'ao 2. A colt.

駰 yin 1. An iron-grey horse.

騭 chih 1. A stallion, to promote, to fix.

駼 t'u 2. A wild ass.

駿 tsun 4. A fine horse, noble, vast, to spread.

8-9

騑 fei 1. An extra horse fastened to the axle with long traces.

騎 ch'i 2. To ride, to sit astride.

騍 k'o 4. Female of horses, mules, etc.

騋 lai 2. A mare.

騀 erh 2. A stallion.

騇 shê 4. A mare.

騌 tsung 1. A horse's mane.

騈 ping 4. A couple, a pair, a band.

騐 yen 4. To inspect, to verify, evidence.

颿 fan 2. A horse racing.

騢 hsia 2. A spotted horse.

騙 p'ien 4. To cheat, to swindle, to mount a horse.

騯 pên 1 To gallop away.

騣 tsung 1. A horse's mane.

騘 ts'ung 1. A piebald horse.

騩 wei 4. An ass.

騖 wu 4. To gallop, boisterous.

10-11

驏 chan 4. A horse rolling himself in the dust.

騭 chih 1. A stallion, to promote, to fix.

騫 ch'ien 1. Glanders, decay, ruin.

騷 sao 1. To rub down a horse, disquiet, griefs.

騸 shan 4. To geld a horse or ass.

騰 t'êng 2. To leap on, to mount, to move out, to differ.

騲 ts'ao 3. A she-ass.

驅 ch'ü 1. To drive away, to expel, forerunner, vanguard.

騾 lo 2. A mule.

驁 ao 2. A vicious horse, indomitable, stubborn.

驂 ts'an 1. The two outside horses of a team of four.

12-13

驍 hsiao 1. A fine horse, brave, strong.

驊 hua 2. A spotted horse.

驕 chiao 1. Haughty, proud.

驌 su 4. A thoroughbred horse

驚 ching 1. Frightened, terrified, to frighten.

驖 t'ieh 3. An iron-gray horse.

驗 yen 4. To verify, evidence fulfilment, effect, proof.

驛 i 4. The government postal service, a courier.

14 &

驢 lü 2. A donkey.

驥 chi 4. A thoroughbred horse.

𩧯 ch'ien 3. Lame.

驤 hsiang 1. A spirited horse, caracoling and cantering, to prance.

䆘 ts'uan 4. To leap, to jump.

驩 huan 1. A gentle, tractable horse, gleeful, frolicksome, to play.

驪 li 2. A fleet horse.

驏 ch'an 3. To ride a horse barebacked.

Rad. 188

骨 

See Lesson 118 A.

骨 ku 2. A bone, framework.

骭 kan 4. Shin-bone, tibia.

骪 ko 1. Arm.

骩 wan 3. Luxation.

骯 ang 1. na 1. Dirty, filthy.

䯁 pa 4. A handle made of bone.

骰 shai 3. Dices.

髛 k'ao 1. The end bone of the spine.

䯵 t'o 2. Anchylosis.

骷 k'u 1. Dry bones, a skeleton, a skull.

骳 p'i 4. Distorted, twisted.

䯋 po 4. The shoulderblade, scapula.

骲 p'ao 2. The tip of an arrow made of bone.

骶 ti 3. The os sacrum.

骴 tzŭ 1. A putrid carcass.

䯏 kua 4. Hyoid bone.

䯒 hsing 1. The thighbone.

骸 hai 2. Bones, skeleton.

骼 ko 1. The arm.

骻 k'ua 3. The bones of the pelvis.

骾 kêng 3. Hard bones, unyielding, firm.

骽 t'ui 3. The thigh.

髁 huai 3. The pelvis or hip bones.

髀 pi 4. The buttocks.

骿 ping 3. Ribs which are joined.

䯈 wan 4. The knee-joint.

髃 yü 2. The clavicle.

䯿 ch'ui 2. The vertebræ.

髈 pang 3. The shoulder.

髆 po 2. p'ai 2. The arm.

髏 lou 2. A skull.

髓 sui 3. Marrow.

體 t'i 3. The limbs; the trunk; the body; substance; style; manner, to conform; respectable.

髑 tu 2. A skull.

髒 tsang 1. Rotten bones; dirty.

髕 pin 4. The patella.

Rad. 189

高

See Lesson 75 B.

高 髙 kao 1. High; lofty; noble; eminent; your, in direct address.

膏 kao 1. Fat, grease.

髞 sao 4. Elevated; roomy.

Rad. 190

See Lesson 112 B.

髟 piao 1. The hair.

髡 k'un 1. To shave the head.

髢 ti 4. Unbound hair.

髣 fang 3. To be like, similar, as.

髦 mao 2. Long hair.

髬 p'ei 1. Dishevelled hair.

髧 tan 3. Tresses or curls.

髮 fa 3. The hair of the human head.

髴 fu 2. Like, nearly.

髯 jan 2. The whiskers.

髳 mao 2. Hairy.

𩬈 t'ai 2. A woman's headdress of false hair.

髫 t'iao 2. The tuft of hair on children's heads.

髭 tzŭ 1. The mustaches.

髻 chieh 1. Chignon of girls, *chua-chieh*.

髶 jung 1. The downy.

髵 **erh** 2. The beard.

髽 **chua** 1. Chignon of girls.

髼 **p'êng** 2. Tangled hair; unkempt.

鬂 **pin** 4. The hair on the temples.

鬄 **t'i** 4. To shave.

鬈 **ch'üan** 2. Curled hair.

鬆 **sung** 1. Dishevelled; loose; lax; to untie.

⿱髟沓 **t'a** 4. The hair on a new-born child's head.

⿱髟采 **ts'ai** 3. A band worn by women.

鬃 **tsung** 1. A wig.

鬍 **hu** 2. The beard.

⿱髟垂 **ch'ui** 2. Hairs hanging on the forehead of an unmarried girl.

⿱髟般 **p'an** 2. The cue coiled around the head.

鬗 **man** 2. A head-dress.

鬖 **san** 1. Dishevelled hair.

⿱髟貴 **k'uei** 4. A ribbon for tying the hair in a knot.

鬚 **hsü** 1. Beard.

鬟 **huan** 2. A slavegirl's hair done up.

⿱髟監 **lan** 2. A mane.

鬢 **pin** 4. The hair on the temples.

鬣 **lieh** 4. Stiff hair, bristles.

鬤 **jang** 2. The hair dishevelled and uncombed.

⿱髟贊 **tsuan** 3. Chignon of married women.

Rad. 191

See Lesson 11 I.

 **tou** 4. To quarrel.

鬧 **ao** 4. A great noise; a bustle, tumult; to scold.

鬨 **hung** 4. The din of battle; to fight.

鬩 **i** 4. A quarrel.

鬮 **chiu** 1. Lots.

鬪 **tou** 4. To quarrel.

鬫 **han** 3. Cries; madness

鬭 **tou** 4. To quarrel.

鬮 **chiu** 1. Lots; to draw, as lots.

Rad. 192

See Lesson 26 C.

鬯 **ch'ang** 4. A sacrificial wine.

鬱 鬰 **yü** 4. Thick; dense; an obstruction.

Rad. 193

See Lesson 155 A.

鬲 **ko** 2. A tripod pot.

融 **jung** 2 Harmony. To melt, cash, etc.

鬴 **fu** 3. A caldron; a large measure.

鬵 **hsün** 2. A boiler.

鬷 **tsung** 1. A caldron.

鬻 **yü** 4. Food; to sell.

Rad. 194

See Lesson 40 C.

鬼 **kuei** 3. Manes; ghosts; devils.

鬽 **mei** 4. Forest sprites.

䰟 魂 **hun** 2. The spiritual soul, the vital principle.

魁 **k'uei** 2. First; chief, eminent; monstrous.

魅 **mei** 4. Dryads.

魃 **po** 4. The demon of drought.

魄 **p'ai** 4. The inferior soul, figure, form.

⿰鬼甫 **fu** 3. A star in *Ursa Major*.

魈 **hsiao** 1. Mountain sprites.

魊 **huo** 4. Spell; delusion.

魌 **ch'i** 1. The demon of pestilence.

魎 **liang** 3. A sprite.

魋 **t'ui** 2. A were-wolf.

魍 **wang** 3. A sprite.

魏 **wei** 4. A proper name; lofty; eminent.

魑 **ch'ih** 1. An elf.

魔 **mo** 2. A devil; a demon.

魒 **p'iao** 1. A star in *Ursa Major*.

魕 **chi** 1. Devilish, magic.

魙 **chien** 4. The death of the ghost of a man.

魘 **yen** 3. Horrid dreams, nightmare.

Rad. 195

See Lesson 142 A.

魚 **yü 2.** A fish, a letter.

𩵖 **ya 4.** A kind of sheatfish.

魜 **jên.** A seal.

魝 **chi 4.** To split fish for drying, to open.

魛 **tao 1.** A kind ot herring.

魟 **kung 1.** Large skate.

魫 **ch'êu 2.** The roe of fish.

魴 **fang 2.** A kind of bream.

𩶘 **tsa 2.** The motion of a fish's mouth and gills.

魪 **chieh 4.** The sole.

𩶃 **kung 1.** Skate.

魯 **lu 3.** Stupid, coarse.

魶 **na 4.** A seal.

魦 **sha 1.** A shark.

魨 **t'un 2.** River pig.

魰 **wên 2.** A flying fish.

魷 **yu 2.** The cuttle-fish.

𩵹 **yü 2.** To fish.

5

鮓 **cha 3.** A condiment of fish.

𩶉 **ch'ih 1.** The mackerel.

鮒 **fu 4.** A fish like perch, that goes in shoals; union, mutual affection.

魽 **han 1.** Bivalve shells.

魺 **ho 1.** A sea-blubber.

魼 **ch'ü 1.** The flounder.

鮎 **nien 2.** The mud-fish.

鮩 **ping 4.** A shell-fish.

鮑 **pao 4.** Salted dried fish, bad smell, bad companies.

鮅 **pi 4.** A kind of bleak.

𩶲 **shan 4.** The eel.

穌 **su 1.** To revive.

鮂 **ch'iu 2.** A kind of pike.

鮐 **t'ai 2.** The *Tetraoden.*

鮀 **t'o 2.** A snake-fish.

𩷁 **yang 1.** A kind of sheat-fish.

6

鮆 **tzŭ 1.** A mullet.

鮫 **chiao 1.** A large shark.

鮰 **hui 2.** A salmon.

鮭 **kui 1.** The fresh-water wide porpoise.

𩶙 **mi 3.** Fish-spawn.

鮞 **erh 2.** The roe of fishes.

鮮 **hsien 1.** Fresh fish, fresh new, bright.
hsien 3. Few, rare.

鮧 **i 2.** *Silurus asotus.*

鮦 **t'ung 2.** *Ophiocephalus.*

鮠 **wei 1.** A kind of shad.

鮪 **wei 3.** A snouted cturgeon.

7

鯊 **sha 1.** A shark.

鯈 **t'iao 2.** A long thin fish.

鯇 **huan 3.** A tench.

鯁 **kêng 3.** Fish-bones.

鮨 **i 2.** A porpoise.

鯀 **kun 3.** A great fish, a proper name.

鯉 **li 3.** The carp.

鮾 **nei 3.** Putrid fish.

鯆 **p'u 1.** The skate.

鮹 **hsiao 1.** An eel.

䱒 **i 4.** Salted fish.

8

鯯 **chih 4.** An anchovy.

䱛 **huo 2.** Alligator.

鯢 **i 2.** A whale.

鯚 **chi 4.** A kind of perch.

鯨 **ching 1.** A whale.

鯝 **ku 4.** The guts of a fish.

鯤 **k'un 1.** A marine monster.

鯠 **lai 2.** A kind of eel.

鯪 **ling 2.** A dace.

鯛 **t'iao 2.** The perch.

鯧 **ch'ang 1.** A conger-eel.

鯫 **tsou 1.** Minnows.

鯖 **ch'ing 1.** Mackerel.

9

鰆 **ch'un 1.** A mullet.

鰒 **fu 2.** Ear-shell, *Haliotis.*

鯸 **hou 1.** A poisonous fish.

鰕 **hsia 1.** Shrimps, prawns.

鰀 **huan 3.** A species of tench.

鰉 **huang 2.** The sturgeon.

鰔 **kan 3.** A kind of mud-fish, the *Pimelodus*.

鰐 **o 4.** The crocodile.

鯿 **pien 1.** The bream.

鰓 **sai 1.** The gills of a fish.

鯹 **hsing 1.** Putrid fish.

鯷 **t'i 2.** The sheat-fish.

鯑 **t'i 2.** A newt; an eft.

鰈 **tieh 2.** A plaice.

鯽 **chi 4.** The bastard carp.

鰍 **ch'iu 1.** The loach, *Cobitis*.

鯼 **tsung 1.** A large sea fish.

鰋 **yen 3.** A cat-fish, silure.

10

鰝 **hao 4.** A large craw-fish.

鰥 **kuan 1.** A huge fish. A bachelor, a widower.

鰣 **shih 2.** The shad, *Alosa Reevesi*.

鰨 **t'a 4.** The dugong.

鰫 **jung 2.** A dace.

[illegible] **ts'ang 1.** The pomfret.

鰦 **tzŭ 1.** A kind ot mackerel.

鰩 **yao 2.** The flying-fish.

鰧 **t'êng 2.** A gurnard.

11

鰵 **min 3.** A perch-like fish.

鰲 **ao 2.** A sea monster.

鱉 **pieh 1.** A turtle.

[illegible] **koei 1.** The fresh-water porpoise.

鰱 **lien 2.** A bream.

鰻 **man 2.** The eel.

鰹 **chien 1.** A kind of mullet.

鱄 **chuan 1.** A kind of salmon.

鰾 **piao 4.** Eish-glue.

12

鱎 **chiao 3.** The culter, a fish peculiar to China.

鱖 **chüeh 4.** A perch.

鱗 **lin 2.** The scales of a fish.

鱔 **shan 4.** The eel.

鱓 **shan 4.** The eel.

鱘 **hsün 2.** The sturgeon.

鱊 **yü 4.** A kind of bleak.

13 &

鱟 **hou 4.** The king-crab, *Limulus Polyphemus*.

鱣 **chan 1.** A sturgeon.

鱝 **fên 4.** A skate.

鱤 **kan 3.** A mullet.

鱠 **k'uai 4.** Stewed fish.

鱧 **li 3.** A mullet.

鰜 **lien 2.** A kind of shad.

[illegible] **ao 4.** A large kind of perch.

鱡 **tsei 2.** The octopus.

鱯 **huo 4.** A large kind of silure.

鱮 **yü 3.** A tench.

鱭 **ch'i 3.** A mullet.

鱵 **chên 1.** A kind of white-bait, *Hemiramphus*.

鱲 **lieh 4.** Perch.

[illegible] **lai 4.** A small kind of goby, the *Trypauchen vagina*.

鱸 **lu 2.** A perch.

鱷 **o 4.** The crocodile.

[illegible] **ts'an 1.** *Trichiurus armatus*.

鱺 **li 2.** A fresh water eel.

鱻 **hsien 1.** Fresh fish, good, new clean.

Rad. 196

鳥 [illegible]

See Lesson 138 A.

鳥 **niao 3.** Birds.

鳦 **ya 2.** Swallow.

鳧 **fu 4.** Ducks.

鳩 **chiu 1.** The wood-pigeon.

鳭 **tiao 1.** The wren.

鳳 **fêng 4.** The phœnix.

鳱 **kan 1.** The magpie.

鳴 **ming 2.** The cry of a bird or animal, to sound.

鳲 **shih 1.** The turtle dove.

[illegible] **tu 3.** The cuckoo.

鳶 **yüan 2.** The kite, *Milvus melanotis*.

4

鳸 **hu 4.** A quail.

鴆 **chên 4.** Poison.

鴟 **ch'i 2.** A pheasant.

鳻 **pan 1.** Wild pigeon.

鴃 **chüeh 2.** A shrike.

鴇 **pao 3.** A bustard.

鴄 **p'i 4.** A wild duck.

鴉 **ya 1.** A raven, a crow.

鴈 **yen 4.** A wild goose.

䲰 **yün 4.** The secretary falcon, *Serpentarius reptilivorus.*

5

鴏 **cha 2.** A grebe.

鴌 **ch'iao 3.** The tailor-bird, *Sylvia sutoria.*

鴛 **yüan 1.** The drake of the mandarin duck.

鴦 **yang 1.** The hen of the mandarin duck.

鴞 **hsiao 1.** An owl, filial impiety.

鴟 **ch'ih 1.** An owl.

鴝 **ch'ü 1.** A species of thrush.

鴣 **ku 1.** A partridge.

鴗 **li 4.** A green king-fisher, *Alcedo bengalensis.*

鴒 **ling 2.** A kind of lark.

鴘 **pien 3.** A hunting falcon.

鴠 **tan 4.** A nightingale.

鴕 **t'o 2.** The ostrich.

鴨 **ya 1.** A duck.

6

鵀 **jên 4.** A head-dress of feathers.

鴷 **lieh 4.** The wood-pecker.

鳶 **yüan 2.** The kite.

鴜 **tzŭ 1.** A cormorant.

鴮 **hu 4.** The pelican.

鴻 **hung 2.** Swan, vast.

鵁 **chiao 1.** The egret.

鳽 **chien 1.** A heron.

鴿 **ko 1.** A domestic pigeon, a dove.

鴰 **kua 1.** A rook.

鴙 **ch'ih 4.** An owl.

鵅 **lao 4.** The rail.

鵔 **sung 1.** A kestrel.

鴳 **an 1.** A quail.

鵂 **hsiu 1.** A sort of owl.

7

鵝 **o 2. wo 2.** The domestic goose.

鵫 **k'an 3.** A nightingale.

鵠 **ku 3.** The snow-goose, a target.

鵑 **chüan 1.** A cuckoo.

鵓 **po 4.** A wood pigeon.

鵜 **t'i 2.** The pelican.

鵌 **t'u 2.** A wood-pecker.

鵒 **yü 4.** The mynah.

8

鶽 **sung 1.** A sparrow-hawk.

鶀 **ch'i 2.** A wild goose.

鵮 **ch'ien 1.** To peck.

鶋 **chü 1.** The jackdaw.

鵴 **chü 2.** The common cuckoo.

鵾 **k'un 1.** Heath-cock.

鷆 **ming 2.** A kind of pheasant.

䳮 **nan 1.** A quail.

鵡 **wu 3.** A cockatoo.

鵬 **p'êng 2.** The rukh, a fabulous bird.

鵯 **p'i 1.** The jackdaw.

鶉 **ch'un 2.** A quail.

鵰 **tiao 1.** The osprey, fishing eagle.

鵽 **to 4.** The sand-grouse.

鶄 **ching 1.** A water-fowl.

鵲 **ch'iao 3.** The magpie, a jay.

鶂 **i 4.** A goose.

鵷 **yüan 1.** The argus pheasant.

9

鶩 **wu 4.** A duck

鶖 **ch'iu 1.** A crane.

鶘 **hu 2.** The pelican.

鶛 **chieh 1.** A quail.

鶪 **ch'ü 4.** The shrike or the cuckoo.

鶒 **ch'ih 4.** A crane.

鶚 **o 4.** The osprey or fish-hawk.

鶗 **t'i 2.** The pelican.

鶟 **tu 4.** A moor-hen.

鶡 **ho 4.** A long-tailed pheasant, *Syrmaticus Reevesi.*

鶢 **yüan 2.** A bird which frequents the seashore.

鶠 **yen 3.** The female of the phœnix.

10

鶯 **ying 1.** The oriole.

鶱 **hsien 1.** To soar high.

鷇 **k'ou 4.** The young of sparrows or swallows.

鶵 **ch'u 2.** A chick, to rear brood.

鶴 **hao** 2. **ho** 2. A crane.

鶻 **hu** 4. A buzzard.

鷄 **chi** 1. Gallinaceous birds, cock, a hen.

鶼 **chien** 1. The spoonbill, *Platalea major*.

鴿 **ko** 1. A parrot.

鶹 **liu** 2. The large horned owl.

鶽 **hsün** 3. A falcon.

鶨 **ch'uan** 4. A penguin.

鷉 **t'i** 1. A species of grebe.

鷏 **t'ien** 2. A wader.

鶬 **ts'ang** 1. A kind of crane.

鷀 **tz'ŭ** 2. The fishing cormorant.

鷂 **yao** 4. A kite, a paper kite.

鷊 **i** 4. A pheasant with a collar, *Tragopan satyrus*.

鷁 **i** 4. A kind of sea bird painted on the sterns of junks.

11

鷖 **i** 1. The widgeon.

鷔 **ao** 2. A bird of ill omen.

鷟 **tsu** 2. A kind of duck.

鷩 **pieh** 4. The golden pheasant.

鷙 **chih** 4. Birds of prey.

鷌 **ma** 2. A wild goose.

[illegible] **chang** 1. A kind of wader.

鷚 **liao** 4. A titlark.

鷓 **chê** 2. The common partridge.

鷗 **ou** 1. A sea gull.

[illegible] **p'iao** 1. To fly lightly, a sea-gull.

鷞 **shuang** 1. The turquoise kingfisher.

12

[illegible] **ch'ang** 3. Downy feathers of long-legged birds.

鷥 **ssŭ** 1. The white egret heron.

鷲 **chiu** 4. A vulture.

鷧 **i** 4. The fishing cormorant.

鷮 **chiao** 1. A pheasant.

鷯 **liao** 2. A wren.

[illegible] **hsiang** 4. The hornbill of Siam.

鷫 **su** 4. Turquoise king-fisher.

鷳 **hsien** 2. The silver pheasant.

[illegible] **têng** 1. A heron.

[illegible] **t'ung** 2. The hornbill.

鷦 **chiao** 1. The wren.

鷸 **yü** 4. A kingfisher.

13 &

鸇 **chan** 1. A sparrow-hawk.

鷽 **hsiao** 2. A blue jay, *Urocissa sinensis*.

鸃 **i** 2. A crow-pheasant.

鸁 **lo** 3. The grebe.

鷺 **lu** 4. A heron.

鸀 **shu** 2. A kind of jay.

鸅 **chai** 2. The white pelican.

鷹 **ying** 1. An eagle.

鸏 **mêng** 2. A toucan.

鸐 **ti** 2. The Tartar pheasant.

鸌 **huo** 4. A corn-crake.

鸓 **lei** 3. The flying squirrel, *Pteromys*.

鸕 **lu** 2. The fishing cormorant.

鸘 **shuang** 1. A crested hawk.

鸚 **ying** 1. A parrot.

鸜 **ch'ü** 1. A species of thrush.

鸛 **kuan** 4. A heron.

鸝 **li** 2. The oriole.

鸞 **luan** 2. Argus pheasant, small bells hung on bridles, imperial.

Rad. 197

See Lesson 41 D.

鹵 **lu** 3. Salt lands, natural salt, rude, incivil.

[illegible] **tan** 4. Without salt, insipid.

鹹 **hsien** 2. Salt, bitter, brackish.

鹻 **chien** 3. Soda.

盬 **ku** 3. Preparation of salt, by evaporation.

鹺 **ts'o** 1. Briny, salt.

[illegible] **chien** 3. Soda, barilla.

鹼 **chien** 3. Barilla.

鹽 **yen** 2. Salt.

Rad 198

See Lesson 136 A.

鹿 **lu** 4. A stag, a deer.

麂 **chi** 3. A large deer.

麀 **yu** 1. The female of the stag, a doe.

塵 **ch'ên** 2. Dust.

麃 **piao** 1. A roebuck.

麈 **chu** 3. The Chinese elk.

麚 **chia** 1. A buck, a male deer.

麅 **p'ao** 2. Fallow-deer.

麆 **ts'u** 1. The fawn of an antelope.

⿸鹿旨 **chi** 3. A large deer.

麋 **mi** 2. The tailed deer, elk, difform.

麏 **yin** 1. A female deer.

麎 **ch'ên** 2. The female of the elk.

麌 **yü** 4. A stag, to herd.

麑 **i** 2. A fawn.

麒 **ch'i** 2. The male unicorn.

麖 **ching** 1. A large deer.

麔 **chiu** 4. The male of the elk.

麇 **ch'ün** 1. A deer, a herd.

麗 **li** 4. Antelopes, elegant, graceful, glorious.

麓 **lu** 4. The foot of a mountain.

⿸鹿委 **wei** 1. The best cut of venison.

麘 **hsiang** 1. The musk deer.

麙 **hsien** 2. An antelope.

麚 **chia** 1. A buck, a stag.

麛 **mi** 2. A fawn.

麝 **shê** 4. The musk deer.

麞 **chang** 1. The hornless river-deer.

麟 **lin** 2. The female of the unicorn.

麤 **ts'u** 1. A herd of antelopes, dust, coarse.

麢 **ling** 2. The chamois.

Rad. 199

See Lesson 13 C.

麥 **ma.** 4. Corn.

麧 **ho** 1. Oat-meal.

⿰麥乇 **t'o** 2. Cakes.

⿰麥弋 **i** 4. Wheat cleaned from shaft.

麩 **fu** 1. Wheat bran.

麪 **mien** 4. Flour; vermicelli.

⿰麥比 **p'i** 2. Broken wheat roasted.

⿰麥末 **mo** 4. Broken grain, grits.

⿰麥它 **t'o** 2. Cakes.

麯 **ch'ü** 1. Leaven.

麰 **mou** 2. Barley.

⿰麥肖 **hsiao** 3. Grits.

麴 **ch'ü** 1. Leaven, yeast.

麨 **ch'ao** 3. Roasted wheat taken for a journey.

麵 **mien** 4. Wheat flour; vermicelli.

⿰麥屑 **hsieh** 4. Grits.

⿰麥連 **lien** 3. Oat-cakes.

⿰麥將 **ch'iang** 4. Broth; paste.

Rad. 200

See Lesson 79 H.

麻 **ma** 2. Plants furnishing textile fibres.

麼 **mo** 1. An interrogative particle.

麾 **hui** 1. A signal flag.

摩 **mo** 1. To feel with the hand.

磨 **mo** 2. To polish; to grind.

⿸麻目 **ma** 2. To look at long; indistinct.

糜 **mi** 2. Rice gruel.

靡 **mei** 2. Laid out; not.

魔 **mo** 2. A devil.

穈 **mei** 2. A kind of millet.

Rad. 201

See Lesson 171 A.

黃 **huang** 2. Yellow; imperial; a surname.

黋 **kuang** 1. Brave; valorous.

黈 **chu** 3. Yellow.

⿱𣪊黃 **huang** 2. The yolk of an egg.

黌 **hung** 2. To learn; a school; an academy.

Rad. 202

See Lesson 121 I.

黍 **shu** 3. The panicled millet.

黎 **li** 2. Black.

⿰黍尼 **ni** 2. To adhere, to stick.

黏 **nien** 2. Glutinous, to stick up.

⿰黍卑 **pai** 4. A panic grass.

⿰黍果 **kua** 3. Pastry; biscuits.

Rad. 203

黑

See Lesson 40 D.

黑 **hei 1.** Black; dark; evil.

墨 **mei 4.** Ink.

黚 **kan 4.** Black spots.

黔 **ch'ien 1.** Brown.

默 **mei 4.** Dark ; retired ; secret ; silent.

黕 **t'ai 4.** Very black.

黜 **ch'o 4.** To degrade, to dismiss.

黛 **tai 4.** Indigo.

點 **tien 3.** A spot, a speck, a dot ; to nod ; to light ; a little, a point ; to set.

黝 **yu 3.** Ashy colour.

黠 **chieh 1.** Black.

䵳 **hui 1.** An ashy colour.

黟 **i 1.** Black; ebony.

黥 **ch'ing 2.** To tattoo; marks.

黧 **li 2.** A dark dun colour.

黨 **tang 3.** A party; club; a cabal.

黦 **yeh 4.** Faded.

黮 **chên 4.** Black ; to smut.

黯 **an 3.** Dark; gloomy.

黳 **tzŭ 1.** Black.

黴 **mei 2.** Microbes, spoiled.

黲 **ts'an 3.** Speckled ; black and white.

黱 **chêng 4.** To become block.

䵞 **tsêng 4.** A black face.

𪒠 **ch'iao 2.** Spots on the face.

黶 **yen 3.** Faded.

黱 **t'êng 2.** Black; obscure.

黷 **tu 4.** To blacken; to spoil.

Rad. 204

黹

See Lesson 35 G.

黹 **chih 3.** Embroidery.

黺 **fên 3.** Embroideries, flowered silk.

黻 **fu 4.** Embroidered; ornamented.

黼 **fu 3.** Embroidery; adorned with figures.

Rad. 205

黽

See Lesson 108 C.

黽 **min 3.** A toad; to make an effort; obscenities.

黿 **yüan 2.** The great sea turtle.

鼂 **ch'ao 2.** A marine animal.

鼄 **chu 1.** The spider.

鼃 **wa 1.** A frog ; obscenities.

鼇 **ao 2.** A huge turtle.

鼈 **pieh 1.** A turtle.

鼉 **t'o 2.** An iguana ; crocodile.

Rad. 206

鼎

See Lesson 127 D.

鼎 **ting 3.** A tripod.

鼏 **mi 2.** A dish covered.

鼐 **nai 4.** Incense tripod.

鼒 **ts'ai 2.** A small tripod.

Rad. 207

鼓

See Lesson 165 C.

鼓 鼔 **ku 3.** A drum ; drumshaped ; bulging; to excite.

鼕 **t'ung 1.** The rattle of drums.

𪔃 **fu 2.** Clangor.

鼖 **fên 2.** A large drum.

鼛 **ta 1.** The sound of little drums.

鼗 **t'ao 2.** A small flat drum with a handle.

鼜 **t'ung 1.** The noise of drums beating.

鼛 **kao 1.** A large drum.

鼙 **p'i 2.** A war-drum.

鼘 **yüan 1.** The roll of drums.

鼞 **t'ang 1.** The roll of drums.

鼟 **t'êng 1.** The roll of drums.

Rad. 208

See Lesson 139 B.

鼠 **shu 3.** A rat.
鼦 **tiao 1.** The sable.
鼢 **fên 3.** A kind of mole, *Scaptochirus moschatus*.
鼨 **chung 1.** A rodent marked with spots.
䶉 **liu 2.** The *Rhyzomys sincnsis*.
鼥 **po 4.** The beaver.
鼪 **shêng 1.** A polecat.
鼫 **shih 4.** The long-tailed marmot.
鼬 **yu 4.** A polecat.
鼵 **tsun 4.** A kind of marmot.
鼯 **wu 2.** Flying squirrel.
䶅 **chui 1.** A rat.
鼷 **hsi 2.** A mouse.
鼸 **ch'ien 3.** A hamster.

Rad. 209

See Lesson 40 C.

鼻 **pi 2.** The nose.
[illegible] [illegible] **ch'iao 4.** A turn-up nose.
鼽 **ch'iu 3.** A cold in the head.
鼾 **han 1.** To snore.
𪖌 **hsi 4.** To snivel.
齁 **hou 1.** To snore.
𪖐 **ch'iu 4.** A pug nose.
𪖙 **t'i 4.** Mucus.
齅 **hsiu 4.** To smell.
齆 **yung 1.** A stoppage of the nose.
齈 **nung 2.** Mucus of the nose.
𪖨 **t'i 4.** To sneeze.
齉 **nang 4.** To speak through the nose.

Rad. 210

See Lesson 174 A.

齊 **ch'i 2.** Even, harmony, order, to equalise, perfect.
齋 **chai 1.** To abstain from, abstinence, a study, a retired life.
齍 **tzŭ 1.** A ritual offering.
齎 **chi 1.** To offer to; to give, offerings.
齏 **chi 1.** To mix, to blend, to compound.

Rad. 211

See Lesson 175 A.

齒 **ch'ih 3.** The front teeth, the mouth, age, to record.
齔 **ch'ên 4.** To shed milk teeth.
齕 **ho 4.** To bite, to gnaw, to cut off, to peculate.
齘 **chieh 4.** To gnash.
齖 **ya 2.** Uneven teeth.
齗 **yin 2.** Gingivitis.
齝 **ch'ih 1.** To chew, to ruminate.
𪗃 **k'o 4.** To crunch with the teeth.
齣 **ch'u 1.** Act of a play, a part.
齡 **ling 2.** Front teeth, age.
齙 **pao 1.** Projecting teeth.
𪗔 **ssŭ 4.** To ruminate.
齠 **t'iao 2.** To shed the teeth.
齟 **chü 4.** Irregular teeth, discordant.
齜 **ts'ŭ 1.** To gnash one's teeth.
齦 **k'ên 3.** To gnaw.
齩 **yao 3.** To bite, to masticate.
齧 **yeh 4. nieh 4.** To bite, to eat.
齪 **ts'u 4.** Narrow, shallow.
齬 **yü 3.** Irrogular teeth.
齮 **ch'i 1.** To bite, to eat.
齯 **i 2.** To cut teeth.
齶 **o 4.** The roof of the mouth.
齲 **chü 3.** A spoiled tooth.
齷 **wo 4.** Crumpled.
齵 **yü 2.** Uneven teeth, irregular.
齻 **tien 1.** To get one's wisdom teeth.
齸 **i 4.** To ruminate, to chew.
齇 **cha 1.** Irregular teeth.
䶦 **ni 4.** Rotten teeth, caries
齼 **ch'u 3.** The teeth set on edge.
𪙏 **chi 1.** To bite, a mouthful.
齾 **yeh 1.** Fragmentary things, remnants.

Rad. 212

龍

See Lesson 140 A.

龍 **lung 2.** A dragon, imperial, glorious.

龐 **p'ang 2.** A palace.

龕 **k'an 1.** A shrine for an idol, a niche.

龔 **kung 1.** To give, to offer, a cult.

Rad. 213

See Lesson 108 B.

龜 **kuei 1.** A tortoise.

[龜焦] **chiao 1.** To scorch a tortoise shell for divination.

Rad. 214

See Lesson 14 H.

龠 **yao 4.** Pandean pipes.

龡 **ch'ui 1.** To play, to blow

龢 **ho 2.** Harmony, concord.

龣 **ch'ang 4.** To sing, a choir, harmony.

龤 **hsieh 2.** Harmony, concord.

龥 **yü 4.** To cry, to pray to, to importune, to exhort

List of difficult Characters.

The following Table contains a selection of the characters whose Radicals are not very obvious Tney are classified by the number of their strokes. The figure after each one denotes its Radical.

2

丁	1
七	1
乃	4
九	5
了	6
刀	18

3

丈	1
上	1
下	1
丫	2
个	2
丸	3
久	4
乞	5
也	5
于	7
亡	8
兀	10
亾	11
凡	16
千	24
叉	29
才	64

4

不	1
丐	1
丏	1
丑	1
中	2
丰	2
丹	3
之	4
予	6
云	7
互	7
五	7
井	7
仁	9
仄	9
今	9
介	9
从	9
允	10
元	10
內	11
公	12
六	12
兮	12
勿	20
化	21
匹	23
升	24
午	24
卞	25
卬	26
厄	27
反	29
叐	29
友	29
及	29
壬	32
壬	33
天	37
夭	37
夫	37
夬	37
孔	39
少	42
尤	43
尹	44
尺	44
屯	45
巴	49
市	50
廿	55
弔	57
王	95

5

且	1
丕	1
世	1
丘	1
丙	1
丱	2
主	3
乍	4
乎	4
乏	4
令	9
以	9
兄	10
仝	11
冉	13
册	13
同	13
冋	13
多	15
凸	17
凹	17
出	17
匆	20
北	21
半	24
卡	25
占	25
卮	26
卯	26
去	28
只	30
史	30
右	30
司	30
央	37
失	37
尔	42
巨	48
左	48
㠯	49
平	51
弁	55
弗	57
必	61
戊	62
未	75
末	75
本	75
正	77
母	80
民	83
永	85
氷	85

由 102
甲 102
申 102

6

丞 1
丟 1
而 1
亘 7
亙 7
亥 8
交 8
亦 8
企 9
兆 10
先 10
光 10
全 11
共 12
再 13
冉 24
危 26
同 30
后 30
吏 30
向 30
合 30
吊 30
在 32
夅 34
夙 36
夷 37
存 39
安 40
寺 41
尖 42
尽 44
州 47
年 51
戌 62
戍 62
成 62
曲 73
曳 73
有 74
朱 75
束 75
此 77
死 78
牟 93
百 106
考 125
西 146

7

两 1
串 2
乱 5
况 7
亨 8
余 9
免 10
兎 10
兵 12
卵 26
含 30
君 30
吳 30
吾 30
告 30
呂 30
坐 32
声 33
夾 37
妥 38
孝 39
巡 47
巫 48
卮 49
弄 55
弟 57
我 62
更 73
東 75
步 77
每 80
求 85
甫 101
男 102
皂 106
矣 111
秀 115
系 120
罕 122
肖 130
臣 13
自 132
艮 138

8

並 1
乘 4
乳 5
事 6
亞 7
亟 7
些 7
享 8
京 8
來 9
兒 10
兔 10
兩 11
其 12
具 12
典 12
函 17
卑 24
卓 24
卒 24
卷 26
卺 26
受 29
叔 29
周 30
命 30
垂 32
夜 36
奇 37
奉 37
奈 37
妻 38
妾 38
季 39
尙 42
巵 43
岡 46
巷 49
幸 51
幷 51
忝 61
所 63
承 64
易 72
東 75
果 75
武 77
氓 83
畀 102
畁 102
直 109
秉 115
罔 122
羌 123
肩 130
肯 130
舀 134
舍 135
表 145
采 165

9

亮 8
俎 9
俞 9
兗 10
兪 11
冑 13

冒 13
冠 14
前 18
南 24
单 24
卸 26
叚 29
叛 29
咫 30
咸 30
哀 30
哉 30
奏 37
奐 37
奔 37
威 38
姜 38
帝 50
幽 52
拜 64
春 72
是 72
曷 73
柰 75
某 75
枼 75
柬 75
柔 75
歪 77
泉 85
為 86
甚 99
畏 102
畆 102
皆 106
盾 109
省 109
看 109
禺 114
竒 117
美 123
者 125
冑 130
胤 130
背 130
胡 130
胥 130
臾 134
臿 134
軍 159
酋 164
重 166

10

乗 4
乘 4
亳 8
倉 9
兼 12
叟 29
哥 30
哭 30
唐 30
垂 32
夏 35
套 37
奚 37
島 46
差 48
師 50
弱 57
恭 61
晉 73
晋 73
書 73
毒 80
泰 85
烏 86
烕 86
烖 86
莆 101
眞 109
真 109
祟 113
秦 115
耋 125
能 130
臭 132
舀 134
芻 140
荆 140
衮 145
衰 145
袁 145
衷 145
豈 151
邕 163
釜 167

11

乾 5
兜 10
冕 13
凰 16
務 19
匏 20
匙 21
匘 21
參 28
啓 30
商 30
啇 30
啎 30
堂 32
執 32
堇 32
婁 38
孰 39
將 41
巢 47
常 50
帶 50
彪 59
旣 71
晝 72
曹 73
望 74
桼 75
柴 75
梟 75
梵 75
毫 82
焉 86
爽 89
牽 93
犀 93
率 96
畢 102
眾 109
章 117
羞 123
脣 130
舂 134
袞 145
雀 172

12

乾 5
傘 9
冕 13
博 24
喜 30
善 30
喪 30
喬 30
單 30
堯 32
報 32
壺 33
壹 33
壻 33
奡 37
孱 39
就 43
巽 49
幾 52
弑 56
彘 58
朝 74
棗 75
棘 75
棄 75

渠 15
毓 80
無 86
爲 87
甦 100
畫 102
異 102
疏 103
登 105
童 117
粵 119
着 123
舒 135
舜 136
衆 143
象 152
辜 160
量 166
集 172

13

亂 5
僉 9
匯 22
嗇 30
嗣 30
壺 33
奧 37
尟 42
尠 42
幹 51
愛 61
暈 72
會 73
業 75
楚 75
歲 77
爺 88
畵 102
禀 113
禽 114
稟 115
羨 123
義 123
聖 128
肅 129
肆 129
舝 136
葬 140
號 441
蜀 142
裏 145
豋 151
農 161
雍 172

14

兢 10
凳 16
凴 16
叠 29
嘉 30
嘏 30
嘗 30
壽 33
夀 33
夥 36
暢 72
朅 73
榦 75
歰 77
爾 89
疑 103
肇 129
膏 130
臧 131
臺 133
與 134
舞 136
蒙 140
裹 145

15

奭 37
慶 61
憂 61
暴 72
樊 75
緜 120
羮 123
膚 130
興 134
舖 135
虢 141
輝 159
靠 175
養 184
魯 195
黎 202

16

器 30
噩 30
奮 37
學 39
整 66
暨 72
燕 86
縣 120
羲 123
舘 135
豫 152
[illegible] 154
賴 154

17

冀 12
徽 60
應 61
糞 119
繇 120
舉 134
褻 145
襄 145
豳 152
賾 154
輿 159
隸 171

18

叢 29
彝 58
斃 66
歸 77
瞿 109
虩 141

19 &

嚮 30
羸 123
嚴 30
競 117
辮 120
釋 165
亹 8
臝 130
囊 30
懿 61
糴 119
聽 128
轡 159
蠲 142
變 149
贛 154
鹽 197
糶 113
纛 120
釁 164
豔 152
鑿 167
鬱 192

A CATALOGUE OF SELECTED DOVER BOOKS
IN ALL FIELDS OF INTEREST

A CATALOGUE OF SELECTED DOVER BOOKS IN ALL FIELDS OF INTEREST

AMERICA'S OLD MASTERS, James T. Flexner. Four men emerged unexpectedly from provincial 18th century America to leadership in European art: Benjamin West, J. S. Copley, C. R. Peale, Gilbert Stuart. Brilliant coverage of lives and contributions. Revised, 1967 edition. 69 plates. 365pp. of text.
21806-6 Paperbound $3.00

FIRST FLOWERS OF OUR WILDERNESS: AMERICAN PAINTING, THE COLONIAL PERIOD, James T. Flexner. Painters, and regional painting traditions from earliest Colonial times up to the emergence of Copley, West and Peale Sr., Foster, Gustavus Hesselius, Feke, John Smibert and many anonymous painters in the primitive manner. Engaging presentation, with 162 illustrations. xxii + 368pp.
22180-6 Paperbound $3.50

THE LIGHT OF DISTANT SKIES: AMERICAN PAINTING, 1760-1835, James T. Flexner. The great generation of early American painters goes to Europe to learn and to teach: West, Copley, Gilbert Stuart and others. Allston, Trumbull, Morse; also contemporary American painters—primitives, derivatives, academics—who remained in America. 102 illustrations. xiii + 306pp. 22179-2 Paperbound $3.00

A HISTORY OF THE RISE AND PROGRESS OF THE ARTS OF DESIGN IN THE UNITED STATES, William Dunlap. Much the richest mine of information on early American painters, sculptors, architects, engravers, miniaturists, etc. The only source of information for scores of artists, the major primary source for many others. Unabridged reprint of rare original 1834 edition, with new introduction by James T. Flexner, and 394 new illustrations. Edited by Rita Weiss. 6⅝ x 9⅝.
21695-0, 21696-9, 21697-7 Three volumes, Paperbound $13.50

EPOCHS OF CHINESE AND JAPANESE ART, Ernest F. Fenollosa. From primitive Chinese art to the 20th century, thorough history, explanation of every important art period and form, including Japanese woodcuts; main stress on China and Japan, but Tibet, Korea also included. Still unexcelled for its detailed, rich coverage of cultural background, aesthetic elements, diffusion studies, particularly of the historical period. 2nd, 1913 edition. 242 illustrations. lii + 439pp. of text.
20364-6, 20365-4 Two volumes, Paperbound $6.00

THE GENTLE ART OF MAKING ENEMIES, James A. M. Whistler. Greatest wit of his day deflates Oscar Wilde, Ruskin, Swinburne; strikes back at inane critics, exhibitions, art journalism; aesthetics of impressionist revolution in most striking form. Highly readable classic by great painter. Reproduction of edition designed by Whistler. Introduction by Alfred Werner. xxxvi + 334pp.
21875-9 Paperbound $2.50

ALPHABETS AND ORNAMENTS, Ernst Lehner. Well-known pictorial source for decorative alphabets, script examples, cartouches, frames, decorative title pages, calligraphic initials, borders, similar material. 14th to 19th century, mostly European. Useful in almost any graphic arts designing, varied styles. 750 illustrations. 256pp. 7 x 10. 21905-4 Paperbound $4.00

PAINTING: A CREATIVE APPROACH, Norman Colquhoun. For the beginner simple guide provides an instructive approach to painting: major stumbling blocks for beginner; overcoming them, technical points; paints and pigments; oil painting; watercolor and other media and color. New section on "plastic" paints. Glossary. Formerly *Paint Your Own Pictures*. 221pp. 22000-1 Paperbound $1.75

THE ENJOYMENT AND USE OF COLOR, Walter Sargent. Explanation of the relations between colors themselves and between colors in nature and art, including hundreds of little-known facts about color values, intensities, effects of high and low illumination, complementary colors. Many practical hints for painters, references to great masters. 7 color plates, 29 illustrations. x + 274pp. 20944-X Paperbound $2.50

THE NOTEBOOKS OF LEONARDO DA VINCI, compiled and edited by Jean Paul Richter. 1566 extracts from original manuscripts reveal the full range of Leonardo's versatile genius: all his writings on painting, sculpture, architecture, anatomy, astronomy, geography, topography, physiology, mining, music, etc., in both Italian and English, with 186 plates of manuscript pages and more than 500 additional drawings. Includes studies for the Last Supper, the lost Sforza monument, and other works. Total of xlvii + 866pp. 7⅞ x 10¾. 22572-0, 22573-9 Two volumes, Paperbound $10.00

MONTGOMERY WARD CATALOGUE OF 1895. Tea gowns, yards of flannel and pillow-case lace, stereoscopes, books of gospel hymns, the New Improved Singer Sewing Machine, side saddles, milk skimmers, straight-edged razors, high-button shoes, spittoons, and on and on . . . listing some 25,000 items, practically all illustrated. Essential to the shoppers of the 1890's, it is our truest record of the spirit of the period. Unaltered reprint of Issue No. 57, Spring and Summer 1895. Introduction by Boris Emmet. Innumerable illustrations. xiii + 624pp. 8½ x 11⅝. 22377-9 Paperbound $6.95

THE CRYSTAL PALACE EXHIBITION ILLUSTRATED CATALOGUE (LONDON, 1851). One of the wonders of the modern world—the Crystal Palace Exhibition in which all the nations of the civilized world exhibited their achievements in the arts and sciences—presented in an equally important illustrated catalogue. More than 1700 items pictured with accompanying text—ceramics, textiles, cast-iron work, carpets, pianos, sleds, razors, wall-papers, billiard tables, beehives, silverware and hundreds of other artifacts—represent the focal point of Victorian culture in the Western World. Probably the largest collection of Victorian decorative art ever assembled—indispensable for antiquarians and designers. Unabridged republication of the Art-Journal Catalogue of the Great Exhibition of 1851, with all terminal essays. New introduction by John Gloag, F.S.A. xxxiv + 426pp. 9 x 12. 22503-8 Paperbound $4.50

THE ARCHITECTURE OF COUNTRY HOUSES, Andrew J. Downing. Together with Vaux's *Villas and Cottages* this is the basic book for Hudson River Gothic architecture of the middle Victorian period. Full, sound discussions of general aspects of housing, architecture, style, decoration, furnishing, together with scores of detailed house plans, illustrations of specific buildings, accompanied by full text. Perhaps the most influential single American architectural book. 1850 edition. Introduction by J. Stewart Johnson. 321 figures, 34 architectural designs. xvi + 560pp.
22003-6 Paperbound $4.00

LOST EXAMPLES OF COLONIAL ARCHITECTURE, John Mead Howells. Full-page photographs of buildings that have disappeared or been so altered as to be denatured, including many designed by major early American architects. 245 plates. xvii + 248pp. 7⅞ x 10¾. 21143-6 Paperbound $3.00

DOMESTIC ARCHITECTURE OF THE AMERICAN COLONIES AND OF THE EARLY REPUBLIC, Fiske Kimball. Foremost architect and restorer of Williamsburg and Monticello covers nearly 200 homes between 1620-1825. Architectural details, construction, style features, special fixtures, floor plans, etc. Generally considered finest work in its area. 219 illustrations of houses, doorways, windows, capital mantels. xx + 314pp. 7⅞ x 10¾. 21743-4 Paperbound $3.50

EARLY AMERICAN ROOMS: 1650-1858, edited by Russell Hawes Kettell. Tour of 12 rooms, each representative of a different era in American history and each furnished, decorated, designed and occupied in the style of the era. 72 plans and elevations, 8-page color section, etc., show fabrics, wall papers, arrangements, etc. Full descriptive text. xvii + 200pp. of text. 8⅜ x 11¼.
21633-0 Paperbound $5.00

THE FITZWILLIAM VIRGINAL BOOK, edited by J. Fuller Maitland and W. B. Squire. Full modern printing of famous early 17th-century ms. volume of 300 works by Morley, Byrd, Bull, Gibbons, etc. For piano or other modern keyboard instrument; easy to read format. xxxvi + 938pp. 8⅜ x 11.
21068-5, 21069-3 Two volumes, Paperbound $8.00

HARPSICHORD MUSIC, Johann Sebastian Bach. Bach Gesellschaft edition. A rich selection of Bach's masterpieces for the harpsichord: the six English Suites, six French Suites, the six Partitas (Clavierübung part I), the Goldberg Variations (Clavierübung part IV), the fifteen Two-Part Inventions and the fifteen Three-Part Sinfonias. Clearly reproduced on large sheets with ample margins; eminently playable. vi + 312pp. 8⅛ x 11. 22360-4 Paperbound $5.00

THE MUSIC OF BACH: AN INTRODUCTION, Charles Sanford Terry. A fine, nontechnical introduction to Bach's music, both instrumental and vocal. Covers organ music, chamber music, passion music, other types. Analyzes themes, developments, innovations. x + 114pp. 21075-8 Paperbound $1.25

BEETHOVEN AND HIS NINE SYMPHONIES, Sir George Grove. Noted British musicologist provides best history, analysis, commentary on symphonies. Very thorough, rigorously accurate; necessary to both advanced student and amateur music lover. 436 musical passages. vii + 407 pp. 20334-4 Paperbound $2.25

JOHANN SEBASTIAN BACH, Philipp Spitta. One of the great classics of musicology, this definitive analysis of Bach's music (and life) has never been surpassed. Lucid, nontechnical analyses of hundreds of pieces (30 pages devoted to St. Matthew Passion, 26 to B Minor Mass). Also includes major analysis of 18th-century music. 450 musical examples. 40-page musical supplement. Total of xx + 1799pp.
(EUK) 22278-0, 22279-9 Two volumes, Clothbound $15.00

MOZART AND HIS PIANO CONCERTOS, Cuthbert Girdlestone. The only full-length study of an important area of Mozart's creativity. Provides detailed analyses of all 23 concertos, traces inspirational sources. 417 musical examples. Second edition. 509pp. (USO) 21271-8 Paperbound $3.50

THE PERFECT WAGNERITE: A COMMENTARY ON THE NIBLUNG'S RING, George Bernard Shaw. Brilliant and still relevant criticism in remarkable essays on Wagner's Ring cycle, Shaw's ideas on political and social ideology behind the plots, role of Leitmotifs, vocal requisites, etc. Prefaces. xxi + 136pp.
21707-8 Paperbound $1.50

DON GIOVANNI, W. A. Mozart. Complete libretto, modern English translation; biographies of composer and librettist; accounts of early performances and critical reaction. Lavishly illustrated. All the material you need to understand and appreciate this great work. Dover Opera Guide and Libretto Series; translated and introduced by Ellen Bleiler. 92 illustrations. 209pp.
21134-7 Paperbound $1.50

HIGH FIDELITY SYSTEMS: A LAYMAN'S GUIDE, Roy F. Allison. All the basic information you need for setting up your own audio system: high fidelity and stereo record players, tape records, F.M. Connections, adjusting tone arm, cartridge, checking needle alignment, positioning speakers, phasing speakers, adjusting hums, trouble-shooting, maintenance, and similar topics. Enlarged 1965 edition. More than 50 charts, diagrams, photos. iv + 91pp. 21514-8 Paperbound $1.25

REPRODUCTION OF SOUND, Edgar Villchur. Thorough coverage for laymen of high fidelity systems, reproducing systems in general, needles, amplifiers, preamps, loudspeakers, feedback, explaining physical background. "A rare talent for making technicalities vividly comprehensible," R. Darrell, *High Fidelity*. 69 figures. iv + 92pp. 21515-6 Paperbound $1.00

HEAR ME TALKIN' TO YA: THE STORY OF JAZZ AS TOLD BY THE MEN WHO MADE IT, Nat Shapiro and Nat Hentoff. Louis Armstrong, Fats Waller, Jo Jones, Clarence Williams, Billy Holiday, Duke Ellington, Jelly Roll Morton and dozens of other jazz greats tell how it was in Chicago's South Side, New Orleans, depression Harlem and the modern West Coast as jazz was born and grew. xvi + 429pp.
21726-4 Paperbound $2.50

FABLES OF AESOP, translated by Sir Roger L'Estrange. A reproduction of the very rare 1931 Paris edition; a selection of the most interesting fables, together with 50 imaginative drawings by Alexander Calder. v + 128pp. 6½x9¼.
21780-9 Paperbound $1.25

ADVENTURES OF AN AFRICAN SLAVER, Theodore Canot. Edited by Brantz Mayer. A detailed portrayal of slavery and the slave trade, 1820-1840. Canot, an established trader along the African coast, describes the slave economy of the African kingdoms, the treatment of captured negroes, the extensive journeys in the interior to gather slaves, slave revolts and their suppression, harems, bribes, and much more. Full and unabridged republication of 1854 edition. Introduction by Malcom Cowley. 16 illustrations. xvii + 448pp. 22456-2 Paperbound $3.50

MY BONDAGE AND MY FREEDOM, Frederick Douglass. Born and brought up in slavery, Douglass witnessed its horrors and experienced its cruelties, but went on to become one of the most outspoken forces in the American anti-slavery movement. Considered the best of his autobiographies, this book graphically describes the inhuman treatment of slaves, its effects on slave owners and slave families, and how Douglass's determination led him to a new life. Unaltered reprint of 1st (1855) edition. xxxii + 464pp. 22457-0 Paperbound $2.50

THE INDIANS' BOOK, recorded and edited by Natalie Curtis. Lore, music, narratives, dozens of drawings by Indians themselves from an authoritative and important survey of native culture among Plains, Southwestern, Lake and Pueblo Indians. Standard work in popular ethnomusicology. 149 songs in full notation. 23 drawings, 23 photos. xxxi + 584pp. 6⅝ x 9⅜. 21939-9 Paperbound $4.50

DICTIONARY OF AMERICAN PORTRAITS, edited by Hayward and Blanche Cirker. 4024 portraits of 4000 most important Americans, colonial days to 1905 (with a few important categories, like Presidents, to present). Pioneers, explorers, colonial figures, U. S. officials, politicians, writers, military and naval men, scientists, inventors, manufacturers, jurists, actors, historians, educators, notorious figures, Indian chiefs, etc. All authentic contemporary likenesses. The only work of its kind in existence; supplements all biographical sources for libraries. Indispensable to anyone working with American history. 8,000-item classified index, finding lists, other aids. xiv + 756pp. 9¼ x 12¾. 21823-6 Clothbound $30.00

TRITTON'S GUIDE TO BETTER WINE AND BEER MAKING FOR BEGINNERS, S. M. Tritton. All you need to know to make family-sized quantities of over 100 types of grape, fruit, herb and vegetable wines; as well as beers, mead, cider, etc. Complete recipes, advice as to equipment, procedures such as fermenting, bottling, and storing wines. Recipes given in British, U. S., and metric measures. Accompanying booklet lists sources in U. S. A. where ingredients may be bought, and additional information. 11 illustrations. 157pp. 5⅝ x 8⅛.
(USO) 22090-7 Clothbound $3.50

GARDENING WITH HERBS FOR FLAVOR AND FRAGRANCE, Helen M. Fox. How to grow herbs in your own garden, how to use them in your cooking (over 55 recipes included), legends and myths associated with each species, uses in medicine, perfumes, etc.—these are elements of one of the few books written especially for American herb fanciers. Guides you step-by-step from soil preparation to harvesting and storage for each type of herb. 12 drawings by Louise Mansfield. xiv + 334pp.
22540-2 Paperbound $2.50